DECISION SUPPORT SYSTEMS AND INTELLIGENT SYSTEMS

DECISION SUPPORT SYSTEMS AND INTELLIGENT SYSTEMS

SEVENTH EDITION

Efraim Turban
Chinese University of Hong Kong

Jay E. Aronson
University of Georgia

Ting-Peng Liang
Chinese University of Hong Kong

with contributions by

Richard V. McCarthy
Quinnipiac University

PEARSON

Prentice
Hall

PEARSON EDUCATION INTERNATIONAL

AVP/Executive Editor: Bob Horan
VP/Publisher: Natalie E. Anderson
Project Manager (Editorial): Kyle Hannon
Editorial Assistant: Robyn Goldenberg
Senior Media Project Manager: Joan Waxman
Marketing Assistant: Danielle Torio
Managing Editor (Production): John Roberts
Production Editor: Suzanne Grappi
Production Assistant: Joe DeProspero
Manufacturing Buyer: Michelle Klein
Design Manager: Maria Lange
Cover Design: Jayne Conte
Cover Illustration/Photo: Photodisc
Manager, Print Production: Christy Mahon
Composition/Full-Service Project Management : Pine Tree Composition, Inc.
Printer/Binder: Hamilton

Credits and acknowledgments borrowed from other sources and reproduced, with permission, in this textbook appear on appropriate page within text.

If you purchased this book within the United States or Canada you should be aware that it has been wrongfully imported without the approval of the Publisher or the Author.

Pearson Education LTD.
Pearson Education Singapore, Pte. Ltd
Pearson Education, Canada, Ltd
Pearson Education-Japan

Pearson Education Australia PTY, Limited
Pearson Education North Asia Ltd
Pearson Educación de Mexico, S.A. de C.V.
Pearson Educación Malaysia, Pte. Ltd

10 9 8 7 6 5 4 3 2 1
ISBN 0-13-123013-1

Dedicated to
my wife, Sharon,
and my children, Marla, Michael, and Stephanie,
with love

To my wife, Lina,
and my daughters, Daphne and Sharon,
with love

To my wife, Jenny,
and my sons, Nigel and David

Efraim Turban (M.B.A., Ph.D., University of California Berkeley) is a visiting professor at City University of Honk Kong. Prior to this he was on the staff of several universities including Lehigh University, Florida International University, and the University of Southern California. Dr. Turban is the author of about 100 refereed papers published in leading journals such as *Management Science, MIS Quarterly* and *Decision Support Systems*. He also the author of 20 books including *Electronic Commerce: A Managerial Perspective and Information Technology for Management*. He is also a consultant to major corporations world wide. Dr. Turban's current areas of interest are Web-based decision support systems, using intelligent agents in electronic commerce systems, and collaboration issues in global electronic commerce.

Jay E. Aronson (M.S., M.S., Ph.D., Carnegie Mellon University) is a professor of Management Information Systems in the Terry College of Business at The University of Georgia. Prior to this he was on the faculty at Southern Methodist University. Dr. Aronson is the author of about 50 refereed papers that have appeared in leading journals including *Management Science, Information Systems Research*, and *MIS Quarterly*. He is the author of three books, and contributes to several professional encyclopedias. He is also a consultant to major international corporations and organizations. Dr. Aronson's current areas of research include knowledge management, collaborative computing, and parallel computing.

Ting-Peng Liang (MA, Ph.D., University of Pennsylvania) is a National Chair Professor of Information Systems at National Sun Yat-sen University in Taiwan and a visiting professor at Chinese University of Hong Kong. Prior to this, he had been on the faculties of University of Illinois (Urbana-Champaign) and Purdue University. Dr. Liang has published more than 50 referred research papers in leading journals such as *Management Science, MIS Quarterly, Decision Support Systems*, and *Journal of MIS*. He is also the author of three books and a consultant to several major companies in the United States and Taiwan. Dr. Liang's current areas for research and teaching include Web-based intelligent systems, electronic commerce, knowledge management, and strategic applications of information technologies.

BRIEF CONTENTS

CONTENTS

OVERVIEW

As we begin the 21st century, we observe major changes in how managers use computerized support in making decisions. As more and more decision-makers become computer and Web literate, decision-support systems (DSS) / business intelligence (BI) is evolving from its beginnings as primarily a personal-support tool, and is quickly becoming a *shared commodity* across the organization. Organizations can now easily use intranets and the Internet to deliver high-value performance-analysis applications to decision-makers around the world. Corporations regularly develop distributed systems, *intranets* and *extranets*, that enable easy access to data stored in multiple locations, and collaboration and communication worldwide. Various information systems are integrated with one other and/or with other Web-based automated systems. Some integration even transcends organizational boundaries. Managers can make better decisions because they have more accurate information at their fingertips.

Today's DSS tools utilize the Web for their graphical user interface that allows users to flexibly, efficiently, and easily view and process data and models with familiar Web browsers. The easy-to-use and readily available capabilities of enterprise information, knowledge and other advanced systems have migrated to the PC and personal digital assistants (PDAs). Managers communicate with computers and the Web using a variety of hand-held wireless devices, including the cell telephone. These devices enable managers to access important information and useful tools, communicate, and collaborate. *Data warehouses* and their analytical tools (e.g., *online analytical processing/OLAP* and *data mining*) dramatically enhance information access across organizational boundaries. Decision support for groups continues to improve with major new developments in *group support systems* for enhancing collaborative work, anytime and anywhere. *Artificial intelligence* methods are improving the quality of decision support, and have become embedded in many applications ranging from antilocking automotive brakes to intelligent Web search engines. *Intelligent agents* perform routine tasks, freeing up time that decision-makers can devote to important work. Developments in *organizational learning* and *knowledge management* deliver the entire organization's expertise to bear on problems anytime and anywhere. The Internet and intranet information-delivery systems enhance and enable all of these decision support systems.

The purpose of this book is to introduce the reader to these technologies, which we call, collectively, *management support systems* (MSS). This book presents the fundamentals of the techniques and the manner in which these systems are constructed and used.

The theme of this totally revised edition is "Web-based, enterprise decision support." In addition to traditional DSS applications, this edition expands the reader's understanding of the world of the Web by providing examples, products, services, and exercises, and by discussing Web-related issues throughout the text. We highlight *Web intelligence/Web analytics*, which parallel business intelligence/business analytics for electronic commerce and other Web applications. The book is supported by a Web site (prenhall.com/turban) containing additional Web Chapters that supplement the text. Most of the specific improvements made in this seventh edition concentrate on three areas: enterprise decision support, artificial intelligence, and Web DSS. Despite the many changes, we have preserved the comprehensiveness and user friendliness that have made the text a market leader. We have also reduced the book's size by eliminating generic material and by moving material to the Web site. Finally, we present accurate and updated material not available in any other text.

DSS and ES courses and portions of courses are recommended jointly by the Association for Computing Machinery (ACM), the Association for Information Systems (AIS), and the Association of Information Technology Professionals (AITP, formerly DPMA) (see *Data Base*, Vol. 28, No. 1, Winter 1997). This course is designed to cover the decision-support and artificial intelligence components of the IS'97 Model Curriculum for information systems. It actually covers more than what is recommended. The text also covers the decision-support and artificial intelligence components of the Information Systems 2000 Model Curriculum draft (www.is2000.org). Another objective is to provide the practicing manager with the foundations and applications of DSS, GSS, knowledge management, ES, neural computing, intelligent agents, and other intelligent systems.

THE SEVENTH EDITION

The seventh edition of this book makes a major departure from the previous editions for the purpose of improving the text.

The major improvements include the following:
- Expansion and major updating of data warehousing, online analytical processing, and data-mining materials in Chapter 5.
- Reordering Chapters 4 and 5 on modeling and data to enable intelligent, detailed coverage of data warehousing and its associated business intelligence development and application.
- Expansion and major updating of the materials on enterprise information systems, including portals, supply chain management, enterprise resource planning/enterprise resource management, customer relationship (resource) management, product life-cycle management, business process management, business activity monitoring, and a reduction in the historical materials in Chapter 8.
- A support Web site organized by chapters to enhance the text materials.
- A major updating of the treatment of knowledge management (Chapter 9).
- Condensing the material on artificial neural networks into a single chapter (Chapter 13).
- Combining the several chapters on expert systems into one.
- Creating a single chapter from those on networked decision support and group support systems (Chapter 7).
- Eliminating the chapter on intelligent systems development from the text and moving it to the book's Web site.
- Updating the theoretical material on decision-making in Chapter 2. This includes material on alternative decision-making models and temperament types.
- Updating the real-world case applications in many of the chapters. These include the IMERYS case applications in Chapters 2, 4, and 6.
- Including major discussions on OLAP, data mining, expert systems, and neural network packages.
- The overall number of chapters was reduced.

- The book is supported by a Web site, prenhall.com/turban, that includes supplementary material organized by chapters.
- The Internet Exercises for each chapter have been expanded. A diversity of exercises provides students with extensive, up-to-date information and a better sense of reality.
- Hands-on exercises provide opportunities to build decision support applications.
- Expanded group exercises and term projects. These enhance the learning experience by providing activities for small groups and longer-term activities. Some term projects involve building systems for real organizations (we have used this approach very successfully for over 15 years in our teaching).
- Updated research findings and references.
- More real-world examples.

THE SUPPLEMENT PACKAGE: www.prenhall.com/turban

A comprehensive and flexible technology-support package is available to enhance the teaching and learning experience. All instructor and student supplements are available on the text Web site: www.prenhall.com/turban.

- *Instructor's Manual.* The Instructor's Manual includes learning objectives for the entire course and for each chapter, answers to the questions and exercises at the end of the chapters, and teaching suggestions (including instructions for projects). Available on the secure faculty section of the Turban Web site.
- *Test Item File and TestGen Software.* The Test Item File is a comprehensive collection of true-false, multiple-choice, fill-in-the-blank, and essay questions. The questions are rated by difficulty level, and the answers are referenced by page number. The Test Item File is available in Microsoft Word and as the computerized Prentice Hall TestGen. TestGen is a comprehensive suite of tools for testing and assessment. It allows instructors to easily create and distribute tests for their courses, either by printing and distributing through traditional methods or by online delivery via a local area network (LAN) server. TestGen features screen wizards to assist you as you move through the program, and the software is backed with full technical support. Both the Test Item File and TestGen software are available on the secure faculty section of the Turban Web site.
- *PowerPoint Slides.* PowerPoint slides are available that illuminate and build on key concepts in the text. Both students and faculty can download the PowerPoint slides from the Turban Web site.
- *Materials for Your Online Course.* Prentice Hall supports our adopters using online courses by providing files ready for upload into both WebCT and Blackboard course management systems for our testing, quizzing, and other supplements. Please contact your local PH representative or email mis_service@prenhall.com for further information on your particular course.

Note: Web site URLs are *dynamic.* As this book went to press, we verified that all the cited Web sites were active and valid. Web sites to which we refer in the text sometimes change or are discontinued because companies change names, are bought or sold, merge, or fail. Sometimes Web sites are down for maintenance, repair, or redesign . Most organizations have dropped the initial "www" designation for their sites, but some still use it. If you have a problem connecting to a Web site that we mention, please be patient and simply run a Web search to try to identify the possible new site. Most times, the new site can be quickly found. We apologize in advance for this inconvenience.

ACKNOWLEDGMENTS

Many individuals have provided suggestions and criticisms since the publication of the first edition. Dozens of students participated in class testing of various chapters, software, and problems, and assisted in collecting material. It is not possible to name everyone who participated in this project; thanks go to all of them. However, certain individuals made significant contributions, and they deserve special recognition.

First, we appreciate the efforts of those individuals who provided formal reviews of the first through sixth editions:

Robert Blanning, Vanderbilt University
Charles Butler, Colorado State University
Warren Briggs, Suffolk University
Sohail S. Chaudry, University of Wisconsin–La Crosse
Kathy Chudoba, Florida State University
Woo Young Chung, University of Memphis
Paul Buddy Clark, South Carolina State University
Pi'Sheng Deng, California State University–Stanislaus
Joyce Elam, Florida International University
Gary Farrar, Jacksonville University
George Federman, Santa Clara City College
Joey George, Florida State University
Paul Gray, Claremont Graduate School
Orv Greynholds, Capital College (Laurel, Md.)
Ray Jacobs, Ashland University
Leonard Jessup, Indiana University
Jeffrey Johnson, Utah State University
Saul Kassicieh, University of New Mexico
Anand S. Kunnathur, University of Toledo
Shao-ju Lee, California State University at Northridge
Hank Lucas, New York University
Jane Mackay, Texas Christian University
George M. Marakas, University of Maryland
Dick Mason, Southern Methodist University
Nick McGaughey, San Jose State University
Ido Millet, Pennsylvania State University–Erie
Benjamin Mittman, Northwestern University
Larry Moore, Virginia Polytechnic Institute and State University
Simitra Mukherjee, Nova Southeastern University
Marianne Murphy, Northeastern University
Peter Mykytyn, Southern Illinois University
Souren Paul, Southern Illinois University
Roger Alan Pick, University of Missouri–St. Louis
W. "RP" Raghupaphi, California State University–Chico
Loren Rees, Virginia Polytechnic Institute and State University
David Russell, Western New England College
Steve Ruth, George Mason University
Vartan Safarian, Winona State University
Glenn Shephard, San Jose State University

Jung P. Shim, Mississippi State University
Randy Smith, University of Virginia
James T. C. Teng, University of South Carolina
John VanGigch, California State University at Sacramento
David Van Over, University of Idaho
Paul J. A. van Vliet, University of Nebraska at Omaha
B. S. Vijayaraman, University of Akron
Diane B. Walz, University of Texas at San Antonio
Paul R. Watkins, University of Southern California
Randy S. Weinberg, Saint Cloud State University
Jennifer Williams, University of Southern Indiana
Steve Zanakis, Florida International University

Second, several individuals contributed material to the text or the supporting material. Major contributors include: the independent consultant Lou Frenzel, whose books, *Crash Course in Artificial Intelligence* and *Expert Systems and Understanding of Expert Systems* (both published by Howard W. Sams, New York, 1987) provide considerable material; Larry Medsker (American University), who contributed substantial material on neural networks; and Richard V. McCarthy (Quinnipiac University), who performed major revisions on Chapters 5 and 8. Elena Karahanna (The University of Georgia) gave us the idea for the Running Case on decision-making in Chapter 2.

Third, the book benefited greatly from the efforts of many individuals who contributed advice and interesting material (such as problems), gave feedback on material, or helped in class testing. These individuals are Warren Briggs (Suffolk University), Frank DeBalough (University of Southern California), Alan Dennis (Indiana University), George Easton (San Diego State University), Janet Fisher (California State University, Los Angeles), David Friend (Pilot Software, Inc.), Paul Gray (Claremont Graduate School), Dustin Huntington (Exsys, Inc.), Elena Karahanna (The University of Georgia), Dave King (Comshare, Inc.), Jim Ragusa (University of Central Florida), Elizabeth Rivers, Alan Rowe (University of Southern California), Steve Ruth (George Mason University), Linus Schrage (University of Chicago), Antonie Stam (University of Missouri), Ron Swift (NCR Corp.), Merril Warkentin (Northeastern University), Paul Watkins (University of Southern California), Ben Mortagy (Claremont Graduate School of Management), Dan Walsh (Bellcore), Richard Watson (University of Georgia), and the many instructors and students who have provided feedback.

Fourth, several vendors cooperated by providing development and/or demonstration software: CACI Products Company (LaJolla, Calif.), California Scientific Software (Nevada City, Calif.), Cognos, Inc. (Ottawa, Ont.), Comshare, Inc. (Ann Arbor, Mich.), DS Group, Inc. (Greenwich, Conn.), Expert Choice, Inc. (Pittsburgh, Pa.), Exsys, Inc. (Albuquerque, N.Mex.), Palisade Software (Newfield, N.Y.), Pilot Software, Inc. (Cambridge, Mass.), Promised Land Technologies (New Haven, Conn.), Ward Systems Group, Inc. (Frederick, Md.), Idea Fisher Systems, Inc. (Irving, Calif.), and Wordtech Systems (Orinda, Calif.).

Fifth, many individuals helped us with administrative matters and editing, proofreading, and preparation. The project began with Jack Repcheck (a former Macmillan editor), who initiated this project with the support of Hank Lucas (New York University). Editing was done by Bob Milch. A major thank you goes to Janet Bond for her efforts in putting the references together, and to Martin Pence for his countless hours in tracking down library material, Web sites, and other information. And thanks are due to Judy Lang, who played a major role in many tasks, including the preparation of the book, the Test Bank, and the Instructor's Manual.

Finally, the Prentice Hall team is to be commended: Executive Editor Bob Horan, who orchestrated this project, Robert Milch, who copyedited the manuscript, the production team, including Suzanne Grappi and Patty Donovan, the staff at Pine Tree Composition, who transformed the manuscript into a book, our editorial project manager, Kyle Hannon, and our media project manager, Joan Waxman.

We would like to thank all these individuals and corporations. Without their help the creation of this book would not have been possible.

J.E.A.

E.T.

T.P.L.

DECISION-MAKING AND COMPUTERIZED SUPPORT

LEARNING OBJECTIVES FOR PART I

❖ Understand how computer technologies can assist managers in their work

❖ Recognize the different types of decision support systems used in practice

❖ Understand the foundations of decision-making

❖ Understand the key issues in decision-making

❖ Understand how the World Wide Web/Internet has affected decision support systems

❖ Learn why computer technologies are necessary for modern decision-making

Management-support systems (MSS) are collections of computer technologies that support managerial work—essentially decision-making. MSS developments follow those of computer technologies, most recently the Internet and the World Wide Web. These technologies have had a profound impact on MSS in terms of their tools and their use. We highlight their effects throughout this text. In Part I, we cover two topics. Chapter 1 contains an overview of the text, including the rationale for the technologies and a brief description of each. In Chapter 2, we present the fundamentals of decision-making, including terminology and an overview of the decision-making process.

Note: Web site URLs are dynamic. As this book went to press, we verified that all the cited Web sites were active and valid. Web sites to which we refer in the text sometimes change or are discontinued because companies change names, are bought or sold, merge, or fail . Sometimes Web sites are down for maintenance, repair, or redesign. Most organizations have dropped the initial "www" designation for their sites, but some still use it. If you have a problem connecting to a Web site that we mention, please be patient and simply run a Web search to try to identify the possible new site. Most times, the new site can be quickly found. We apologize in advance for this inconvenience.

CHAPTER

1

MANAGEMENT SUPPORT SYSTEMS: AN OVERVIEW

LEARNING OBJECTIVES

❖ Understand how computer technologies can assist managers in their work

❖ Learn the basic concepts of decision-making

❖ Learn the basic concepts of decision support systems

❖ Recognize the different types of decision support systems used in practice

❖ Recognize when a certain decision support system is applicable to a specific type of problem

❖ Understand how the World Wide Web/Internet has affected decision support systems

This book is about emerging and advanced computer technologies for supporting the solution of managerial problems. These technologies continually change how organizations are structured, reengineered, and managed. This introductory chapter provides an overview of the book and covers the following topics:

1.1 OPENING VIGNETTE: HARRAH'S MAKES A GREAT BET[1]

THE PROBLEM

Gaming is highly competitive and profitable. Many people want to gamble, and every casino wants to attract their business. In the early 1990s, gambling on riverboats and Native American reservations was legalized. Major operators moved into these new markets. Between 1990 and 1997, Harrah's tripled its number of casinos. As the new markets grew more competitive, the business reached the point of diminishing returns. Harrah's early arrival was often usurped by newer, grander, more extravagant casinos nearby. Each Harrah's casino operated and marketed itself independently from the others. The managers of each property felt that they owned certain customers, and customers were treated differently at other Harrah's properties.

Customer service had not changed much since the 1970s. Casino managers had long recognized the importance of *building relationships* with their most profitable clientele. They reserved *star* treatment for the high-rollers, but only gave an occasional free drink to the folks playing machines. However, by the end of the 1980s, slot machines surpassed table games as the major casinos' largest source of income. In 1997, executives at Harrah's recognized that devising a means to keep their 25 million slot players loyal to Harrah's was the *key to profitability*.

THE SOLUTION

Harrah's approaches each new customer as a *long-term acquaintance*. The company analyzed gigabytes of customer data collected by player-tracking systems during the previous five years with data mining techniques. Executives found that the 30 percent of their customers who spent between $100 and $500 per visit accounted for 80 percent of company revenue—and almost 100 percent of profits. These gamblers were typically locals who visited regional Harrah's properties frequently.

Harrah's developed a *Total Rewards Program*. It distributes *Harrah's Total Rewards Cards* to its customers, which they use to pay for slots, food, and rooms operated by the Harrah's, Players, Rio, and Showboat brands. The company uses magnetic strips on the cards to capture gaming information on every customer, and offers comps (free drinks, meals, hotel rooms, etc.) and other incentives based on the amount of money inserted into machines, not the amount won. The card tracks how long customers play, how much they bet, what games they prefer, and whether they win or lose. It creates a "profitability profile" that estimates a customer's value to the company. Harrah's publishes clear criteria for comping players free rooms and upgrades, and makes them accessible and redeemable.

Harrah's electronically linked all of its players clubs so that when gamblers at one location go to another, they can redeem their Reward points for free meals, rooms, or shows. Harrah's can actively market its casino "family" to Total Rewards Customers. The airlines have been doing this for years. Now Harrah's could establish close relationships with its most profitable customers and develop brand loyalty.

Harrah's system works as follows:

---

[1]Adapted from J.A. Nickell, "Welcome to Harrah's," *Business 2.0*, April 2002; and C. Rosen, "Harrah's Bets on Loyalty Program," *InformationWeek*, October 30, 2000.

- *Magnetic card readers* on all its gaming machines read a customer ID number from each card and flash a personalized greeting with the customer's current tally of Reward points.
- *Electronic gaming machines* are computerized and networked. Each machine captures transaction data and relays it to Harrah's mainframe servers.
- *Onsite transaction systems* at each casino property store all casino, hotel, and dining transaction data.
- A *national data warehouse* links the casinos' computer systems and customer data to a single server that tallies customer history and Reward points.
- *Predictive analysis software* programs produce nearly instantaneous customer profiles. The company can design and track marketing initiatives and their results.
- A *Web site* keeps customers informed, connected, and entertained.

The **data warehouse**, a large, specialized database, maintains demographic and spending-pattern data on all customers. **Data mining** techniques, also called **business intelligence** (**business analytics,** or analytical methods), are used to analyze the data and identify classes of profitable customers to target for future business at all properties. Together, these methods are combined into a **customer relationship management (CRM)** system, a **decision support system (DSS)** that helps managers make sales and marketing decisions.[2] The Harrah's Web site links customer information, the brand-loyalty program, the properties, specials, and other relevant data.

Data are collected at each property by **transaction processing systems (TPS)** and moved to a centralized data warehouse, where they are analyzed. Age and distance from the casino are critical predictors of frequency, coupled with the kind of game played and how many coins are played per game. For example, the *perfect player* is a 62-year-old woman who lives within 30 minutes of Kansas City, Missouri, and plays dollar video poker. Such customers typically have substantial disposable cash, plenty of time on their hands, and easy access to a Harrah's riverboat casino.

The system identifies high-value customers and places them in corresponding demographic segments (all told there are 90). Customers who live far away typically receive direct-mail discounts or comps on hotel rooms or transportation, while drive-in customers get food, entertainment, or cash incentives. Most offers have tight expiration dates to encourage visitors to either return sooner or switch from a competitor. For each direct-marketing pitch, the company tracks response rates and returns on investment, and adjusts its future campaigns according to the results.

THE RESULTS

Slots and other electronic gaming machines account for most of Harrah's $3.7 billion in revenue and more than 80 percent of its operating profit. Largely on the strength of its new tracking and data mining system for slot players, Harrah's has recently emerged as the second-largest operator in the United States, with the highest three-year investment return in the industry. The Total Rewards program has generated $20 million in annual cost reductions by identifying unprofitable customers and treating them as such. In 2001, the Harrah's network linked more than 40,000 gaming machines

---

[2]The acronym *DSS* is treated as both singular and plural throughout this book. Similarly, other acronyms, such as *MIS* and *EIS*, designate both plural and singular forms.

in twelve states and created brand loyalty. In just the first two years of the Total Rewards program, revenue increased by $100 million from customers who gambled at more than one Harrah's casino. Since 1998, each percentage-point increase in Harrah's share of its customers' overall gambling budgets has coincided with an additional $125 million in shareholder value. The company's record earnings of $3.7 billion in 2001 were up 11 percent from 2000. More than half of the revenue at Harrah's three Las Vegas casinos now comes from players the company already knows from its casinos outside of Nevada.

❖ QUESTIONS FOR THE OPENING VIGNETTE

1. How did Harrah's end up with a major problem on its hands?
2. Why was it important to collect data on customers?
3. How do DSS technologies (data mining, data warehouse, customer resource management, etc.) help managers identify customer profiles and their profitability?
4. What was the impact of the Harrah's customer-loyalty program?
5. *Open-ended:* How could a retail store effectively develop methods and systems like those used by Harrah's to boost profitability and market share?

1.2 MANAGERS AND DECISION-MAKING

The opening vignette illustrates how Harrah's developed and uses a computerized decision support system to maintain customer loyalty, expand its market, and cross-market its properties. Harrah's was an underperformer in the market until the DSS was deployed. It is now an industry leader, operating successfully in an extremely competitive market. Some of the points demonstrated by this vignette are:

- The nature of the competition in the gaming industry makes it necessary to use computerized decision support tools to succeed and to survive.
- The company uses the World Wide Web extensively for its interface. Analysts, marketing specialists, and even customers can access the system directly through the World Wide Web.
- The system is based on data organized in a special data warehouse to allow easy processing and analysis.
- The major technologies used are data mining (business intelligence//business analytics) systems to identify profitable customer classes (analysis) and a customer-relationship management (CRM) system to market promotions, monitor sales, and identify problems and new opportunities. The data-mining methods may include regression analysis, neural networks, cluster analysis, and optimization approaches.
- The DSS is used in making a variety of marketing decisions, ranging from determining which customers are most profitable to how to promote the properties to all customers. Promotions can be made on a day-to-day basis.
- Decision support is based on a vast amount of internal and external data.
- The DSS analysis software applications are separate from the transaction processing system (TPS), yet they use much of the TPS data.
- Statistical and other quantitative models are used in the CRM.
- The managers are ultimately responsible for all decisions.

Airlines, retail organizations, banks, service companies, and others have successfully used many of Harrah's methods. The vignette demonstrates that to run an effective business today in a competitive environment, real-time, targeted, computerized decision support is essential. This is the major theme of the book.

THE NATURE OF MANAGERS' WORK

To better understand the support information systems can give managers, it is useful to look at the nature of managers' work. Mintzberg's (1980) classic study of top managers and several replicated studies suggest that managers perform 10 major roles that can be classified into three major categories: interpersonal, information, and decisional (see Table 1.1).

To perform these roles, managers need information that is delivered, efficiently and in a timely manner, to personal computers on their desktops, to mobile computers, and even to computers embedded in PDAs (personal digital assistants) and cell telephones. This information is delivered by computers that function as servers, generally via Web technologies (Shim et al., 2002; see also Gregg, 2002; Hall, 2002; Hoch and Kunreuther, 2001; and Langseth and Vivatrat, 2002). In addition to obtaining information necessary to better perform their roles, managers use computers directly

TABLE 1.1	Mintzberg's 10 Management Roles
Role	*Description*
Interpersonal	
Figurehead	Symbolic head; obliged to perform a number of routine duties of a legal or social nature
Leader	Responsible for the motivation and activation of subordinates; responsible for staffing, training, and associated duties
Liaison	Maintains self-developed network of outside contacts and informers who provide favors and information
Informational	
Monitor	Seeks and receives a wide variety of special information (much of it current) to develop a thorough understanding of the organization and environment; emerges as the nerve center of the organization's internal and external information
Disseminator	Transmits information received from outsiders or from subordinates to members of the organization; some information factual, some involving interpretation and integration
Spokesperson	Transmits information to outsiders on the organization's plans, policies, actions, results, and so forth; serves as an expert on the organization's industry
Decisional	
Entrepreneur	Searches the organization and its environment for opportunities and initiates improvement projects to bring about change; supervises design of certain projects
Disturbance handler	Responsible for corrective action when the organization faces important, unexpected disturbances
Resource allocator	Responsible for the allocation of organizational resources of all kinds—in effect the making or approving of all significant organizational decisions
Negotiator	Responsible for representing the organization at major negotiations

Source: Adapted from Mintzberg (1980) and Mintzberg (1993).

to support and improve decision-making, a key task that is part of most of these roles.

1.3 MANAGERIAL DECISION-MAKING AND INFORMATION SYSTEMS

We begin by examining the two important topics of managerial decision-making and information systems.

Management is a process by which organizational goals are achieved using resources. The resources are considered inputs, and attainment of goals is viewed as the output of the process. The degree of success of the organization and the manager's job is often measured by the ratio of outputs to inputs. This ratio is an indication of the organization's **productivity.**

Productivity is a major concern for any organization because it determines the well-being of the organization and its members. Productivity is also a a very important issue at the national level. National productivity is the aggregate of the productivity of all the people and organizations in the country, and it determines the country's standard of living, employment level, and economic health. The level of productivity, or the success of management, depends on the performance of managerial functions, such as planning, organizing, directing, and controlling. In addition, the Web improves productivity by providing, among other things, data, environmental scanning, and portals that lead to better decisions, and thus, increased productivity. To perform their functions, managers are engaged in a continuous process of making decisions.

All managerial activities revolve around decision-making. *The manager is primarily a decision-maker* (see DSS in Focus 1.1). Organizations are filled with decision-makers at various levels.

For years, managers considered decision-making purely an art—a talent acquired over a long period through experience (learning by trial and error). Management was

---

DSS IN FOCUS 1.1

DECISION-MAKING ABILITY RATED FIRST IN SURVEY

In almost any survey of what constitutes good management, the ability to make clear-cut decisions when needed is prominently mentioned. It is not surprising, therefore, to learn that the ability to make crisp decisions was rated first in importance in a study of 6,500 managers in more than 100 companies, many of them large blue-chip corporations.

Managers starting a training course at Harbridge House, a Boston-based firm, were asked how important it was for managers to follow certain managerial practices. They also were asked how well, in their estimation, managers performed these practices.

From a statistical distillation of these answers, Harbridge ranked making clear-cut decisions when needed as the most important of 10 managerial practices. Unfortunately, the respondents concluded that only 20 percent of the managers performed well on this.

Ranked second in managerial importance was getting to the heart of problems rather than dealing with less important issues, a finding that shows up in similar studies. Most of the remaining eight management practices were related directly or indirectly to decision-making.

This situation is timeless. See any recent survey in *CIO*, *Datamation*, or *InformationWeek*.

considered an art because a variety of individual styles could be used in approaching and successfully solving the same types of managerial problems. These styles were often based on creativity, judgment, intuition, and experience rather than on systematic quantitative methods grounded in a scientific approach.

However, the environment in which management operates changes rapidly. Business and its environment are growing more complex every day. Figure 1.1 shows the changes in major factors that affect managerial decision-making. As a result, decision-making today is more complicated. It is more difficult to make decisions for several reasons. First, the number of available alternatives is much larger than ever before because of improved technology and communication systems, especially the Web/Internet and its search engines. As more data and information become available, more alternatives can be identified and explored. Despite the speed at which data and information can be accessed, the decision-making alternatives must be analyzed. This takes (human-scale = slow) time and thought. Despite having more and better information than ever before, time pressure prevents decision-makers from gathering all that they need and from sharing it (Hoch et al., 2001; Tobia, 2000). Second, the cost of making errors can be large because of the complexity and magnitude of operations, automation, and the chain reaction that an error can cause in many parts of the organization. Third, there are continuous changes in the fluctuating environment and more uncertainty in several impacting elements. Finally, decisions must be made quickly to respond to the market. Advances in technology, notably the Web, have dramatically increased the speed at which we obtain information and the expected speed at which we make our decisions. There is an expectation that we can respond instantly to changes in the environment.

Because of these trends and changes, it is nearly impossible to rely on a trial-and-error approach to management, especially for decisions involving the factors shown in Figure 1.1. Managers must be more sophisticated: They must use the new tools and techniques of their fields. Some of these tools and techniques are the subject of this book. Using them to support decision-making can be extremely rewarding in making effective decisions (Vitt et al., 2002). For an example of Web-based technology creating effective decision-making by Imperial Sugar's customers and vendors, see DSS in Action 1.2.

FIGURE 1.1   Factors Affecting Decision Making

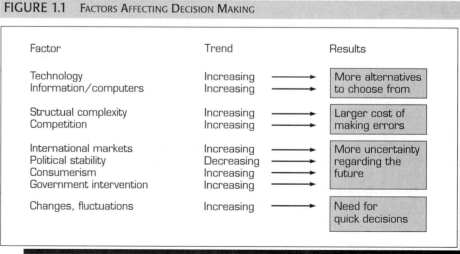

IMPERIAL SUGAR SWEETENS
THE DEAL WITH WEB SERVICES

Imperial Sugar (based in Sugarland, Texas) is the largest sugar refiner in the United States ($1.6 billion in sales in 2001). Nevertheless, the company was in the red in 2000 and 2001, with losses totaling more than $372 million. At the start of 2001, sugar prices collapsed, leading Imperial Sugar to file for bankruptcy protection. As a major part of Imperial's recovery program, CEO George Muller decided to use technology to improve the company's situation. His first effort involved integrating Imperial directly into its customers' supply chains by giving them direct access to order-status information on their orders via the Web. This would result in lower selling costs, and in consequence Imperial hoped to obtain a bigger share of its customers' business. The system would change the mostly personal relationships between Imperial's 20 customer service representatives and 40 large customers and brokers, representing more than 800 different customer offices. Decision-making at the company and for its customers would never be the same. In a commodity-based business, adding value is the only thing that differentiates one firm from another. This system added value!

The cost of the XML-based project was well less than $500,000. Just as Imperial emerged from bank-ruptcy in August, the self-service application was rolled out. Before the self-service system, a customer service representative might spend as many as five hours per day on the phone handling customer inquiries. Now, the time spent on status inquiries dropped to two hours or less. By halving the phone workload, Imperial nearly doubled its effective salesforce (in person-hours)—and its customer service representatives were able to take a more consultative approach to sales. Online order tracking gives customers 24-hour access to information about coming shipments, helping them to plan their production better.

Following system deployment, the company generated its first operating profit in six quarters: $669,000 on net sales of $322.3 million. In the long term, Imperial plans to do *collaborative forecasting of demand* with its customers to lower its inventory costs. By making the purchasing process easier, Imperial also plans to *analyze its customers' needs* to boost overall revenue, thus creating an effective revenue- management system. Finally, customers can order directly over the Web.

Source: Adapted from S. Gallagher, "Imperial Sugar Rebuilds on Web Services," *Baseline*, March 18, 2002.

1.4 MANAGERS AND COMPUTER SUPPORT

The impact of computer technology on organizations and society is increasing as new technologies evolve and current technologies expand. More and more aspects of organizational activities are characterized by interaction and cooperation between people and machines. From traditional uses in payroll and bookkeeping functions, computerized systems are now penetrating complex managerial areas ranging from the design and management of automated factories to the application of artificial intelligence methods to the evaluation of proposed mergers and acquisitions. Nearly all executives know that information technology is vital to their business and extensively use technologies, especially Web-based technologies.

Computer applications have moved from transaction processing and monitoring activities to problem analysis and solution applications, where much of the activity is handled over the Web (see Geoffrion and Krishnan, 2001). Topics such as data warehousing, data mining, online analytical processing, and the use of the Web via the Internet, intranets and extranets for decision support are the cornerstones of high-tech modern management at the start of the twenty-first century. Managers must have high-speed, networked information systems to assist them directly with their most important task: making decisions (see Hoch, 2001).

1.5 COMPUTERIZED DECISION SUPPORT AND THE SUPPORTING TECHNOLOGIES

A computerized decision support system may be needed for various reasons. For example:

- *Speedy computations.* A computer lets the decision-maker perform many computations quickly and at a low cost. Timely decisions are critical for many situations, ranging from a physician in an emergency room to a stock trader on the trading floor.

- *Improved communication.* Groups can collaborate and communicate readily with Web-based tools. Collaboration is especially important along the supply chain, where customers all the way through to vendors must share information.

- *Increased productivity.* Assembling a group of decision-makers, especially experts, may be costly. Computerized support can reduce the size of the group and enable its members to be at different locations (saving travel costs). In addition, the productivity of staff support (such as financial and legal analysts) may be increased. Productivity may also be increased by using optimization tools that determine the best way to run a business. See the Chapter 4 Case Applications; Sodhi, 2001; Keskinocak and Tayur, 2001, Geoffrion and Krishnan, 2001; Warren et al., 2002.

- *Technical support.* Many decisions involve complex computations. Data can be stored in different databases and at Web sites anywhere in the organization and even possibly outside the organization. The data may include text, sound, graphics, and video. It may be necessary to transmit them quickly from distant locations. Computers can search, store, and transmit needed data quickly, economically, and transparently.

- *Data warehouse access.* Large data warehouses, like the one operated by Wal-Mart, contain petabytes of data. Special methods, and sometimes parallel computing, are needed to organize and search the data.

- *Quality support.* Computers can improve the *quality* of the decisions made. For example, more data can be accessed, more alternatives can be evaluated, risk analysis can be performed quickly, and the views of experts (some of whom are in remote locations) can be collected quickly and at a lower cost. Expertise can even be derived directly from a computer system through artificial intelligence methods. With computers, decision-makers can perform complex simulations, check many possible scenarios, and assess diverse impacts quickly and economically (see Saltzman and Mehrotra, 2001). All these capabilities lead to better decisions.

- *Competitive edge: enterprise resource management and empowerment.* Competitive pressures make the job of decision-making difficult. Competition is based not just on price but on quality, timeliness, customization of products, and customer support. Organizations must be able to frequently and rapidly change their mode of operation, reengineer processes and structures, empower employees, and innovate. Decision-support technologies such as expert systems can create meaningful empowerment by allowing people to make good decisions quickly, even if they lack some knowledge. **Enterprise resource management (ERM)** systems are a type of decision support system that describes an entire organization, and help manage it. Finally, optimizing the supply chain requires special tools (see Keskinocak and Tayur, 2001; and Sodhi, 2001).

- *Overcoming cognitive limits in processing and storage.* According to Simon (1977), the human mind has only a limited ability to process and store information.

People may sometimes find it difficult to recall and use information in an error-free fashion.

Most decision-support methods provide for quick data queries and use models to convert the data into usable information for consideration by a decision-maker. For example, data can be fed into a forecasting model where they are converted into a forecast. The resulting forecast may be used as information for decision-making. It may be further converted by another model, thereby providing additional information for decision-making.

COGNITIVE LIMITS

The term **cognitive limits** indicates that an individual's problem-solving capability is limited when a wide range of diverse information and knowledge is required. Pooling several individuals may help, but problems of coordination and communication may arise in workgroups. Computerized systems enable people to quickly access and process vast amounts of stored information. Computers can also improve coordination and communication for group work, as is done in **group support systems (GSS), knowledge management systems (KMS),** and several types of **enterprise information systems (EIS).** The Web has contributed both to this problem and to its solution. For example, many of us are hit daily with a barrage of e-mail. Intelligent agents (a type of artificial intelligence) as part of an e-mail client system can effectively filter out the undesired e-mail messages.

DECISION SUPPORT TECHNOLOGIES

Decision support can be provided by one or more decision support technologies. The major decision support technologies are listed in DSS in Focus 1.3 together with the relevant chapter in this book. They are described briefly in this chapter. Related decision support technologies are described on the book's Web site (prenhall.com/turban) in Web Chapters. Which of these technologies should be used depends on the nature of the problem and the specific decision support configuration.

In this text, the term **management support system (MSS)** refers to the application of any technology, either as an independent tool or in combination with other information technologies, to support management tasks in general and decision-making in particular. This term may be used interchangeably with decision support system (DSS) and business intelligence (BI) system.

1.6 A FRAMEWORK FOR DECISION SUPPORT

Before describing specific management support technologies, we present a classic framework for decision support. This framework provides several major concepts that will be used in forthcoming definitions. It also helps to cover several additional issues, such as the relationship between the technologies and the evolution of computerized systems. Gorry and Scott Morton (1971), who combined the work of Simon (1977) and Anthony (1965), proposed this framework, shown as Figure 1.2.

DSS IN FOCUS 1.3

MANAGEMENT SUPPORT SYSTEM TECHNOLOGIES (TOOLS)

- Decision support systems (DSS) (Chapter 3)
- Management science (MS)/operations research (OR) models and techniques (Chapter 4)
- Business analytics (Chapter 4)
- Data mining (Chapter 5)
- Data warehousing (Chapter 5)
- Business intelligence (Chapter 5)
- Online analytical processing (OLAP) (Chapter 5)
- Computer-assisted systems engineering (CASE) tools (Chapter 6)
- Group support systems (GSS)/collaborative computing (Chapter 7)
- Enterprise information systems (EIS) and enterprise information portals (EIP) (Chapter 8)
- Enterprise resource management (ERM)/enterprise resource planning (ERP) systems (Chapter 8)
- Customer resource management (CRM) systems (Chapter 8)
- Supply-chain management (SCM) (Chapter 8)
- Knowledge management systems (KMS) and knowledge management portals (KMP) (Chapter 9)
- Expert systems (ES) (Chapters 10 and 11)
- Artificial neural networks (ANN), genetic algorithms, fuzzy logic, and hybrid intelligent support systems (Chapter 12)
- Intelligent systems over the Internet (intelligent agents) (Chapter 13)
- Electronic Commerce DSS (Chapter 14)

The left side of Figure 1.2 is based on Simon's idea that decision-making processes fall along a continuum that ranges from highly structured (sometimes called *programmed*) to highly unstructured (*nonprogrammed*) decisions. Structured processes are routine, and typically repetitive problems for which standard solution methods exist. **Unstructured** processes are fuzzy, complex problems for which there are no cut-and-dried solution methods. Simon also describes the decision-making process with a three-phase process of intelligence, design, and choice (see Chapter 2).

> *Intelligence:* searching for conditions that call for decisions
> *Design:* inventing, developing, and analyzing possible courses of action
> *Choice:* selecting a course of action from those available

An *unstructured problem* is one in which none of these three phases is structured. Decisions in which some but not all of the phases are structured are called **semistructured** by Gorry and Scott Morton.

In a *structured problem*, the procedures for obtaining the best (or at least a good-enough) solution are known. Whether the problem involves finding an appropriate inventory level or choosing an optimal investment strategy, the objectives are clearly defined. Common objectives are cost minimization and profit maximization. The manager can use the support of clerical, data processing, or management science models. Management support systems such as DSS and **expert systems** can be useful at times. In an *unstructured problem*, human intuition is often the basis for decision-making. Typical unstructured problems include planning new services, hiring an executive, and choosing a set of research and development projects for the next year. Only part of an unstructured problem can by supported by advanced decision support tools, such as expert systems (ES), **group support systems (GSS),** and knowledge management systems (KMS). Gathering information via the Web is helpful in solving unstructured problems. *Semistructured problems* fall between structured and unstructured prob-

Type of Decision	Type of Control			Technology Support Needed
	Operational Control	**Managerial Control**	**Strategic Planning**	
Structured	Accounts receivable, account payable, order entry **1**	Budget analysis, short-term forecasting, personnel reports, make-or-buy **2**	Financial management (investment), warehouse location, distribution systems **3**	Management information system, management science models, transaction processing
Semistructured	Production scheduling, inventory control **4**	Credit evaluation, budget preparation, plant layout, project scheduling, reward system design, inventory categorization **5**	Building new plant, mergers and acquisitions, new product planning, compensation planning, quality assurance planning, HR policies, inventory planning **6**	DSS, KMS, GSS, CRM, SCM
Unstructured	Selecting a cover for a magazine, buying software, approving loans help desk **7**	Negotiating, recruiting an executive, buying hardware, lobbying **8**	R & D planning, new technology development, social responsibility planning **9**	GSS, KMS ES, neural networks
Technology Support Needed	Management information system, management science	Management science, DSS, ES, EIS, SCM CRM, GSS, SCM	GSS, CRM EIS, ES, neural networks, KMS	

FIGURE 1.2   DECISION SUPPORT FRAMEWORKS

lems, having some structured elements and some unstructured elements. Solving them involves a combination of both standard solution procedures and human judgment. Keen and Scott Morton (1978) mention trading bonds, setting marketing budgets for consumer products, and performing capital acquisition analysis as semistructured problems. DSS provides models for the portion of the decision-making problem that is structured. For these, a DSS can improve the quality of the information on which the decision is based by providing not only a single solution but also a range of alternative solutions along with their potential impacts. These capabilities help managers to better understand the nature of problems and thus to make better decisions.

The second half of this framework (Figure 1.2, top) is based on Anthony's (1965) taxonomy, which defines three broad categories that encompass all managerial activities: *strategic planning*, defining long-range goals and policies for resource allocation; *management control*, the acquisition and efficient use of resources in the accomplishment of organizational goals; and *operational control*, the efficient and effective execution of specific tasks.

Anthony and Simon's taxonomies are combined in the nine-cell decision support framework shown in Figure 1.2. The right-hand column and the bottom row indicate the technologies needed to support the various decisions. Gorry and Scott Morton suggested, for example, that for **semistructured decisions** and **unstructured decisions,** conventional management information systems (MIS) and **management science (MS)** approaches are insufficient. Human intellect and a different approach to computer technologies are necessary. They proposed the use of a supportive information system, which they called a decision support system (DSS).

The more structured and operational control-oriented tasks (cells 1, 2, and 4) are performed by low-level managers, whereas the tasks in cells 6, 8, and 9 are the responsibility of top executives or highly trained specialists. This means that KMS, neural computing, and ES are more often applicable for people tackling specialized, complex problems.

The Gorry and Scott Morton framework classifies problems and helps us select appropriate tools. However, there are times when a structured approach may help in solving unstructured tasks, and vice versa. In addition, combinations of tools may be used.

COMPUTER SUPPORT FOR STRUCTURED DECISIONS

Structured and some semistructured decisions, especially of the operational and managerial control type, have been supported by computers since the 1960s. Decisions of this type are made in all functional areas, especially in finance and production (operations management).

Such problems, which are encountered often, have a high level of structure. It is therefore possible to abstract and analyze them and classify them into specific classical problem types. For example, a make-or-buy decision belongs in this category. Other examples are capital budgeting, allocation of resources, distribution problems, procurement, planning, and inventory control. For each type of problem, an easy-to-apply prescribed model and solution approach have been developed, generally as quantitative formulas. This approach is called management science (MS) or **operations research (OR).**

MANAGEMENT SCIENCE

The management science approach adopts the view that managers follow a systematic process in solving problems. Therefore, it is possible to use a scientific approach to automate portions of managerial decision-making. The systematic process involves the following steps:

1. Defining the problem (a decision situation that may deal with some difficulty or with an opportunity).
2. Classifying the problem into a standard category.
3. Constructing a mathematical model that describes the real-world problem.
4. Finding possible solutions to the modeled problem and evaluating them.
5. Choosing and recommending a solution to the problem.

The management science process is based on mathematical modeling (algebraic expressions that describe the problem). Modeling involves transforming the real-world problem into an appropriate prototype structure (model). There are computerized methodologies that find solutions to this model quickly and efficiently. Some of these are deployed directly over the Web (e.g., Fourer and Goux, 2001). Less structured problems can be handled only by a DSS that includes customized modeling capabilities. For example, in a bookstore, the given annual demand for a particular kind of book implies that a standard inventory management model could be used to determine the number of books to order, but human judgment is necessary to predict demand and order quantities that vary over time for blockbuster authors, such as John Grisham and Stephen King.

Since the development of the Internet and World Wide Web servers and tools, there have been dramatic changes in how decision-makers are supported. Most importantly, the Web provides (1) access to a vast body of data available around the world, and (2) a common, user-friendly graphical user interface (GUI), which is easy to learn and use and readily available. At the structured operational level (1), these are the most critical Web impacts. As enhanced collaboration becomes more important, we find the inclusion of enterprise systems that include **supply chain management,** customer relationship management, and knowledge management systems.

1.7 THE CONCEPT OF DECISION SUPPORT SYSTEMS

In the early 1970s, Scott Morton first articulated the major concepts of DSS. He defined DSS as "interactive computer-based systems, which help decision-makers utilize data and models to solve unstructured problems" (Gorry and Scott Morton, 1971). Another classic DSS definition, provided by Keen and Scott Morton (1978), is:

> Decision support systems couple the intellectual resources of individuals with the capabilities of the computer to improve the quality of decisions. It is a computer-based support system for management decision makers who deal with semistructured problems.

Note that the term decision support system, like management information system and other terms in the field of Management support systems (MSS), is a content-free expression; that is, it means different things to different people. Therefore, *there is no universally accepted definition of DSS.* We present the major definitions in Chapter 3.

DSS AS AN UMBRELLA TERM

DSS is used by some as a specific tool. The term DSS is also sometimes used as an umbrella term to describe any computerized system that supports decision-making in an organization. An organization may have a knowledge management system to guide all its personnel in their problem-solving, it may have separate DSS for marketing, finance, and accounting, a supply chain management (SCM) system for production, and several expert systems for product repair diagnostics and help desks. DSS encompasses them all. In contrast, a narrow definition refers to a specific technology (see Chapter 3).

DSS in Action 1.4 demonstrates some of the major characteristics of a decision support system. The initial risk analysis was based on the decision-maker's definition of the situation using a management science approach. Then the executive vice president, using his experience, judgment, and intuition, felt that the model should be scrutinized. The initial model, although mathematically correct, was incomplete. With a regular simulation system, a modification would have taken a long time, but the DSS provided a quick analysis. Furthermore, the DSS was flexible and responsive enough to allow managerial intuition and judgment to be incorporated into the analysis. A similar incident occurred at American Airlines in the 1980s. Through a detailed and complex analysis, analysts determined that the airline could save hundreds of millions of dollars

DSS IN ACTION 1.4

THE HOUSTON MINERALS CASE

Houston Minerals Corporation was interested in a proposed joint venture with a petrochemical company to develop a chemical plant. Houston's executive vice president responsible for the decision wanted an analysis of the risks involved in the areas of supplies, demands, and prices. Bob Sampson, manager of planning and administration, and his staff built a DSS in a few days by means of a specialized planning language. The results strongly suggested that the project should be accepted.

Then came the real test. Although the executive vice president accepted the validity and value of the results, he was worried about the project's downside risk: the chance of a catastrophic outcome. As Sampson tells it, he said something like this: "I know how much work you have already done, and I am ninety-nine percent confident with it. However, I would like to see this in a different light. I know we are short of time, and we have to get back to our partners with our yes or no decision."

Sampson replied that the executive could have the risk analysis he needed in less than an hour. He continued. "Within twenty minutes, there in the executive boardroom, we were reviewing the results of his what-if? questions. The results led to the eventual dismissal of the project, which we otherwise would probably have accepted."

Source: Based on information provided by Comshare, Inc.

annually in fuel costs by using altitude profiles. An airplane could ascend optimally to its cruising altitude as a function of meteorological conditions, its route, and other traffic. A second analysis requested by the CEO confirmed that the initial analysis was indeed correct. The CEO felt more comfortable about the solution to this fuzzy problem. However, in this case the delay in implementing the decision cost the airline several million dollars.

How can a thorough risk analysis like the one in DSS in Action 1.4 be performed so quickly? How can the judgment factors be elicited, quantified, and worked into a model? How can the results be presented meaningfully and convincingly to the executive? What are "what-if" questions? How can the Web be used to access appropriate data and models, and integrate them? We provide answers to these questions throughout this book.

WHY USE A DSS?

Surveys have identified the many reasons why major corporations have developed large-scale decision support systems. These include:

Companies work in an unstable or rapidly changing economy.
There are difficulties in tracking the numerous business operations.
Competition has increased.
Electronic commerce.
Existing systems do not support decision-making.
The Information systems department is too busy and cannot address all
    management inquiries.
Special analysis of profitability and efficiency is needed.
Accurate information is needed.
DSS is viewed as an organizational winner.
New information is needed.

Management mandates a DSS.
Higher decision quality.
Improved communication.
Improved customer and employee satisfaction.
Timely information is provided.
Cost reduction is achieved (cost and timesaving, increased productivity).

Another reason for DSS development is the high level of computer and Web literacy among managers. Most end-users are not programmers, so they need easy-to-use development tools and procedures. They need access to data in an understandable format and the ability to manipulate them in meaningful ways. These are provided by Web-based DSS.

In the early days of DSS, managers did not depend on numbers. Many managers preferred to manage by intuition. As time went by, managers did indeed use MIS-generated reports, but the gut feel of what was right was what was important in solving a problem. As PC technology advanced, a new generation of managers evolved—one that was comfortable with computing and knew that the technology helped them make intelligent business decisions faster. During the 1990s, the business intelligence technologies industry grew steadily, with revenues reaching into the low billions, according to an IDC report from the period. Now, new tools like online analytical processing, data warehousing, data mining, enterprise information systems, and knowledge management systems, delivered via Web technology, promise managers easy access to tools, models, and data for decision-making. These tools are also described under the names

---

DSS IN ACTION 1.5

HELPING ATLANTIC ELECTRIC COMPANY SURVIVE IN THE FREE MARKETPLACE

Atlantic Electric Company of New Jersey was losing the monopoly it once held. Some of its old clients were already buying electricity from a new, unregulated type of competitor: an independent co-generator that generated its own electricity and sold its additional capacity to other companies at low prices. The competitor found easy-to-serve commercial accounts. Atlantic Electric Company was even in danger of losing its residential customer base because the local regulatory commission was about to rule that these customers would be better served by another utility.

To survive, the company had to become the least expensive provider in its territory. One way to do this was to provide employees with the information they needed to make more up-to-date and accurate business decisions. The old information technology included a mainframe and a corporate network for mainframe access. However, this system was unable to meet the new challenge. It was necessary to develop user applications, in a familiar format, and to do it rapidly with minimum cost. This required a PC-based decision support system that currently runs on the corporate intranet.

Some of the applications developed include

- A DSS for fuel-purchasing decisions
- A DSS for customized rates, based on a database for customers and their electricity usage pattern
- A DSS for substation design and transmission
- A cash-management DSS for the finance department

The implementation of these and other DSS applications helped the company to survive and successfully compete in its field. By 2000, the company had deployed the DSS applications on its intranet, an internal Internet-based system that includes Web servers and uses Web browsers for access (see atlanticelectric.com).

of business intelligence and business analytics. See Hapgood (2001) for details. See also Cohen et al. (2001), Hoch et al. (2001), Powers (2002), and Vitt et al. (2002).

The overall results of using a DSS can be impressive, as indicated by the Atlantic Electric Company case (see DSS in Action 1.5).

We next describe some of the most important DSS technologies. In Table 1.2, we describe how the World Wide Web has affected important DSS technologies, and vice versa. In most cases, the communications capabilities of the Internet/Web have affected managers' practices in terms of accessing data and files, and of communicating with one other. The Web readily permits collaboration through communication. Data (including text, graphics, video clips, etc.) are stored on Web servers or legacy (older mainframe) systems that deliver data to the Web server and then to the client Web browser. The Web browser and its associated technologies and scripting languages have raised the bar in terms of processing on the client side, and presenting information to the user. High-resolution graphics through a powerful GUI is the norm for how we interact with computer systems.

1.8 GROUP SUPPORT SYSTEMS

Groups make many major decisions in organizations. Getting a group together in one place and at one time can be difficult and expensive. Furthermore, traditional meetings can last a long time, and any resulting decisions may be mediocre.

Attempts to improve the work of groups with the aid of information technology have been described as collaborative computing systems, groupware, electronic meeting systems, and GSS (see DSS in Action 1.6). Most groupware currently runs over the Web and provides both videoconferencing and audio conferencing, in addition to meeting tools like electronic brainstorming, voting, and document sharing. Groupware includes Groupsystems, Groove, PlaceWare, WebEx. NetMeeting, and even distance learning courseware tools, such as Blackboard.

1.9 ENTERPRISE INFORMATION SYSTEMS

Enterprise information systems (EIS) evolved from executive information systems combined with Web technologies. Enterprise information *portals* are now utilized to view information that spans the entire organization. Enterprise information systems give access to relevant enterprise-wide information that individuals need to perform their tasks.

- Provide an organizational view of operations
- Provide an extremely user-friendly interface through portals, sometimes compatible with individual decision styles
- Provide timely and effective corporate level tracking and control
- Provide quick access to detailed information behind text, numbers, or graphics through *drill-down*
- Filter, compress, and track critical data and information
- Identify problems (opportunities).

TABLE 1.2   MSS Technologies and the Web

MSS Technology	Web Impact	Effect on the Web
Database Management Systems (DBMS) and Management Information Systems (MIS)	Improved, Universal Graphical User Interfaces (GUI) Quick Access to Data Anywhere, Anytime, In Many Formats Improved Communication of Data and Results	Database Web servers provide information directly rather than accessing data stored on legacy systems Database organization helps in Web database design and development
Model-base management systems (MBMS) and models (business analytics)	Access and interface Models and solution methods easily distributed Java applets of optimization and simulation code Access to information about models and solution methods	Better network design through optimization and simulation Improved network infrastructure design Optimal message routing Improved integrated circuit and circuit board design
Revenue management	Improved data access and interface Improved data gathering More accurate, advanced economic and forecasting models and data	Accurate, dynamic pricing of Web services and software
Online analytical processing (OLAP)/ Business intelligence (BI)	Improved data access and interface Better access to solution and visualization tools Better communication-can utilize parallel processing	Analysis of network design and loads on Web sites-more effective Web sites
Data mining (BI) (includes models)	Improved data access and interface Better access to solution tools Better communication-can utilize parallel processing	Identify relationships among customers and other factors that indicate loads on Web sites-more effective Web sites
Data warehousing	Improved data access and interface	Need to handle large amounts of data, graphs, charts, etc.
Geographic information systems (GIS)	Improved data access and interface Improved communication Improved visualization	Accurate geographic data leads to more effective network design and efficient message passing
Systems development tools and methods: Computer-aided systems engineering (CASE)	Improved data access and interface and data	Design of Web applications follows a defined path Diagrams and methodologies are applied to network, database and server design and development
Group support systems (GSS)	Provides access to data, information, and models Enables communication and collaboration	Older systems via telephone and LANs indicated how the Web could provide these capabilities Collaborative network and e-commerce site design Access to experts on e-commerce
Enterprise information systems (EIS)/ Enterprise information portals	Access to relevant information in many formats Web browsers provide GUIs that appeal to executives with drill-down capability Communication capabilities with others in the organization	Intranet structuring Financial decisions regarding the Web's design, equipment, and use Identification of strategic Web use

(continued)

TABLE 1.2   MSS Technologies and the Web (*continued*)

MSS Technology	*Web Impact*	*Effect on the Web*
Enterprise resource planning (ERP)/ Enterprise resource management (ERM)	Access to data and the interface enabled their expansion	Used by e-commerce firms for operations
Customer relationship (resource) management (CRM)	Access to data and the interface Enabled their development and expansion	Increased load due to customer reach Provides new products and technologies that customers want
Supply chain management (SCM)	Improved communication and collaboration along the supply chain Web tools have become embedded in SCM Access to optimization tools	Improved production of Web hardware and software Improved communication of problems from customers to vendors helps in identifying problems with the Web
Knowledge management systems (KMS)	Provides the communication, collaboration, and storage technologies—anytime, anywhere Access to legacy systems Provides collaboration needed for knowledge gathering	Designers and developers can access and share knowledge and information about Web infrastructure for improvements
Executive information systems (EIS)	Provides improved access to a information in a variety of formats Improved, standardized GUI Drill-down into legacy systems and Web database servers	In the late 1970s, EIS already incorporated user-seductive GUI interfaces, and access to information in a variety of formats EIS also incorporated a client/server architecture—adopted by Web systems Showed what computers were capable of These capabilities were eventually incorporated into all Web-based systems
Expert systems (ES)	Improved interface and access to knowledge Access to experts Deployable applets for system development and deployment	Provides expertise in network and circuit design and troubleshooting
Artificial neural networks (ANN)	Deployable applets for system development and deployment	Detects credit card and other fraud in e-commerce Identifies Web use patterns
Genetic algorithms (GA)	Deployable applets for system development and deployment	Solves dynamic message routing and design problems
Fuzzy logic (FL)	Deployable applets for system development and deployment	Solves dynamic message routing and design problems
Intelligent agents (IA)	Enables them to travel and run on different sites, especially enabling automatic negotiations	Enables intelligent Web search engines, efficient message passing
Electronic commerce (e-commerce)	Enabled by the Web	Web products and services

Notes: Some technologies listed are not strictly MSS technologies, but they are used by decision-makers.

All technologies have improved user interfaces and transparent or at least easier access to data.

This table contains a sample of impacts.

DSS IN ACTION 1.6

GROUPSYSTEMS ENHANCE TRAINING
OF THE HONG KONG POLICE FORCE (HKPF)

THE PROBLEM

The HKPF runs management skills training courses for its police officers. These involve deliberation of topics central to police work, with officers expected to reach a decision and develop an action plan. The police have traditionally used face-to-face discussion and "butcher paper" for these sessions but found that discussions lacked depth and that a minority of "loud" officers dominated many sessions.

THE SOLUTION

The course director (a senior officer), turned to GroupSystems software (Groupsystems.com, Tucson, Arizona) to enhance the quality of the training provided. Officers, in groups of five to eight, brainstormed issues online before voting on key solution components and developing action plans. Topics include the repatriation of Vietnamese migrants and combating CD-ROM piracy. The course director used GroupSystems to inject his own contributions into the discussions as they were in progress, modifying the problem context and increasing the realism of the material. Officers were expected to incorporate these new challenges on the fly.

THE RESULTS

The officers, despite their lack of familiarity with GroupSystems, expressed general approval of the software, believing that their learning experience had been significantly enhanced and that their skills in eliciting and discussing critical issues had been developed remarkably. The course director was similarly satisfied, acknowledging that more had been accomplished than would normally be possible given session constraints. No officer rated the sessions negatively, even though some admitted their computer phobia and inability to type effectively. All used the system to contribute valuable ideas, and the dominance of individual officers was much reduced. These positive impacts occur routinely, as is evident from success stories on groupware vendor Web sites.

Source: Contributed by Robert Davison, City University of Hong Kong (Jan. 2000). Used with permission.

In DSS in Action 1.7, we describe how Cisco's sales department uses its enterprise information system, which hooks into its supply chain management system, to alert managers about possible problems as they occur in real time.

There are several important specialized enterprise information systems. These include **enterprise resource management (ERM)** systems/**enterprise resource planning (ERP)** systems, customer relationship management (CRM) systems, and supply chain management (SCM) systems.

Strong global competition drives companies to find ways to reduce costs, improve customer service, and increase productivity. One area where substantial savings are realized is the streamlining of the various activities conducted along the supply chain, both inside a company and throughout the extended supply chain that includes its suppliers, business partners, and customers (e.g., Sodhi, 2001; Sodhi and Aichlmayr, 2001). Using various information technologies and decision support methodologies, companies attempt to integrate as many information support systems as possible. Two major concepts are involved. First, **enterprise resource planning (ERP)** (also called enterprise resource management) tries to integrate, within one organization, repetitive transaction processing systems, such as ordering, producing, packaging, costing, delivery, and billing. Such integration involves many decisions that can be facilitated by DSS or provide a fertile ground for DSS applications. Second, supply chain management (SCM) attempts to improve tasks within the various segments of the supply chain, such as manufacturing and human resource management, as well as along the entire extended chain. The previously described decision support tools can enhance SCM, especially management science

DSS IN ACTION 1.7

CISCO'S ENTERPRISE INFORMATION SYSTEM / PORTAL: A DIGITAL DASHBOARD DRIVES THE COMPANY

Ideally, everyone in an organization should have access to the real-time information that is needed for decision-making. At Cisco, "The whole corporation is moving to real time," says Mike Zill, director of sales and finance information technology. "It's difficult to have the applications stay in batch when the architecture is message-based."

Sales department managers use a Web-based "dashboard," or enterprise information portal (a graphical user-interface-based view), from OneChannel Inc. (Mountain View, California). The dashboard gives them real-time views of their accounts' activities. Just as a red light appears on a car's dashboard when there is a problem, the software triggers an alert when a business condition hits a predetermined threshold, sending a message or warning to the user's dashboard. For example, if

Cisco's sales department has a top-ten list of new products it wants sold, the application will let the Cisco manager know the instant the distributor's sales fall outside target levels.

Cisco had to build deep hooks into its supply chain. Once it receives the data, Cisco couples them with real-time Web-based inventory information and processes them using analytics software from Hyperion Solutions Corp. in Sunnyvale, California. Channel managers can then query the Hyperion software in detail through the OneChannel dashboard to find the underlying causes of any problem.

Source: Adapted from M. Hall, "Web Analytics: Get Real." *ComputerWorld*, Vol. 36, No. 14, April 1, 2002, pp. 42–43.

methods that can be used to optimize the supply chain (see Keskinocak and Tayur, 2001), and group support systems that enhance collaboration from vendors through to customers. SCM involves many nonroutine decisions. These topics are related to enterprise systems, such as organizational decision support systems, EIS, and intranet applications. They are also related to interorganizational systems and concepts. such as customer relationship management (CRM) (Swift, 2001), extranets, and virtual organizations. Related to these are revenue management systems, which utilize demand and pricing forecasts to establish the right product at the right price at the right time at the right location in the right format for the right customer (see Cross, 1997; Smith et al., 2001; and e-optimization.com, 2002).

Web technologies are critical for the success of EIS, SCM, CRM, and now revenue management. The Web provides access to terabytes of data in data warehouses and business intelligence / business analytics tools like those in **online analytical processing (OLAP)** and data mining, which are used to establish relationships that lead to higher profitability (Callaghan, 2002). Data access, communication, and collaboration are critical in making MSS technologies work.

Closely interrelated to these is electronic commerce (e-commerce), which includes not only electronic markets, but also interorganizational electronic systems, Web-based customer services, intraorganizational applications, and business-processes reengineering. Of course, the Web and its associated technologies are critical for all aspects of e-commerce and its success. See DSS in Action 1.2.

1.10 KNOWLEDGE MANAGEMENT SYSTEMS

Past knowledge and expertise can often be used to expedite decision-making. It does not make sense to reinvent the wheel each time a decision-making situation is encountered. The knowledge accumulated in organizations over time can be used to solve identical or similar problems. There are several important issues to address: where to find knowledge, how to classify it, how to ensure its quality, how to store it, how to maintain it, and how to use it. Furthermore, it is important to motivate people to contribute their knowledge, because much knowledge is usually not documented. Moreover, when people leave an organization, they take their knowledge with them. Knowledge management systems (KMS) and their associated technologies deal with these issues. Knowledge is organized and stored in a **knowledge repository,** a kind of textual database. When a problem has to be solved, or an opportunity to be assessed, the relevant knowledge can be found and extracted from the knowledge repository. **Knowledge management systems** have the potential to dramatically leverage knowledge use in an organization. Documented cases indicate that *returns on investment are as high as a factor of 25 within one to two years* (see Housel and Bell, 2001). Web technologies feature prominently in almost all KMS. Web technologies provide the communication, collaboration, and storage capabilities so needed by KMS.

There are many kinds of knowledge management systems, and they can be used to support decision-making in several ways, including allowing employees direct access to usable knowledge and to people who have the knowledge. One important application is described in DSS in Action 1.8.

1.11 EXPERT SYSTEMS

When an organization has a complex decision to make or a problem to solve, it often turns to experts for advice. The experts it selects have specific knowledge about and experience in the problem area. They are aware of the alternatives, the chances of success, and the benefits and costs the business may incur. Companies engage experts for

---

DSS IN ACTION 1.8

XEROX CORPORATION'S KNOWLEDGE BASE HELPS THE COMPANY SURVIVE

With decreasing demand for copying, Xerox Corporation has been struggling to survive the digital revolution. Championed by Cindy Casslman, the company pioneered an intranet-based knowledge repository in 1996, with the objective of delivering information and knowledge to the company's employees. A second objective was to create a sharing virtual community. Known as the first knowledge base (FKB), the system was designed initially to support salespeople so that they could quickly answer customers' queries. Before FKB, it frequently took hours of investigation to collect information to answer one query. Since each salesperson had to deal with several queries simultaneously, clients sometimes had to wait days for a reply. Now a salesperson can log on to the KMS and in a few minutes provide answers to the client. Customers tend to have similar questions, and when a solution to an inquiry is found, it is indexed so that it can be quickly found when needed by another salesperson. An average saving of two days per inquiry was realized. In addition to improved customer service, the accumulated knowledge is analyzed to learn about products' strengths and weaknesses, customer demand trends, and so on. Employees now share their knowledge and help each other. Xerox had a major problem when it introduced the FKB; it had to persuade people to share and contribute knowledge as well as to go on the intranet and use the knowledge base. This required an *organizational culture change* that took several years to implement. The FKB continues to evolve and expand rapidly (which is not unusual in KMS implementations). People in almost every area of the company, worldwide, are now making much faster and frequently better decisions.

advice on such matters as what equipment to buy, mergers and acquisitions, major problem diagnostics in the field, and advertising strategy. The more unstructured the situation, the more specialized (and expensive) the advice is. **Expert systems** attempt to mimic human experts' problem-solving abilities.

Typically, an expert system (ES) is a decision-making or problem-solving software package that can reach a level of performance comparable to—or even exceeding—that of a human expert in some specialized and usually narrow problem area. The basic idea behind an ES, an applied artificial intelligence technology, is simple. **Expertise** is transferred from the expert to a computer. This knowledge is then stored in the computer, and users run the computer for specific advice as needed. The ES asks for facts and can make inferences and arrive at a specific conclusion. Then, like a human consultant, it advises nonexperts and explains, if necessary, the logic behind the advice. Expert systems are used today in thousands of organizations, and they support many tasks. For example, see AIS (Artificial Intelligence Systems) in Action 1.9. Expert systems are often integrated with or even embedded in other information technologies. Most new ES software is implemented in Web tools (e.g., Java applets), installed on Web servers, and use Web-browsers for their interfaces. For example, Corvid Exsys is written in Java and runs as an applet.

1.12 ARTIFICIAL NEURAL NETWORKS

The application of the technologies mentioned above was based on the use of explicit data, information, or knowledge stored in a computer and manipulated as needed. However, in the complex real world we may not have explicit data, information, or knowledge. People often must make decisions based on partial, incomplete, or inexact information. Such conditions are created in rapidly changing environments. Decision-makers use their experiences to handle these situations; that is, they recall similar experiences and learn from them what to do with similar new situations for which exact replicas are unavailable. When this approach to problem-solving is computerized, we call it **machine learning,** and its primary tools are **artificial neural networks (ANN)** and case-based reasoning.

Neural computing, or an artificial neural network (ANN), uses a pattern-recognition approach to problem-solving, and they have been employed successfully in many business applications (Fadlalla and Lin, 2001; Haykin, 1999; Ainscough et al., 1997). An ANN *learns* patterns in data presented during training and can apply what it has learned to new cases. One important application is that of bank loan approval. An ANN can learn to identify potential loan defaulters from patterns. One of the most successful applications of an ANN is in detecting unusual credit card spending patterns, thus identifying fraudulent charges. This is especially important for the many Web-based transactions of e-commerce (see AIS in Action 1.10).

1.13 ADVANCED INTELLIGENT DECISION SUPPORT SYSTEMS

At the cutting edge of applied artificial intelligence are several exciting technologies that assist decision-makers. These include genetic algorithms, fuzzy logic, and intelligent agents (IA).

Genetic algorithms solve problems in an evolutionary way. They mimic the process of evolution and search for an extremely good solution. Survival of the fittest guides this method. Genetic algorithms have been used to maximize advertising profit at tele-

AIS IN ACTION 1.9

EXPERT SYSTEMS PROVIDE USEFUL ADVICE

Suppose you manage an *engineering firm* that bids on many projects. Each project is, in a sense, unique. You can calculate your expected cost, but that is not sufficient to determine your bid. You have background information on your likely competitors and their bidding strategies. Something is known about the risks: possible technical problems, political delays, material shortages, or other sources of trouble. An experienced proposal manager can generally put all this together and arrive at a sound judgment concerning terms and bidding price. However, you do not have that many experienced proposal managers. This is where expert systems become useful. An expert system can capture the lines of thinking the experienced proposal managers can follow. It can also catalog information gained on competitors, local risks, and so on, and can incorporate your policies and strategies concerning risk, pricing, and terms. It can help your inexperienced proposal managers develop an informed bid consistent with your policy.

A *bank loan officer* must make many decisions daily about who is a good credit risk and who is not. Once information is gathered about a client, an expert can readily estimate the likelihood that he or she will pay back a loan or default on it. Sometimes a loan officer is busy, unavailable, or even new to the job. A Web-based expert system can help. All the needed data are captured and placed into a database. An expert system can then determine the likelihood of a good risk. Furthermore, it can determine what the potential borrower can do to improve his or her likelihood of obtaining a loan (e.g., pay off some credit cards, ask for a smaller loan or higher interest rate). A final benefit is

that an expert system can indicate when it does not know, and the loan officer can focus only on these difficult cases rather than the easy yes/no decisions.

Suppose you are a *life insurance agent*, and you are a good one; however, your market has changed. You are no longer competing only with other insurance agents. You are also competing with banks, brokers, money market fund managers, and the like. Your company now carries a whole array of products, from universal life insurance to venture capital funds. Your clients have the same problems as ever, but they are more inquisitive, more sophisticated, and more conscious of tax avoidance and similar considerations. How can you give them advice and put together a sensible package for them when you are more confused than they are? How can you provide service to your customers and market new services to existing and new customers over the Web? Try an expert system for support.

Financial planning systems and estate planning guides have been part of the insurance industry's marketing kit for a long time. However, sensible financial planning takes more skill than the average insurance agent has or can afford to acquire. This is one reason why the fees of professional planners are as high as they are. A number of insurance companies have been investing heavily in artificial intelligence techniques in the hope that these techniques can be used to build sophisticated, competitive, knowledge-based financial planning support systems to assist their agents in helping their clients.

Source: Part is condensed from a publicly disclosed project description of Arthur D. Little, Inc.

vision stations, and facilities layout among other applications. Genetic algorithms have been implemented directly in Java applets (and other Web technology), and in spreadsheets (e.g., evolver from Palisade Software).

Fuzzy logic approaches problems the way people do. It can handle the imprecise nature of how humans communicate information. For example, you might say, "The weather is really hot!" on a hot day. Consider how *hot* is *hot*? Would one degree cooler still be *really hot*, or simply *hot*? This imprecision can be handled mathematically in a precise way to assist decision-makers in solving problems with imprecise statements of their parameters. Usually fuzzy logic methods are combined with other artificial intelligence methods, such as expert systems and artificial neural networks, to boost their accuracy in their decision-making.

Intelligent agents (intelligent software agents, softbots) help in automating various tasks, increasing productivity and quality. Most intelligent systems include expert sys-

AIS IN ACTION 1.10

SUMITOMO CREDIT SERVICE: AN EXPANDING WORLD MARKET

With close to 18 million cardholders and 1.8 million merchants nationwide, the Sumitomo Credit Service Co., Ltd., was the leading credit card issuer in Japan in 2000. Sumitomo Credit Service is recognized as an innovator in the Japanese consumer credit industry, both for its international business strategy and its early adoption of technical advances in card processing.

When credit card fraud became a critical issue in the Japanese market in 1996, Sumitomo Credit Service decided to implement Falcon, a neural network–based system from HNC Software. The system excelled in identifying fraud patterns that had gone undetected before. HNC had never before implemented a Japanese version of Falcon, complete with features specific to the Japanese market, such as the double-byte architecture necessary for Japanese characters.

Sumitomo Credit Service was the first issuer in Japan to implement predictive software solutions, and the enhanced power to predict fraud has become Sumitomo Credit Service's competitive advantage in the security and risk-management area. A neural network, as we will see in Chapters 12, uses historical data to predict the future behavior of systems, people, and markets to meet the growing demand for predictive analysis to provide effective consumer business strategies.

Source: Compiled from HNC Software Web Site: hnc.com, San Diego, CA, 2000.

tems or another intelligent component. Intelligent agents play an increasingly important role in electronic commerce (Turban and King, 2003). Like a good human agent (travel agent, real estate agent, etc.), these systems learn what you want to do, and eventually take over and can perform many of your mundane tasks.

1.14 HYBRID SUPPORT SYSTEMS

The objective of a **computer-based information system (CBIS),** regardless of its name or nature, is to assist management in solving managerial or organizational problems faster and better than is possible without computers. To attain this objective, the system may use one or more information technologies. Every type of CBIS has certain advantages and disadvantages. By integrating technologies, we can improve decision-making, because one technology can provide advantages where another is weak.

Machine repair provides a useful analogy. The repair technician diagnoses the problem and identifies the best tools to make the repair. Although only one tool may be sufficient, it is often necessary to use several tools to improve results. Sometimes there may be no standard tools. Then special tools must be developed, like a ratchet tip at the end of a screwdriver handle, or a screwdriver blade at the end of a ratchet wrench to reach into those hard to get places. The managerial decision-making process described in DSS in Action 1.11 illustrates the combined use of several MSS technologies in solving a single enterprise-wide problem. United Sugars is a competitor of Imperial Sugar (DSS in Action 1.2).

Many complex problems require several MSS technologies, as illustrated in the opening vignette and throughout this book. A problem-solver can employ several tools in different ways, such as:

- Use each tool independently to solve different aspects of the problem.
- Use several loosely integrated tools. This mainly involves transferring data from one tool to another (e.g., from an ES to a DSS) for further processing.

DSS IN ACTION 1.11

UNITED SUGARS CORPORATION OPTIMIZES PRODUCTION, DISTRIBUTION, AND INVENTORY CAPACITY

United Sugars Corporation (Bloomington, Minnesota) is a grower-owned cooperative that sells and distributes sugar products for its member companies. United has a 25 percent U.S. market share and sales of more than $1 billion annually. When the United States Sugar Corporation in southern Florida joined the cooperative, United Sugars decided to revise its marketing and distribution plans to gain access to new markets and serve existing ones more efficiently. Improvements in managing the supply chain and in the supply chain's design were in order.

A strategic model was developed to identify the minimum-cost solution for packaging, inventory, and distribution. The company's ERP system (SAP) and a legacy database system provided data for the mathematical model. This first model contains about a million decision variables and more than 250,000 relationships.

A Web-based GIS graphically displays reports optimal solutions. A map of the United States indicates the location of plants, warehouses, and customers. Each one is a hotspot that links to additional information about the solution.

This model is used to schedule production and distribution. Results are uploaded into the ERP to support operational decisions. The results of the strategic model drive the generation of subsequent models for inventory analysis. These models simulate a variety of inventory situations, through what-if analyses, and help analysts reduce overall inventory. All results are displayed in a variety of formats in a Web browser.

The hybrid DSS consisting of several optimization and simulation models, an ERP, and Web interfaces optimizes the supply chain at United Sugars.

Source: Adapted from Cohen et al. (2001).

- Use several tightly integrated tools (e.g., a fuzzy neural network). From the user's standpoint, the tool appears as one hybrid system.

The goal of using **hybrid computer systems** is the *successful solution* of managerial problems as is illustrated in DSS in Action 1.11.

In addition to performing different tasks in the problem-solving process, tools can support each other. For example, an expert system can enhance the modeling and data management of a DSS. A neural computing system or a GSS can support the knowledge acquisition process in building an expert system. Expert systems and artificial neural networks play an increasingly important role in enhancing other MSS technologies by making them *smarter*. The components of such systems include not only MSS, but also management science, statistics, and a variety of computer-based tools.

EMERGING TECHNOLOGIES AND TECHNOLOGY TRENDS

A number of emerging technologies directly and indirectly influence decision support systems. The World Wide Web has influenced many aspects of computer use, and therefore of DSS.

As technology advances, the speed of computation increases, leading to greater computational capability, while the physical size of the computer decreases. Every few years there is a several-factor change in these parameters. Purchasing a personal computer may seem expensive to a student, but its capabilities far exceed those of many legacy mainframes only a few years old. Many important *new* technologies have been around for decades. However, owing to the interconnectivity available through the Web, successful commercial implementation has now become feasible. Some specific technologies to watch (Vaughan, 2002) include grid computing, rich client interfaces, model-driven architecture, wireless computing, and agents, algorithms, and heuristics.

- *Grid computing*. Although a hot area, this has been around for decades. The basic idea is to cluster computing power in an organization and utilize unused cycles for problem-solving and other data-processing needs. This lets an organization get full use of its in-house number-crunching power. Some firms utilize unused cycles on employee desktops, whereas other firms simply replace their supercomputers with PC clusters. For example, CGG, an oil firm, replaced its supercomputers with a cluster of more than 6,000 PCs that is expected to grow to 10,000. These cost less than a supercomputer, but special software is needed to manage it (see Nash, 2002).
- *Rich client interfaces*. Customers and employees expect data and tool access to be pleasant to use and correct. In time, expectations have risen. As servers increase in capability, browser technology improves. GUIs, especially for Web access, improve continuously.
- *Model-driven architecture*. Software reuse and machine-generated software via computer-aided software engineering (CASE) tools are becoming more prevalent. The standardization of model vocabularies around UML has led developers to believe that code generation is feasible. However, even if code is 90 percent correct, the extra human effort required to fix the 10 percent to make it work may eliminate any benefits.
- *Wireless computing* (also *mobile computing*). The move to m-commerce is evolving because cellular telephones and wireless PC cards are so inexpensive. Mobile devices are being developed along with useful software to make this new approach work. A number of firms, such as FedEx, have been using mobile computing to gather data on packages to track shipping and analyze patterns.
- *Agents, algorithms, and heuristics*. Intelligent agents, though embedded in Web search engines for years, are being developed to function within devices and other software. They help users and assist in e-commerce negotiations. Algorithms and heuristics for improving system performance are being distributed as part of Java middleware and other platforms. For example, how to route a message over the Web may be computed by an algorithm embedded in an instant messenger system.

Gartner Inc. (Anonymous, 2002) recommends that enterprises in an economic slowdown select technologies that support their core business initiatives. This is generally good advice for any economic situation. In good times, money can be spent on exploring new technology impacts. All the items on Gartner's emerging-technologies list involve the Web. Here are Gartner's four emerging-technology trends to watch:

- *Customer self-service*. By 2005, it is expected that more than 70 percent of customer-service interaction for information and remote transactions will be automated. Web sites will have to provide the services that customers need and move the "products" that firms want to sell. There is an expectation of high returns on investment, better customer reach, and improved service quality. This will lead to increased competitiveness and savings that can be passed on to customers. DSS in Action 1.12 describes an example of how Palm Inc. deployed a portal that provides excellent customer service.
- *Web services*. The world has moved to the Web. Firms want a Web presence. Regardless of your industry, there is some aspect of what you do that can and should be put onto an e-commerce Web site. At a bare minimum, customers

---

DSS IN ACTION 1.12

PALM PROVIDES IMPROVED CUSTOMER SERVICE WITH A WEB PORTAL

Palm Inc. faced a problem with its Web site. Customers would access it, look over the various models of PDAs (personal digital assistants), get thoroughly confused, and order nothing. Something had to be done. In March 2002, Palm launched Active Sales Assistant, created by Active Decisions, to assist customers in comparing and deciding among Palm products. Customers identify the important features. The Assistant drills down and asks for more information from the customer if specific features were not identified (e.g., a color or monochrome screen display may not be important initially, but price may make it more significant when choosing between a pair of PDAs). When

the Assistant was pilot tested for a month, Palm discovered that customers preferred it to navigating on their own. Customers generally purchased an item, usually a higher-priced one than they initially intended. Aspects of fuzzy logic and economic utility functions are used in an internal model that helps the customers. The system learns what the user wants and attempts to identify the best fit. After implementing Active Decisions, revenues were up 20 percent.

Source: Adapted from Marvin Pyles, "A Fistful of Dollars: How Palm Increased Revenues 20 Percent," *Customer Relationship Management*, November 2002, pp. 54–55.

---

expect contact information and advertising. They want to be able to find you and see what you sell.
- *Wearable computers*. By 2007, more than 60 percent of the U.S. population between ages 15 and 50 will carry or wear a wireless computing and communications device at least six hours a day. The prevalence of these devices will definitely lead to significant commerce and service opportunities.
- *Tagging the world*. By 2008, more than $90 billion of business-to-consumer (B2C) purchase decisions and $350 billion of business-to-business (B2B) purchase decisions will be based on *tags*. Tags contain information and opinions about purchasable items. The flood of information, products, and services is spurring a focus on organizing and labeling choices to help buyers find, prioritize, and select items. The growing tagging industry will modify buying behavior and help create new industries in advisory and market research services.

1.15 PLAN OF THE BOOK

The 15 chapters of the book are organized in six parts (Figure 1.3).

PART I: BUSINESS INTELLIGENCE: DECISION-MAKING AND COMPUTERIZED SUPPORT
In Chapter 1, we provide an introduction, definitions, and an overview of decision support systems. In Chapter 2, we describe the process of managerial decision-making and DSS impacts.

PART II: DECISION SUPPORT SYSTEMS
Chapter 3 provides an overview of DSS and its major components. Chapter 4 describes the difficult topic of (mathematical) modeling and analysis. We describe both structured models and modeling tools. We also describe how unstructured problems can be modeled. In Chapter 5, we build on the modeling and analysis concepts, combine them

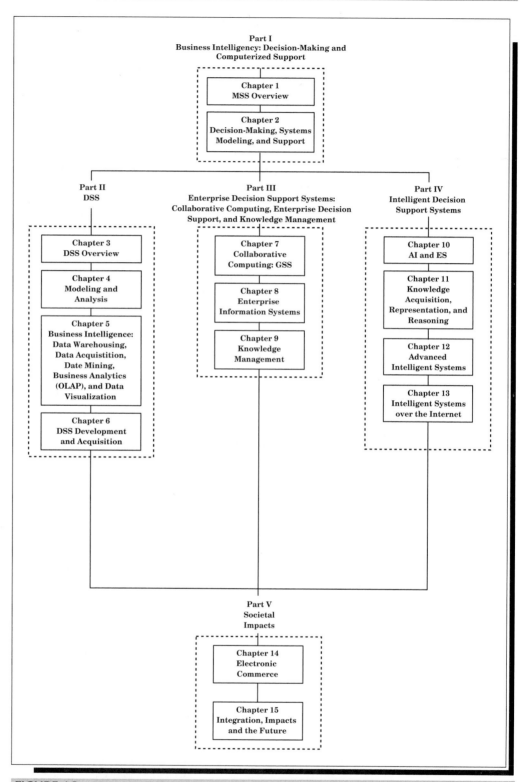

FIGURE 1.3   PLAN OF THE BOOK

with database concepts, resulting in modern business intelligence technologies and tools. These include **data warehousing, data acquisition, data mining,** online analytical processing (OLAP), and visualization. In Chapter 6, we describe DSS development and acquisition processes, and technologies.

PART III: ENTERPRISE DECISION SUPPORT SYSTEMS: COLLABORATIVE COMPUTING, ENTERPRISE DECISION SUPPORT, AND KNOWLEDGE MANAGEMENT

Chapter 7 deals with the support provided to groups working either in the same room or at different locations, especially via the Web. Chapter 8 covers the topic of enterprise decision support systems, including EIS, ERP/ERM, CRM, SCM, BPM, BAM, and PLM. Many decision-making problems require access to enterprise-wide data, policies, rules, and models; the decisions can then affect employees throughout the organization. The last chapter in this part is an in-depth discussion on knowledge management systems (KM), an exciting, enterprise-level DSS that can leverage large gains in productivity. Again, the Web plays a key role.

PART IV: INTELLIGENT SYSTEMS

The fundamentals of artificial intelligence and expert systems are the subject of Chapter 10. Methods of knowledge acquisition, representation, and reasoning are covered in Chapter 11. Advanced intelligent systems including artificial neural networks, genetic algorithms, fuzzy logic, and hybrids are the subjects of Chapter 12. Chapter 13 covers how intelligent systems work over the Internet, including intelligent agents.

PART V: SOCIETAL IMPACTS

Chapter 14 is an introduction to electronic commerce, the role of the Web, and the role that DSS technologies play. Finally, MSS integration, societal impacts, and its future are covered in Chapter 15.

❖ WEB SITE

This book's Web site, prenhall.com/turban, contains supplemental textual material organized as Web Chapters. The topics of these chapters are listed on the Web site in its *Web Table of Contents*. There is at least one chapter describing "New Developments in Decision Support Systems and Artificial Intelligence." The Web site also contains the book's PowerPoint presentations.

❖ CHAPTER HIGHLIGHTS

- The rate of computerization is increasing rapidly, and so is its use for managerial decision support.
- Managerial decision-making has become complex. Intuition and trial-and-error methods may not be sufficient.
- The time frame for making decisions is shrinking, whereas its global nature is expanding, necessitating the development and use of computerized decision support systems.
- Management support systems are technologies designed to support managerial work. They can be used independently or in combination.
- Computerized support for managers is often essential for the survival of organizations.
- A decision support framework divides decision situations into nine categories, depending on the degree of structuredness and managerial activities. Each category is supported differently.
- Structured decisions are supported by standard quantitative analysis methods, such as management science, and by MIS.
- Decision support systems (DSS) use data, models, and possibly knowledge for the solution of semistructured and unstructured problems.

- Business intelligence methods utilize both analytical tools and database systems that include data warehouses, data mining, online analytical processing, and data visualization.
- Group support systems (GSS) support group work processes.
- Enterprise information systems (EIS) give access to the specific enterprise-wide information that individuals need to perform their tasks.
- Enterprise resource planning (ERP)/enterprise resource management (ERM), customer relationship management (CRM) systems, and supply chain management (SCM) systems are all types of enterprise information systems.
- Enterprise resource planning and supply chain management are correlated with decision support systems, electronic commerce, and customer relationship management.
- Knowledge management systems (KMS) capture, store, and disseminate important expertise throughout an organization.

- Knowledge repositories contain knowledge that can be reused to support complex decisions.
- Expert systems are advisory systems that attempt to mimic experts; they apply knowledge directly to problem-solving.
- Neural computing is an applied artificial intelligence technology that attempts to exhibit pattern recognition by learning from experience.
- Advanced intelligent decision support systems, such as genetic algorithms, fuzzy logic, and intelligent (software) agents, enhance productivity and quality.
- All MSS technologies are interactive and can be integrated among themselves and with other CBIS into hybrid computer systems.
- Web technology and the Internet, intranets, and extranets play a key role in the development, dissemination, and use of MSS.

❖ KEY WORDS

- artificial neural networks (ANN)
- business analytics
- business intelligence
- cognitive limits
- computer-based information system (CBIS)
- customer relationship management (CRM)
- data mining
- decision support systems (DSS)
- electronic commerce (e-commerce)
- enterprise information system (EIS)
- enterprise resource management (ERM)

- enterprise resource planning (ERP)
- expert system (ES)
- expertise
- fuzzy logic
- genetic algorithms
- group support systems (GSS)
- intelligent agent (IA)
- hybrid (integrated) computer systems
- knowledge management systems (KM)
- knowledge repository
- machine learning

- management information system (MIS)
- management science (MS)
- management support system (MSS)
- operations research (OR)
- organizational knowledge repository
- productivity
- semistructured decisions
- structured decisions
- supply chain management (SCM)
- transaction processing system (TPS)
- unstructured decisions

❖ QUESTIONS FOR REVIEW

1. What caused the latest revolution in management use of computers? List at least two causes.
2. List and define the three phases of the decision-making process (according to Simon).
3. Define DSS.
4. Discuss the major characteristics of DSS.
5. List five major benefits of DSS.
6. Why is management often equated with decision-making?
7. Discuss the major trends that affect managerial decision-making.
8. Define management science.

9. Define structured, semistructured, and unstructured decisions.
10. Categorize managerial activities (according to Anthony).
11. Define group support systems.
12. Relate DSS to EIS, ERP/ERM, SCM, and the Web.
13. Define knowledge management.
14. Define expert system.
15. List the major benefits of ES.
16. Define neural computing.
17. Define intelligent agents.
18. What is a hybrid support system?

❖ QUESTIONS FOR DISCUSSION

1. Give additional examples for the contents of each cell in Figure 1.2.
2. Design a computerized system for a brokerage house that trades in securities, conducts research on companies, and provides information and advice to customers (such as "buy," "sell," and "hold"). In your design, clearly distinguish seven parts: TPS, MIS, DSS, EIS, GSS, KMS, CRM, ES, and ANN. Be sure to discuss input and output information. Assume that the brokerage company is a small one with only 20 branches in four different cities.
3. Survey the literature of the last six months to find one application of each MSS technology discussed. Summarize the applications on one page and submit it with a copy of the articles.
4. Observe an organization with which you are familiar. List three decisions it makes in each of the following categories: strategic planning, management control (tactical planning), and operational planning and control.
5. What capabilities are provided by ANN and not by any other MSS?
6. Describe how hybrid systems might help a manager in decision-making.
7. Indicate which MSS can be used to assist a manager in fulfilling Mintzberg's 10 management roles. How and why can they help? Be specific.
8. Discuss the relationships among EIS, ERP/ERM, SCM, and CRM.
9. Why is e-commerce related to EIS and decision support?
10. Why is the role of knowledge management so important for decision support? Discuss an example of how the two can be integrated.
11. Describe how the World Wide Web affects MSS, and vice versa.

❖ EXERCISE

1. Write a report (5–10 pages) describing how your company, or a company you are familiar with, currently uses computers and information systems, including Web technologies and the Web itself, in decision-making. In light of the material in this chapter, describe how you could use such support systems if they were readily available (which ones are available to you and which ones are not?).

❖ GROUP ASSIGNMENTS AND ROLE-PLAYING

1. Find information on the proactive use of computers to support ad hoc decisions versus transaction processing systems (TPS). Each member of the group should choose an application in a different industry (retail, banking, insurance, food, etc.). Be sure to include the impacts of the Web/Internet. Summarize the findings and point out the similarities and differences of the applications. Use as sources companies where students are employed, trade magazines, Internet newsgroups, and vendor Web sites. Finally, prepare a class presentation on the findings.

❖ INTERNET EXERCISES

1. Search the Internet for material regarding the work of managers, the need for computerized support, and the role decision support systems play in providing such support. What kind of references to consulting firms, academic departments, and programs do you find? What major areas are represented? Select five sites that cover one area and report your findings.
2. Explore the *public areas* of dssresources.com. Prepare a list of its major available resources. You may want to refer to this site as you work through the book.
3. Look at the Web Chapters on the book's Web site (prenhall.com/turban). Describe in a one-page summary report how they relate to the chapters in the text.
4. Access sap.com and peoplesoft.com and find information on how enterprise resource planning (ERP) software helps decision-makers. In addition, examine how these software products utilize Web technology, and the Web itself.
5. Access intelligententerprise.com. For each topic cited in this chapter, find some interesting development reported on the site and prepare a report.
6. Search the Web for DSS, business intelligence, business analytics, OLAP, data mining, and data warehousing. Identify similarities and differences among these items based on what you find.

ABB AUTOMATION MAKES FASTER AND BETTER DECISIONS WITH DSS

INTRODUCTION

ABB is a global leader in power and automation technologies that enable utility and industry customers to improve performance while lowering environmental impact. ABB has approximately 152,000 employees in more than 100 countries. It is constantly developing new *automation technology* solutions to help its customers to optimize their productivity. These solutions include simulation, control and optimization strategies, the interaction between people and machines, embedded software, mechatronics, monitoring, and diagnosis. The intent is to develop a common industrial IT architecture for real-time solutions across the business enterprise.

THE DECISION SUPPORT SYSTEM SOLUTION

ABB has expertise in developing such systems, and it developed one for its own use in a textile division. ABB Automation's decision support system captures and manages information from ABB's Range MES package for managers to use in their analysis and decision-making. The primary purpose of the DSS is to provide managers with technology and tools for data warehousing, data mining, and decision support, ideally leading to better and faster decision-making.

The system provides

- Storage of production data from a distributed control system (DCS) in a data warehouse
- Data capture without burdening the control system hardware
- Site-wide access to data for decision support through data visualization tools (a Web-based interface) that are easily used by nontechnical site staff
- Pre-configured windows to the data (for structured queries)
- Capability to access data for ad hoc reports and data analysis
- Access to real-time operating data (for analysis).

DETAILS OF THE DSS AND ITS USE

The DSS provides a method for flexible-term storage (warehousing) and analysis of important data. It is part of the Managerial Supervisory Control System (MSS) and summarizes data for each process area in a plant. In addition to DSS, MSS includes lot-tracking, history, and process data. The DSS has a flexible, accessible architecture facilitating generation of reports, information searches and flexible term data storage that is easily accessible.

A Web-based dashboard (an enterprise information portal) is used for views in the data warehouse. The production system status (overall efficiency and of each lot and summary data) can be monitored graphically in near real-time. Equipment failures, off-quality production, and their causes are quickly identified and rectified. Process improvements through time are tracked. Analysis is performed by through data mining and online analytical processing (OLAP) technologies by accessing production data from the data warehouse. Resource consumption, energy consumption and other production factors are also monitored.

RESULTS

The DSS enables the user to make decisions for more consistent and efficient operation and to monitor and manage costs of producing high-quality goods. It provides a near real-time display of operating data, detailing range stops and associated downtime, to eliminate major causes of downtime.

The ultimate challenge is to improve management of the manufacturing process by *leveraging* the large quantities of production data available. The DSS gives managers plant-wide access to relevant plant-floor production data leading to *more informed decisions* and *increased profits*.

Sources: Based on Anonymous, "ABB: Decision Support System," *Textile World*, Vol. 150, No. 4, 52–54, April 2000; and the ABB Web site, abb.com.

CASE QUESTIONS

1. Identify the model, data, and user interface components of the ABB DSS.
2. What DSS technologies does ABB Automation use to improve productivity?
3. How does ABB Automation use DSS to make faster and better decisions?
4. Why are the decisions faster and better?
5. How could artificial intelligence systems, such as expert systems or artificial neural networks, be integrated into ABB's DSS?
6. Consider the DSS material in the chapter: What is meant by leveraging production data to improve the management of the manufacturing process?

DECISION-MAKING SYSTEMS, MODELING, AND SUPPORT

LEARNING OBJECTIVES

❖ Understand the conceptual foundations of decision-making

❖ Understand the systems approach

❖ Understand Simon's four phases of decision-making: intelligence, design, choice, and implementation

❖ Recognize the concepts of rationality and bounded rationality, and how they relate to decision-making

❖ Differentiate between the concepts of *making* a choice and *establishing* a principle of choice

❖ Recognize how decision style, cognition, management style, personality (temperament), and other factors influence decision-making

❖ Learn how DSS support for decision-making can be provided in practice

The major focus of this book is the computerized support of decision-making. The purpose of this chapter is to describe the conceptual foundations of decision-making and the systems approach, and how support is provided. In addition to the opening vignette, we use the *MMS Running Case* throughout the chapter to illustrate the process of decision-making in industry. This *Running Case* is concluded in Case Application 2.4. This chapter covers

2.1 OPENING VIGNETTE: STANDARD MOTOR PRODUCTS SHIFTS GEARS INTO TEAM-BASED DECISION-MAKING[1]

INTRODUCTION

Decision-making is complex—very complex; and it involves people and information. In most organizations, when you pay people to work, they work—and don't think. But when you pay people to think, they think, and when you empower them to make decisions, they make good ones. The benefits to the bottom line can be huge. You leverage the intellectual assets of your organization in ways that you might not have thought possible. The Standard Motor Products (SMP) plant, in Edwardsville, Kansas, makes and distributes after-market automotive products. Team decision-making by the workers works. A change in work culture and understanding made it possible.

A SAMPLE DAY AT SMP

June 11, 6 a.m., a workday: Inside the plant, Brenda Craig pages through the day's order sheets, figuring out what her co-workers should do today. She's not the boss, but the scheduler for her work team this month.

Over the next year, everyone on her 12-member team will rotate through all of the group's tasks. Each will get to determine how many man-hours are needed to load overnight orders onto delivery trucks. The team meets briefly to decide duties. They quickly estimate whether overtime might be needed and whether other work teams need help or can help them.

Everybody on the team is responsible for handling the orders. Everyone understands what needs to be done. The workers are not task-driven. They *think!* They *make decisions!* And everybody is responsible for identifying when members gets off track and helping them get their act together.

STANDARD MOTOR PRODUCTS' SELF-DIRECTED TEAM CULTURE

The team system thrives in what could be, but is not, a divisive environment. About 55 percent of the workers are union members. There is still a management hierarchy at SMP. But general manager Thom Norbury and the other six members of the plant's core leadership team rarely interfere with work teams' decisions. Usually, team representatives debate options and choose well, Norbury says. The whole process utilizes the *talents* of the employees.

Former plant general manager Joe Forlenza believed that workers could make organization-savvy decisions. When Forlenza was growing up, he saw people managing their own lives under all kinds of circumstances. He says that, "I . . . saw that anybody with a brain is wasted if they don't use it." Some SMP managers said that empowerment would not work, especially under union contracts. A decade later, the empowered workplace thrives at SMP.

Forlenza examined team-coordinated decision-making and began shifting responsibilities and eliminating midlevel supervisory jobs. Some managers left voluntarily; some were *invited* to do so. After the first year, plant productivity dropped. Since this

---

[1]*Source:* Adapted from Diane Stafford, "Team-Based Decision-Making Works at Edwardsville, Kan., Auto Products Plant," *Knight Ridder Tribune Business News*, June 11, 2002, p. 1; and public domain publications.

was expected (Joe had studied how this works in practice), he *remained committed to the change*, and by the end of the second year, productivity was back up and improving. It continues to improve today.

LEADERSHIP COMMITMENT TO CHANGE

The Edwardsville plant succeeded where other companies failed because of a rare top-down commitment. Joe made a long-term commitment to teach his teams to mature, and to make good decisions for the organization and for themselves. Some of the old management team couldn't conform, but fortunately many did. When the trust level between employer and employee is low, there are problems. Also, some employees have trouble assuming responsibility on the job. Unfortunately, many American businesses have taught their workers that they are not paid to think—so they don't.

In general, about 10 percent of workers cannot function in a team environment. This is sometimes because of personality issues, or because they are top performers or bottom performers who refuse to cooperate with a team. These people must be let go when building a team culture, to eliminate resentment. Norbury says that self-directed work teams require continuous commitment. Otherwise, stress can easily cause managers to revert to old behaviors. Leadership commitment is a *critical factor* in instituting any organizational change.

TEAM DECISION-MAKING

At SMP, a team knows its schedule, goals, and financial situation. The team has a lot more *information* about the business than workers typically do. Teams know whether they are making good decisions because they have access to financial data that were previously only available to management. They measure productivity and calculate their rewards. The teams strive to be self-managed. Most of the teams in the plant have made it to the highest self-empowerment level. Team members provide *feedback* to one other daily. Feedback recipients accept criticism in a *no excuses* manner. Most of them already know what feedback to expect.

RESULTS

Since the team approach was instituted, there has been less friction between management and union representatives. They often resolve issues through flexible letters of understanding instead of binding contracts. Such decisions are much easier to negotiate. People are much happier. Workers are responsible for scheduling shipments, determining overtime, scheduling shifts, work assignments, and so on. Team members are responsible for making decisions when production falls off. Most managerial decision-making has moved to the self-directed teams. The workers need little supervision. Overall, empowered workers, when rewarded appropriately, make good decisions.

❖ QUESTIONS FOR THE OPENING VIGNETTE

1. Why do you think workers in many organizations are paid to *do*, rather than to *think*? Does this make sense? Why or why not?

2. Why do you think productivity dropped in the first year of the team-based program? Explain.

3. Why is leadership commitment to change important? Explain.

4. How are decisions handled in the team approach? Consider the following:
   a. How do teams identify problems?
   b. How do teams approach problems?

   c. How do teams choose solutions?

   d. How do teams implement solutions?

5. How do teams handle conflicting objectives?

6. What are some of the possible impacts on decision-making if someone who is not a team player is a member of a team? Could this be why many of the midlevel managers were convinced to leave? Explain.

7. Technology is used to access information and data. Describe how information technology can help the teams.

8. What is the impact on decision-making of giving people responsibility for their own work? Why are self-directed team members happier than workers under a traditional hierarchy?

2.2 DECISION-MAKING: INTRODUCTION AND DEFINITIONS

The opening vignette demonstrated some aspects of a typical business decision:

- The decision is often made by a group.
- Group members may have biases.
- Empowering a group leads to better decisions.
- Individuals may also be responsible for making a decision.
- There may be many (hundreds or even thousands) of alternatives to consider.
- The results of making a business decision usually materialize in the future. No one is a perfect predictor of the future, especially in the long run.
- Decisions are interrelated. A specific decision may affect many individuals and groups within the organizational system.
- Decision-making involves a process of thinking about the problem leading to the need for data and modeling of the problem (loosely speaking: understanding the relationships among its different aspects). This leads to interpretation and application of knowledge.
- Feedback is an important aspect of decision-making.

Additionally,

- Groupthink (buy-in by group members without any thinking) can lead to bad decisions.
- There can be several, conflicting objectives.
- Many decisions involve risk. Different people have different attitudes toward risk.
- Decision-makers are interested in evaluating what-if scenarios.
- Experimentation with the real system (i.e., develop a schedule, try it, and see how well it works—trial and error) may result in failure.
- Experimentation with the real system is possible only for one set of conditions at a time and can be disastrous.
- Changes in the decision-making environment may occur continuously, leading to invalidating assumptions about the situation (e.g., deliveries around holiday times may increase, requiring a different view of the problem).
- Changes in the decision-making environment may affect decision quality by imposing time pressure on the decision-maker.
- Collecting information and analyzing a problem takes time and can be expensive. It is difficult to determine when to stop and make a decision.

- There may not be sufficient information to make an intelligent decision.
- There may be too much information available (information overload).

Ultimately, we want to help decision-makers make better decisions (see Churchman 1982; Hoch, 2001; Hoch and Kunreuther, 2001; Hoch, Kunreuther with Gunther, 2001; Kleindorfer, 2001; Mora, Forgionne and Gupta, 2002; Power, 2002; Roth and Mullen, 2002; Shim et al., 2002; Shoemaker and Russo, 2001; Simon, 2000; Verma and Churchman, 1998; Vitt, Luckevich, and Misner, 2002). However, making better decisions does not necessarily mean making faster decisions. The fast-changing business environment often requires faster decisions, which may be detrimental to decision quality (see DSS in Focus 2.1). To determine how real decision-makers make decisions, we must first understand the process and the important issues of decision-making. Then we can understand appropriate methodologies for assisting decision-makers and the contribution that information systems can make. Only then can we develop decision support systems to help decision-makers.

This chapter is organized along the three key words that form the term DSS: *decision*, *support*, and *systems*. One does not simply apply information technology tools blindly to decision-making. Rather, support is provided through a rational approach that simplifies reality and provides a relatively quick and inexpensive means of considering various alternative courses of action to arrive at the best (or at least a very good) solution to the problem.

DECISION-MAKING

Decision-making is a process of choosing among alternative courses of action for the purpose of attaining a goal or goals. According to Simon (1977), *managerial decision-making is synonymous with the whole process of management*. Consider the important managerial function of planning. Planning involves a series of decisions: What should be done? When? Where? Why? How? By whom? Managers set goals, or plan; hence, planning implies decision-making. Other managerial functions, such as organizing and controlling, also involve decision-making.

DECISION-MAKING AND PROBLEM-SOLVING

A problem occurs when a system does not meet its established goals, does not yield the predicted results, or does not work as planned. Problem-solving may also deal with identifying new opportunities. Differentiating the terms **decision-making** and **problem-**

DSS IN FOCUS 2.1

WHEN DECISION-MAKING IS FAST, THE FAST CAN GET HURT

Fast decision-making requirements may be detrimental to decision quality. Managers were asked which areas suffered most. Here is what they said:

Personnel/HR	27%
Budgeting/finance	24%
Organizational structuring	22%
Quality/productivity	20%
IT selection and installation	17%
Process improvement	17%

Source: Condensed from D.J. Horgan, "Management Briefs: Decision Making: Had We But World Enough and Time," *CIO*, November 15, 2001.

solving can be confusing. One way to distinguish between the two is to examine the phases of the decision process. These phases are (1) intelligence, (2) design, (3) choice, and (4) implementation. Some consider the entire process (phases 1–4) as problem-solving, with the **choice phase** as the real decision-making. Others view phases 1–3 as formal decision-making ending with a recommendation, whereas problem-solving additionally includes the actual implementation of the recommendation (phase 4). We use the terms decision-making and problem-solving interchangeably.

DECISION-MAKING DISCIPLINES

Decision-making is directly influenced by several major disciplines, some behavioral and some scientific in nature. We must be aware of how their philosophies can affect our ability to make decisions and provide support. Behavioral disciplines include

- Anthropology
- Law
- Philosophy
- Political science
- Psychology
- Social psychology
- Sociology.

Scientific disciplines include

- Computer science
- Decision analysis
- Economics
- Engineering
- Hard sciences: biology, chemistry, physics, etc.
- Management science/operations research
- Mathematics
- Statistics.

Each discipline has its own set of assumptions about reality and methods. Each also contributes a unique, valid view of how people make decisions. Finally, there is a lot of variation in what constitutes a successful decision in practice. For example, we provide a sample of the "75 greatest management decisions ever made" in DSS in Action 2.2. All of these were successful for a number of reasons, some serendipitous. Other great decisions, such as building the Great Wall of China, made good sense at the time (it is considered a success; see the list), but actually *failed in practice* because of bad managerial practices. Other decisions failed as well. See DSS in Action 2.2.

2.3 SYSTEMS

The acronyms *DSS*, *GSS*, *EIS*, and *ES* all include the term *system*. A **system** is a collection of objects such as people, resources, concepts, and procedures intended to perform an identifiable function or to serve a goal. For example, a university is a system of students, faculty, staff, administrators, buildings, equipment, ideas, and rules with the goal of educating students, producing research, and providing service to the community (another system). A clear definition of the system's goal is a critical consideration

DSS IN ACTION 2.2

THE 75 GREATEST MANAGEMENT DECISIONS EVER MADE

Management Review asked experts for their nominations of the 75 greatest management decisions ever made. The resulting list is both eclectic and eccentric. All the decisions were *successful* and had *major impact*. Here is a sample:

- Walt Disney listened to his wife, Lillian, and named his cartoon mouse Mickey instead of Mortimer. Entertainment was never the same after Mickey and Minnie debuted in *Steamboat Willie* in 1928.

- As ambassador to France in the 1780s, Benjamin Franklin, spent his time encouraging the emigration of skilled workers to the United States—an early instance of poaching staff.

- Around 59 B.C., Julius Caesar kept people up to date with handwritten sheets that were distributed in Rome and, it is thought, with wall posters. The greatness of leaders has been partly measured ever since by their ability to communicate.

- Ignoring market research, Ted Turner launched the Cable News Network in 1980. No one thought a 24-hour news network would work.

- During World War II, Robert Woodruff, president of Coca-Cola, committed to selling bottles of Coke to members of the armed services for a nickel. Customer loyalty never came cheaper.

- In 1924 Thomas Watson, Sr., changed the name of the Computing-Tabulating-Recording Company to International Business Machines. The company had no international operations, but it was a bold statement of ambitions.

- In 1981 Bill Gates decided to license MS/DOS to IBM, while IBM ceded control of the licenses for all non-IBM PCs. This laid the foundation for Microsoft's huge success and IBM's fall from grace. (IBM's decision here could be listed as one of the 75 worst management decisions ever made.)

- The Chinese Qin Dynasty (221–206 B.C.) produced the Great Wall—a fantastic feat of management and engineering. The Chinese also developed what is reputed to have been the first reliable system of weights and measures, thereby aiding commercial development.

- In the nineteenth century, Andrew Carnegie decided to import British steel and steelmaking processes to America to build railway bridges made of steel instead of wood. The imported skills ignited the U.S. steel industry, and Carnegie became a steel baron.

- Queen Isabella of Spain decided to sponsor Columbus' voyage in 1492. This was a very risky situation that had a high payoff—the discovery of a New World.

Source: Adapted from Stuart Crainer, *The 75 Greatest Management Decisions Ever Made:... And 21 of the Worst*, MJF Books, New York, 2002. Also see Anonymous, "Top 75: The Greatest Management Decisions Ever Made," *Management Review*, Vol. 87, No. 10, November, 1998, pp. 20–23; and Stuart Crainer, "The 75 Greatest Management Decisions Ever Made," *Management Review*, Vol. 87, No. 10, November 1998, pp. 16–19.

in the design of a management support system (MSS). For example, the purpose of an air defense system is to protect ground targets, and not just to destroy attacking aircraft or missiles.

The notion of levels (i.e., a hierarchy) of systems reflects the fact that all systems are actually subsystems because every system is contained within some larger system. For example, a bank includes such subsystems as a commercial loan department, a consumer loan department, a savings department, and an operations department. The bank itself may also be a branch that is part of a collection of other banks, and these banks may collectively be a subsidiary of a holding corporation, such as the Bank of America, which is a subsystem of the California banking system, which is part of the national banking system, which is part of the national economy, and so on. The interconnections and interactions among the subsystems are called **interfaces**.

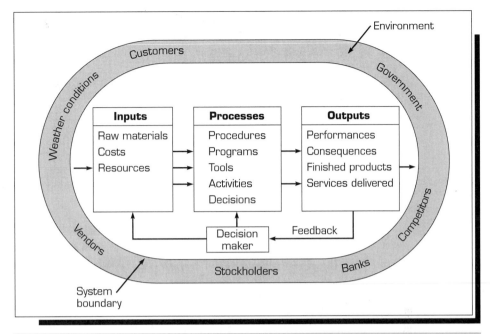

FIGURE 2.1   THE SYSTEM AND ITS ENVIRONMENT

THE STRUCTURE OF A SYSTEM

Systems (Figure 2.1) are divided into three distinct parts: inputs, processes, and outputs. They are surrounded by an environment and often include a feedback mechanism. In addition, a human decision-maker is considered part of the system.

INPUTS

Inputs are elements that enter the system. Examples of inputs are raw materials entering a chemical plant, students admitted to a university, and data input into a Web page for a database query.

PROCESSES

Processes are all the elements necessary to convert or transform inputs into outputs. For example, a process in a chemical plant may include heating the materials, using operating procedures, using a material-handling subsystem, and using employees and machines. In a university, a process may include holding classes, doing library work, and Web searching. In a computer, including a Web-based one, a process may include activating commands, executing computations, and storing information.

OUTPUTS

Outputs are the finished products or the consequences of being in the system. For example, fertilizers are one output of a chemical plant, educated people are one output of a university, and reports may be the outputs of a computer system. A Web server may produce a Web page dynamically, based on its inputs and processes.

FEEDBACK

There is a flow of information from the output component to the decision-maker concerning the system's output or performance. Based on the outputs, the decision-maker, who acts as a control, may decide to modify the inputs, the processes, or both. This information flow, appearing as a closed loop (Figure 2.1), is called *feedback*. This is how real systems monitoring occurs. The decision-maker compares the outputs to the expected outputs and adjusts the inputs and possibly the processes to move closer to the output targets.

The Environment

The environment of the system is composed of several elements that lie outside it in the sense that they are not inputs, outputs, or processes. However, they affect the system's performance and consequently the attainment of its goals. One way to identify the elements of the environment is by posing two questions (Churchman, 1975; also see Gharajedaghi, 1999):

- Does the element matter relative to the system's goals?
- Is it possible for the decision-maker to significantly manipulate this element?

If and only if the answer to the first question is yes, and the answer to the second is no, is the element in the environment. Environmental elements can be social, political, legal, physical, or economic. Often they consist of other systems. For a chemical plant, suppliers, competitors, and customers are elements of the environment. A state university may be affected by rules and laws passed by the state legislature, but for the most part the legislature is part of the environment, since the university system probably has no direct impact on it. In some cases, they may interact, though, and the environment is redefined. A DSS designed to set tuition rates would not normally interact directly with the state government. For a computer system, the environment is anything that is not part of the system. It can include other systems with which it interacts, users that provide input, and users who examine output.

The Boundary

A system is separated from its environment by a *boundary*. The system is inside the boundary, whereas the environment lies outside. A boundary can be physical (e.g., the system is a department with a boundary defined by Building C; in the case of your bodily system, the boundary is your skin), or it can be some nonphysical factor. For example, a system can be bounded by time. In such a case, we can analyze an organization for a period of only 1 year.

The boundary of an information system is usually defined by narrowing the system's scope to simplify its analysis. In other words, the boundary of an information system, especially a decision support system, is by design. Boundaries are related to the concepts of closed and open systems.

Closed and Open Systems

Because every system is a subsystem of another, it may seem as if the process of system analysis will never end. Therefore, one must confine a system analysis to defined, manageable boundaries. Such confinement is called *closing* the system.

A *closed system* is at one extreme of a continuum that reflects the degree of independence of systems (an *open system* is at the other extreme). A closed system is totally independent, whereas an open system is very dependent on its environment. An open system accepts inputs (information, energy, materials) from the environment and may deliver outputs to the environment.

When determining the impact of decisions on an open system, we must determine its relationship with the environment and with other systems. In a closed system, we need not do this because the system is considered to be isolated. Many computer systems, such as transaction processing systems (TPS), are considered closed systems. Generally, closed systems are fairly simple in nature.

A special type of closed system called a *black box* is one in which inputs and outputs are well defined, but the process itself is not specified. Many managers are not concerned with how a computer works, especially when it is accessed via the Web. Essentially, they prefer to treat computers as black boxes, like a telephone or an elevator. Managers simply use these devices independent of the operational details because they understand the results or consequences of how the devices function. Their tasks do not require them to understand how the devices work. This concept leads to the development of commercially successful expert systems, data mining, and online analytical processing.

Decision-support systems attempt to deal with systems that are fairly open. Such systems are complex, and during when analyzing them one must determine the impacts on and from the environment. Consider the two inventory systems outlined in Table 2.1. We compare a well-known inventory model, the economic order quantity (EOQ) model, for a fairly closed system, with a hypothetical DSS for an inventory system for an open system. The closed system is very restrictive in terms of its assumptions and thus its applicability.

SYSTEM EFFECTIVENESS AND EFFICIENCY

Systems are evaluated and analyzed in terms of two major performance measures: effectiveness and efficiency.

- **Effectiveness** is the degree to which goals are achieved. It is therefore concerned with the outputs of a system (e.g., total sales or earnings per share).
- **Efficiency** is a measure of the use of inputs (or resources) to achieve outputs (e.g., how much money is used to generate a certain level of sales).

Peter Drucker proposed the following interesting way to distinguish between the two terms:

Effectiveness is doing the right thing.
Efficiency is doing the thing right.

	TABLE 2.1 A Closed Versus an Open Inventory System	
Factor	*Management Science: EOQ (Closed System)*	*Inventory DSS (Open System)*
Demand	Constant	Variable—influenced by many factors
Unit cost	Constant	May change daily
Lead time	Constant	Variable, difficult to predict
Vendors and users	Excluded from analysis	May be included in analysis
Weather and other environmental factors	Ignored	May influence demand and lead time

DSS IN ACTION 2.3

THE WEB CHANGES THE FACE OF POLITICAL DECISION-MAKING

Getting informed is one of the most difficult things for the public to do during an election campaign. The Web provides new avenues for the dissemination of information about political candidates. For example, the University of Nevada, Reno (UNR), has launched a Web site called Nevada Votes! (nevadavotes.unr.edu) to help citizens make informed decisions in upcoming state elections (from the U.S. Congress to municipal offices). The site is a collaborative effort of university libraries, campus IT, and the campus National Public Radio affiliate, KUNR. It includes statewide election district maps, profiles on more than 350 candidates, photos, streaming audio files with candidate statements, PAC contributions, initiatives, referenda, political parties, and voter registration. In addition to policy views, the profiles include the candidates' responses to questions about their role models, their favorite books, and many other matters.

Source: Adapted from Susan DiMattia, "Nevada U. Provides Election Information," *Library Journal,* Vol. 127, No. 16, October 1, 2002, p. 17.

An important characteristic of management support system is their emphasis on the effectiveness, or "goodness," of the decision produced, rather than on the computational efficiency of obtaining it—usually a major concern of a transaction processing system. Most Web-based decision support systems are focused on improving decision effectiveness. Efficiency may be a byproduct.

Measuring the effectiveness and efficiency of many managerial systems is a major problem. This is especially true for systems that deliver human services (education, health, recreation), which often have several qualitative and conflicting goals and are subject to much external influence because of funding and political considerations. For an example of how the Web has influenced political decision-making in a large way, see the example described in DSS in Action 2.3. This is also true for DSS. How does one measure a manager's confidence about making a better decision? Even so, many attempts have been made to quantify DSS effectiveness and efficiency. This is necessary to gain managerial support and the resources to develop them.

INFORMATION SYSTEMS

An information system collects, processes, stores, analyzes, and disseminates information for a specific purpose. Information systems are at the heart of most organizations. For example, banks and airlines would be unable to function without their information systems. With the advent of electronic businesses (e-businesses), if there is no information system, especially through the Web, there is no business. Information systems accept inputs and process data to provide information to decision-makers and help them communicate the results. Most consumers and decision-makers now expect a World Wide Web presence and activities (see DSS in Action 2.4 for how customers used and evaluated bank Web sites; and Agosto, 2002, who evaluated the role of personal preference in how Web sites are used and evaluated). Information systems and a Web presence for e-commerce have become critical for many organizations that in the past did not rely on them (see DSS in Action 2.5). Dun & Bradstreet's D&B Global DecisionMaker is a Web-based automated credit decision-making service. It offers its customers a simple, fast credit-decision solution. See Anonymous (2002) for

DSS IN ACTION 2.4

THE WEB RAISES THE BAR FOR CONSUMER EXPECTATIONS IN DECISION-MAKING

Information search is the primary reason for most Internet use. Companies must understand consumers' information requirements to ensure Web site effectiveness in aiding consumer decision-making. Kathryn Waite and Tina Harrison performed a study to determine the factors that contribute to customer satisfaction and dissatisfaction with current online information provision by retail banks in Britain. Since the highest Internet use is found in the finance and insurance sectors (over 70 percent of businesses have their own or a third-party Web site), retail banks were studied. An analysis of the most and least important attributes revealed that those contributing to decision-making convenience are preferred over the technological entertainment value. Certain Web site features and design are most likely to attract and retain customers. Specifically, when it comes to banking, people want to be able to conduct their business and find out what they want to know—not to be entertained.

Source: Adapted from K. Waite and T. Harrison, "Consumer Expectations of Online Information Provided by Bank Websites," *Journal of Financial Services Marketing*, Vol. 6, No. 4, June 2002, pp. 309–322.

details. Domaszewicz (2002) describes how health care decisions are supported by Web-based DSS.

2.4 MODELS

A major characteristic of a decision support system is the inclusion of at least one model. The basic idea is to perform the DSS analysis on a model of reality rather than on the real system. A model is a simplified representation or abstraction of reality. It is usually simplified because reality is too complex to describe exactly and because much of the complexity is actually irrelevant in solving the specific problem. Models can represent systems or problems with various degrees of abstraction. They are classified, based on their degree of abstraction, as either iconic, analog, or mathematical.

ICONIC (SCALE) MODELS

An **iconic model**—the least abstract type of model—is a physical replica of a system, usually on a different scale from the original. An iconic model may be three-dimensional, such as that of an airplane, car, bridge, or production line. Photographs are two-dimensional iconic-scale models.

ANALOG MODELS

An **analog model** behaves like the real system but does not look like it. It is more abstract than an iconic model and is a symbolic representation of reality. Models of this type are usually two-dimensional charts or diagrams. They can be physical models, but the shape of the model differs from that of the actual system. Some examples include

DSS IN ACTION 2.5

POLITICAL ADVOCACY VIA THE WEB

What makes an advocacy group's Web site work? How can an advocacy group develop a site to reach its constituency? Heather Sehmel studied these questions and more. To make better decisions, people working in small organizations need to know more about the processes through which they make decisions about the use of Web sites as part of their comprehensive communication effort. Many advocacy Web sites do not exploit the Web to the fullest. Many miss out on the ability to create dialogue or provide personalized information. Heather Sehmel looked into the following questions:

1. How, by whom, and for what reasons are decisions made about how to use the group's Web site?

2. How does the site meet the goals and reflect the values of its developers?

3. How does the site reflect or fail to reflect common goals of environmental advocacy communication?

4. What other documents and communications relate to the advocacy campaign? How, if at all, might these documents interact with or lead individuals to interact with the Web site?

5. Who visits the Web site and why? How do site visitors use the site?

Sehmel's investigation of an Austin-based advocacy group led her to discover that the group encountered many of the common barriers to organizational decision-making. One of the major barriers to the group's making good decisions about how to use its Web site was the inability of its employees to know the alternatives available to them and/or the consequences of the alternatives. Another major barrier was the lack of feedback about the choices they made, which would have enabled them to become more expert rhetoricians on the Web. The following factors contributed to these problems:

- The group's employees were not trained in Web design, but instead mainly learned about Web communication through their visits to Web sites, an imperfect method.

- The Webmaster perceived herself, and the rest of the staff perceived her, largely as a technical expert, not an expert in Web rhetoric.

- The group had limited knowledge of its Web audience.

- The group had little feedback about the success of its Web communications.

- The group's employees had limited time.

- The group's financial resources were limited.

- The group had to make fast responses to rapidly changing political situations.

- It had to collaborate with other advocacy groups.

Source: Adapted from Heather Sehmel, "Websites and Advocacy Campaigns: Decision-Making, Implementation, and Audience in an Environmental Advocacy Group's Use of Websites as Part of Its Communication Campaigns," *Business Communication Quarterly*, June 2002.

- Organization charts that depict structure, authority, and responsibility relationships
- Maps on which different colors represent objects, such as bodies of water or mountains
- Stock market charts that represent the price movements of stocks
- Blueprints of a machine or a house
- Animations, videos, and movies

MATHEMATICAL (QUANTITATIVE) MODELS

The complexity of relationships in many organizational systems cannot be represented by icons or analogically because such representations would soon become cumbersome, and using them would be time-consuming. Therefore, more abstract models are described mathematically. Most DSS analyses are performed numerically with mathematical or other quantitative models.

THE BENEFITS OF MODELS

A management-support system uses models for the following reasons:

- Model manipulation (changing decision variables or the environment) is much easier than manipulating the real system. Experimentation is easier and does not interfere with the daily operation of the organization.
- Models enable the compression of time. Years of operations can be simulated in minutes or seconds of computer time.
- The cost of modeling analysis is much less than the cost of a similar experiment conducted on a real system.
- The cost of making mistakes during a trial-and-error experiment is much less when models are used rather than real systems.
- The business environment involves considerable uncertainty. With modeling, a manager can estimate the risks resulting from specific actions.
- Mathematical models enable the analysis of a very large, sometimes infinite, number of possible solutions. Even in simple problems, managers often have a large number of alternatives from which to choose.
- Models enhance and reinforce learning and training.
- Models and solution methods are readily available over the Web.
- There are many Java applets (and other Web programs) that readily solve models.

Advances in computer graphics, especially through Web interfaces and their associated object-oriented programming languages, have led to an increased tendency to use iconic and analog models to complement MSS mathematical modeling. For example, visual simulation combines all three types of models. Case Application 2.3 contains an interesting description of a multicriteria model that involves both qualitative and quantitative criteria. We provide a preview of the modeling process in a Web Chapter. We defer our detailed discussion on models until Chapter 4.

2.5 PHASES OF THE DECISION-MAKING PROCESS

It is advisable to follow a systematic decision-making process. Simon (1977) says that this involves three major phases: intelligence, design, and choice. He later added a fourth phase, implementation. Monitoring can be considered a fifth phase—a form of feedback. However, we view monitoring as the **intelligence phase** applied to the **implementation phase**. Simon's model is the most concise and yet complete characterization of rational decision-making. A conceptual picture of the decision-making process is shown in Figure 2.2.

There is a continuous flow of activity from intelligence to design to choice (bold lines), but at any phase there may be a return to a previous phase (feedback). Modeling is an essential part of this process. The seemingly chaotic nature of following a haphazard path from problem discovery to solution by decision-making can be explained by these feedback loops.

The decision-making process starts with the intelligence phase. Reality is examined, and the problem is identified and defined. **Problem ownership** is established as well. In the design phase, a model that represents the system is constructed. This is

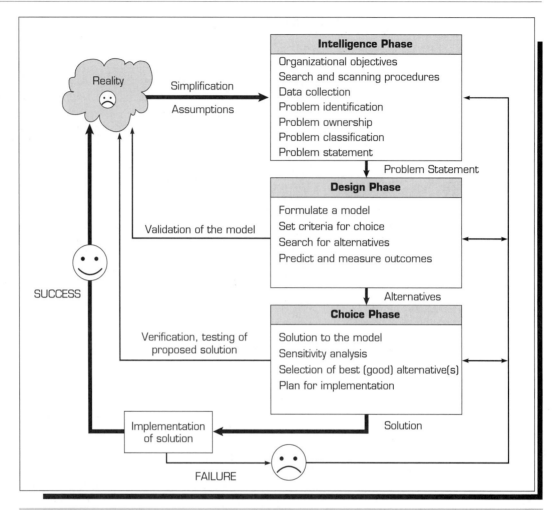

FIGURE 2.2　THE DECISION-MAKING/MODELING PROCESS

done by making assumptions that simplify reality and writing down the relationships among all the variables. The model is then validated, and criteria are determined in a principle of choice for evaluation of the alternative courses of action that are identified. Often the process of model development identifies alternative solutions, and vice versa. The choice phase includes selection of a proposed solution to the model (not necessarily to the problem it represents). This solution is tested to determine its viability. Once the proposed solution seems reasonable, we are ready for the last phase: implementation of the decision (*not necessarily of a system*). Successful implementation results in solving the real problem. Failure leads to a return to an earlier phase of the process. In fact, we can return to an earlier phase during any of the latter three phases. The decision-making situations described in Case Applications 2.1, 2.2, and 2.3 follow Simon's four-phase model, as do almost all decision making situations. We next discuss the decision-making process in detail, illustrated by the *MMS Running Case* in the DSS in Action boxes. Case Application 2.4 contains the summary and conclusion and Case Questions for the *MMS Running Case*.

Note that there are many other decision-making models. Notable among them is the Kepner-Tregoe (1965) method, which has been adopted by many firms because the tools and methods are readily available from Kepner-Tregoe, Inc. (also see Bazerman,

TABLE 2.2 Simon's Four Phases of Decision-Making and the Web

Phase	Web Impacts	Impacts On The Web
1. Intelligence	Access to information to identify problems and opportunities from internal and external data sources Access to AI methods and other data-mining methods to identify opportunities Collaboration through GSS and KMS Distance learning can provide knowledge to add structure to problems	Identification of opportunities for e-commerce, Web infrastructure, hardware and software tools, etc. Intelligent agents lessen the burden of information overload Smart search engines
2. Design	Access to data, models, and solution methods Use of OLAP, data mining, data warehouses Collaboration through GSS and KMS Similar solutions available from KMS	Brainstorming methods (GSS) to collaborate in Web infrastructure design Models and solutions of Web infrastructure issues
3. Choice	Access to methods to evaluate the impacts of proposed solutions	DSS tools examine and establish criteria from models to determine Web, intranet, and extranet infrastructure DSS tools determine how to route messages
4. Implementation	Web-based collaboration tools (GSS) and KMS can assist in implementing decisions. Tools monitor the performance of e-commerce and other sites, intranet, extranet, and the Internet itself	Decisions were implemented on browser and server design and access: these ultimately determined how to set up the various components that have evolved into the Internet

2001). We have found that these alternative models readily map into the Simon four-phase model. These alternative methods are described in a Web Chapter on the book's Web site (prenhall.com/turban). We next turn to a detailed discussion of the four phases. Web impacts on the four phases, and vice versa, are shown in Table 2.2

2.6 DECISION-MAKING: THE INTELLIGENCE PHASE

Intelligence in decision-making involves scanning the environment, either intermittently or continuously. It includes several activities aimed at identifying problem situations or opportunities. (It may also include monitoring the results of the implementation phase of a decision-making process.) See DSS in Action 2.6 for the first of the *MMS Running Case* situations.

PROBLEM (OR OPPORTUNITY) IDENTIFICATION

The intelligence phase begins with the identification of organizational goals and objectives related to an issue of concern (e.g., inventory management, job selection, lack of

MMS RUNNING CASE: THE INTELLIGENCE PHASE

INTRODUCTION

MMS Rent-a-Car, based in Atlanta, Georgia, has outlets at major airports and cities throughout North America. Founded by CEO Elena Markum some seven years ago, it has seen fast growth over the last few years, mainly because it offers quality service, fast, at convenient locations. MMS is highly competitive, able to offer cars at slightly lower rates than its competitors, because most of its airport facilities are located near but not at the airport. A keen user of information systems, MMS tracks competitors' prices, stored in a large data warehouse, through its Web-based enterprise information system portal, CLAUDIA (Come Learn About statUs for Deals and Information on Autos). CLAUDIA also tracks sales, fleet status, other internal status information, and external information about the economy and its relevant components. CLAUDIA has been a great success in keeping MMS competitive.

PROBLEMS

Elena has called a meeting of her vice presidents to discuss a problem that she noticed yesterday while tapping into CLAUDIA. Rentals are off about 10 percent nationally from the MMS projections for last month. Furthermore, CLAUDIA's forecasts indicate that they will continue to decrease. Elena wants to know why. This morning, the following VPs are present:

Sharon Goldman, Marketing (CMO)

Michael Lee, Operations (COO)

Marla Dana, Fleet Acquisitions (CFAO)

Tonia van de Stam, Information Systems (CIO)

Mark Lams, Knowledge Systems (CKO)

Jelene Thompson, Accounting (CAO)

Rose Franklin, Finance (CFO)

THE FIRST MEETING

Elena calls the meeting to order:

ELENA: Thank you all for coming on such short notice. I'm glad that we could schedule this meeting through our new scheduling module of CLAUDIA. I know you have all read my e-mail about our latest problem—sales are off by 10 percent. Basically, this will put us in the red for the year if it continues for another four months. CLAUDIA's forecasting system, that links to our revenue management system (RMS), indicates that sales will continue to decrease for the next four months even after we adjust prices. Folks, what's going on? I want to know what has caused this problem, how we can fix it, and how we can prevent it from happening again. Aside from solving the problem, I want to develop some knowledge about it and use it as an opportunity to improve our business.

MARLA: Frankly, Elena, I don't understand it! I noticed a slight dip in sales two months ago, but was so busy with our new fleet acquisitions that I planned to go back and look into what happened when I finished replacing the fleet later this week. I should have passed word on to our analysts to have a look back then. Sorry.

ELENA: No problem, Marla. I should have noticed it myself. I'm glad you were at least aware and ready to move on it. So, we have evidence of a problem. What else do we have?

SHARON: My up-to-date reports from the travel industry indicate that over the last six months there has been a slight increase in business overall. More people are flying for business meetings, conventions, trade shows, and pleasure. And the same proportion of them is renting cars in North America. This is true for all of our primary markets—major cities and airports, but not for our secondary markets in the smaller cities, where most rentals are for business. Overall, business should be up. Vacation business is up quite a bit from the central Florida theme parks advertising specials, and major conventions. Both political party conventions were held in major cities. Data indicate that our rentals did not increase while the total market did. Our earlier forecasts indicated that business should have increased, our rental rates reflect this, as does our increased fleet size, by 15 percent. The cars should be moving—but they're not!

ELENA: How about the advertising impacts?

ROSE: Our financials indicate that we have been spending more on advertising in our primary markets. Yet those are where our sales are dropping fastest.

JELENE: I agree. Though our records were about three weeks behind, now they are up date to, and will stay up to date thanks to our upgrade to CLAUDIA. I'm looking at the current data right now on our secure wireless network, and we're definitely down.

ELENA: OK. Our advertising expenditures are up. That's because we made that deal with Gold Motors Corporation (GMC). We just finished replacing our entire fleet with GMC cars and vans, right, Marla?

MARLA: Absolutely! The cars are much more reliable and cheaper to maintain than the ones that had the transmissions burning out every 45,000 miles [72,000 km.]. These cars and vans are the national best-sellers, have great reputations, and are of high quality. They have the highest safety records in most categories. All of the standard models came in first: subcompacts, compacts, mid-size, full-size, and mini-vans. About six weeks ago we started getting in the hot new GMC Spider 1600 convertible. We have an exclusive deal on this hot little number. It looks like the sporty 1971 Fiat Spider, but is built to new quality standards. It's fun to drive—they let me have one for a year before we got the fleet in! They are expensive, and GMC owns the domestic market. We should be able to rent these out all the time. We have five at each agency across the country, and by year's end we should have ten.

SHARON: We got an exclusive with them for the next three years. They only give the fleet discount to us, we feature their cars in our advertising, and they feature us in theirs. And the Spider came

to us right off the new assembly line in Pittsburgh.

ELENA: I have one of the Spiders, too. So I suspect that they're constantly rented out, aren't they?

MICHAEL: Well, no. Only about half of them are rented. The rental rates were supposed to be set pretty high, but our RMS recommends setting it at the same price as a compact. We hedged a little and set the price to about 10 percent higher. Some local agency offices are overriding the system and setting the prices 15 percent less and they still can't move them.

ELENA: How about the other classes of cars?

MICHAEL: Rentals down about 8 percent nationally on all the other ones.

ELENA: So sales are down 8 percent for everything but the Spider, and the Spider, which should be a hot seller, is off by 50 percent. I know from CLAUDIA that our inventory is OK. All the new cars came in on schedule, and we were able to sell the used cars through electronic auction sites and carmax.com. Folks, we definitely have a big problem.

MICHAEL: As COO, I see that this is primarily my problem, though all of you here are involved. We've never had this happen before, so I really don't know how to classify the problem. But I think we can get at most of the information we need. This situation is only a symptom of the problem. We need to identify the cause so we can correct the problem. I want some time to get my analysts, and Tonia's, moving on it. I will need some major help from Sharon's people, and probably a bit from everyone. Sharon and I talked before the meeting. We both have a feeling that there is something wrong with how we are marketing the new cars, but we don't have enough information just yet to identify it. I hope that once we solve this problem we'll have a nice piece of strategic knowledge for Mark to put into the KMS. I'll tentatively schedule a meeting through CLAUDIA next week as close to this time as possible, depending on people's previous commitments. I'll e-mail the major results as we go. I'm sure we'll know something before the next meeting.

ELENA: Thanks Michael. OK, folks! We know we have a serious problem. We've seen its effects. Michael will assume ownership and move ahead. I also want our IS analysts looking at data even before anyone requests them. That includes any weird economic trends or events, and look at the underlying structure and parameters of our forecasting models. OK, Tonia? Sharon, you look into the advertising. See if there are any external events or trends or reports on the cars that could affect our rentals. The RMS has been accurate until now. It's been able to balance price, supply, and demand, but something happened. Thank you all and have a great day.

Source: This fictional decision-making case is loosely based on several real situations. Thanks to Professor Elena Karahanna at The University of Georgia for inspiring it.

or an incorrect Web presence) and determination of whether they are being met. Problems occur because of dissatisfaction with the status quo. Dissatisfaction is the result of a difference between what we desire (or expect) and what is occurring. In this first phase, one attempts to determine whether a problem exists, identify its symptoms, determine its magnitude, and explicitly define it. Often, what is described as a problem (such as excessive costs) may be only a symptom (measure) of a problem (such as improper inventory levels). Because real-world problems are usually complicated by many interrelated factors, it is sometimes difficult to distinguish between the symptoms and the real problem, as is described in DSS in Action 2.6. New opportunities and problems certainly may be uncovered while investigating the cause of the symptoms.

The existence of a problem can be determined by monitoring and analyzing the organization's productivity level. The measurement of productivity and the construction of a model are based on real data. The collection of data and the estimation of future data are among the most difficult steps in the analysis. Some issues that may arise during data collection and estimation, and thus plague decision-makers, are

- Data are not available. As a result, the model is made with, and relies on, potentially inaccurate estimates.
- Obtaining data may be expensive.
- Data may not be accurate or precise enough.
- Data estimation is often subjective.
- Data may be insecure.
- Important data that influence the results may be qualitative (soft).
- There may be too many data (information overload).
- Outcomes (or results) may occur over an extended period. As a result, revenues, expenses, and profits will be recorded at different points in time. To overcome this difficulty, a present-value approach can be used if the results are quantifiable.
- It is assumed that future data will be similar to historical data. If not, the nature of the change has to be predicted and included in the analysis.

Once the preliminary investigation is completed, it is possible to determine whether a problem really exists, where it is located, and how significant it is. A key issue is whether an information system is reporting a problem or only the symptoms of a problem. For example, in the *MMS Running Case*, sales are down; there is a problem; but the situation, no doubt, is symptomatic of the problem.

PROBLEM CLASSIFICATION

Problem classification is the conceptualization of a problem in an attempt to place it in a definable category, possibly leading to a standard solution approach. An important approach classifies problems according to the degree of structuredness evident in them.

PROGRAMMED VERSUS NONPROGRAMMED PROBLEMS

Simon (1977) distinguished two extremes regarding the structuredness of decision problems. At one end of the spectrum are well-structured problems that are repetitive and routine and for which standard models have been developed. Simon calls these **programmed problems**. Examples of such problems are weekly scheduling of employees, monthly determination of cash flow, and selection of an inventory level for a specific item under constant demand. At the other end of the spectrum are unstructured problems, also called **nonprogrammed problems**, which are novel and nonrecurrent. For example, typical unstructured problems include merger and acquisition decisions, undertaking a complex research and development project, evaluating an electronic commerce initiative, determination about what to put on a Web site (see DSS in Action 2.5), and selecting a job. Semistructured problems fall between the two extremes. In the *Running Case*, the problem seems unstructured. With analysis, it should become semistructured. Hopefully, over time, it will become structured. Generally, a structured or semistructured problem tends to gain structure as it is solved (see DSS in Action 2.7).

PROBLEM DECOMPOSITION

Many complex problems can be divided into subproblems. Solving the simpler subproblems may help in solving the complex problem. Also, seemingly poorly structured problems sometimes have highly structured subproblems. Just as a semistructured problem results when some phases of decision-making are structured while other phases are unstructured, so when some subproblems of a decision-making problem are

---

DSS IN FOCUS 2.7

KNOWLEDGE CAN STRUCTURE AN UNSTRUCTURED PROBLEM

A decision-maker must recognize that problems can be unstructured when there is only minimal or even no knowledge and information about them. Developing knowledge about a problem can add structure to unstructured or semistructured problems. This is partly why the prototyping development process for DSS has proven successful in practice (see Chapter 6). This also explains the difference between being an expert and being a novice in a particular field. For example, if you know little about the restaurant business except that

you want to open a restaurant, determining an appropriate location for your restaurant is unstructured. If you seek out expert knowledge and demographic information, you will add structure to the problem through learning. Alternatively, if you are responsible for choosing locations for a large chain of restaurants, determining where to put the 2,000th restaurant is a very structured problem to which known data and models from your organization are applied.

structured with others unstructured, the problem itself is semistructured. As a DSS is developed and the decision-maker and development staff learn more about the problem, it gains structure. Decomposition also facilitates communication among decision-makers. Decomposition is one of the most important aspects of the Analytical Hierarchy Process (AHP) (Forman and Selly, 2001; Saaty, 1999) which helps decision-makers incorporate both qualitative and quantitative factors into their decision-making models. See Case Application 2.3. In the *Running Case*, there are several aspects to be investigated: advertising, sales, new car acquisition, and so on. Each of them is a subproblem that interacts with the others.

PROBLEM OWNERSHIP

In the intelligence phase, it is important to establish problem ownership. A problem exists in an organization only if someone or some group takes on the responsibility of attacking it and if the organization has the ability to solve it. For example, a manager may feel that he or she has a problem because interest rates are too high. Since interest rate levels are determined at the national and international levels, and most managers can do nothing about them, high interest rates are the problem of the government, not a problem for a specific company to solve. The problem companies actually face is how to operate in a high-interest-rate environment. For an individual company, the interest- rate level should be handled as an uncontrollable (environmental) factor to be predicted.

When problem ownership is not established, either someone is not doing his or her job, or the problem at hand has yet to be identified as belonging to anyone. It is then important for someone to either volunteer to "own" it or assign it to someone. This was done, very clearly, in the *MMS Running Case*.

The intelligence phase ends with a formal problem statement.

2.7 DECISION-MAKING: THE DESIGN PHASE

The **design phase** involves finding or developing and analyzing possible courses of action. These include understanding the problem and testing solutions for feasibility. A model of the decision-making problem is constructed, tested, and validated. See the *MMS Running Case* in DSS in Action 2.8.

Modeling involves conceptualizing the problem and abstracting it to quantitative and/or qualitative form. For a mathematical model, the variables are identified and their mutual relationships are established. Simplifications are made, whenever necessary, through assumptions. For example, a relationship between two variables may be assumed to be linear even though in reality there may be some nonlinear effects. A proper balance between the level of model simplification and the representation of reality must be obtained because of the benefit/cost trade-off. A simpler model leads to lower development costs, easier manipulation, and a faster solution but is less representative of the real problem and can produce inaccurate results. On the other hand, a simpler model generally requires fewer data, or the data are aggregated and easier to obtain.

The process of modeling is a combination of art and science. As a science, there are many standard model classes available, and with practice an analyst can determine

MMS RUNNING CASE: THE DESIGN PHASE

Later on the day of the first meeting, Michael Lee as his top analyst, Stephanie Elberson, to look into what might have happened. Michael recognized that it was too early to start looking into criteria, solutions, and more (he had studied decision-making in a DSS course in his MBA program). He was still trying to understand the problem and separate the problem that could be analyzed from the symptoms. He wanted to make the connection between the two, but he felt that something was fundamentally wrong and CLAUDIA could not identify it. A good decision-maker relies on judgment and has a good "feel" for what makes sense and what does not. Michael was one of the best.

Stephanie put together a team of analysts and started formulating areas to investigate. One member of the team, Dot Frank, worked closely with Sharon's analyst, Phil Abrams, to establish the accuracy of the forecasting model. Amy Lazbin, on Stephanie's team, looked into databases of operational data available internally and economic data available through subscription services. The latter data focused on the auto rental, automobile, and general economic areas. The analysis team initially set the data-mining tools on automatic to establish relationships in the data. For the most part, Amy was able to verify most of the relationships and assumptions that were already in the forecasting models and the revenue-management system. Nothing new popped up from the artificial neural networks, clustering analysis algorithms, and statistical regression models. The pricing model and the forecasting models were all right, though there were some new fluctuations and the errors were higher when the team looked into how well they had performed over the last two months as this new problem arose. The team noticed that the neural networks outperformed the regression-based systems a bit, so they set up an IS and marketing group to look into how they could improve the regression-based models with neural networks. (This was a new opportunity, which led them to return to the intelligence phase with a new set of issues.)

Stephanie was puzzled. She met with Michael two days later to discuss what she was going to do next. She also invited the marketing team and the IS team to each send someone to the meeting. Phil Abrams and Marina Laksey (from IS) joined the team at this point. The meeting was held in the EMC (electronic meeting center), where they would be able to analyze data and use the group-support system (GSS). Here's how the meeting went:

STEPHANIE: Thank you all for coming today. As you know, we are working hard on the problem—or rather the symptoms—to try to get to the heart of the problem. Data-mining tools helped a bit, but there is something fundamentally wrong and we have yet to find it. Any ideas?

MARINA: Stephanie, we used the data-mining tools and looked at most, if not all, of the data we normally look at. And we usually look at standard views through our spreadsheet-type interface. I know we have to look "outside the box." First off, the four of us need to fire up our new, powerful OLAP (online analytical processing) software, DOT (Data on Time). It taps into our data warehouse and other data, but it goes beyond data mining by allowing us to poke about in the data. We just got the software in two weeks ago, and I have already gone through the training course. It has many of the features that CLAUDIA has, but allows us to look into multidimensional data from any of our data sources in any "slice" we choose. It also lets us link into other databases and data marts like the one that marketing has. Let me start it up!

PHIL: I agree. I learned how to use the OLAP software on my own, and I've developed some interesting views of our marketing data that show relationships we did not believe possible. The graphics are almost automatic. Let's try it!

The team saw the bumps in the data, but had no idea what had caused them. At least they could see them. When they tapped into the advertising plans, they noticed a slight inverse relationship with sales and advertising. When they asked Phil about it, he said:

PHIL: Sales dropped two weeks after our new joint-marketing campaign began. We heavily advertised the new cars. Every national and local TV commercial prominently displayed the Spider.

We have data on that in our marketing databases. I know you don't normally look at that. Here, let me bring them up. Hmmm! We show how much air time each commercial played where, and what was in them. Let me do a little slicing and aggregating here. Aha! I see. We are mostly advertising the cars nationally. Sales are very weak in primary markets, but also a bit weak in secondary markets. Ah! Ah! Ah! One problem we have is that of distribution. We have over half the cars in the wrong places. We need to move all the Spiders from the secondary markets to the primary markets. But I think we have another problem—the pricing, supply, and demand data that we are using to predict rentals don't make sense. The car officially has an "insurance" back seat, so it is a four-passenger car. But you'd be lucky to get a carry-on suitcase back there. Since we didn't have data on it, someone in our group entered it as a four-seat compact with two doors. The system thinks it is a car ideal for a small family or a single businessperson on a budget. These rent well in the Midwest in the secondary markets, but badly in the convention areas, where there are men who are going through their midlife crises and single women who like to rent sporty cars. We have a lot of analyses to do here on where we are advertising what. I'm not sure who rents what where, but I suspect that we can target our ads better once we determine our market clusters, like males in Nebraska, 45 years old, traveling to San Diego for trade conferences. We have the data, we just need to apply them better.

MICHAEL: Hold on. Before I start moving cars around, we need to analyze this a bit more. We've never had a car like the Spider, so we need to investigate its properties and which categories of customers would ideally want it. Part of the solution jumped at us. But what are we trying to do? If I remember correctly, a few years ago we ran a "try before you buy" promotion in conjunction with our previous car supplier. People could rent our excess

stock on our off-days for half the rental rate for up to three days. If they bought the car from a dealer in the area, they got the rental price back. If not, they had fun with the car. It worked well. We noticed that people who liked the car they rented had a tendency to rent them again, especially in our primary markets. We have a lot to look into.

I want to recap what we have. We know that our goal is to maximize net profit. This is clearly our principle of choice. We need to come up with criteria that describe the impact of alternatives and determine how they affect our bottom line. Our revenue management system sets prices so that we can ideally do that. We have some errors in our marketing database, we must rethink how we advertise and how we distribute our stock. OK. I meet with the VP team in a couple of days. I'm going to e-mail them information about what we've uncovered and where to find the data. First I'll talk to Sharon so she can get busy with some ideas on marketing.

AT A MEETING TWO DAYS LATER: SAME PLACE, SAME PEOPLE

STEPHANIE: Good morning. Those of us in the trenches think we've got it! Here's what's going on. We have several problems, each of which we have developed some alternatives for. We're going to discuss what we think are the best ones for each situation. Some we can implement right away, others will take some time.

Let's start with our objective—to maximize profit. *Our principle of choice is one of profit maximization.* This part of the problem was easy. Our RMS recognizes this and adjusts prices automatically to maximize profit on an annual basis. There are some errors in the price elasticity curve for the Spider, but in general, the real question now is how to manage demand. Our advertising influences demand, as does our inventory. We need for the right product to appeal to the right customers. There are many criteria that we need to measure, from quality to color to size, and customer service, car availability, etc., in terms of how they affect rentals. We are doing this, but need to do a better job of it in order to track our rentals. We have a team analyzing this right now. In a few weeks, they will have some concrete recommendations for system upgrades to the revenue management system.

Our symptoms indicate the following *real* problems and alternatives, among which we can choose:

Data accuracy:

We need to change the profile of the Spider from a compact to a sports car. We need to develop the RMS profile from what little data we've got. Fortunately, we can tap into market data that our faculty consultants at UGA have gathered for us in their research. One of the faculty members drives a Spider as well.

Inventory Imbalance:

We have done some analysis to determine what the real demand for the Spider is, and how it affects the demand for other cars, and vice versa. We built an **optimization** model and solved it. Based on our current advertising, we have determined that by moving about 15 percent of our fleet around (and not too far), we can take care of most of the demand imbalance. We recommend moving all the Spiders from secondary to primary markets right away. We also want to move some of our minivans and full-size cars around. Later, we can adjust advertising to push some secondary market demand.

Advertising imbalance:

We advertise where our customers are, but they rent elsewhere, and for different reasons. We need to do a better job of identifying customer homes to determine what to advertise where. Our analysis shows rentals are off partly because we indicate that we have the Spider. Young to middle-aged men and single women want to rent it, but we stock out where they are going. For example, we discovered that middle-aged men and women from the Midwest rent compacts in the secondary Midwest markets, but in the primary markets on the coasts want to rent the Spider. We are still analyzing effects like this, and should be able to complete the work in about a week to determine how to realign our advertising efforts.

Try before you buy:

This actually is an opportunity, not a problem. When we saturate Spider demand in primary markets, we should get some additional Spiders in the secondary markets and reestablish the "try before you buy" campaign. This car will be a real boon in this effort. Sharon's group has already established a cooperative agreement with GMC. They're interested, and it should boost our profitability on these cars by 18 percent.

Discount substitutes:

We discovered that many customers called or got on our Web site to rent the Spider. When they found out that we didn't have one for them, rather than rent a different car, many were so annoyed that they rented a car from one of our competitors, usually a Toyota MR-2. This happened in almost all of our primary markets. In our secondary markets, people really didn't want the Spider, but instead wanted full-size cars. Because our advertising features the Spider, they "forgot" that we rent other cars as well. Actually, *we forgot to remind them.* Our advertising is backfiring on us. We should immediately discount substitutes for the Spider until we get the Spiders in place next week.

Florida Theme Park Demand:

We have a unique opportunity here. Florida theme parks have been advertising heavily in Europe because the euro is strong relative to the dollar. We must increase advertising in Europe either with the theme parks or separately. Phil is confident that we can run a joint campaign. Marketing will look into this, and how we might be able to get customers to pay in advance in euros. To do this we may need to move minivans to Florida from as far away as Tennessee.

What it boils down to is that we want to be more aggressive in balancing our stock to meet demand, and tie this into the RMS and advertising. We also want to refine our advertising model to handle new types of cars like sports cars and update demand data more frequently.

Michael, this is what we want to present to the VPs on Monday. Is that OK?

MICHAEL: Perfect! We have identified the real problems and have good alternatives. I really appreciate the *completed staff work* (à la Napoleon). If this all works out, the end-of-the-year bonuses for this team should be excellent. Let's go have lunch! I'm buying!

which one is applicable to a given situation. As an art, a level of creativity and finesse is required when determining what simplifying assumptions can work, how to combine appropriate features of the model classes, and how to integrate models to obtain valid solutions. In the *MMS Running Case*, the problem at hand was very vague.

Decision-makers sometimes develop mental models, especially in time-pressure situations (see DSS in Action 2.9). Mental models help frame the decision-making situation, a topic of cognition theory (see Shoemaker and Russo, 2001). The team investigated the data in order to develop an understanding that was more of a mental model of the situation. Models were indeed used and tested, but not described in the *Running Case*. Data mining, OLAP, and revenue management software have many models embedded in them (see Cross, 1997; Swift, 2001).

DSS IN ACTION 2.9

TO FLY OR NOT TO FLY? THAT IS THE QUESTION: PRESSURE TO FLY FOR THE WRONG REASONS

When pilots find themselves pressured to perform, there is a chance that good judgment and safety will be compromised. How can a pilot determine whether it is safe to fly? Pilots like to think that they have good judgment, and that regardless of the situation, they will always make the right call. They train, practice, and follow the rules. But despite experience and professionalism, flight crews sometimes still get into deep trouble. This may be especially so when the choice to fly or not is framed in the context of a life-and-death situation for a passenger (e.g., if an air-ambulance is needed, the crew might not see dangerous weather as a high risk). Without a doubt, emotions enter the decision-making picture, and they compromise safety (Hoch and Kunreuther, 2001).

The emotional aspects of the mission in air-ambulance operations often create strong pressure to fly, even in marginal conditions. "Whether it's a sick passenger or a bag of rocks, we should be flying the same and making the same decisions," says Ed Phillips, aviation services manager for Life Star Air Ambulance (Hartford, Connecticut). "But if the pilot has a 10-year-old son, and hears that it's a 10-year-old boy who's been injured in the town next to his, [he's going to want] to fly . . . no matter what." Phillips explains further, "One way we take the pressure off is to leave out the details of the mission. We give the pilots only the locations, and let them make the go/no-go decision. If they decide to take the mission, we can give them the details once they're in the air." At Air Methods (Jackson County, Georgia), the crew makes a decision about flying before they know the condition of the patient. The pilot does not have any medical training;

so once airborne, he or she ideally flies with the same calm speed on any call. On the corporate side, pressure to fly may come from an executive who needs to be somewhere fast. There are also issues of personal fitness. Alcohol and medications affect judgment. But job and economic pressures can come to bear. There are cases where fatigue and poor weather have unfortunately led to crashes. Time pressure in conjunction with other factors can lead to dangerous conditions.

For a pilot to refocus judgment to alleviate the pressure to fly, the solution is simple. The pilot must try to separate the aviation decision-making from outside influences. Customers must be apprised of the reason that a flight may be delayed or cancelled. Passengers need to be made aware of flight regulations in a clear, written format. *Pilots should not bend the rules.* CRM (crew resource management) can be used to identify customer personalities and show ways to deal with them that deflect the pressure. Ill pilots should not fly. There are self-assessment tools that help pilots determine whether they are fit. Finally, the chief pilot must back a pilot's decision not to fly. This may require a major change in corporate culture.

Pilots tend to be very task-oriented and goal-driven. They tend to put more pressure on themselves than most other people do. But the real job is not transporting people. The most important job of a pilot is decision-making.

Source: Adapted from Robert N. Rossier, "Pressured to Perform: Flying for the Wrong Reasons," *Business & Commercial Aviation*, Vol. 90, No. 6, June 2002, 62–69; and Allison Floyd, "Flights Save Time and Lives," *Athens Banner-Herald*, Vol. 170, No. 3, pp. A1, A5.

Models have **decision variables** that describe the alternatives a manager must choose among (like how many cars to deliver to an specific rental agency, how to advertise at specific times, or which Web server to buy or lease), a result variable or a set of result variables (like profit, revenue, or sales) that describes the objective or goal of the decision-making problem, and uncontrollable variables or parameters (like economic conditions) that describe the environment. The process of modeling involves determining the (usually mathematical, sometimes symbolic) relationships among the variables. These topics are discussed in depth in Chapter 4.

SELECTION OF A PRINCIPLE OF CHOICE

A **principle of choice** is a criterion that describes the acceptability of a solution approach. In a model, it is a result variable. Selecting a principle of choice is not part of the choice phase but involves how we establish our decision-making objective(s) and how it is (they are) incorporated into the model(s). Are we willing to assume high risk, or do we prefer a low-risk approach? Are we attempting to optimize or satisfice? It is also important to recognize the difference between a criterion and a constraint (see DSS in Focus 2.10). Among the many principles of choice, *normative* and *descriptive* are of prime importance.

NORMATIVE MODELS

Normative models are those in which the chosen alternative is demonstrably the best of all possible alternatives. To find it, one should examine all the alternatives and prove that the one selected is indeed the best, which is what one would *norm*ally want. This process is basically **optimization**. In operational terms, optimization can be achieved in one of three ways:

DSS IN FOCUS 2.10

THE DIFFERENCE BETWEEN A CRITERION AND A CONSTRAINT

Many people new to the formal study of decision-making inadvertently confuse the concepts of criterion and constraint. Often this is because a criterion may imply a constraint, either implicit or explicit, thereby adding to the confusion. For example, in Case Application 2.3, there is a distance criterion, where the decision-maker does not want to travel too far from home. However, there is an implicit constraint that the alternatives from which he selects must be within a certain distance from his home. This constraint effectively says that if the distance from home is greater than a certain amount, then the alternative is not feasible, or rather that the distance to an alternative must be less than or equal to a certain number (this would be a formal relationship in some models; in the model of the case, it reduces the search, considering fewer alternatives). This is similar to the in-class examples of university selection, where schools beyond a single day's driving distance were not considered by most people, and, in fact, the utility function (criterion value) of distance started out low close to home, peaked at about 70 miles (about 100 km)—the distance between Atlanta and Athens, Georgia—and sharply dropped off thereafter. (See the Web Chapter "Select a College/University with an Interactive Multiple-Goal DSS.")

- Get the highest level of goal attainment from a given set of resources. For example, which alternative will yield the maximum profit from an investment of $10 million?
- Find the alternative with the highest ratio of goal attainment to cost (e.g., profit per dollar invested) or maximize productivity.
- Find the alternative with the lowest cost (or smallest amount of other resources) that will meet an acceptable level of goals. For example, if your task is to select hardware for an intranet with a minimum bandwidth, which alternative will accomplish this goal at the least cost?

Normative decision theory is based on the following assumptions of *rational decision-makers*:

- Humans are economic beings whose objective is to maximize the attainment of goals; that is, the decision-maker is rational. (More of a good thing [revenue, fun] is better than less; less of a bad thing [cost, pain] is better than more.)
- For a decision-making situation, all viable alternative courses of action and their consequences, or at least the probability and the values of the consequences, are known.
- Decision-makers have an order or preference that enables them to rank the desirability of all consequences of the analysis (best to worst).

Kontoghiorghes, Rustem, and Siokos (2002) describe the rational approach to decision-making, especially as it relates to using models and computing.

Are decision-makers really rational? See DSS in Focus 2.11; also Schwartz (1998), and Halpern and Stern (1998) for anomalies in rational decision-making. Though there may be major anomalies in the presumed rationality of financial and economic behavior, we take the view that these could be caused by incompetence, lack of knowledge, multiple goals that are framed inadequately, misunderstanding of a decision-maker's true expected utility, and time-pressure impacts. For more on rationality, see Gharajedaghi (1999), Larrson (2002), Ranganathan and Sethi (2002), and Verma and Churchman (1998).

There are other anomalies, often caused by time pressure. For example, Stewart (2002) describes a number of researchers who are working with intuitive decision-making. The idea of "thinking with your gut" is obviously a heuristic approach to decision-making. It works well for firefighters and military personnel on the battle-

DSS IN FOCUS 2.11

ARE DECISION-MAKERS REALLY RATIONAL?

Some researchers question the rationality concept. There are countless cases of individuals and groups behaving irrationally in real-world and experimental decision-making situations. For example, suppose you need to take a bus to work every morning and the bus leaves at 7:00 a.m. Therefore, if it takes you one hour to wake up, prepare for work, and get to the bus stop, you should always awaken at or before 6:00 a.m. However, sometimes (perhaps many times) you may sleep until 6:30, knowing that you will miss breakfast and not perform well at work. Or you may be late and arrive at the bus stop at 7:05, hoping that the bus will be late. So, why are you late? Multiple objectives and hoped-for goal levels may lead to this situation. Or your true expected utility for being on time might simply indicate that you should go back to bed most mornings!

field. One critical aspect of decision-making in this mode is that many scenarios have been thought through in advance. Even when a situation is new, it can quickly be matched to an existing one on the fly, and a reasonable solution can be obtained. See Stewart (2002) for details. See Luce et al. (2001) for a description of how emotions affect decision-making, and Pauly (2001) for a description of inconsistencies in decision-making. Bonabeau and Meyer (2001) describe a decision-making approach called swarm intelligence. It is based on chaos theory and has its roots in the way an anthill functions successfully. There is a certain rationality underlying its approach. Daniel Kahneman and Amos Tversky received the Nobel Prize in Economics in 2002 for their work on what appears to be irrationality in decision-making. We believe that the irrationality is caused by the factors listed above. For example, Tversky, Slovic, and Kahneman (1990) investigate the causes of preference reversal, which is a known problem in applying the analytical hierarchy process to problems. They conducted experiments to investigate the phenomenon. However, some criterion or preference is generally omitted from the analysis. Ratner, Kahn, and Kahneman (1999) investigated how variety can cause individuals to choose less-preferred options even though they will enjoy them less. In this case, variety clearly has value, is part of a decision-maker's utility, and is a criterion and/or constraint that should be considered in decision-making.

In the *MMS Running Case*, rationality prevailed. Maximizing profit was clearly the principle of choice. However, have a look at the situation faced by the Lafko family described in DSS in Action 2.12. Rationality is present, but it may be preventing the family from obtaining and implementing a viable decision.

SUBOPTIMIZATION

By definition, optimization requires a decision-maker to consider the impact of each alternative course of action on the entire organization because a decision made in one area may have significant effects (positive or negative) in other areas. Consider a marketing department that implements an e-commerce site. Within hours, orders far exceed production capacity. The production department, which plans its own schedule, cannot meet demand. It may gear up for as high demand as is possible to meet. Ideally and independently, the department should produce only a few products in extremely large quantities to minimize manufacturing costs. However, such a plan may result in large, costly inventories and marketing difficulties caused by the lack of a variety of products, especially if customers start to cancel orders since that were not met in a timely way. This situation illustrates the sequential nature of decision-making (see Borges, Pino, and Valle 2002; Sun and Giles, 2001).

A systems point of view assesses the impact of all decisions on the entire system. Thus, the marketing department should make its plans in conjunction with other departments. However, such an approach may require a complicated, expensive, time-consuming analysis. In practice, the MSS builder may close the system within narrow boundaries, considering only the part of the organization under study (the marketing and/or production department in this case), and incorporate relationships into the model that assume away certain complicated relationships describing interactions with and among the other departments. The other departments can be aggregated into simple model components. Such an approach is called **suboptimization**.

If a suboptimal decision is made in one part of the organization without considering the details of the rest of the organization, then an optimal solution from the point of view of that part may be inferior for the whole. However, suboptimization may still be a very practical approach to decision-making, and many problems are first approached from this perspective. It is possible to reach tentative conclusions (and

---

DSS IN ACTION 2.12

DECISION-MAKING BETWEEN A ROCK AND A HARD PLACE; OR, WHAT CAN YOU DO WHEN THERE ARE NO GOOD OR EVEN FEASIBLE ALTERNATIVES?

Fred J. Lafko, an entrepreneur in Poughkeepsie, New York, had a vision in the early 1980s. He bought the *Alexander Hamilton*, a side-wheeler ship used by the Hudson River Day Line from the early 1900s until the latter part of the twentieth century (you can see image at farberantiques.com/hudson.html). Lafko planned to move the ship from the New York City area to Poughkeepsie and make it into a tourist site. He would build a trendy restaurant, shops, and offices into it and moor it along the banks of the Hudson River. As it happens, the *Alexander Hamilton* was one of the few ships listed as a National Historical Monument. This was because of its unique engine design. It was the last ship of its type that could sail. Lafko arranged to have it moved to Poughkeepsie, but unfortunately the ship ran aground on a sandbar in the river. Experts said he would have to wait until the next major high tide (when the moon was full) to pull it off. He arranged for tugboats to pull the ship off the sandbar. Unfortunately the tugboats were late. A month later, he arranged to have them come a day early, and they successfully pulled the *Alexander Hamilton* off the sandbar. Fred arranged to have the ship tied up at the U.S. Navy's Sulko Pier so that he could assess the damage. Once the ship was made seaworthy, he arranged again to tow it to Poughkeepsie. Before the ship could be moved a hurricane sunk it, just below the water line. Shortly after,

Fred Lafko unfortunately died, and his brother Jack, who handled his estate, did nothing about the ship, much to the consternation of Fred's six grown children and the Navy, which wanted its pier back.

In the summer of 2002 Jack died. Fred's children had to make a decision about the ship. After 20 years underwater, there is probably very little left of it worth salvaging. But since the ship is a National Historical Monument, they cannot simply cut it up and scrap it. They also cannot remove the engine. The conventional way to lift the ship out of the water is to build a water-tight fence around it and pump out the silt. The U.S. Environmental Protection Agency will not allow this, because the silt would pollute the river (even thought that is where the silt is now). Other salvage methods are very dangerous or expensive. The Navy will not take ownership of the ship (because then it would have to deal with the problem directly), and it is not clear if the children can donate the ship to anyone else or to another agency interested in preserving the past. No one will buy the ship because of all the complications. There do not appear to be any good or even feasible decisions. What can Fred's family do?

Source: Dennis Lafko, one of Fred's sons, as told to Jay Aronson on a flight from Atlanta to Colorado Springs, July 2002.

---

generally usable results) by analyzing only a portion of a system without getting bogged down in too many details. Once a solution is proposed, its potential effects on the remaining departments of the organization can be tested. If no significant negative effects are found, the solution can be implemented.

Suboptimization may also apply when simplifying assumptions are used in modeling a specific problem. There may be too many details or too many data to incorporate into a specific decision-making situation, and so not all of them are used in the model. If the solution to the model seems reasonable, it may be valid for the problem and thus be adopted. For example, in a production department, parts are often partitioned into A/B/C inventory categories. Generally, A items (large gears, whole assemblies) are expensive (say, $3,000 or more apiece), built to order in small batches, and inventoried in low quantities; C items (nuts, bolts, screws) are very inexpensive (say, less than $2) and ordered and used in very large quantities; and B items fall in between. All A items can be handled by a detailed scheduling model and physically monitored closely by management; B items are generally somewhat aggregated, their groupings are scheduled, and management reviews these parts less frequently; and C items are not scheduled but are simply acquired or built based on a policy defined by management with a simple EOQ ordering system that assumes constant annual demand. The policy might be reviewed once a year. This situation applies when determining all criteria or modeling the entire problem becomes prohibitively time-consuming or expensive.

Suboptimization may also involve simply bounding the search for an optimum (e.g., by a heuristic) by considering fewer criteria or alternatives or by eliminating large portions of the problem from evaluation. If it takes too long to solve a problem, a good-enough solution found so far may be used and the optimization effort terminated.

DESCRIPTIVE MODELS

Descriptive models describe things as they are, or as they are believed to be. These models are typically mathematically based. Descriptive models are extremely useful in DSS for investigating the consequences of various alternative courses of action under different configurations of inputs and processes. However, because a descriptive analysis checks the performance of the system for a given set of alternatives (rather than for *all* alternatives), there is no guarantee that an alternative selected with the aid of a descriptive analysis is optimal. In many cases, it is only satisfactory. **Simulation** is probably the most common descriptive modeling method. Simulation has been applied to many areas of decision-making. Computer and video games are a form of simulation. An artificial reality is created, and the game player lives within it. Virtual reality is also a form of simulation. The environment is simulated, not real. A common use of simulation is in manufacturing. Again, consider the production department of a firm with complications caused by the marketing department. The characteristics of each machine in a job shop along the supply chain can be described mathematically. Relationships can be established based on how each machine physically runs and relates to others. Given a trial schedule of batches of parts, one can measure how batches flow through the system and the utilization statistics of each machine. Alternative schedules may then be tried, and the statistics recorded, until a reasonable schedule is found. Marketing can examine access and purchase patterns on its Web site. Simulation can be used to determine how to structure a Web site for improved performance and to estimate future purchases. Both departments have used primarily experimental modeling methods.

Classes of descriptive models include

- Complex inventory decisions
- Environmental-impact analysis
- Financial planning
- Information flow
- Markov analysis (predictions)
- Scenario analysis
- Simulation (alternative types)
- Technological forecasting
- Waiting line (queuing) management.

There are a number of nonmathematical descriptive models for decision-making. One is the cognitive map (Eden and Ackermann, 2002; Jenkins, 2002). A cognitive map can help a decision-maker sketch out the important qualitative factors and their causal relationships in a messy decision-making situation. It helps the decision-maker (or decision-making group) focus on what is relevant and what is not, and the map evolves as more is learned about the problem. The map can help the decision-maker understand issues better, focus better, and reach closure. One interesting software tool for cognitive mapping is Decision Explorer (Banxia Software Ltd., Glasgow, Scotland, banxia.com; try the demo).

Another descriptive decision-making model is the use of narratives to describe a decision-making situation. A narrative is a story that, when told, helps a decision-maker uncover the important aspects of the situation and leads to better understanding and framing. It is extremely effective when a group is making a decision and can lead to a more common frame. Juries in court trials typically use narrative-based approaches in reaching verdicts (see Allan, Fairtlough, and Heinzen, 2002; Beach, 1997; Denning, 2000; and the film *12 Angry Men*).

GOOD ENOUGH OR SATISFICING

According to Simon (1977), most human decision-making, whether organizational or individual, involves a willingness to settle for a satisfactory solution, "something less than the best." When **satisficing**, the decision-maker sets up an aspiration, goal, or desired level of performance and then searches the alternatives until one is found that achieves this level. The usual reasons for satisficing are time pressure (decisions may lose value over time), the ability to achieve optimization (solving some models could take longer than until when the sun is supposed to become a supernova), as well as recognition that the marginal benefit of a better solution is not worth the marginal cost to obtain it. (This is like searching the Web. You can look at only so many Web sites before you run out of time and energy.) In this situation, the decision-maker is behaving rationally, though in reality he or she is satisficing. Essentially, *satisficing is a form of suboptimization.* There may be a best solution, an optimum, but it is difficult, if not impossible, to attain. With a normative model, too much computation may be involved; with a descriptive model, it may not be possible to evaluate all the sets of alternatives.

Related to satisficing is Simon's idea of *bounded rationality.* Humans have a limited capacity for rational thinking; they generally construct and analyze a simplified model of a real situation by considering fewer alternatives, criteria, and/or constraints. Their behavior with respect to the simplified model may be rational. However, the rational solution for the simplified model may not be rational for the real-world problem. Rationality is bounded not only by limitations on human processing capacities but also by individual differences, such as age, education, knowledge, and attitudes. Bounded rationality is also why many models are descriptive rather than normative. This may also explain why so many good managers rely on intuition, an important aspect of good decision-making (see Stewart, 2002; Pauly, 2001). Agosto (2002) investigated bounded rationality and satisficing in "young people's" Web-based decision-making. Agosto was interested in how adolescents handle time constraints, information overload, and personal preferences, all factors that lead to satisficing. The research study indicates that reduction (filtering out information) and termination (early stopping) are two major satisficing behaviors. And personal preference plays a major role in Web site evaluation, especially in graphic/multimedia and subject-content preferences. Mingers and Rosenhead (2000) describe moving away from mathematical models and toward a facilitated, "enriched" decision-making process that involves group processes. This may make the decision-makers feel good about the process, but it ignores the fact that many models embedded in DSS are available just for the taking. Organizations that do not use the models may feel good, but firms that utilize the models (even in a facilitated environment) will definitely make more effective decisions. When tools are available and are effective, they should be used for competitive advantage.

DEVELOPING (GENERATING) ALTERNATIVES

A significant part of the process of model building is generating alternatives. In optimization models (such as linear programming), the alternatives may be generated automatically by the model. In most MSS situations, however, it is necessary to generate alternatives manually. This can be a lengthy process that involves searching and creativity. It takes time and costs money. Issues such as when to stop generating alternatives can be very important. Too many alternatives can be detrimental to the process of decision-making. A decision-maker may suffer from information overload. See DSS in Action 2.13. Cross (2001) describes a new initiative for administrators in higher-education institutions to handle *information overload*. The National Learning Infrastructure Initiative (NLII) Institute Readiness Program (READY) provides a way to organize and communicate information about the incorporation of technology into higher education. The Web-based READY portal filters through large amounts of information to select only relevant items for alternative selection. Generating alternatives is heavily dependent on the availability and cost of information and requires expertise in the problem area. This is the least formal aspect of problem-solving. Alternatives can be generated and evaluated with heuristics. The generation of alternatives from either individuals or groups can be supported by electronic brainstorming software in a Web-based GSS.

Note that the search for alternatives usually comes after the criteria for evaluating the alternatives are determined. This sequence can reduce the search for alternatives and the effort involved in evaluating them, but identifying potential alternatives can sometimes aid in identifying criteria. Identifying criteria and alternatives proved difficult in the *MMS Running Case*. The analysts first had to identify the many *problems*. Once the problems were identified, years of experience and access to information through the CLAUDIA portal made it easy for the team to develop obvious solutions and establish their value to the bottom line.

The outcome of every proposed alternative must be established. Depending upon whether the decision-making problem is classified as one of certainty, risk, or uncer-

---

DSS IN ACTION 2.13

TOO MANY ALTERNATIVES SPOILS THE BROTH

The following decision-making situation was overheard on a bus ride at a national meeting:

A major university was in the process of moving its distance learning activities to the Web. A professor was assigned the task of looking into the possible alternatives. He created a list of 23 companies in a report. He included detailed descriptions of the alternatives and what the university needed. There was extensive documentation. He wanted to be thorough, even though not all of the alternatives were appropriate for the university (constraints clearly would have cut the list down). He felt it was a good report.

The day before the decision was to be made, a salesman for such products stopped by the president's office. The president picked this company's product. As was overheard on the bus: "Studies on decision-making show that when you give someone too many options to choose from, plus a deadline, he or she usually freezes and is likely to choose the last one mentioned."

Three to five alternatives seem to be about right. An executive summary would have been a good idea. After all, they were trying to solve a problem, not survey the marketplace. Even using a software tool to compare these few valid alternatives would have been a good idea. Perhaps Expert Choice could have been used. See Case Application 2.3.

Source: Modified and condensed from S.M. Johnstone, "Decision Support for Distance Learning Solutions: Help is Online," *Syllabus*, October 2001.

DSS IN FOCUS 2.14

HOW DO PEOPLE REALLY VIEW RISK?

Professor Adam Goodie at The University of Georgia has empirically demonstrated how people view risk in decision-making. "When people are called to gamble on a random event, where there's a very large probability of something small but good happening and a very low probability of something big and bad happening, they don't want to do it," Goodie says. "If it's something they have control over, like their own knowledge of the world, *then they insist on doing it.* That has significance for all sorts of decisions we make in our lives." The most obvious example is the debate over airline travel since the events of September 11, Goodie says. "People aren't afraid of driving, but they're afraid of flying, even though air travel is statistically much safer per mile traveled," he says. "But

people feel safer if they're driving because they have control over the sources of risk and uncertainty."

A sense of control is a key factor in determining whether people take risks or avoid them. People are more willing to take risks when they feel they can control the outcome of a situation—*even if they have over-estimated their likelihood of success.* People are often overconfident about their knowledge. This may explain why slot machines require the player to pull a lever. It may give the player a feeling of control.

Source: For more information, see A. Mann, "Risky Business," *Columns* (UGA Faculty Newsletter), February 11, 2002, p. 3; Goodie (2001).

tainty, different modeling approaches may be used (see Drummond, 2002; Koller, 2000). These are discussed in Chapter 4. See DSS in Focus 2.14 for a description of how people really view risk.

MEASURING OUTCOMES

The value of an alternative is evaluated in terms of goal attainment. Sometimes an outcome is expressed directly in terms of a goal. For example, profit is an outcome, profit maximization is a goal, and both are expressed in dollar terms. An outcome such as customer satisfaction may be measured by the number of complaints, by the level of loyalty to a product, or by ratings found by surveys. Ideally, one would want to deal with a single goal, but in practice it is not unusual to have multiple goals (see Barba-Romero, 2001; Koksalan and Zionts, 2001). When groups make decisions, each group participant may have a different agenda. For example, executives may want to maximize profit, marketing may want to maximize market penetration, operations may want to minimize costs, while stockholders may want to maximize the bottom line. Typically these goals conflict, so special multiple-criteria methodologies have been developed to handle this. One such method is the analytic hierarchy process, outlined in Case Application 2.3 and the Web Chapter on college/university selection.

SCENARIOS

A **scenario** is a statement of assumptions about the operating environment of a particular system at a given time; that is, a narrative description of the decision-situation setting. A scenario describes the decision and uncontrollable variables and parameters for a specific modeling situation. It also may provide the procedures and constraints for the modeling.

Scenarios originated in the theater. The term was borrowed for war gaming and large-scale simulations. Scenario planning and analysis is a DSS tool that can capture a whole range of possibilities. A manager can construct a series of scenarios (what-if cases), perform computerized analyses, and learn more about the system and decision-making problem while analyzing it. Ideally, the manager can identify an excellent, possibly optimal, solution to the model of the problem.

A scenario is especially helpful in simulations and what-if analysis. In both cases, we change scenarios and examine the results. For example, one can change the anticipated demand for hospitalization (an input variable for planning), thus creating a new scenario. Then one can measure the anticipated cash flow of the hospital for each scenario.

Scenarios play an important role in MSS because they

- Help identify opportunities and problem areas
- Provide flexibility in planning
- Identify the leading edges of changes that management should monitor
- Help validate major modeling assumptions
- Allow the decision-maker to explore the behavior of a system through a model
- Help to check the sensitivity of proposed solutions to changes in the environment as described by the scenario

POSSIBLE SCENARIOS

There may be thousands of possible scenarios for every decision situation. However, the following are especially useful in practice:

- The worst possible scenario
- The best possible scenario
- The most likely scenario
- The average scenario

The scenario determines the context of the analysis to be performed. Scenarios were used in the *MMS Running Case* in establishing the value of each alternative.

ERRORS IN DECISION-MAKING

The model is the critical component in the decision-making process, but one may make a number of errors in its development and use. Validating the model before it is used is critical. Gathering the right amount of information, with the right level of precision and accuracy, to incorporate into the decision-making process is also critical. Sawyer (1999) describes "the seven deadly sins of decision-making," most of which are behavior- or information-related. We summarize these "sins" in DSS in Focus 2.15.

2.8 DECISION-MAKING: THE CHOICE PHASE

Choice is the *critical act* of decision-making. The choice phase is the one in which the actual decision is made and where the commitment to follow a certain course of action is made. The boundary between the design and choice phases is often unclear because certain activities can be performed during both of them and because one can return frequently from choice activities to design activities. For example, one can generate new alternatives while performing an evaluation of existing ones. The choice phase includes the search, evaluation, and recommendation of an *appropriate* solution to the model. A solution to a model is a specific set of values for the decision variables in a selected alternative. In the *MMS Running Case* (see DSS in Action 2.16), choices were evaluated as to their viability and profitability. A choice was made to correct data errors and to move a specific number of cars from one set of locations to another. The

---

DSS IN FOCUS 2.15

THE SEVEN DEADLY SINS OF DECISION-MAKING

Sawyer (1999) describes what she calls "the seven deadly sins of decision-making." These are common pitfalls of decision-making that decision-makers often unwittingly encounter. They are all interrelated. The seven deadly sins are:

1. Believing that you already have all the answers (no attempt is made to seek outside information or expertise)

2. Asking the wrong questions (you need the right information to make an informed decision)

3. The old demon ego (a decision-maker feels he or she is right and refuses to back down from a bad policy or decision)

4. Flying-by-the-seat-of-your-pants saves money—doesn't it? (by not seeking out information, an organization saves money—and makes bad decisions)

5. All aboard the bandwagon: if it works for them, it'll work for us (copying someone else's ideas really involves understanding why and how they work)

6. Hear no evil (discourage and ignore negative advice—kill the messenger with the bad news)

7. Hurry up and wait: making no decision can be the same as making a bad decision (procrastination is not necessarily a good managerial technique).

Of course, all of these lead to bad decisions that lead to unnecessary and high costs for firms and individuals (including getting fired). Many of these "sins" clearly involve behavioral issues and lack of information and expertise that leads to less objectivity in the decision-making process. These "sins" often appear in the press and on the Web as ways *not* to make decisions.

Source: Based on D.C. Sawyer, *Getting It Right: Avoiding the High Cost of Wrong Decisions*, Boca Raton, FL: St. Lucie Press, 1999.

---

advertising plan was modified, and new data and features were to be added to the firm's DSS.

Note: Solving the model is not the same as solving the problem the model represents. The solution to the model yields a recommended solution to the problem. The problem is considered solved only if the recommended solution is *successfully implemented*.

Solving a decision-making model involves searching for an appropriate course of action. These search approaches include **analytical techniques** (solving a formula), **algorithms** (step-by-step procedures), heuristics (rules of thumb), and blind search (shooting in the dark, ideally in a logical way). These are covered in Chapter 4.

Each alternative must be evaluated. If an alternative has multiple goals, these must all be examined and balanced off against the others. **Sensitivity analysis** is used to determine the robustness of any given alternative (slight changes in the parameters should ideally lead to slight or no changes in the alternative chosen). **What-if analysis** is used to explore major changes in the parameters. Goal seeking helps the manager determine values of the decision variables to meet a specific objective. All of this is covered in Chapter 4.

2.9 DECISION-MAKING: THE IMPLEMENTATION PHASE

In *The Prince*, Machiavelli astutely noted some 500 years ago that there was "nothing more difficult to carry out, nor more doubtful of success, nor more dangerous to handle, than to initiate a new order of things." The implementation of a proposed solution to a problem is, in effect, the initiation of a new order of things, or the introduction of

DSS IN ACTION 2.16

MMS RUNNING CASE: THE CHOICE PHASE

Monday's Meeting: With All Vice Presidents, Stephanie, and Her Team

ELENA: Thank you again for coming. Stephanie, Michael tells me you're on to something. Let's hear what you have to say.

STEPHANIE: Well, we think we've discovered what to do. But first let me outline what the *real* problems are, and some suggested solutions and why these are appropriate solutions.

Next Stephanie essentially outlines the details from the meeting described in DSS in Action 2.8. There is a little discussion to clarify a few points.

ELENA: Amazing. I'm glad Mark recommended acquiring DOT three months ago. Though expensive, it's already paid off. Can you get me specifics on the bottom line for each alternative?

STEPHANIE: Not accurate ones for each just yet. Some will take up to a couple of weeks. We do have estimates on all of them. Here are the results in my PowerPoint presentation.

ELENA: Hmmm. OK. I want those data on the Spider updated immediately, and some of them moved to where they'll rent.

MARLA: It's already done. I took steps right away once Michael told me what happened. After all, it's my responsibility. I already gave some updated data to IS. They've adjusted the revenue management system. Preliminary data indicate that they have improved our profitability already. In a couple of markets where it was relatively inexpensive, I have moved some cars around based on the DSS model's recommendation. It worked! I think we should make the major changes recommended by the solution to the model. My estimates, just from these few markets, are that it will work just as the model predicts.

SHARON: We're looking into how to modify our marketing and tie it into the revenue-management system. We're also running models on how European marketing should work. We'll know in a week what to do.

ELENA: Excellent! Here's where we stand. We're going to adjust the profile data of the Spider and all models frequently, move cars around, and discount substitutes until we can get the imbalance fixed. We'll decide on what to do about the other issues after the rest of the analysis is completed.

change. And change must be managed. User expectations must be managed as part of change management.

The definition of implementation is somewhat complicated because implementation is a long, involved process with vague boundaries. Simplistically, implementation means putting a recommended solution to work, *not necessarily the implementation of a computer system.* Many generic implementation issues, such as resistance to change, degree of support of top management, and user training, are important in dealing with management support systems. In the *MMS Running Case* (DSS in Action 2.17), implementation was a little fuzzy. Some decisions were pilot-tested by the people responsible for that aspect of decision-making before the decision was implemented nationally. Essentially for MMS, implementation involved updating computer systems, testing models and scenarios for impacts, and physically moving the cars from some locations to others. The computer system updates ideally should involve some kind of formal information system development approach, while the actual implementation of the decision may not. Implementation is covered in detail in Chapter 6. The decision-

---

MMS RUNNING CASE: THE IMPLEMENTATION PHASE

The implementation of the first couple of decisions was relatively easy. Transport vehicles were rented and cars were moved. Discounts were easy to establish for substitute cars, because this could be done as routinely as when there was a normal stockout. A customer would first be offered the opportunity to upgrade. If the customer turned it down, the upgrade would be offered free. This work 95 percent of the time, even in the case of the Spider. Sales were up, and the company was projected to be profitable with these small changes.

Elena got the results of the additional analyses. They all made sense. She decided, with the advice of her VPs and the analysts, to go ahead with all the recommendations, but held back on European marketing until a presence in Europe could be established in major markets. The "try before you buy" campaign would be started once there were 15 Spiders in most major markets and three in each secondary market. She also approved adding new data and features to CLAUDIA.

Once the advertising effort was refined and tied into the revenue management system, profits soared. Every member of Stephanie's team and all the VPs involved got a generous end-of-year bonus, an extra week's vacation, and a gift of a free GMC Spider.

---

making process, though conducted by people, can be improved with computer support, the subject of the next section.

2.10 HOW DECISIONS ARE SUPPORTED

In Chapter 1 we discussed the need for computerized decision support and briefly described some decision aids. Here we relate specific management support system technologies to the decision-making process (Figure 2.3).

FIGURE 2.3   DSS SUPPORT

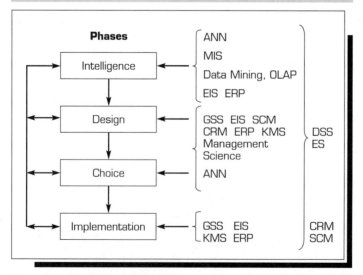

Source: Based on Sprague, R. H., Jr., "A Framework for the Development of DSS." *MIS Quarterly,* Dec. 1980, Fig. 5, p. 13.

SUPPORT FOR THE INTELLIGENCE PHASE

The primary requirement of decision support for the intelligence phase is the ability to scan external and internal information sources for opportunities and problems and to interpret what the scanning discovers. Web tools and sources are *extremely* useful for environmental scanning. Web browsers provide useful front ends for a variety of tools, from OLAP to data mining and data warehouses. Data sources may be internal and external. Internal sources may be accessed via a corporate intranet. External sources are many and varied. For a list of many Web sites with global macroeconomic and business data, see Hansen (2002).

Decision support technologies can be very helpful. For example, an enterprise information system can support the intelligence phase by continuously monitoring both internal and external information, looking for early signs of problems and opportunities through a Web-based enterprise information portal, as in the *MMS Running Case* (also see DSS in Action 2.18 for an example in the pharmaceutical industry). Similarly, (automatic) data mining (which may include expert systems, CRM, and neural networks) and (manual) online analytic processing (OLAP) also support the intelligence phase by identifying relationships among activities and other factors. These relationships can be exploited for competitive advantage (e.g., CRM identifies classes of customers to approach with specific products and services; see Sparacino and O'Reilly, 2000). A knowledge management system can be used to identify similar past situations and how they were handled. Group support systems can be used to share information and for brainstorming. Artificial neural networks can be used to identify the best takeover targets, as was demonstrated for banks by Shawver and Aronson

---

DSS IN ACTION 2.18

PHARMACEUTICAL FIRMS ANALYZE AND VISUALIZE WITH WEB PORTALS INTO DATA

Infinity Pharmaceuticals, Inc. (Boston) speeds drug development by facilitating the process of evaluating new chemicals through real-time Web analytics. Researchers need to generate statistical models of how compounds will behave in a given chemical assay. With so many different models, the more real-time and interactive a researcher is, the more effective he or she will be. Data integration of chemical models databases with outside sources, such as databases of chemical compounds, and a consistent interface are critical. Infinity's IT staff solved the problem by building a real-time system using Web services as its application model. XML interfaces are coded into every program. The design also includes a standardized metadata model, to which Infinity maps its data dictionaries. Data integration is done upfront. The Spotfire.net (Spotfire Inc., Cambridge, Massachusetts) decision-analytics portal uses Web connectivity to provide scientific decision-making communities with a unified workspace to access large amounts of complex chemical-structure or gene-expression data, visually explore and analyze these data, and share results. Spotfire.net automatically generates interactive query devices for rapid identification of trends, anomalies, outliers, and patterns. Researchers can view and maneuver data in 3-D by selecting different visualization types or displaying multiple variables on the same screen. Spotfire.netprovides algorithms for data mining and basic statistical analysis via the Web to the user's desktop. These include decision tree analysis, principal components analysis, K-means clustering, hierarchical clustering, and other statistical calculations, such as boxplots. Millions of compounds can be analyzed and visualized in seconds.

Sources: Adapted from Mark Hall, "Web Analytics: Get Real," *ComputerWorld*, Vol. 36, No. 14, April 1, 2002, 42–43; Julia Boguslavsky, "Visualize Large Data Sets Online," *Research & Development*, Vol. 42, No. 9, September 2000, p. 59.

(2003). The Web provides consistent, familiar interface tools via portals and access to critical, often fuzzy information necessary to identify problems and opportunities.

Expert systems, on the other hand, can render advice regarding the nature of the problem, its classification, its seriousness, and the like. ES can advise on the suitability of a solution approach and the likelihood of successfully solving the problem. One of the primary areas of ES success is interpreting information and diagnosing problems. This capability can be exploited in the intelligence phase. Even intelligent agents can be used to identify opportunities (see Desouza, 2001).

Another area of support is reporting. Both routine and ad hoc reports can aid in the intelligence phase. For example, regular reports can be designed to assist in the problem-finding activity by comparing expectations with current and projected performance. Web-based OLAP tools are excellent at this task (see DSS in Action 2.18). So are electronic document management systems.

Much of the information used in seeking new opportunities is qualitative or soft. This indicates a high level of unstructuredness in the problems, thus making DSS quite useful in the intelligence phase. For example, see DSS in Action 2.19, where Union Pacific seeks out opportunities in the avalanche of data that it *must* collect by law.

The Web and advanced database technologies have created a glut of data and information available to decision-makers—so much that it can detract from the quality and speed of decision-making. Fortunately, intelligent agents and other artificial intelligence tools can lessen the burden. In DSS in Focus 2.20, we describe the issues that managers are grappling with in the digital age of decision-making.

SUPPORT FOR THE DESIGN PHASE

The design phase involves generating alternative courses of action, discussing the criteria for choice and their relative importance, and forecasting the future consequences of using various alternatives. Several of these activities can use standard models provided by a decision support system (such as financial and forecasting models, available as applets). Alternatives for structured problems can be generated through the use of either standard or special models. However, the generation of alternatives for complex problems requires expertise that can only be provided by a human, brainstorming software, or an expert system. OLAP and data mining software are quite useful in identifying relationships that can be used in models (see the *MMS Running Case*). Most DSS

DSS IN ACTION 2.19

UNION PACIFIC RAILROAD: IF YOU'RE COLLECTING DATA, YOU SHOULD USE IT PROFITABLY!

Union Pacific is required by law to collect dozens of gigabytes of data every month about rail conditions, but a competitive spirit is why the company *leverages* those data, stored in several incompatible formats in various relational and mainframe systems, for its business intelligence initiative. Using reporting, analysis, and query applications, decision-makers can find the needed and appropriate information from existing systems and derive answers from composite, incompatible data—without waiting for daily or monthly batch loads into a centralized data warehouse.

Source: Modified from Anonymous, "Smarter, Faster, More Profitable: 20 Organizations That Get It," *IntelligentEnterprise*, Oct. 4, 2001, pp. 18–19.

DSS IN FOCUS 2.20

DECISION-MAKING IN THE DIGITAL AGE

Kepner-Tregoe, Inc. (Princeton, New Jersey) surveyed managers and workers across the United States to determine how they are coping with the need for faster decision-making and how companies are balancing the requirement for speed with the concomitant need for quality.

Decision-makers are under pressure to keep up but in the process are too often sacrificing the quality of decision-making. *Digital age* decision-makers are not making the most of what is available. Decision-makers are often unable to gather sufficient information, they're doing a poor job of sharing that information, and they're failing to involve the right people in the decision process. Here are the key findings:

- **More decisions are being made in less time.**
  Both managers and workers must make more decisions in the same or less time. Sixty-five percent of workers and 77 percent of managers say that they must make more decisions every day. At the same time, most also agree that the amount of time they have to make these decisions has either decreased on stayed the same.

- **Respondents are missing opportunities.**
  Despite the pressure to make speedy decisions, nearly three-quarters of workers and four-fifths of managers say they miss opportunities because they don't make decisions quickly enough. Most agree that decisions are frequently not implemented in a timely manner.

- **Many feel as if they are losing the race.**
  When asked to compare the speed of their organization's decision-making to that of rivals, only one-quarter of workers and less than one-third of managers said they are moving faster than their competition.

- **Many barriers to speed are human.**
  Workers and managers closely agreed that the need for multiple approvals is the most frequently

encountered barrier. Other common roadblocks are organizational politics, changing priorities, and getting people to agree up front on what they want the decision to accomplish.

- **Information technology clearly has a widespread influence.**
  When asked specifically where IT has become the most important source of information for decision-making, both workers and managers listed budgeting/finance, purchasing and customer service, followed closely by daily product management, quality/productivity, personnel/human resources, and process improvement.

- **Sources of information are constantly changing.**
  When asked where they get the information upon which they base their decisions today (compared to three years earlier), both workers and managers described a major shift from real to virtual sources. The most dramatic change has been in the increased use of e-mail. Most also agree not only that the quantity of information has increased, but that the quality of the information has increased as well.

- **Decision-making amnesia is rampant.**
  Organizations are *not very effective* at preserving their decision-making experiences. Of those who said that their organizations have a system in place to house decision criteria, 77 percent of workers and 82 percent of managers said they couldn't assess the utility of their database.

Decision-leading firms have figured out ways to counter these deficiencies. See the source for details.

Source: Modified from D.K. Wessel, "Decision Making in the Digital Age," *DM Review 2002 Resource Guide, DM Review,* December 2001.

have quantitative analysis capabilities, and an internal ES can assist with qualitative methods as well as with the expertise required in selecting quantitative analysis and forecasting models. A knowledge management system should certainly be consulted to determine whether such a problem has been encountered before, or whether there are experts on hand who can provide quick understanding and answers. Customer relationship management systems, revenue management systems (as in the *MMS Running Case*), enterprise resource planning, and supply chain management systems software

are useful in that they provide models of business processes that can test assumptions and scenarios. If the problem requires brainstorming to help identify important issues and options, a group support system may prove helpful. Tools that provide cognitive mapping can also help. All of these tools may be accessed via the Web. Cohen, Kelly, and Medaglia (2001) describe several Web-based tools that provide decision support, mainly in the design phase, by providing models and reporting of alternative results. Each of their cases has saved millions of dollars annually by utilizing these tools. Web-based DSS are helping engineers in product design as well as decision-makers solving business problems. See DSS in Action 2.21.

SUPPORT FOR THE CHOICE PHASE

In addition to providing models that rapidly identify a best or good enough alternative, a decision support system can support the choice phase through the what-if and goal-seeking analyses. Different scenarios can be tested for the selected option to reinforce the final decision. Again, a knowledge management system helps identify similar past experiences; CRM, ERP, and SCM systems are used to test the impacts of the decisions in establishing their value leading to an intelligent choice. An expert system can be used to assess the desirability of certain solutions as well as to recommend an appropriate solution. If a group makes the decision, a group support system can provide support to lead to consensus.

SUPPORT FOR THE IMPLEMENTATION PHASE: MAKING THE DECISION HAPPEN

The DSS benefits provided during implementation may be as important as or even more important than those in the earlier phases. DSS can be used in implementation activities such as decision communication, explanation, and justification.

Implementation phase DSS benefits are partly due to the vividness and detail of analyses and reports. For example, one chief executive officer (CEO) gives employees and external parties not only the aggregate financial goals and cash needs for the near

---

DSS IN ACTION 2.21

WEB-BASED DSS ASSIST ENGINEERS IN PRODUCT DESIGN

Though not a business decision-making situation, engineering organizations must solve product and service *design* problems. 3Ga Corp. has developed 3G.web .decisions, an Internet technology that accelerates the product-design process. 3G.web.decisionswas developed on the Java, XML, and Microsoft.NET platforms. It lets project engineers use their Web browsers to access and reuse parametric CAD and engineering data to support design change recommendations. Any member of a product-design team can simulate the impact of parametric engineering changes on the fit, form, and functional behavior of a design. Hundreds of design alternatives can be evaluated in real time. Team members collectively determine which configuration is the most cost-effective, highest quality, and easiest to produce. The software supports models from several standard data package formats.

Source: Adapted from Anonymous, "Validating Design Decisions On-Line," *Computer-Aided Engineering*, Vol. 20, No. 4, April, 2000, p. 24.

term but also the calculations, intermediate results, and statistics used in determining the aggregate figures. In addition to communicating the financial goals unambiguously, the CEO signals other messages. Employees know that the CEO has thought through the assumptions behind the financial goals and is serious about their importance and attainability. Bankers and directors are shown that the CEO was personally involved in analyzing cash needs and is aware of and responsible for the implications of the financing requests prepared by the finance department. Each of these messages improves decision implementation in some way. In the Opening Vignette, team members had access to information in order to make decisions, and information about the results of the decisions. The same is true in the *MMS Running Case*. KMS, EIS, ERP, CRM, and SCM are all useful in tracking how well the implementation is working. GSS is useful for a team to collaborate in establishing implementation effectiveness. For example, a decision might be made to get rid of unprofitable customers. An effective CRM can identify classes of customers to get rid of, identify the impact, and then verify that it really worked that way (see Murphy, 2002; Swift, 2001).

All phases of the decision-making process can be supported by improved communication by collaborative computing through GSS and KMS. Computerized systems can facilitate communication by helping people explain and justify their suggestions and opinions. Quantitative support can also be quickly provided for analyzing various possible scenarios while a meeting is in session (either in person or virtually).

Decision implementation can also be supported by expert systems. An ES can be used as an advisory system regarding implementation problems (such as handling resistance to change). Finally, an ES can provide training that may smooth the course of implementation.

Impacts along the value chain, though reported by an enterprise information system through a Web-based enterprise information portal, are typically identified by SCM and ERP systems. CRM systems report and update internal records based on the impacts of the implementation. And then these inputs are used to identify new problems and opportunities—a return to the intelligence phase.

NEW TECHNOLOGY SUPPORT FOR DECISION-MAKING

Web-based systems clearly have influenced how decision-making is supported. With the development of m-commerce (mobile commerce), more and more personal devices (personal digital assistants, cell phones, tablet computers, laptop computers) can access information sources, and users can respond to systems with information updates, collaboration efforts, and decisions. This is especially important for salespeople, who can be more effective if they can access their CRM while on the road and then enter orders. Constant access to corporate data, inventory and otherwise, can only help them in their work. Overall, wireless devices are taking on greater importance in the enterprise, generally by accessing specialized Web servers that provide data and communication directly to the m-commerce device. East Bay Restaurant Supply (Oakland, California) reports that though it has not evaluated the effectiveness of providing instantaneous information to all its sales reps, it has saved $45,000 by providing each of its 15 reps with a Palm Pilot instead of a notebook computer. (For details on how East Bay Restaurant Supply and other firms have initiated m-commerce efforts, see McVicker, 2001.) Finally, advanced artificial intelligence technologies can be utilized in decision-making. Camacho et al. (2001) describe how travel planning in e-tourism can be handled by intelligent agents; Desouza (2001) surveys applications of intelligent agents for competitive intelligence.

The Web provides a vehicle to disseminate knowledge and information about decision-making and DSS. We list some of the many sources for decision-making support and theory in Table 2.3.

2.11 PERSONALITY TYPES, GENDER, HUMAN COGNITION, AND DECISION STYLES

PERSONALITY (TEMPERAMENT) TYPES

Many studies indicate that there is a strong relationship between personality and decision-making. Personality type influences general orientation toward goal attainment, selection of alternatives, treatment of risk, and reactions under stress. It affects a decision-maker's ability to process large quantities of information, time pressure, and reframing. It also influences the rules and communication patterns of an individual decision-maker. For example, see Harrison (1999).

People are *not* alike. In the 1920s, Carl Jung (1923) described how people are fundamentally different, though they all have the same set of instincts that drive them internally. Actually, **personality (temperament) types** were described in ancient Greece by Hippocrates (Keirsey, 1998; Montgomery, 2002), and were surely known long before that. In the 1950s, Myers and Briggs revived Jung's research and developed the well-known Myers–Briggs Type Indicator (Quenk, 1999), along with an interpretation of each type (Berens et al., 2002; Montgomery, 2002; Myers and Myers, 1999). The Myers–Briggs temperament types are described briefly in DSS in Focus 2.22.

There is a long, detailed Myers–Briggs test that can be administered only by a professional counselor (contact the Center for Applications of Psychological Type, capt.org); however, Keirsey and Bates (1984) have published a shorter, readily available questionnaire to determine one's type, along with a detailed description of the types and how they are motivated, act, and interact.

Birkman (1995) developed a personality typing called "True Colors" (be aware that there are several different "colors" types in books and on the Web). His personality typing follows the basic Jungian structure, but the establishment of one's personality type requires answering 16 simple, true/false questions. One author has used this personality typing in his classes since 1998, and of the more than 1,000 students who have been typed, few have claimed that the types did not match their own sense of their personalities. The color types can be quickly established, discussed, and used to build teams in classes and, more important, in decision-making environments. Birkman's True Colors typing is briefly described in DSS in Focus 2.23.

Temperament helps describe how one can best attack decision-making problems because certain activities are better handled by each type. It also indicates how each type relates to each of the other types, describing positive communication patterns, work patterns, and so on. This information can be helpful in determining the best way to interact with your significant other. The most important issue to understand in identifying and using temperament types is that there is no right or wrong, or good or bad type. People simply have different personality types. People of different types act and react differently in different situations (e.g., under stress, under normal conditions), have different motivational needs and values, conceptualize differently, and readily adopt certain roles in the decision-making process. Each type has preferred ways of learning and explaining (important for college careers and training). People of each type are communicated with in different "best" ways, and thus there are differences in

TABLE 2.3   Web Sources for Decision-Making Support Sampler

Web Site	Content Sample	Organization
www.ubmail.ubalt.edu/~harsham/	An extensive bibliography on decision-making tools: "Applied Management Science: Making Good Strategic Decisions" (www.ubmail.ubalt.edu/~harsham/opre640/opre640.htm); "Decision Science Resources" (www.ubmail.ubalt.edu/~harsham/refop/Refop.htm); "Compendium of Decision-making Web Site Reviews" (www.ubmail.ubalt.edu/~harsham/opre640a/partI.htm)	Hossein Arsham, University of Baltimore
www.mindtools.com	Information about decision-making, decision trees, decision analysis, and creativity	Mind Tools Community
faculty.fuqua.duke.edu/daweb/	Contact point for decision analysis research. "Lexicon of Decision-making," by Tom Spradlin	Decision Analysis Society Home Page
psych.fullerton.edu/mbirnbaum/dec.html	Applied research site. Contains online Decision Research Center experiments	Decision Research Center
www.sjdm.org	Society for Judgment and Decision-Making References and meetings on judgment and decision-making	Psychology Department, California State University, Fullerton
www.smdm.org	Contact point for promoting rational and systematic approaches to decision-making that will improve the health and clinical care of individuals and assist in health policy formation	Society for Medical Decision Making
www.cdm.lcs.mit.edu	Description of projects and references on providing better health care through applied artificial intelligence	The Clinical Decision-making Group at the Laboratory for Computer Science at MIT
dieoff.com/page163.htm	"Decision-making and Problem Solving" by Herbert A. Simon and Associates	Brain Food, Jay Hanson
www.aol.com/progresssite/	Building a collection of cases on decision-making	Progress Research Project with Brunel University
www.ncedr.org	Produces and disseminates scientific and operational advances of direct use to subnational environmental decision-makers.	National Center for Environmental Decision-Making Research
www.iiasa.ac.at/Research/DAS/research/res98/node5.html	Project on the development, testing, and use of Web-based systems for decision-making and negotiations	International Institute for Applied Systems Analysis (IIASA)
www.ethics.ubc.ca/resources/dec-mkg/	Applied Ethics Resources on WWW References and software for ethical decision-making A Framework for Ethical Decision-Making software	Centre for Applied Ethics
www.scu.edu/ethics/practicing/decision/	Articles on ethical decision-making	Markkula Center for Applied Ethics at Santa Clara University
www.banxia.com	Cognitive map bibliography and software	Banxia
www.terry.uga.edu/mcdm/	Contact organization for researchers	International Society on Multiple Criteria Decision Making
Various	Good source of Web sites with global macroeconomic and business data	Hansen (2002)

DSS IN FOCUS 2.22

MYERS–BRIGGS TEMPERAMENT TYPES

The Myers–Briggs temperament types are characterized along four dimensions, four pairs of so-called preferences:

- Extraversion (E) to Intraversion (I)
- Sensation (S) to Intuition (N)
- Thinking (T) to Feeling (F)
- Perceiving (P) to Judging (J).

There are 16 main types (combinations) and an additional 32 mixed types. Types change over time and depend a bit on mood and situation. Some simple words that describe people of each type are

- Extraversion: sociable
- Introversion: territorial
- Sensation: practical
- Intuition: innovative
- Thinking: impersonal
- Feeling: personal

- Perceiving: open
- Judging: closure.

If one examines the entire population, the types are distributed approximately as shown below:

- Extraversion (75 percent) to Intraversion (25 percent)
- Sensation (75 percent) to Intuition (25 percent)
- Thinking (50 percent) to Feeling (50 percent)
- Perceiving (50 percent) to Judging (50 percent).

According to Jung, one need not be one or the other of each pair but can exhibit traits of both. Through learning, it is possible for an introvert to behave like an extrovert (as do many college faculty), and for an extrovert to behave like an introvert (as do some college students).

Source: Based partly on Berens (2000), Berens et al. (2002), Myers (1998), Keirsey (1998), Keirsey and Bates (1984), Montgomery (2002).

DSS IN FOCUS 2.23

TRUE COLORS TEMPERAMENT TYPES

The True Colors temperament types are Red, Green, Yellow, and Blue. The colors have no *formal meaning* but are simply used to differentiate the types. The colors appear on the following grid:

Red	Green
Yellow	Blue

Some traits are shared up and down the columns (Red and Yellow, Green, and Blue), whereas others are shared across the rows (Red and Green, Yellow and Blue). Diagonal colors have little in common in their makeup. Green types like to communicate directly and work with people. They like to work in groups and to get people excited about what they are doing. Marketing specialists have a tendency to be Green. Red types also like to communicate directly but stay focused

on the task at hand, as do Yellow types. Red types tend to volunteer to be group leaders and stay excited about and focused on getting a job done. Yellow types are most comfortable with indirect communication and like to deal with details (they make great accountants and programmers). Blue types also prefer indirect communication and are innovative, introspective, and creative but are easily distracted and may need people nearby to keep them focused. Blue types make great researchers but often have to be reminded to stay on track with their projects. When a team is formed with members of all the different color types, the team tends to be very creative and productive. One author always has his students take the True Colors test and uses the results to help establish class teams.

Source: Based partly on Birkman (1995).

the way they work in teams, in the way they lead teams, in how they frame problems, and also in their cognitive and decision styles. Since each type can be best reached differently, it is important in developing *shared frames* to use an appropriate approach for each type. Finally, it is important to have a balanced team made up of various types to best get the work done. Some types are better thinkers, others are better doers, and so on. Each type can contribute actively to teamwork. Personality type clearly influences one's cognitive style and decision style. See DSS in Action 2.24 and Pearman (1998). For more information on the Myers–Briggs Type Indicator, see Keirsey (1998); Keirsey and Bates (1984); and keirsey.com; for more information on True Colors typing, see Birkman (1995) and birkman.com.

GENDER

Psychological empirical testing sometimes indicates that there are (slight) gender differences and gender similarities in decision-making, including such factors as boldness, quality, ability, risk-taking attitudes, and communication patterns. Powell and Johnson (1995) observe that decision-support systems are designed on the assumption of no gender differences, but people of each gender may take decisions in different ways and have different information style preferences. Their extensive review of the recent literature suggests that gender differences are associated with abilities and motivation, risk attitude and confidence, as well as decision style. Men are more inclined to take risks than women in a variety of situations, a difference which does not stem from differences in the perceived probability of success (Smith, 1999). Where gender differences exist (i.e., have statistical significance) they are very small (Smith, 1999). The results are essentially inconclusive, and so it is unwise to attempt to characterize either males or females as better or worse decision-makers.

COGNITION THEORY

Cognition is the set of activities by which a person resolves differences between an internalized view of the environment and what actually exists in the environment. In other words, it is the ability to perceive and understand information. Cognitive models are attempts to explain or understand human cognitive processes. Such models explain, for instance, how people revise formerly held opinions to conform with the

---

DSS IN ACTION 2.24

TEMPERAMENT DOES INFLUENCE DECISION STYLE

The influence of a manager's decision style in strategic decision-making was examined in an experimental setting. Simulated decisions were used for 79 executive-level hospital managers and 89 hospital middle managers. They first took a Myers–Briggs type-indicator test to determine their decision styles. Then the managers were asked to evaluate a set of projects keyed to their individual styles. Decision style influenced their views of adoption and risk. The decisions of top executives were more style-dependent than those of middle managers. The *judicial* top executive was found to be *action-*

oriented, and the *systematic* top executive was found to be *action-averse*. The *speculative* and *heuristic* top executives took nearly identical *neutral* positions. Top executives with a *sensate* style were similar to top executives with a *pure systematic* style, and top executives with a *feeling* style were similar to top executives with a *pure judicial* style.

Source: Modified from P.C. Nutt, "Strategic Decisions Made by Top Executives and Middle Managers with Data and Process Dominant Styles," *Journal of Management Studies*, Vol. 27, No. 2, March 1990, pp. 173–194.

choices they have made. Elkins (2000) discusses how we can observe and learn better for improved problem-framing and, ultimately, decision-making.

COGNITIVE STYLE

Cognitive style is the subjective process through which people perceive, organize, and change information during the decision-making process. Cognitive style, sometimes called *management style*, is important because in many cases it determines a person's preference for the human–machine interface. For example, should data be raw or aggregate, or should they be tabulated or presented as graphs? Should data be presented as auditory, visual, or action-oriented (Markova, 1996; Wallington, 2001).

There is no one best style. Each has its own unique strengths and weaknesses. A good manager can utilize more than one style. Flexibility is a definite advantage because your preferred style may not mesh well with the needs of other people (Wallington, 2001). But meshing the strengths of complementary styles can lead to more effective collaboration.

Furthermore, cognitive styles affect preferences for qualitative versus quantitative analysis as well as for decision-making aids. In this way, cognitive style affects the way an individual frames a decision-making situation so as to understand it better. Simply put, a frame "provides the context within which information is used, and different frames put the focus on different kinds of information" (Beach, 1997; also see Shoemaker and Russo, 2001). In other words, a frame is the decision-maker's interpretation of the situation. A frame provides a mental model for the decision-maker. As a problem is analyzed, it can be reframed in light of new information. When a group is involved in decision-making, it is desirable to have shared frames that involve some level of common organizational culture. If frames are not shared sufficiently, the group will have trouble developing a consensus. Are there cultural differences that vary by country and affect management styles? See DSS in Focus 2.25.

Research on cognitive styles is directly relevant to the design of management information systems. MIS and transaction processing systems tend to be designed by people who perceive the decision-making process as systematic. Systematic managers are generally willing to use such systems; they are typically looking for a standard technique and view the system designer as an expert with a catalog of methods. However, such systems do not conform to the natural style of a heuristic decision-maker. For such an individual, a system should allow for exploration of a wide range of alternatives, permit changes in priorities or in processing, allow the user to shift easily between

---

DSS IN FOCUS 2.25

MANAGEMENT STYLES AROUND THE WORLD

There are substansive cultural differences in the way decisions are made in different countries. In effect, *countries have management styles.* Albaum and Herche (1999) tested dimensions of management style, including cautious autonomy, quantitative planning, market listening, lone planning, and lone implementation. Four of these five dimensions (all but cautious autonomy) distinguish unique characteristics of the management style of marketing managers in the nations studied (Spain, Netherlands, Denmark, Finland, and France). For example, French managers clearly showed a distinctive style in that they paid more attention to quantitative information, listened to markets, were driven by data, and placed a lower priority on individual implementation.

_____

Source: Adapted from Albaum and Herche (1999).

TABLE 2.4   Cognitive-style Decision Approaches

Problem-solving Dimension	Heuristic	Analytic
Approach to learning	Learns more by acting than by analyzing the situation and places more emphasis on feedback	Employs a planned sequential approach to problem solving; learns more by analyzing the situation than by acting and places less emphasis on feedback
Search	Uses trial and error and spontaneous action	Uses formal rational analysis
Approach to analysis	Uses common sense, intuition, and feelings	Develops explicit, often quantitative, models of the situation
Scope of analysis	Views the totality of the situation as an organic whole rather than as a structure constructed from specific parts	Reduces the problem situation to a set of underlying causal functions
Basis for inferences	Looks for highly visible situational differences that vary with time	Locates similarities or common alities by comparing objects

levels of detail, and permit some user control over the output form (visual, verbal, graphic, etc.). This is precisely what a decision support system attempts to do (Table 2.4).

Although cognitive style is a useful concept, it may be overemphasized in the MIS literature. It is difficult to take cognitive style into consideration for information systems and decision-making. For one thing, cognitive style is not distinct; it varies along a continuum. Many people are not completely heuristic or analytic but are somewhere in between. Related to cognitive style are the concepts of personality (temperament) type and decision style.

Research on cognitive and management styles states an obvious fact: in general, when a decision support system (or any information system) matches a manager's cognitive style, the DSS is more effective (see Lu, Yu, and Lu, 2001). Furthermore, when the DSS matches a manager's problem-solving mode (a cognitive model that characterizes the problem-solving process of a manager; this includes reasoning, analogizing, creating, optimizing), the DSS is more successful (see Van Bruggen and Wierenga, 2001). Clearly, the task at hand indicates what mode is needed. This is critical when deploying Web-based DSS and especially for appealing to e-commerce customers (see DSS in Action 2.4). In keeping with the idea of problem-solving mode, Hoenig (2001) describes six essential skills of problem-solving, each related to a specific *problem-solving personality*. These are described in DSS in Focus 2.26.

DECISION STYLE

Decision style is the manner in which decision-makers think and react to problems. This includes the way they perceive, their cognitive response, and how values and beliefs vary from individual to individual and from situation to situation. As a result, people make decisions differently. Although there is a general process of decision-making, it is far from linear. People do not follow the same steps of the process in the same sequence, nor do they use all the steps. Furthermore, the emphasis, time allotment, and priorities given to each step vary significantly, not only from one person to another but

---

DSS IN FOCUS 2.26

ARE THERE PROBLEM-SOLVING PERSONALITIES?

Hoenig feels that solving any problem involves six essential skills. The more you can master, the better the ultimate result. The six essential skills are generating mind-set, acquiring knowledge, building relationships, managing problems, creating solutions, and delivering results. The tougher, larger, and more demanding a problem or opportunity, and the faster and more competitive your environment, the more important they become.

Each of the six essentials represents a package of habits, skills, and knowledge that effectively comprise a *problem-solving personality*. Each personality draws its strength from a variety of specialties and professions. The six personalities serve as a convenient way to assess oneself and others in the workplace, to identify one's own personal mixture of strengths and weaknesses and how to develop a complete problem-solving capability. Great problem-solvers know the strengths and weaknesses of the different personality types. They build teams that compensate for their weakness, creating wholes that are equal to or greater than the sum of their parts. The problem-solving personalities (and skills) are

- The *Innovator* (generating mind-set) focuses on moving from self-doubt to innovation by developing potent ideas and attitudes, above all through seeking out alternative points of view.

- The *Discoverer* (acquiring knowledge) concentrates on moving from innovation to insight by asking the right questions and getting good, timely information.

- The *Communicator* (building relationships) covers how to move from insight to community by cultivating quality communication and interaction, and so creating an ever expanding circle of relationships based on service, loyalty, and identity.

- The *Playmaker* (managing problems) focuses on moving from building a community to giving the community a sense of direction and clear priorities by choosing destinations and strategies.

- The *Creator* (creating solutions) shows how to move from leadership to power by designing, building, and maintaining optimal solutions.

- The *Performer* (delivering results) concentrates on moving from power to sustainable advantage through intuitive and disciplined implementation.

The difference between the best and the worst problem-solvers is how many of the six essentials they can cultivate (by themselves and/or with others) and how deeply the skills are understood—individually and collectively. To become an expert problem-solver, one must understand the six essentials, practice them, master them at one level and then move on toward the limits of one's potential. An interesting aspect of these skills and personalities is to consider how they mesh with Simon's four phases of decision-making.

Source: Abstracted from C. Hoenig, "Means to an End," *CIO,* November 1, 2000, p. 204. Also see C. Hoenig. *From the Problem Solving Journey.* Perseus Publishing, Cambridge, MA, 2000.

---

also from one situation to the next. The manner in which managers make decisions (and the way they interact with other people) describes their decision style. Because decision styles depend on the factors described earlier, there are many decision styles. Personality temperament tests are often used to determine decision styles. Since there are many such tests, it is important to try to equate them in determining decision style. However Leonard et al. (1999) discovered that the various tests measure somewhat different aspects of personality, so they cannot be equated.

In addition to the heuristic and analytic styles mentioned earlier, one can distinguish autocratic versus democratic styles; another style is consultative (with individuals or groups). Of course, there are many combinations and variations of styles. For example, one can be analytic and autocratic, or consultative (with individuals) and heuristic.

For a computerized system to successfully support a manager, it should fit the decision situation as well as the decision style. Therefore, the system should be flexible and adaptable to different users. The ability to ask what-if and goal-seeking questions provides flexibility in this direction. A Web-based interface using graphics is a desirable feature in supporting certain decision styles. If a management support system is to support varying styles, skills, and knowledge, it should not attempt to enforce a specific process. Rather, it should help decision-makers use and develop their own styles, skills, and knowledge.

Different decision styles require different types of support. A major factor that determines the type of required support is whether the decision-maker is an individual or a group. Individual decision-makers need access to data and to experts who can provide advice, while groups additionally need collaboration tools. Web-based MSS can provide support to both.

There is a lot of information on the Web about cognitive style and decision style (e.g., see Birkman International Inc. at birkman.com; and the Keirsey Temperament Sorter and Keirsey Temperament Theory Web site at keirsey.com). Many personality/temperament tests are available to help managers identify their own styles and those of their employees. Identifying an individual's style can help establish the most effective communication patterns and ideal tasks for which he or she is suited.

2.12 THE DECISION-MAKERS

Decisions are often made by individuals, especially at lower managerial levels and in small organizations. There may be conflicting objectives even for a sole decision-maker. For example, in an investment decision, an individual investor may consider the rate of return on the investment, liquidity, and safety as objectives. Finally, decisions may be fully automated (but only after a human decision-maker decides to do so!).

Our discussion of decision-making focused on an individual decision-maker. The Opening Vignette described both individual and group decision-making, with groups taking responsibility for both. Most major decisions in medium-sized and large organizations are made by groups. Obviously, there are often conflicting objectives in a group decision-making setting. Groups can be of variable size and may include people from different departments or from different organizations. Collaborating individuals may have different cognitive styles, personality types, and decision styles. Some clash, whereas others are mutually enhancing. Consensus can be a difficult political problem (see DSS in Action 2.27). Therefore, the *process* of decision-making by a group can be very complicated. Computerized support (Chapter 7) can greatly enhance group

---

DSS IN ACTION 2.27

GROUP CONSENSUS:
THE 23-MILE-PER-HOUR SPEED LIMIT

Consensus by a group can lead to the implementation of unusual and potentially unrealistic solutions. For example, there is a condominium complex in Lake Worth, Florida, where the residents could not agree on a "reasonable" speed limit. They finally came to a consensus that was a compromise value close to the average of the group members' individual suggestions. The speed limit was set at 23 mph (13.8 kph), whereas 20 mph (12 kph) or 25 mph (15 kph) would have been an acceptable and especially anticipated solution for most drivers.

decision-making. Computer support can be provided at an even broader level, enabling members of whole departments, divisions, or even entire organizations to collaborate online. Such support has evolved over the last few years into enterprise information systems and includes group support systems (GSS), enterprise resource management (ERM)/enterprise resource planning (ERP), supply-chain management (SCM), knowledge management systems (KMS), and customer relationship management (CRM) systems.

❖ CHAPTER HIGHLIGHTS

- Managerial decision-making is synonymous with the whole process of management.
- Problem-solving is also opportunity evaluation.
- A system is a collection of objects, such as people, resources, concepts, and procedures, intended to perform an identifiable function or to serve a goal.
- Systems are composed of inputs, outputs, processes, and decision-makers.
- All systems are separated from their environment by a boundary that is often imposed by the system designer.
- Systems can be open, interacting with their environment, or closed.
- DSS deals primarily with open systems.
- A model is a simplified representation or abstraction of reality.
- Models are used extensively in MSS; they can be iconic, analog, or mathematical.
- Decision-making involves four major phases: intelligence, design, choice, and implementation.
- In the intelligence phase, the problem (opportunity) is identified, classified, and decomposed (if needed), and problem ownership is established.
- In the design phase, a model of the system is built, criteria for selection are agreed on, alternatives are generated, results are predicted, and a decision methodology is created.
- There is a trade-off between model accuracy and cost.

- Rationality is an important assumption in decision-making. Rational decision-makers can establish preferences and order them consistently.
- In the choice phase, alternatives are compared and a search for the best (or a good enough) solution is launched. Many search techniques are available.
- In implementing alternatives, one should consider multiple goals and sensitivity-analysis issues.
- Satisficing is a willingness to settle for a satisfactory solution. In effect, satisficing is suboptimizing. Bounded rationality results in decision-makers satisificing.
- Computer systems, especially those that are Web-based, can support all phases of decision-making by automating many of the required tasks or by applying artificial intelligence.
- Personality types may influence decision-making capabilities and styles.
- Human cognitive styles may influence human–machine interaction.
- Human decision styles need to be recognized in designing MSS.
- There are inconclusive results on how gender differences influence decision-making and computer use in decision-making.
- Individual and group decision-making can both be supported by MSS.

❖ KEY WORDS

- algorithm
- analog model
- analytical techniques
- choice phase
- cognitive style (cognition)
- decision-making
- decision style
- decision variables
- descriptive models
- design phase
- effectiveness
- efficiency
- iconic model
- implementation phase
- inputs
- intelligence phase
- interfaces
- nonprogrammed problem
- normative models
- optimization
- personality (temperament) type
- principle of choice
- problem ownership
- problem-solving
- programmed problem
- satisficing
- scenario
- sensitivity analysis
- simulation
- suboptimization
- system
- what-if analysis

❖ QUESTIONS FOR REVIEW

1. Review what is meant by decision-making versus problem-solving. Compare the two, and determine whether or not it makes sense to distinguish them.
2. Define a system.
3. List the major components of a system.
4. Explain the role of feedback in a system.
5. Define the environment of a system.
6. Define open and closed systems. Give an example of each.
7. Define efficiency, define effectiveness, and compare and contrast the two.
8. Define the phases of intelligence, design, choice, and implementation.
9. Distinguish a problem from its symptoms.
10. Define programmed (structured) versus nonprogrammed (unstructured) problems. Give one example in each of the following areas: accounting, marketing, human resources.
11. List the major components of a mathematical model.
12. Define optimization and contrast it with suboptimization.
13. Compare the normative and descriptive approaches to decision-making.
14. Define rational decision-making. What does it really mean to be a rational decision-maker?
15. Why do people exhibit bounded rationality when problem-solving?
16. Define a scenario. How is it used in decision-making?
17. How can a DSS support the implementation of a decision?
18. Define implementation.
19. What is a personality (temperament) type? Why is it an important factor to consider in decision-making.
20. Define cognition and cognitive style.
21. Define decision style.
22. Compare and contrast decision-making by an individual with decision-making by a group.

❖ QUESTIONS FOR DISCUSSION

1. Specify in a table the inputs, processes, and outputs of the following systems. Determine what is required for each system to be efficient and effective.
   a. Post office
   b. Elementary school
   c. Grocery store
   d. Farm
2. List possible kinds of feedback for the systems in the preceding question. Explain how feedback is essentially part of Simon's intelligence decision-making phase.
3. A hospital includes dietary, radiology, housekeeping, and nursing (patient care) departments, and an emergency room. List and describe four system interfaces between pairs of these departments.
4. How would you measure the productivity of
   a. A letter carrier
   b. A salesperson
   c. A professor
   d. A social worker
   e. A student
   f. A farmer
5. Give an example of five elements in the environment of a university.
6. Analyze a managerial system of your choice and identify the following:
   a. The components, inputs, and outputs
   b. The boundary
   c. The environment
   d. The processes
   e. The system's goals
   f. The feedback
7. What are some of the measures of effectiveness in a toy manufacturing plant, a restaurant, an educational institution, and the U.S. Congress?
8. Assume that a marketing department is an open system. How would you close this system?
9. Your company is considering opening a branch in China. List typical activities in each phase of the decision to open or not to open (intelligence, design, choice, implementation).
10. You are about to sell your car. What principles of choice are you most likely to use in deciding whether to offer or reject offers? Why?
11. You are about to buy a car. Follow Simon's four-phase model and describe your activities at each step.
12. The use of scenarios is popular in computerized decision-making. Why? For what types of decisions is this technique most appropriate?
13. Explain, through an example, the support given to decision-makers by computers in each phase of the decision process.
14. Some experts believe that the major contribution of DSS is to the implementation of the decision. Why is this so?

15. Explain how personality type, gender, cognitive style, and decision style are related. How might these concepts affect the development of decision support systems?

16. Table 2.4 shows the major differences between heuristic and analytic cognitive styles.
    a. Do you consider yourself heuristic or analytic? Why?
    b. Assume you are making a presentation to two managers—one heuristic, the other analytic—regarding a decision about adding a service by the bank you work for. How would you appeal to their cognitive styles? (Be specific.)

17. Decision-making styles vary from analytic to heuristic-intuitive. Does a decision-maker consistently use the same style? Give examples from your own experience.

18. Most managers are capable of using the telephone without understanding or even considering the electrical and magnetic theories involved. Why is it necessary for managers to understand MSS tools to use them wisely?

❖ EXERCISES

1. Consider the "75 greatest management decisions ever made" described in DSS in Action 2.2. From the articles, examine a subset of five decisions. Compare and contrast them: Identify the similarities and differences. How do you think the intelligence phase was handled for each?

2. Early in the chapter, we mention the Great Wall of China as a major blunder. Investigate it. Study the history of the Great Wall. Look up why it was constructed, how it was done, how long it took, and similar facts. Why did it fail to meet its primary objective? Identify four other equally major blunders, and explain what happened in each case.

3. According to Warren Bennis and Burt Nanus (*Leaders*, HarperCollins, New York, 1997), "Managers are people who do things right and leaders are people who do the right thing. The difference may be summarized as activities of vision and judgment—*effectiveness*—versus activities of mastering routines—*efficiency*" (also see David Baron, *Moses on Management*, Pocket Books, New York, 1999). Explain how this relates to decision-making, managers, executives and systems.

4. Comment on Simon's (1977) philosophy that managerial decision-making is synonymous with the whole process of management. Does this make sense or not? Explain. Use a real-world example in your explanation.

5. Consider a situation in which you have a preference for where you go to college; you want to be not too far away from home and not too close. Why might this situation arise? Explain how this situation fits in with rational decision-making behavior.

6. When you were looking for a college program, somehow you were able to decide on going where you are now. Examine your decision-making process and describe it in a report. Explain how you eliminated the many thousands of programs around the world, and then in your own country or region. What criteria were important? What was your final set of alternatives? And how did you decide among them? Compare your results with those of others in the class.

7. You are about to buy a car. What criteria are important? What specific choices do you have, and how will you limit your choices? Read Case Application 2.3 and structure your problem within the AHP framework. Does this make intuitive sense? Explain why it does or does not.

8. Consider the A/B/C parts inventory management and scheduling situation described under suboptimization). Describe how management of the A items might be viewed as a nonprogrammed (unstructured or least-structured) problem, management of the B parts as a semistructured problem, and management of the C parts as a programmed (structured) problem.

9. Stories about suboptimization issues abound in some formerly centrally planned national economies in which the output of factories was measured by seemingly useful measures, with unexpected and disastrous results. Specifically, a ball-bearing factory's output was measured by the total weight of the ball bearings produced, and so the plant manager decided to produce one very large ball bearing each month. There was a shoe factory where output was measured by the number of left shoes, and so the plant manager decided to make *only left shoes* to double the factory's official output. Explain in detail how the measure of the result variable (output) of a subsystem can lead to bad decisions that lead to suboptimized results for the entire system, and what the conse-

quences might be. Think in terms of what it means to *establish a principle of choice*. This is not unique to centrally planned economies but can happen in any organization. Give an example from your personal or professional life in which this happened.

10. Explain how Hoenig's (2001) problem-solving personalities (see DSS in Focus 2.26) each focus in on each of Simon's four phases of decision-making.

11. According to H.L. Mencken (1880–1956), "For every problem there is one solution which is simple, neat and wrong." Explain this statement in the light of the decision-making material in this chapter and examples with which you are familiar.

❖ GROUP ASSIGNMENTS AND ROLE-PLAYING

1. Interview a person who was recently involved in making a business decision. Try to identify
   a. The scope of the problem solved
   b. The people involved in the decision (explicitly identify the problem owners)
   c. Simon's phases (you may have to ask specific questions, such as how the problem was identified)
   d. The alternatives (choices) and the decision chosen
   e. How the decision was implemented
   f. How computers were used to support the decision-making or why they were not used.

   Produce a detailed report describing an analysis of the above and clearly state how closely the real-world decision-making process compares to Simon's suggested process. Clearly identify how computers were used or why they were not used.

2. Have everyone in your group perform a personality type test—either the Myers–Briggs (Keirsey and Bates, 1984) or the True Colors (Birkman, 1995) type. Compare the results and see if they match up well with each member's modus operandus. For each member, how does their type describe the way they make decisions? Is the group made up of different or similar types? How will this help or hinder the group's ability to function? Based on the types, what could each member bring to the table for better group performance? What special things will the group need to consider to enhance communication in the group so that it will function effectively?

3. *Personality Discussion and Role-Play:* For any movie or television show that has four or more main characters (we suggest the popular *Friends* show), identify the temperament type of each character. Describe how each character interacts with the others, and describe how this maps into the personality types described by either Myers–Briggs or True Colors. Get the members of your group to behave like the characters in a real situation (go to a coffeehouse, as in *Friends*). Later describe the experience.

4. Develop a cognitive map of the decision-making problem of selecting a job, or a university program using Decision Explorer (Banxia Software Ltd., banxia.com). Describe your thought processes and how you developed the map.

5. Compare the results for gender differences and similarities described by Smith (1999) and Leonard et al. (1999) with the case of gender differences described by R. L. Fox, and R. A. Schuhmann in "Gender and Local Government: A Comparison of Women and Men City Managers" (*Public Administration Review*, Vol. 59, No. 3, May/June, 231–242, 1999). Do the results for city managers match those found in the other literature? If so, in what ways?

6. Watch the movie *12 Angry Men* (1957) starring Henry Fonda. Comment on the group decision-making process followed by the jury. Explain how this is a demonstration of group decision-making. Does it fit into Simon's four-phase model? Explain why or why not, citing examples from the movie.

7. Watch the movie *The Bachelor* (1999) starring Chris O'Donnell. In it, a man must marry by a deadline to inherit $100 million. There are many alternatives, but the *criteria* are quite fuzzy. Watch the scene toward the end of the movie where about a thousand brides converge on a church and want to know "What are the criteria?" Explain how the main character describes his criteria, and what they are. Explain why they are quite vague. Explain what his criteria really are. Given enough time, compare your answers to S. Piver, *The Hard Questions: 100 Essential Questions to Ask Before You Say "I Do"* (New York: J.P. Tarcher, 2000).

8. Sometimes you find yourself between the proverbial rock and hard place. All the alternatives (discovered so far) are bad or infeasible. Then you have a *real problem*. Examine the decision-making situation about the *Alexander Hamilton*, described in DSS in Action 2.12. Explore the situation regarding the ship, and suggest some possible alternatives and why they are feasible. E-mail good suggestions to Jay Aronson at *jaronson@uga.edu* so he can forward them to Dennis Lafko.

❖ INTERNET EXERCISES

1. Search the Web for material on managerial decision-making. What general classes of materials can you identify in a sample of 10 sites?

2. Many colleges and universities post their course catalogs, course descriptions, and syllabi on the Web. Identify a sample of 10 decision-making courses that are posted and compare their topical material. What is the major focus of these courses? What percentage of them includes computerized support? In which departments or colleges are they typically found?

3. Search the Web for companies and organizations that provide computerized support for managerial decision-making. Take a sample of five software vendors and characterize their products based on specific functional market area (marketing, manufacturing, insurance, transportation, etc.), level of managerial support (strategic, tactical, operational, transactional), type of computerized tool (e.g., DSS, data mining, business intelligence, OLAP, EIS, ES, ANN, cluster analysis), and how they utilize Web technologies. Take a sample of 10 nonvendors (e.g., consultants). What kinds of support do they provide?

4. Some companies and organizations have downloadable demo or trial versions of their software products on the Web so that you can copy and try them out on your own computer. Others have online demos. Find one that provides decision support, try it out, and write a short report about it. You should include details about the intended purpose of the software, how it works, and how it supports decision-making.

5. Visit the teradatauniversitynetwork.com Web site. Explore the public areas. Describe five of the types of decision-making studies and cases that are listed.

CLAY PROCESS PLANNING AT IMERYS: A CLASSICAL CASE OF DECISION-MAKING

Part 1: The Go/No Go Decision for the Process OPtimization (POP) DSS

INTRODUCTION

IMERYS (formerly English China Clay International, ECCI) in Sandersville, Georgia, mines crude kaolin (China) clay and processes it into a wide variety of products (dry powders, slurries, etc.) that add gloss to paper, cardboard, paint, wallpaper, and other materials. Kaolin clay is also used to make ceramics, tableware, and sculptures. It can also be used for processing aluminum, making toothpaste, and as a medication for soothing stomach upset (yes, the crude clay is edible right from the ground). Between 50 and 100 million years ago, during the Cretaceous and Tertiary geological periods, kaolin deposits formed on the Atlantic seacoast along the Fall Line that crosses central Georgia. In 1880 the first clays were mined and processed, and since then the industry has expanded dramatically. The total annual economic impact in Georgia was $824 million in 1996. Georgia's total kaolin production capacity was about 8.3 million tons (half the world's production), of which some 6.8 million tons were processed in 2001. This represents the bulk of kaolin processing in the United States. Major deposits are also mined and processed in Brazil, China (PRC), the Czech Republic, France, Germany, and the United Kingdom. Georgia supplies more than half the kaolin used by papermakers worldwide. The middle-Georgia kaolin deposits are the largest in the world. Sandersville is called the *kaolin capital of the world*. See the China Clay Producers Association (kaolin.com) and IMERYS (imerys.com) Web sites for more information on the geology, history, mining, products, and economic impacts of kaolin clay.

THE SITUATION

In late 1998, as part of a continuous improvement initiative, ECCI managers, engineers, and IS analysts met to determine the feasibility of applying mathematical programming (optimization) to clay mining and production. The need to process lower-quality crude clays, the depletion of higher-quality crude clays, and some new processing methods prompted a fresh look at the various aspects of clay processing and scheduling.

Several members of the continuous-improvement initiative team had previously been involved in the develop-

ment of large, complex linear and mixed-integer programming models for kaolin clay production planning at other organizations (the models were used mostly for capacity planning and had several thousand relationships and variables). None of these models had taken the clay all the way from the mines to the customer in the detail that would ideally be required now. Also, determining blends of clays had never been modeled before.

DECISION-MAKING: DECISION NUMBER 1: GO/NO GO

The initial decision-making process began with the continuous-improvement team recognizing that there was an opportunity, exploring potential impacts, and taking ownership of the problem (intelligence). The ECCI team was charged with exploring any potential improvement methodology. Such improvements could include making better decisions, making faster decisions, and so on. Initially, there was no way to know that such an approach would really work, but some team members were familiar with mathematical programming and knew that it was certainly worth exploring because it had produced favorable results for other problems in other organizations with which they had been associated. The next step was to seek out additional knowledge, information, and expertise and establish the likelihood of success. This included meeting with managers and other potential users who needed accurate production plans to determine what new sales could be accepted and how they could be made. The decision to pursue the development of a system was based on mental and simple spreadsheet models, and past experience (design). Influencing the decision was the fact that the IS department was implementing a forecasting model that was part of a staged development enterprise resource planning (ERP) system. Given a set of forecasts, this new mathematical programming model, as part of a decision-support system, could potentially drive the ERP in overall organizational planning. This was decision-making under uncertainty, where the risk of failure (or success) had yet to be assessed. Analysts find these problems most challenging because they eventually may have to build a system that has never been developed before. Following a workshop, the team decided that the initiative had merit, and recognizing that the project would be a major initiative requiring substantial resources in personnel and money, they reached a consensus and decided to proceed with development of the system (choice). The implementation phase involved assembling a formal team to move forward with development of the decision-support system. The consequences of the decision follow in the subsequent IMERYS case narratives.

And so ECCI committed resources to a new initiative for developing a decision-support system to assist members of the organization in decision-making. The development team now had to understand how clay is processed and develop a methodology to assist the decision-makers. The scope of the project evolved as new information was learned.

CASE QUESTIONS

1. Why did the continuous-improvement team start exploring the use of mathematical programming for clay process planning?
2. Why do you think that earlier models and systems developed to solve similar types of problems were not directly applicable in this case?

3. For this first go/no go problem, describe how the decision was made. Relate your explanation to Simon's four-phase decision-making model. Do you think that this was a crucial decision in light of this project?
4. In 1999, the industry experienced a downturn. How could using a model like the one that ECCI decided to develop help it compete?

CASE APPLICATION 2.2

CLAY PROCESS PLANNING AT IMERYS: A CLASSICAL CASE OF DECISION-MAKING

Part 2: The Decisions of the Process OPtimization (POP) DSS

KAOLIN PROCESSING

Kaolin production involves mining a variety of crude clays followed by a number of purification, grinding, separation, heating, blending, and other steps (for a description of typical steps, see kaolin.com). Different crude clay recipes can be used to produce similar and different final products; and, at a number of points in production, alternative blends can be used in creating final products with identical properties (brightness, gloss, etc.). Some processes can be performed on different pieces of equipment, and sometimes there are several units of similar equipment that can be aggregated into a single one (to simplify the model). Further complicating the decision-making situation, different initial crude blends typically require different rates for several pieces of equipment used for different processes. For example, a lower percentage of a *fine* (smaller-particle-size) crude clay blended with *coarse* clays generally requires additional time (a slower rate) to crush the coarser clay sufficiently for further processing. Costs per hour, costs per ton, recovery factors (which may vary by clay), and rate (in tons per hour) are specified for

each process for each clay for each recipe (blend). These data are estimates because the times vary with subtle changes in the clay, depending on the mine, and even the particular pit in the mine from which the clay is extracted.

ALTERNATIVE RECIPES AND NEW PROBLEMS

One of the problems facing ECCI in late 1999 was that some of the mines with high-quality crude clays were almost depleted. Alternative crude recipes, process adjustments, and new processes had to be instituted to produce final clays identical in quality to existing products. New final clay products (pure and blends) are continually being developed as well. The clays also follow different step orderings through the production process, depending on their major class of products. One class of clays is wet; the other is dry. Within each major class are several pure finished products, and hundreds of blends of these are needed to obtain the desired properties required by customers in the global marketplace. Kaolin (dry) clays have three major products with about 20 final blends, while hydrous (wet) clays have six major products with several hundred final blends. Clays may also be processed at different plants. There are transfers of clays from other plants, some of which were initially modeled in this phase of the project, while others were placed on hold. Some crude clays and finished clays can be purchased on the open market, while others cannot (these are uniquely produced by ECCI in Sandersville). Chemicals are added at a number of different steps in the process. There is a direct relationship between chemical use and the processing rates of several pieces of equipment. The use of more chemicals may typically require less processing time in one or more production steps. ECCI ships finished products to customers on every continent. They also maintain warehouses on several continents. They ship products by rail, truck, and ship.

Clearly, there are many decisions to be made, hence many decision variables. There are many constraints due to time and tonnage capacity limits, and these vary depending on the rates. There are many constraints that describe the flows through each process; and many that relate the flows from each piece of equipment to the others. There are many intermediate variables representing the amount of clay that flows from the output of one process to the input of another. There are many combinations of clays, dramatically increasing the number of decision variables. The result variable is profit, which is to be maximized. Also, certain assumptions that bound rationality must be made, in order to develop a reasonable-sized model that can be solved in a finite amount of time. For example, although the model can be assumed to be linear, within the normal operating parameters of the plants, the engineers and scientists who design and run the processes have indicated that there are some subtle nonlinearities.

DECISION-MAKING: DECISION NUMBER 2: OPTIMAL CLAY PROCESSING

The primary goal is to determine the optimal way (i.e., maximizing net profit) to process clays all the way from the mines to the customers. This model can determine how the clays should be optimally blended, and at which stages, and which equipment should run at capacity. Later, capacity expansion can be added to the model to determine which equipment should have additional production capacity, again to maximize profit. The model can also determine which demand from the open market has to be met if existing capacity proves insufficient.

The overall decision-making problem is: given a set of demands for final clay products (possibly obtained from a forecasting system), determine how to process the clay optimally (maximize net profit). This involves determining

- A time horizon (typically 1 year, 3 months, or 2 weeks)
- Which mines to use, which clays from these mines to extract, and how much to extract

- Which crude blends to use
- Which processes to run the clays through and at which rates
- Chemicals to be used and where they should be used
- Which intermediate blends to use
- How best to blend the finished products.

These decisions involved establishing standard rates and costs for equipment for the various clays, as well as determining which specific pieces of equipment could be utilized for specific clays. Because a new process was coming online in late 1999, it was modeled as well, along with discontinuing use of the old crude clays, as they would soon be depleted, and activating new ones.

Given a set of demands for finished clay products, specific decisions included

1. How much of each kind of crude clay to mine (before and after the depletion of high-quality grades)
2. What crude blends (recipes) to use (which impacts certain equipment process rates)
3. Which production processes to use for crude clay blends
4. How to further blend processed crude clay blends into intermediate clays (which impacts certain equipment process rates)
5. Which specific processes to use on intermediate clays
6. How to recycle coproducts back into the production stream
7. How to blend intermediate clays into final clays
8. What demands to really meet from existing production capacity
9. How much clay should be purchased from external sources to blend into intermediate and final products
10. How much of each chemical should be used
11. Which final processes to use on final clay blends
12. Which final demands should be met by external market purchases or by production at other plants in the organization.

A linear programming model can support this kind of decision-making within a DSS. Data gathering for the model and integrating the two could (and did) prove difficult and time-consuming. Development of the Process OPtimization (POP) linear programming model and the DSS are described as case applications in Chapters 4 and 6.

THE PROTOTYPING APPROACH

Early in the project it was decided that a DSS prototyping approach would be used. One small calcine (dry) plant would be modeled first to develop the necessary features, familiarize the team members with the tools and methodologies, and establish the database structures that would guide the rest of the system development.

NEW COMPLICATIONS

Impacting directly on the POP project, IMATEL, a French mining consortium, purchased ECCI and in early 1999 and merged it into their holdings under the name IMERYS later in the year. These holdings included the Dry Branch Kaolin Company located in Dry Branch, Georgia. The European Community (EC) approval agency quickly approved the purchase, but the U.S. Justice Department added some restrictions: some of the ECCI plant processing operations had to be quickly sold to obtain approval. It turns out that this included our test plant.

CASE QUESTIONS

1. Why was it important for the model to handle blends and recipes?
2. The linear programming model to be developed will describe several plants and be rather large. The version of the model that represented two plants had on the order of 10,000 constraints and 40,000 variables (the version deployed in July 2002 had over 80,000 constraints and 150,000 variables). How does one go about verifying that the model is correct, that is, getting the right answer? How can one "manage" the data? Who should be allowed to update the model structure? Update the demands? Update other aspects? Why?
3. Pick three decisions listed and explain their importance to the company.
4. Why was a prototyping (evolutionary design) approach adopted by the team? Did this make sense? Why or why not?
5. How could the external event of the purchase of ECCI by IMATEL and its merger into IMERYS affect the model and the system development? Why was this an important event with regard to the DSS and the model?
6. The mining and materials-processing industries typically lag behind other industries in the development and use of DSS and modeling. Why do you think this is so, and what can be done to advance these industries so that they can and will use advanced tools?

CASE APPLICATION 2.3

KEY GRIP SELECTS FILM PROJECTS BY AN ANALYTICAL HIERARCHY PROCESS

INTRODUCTION

In the motion picture industry, the workers called grips are "intelligent muscle on set." Grips are responsible for setting up lights, cameras, and other materials on the set. Not just muscle is required, however. Grips must be able to make decisions as to how best to do setups, which can be quite complex. In fact, many grips have a B.A. or M.A. degree in theater. The *key grip* is responsible for all the grips on the set and is essentially their manager, as well as a liaison between the other grips and the production company. The primary concern of the key grip is safety on the set.

Charles N. Seabrook, of Charleston, South Carolina, is a key grip, an important job in the filmmaking industry. Charles has been in the business for nearly 20 years and has an excellent reputation. He is one of the best.

Consequently, he often has problems deciding which job offer (movie) to accept. Even when there are no competing offers, he sometimes has to decide whether or not he wants to work a particular job.

The Analytical Hierarchy Process (AHP) (Forman and Selly, 2001; Saaty, 1999) is an excellent method for selecting competing activities using distinct criteria. The criteria can be quantitative or qualitative in nature, and even quantitative criteria are handled by a decision-maker's preference structure rather than numerically. To develop a DSS to solve Seabrook's recurrent (institutional) problem, we developed an AHP model in Expert Choice (Expert Choice, Inc.; a downloadable demo is available at expertchoice.com). Our decision-making approach fits the Simon four-phase model. We decided to

---

Contributed by the MAccAttack student team: M. Adams, P. Lambeth, C. Maxwell, and M. Whitmire, The University of Georgia, Athens, Georgia, 2000.

use the Ratings Module of Expert Choice to formulate a model to aid Seabrook in his decision-making.

CRITERIA

Our first step was to interview Seabrook regarding the general aspects of his professional life and how he goes about making decisions. Then we interviewed him to establish the important criteria for job selection. Initially, he stated the following eight potential criteria:

- **Location of filming.**
  The distance from Seabrook's home in Charleston, South Carolina.
- **Time away from family.**
  Seabrook is dedicated to his family and prefers not to spend long periods away from home.
- **Reputation of the production company.**
  The company producing the film plays an important part in how well people get along on the set and how well the filming is organized.
- **Film budget.**
  Often, if a film has a low budget, there are problems in obtaining equipment and general dissatisfaction among the crew.
- **Pay.**
  Obviously, the hourly rate paid to Seabrook is a high priority.
- Union involvement.
  If the union is involved in the film, working conditions are usually better and, more important, employee benefits are paid.
- **Quality of best boy available.**
  The best boy is the key grip's assistant and is heavily involved in the large amount of paperwork required on the set. Having a reliable best boy is crucial to the film. However, later we learned that this criterion is not necessary, because Seabrook does not accept a film if his regular best boy, Jack Gilchrist, is not available.
- **Quality of grips available for hire.**
  A film often functions as a virtual company with technically qualified individuals hired to do particular jobs. If there is a lack of competent grips available, the key grip's tasks become much more difficult.

After further discussion, the criteria were reduced to a more manageable set of five, for which further clarifications of their definitions were developed. The final five were

- **Location of filming.**
  This implies that there will be time away from family, as the distance from home determines the amount of time he is away.
- *Pay.*

- **Working conditions.**
  This factor includes how lenient the budget is, as well as how many days per week and hours per day are required. Because this also determines how much overtime is available, it is closely tied to pay.
- **Union involvement.**
- **Reputation of production company.**

Note that in developing the criteria, we did not discuss specific alternative choices.

AHP: EXPERT CHOICE MODELS AND DEVELOPMENT

The structure of an AHP model as implemented in Expert Choice is that of an inverted tree. There is a single *goal* node at the top that represents the goal of the decision-making problem. One hundred percent of the weight of the decision is in this node. Directly under the goal are leaf nodes representing all the *criteria*, both qualitative and quantitative. The weight of the goal must be partitioned among the criteria nodes as ratings. There are several methods built into Expert Choice to do this. All are based on comparing all pairs of criteria to establish how the weight of the goal is to be distributed. The software also provides a measure of the inconsistency of the comparisons. Thus, if the decision-maker prefers criterion 1 to criterion 2 at a certain preference level (say, moderate) and compares criterion 1 to criterion 3 identically, then for consistency in decision-making, he or she should compare criteria 2 and 3 as equally preferred. After the decision-maker completes the comparisons, the weight of the decision-making problem is distributed among the criteria in accordance with the preference structure derived from the pairwise comparisons. Expert Choice provides an inconsistency ratio indicating how *consistent* the decision-maker is in making judgments.

There are two ways to build the model. If the problem is ad hoc (occurs one time) and there are few alternatives (say, seven plus or minus two), then the decision-maker enters the *choice nodes* (alternatives) beneath the first criterion and replicates them to all its peers (the other criteria). Then the decision-maker pairwise compares the choices under the first criterion, under the second one, and so on, until all are compared. From each set of comparisons, Expert Choice divides the problem's weight in the specific criterion among the choices and calculates an inconsistency ratio within the criterion. Once all the choices have been compared, the results are synthesized, the choice with the most weight becomes the "expert choice," and the inconsistency ratio indicates how trustable the decision is (0 indicates perfectly consistent; 1 indicates perfectly inconsistent).

If the problem is recurring or there are many alternatives to select among, the ratings model can be used. The leaf nodes below each criterion describe the scale for each criterion. For example, working conditions might be characterized as excellent, good, fair, or poor. The decision-maker pairwise compares these scale characterizations just like choices. Excellent is clearly preferred to good, good to fair, and fair to poor. The weights of these characterizations establish a scale for a specific movie project.

Once all the criteria have their scales and have been pairwise compared, we switch to the ratings model, where each choice is represented by the rows of a spreadsheet-like framework and a column represents each criterion. The decision-maker then clicks on the appropriate rating for each criterion for each movie. Once all criteria ratings are selected, a value for the alternative is computed. The decision-maker may decide to accept movies only if their values exceed a minimum level, or may sort the choices and select the most highly rated one. Regardless of which method is used, the AHP, essentially as implemented in Expert Choice, extracts the decision-maker's utility function through the decision-maker's preferences.

MODEL BUILDING

The goal and five criteria were entered into our Expert Choice model, and a rating scale was determined for each of the criteria by Seabrook. The screenshot in Figure 2.4 shows the goal (Which movie to choose?), the five criteria, and the scale for each.

A pairwise comparison analysis was then performed, and the priorities were determined. At this point, another conference with Seabrook allowed us to fine-tune the priorities. The results are shown in the screenshot in Figure 2.5 and also in the weights in the criteria nodes in Figure 2.4. Note the overall inconsistency ratio of 0.07. Attempts to reduce this number led to priorities that Seabrook felt did not match his preferences, and so we returned to the earlier values. Generally, if the ratio is less than 0.1, the comparisons can be considered consistent.

Next, we pairwise compared the ratings scales beneath each criterion. Finally, we switched to the Ratings Module and contacted Seabrook again to obtain a set of usable real-world data on movies he had considered in the past to validate the model. We prepared a survey form for him to rate the last four jobs he had been offered. It was a simple circle-the-correct-response survey. The data were entered into the model, with the ratings results shown in Figure 2.6.

RESULTS

The names of the movies are omitted for confidentiality, but the results matched Seabrook's decisions. Movie 1, with a rating of only 0.279, was rejected by both the model and. Seabrook. Seabrook accepted all of the other three movies and, as a result, felt that the ideal cutoff rating should be set to 0.4, since the lowest rated accepted movie was only 0.001 points less than that. This level may change when Seabrook adopts the model, for he will be able to update the model as his priorities change. One month following the initial model and system development, we installed Expert Choice on Seabrook's computer and provided training to ensure that he could use the model to its fullest potential. He is very pleased with the system and has incorporated it into his decision-making process.

FIGURE 2.4   EXPERT CHOICE MODEL SHOWING THE CRITERIA AND THEIR RATING SCALES

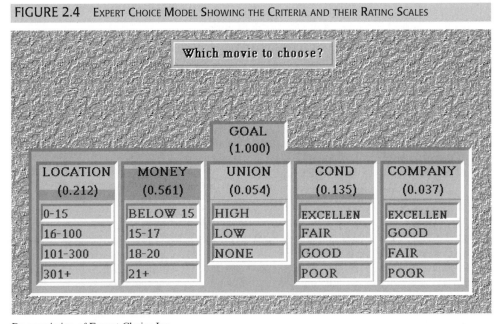

By permission of Expert Choice Inc.

FIGURE 2.5   EXPERT CHOICE RESULTS OF PAIRWISE COMPARISONS FOR THE CRITERIA

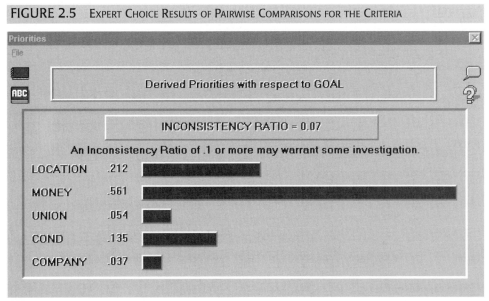

By permission of Expert Choice Inc.

CONCLUSION

Charles Seabrook can now use a specific DSS application that provides assistance in his rational decision-making process of determining which job offers he should accept or reject. Up until now, he used the same criteria as are in the model. But he used a mental model in which it can be difficult, if not impossible, to consider all criteria while simultaneously weighing the importance of each. Using the AHP through Expert Choice to transfer his knowledge and preferences into a formal decision-making model leads to more consistent and higher-quality decision-making. Previously, Seabrook generally made decisions based on one factor that was overwhelmingly good or bad. Now, he is able to weigh the importance of *all* the factors in a rational way.

FIGURE 2.6   EXPERT CHOICE RATINGS MODEL WITH SAMPLE, REAL-WORLD DECISION MAKING RESULTS

LOCATION			
0-15 1 (1.000)	16-100 2 (.637)	101-300 3 (.212)	301+ 4 (.066)

	Alternatives	TOTAL	LOCATION . . .2123	MONEY . . .5610	UNION . . .0537	COND . . .1355	COMPANY . . .0374
1	Movie 1	0.279	16-100	15-17	NONE	GOOD	GOOD
2	Movie 2	1.000	0-15	21+	HIGH	EXCELLEN	EXCELLEN
3	Movie 3	0.399	16-100	18-20	HIGH	GOOD	GOOD
4	Movie 4	0.409	0-15	BELOW 15	NONE	EXCELLEN	EXCELLEN
5							
6							
7							
8							
9							
10							

By permission of Expert Choice Inc.

CASE QUESTIONS

1. Do you think that Seabrook really used *all* eight criteria in his decision-making before this DSS was developed? Why or why not? How much information would be needed if he were selecting from among 12 movies and used all eight criteria? Is this a feasible way to go about working with information? Why or why not?
2. Describe how the process and model fit into the Simon four-phase decision-making model.
3. Explain the differences between the "standard" AHP model with goal/criteria/choices and the ratings AHP model with goal/criteria/ratings scales/choices.
4. Why was it more appropriate to use the ratings-model approach than the standard one?
5. How did the AHP Expert Choice model assist Seabrook in providing a more rational framework in his decision-making?
6. Do you think that this project would have been as successful if the development team had not worked closely with the decision-maker? Why or why not?

CASE APPLICATION 2.4

MMS RUNNING CASE: SUMMARY AND CONCLUSION

MMS ran into new problems when it changed its fleet. CLAUDIA was not equipped to handle new cars, unlike others from past experience, and did not track events as well as trends. Simon's four phases of decision-making, along with feedback, were followed, even though the problems were not really identified in the first phase. Successful problem-solving was ultimately accomplished using Web-based DSS.

CASE QUESTIONS

1. What is meant by a symptom versus a problem? Relate these ideas to the case.
2. Why is problem ownership so important?
3. Even though the problem was not identified at the end of the intelligence phase, what was?
4. How was the design phase performed?
5. The choice phase seemed like a combination of design, choice, and implementation. Is this a problem?
6. The implementation phase seemed to involve elements of all the phases. Is this a problem?
7. How were new problems or opportunities handled as they arose?
8. Why do you suppose some alternatives were either modified or postponed?

DECISION SUPPORT SYSTEMS

LEARNING OBJECTIVES FOR PART II

❖ Understand the foundations, definitions, and capabilities of decision support systems

❖ Describe DSS components and technology levels

❖ Explain the importance of databases and database management

❖ Explain the importance of models and model management

❖ Understand how DSS are developed

❖ Understand DSS success and failure factors

❖ Understand collaboration, and group support systems and their impacts

❖ Understand knowledge management systems and their impacts

In Part II, we concentrate on decision support methodology, technology components, and development. Throughout we highlight the major impacts of the World Wide Web on DSS. Chapter 3 provides an overview of DSS: its characteristics, structure, use, and types. Two of the major components of DSS are presented in Chapter 4 (Modeling and Analysis) and Chapter 5 (Modern DSS/Business Intelligence Data Management). Chapter 6 covers the DSS development process.

DECISION SUPPORT SYSTEMS: AN OVERVIEW

LEARNING OBJECTIVES

❖ Understand possible DSS configurations

❖ Describe DSS characteristics and capabilities

❖ Understand DSS components and how they integrate

❖ Describe the components and structure of each DSS component: the data-management sub-system, the model-management subsystem, the user-interface (dialog) subsystem, the knowl-edge-based management subsystem, and the user

❖ Explain how the World Wide Web has affected DSS, and vice versa

❖ Explain the unique role of the user in DSS versus MIS

❖ Describe the DSS hardware platforms

❖ Understand the important DSS classifications

In Chapter 1 we introduced DSS and stressed its support in the solution of complex managerial problems. The methodology of decision-making was presented in Chapter 2. In this chapter we show how DSS superiority is achieved by examining its capabilities, structure, and classifications in the following sections:

3.1 OPENING VIGNETTE: SOUTHWEST AIRLINES FLIES IN THE FACE OF COMPETITION THROUGH DSS[1]

INTRODUCTION

About a year after the September 11, 2001 disaster and the resulting plunge in airline revenues, Southwest Airlines was so pleased with the performance of its *business intelligence/DSS applications* for financial management that it expanded deployment to include flight operations and maintenance. In the middle of a crisis, Southwest Airlines successfully deployed its Hyperion Solutions Corp. Essbase online analytical processing (OLAP) application and Pillar budgeting software. Southwest can accurately make financial forecasts in facing the severe market downturn. Southwest has exploited its business intelligence applications successfully.

PROBLEMS MANY COMPANIES FACE

Most companies do not adequately tie their financial applications into an OLAP system, analyze their data, and then meaningfully present it to business personnel. Southwest's success resulted from its ability to tie its enterprise resource planning applications to its OLAP software and then present relevant financial data and scenarios to its decision-makers.

THE SITUATION

Right after the terrorist attacks, the airline was operating "in a world of complete uncertainty," said Mike Van de Ven, vice president of financial planning and analysis at Southwest. "We were asked to give some sort of financial insight for a variety of decisions the company might make."

Prior to the roughly $1 million installation of Essbase from Hyperion (Sunnyvale, California) in 1999, Southwest analysis personnel wrote queries by hand, spending about a half hour running them, and then put the figures into spreadsheets for additional analysis. The total time could take up to four hours.

RESULTS

Essbase has cut the analysis time to as little as two minutes, leading to massive savings. After running worst- and best-case scenarios and creating forecasts, Southwest developed an action plan to stabilize its finances. It helped answer questions like, "How fast would we burn through our cash?" As of July 2002, the forecasts have been within 2 percent of actual values.

---

[1]*Sources:* Based on Marc L. Songini, "Southwest Expands Business Tools' Role," *ComputerWorld*, Vol. 36, No. 29, July 15, 2002, p. 6; Trebor Banstetter, "Southwest Airlines Posts $75 Million Fourth-Quarter Profit," *Knight Ridder Tribune Business News*, October 18, 2002; Trebor Banstetter, "Southwest Airlines Sees Passenger Traffic Rise," *Knight Ridder Tribune Business News*, October 3, 2002; and Bill Hensel, Jr., "Dallas-Based Southwest Airlines Adds Flights, Drops Fares," *Knight Ridder Tribune Business News*, August 28, 2002.

Analysts can access both operational and financial data to analyze and identify the impact of one set on the other. Relationships can be found to improve forecasting. Overall, the application has paid for itself just through the savings from automating the data-collection processes.

Southwest has better control over its cost structure than the network carriers do. It is the largest airline that has remained profitable since the travel industry began to slump in 2001. The airlines overall lost $7 billion in 2001 and was expected to lose at least as much in 2002. Southwest Airlines may have been one of the only carriers to make a profit in 2002. Southwest Airlines is still growing (though cautiously), despite the massive market downturn and showed a $75 million profit in the fourth quarter of 2002. Southwest's new business intelligence tools help decision-makers accurately predict their markets and decide which ones to expand into.

❖ QUESTIONS FOR THE OPENING VIGNETTE

1. What kinds of models do you suppose Southwest Airlines used in its OLAP?
2. How can business intelligence like that utilized by Southwest Airlines lead to higher profits and a more competitive position in the marketplace?
3. Explain how the benefits were obtained.
4. Why don't most companies do what Southwest Airlines did?
5. Explain how these ideas could be used in other industry segments (e.g., retail, insurance, oil and gas, universities).

3.2 DSS CONFIGURATIONS

The opening vignette illustrates the versatility of a DSS/**business intelligence system**. Specifically, it shows a support system with the following characteristics:

- It supports individual members and an entire team.
- It is used repeatedly and constantly.
- It has three major components: data, models. and a user interface.
- It uses subjective, personal, and objective data.
- It is used in the private sector.
- It helps the user to make faster, smarter, better decisions.

Though not mentioned, the user interface and database access were, no doubt, implemented with Web/Internet technologies.

This vignette demonstrates some of the potential diversification of DSS. Decision support can be provided in many different configurations. These configurations depend on the nature of the management-decision situation and the specific technologies used for support. These technologies are assembled from four basic components (each with several variations): *data, models, user interface*, and (optionally) *knowledge*, often deployed over the Web. Each of these components is managed by software that either is commercially available or must be programmed for the specific task. The manner in which these components are assembled defines their major capabilities and the nature of the support provided. For example, models are emphasized in a model-oriented DSS. Such models can be customized with a spreadsheet or a programming language or can be provided by standard algorithm-based tools that include linear programming. Similarly, in a data-oriented DSS, a database and its management play the major roles. In the situation in the opening vignette, both approaches were used. In this chapter we will explore all of these and related topics, but first we revisit the definitions of a DSS.

3.3 WHAT IS A DSS?

The early definitions of a DSS identified it as a system intended to support managerial decision-makers in semistructured decision situations. DSS were meant to be an adjunct to decision-makers to extend their capabilities but not to replace their judgment. They were aimed at decisions where judgment was required or at decisions that could not be completely supported by algorithms. Not specifically stated, but implied in the early definitions, was the notion that the system would be computer-based, would operate interactively online, and preferably would have graphical output capabilities. The early definitions were open to several interpretations. Soon several other definitions appeared that caused considerable disagreement as to what a DSS really is. We discuss these definitions next.

DSS DEFINITIONS

Little (1970) defines DSS as a "model-based set of procedures for processing data and judgments to assist a manager in his decision-making." He argues that to be successful, such a system must be simple, robust, easy to control, adaptive, complete on important issues, and easy to communicate with. Alter (1980) defines DSS by contrasting them with traditional electronic data processing (EDP) systems on five dimensions, as shown in Table 3.1.

Moore and Chang (1980) argue that the structuredness concept, so much a part of early DSS definitions (i.e., that DSS can handle semistructured and unstructured situations), is not meaningful in general; a problem can be described as structured or unstructured only with respect to a particular decision-maker or a specific situation (i.e., structured decisions are structured because we choose to treat them that way). Thus, they define DSS as extendible systems capable of supporting ad hoc data analysis and decision modeling, oriented toward future planning, and used at irregular, unplanned intervals.

TABLE 3.1	DSS Versus EDP	
Dimension	*DSS*	*EDP*
Use	Active	Passive
User	Line and staff management	Clerical
Goal	Effectiveness	Mechanical efficiency
Time horizon	Present and future	Past
Objective	Flexibility	Consistency

Source: Based on Alter (1980).

Bonczek et al. (1980) define a DSS as a computer-based system consisting of three interacting components: a language system (a mechanism to provide communication between the user and other components of the DSS), a knowledge system (a repository of problem domain knowledge embodied in DSS as either data or procedures), and a problem-processing system (a link between the other two components, containing one or more of the general problem-manipulation capabilities required for decision-making). The concepts provided by this definition are important for understanding the relationship between DSS and knowledge.

Finally, Keen (1980) applies the term DSS "to situations where a 'final' system can be developed only through an adaptive process of learning and evolution." Thus, he defines a DSS as the product of a developmental process in which the DSS user, the DSS builder, and the DSS itself are all capable of influencing one another, resulting in system evolution and patterns of use.

These definitions are compared and contrasted by examining the various concepts used to define DSS (Table 3.2). It seems that the basis for defining DSS has been developed from the perceptions of what a DSS does (e.g., support decision-making in unstructured problems) and from ideas about how the DSS's objective can be accomplished (e.g., components required, appropriate usage pattern, necessary development processes).

Unfortunately, the formal definitions of DSS do not provide a consistent focus because each tries to narrow the population differently. Furthermore, they collectively ignore the central purpose of DSS, that is, *to support and improve decision-making*. In later DSS definitions, the focus seems to be on inputs rather than outputs. A very likely reason for this change in emphasis is the difficulty of measuring the outputs of a DSS (e.g., decision quality or confidence in the decision made).

A DSS APPLICATION

A DSS is usually built to support the solution of a certain problem or to evaluate an opportunity. As such it is called a **DSS application**. In DSS in Focus 3.1 we provide a working definition that includes a range from a basic to an ideal DSS application. Later in this chapter the various configurations of DSS are explored. However, it is beneficial first to deal with the characteristics and capabilities of DSS, which we present next.

We show a typical Web-based DSS architecture in Figure 3.1. This DSS structure utilizes models in business intelligence work. Processing is distributed across several servers in solving large analytical problems. This multitiered architecture uses a Web browser to run programs on an application server. The server accesses data to construct one or more models. Data may also be provided by a data server that optionally extracts data from a data warehouse or a legacy mainframe system. When the user requires that the model be optimized, the model, populated with the data, is transferred to an optimization server. The optimization server may access additional data

TABLE 3.2 Concepts Underlying DSS Definitions	
Source	*DSS Defined in Terms of*
Gorry and Scott-Morton (1971)	Problem type, system function (support)
Little (1970)	System function, interface characteristics
Alter (1980)	Usage pattern, system objectives
Moore and Chang (1980)	Usage pattern, system capabilities
Bonczek et al. (1989)	System components
Keen (1980)	Development process

WHAT IS A DSS APPLICATION?

A DSS is an approach (or methodology) for supporting decision-making. It uses an interactive, flexible, adaptable CBIS especially developed for supporting the solution to a specific nonstructured management problem. It uses data, provides an easy user interface, and can incorporate the decision-maker's own insights.

In addition, a DSS usually uses models and is built (often by end-users) by an interactive and iterative process. It supports all phases of decision-making and may include a knowledge component.

Finally, a DSS can be used by a single user on a PC or can be Web-based for use by many people at several locations.

from the data server, solves the problem, and provides the solution directly to the user's Web browser. Generated solution reports, which the application server may massage to make them readable by managers, may be sent directly to appropriate parties via e-mail or may be made available through another Web portal as part of this enterprise information system. The Web-based DSS described in Case Application 3.2 is structured along these lines, as is the application described in DSS in Action 3.2. See Cohen, Kelly, and Medaglia (2001) for further examples of several Web-based applications that utilize this type of architecture. Similar architectures are described by Dong, Sundaram, and Srinivasan (2002), Gachet (2002), and Forgionne et al. (2002).

FIGURE 3.1 MULTITIERED ARCHITECTURE FOR INCORPORATING OPTIMIZATION, SIMULATION, AND OTHER MODELS INTO WEB-BASED DSS

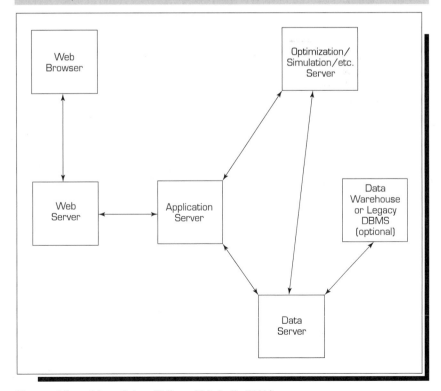

(*Source:* Adapted from Cohen, Kelly, and Medaglia, 2001.)

CAMERON AND BARKLEY COMPANY'S WEB-BASED DSS REDUCES INVENTORIES AND IMPROVES PERFORMANCE

Cameron and Barkley (Cambar) Company (Charleston, South Carolina) distributes industrial, electrical, and electronic supplies throughout the United States. Nearly one-half million products comprise Cambar's inventory. Cambar needed to reduce its inventory without sacrificing its level of customer service. These two goals are contradictory, yet occur often in practice. The company needed to manage and improve its product inventory and improve the accuracy of demand forecasts—the key to inventory reduction. By analyzing demand data, several good ordering rules were identified. Next a prototype inventory-planning and management system was developed, tested, and deployed. The buyers, who managed the inventory, had the goal of maintaining high enough inventory levels to meet strict levels of customer service. But too high invokes inventory carrying costs; capital is tied up in inventory, and there are costs of maintaining it. Buyers used judgmental and simple demand forecasts to determine these lev-

els. They had a tendency to overstock and far missed the goal of a minimum of four inventory turns per year.

Then Cambar developed the Inventory-Replenishment Planner (IRP). This model utilizes the architecture shown in Figure 3.1. A Web interface captures user interactions, saves the business information, and builds a model utilizing data from a data server on the application server. The model approximates lead-time demand and minimizes ordering and fixed costs subject to required service levels. The model is solved on the optimization/simulation server with two heuristics. The effects are evaluated on the optimization/simulation server by simulating the effect of policies to evaluate their effectiveness. Results are captured by the application server and handed off to the Web server, which generates meaningful reports to determine what and when to order.

Source: Adapted from Cohen, Kelly, and Medagli (2001).

3.4 CHARACTERISTICS AND CAPABILITIES OF DSS

Because there is no consensus on exactly what a DSS is, there is obviously no agreement on the standard characteristics and capabilities of DSS. The capabilities in Figure 3.2 constitute an ideal set, some members of which were described in the definitions as well as in the opening vignette. The term *business intelligence* is synonymous with DSS but has become tightly aligned with Web implementations (see DSS in Focus 3.3; also see Callaghan, 2002; Hall, 2002a,b; Harreld, 2002; d Ocken, 2002). **Business analytics** is another term that implies the use of models and data to improve an organization's performance or competitive posture. In business analytics, the focus is on the use of models, even if they are deeply buried inside the system. In fact, PricewaterhouseCoopers (PwC) estimates that only 10 to 20 percent of users access DSS tools. To reach the rest, business analytics must be embedded in core IT solutions (see Hall, 2000b). Hall (2002a) describes *Web analytics*, an approach to using business analytics tools on real-time Web information to assist in decision-making. Most of these applications are related to e-commerce, while others are being initiated in product development and supply chain management.

The key DSS characteristics and capabilities (Figure 3.2) are:

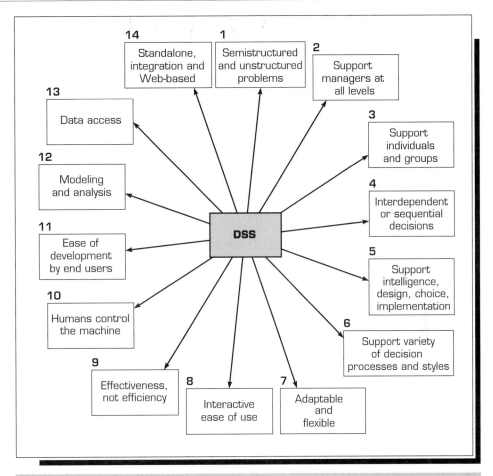

FIGURE 3.2   KEY CHARACTERISTICS AND CAPABILITIES OF DSS

DSS IN FOCUS 3.3

WHAT IS BUSINESS INTELLIGENCE?

Business intelligence (BI) is a collection of technical and process innovations across the data warehousing and business intelligence space. Proactive BI focuses on decision-making acceleration by leveraging existing BI infrastructure to identify, calculate, and distribute up-to-the-moment, mission-critical information. Through the application of these techniques and technologies, the reach and value of data warehouse and BI systems can be increased by one or more orders of magnitude. Business success today requires intelligent data use.

Proactive BI has five components: real-time warehousing, automated anomaly and exception detection, proactive alerting with automatic recipient determination, seamless follow-through workflow, and automatic learning and refinement. Wireless technologies have a key role to play in increasing the value and efficiency of several of these components.

Business analytics implies the use of models in business intelligence. These models may be manual, as in OLAP, or automatic, as in data mining.

Sources: Some material adapted from Langseth and Vivatrat, 2002; also see Ocken, 2002; Rothrock (2002).

1. Support for decision-makers, mainly in semistructured and unstructured situations, by bringing together human judgment and computerized information. Such problems cannot be solved (or cannot be solved conveniently) by other computerized systems or by standard quantitative methods or tools.

2. Support for all managerial levels, ranging from top executives to line managers.

3. Support for individuals as well as to groups. Less-structured problems often require the involvement of individuals from different departments and organizational levels or even from different organizations. DSS support virtual teams through collaborative Web tools.

4. Support for interdependent and/or sequential decisions. The decisions may be made once, several times, or repeatedly.

5. Support in all phases of the decision-making process: intelligence, design, choice, and implementation.

6. Support in a variety of decision-making processes and styles.

7. Adaptivity over time. The decision-maker should be reactive, able to confront changing conditions quickly, and able to adapt the DSS to meet these changes. DSS are flexible, and so users can add, delete, combine, change, or rearrange basic elements. They are also flexible in that they can be readily modified to solve other, similar problems.

8. User feeling of at-homeness. User-friendliness, strong graphical capabilities, and a natural language interactive human–machine interface can greatly increase the effectiveness of DSS. Most new DSS applications use Web-based interfaces.

9. Improvement of the effectiveness of decision-making (accuracy, timeliness, quality) rather than its efficiency (the cost of making decisions). When DSS are deployed, decision-making often takes longer, but the decisions are better.

10. Complete control by the decision-maker over all steps of the decision-making process in solving a problem. A DSS specifically aims to support and not to replace the decision-maker.

11. End-users are able to develop and modify simple systems by themselves. Larger systems can be built with assistance from information system (IS) specialists. OLAP (online analytical processing) software in conjunction with data warehouses allows users to build fairly large, complex DSS.

12. Models are generally utilized to analyze decision-making situations. The modeling capability enables experimenting with different strategies under different configurations. In fact, the *models make a DSS different from most MIS*.

13. Access is provided to a variety of data sources, formats, and types, ranging from geographic information systems (GIS) to object-oriented ones.

14. Can be employed as a standalone tool used by an individual decision-maker in one location or distributed throughout an organization and in several organizations along the supply chain. It can be integrated with other DSS and/or applications, and can be distributed internally and externally, using networking and Web technologies.

These key DSS characteristics and capabilities allow decision-makers to make better, more consistent decisions in a timely manner, and they are provided by the major DSS components, which we describe next.

3.5 COMPONENTS OF DSS

A DSS application can be composed of the subsystems shown in Figure 3.3.

Data-management subsystem. The data management subsystem includes a database that contains relevant data for the situation and is managed by software called the **database management system (DBMS).**[2] The data management subsystem can be interconnected with the corporate **data warehouse**, a repository for corporate relevant decision-making data. Usually the data are stored or accessed via a database Web server.

Model management subsystem. This is a software package that includes financial, statistical, management science, or other quantitative models that provide the system's analytical capabilities and appropriate software management. Modeling languages for building custom models are also included. This software is often called a **model base management system (MBMS).** This component can be connected to corporate or external storage of models. Model solution methods and management systems are implemented in Web development systems (like Java) to run on application servers.

User interface subsystem. The user communicates with and commands the DSS through this subsystem. The user is considered part of the system. Researchers assert that some of the unique contributions of DSS are derived from the intensive interaction between the computer and the decision-maker. The Web browser provides a familiar, consistent graphical user interface structure for most DSS.

Knowledge-based management subsystem. This subsystem can support any of the other subsystems or act as an independent component. It provides intelligence to

FIGURE 3.3 A SCHEMATIC VIEW OF DSS

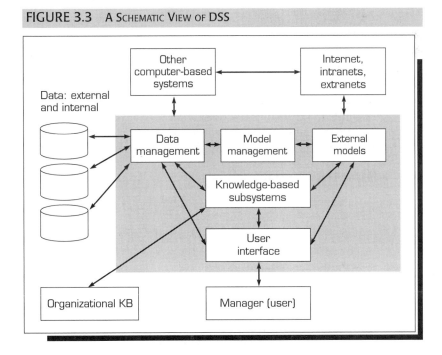

---

[2]DBMS is both singular and plural (system and systems), as are many acronyms in this text.

augment the decision-maker's own. It can be interconnected with the organization's knowledge repository (part of a knowledge management system), which is sometimes called the **organizational knowledge base.** Knowledge may be provided via Web servers. Many artificial intelligence methods have been implemented in Web development systems like Java, and are easy to integrate into the other DSS components.

By definition, a DSS must include the three major components of a DBMS, MBMS, and user interface. The knowledge-based management subsystem is optional, but can provide many benefits by providing intelligence in and to the three major components. As in any management information system, the user may be considered a component of DSS.

These components form the DSS application system, which can be connected to the corporate intranet, to an extranet, or to the Internet. Typically the components communicate via Internet technology. Web browsers typically provide the user interface. The schematic view of a DSS and the above components shown in Figure 3.2 provides a basic understanding of the general structure of a DSS. In Table 3.3, we provide a sampling of the impacts of the Web on DSS components, and vice versa. These impacts have been substantial, because improvements in what began as the Internet have had a major effect on how we access, use, and think of DSS. Next, we present a more detailed look at each component; we provide details in Chapters 4–9.

3.6 THE DATA MANAGEMENT SUBSYSTEM

The data-management subsystem is composed of the following elements:

- DSS database
- Database management system
- Data directory
- Query facility.

These elements are shown schematically in Figure 3.4 (in the shaded area). The figure also shows the interaction of the data management subsystem with the other parts of the DSS, as well as its interaction with several data sources. A brief discussion of these elements and their function follows; further discussion is provided in Chapter 5. In DSS in Action 3.4, the primary focus of the DSS is on the database.

THE DATABASE

A **database** is a collection of interrelated data organized to meet the needs and structure of an organization and can be used by more than one person for more than one application. There are several possible configurations for a database. In many DSS instances, data are ported from the data warehouse or a legacy mainframe database system through a database Web server (see DSS in Action 3.2 and 3.4). For other DSS applications, a special database is constructed as needed. Several databases can be used in one DSS application, depending on the data sources. Generally users expect to utilize a Web browser for access, and database Web servers deliver the data regardless of the source. For examples, see DSS in Action 3.2 and 3.4.

The data in the DSS database, as shown in Figure 3.4, are extracted from internal and external data sources, as well as from personal data belonging to one or more users. The extraction results go to the specific application's database or to the corpo-

TABLE 3.3   DSS Components and Web Impacts

Phase	Web Impacts	Impacts on the Web
Database Management System (DBMS)	Consistent, friendly, graphical user interface Provides for a direct mechanism to query databases Provides a consistent communication channel for data, information, and knowledge Data access through m-commerce devices Intranets and extranets Web-based development tools New programming languages and systems Proliferation of database use throughout organizations-made enterprise-wide systems feasible Access to information about databases	A means to conduct e-commerce (transactions must be stored and acted upon) Database Web servers Stores data about the Web for analysis using models to determine effectiveness and efficiency
Model Base Management System (MBMS)	Access to models and solution methods implemented as Java applets and other Web development systems Use of models by untrained managers because they are so easy to use Access to Web-based AI tools to suggest models and solution methods in DSS Access to information about models	Improved infrastructure design and updates Models and solutions of Web infrastructure issues Models of Web message routing improves performance Forecasting models predict viability of hardware and software choices
User Interface Dialog (UI) System	Web browsers provide a flexible, consistent, and familiar DSS graphical user interface Access to information about user interfaces Experimental user interfaces are tested and distributed via the Web	Initial graphical user interfaces and the computer mouse helped define how a Web browser should work Speech recognition and generation are deployed over the Web
Knowledge-base Management System (KBMS)	Access to AI methods Access to information about AI methods Access to knowledge Web-based AI tools are deployed as Java applets or as other Web development system tools	AI methods readily handle network design issues and message routing Expert systems diagnose problems and workarounds for failures in the Internet Expert systems diagnose hardware problems and recommend specific repairs Intelligent search engines learn user patterns

rate data warehouse (Chapter 5), if it exists. In the latter case, it can be used for other applications.

Internal data come mainly from the organization's transaction processing system. A typical example of such data is the monthly payroll. Depending on the needs of the DSS, operational data from functional areas, such as marketing (e.g., Web transactions from e-commerce), might be included. Other examples of internal data are machine maintenance scheduling and budget allocations, forecasts of future sales, costs of out-of-stock items, and future hiring plans. Internal data can be made available through Web browsers over an **intranet,** an internal Web-based system.

External data include industry data, marketing research data, census data, regional employment data, government regulations, tax rate schedules, and national economic data. These data can come from government agencies, trade associations, market research firms, econometric forecasting firms, and the organization's own efforts to col-

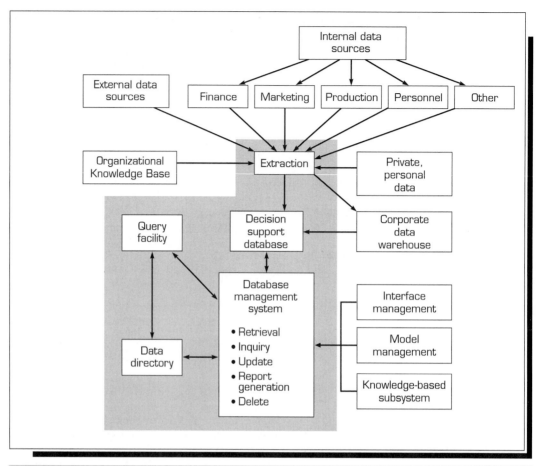

FIGURE 3.4   THE STRUCTURE OF THE DATA MANAGEMENT SUBSYSTEM

DSS IN ACTION 3.4

ROADWAY DRIVES LEGACY APPLICATIONS ONTO THE WEB

It was time for Roadway Express Inc. (Akron, Ohio) to move from a mainframe *green screen* to the more popular Web browser interface. The existing system could handle data requests and updates, but it looked old and did not present customers with a good impression of the company. So Roadway, rather than reinvent the wheel, polished its surface instead. Roadway's Web design group developed a Web server front-end for access to mainframe scheduling and tracking data. The Janus Web Server (Sirius Software Inc., Cambridge, Massachusetts) front-ends the mainframe, allowing Roadway to reuse its existing transportation-management and administrative systems. The link between the two systems is so seamless that users don't realize they are using 14-year-old technology. Customers can access the system and generate reports on their own shipments. Roadway's Web site is one of the most sophisticated and capable on the market.

Source: Adapted from Linda Rosencrance, "Roadway Drives Legacy Apps onto the Web," *ComputerWorld*, April 9, 2002, p. 48.

lect external data. Like internal data, external data can be maintained in the DSS database or accessed directly when the DSS is used. External data are provided, in many cases, over the **Internet** (e.g., from computerized online services or as picked up by search engines). As we mentioned in Chapter 2, Hansen (2002) provides a list of many Web sites with global macroeconomic and business data.

Private data can include guidelines used by specific decision-makers and assessments of specific data and/or situations.

DATA ORGANIZATION

Should a DSS have a standalone database? It depends. In small, ad hoc DSS, data can be entered directly into models, sometimes extracted directly from larger databases. In large organizations that use extensive amounts of data, such as Wal-Mart, AT&T, and American Air Lines, data are organized in a data warehouse and used when needed (Agosta, 2002; Inmon, 2002; Inmon et al. 2000, 2001, 2002; Marakas, 2003). Some large DSS have their own fully integrated, multiple-source DSS databases. A separate DSS database need not be physically separate from the corporate database. They can be stored together physically for economic reasons. Some OLAP systems extract data, whereas others manipulate the data in the external database directly. Later, in DSS in Action 3.8, we describe a spreadsheet-oriented DSS for production planning and scheduling (see Respicio, Captivo, and Rodrigues, 2002). The DSS has a separate database, essentially in an Excel spreadsheet, that is populated with data extracted from a legacy database. Updates to the legacy database based on the DSS solutions are uploaded back.

A DSS database can also share a DBMS with other systems. A DSS database can include multimedia objects (e.g., pictures, maps, sounds) (Castelli and Bergman, 2002). Object-oriented databases in XML have been developed and used in DSS. These are becoming more important as m-commerce applications are deployed, because XML is becoming the standard, consistent data translation method for m-commerce devices (e.g., PDAs, cell telephones, notebook computers, tablet computer). The XML format is also used for standard Web browser access to data.

EXTRACTION

To create a DSS database or a data warehouse, it is often necessary to capture data from several sources. This operation is called **extraction**. It basically consists of importing of files, summarization, standardization filtration, and condensation of data. Extraction also occurs when the user produces reports from data in the DSS database. As will be shown in Chapter 5, the data for the warehouse are extracted from internal and external sources. The extraction process is frequently managed by a DBMS. *This extraction process is not trivial!* MIS professionals generally structure this process so that users need not deal with the complicated details. Much effort is required to structure the extraction process properly. To extract data, an exact query must be made to several related data tables that may span several independent databases. The pieces to be extracted must be "reconnected" so that a useful DSS database results. OLAP software like Temtec's Executive Viewer requires these actions before the OLAP may be used.

DATABASE MANAGEMENT SYSTEM

A database is created, accessed, and updated by a DBMS. Most DSS are built with a standard commercial relational DBMS that provides capabilities (see DSS in Focus 3.5).

THE CAPABILITIES OF A RELATIONAL DBMS IN A DSS

- Captures or extracts data for inclusion in a DSS database
- Updates (adds, deletes, edits, changes) data records and files
- Interrelates data from different sources
- Retrieves data from the database for queries and reports (e.g., using SQL via the Web)
- Provides comprehensive data security (e.g., protection from unauthorized access and recovery capabilities)

- Handles personal and unofficial data so that users can experiment with alternative solutions based on their own judgment
- Performs complex data manipulation tasks based on queries
- Tracks data use within the DSS
- Manages data through a data dictionary

An effective database and its management can support many managerial activities; general navigation among records, support for creating and maintaining a diverse set of data relationships, and report generation are typical examples. However, the real power of a DSS occurs when data are integrated with its models. (See DSS in Actions 3.2 and 3.8.)

THE QUERY FACILITY

In building and using DSS, it is often necessary to access, manipulate, and query data. The **query facility** performs these tasks. It accepts requests for data from other DSS components (Figure 3.4), determines how the requests can be filled (consulting the data directory if necessary), formulates the detailed requests, and returns the results to the issuer of the request. The query facility includes a special query language (e.g., SQL). Important functions of a DSS query system are selection and manipulation operations (e.g., the ability to follow a computer instruction, such as "Search for all sales in the Southeast Region during June 2004 and summarize sales by salesperson"). Though transparent to the user, this is a very important activity. All the user may see is a screen with a simple request for data, and following the click of a button, the user gets the results neatly formatted in a table in a dynamic HTML (or other Web-structured) page displayed on the screen.

THE DIRECTORY

The data **directory** is a catalog of all the data in the database. It contains data definitions, and its main function is to answer questions about the availability of data items, their source, and their exact meaning. The directory is especially appropriate for supporting the intelligence phase of the decision-making process by helping to scan data and identify problem areas or opportunities. The directory, like any other catalog, supports the addition of new entries, deletion of entries, and retrieval of information on specific objects.

All of the database elements have been implemented on database Web servers that respond to Web browser screens. The Web has dramatically changed the way we access, use, and store data.

3.7 THE MODEL MANAGEMENT SUBSYSTEM

The model management subsystem of the DSS is composed of the following elements:

- Model base
- Model base management system
- Modeling language
- Model directory
- Model execution, integration, and command processor.

These elements and their interfaces with other DSS components are shown in Figure 3.5. The definition and function of each of these elements are described next.

MODEL BASE

A **model base** contains routine and special statistical, financial, forecasting, management science, and other quantitative models that provide the analysis capabilities in a DSS. The ability to invoke, run, change, combine, and inspect models is a *key DSS capability that differentiates it from other CBIS*. The models in the model base can be divided into four major categories: strategic, tactical, operational, and analytical. In addition, there are model building blocks and routines.

Strategic models are used to support top management's strategic planning responsibilities. Potential applications include devising an e-commerce venture, developing corporate objectives, planning for mergers and acquisitions, plant location selection,

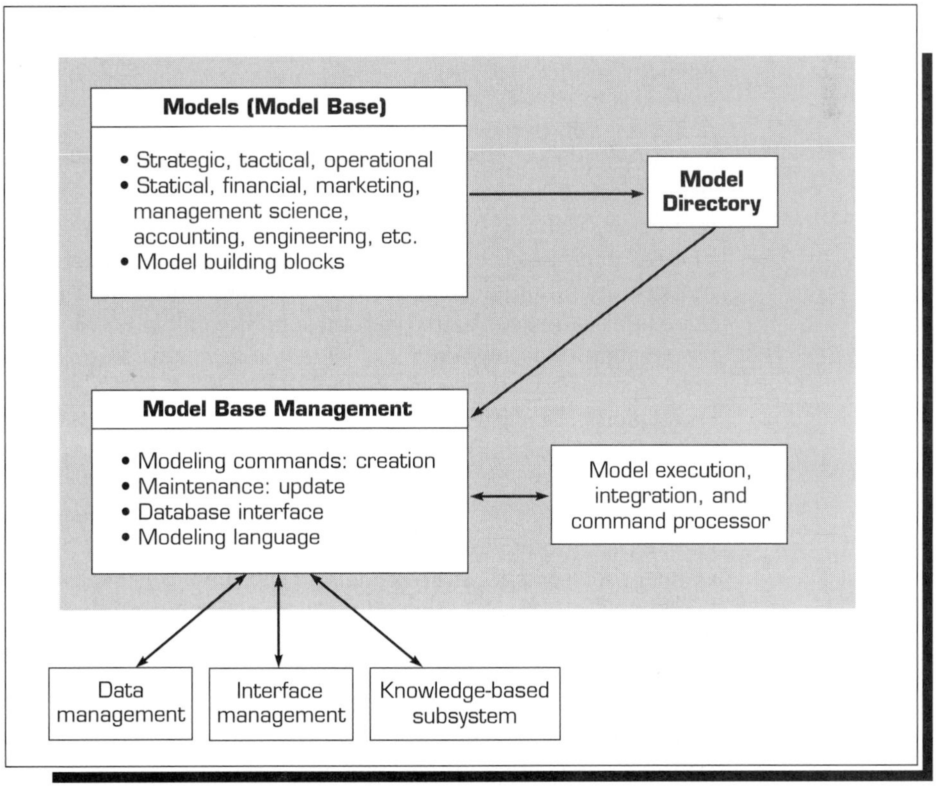

FIGURE 3.5   THE STRUCTURE OF THE MODEL MANAGEMENT SUBSYSTEM

environmental impact analysis, and nonroutine capital budgeting. One example of a DSS strategic model is that of Southwest Airlines in the Opening Vignette. Southwest used the system to create accurate financial forecasts so that it could identify strategic opportunities. Another is described in the IMERYS Case Applications at the end of Chapters 2, 4, and 6. The large-scale linear programming model is at the heart of the POP DSS that allows executives of the company to plan large, expensive equipment needs as many years ahead as needed.

Tactical models are used mainly by middle management to assist in allocating and controlling the organization's resources. Examples of tactical models include selecting a Web server, labor requirement planning, sales promotion planning, plant-layout determination, and routine capital budgeting. Tactical models are usually applicable only to an organizational subsystem, such as the accounting department. Their time horizons vary from one month to less than two years. Some external data are needed, but the greatest requirements are for internal data. When the IMERYS POP DSS is used by managers in three- month to one-year time horizons, it is used as a tactical tool that determines how much clay they can produce to meet predicted market demand.

Operational models are used to support the day-to-day working activities of the organization. Typical decisions involve e-commerce transaction acceptance (purchases, etc.), approval of personal loans by a bank, production scheduling, inventory control, maintenance planning and scheduling, and quality control. Operational models mainly support first-line managers' decision-making with a daily to monthly time horizon. These models normally use only internal data. An excellent example of an operational model is the one developed by a large U.S. national bank with hundreds of branches (the officers of the bank wish it to remain anonymous). The bank developed an artificial neural network model to determine whether or not specific loan applicants should be given loans. The accurate predictions of the system allowed the bank to hold back on hiring additional loan officers, saving the bank some $200,000 in its first year of operation for a development cost of about $300,000. The POP DSS at IMERYS is used operationally to determine exactly which clays to produce when over a two-week time horizon, over which the demand is known from actual contracted sales.

Analytical models are used to perform some analysis on the data. They include statistical models, management science models, data mining algorithms (see Chapter 4, and Hand, Mannila, and Smyth, 2001; Han and Kamber, 2000), financial models, and more. Sometimes they are integrated with other models, such as strategic planning models. The foundations of *business analytics* (the term was coined in the early 2000s) encompass all these analytical models. Typically, business analytics tools are Web-based, and that is why the term *Web analytics* was coined. These tools may readily be applied to Web systems; one example of their use is for administering and monitoring e-commerce. Business analytics software is generally easy to use. It includes OLAP, which is designed for use by managers or executives, as opposed to analysts, and data mining (see Hall, 2002a, 2002b; Langseth and Vivatrat, 2002).

The models in the model base can also be classified by functional areas (e.g., financial models, production control models) or by discipline (e.g., statistical models, management science allocation models). The number of models in a DSS can vary from a few to several hundred. Examples of DSS with several integrated models are described in DSS in Actions 3.2, 3.8, and the Web Chapter on Procter & Gamble's redesign of its distribution system. Models in DSS are basically mathematical; that is, they are expressed by formulas. These formulas can be preprogrammed in DSS development tools such as Excel. They can be written in a spreadsheet and stored for future use, or they can be programmed for only one use.

MODEL BUILDING BLOCKS AND ROUTINES

In addition to strategic, tactical, and operational models, the model base can contain **model building blocks** and routines. Examples include a random number generator routine, a curve- or line-fitting routine, a present-value computational routine, and regression analysis. Such building blocks can be used in several ways. They can be employed on their own for such applications as data analysis. They can also be used as components of larger models. For example, a present-value component can be part of a make-or-buy model. Some of these building blocks are used to determine the values of variables and parameters in a model, as in the use of regression analysis to create trend lines in a forecasting model. Such building blocks are available in DSS commercial development software, such as the functions and add-ins of Excel, and in the general modeling structures of OLAP and data mining software. Since model solution methods have been implemented directly in Java and other Web development systems, access and integration of models has been simplified.

MODELING TOOLS

Because DSS deal with semistructured or unstructured problems, it is often necessary to customize models using programming tools and languages. Some examples of these are C++ and Java. OLAP software may also be used to work with models in data analysis. A Web-based system that uses a cluster analysis model for recommending movies is described in DSS in Action 3.6. For small and medium-sized DSS or for less complex ones, a spreadsheet (e.g., Excel) is usually used. We will use Excel for many key examples.

THE MODEL BASE MANAGEMENT SYSTEM

The functions of model base management system (MBMS) software are *model creation* using programming languages, DSS tools and/or subroutines, and other building blocks; *generation of new routines* and reports; *model updating* and *changing*; and

---

DSS IN ACTION 3.6

A WEB-BASED DSS CLUSTER ANALYSIS METHOD MATCHES UP MOVIES AND THEATER-GOERS

NetFlix.com (Los Gatos, California) provides movie recommendations to its 500,000 subscribers. The recommendations are provided by the subscribers themselves. But how do you go about identifying which movies are similar, so that you can make recommendations ("Customers who liked movie X also liked movie Y")? Canned software cannot evaluate the many subjective, on-the-fly reviews provided by tens of thousands of critics. NetFlix needed to do this to remain competitive. Enter *cluster analysis*. Mathematicians encoded cluster analysis software to define movie clusters, relate opinions to the clusters, evaluate thousands of ratings per second, and factor in current Web site behavior to deliver a specially configured Web page before a customer can click again. The real-time analytics can also tell marketing managers what Web page design is working best for a given promotion. They can then change the Web page design immediately, based on the dynamic feedback. Cluster analysis is a very effective modeling tool that is used in customer relationship management systems (CRM) when trying to determine which products appeal to which customers.

Source: Adapted from Mark Hall, "Web Analytics: Get Real," *ComputerWorld*, Vol. 36, No. 14, April 1, 2002, pp. 42–43.

MAJOR FUNCTIONS OF THE MBMS

- Creates models easily and quickly, either from scratch or from existing models or from the building blocks
- Allows users to manipulate models so that they can conduct experiments and sensitivity analyses ranging from what-if to goal-seeking
- Stores, retrieves, and manages a wide variety of different types of models in a logical and integrated manner
- Accesses and integrates the model building blocks

- Catalogs and displays the directory of models for use by several individuals in the organization
- Tracks model data and application use
- Interrelates models with appropriate linkages with the database and integrates them within the DSS
- Manages and maintains the model base with management functions analogous to database management: store, access, run, update, link, catalog, and query
- Uses multiple models to support problem solving

---

model data manipulation. The MBMS is capable of interrelating models with the appropriate linkages through a database (see DSS in Focus 3.7.)

THE MODEL DIRECTORY

The role of the model directory is similar to that of a database directory. It is a catalog of all the models and other software in the model base. It contains model definitions, and its main function is to answer questions about the availability and capability of the models.

MODEL EXECUTION, INTEGRATION, AND COMMAND

The following activities are usually controlled by model management. *Model execution* is the process of controlling the actual running of the model. *Model integration* involves combining the operations of several models when needed (e.g., directing the output of one model, say forecasting, to be processed by another one, say a linear programming planning model; see the IMERYS Case Applications 2.2 and 4.1, and DSS in Actions 3.2 and 3.8) or integrating the DSS with other applications. Portucel Industrial (a major Portuguese paper producer) uses a DSS that contains six integrated models: three capacity planning and scheduling models, two cutting plan models, and one demand forecasting model. (Respicio, Captivo, and Rodrigues, 2002; see DSS in Action 3.8).

A *model command processor* is used to accept and interpret modeling instructions from the user interface component and route them to MBMS, model execution, or integration functions.

An interesting question for a DSS might be: Which models should be used for what situations? Such model selection cannot be done by the MBMS because it requires expertise and therefore is done manually. This is a potential automation area for a *knowledge component* to assist the MBMS.

Another interesting, more subtle question is: What method should be used to solve a particular problem in a specific model class? For example, an assignment problem (say assigning 10 jobs to 10 people) is a type of transportation problem, which is a type of network flow problem, which is a type of linear programming problem, which is a type of mathematical optimization problem. Special solution methods are generally more efficient when dealing with more specialized structures. In other words, special methods for

PORTUCEL INDUSTRIAL'S SPREADSHEET-BASED DSS FOR PRODUCTION PLANNING AND SCHEDULING IN THE PAPER INDUSTRY

Paper production planning and scheduling on a global level is a difficult problem. The tools necessary for solving it are typically quite difficult to understand and handle, and are rarely integrated in practice. Portucel Industrial (Portugal) developed a PC-based, spreadsheet DSS that utilizes six integrated models for paper production and scheduling. The system interacts with a human decision-maker who provides judgments as to the feasibility of plans. An exponential smoothing forecasting model (1) predicts product demands. Charts are produced for human interpretation. Three models perform capacity planning and scheduling. One model (2) assigns stock to client orders; a second (3) determines the acceptability of an order through effective capacity/aggregate demand ratio analysis; while the third (4) decomposes the problem into two subproblems to perform capacity planning and the actual scheduling. The next two models are used to determine how to cut the rolls of paper. The first (5) solves a cutting stock problem to determine the actual widths of the rolls to cut to meet all the orders. The second model (6) assigns the items to client orders in an attempt to minimize order spread (limit the waste). As these problems are solved,

the user may perform what-if analyses. These models are integrated in a PC-based DSS that exchanges data with the company's information system. Data are extracted daily from the IS into files that the spreadsheet-based system can import. The DSS generates local files for cutting plans, assignment of stock to client orders, and changes on active orders or proposed orders. The DSS exports these files to the IS, which updates the main database accordingly. Information about the cuts is automatically sent to the cutting machine on the shop floor.

The DSS provides many benefits. It is an easy-to-use tool that quickly generates and evaluates alternative solutions. The decision-maker can match these solutions against his or her knowledge and expertise. More rational and therefore better production decisions are made. Overall, costs are down and information is better organized. Production planning is better coordinated, leading to reduced lead times and an improvement in customer service.

Source: Adapted from Respicio, Captivo, and Rodrigues (2002).

solving an assignment problem should work better than applying transportation problem algorithms to it, and so on. But this is not always true. And to complicate matters, there may be many ways to solve a specific problem depending upon its characteristics. Again, there is potential for the knowledge component to assist in selecting an appropriate solution method. In the late 1990s, the elements of the model base management system migrated to Web-based systems, deployed as Java applets or modules of other Web development systems (see Fourer and Goux, 2002; Geoffrion and Krishnan, 2001).

3.8 THE USER INTERFACE (DIALOG) SUBSYSTEM

The term **user interface** covers all aspects of communication between a user and the DSS or any MSS. It includes not only the hardware and software but also factors that deal with ease of use, accessibility, and human–machine interactions. Some MSS experts feel that the user interface is the most important component because it is the source of many of the power, flexibility, and ease-of-use characteristics of MSS (Sprague and Watson, 1996a). Others state that the user interface is the system from the user's standpoint because it is the only part of the system that the user sees (Whitten, Bentley, and Dittman 2001). A difficult user interface is one of the major reasons why managers do not use computers and quantitative analyses as much as they could, given the availability of these technologies. The Web browser has been recognized as an effective DSS graphical user interface because it is flexible, user friendly, and a gateway to almost all sources of necessary information and data (see Meredith, 2002). For a historical perspective and gallery of the graphical user interface, see Nathan Lineback's *Toasty Technology Web Page* (toastytech.com/guis/). For advances in interface research, see the PARC Inc. *User Interface @PARC* Web Page (www2.parc.com/istl/projects/uir/).

MANAGEMENT OF THE USER INTERFACE SUBSYSTEM

The user interface subsystem is managed by software called the **user interface management system (UIMS)**. The UIMS is composed of several programs that provide the capabilities listed in DSS in Focus 3.10. The UIMS is also known as the dialog generation and management system.

THE USER INTERFACE PROCESS

The user interface process for an MSS is shown schematically in Figure 3.6. The user interacts with the computer via an action language processed by the UIMS. In

FIGURE 3.6   SCHEMATIC VIEW OF THE USER INTERFACE SYSTEM

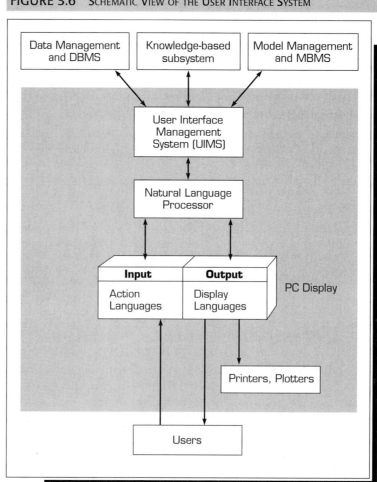

MAJOR CAPABILITIES OF THE UIMS

- Provides a graphical user interface, frequently using a Web browser
- Accommodates the user with a variety of input devices
- Presents data with a variety of formats and output devices
- Gives users help capabilities, prompting, diagnostic, and suggestion routines, or any other flexible support
- Provides interactions with the database and the model base
- Stores input and output data
- Provides color graphics, three-dimensional graphics, and data plotting

- Has windows that allow multiple functions to be displayed concurrently
- Can support communication among and between users and builders of MSS
- Provides training by example (guiding users through the input and modeling processes)
- Provides flexibility and adaptiveness so the MSS can accommodate different problems and technologies
- Interacts in multiple, different dialog styles
- Captures, stores, and analyzes dialog usage (tracking) to improve the dialog system; tracking by user is also available

advanced systems, the user interface component includes a natural language processor or can use standard **objects** (e.g., pull-down menus, buttons, Internet browser) through a **graphical user interface (GUI).** The UIMS provides the capabilities listed in DSS in Focus 3.9 and enables the user to interact with the model-management and data management subsystems. A DSS user interface can be accessed from a cell telephone via either voice or the display panel. New, mobile DSS are being deployed directly on personal digital assistants (PDAs) that have a large memory, a quality graphical display, and wireless links through a built-in cell telephone or a direct Internet connection. PDAs can readily recognize a modified form of handwriting (e.g., Graffiti for Palm Pilots, palm.com). Advances in speech recognition technology create DSS interface opportunities (see DSS in Action 3.10). For example, Adomo provides a Mobile Communication Server that accesses Microsoft applications directly by voice over the telephone. These types of systems allow employees access to corporate applications directly over any telephone (Cohn, 2002). See Friley (2002) and Waters (2002) for more on speech recognition and associated technologies.

GIVING VOICE TO DSS APPLICATIONS

There are many reasons to build speech recognition and voice generation into DSS. One, of course, is for access of DSS via telephone. Another is accurate language translation—both verbal and textual. A third and most important one is that speech is a very natural way for humans to interact with one other. However, most computers do not *understand* the fuzzy nuances of human speech. For a computer to *interpret* the words of speech is relatively easy, but understanding the *meaning* is fairly difficult. Artificial intelligence methods are often used. The good news is that speech recognition technologies have come a long way in the last decade (e.g., watch the captioning on CNN when a live story is broadcast). The bad news, however, is that they still have a long way to go before they can be used seamlessly in applications.

NEW USER INTERFACE DEVELOPMENTS

We have already mentioned voice/speech and handwriting recognition for its use for input, as well as direct translation of text into voice (which can even include gestures by a face on the screen—see annanova.com for an artificial newscaster). There are a number of new user-interface developments, mostly in laboratories, that may have an effect on how we use computers in decision-making and other tasks. For example, scientists are developing automatic, real-time, natural language translation (this requires speech recognition and generation), something that has challenged scientists and linguists for decades. As this book went to print, Sphinx (speech recognizer) and Carnival (speech synthesizer), developed at Carnegie Mellon's Language Technologies Institute, are making such language translation a reality. The quality and size of visual output displays are physically limited by the size of molecules. Even so, displays are getting better and better. Even PDAs and picture cell telephones have crisp images. Holographic displays that require neither specialized hardware nor glasses are just leaving the labs. LCD panels developed at Phillips Research have this capability. Scientists have experimented with helmets that detect brainwaves. Such a device could allow a quadriplegic the ability to interface with a computer. Tactile interfaces have been a bit of a problem. Immersion Corp.'s Cyberforce System includes a spandex glove that simulates the tactile sense that doctors get when performing surgery. This *haptic* interface allows surgeons to simulate their work before actually performing a real operation. In this way, medical students can experience virtual operations that feel so real that they have essentially performed the real thing. For videoconferencing, Microsoft has developed RingCam, an omnidirectional video camera that allows off-site meeting goers to view the entire room as if they were really at the meeting. It utilizes eight microphones and five small cameras. Finally, see DSS in Action 3.11 for a description of a *gesture interface* that utilizes holographic displays. See PC Magazine (2002) and Rhey (2002) for information on some of these developments.

NEW DEVELOPMENTS IN DECISION SUPPORT SYSTEMS

We conclude the sections on the three major DSS components with some recent technology and methodology developments that affect DSS and decision-making. In the

---

DSS IN ACTION 3.11

GESTURES IN THE AIR FOR INPUT

Spice (2002) reports on a human-automobile interface being developed at Carnegie Mellon University (Pittsburgh). Hand gestures (pointing, waving, etc.) toward icons projected onto the windshield are captured by cameras in the car and translated directly into instructions for adjusting the radio, putting someone on hold on your cell phone, or programming the on-board navigation system. This gesture interface can assist drivers in getting past the distractions caused by many electronic devices, whether a part of the car or brought on board. The goal is to increase safety. However, this new interface has implications for com-

puter interfaces in general. The next generation of PC interfaces may well be holographic in nature (see the "New Developments in DSS" subsection) or simply projected, and would be programmable. Gestures could be detected, instead of using hardware like a mouse or keyboard. There would be no moving parts, and the user would be able to use a set of preprogrammed gestures or could customize the system accordingly. In virtual reality settings, the "glove" that detects motion might become a relic. In addition to DSS, video games should benefit from the gesture interface technology.

preceding subsection, we described new technologies for the interface. Many developments in DSS components are the result of new developments in data warehousing, data mining, online analytical processing (OLAP), and World Wide Web technologies. Most DSS today access data from a data warehouse, and use models from OLAP or data mining tools. Data warehouses can provide petabytes of sales data for a retail organization. Data mining and OLAP systems provide integration with the data warehouse, the models, and often a very friendly user interface for DSS. Web communication technologies (Internet, intranets, extranets) provide links among the components, especially for accessing data sources and knowledge. Web browsers or Web-like user interfaces link users to the DSS. Web technologies enable virtual teams to collaborate, and provide access to integrated data, models, and knowledge components. For example, see DSS in Action 3.12 and the virtual environment of Andrienko, Andrienko, and Jankowski (2002). The Web has become the center of activity in developing DSS. Web-based DSS have reduced technological barriers and made it easier and less costly to make decision-relevant information and model-driven DSS available to managers and staff users in geographically distributed locations, especially through mobile devices. See Andrienko, Andrienko, and Jankowski (2002), Dong, Sundaram, and Srinivasan (2002), Eom (2002), Gachet (2002), Gregg (2002), Shim et al. (2002). We discuss some of these developments in Chapter 5.

There is also a clear link between hardware and software capabilities and improvements in DSS. Hardware continues to shrink in size while increasing in speed and other capabilities. However, we are reaching some physical limitations as to size and speed. Quantum computing (based on subatomic particle motion and charges) promises to break this barrier. By the end of 2002, a quantum system was capable of factoring the number 15. Though this seems to be a simple problem, it demonstrates the possibilities that quantum computing offers—very tiny, powerful computers. Artificial intelligence (see the next section) is making inroads in improving DSS. Faster, intelligent search engines are an obvious outcome. There are many others. For example, Desouza (2001) surveys applications of intelligent agents for competitive intelligence.

A fresh look at DSS evaluation was proposed by Phillips-Wren and Forgionne (2002). They developed an Analytical Hierarchy Process approach (see Chapter 2) toward evaluating Web-based real-time decision support systems in terms of criteria based on data, time, and effectiveness.

DSS IN ACTION 3.12

BLACKBOARD: A DSS FOR E-LEARNING

Blackboard Inc. (www.blackboard.com) offers a complete Web-based suite of enterprise software products and services that power a total "e-Education Infrastructure" for schools, colleges, universities, and other education providers. Blackboard solutions deliver the promise of the Internet for online teaching and learning, campus communities, auxiliary services, and integration of Web-enabled student services and back office systems. Blackboard provides a means of communication, collaboration, access to course materials (text,

data, software, etc.) and course tools (gradebook/grade reporting, e-mail, etc.), and so on. Essentially, Blackboard is a DSS for a course instructor and students. Blackboard is a course *portal* in the same sense as an enterprise information portal.

Sources: Blackboard, Inc. Web Site, www.blackboard.com, blackboard, Inc., Washington, DC, and Jay E. Aronson's personal experience using Blackboard for course management and delivery.

Some DSS in the future may include emotions, mood, tacit values, and other soft factors. This may be extremely important in dealing with health care choices, when the DSS is utilized by doctors, nurses, other caregivers, and patients. Though some of these factors were incorporated into the second generation of executive information systems, their importance is often overlooked.

Meredith (2002) proposed developing a multimedia, Internet-based DSS of this kind.

See Mora, Forgionne, and Gupta (2002) for a look at the future of DSS, and PC Magazine (2002) and Rhey (2002) for information on some technology developments.

3.9 THE KNOWLEDGE-BASED MANAGEMENT SUBSYSTEM

Many unstructured and even semistructured problems are so complex that their solutions require expertise. This can be provided by an expert system or other intelligent system. Therefore, more advanced DSS are equipped with a component called a *knowledge-based management subsystem.* This component can supply the required expertise for solving some aspects of the problem and provide knowledge that can enhance the operation of other DSS components.

Silverman (1995) suggests three ways to integrate knowledge-based expert systems (ES) with mathematical modeling: knowledge-based decision aids that support the steps of the decision process not addressed by mathematics (e.g., selecting a model class or a solution methodology); intelligent decision modeling systems that help users build, apply, and manage libraries of models; and decision analytic expert systems that integrate theoretically rigorous methods of uncertainty into expert system knowledge bases.

The knowledge component consists of one or more intelligent systems. Like database and model management software, knowledge-base management software provides the necessary execution and integration of the intelligent system. *Caution:* a knowledge management system is typically a text-oriented DSS; not a knowledge-based management system.

A decision support system that includes such a component is called an intelligent DSS, a DSS/ES, an expert-support system, active DSS, or knowledge-based DSS (see DSS in Action 3.13 for an example that includes both an expert system and an artificial neural network in a Web-based package written in Java). Most data mining applications include intelligent systems, such as artificial neural networks and rule induction methods for expert systems, to search for potentially profitable patterns in data. Many OLAP systems include artificial neural networks and data induction tools that extract rules for expert systems.

3.10 THE USER

The person faced with the decision that an MSS is designed to support is called the *user,* the *manager,* or the *decision-maker.* However, these terms fail to reflect the heterogeneity that exists among the users and usage patterns of MSS (Alter, 1980). There are differences in the positions that users occupy, their cognitive preferences and abilities, and their ways of arriving at a decision (decision styles). The user can be an individual or a group, depending upon who is responsible for the decision. The user, though not listed as a major component of DSS, by definition provides the *human intellect.* The

DSS IN ACTION 3.13

IAP SYSTEM'S INTELLIGENT DSS DETERMINES THE SUCCESS OF OVERSEAS ASSIGNMENTS AND LEARNS FROM THE EXPERIENCE

Overseas assignments for managers and executives can be an exciting adventure for the entire family; or a disaster. If an assignment is a failure, the cost of replacing the manager, and the impact on his or her family, can cost well over a quarter of a million dollars. Many companies (e.g., Coca-Cola) require employees to have overseas assignments before they can move into high executive positions. The critical issue is to be able to predict whether or not a specific assignment will be a good or bad experience for the manager and his or her family.

Enter Intelligent DSS. The International Assignment Profile (IAP) is a new, state-of-the-art method for use in ex-pat preparation (or selection) that collects key, comprehensive information about the family and compares their answers to known conditions in the anticipated international location.

IAP increases the human and business success of international assignments by spotting key issues and pinpointing the weak links or problems that could compromise an international relocation or assignment while there is still time to plan and prevent problems.

IAP's goals include:

- Better preparation for transfer
- Faster adjustment to international locations
- Significant reduction in compromised assignments
- No failed assignments

IAP is written in Exsys Corvid, a Web-based expert system shell (www.exsys.com). Through feedback from past assignments, artificial neural networks learn emerging patterns. IAP uses modern technology and *artificial intelligence* to assist companies in making more accurate, less stressful foreign placements and international relocations. The employee *and* his or her spouse complete the IAP interview process on the Web or on their computer. The system analyzes the information, detects and isolates critical patterns that might jeopardize the business purpose of the relocation, and produces a report for planning and problem prevention.

IAP produces a detailed list of exactly what issues need to be resolved and what planning needs to be done to ensure success. When the entire family is happy, the assignment succeeds. For a large firm, using IAP can readily save millions of dollars per year.

Source: Adapted from the International Assignment Profile Systems, Inc., Houston, TX Web site iapsystems.com, November 2002.

---

user, as the person or people primarily responsible for making the decision, provides expertise in guiding the development and use of a DSS. This intellectual capability is critical to the system's success and proper use. If the main user of a DSS is replaced by another, less knowledgeable user (in terms of the decision-making problem and environment), the DSS will generally be less effective.

An MSS has two broad classes of users: managers and staff specialists. Staff specialists, such as financial analysts, production planners, and marketing researchers, outnumber managers by about three to two, and use computers by a much larger ratio. When designing an MSS, it is important to know who will actually have hands-on use of it. In general, managers expect systems to be more user-friendly than do staff specialists. Staff specialists tend to be more detail-oriented, are more willing to use complex systems in their day-to-day work, and are interested in the computational capabilities of the MSS. That is why the first users of OLAP were staff specialists. Often, staff analysts are the intermediaries between management and the MSS.

An **intermediary** allows the manager to benefit from the decision support system without actually having to use the keyboard. Several types of intermediaries reflect different support for the manager:

1. **Staff assistants** have specialized knowledge about management problems and some experience with decision support technology.
2. **Expert tool users** are skilled in the application of one or more types of specialized problem-solving tools. An expert tool user performs tasks that the problem solver does not have the skill or training to perform.
3. **Business (system) analysts** have a general knowledge of the application area, a formal business administration education (not in computer science), and considerable skill in using DSS construction tools.
4. **Facilitators in a group support system** control and coordinate the use of software to support the work of people working in groups. The facilitator also is responsible for the conduct of work-group sessions.

Within the categories of managers and staff specialists, there are important subcategories that influence MSS design. For example, managers differ by organizational level, functional area, educational background, and need for analytic support. Staff specialists differ respect to education, functional area, and relationship to management.

Today's users are typically very hands-on oriented both in creating and using DSS (say through an OLAP), though they may need help from analysts in initially setting up access to needed data.

3.11 DSS HARDWARE

Decision support systems have evolved simultaneously with advances in computer hardware and software technologies. Hardware affects the functionality and usability of the MSS. The choice of hardware can be made before, during, or after the design of the MSS software, but it is often determined by what is already available in the organization. Typically, MSS run on standard hardware. The major hardware options are the organization's servers, mainframe computers with legacy database-management systems, a workstation, a personal computer, or a client/server system. Distributed DSS runs on various types of networks, including the Internet, intranets, and extranets (see Gachet, 2002; Gregg et al., 2002). Access may be provided for a number of mobile devices, including notebook PCs, tablet PCs, PDAs, and cell telephones. This portability has become critical for deploying decision-making capability (business intelligence) in the field, especially for salespersons (see Rothrock, 2002). A de facto hardware standard is that of a Web server through which the database management system provides data accessed from existing databases on the server, data warehouses, or legacy databases. Users access the DSS by client PCs (or other mobile devices) on which Web browsers are running. Models are provided directly through packages running on either the server, the mainframe, or some other external system, or even on the client PC. See Figure 3.1 for the architecture of what has become the typical DSS/business intelligence hardware configuration.

3.12 DSS CLASSIFICATIONS

There are several ways to classify DSS applications. The design process, as well as the operation and implementation of DSS, depends in many cases on the type of DSS involved. However, remember that not every DSS fits neatly into one category. We present representative classification schemes next.

ALTER'S OUTPUT CLASSIFICATION

Alter's (1980) classification is based on the "degree of action implication of system outputs" or the extent to which system outputs can directly support (or determine) the decision. According to this classification, there are seven categories of DSS (Table 3.4). The first two types are *data-oriented*, performing data retrieval or analysis; the third deals both with data and models. The remaining four are *model-oriented*, providing simulation capabilities, optimization, or computations that suggest an answer.

HOLSAPPLE AND WHINSTON'S CLASSIFICATION

Holsapple and Whinston (1996) classify DSS into the following six frameworks: text-oriented DSS, database-oriented DSS, spreadsheet-oriented DSS, solver-oriented DSS, rule-oriented DSS, and compound DSS.

TEXT-ORIENTED DSS

Information (including data and knowledge) is often stored in a textual format and must be accessed by decision-makers. Therefore, it is necessary to represent and process text documents and fragments effectively and efficiently. A text-oriented DSS supports a decision-maker by electronically keeping track of textually represented information that could have a bearing on decisions. It allows documents to be electronically created, revised, and viewed as needed. Information technologies such as Web-based document imaging, hypertext, and intelligent agents can be incorporated into text-oriented DSS applications. There are many text-oriented DSS applications. Among them are electronic document management systems, knowledge- management, content management, and business rules systems. Content management systems (CMS) are used to manage the material posted on Web sites. Consistency, version control, accuracy, and proper navigation are handled directly by the system. See DSS in Action 3.14. Many freight and shipping companies (e.g., FedEx and UPS) use text-based DSS to coordinate shipping, help customers determine the best means to ship, and help customers and the company to track packages (see DSS in Action 3.4). In fact, FedEx has deployed a wireless handheld PC version of its system from which it expects to save $20 million in annual costs (see Brewin, 2002).

DATABASE-ORIENTED DSS

In this type of DSS, the database organization plays a major role in the DSS structure. Early generations of database-oriented DSS mainly used the *relational* database configuration. The information handled by relational databases tends to be voluminous, descriptive, and rigidly structured. A database-oriented DSS features strong report generation and query capabilities. Hendricks (2002) describes how the government of The Netherlands provides Web-based property management for intelligent decision-making. The system is primarily data-oriented and assists the government agency through standard and GIS databases in the effective use of its large portfolio of prop-

TABLE 3.4   Characteristics of Different Classes of Decision Support Systems

Orientation	Category	Type of Operation	Type of Task	User	Usage Pattern	Time
Data	File drawer systems	Access data items	Operational	Nonmanagerial line personnel	Simple inquiries	Irregular
	Data analysis systems	Ad hoc analysis of data files	Operational analysis	Staff analyst or managerial line personnel	Manipulation and display of data	Irregular or periodic
Data or Models	Analysis information systems	Ad hoc analysis involving multiple databases and small models	Analysis, planning	Staff analyst	Programming special reports, developing small models	Irregular, on request
Models	Accounting models	Standard calculations that estimate future results on the basis of accounting definitions	Planning, budgeting	Staff analyst or manager	Input estimates of activity; receive estimated monetary results as output	Periodic (e.g., weekly, monthly, yearly)
	Representational models	Estimating consequences of particular actions	Planning, budgeting	Staff analyst	Input possible decision; receive estimated results as output	Periodic or irregular (ad hoc analysis)
	Optimization models	Calculating an optimal solution to a combinatorial problem	Planning, resource allocation	Staff analyst	Input constraints and objectives; receive answer	Periodic or irregular (ad hoc) analysis
	Suggestion models	Performing calculations that generate a suggested decision	Operational	Nonmanagerial line personnel	Input a structured description of the decision situation; receive a suggested decision as output	Daily or periodic

Source: Condensed from Alter (1980), pp. 90–91.

erties. (Also see the Government Buildings Agency Property Management Web site: www.rijksgebouwendienst.nl.) DSS in Action 3.15 contains another example.

SPREADSHEET-ORIENTED DSS

A spreadsheet is a modeling system that allows the user to develop models to execute DSS analysis. These models not only create, view, and modify procedural knowledge[3]

[3]Procedural knowledge is generic knowledge regarding problem-solving procedures. In contrast, descriptive or declarative knowledge relates to the specific knowledge domain of the problem to be solved.

NOVANT HEALTH'S CONTENT MANAGEMENT SYSTEM CREATES HEALTHY DOCUMENTS

At Novant Health (NC), a nonprofit health care system, 13,000 employees were generating and accumulating tons of documents on policy and procedures manual, patient education materials, and administrative and regulatory documents that needed to be posted to the organization's Web site by homemade tools. Ultimately, they implemented the Interwoven TeamSite enterprise CMS. Since then, the IT department has been transformed to one that manages corporate information rather than maintain individual pages.

Source: Adapted from John Clymon, "From Chaos to Control," *PC Magazine*, September 17, 2002, pp. 125–133.

but also instruct the system to execute their self-contained instructions (macros). Spreadsheets are widely used in end-user developed DSS. (For examples, see Buehlmann, Ragsdale, and Gfeller, 2000; LeBlanc, Randalls, and Swann, 2000; Respicio, Captivo, and Rodrigues, 2002 [summarized in DSS in Action 3.8].) The most popular end user tool for developing DSS is Microsoft Excel. Excel includes dozens of statistical packages, a linear programming package (solver), and many financial and management science models.

Because packages such as Excel can include a rudimentary DBMS or can readily interface with one, they can handle some properties of a database-oriented DSS, especially the manipulation of descriptive knowledge. Some spreadsheet development tools include what-if analysis and goal-seeking capabilities, and these are revisited in Chapter 4. A spreadsheet-oriented DSS is a special case of a solver-oriented DSS.

DATABASE-ORIENTED DSS: GLAXO WELLCOME ACCESSES LIFE-SAVING DATA

When Glaxo Wellcome revealed that a combination of two of its drugs, Epivir and Retrovir, was effective in treating AIDS, doctors began writing prescriptions en masse almost overnight. Such a tidal wave of demand could have resulted in lower inventories to pharmaceutical wholesalers and shortages.

Thanks to a data warehouse application, however, market analysts at Glaxo Wellcome were able to track the size and sources of demand and generate reports within hours, even minutes. The result: Wholesalers around the world never ran out of Epivir and Retrovir.

Called GWIS (Glaxo Wellcome Information System), the data warehouse application was built with MicroStrategy Inc.'s DSS relational online analytical processing (ROLAP) technology. GWIS works directly with data stored in a relational database-management system, integrating internal data with data from external sources.

The application was rolled out in June 1996 to 150 employees in Glaxo Wellcome's marketing analysis department. Users can analyze sales, inventory, and prescription data for drugs on the fly, helping Glaxo Wellcome streamline its distribution process and cut operational costs. An additional IS benefit is that users can access information from various databases and computers. They no longer create local databases on their PCs which ultimately interfere with data integrity or require IT support. GWIS helps the IT organization design and manage the disparate data sources.

Source: Condensed from B. Fryer, "Fast Data Relief," *InformationWeek*, December 2, 1996, pp. 133–136; and www.microstrategy.com/customersuccesses, January 2000.

SOLVER-ORIENTED DSS

A solver is an algorithm or procedure written as a computer program for performing certain computations for solving a particular problem type. Examples of a solver can be an economic order quantity procedure for calculating an optimal ordering quantity or a linear regression routine for calculating a trend. A solver can be commercially programmed in development software. For example, Excel, includes several powerful solvers—*functions* and *procedures*—that solve a number of standard business problems. The DSS builder can incorporate the solvers in creating the DSS application. Solvers can be written in a programming language such as C++; they can be written directly on or can be an *add-in* tool in a spreadsheet, or they can be embedded in a specialized modeling language, such as Lingo. More complicated solvers, such as linear programming, used for optimization, are commercially available and can be incorporated in a DSS. For examples, see the Case Applications and examples in Chapter 4.

RULE-ORIENTED DSS

The knowledge component of DSS described earlier includes both procedural and inferential (reasoning) rules, often in an expert system format. These rules can be qualitative or quantitative, and such a component can replace quantitative models or can be integrated with them. For example, Bishop (1991) describes the integration of an assignment algorithm implementation (a form of linear programming) (Chapter 4) with that of an expert system for redirecting in-flight airplanes, flight crews, and passengers in the event that a major hub airport is knocked out of commission. Also see DSS in Action 3.17.

COMPOUND DSS

A compound DSS is a hybrid system that includes two or more of the five basic structures described earlier. See DSS in Action 3.16 for an example of a compound DSS.

DSS IN ACTION 3.16

COMPOUND DSS: FINANCIAL REPORTING, DECISION SUPPORT, AND EIS HELP T&N PREDICT THE FUTURE

T&N is a leading world supplier of high-quality automotive components, as well as engineering and industrial materials. The company has an annual turnover of more than $4.1 billion and employs 43,000 people throughout the world. The company formed an independent finance advisory division to improve company performance.

Operating units wanted detailed information at the product level; product groups wanted broader detail; management wanted strategic high-level summary and exception information (requiring three systems: financial reporting, decision support, and executive information), but all data had to be consistent.

A comprehensive MSS was initiated in the mid-1990s. Data are transmitted by e-mail to the Manchester (England) headquarters for the production of group accounts. This includes all accounting data, profit and loss, analysis of expenditure, cash flow, and balance sheets.

T&N also stores explanation text in the database. The DSS is installed at all main consolidation points in the group, allowing rapid collection and aggregation of the data. The data are not seen simply as historical information, however. They are increasingly being used to help predict the future. T&N uses financial models and such techniques as simulation, stochastic forecasting, and statistical analysis of variance based on accurate information. This enables the firm to track resources more directly. The success of the DSS led to the completed implementation of an enterprise information system.

Source: Based on material at Comshare's Web site, comshare.com.

INTELLIGENT DSS

The so-called intelligent or knowledge-based DSS has attracted a lot of attention. The rule-oriented DSS that we described above can be divided into six types: descriptive, procedural, reasoning, linguistic, presentation, and assimilative. The first three are termed "primary" types, and the remainder are derived from them. Intelligent DSS are discussed in Parts IV and V of this book.

OTHER CLASSIFICATIONS OF DSS

There are several other classifications of DSS, such as the following.

INSTITUTIONAL AND AD HOC DSS

Institutional DSS (Donovan and Madnick, 1977) deal with decisions of a recurring nature. A typical example is a portfolio management system (PMS), which has been used by several large banks for supporting investment decisions. An institutionalized DSS can be developed and refined as it evolves over a number of years because the DSS is used repeatedly to solve identical or similar problems. It is important to

---

DSS IN ACTION 3.17

INSTITUTIONAL DSS: THE UNIVERSITY OF GEORGIA USES A WEB-BASED DSS FOR THE COURSE APPROVAL PROCESS

When the University of Georgia moved from the quarter to the semester system in 1998, there was a need to revamp the entire curriculum. Every course had to go through the entire course approval process, involving a lengthy paper trail with approve/modify/reject decisions made at every step. The workflow clearly needed to be automated, and decision-making embedded in the process. The Course Approval Process Automatic (CAPA) system was developed to support semester conversion issues with a work coordination and automation solution that used specific technology. Its objectives were to coordinate a decision-making process that involved multiple committees, dean's offices, departmental offices, the graduate school, and the vice president of academic affairs.

CAPA is a Web-based (intranet) system. It uses a two-tiered architecture. The Web server provides information to users, and the SQL database runs on another system in the background. Comments, approval, denial, or more work decisions are made every step of the way, and the results are recorded in the database.

The reason for using a Web server was so that the university could freely provide Web browsers for clients (access software for PCs on the various local area networks on campus). No additional hardware or software costs would be incurred by individual colleges and departments.

The principal benefits of CAPA are as follows:

- CAPA saves time and is cost-effective, especially for users.
- CAPA is flexible enough to support various related applications and is extensible, to support additional requirements.
- CAPA requires little or no user training and no new hardware or software.
- CAPA addresses long-term maintenance, management, and upgrade issues.

Appropriate information on courses can be accessed from the database to assist decision-makers at the departmental, college, and university levels. Information is current, and decisions on the courses are based on current information. Since the semester conversion, the CAPA system is the only course approval process at The University; no paper is used. And, the officially recognized courses and programs of study are those in CAPA, not in the annually printed bulletin. The University has since moved a number of other institutional systems to the Web, including registration and mid-semester course withdrawal.

remember that an institutional DSS may not be used by everyone in an organization; it is the *recurring nature of the decision-making problem* that determines whether a DSS is institutional versus ad hoc. See DSS in Action 3.17 for a description of an institutional DSS.

Ad hoc DSS deal with specific problems that are usually neither anticipated nor recurring. Ad hoc decisions often involve strategic planning issues and sometimes management control problems. Justifying a DSS that will be used only once or twice is a major issue in DSS development. Countless ad hoc DSS applications have evolved into institutional DSS. Either the problem recurs and the system is reused, or others in the organization have similar needs that can be handled by the former ad hoc DSS. See DSS in Action 3.18 for a description of an ad hoc DSS that evolved into an institutional DSS.

PERSONAL, GROUP, AND ORGANIZATIONAL SUPPORT

The support given by DSS can be separated into three distinct, interrelated categories (Hackathorn and Keen, 1981):

Personal Support   Here the focus is on an individual user performing an activity in a discrete task or decision. The task is fairly independent of other tasks. The situation described in DSS in Action 3.18 started with the development of a personal support DSS.

DSS IN ACTION 3.18

AD HOC VISUAL BASIC DSS HELPS CLOSE THE DEAL AND BECOMES AN INSTITUTIONAL DSS

No one needs to convince real estate agent Jim Rauschkolb about the value of information technology. A bad math error in 1980 turned him into a computer programmer and forever changed the way he sells property. In 1980 he sold a family's home and calculated, with a pencil and paper at their dining room table, what they were going to net. At the closing, he discovered that his calculations were off by $1,800, which came out of his pocket. When this happened, Rauschkolb set out to develop a computer system that would remember every line item that needed to be calculated, do the math, and manage the increasingly complex interdependencies between details, such as the net gain from the sale of a home and the down payment on a new property. He learned how to program and built an ad hoc DSS. By using the software, he found that it was much easier to get people to sign a contract. He could show customers all the financial details up front in an easy-to-understand fashion, including whether they qualified for a mortgage. Furthermore, the calculations were done quickly and accurately. Rauschkolb, now a vice president in the

Century 21 office in Orinda, California, continued to use DSS and computers. In the late 1990s he needed to integrate applications and port them to a client/server development environment. Rauschkolb has ported three of his applications to Visual Basic (VB), with more on the way. One copyrighted application calculates the accurate cost of buying a house by analyzing sale price, equity, down payment, monthly mortgage, interest, income, and other factors. This process takes some agents hours to complete; Rauschkolb's program delivers accurate results in minutes. Having ported his applications to VB, Rauschkolb is now making the next logical move: distributing his programs to other agents for their PCs. He has packaged several of his applications with Web capabilities. What started as revenge against a math error ended as an outstanding Web DSS application—and the ad hoc application became an institutional DSS. And now it can be ported to .Net and to the Web.

Source: Condensed from R. Levin, "Visual Basic Helps Close the Deal," *InformationWeek*, November 4, 1996, pp. 16A–17A.

Group Support   The focus here is on a group of people, all of whom are engaged in separate but highly interrelated tasks. An example is a typical finance department in which one DSS can serve several employees all working on the preparation of a budget. If the use of an ad hoc DSS spreads, it becomes a group support DSS. Note that this is *not the same as* a group support system that provides collaboration and communication capabilities to a group working together.

Organizational Support   Here the focus is on organizational tasks or activities involving a sequence of operations, different functional areas, possibly different locations, and massive resources. The Web-based CAPA system described in DSS in Action 3.17 at The University of Georgia provides organizational support for faculty, staff, and students.

INDIVIDUAL DSS VERSUS A GROUP SUPPORT SYSTEM (GSS)

Several DSS researchers and practitioners (such as Keen, 1980) point out that the fundamental model of a DSS—the lonely decision-maker striding down the hall at high noon to make a decision—is true only for minor decisions. In most organizations, be they public, private, Japanese, European, or American, most major decisions are made collectively. Working in a group can be a complicated process, and it can be supported by computers in what is called a **group support system (GSS)**. The Blackboard distance-learning system (DSS in Action 3.12; blackboard.com) provides support to all individuals and groups involved in a course. As a content management system it provides support to the group of students taking the course: it stores and distribute course materials. It supports the individual instructor through an online gradebook and a number of other tools that faculty need in course management. And, it functions as a GSS through its discussion lists, e-mail feature, and virtual classroom.

Note: The term *group support* introduced earlier should not be confused with the concept of group support system (GSS). In group support, the decisions are made by individuals whose tasks are interrelated. Therefore, they check the impact of their decision on others but do not necessarily make decisions as a group. In GSS, each decision (sometimes only one decision) is made by a group. Blackboard, just mentioned, is exceptional in that it does both.

CUSTOM-MADE SYSTEMS VERSUS READY-MADE SYSTEMS

Many DSS are custom-made for individual users and organizations (e.g., the Opening Vignette and the real estate DSS application in DSS in Action 3.18). However, a comparable problem may exist in similar organizations. For example, hospitals, banks, and universities share many similar problems. Similarly, certain nonroutine problems in a functional area (e.g., finance or accounting) can repeat themselves in the same functional area of different organizations. Therefore, it makes sense to build generic DSS that can be used (sometimes with modifications) in several organizations. Such DSS are called ready-made and are sold by various vendors (e.g., Cognos, Temtec, Teradata). Essentially, the database, models, interface, and other support features are built in: just add an organization's data and logo. For example, the IAP Systems application described in DSS in Action 3.13 is a ready-made DSS. The real estate applications described in DSS in Action 3.18 can also be viewed as a ready-made DSS, as can Blackboard. Recently, the number of ready-made DSS has been increasing because of their flexibility and low cost to develop them using Internet technologies for database access and communications, and Web browsers for interfaces (see DSS in Action 3.13).

One complication in terminology results when an organization develops an institutional system but, because of its structure, uses it in an ad hoc manner. An organization can build a large data warehouse but then use OLAP tools to query it and perform ad hoc analysis to solve nonrecurring problems. The DSS exhibits the traits of ad hoc and institutional systems, and also of custom and ready-made systems. We describe such a Web-based system in Case Application 3.2. Several ERP, CRM, KM, and SCM companies offer DSS applications online. These kinds of systems can be viewed as ready-made, though typically they require modifications (sometimes major) before they can be used effectively. See Chapter 8.

DSS AND THE WEB

Two recent developments in computer technology provide fertile ground for new or enhanced DSS applications. The first is Web technologies (Internet, intranet, and extranets), and the second is enterprise software, such as KM, ERP, CRM, and SCM (see Chapter 8). The power and capabilities of the World Wide Web are having a dramatic impact on DSS development, application, and use patterns. The link between the Web and DSS may be considered in two main categories: DSS development (Chapter 6) and DSS use.

DSS DEVELOPMENT

The Web can be used for collecting both external and internal (intranet) data for the DSS database. The Web can be used for communication and collaboration among DSS builders, users, and management. In addition, the Web can be used to download DSS software, use DSS applications provided by the company, or buy online from application service providers (ASPs). For example, see Fourer and Goux (2002) and Geoffrion and Krishnan (2001).

All major database vendors (e.g., IBM, Microsoft, Oracle, Sybase) provide Web capabilities by running directly on Web servers. Data warehouses, and even legacy systems running on mainframes or ported to small RISC workstations can be accessed through Web technologies. Typically models are solved on fast machines, but lately they have been ported to Web servers, either running in the background or accessed from other systems, such as mainframes. Optimization, simulation, statistics systems, and expert systems have been programmed to run in Java (see Fourer and Goux, 2002). These developments simplify access to data, models, and knowledge, and simplify their integration. Enterprise information systems/portals and OLAP systems provide powerful tools with which to develop DSS applications, generally via Web tools.

New software development tools, such as Java, PHP, and .Net, provide powerful on-screen objects (buttons, textboxes, etc.) for interfacing with databases and models. These readily open up direct access to the Web for the DSS developer. In many ways this simplifies the developer's tasks, especially by providing common development tools and a common interface structure through Web browser technologies.

DSS USE

The standard DSS interface is now the Web browser, or at least a similar-looking screen. Web browser technologies have changed our expectations of how software should look and feel. Many DSS provide drill-down capabilities (to look into data for the source of problems) and a traffic light display (green = OK, red = problems, yellow = problem brewing; see TemTec's Executive Viewer software). DSS is used on

FIGURE 3.7   SUMMARY OF DSS CAPABILITIES

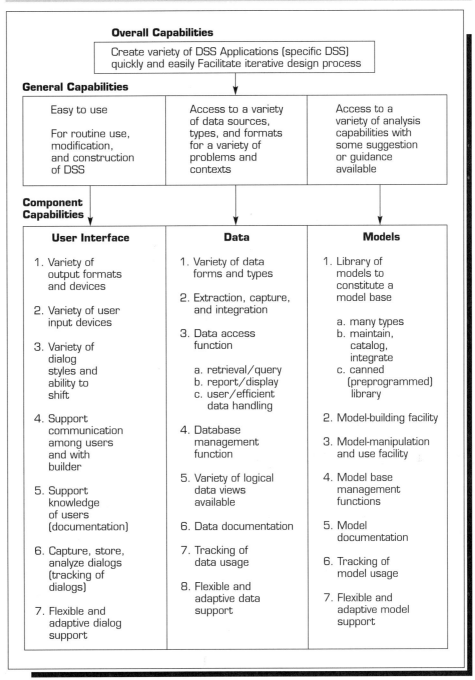

Source: Based on Ralph Sprague and Eric Carlson, *Building Effective Decision Support Systems,* 1982, p. 313. Reprinted by permission of Prentice-Hall, Inc.

the Web in several ways. First, users can go on the intranet and activate ready-made DSS applications. All they need do is to enter some data, or specify dates and other information. The DSS is then run and they can see the results. For example, see Stihl's Chain Saw Assistant (www.stihlusa.com), which helps you select a chain saw (there are many product selection guides online). Second, they can get online advice and help on how to use the DSS applications. Third, they communicate with others regarding the interpretation of the DSS results. Finally, they can collaborate in implementing solutions generated by the DSS model. Web tools provide communication and collaboration capabilities for GSS and KMS, as well as for content management systems, EIS, CRM, and SCM.

3.13 SUMMARY

We have introduced the fundamentals of DSS. We began the chapter with a discussion of the Southwest Airlines vignette. We then covered the key DSS characteristics and capabilities. We summarize the major capabilities of DSS components (excluding the knowledge component) in Figure 3.7. For further details, see Daniel Power's DSS Web tour at dss.cba.uni.edu/tour/dsstour.html.

❖ CHAPTER HIGHLIGHTS

- There are several definitions of DSS.
- A DSS, also known as a business intelligence system, is designed to support complex managerial problems that other computerized techniques cannot. DSS is user-oriented, uses data, and models.
- DSS can provide support in all phases of the decision-making process and to all managerial levels for individuals, groups, and organizations.
- DSS is a user-oriented tool. Many applications can be constructed by end users.
- DSS can improve the effectiveness of decision-making, decrease the need for training, improve management control, facilitate communication, save effort by the user, reduce costs, and allow for more objective decision-making.
- The major components of a DSS are a database and its management, a model base and its management, and a user-friendly interface. An intelligent (knowledge-based) component can also be included. The user is also considered to be a component.
- The components of DSS are typically interconnected via Internet technologies. Web browsers are typically used as user interfaces.
- Data warehouses, data mining, and online analytical processing (OLAP) have made it possible to develop DSS quickly and easily.

- The data management subsystem usually includes a DSS database, a DBMS, a data directory, and a query facility.
- Data are extracted from several sources, internal and external.
- The DBMS provides many capabilities to the DSS, ranging from storage and retrieval to report generation.
- The model base includes standard models and models specifically written for the DSS.
- Custom-made models can be written in third- and fourth-generation languages, in special modeling languages, and in Web-based development systems (Java, etc.).
- The user interface (or dialog) is of utmost importance. It is managed by software that provides the needed capabilities. Web browsers often provide a friendly, consistent, and common DSS graphical user interface.
- The DSS is supplemented by the user's intellectual capabilities. The user is knowledgeable about the problem being solved.
- DSS can be used directly by managers (and analysts), or it can be used via intermediaries.
- DSS applications can be delivered and run on the Web. It is convenient to distribute them to remote locations.

❖ KEY WORDS

- ad hoc DSS
- business (system) analyst
- business analytics
- business intelligence
- data warehouse
- database
- database management system (DBMS)
- directory
- DSS application
- expert tool user

- extraction
- facilitator (in GSS)
- graphical user interface (GUI)
- group support system (GSS)
- institutionalized DSS
- intermediary
- Internet
- intranet
- model base
- model base management system (MBMS)

- model building blocks
- object
- operational models
- organizational knowledge base
- query facility
- staff assistant
- strategic models
- tactical models
- user interface
- user interface management system (UIMS)

❖ QUESTIONS FOR REVIEW

1. Provide two definitions of DSS. What do they have in common? What features differentiate them?
2. Why do people attempt to narrow the definition of DSS?
3. Give your own definition of DSS. Compare it to the definitions in Question 1.
4. List the major components of DSS and briefly define each of them.
5. What are the major functions (capabilities) of DBMS?
6. What is extraction?
7. What is the function of a query facility?
8. What is the function of a directory?
9. Models are classified as strategic, tactical, or operational. What is the purpose of such a classification? Give an example of each.
10. List some of the major functions of an MBMS.
11. Compare the features and structure of the MBMS to those of the DBMS.
12. Why is model selection for DSS difficult?
13. Define a text-oriented DSS.
14. What is the major purpose of a user interface system?
15. What are the major functions of a dialog (interface) management system?
16. List and describe the major classes of DSS users.
17. What types of support are provided by DSS?
18. Define the term ready-made DSS.
19. Compare a custom-made DSS with a ready-made DSS. List the advantages and disadvantages of each.
20. Search for a ready-made DSS. What type of industry is its market? Why is it a ready-made DSS?

❖ QUESTIONS FOR DISCUSSION

1. Review the major characteristics and capabilities of DSS. Relate each of them to the major components of DSS.
2. List some internal data and external data that could be found in a DSS for selecting a portfolio of stocks for an investor.
3. List some internal and external data in a DSS that would be constructed for a decision regarding a hospital expansion.
4. Provide a list of possible strategic, tactical, and operational models for a university, a restaurant, and a chemical plant.
5. Show the similarities between DBMS and MBMS. What is common to both and why? What are the differences and why?
6. Explain why DSS was the first MIS ever defined as requiring a computer.
7. Explain why a DSS needs a database management system, a model-management system, and a user interface, but *not* a knowledge-base management system.
6. Compare an individual DSS to a group DSS.
7. What are the benefits and the limitations of Holsapple and Whinston's classification approach?
8. Why do managers use intermediaries? Will they continue to use them in the future? Why or why not?
9. Explain why the user may be considered a component of the DSS.
10. Discuss the potential benefits that a DSS application can derive from the Web in terms of both developers and users.
11. Explain how the Web has impacted the components of DSS, and vice versa.

❖ EXERCISES

1. Susan Lopez has been made director of the transportation department at a medium-sized university. She controls the following vehicles: 17 sedans, 15 vans, and 3 trucks. The previous director was fired because there were too many complaints about vehicles not being available when needed. Susan has been told not to expect any increase in the budget for the next two years (meaning no replacement or additional vehicles). Susan's major job is to schedule vehicles for employees and to schedule the maintenance and repair of these vehicles. All this was done manually by her predecessor. Your job is to consult with Susan regarding the possibility of using a DSS to improve the situation. Susan has a top-end PC and the newest version of Microsoft Office, but she uses the computer only as a word processor. She has access to the university's intranet and to the Internet. Answer the following questions:
   a. Can the development and use of a DSS be justified? (That is, what can the DSS do to support Susan's job?)
   b. What will be included in the data management, model management, and interface?
   c. What type of support do you expect this DSS to render?
   d. How would you classify this DSS?
   e. Does it make sense to have a knowledge component?
   f. Should the DSS be built, or should one be rented online? Why?
   g. Should Susan disseminate the DSS to others on the intranet? Why or why not?
2. Consider the following two banking situations. A bank's marketing staff realizes that check-processing data which banks too often purge after a short period (60–90 days) could yield valuable information about customers' loan payment patterns and preferences.

The bank starts to retain these data using information discovery tools running on an advanced parallel-processing system to sort through checking account activity data to identify homeowner customers who pay mortgages by check on the fifth, sixth, or seventh day of the month. The bank targets these customers with a special home equity loan to consolidate debts, with automatic payment for the loan and the mortgage on the first of the month. The bank uses data mining tools to study levels of activity by affluent users over time in multiple channels: branches, automated teller machines (ATMs), telephone centers, and point-of-sale systems throughout all the regions the bank serves. It then takes the analysis to a second level: determining the profitability per transaction in each channel. Based on this initiative, the bank undertakes a comprehensive reengineering effort. Discovering that ATM and telephone banking are increasingly active and profitable, the management decides to focus resources and marketing efforts in expanding these channels. It decides to close full-service branches with low activity but replaces some with standalone ATM machines to continue providing customer service. Because some branches are still highly profitable and heavily used, management decides to expand the services offered at these locations. In both situations, identify the DSS applications that are used. Classify them according to the Alter scheme and according to the Holsapple and Whinston scheme.
3. Find literature about an actual DSS application (use professional journals, ABI Inform, customer success stories on DSS vendors' sites, or the Internet for your search). In this application, identify the reasons for the DSS, the major components, the classification (type) of the DSS, the content of the model, and the development process and cost.

❖ GROUP PROJECT

1. Design and implement a DSS for either the problem described in Exercise 1 or a similar real-world problem. Clearly identify data sources and model types, and document the problems your group encountered while developing the DSS.

❖ INTERNET EXERCISES

1. Search the Internet for literature about DSS/business intelligence/business analytics.
2. Identify a DSS/business intelligence/business analytics software vendor. Obtain information about its products. Write up your findings about its products in a report.
3. On the World Wide Web, find a DSS/business intelligence/business analytics software vendor with downloadable demo software. Download the software, install it, and test it. Report your findings to the class and demonstrate the software's capabilities.

4. On the World Wide Web, identify a course syllabus and materials for a DSS/ business intelligence/ business analytics course at another college or university. Compare the course description to your own course. Repeat this assignment using a DSS/ business intelligence/business analytics course syllabus from a university in another country. Use www.isworld.org.

5. On the Web, identify several product selection guides that recommend specific products for you. Use five to ten of these, examine their positive and negative points, and describe their features and use in a report.

6. Explore the teradatauniversity.com site. In a report, describe at least three interesting DSS applications and three interesting DSS areas (CRM, SCM, etc.) that you have discovered there.

THE ADVANTAGE OF PETROVANTAGE: BUSINESS INTELLIGENCE/DSS CREATES AN E-MARKETPLACE

BACKGROUND

Aspen Tech supplies software to the process industries, and has carved out an important niche that in 2001 led to annual revenues of about $380 million. With the release of PetroVantage, the 21-year-old company plans to streamline the processes for potentially lucrative industry petroleum. "The opportunity for companies to extract value using PetroVantage, from well head to gas pump, is substantial," said David McQuillin, Aspen Tech's chief operating officer and chief executive–elect. "The key part of this application is the trading and logistics capabilities." PetroVantage can save companies hundreds of thousands of dollars per day.

Industry analysts say the logistics of delivering petroleum from the wellhead to the consumer are among the most complicated of any industry. There are 500 types of crude oil, each with different characteristics; each refinery is unique, concentrating on different blends and end-product uses. Deciding what oil to buy and how to transport it involves an arcane process in which 20 to 25 worldwide traders make decisions that affect the international distribution process. These traders must integrate information on type, bulk, docking, refining, and delivery. They must know how much oil is coming out of the earth, where the ships are to transport it, what refineries can process the product, and what ports can accept the cargo. Then decisions must be made on how to transport the refined product to distributors. Critical analysis of these worldwide systems can be flawed, resulting in delays and losses. PetroVantage officials see an opportunity to launch a Web-based solution to modernize this immense process. "The world does more with petroleum than any other substance except water," said Chuck Moore, vice president of the petroleum business group at Aspen Tech. "We think there's a big opportunity here, especially because we will be leveraging some of the strengths of Aspen Tech."

THE DSS

PetroVantage is a suite of applications that enable a company to determine the best place to buy crude oil or any elements that make up different fuel mixtures, where to refine it, how to ship it, and how to distribute it to the retail sites. Engineers use parts of the application for every aspect of refinery or plant operations, including the design, building, cost, training, infrastructure and equipment, and maintenance of a facility. IBM provides the hardware, software, Web-hosting, and implementation infrastructure.

PetroVantage has developed online models that incorporate the attributes of about 600 of the world's 700 oil refineries. These attributes include production capacity and products produced. The marketplace provides an online platform for negotiating crude oil and oil products sales, evaluating deals, managing logistics, and linking key participants in complex crude oil trades. Traders use the system to buy, sell, and swap the physical barrel of crude oil and crude oil products, such as gasoline or jet fuel. The site's advantage lies in its ability to manage so many functions.

Decision support functions are what differentiate PetroVantage from other oil industry e-marketplaces, such as HoustonStreet.com and Altra Energy Technologies. The platform is unique because these kinds of decision support tools need to be based on some very complex models of what you can do with the crude oil.

The suite of applications falls into four main categories: end-to-end supply planning, refining solutions, fuel marketing, and, recently added, exploration and production. Perhaps the greatest return would be seen by those most familiar with procuring, trading, transporting, and storing oil and fuel. Moore said that 70 percent of fuel and crude oil distribution in the United States is handled by Aspen Tech's systems.

Developed from Anonymous, "PetroVantage Launches Commercial Software," *National Petroleum News*, Jan 2002, Vol. 94, No. 1, p. 54; William Copeland, "Accurate Inventory Tracking Means Opportunities Gained," *World Refining*, Vol. 11, No. 9, November 2001, p. 48; Matthew French, "Aspen Tech Fuels Up Its PetroVantage Product at Citgo," *Mass High Tech*, Vol. 20, No. 35, September 2, 2002, p. 8; Dyke Hendrickson, "Online Oil Exchange Heats Up," *Mass High Tech*, Vol. 18, No. 39, September 25, 2000, p. 1; Lewis, David, "Oil Exchange Lassos Big User—Occidental Joins Nine Other Customers in Pilot Test of E-marketplace," *InternetWeek*, Special Issue 872, August 6, 2001, p. 42.

PETROVANTAGE DEVELOPMENT AND PILOT TESTING

PetroVantage was pilot-tested by Citgo from early to mid-2002. The Tulsa, Oklahoma, company announced in September 2002 that it would deploy the PetroVantage across its entire enterprise to figure out cost-cutting measures and meet customer demands at 14,000 retail locations in 47 states. While the application isn't actually used at the retail level, all of the decision-making that takes place in the chain of command prior to that could rely on PetroVantage.

Williams R&M signed up with PetroVantage in the spring of 2001, and subsequently joined the PetroVantage Foundation Client Program. Williams R&M operates a refinery in Memphis with a capacity of 165,000 barrels per day. It pilot-tested PetroVantage to optimize its processing decisions, as well as crude oil logistics and refined-products distribution.

Occidental's marketing subsidiary, Occidental Energy Marketing Inc., joined another nine oil companies—including the $11.6 billion Williams Cos. and spin-off Williams Energy Partners, as well as Midwest independent oil refiner Premcor—in testing PetroVantage in 2002. Occidental thinks the marketplace can help it wring better profit margins from crude oil trading. Occidental sells crude oil to wholesalers and brokers, as well as directly to refineries run by companies such as ExxonMobil.

The pilot program went well throughout 2001 and 2002, but the platform's long-term viability depends on other factors, especially the participation of the largest oil companies. PetroVantage is working to include futures and options, which some trading firms use to hedge against fluctuations in the price of oil.

RESULTS

The platform went live in September 2002. Its first commercial customers were Citgo, Premcor, Enron, and Williams Energy Partners. PetroVantage officials predict that their platform has the potential to achieve $20 billion to $30 billion in annual savings from the oil industry's logistics and trading costs of $150 billion per year through its collaborative software solution.

Moore says, "If a company deals in a million barrels a day and you can save them even a few cents on each barrel, you're talking about a return of hundreds of thousands of dollars per day saved. Citgo deals in a *million barrels per day and 7 billion gallons of fuels per year*."

Michael Cimino used to work in the trading and procurement of space, and now ensures its usability and mar-

ketability. "A trader using this software has a tremendous advantage over one who isn't," Cimino said. "A buyer can find, across the global market, a number of sellers and be able to determine within minutes what would be the best investment, based on what he or she already has and what they need."

Moore said that even market anomalies can be better dealt with using PetroVantage. The test came shortly after September 11, "When the airplanes around the country were grounded, oil and fuel companies were swimming in jet fuel, and had nowhere to unload it." Moore explained, "Using our solution, [a customer] was able to find the right deals to mix the fuel they had and turn it into diesel and home heating oil, and get it out of their hands. . . . [A] process that normally takes several weeks was reduced to several days."

The Williams Cos. uses PetroVantage to simplify the trading process. Without PetroVantage, crude traders today might buy and sell on "several different electronic platforms, with a telephone in each ear to several brokers and the fax and e-mail going back and forth." "We like being able to go to a single site and pull everything together: what it costs to buy the components that make gasoline, the cost of arranging a barge or a ship, what kind of [storage] tankerage is available once it gets to port and what that's going to cost," said Bill Copeland, manager of terminal services for Williams Energy Partners. Williams also optimizes the scheduling of storage tanks to boost its terminals' profits. Occidental Marketing uses the e-marketplace to seek the best refineries to buy its oil at the most favorable price at a given time.

The PetroVantage collaborative software solution replaces the time-consuming data-gathering tasks and multiple approximations used in many of today's key trading and logistics decisions with fast and accurate optimization tools integrated with continuously updated data. It enables companies to identify costly deviations in operations, logistics, and deal margins. At the same time, it provides a means for faster and better coordination of responses from the many individuals across multiple companies and locations that are required to drive higher profitability in critical operations.

PetroVantage represents the next generation of digital marketplaces. "The company will offer a collaborative workflow environment that enables the petroleum industry to integrate state-of-the-art decision-support technology with an intuitive transaction platform, a feature no other petroleum industry marketplace currently offers" (PetroVantage Literature).

CASE QUESTIONS

1. How did the DSS/business intelligence tools provided by PetroVantage create and then assist decision-makers in the electronic marketplace?
2. Why was it important to perform pilot-testing with PetroVantage for almost two years?
3. How are customer supply chains integrated into PetroVantage?

4. What other features should be included in PetroVantage, and why?
5. Discuss the kinds of problems that can occur if the largest oil companies opt not to become customers of PetroVantage.
6. How could such a system provide benefits in other industries? Which are natural fits, which are not?

CASE APPLICATION 3.2

FEDEX TRACKS CUSTOMERS ALONG WITH PACKAGES

INTRODUCTION

Federal Express Corp. is well-known for keeping track of its ever-moving overnight packages. It's one of the most important things the company does. In fact, there's only one thing that's more important for FedEx to track—its customer base. Until recently, FedEx wasn't doing a great job of quickly getting its business managers the information they needed to keep up with the company's fast-moving customers.

FedEx maintains a network of 46,000 U.S. drop-off points. But the company was not always sure that those points were in exactly the right (optimal) locations. New customers appear, old customers disappear, and some customers relocate. As businesses move from urban centers to suburban business parks, and as more and more individuals telecommute, FedEx wants its drop points, from large service centers to drop boxes, to be conveniently located for customers. But until recently FedEx managers did not have easy access to traffic information about its drop locations.

FedEx has a proprietary, mainframe-based Cosmos tracking and billing application that collects massive amounts of operational data, including where packages are picked up. But FedEx analysts could not easily access the data. Analysts submitted requests for custom reports (ad hoc use) to a staff of eight programmers, then waited for up to two weeks for a report. FedEx was using a mainframe version of Information Builders' FOCUS decision-support database to produce the reports. The old system did not support quick decision-making.

THE SOLUTION

FedEx decided to give analysts direct access to information. In June, the company deployed a Web-based version of the FOCUS database, WebFOCUS. The new system runs on the company's intranet and has a self-service data warehouse to help company executives make up-to-the-minute decisions about where it should locate the service centers and drop boxes that customers use every day. Data are downloaded from the Cosmos mainframe system to the WebFOCUS server running Windows NT. Analysts can query the data either by using a set of preconfigured reports (institutional use/ready-made DSS) or by creating their own ad hoc queries (ad hoc use/custom-made DSS).

FedEx evaluated several Web-based decision-support systems. It selected WebFOCUS primarily because the company already had programmers with FOCUS experience. That helped FedEx get an initial release of the intranet-based application deployed in just three weeks.

RESULTS

The self-service, intranet-based decision support system application makes it easier to get a more complete view of population shifts and other customer trends by combining the company's own drop point usage data with demographic data purchased from vendors. Programmers who had previously been developing reports from FedEx's mainframe FOCUS database have integrated external

---

Based on material at Information Builders, Inc. Web site informationbuilders.com, November 2002.

data with the WebFOCUS data to allow analysts to anticipate and more accurately track customer trends.

Being able to anticipate customer trends is increasingly critical not only to FedEx also but to other companies in the distribution and logistics business. As companies such as FedEx try to link their distribution services directly into the supply chain operations of their large corporate customers, they need to make sure they have the support centers, trucks, and people in the right place at the right time.

FedEx expanded the system in several ways. First, the WebFOCUS database was extended to store 25 months of data instead of the original three months of historical shipment information. That increased the data warehouse's capacity from 21 million records to 260 million records, requiring a hardware upgrade.

FedEx is also improving the system's reporting capabilities. The company is rolling out the managed reporting features of WebFOCUS to allow analysts to schedule and create more predefined reports. FedEx is also deploying new applications in Information Builders' Cactus development tool to allow analysts to update and enhance drop-point data in the WebFOCUS database, not just read it. With the new self-service data warehouse and planned enhancements, FedEx will have a better handle on tracking its fast-moving customers.

Redeploying the decision-support application on the intranet has already paid off in quicker access to information and quicker decisions. Analysts using WebFOCUS can tap directly into up-to-the-minute drop site usage data from any PC running a Web browser and get reports on their screens seconds instead of weeks. FedEx can more actively manage the location of its service centers and drop points as populations shift and customer habits change. The payoff is better customer service and lower operating costs.

In addition to more accurately tracking drop point usage, FedEx analysts can get fresh information on the profitability of each service center and drop box. Doing a better job of placing them will help cut costs and increase revenue. Have a look at the FedEx video on Information Builders' Web site (informationbuilders.com).

CASE QUESTIONS

1. Describe the benefits of the FedEx system. What other benefits might FedEx obtain with other features?

2. Why is it important for a company like FedEx to manage its drop locations effectively?

3. Describe the benefits of switching from FOCUS to WebFOCUS. Do you think this was the right approach? Why or why not?

4. How can the FedEx approach taken in this case be applied to other industries?

CHAPTER 4

MODELING AND ANALYSIS

LEARNING OBJECTIVES

- ❖ Understand the basic concepts of MSS modeling
- ❖ Describe how MSS models interact with data and the user
- ❖ Understand the different model classes
- ❖ Understand how to structure decision-making of a few alternatives
- ❖ Describe how spreadsheets can be used for MSS modeling and solution
- ❖ Explain what optimization, simulation, and heuristics are, and when and how to use them
- ❖ Describe how to structure a linear programming model
- ❖ Become familiar with some capabilities of linear programming and simulation packages
- ❖ Understand how search methods are used to solve MSS models
- ❖ Explain the differences between algorithms, blind search, and heuristics
- ❖ Describe how to handle multiple goals
- ❖ Explain what is meant by sensitivity, automatic, what-if analysis, and goal seeking
- ❖ Describe the key issues of model management

In this chapter, we describe the model base and its management, one of the major components of DSS. We present this material with a note of caution: modeling can be a very difficult topic and is as much an art as a science. The purpose of this chapter is not necessarily for the reader to *master the topics* of modeling and analysis. Rather, the material is geared toward *gaining familiarity* with the important concepts as they relate to business intelligence/DSS. We walk through some basic concepts and definitions of modeling before introducing the influence diagram, which can aid a decision-maker in sketching a model of a situation and even solving it. We next introduce the idea of modeling directly in spreadsheets. Only then do we describe the structure of some successful time-proven models and methodologies: decision analysis, decision trees, optimization, search methods, heuristic programming, and simulation. We next touch on some recent developments in modeling tools and techniques and conclude with some important issues in model-base management. We defer our discussion on the database and its management until the next chapter. We have found that it is necessary to understand models and their use before attempting to learn how to utilize data warehouses, OLAP, and data mining effectively.

The chapter is organized as follows:

4.1 OPENING VIGNETTE: DUPONT SIMULATES RAIL TRANSPORTATION SYSTEM AND AVOIDS COSTLY CAPITAL EXPENSE[1]

DuPont used simulation to avoid costly capital expenditures for rail car fleets as customer demands changed. Demand changes could involve rail car purchases, better management of the existing fleet, or possibly fleet size reduction. The old analysis method, past experience, and conventional wisdom led managers to feel that the fleet size should be increased. The real problem was that DuPont was not using its specialized rail cars efficiently or effectively, not that there were not enough of them. There was immense variability in production output and transit cycle time, maintenance scheduling, and order sequencing. This made it difficult, if not impossible, to handle all the factors in a cohesive and useful manner leading to a good decision.

The fleets of specialized rail cars are used to transport bulk chemicals from DuPont to manufacturers. The cost of a rail car can vary from $80,000 for a standard tank car to more than $250,000 for a specialized tanker. Because of the high capital expense, effective and efficient use of the existing fleet is a must.

Instead of simply purchasing more rail cars, DuPont developed a ProModel simulation model (ProModel Corporation, Orem, Utah, www.promodel.com) that represented the firm's entire transportation system. It accurately modeled the variability inherent in chemical production, tank car availability, transportation time, loading and unloading time, and customer demand. A simulation model can provide a virtual environment in which experimentation with various policies that affect the physical transportation system can be performed before real changes are made. Changes can be made quickly and inexpensively in a simulated world because relationships among the components of the system are represented mathematically. It is not necessary to purchase expensive rail cars to determine the effect.

---

[1]Adapted from Web site of ProModel Corporation, Orem, Utah, www.promodel.com, 2002.

ProModel allowed the company to construct simulation models easily and quickly (the first one took just two weeks to develop) and to conduct **what-if analyses.** It also included extensive graphics and animation capabilities. The simulation involved the entire rail transportation system. Many scenarios were developed, and experiments were run. DuPont experimented with a number of conditions and scheduling policies. Development of the simulation model helped the decision-making team understand the entire problem (see Banks et al.; 2001; Evans and Olson, 2002; Harrell et al., 2000; Law et al., 2000; Ross, 2003; Seila, Tadikamalla, and Ceric, 2003). The ProModel simulation accurately represented the variability associated with production, availability of tank cars, transportation times, and unloading at the customer site.

With the model, the entire national distribution system can be displayed graphically (visual simulation) under a variety of conditions—especially the current ones and forecasted customer demand. The simulation model helped decision-makers identify bottlenecks and other problems in the real system. By experimenting with the simulation model, the real issues were easily identified. The results convinced decision-makers that a capital expense was unjustified. In fact, the needed customer deliveries could still be made after downsizing the fleet. Simulation drove this point home hard. After only two weeks of analysis, DuPont saved $500,000 in capital investment that year.

Following the proven success of this simulation model, DuPont has started performing logistics modeling on a variety of product lines, crossing division boundaries and political domains. Simulation dramatically improved DuPont's logistics. The next step focused on international logistics and logistics support for new market development. Savings in these areas can be substantially higher.

❖ QUESTIONS FOR THE OPENING VIGNETTE

1. Why did the decision-makers initially feel that fleet expansion was the right decision?

2. How do you think the decision-makers learned about the real system through model development? As a consequence, were they able to focus better on the structure of the real system? Do you think their involvement in model building helped them in accepting the results? Why or why not?

3. Explain how simulation was used to evaluate the operation of the rail system before the changes were actually made.

4. How could the time compression capability of simulation help in this situation?

5. Simulation does not necessarily guarantee that an analyst will find the best solution. Comment on what this might mean to DuPont.

6. Once the system indicated that downsizing was a viable alternative, why do you think the managers bought into the system? Do you think that this is why the development team continues to work on other logistics problems? Explain.

4.2 MSS MODELING

The opening vignette illustrates a complex decision-making problem for which conventional wisdom dictated an inferior decision alternative. By accurately modeling the rail transportation system, decision-makers were able to experiment with different policies and alternatives quickly and inexpensively. Simulation was the modeling approach used. The DuPont simulation model was implemented with commercial software, which is typical. The simulation approach saves DuPont a substantial amount of money annually. Instead of investing in expensive rail cars and then experimenting with how best to use them (also quite expensive), all the work was performed on a computer, initially in two weeks. Before the first flight to the moon, the National Aeronautics and Space Administration (NASA) performed countless simulations. NASA still simulates space shuttle missions. General Motors now simulates all aspects of new car development and testing (see Gallagher, 2002; Gareiss, 2002; Witzerman, 2001). And Pratt & Whitney uses a simulated (virtual reality) environment in designing and testing engines for jet fighters (Marchant, 2002). It is extremely easy to change a model of a physical system's operation with computer simulation.

The DuPont simulation model was used to learn about the problem at hand, not necessarily to derive new alternative solutions. The alternative solutions were known, but were untested until the simulation model was developed and tested. Some other examples of simulation are given by Van der Heijden et al. (2002) and Rossetti and Selandar (2001). Van der Heijden et al. (2002) used an object-oriented simulation to design an automated underground freight transportation system at Schiphol Airport (Amsterdam). Rossetti and Selandar (2001) developed a simulation model that compared using human couriers to robots in a university hospital. The simulation showed that the hospital could save over $200,000 annually by using the robots. Simulation models can enhance an organization's decision-making process and enable it to see the impact of its future choices. For example, Fiat saves $1 million annually in manufacturing costs through simulation. The 2002 Winter Olympics (Salt Lake City, Utah) used simulation to design security systems and bus transportation for most of the venues. The predictive technology enabled the Salt Lake Organizing Committee to model and test a variety of scenarios, including security operations, weather, and transportation-system design. Its their highly variable and complex vehicle-distribution network. Savings were over $20 million per year. Benefits included lower costs and improved customer service. (See promodel.com for details.)

Modeling is a key element in most DSS/business intelligence (also business analytics) and a necessity in a model-based DSS. There are many classes of models, and there are often many specialized techniques for solving each one. Simulation is a common modeling approach, but there are several others. For example, consider the optimization approach taken by Procter and Gamble (P&G) in redesigning its distribution system (Web Chapter). P&G's DSS for its North America supply chain redesign includes several models:

- A generating model (based on an algorithm) to make transportation cost estimates. This model is programmed directly in the DSS.
- A demand forecasting model (statistically based).
- A distribution center location model. This model uses aggregated data (a special modeling technique) and is solved with a standard linear/integer optimization package.
- A transportation model (specialization of a linear programming model) to determine the *best* shipping from product sources to distribution centers (fed to it from the previous model) and hence to customers. It is solved using commercial software and is loosely integrated with the distribution location model. These two problems are solved sequentially. The DSS must interface with commercial software and integrate the models.
- A financial and risk simulation model that takes into consideration some qualitative factors that require important human judgment.
- A geographic information system (effectively a graphical model of the data) for a user interface.

The Procter & Gamble situation demonstrates that a DSS can be composed of several models, some standard and some custom built, used collectively to support strategic decisions in the company. It further demonstrates that some models are built directly in the DSS software development package, some need to be constructed externally to the DSS software, and others can be accessed by the DSS when needed. Sometimes a massive effort is necessary to assemble or estimate reasonable model data (about 500 P&G employees were involved over the course of about a year), that the models must be integrated, that models may be decomposed and simplified, that sometimes a suboptimization approach is appropriate, and finally, that human judgment is an important aspect of using models in decision-making.

As is evident from the P&G situation and the IMERYS situation described in Case Application 4.1, modeling is not a simple task [also see Stojkovic and Soumis (2001), who developed a model for scheduling airline flights and pilots; Gabriel, Kydes and Whitman (2001), who model the U.S. national energy-economic situation; and Teradata (2003), which describes how Burlington Northern Santa Fe Corporation optimizes rail car performance through **mathematical (quantitative) models** embedded in its OLAP tool]. The model builder must balance the model's simplification and representation requirements so that it will capture enough of reality to make it useful for the decision-maker.

Applying models to real-world situations can save millions of dollars, or generate millions of dollars in revenue. At American Airlines (AMR, Corp.), models were used extensively in SABRE through the American Airlines Decision Technologies (AADT) Corp. AADT pioneered many new techniques and their application, especially that of revenue management. For example, optimizing the altitude ascent and descent profile for its planes saved several million dollars per week in fuel costs. AADT saved hundreds of millions of dollars annually in the early 1980s, and eventually its incremental revenues exceeded $1 billion annually, exceeding the revenue of the airline itself (see Horner, 2000; Mukherjee, 2001; Smith et al., 2001; DSS in Action 4.1). Trick (2002) describes how Continental Airlines was able to recover from the 9/11 disaster by using a system developed for snowstorm recovery. This system was instrumental in saving millions of dollars.

DSS IN ACTION 4.1

United Airlines is in the process of creating a new generation of model-based DSS tools for planning, scheduling, and operations. United plans a major integration effort to determine the optimal schedule that can be designed and managed to maximize profitability. The key to integration and collaboration is a Web-based system called 1PLAN that provides a platform for planners, schedulers, and other analysts across the airline to collaborate during the decision support process. It uses a suite of decision support tools:

1. SIMON optimally designs a flight network and fleet assignment simultaneously.

2. ARM uses neighborhood search techniques for optimal multi-objective fleet assignment.

3. AIRSIM uses advanced statistical tools to predict airline reliability.

4. SKYPATH performs optimal flight planning for minimizing fuel burn on flights.

5. CHRONOS enables dynamic multi-objective operations management.

Source: Adapted from Mukherjee (2001) .

Some major modeling issues include problem identification and environmental analysis, variable identification, forecasting, the use of multiple models, model categories (or appropriate selection), model management, and knowledge-based modeling.

IDENTIFICATION OF THE PROBLEM AND ENVIRONMENTAL ANALYSIS

This issue was discussed in Chapter 2. One very important aspect is **environmental scanning and analysis**, which is the monitoring, scanning, and interpretation of collected information. No decision is made in a vacuum. It is important to analyze the scope of the domain and the forces and dynamics of the environment. One should identify the organizational culture and the corporate decision-making processes (who makes decisions, degree of centralization, and so on). It is entirely possible that environmental factors have created the current problem. **Business intelligence** (business analytics) **tools** can help identify problems by scanning for them (see Hall, 2002a, 2000b; Whiting, 2003; the MSS Running Case in DSS in Action 2.6; and DSS in Action 3.6, where we describe how NetFlix.com creates usable environmental information for moviegoers). The problem must be understood, and everyone involved should share the same frame of understanding because the problem will ultimately be represented by the model in one form or another (as was done in the opening vignette). Otherwise, the model will not help the decision-maker.

VARIABLE IDENTIFICATION

Identification of the model's variables (decision, result, uncontrollable, etc.) is critical, as are their relationships. Influence diagrams, which are graphical models of mathematical models, can facilitate this process. A more general form of an influence diagram, a cognitive map, can help a decision-maker to develop a better understanding of the problem, especially of variables and their interactions.

FORECASTING

Forecasting is essential for construction and manipulation of models because when a decision is implemented, the results usually occur in the future. DSS are typically designed to determine what will be, rather than as traditional MIS, which report what is or what was (Chapter 3). There is no point in running a what-if analysis (sensitivity) on the past because decisions made then have no impact on the future. In Case Application 4.1, the IMERYS clay processing model is "demand-driven." Clay demands are forecasted so that decisions about clay production that affect the future can be made. Forecasting is getting "easier" as software vendors automate many of the complications of developing such models. For example, SAS has a High Performance Forecasting system that incorporates its predictive analytics technology, ideally for retailers. This software is more automated than most forecasting packages.

E-commerce has created an immense need for forecasting and an abundance of available information for performing it. E-commerce activities occur quickly, yet information about purchases is gathered and should be analyzed to produce forecasts. Part of the analysis involves simply predicting demand; but product life-cycle needs and information about the marketplace and consumers can be utilized by forecasting models to analyze the entire situation, ideally leading to additional sales of products and services (see Gung, Leung, Lin, and Tsai, 2002).

Hamey (2003) describes how firms attempt to predict who their best (i.e., most profitable) customers are and focus in on identifying products and services that will appeal to them. Part of this effort involves identifying lifelong customer profitability. These are important aspects of how customer relationship management and revenue-management systems work.

Further details on forecasting can be found in a Web Chapter (prenhall.com/turban). Also see Faigle, Kern, and Still (2002).

MULTIPLE MODELS

A decision support system can include several models (sometimes dozens), each of which represents a different part of the decision-making problem. For example, the Procter & Gamble supply chain DSS includes a location model to locate distribution centers, a product-strategy model, a demand forecasting model, a cost generation model, a financial and risk simulation model, and even a GIS model. Some of the models are standard and built into DSS development generators and tools. Others are standard but are not available as built-in functions. Instead, they are available as free-standing software that can interface with a DSS. Nonstandard models must be constructed from scratch. The P&G models were integrated by the DSS, and the problem had multiple goals. Even though cost minimization was the stated goal, there were other goals, as is shown by the way the managers took political and other criteria into consideration when examining solutions before making a final decision. Sodhi and Aichlmayr (2001) indicate how Web-based tools can be readily applied to integrating and accessing supply chain models for true supply chain optimization. Also see DSS in Action 4.1 for how United Airlines is integrating its models into a major DSS tool.

MODEL CATEGORIES

Table 4.1 classifies DSS models into seven groups and lists several representative techniques for each category. Each technique can be applied to either a static or a dynamic model (Section 4.3), which can be constructed under assumed environments of certainty, uncertainty, or risk (Section 4.4). To expedite model construction, one can use special decision analysis systems that have modeling languages and capabilities embedded in them. These include fourth-generation languages (formerly financial planning languages) such as Cognos PowerHouse.

MODEL MANAGEMENT

Models, like data, must be managed to maintain their integrity and thus their applicability. Such management is done with the aid of model base management systems (Section 4.16).

KNOWLEDGE-BASED MODELING

DSS uses mostly quantitative models, whereas expert systems use qualitative, knowledge-based models in their applications. Some knowledge is necessary to construct solvable (and therefore usable) models. We defer the description of knowledge-based models until later chapters.

CURRENT TRENDS

There is a trend toward making MSS models completely transparent to the decision-maker. In **multidimensional modeling** and some other cases, data are generally shown in a spreadsheet format (Sections 4.6 and 4.15), with which most decision-makers are familiar. Many decision-makers accustomed to slicing and dicing data cubes are now

TABLE 4.1	Categories of Models	
Category	*Process and Objective*	*Representative Techniques*
Optimization of problems with few alternatives (Section 5.7)	Find the best solution from a small number of alternatives	Decision tables, decision trees
Optimization via algorithm (Section 5.8 and 5.9)	Find the best solution from a large or an infinite number of alternatives using a step-by-step improvement process	Linear and other mathematical programming models, network models
Optimization via an analytic formula (Section 5.9)	Find the best solution in one step using a formula	Some inventory models
Simulation (Sections 5.12 and 5.14)	Finding a good enough solution or the best among the alternatives checked using experimentation	Several types of simulation
Heuristics (Section 5.12)	Find a good enough solution using rules	Heuristic programming, expert systems
Predictive models (Web Chapter)	Predict the future for a given scenario	Forecasting models, Markov analysis
Other models	Solve a what-if case using a formula	Financial modeling, waiting lines

using online analytical processing (OLAP) systems that access data warehouses (see the next chapter). Although these methods may make modeling palatable, they also eliminate many important and applicable model classes from consideration, and they eliminate some important and subtle solution interpretation aspects. Modeling involves much more than just data analysis with trend lines and establishing relationships with statistical methods. This subset of methods does not capture the richness of modeling, some of which we touch on next, in several Web Chapters, and in Case Application 4.1.

4.3 STATIC AND DYNAMIC MODELS

DSS models can be classified as static or dynamic.

STATIC ANALYSIS

Static models take a single snapshot of a situation. During this snapshot everything occurs in a single *interval*. For example, a decision on whether to make or buy a product is static in nature (see the Web Chapter on Scott Housing's decision-making situation). A quarterly or annual income statement is static, and so is the investment decision example in Section 4.7. The IMERYS decision-making problem in Case Application 4.1 is also static. Though it represents a year's operations, it occurs in a fixed time frame. The time frame can be "rolled" forward, but it is nonetheless static. The same is true for the P&G decision-making problem (Web Chapter). In the latter case, however, the impacts of the decisions may last over several decades. Most static decision-making situations are presumed to repeat with identical conditions (as in the BMI linear programming model described later). For example, process simulation begins with *steady-state,* which models a static representation of a plant to find its optimal operating parameters. A static representation assumes that the flow of materials into the plant will be continuous and unvarying. Steady-state simulation is the main tool for process design, when engineers must determine the best trade-off between capital costs, operational costs, process performance, product quality, environmental and safety factors. (Boswell, 1999)

The stability of the relevant data is assumed in a static analysis.

DYNAMIC ANALYSIS

There are stories about model builders who spend months developing a complex, ultra-large-scale, hard-to-solve static model representing a week's worth of a real-world decision-making situation like sausage production. They deliver the system and present the results to the company president, who responds, "Great! Well, that handles one week. Let's get started on developing the 52-week model."[2]

Dynamic models represent scenarios that change over time. A simple example is a 5-year profit-and-loss projection in which the input data, such as costs, prices, and quantities, change from year to year.

Dynamic models are *time-dependent.* For example, in determining how many checkout points should be open in a supermarket, one must take the time of day into consideration, because different numbers of customers arrive during each hour. Demands must be forecasted over time. The IMERYS model can be expanded to include multiple time periods by including inventory at the holding tanks, warehouses, and mines. Dynamic simulation, in contrast to steady-state simulation, represents what happens when conditions vary from the steady state over time. There might be variations in the raw materials (e.g., clay) or an unforeseen (even random) incident in some of the processes. This methodology is used in plant control design (Boswell, 1999).

Dynamic models are important because they use, represent, or generate trends and patterns over time. They also show averages per period, moving averages, and comparative analyses (e.g., profit this quarter against profit in the same quarter of last year). Furthermore, once a static model is constructed to describe a given situation—say, product distribution can be expanded to represent the dynamic nature of the problem (e.g., IMERYS). For example, the transportation model (a type of network flow model) describes a static model of product distribution. It can be expanded to a dynamic network flow model to accommodate inventory and backordering (Aronson, 1989). Given a static model describing one month of a situation, expanding it to 12 months is conceptually easy. However, this expansion typically increases the model's complexity dramatically and makes it harder, if not impossible, to solve. Also see Xiang and Poh (2002).

4.4 CERTAINTY, UNCERTAINTY, AND RISK[3]

Part of Simon's decision-making process described in Chapter 2 involves evaluating and comparing alternatives, during which it is necessary to predict the future outcome of each proposed alternative. Decision situations are often classified on the basis of

---

[2]Thanks to Dick Barr of Southern Methodist University, Dallas, Texas, for this one.

[3]Parts of Sections 4.4, 4.5, and 4.7, 4.9, 4.12, and 4.13 were adapted from Turban and Meredith (1994).

what the decision-maker knows (or believes) about the forecasted results. Customary, we classify this knowledge into three categories (Figure 4.1), ranging from complete knowledge to total ignorance. These categories are

- Certainty
- Risk
- Uncertainty

When we develop models, any of these conditions can occur, and different kinds of models are appropriate for each case. We discuss both the basic definitions of these terms and some important modeling issues for each condition.

DECISION-MAKING UNDER CERTAINTY

In decision-making under **certainty**, it is *assumed* that complete knowledge is available so that the decision-maker knows exactly what the outcome of *each course of action* will be (as in a deterministic environment). It may not be true that the outcomes are 100 percent known, nor is it necessary to really evaluate *all* the outcomes, but often this assumption simplifies the model and makes it tractable. The decision-maker is viewed as a perfect predictor of the future because it is assumed that there is only one outcome for each alternative. For example, the alternative of investing in U.S. Treasury bills is one for which there is complete availability of information about the future return on the investment. Such a situation occurs most often with structured problems with short time horizons (up to 1 year). Another example is that every time you park downtown, you get a parking ticket because you exceed the time limit on the parking meter—although once it did not happen. This situation can still be treated as one of decision-making under certainty. Some problems under certainty are not structured enough to be approached by analytical methods and models; they require a DSS approach.

Certainty models are relatively easy to develop and solve, and can yield optimal solutions. Many financial models are constructed under assumed certainty, even though the market is anything but 100 percent certain. Problems that have an infinite (or a very large) number of feasible solutions are extremely important and are discussed in Sections 4.9 and 4.12.

DECISION-MAKING UNDER UNCERTAINTY

In decision-making under **uncertainty**, the decision-maker considers situations in which several outcomes are possible for each course of action. In contrast to the risk situation, in this case the decision-maker does not know, or cannot estimate, the proba-

FIGURE 4.1   THE ZONES OF DECISION MAKING

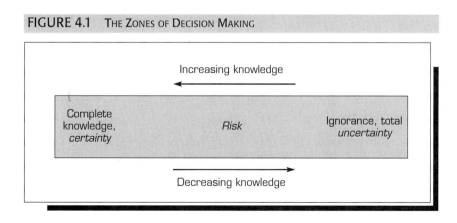

bility of occurrence of the possible outcomes. Decision-making under uncertainty is more difficult because of insufficient information. Modeling of such situations involves assessment of the decision-maker's (or the organization's) attitude toward risk (see Nielsen, 2003).

Managers attempt to avoid uncertainty as much as possible, even to the point of assuming it away. Instead of dealing with uncertainty, they attempt to obtain more information so that the problem can be treated under certainty (because it can be "almost" certain) or under calculated (assumed) risk. If more information is not available, the problem must be treated under a condition of uncertainty, which is less definitive than the other categories.

DECISION-MAKING UNDER RISK (RISK ANALYSIS)

A decision made under **risk**[4] (also known as a probabilistic or stochastic decision-making situation) is one in which the decision-maker must consider several possible outcomes for each alternative, each with a given probability of occurrence. The long-run probabilities that the given outcomes will occur are assumed to be known or can be estimated. Under these assumptions, the decision-maker can assess the degree of risk associated with each alternative (called *calculated* risk). Most major business decisions are made under assumed risk. **Risk analysis** can be performed by calculating the expected value of each alternative and selecting the one with the best expected value. Several techniques can be used to deal with risk analysis (see Drummond, 2001; Koller, 2000; Laporte, Louveeaux, and Van Hamme, 2002). They are discussed in Sections 4.7 and 4.13.

4.5 INFLUENCE DIAGRAMS

Once a decision-making problem is understood and defined, it must be analyzed. This can best be done by constructing a model. Just as a flowchart is a graphical representation of computer program flow, an influence diagram is a map of a model (effectively a model of a model). An **influence diagram** is a graphical representation of a model used to assist in model design, development, and understanding. An influence diagram provides visual communication to the model builder or development team. It also serves as a framework for expressing the exact nature of the relationships of the MSS model, thus assisting a modeler in focusing on the model's major aspects, and can help eliminate the less important from consideration. The term *influence* refers to the dependency of a variable on the level of another variable. Influence diagrams appear in several formats. The following description has evolved into a standard format (see the Decision Analysis Society Web site, faculty.fuqua.duke.edu/daweb/dasw6.htm; the Hugin Expert A/S (Aalborg, Denmark) Web site, developer.hugin.com/tutorials/ ID_example/; and the Lumina Decision Systems (Los Gatos, California) Web site, www.lumina.com/software/ influencediagrams.html):

---

[4]Our definitions of the terms *risk* and *uncertainty* were formulated by F. H. Knight of the University of Chicago in 1933. There are other, comparable definitions in use.

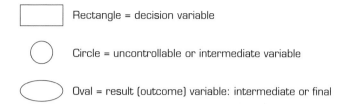

Rectangle = decision variable

Circle = uncontrollable or intermediate variable

Oval = result (outcome) variable: intermediate or final

The variables are connected with arrows that indicate the direction of influence (relationship). The shape of the arrow also indicates the type of relationship. The following are typical relationships:

- Certainty

- Uncertainty

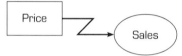

- Random (risk) variable: place a tilde (~) above the variable's name.

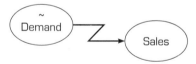

- Preference (usually between outcome variables): a double-line arrow $\Rightarrow$.
- Arrows can be one-way or two-way (bidirectional), depending on the direction of influence of a pair of variables.

Influence diagrams can be constructed with any degree of detail and sophistication. This enables the model builder to map all the variables and show all the relationships in the model, as well as the direction of the influence. They can even take into consideration the dynamic nature of problems (see Glaser and Kobayashi, 2002; Xiang and Poh, 2002).

Example
Consider the following profit model:
Profit = income − expenses
Income = units sold * unit price
Units sold = 0.5 * amount used in advertisement
Expenses = unit cost * units sold + fixed cost

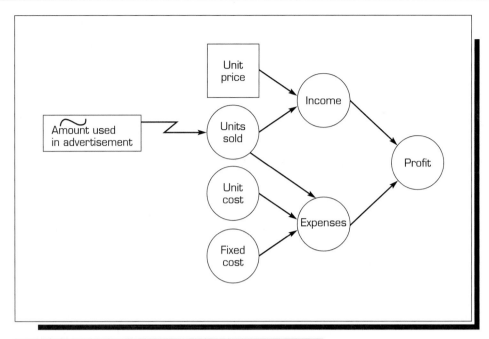

FIGURE 4.2   AN INFLUENCE DIAGRAM FOR THE PROFIT MODEL

An influence diagram for this simple model is shown in Figure 4.2.

SOFTWARE

There are several software products that create and maintain influence diagrams. The solution process of these products transforms the original problem into graphical form. Representative products are

- *Analytica* (Lumina Decision Systems, Los Altos, California, lumina.com). Analytica supports hierarchical diagrams, multidimensional arrays, integrated documentation, and parameter analysis.
- *DecisionPro* (Vanguard Software Corporation, Cary, North Carolina, vanguardsw.com). DecisionPro builds near-influence diagrams. The user decomposes a problem into a hierarchical tree structure (thus defining the relationships among variables). At the bottom, the variables are assigned values, or their values can be randomly generated. DecisionPro is an integrated tool that includes a wide range of decision-making techniques: linear programming, simulation, forecasting, and statistical analysis.
- *DATA and Data Pro* (TreeAge Software Inc., Williamstown, Massachusetts, treeage.com). DATA includes influence diagrams, decision trees, simulation models, and others. It integrates with spreadsheets and Web pages.
- *iDecide* (Definitive Software Inc., Broomfield, Colorado, definitivesoftware.com). Definitive Software's iDecide creates influence diagram-based decision models with bidirectional integration with Excel spreadsheets. The models can go directly from influence diagrams to Monte Carlo methods.

- *PrecisionTree* (Palisade Corporation, Newfield, New York, palisade.com). PrecisionTree creates influence diagrams and decision trees directly in an Excel spreadsheet.

See faculty.fuqua.duke.edu/daweb/dasw6.htm for more. Downloadable demos are available from each vendor's Web site. All of these Web-enabled systems create models with a treelike structure in such a way that the model can be easily developed and understood. Influence diagrams help focus on the important variables and their interactions. In addition, these software systems can generate a usable model and solve it without converting it for solution by a specialized tool. For example, Analytica lets the model builder describe blocks of the model and how they influence the important result variables. These submodel blocks are disaggregated by a model builder constructing a more detailed model. Finally, at the lowest level, variables are assigned values (see the Lumina Decision Systems Web site, lumina.com). In Figure 4.3a, we show an example of a marketing model in Analytica. This model includes a price submodel and a sales submodel, which appear in Figures 4.2b and 4.2c, respectively.

See the "2002 Decision Analysis Survey" in *OR/MS Today*, June 2002 (updated annually and available online at lionhrtpub.com/orms/) for a survey of decision-analysis software that includes influence diagrams. Also see Maxwell (2002). We next turn to an important implementation vehicle for models: the spreadsheet.

FIGURE 4.3A ANALYTICA INFLUENCE DIAGRAM OF A MARKETING PROBLEM: THE MARKETING MODEL

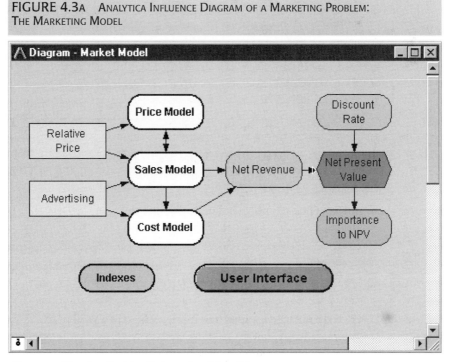

Courtesy of Lumina Decision Systems, Los Altos, CA.

FIGURE 4.3B   THE PRICE SUBMODEL

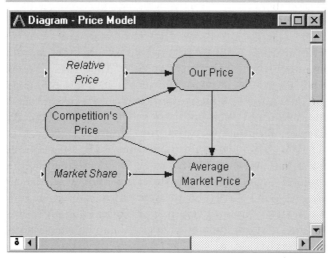

Courtesy of Lumina Decision Systems, Los Altos, CA.

FIGURE 4.3C   THE SALES SUBMODEL

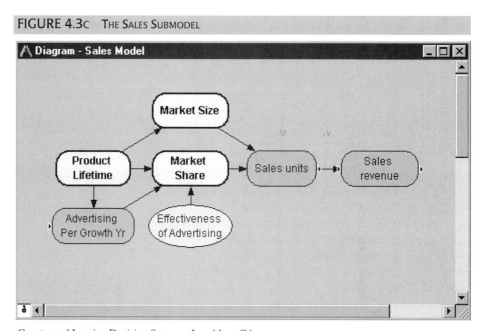

Courtesy of Lumina Decision Systems, Los Altos, CA.

4.6 MSS MODELING WITH SPREADSHEETS

Models can be developed and implemented in a variety of programming languages and systems. These range from third-, fourth-, and fifth-generation programming languages to CASE systems and other systems that automatically generate usable software. We focus primarily on *spreadsheets* (with their add-ins), modeling languages, and transparent data analysis tools.

With their strength and flexibility, spreadsheet packages were quickly recognized as easy-to-use implementation software for the development of a wide range of applications in business, engineering, mathematics, and science. As spreadsheet packages evolved, add-ins were developed for structuring and solving specific model classes. These add-ins include Solver (Frontline Systems Inc., Incline Village, Nevada) and What'sBest! (a version of Lindo, Lindo Systems Inc., Chicago, Illinois) for performing linear and nonlinear optimization, Braincel (Promised Land Technologies, Inc., New Haven, Connecticut) for artificial neural networks, Evolver (Palisade Corporation, Newfield, New York) for genetic algorithms, and @Risk (Palisade Corporation, Newfield, New York) for performing simulation studies. Because of fierce market competition, the better add-ins are eventually incorporated directly into the spreadsheets (e.g., Solver in Excel is the well-known GRG-2 nonlinear optimization code).

The spreadsheet is the most popular *end-user modeling tool* (Figure 4.4) because it incorporates many powerful financial, statistical, mathematical, and other functions. Spreadsheets can perform model solution tasks like linear programming and regression analysis. The spreadsheet has evolved into an important tool for analysis, planning, and modeling. (See Denardo, 2001; Hsiang, 2002; Monahan, 2000; Winston and Albright, 2000.)

Other important spreadsheet features include what-if analysis, goal seeking, data management, and programmability (*macros*). It is easy to change a cell's value and immediately see the result. Goal seeking is performed by indicating a target cell, its desired value, and a changing cell. Rudimentary database management can be performed, or parts of a database can be imported for analysis (which is essentially how OLAP works with multidimensional data cubes; in fact, most OLAP systems have the

FIGURE 4.4   EXCEL SPREADSHEET STATIC MODEL EXAMPLE OF A SIMPLE LOAN CALCULATION OF MONTHLY PAYMENTS

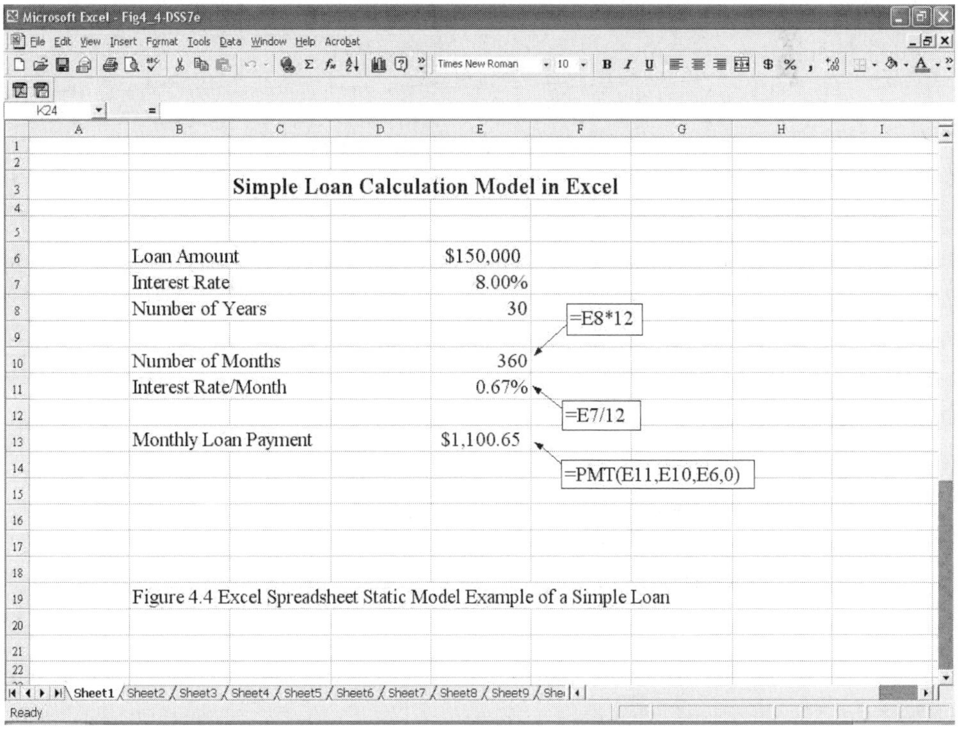

Figure 4.4 Excel Spreadsheet Static Model Example of a Simple Loan

look-and-feel of advanced spreadsheet software once the data are loaded). The programming productivity of building DSS can be enhanced with the use of templates, macros, and other tools.

Most spreadsheet packages provide fairly seamless integration by reading and writing common file structures that allow easy interfacing with databases and other tools. Microsoft Excel and Lotus 1-2-3 are the two most popular spreadsheet packages.

In Figure 4.4 we show a simple loan calculation model (the boxes on the spreadsheet describe the contents of the cells containing formulas). A change in the interest rate (performed by typing in a new number in cell E7) is immediately reflected in the monthly payment (in cell E13). The results can be observed and analyzed immediately. If we require a specific monthly payment, goal seeking (Section 4.10) can be used to determine an appropriate interest rate or loan amount.

Static or dynamic models can be built in a spreadsheet. For example, the monthly loan calculation spreadsheet shown in Figure 4.4 is static. Although the problem affects the borrower over time, the model indicates a single month's performance, which is replicated. A dynamic model, on the other hand, represents behavior over time. The loan calculations in the spreadsheet shown in Figure 4.5 indicate the effect of prepayment on the principal over time. Risk analysis can be incorporated into spreadsheets by using built-in random number generators to develop simulation models (see Section 4.13, and the Web Chapters describing an economic order-quantity simulation model under assumed risk and a spreadsheet simulation model of cash flows).

LeBlanc, Randalls, and Swann (2000) describe an excellent example of a model-based DSS developed in a spreadsheet. It assigns managers to projects for a major construction firm. By using the system, the company did not have to replace a manager

FIGURE 4.5   EXCEL SPREADSHEET DYNAMIC MODEL EXAMPLE OF A SIMPLE LOAN CALCULATION OF MONTHLY PAYMENTS AND THE EFFECTS OF PREPAYMENT

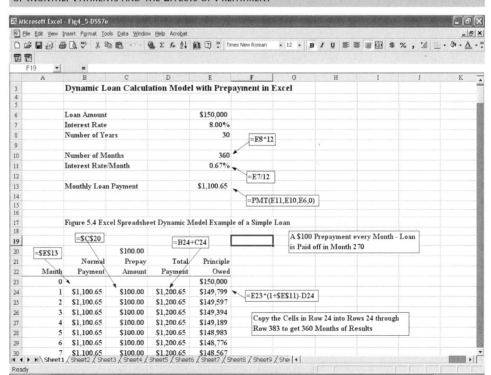

who resigned and thus substantially reduced travel costs. Buehlmann, Ragsdale, and Gfeller (2000) describe a spreadsheet-based DSS for wood panel manufacturing. This system handles many complex real-time decisions in a dynamic shop floor environment. Portucel Industrial developed a complete spreadsheet-based DSS for planning and scheduling paper production. See DSS in Action 3.8 and Respicio, Captivo, and Rodrigues (2002).

Spreadsheets were developed for personal computers, but they also run on larger computers. The spreadsheet framework is the basis for multidimensional spreadsheets and OLAP tools, which are described in the next chapter.

4.7 DECISION ANALYSIS OF A FEW ALTERNATIVES (DECISION TABLES AND DECISION TREES)

Decision situations that involve a finite and usually not too large number of alternatives are modeled by an approach called **decision analysis** (see Arsham, 2003a, 2003b; and the Decision Analysis Society Web site, faculty.fuqua.duke.edu/daweb/). Using this approach, the alternatives are listed in a table or a graph with their forecasted contributions to the goal(s) and the probability of obtaining the contribution. These can be evaluated to select the best alternative.

Single-goal situations can be modeled with **decision tables** or **decision trees**. Multiple goals (criteria) can be modeled with several other techniques described later.

DECISION TABLES

Decision tables are a convenient way to organize information in a systematic manner. For example, an investment company is considering investing in one of three alternatives: bonds, stocks, or certificates of deposit (CDs). The company is interested in one goal: maximizing the yield on the investment after one year. If it were interested in other goals, such as safety or liquidity, the problem would be classified as one of *multi-criteria decision analysis* (Koksalan and Zionts, 2001) (see DSS in Action 3.2 and 4.1; Dias and Climaco, 2002).

The yield depends on the state of the economy sometime in the future (often called the *state of nature*), which can be in solid growth, stagnation, or inflation. Experts estimated the following annual yields:

- If there is solid growth in the economy, bonds will yield 12 percent, stocks 15 percent, and time deposits 6.5 percent.
- If stagnation prevails, bonds will yield 6 percent, stocks 3 percent, and time deposits 6.5 percent.
- If inflation prevails, bonds will yield 3 percent, stocks will bring a loss of 2 percent, and time deposits will yield 6.5 percent.

The problem is to select the one best investment alternative. These are assumed to be discrete alternatives. Combinations such as investing 50 percent in bonds and 50 percent in stocks must be treated as new alternatives.

The investment decision-making problem can be viewed as a *two-person game* (see Kelly, 2002). The investor makes a choice (a move) and then a state of nature occurs (makes a move). The payoff is shown in a table representation (Table 4.2) of a

TABLE 4.2   Investment Problem Decision Table Model

	State of Nature (Uncontrollable Variables)		
Alternative	*Solid Growth (%)*	*Stagnation (%)*	*Inflation (%)*
Bonds	12.0	6.0	3.0
Stocks	15.0	3.0	−2.0
CDs	6.5	6.5	6.5

mathematical model. The table includes *decision variables* (the alternatives), *uncontrollable variables* (the states of the economy, e.g., the environment), and *result variables* (the projected yield, e.g., outcomes). All the models in this section are structured in a spreadsheet framework.

If this were a decision-making problem under certainty, we would know what the economy will be and could easily choose the best investment. But this is not the case, and so we must consider the two situations of uncertainty and risk. For uncertainty, we do not know the probabilities of each state of nature. For risk, we assume that we know the probabilities with which each state of nature will occur.

TREATING UNCERTAINTY

There are several methods of handling uncertainty. For example, the *optimistic approach* assumes that the best possible outcome of each alternative will occur and then selects the best of the bests (stocks). The *pessimistic approach* assumes that the worst possible outcome for each alternative will occur and selects the best of these (CDs). Another approach simply assumes that all states of nature are equally likely. See Clemen and Reilly (2000), Goodwin and Wright (2000), Kontoghiorghes, Rustem, and Siokos (2002). There are serious problems with every approach for handling uncertainty. Whenever possible, the analyst should attempt to gather enough information so that the problem can be treated under assumed certainty or risk.

TREATING RISK

The most common method for solving this **risk analysis** problem is to select the alternative with the greatest expected value. Assume that experts estimate the chance of solid growth at 50 percent, that of stagnation at 30 percent, and that of inflation at 20 percent. Then the decision table is rewritten with the known probabilities (Table 4.3). An expected value is computed by multiplying the results (outcomes) by their respective probabilities and adding them. For example, investing in bonds yields an expected return of 12(0.5) + 6(0.3) + 3(0.2) = 8.4 percent.

This approach can sometimes be a dangerous strategy, because the "utility" of each potential outcome may be different from the "value." Even if there is an infinitesimal chance of a catastrophic loss, the expected value may seem reasonable, but the investor

TABLE 4.3   Decision Under Risk and Its Solution

Alternative	*Solid Growth, .50(%)*	*Stagnation, .30(%)*	*Inflation, .20(%)*	*Expected Value (%)*
Bonds	12.0	6.0	3.0	8.4 (maximum)
Stocks	15.0	3.0	−2.0	8.0
CDs	6.5	6.5	6.5	6.5

may not be willing to cover the loss. For example, suppose a financial advisor presents you with an "almost sure" investment of $1,000 that can double your money in one day, then says, "Well, there is a .9999 probability that you will double your money, but unfortunately there is a .0001 probability that you will be liable for a $500,000 out-of-pocket loss." The expected value of this investment is

$$0.9999 \, (\$2,000 - \$1,000) + .0001 \, (-\$500,000 - \$1,000) = \$999.90 - \$50.10 = \$949.80$$

The potential loss could be catastrophic for any investor who is not a billionaire. Depending on the investor's ability to cover the loss, an investment has different expected utilities. Remember that the investor makes the decision only *once*.

DECISION TREES

An alternative representation of the decision table is a decision tree (Mind Tools Community, www.mindtools.com). A decision tree shows the relationships of the problem graphically and can handle complex situations in a compact form. However, a decision tree can be cumbersome if there are many alternatives or states of nature. DATA (TreeAge Software Inc., Williamstown, Massachusetts, treeage.com) and PrecisionTree (Palisade Corporation, Newfield, New York, palisade.com) include powerful, intuitive, and sophisticated decision tree analysis systems. Several other methods of treating risk are discussed later in the book. These include simulation, certainty factors, and fuzzy logic.

A simplified investment case of **multiple goals** is shown in Table 4.4. The three goals (criteria) are yield, safety, and liquidity. This situation is under assumed certainty; that is, only one possible consequence is projected for each alternative (the more complex cases of risk or uncertainty could be considered). Some of the results are qualitative (such as low and high) rather than numeric.

Rosetti and Selandar (2001) discuss the multicriteria approach to analyzing hospital-delivery systems. Their method captures the decision-maker's beliefs through a series of sequential, rational, and analytic processes. They used the Analytic Hierarchy Process (AHP) (Forman and Selly 2001; Saaty 1999; Palmer 1999). Phillips-Wren and Forgionne (2002) describe a multiple-objective approach based on the AHP to evaluating DSS. Raju and Pillai (1999) applied a multicriteria model to river-basin planning. Another example of a DSS designed for handling multiple-goal decision-making is described by Murthy et al. (1999). They developed a fairly complex paper manufacturing and scheduling DSS that saved a substantial sum of money annually. Barba-Romero (2001) describe a government DSS that utilizes a multicriteria model in acquiring data processing systems. In DSS in Action 3.2, we describe a Web-based multicriteria problem for the Cameron and Barkley Company. The buyers faced the conflicting goals of minimizing inventory and maintaining high levels of customer service. There are many decision analysis and multicriteria decision-making software packages, including DecisionPro (Vanguard Software Corporation, vanguardsw.com), Expert Choice, Expert Choice 2000 2nd Edition for Groups, and the Web-based special versions for strategic planning, human resources, procurement, and more (Expert

TABLE 4.4   Multiple Goals

Alternative	Yield (%)	Safety	Liquidity
Bonds	8.4	High	High
Stocks	8.0	Low	High
CDs	6.5	Very high	High

Choice Inc., expertchoice.com), Hipre and the Java Applet Web-Hipre (Systems Analysis Laboratory, Helsinki University of Technology, hipre.hut.fi; see Mustajoki and Hamalainen, 2000), and Logical Decisions for Windows and for Groups (Logical Decisions Group, logicaldecisions.com). Demo software versions of all these systems are available on the Web. Akarte et al. (2001) describe how a Web-based implementation of the Analytic Hierarchy Process was used to solve a multicriteria problem in vendor selection. See the Scott Homes Web Chapter for an example of the use of Expert Choice in solving a similar multicriteria problem. Recent multicriteria research is described in Koksalan and Zionts (2001).

See Clemen and Reilly (2000), Goodwin and Wright (2000), and the Decision Analysis Society Web site (faculty.fuqua.duke.edu/daweb/) for more on decision analysis. Although quite complex, it is possible to apply mathematical programming (Section 4.9) directly to decision-making situations under risk (Sen and Higle, 1999).

4.8 THE STRUCTURE OF MSS MATHEMATICAL MODELS

We present the topics of MSS mathematical models (mathematical, financial, engineering, etc.). These include the components and the structure of models.

THE COMPONENTS OF MSS MATHEMATICAL MODELS

All models are made up of three basic components (Figure 4.6): **decision variables**, **uncontrollable variables** (and/or **parameters**), and **result (outcome) variables**. Mathematical relationships link these components together. In nonquantitative models, the relationships are symbolic or qualitative. The results of decisions are determined by the decision made (value of the decision variables), the factors that cannot be controlled by the decision-maker (in the environment), and the relationships among the variables. The modeling process involves identifying the variables and relationships among them. Solving a model determines the values of these and the result variable(s).

Result variables reflect the level of effectiveness of the system; that is, they indicate how well the system performs or attains its goal(s). These variables are outputs. Examples of result variables are shown in Table 4.5. Result variables are considered *dependent variables*. Intermediate result variables are sometimes used in modeling to identify intermediate outcomes. In the case of a dependent variable, another event must occur first before the event described by the variable can occur. Result variables

FIGURE 4.6 THE GENERAL STRUCTURE OF A QUANTITATIVE MODEL

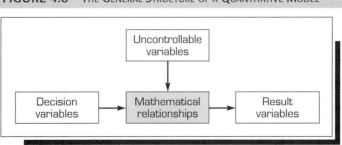

TABLE 4.5 Examples of the Components of Models

Area	Decision Variables	Result Variables	Uncontrollable Variables and Parameters
Financial investment	Investment alternatives and amounts How long to invest When to invest	Total profit, risk Rate of return (ROI) Earnings per share Liquidity level	Inflation rate Prime rate Competition
Marketing	Advertising budget Where to advertise	Market share Customer satisfaction	Customers' income Competitors' actions
Manufacturing	What and how much to produce Inventory levels Compensation programs	Total cost Quality level Employee satisfaction	Machine capacity Technology Materials prices
Accounting	Use of computers Audit schedule	Data processing cost Error rate	Computer technology Tax rates Legal requirements
Transportation	Shipments schedule Use of *smart cards*	Total transport cost Payment float time	Delivery distance Regulations
Services	Staffing levels	Customer satisfaction	Demand for services

depend on the occurrence of the decision and the uncontrollable **independent variables**.

DECISION VARIABLES

Decision variables describe alternative courses of action. The decision-maker controls the decision variables. For example, for an investment problem, the amount to invest in bonds is a decision variable. In a scheduling problem, the decision variables are people, times, and schedules. Other examples are listed in Table 4.5.

UNCONTROLLABLE VARIABLES OR PARAMETERS

In any decision-making situation, there are factors that affect the result variables but are not under the control of the decision-maker. Either these factors can be fixed, in which case they are called parameters, or they can vary (variables). Examples are the prime interest rate, a city's building code, tax regulations, and utilities costs (others are shown in Table 4.5). Most of these factors are uncontrollable because they are in and determined by elements of the system environment in which the decision-maker works. Some of these variables limit the decision-maker and therefore form what are called the constraints of the problem.

INTERMEDIATE RESULT VARIABLES

Intermediate result variables reflect intermediate outcomes. For example, in determining machine scheduling, spoilage is an intermediate result variable, and total profit is the result variable (spoilage is one determinant of total profit). Another example is employee salaries. This constitutes a decision variable for management. It determines

employee satisfaction (intermediate outcome), which in turn determines the productivity level (final result).

THE STRUCTURE OF MSS MATHEMATICAL MODELS

The components of a quantitative model are linked together by mathematical (algebraic) expressions—equations or inequalities.

A very simple financial model is $P = R - C$, where P = profit, R = revenue, and C = cost. The equation describes the relationship among these variables.

Another well-known financial model is the simple present-value cash flow model,

$$P = \frac{F}{(1 + i)^n}$$

where P = present value, F = a future single payment in dollars, i = interest rate (percentage), and n = number of years. With this model, one can readily determine the present value of a payment of \$100,000 to be made five years from today, at a 10 percent (0.1) interest rate, to be

$$P = \frac{100,000}{(1 + 0.1)^5} = \$62,092$$

We present more interesting, complex mathematical models in the following sections.

4.9 MATHEMATICAL PROGRAMMING OPTIMIZATION

The basic idea of optimization was introduced in Chapter 2. **Linear programming (LP)** is the best-known technique in a family of optimization tools called mathematical programming. It is used extensively in DSS (see DSS in Action 4.2). Linear programming models have many important applications in practice. For examples, see the Web Chapter on Procter and Gamble, where several linear programming problems were used, and IMERYS Case Application 4.1.

MATHEMATICAL PROGRAMMING

Mathematical programming is a family of tools designed to help solve managerial problems in which the decision-maker must allocate scarce resources among competing activities to optimize a measurable goal. For example, the distribution of machine time (the resource) among various products (the activities) is a typical allocation problem. Linear programming (LP) allocation problems usually display the following characteristics.

LP Characteristics
- A limited quantity of economic resources is available for allocation.
- The resources are used in the production of products or services.
- There are two or more ways in which the resources can be used. Each is called a solution or a program.
- Each activity (product or service) in which the resources are used yields a return in terms of the stated goal.
- The allocation is usually restricted by several limitations and requirements called constraints.

DSS IN ACTION 4.2

EFES MALT PLANT LOCATION OPTIMIZATION

Efes Beverage Group (Efes), a beer company in Turkey, wanted to determine the best locations for new malt plants. In an earlier project, Efes had used a mathematical programming model to determine where to locate new breweries. As some of these new breweries were being constructed, Efes managers asked the same team to help.

Various sites were evaluated as possible locations for new malt plants. An economic analysis revealed the inferiority of some alternatives that some managers had championed. To evaluate the remaining possibilities, a mixed-integer programming model was developed that considered both the location of new malt plants and the distribution of barley and malt. It considered the long-run effects of the decisions and minimized the present value of total costs. The model readily identified locations for the new malt plants. With the user-friendly optimization software, sensitivity analyses were conducted to determine the impact of forcing the selection of certain favored sites. Some were deemed acceptable, while others caused large increases in the optimal overall system cost (about $19 million). Efes used the model for distribution decisions. As a next step, the location and distribution decisions can be linked (as in Case Application 4.1).

Source: Condensed and modified from M. Koksalan and H. Sural, "Efes Beverage Group Makes Location and Distribution Decisions for Its Malt Plants," *Interfaces*, Vol. 29, No. 2, March/April 1999, pp. 89–103.

The LP allocation model is based on the following rational economic assumptions:

LP Assumptions

- Returns from different allocations can be compared; that is, they can be measured by a common unit (e.g., dollars or utility).
- The return from any allocation is independent of other allocations.
- The total return is the sum of the returns yielded by the different activities.
- All data are known with certainty.
- The resources are to be used in the most economical manner.

Allocation problems typically have a large number of possible solutions. Depending on the underlying assumptions, the number of solutions can be either infinite or finite. Usually, different solutions yield different rewards. Of the available solutions, at least one is the best, in the sense that the degree of goal attainment associated with it is the highest (i.e., the total reward is maximized). This is called an optimal solution, and can be found by using a special algorithm.

LINEAR PROGRAMMING (LP)

Every LP problem is composed of *decision variables* (whose values are unknown and are searched for), an *objective function* (a linear mathematical function that relates the decision variables to the goal, measures goal attainment, and is to be optimized), *objective function coefficients* (unit profit or cost coefficients indicating the contribution to the objective of one unit of a decision variable), *constraints* (expressed in the form of linear inequalities or equalities that limit resources and/or requirements; these relate the variables through linear relationships), *capacities* (which describe the upper and sometimes lower limits on the constraints and variables), and *input–output (technology) coefficients* (which indicate resource utilization for a decision variable). See DSS in Focus 4.3.

THE LP PRODUCT-MIX MODEL FORMULATION

MBI Corporation manufactures special-purpose computers. A decision must be made: How many computers should be produced next month at the Boston plant? Two types of computers are considered: the CC-7, which requires 300 days of labor and $10,000 in materials, and the CC-8, which requires 500 days of labor and $15,000 in materials. The profit contribution of each CC-7 is $8,000, whereas that of each CC-8 is $12,000. The plant has a capacity of 200,000 working days per month, and the material budget is $8 million per month. Marketing requires that at least 100 units of the CC-7 and at least 200 units of the CC-8 be produced each month. The problem is to maximize the company's profits by determining how many units of the CC-7 and how many units of the CC-8 should be produced each month. Note that in a real-world environment it could possibly take months to obtain the data in the problem statement, and while gathering the data, the decision-maker would no doubt uncover facts about how to structure the model to be solved. This was true for the situation described in IMERYS Case Applications 2.1 and 2.2. Web-based tools for gathering data can help (see DSS in Action 2.6).

MODELING

A standard linear programming (LP) model can be developed (see DSS in Focus 4.3). It has three components:

Decision variables:

X_1 = units of CC-7 to be produced
X_2 = units of CC-8 to be produced

Result variable:

Total profit = Z. The objective is to maximize total profit: $Z = 8{,}000X_1 + 12{,}000X_2$

Uncontrollable variables (constraints):

Labor constraint: $300X_1 + 500X_2 \leq 200{,}000$ (in days)
Budget constraint: $10{,}000X_1 + 15{,}000X_2 \leq 8{,}000{,}000$ (in dollars)
Marketing requirement for CC-7: $X_1 \geq 100$ (in units)
Marketing requirement for CC-8: $X_2 \geq 200$ (in units)

This information is summarized in Figure 4.7.

The model also has a fourth, hidden component. Every linear programming model has some internal intermediate variables that are not explicitly stated. The labor and

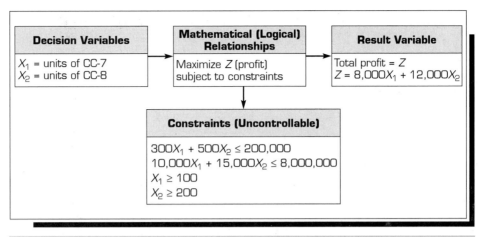

FIGURE 4.7   MATHEMATICAL MODEL OF A PRODUCT MIX EXAMPLE

budget constraints may each have some "slack" in them when the left-hand side is strictly less than the right-hand side. These slacks are represented internally by slack variables that indicate excess resources available. The marketing requirement constraints may each have some "surplus" in them when the left-hand side is strictly greater than the right-hand side. These surpluses are represented internally by surplus variables indicating that there is some room to adjust the right-hand sides of these constraints. These slack and surplus variables are intermediate. They can be of great value to the decision-maker because linear programming solution methods use them in establishing sensitivity parameters for economic what-if analyses.

The product-mix model has an infinite number of possible solutions. Assuming that a production plan is not restricted to whole numbers—a reasonable assumption in a monthly production plan—we want a solution that maximizes total profit: an optimal solution.

Fortunately, Excel comes with the add-in Solver that can readily obtain an optimal (best) solution to this problem. We enter these data directly into an Excel spreadsheet, activate Solver, and identify the goal (set Target Cell equal to Max), decision variables (By Changing Cells), and constraints (Total Consumed elements must be less than or equal to Limit for the first two rows and must be greater than or equal to Limit for the third and fourth rows). Also, in Options, activate the boxes Assume Linear Model and Assume Non-negative, and then *solve* the problem. Next, select all three reports—Answer, Sensitivity, and Limits—to obtain an optimal solution of $X_1 = 333.33$, $X_2 = 200$, Profit = \$5,066,667 as shown in Figure 4.8. Solver produces three useful reports about the solution. Try it.

The evaluation of the alternatives and the final choice depend on the type of criteria we have selected. Are we trying to find the best solution? Or will a "good enough" result be sufficient? (See Chapter 2.)

Linear programming models (and their specializations and generalizations) can be specified directly in a number of user-friendly modeling systems. Two of the best known are Lindo and Lingo (Lindo Systems Inc., Chicago, Illinois, lindo.com; demos are available from the Lindo Web site) (Schrage, 1997). Lindo is a linear and integer programming system. Models are specified in essentially the same way that they are defined algebraically. Based on the success of Lindo, the company developed Lingo, a modeling language that includes the powerful Lindo optimizer plus extensions for solving nonlinear problems. The IMERYS DSS (Case Application 4.1) was implemented using Lingo

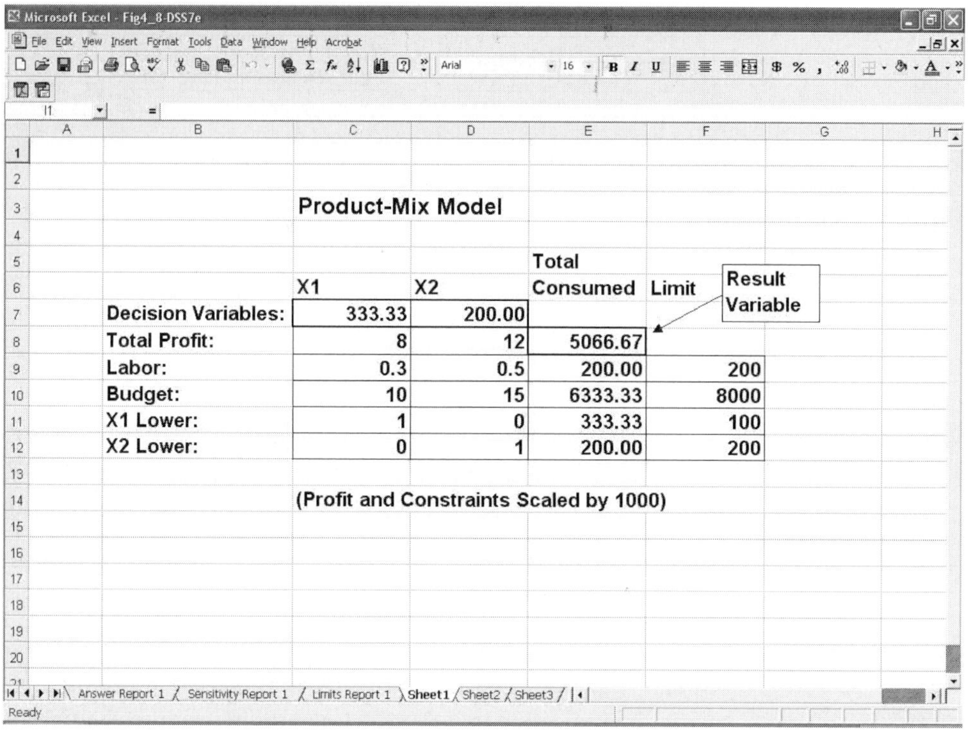

	X1	X2	Total Consumed	Limit
Decision Variables:	333.33	200.00		
Total Profit:	8	12	5066.67	
Labor:	0.3	0.5	200.00	200
Budget:	10	15	6333.33	8000
X1 Lower:	1	0	333.33	100
X2 Lower:	0	1	200.00	200

FIGURE 4.8 Excel Solver Solution to the Product-Mix Example

as its model generator and solver. Lindo and Lingo models and solutions of the product-mix model are shown, respectively, in DSS in Focus 4.4 and 4.5.

The uses of mathematical programming, especially of linear programming, are fairly common in practice. There are standard computer programs available. Optimization functions are available in many DSS integrated tools, such as Excel. Also, it is easy to interface other optimization software with Excel, database management systems, and similar tools. Optimization models are often included in decision support implementations, as shown in DSS in Action 4.2. More details on linear programming, a description of another classic LP problem called the *blending problem*, and an Excel spreadsheet formulation and solution are described in a Web Chapter.

The most common optimization models can be solved by a variety of mathematical programming methods. They are:

- Assignment (best matching of objects)
- Dynamic programming
- Goal programming
- Investment (maximizing rate of return)
- Linear and integer programming
- Network models for planning and scheduling
- Nonlinear programming
- Replacement (capital budgeting)
- Simple inventory models (e.g., economic order quantity)
- Transportation (minimize cost of shipments).

DSS IN FOCUS 4.4

LINDO EXAMPLE: THE PRODUCT-MIX MODEL

Here is the Lindo version of the product-mix model. Note that the model is essentially identical to the algebraic expression of the model.

<<The Lindo Model:>>

```
MAX      8000 X1 + 12000 X2
SUBJECT TO
    LABOR)      300 X1 + 500 X2 <= 200000
    BUDGET)    10000 X1 + 15000 X2 <= 8000000
   MARKET1)    X1 >=   100
   MARKET2)    X2 >=   200
END
```

<<Generated Solution Report>>

```
LP OPTIMUM FOUND AT STEP       3

        OBJECTIVE FUNCTION VALUE

     1)     506667.00

VARIABLE          VALUE          REDUCED COST
      X1       333.333300            .000000
      X2       200.000000            .000000

      ROW    SLACK OR SURPLUS       DUAL PRICES
    LABOR)         .000000          26.666670
   BUDGET)  1666667.000000            .000000
  MARKET1)      233.333300            .000000
  MARKET2)         .000000       -1333.333000

NO. ITERATIONS=        3

RANGES IN WHICH THE BASIS IS UNCHANGED:

                   OBJ COEFFICIENT RANGES
VARIABLE          CURRENT         ALLOWABLE         ALLOWABLE
                    COEF          INCREASE          DECREASE
      X1       8000.000000         INFINITY        799.999800
      X2      12000.000000      1333.333000          INFINITY

                   RIGHT-HAND-SIDE RANGES
   ROW            CURRENT         ALLOWABLE         ALLOWABLE
                    RHS           INCREASE          DECREASE
  LABOR     200000.000000     50000.000000      70000.000000
  BUDGET   8000000.000000         INFINITY    1666667.000000
 MARKET1       100.000000       233.333300          INFINITY
 MARKET2       200.000000       140.000000        200.000000
```

LINGO EXAMPLE: THE PRODUCT-MIX MODEL

Here is the Lingo version of the product-mix model. Note the specialized modeling-language commands, SET definitions, and DATA definitions. Though this model is much more complex than the Lindo version, it is much more powerful in that additional computers or resources can be added by simply augmenting the DATA and SET sections. The model itself is unchanged. In models that interact with databases, the data in the database are simply modified and the model file does not change. This approach was used in IMERYS Case Application 4.1.

<<The Model>>>

```
MODEL:
! The Product-Mix Example;
SETS:
COMPUTERS / CC7, CC8 / : PROFIT, QUANTITY, MARKETLIM ;
RESOURCES / LABOR, BUDGET / : AVAILABLE ;
RESBYCOMP (RESOURCES, COMPUTERS) : UNITCONSUMPTION ;
ENDSETS
DATA:
PROFIT MARKETLIM =
  8000, 100,
 12000, 200;
AVAILABLE = 200000, 8000000 ;
UNITCONSUMPTION =
 300, 500,
 10000, 15000 ;
ENDDATA
MAX = @SUM (COMPUTERS: PROFIT * QUANTITY) ;
@FOR ( RESOURCES ( I):
  @SUM( COMPUTERS( J):
    UNITCONSUMPTION ( I,J) * QUANTITY (J)) <=
AVAILABLE( I)) ;
@FOR( COMPUTERS( J):
    QUANTITY (J) >= MARKETLIM( J)) ;
! Alternative
@FOR( COMPUTERS( J) :
  @BND (MARKETLIM(J), QUANTITY (J) , 1000000)) ;
```

<<(Partial) Solution Report>>

```
 Global optimal solution found at step:           2
 Objective value:                        5066667.
             Variable           Value        Reduced Cost
            PROFIT( CC7)       8000.000        0.0000000
            PROFIT( CC8)       12000.00        0.0000000
          QUANTITY( CC7)       333.3333        0.0000000
          QUANTITY( CC8)       200.0000        0.0000000
         MARKETLIM( CC7)       100.0000        0.0000000
         MARKETLIM( CC8)       200.0000        0.0000000
        AVAILABLE( LABOR)      200000.0        0.0000000
        AVAILABLE( BUDGET)     8000000.        0.0000000
```

```
UNITCONSUMPTION( LABOR, CC7)        300.0000            0.0000000
UNITCONSUMPTION( LABOR, CC8)        500.0000            0.0000000
UNITCONSUMPTION( BUDGET, CC7)       10000.00            0.0000000
UNITCONSUMPTION( BUDGET, CC8)       15000.00            0.0000000

                      Row      Slack or Surplus        Dual Price
                        1          5066667.            1.000000
                        2          0.0000000           26.66667
                        3          1666667.            0.0000000
                        4          233.3333            0.0000000
                        5          0.0000000           -1333.333
```

Some important recent applications of mathematical programming include its application to Internet network design (Gourdin, 2001) and the cell telephone frequency allocation problem (Bourjolly et al., 2001). Obtaining an optimal solution to both of these problems has a critical impact on how well the Internet/Web functions, and on how effective e-commerce and m-commerce can be. Other examples include those found in production/operations management (e.g., the lot-sizing problem; see Wolsey, 2002), and the knapsack problem (stuff a knapsack with the highest-valued items without exceeding its weight limit), which is used to determine which experiments to take aboard spacecraft (see Erlebach, Kellerer, and Pferschy, 2002). Bossaerts, Fine, and Ledyard (2000) describe how an integer programming package, available over the Web, is used by the Bond Connect online marketplace for fixed-income security analysis to help match and price trades in a combinatorial auction setting. Geoffrion and Krishnan (2001) describe how mathematical modeling is moving to the Web. For example, MathML, is a markup language for mathematical processing (www.w3.org/Math/).

4.10 MULTIPLE GOALS, SENSITIVITY ANALYSIS, WHAT-IF, AND GOAL SEEKING

The search process described earlier is coupled with evaluation. Evaluation is the final step that leads to a recommended solution.

MULTIPLE GOALS

The analysis of management decisions aims at evaluating, to the greatest possible extent, how far each alternative advances management toward its goals. Unfortunately, managerial problems are seldom evaluated with a single simple goal like profit maximization. Today's management systems are much more complex, and one with a single goal is rare. Instead, managers want to attain *simultaneous goals*, some of which may conflict. Different stakeholders have different goals. Therefore, it is often necessary to analyze each alternative in light of its determination of each of several goals (see Koksalan and Zionts, 2001).

For example, consider a profit-making firm. In addition to earning money, the company wants to grow, develop its products and employees, provide job security to its workers, and serve the community. Managers want to satisfy the shareholders and at the same time enjoy high salaries and expense accounts, and employees want to increase their take-home pay and benefits. When a decision is to be made, say, about an investment project, some of these goals complement each other, whereas others conflict.

Many quantitative models of decision theory are based on comparing a single measure of effectiveness, generally some form of "utility" to the decision-maker. Therefore, it is usually necessary to transform a multiple-goal problem into a single-measure-of-effectiveness problem before comparing the effects of the solutions. This is a common method for handling multiple goals in a linear programming model. For example, see DSS in Focus 4.6, in which we have modified the MBI model into a *goal programming* model.

Certain difficulties may arise when analyzing multiple goals:

- It is usually hard to obtain an explicit statement of the organization's goals.
- The decision-maker may change the importance assigned to specific goals over time or for different decision scenarios.
- Goals and subgoals are viewed differently at various levels of the organization and within different departments.
- Goals change in response to changes in the organization and its environment.
- The relationship between alternatives and their role in determining goals may be difficult to quantify.
- Complex problems are solved by groups of decision-makers, each of whom has a personal agenda.
- Participants assess the importance (priorities) of the various goals differently.

Several methods of handling multiple goals can be used when working with MSS. The most common ones are

- Utility theory
- Goal programming
- Expression of goals as constraints using linear programming
- A point system

Some methods even work interactively with the decision-maker in searching the solution space for an alternative that provides for required attainment of all goals while searching for an "efficient" solution. The Web Chapters on Scott Homes and Selecting a College/University contain examples. Also see Ehrgott and Gandibleaux (2002). New methods are continually being developed for handling multiple goals. For example, see Koksalan and Zionts (2001) and Erlebach, Kellerer, and Pferschy (2002).

SENSITIVITY ANALYSIS

A model builder makes predictions and assumptions regarding the input data, many of which deal with the assessment of uncertain futures. When the model is solved, the results depend on these data. **Sensitivity analysis** attempts to assess the impact of a change in the input data or parameters on the proposed solution (the result variable).

Sensitivity analysis is extremely important in MSS because it allows flexibility and adaptation to changing conditions and to the requirements of different decision-making situations, provides a better understanding of the model and the decision-making situation it attempts to describe, and permits the manager to input data so that confidence in the model increases. Sensitivity analysis tests such relationships as

THE GOAL PROGRAMMING MBI MODEL

In a goal programming model, all goals are represented as constraints that have target values for the left-hand side. For example, the labor constraint has a target value of 200,000 days. If the target is met, there is no penalty. If we use more than 200,000 days of labor, we are over our goal, and there is a penalty for the deviation. If we are under our goal (i.e., we use less labor than the target amount), there may also be a penalty, perhaps wages must be paid for no production. The same is true of the budget constraint. In this model, we convert the objective of maximizing profit to a goal of profit meeting or exceeding a target level of $5 million. If we are under our goal, there is a penalty; but if we are over our goal, there is no penalty. Penalties are imposed by weights indicating the importance of each of the multiple objectives and the importance of each being over or under our goal. The marketing constraints here are not goals, but required limits.

Profit goal: $8,000\ X_1 + 12,000\ X_2 - OVER_1 + UNDER_1 = 5,000,000$

Labor goal: $300\ X_1 + 500\ X_2 - OVER_2 + UNDER_2 = 200,000$

Budget goal: $10,000\ X_1 + 15,000\ X_2 - OVER_3 + UNDER_3 = 8,000,000$

Marketing requirement for CC-7: $X_1 \geq 100$

Marketing requirement for CC-8: $X_2 \geq 200$

The objective is to minimize a weighted sum of the OVER and UNDER variables. For a particular solution, the UNDER and OVER variables indicate the amount the left-hand side of the goal constraint value varies from the target. Below is a Lingo model and solution. The budget is right on target (it had the highest weights in the objective). The profit is outstanding. We produce 500 units of CC-7 ($=X_1$), and 200 units of CC-8 ($=X_2$). We exceeded the $5 million by $1.4 million ($= OVER_1$), which leads to a total profit of $6.4 million, which is $1.3 million greater than before. But because $OVER_2$ is 50,000, we are using an additional 50,000 hours of labor. Since the weight in the objective for $OVER_2$ reflects the marginal cost of obtaining additional labor, this solution is an improvement over the standard linear programming one.

```
! Lingo Goalprodmixsimple Model ;
MIN   =   0 * OVER1 + 1000 * UNDER1 +
         50 * OVER2 +   10 * UNDER2 +
        100 * OVER3 +   20 * UNDER3 ;
<PROFIT> 8000 * X1 + 12000 * X2 - OVER1 + UNDER1 = 5000000 ;
<LABOR>   300 * X1 +   500 * X2 - OVER2 + UNDER2 = 200000 ;
<BUDGET> 10000 * X1 + 15000 * x2 - OVER3 + UNDER3 = 8000000 ;
<MARKET1>  X1 >=   100 ;
<MARKET2>  X2 >=   200 ;
```

<<< Lingo Goalprodmixout Solution (Variables only) >>>

Variable	Value	Reduced Cost
OVER1	1400000.	0.0000000
UNDER1	0.0000000	1000.000
OVER2	50000.00	0.0000000
UNDER2	0.0000000	60.00000
OVER3	0.0000000	101.5000
UNDER3	0.0000000	18.50000
X1	500.0000	0.0000000
X2	200.0000	0.0000000

- The impact of changes in external (uncontrollable) variables and parameters on outcome variable(s)
- The impact of changes in decision variables on outcome variable(s)
- The effect of uncertainty in estimating external variables
- The effects of different dependent interactions among variables
- The robustness of decisions under changing conditions.

Sensitivity analyses are used for

- Revising models to eliminate too large sensitivities
- Adding details about sensitive variables or scenarios
- Obtaining better estimates of sensitive external variables
- Altering the real-world system to reduce actual sensitivities
- Accepting and using the sensitive (and hence vulnerable) real world, leading to the continuous and close monitoring of actual results

The two types of sensitivity analyses are automatic and trial-and-error.

AUTOMATIC SENSITIVITY ANALYSIS

Automatic sensitivity analysis is performed in standard quantitative model implementations such as linear programming. For example, it reports the range within which a certain input variable or parameter value (e.g., unit cost) can vary without making any significant impact on the proposed solution. Automatic sensitivity analysis is usually limited to one change at a time, and only for certain variables. However, it is very powerful because of its ability to establish ranges and limits very fast (and with little or no additional computational effort). For example, automatic sensitivity analysis is part of the linear programming (LP) solution report for the MBI Corporation product-mix problem described earlier. Sensitivity analysis is provided by both Solver and Lindo. If the right-hand side of the marketing constraint on CC-8 could be decreased by one unit, then the net profit would increase by $1,333.33. This is valid for the right-hand side decreasing to zero. For details see Hillier and Lieberman (2003), Taha (2003), and Taylor (2002).

TRIAL AND ERROR

The impact of changes in any variable, or in several variables, can be determined through a simple trial-and-error approach. You change some input data and solve the problem again. When the changes are repeated several times, better and better solutions may be discovered. Such experimentation, which is easy to conduct when using appropriate modeling software like Excel, has two approaches: what-if analysis and goal seeking.

WHAT-IF ANALYSIS

What-if analysis is structured as *What will happen to the solution if an input variable, an assumption, or a parameter value is changed?*

Here are some examples:

- What will happen to the total inventory cost if the cost of carrying inventories increases by 10 percent?
- What will be the market share if the advertising budget increases by 5 percent?

Assuming the appropriate user interface, it is easy for managers to ask the computer model these types of questions and get immediate answers. Furthermore, they

FIGURE 4.9   EXAMPLE OF "WHAT-IF" ANALYSIS DONE IN EXCEL WORKSHEET

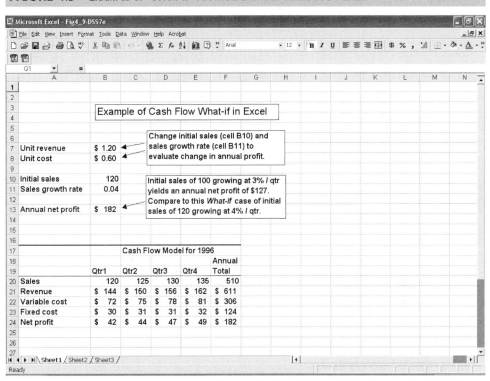

Initially, initial sales were 100 growing at 3 percent per quarter yielding an annual net profit of $127. By changing the initial sales cell to 120 and the sales growth rate to 4 percent, the annual net profit rose to $182.

can perform multiple cases and thereby change the percentage, or any other data in the question, as desired. All this is done directly, without a computer programmer.

Figure 4.9 shows a spreadsheet example of a what-if query for a cash flow problem. The user changes the cells containing the initial sales (from 100 to 120) and the sales growth rate (from 3 percent to 4 percent per quarter). The computer immediately recomputes the value of the annual net profit cell (from $127 to $182). What-if analysis is common in expert systems. Users are given the opportunity to change their answers to some of the system's questions, and a revised recommendation is found.

GOAL SEEKING

Goal seeking analysis calculates the values of the inputs necessary to achieve a desired level of an output (goal). It represents a backward solution approach. Some examples of goal seeking are:

- What annual R&D budget is needed for an annual growth rate of 15 percent by 2005?
- How many nurses are needed to reduce the average waiting time of a patient in the emergency room to less than 10 minutes?

An example of goal seeking is shown in Figure 4.10. Initially, initial sales were 100 growing at 3 percent per quarter, yielding an annual net profit of $127. By changing the

FIGURE 4.10 GOAL-SEEKING ANALYSIS

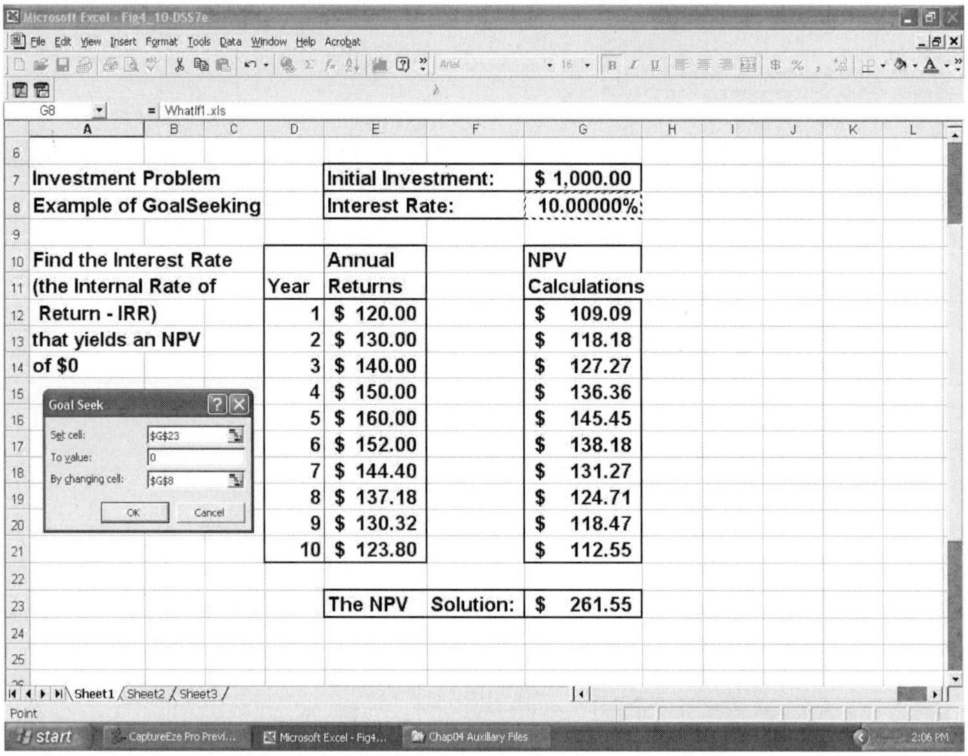

	A	B	C	D	E	F	G	H	I	J	K
6											
7	Investment Problem				Initial Investment:		$ 1,000.00				
8	Example of GoalSeeking				Interest Rate:		10.00000%				
9											
10	Find the Interest Rate				Annual		NPV				
11	(the Internal Rate of			Year	Returns		Calculations				
12	Return - IRR)			1	$ 120.00		$ 109.09				
13	that yields an NPV			2	$ 130.00		$ 118.18				
14	of $0			3	$ 140.00		$ 127.27				
15				4	$ 150.00		$ 136.36				
16				5	$ 160.00		$ 145.45				
17				6	$ 152.00		$ 138.18				
18				7	$ 144.40		$ 131.27				
19				8	$ 137.18		$ 124.71				
20				9	$ 130.32		$ 118.47				
21				10	$ 123.80		$ 112.55				
22											
23					The NPV	Solution:	$ 261.55				

Goal Seek dialog box:
Set cell: G23
To value: 0
By changing cell: G8

The goal to be achieved is NPV equal to zero, which determines the internal rate of return (IRR) of this cash flow including the investment. We set the NPV cell to value 0 by changing the interest rate cell. The answer is 38.77059 percent.

initial sales cell to 120 and the sales growth rate to 4 percent, the annual net profit rose to $182.

COMPUTING A BREAK-EVEN POINT USING GOAL SEEKING

Some modeling software packages can directly compute break-even points, an important application of goal seeking. This involves determining the value of the decision variables (e.g., quantity to produce) that generate zero profit. For example, in a financial planning model in Excel, the internal rate of return is the interest rate that produces a net present value of zero.

In many decision support systems, it can be difficult to conduct sensitivity analysis because the prewritten routines usually present only a limited opportunity for asking what-if questions. In a DSS, the what-if and the goal-seeking options must be easy to perform.

The goal to be achieved is NPV equal to zero, which determines the internal rate of return (IRR) of this cash flow including the investment. We set the NPV cell to value 0 by changing the interest rate cell. The answer is 38.77059 percent.

4.11 PROBLEM-SOLVING SEARCH METHODS

SEARCH APPROACHES

When problem-solving, the choice phase involves a search for an appropriate course of action (among those identified during the design phase) that can solve the problem. There are several major search approaches, depending on the criteria (or criterion) of choice and the type of modeling approach used. These search approaches are shown in Figure 4.11. For normative models, such as mathematical programming-based ones, either an analytical approach is used or a complete, exhaustive enumeration (comparing the outcomes of all the alternatives) is applied. For descriptive models, a comparison of a limited number of alternatives is used, either blindly or by employing heuristics. Usually the results guide the decision-maker's search.

ANALYTICAL TECHNIQUES

Analytical techniques use mathematical formulas to derive an optimal solution directly or to predict a certain result. Analytical techniques are used mainly for solving structured problems, usually of a tactical or operational nature, in areas such as resource allocation or inventory management. Blind or heuristic search approaches are generally employed to solve more complex problems.

ALGORITHMS

Analytical techniques may use algorithms to increase the efficiency of the search. An algorithm is a step-by-step search process (Figure 4.12) for obtaining an optimal solution. (Note: there may be more than one optimum, so we say *an* optimal solution rather than *the* optimal solution.) Solutions are generated and tested for possible improvements. An improvement is made whenever possible, and the new solution is subjected to an improvement test based on the principle of choice (objective value found). The process continues until no further improvement is possible. Most mathematical programming problems are solved by efficient algorithms (see Armstrong, 2001). Web search engines use algorithms to speed up the search and produce accurate results. Monika Henzinger developed the algorithms that Google uses in its searches. Google's algorithms are so good that Yahoo pays $7 million annually to use them (see Patton, 2002/2003).

BLIND SEARCH

In conducting a search, a description of a desired solution may be given. This is called a goal. A set of possible steps leading from initial conditions to the goal is called the search steps. Problem-solving is done by searching through the space of possible solutions. The first of these search methods is blind search. The second is heuristic search, discussed in the next section.

Blind search techniques are arbitrary search approaches that are not guided. There are two types of blind searches: a *complete enumeration*, for which all the alternatives are considered and therefore an optimal solution is discovered; and an *incomplete*, partial search, which continues until a good-enough solution is found. The latter is a form of suboptimization.

There are practical limits on the amount of time and computer storage available for blind searches. In principle, blind search methods can eventually find an optional

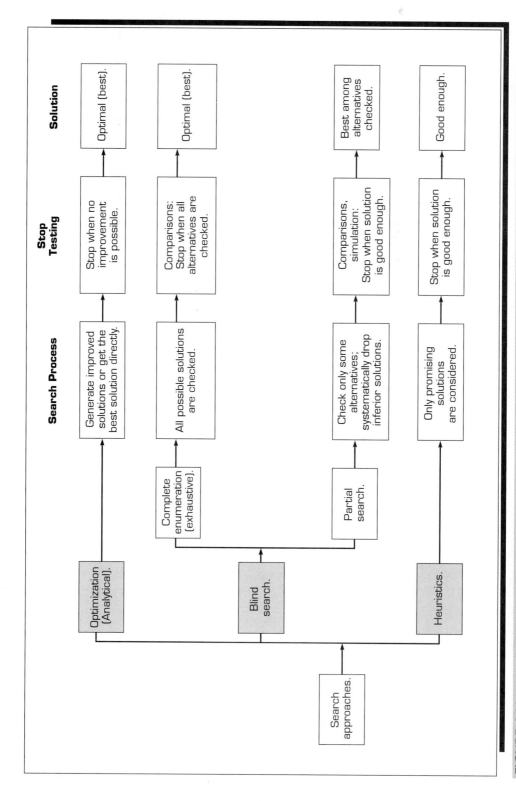

Search Process

Stop Testing

Solution

Optimization (Analytical).

→ Generate improved solutions or get the best solution directly. → Stop when no improvement is possible. → Optimal (best).

Blind search.

→ Complete enumeration (exhaustive). → All possible solutions are checked. → Comparisons: Stop when all alternatives are checked. → Optimal (best).

Heuristics.

→ Partial search. → Check only some alternatives; systematically drop inferior solutions. → Comparisons, simulation: Stop when solution is good enough. → Best among alternatives checked.

→ Only promising solutions are considered. → Stop when solution is good enough. → Good enough.

Search approaches.

FIGURE 4.11 FORMAL SEARCH APPROACHES

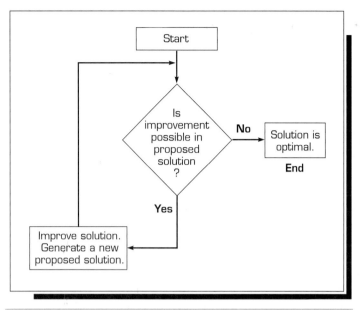

FIGURE 4.12   THE PROCESS OF USING AN ALGORITHM

solution in most search situations, and in some situations the scope of the search can be limited; however, the method is not practical for solving very large problems because too many solutions must be examined before an optimal solution is found.

HEURISTIC SEARCH

For many applications, it is possible to find rules to guide the search process and reduce the amount of necessary computations. This is done by heuristic search methods, which we describe next.

4.12 HEURISTIC PROGRAMMING

The determination of **optimal solutions** to some complex decision problems could involve a prohibitive amount of time and cost or may even be impossible. Alternatively, the simulation approach (Section 4.13) may be lengthy, complex, inappropriate, and even inaccurate. Under these conditions it is sometimes possible to obtain satisfactory solutions more quickly and less expensively by using **heuristics.**

Heuristics (from the Greek word for *discovery*) are decision rules governing how a problem should be solved. Usually, heuristics are developed on the basis of a solid, rigorous analysis of the problem, sometimes involving carefully designed experimentation. In contrast, guidelines are usually developed as a result of a trial-and-error experience. Some heuristics are derived from guidelines. *Heuristic searches* (or *programming*) are step-by-step procedures (like algorithms) that are repeated until a satisfactory solution is found (unlike algorithms). In practice, such a search is much faster and cheaper than a blind search, and the solutions can be very close to the best ones. In fact, problems that theoretically can be solved to optimality (but with a very long solution time) are in practice sometimes solved by heuristics, which can guarantee

TABLE 4.6 Examples of Heuristics	
Sequence jobs through a machine	Do the jobs that require the least time first.
Purchase stocks	If a price-to-earnings ratio exceeds 10, do not buy the stock.
Travel	Do not use the freeway between 8 and 9 a.m.
Capital investment in high-tech projects	Consider only projects with estimated payback periods of less than 2 years.
Purchase of a house	Buy only in a good neighborhood, but buy only in the lower price range.

a solution within a few percent of the optimal objective value. For details and advances, see Glover and Kochenberger (2001). Examples of heuristics are given in Table 4.6.

Decision-makers use heuristics or rules of thumb for many reasons, some more reasonable than others. For example, decision-makers may use a heuristic if they do not know the best way to solve a problem or if optimization techniques have not yet been developed. A decision-maker might not be able to obtain all the information necessary, or the cost of obtaining the information or developing a complex model may be too high. This was done in the Cameron and Barkley Company's Web-based DSS for reducing inventories and improving overall service performance, described in DSS in Action 3.2; see Cohen, Kelly, and Medagli (2001).

The heuristic process can be described as developing rules to help solve complex problems (or intermediate subproblems to discover how to set up subproblems for final solution by finding the most promising paths in the search for solutions), finding ways to retrieve and interpret information on the fly, and then developing methods that lead to a computational algorithm or general solution.

Although heuristics are employed primarily for solving ill-structured problems, they can also be used to provide satisfactory solutions to certain complex, well-structured problems much more quickly and cheaply than optimization algorithms (e.g., large-scale combinatorial problems with many potential solutions to explore) (Sun et al., 1998). The main difficulty in using heuristics is that they are not as general as algorithms. Therefore, they can normally be used only for the specific situation for which they were intended. Another problem with heuristics is that they may produce a poor solution. Heuristics are often stated like algorithms. They can be step-by-step procedures for solving a problem, but there is no guarantee that an optimal solution will be found.

> It is critical to realize that heuristics provide time-pressured managers and other professionals with a simple way of dealing with a complex world, producing correct or partially correct judgments more often than not. In addition, it may be inevitable that humans will adopt some way of simplifying decisions. The only drawback is that individuals frequently adopt . . . heuristics without being aware of them. (Bazerman, 2001)

Heuristic programming is the approach of using heuristics to arrive at feasible and "good enough" solutions to some complex problems. Good enough is usually in the range of 90–99.9 percent of the objective value of an optimal solution. Heuristics can be quantitative, and so can play a major role in the DSS model base, where heuristics were used to solve a complex integer programming problem. They can also be qualitative, and then can play a major role in providing knowledge to expert systems.

METHODOLOGY

Heuristic thinking does not necessarily proceed in a direct manner. It involves searching, learning, evaluating, judging, and then re-searching, relearning, and reappraising as exploring and probing take place. The knowledge gained from success or failure at some point is fed back to and modifies the search process. It is usually necessary either to redefine the objectives or the problem or to solve related or simplified problems before the primary one can be solved.

Tabu search heuristics (Glover and Kochenberger, 2001) are based on intelligent search strategies to reduce the search for high-quality solutions in computer problem-solving. Essentially, the method "remembers" what high-quality and low-quality solutions it has found and tries to move toward other high-quality solutions and away from the low-quality ones. The tabu search methodology has proved successful in efficiently solving many large-scale combinatorial problems (e.g., the fixed-charge transportation problem; see Sun et al., 1998). Tabu search heuristics were part of Bourjolly et al.'s (2001) method for allocating cell telephone frequencies in Canada.

Genetic algorithms (Reeves and Rowe, 2002; Sarker et al., 2002) start with a set of randomly generated solutions and recombine pairs of them at random to produce offspring (modeled on the evolution process). Only the best offspring and parents are kept to produce the next generation. Random mutations may also be introduced. Some new applications are described by Ursem, Filipic and Krink (2002) for greenhouse control, and by Borgulya (2002) for machine scheduling. Genetic algorithms are described in depth in a later chapter.

WHEN TO USE HEURISTICS

Heuristic application is appropriate in the following situations:

- The input data are inexact or limited.
- Reality is so complex that optimization models cannot be used.
- A reliable exact algorithm is not available.
- Complex problems are not economical for optimization or simulation or consume excessive computation time.
- It is possible to improve the efficiency of the optimization process (e.g., by producing good starting solutions).
- Symbolic rather than numerical processing is involved (as in expert systems).
- Quick decisions must be made and computerization is not feasible (some heuristics do not require computers).

ADVANTAGES AND LIMITATIONS OF HEURISTICS

The major advantages of heuristics are the following:

- They are simple to understand and therefore easier to implement and explain.
- They help train people to be creative and develop heuristics for other problems.
- They save formulation time.
- They save computer programming and storage requirements.
- They save computational time and thus real time in decision-making. Some problems are so complex that they can be solved only with heuristics.
- They often produce multiple acceptable solutions.
- Usually it is possible to state a theoretical or empirical measure of the solution quality (e.g., how close the solution's objective value is to an optimal one, even though the optimal value is unknown).

- They can incorporate intelligence to guide the search (e.g., tabu search). Such expertise may be problem specific or based on an expert's opinions embedded in an expert system or search mechanism.
- It is possible to apply efficient heuristics to models that could be solved with mathematical programming. Sometimes heuristics are the preferred method, and other times heuristic solutions are used as initial solutions for mathematical programming methods.

The primary limitations of heuristics are the following:

- An optimal solution cannot be guaranteed. Sometimes the bound on the objective value is very bad.
- There may be too many exceptions to the rules.
- Sequential decision choices may fail to anticipate the future consequences of each choice.
- The interdependencies of one part of a system can sometimes have a profound influence on the whole system.

Heuristic algorithms that function like algorithms but without a guarantee of optimality can be classified as follows (Camm and Evans, 2000):

- *Construction heuristics.* These methods build a feasible solution by adding components one at a time until a feasible solution is obtained. For example, in a traveling salesperson problem, always visit the next unvisited city that is closest.
- *Improvement heuristics.* These methods start with a feasible solution and attempt to successively improve on it. For example, in a traveling salesperson solution, attempt to swap two cities.
- *Mathematical programming.* This method is applied to less constrained (relaxed) models in the hope of obtaining information about an optimum to the original one. This technique is often used in integer optimization.
- *Decomposition.* This approach involves solving a problem in stages. In the P&G Web Chapter, the distribution problem was solved and then used in solving the product-strategy problem.
- *Partitioning.* This method involves dividing a problem up into smaller, solvable pieces and then reassembling the solutions to the pieces. This technique can be applied to large traveling salesperson problems. The country can be divided into four regions, each problem solved, and then the solutions connected together.

Vehicle routing has benefited from the development and use of efficient heuristics (e.g., Applegate et al., 2002; Belenguer, Martinez, and Mota, 2000; Foulds and Thachenkary, 2001; LaPorte et al., 2002; Liu and Shen, 1999; Gendreau et al., 1999), as has university course, classroom, and faculty scheduling (see Foulds and Johnson, 2000). Karaboga and Pham (1999) and Glover and Kochenberger (2001) discuss modern heuristic methods (tabu search, genetic algorithms, and simulated annealing). Also see Nance and Sargent (2002).

4.13 SIMULATION

To simulate means to assume the appearance of the characteristics of reality. In MSS, **simulation** is a *technique for conducting experiments (e.g., what-if analyses) with a computer on a model of a management system.*

Typically there is some randomness in the real decision-making situation. Because DSS deals with semistructured or unstructured situations, reality is complex, which may not be easily represented by optimization or other models but can often be handled by simulation. Simulation is one of the most commonly used DSS methods.

MAJOR CHARACTERISTICS OF SIMULATION

Simulation is not strictly a type of model; models generally *represent* reality, whereas simulation typically imitates it. In a practical sense, there are fewer simplifications of reality in simulation models than in other models. In addition, simulation is a technique for *conducting experiments*. Therefore, it involves testing specific values of the decision or uncontrollable variables in the model and observing the impact on the output variables. In the Opening Vignette, the DuPont decision-makers had initially chosen to purchase more rail cars, whereas an alternative involving better scheduling of the existing cars was developed, tested, found to have excess capacity, and saved money.

Simulation is a *descriptive* rather than a normative method. There is no automatic search for an optimal solution. Instead, a simulation model describes or predicts the characteristics of a given system under different conditions. Once the values of the characteristics are computed, the best of several alternatives can be selected. The simulation process usually repeats an experiment many, many times to obtain an estimate (and a variance) of the overall effect of certain actions. For most situations, a computer simulation is appropriate, but there are some well-known manual simulations (e.g., a city police department simulated its patrol car scheduling with a carnival game wheel).

Finally, simulation is normally used only when a problem is too complex to be treated by numerical optimization techniques. **Complexity** here means either that the problem cannot be formulated for optimization (e.g., because the assumptions do not hold), the formulation is too large, there are too many interactions among the variables, or the problem is stochastic in nature (exhibits risk or uncertainty). Designing and testing a new model of an automobile is extremely complex. That is one reason why General Motors utilizes simulation throughout the entire design process (see Gallagher, 2002; Gareiss, 2002; Witzerman, 2001). The success of General Motors may have prompted Daimler-Chrysler to move in this direction. By 2005, its Digital Factory, which utilizes simulation and visualization tools, will have helped to design, build, and retrofit all of its plants (see Hoffman, 2002).

ADVANTAGES OF SIMULATION

Simulation is used in MSS for the following reasons:

- The theory is fairly straightforward.
- A great amount of *time compression* can be attained, quickly giving the manager some feel as to the long-term (1- to 10-year) effects of many policies.
- Simulation is descriptive rather than normative. This allows the manager to pose what-if questions. Managers can use a trial-and-error approach to problem-solving and can do so faster, cheaper, more accurately, and with less risk (see the opening vignette).
- The manager can experiment to determine which decision variables and which parts of the environment are really important, and with different alternatives.
- An accurate simulation model requires an intimate knowledge of the problem, thus forcing the MSS builder to constantly interact with the manager. This is desirable for DSS development because the developer and manager both gain a

better understanding of the problem and the potential decisions available (Eldabi et al., 1999) (see the opening vignette).

- The model is built from the manager's perspective.
- The simulation model is built for one particular problem and typically cannot solve any other problem. Thus, no generalized understanding is required of the manager; every component in the model corresponds to part of the real system.
- Simulation can handle an extremely wide variety of problem types, such as inventory and staffing, as well as higher-level managerial functions, such as long-range planning.
- Simulation generally can include the real complexities of problems; simplifications are not necessary. For example, simulation can use real probability distributions rather than approximate theoretical distributions.
- Simulation automatically produces many important performance measures.
- Simulation is often the only DSS modeling method that can readily handle relatively unstructured problems.
- There are some relatively easy-to-use (Monte Carlo) simulation packages. These include add-in spreadsheet packages (@Risk), the influence diagram software mentioned earlier, Java-based (and other Web development) packages, and the visual interactive simulation systems to be discussed shortly.

DISADVANTAGES OF SIMULATION

The primary disadvantages of simulation are the following:

- An optimal solution cannot be guaranteed, but relatively good ones are generally found.
- Simulation model construction can be a slow and costly process, although newer modeling systems are easier to use than ever.
- Solutions and inferences from a simulation study are usually not transferable to other problems because the model incorporates unique problem factors.
- Simulation is sometimes so easy to explain to managers that analytic methods are often overlooked.
- Simulation software sometimes requires special skills because of the complexity of the formal solution method.

THE METHODOLOGY OF SIMULATION

Simulation involves setting up a model of a real system and conducting repetitive experiments on it. The methodology consists of the steps shown in Figure 4.13.

PROBLEM DEFINITION
The real-world problem is examined and classified. Here we specify why a simulation approach is appropriate. The system's boundaries, environment, and other such aspects of problem clarification are handled here.

CONSTRUCTION OF THE SIMULATION MODEL
This step involves determination of the variables and their relationships, and data gathering. Often the process is described by a flowchart, and then a computer program is written.

TESTING AND VALIDATING THE MODEL
The simulation model must properly represent the system under study. Testing and validation ensure this.

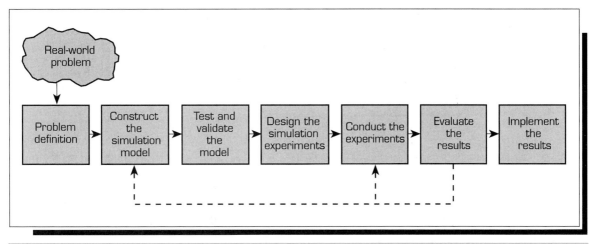

FIGURE 4.13   THE PROCESS OF SIMULATION

DESIGN OF THE EXPERIMENT

Once the model has been proven valid, an experiment is designed. Determining how long to run the simulation is part of this step. There are two important and conflicting objectives: accuracy and cost. It is also prudent to identify typical (mean and median cases for random variables), best-case (e.g., low-cost, high-revenue), and worst-case (e.g., high-cost, low-revenue) scenarios. These help establish the ranges of the decision variables and environment in which to work and also assist in debugging the simulation model.

CONDUCTING THE EXPERIMENT

Conducting the experiment involves issues ranging from random-number generation to result presentation.

EVALUATING THE RESULTS

The results must be interpreted. In addition to standard statistical tools, sensitivity analyses can also be used.

IMPLEMENTATION

The implementation of simulation results involves the same issues as any other implementation. However, the chances of success are better because the manager is usually more involved in the simulation process than with other models. Higher levels of managerial involvement generally lead to higher levels of implementation success.

Many simulation packages are Web ready. They typically are developed along the lines of the DSS architecture shown in Figure 3.1, where a user connects to the main server through a Web browser. This server connects to optimization servers, database servers, and they in turn may connect to data warehouses, which populate the models. For example, see Pooley and Wilcox (2000) for a description of a Java-based simulation system. Also see major vendors' Web sites.

TYPES OF SIMULATION

PROBABILISTIC SIMULATION

In probabilistic simulation, one or more of the independent variables (e.g., the demand in an inventory problem) are probabilistic. They follow certain probability distributions, which can be either discrete distributions or continuous distributions.

TABLE 4.7   Discrete Versus Continuous Probability Distributions

Daily Demand	Discrete Probability	Continuous Probability
5	.10	Daily demand is normally
6	.15	distributed with a
7	.30	mean of 7 and a
8	.25	standard deviation
9	.20	of 1.2.

- *Discrete distributions* involve a situation with a limited number of events (or variables) that can take on only a finite number of values.
- *Continuous distributions* are situations with unlimited numbers of possible events that follow density functions, such as the normal distribution.

The two types of distributions are shown in Table 4.7. Probabilistic simulation is conducted with the aid of a technique called Monte Carlo, which was used in the opening vignette situation.

TIME-DEPENDENT VERSUS TIME-INDEPENDENT SIMULATION

Time-independent refers to a situation in which it is not important to know exactly when the event occurred. For example, we may know that the demand for a certain product is three units per day, but we do not care *when* during the day the item is demanded. In some situations, time may not be a factor in the simulation at all, such as in steady-state plant control design (Boswell, 1999). On the other hand, in waiting-line problems applicable to e-commerce, it is important to know the precise time of arrival (to know whether the customer will have to wait). This is a *time-dependent* situation.

SIMULATION SOFTWARE

There are hundreds of simulation packages for a variety of decision-making situations. Most run as Web-based systems (see Dembo et al., 2000). PC software packages include Analytica (Lumina Decision Systems, lumina.com), and the Excel add-ins Crystal Ball (Decisioneering, decisioneering.com) and @Risk (Palisade Software, palisade.com). Web-based systems include WebGPSS (GPSS, webgpss.hk-r.se), SIMUL8 (SIMUL8 Corporation, SIMUL8.com), and Silk (ThreadTec, Inc., threadtec.com).

VISUAL SIMULATION

The graphical display of computerized results, which may include animation, is one of the more successful developments in computer–human interaction and problem-solving. We describe this in the next section.

OBJECT-ORIENTED SIMULATION

There have been some advances in the area of developing simulation models using the object-oriented approach (e.g., Yun and Choi, 1999). Yun and Choi (1999) describe an object-oriented simulation model for container-terminal operation analysis. Each piece of equipment at the terminal maps into an object representation in the simulation model. SIMPROCESS (CACI Products Company, caciasl.com) is an object-oriented process modeling tool that lets the user create a simulation model with screen-based objects. Unified modeling language (UML) is a modeling tool that was designed for object-oriented and object-based systems and applications. Since UML is object-oriented, it could be used in practice for modeling complex, real-time systems. UML is particularly well suited for modeling. A real-time system is a software system that maintains an ongoing, timely interaction with its environment; examples include many DSS and information and communication systems (Selic, 1999).

SIMULATION EXAMPLE

We show an example of a spreadsheet-based economic order quantity simulation model and a spreadsheet simulation model for evaluating a simple cash-flow problem in a Web Chapter. DSS in Action 4.7 describes a case study of applying simulation to IT network design. CACI Products Company now provides COMNET III, a simulation system specifically for analyzing these types of IT network design problems. Saltzman and Mehrotra (2001) used a simulation approach to analyze a call center. Jovanovic (2002) determines how to schedule tasks in distributed systems via simulation. This is important when managing grid computer networks. Dronzek (2001) used simulation to improve critical care in a military hospital.

He analyzed proposed changes in a health care system using simulation modeling to determine the impact of potential changes without disrupting the established process of care or disturbing staff, patients, or the facility. Credit Suisse First Boston uses an ASP simulation system to predict the risk and reward potential of investments (see Dembo et al., 2000). General Motors (see Gallager, 2002; Gareiss, 2002; Witzerman, 2001) delays constructing physical models of automobiles until late in the design process, since simulation is cheaper and produces more accurate results in testing new products. This includes crash tests and wind tunnel tests. Witzerman (2001) describes how GM's paint shop robots are simulated for improved performance. These tools are very effective and have led to major improvements. It now takes only 18 months to develop a new vehicle, down from 48 months. Engineering productivity is way up, as is quality. Also see Marchant (2002).

4.14 VISUAL INTERACTIVE MODELING AND VISUAL INTERACTIVE SIMULATION

CONVENTIONAL SIMULATION

Simulation is a well-established, useful method for gaining insight into complex MSS situations. However, simulation does not usually allow decision-makers to see how a solution to a complex problem evolves over (compressed) time, nor can they interact with it. Simulation generally reports statistical results at the end of a set of experiments. Decision-makers are thus not an integral part of simulation development and experimentation, and their experience and judgment cannot be used directly in the study. If the simulation results do not match the intuition or judgment of the decision-maker, a *confidence gap* in the use of the model occurs.

One of the most exciting developments in computer graphics is **visual interactive modeling (VIM)** (see DSS in Action 4.8). The technique has been used with great success for DSS in the area of operations management. Decision-makers who used VIM in

PACIFIC BELL USES SIMULATION TO DESIGN AN IT NETWORK

Decision support simulation software for networks and networked applications can be used to experiment with multiple what-if scenarios. Then IT can determine a best solution before making blind commitments or sinking resources into large projects without a thorough understanding of the expected outcome. Simulations help IT determine how the infrastructure would react to a given scenario, such as increased network traffic, new transport technologies, topology changes, and new prioritized applications like ERP and voice-over Internet protocol (IP). The value of a decision-support tool is its ability to deliver reliable, timely, and verifiable data about result variables, leading to confident, resource-saving decisions—critical during initial IT system design and implementation, when trade-offs can be weighed and cost considerations examined before committing heavily to a project.

Pacific Bell, a subsidiary of SBC Communications, Inc. (SBC), collaborated with a large government agency in southern California to design a network to support more than 80,000 employees at hundreds of sites. Throughout the southern California project, SBC and the government utilized IT DecisionGuru, a modeling and simulation tool from MIL 3 Inc. (Washington, D.C.).

The challenge for the SBC/government team was to design a network backbone to link thousands of nodes at every site into a network capable of supporting data, video, and voice and to support future growth. The design team first built a baseline model of projected "typical" network activity. Then it used its simulation software to explore the relative performance gains offered by various architecture options. This process enabled the design team to visualize all relevant network performance indicators.

After running several simulations, it was determined that a network consisting of only ATM OC-3 links would have very low utilization. While perfectly acceptable from a performance perspective, it would be very expensive. But a network with only T1 links performs poorly at a lower cost. The best solution combined the cost efficiency of T1 lines with the bandwidth of ATM links, as the simulation indicated. This middle-of-the-road strategy saved a lot of money and avoided potentially costly impacts from poor performance.

The most critical issue was the sizing of the dedicated wide area network (WAN) links. There was a trade-off between overprovisioned service, for which excess capacity would cost hundreds of thousands of dollars unnecessarily, and underprovisioning, which could cause unacceptably poor network performance. By simulating the key decision elements, the SBC/government team designed an efficient architecture to handle anticipated bandwidth needs at an acceptable cost. Without sacrificing service levels, the government reduced its expected WAN costs by more than 25 percent, translating into millions of dollars saved per year.

SBC also benefited in much the same way that any internal IT organization can benefit from simulation. It built credibility with business decision-makers by providing quantifiable data to support its recommendations, making government decision-makers much more comfortable that SBC could deliver the service levels it promised.

Source: Based on S. Toborg and M. Cohen, "Benefits and Savings Accrue with Simulation," *Communications News,* Vol. 36, No. 9, Sept. 1999, pp. 34–36.

their decision-making were surveyed and found to have a high level of support for and interest in these models (Bell et al., 1999). This technique has several names and variations, including *visual interactive problem-solving*, *visual interactive modeling*, and *visual interactive simulation*.

Visual interactive modeling uses computer graphic displays to present the impact of different managerial decisions. It differs from regular graphics in that the user can adjust the decision-making process and see the results of the intervention. A visual model is a graphic used as an integral part of decision-making or problem-solving, not just as a communication device. The VIM displays the effect of different decisions in graphic form on a computer screen, as was done through the GIS in the P&G supply chain redesign through optimization (Web Chapter). Some people respond better to graphical displays, and this

DSS IN ACTION 4.8

VISUAL INTERACTIVE SIMULATION: U.S. ARMY HOSPITAL USES ANIMATED SIMULATION OF A FAMILY PRACTICE CLINIC

The U.S. Army Hospital in Heidelberg, Germany, used animated simulation to develop viable alternatives for their family practice clinic. The clinic was attempting to examine different staffing alternatives, determine the best patient and staff flow scheme, and increase productivity to provide sufficient capacity. An animated simulation model was developed. The current environment, as represented by the status quo model, could not provide the needed capacity of outpatient visits. Alternative models were developed, two of which were good possibilities. The two alternative models, an all-physician model (the "physician model") and a combination model with both physicians and nonphysician providers (the "combo model"), were run and compared, and neither could handle the patient load. A process change in parallel patient screening was developed to increase patient throughput and to increase capacity. Then both models could meet clinic capacity requirements, both in the newly planned clinic and in the current one. Based on the simulation, the physician and combo models were selected for the health care operation in a phased-in plan from the former to the latter.

The simulation gave the decision-makers insight into provider and support staff use rates, down time, and

small but significant process improvements. The all-physician model was recommended as a short-term arrangement after considering cost, supervisory issues, and provider availability. Changes at the clinic were to take place in the near future, and phasing in the non-physician providers would take some time.

Although the physician model was selected as a short-term arrangement to meet the needs of the community and health care system, the simulation model showed that much more work and evaluation of patient wait times had to be conducted to decrease the wait for customers. Management had determined the number of physicians and staff members needed to meet patient capacity needs, the necessary size of the waiting area, the necessary provider scheduling changes, and the process changes necessary to meet the capacity requirement, patient expectations, and organizational goals via simulation. The move to the renovated area was successful and had the additional results of impaneling the beneficiaries in the community. A migration plan was adopted based on further simulation runs.

Source: Adapted from Ledlow et al. (1999).

---

type of interaction can help managers learn about the decision-making situation. For example, Swisher et al. (2001) applied an object-oriented visual simulation to examining the functioning of a physician clinic environment within a physician network to provide high-quality, cost-effective healthcare in a family practice. The simulation system identified the most important input factors that significantly affected performance. These inputs, when properly managed, led to lower costs and higher service levels.

VIM can represent a static or a dynamic system. Static models display a visual image of the result of one decision alternative at a time. Dynamic models display systems that evolve over time, and the evolution is represented by animation. A snapshot example of a generated animated display of traffic at an intersection, from the Orca Visual Simulation Environment (Orca Computer Inc., Blacksburg, Virginia, orcacomputer.com), is shown in Figure 4.14. The Orca Web site shows several animations that were generated by its simulation system.

VISUAL INTERACTIVE SIMULATION

Visual simulation is one of the most exciting dynamic VIMs. It is a very important DSS technique because simulation is a major approach in problem-solving. **Visual interactive simulation (VIS)** allows the end user to watch the progress of the simulation model in an animated form on graphics displays.

FIGURE 4.14 EXAMPLE OF A GENERATED IMAGE OF TRAFFIC AT AN INTERSECTION FROM THE ORCA VISUAL SIMULATION ENVIRONMENT

Courtesy of Orca Computer, Inc., Blacksburg, VA

The basic philosophy of VIS is that decision-makers can interact with the simulated model and watch the results develop over time (see the Web demos at Orca Computer Inc., orcacomputer.com). The user can try different decision strategies online. Enhanced learning, both about the problem and about the impact of the alternatives tested, can and does occur. Decision-makers can also contribute to model validation. They will have more confidence in its use because of their own participation in its development and use. They are also in a position to use their knowledge and experience to interact with the model to explore alternative strategies. Ledlow et al. (1999) describe how the U.S. Army Hospital in Heidelberg, Germany, used animated simulation to develop viable alternatives for its family practice clinic (see DSS in Action 4.8).

Animated VIS software systems are provided by Orca Computer, Inc., GPSS/PC (Minuteman Software), and VisSim (Visual Solutions). The latest visual simulation technology is coupled with the concept of virtual reality, where an artificial world is created for a number of purposes, from training to entertainment to viewing data in an artificial landscape. For example, Harris Corp. has developed a visual interactive simulation system for the U.S. military. The system lets ground troops gain familiarity with terrain or a city so that they can very quickly orient themselves. It also is used by pilots to gain familiarity with targets by simulating attack runs. The software includes GIS coordinates. (CNN Television Report, Nov. 16, 2002.)

VISUAL INTERACTIVE MODELS AND DSS

VIM in DSS has been used in several operations management decisions. The method consists of priming a visual interactive model of a plant (or company) with its current status. The model then runs rapidly on a computer, allowing management to observe how a plant is likely to operate in the future.

Waiting-line management (queuing) is a good example of VIM. Such a DSS usually computes several measures of performance (e.g., waiting time in the system) for the various decision alternatives. Complex waiting-line problems require simulation. VIM can display the size of the waiting line as it changes during the simulation runs and can also graphically present the answers to what-if questions regarding changes in input variables.

The VIM approach can also be used in conjunction with artificial intelligence. Integration of the two techniques adds several capabilities that range from the ability to build systems graphically to learning about the dynamics of the system. High-speed parallel computers such as those made by Silicon Graphics Inc. and Hewlett-Packard make large-scale, complex, animated simulations feasible in real time (the movie *Toy Story* and its sequel were essentially long VIMs). The *grid computing paradigm* may help in large-scale simulations.

General-purpose commercial dynamic VIM software is readily available. For information about simulation software, visual and otherwise, see The IMAGE Society Inc. Web site (public.asu.edu), the Society for Computer Simulation International Web site (scs.org), and the annual software surveys at the *OR/MS Today* Web site (lionhrtpub.com/orms/).

4.15 QUANTITATIVE SOFTWARE PACKAGES

Some DSS tools offer several built-in subroutines for constructing quantitative models in areas such as statistics, financial analysis, accounting, and management science. These models can be activated by a single command, such as

- *MOVAVG.* This function calculates a moving average estimated forecast of a time series of data. It might be embedded in a production planning model to generate demand.
- *NPV.* This function calculates the net present value of a series of future cash flows for a given interest rate. It could be part of a make-versus-buy model.

OLAP systems are essentially a collection of optimization, simulation, statistical, and artificial intelligence packages that access large amounts of data for analysis. (For example, Oracle Financials Suite provides business intelligence and risk management applications; see Ferguson, 2002.) In addition, many DSS tools can easily interface with powerful standard quantitative stand-alone software packages. A DSS builder can increase his or her productivity by using **quantitative software packages** (preprogrammed models sometimes called "ready-made") rather than "reinventing the wheel." Some of these models are building blocks of other quantitative models. For example, a regression model can be part of a forecasting model that supports a linear programming planning model (as in the P&G Web Chapter and IMERYS Case Application 4.1). Thus, a complicated model can easily be integrated with many sets of data. The Lingo modeling language described earlier for optimization problems can be designed with a SET definition section and a DATA section. The sets and data can be fed from a database, while the actual Lingo model lines do not explicitly state any dimension or data aspects. While spreadsheets have the same capability, data must be carefully inserted. For a comprehensive resource directory of these types of systems, see the *OR/MS Today* Web site (lionhrtpub.com/orms/). Since the Web has promoted the widespread use of modeling, optimization, simulation, and related techniques, we list a sampling of Web impacts on these areas, and vice versa, in Table 4.8.

Data mining tools are utilized for customer segmentation analysis. These tools automate much of the tedious nature of using standard optimization packages by providing convenient and powerful ways to analyze sales. These customer analytic tools are available from Cognos, Inc. (cognos.com), DigiMine Inc. (digimine.com), Hyperion Solutions Corp. (hyperion.com), IBM (ibm.com), Informatica Corp. (informatica.com), Megaputer Intelligence, Inc. (megaputer.com), Oracle Corp. (oracle.com), and Teradata (teradata.com). (See Pallatto, 2003.)

These tools are improving in capability, portability, and usability almost daily. Similar to developments in enterprise resource planning systems for operational applications, new OLAP-type ADP (Analytical Development Platforms) plug-and-develop capabilities enable developers to build sophisticated applications with a unique look, feel, and functionality in a few days or weeks. Vendors include AlphaBlox, Proclarity, and Business Objects (see Callaghan, 2003). Object models are automatically created in graphical, configurable, Web-ready components. See Eckerson (2003) and Fourer and Goux (2001) for details. Finally, Hossein Arsham (2003a, 2003b) maintains an extensive bibliography on decision-making tools and decision sciences resources.

STATISTICAL PACKAGES

Several statistical functions are built into various DSS tools, such as mean, median, variance, standard deviation, kurtosis, t-test, chi-square, various types of regression (linear, polynomial, and stepwise) correlations, forecasting, and analysis of variance. Web-based statistics packages include STATLib (lib.stat.cmu.edu), StatPages.net (statpages.net), StatPoint Internet Statistical Computing Center (sgorp.com/on-line_computing.htm), and SticiGui (stat.Berkeley.edu/~stark/SticiGui/).

Regression analysis is a powerful statistical curve-fitting technique. An example of an SPSS run that quickly analyzed a set of data appears in a Web Chapter. The run was triggered with a single click of a button, the results were clearly delineated in the report, and the report was automatically formatted. These features can readily enhance a DSS developer's capabilities.

More power can be obtained from stand-alone statistical packages, some embedded in OLAP, which can readily interface with spreadsheets (Excel). Typical packages include SPSS and Systat (SPSS Inc., Chicago, Illinois, spss.com), Minitab (Minitab Inc., State College, Pennsylvania, minitab.com), SAS (SAS Institute Inc., Cary, North Carolina, sas.com), and TSP (TSP International, Palo Alto California, tspintl.com). StatPac Inc. (statpac.com, Minneapolis, Minnesota) includes survey analysis software in its StatPac package. Most spreadsheets also contain sophisticated statistical functions and routines.

Statistical software is now considered more a decision-making tool than a sophisticated analytical tool in the decision-making process. It is even embedded in Web-ready data mining and OLAP tools, and so the user is unaware that sophisticated statistical methods are being used. This subtle change in the user's focus has occurred because of the maturity of well-accepted technology and the low cost and high performance of computers. This has clearly led to a greater acceptance of statistical methodologies.

TABLE 4.8   Models and Web Impacts

Modeling Topic	Web Impacts	Impacts on the Web
Models	Application servers provide access to models and their solution methods in a consistent, friendly, graphical user interface Provides for a direct mechanism to query solutions Provides a channel to integrate models and models with data Provides a consistent communication channel New programming languages and systems Intranets and extranets influence the use of models in supply chain management, customer relationship management and revenue management Proliferation of model use throughout organizations-makes enterprise-wide systems like SCM and CRM feasible and practical Access to information about models Makes models usable for e-commerce settings	Describes the Internet/Web, intranet and extranet structures as networks Describes how to optimize Web performance-sites and message routing from site to site and bandwidth allocation Provides a means to analyze e-commerce (transactions and other processes can be analyzed) to determine effectiveness and efficiency Model base application servers Models to evaluate tradeoffs among service levels and types Forecasting models predict viability of hardware and software choices Forecasting models predict network performance and e-commerce activity Improved component and other hardware selection
Mathematical Programming (Optimization)	All of the above Access to models and solution methods implemented as Java applets and other Web development systems Use of models by untrained managers because they are so easy to use Access to Web-based AI tools to suggest models and solution methods in DSS Access to information about models	All of the above Improved infrastructure design and updates Traveling salesman model (vehicle routing) solutions improve dynamic message routing; also improved integrated circuit and circuit board design Internet communication readily enables grid computing
Heuristics	All of the above	All of the above Establish rules rather than optimize to determine how to structure networks and message routing
Simulation	All of the above Improved visualization and delivery of results Distributed processing	Simulation of difficult, probabilistic models lead to better performance Simulation of Web traffic Simulation of Web site activities for better e-commerce performance
Model Management Systems	Access to Web-based programming tools, AI methods, and application servers that perform model management New Web-based model management systems	AI-based methods for model management have improved Web performance by improving the effectiveness and efficiency of the network infrastructure

MANAGEMENT SCIENCE (ANALYTICAL MODELING) PACKAGES

There are several hundred management science packages on the market for models ranging from inventory control to project management. Several DSS generators include optimization and simulation capabilities. Lists of representative management science packages can be found in management science publications (e.g., *OR/MS Today* and *INFORMS OnLine*, www.informs.org). Lionheart Publishing Inc. (lionhrtpub.com/orms/) has software surveys on the *OR/MS* Web site on statistical analysis, linear programming (Fourer, 2001), simulation, decision analysis, forecasting, vehicle routing, and spreadsheet add-ins (Grossman, 2002). Newer releases have Java (or other Web server software) interfaces so they can be readily provided via Web servers and browsers. For example, Sunset Software Technology's (www.sunsetsoft. com) XA consists of Java-based linear, mixed integer, and other solvers. Related software incorporates management science and statistics methods directly into OLAP and data mining systems. Boguslavsky (2000) describes how visualization and analytical methods have been partly automated into the Web-based Spotfire.net. The system has been used to accelerate drug and gene discovery, among other things (see DSS in Action 2.18). Several Web-based systems have been designed for solving complex, multicriteria problems. These include Nimbus (see Miettinen and Makela, 2000). The ILOG software components (ilog.com/industries/ebusiness/) are available for mathematical programming, and many can be embedded in Web environments. OR-Objects (opsresearch.com/OR-Objects/) is a freeware collection of over 500 Java classes for operations research application development. More information about techniques and packages may be found at the INFORMS Web site (www.informs.org) and Michael Trick's Operations Research Page (mat.gsia.cmu.edu). The Optimization Software Guide (www.mcs.anl.gov/otc/Guide/SoftwareGuide/) and the Decision Tree for Optimization Software (plato.la.asu.edu/guide.html) are two major Web resources for optimization and optimization packages. Geoffrion and Krishnan (2001) describe several ASPs for optimization.

Fourer and Goux (2001) describe many Web-based packages and resources. For example, GIDEN (giden.iems.nwu.edu) is a Java applet that provides visual representations and solutions to network flow problems. TSPfast (home.wxs.nl/~onno .waalewijn/tspfast.html) and TSPx (home.wxs.nl/~onno.waalewijn/tspx.html) are Java applets that solve traveling salesperson problems. In the area of Web-based servers, the NEOS Server for Optimization (www-neos.mcs.anl.gov/neos/) is one of the most ambitious efforts. Over two dozen solvers are there (see Figure 3.1 for how this fits into a Web-based optimization package).

Win QSB (Chang, 2000) is an example of a fairly comprehensive and robust academic management science package. Lindo and Lingo (Lindo Systems Inc.), IBM's Optimization System Library (OSL), and CPLEX (CPLEX Optimization Inc.) are commercial ones. Simulation packages include GPSS (and GPSS/PC), ProModel (ProModel Corporation), SLAM (Pritsker Corporation), and SIMULA and SIMSCRIPT (CACI Products Company). Many academic packages are available directly from their authors and via the Web (see the Society for Computer Simulation International Web site, scs.org; and Pooley and Wilcox, 2000).

REVENUE MANAGEMENT

An exciting application area for DSS modeling and tools (typically Web-based) has developed along with the service industries. Revenue management (yield management) involves models that attempt to stratify an organization's customers, estimate demands, establish prices for each category of customer, and dynamically model all.

Until a flight takes off, an airline seat is available, but once the flight leaves, the seat cannot be inventoried. Through revenue management methods, an airline might have several hundred different fares for its coach seats on a single flight. Revenue management involves creating detailed economic models and forecasts for each product. It is important to determine an appropriate price at an appropriate time for an appropriate class of customers. In essence, the crucial part of revenue management involves selling the right product in the right format to the right customer through the right channel at the right time at the right price. Another part involves knowing when to turn away a customer because a "better" (higher-paying) customer will appear with a significantly high enough probability. Many models are used in revenue management. For example, the Co-operative Desjardins Movement (Bank) in Quebec used cluster analysis (Goulet and Wishart, 1996) to classify all of its 4.2 million members to better serve them and provide appropriate products to appropriate customers. Consequently, they have been able to retain members' loyalty and capture more market share, generating more income. At the heart of revenue-management systems are forecasting models (discussed earlier), and dynamic pricing models based on economics (see Kephart, Hanson, and Greenwald, 2000).

The largest developer and user of revenue management methods was initially the airline industry (see Cross, 1997; Smith et al., 2001), but recent advances have expanded the field to a number of areas. The next "batch" of firms to adopt airline-related revenue management methods were in other travel-related industries, such as railroad, hotels, and rental car agencies, but revenue management eventually expanded to include broadcasting, retail manufacturing, and power generation (see Cross, 1997). And now other industries that distribute products through Internet channels have product-planning problems similar to those the airlines faced. They need models to track product visibility, adjust products to the channels, and estimate the impact on demand and revenue; that is, revenue management with dynamic pricing (see Geoffrion and Krishnan, 2001).

Tedechi (2002) describes how Saks uses price optimization, a form of revenue management, to determine the appropriate time to mark down items in the department store. Gross margins can be improved by some 10 percent. Sliwa (2003) describes the concept of *price optimization*—essentially revenue management. Mantrala and Rao (2001) describe a DSS that utilizes a complex model to determine order quantities and markdowns for fashion goods. This model is similar to those utilized in price optimization systems. Hicks (2000) and Hamey (2003) describe further how retailers are attempting to identify their best customers. Revenue management principles can even be applied to auctions, which are big business on the Web (see Baker and Murthy, 2002). For further details on revenue management, see Lahoti (2002) and Cross (1997). See e-optimization.com (2002), Boyd (1998), Kelly (1999), and Horner (2000) for discussions of revenue management in the airline industry. Baker and Collier (1999) describe an example in the hotel industry; Oberwetter (2001) explains how it is used in the movie industry. Web-based revenue-management systems have been applied in the cargo freight arena. OptiYield-RT (www.logistics.com) is a real-time Web-based yield-management system for truckload carriers. NeoYield (NeoModal.com) handles ocean carriers in an ASP framework (see Geoffrion and Krishnan, 2001). Home Depot uses integer programming models in an Internet-based combinatorial bidding application for contracting transportation costs (see Keskinocak and Tayur, 2001).

For more on revenue management, especially Web-based tools, see the Manugistics Group, Inc. (www.manugistics.com), PROS Revenue Management, Inc. (prosrm.com), Sabre Inc. (sabre.com), and Revenue Management Systems, Inc. (www.revenuemanagement.com) Web sites.

OTHER SPECIFIC DSS APPLICATIONS

The number of DSS application software products is continually increasing. A number of these are spreadsheet add-ins, such as What's Best! (linear programming, Lindo Systems Inc., Chicago, Illinois, lindo.com), Solver (linear programming, Frontline Systems Inc., Incline Village, Nevada, frontsys.com), @Risk (simulation, Palisade Corporation, Newfield, New York, palisade.com), BrainCel (neural network, Promised Land Technologies Inc., New Haven, Connecticut, promland.com), and Evolver (genetic algorithm, Palisade Corporation) (see Grossman, 2002). Sometimes it is necessary to modify the source code of the package to fit the decision-maker's needs. Some actually produce source code from the development language specifically for Web deployment. For example, many neural network packages can produce a deployable version of their internal user-developed models in the C programming language. Finally, there are some industry-specific packages. One example is the workforce management optimization software from ORTEC International, USA, Inc. (www.ortec.com). This software handles shift scheduling with real-time control. Results are displayed graphically.

4.16 MODEL BASE MANAGEMENT

In theory, a **model base management system (MBMS)** is a software package with capabilities similar to those of a DBMS. There are dozens of commercial DBMS packages, but unfortunately there are no comprehensive model base management packages on the market. However, there are commonalities between the two, and thus ideas from DBMS have been applied in model management (see Tsai, 2001). Limited MBMS capabilities are provided by some spreadsheets and other model-based DSS tools and languages. There are no standardized MBMS for a number of reasons:

- While there are standard model classes (like standard database structures: relational, hierarchical, network, object-oriented), there are far too many of them, and each is structured differently (e.g., linear programming vs. regression analysis).
- Given a problem, several different classes of models and techniques may apply. Sometimes trial and error is the only way to determine which work best.
- Each model class may have several approaches for solving problems in the class, depending on problem structure, size, shape, and data. For example, any linear programming problem can be solved by the simplex method, but there is also the interior point method. Method specializations can work better than the standard methods if they match the model.
- Every organization uses models somewhat differently.
- MBMS capabilities (e.g., selecting which model to use, how to solve it, and what parameter values to use) require expertise and reasoning capabilities, which can be made available in expert systems and other artificial intelligence approaches.

Eom (1999) indicates that model management research includes several topics, such as model base structure and representation, the structured modeling approach, model base processing, model integration, and application of artificial intelligence to model integration, construction, and interpretation. It is critical to develop notions of how to apply artificial intelligence to MBMS. Dolk (2000) discusses how model management and data warehouses can and should be integrated. Wu (200) describes a model management system for test construction DSS. And Huh (2000) describes how collaborative model management can be done.

An effective model base management system makes the structural and algorithmic aspects of model organization and associated data-processing transparent to users of the MBMS (e.g., the P&G Web Chapter; and IMERYS Case Application 4.1) (Orman, 1998). Web capabilities are a must for an effective MBMS. The MBMS should also handle model integration (model-to-model integration, like a forecasting model feeding a planning model; data-to-model integration; and vice versa).

Some desirable MBMS capabilities include the following:

- **Control.** The DSS user should be provided with a spectrum of control. The system should support both fully automated and manual model selection, depending on which seems most helpful for an intended application. The user should also be able to use subjective information.
- **Flexibility.** The DSS user should be able to develop part of the solution using one approach and then be able to switch to another modeling approach if desired.
- **Feedback.** The MBMS should provide sufficient feedback to enable the user to know the state of the problem-solving process at any time.
- **Interface.** The DSS user should feel comfortable with the specific model from the MBMS in use. The user should not have to laboriously supply inputs.
- **Redundancy reduction.** Sharing models and eliminating redundant storage, as in a data warehouse, can accomplish this.
- **Increased consistency.** This can occur when decision-makers share the same model and data (designed into the IMERYS DSS).

To provide these capabilities, it appears that an MBMS design must allow the DSS user to

- *Access and retrieve existing models*
- *Exercise and manipulate existing models,* including model instantiation, model selection, model synthesis, and the provision of suitable model outputs
- *Store existing models,* including model representation, model abstraction, and physical and logical model storage
- *Maintain existing models* as appropriate for changing conditions
- *Maintain standard cases* for models as appropriate for changing conditions
- *Construct new models* with reasonable effort when they are needed, usually by building new models using existing models as building blocks.

There are a number of additional requirements for these capabilities. For example, there must be appropriate communication and data changes among models that have been combined. In addition, there must be a standard method for analyzing and interpreting the results obtained from using a model. This can be accomplished in a number of ways (e.g., by OLAP or expert systems).

As a result of required e-commerce and Internet speeds, accurate models must be developed faster. Data must be ready to load them, and decisions based on solution results should be implemented quickly. We must use high-level modeling languages and tools in the modern business environment. Risk goes up because even the most successful models require major refining, and some are never accurate enough to deploy. *Model petrification* refers to an organization's loss of understanding of models after the development team leaves. As with any MIS, the understanding of models utilized in practice must be maintained to obtain the full benefits of them. Models, like any code, must be documented and responsibility passed on. See Smith, Gunther, and Ratliff (2001).

Model management is quickly moving to the Web in the ASP (application service provider) format. LogicTools (logic-tools.com), MultiSimplex (multisimplex.com) (watch the online demo), and the Web-based Model Management System—MMM (meta-mmm.wiwi.hu-berlin.de) are three examples. Dotti et al. (2000) describe a Web architecture for metaheuristics.

The MBMS does directly influence the capability of a DSS to support decision-maker. For example, in an experimental study, Chung (2000) determined that the adequacy of the modeling support provided by a MBMS influences the decision-maker's problem-solving performance and behavior. Decision-makers who receive adequate modeling support from MBMS outperformed those without such support. Also, the MBMS helped turn the decision-makers' perception of problem-solving from a number-crunching task into the development of solution strategies, consequently changing their decision-making behavior. This is important as OLAP and data mining tools attempt to improve decision-making (see the next chapter).

MODELING LANGUAGES

There are a number of specialized modeling languages that act as front ends to the software that actually performs optimization or simulation. They essentially front-end the working or algorithmic code and assist the manager in developing and managing models. Some popular mathematical programming modeling languages include Lingo, AMPL, and GAMS.

RELATIONAL MODEL BASE MANAGEMENT SYSTEM

As is the case with a relational view of data, in a **relational model base management system (RMBMS)** a model is viewed as a virtual file or virtual relation. Three operations are needed for relational completeness in model management: execution, optimization, and sensitivity analysis. Web interfaces are instrumental in model access. Web application servers provide smooth access to models, data to populate the models, and solution methods. Essentially, they perform model management. Typically, the architecture shown in Figure 3.1 is used in practice. A modern, effective DSS can be developed with Web components.

OBJECT-ORIENTED MODEL BASE
AND ITS MANAGEMENT

Using an object-oriented DBMS construct, it is possible to build an **object-oriented model base management system (OOMBS)** that maintains logical independence between the model base and the other DSS components, facilitating intelligent and stabilized integration of the components. Essentially, all the object-oriented concepts embedded in the GUI can apply to model management. As was described for a relational model management system, Web application servers are utilized similarly for object-oriented model base management systems. Du (2001) developed an object-oriented paradigm to develop an evolutionary vehicle routing system. He used a component assembly model.

MODELS FOR DATABASE AND MIS DESIGN AND THEIR MANAGEMENT

Models describing efficient database and MIS design are useful in that the deployed systems will function optimally. These models include data diagrams and entity-relationship diagrams, which are managed by computer-aided systems engineering (CASE). They graphically portray how data are organized and flow in a database design and work much like the situation described in the opening vignette. A model is developed to describe and evaluate an untried alternative. Then, when the decision is implemented, the real system behaves as if the decision-makers have had many years of experience in running the new system with the implemented alternative. Thus, the model building and evaluation are training tools for the DSS team members.

❖ CHAPTER HIGHLIGHTS

- Models play a major role in DSS. There are several types of models.
- Models can be either static (a single snapshot of a situation) or dynamic (multiperiod).
- Analysis is conducted under assumed certainty (most desirable), risk, or uncertainty (least desirable).
- Influence diagrams graphically show the interrelationships of a model. They can be used to enhance the presentation of spreadsheet technology.
- Influence diagram software can also generate and solve the model.
- Spreadsheets have many capabilities, including what-if analysis, goal seeking, programming, database management, optimization, and simulation.
- Decision tables and decision trees can model and solve simple decision-making problems.
- Mathematical programming is an important optimization method.
- Linear programming is the most common mathematical programming method. It attempts to find an optimal allocation of limited resources under organizational constraints.
- The major parts of a linear programming model are the objective function, the decision variables, and the constraints.
- Multiple criteria decision-making problems are difficult but not impossible to solve.
- The Analytic Hierarchy Process (e.g., Expert Choice software) is a leading method for solving multicriteria decision-making problems.
- What-if and goal seeking approaches are the two most common methods of sensitivity analysis.

- Heuristic programming involves problem-solving using general rules or intelligent search.
- Simulation is a widely used DSS approach involving experimentation with a model that represents the real decision-making situation.
- Simulation can deal with more complex situations than optimization, but it does not guarantee an optimal solution.
- Visual interactive simulation (VIS) allows a decision-maker to interact directly with the model.
- VIS can show simulation results in an easily understood manner.
- Visual interactive modeling (VIM) is an implementation of the graphical user interface (GUI). It is usually combined with simulation and animation.
- Many DSS development tools include built-in quantitative models (financial, statistical) or can easily interface with such models.
- Model base management systems perform tasks analogous to those performed by DBMS.
- Unlike DBMS, there are no standard MBMS because of the many classes of models, their use, and the many techniques for solving them.
- Artificial intelligence techniques can be effectively used in MBMS.
- Models are useful for creating information systems.
- The Web has had a profound impact on models and model management systems, and vice versa.
- Web application servers provide model management capabilities to DSS.

❖ KEY WORDS

- business intelligence
- certainty
- complexity

- decision analysis
- decision table
- decision tree

- dynamic models
- environmental scanning and analysis

- forecasting
- genetic algorithms
- goal-seeking analysis
- heuristic programming
- heuristics
- independent variables
- influence diagram
- linear programming (LP)
- mathematical (quantitative) model
- mathematical programming
- model base management system (MBMS)
- multidimensional modeling
- multiple goals
- object-oriented model base management system (OOMBMS)
- optimal solution
- parameters
- quantitative software packages
- regression analysis
- relational model base management system (RMBMS)
- result (outcome) variable
- risk
- risk analysis
- sensitivity analysis
- simulation
- static models
- tabu search
- uncertainty
- uncontrollable variables
- visual interactive modeling (VIM)
- visual interactive simulation (VIS)
- what-if analysis

❖ QUESTIONS FOR REVIEW

1. What are the major types of models used in DSS?
2. Distinguish between a static model and a dynamic model. Give an example of each.
3. What is an influence diagram? What is it used for?
4. What is a spreadsheet?
5. What makes a spreadsheet so conducive to the development of DSS?
6. What is a decision table?
7. What is a decision tree?
8. What is an allocation problem?
9. List and briefly discuss the three major components of linear programming.
10. What is the role of heuristics in modeling?
11. Define visual simulation and compare it to conventional simulation.
12. Define visual interactive modeling (VIM).
13. What is a model base management system?
14. Explain why the development of a generic model base management system is so difficult.

❖ QUESTIONS FOR DISCUSSION

1. What is the relationship between environmental analysis and problem identification?
2. What is the difference between an optimistic approach and a pessimistic approach to decision-making under assumed uncertainty?
3. Explain why solving problems under uncertainty sometimes involves assuming that the problem is to be solved under conditions of risk.
4. Explain the differences between static and dynamic models. How can one evolve into the other?
5. Explain why an influence diagram can be viewed as a model of a model.
6. Excel is probably the most popular spreadsheet software for the PC. Why? What can you do with this package that makes it so attractive?
7. Explain how OLAP provides access to powerful models in a spreadsheet structure.
8. What is the difference between decision analysis with a single goal and decision analysis with multiple goals (criteria)?
9. Explain how linear programming can solve allocation problems.
10. What are the advantages of using a spreadsheet package to create and solve linear programming models? What are the disadvantages?
11. What are the advantages of using a linear programming package to create and solve linear programming models? What are the disadvantages?
12. Give examples of three heuristics with which you are familiar.
13. Describe the general process of simulation.
14. List some of the major advantages of simulation over optimization, and vice versa.
15. What are the advantages of using a spreadsheet package to perform simulation studies? What are the disadvantages?
16. Compare the methodology of simulation to Simon's four-phase model of decision making. Does the methodology of simulation map directly into Simon's model? Explain.
17. Many computer games can be considered visual simulation. Explain why.
18. Explain why VIM is particularly helpful in implementing recommendations derived by computers.

19. Compare the linear programming features available in spreadsheets (e.g., Excel Solver) to those in quantitative software packages (e.g., Lindo).

20. There are hundreds of DBMS packages on the market. Explain why there are no packages for model base management systems (MBMS).

21. Does Simon's four-phase decision-making model fit into most of the modeling methodologies described? How or how not?

❖ EXERCISES

1. Create the spreadsheet models shown in Figures 4.3 and 4.4.
   a. What is the effect of a change in the interest rate from 8 percent to 10 percent in the spreadsheet model shown in Figure 4.4?
   b. For the original model in Figure 4.4, what interest rate is required to decrease the monthly payments by 20 percent? What change in the loan amount would have the same effect?
   c. In the spreadsheet shown in Figure 4.5, what is the effect of a prepayment of $200 per month? What prepayment would be necessary to pay off the loan in 25 years instead of 30 years?

2. *Class exercise.* Build a predictive model. Everyone in the class should write their weight, height, and gender on a piece of paper (no names please!). If the sample is too small (you will need about 20–30 students), add more students from another class.
   a. Create a regression (causal) model for height versus weight for the whole class, and one for each gender. If possible, use a statistical package like SPSS and a spreadsheet (Excel) and compare their ease of use. Produce a scatterplot of the three sets of data.
   b. Do the relationships appear linear (based on the plots and the regressions)? How accurate were the models (how close to 1 is the value of R^2)?
   c. Does weight cause height, does height cause weight, or does neither really cause the other? Explain.
   d. How can a regression model like this be used in building or aircraft design? Diet or nutrition selection? A longitudinal study (say, over 50 years) to determine whether students are getting heavier and not taller, or vice versa?

3. It has been argued in a number of different venues that a higher education level indicates a greater average income. The real question for a college student might be: should I stay in school?
   a. Using publicly available U.S. Census data for the 50 states and Washington, D.C., develop a linear regression model (causal forecasting) to see whether this relationship is true. (Note that some data massaging may be necessary.) How high was the R^2 value (a measure of quality of fit)? Don't forget to scatterplot the data.
   b. Does the relationship appear to be linear? If not, check a statistics book and try a nonlinear function. How well does the nonlinear function perform?
   c. Which five states have the highest average incomes, and which five states have the highest average education levels? From this study, do you believe that a higher average education level tends to "cause" a higher average income? Explain.
   d. If you have studied (or will study) neural networks, using the same data, build a neural network prediction model and compare it to your statistical results.

4. Set up spreadsheet models for the decision table models of Section 4.7 and solve them.

5. Solve the MBI product-mix problem described in the chapter (use either Excel's Solver or a student version of a linear programming solver such as Lindo or Win QSB. Lindo is available from Lindo Systems, Inc., at lindo.com; others are also available—search the Web. Examine the solution (output) reports for the answers and sensitivity report. Did you get the same results as those reported in this chapter? Try the sensitivity analysis outlined in the chapter; that is, lower the right-hand side of the CC-8 marketing constraint by one unit from 200 to 199. What happens to the solution when you solve this modified problem? Eliminate the CC-8 lower bound constraint entirely (this can be done easily by either deleting it in Solver or setting the lower limit to zero) and re-solve the problem. What happens? Using the original formulation, try modifying the objective function coefficients and see what happens.

6. Assume that you know that there is one irregular coin (either lighter or heavier) among 12. Using a two-pan scale, you must find that coin (is it lighter or heavier?) in no more than three tests. Solve this problem and explain the weighing strategy that you use. What approach to problem-solving is used in this case?

7. Use a roadmap of the United States (or your own country). Starting from where you are now, identify a

location on the other side and plot out a route to go from here to there. What (heuristic) rules did you use in selecting your route? Did you identify a shortest route or a fastest route? Explain why. How does your route compare to published distances (if available) between the locations?

8. Use Expert Choice software to select your next car. Evaluate cars on ride (from poor to great), looks (from attractive to ugly), and acceleration (seconds from 0 to 60 mph; 100 kph). Consider three final cars on your list and develop each of the items in parts (a)–(e).

   a. A problem hierarchy
   b. A comparison of the importance of the criteria against the goal
   c. A comparison of the alternative cars for each criterion
   d. An overall ranking (a synthesis of leaf nodes with respect to the goal)
   e. A sensitivity analysis
   f. Maintain the inconsistency ratio lower than 0.1. If you initially had an inconsistency index greater than 0.1, what caused it to be that high? Would you really buy the car you selected? Why or why not?
   g. Develop a spreadsheet model using estimated preference weights and estimates for the intangible items, each on a scale from 1 to 10 for each car. Compare the conclusions reached with this method to those found using the Expert Choice model. Which one more accurately captures your judgments and why?

9. Build an Expert Choice model to select the next president of the United States (if it is not an election year or you do not live in the United States, use a relevant election). Whom did you choose? Did your solution match your expectations?

10. *Job Selection using Expert Choice.* You are in the job market (use your imagination if necessary). List the names of four or five different companies that have offered you a job (or from which you expect to get an offer). (As an alternative, your instructor may assign graduate or undergraduate program selection.) Write down all the factors that may influence your decision as to which job offer you will accept. Such factors may include geographic location, salary, benefits, taxes, school system (if you have children), and potential for career advancement. Some of these factors (criteria, attributes) may have subcriteria. For instance, location may be subdivided into climate, urban concentration, cost of living, and so on. If you do not yet have a salary figure associated with a job offer, guess a reasonable figure. Perhaps your classmates can help you determine realistic figures.

    a. Model this problem in a spreadsheet (Excel) using some kind of weighted average methodology (you set the criteria weights first) (see the current *Rand-McNally Places Rated Almanac* for an example).
    b. Construct an Expert Choice model for your decision problem and use the pairwise comparisons to arrive at the best job opportunity.
    c. Compare the two approaches. Do they yield the same results? Why or why not?
    d. Write a short report (one or two typed pages) explaining the results, including those of the weighted average methodology, and for Expert Choice, explain each criterion, subcriterion (if any), and alternative. Describe briefly which options and capabilities of Expert Choice you used in your analysis and show the numerical results of your analysis. For this purpose, you may want to include printouts of your AHP tree, but make sure you circle and explain the items of interest on the printouts. Discuss the nature of the trade-offs you encountered during the evaluation process. You may want to include a meaningful sensitivity analysis of the results (optional).
    e. *To think about:* Was the Expert Choice analysis helpful in structuring your preferences? Do you think it will be a helpful aid in your actual decision-making process? Comment on all these issues in your report.

11. For the last few multicriteria decision making exercises, set each up and solve it using Web-Hipre (hipre.hut.fi, Systems Analysis Laboratory, Helsinki University of Technology, Helsinki, Finland), a Web-enabled implementation of the Analytic Hierarchy Process. How does Web-Hipre compare to Expert Choice in functionality and use?

12. *Heuristic study: the traveling salesperson problem.* On a map of the United States mark all the state capitals in the continental United States (exclude Hawaii and Alaska but include Washington, D.C.). Starting from any state capital, identify the paths you would follow to visit each of the cities exactly once with a return to the starting capital while attempting to minimize the total distance traveled. How can you do this? What would you do differently if you were allowed to visit each city more than once. If you can find the distances in a table (e.g., on a roadmap of the United States), try to do the same using the 49 by 49 entry table. How hard is it to get the data and organize it? Can you eliminate some data? If so, how or why? If not, why not? Which approach is easier? Do you appreciate the graphic approach more? What does this tell you in terms of developing DSS models for managers?

❖ GROUP PROJECTS

1. *Software demonstration.* Each group is assigned a different state-of-the-art DSS software product to review, examine, and demonstrate in class. The specific packages depend on your instructor and the group interests. You may need to download the demo from a vendor's Web site, depending on your instructor's directions. Be sure to get a running demo version, not a slide show. Do a half-hour in-class presentation, which should include an explanation of *why the software is appropriate* for assisting in decision-making, a *hands-on demonstration* of selected important capabilities of the software, and your *critical evaluation* of the software. Try to make your presentation interesting and instructive to the whole class. The main purpose of the class presentation is for class members to see as much state-of-the-art software as possible, both in breadth (through the presentations by other groups) and in depth (through the experience you have in exploring the ins and outs of one particular software product). Write a report (5–10 pages) on your findings and comments regarding this software. Include screen shots in your report. Would you recommend this software to anyone? Why or why not?

2. *Expert Choice software familiarity.* Have a group meeting and discuss how you chose a place to live when you relocated to start your college program (or relocated to where you are now). What factors were important for each individual then, and how long ago was it? Have the criteria changed? As a group, identify the five to seven most important criteria used in making the decision. Using the current group members' living arrangements as choices, develop an Expert Choice model describing this decision-making problem. Do not put your judgments in yet. You should each solve the EC model independently. Be careful to keep the inconsistency ratio less than 0.1. How many of the group members selected their current home using the software? If so, was it a close decision, or was there a clear winner? If some group members did not choose their current homes, what criteria made the result different (spouses of group members are not part of the home)? Did the availability of better choices that meet their needs become known? How consistent were your judgments? Do you think that you would really prefer to live in the winning location? Why or why not? Finally, average the results for all group members (by adding up the synthesized weights for each choice and dividing by the number of group members). This is one way TeamEC works. Is there a clear winner? Whose home is it and why did it win? Were there any close second choices? Turn in your results in a summary report (up to two typed pages), with copies of the individual Expert Choice runs.

❖ MAJOR GROUP TERM PROJECT 1

Identify a decision-making problem in a real organization and apply the Analytic Hierarchy Process Method via Expert Choice software to it. Find a business or organization, preferably one where you (or someone in your group) are working, used to work, or know an employee or owner. Otherwise, you might consider campus organizations or departments with which you are affiliated. Essentially, you need a contact willing to spend a little time with your group. The problem should involve clear choices (you may need to identify these) and some intangible aspects (not all factors should be strictly quantitative). You will have to spend some time learning about the problem at hand. Interview the decision-maker, identify important criteria and choices, and build an Expert Choice model. Try your judgments in solving the problem with the prototype (record the results), and then use the expert's (decision-maker's) judg-

ments. Get the expert's opinion of how the software helped or hindered the decision-making process. This project has worked very well in practice: students and decision-makers have expressed the opinion that they were very satisfied with the activities and results (see the Scott Homes Web Chapter for an example of a term project like this one).

The four deliverables are as follows:

1. *One-page proposal.* Turn in a one-page proposal describing the Expert Choice project you intend to do. Indicate the project title, the client, and the expected results. This proposal should be due no later than five weeks before the final due date for the project.

2. *Intermediate progress report (maximum—two pages typed).* In this short report, describe the nature of your application and indicate how far along you are. Experience shows that you may be in trouble if you wait too long to work on

this group project, so start working seriously on it as soon as you can. The short report should be due three weeks before the final due date for the project. Your instructor may require additional intermediate progress reports.

3. and 4. *Final project presentation and report (maximum—10 typed pages excluding appendices with screen shots).* This report must include a letter (on a letterhead) from the client indicating his or her opinion of the project and interaction with your group (two sentences are sufficient). Will the client use the method or the software? Does the client believe the choice? Why

or why not? Can the client save money by implementing the suggestion? Does the client obtain other benefits by doing so? How closely does the suggestion match what the client is doing (or wants to do)? What, if any, were the limitations imposed by the software? How did they affect your ability to do the project? What was the most difficult part of working on the project? The group presentations (20 minutes per group) should be scheduled during the last week of the course, with the report due at the same time.

❖ MAJOR GROUP TERM PROJECT 2

With the outline provided for the first project, use a decision support methodology and a software package that your instructor provides or recommends.

This could involve developing an optimization-based DSS, a database-based DSS, a document-based DSS, or a Web-based DSS.

❖ MAJOR GROUP TERM PROJECT 3

Develop a real-world DSS that links a database to a transportation (or other type of linear programming) model through a user interface (Lingo and Microsoft Access are recommended, as are Excel with Solver and Access). The database should contain raw data about the potential transportation

routes, along with supply and demand points. The database should also handle the user interface and provide managerially meaningful descriptions of the routes after the optimization system is called. There is a Web Chapter that describes this project.

❖ INTERNET EXERCISES

1. Search the Internet and identify software packages for linear programming, simulation, inventory control, project management, statistics, forecasting, and financial modeling. What types of organizations provide these packages? Are any free?
2. Investigate ProModel (or a similar simulation package) on the Web. What features do you think DuPont used in its modeling and analysis (as discussed in the opening vignette)? Download the demo version and implement the cash flow simulation model in the Web Chapter. How does it compare to the Excel version?
3. Repeat Exercise 2 using @Risk.
4. Search the Web for the newest software packages and books on DSS modeling. What appears to be the major focus of each? Prepare a short report.
5. Do a Web search to identify companies and products for decision analysis. Find at least one demo package,

download it (or try it online if possible), and write a report on your experience.
6. Use the Internet to obtain demo software from management science or statistics vendors (try the SAS Institute Inc., SPSS Inc., CACI Products Company, and Lindo Systems Inc.). Also, be sure to look for shareware (fully functional packages that can be tried for a limited time for free). Try some of the packages and write a report on your findings.
7. Identify a company involved in animation or visual interactive simulation over the Web. Are any of the products Web-ready? Do any of them provide virtual reality capabilities or real-time online simulations? Do any of them utilize holographic 3-D imaging, virtual reality capabilities, or real-time online simulations? Try one if you can and write a brief report on your experiences.

❖ TERM PAPER

Select a current DSS technology or methodology. Get your instructor's approval. Write a report detailing the origins of the technology, what need prompted development of the technology, and what the future holds for it over the next two, five, or ten years (the number of pages is up to your instructor). Use electronic sources, if possible, to identify companies providing the technology. If demo software is available, acquire it and include the results of a sample run in your paper.

CLAY PROCESS PLANNING AT IMERYS: A CLASSICAL CASE OF DECISION MAKING

Part 3: The Process Optimization Model

INTRODUCTION

This case application continues the effort described in Case Applications 2.1 and 2.2. The Process OPtimization (POP) development team at English China Clay International (ECCI, which became IMERYS) in Sandersville, Georgia, developed a large-scale mathematical programming model that describes its clay processing operation from the mines to the finished product. Here we describe the structure of the POP model: a large-scale, generalized, multicommodity network flow model with side constraints. We further describe how the data and model are managed. Finally, we describe how the model is and will be used. The prototyping development process followed in developing the POP DSS is described in detail in Case Application 6.1.

THE PLANTS

The scope of the first phase of the project originally called for developing an integrated model representing four plants—two hydrous plants, a large calcine plant, and a small calcine plant—but did not represent the mines (calcine is dry clay, and hydrous has more moisture; different products are made from each, and almost any set of clays can be blended to generate a final product with unique properties). The mining portion of the model was added later. While development of the model for the small calcine plant was underway, ECCI was purchased by IMATEL (France), and eventually one hydrous plant, about one-fifth of the large calcine plant, and the small calcine plant were sold per a U.S. Justice Department ruling. As outlined in Case Application 6.1, we had completed development of the model of both calcine plants at that time. For validation purposes, we kept the plants in the model until it became operational. The POP DSS model deployed in late 1999 represented one hydrous plant, the large calcine plant, and the small calcine plant. Later, we replaced the small plant with external market purchases and demands for intermediate clays that were shipped to it.

THE MODEL BUILDING BLOCKS

The decision variables include which mines to excavate, how much and what kind of crude clays to extract from each one, how to blend crude clays, which equipment to process the clay on, the speed at which to process the clay, what intermediate blends (recipes) to use, what final blends to use, what demands to meet (or not meet if necessary), what final clays to purchase from the open market, and so on.

Fortunately, the multicommodity network flow problem represents flow problems of many commodities (e.g., different clays) through common links (arcs) that generally have capacity limits. The model can be represented graphically, making it easy to sketch and understand. Ours is a generalized model; that is, each link that allows flow has a multiplier (a recovery factor for a process) between 0 and 1 indicating how much of the flow actually reaches the node at the end of the link. This is used to model *losses* that result from chemical and physical transformation of the clays. In addition, there are some side constraints that enforce blends and enforce mutual capacities on the links (e.g., the total flow through each arc for all commodities cannot exceed the capacity in terms of flow or time). This is a static model.

Developing a standard set of building blocks made it easier for the team to develop and implement the model. Given a particular clay, there are several model building blocks, but the most important one is the process. These are entities that represent a type of equipment processing the clay. For example, transporting the clay from a mine to a particular plant is a process. Another process is grinding. Other building blocks, such as a holding tank, follow naturally from the process definition. Some processes are simply represented as a pair of nodes: a source (a supply, e.g., a mine), a sink (the demand for a finished clay), and a link that allows flow between pairs of building blocks. Every process has a set of clays that can flow through it. For each clay flowing through a process, the following data must be specified: the rate of flow (in tons per hour, which varies by clay), a unit cost per ton for processing, a unit cost per hour utilized, a recovery factor (the multiplier between 0 and 1), a capacity limit on the flow, and a capacity limit on the processing time.

The basic building block of a simple process consists of two nodes and a single arc. The first node is the feed node. Any preceding processes can feed the clay into the process through this node. The second node is the product node. This is where the processed clay arrives and is ready for transport to its next destination. The decision variable is to determine the flow through the process (on the arc). A simple process looks like

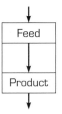

Complex processes have two or more distinct products (e.g., a categorizing process divides clay into small and large particle sizes, each of which is processed differently afterward; so each product has a different recovery factor, while the rate and unit costs of processing are unchanged. A complex process has an intermediate node (the process set node), a product node for each one, and arcs to link them. It looks like

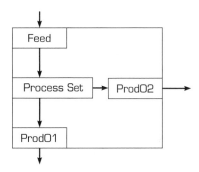

Chemicals that alter the clays' properties are added to the clays in different processes. The amount used is proportional to the flow (in pounds per ton), and, depending on the rate the process uses, different chemical amounts can be involved. Alternative processing for the same clay may lead to the use of different chemicals.

Clays can flow from plant to plant, from the *economy* into the plant, from mine to plant, and so on. The model is then built by connecting these processes with arcs that transport the clays. These arcs represent any transporting of clays. There are about 15 crude clays, five families of hydrous clays, and three main calcine products. Though few in number, these clays can be combined with each other and with clays obtained from other plants or on the open market to produce several hundred different final clays. There are hundreds of ways to blend the crudes to form any of the hydrous family clays. Each family goes through the production process in several different ways. There are different ways to process each particular clay, and different blends and chemical amounts can be used. The model was to determine the optimal blends to use.

The model, when solved, determines the clay flows (decision variables, in tons) and the time consumed for each clay in each process. These values are capacitated, and the total flow and total time consumed are also capacitated, both because of physical limitations of the process-

ing equipment and the required characteristics of the finished products. The recipes used and which processes are running at capacity are of great interest to the company for planning purposes. The mining operations are also a "process," as is meeting the demand for each clay.

The objective is to maximize profit. Each finished product clay has a unit price for every form of it that is sold (slurry, bulk, bag, etc.). More than 2.3 million tons of crude clay processing annually was modeled.

MODELING DIFFICULTIES

What made this model difficult to construct and interesting was the large size (initially more than 8,000 constraints and 35,000 variables; by 2003 there were over 80,000 constraints and 170,000 variables) and the fact that several different process characteristics were estimated because the processes had not yet been constructed. There were also points in the processing where by-products were fed back into the system to an earlier step (clay recoveries).

Once the small calcine plant and a portion of the large calcine plant were sold, the flows into these portions of the model were turned off by setting the capacity of the calcining process equal to zero, and open market purchases were added for some final products. A second hydrous plant was never modeled. Later, the size of the model increased by 50 percent as other plants and clays were added.

THE LINGO MODELING LANGUAGE AND THE ACCESS DATABASE INTEGRATION

The model was developed in Lingo (a modeling language from Lindo Systems Inc., lindo.com), which integrates directly with a Microsoft Access database of more than 10 relational tables through the Microsoft @ODBC interface. The Lingo model lines are specified independently from the data link statements (links). The Process OPtimization Lingo model is populated with data from the database, generates the model, solves it, and loads the solution directly back into the database automatically. Lingo model lines generally look like shorthand for the algebra of mathematical programming, thus providing a familiar vehicle for model building. For example, the Lingo model line for the supply constraints of a transportation problem (from factories to customers) might be

@FOR(FACTORY(I):
    @SUM(CUSTOMER(J): FLOW(I, J))
        <= CAPACITY(I));

which means: For every FACTORY(I), SUM all the flows from supply node I to demand node J over all CUSTOMER(J) (all customers), (FLOW(I,J)), and set that value to be less than or equal to the available CAPACITY(I) at FACTORY(I). There are special data statements specifying all necessary data to identify the sets FACTORY, CUSTOMER, and CAPACITY. The POP model's mining portion looks very much like a modified transportation problem. Limits on blends can be specified (e.g., clay B must constitute between 80 and 95 percent of the blend).

POP DSS USE

The DSS, written as a menu-oriented Access database table, manages the data in the system. A particular scenario is set up in the Access tables through a friendly graphical user interface (GUI) screen. The user sets the demands, makes other adjustments to the processes, and then activates Lingo with the click of a button. Lingo automatically generates the entire model from its compact representation and the data as specified in the database, and solves it. Lingo loads its solution back into the database and returns control to the menu-oriented GUI. Access programs then produce managerially meaningful graphs of utilization and reports on clay extraction and processing. Trouble spots are identified, the case can be saved, and another scenario can be run.

For a fixed time period (one year, one quarter, two weeks, etc.), the solution to the model indicates which mines are active, how much clay is mined from each mine, to which processing unit the clay is shipped from the mines, and the appropriate crude blends (recipes) to be used. It determines all the clay flows throughout the entire system and which clays to purchase from the market. The model quickly identifies which processes are running at capacity and indicates the potential increase in profit that could be obtained if these capacities could be increased (through sensitivity analysis). Sometimes there are underutilized processes that could handle some of the load of the limited processes but are somewhat inefficient at doing so. Plant managers are reluctant to use these processes but carefully examine them and sometimes activate them.

The model also indicates how to handle the situation now that some of the higher-quality clay mines are depleted and new processes have been introduced. Finally, underutilization of some processes indicates that some final products, normally produced at other plants (not yet in the model), could be produced at the plants represented by the model. Several of these clays have already been added to POP.

The most interesting aspect of the model is that the engineers and managers who structure the plants were doing an excellent job of keeping them fine-tuned without access to these analytical tools. The model did recommend using different mines from time to time, and it has provided guidance on how to manage the mines for ten years. The total amount of clay being processed is about the same as what the model solution recommends, which certainly helped to validate the model. What the model is best used for is determining how to handle the resources that are 100 percent utilized (bottlenecks) and how to handle new and unexpected situations, such as new clays, new demands, and new processes. It also provides answers quickly and easily, thus guiding managers and engineers in their decision-making. When a plant was closed in 2001, the production and demand for its products were moved to the main hydrous plant that was already in the POP DSS. POP accurately determined the blends that indicated how to handle this record throughput optimally. Even the plant manager, initially skeptical, agreed that his plant could handle the load once he saw POP's recommendations.

As mentioned in Case Application 2.2, the cost of operating a new process was determined, thus guiding budgeting decisions for the next fiscal year. The model is used for annual planning. It is also used in the short term for scheduling specific large orders in with the forecasted demands. Essentially, the POP DSS is used for strategic planning (1–5 years), tactical planning (3–6 months), and operational planning (2 weeks). A simple factor is changed to generate a model that spans any needed time frame.

SUMMARY AND CONCLUSIONS

The POP model as part of the POP DSS at IMERYS is helping to guide planning on an annual, quarterly, and even weekly basis. It helps decision-makers determine which options are most viable in terms of meeting clay demand at a maximum profit. Planning for millions of tons of clay processing is not a trivial task, and the POP DSS handles it readily and quickly. POP continues to expand to include other IMERYS plants and mines. The POP DSS is a success.

CASE QUESTIONS

1. What is the POP DSS used for?
2. What are the benefits of using a network-based model?
3. What are the benefits of the POP DSS?
4. How can what-if cases (scenarios) be used to determine whether to add extra processing equipment instead of adjusting existing processes and chemical use?
5. Could other firms that process materials use a system like this? Why or why not?
6. How could a demand forecasting model be integrated with POP? (A question to think about—not in this case application.)
7. How could the results of the POP DSS guide an enterprise resource planning (ERP) system? (A question to think about—not described in this case application.)

5

BUSINESS INTELLIGENCE: DATA WAREHOUSING, DATA ACQUISITION, DATA MINING, BUSINESS ANALYTICS, AND VISUALIZATION

LEARNING OBJECTIVES

❖ Describe issues in data collection, problems, and quality.

❖ Describe the characteristics and organization of database management systems.

❖ Explain the importance and use of a data warehouse and data mart.

❖ Describe business intelligence/business analytics and their importance to organizations.

❖ Describe how online analytical processing (OLAP), data mining, data visualization, multidimensionality, and real-time analytics can improve decision-making.

❖ Explain how the Web impacts database technologies and methods, and vice versa.

❖ Describe how database technologies and methods as part of business intelligence/business analytics improve decision-making.

❖ Describe Web intelligence/Web analytics and their importance to organizations.

Many organizations have amassed vast amounts of data that employees use to unlock valuable secrets to enable the organization to compete successfully. Some organizations do this extremely well, but others are quite ineffective. To use analytic tools to improve organizational decision-making, a foundational data architecture and enterprise architecture must be in place to facilitate effective decision analysis. Enabling decision analysis through access to all relevant information is known as *business intelligence*. Business intelligence includes data warehousing, online analytical processing, data mining, and visualization and multidimensionality. The outline of this chapter is as follows:

5.1 OPENING VIGNETTE: INFORMATION SHARING A PRINCIPAL COMPONENT OF THE NATIONAL STRATEGY FOR HOMELAND SECURITY[1]

Data warehouses provide a strategic data architecture to enable decision support analysis. Data warehousing enables data mining, the ability to automatically synthesize vast amounts of information in order to discover *hidden truths* within the data. Data portals have emerged as the next generation in Web-enabled data warehouses. One of the most significant data portals has been developed in direct response to the terrorist attacks on the United States on September 11, 2001.

The National Strategy for Homeland Security of the United States includes a National Vision for the sharing of information related to the detection of terrorist activities. It states,

> We will build a national environment that enables the sharing of essential homeland security information. We must build a *system of systems* that can provide the right information to the right people at all times. Information will be shared "horizontally" across each level of government and "vertically" among federal, state and local governments, private industry and citizens. With the proper use of people, processes, and technology, homeland security officials throughout the United States can have complete and common awareness of threats and vulnerabilities as well as knowledge of the personnel and resources available to address these threats. Officials will receive the information they need so they can anticipate threats and respond rapidly and effectively.

The goal of the project is to create a workable model for integrating knowledge that resides across many disparate data sources, while ensuring that privacy and civil liberties are adequately safeguarded. The five major initiatives that are identified within the strategy include:

1. To integrate information sharing across the federal government
2. To extend the integration of information sharing across state and local governments, private industry, and citizens
3. To adopt common metadata standards of electronic information relevant to homeland security
4. To improve public safety communication
5. To ensure reliable public health information.

---

[1]Modified from the National Strategy for Homeland Security Web site, www.whitehouse.gov/homeland/book/index.html.

These goals can only be accomplished if there is a means to facilitate the sharing of information among numerous agencies that currently maintain independent data silos. Border security alone engages eleven agencies. For the entire data warehouse project, approximately 80 percent of the architecture will be in place in 18 months, while the complete implementation will phase in over three to five years. Ultimately the data warehouse will lead to increased security for the United States. It will be a model for how all countries can interact to protect their borders and ensure the safety of their citizenry. This ambitious project is not without challenges. For example, data will need to be mined from immigration records, treasury records (dealing with the exchange of large sums of money), and FBI (criminal) records. The data exist in different formats and data types; a major effort is underway to establish a means to link and search through these data to identify potential threats and crimes.

❖ QUESTIONS FOR THE OPENING VIGNETTE

1. Identify the challenges faced by the Office of Homeland Security in integrating disparate databases.
2. Identify the sources of information that will be required to make the information in this data portal useful.
3. What are the expected benefits?
4. Identify decisions supported by this data portal.
5. What decision support tools and techniques can be used to identify potential terrorist activities?
6. What would you recommend to the Office of Homeland Security to improve the capabilities of this data portal?

5.2 THE NATURE AND SOURCES OF DATA

In order to understand a situation, a decision-maker needs data, information, and knowledge. These must be integrated and organized in a manner that makes them useful. Then the decision-maker must be able to apply analysis tools (online analytical processing (OLAP), data mining, etc.) so that the data, information, and knowledge can be utilized to full benefit. These analysis tools fall under the general heading of business intelligence (BI) and business analytics (BA) (see Chapters 3 and 4). New tools allow decision-makers and analysts to readily identify relationships among data items that enable understanding and provide a competitive advantage. For example, a customer-relationship (resource) management (CRM) system allows managers to better understand their customers. They can then determine a likely candidate for a particular product or service at a specific price (see Chapter 8). Marketing efforts are improved and sales are maximized. All enterprise information systems (e.g., CRM, executive information systems, content-management systems, revenue management systems, enterprise resource planning/enterprise resource management systems, supply chain management systems, knowledge management systems) utilize database management systems, data warehouses, OLAP, and data mining as their foundation (see Chapters 8 and 9). These business intelligence/business analytic (and Web intelligence/Web analytic) tools enable the modern enterprise to compete successfully. In the right hands, these tools provide great decision-makers with great capabilities. For example, see Case Application 5.2, which indicates how a firm developed and then utilized databases in an extremely competitive manner.

The Opening Vignette illustrates what can go wrong in the extreme when you do not gather data to track the activities of individuals and organizations that impact your organization (in a business environment, these are customers, potential customers and the competition). The critical issue for the U.S. Department of Homeland Security is to gather and analyze data from disparate sources. These data must be integrated in a data warehouse and analyzed automatically via data-mining tools or by analysts using OLAP tools. Of course, abuses can occur in the process of collecting and utilizing such a massive amount of data (see DSS in Focus 5.1).

The impact of tracking data and then exploiting them for competitive advantage can be enormous. Entire industries, such as travel, banking, and all successful e-commerce ventures, rely totally on their data and information content to flourish. Experian Automotive has developed a business opportunity from modern database, extraction and integration tools (see DSS in Action 5.2).

Songini (2002) provides an excellent description of databases, data, information, metadata, OLAP, repository, and data mining. Major database vendors include IBM, Oracle, Informix, Microsoft, and Sybase. Database vendors are reviewed on a regular basis by the trade press. For example, see Whiting (2000) and the "Annual Product Review" issue of *DM Review* (www.dmreview.com) every July.

All decision-support systems use data, information, and/or knowledge. These three terms are sometimes used interchangeably and may have several definitions. A common way of looking at them is as follows:

- **Data.** Items about things, events, activities, and transactions are recorded, classified, and stored but are not organized to convey any specific meaning. Data items can be numeric, alphanumeric, figures, sounds, or images.
- **Information.** Data that have been organized in a manner that gives them meaning for the recipient. They confirm something the recipient knows, or may have

---

DSS IN FOCUS 5.1

HOMELAND SECURITY PRIVACY AND COST CONCERNS

The U.S. government plans to apply analytic technologies on a global scale in the war on terrorism, but will they prove an effective weapon? In the first year and a half after September 11, 2001, supermarket chains, home improvement stores, and others voluntarily handed over massive amounts of customer records to federal law enforcement agencies, almost always in violation of their stated privacy policies. Many others responded to court orders for information, as required by law. The government has a right to gather corporate data under legislation passed after September 11, 2001.

The FBI now mines enormous amounts of data looking for activity that could indicate a terrorist plot or crime. Transaction data are where law-enforcement agencies expect to find results. American businesses are stuck in the middle. Some have to create special systems to generate the data required by law-enforcement agencies. An average-size company will spend an average of $5 million for a system. On the other hand, not complying can cost more. Western Union was fined $8 million in December 2002 for not complying properly.

Privacy issues abound. Since the government is acquiring personal data to detect suspicious patterns of activity, there is the prospect of abuse and illegal use of the data. There may be significant privacy costs involved. There are major problems with violating people's freedoms and rights. There is a need for an oversight organization to "watch the watchers." The DHS must not mindlessly acquire data. It should only acquire pertinent data and information that can be mined to identify patterns that potentially could lead to stopping terrorist activities.

Source: Partly adapted from John Foley, "Data Debate." *InformationWeek*, May 19, 2003, pp. 22–24; S. Grimes, "Look Before You Leap," *Intelligent Enterprise*, June 2003; Ben Worthen, "What to Do When Uncle Sam Wants Your Data," *CIO*, April 15, 2003, pp. 56–66.

DATABASE TOOLS OPEN UP NEW REVENUE OPPORTUNITIES FOR EXPERIAN AUTOMOTIVE

Experian Automotive has developed new business opportunities from data tools that manage, extract, and integrate. Experian has developed a system with a huge database (the world's 10th largest) to track automobile sales data. The acquired data are external and come from public records of automobile sales. Experian draws on these data to provide the ownership history of any vehicle bought or sold in the United States for an inexpensive fee per query via the Web. There is a massive market for this service, especially from car dealerships. Experian also focuses on automobile parts companies to identify recalls and consider how to target automobile parts sales.

Source: Adapted from Pimm Fox, "Extracting Dollars from Data," *ComputerWorld,* April 15, 2002, p. 42.

"surprise" value by revealing something not known. An MSS application processes data items so that the results are meaningful for an intended action or decision.

- ***Knowledge.*** Knowledge consists of data items and/or information organized and processed to convey understanding, experience, accumulated learning, and expertise that are applicable to a current problem or activity. Knowledge can be the application of data and information in making a decision. (See Chapters 9 and 10.)

MSS data can include documents, pictures, maps, sound, video, and animation. These data can be stored and organized in different ways before and after use. They also include concepts, thoughts, and opinions. Data can be raw or summarized. Many MSS applications use summary or extracted data that come from three primary sources: internal, external, and personal.

INTERNAL DATA

Internal data are stored in one or more places. These data are about people, products, services, and processes. For example, data about employees and their pay are usually stored in the corporate database. Data about equipment and machinery can be stored in the maintenance department database. Sales data can be stored in several places: aggregate sales data in the corporate database, and details at each region's database. An MSS can use raw data as well as processed data (e.g., reports and summaries). Internal data are available via an organization's intranet or other internal network.

EXTERNAL DATA

There are many sources of external data. They range from commercial databases to data collected by sensors and satellites. Data are available on CDs and DVDs, on the Internet, as films and photographs, and as music or voices. Government reports and files are a major source of external data, most of which are available on the Web today (e.g., see www.ftc.gov, the U.S. Federal Trade Commission). External data may also be available by using GIS (geographic information systems, see Section 5.13), from federal census bureaus, and other demographic sources that gather data either directly from customers or from data suppliers. Chambers of commerce, local banks, research institutions, and the like, flood the environment with data and information, resulting in *information overload* for the MSS user. Data can come from around the globe. Most external data are irrelevant to a specific MSS. Yet many external data must be monitored and captured to ensure that important items are not overlooked. Using intelligent scanning and interpretation agents may alleviate this problem. For tips on how to manage external data, see Collett (2002).

PERSONAL DATA AND KNOWLEDGE

MSS users and other corporate employees have expertise and knowledge that can be stored for future use. These include subjective estimates of sales, opinions about what competitors are likely to do, and interpretations of news articles. What people really know and methodologies to capture, manage, and distribute it are the subject of *knowledge management* (Chapter 9).

5.3 DATA COLLECTION, PROBLEMS, AND QUALITY

The need to extract data from many internal and external sources complicates the task of MSS building. Sometimes it is necessary to collect raw data in the field. In other cases, it is necessary to elicit data from people or to find it on the Internet. Regardless of how they are collected, data must be validated and filtered. A classic expression that sums up the situation is "Garbage in, garbage out" (GIGO). Therefore, *data quality* (DQ) is an extremely important issue.

METHODS FOR COLLECTING RAW DATA

Raw data can be collected manually or by instruments and sensors. Representative data collection methods are time studies, surveys (using questionnaires), observations (e.g., using video cameras; see Exercise 9), and soliciting information from experts (e.g., using interviews; see Chapter 11). In addition, sensors and scanners are increasingly being used in data acquisition. Probably the most reliable method of data collection is from point-of-purchase inventory control. When you buy something, the register records sales information with your personal information collected from your credit card. This has enabled Wal-Mart, Sears, and other retailers to build complete, massive (petabyte-sized) data warehouses in which they collect and store business intelligence data about their customers. This information is then used to identify customer buying patterns to manage local store inventory and identify new merchandising opportunities. It also helps the retail organization manage its suppliers.

Ewalt (2003) describes how PDAs are utilized to collect and utilize data in the field. Logistics companies have been using PDAs for some time. Menlo Worldwide Forwarding, a global freight company, recently equipped over 800 drivers with PDAs. Radio links are used to dispatch drivers to pick up packages. The driver scans a bar code label on the package into the PDA, which then beams tracking data back to the home office.

The need for reliable, accurate data for any MSS is universally accepted. However, in real life, developers and users face ill-structured problems in "noisy" and difficult environments. There is a wide variety of hardware and software for data storage, communication, and presentation, but much less effort has gone into developing methods for MSS data capture in less tractable decision environments. Inadequate methods for dealing with these problems may limit the effectiveness of even sophisticated technologies in MSS development and use. Some methods involve physically capturing data via bar codes or by RFID (radio-frequency identification tag) technology. An RFID electronic button sends an identification signal with some data (several kilobytes when these devices were new) directly to a nearby receiver. A packing crate, or even an individual consumer product, can readily be identified. In the early 2000s, manufacturers, airlines, and retailers were experimenting with utilizing RFID devices for security, speeding up processing in receiving, and customer checkout. Wal-Mart Stores Inc. announced in June 2003 that by January 2005 its 100 key suppliers must use RFID to track pallets of goods through its supply chain. See DSS in Action 5.3. Swatch incorporates the device into select watch models so that ski lift passes at ski resorts are automatically encoded into it. The resort can readily identify the types of slopes you like to ski and share the information with its other properties.

DSS IN ACTION 5.3

RFID TAGS HELP AUTOMATE DATA COLLECTION AND USE

In June 2003, Wal-Mart Stores Inc. announced that by 2005 its 100 key suppliers must use RFID to track pallets of goods through its supply chain. Wal-Mart considers this much more than a company-specific effort and urged all retailers and suppliers to embrace RFID and related standards. Wal-Mart's initiative should result in deploying about 1 *billion* RFID tags to track and identify items in the individual crates and pallets. Wal-Mart will first concentrate on using the technology to improve inventory management in its supply chain. Wal-Mart's decision to deploy the technology should legitimize it and push it into the mainstream. The Wal-Mart deadline will definitely speed adoption by the industry.

The RFID unit price must be 5 cents (United States) or less for the Wal-Mart initiative to be cost-effective. In mid-2003, the RFID tags cost between 30 to 50 cents. Based on a 5 cent per tag cost, the outlay for the tags alone will total $50 million. In 2003, the readers sold for $1000 or more.

Wal-Mart is not the only retailer moving toward RFID. Marks & Spencer PLC, one of Britain's largest retailers, utilizes RFID technology in its food supply-chain operations. Each of 3.5 million plastic trays used to ship products has an RFID tag on it. Procter & Gamble Co. experimented with RFID for more than six months in 2003, running tests with several retailers.

In 2003, Delta Airlines started tests of using RFID to identify baggage while bags are loaded and unloaded on airport tarmacs. Delta will load data into the tags as the bar code is printed. Testing is critical because of potential interference from other airport wireless systems. Delta expected to see a higher level of accuracy than from the existing bar-code system. Even so, Delta delivers 99 percent of the 100 million or so bags it handles each year. But it still costs Delta a small fortune to find missing bags.

RFID tags have been utilized to track the movement of pharmaceuticals through Europe's "gray" (i.e., semi-legal) markets. At the time, medicines were generally much less expensive in southern Europe than in northern Europe, so unscrupulous wholesalers traveled south to buy them for resale in the north. RFID tags were installed inside the labels. When a vendor representative visited the dishonest wholesalers, he was able to identify the source of their stock once he got within 3 meters of the containers. All contracts with these wholesalers were immediately cancelled.

Others possible uses of RFID include embedding them in badges so that doors will automatically unlock for an authorized person, and providing access to movies and other events (through a watch-embedded or card-embedded RFID tag). They could be embedded in automobiles for automatic toll charges (as in the City of London, see Exercise 9), used in automobiles to store an entire maintenance and repair record (this is currently done for industrial fork lifts), or even under the skin for identification (by ATMs, museums, transit systems, admission to any facility, or law enforcement officials). Some pet owners have had these tags surgically embedded under their pet's skin for identification if lost or stolen. Eventually, consumer product packages and suitcases may be manufactured to contain RFID tags so that when you walk out of a store, readers detect what you have selected, and your account will automatically be charged for what you have, through an RFID tag either under your skin or in a credit card.

Source: Partly adapted from Bob Brewin, "Delta to Test RFID Tags on Luggage," *ComputerWorld*, Vol. 37, No. 25, June 23, 2003, p. 7; Chris Murphy and Mary Hayes, "Tag Line," *InformationWeek*, June 15, 2003, pp. 18–20; Jaikumar Vijayan and Bob Brewin, "Wal-Mart Backs RFID Technology." *ComputerWorld*, Vol. 37, No. 24, June 16, 2003, pp. 1, 14.

Even biometric (scanning) devices are used to collect real-world data. Biometric systems detect various physical and behavioral features of individuals and assess them to authenticate the identities of visitors and immigrants entering the United States. Databases and data mining methods are also used. Some $400 million was spent on biometrics for U.S. border control in 2003. See Verton (2003).

DATA PROBLEMS

All computer-based systems depend on data. The quality and integrity of the data are critical if the MSS is to avoid the GIGO syndrome. MSS depend on data because compiled data that make up information and knowledge are at the heart of any decision-making system.

The major DSS data problems are summarized in Table 5.1 along with some possible solutions. Data must be available to the system or the system must include a data-acquisition subsystem. Data issues should be considered in the planning stage of system development. If too many problems are anticipated, the costs of solving them can be estimated. If they are excessive, the MSS project should not be undertaken or should be put on hold until costs and problems decrease.

DATA QUALITY

Data quality (DQ) is an extremely important issue because quality determines the usefulness of data as well as the quality of the decisions based on them. Data in organizational databases are frequently found to be inaccurate, incomplete, or ambiguous. The

TABLE 5.1   Data Problems

Problem	Typical Cause	Possible Solutions
Data are not correct.	Data were generated carelessly. Raw data were entered inaccurately. Data were tampered with.	Develop a systematic way to enter data. Automate data entry. Introduce quality controls on data generation. Establish appropriate security programs.
Data are not timely.	The method for generating data is not rapid enough to meet the need for data.	Modify the system for generating data. Use the Web to get fresh data.
Data are not measured or indexed properly.	Raw data are gathered inconsistently with the purposes of the analysis. Use of complex models.	Develop a system for rescaling or recombining improperly indexed data. Use a data warehouse. Use appropriate search engines. Develop simpler or more highly aggregated models.
Needed data simply do not exist.	No one ever stored data needed now. Required data never existed.	Predict what data may be needed in the future. Use a data warehouse. Generate new data or estimate them.

Source: Based on Alter (1980), p. 130. Alter, S. L. (1980). *Decision Support Systems: Current Practices and Continuing Challenges.* Reading, MA: Addison-Wesley.

economic and social damage from poor-quality data costs billions of dollars (Redman, 1998).

The Data Warehousing Institute (TDWI) estimated in 2001 that poor-quality customer data caused U.S. businesses $611 billion a year in postage, printing, and the staff overhead to deal with the mass of erroneous communications and marketing (from a TDWI report: Wayne Erickson, "Data Quality and the Bottom Line www.dw-institute.com/dqreport/). Frighteningly, the real cost of poor-quality data is much higher. Organizations can frustrate and alienate loyal customers by incorrectly addressing letters or failing to recognize them when they call, or visit a store or Web site. Once a company loses its loyal customers, it loses its base of sales and referrals, as well as future revenue potential. See Eckerson (2002a). Some typical costs include those of rework, lost customers, late reporting, wrong decisions, wasted project activities, slow response to new needs (missed opportunities), and delays in implementing large projects that depend on existing databases (Olson, 2003a, 2003b).

Data quality is one of those topics that everyone knows is important but tends to neglect. Data quality often generates little enthusiasm and is typically viewed as a maintenance function. Firms have clearly been willing to accept poor data quality. Companies can even survive and flourish with poor data quality. It is not considered a life-and-death issue, but sometimes it can be. Data inaccuracies can be extremely costly (see Olson, 2003a, 2003b). Even so, most firms manage data quality in a casual manner (Eckerson, 2002a). According to Hatcher (2003), data quality is a major problem in data warehouse development and business intelligence/business analytics utilization. Data quality can delay the implementation of a warehouse or a data mart six months or more. Inaccurate data stored in a data warehouse and then reported to someone will instantly kill a user's trust in the new system.

A recent TDWI (The Data Warehouse Institute) survey uncovered the sources of dirty data. These are shown in Table 5.2. Unsurprisingly, respondents to TDWI's survey cite data-entry errors by employees as the primary cause of dirty data.

Data quality was often overlooked in the early days of data warehousing. Many of the original decisions about data quality now need to be revisited by data warehouse practitioners in order to keep pace with the demands of enterprise decision-making (see Canter, 2002). For an example of an organization that suffered because of data quality, see DSS in Action 5.4.

Strong et al. (1997) conducted extensive research on data quality problems and divided them into the following four categories and dimensions:

TABLE 5.2 Source of Data Quality Problems

Source of Data Quality Problem	Percent Response
Data entry by employees	76
Changes to source systems	53
Data migration or conversion projects	48
Mixed expectations by users	46
External data	34
Systems errors	26
Data entry by customers	25
Other	12

Source: Adapted from Wayne Eckerson, "Data Quality and the Bottom Line," *Application Development Trends,* May 2002, pp. 24–30.

DSS IN ACTION 5.4

DATA QUALITY IS THE CULPRIT IN MONTANA PRISONS

Data quality held the Montana Department of Corrections prisoner for years. As IT systems aged, data entry errors in reports built up. Required forms that were submitted to state and federal authorities could not pass a lie detector test. Even though the department's IS group spent countless hours of manual effort in attempting to maintain some level of reporting integrity, overall confidence in data quality was low. The issue came to breakout proportions when, in 1997, the department lost a $1 million federal grant. The guilty party was its information systems, which lacked business rules and a data dictionary. The systems could not accurately forecast how many of any type of offender would be incarcerated. Fortunately, no offenders were lost in the data shuffle, but there was no way to predict demand for prison "services" to "customers" over the next two to five years.

By mid-1999, a major effort focused on cleaning up the prison information systems through quality and accurate data was completed. By 2001, the department's information systems gatekeepers (everyone who entered and maintained data) had developed a culture of data quality. Though not unusual, it is important to note that some 15 to 20 percent of a company's operating revenue may be spent on workarounds or repairs of data-quality problems. And some organizations, like the Montana Department of Corrections, have created full-time positions devoted to ensuring data quality.

Source: Adapted from Beth Stackpole, "Dirty Data Is the Dirty Little Secret That Can Jeopardize Your CRM Effort," *CIO,* February 15, 2001, pp. 101–114.

- ***Contextual DQ:*** Relevancy, value added, timeliness, completeness, amount of data
- ***Intrinsic DQ:*** accuracy, objectivity, believability, reputation
- ***Accessibility DQ:*** accessibility, access security
- ***Representation DQ:*** interpretability, ease of understanding, concise representation, consistent representation.

Strong et al. (1997) developed a framework that presents the major issues and barriers in each of the categories. They suggested that once the major variables and relationships in each category are identified, an attempt can be made to find out how to better manage the data. Some of the problems are technical ones, such as capacity, while others relate to potential computer crimes. For a comprehensive discussion, see Wang (1998).

Data quality is important, especially for CRM, ERP, and other enterprise information systems. The problem is that data warehousing, e-business, and CRM projects often expose poor-quality data because they require companies to extract and integrate data from multiple operational systems that are often peppered with errors, missing values, and integrity problems. These problems do not show up until someone tries to summarize or aggregate the data. See Dyché (2001).

Improved data quality is the result of a business improvement process designed to identify and eliminate the root causes of bad data. Data warehouse applications require data cleansing every time the warehouse is populated or updated. See King (2002). To improve data quality and maintain accuracy requires an active data quality assurance program. Berg and Heagele (1997) provide a management perspective and model for improving data quality. We describe their *data quality action plan*, which provides a framework, in DSS in Focus 5.5. Some specific major benefits from examples of improving data quality include integrating the information systems of two businesses that merged after an acquisition. Instead of a three-year effort, it was completed in one year. Another example is that of getting a CRM system completed and serving the sales and marketing organizations in one year instead of working on it for three years

DSS IN FOCUS 5.5

A DATA QUALITY ACTION PLAN

A data quality action plan is a recommended framework for guiding data quality improvement. Here are the steps to follow:

1. Determine the critical business functions to be considered.
2. Identify criteria for selecting critical data elements.
3. Designate the critical data elements.
4. Identify known data-quality concerns for the critical data elements, and their causes.
5. Determine the quality standards to be applied to each critical data element.
6. Design a measurement method for each standard.

7. Identify and implement quick-hit data quality improvement initiatives.
8. Implement measurement methods to obtain a data-quality baseline.
9. Assess measurements, data quality concerns, and their causes.
10. Plan and implement additional improvement initiatives.
11. Continue to measure quality levels and tune initiatives.
12. Expand process to include additional data elements.

Source: Adapted from Berg and Heagele (1997).

and then canceling it (see Olson, 2003a, 2003b). The Montana Department of Corrections situation described in DSS in Action 5.4 recovered from its low-quality data problem by developing a culture of quality through a data quality assurance plan.

We describe some best practices for data quality in DSS in Focus 5.6. Practitioners have identified these as important for an organization to maintain a high level of data quality and integrity.

Data-quality issues, methods, and solutions are discussed in great detail by Berson et al. (2000), Canter (2002), Dasu and Johnson (2003), Dravis (2002), Dyché (2001),

DSS IN FOCUS 5.6

BEST PRACTICES FOR DATA QUALITY

Here are some best practices for ensuring data quality in practice.

- ***Data scrubbing is not enough.*** Data cleansing software only handles a few issues: inaccurate numbers, misspellings, incomplete fields. Comprehensive data-quality programs approach data standardization so that information can maintain its integrity.

- ***Start at the top.*** Top management must be aware of data quality issues and how they impact the organization. They must buy into any repair effort, because resources will be needed to address long-standing issues.

- ***Know your data.*** Understand what data you have, and what they are used for. Determine the

appropriate level of precision necessary for each data item.

- ***Make it a continuous process.*** Develop a culture of data quality. Institutionalize a methodology and best practices for entering and checking information.

- ***Measure results.*** Regularly audit the results to ensure that standards are being enforced and to estimate impacts on the bottom line.

Source: Adapted from Beth Stackpole, "Dirty Data Is the Dirty Little Secret That Can Jeopardize Your CRM Effort," *CIO*, February 15, 2001, pp. 101–114.

Eckerson (2002a), King (2002), Loshin (2001, 2003), Olson. (2003a, 2003b), Stackpole (2001), Stodder (2002), and Theodoratos and Bouzeghoug (2001).

DATA INTEGRITY

One of the major issues of DQ is **data integrity**. Older filing systems may lack integrity. That is, a change made in the file in one place may not be made in the file in another place or department. This results in conflicting data. Data quality specific issues and measures depend on the application of the data. This is an especially important issue in collaborative computing environments (Chapter 7), such as the one provided by Lotus Notes/Domino and Groove. In the area of the data warehouse, for example, Gray and Watson (1998) distinguish the following five issues:

- *Uniformity.* During data capture, uniformity checks ensure that the data are within specified limits.
- *Version.* Version checks are performed when the data are transformed through the use of metadata to ensure that the format of the original data has not been changed.
- *Completeness check.* A completeness check ensures that the summaries are correct and that all values needed to create the summary are included.
- *Conformity check.* A conformity check makes sure that the summarized data are "in the ballpark." That is, during data analysis and reporting, correlations are run between the value reported and previous values for the same number. Sudden changes can indicate a basic change in the business, analysis errors, or bad data.
- *Genealogy check or drill down.* A genealogy check or drill down is a trace back to the data source through its various transformations.

DATA ACCESS AND INTEGRATION

A decision-maker typically needs access to multiple sources of data that must be integrated (see the Opening Vignette and Case Applications 5.1 and 5.2). Before data warehouses, data marts, and business intelligence software, providing access to data sources was a major, laborious process. Even with modern Web-based data management tools, recognizing what data to access and providing it to the decision-maker is a nontrivial task that requires database specialists. As data warehouses grow in size, the issues of integrating data exasperate. This is especially important for the Department of Homeland Security. See Chabrow (2002) and DSS in Action 5.7 for how the DHS is working on a massive enterprise data and application integration project.

The needs of business analytics continue to evolve. In addition to historical, cleansed, consolidated, and point-in-time data, business users increasingly demand access to real-time, unstructured, and/or remote data. In addition, everything has to be integrated with the contents of their existing data warehouse. See Devlin, 2003. Moreover, access via PDAs and through speech recognition and synthesis is becoming more commonplace, further complicating integration issues (see Edwards, 2003).

Fox (2003) describes active information models for data transformation in developing an enterprise-wide system. These models take into consideration the necessary transformation logic to custom-developed high cost applications. Further, they must include the semantic and syntactic differences between schemas. This is especially important when corporate mergers occur and parallel applications must be integrated. Enterprise data resources can take many different forms: Relational Database (RDB) tables, XML documents, Electronic Data Interchange (EDI) messages, COBOL records, and so on. Independent Software Vendor (ISV) applications, such as enter-

HOMELAND SECURITY DATA INTEGRATION

Steve Cooper, special assistant to the president and CIO of the U.S. Department of Homeland Security (DHS), is responsible for determining which existing applications and types of data can help the organization meet its goal, migrating the data into a secure, usable, state-of-the-art framework, and integrating the disparate networks and data standards of 22 federal agencies, with 170,000 employees, that merged to form the DHS. This task is to be completed by mid-2005. The real problem is that federal agencies have historically operated autonomously, and their IT systems were not designed to interoperate with one another. Essentially, the DHS needs to link silos of data together.

The DHS has one of the most complex information-gathering and data migration projects under way in the federal government. The challenge of moving data from legacy systems (see Case Application 5.2), within or across agencies, is something all departments must address. Complicating the issue is the plethora of rapidly aging applications and databases throughout government. Data integration improvement is under way at the federal, local, and state levels. The government is utilizing tools from the corporate world.

Major problems have occurred because each agency has its own set of business rules that dictate how data are described, collected, and accessed. Some of the data are unstructured and not located in relational databases, and they cannot be easily manipulated and analyzed. Commercial applications will definitely be used in this major integration. Probably the bulk of the effort will be accomplished with data warehouse and data-mart technologies. Informatica, among other software vendors, has developed data integration solutions that enable organizations to combine disparate systems to make information more widely accessible throughout an organization. Such software may be ideal for such a large-scale project.

The idea is to decide on and create an enterprise architecture (see Case Application 5.2) for federal and state agencies involved in homeland security. The architecture will help determine the success of homeland defense. The first step in migrating data is to identify all the applications and data in use. After identifying applications and databases, the next step is to determine which to use and which to discard. Once an organization knows which data and applications it wants to keep, the difficult process of moving the data starts. First, it is necessary to identify and build on a common thread in the data. Another major challenge in the data-migration arena is security, especially when dealing with data and applications that are decades old.

Homeland Security will definitely have an information-analysis and infrastructure-protection component. This may be the single most difficult challenge for the DHS. Not only will Homeland Security have to make sense of a huge mountain of intelligence gathered from disparate sources, but then it will have to get that information to the people who can most effectively act on it. Many of them are outside the federal government.

Even the central government recognizes that data deficiencies may plague the DHS. Moving information to where it is needed, and doing so when it is needed, is critical and exceedingly difficult. Some 650,000 state and local law enforcement officials "operate in a virtual intelligence vacuum, without access to terrorist watch lists provided by the State Department to immigration and consular officials," according to the October 2002 Hart–Rudman report, "America Still Unprepared— America Still in Danger," sponsored by the Council on Foreign Relations. The task force cited the lack of intelligence sharing as a critical problem deserving immediate attention. "When it comes to combating terrorism, the police officers on the beat are effectively operating deaf, dumb and blind," the report concluded.

DARPA, the Defense Advanced Research Projects Agency, spent $240 million on combined projects on Total Information Awareness, to develop ways of treating worldwide, distributed legacy databases as if they were a single, centralized database.

Sources: Adapted from Eric Chabrow, "One Nation, Under I.T." *InformationWeek*, No. 914, November 11, 2002, pp. 47–50; Todd Datz, "Integrating America," *CIO*, December 2002, p. 44–51; John Foley, "Data Debate." *InformationWeek*, May 19, 2003, pp. 22–24; Amy Rogers Nazarov, "Informatica Seeks Partners to Gain Traction in Fed Market." *CRN*, June 9, 2003, p. 39; Patrick Thibodeau, "DHS Sets Timeline for IT Integration," *ComputerWorld*, June 16, 2003, p. 7; Katherine McIntire Peters, "5 Homeland Security Hurdles," *Government Executive*, Vol. 35, No. 2, pp. 18–21, February 2003; Amy Rogers, "Data Sharing Key to Homeland Security Efforts," *CRN*, No. 1019, November 4, 2002, pp. 39–40; and Karen D. Schwartz, "The Data Migration Challenge," *Government Executive*, Vol. 34, No. 16, December 2002, pp. 70–72.

prise resource planning, customer relationship management software, and in-house-developed software, define their own input and output schemas. Often, different schemas hold similar information structured differently. The information model is central in that it represents a neutral semantic view of the enterprise. See Fox (2003) for details. Case Application 5.2 describes how a firm developed an infrastructure for integrating data from disparate sources. DSS in Focus 5.8 describes the processes of extract, transform, and load (ETL), which are the basis for all data-integration efforts.

Many integration projects involve enterprise-wide systems. In DSS in Focus 5.9, we provide a checklist of what works and what does not work when attempting such a project. See Orovic (2003) for details and impacts. Also see Chapter 6 for details on DSS implementation.

Integrating data properly from various databases and other disparate sources is difficult. But when not done properly, it can lead to disaster in enterprise-wide systems like CRM, ERP, and supply chain projects (Nash, 2002). See DSS in Focus 5.10 for issues relating to data cleansing as a part of data integration. Also see Dasu and Johnson (2003). Madsen (2003) describes how a real-time delivery infrastructure (see Section 5.12) allows an enterprise to easily integrate applications on a repeatable basis and yet remain flexible enough to accommodate change.

The following authors discuss data integration issues, models, methods, and solutions: Balen (2000), Calvanese et al. (2001), Devlin (2003), Erickson (2003), Fox (2003), Holland (2000), McCright (2001), Meehan (2002), Nash (2002), Orovic (2003), Vaughan (2003), Pelletier, Pierre, and Hoang (2003), and Whiting (2002).

DATA INTEGRATION VIA XML

XML is quickly becoming the standard language for database integration and data transfer (Balen, 2000). By 2004, some 40 percent of all e-commerce transactions occurred over XML servers. This was up from 16 percent in 2002 (see Savage, 2001). XML may revolutionize electronic data exchange by becoming the *universal data translator* (Savage, 2001). Systems developers must be extremely careful because XML *cannot overcome poor business logic*. If the business processes are bad, no data integration method will improve them.

Even though XML is an excellent way to exchange data among applications and organizations, a critical issue is whether it can function well as a native database format in practice. XML is a mismatch with relational databases: it works, but is hard to maintain. There are difficulties in performance, specifically in searching large databases.

DSS IN FOCUS 5.8

WHAT IS ETL?

Extract, transform, and load (ETL) programs periodically extract data from source systems, transform them into a common format, and load them into the target data store, typically a data warehouse or data mart. ETL tools also typically transport data between sources and targets, document how data elements change as they move between source and target (e.g., metadata), exchange metadata with other applications as needed, and administer all run-time processes and operations (e.g., scheduling, error management, audit logs, statistics). ETL is extremely important for data integration and data warehousing.

Source: Adapted from Wayne Erickson, "The Evolution of ETL," in *What Works: Best Practices in Business Intelligence and Data Warehousing,* Vol. 15, The Data Warehousing Institute, Chatsworth, CA, June, 2003.

DSS IN FOCUS 5.9

WHAT TO DO AND WHAT NOT TO DO WHEN IMPLEMENTING AN ENTERPRISE-WIDE INTEGRATION PROJECT

WHAT TO DO:

1. Think globally and act locally. Plan enterprise-wide; implement incrementally.
2. Define integration framework components.
3. Focus on business-driven goals with high cost and low technical complexity.
4. Treat the enterprise system as your strategic application.
5. Pursue reusable, template-based approaches to development.
6. Use prototyping as the project estimate generator.
7. Think of integration at different levels of abstraction.
8. Expect to build application logic into the enterprise infrastructure.
9. Assign project responsibility at the highest corporate level and negotiate, negotiate, negotiate.
10. Plan for message logging and warehouse to track audit and recovery.

WHAT NOT TO DO:

1. Critique business strategy through the enterprise architecture. Instead evaluate the impact of the business strategy on IT.

2. Purchase more than you need for a given phase.
3. Substitute an enterprise application architecture for a data warehouse.
4. Force usage of near-real-time message-based integration unless it is absolutely mandatory.
5. Assume that existing process models will suffice for process integration; they are not the same.
6. Plan to change your business processes as part of the enterprise application implementation.
7. Assume that all relevant knowledge resides within the project team.
8. Be driven by centralizing any enterprise-level business objects as part of the enterprise application implementation.
9. Be intrusive into the existing applications.
10. Use ad hoc process and message modeling techniques.

Source: Adapted from V. Orovic, "To Do & Not to Do," *eAI Journal*, June, 2003, pp. 37–43.

XML uses a lot of space. Even so, there are native XML database engines. See DeJesus (2000) for more on these.

DATA INTEGRATION SOFTWARE

Developers of document and data capture and management software are increasingly utilizing XML to transport data from sources to destinations. For example, Captiva Software Corp., RTSe USA Inc., Kofax Image Products Inc., and Tower Software all utilize XML to move and upload documents to the Web, intranets, and wireless applications. RosettaNet XML Solutions create standard B2B protocols that increase supply chain efficiency. BizTalk Server 2000 uses XML to help companies manage their data, conduct data exchanges with e-commerce partners more easily, and lower costs (Savage, 2001). The ADT (formerly InfoPump) data-transformation tools from Computer Associates track changes in data and applications. The software lets companies extract and transform data from up to 30 sources including relational databases, mainframe IMS and VSAM files, and applications, and load them into a database or data warehouse. Vaughan (2003) provides a list of software tools that use XML to extract and transform data.

DSS IN FOCUS 5.10

ENTERPRISE DATA HOUSE CLEANING

Every organization has redundant data, wrong data, missing data, and miscoded data, probably buried in systems that do not communicate much. This is the attic problem familiar to most homeowners: Throw in enough boxes of seasonal clothes, holiday trim, family-history documents, and other important items, and soon the mess is too big to manage. It happens at companies, too. Multiple operating units, manufacturing plants, and other facilities may all run different vendors' applications for sales, human resources, and other tasks. The mix of disparate data makes for a pile of unsorted and unreconciled information. Integration becomes a major effort.

CLEANING HOUSE:

Before any data can be cleansed, your IT department must create a plan for finding and collecting all the data and then decide how to manage them. Practitioners offer this advice:

1. Decide what types of information must be captured. Set up a small data-mapping committee to do this.

2. Find mapping software that can harvest data from many sources, including legacy applications, PC files, HTML documents, unstructured sources, and enterprise systems. Several vendors have developed such software.

3. Start with a high-payoff project. The first integration project should be in a business unit that generates high revenue. This helps obtain upper-management buy-in.

4. Create and institutionalize a process for mapping, cleansing, and collating data. Companies must continually capture information from disparate sources.

Source: Adapted from Kim S. Nash, "Merging Data Silos," *ComputerWorld*, April 25, 2002, pp. 30–32.

5.4 THE WEB/INTERNET AND COMMERCIAL DATABASE SERVICES

External data pour into organizations from many sources. Some of the data come on a regular basis from business partners through collaboration (e.g., collaborative supply-chain management; see Chapters 7 and 8). The Internet is a major source of data.

- The **Web/Internet**. Many thousands of databases all over the world are accessible through the Web/Internet. A decision-maker can access the home pages of vendors, clients, and competitors, view and download information, or conduct research. The Internet is the major supplier of external data for many decision situations.

- Commercial data banks. An **online (commercial) database** service sells access to specialized databases. Such a service can add external data to the MSS in a timely manner and at a reasonable cost. For example, GIS data must be accurate; regular updates are available. Several thousand services are currently available, many of which are accessible via the Internet. Table 5.3 lists several representative services.

The collection of data from multiple external sources may be complicated. Products from leading companies, such as Oracle, IBM, and Sybase, can transfer information from external sources and put it where it is needed, when it is needed, in a usable form.

Since most sources of external data are on the Web, it makes sense to use intelligent agents to collect and possibly interpret external data. Pelletier, Pierre, and Hoang (2003) describe a multi-agent system designed for intelligent information retrieval from het-

TABLE 5.3   Representative Commercial Database (Data Bank) Services

CompuServe (compuserve.com) and The Source. Personal computer networks providing statistical data banks (business and financial market statistics) as well as bibliographic data banks (news, reference, library, and electronic encyclopedias). CompuServe is the largest supplier of such services to personal computer users.

Compustat (compustat.com). Provides financial statistics about tens of thousands of corporations. Data Resources Inc. offers statistical data banks for agriculture, banking, commodities, demographics, economics, energy, finance, insurance, international business, and the steel and transportation industries. DRI economists maintain a number of these data banks. Standard & Poor's is also a source. It offers services under the U.S. Central Data Bank.

Dow Jones Information Service. Provides statistical data banks on stock market and other financial markets and activities, and in-depth financial statistics on all corporations listed on the New York and American stock exchanges, plus thousands of other selected companies. Its Dow Jones News/Retrieval System provides bibliographic data banks on business, financial, and general news from the *Wall Street Journal, Barron's,* and the Dow Jones News Service.

Lockheed Information Systems. The largest bibliographic distributor. Its DIALOG system offers extracts and summaries of hundreds of different data banks in agriculture, business, economics, education, energy, engineering, environment, foundations, general news publications, government, international business, patents, pharmaceuticals, science, and social sciences. It relies on many economic research firms, trade associations, and government agencies for data.

Mead Data Central (www.mead.com). This data bank service offers two major bibliographic data banks. Lexis provides legal research information and legal articles. Nexis provides a full-text (not abstract) bibliographic database of hundreds of newspapers, magazines, and newsletters, news services, government documents, and so on. It includes full text and abstracts from the *New York Times* and the complete 29-volume *Encyclopedia Britannica.* Also provided are the Advertising & Marketing Intelligence (AMI) data bank and the National Automated Accounting Research System.

erogeneous distributed sources. The system uses software agents and is ideal for intelligent integration. For another example of how this is performed, see Liu et al. (2000).

THE WEB AND CORPORATE DATABASES AND SYSTEMS

Developments in **document management systems (DMS)** and **content management systems (CMS)** include the use of Web browsers by employees and customers to access vital information. Critical issues have become more critical in Web-based systems (see Gates, 2002; Rapoza, 2003). It is important to maintain accurate, up-to-date versions of documents, data, and other content, since otherwise the value of the information will diminish. Real-time computing, especially as it relates to DMS and CMS, has become a reality. Managers expect their DMS and CMS to produce up-to-the-minute accurate documents and information about the status of the organization as it relates to their work (see Gates, 2002; Raden, 2003a, 2003b). This real-time access to data introduces new complications in the design and development of data warehouses and the tools that access them. See Section 5.12 for details. Other Web developments include Pilot Software's Decision Support Suite (pilotsw.com) combined with BlueIsle Software's InTouch (blueisle.com) and group support systems deployed via Web browsers (e.g., Lotus Notes/Domino and Groove), and database management systems that provide data directly in a format that a Web browser can display with delivery over the Internet or an intranet. Pilot's Internet Publisher is a standalone Web product, as is DecisionWeb from Comshare (comshare.com).

The "big three" vendors of relational database management systems—Oracle, Microsoft, and IBM—all have core database products to accommodate a world of

client/server architecture and Internet/intranet applications that incorporate nontraditional, or rich, multimedia data types. So do other firms in this area. Oracle's Developer/2000 is able to generate graphical client/server applications in PL/SQL code, Oracle's implementation of structured query language (SQL), as well as in COBOL, C++, and HTML. Other tools provide Web browser capabilities, multimedia authoring and content scripting, object class libraries, and OLAP routines. Microsoft's .Net strategy supports Web-based business intelligence.

Among the suppliers of Web site and database integration are Spider Technologies (spidertech.com), Hart Software (hart.com), Next Software Inc. (next.com), NetObjects Inc. (netobjects.com), Oracle Corporation (oracle.com), and OneWave Inc. (onewave.com). These vendors link Web technology to database sources and to legacy database systems.

The use of the Web has had a far-reaching impact on collaborative computing in the form of groupware (Chapter 7), enterprise information systems (Chapter 8), knowledge-management systems (Chapter 9), document management systems, and the whole area of interface design, including the other enterprise information systems: ERP/ERM, CRM, PLM, and SCM.

5.5 DATABASE MANAGEMENT SYSTEMS IN DECISION SUPPORT SYSTEMS/BUSINESS INTELLIGENCE

The complexity of most corporate databases and large-scale independent MSS databases sometimes makes standard computer operating systems inadequate for an effective and efficient interface between the user and the database. A **database management system (DBMS)** supplements standard operating systems by allowing for greater integration of data, complex file structure, quick retrieval and changes, and better data security. Specifically, a DBMS is a software program for adding information to a database and updating, deleting, manipulating, storing, and retrieving information. A DBMS combined with a modeling language is a typical system-development pair used in constructing decision support systems and other management-support systems. DBMS are designed to handle large amounts of information. Often, data from the database are extracted and put in a statistical, mathematical, or financial model for further manipulation or analysis. Large, complex DSS often do this.

The major role of DBMS is to manage data. By *manage*, we mean to create, delete, change, and display the data. DBMS enable users to query data as well as to generate reports. For details, see Ramakrishnan and Gehrke (2002). Effective database management and retrieval can lead to immense benefits for organizations, as is evident in the situation of Aviall Inc., described in DSS in Action 5.11.

Unfortunately, there is some confusion about the appropriate role of DBMS and spreadsheets. This is because many DBMS offer capabilities similar to those available in an integrated spreadsheet such as Excel, and this enables the DBMS user to perform DSS spreadsheet work with a DBMS. Similarly, many spreadsheet programs offer a rudimentary set of DBMS capabilities. Although such a combination can be valuable in some cases, it may result in lengthy processing of information and inferior results. The add-in facilities are not robust enough and are often very cumbersome. Finally, the computer's available RAM may limit the size of the user's spreadsheet. For some applications, DBMS work with several databases and deal with many more data than a spreadsheet can.

DSS IN ACTION 5.11

AVIALL LANDS $3 BILLION DEAL

How important is effective data management and retrieval? Aviall Inc. attributes a $3 billion spare parts distribution contract that it won to its IT infrastructure. The ten-year contract requires the company to distribute spare parts for Rolls-Royce aircraft engines. The ability to offer technology-driven services, such as sales forecasting, down to the line-item level was cited as one of the reasons why Aviall was successful. It recently linked information from its ERP, supply chain management, customer-relationship management, and

e-business applications to provide access to its marine and aviation parts inventory and distribution (at a cost of some $30 to $40 million). The system is expected to pay for itself by cutting costs associated with "lost" inventory. Timely access to information is proving to be a competitive resource that results in a *big payoff.*

Source: Adapted from Marc L. Songini, "Distribution Deal Prods Tight IT Ties Between Aviall, Rolls-Royce," *ComputerWorld,* January 14, 2002.

For DSS applications, it is often necessary to work with both data and models. Therefore, it is tempting to use only one integrated tool, such as Excel. However, interfaces between DBMS and spreadsheets are fairly simple, facilitating the exchange of data between more powerful independent programs. Web-based modeling and database tools are designed to seamlessly interact (Fourer, 2001).

Small to medium DSS can be built either by enhanced DBMS or by integrated spreadsheets. Alternatively, they can be built with a DBMS program and a spreadsheet program. A third approach to the construction of DSS is to use a fully integrated DSS generator (Chapter 6).

5.6 DATABASE ORGANIZATION AND STRUCTURES

The relationships between the many individual records stored in a database can be expressed by several logical structures (see Kroenke, 2002; Mannino, 2001; McFadden et al., 2002; Post, 2002; and Riccardi, 2003). DBMS are designed to use these structures to perform their functions. The three conventional structures—relational, hierarchical, and network—are shown in Figure 5.1.

RELATIONAL DATABASES

The relational form of DSS database organization, described as tabular or flat, allows the user to think in terms of two-dimensional tables, which is the way many people see data reports. Relational DBMS allow multiple access queries. Thus, a data file consists of a number of columns proceeding down a page. Each column is considered a separate field. The rows on a page represent individual records made up of several fields, the same design that is used by spreadsheets. Several such data files can be related by means of a common data field found in two (or more) data files. The names of common fields must be spelled exactly alike, and the fields must be the same size (the same number of bytes) and type (e.g., alphanumeric or dollar). For example, in Figure 5.1 the data field Customer Name is found in both the customer and the usage file, and thus they are related. The data field Product Number is found in the product file and the

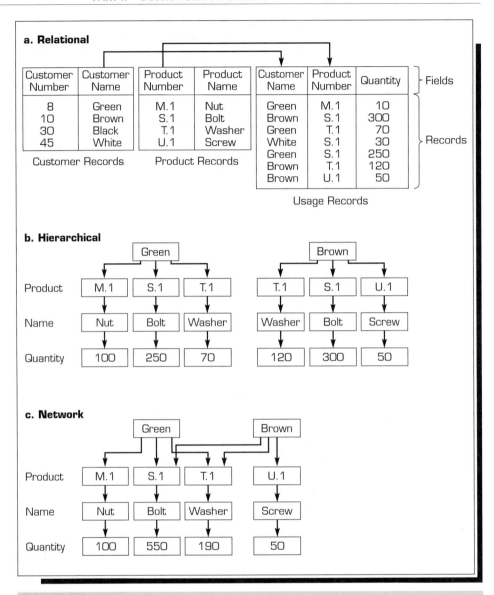

FIGURE 5.1 DATABASE STRUCTURES

usage file. It is through these common linkages that all three files are related and in combination form a **relational database**.

The advantage of this type of database is that it is simple for the user to learn, is easily expanded or altered, and can be accessed in a number of formats not anticipated at the time of the initial design and development of the database. It can support large amounts of data and efficient access. Many data warehouses are organized this way.

HIERARCHICAL DATABASES

A hierarchical model orders data items in a top-down fashion, creating logical links between related data items. It looks like a tree or an organization chart. It is used mainly in transaction processing, where processing efficiency is a critical element.

NETWORK DATABASES

The network database structure permits more complex links, including lateral connections between related items. This structure is also called the CODASYL model. It can save storage space through the sharing of some items. For example, in Figure 5.1, Green and Brown share S.1 and T.1.

OBJECT-ORIENTED DATABASES

Comprehensive MSS applications, such as those involving computer-integrated manufacturing (CIM), require accessibility to complex data, which may include pictures and elaborate relationships. Such situations cannot be handled efficiently by hierarchical, network, or even relational database architectures, which mainly use an alphanumeric approach. Even the use of SQL to create and access relational databases may not be effective. For such applications, a graphical representation, such as the one used in objected-oriented systems, may be useful.

Object-oriented data management is based on the principle of object-oriented programming (see details in the Web Chapter; also see Moore and Britt, 2001). Object-oriented database systems combine the characteristics of an object-oriented programming language, such as Veritos or UML, with a mechanism for data storage and access. The object-oriented tools focus directly on the databases. An **object-oriented database management system (OODBMS)** allows one to analyze data at a conceptual level that emphasizes the natural relationships between objects. Abstraction is used to establish inheritance hierarchies, and object encapsulation allows the database designer to store both conventional data and procedural code within the same objects.

An object-oriented data management system defines data as objects and encapsulates data along with their relevant structure and behavior. The system uses a hierarchy of classes and subclasses of objects. Structure, in terms of relationships, and behavior, in terms of methods and procedures, are contained within an object.

The worldwide relational and object-relational database management systems software market is expected to grow to almost $20 billion by 2006, according to IDC (The Day Group, 2002). Object-oriented database managers are especially useful in distributed DSS for very complex applications. Object-oriented database systems have the power to handle the complex data used in MSS applications. For a descriptive example, see DSS in Action 5.12. Trident Systems Group Inc. (Fairfax, Virginia) has developed a large-scale object-oriented database system for the U.S. Navy (see Sgarioto, 1999).

MULTIMEDIA-BASED DATABASES

Multimedia database management systems (MMDBMS) manage data in a variety of formats, in addition to the standard text or numeric field. These formats include images, such as digitized photographs, and forms of bit-mapped graphics, such as maps or .PIC files, hypertext images, video clips, sound, and virtual reality (multidimensional images). Cataloguing such data is tricky. Accurate and known key words must be used. It is critical to develop effective ways to manage such data for GIS and for many other Web applications. Managing multimedia data continues to become more important for business intelligence (see D'Agostino, 2003).

Most corporate information resides outside the computer in documents, maps, photos, images, and videotapes. For companies to build applications that take advantage of such rich data types, a special database management system with the ability to manage and manipulate multiple data types must be used. Such systems store rich mul-

G. PIERCE WOOD MEMORIAL HOSPITAL OBJECTS

Glenn Palmier, data processing manager for G. Pierce Wood Memorial Hospital (GPW), was not happy that the vendor of his database-management systems, InterSystems Corp., was upgrading to an object-oriented architecture in its core product, CACHE. At the time, GPW had 45 different systems developed over 15 years at the state mental health facility in Arcadia, Florida. Smooth operations and fast data access were critical to GPW. The vendor moved quickly, reducing a five-year conversion plan to eight months. By then, GPW had converted all its systems to be object-oriented and Web-based. GPW focused on data usability in the conversion process. Databases were updated to

work better in the new object-oriented environment. After reengineering the databases and upgrading, the new systems ran faster than ever before. For example, the old system required almost two hours to perform a certain query. The new system takes less than a minute. Personnel have been easily and quickly trained in the new systems, and the use of Web browsers to access data fits perfectly into the state's Internet strategy.

Source: Adapted from Jon William Toigo, "Objects Are Good for Your Mental Health." *Enterprise Systems*, June 2001, pp. 34-35.

---

timedia data types as *binary large objects* (BLOBS). Database management systems are evolving to provide this capability (McFadden et al., 2002). It is critical to design the management capability upfront, with scalability in mind. For a lucky example of a situation that was not developed as such, but worked, Hurwicz (2002) describes NASA's experience when it endeavored to download and catalogue images from space for educational purposes, as envisioned by astronaut Sally Ride. Fortunately, there was time and volunteer effort enough to redesign the cataloguing mechanism on the Web-based, multimedia database system. See Hurwicz (2002) for details about the development issues, and the EarthKAM Web site (www.earthkam.ucsd.edu) for direct access to the online, running database system. Note that similar problems can occur in data warehouse design and development.

For Web-related applications of multimedia databases, see Maybury (1997), and multimedia demonstrations on the Web, including those of Macromedia's products and Visual Intelligence Corporation. Also see DSS in Action 5.13. In DSS in Action 5.14, we describe how an animated film production company utilized several multimedia databases to develop the *Jimmy Neutron: Boy Genius* film. The databases and managerial techniques have since led to lower overall production costs for the animated television series.

Some computer hardware (including the communication system with the database) may not be capable of playback in real-time. A delay with some buffering might be necessary (e.g., try any audio or video player in Windows). Intel Corporation's Pentium processor chips incorporate multimedia extension (MMX) technology for processing multimedia data for real-time graphics display. Since then, this and similar technologies have been embedded in many CPU and auxiliary processor chips.

DOCUMENT-BASED DATABASES

Document-based databases, also known as electronic document management (EDM) systems (Swift, 2001), were developed to alleviate paper storage and shuffling. They are used for information dissemination, form storage and management, shipment tracking, expert license processing, and workflow automation. Many content management systems (CMS) are based on EDM. In practice, most are implemented in Web-based sys-

DSS IN ACTION 5.13

MULTIMEDIA DATABASE
MANAGEMENT SYSTEMS: A SAMPLER

IBM developed its DB2 Digital Library multimedia server architecture for storing, managing, and retrieving text, video, and digitized images over networks. Digital Library consists of several existing IBM software and hardware products combined with consulting and custom development (see ibm.com). Digital Library will compete head to head with multimedia storage and retrieval packages from other leading vendors.

MediaWay Inc. (mediaway.com) claims that its multimedia database management system can store, index, and retrieve multimedia data (sound, video, graphics) as easily as relational databases handle tabular data. The DBMS is aimed at companies that want to build what MediaWay calls *multimedia cataloging applications* that manage images, sound, and video across multiple back-end platforms. An advertising agency, for example, might want to use the product to build an application that accesses images of last year's advertisements stored on several servers. It is a client/server implementation. MediaWay is not the only vendor to target this niche, however. Relational database vendors, such as Oracle Corporation and Sybase Inc., have incorporated multimedia data features in their database servers. In addition, several desktop software companies promote client databases for storing scanned images. Among the industries that use this technology are health care, real estate, retailing, and insurance.

Source: Condensed and adapted from the Web sites and publicly advertised information of various vendors.

DSS IN ACTION 5.14

JIMMY NEUTRON: THE "I CAN FIX THAT" DATABASE

Producers and animators working on the film *Jimmy Neutron: Boy Genius* tracked thousands of frames on four massive databases. DNA Productions (Irving, Texas), the animation services company that worked with Nickelodeon and screenwriter and director Steve Oedekerk to produce the film, addressed the problem of assembling the 1800 shots that comprise the 82-minute film by logging and tracking them in four FileMaker Pro databases. One tracked initial storyboards, another tracked the shots assigned to individual artists, the third tracked the progress of each frame throughout the production process, and the fourth tracked retakes (changes to completed shots). At the film's completion, there were 20,000 entries. Each record tracked information about each shot dating back to the beginning of the project. The databases enabled the film to be completed in a mere eighteen months. The best part is that everyone had access to the shots instantly, instead of having to track down an individual or walk over to a large 4 by 8 foot (1.3 by 2.6 meter) board and look for it. Since making the film, the *Jimmy Neutron* TV series continues to utilize the database technology.

Source: Adapted from Stephanie Overby, "Animation Animation," *CIO*, 2002, May 15, 2002, pp. 22–24.

tems. See Bolles (2003), Gates (2002), and Rapoza (2003). Since EDM uses both object-oriented and multimedia databases, document-based databases were included in the preceding two sections. What is unique to EDM are the implementation and the applications. McDonnell Douglas Corporation distributes aircraft service bulletins to its customers around the world through the Internet. The company used to distribute a staggering volume of bulletins to over 200 airlines, using over 4 million pages of documentation every year. Now it is all on the Web, saving money and time both for the company and for its customers. Motorola uses DMS not only for document storage and retrieval but also for small-group collaboration and company-wide knowledge sharing. It has developed virtual communities where people can discuss and publish information, all with the Web-enabled DMS.

Web-enabled document management systems have become an efficient and cost effective delivery system. American Express now offers its customers the option of receiving monthly billing statements online, including the ability to download statement detail, retrieve prior billing cycles, and view activity that has been posted but not yet billed. As this option grows in popularity, it will reduce production and mailing costs. Xerox Corporation developed its first knowledge management system on its EDM platform (see Chapter 9).

INTELLIGENT DATABASES

Artificial intelligence (AI) technologies, especially Web-based intelligent agents and artificial neural networks (ANN), simplify access to and manipulation of complex databases. Among other things, they can enhance the database management system by providing it with an inference capability, resulting in an **intelligent database**.

Difficulties in integrating ES into large databases have been a major problem even for major corporations. Several vendors, recognizing the importance of integration, have developed software products to support it. An example of such a product is the Oracle relational DBMS, which incorporates some ES functionality in the form of a query optimizer that selects the most efficient path for database queries to travel. In a distributed database, for example, a query optimizer recognizes that it is more efficient to transfer two records to a machine that holds 10,000 records than vice versa. (The optimization is important to users because with such a capability they need to know only a few rules and commands to use the database.) Another product is the INGRES II Intelligent Database.

Intelligent agents can enhance database searches, especially in large data warehouses. They can also maintain user preferences (e.g., amazon.com) and enhance search capability by anticipating user needs. These are important concepts that ultimately lead to ubiquitous computing. See DSS in Focus 5.15 for details of recent developments in intelligent agents.

DSS IN FOCUS 5.15

THE BOTS OF THE FUTURE

There are plenty of software agents in use today. They are found in help systems, search engines, and comparison-shopping tools. During the next few years, as technologies mature and agents radically increase their value by communicating with one another, they will significantly affect an organization's business processes. Training, decision support, and knowledge sharing will be affected, but experts see procurement as the killer application of business-to-business agents. Intelligent software agents (bots) feature triggers that allow them to execute without human intervention. Most agents also feature adaptive learning of users' tendencies and preferences and offer personalization based on what they learn about users.

One goal of software agent developers is to develop machines that perform tasks that people do not want to do. Another is to delegate to machines tasks at which they are vastly superior to humans, such as comparing the price, quality, availability, and shipping cost of items.

BotKnowledge.com Agents can automatically perform intelligent searches, answer questions, tell you when an event occurs, individualize news delivery, tutor, and comparison shop.

Agents migrate from system to system, communicating and negotiating with each other. They are evolving from facilitators into decision-makers.

Source: Adapted from S. Ulfelder, "Undercover Agents," *ComputerWorld*, June 5, 2000.

One of IBM's main initiatives in commercial AI provides a knowledge-processing subsystem that works with a database, enabling users to extract information from the database and pass it to an expert system's knowledge base in several different knowledge representation structures. Databases now store photographs, sophisticated graphics, audio, and other media. As a result, access to and management of databases are becoming more difficult, and so are the accessibility and retrieval of information. The use of intelligent systems in database access is also reflected in the use of natural language interfaces which can be used to help nonprogrammers retrieve and analyze data.

5.7 DATA WAREHOUSING

The Opening Vignette demonstrates a scenario in which a **data warehouse** can be utilized to support decision-making, analyzing large amounts of data from various sources to provide rapid results to support a critical process. The necessary data are scattered across many government agencies, and consolidating the data to make them available when needed will entail serious organizational and technical challenges.

Organizations, private and public, continuously collect data, information, and knowledge at an increasingly accelerated rate and store them in computerized systems. Updating, retrieving, using, and removing this information becomes more complicated as the amount increases. At the same time, the number of users that interact with the information continues to increase as a result of improved reliability and availability of network access, especially including the Internet. Working with multiple databases is becoming a difficult task that requires considerable expertise (see DSS in Action 5.16). Data for the data warehouse are brought in from various external and internal

---

DSS IN ACTION 5.16

DATA WAREHOUSING SUPPORTS FIRST AMERICAN CORPORATION'S CORPORATE STRATEGY

First American Corporation changed its corporate strategy from a traditional banking approach to one that was centered on customer relationship management. This enabled First American to transform itself from a company that lost $60 million in 1990 to an innovative financial services leader a decade later. The successful implementation of this strategy would not have been possible without a data warehouse called VISION that stored information about customer behaviors, such as products used, buying preferences, and client value positions. VISION provided:

- Identification of the top 20 percent of profitable customers
- Identification of the 40–50 percent of unprofitable customers
- Retention strategies

- Lower-cost distribution channels
- Strategies to expand customer relationships
- Redesigned information flows.

Access to information through a data warehouse can enable both evolutionary and revolutionary change. First American Corporation was able to achieve revolutionary change, transforming itself into the *Sweet 16* of financial services corporations.

Source: Adapted from B. Cooper, H. J. Watson, B. H. Wixom, and D. Goodhue, "First American Tennessee Case Study," *MIS Quarterly*, 2004, forthcoming. Also presented as "Data Warehousing Supports Corporate Strategy at First American Corporation." SIM International's Best Paper Contest Recipients, 1999.

resources and are cleansed and organized in a manner consistent with the organization's needs. Once the data are populated in the data warehouse, data marts may be loaded for a specific area or department. Often, the data marts are bypassed, and business intelligence tools on client PCs simply load and manipulate local data cubes. Data warehouses can be described as subject-oriented, integrated, time-variant, non-normalized, non-volatile collections of data that support analytical decision-making. See Figure 5.2 for the data warehouse framework and views. Edelstein (1997) presents a good general introduction to data warehousing. Mannino (2001) discusses data warehouse technology and management.

Since enterprise information management solutions aggregate or consolidate report information and electronic documents created by any application running on any platform, the enterprise information management solution extends the access to information and reports processed from the data warehouse (see Mullin, 2002). An enterprise data warehouse is a comprehensive database that supports all decision analysis required by an organization by providing summarized and detailed information. As implied in this definition, the data warehouse has access to all information *relevant* to the organization, which may come from many different sources, both internal and external. See Figure 5.2 for how data work their way into the data warehouse (on the left), for further analysis by tools (to the right).

A data warehouse begins with the physical separation of a company's operational and decision support environments. At the heart of many companies lies a store of *operational data*, usually derived from critical mainframe-based online transaction processing (OLTP) systems, such as order entry point of sales applications. Many legacy

FIGURE 5.2   Data Warehouse Framework and Views

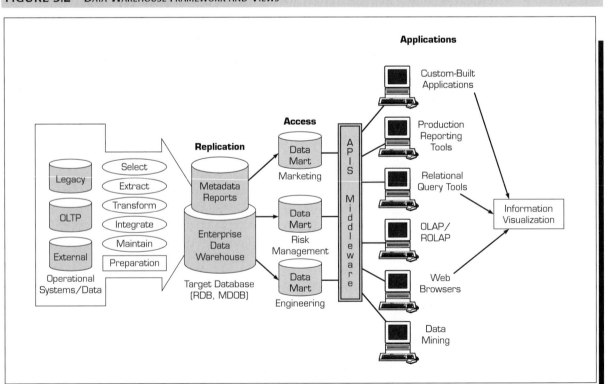

OLTP systems were implemented primarily in COBOL (especially banking systems), and still operate in a customer information control system (CICS) environment. OLTP systems for financial and inventory management and control, for example, also produce operational data. (Many firms are implementing Web front ends for such *legacy* systems. This could be a major and costly mistake. See Case Application 5.2 and Chapter 6.) In the operational environment, data access, application logic tasks, and data-presentation logic are tightly coupled together, usually in non-relational databases. OLTP data are usually detail data that control a specific event, such as the recording of a sales transaction, and are generally not summarized. These non-relational data stores are not very conducive to data retrieval for decision support/business intelligence/business analytic applications. However, decision support information must be made accessible to management. *It is important to physically separate the data warehouse from the OLTP system.*

CHARACTERISTICS OF DATA WAREHOUSING

The major characteristics of data warehousing are as follows:

- *Subject-oriented.* Data are organized by detailed subject (e.g., by customer, policy type, and claim in an insurance company), containing only information relevant for decision support. Subject orientation enables users to determine not only how their business is performing, but why. A data warehouse differs from an operational database in that most operational databases have a product orientation and are tuned to handle transactions that update the database; subject orientation provides a more comprehensive view of the organization.
- *Integrated.* Data at different source locations may be encoded differently. For example, gender data may be encoded as 0 and 1 in one place and "m" and "f" in another. In the warehouse they are *scrubbed* (cleaned) into one format so that they are standardized and consistent. Many organizations use the same terms for data of different kinds. For example, "net sales" may mean net of commission to the marketing department but gross sales returns to the accounting department. Integrated data resolve inconsistent meanings and provide uniform terminology throughout the organization. Also, data and time formats vary around the world.
- *Time-variant (time series).* The data do not provide the current status. They are kept for five or ten years or more and are used for trends, forecasting, and comparisons. There is a *temporal* quality to a data warehouse. *Time is the one important dimension that all data warehouses must support.* Data for analysis from multiple sources contain multiple time points (e.g., daily, weekly, monthly views).
- *Nonvolatile.* Once entered into the warehouse, data are read-only, they cannot be changed or updated. Obsolete data are discarded, and changes are recorded as new data. This enables the data warehouse to be tuned almost exclusively for data access. For example, large amounts of free space (for data growth) typically are not needed, and database reorganizations can be scheduled in conjunction with the load operations of a data warehouse.
- *Summarized.* Operational data are aggregated, when needed, into summaries.
- *Not normalized.* Data in a data warehouse are generally not normalized and highly redundant.
- *Sources.* All data are present; both internal and external.
- *Metadata.* **Metadata** (defined as *data about data*) are included.

METADATA

We include a discussion of metadata in the data warehousing section because they have major impacts on how data warehouses function. As mentioned earlier, the term metadata refers to data about data. Metadata describe the structure of and some meaning about the data, thereby contributing to their effective or ineffective use.

Marco (2001) indicates that metadata hold the key to resolving the challenge of making users comfortable with technology. Executives realize that knowledge differentiates corporations in the information age. Metadata involve knowledge, and capturing and making them accessible throughout an organization have become important success factors. With metadata and a metadata repository, organizations can dramatically improve their use of both information and application development processes. Building a metadata repository should be mandatory for many organizations. Business metadata benefits include the reduction of IT-related problems, increased system value to the business, and improved business decision-making.

According to Kassam (2002), *business metadata* comprises information that increases our understanding of traditional (i.e., structured) data reported. The primary purpose of metadata should be to provide context to the data; that is, enriching information leading to knowledge. Business metadata, though difficult to provide efficiently, releases more of the potential of structured data. The context need not be the same for all users. In many ways, metadata assist in the conversion of data and information into knowledge (see Chapter 9). Metadata form a foundation for a *metabusiness* architecture (see Bell, 2001). Tannenbaum (2002) describes how to identify metadata requirements. Vaduva and Vetterli (2001) provide an overview of metadata management for data warehousing.

Semantic metadata are metadata that describe contextually relevant or domain-specific information about content, in the right context, based on an industry-specific or enterprise-specific custom metadata model or ontology. Basically, this involves putting a level of understanding into metadata. Text mining (Section 5.11) may be a viable way to capture semantic metadata. See Sheth (2003) for details. ADT Enterprise Metadata Edition from Computer Associates extends the capabilities of ADT (described in the *Data Access and Integration* subsection of Section 5.3) to include metadata management capabilities (see Whiting, 2002).

DATA WAREHOUSING ARCHITECTURE AND PROCESS

There are several basic architectures for data warehousing. Two-tier and three-tier architectures are quite common, but sometimes there is only one tier. McFadden, Hoffer, and Prescott (2003) distinguished among these by dividing the data warehouse into three parts:

1. The data warehouse itself, which contains the data and associated software
2. Data acquisition (back-end) software, which extracts data from legacy systems and external sources, consolidates and summarizes them, and loads them into the data warehouse
3. Client (front-end) software, which allows users to access and analyze data in the warehouse (e.g., a DSS/BI/BA engine)

In three-tier architecture, operational systems contain the data and the software for data acquisition in one tier (server), the data warehouse is another tier, and the third tier includes the decision support/business intelligence/business analytics engine (i.e., the application server) and the client. The advantage of this architecture is its sep-

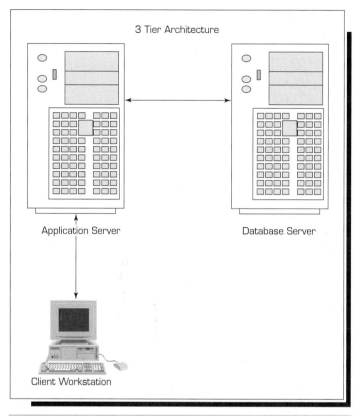

3 Tier Architecture

Application Server

Database Server

Client Workstation

FIGURE 5.3   ARCHITECTURE OF A 3-TIER DATA WAREHOUSE

aration of the functions of the data warehouse, which eliminates resource constraints and makes it possible to easily create data marts. See Figure 5.3.

The Vanguard Group moved to a Web-based three-tier architecture for its enterprise architecture to integrate all its data and provide customers with the same views of data as internal users (see Dragoon, 2003b). Likewise, Hilton migrated all of its independent client/server systems to a three-tier data warehouse using a Web design enterprise system. This change involved an investment of $3.8 million (excluding labor) and affected 1500 users. It increased processing efficiency (speed) by a factor of 6. Hilton expects to save $4.5 to $5 million annually. Hilton plans to experiment with Dell's clustering technology next (see Anthes, 2003.)

In two-tier architecture, the DSS engine is on the same platform as the warehouse. Therefore, it is more economical than the three-tier structure. See Figure 5.4. See Mimno (1997) for more on data warehouse architectures.

Web architectures are similar in structure, requiring a design choice for housing the Web data warehouse with the transaction server or as a separate server(s). Page loading speed is an important consideration in designing Web-based applications; therefore server capacity must be carefully planned for.

There are several issues to consider when deciding which architecture to use. Among them are:

1. Which database management system to use? Most data warehouses are built using relational database management systems. Oracle (Oracle Corporation),

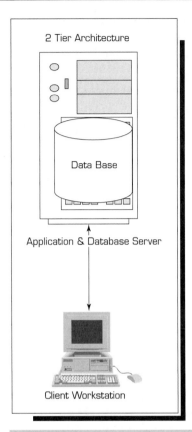

FIGURE 5.4   ARCHITECTURE OF A 2-TIER DATA WAREHOUSE

SQL Server (Microsoft), and DB2 (IBM) are most commonly used. Each of these products supports both client-server and Web-based architectures.

2. Will parallel processing and/or partitioning be utilized? Parallel processing enables multiple CPU's to process data warehouse query requests simultaneously and provides scalability. Data warehouse designers need to decide whether the database tables will be partitioned (split into smaller tables) for access efficiency and what the criteria will be. This is an important consideration that is necessitated by the large amounts of data contained in a typical data warehouse. Teradata has adopted this approach.

3. Will data migration tools be used to load the data warehouse?

4. What tools will be used to support data retrieval and analysis?

DATA WAREHOUSE DEVELOPMENT

A typical data warehouse structure is shown in Figure 5.2. The process of migrating data to a data warehouse involves the extraction of data from *all* relevant sources. Data sources may consist of files extracted from OLTP databases, spreadsheets, personal databases (e.g., Microsoft Access), or external files. Typically, all of the input files are written to a set of staging tables, which are designed to facilitate the load process. A data warehouse contains numerous business rules that define such things as how the data will be used, summarization rules, standardization of encoded attributes, and calculation rules. Any data quality issues pertaining to the source files need to be corrected before the data are loaded into the data warehouse. One of the benefits of a well-designed data warehouse is that these rules can be stored in a metadata repository and applied to the data warehouse centrally. This differs from an OLTP approach, which typically has data and business rules scattered throughout the system. The load process into a data warehouse can be performed either through data-transformation tools that provide a graphical user interface to aid in the development and maintenance business rule development or through more traditional methods by developing programs or utilities to load the data warehouse using programming languages such as PL/SQL, C++, or .Net. This decision does not come lightly for organizations. There are several issues that affect whether an organization will purchase data transformation tools or build the transformation process itself. These include:

1. Data transformation tools are expensive.
2. They may have a long learning curve.
3. It is difficult to measure how the IT organization is doing until it has learned to use the tools.

In the long run, a transformation-tool approach should simplify the maintenance of an organization's data warehouse. Transformation tools can also be effective in detecting and scrubbing; removing any anomalies in the data. OLAP and data-mining tools rely on how well the data are transformed.

STAR SCHEMAS

The data warehouse design is based upon the concept of **dimensional modeling**. Dimensional modeling is a retrieval-based model that supports high-volume query access. The star schema is the means by which dimensional modeling is implemented. A star schema contains a central *fact table*. A fact table contains the attributes needed to perform decision analysis, descriptive attributes used for query reporting, and foreign keys to link to dimension tables. The decision analysis attributes consist of performance measures, operational metrics, aggregated measures, and all other metrics needed to analyze the organization's performance. In other words, the fact table primarily addresses *what* the data warehouse supports for decision analysis. Surrounding the central fact tables (and linked via foreign keys) are **dimension tables**. Dimension tables contain attributes that describe the data contained within the fact table. Dimension tables address *how* data will be analyzed. Some examples of dimensions that would support a product fact table are location, time, and size. An example of a star schema is presented in Figure 5.5.

The **grain** of a data warehouse defines the highest level of detail that is supported. The grain will indicate whether the data warehouse is highly summarized or also includes detailed transaction data. If the grain is defined too high, then the warehouse may not support detail requests to **drill down** into the data. Drill down analysis is the process of probing beyond a summarized value to investigate each of the detail transactions that comprise the summary. A low level of granularity will result in more data being stored in the warehouse. Larger amounts of detail may impact the performance of queries by making the response times longer. Therefore, during the scoping of a data warehouse project, it is important to identify the right level of granularity that will be needed. See Tennant (2002) for a discussion of granularity issues in metadata.

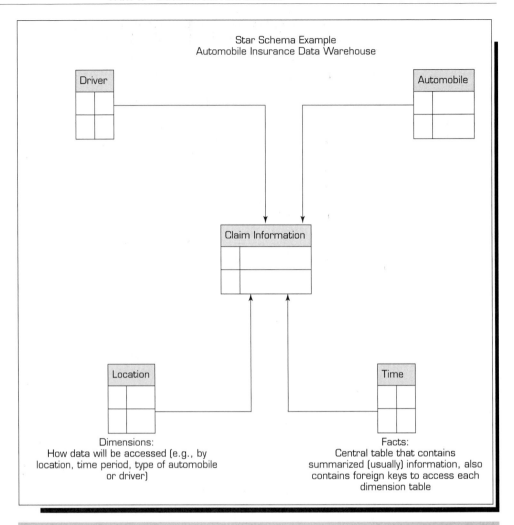

FIGURE 5.5   STAR SCHEMA

IMPLEMENTING DATA WAREHOUSING

Research by McKinsey and Co. indicates that much of the money invested in IT is wasted. IDC estimates that the world invested $5.6 trillion in IT during the 1990s ($2.6 trillion in the United States). IT investment had no impact on productivity in 53 of the 59 economic sectors of the McKinsey study. (We discuss IT effectiveness in Chapter 6.) However, McKinsey reports that IT investment can have an effective return on investment if applications are tied to specific business processes and linked to performance indicators (see Blair, 2003). This is critical in data warehouse and other large-scale database implementations. They must be useful, not just repositories of endless, useless data. They must drive business applications in ERP/ERM, revenue management, SCM, CRM, and so on.

Implementing a data warehouse is generally a massive effort that must be planned and executed according to established methods. In Chapter 6, we discuss these methods in detail. Here we discuss specific ideas and issues as they relate to data warehousing. Eckerson (2002b, 2003) describes the four major ways to develop a data ware-

DSS IN FOCUS 5.17

THE FOUR MAJOR APPROACHES
TO BUILDING A DATA WAREHOUSE

There are four major approaches to building a data warehousing environment: (1) top-down, (2) bottom-up, (3) hybrid, and (4) federated. Most organizations follow one or another of these approaches. In the top-down approach, the data warehouse is the center of the analytic environment. It is carefully designed and implemented. The design and implementation of all other aspects of business intelligence are based on it. This approach provides an integrated, flexible architecture to support later analytic data structures. In the bottom-up approach, the goal is to deliver business value by deploying multidimensional data marts quickly. Later these are organized into a data warehouse. The hybrid approach attempts to blend the first two

approaches. The federated approach is a concession to the natural forces that undermine the best plans for developing a perfect system. It uses all possible means to integrate analytical resources to meet changing needs or business conditions. Essentially, the federated approach involves integrating disparate systems (see the Opening Vignette and DSS in Action 5.7).

Sources: Adapted from Wayne Eckerson, "Four Ways to Build a Data Warehouse," _Application Development Trends,_ May 2002, pp. 20–21; Wayne Eckerson, "Four Ways to Build a Data Warehouse," _What Works: Best Practices in Business Intelligence and Data Warehousing,_ Vol. 15, The Data Warehousing Institute, Chatsworth, CA, June, 2003, pp. 46–49.

house. These include (1) top-down, (2) bottom-up, (3) hybrid, and (4) federated. We summarize these in DSS in Focus 5.17.

The federated approach is probably the least well known. Federation is often viewed as a form of information integration. It complements the traditional ETL and replication approaches by creating and maintaining a logical view of a single warehouse or mart, whereas the data reside in separate systems. See Devlin (2003) for details. One approach that is currently under development matches the notions that underlie peer-to-peer networks. Semantic Webs are used to wrap data into containers that reside in repositories in information space. This approach may be the solution to the massive data integration problem facing the Department of Homeland Security. See King (2003) for details.

Weir (2002) describes the best practices for implementing a data warehouse. We summarize these in DSS in Focus 5.18. Disaster may strike if one does not follow in the path of successful implementations. Adelman and Moss (2001) describe the risks confronting data warehouse projects. See DSS in Focus 5.19. Practitioners have unearthed a wealth of mistakes that have been made in the development of data warehouses. We summarize these in DSS in Focus 5.20. The three DSS in Focus boxes are, of course, interrelated. Watson et al. (1999) further discusses how such mistakes can lead to data warehouse failures.

Watson and Haley (1998) identified data warehouse projects as either data-centric or application-centric. A data-centric warehouse is based upon a data model that is independent of any application. It is designed to support a variety of user needs and applications. The methodological approach to designing a data-centric warehouse involves data modeling with a group of business experts who are familiar with the different information views needed to support the business. This consists of a top-down approach in producing specifications of information needs so as to not leave data behind. It is broad in scope and requires knowledge of current and anticipated data needs. A mapping approach should be used to provide a structured approach to classification of data. Data-centric warehouses should support flexibility because enterprise information constantly needs change based upon changes in the underlying business.

DSS IN FOCUS 5.18

BEST PRACTICES FOR DATA WAREHOUSE IMPLEMENTATION

Here is a list of best practices for implementing a data warehouse. They have been demonstrated in practice and constitute an excellent set of guidelines to follow.

- The project must fit with corporate strategy and business objectives.
- There must be complete buy-in to the project (executives, managers, users).
- Manage expectations.
- The data warehouse must be built incrementally.
- Build in adaptability.

- The project must be managed by both IT and business professionals.
- Develop a business/supplier relationship.
- Only load data that have been cleaned and are of a quality understood by the organization.
- Do not overlook training requirements.
- Be politically aware.

_____

Source: Adapted from Robert Weir, "Best Practices for Implementing a Data Warehouse," *Journal of Data Warehousing*, Vol. 7, No. 1, Winter, 2002, pp. 21–29.

The more dynamic the business, the greater the possibility that data needs will change during the development of the data warehouse. An application-centric warehouse is one initially designed to support a single initiative or small set of initiatives. This is a preferred approach for independent data mart development (see Section 5.8). The advantage of an application-centric approach is that it provides a more focused scope, and therefore increases the likelihood of successful data warehouse implementation. Its biggest disadvantage, however, is that critical data needs may be left out during the initial development, and therefore multiple iterations may be necessary.

DSS IN FOCUS 5.19

DATA WAREHOUSE RISKS

There are many risks in data warehouse projects. Most of them are also found in other IT projects (see Chapter 6), but they are more serious here because data warehouses are large-scale, expensive projects. Each risk should be assessed at the inception of the project. See the source for information on details and how to mitigate the risks:

- No mission or objective
- Quality of source data is not known
- Skills are not in place
- Inadequate budget
- Lack of supporting software
- Source data are not understood
- Weak sponsor
- Users are not computer literate
- Political problems, turf war

- Unrealistic user expectations
- Architectural and design risks
- Scope creep and changing requirements
- Vendors out of control
- Multiple platforms
- Key people may leave the project
- Loss of the sponsor
- Too much new technology
- Having to fix an operational system
- Geographically distributed environment
- Team geography, language culture

_____

Source: Adapted from Sid Adelman and Larissa Moss, "Data Warehouse Risks," *Journal of Data Warehousing*, Vol. 6, No. 1, Winter, 2001, pp. 9–15.

MISTAKES TO AVOID IN DEVELOPING A SUCCESSFUL DATA WAREHOUSE

When developing a successful data warehouse, watch out for these problems (see the explanations about each one):

1. *Starting with the wrong sponsorship chain.* You need an executive sponsor with influence over the necessary resources to support and invest in the data warehouse. You also need an executive *project driver*, someone who has earned the respect of other executives, has a healthy skepticism about technology, and is decisive but flexible. And you need an IS/IT manager to head up the project (the you in the project).

2. *Setting expectations that you cannot meet and frustrating executives at the moment of truth.* There are two phases in every data warehousing project: Phase 1 is the selling phase, where you internally market the project by selling the benefits to those who have access to needed resources. Phase 2 is the struggle to meet the expectations described in phase 1. For a mere $1–7 million, you can hopefully deliver.

3. *Engaging in politically naive behavior.* Do not simply state that a data warehouse will help managers make better decisions. This may imply that you feel they have been making bad decisions until now. Sell the idea that they will be able to get the information they need to help in decision-making.

4. *Loading the warehouse with information just because it was available.* Do not let the data warehouse become a data landfill. This would unnecessarily slow down the use of the system. There is a trend toward real-time computing and analysis. Data warehouses must be shut down to load data in a timely way.

5. *Believing that data warehousing database design is the same as transactional database design.* In general, it is not. The goal of data warehousing is to access aggregates rather than a single or a few records, as in transaction-processing systems. Content is also different, as is evident in how data are organized. Database management systems tend to be nonredundant, normalized, and relational, whereas data warehouses are redundant, unnormalized, and multidimensional.

6. *Choosing a data warehouse manager who is technology-oriented rather than user-oriented.* One key to data warehouse success is to understand that the users must get what they need, not advanced technology for technology's sake.

7. *Focusing on traditional internal record–oriented data and ignoring the value of external data and of*

text, images, and, perhaps, sound and video. Data come in many formats and must be made accessible to the right people at the right time in the right format. They must be catalogued properly.

8. *Delivering data with overlapping and confusing definitions.* Data cleansing is a critical aspect of data warehousing. This includes reconciling conflicting data definitions and formats organization-wide. Politically, this may be difficult, because it involves change, typically at the executive level.

9. *Believing promises of performance, capacity, and scalability.* Data warehouses generally require more capacity and speed than is originally budgeted for. Plan ahead to scale up.

10. *Believing that your problems are over once the data warehouse is up and running.* DSS/business intelligence projects tend to evolve continually (see Chapter 6). Each deployment is an iteration of the prototyping process. There will always be a need to add more and different data sets to the data warehouse, as well as additional analytic tools for existing and additional groups of decision-makers. High energy and annual budgets must be planned for because success breeds success. Data warehousing never ends.

11. *Focusing on ad hoc data mining and periodic reporting instead of alerts.*

The natural progression of information in a data warehouse is

1. *Extract* the data from legacy systems, clean them, and feed them to the warehouse;

2. *Support* ad hoc reporting until you learn what people want; and then

3. *Convert* the ad hoc reports into regularly scheduled reports.

This may be natural, but it is not optimal or even practical. Managers are busy and need time to read reports. *Alert systems* are better and can make a data warehouse mission critical. Alert systems monitor the data flowing into the warehouse and inform all key people with a need to know as soon as a critical event occurs.

Source: Adapted from R. C. Barquin, A. Paller, and H. Edelstein, "Ten Mistakes to Avoid for Data Warehousing Managers," Chapter 7 in R. Barquin and H. Edelstein. (eds.). *Building, Using, and Managing the Data Warehouse*, Upper Saddle River, NJ: Prentice Hall PTR, 1997.

Wixom and Watson (2001) defined a research model for data warehouse success that identified seven important implementation factors that can be categorized into three criteria (organizational issues, project issues, and technical issues). The factors are:

1. Management support
2. Champion
3. Resources
4. User participation
5. Team skills
6. Source systems
7. Development technology

In many organizations, a data warehouse will only be successful if there is strong senior *management support* for its development and a *project champion* (see the best practices, risks, and mistakes described above). Although one might argue that this would be true for any information technology project, it is especially important for a data warehouse. The successful implementation of a data warehouse results in the establishment of an architectural framework that may allow for decision analysis throughout an organization and in some cases also provides comprehensive supply-chain management by granting access to an organization's customers and suppliers. The implementation of Web-based data warehouses (*Webhousing*) has facilitated ease of access to vast amounts of data, but it is difficult to determine the *hard benefits* associated with a data warehouse. Hard benefits are defined as benefits to an organization that can be expressed in monetary terms. Many organizations have limited information-technology resources and must prioritize which projects will be worked on first. Management support and a strong project champion can help ensure that a data warehouse project will receive the resources necessary for successful implementation. Data warehouse *resources* can be a significant cost, in some cases requiring high-end processors and large increases in direct-access storage devices (DASD). Web-based warehouses may also have special security requirements to ensure that only authorized users have access to the data.

User participation in the development of data and access modeling is a critical success factor in data warehouse development. During data modeling, expertise is required to determine what data are needed, define business rules associated with the data, and decide what aggregations and other calculations may be necessary. Access modeling is needed to determine how data are to be retrieved from a data warehouse, and will assist in the physical definition of the warehouse by helping to define which data require indexing. It may also indicate whether dependent data marts are needed to facilitate information retrieval. The *team skills* needed to develop and implement a data warehouse require in-depth knowledge of the database technology and development tools utilized. **Source systems** and **development technology**, as mentioned previously, reference the many inputs and the process used to load and maintain a data warehouse.

MASSIVE DATA WAREHOUSES AND SCALABILITY

In addition to flexibility, a data warehouse needs to support scalability. The main issues pertaining to scalability are the amount of data in the warehouse, how quickly the warehouse is expected to grow, the number of concurrent users, and the complexity of user queries. A data warehouse must scale both horizontally and vertically. The warehouse will grow as a function of data growth and the need to expand the warehouse to support new business functionality. Data growth may be caused by the addition of current cycle data (e.g., this month's results) and/or historical data.

Hicks (2002) describes huge databases and data warehouses. In 2002, the Wal-Mart data warehouse was estimated to have a 200-terabyte capacity. The first petabyte-capacity data warehouse was made available in early 2004. Because of the storage required to archive its news footage, CNN plans to be one of the first organizations to install a petabyte-sized data warehouse (see Newman, 2002).

Given that the size of data warehouses is expanding at an exponential rate, *scalability* is an important issue. Good scalability means that queries and other data-access functions will grow (ideally) linearly with the size of the warehouse. In practice, specialized methods have been developed to create scalable data warehouses. Nance (2001) describes scalability issues in data warehouse situations. Scalability is difficult in managing hundreds of terabytes or more. Terabytes of data have considerable inertia, occupy a lot of physical space, and require powerful computers. Some firms utilize parallel processing, others use clever indexing and search schemes to manage their data. Some spread their data across different physical data stores. As data warehouses approach the petabyte size, better and better solutions to scalability continue to be developed.

Deng (2003) describes the importance of effective indexing for data warehouses. Correct indexing can definitely lead to efficient searches through massive amounts of data. As a data warehouse is designed, it is important to consider correct indexing to help solve scalability problems. Hall (2002) also addresses scalability issues. Sears is an industry leader in deploying and utilizing massive data warehouses. See DSS in Action 5.21 for details.

USERS, CAPABILITIES, AND BENEFITS

Analysts, managers, executives, administrative assistants, and professionals are the major end-users of data warehouses. A data warehousing solution should provide ready access to critical data, insulate operation databases from ad hoc processing that can slow TPS systems, and provide high-level summary information as well as data drill-down capabilities. These properties can improve business knowledge, provide competitive advantage, enhance customer service and satisfaction, facilitate decision-making, improve worker productivity, and help streamline business processes.

DATA WAREHOUSING APPLICATIONS

Allan (2001) provides an excellent example of a data warehouse. He addresses issues associated with the modeling of student record data for use in the student record data mart portion of a data warehouse for a college or university. Ryder uses its data warehouse for logistics. See DSS in Action 5.22.

DSS IN ACTION 5.21

THE SEARS DATA WAREHOUSE GROWS

By April 2002, Sears, Roebuck and Co. had deployed 95 terabytes of new storage capacity, tripling its capacity. This allowed Sears to consolidate two key data warehouses and build a storage area network that handles its inventory and sales data warehouse with its customer information.

With the system, Sears can perform effective targeted promotional mailings. About 5,000 Sears employ-ees use the data warehouse for analytical purposes. They can get daily product-sales information, analyze the purchases of individual customers, and correlate them with previous purchases.

Source: Adapted from Lucas Mearian, "Sears Triples Its Storage Capacity," *ComputerWorld*, February 28, 2002, pp. 1, 53.

DSS IN ACTION 5.22

RYDER RIDES INTO E-LOGISTICS

With a new data warehouse, Ryder Systems Inc. has revamped its e-commerce strategy to match more than 1000 fleet customers and common carriers with freight that needs to be moved immediately. The effort is aimed at expanding Ryder's fleet-management supply-chain business. The system uses a transportation analytics package based on technology from NCR Corp.'s

Teradata data warehouse division and MicroStrategy Inc., a business analytics software vendor. The new system will let shippers place orders online and let carriers book orders in real-time. More is planned for the future.

Source: Adapted from Steve Konicki, "Ryder Trucks into New E-logistics Strategy," *InformationWeek,* June 11, 2001, p. 40.

DSS IN ACTION 5.23

WAL-MART IDENTIFIES AND MEETS UNEXPECTED CUSTOMER DEMAND THROUGH A DATA WAREHOUSE

One instance of timely information being crucial to Wal-Mart took place after the attacks of September 11, 2001. Wal-Mart was able to quickly identify the buying patterns of its customers on the day of the attacks as the demand for weapons, bottled water, and survival gear increased, and then shifted to American flags the day afterwards. Wal-Mart was able to meet customer demand rapidly and could plan accordingly. It was able

to project that customers were delaying normal purchases for a few days, and expected and met the unusual higher demand afterwards.

Source: Adapted from C. Newman, "Teradata: Your Next Best Action with Your Customers," *Teradata Magazine,* Quarter 3, 2002.)

Wal-Mart is an undisputed leader in the data warehouse area. Westerman (2000) describes the effective Wal-Mart model. DSS in Action 5.23 is a small example of the effective use of Wal-Mart's data warehouse.

The major data warehouse vendors are Carleton, IBM, Informix, Microsoft, NCR, Oracle, Red Brick, and Sybase. For more on data warehousing, see Adelman and Moss (2001), Allan (2001), Barquin and Edelstein (1997a, 1997b), Barquin, Paller, and Edelstein (1997), Deng (2003), Eckerson (2002b, 2003), Edelstein (1997), Hall (2002), Konicki (2001), Mannino (2001), Mearian (2002), Mimno (1997), Mullin (2002), Nance (2001), Newman (2002), Watson and Haley (1998), Watson et al. (1999), Weir (2002), Westerman (2000), and Wixom and Watson (2001).

5.8 DATA MARTS

A **data mart** is a subset of the data warehouse, typically consisting of a single subject area (e.g., marketing, operations). A data mart can be either *dependent* or *independent*. A **dependent data mart** is a subset that is created directly from the data warehouse. It has the advantages of using a consistent data model and providing quality data. Dependent data marts support the concept of a single enterprise wide data model, but the data warehouse must be constructed first. A dependent data mart ensures that the end-user is viewing the same version of the data that is accessed by all other data warehouse users.

The high cost of data warehouses limits their use to large companies. As an alternative, many firms use a lower-cost, scaled-down version of a data warehouse referred to as an **independent data mart**. An independent data mart is a small warehouse designed for a strategic business unit (SBU) or a department, but its source is not an enterprise data warehouse.

The advantages of data marts include the following:

- The cost is low in comparison to an enterprise data warehouse (under $100,000 vs. $1 million or more).
- The lead time for implementation is significantly shorter, often less than 90 days.
- They are controlled locally rather than centrally, conferring power on the user.
- They contain less information than the data warehouse and hence have more rapid response and are more easily understood and navigated than an enterprise-wide data warehouse.
- They allow a business unit to build its own decision support systems without relying on a centralized IS department.
- An independent data mart can serve as a proof of concept prior to investing the resources needed to develop a comprehensive enterprise data warehouse. This will generate a quicker return on investment by realizing benefits sooner.

There are several types of data marts:

1. Replicated (dependent) data marts. Sometimes it is easier to work with smaller parts of the warehouse. In such cases one can replicate functional subsets of the data warehouse in smaller databases, each of which is dedicated to certain areas, as shown in Figure 5.2. In this case the data mart is an addition to the data warehouse.
2. Independent data marts. A company can have one or more independent data marts without having a data warehouse. In such cases there is a need to integrate the data marts. This is possible only if each data mart is assigned a specific set of information for which it is responsible. The IS department specifies the rules to the metadata so that the information kept by each mart is compatible with that provided by all the other marts. When this is not done, the data marts are difficult to integrate, creating potentially serious fragmentation problems for the organization.

5.9 BUSINESS INTELLIGENCE/BUSINESS ANALYTICS

Now that we know about databases, data warehouses, data marts, and the analytical decision-making methods discussed in Chapter 4, we are ready to discuss business intelligence/business analytics intelligently.

Business intelligence describes the basic architectural components of a business intelligence environment, ranging from traditional topics, such as business process modeling and data modeling, to more modern topics, such as business rule systems, data profiling, information compliance and data quality, data warehousing, and data mining (see Loshin, 2003).

Business intelligence involves acquiring data and information (and perhaps even knowledge, see Chapter 9) from a wide variety of sources and utilizing them in decision-making. Technically, **business analytics** adds an additional dimension to business intelligence: models and solution methods. These are often buried so deep within the tools, however, that the analyst need not get his or her hands "dirty." Typically, the

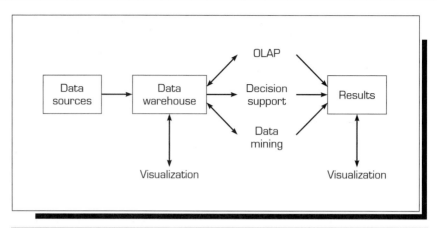

FIGURE 5.6   THE ACTIVITIES OF BUSINESS INTELLIGENCE

terms are used interchangeably. We show the activities of business intelligence in Figure 5.6. Business intelligence methods and tools are highly visual in nature. They provide charts and graphs of multidimensional data with the click of a mouse. These methods generally access data from data warehouses and deposit them into a local, multidimensional database system. *Online analytical processing (OLAP)* methods allow an analyst, or even (less typically) a manager to slice and dice the data, while observing graphs and tables that reflect the dimensions being observed. Models may be applied to the data for forecasting or to identify opportunities (for software examples, see Temtec Executive Viewer, Cognos Impromptu and PowerPlay, and IBM Cube Views). **Data mining** methods apply statistical and deterministic models, and artificial intelligence methods to data, perhaps guided by an analyst (or manager), to identify hidden relationships or induce/discover knowledge among the various data or text elements (for software examples, see IBM DB2 Intelligent Miner Scoring, Angoss KnowledgeSeeker, Megaputer Intelligence PolyAnalyst, and SAS Enterprise Miner). Data mining is also highly visual in the way results are displayed. Graphs and charts typically display results. Thus the key difference between OLAP and data mining is that data mining runs (mostly) automatically, while OLAP is driven. As tools improve in ease of use, more and more managers utilize them, resulting in a trend to move business intelligence from the analyst to the user (manager). This introduces a new problem: Managers sometimes do not fully understand business intelligence/business analytics methods. In consequence, their focus may be on visualization rather than application of appropriate and accurate analysis tools. With both tools, it is important to recognize that systems analysts are generally required to set up the access to the data to be analyzed. This involves dealing with data cleansing and integration, a task best left to IS specialists. See the Opening Vignette and DSS in Action 5.7.

All managers and executives should be using business intelligence systems, but some find the data irrelevant or the tools too complicated to use. Sometimes managers are not trained properly. Distributing information from analytics throughout a company is a major challenge; most businesses want a greater percentage of the enterprise to leverage analytics, but most of the challenges around technology involve culture, people, and processes (see Hatcher, 2003). A critical issue is to align BI systems to business needs. If the system does not provide useful information, it is considered useless. See DSS in Focus 5.24 for details of a recent study on how executives currently utilize business intelligence tools.

DSS IN FOCUS 5.24

ARE BUSINESS INTELLIGENCE SYSTEMS MAKING FIRMS SMARTER?

More than 570 IT executives responded to *CIO Insight*'s Business Intelligence Research Study. *CIO Insight* discovered some interesting facts about the current state of business intelligence.

- Most notably, the use of business intelligence technologies is high, and growing.
- Larger companies are somewhat more likely than smaller companies to use BI.
- In 2002, successful companies spent almost 50 percent more on BI technology than unsuccessful companies. BI seems to be necessary (but not sufficient) for success.
- The government utilizes virtually every market intelligence technology at significantly higher rates than any other sector of the economy.
- The technologies used to collect, aggregate, analyze, and report on competitive intelligence along with the percentage response in parentheses are: reporting tools (82.1), automated data/information

feeds (79), intranets/portals (70.4), data warehousing (69.8), content management (63), data-visualization software (41.4), specialty search engines (41.4), work-flow software (41.4), and harvesting (e.g., intelligent agents) (38.9).

- Just 49 percent of less successful companies are happy with their competitive intelligence efforts.
- Some 88 percent of companies have confidence in the accuracy of the customer information they gather.
- Dissatisfaction with BI usually derives from difficulty in distributing the results.
- CIOs want to move firms to the real-time enterprise.

Source: Adapted from "The 2003 CIO Insight Business Intelligence Research Study: Are Your BI Systems Making You Smarter?" *CIO Insight*, No. 26, May 23, 2003.

In the first 50 years of computing history, computing systems have had a deep and comprehensive infusion into various business domains. Computing systems are now an indispensable infrastructure with which we run, manage, and coordinate business operations. In the first decade of the new millennium, we see a new era of ubiquitous computing systems. Analytics will interweave most, if not all, enterprise systems (Delic and Dayal, 2003). Decision-makers throughout every enterprise need an IT architecture that serves their needs, rather than the other way around. Delic and Dayal (2003) provide an impressive view of emerging enterprise analytic systems (see Chapter 8) that use business intelligence/business analytics requirements as their basis.

According to an IDC report issued in the fall of 2002, organizations that have successfully implemented and used analytic applications have realized returns ranging from 17 percent to more than 2000 percent, with a median ROI of 122 percent ("The Financial Impact of Business Analytics," IDC, October 2002; also see Kaliebe, 2003). Even so, more than half of all business intelligence projects fail. As with data warehousing, business intelligence activities should be regarded, not simply as another set of IT projects, but as a constantly evolving strategy, vision, and architecture that continuously seeks to align an organization's operations and direction with its strategic business goals. We discuss the notion that BI/DSS are never really complete in Chapter 6. They continue to evolve. Companies achieve success when they do the following (see Atre, 2003):

- Make better decisions with greater speed and confidence.
- Streamline operations.
- Shorten product development cycles.

- Maximize value from existing product lines and anticipate new opportunities.
- Create better, more focused marketing as well as improved relationships with customers and suppliers.

Organizations must understand and address many critical challenges for business intelligence success. We describe these in DSS in Focus 5.25.

Business intelligence tools (both data mining and OLAP) have been used to identify white-collar theft in organizations. They are able to identify inflated invoices, embezzlement, customer impersonation, and similar offenses. The estimate of total fraud in the United Kingdom is almost $30 billion (U.S.). Frauds committed by employees cause median losses of $60,000, while frauds committed by managers or executives cause median losses of $250,000. When managers and employees conspire, the median loss rises to $500,000. If all internal data systems are integrated with a data warehouse for fraud analysis so they can be compared to external fraud-related data. Patterns and anomalies become more readily identifiable. Suspicious activities can be isolated, measured, and tracked. See Dorrington (2003) for details.

Williams-Sonoma saves millions with targeted marketing, multichannel branding using the SAS data mining software, Enterprise Miner, along with a suite of CRM applications from SAS. The new marketing system models and explores customer data from more than 30 million households to help the retailer create a personalized, cohesive shopping experience across multiple channels and multiple brands. See Bolen (2003) for details. Callaghan (2003a) describes how SPSS Predictive Web Analytics and SAS Web can be utilized to predict customer Web behavior and develop customer segmentation models (clusters) that lead to better business performance. Retailers frequently use business intelligence tools, as we show in DSS in Action 5.26.

New forms of business intelligence continue to emerge. Performance management systems (PMS) are one of the new forms. These are business intelligence tools that provide scorecards and other relevant information with which decision-makers can determine their level of success in reaching their goals. Two tools include Business

---

TEN CRITICAL CHALLENGES FOR BUSINESS INTELLIGENCE SUCCESS

There are 10 reasons why business intelligence projects fail. Organizations must understand and address these 10 critical challenges for success:

1. Failure to recognize BI projects as cross-organizational business initiatives, and to understand that as such they differ from typical standalone solutions.
2. Unengaged or weak business sponsors.
3. Unavailable or unwilling business representatives.
4. Lack of skilled and available staff, or suboptimal staff utilization.
5. No software release concept (no iterative development method).

6. No work breakdown structure (no methodology).
7. No business analysis or standardization activities.
8. No appreciation of the impact of dirty data on business profitability.
9. No understanding of the necessity for and the use of metadata.
10. Too much reliance on disparate methods and tools.

Source: Adapted from Shaku Atre, "The Top 10 Critical Challenges for Business Intelligence Success." *ComputerWorld,* White Paper/Special Advertising Supplement, Vol. 37, No. 26, June 30, 2003.

DSS IN ACTION 5.26

RETAIL MAKES STEADY
BUSINESS INTELLIGENCE PROGRESS

Hudson's Bay Co. turned 333 in May 2003. Despite its age, Hudson's Bay upgraded its information systems to give executives, store managers, and key suppliers methods to analyze reams of sales and customer data. The challenge the firm faces is to determine how to transform the data into useful information. The firm uses two data warehouses and business intelligence tools from the Teradata division of NCR Corp. to track and make decisions on product inventory and sales.

Most brick-and-mortar retailers lag other industries in business intelligence. Notable exceptions include Wal-Mart Stores Inc. and Sears. Other retailers continue to make impressive strides.

At Harry Rosen Inc., a chain of 17 men's clothing stores, executives use Cognos Inc.'s data analysis tools integrated into a merchandising system. There are more than a dozen sales and inventory reports for analyzing sales that help the firm identify sales trends, manage inventory, and improve gross profit margins.

Other retailers are looking for similar ways to obtain a competitive edge. Putting the right products in the right place at the right time at the right price (see revenue management in Chapter 4) is the goal of retail-

ers. Doing it right determines who succeeds, and who fails.

Using business intelligence and analysis tools from BusinessObjects SA, TruServ Corp. (the parent company of True Value Hardware and Taylor Rental) reduced its "red zone" inventory (products that have not sold in one-half year) by $50 million over two years by analyzing product stockpiles. For about a year, the system has also identified products sitting in its 14 distribution centers that might sell better in other parts of the country.

Stores are learning from online retailers about how to perform analytic investigations of customer performance. For example, J. Crew Group and Nordstrom Inc. use DigiMine to analyze online sales. Nordstrom had a situation where online shoppers were searching for navel rings just like the one that a model wore in an advertisement. Nordstrom was able to quickly obtain the rings for both its stores and online customers, even though it had not carried the product beforehand.

Source: Adapted from Rick Whiting, "Business-Intelligence Buy-In," *InformationWeek*, May 12, 2003, pp. 56–60.

Objects S.A. Performance Manager and the SAS Institute, Inc. Activity-Based Management 6.0. Both provide Web-enabled analysis. Business Objects S.A. Performance Manager software includes goal management, scorecards, and strategy maps, and enables customers to align goals and performance with enterprise strategy. The SAS Institute, Inc. Activity-Based Management 6.0 provides cost and productivity analysis of customers, products, services, or business processes. See Callaghan (2003c) for details.

DASHBOARDS

Dashboards provides managers with exactly the information they need in the correct format at the correct time. Business intelligence systems are the foundation of dashboards, which have evolved from executive information systems into enterprise information systems that access data warehouses via OLAP systems (see Chapter 8 and Leon, 2003). Dashboards can impact on communications and company politics. Dashboards and scorecards measure and display what is important. Each individual, ideally, can focus on what is important to him or her. Essentially a dashboard is a preset OLAP display. See Figure 5.7 for an example of Brio Performance Suite's "CEO Dashboard." MQSoftware, Inc.'s Q Pasa! Business Dashboard provides real-time views of data. Cognos Visualizer Series 7 is another example of a corporate dashboard that helps give managers insight to make better decisions. It is part of Cognos Business

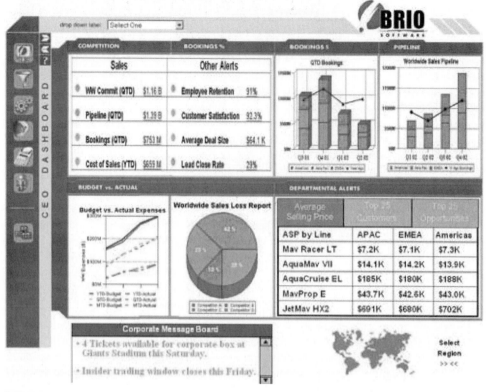

FIGURE 5.7   SCREEN SHOT FROM BIO PERFORMANCE SUITE DIGITAL DASHBOARD

Courtesy of Brio Software Inc.

Intelligence. Business intelligence dashboards have spread to various nonfinancial departments of firms, including sales and customer service. See Table 5.4 for details of how dashboards have spread through organizations.

At Southwest Airlines, they call digital dashboards *cockpits*. Individuals get customized views of the information they need for their work. At Honeywell Inc.'s Specialty Materials Division in Morristown, New Jersey, Cognos Inc. dashboards give everyone in sales a clear view into daily business performance. Sales representatives can see their own sales statistics, but they can also see how others are doing, as can managers. This has led not only to a move from monthly and quarterly data views to daily views. Now the firm has a common definition and view of all information.

TABLE 5.4   Departments with Dashboards

Department	*Percent*
Sales	21.1
Finance	18.8
Customer service	14.3
Manufacturing/operations	12
Supply chain management	10.5
Human resources	8.3

Source: Adapted from M. Leon, "Dashboard Democracy," *ComputerWorld,* June 16, 2003.

BUSINESS INTELLIGENCE ASSESSMENT

A business intelligence assessment is a low-cost, action-able examination of the three areas critical to the implementation of any business intelligence initiative:

- **Business needs analysis:** Analyze the underlying strategic and tactical business goals and objectives that are driving the development of the BI solution, including whether executive sponsorship and funding are available.
- **Organizational analysis:** Analyze the existing business and technical organizational structures, including the level of IT/business partnering in place, the organization's culture and leadership style, its understanding of BI concepts, whether roles and responsibilities have been established, and whether people with the appropriate amount of time and skills are in place.

- **Technical/methodology analysis:** Analyze whether the appropriate technical infrastructure and development methodologies are in place, including all related hardware and software, the quality and quantity of the source data, and the methodology and change-control process.

The assessment forces an organization to examine strengths and weaknesses within these three areas and makes recommendations about how to fix potential problem areas. Ideally perform such an analysis before developing a costly set of systems, including data warehouses, OLAP, and data mining. The assessment itself helps build awareness and support for the initiative.

Source: Adapted from T. Burzinski, "The Case for Business Intelligence Assessments," *DM Review*, July 2002.

Burzinski (2002) recommends performing a business intelligence assessment before implanting any business intelligence initiative. See DSS in Focus 5.27 for details. The development of business intelligence and data warehousing initiatives over the last decade has led to many issues and their solution. We describe critical lessons learned in DSS in Focus 5.28.

The Web has had a profound impact on how these tools function and what they are utilized for. The visual nature of most business intelligence tools is often based on Web-browser interfaces. As Web use and e-commerce increase, there is more of a demand for gathering and analyzing data from the *clickstream*, to identify where cus-

CRITICAL LESSONS IN BUSINESS INTELLIGENCE AND DATA WAREHOUSING

The first 10 years of business intelligence and data warehousing initiatives have resulted in many successful, high-return applications of information technology. Here are some critical lessons that should be followed and examined to help ensure success:

- Create stability in the basic structures of data fundamental for providing business intelligence and running the business.
- Ensure that each data element stands on its own as a fact or attribute.

- Keep an enterprise-wide focus, not a departmental, regional, or other category focus.
- Make business intelligence not simply the analytical report, but the information a manager or executive needs to make informed decisions.
- Use several different business intelligence technologies that integrate well.

Source: Adapted from Richard Skriletz, "New Directions for Business Intelligence," *DM Review*, April 2002, p. 10.

tomers go on a Web site, where they came from, where they go afterwards, and what they buy or don't buy. (These systems are often called Web intelligence/Web analytics; see Section 5.14.) Combining this with census data and geographic information systems, a firm can identify what to target market to existing and potential new customers. We indicate database and business intelligence technologies and Web impacts in Table 5.5.

Kurtyka (2003) discusses issues that relate to organizational learning and business intelligence. Smith (2001) describes a method for the strategic assessment of business intelligence tools. He provides an analysis of a large sample of tools. See Smith (2001) for details. Determining which tool to use has significant consequences on the decision analysis features that will be supported. We have purposely separated data mining tools from the OLAP discussion. Topics and issues pertaining to OLAP, data mining, and the Web are discussed in the remainder of the chapter.

For more on business intelligence, see Bolen (2003), Burzinski (2002), Callaghan (2003a), Delic and Dayal (2003), Dorrington (2003), Kaliebe (2003), Kurtyka (2003), Leon (2003), Loshin (2003), Pallatto (2002a,b), Smith (2001), Songini (2003), Ulfelder (2000a), Vitt, Luckevich, and Misner (2002), and Whiting (2003).

TABLE 5.5　　Database and Business Intelligence Technologies, and Web Impacts

Knowledge Management	Web Impacts	Impacts on the Web
Databases	Consistent, friendly, graphical user interface Web database servers provide efficient and effective data storage and retrieval Convenient, fast and direct access to data on servers Multimedia data storage and retrieval expectations have become a reality Developments in search engines are directly applicable to database technologies	Data captured and shared are utilized in improving Web site design and performance Web servers are developed and sold specifically for database applications
Data warehouse and data mart	Same as above Distributed properties of Web servers have led to distributed data warehouses and data marts The distributed properties have led to improvements in data integration Improvements in technology help solve scalability problems	Same as above Led to the proliferation of Web technologies to provide massive communication for data warehouse use
OLAP	Same as above Here the Web-based graphics are critical to understanding results Access to analytical models and methods to solve business, engineering and other problems	Same as above Improvements in Web e-commerce and other sites Improvements in Web/Internet technologies
Data mining	Same as above Helps to automate the analytical methods	Same as above

5.10 ONLINE ANALYTICAL PROCESSING (OLAP)

For many years IT concentrated on building mission-critical systems that mainly supported corporate transaction processing. Such systems must be virtually fault-tolerant and provide rapid response. An effective solution was provided by online transaction processing (OLTP), which centers on a distributed relational database environment. The latest developments in this area are the utilization of ERP and SCM software for transaction processing tasks, CRM applications, and integration with Web-based technologies and intranets. Many tools were created for developing OLTP applications; the INFORMIX OnLine Dynamic Server (informix.com) is an example of an effective tool.

Access to data is often needed by both OLTP and MSS applications. Unfortunately, trying to serve both types of requests may be problematic (Gray and Watson, 1998). Therefore, some companies elect to separate databases into OLTP types and OLAP types. The OLAP type is based on the data warehouse.

Even so, Gonzales and Robinson (2003) indicate that for OLAP to work properly, the relational database management system must be optimized to support OLAP instead of directly utilizing pure, multidimensional data cubes. The database must be integrated with the centralized, cohesive, and consistent control of multidimensional data across the enterprise. To make the database aware of the higher-level data organization OLAP requires, the database catalogs need a set of higher-level objects that relate directly to OLAP and business models. In effect, these objects will take the existing atomic entities and compound them to make dimensional entities, such as attributes, facts, relationships, hierarchies, and dimensions. Once these high-level objects are defined, the new information can be stored and managed as part of the catalogs (see Gonzales and Robinson, 2003). In effect, managing metadata becomes part of a relational database management system in order to make it "OLAP aware."

The term **online analytical processing (OLAP)** refers to a variety of activities usually performed by end-users in online systems (see DSS in Action 5.29). There is no

---

DSS IN ACTION 5.29

OUTOKUMPU COPPER PRODUCTS

Outokumpu Copper Products (Finland) processes millions of kilograms of base metals each year that are used in such products as belt buckles, drinking water tanks, and radiators. Its products serve industrial, electronic, mining and metal, transport, and construction companies worldwide. Outokumpu has four divisions with 13 business lines operating independently in Europe, America, and Asia. Determining the profit margin of a product, how to lower production costs, customer turnover, and profitability are critical business issues. Integrating and analyzing information from each business unit presented a tremendous challenge, because the markets in the different divisions operate with such specific requirements that a generic information system did not seem possible. The solution was to build a data warehouse and use a Web-based OLAP server. The database utilized Hyperion's Essbase. Two models were quickly built to support customer profitability and products, and one to report on the delivery performance. They used Executive Viewer, an OLAP front-end from Temtec Corporation (try the online demo at www.temtec.com). Executive viewer is Web-based and integrates with numerous databases including Hyperion Essbase. It allowed the company to develop an application to quickly select information by market, product, or customer and supports drill-through analysis. The results have been the implementation of a flexible analytical tool that has met widespread acceptance throughout the organization.

Source: Condensed from Case: "Outokumpu Copper Products—Finland," www.temtec.com, 2003.

DSS IN ACTION 5.30

COGNOS OLAP TOOLS BENEFIT ALLIED BUILDING

Allied Building Products Corporation has grown its building materials distribution company by increasing market share and customers. Allied implemented *Cognos Finance*, a business intelligence (BI) solution from Cognos, in under 90 days. As a result, Allied was able to standardize data company-wide and automate processing to deliver a single coordinated view of financial performance. Cognos Finance allows Allied to reduce manual labor in producing reports, and at the same time provides access to budgets, forecasts, and actuals across all of its branch operations. This enabled an integrated view of information and accelerated accurate financial reporting.

Source: Adapted from "Allied Building Products Corporation Monitors Corporate Performance with Cognos Finance," Cognos, Inc., cognos.com, 2003.

agreement on what activities are considered OLAP. Usually one includes such activities as generating queries (see DSS in Action 5.30), requesting ad hoc reports and graphs, conducting statistical analyses, and building DSS and multimedia applications. Some include executive and/or enterprise information systems and data mining. Essentially, OLAP provides modeling and visualization capabilities to large data sets, either to database management systems or, more often, data warehouse systems. OLAP is different from data mining in that users can ask specific, open-ended questions. Users, typically analysts, run OLAP systems. They drive OLAP, whereas data mining looks for relationships, with some direction from the analyst. OLAP is generally facilitated by working with the data warehouse (or with the data mart or a multidimensional warehouse) and with a set of OLAP tools. These tools can be **query tools,** spreadsheets, data mining tools, data visualization tools, and the like. For a list of OLAP tools, see Costanza (2000), Alexander (2003), Karpinski (1999), and periodic reviews in the software sections of *PCWeek, DM Review, InternetWeek, Intelligent Enterprise,* and *Software Review.* The major vendors of these tools include BusinessObjects S.A., Brio Software Inc., Computer Associates, Cognos Inc., Comshare, Crystal Decisions Inc., Hyperion Software Corporation, Informatica Corp., Information Builders, IBM, Intersolve, Microstrategy Corporation, Oracle, SAS Institute Inc., Software A&G, and Temtec. The multidimensional nature of almost all OLAP systems is described in Section 5.12.

ING Antai Insurance Co. (Taiwan) uses IBM's OLAP Server to analyze large amounts of data to detect fraudulent claims and speed up the processing of claims. It takes only a couple of days to analyze data that previously took several weeks. As the tools and hardware improve, claims can be analyzed instantaneously. The cost of processing claims is greatly reduced. See Raden (1997). TCF Bank utilizes OLAP to provide information directly to those who need it. The bank now understands its customer base more accurately for targeting its marketing efforts. See DSS in Action 5.31 for details. We cover more material in Section 5.11 and in Case Application 5.3 on how banks utilize business intelligence/business analytic tools for similar tasks.

SQL FOR QUERYING

Structured query language (SQL) is a standard data language for data access and manipulation in relational database management systems. It is an English-like language consisting of several layers of increasing complexity and capability. SQL is used for online access to databases, DBMS operations from programs, and database admin-

TCF BANK'S OLAP AND DATA MINING

One of the largest regional banks in the midwestern region of the United States, TCF Bank has more than 390 branches in six states and serves customers from all income groups. TCF Bank has $12.2 billion in assets and operates the fourth-largest supermarket branch-banking system in the country. TCF focuses on being a convenient one-stop shop for customers; it is one of the few banks in the United States that is open 12 hours per day, seven days per week, including holidays.

Users in the bank's major groups (retail banking, consumer loans, mortgage banking, brokerage) found that the IT reports were not meeting their needs. Instead, they had to develop custom processes to download files from IT and then load the data into spreadsheets for further analysis. The time required to create a standard graph report was close to a month. It might take six weeks to generate a customer marketing list.

The information management department needed to come up with a new process to enable users to gain customer insight so as to uncover opportunities and effectively offer new services to customers. TCF adopted Informatica PowerCenter and PowerAnalyzer in mid-2002. PowerAnalyzer's report-creating wizard, metrics-based reporting, and analysis-path drill down features were important ease-of-use functions in the adoption decision. A number of key-indicator starter reports for user dashboards were developed. In a week, 550 loan officers and executives were using these and other reports on a daily basis.

With the new OLAP system, which includes a cross-sell application, TCF is able to identify classes of customers to approach with specific services and products. This is especially critical in identifying the needs of new customers. In addition, reports are generated immediately, so further analysis can be performed.

Source: Adapted from Ted Ledman, "TCF Bank," *What Works: Best Practices in Business Intelligence and Data Warehousing,* Vol. 15, The Data Warehousing Institute, Chatsworth, CA, June 2003, p. 10.

istration functions. It is also used for data access and manipulation functions of some leading DBMS software products (e.g., Oracle, IBM's DB2, Ingres).

Since SQL is nonprocedural and fairly user-friendly, many end-users can use it for their own queries and database operations. SQL can be employed for programs written in any standard programming language; thus, it facilitates software integration. Support of DSS/business intelligence is accomplished in the warehouse with products from vendors such as Brio, BusinessObjects, Cognos, Pilot Software, and SAS. SQL is a fairly simplistic OLAP tool. The real strength of OLAP is in its major analytic capabilities.

OLAP TOOLS

Using SQL and other conventional data access and analysis tools is helpful, but not sufficient, for OLAP. In OLAP a special class of tools is used, known as decision support/business intelligence/business analytic front ends, data-access front ends, database front ends, and visual information access systems. These methods go well beyond spreadsheets in power and results. They tools are intended to empower users.

OLAP tools have characteristics that distinguish them from reporting tools designed to support traditional OLTP reporting applications. The characteristics of OLAP tools were succinctly defined by E. F. Codd and associates (1993); Codd is considered to be the "inventor" of the relational database model. The twelve rules for OLAP tools are summarized in Table 5.6 (see Raden, 1997). They defined four types of processing that are performed by analysts within an organization:

1. Categorical analysis is a static analysis based upon historical data. It is based upon the premise that past performance is an indicator of the future. This is the primary analysis supported by OLTP transaction-based databases.

TABLE 5.6   OLAP Product Evaluation Rules: Codd's Twelve Rules for OLAP

Multidimensional Conceptual View
Transparency
Accessibility
Consistent Reporting Performance
Client-Server Architecture
Generic Dimensionality
Dynamic Sparse Matrix Handling
Multi-User Support
Unrestricted Cross-dimensional Operations
Intuitive Data Manipulation
Flexible Reporting
Unlimited Dimensions and Aggregation Levels

Source: Adapted from "Providing OLAP to User-Analysts: An IT Mandate," Codd & Associates, White Paper, hyperion.com. Also see Radin (1997).

2. Exegetical analysis is also based upon historical data, adding the ability to perform drill down analysis. Drill down analysis is the ability to query further into the data to determine the detail data that were used to determine a derived value.
3. Contemplative analysis allows a user to change a single value to its impact.
4. Formulaic analysis permits changes to multiple variables.

Vendors in the BI arena are maneuvering to empower end users with the ability to customize analytic applications to meet evolving business needs. These include Spotfire (DecisionSite analytics platform), Business Objects (Enterprise BI Suite), and QlikTech (QlikTech). See Haverstein (2003b).

There are hundreds of OLAP tools available today. They share many features but also provide some distinct differences (see DSS in Action 5.30). An example of OLAP output is shown in Figure 5.8, the result of a Cognos Impromptu Version 7.0 query.

Temtec Executive Viewer provides all the expected OLAP features, including multidimensional views of data, dimension expansion and collapse, dynamic column selection, automatic calculations (sums, etc.), automatic charting and graphing, physical maps to display data (Figure 5.9), and instantaneous drilldown and rollup. Executive Viewer utilizes the idea of traffic lights in its display of data. We show an example of this in Figure 5.10. Note the shading in the last, variance column. The value of –2.57 is shaded in red, indicating "stop, there is a problem"; the 4.64 is shaded in yellow indicating "caution, a problem may be developing"; and the rest of the numbers are shaded in green, indicating that it is safe to proceed forward. Try Executive Viewer online (www.temtec.com) using the demo book (where data are integrated into a multidimensional framework).

We show screen shots of the Brio Performance Suite in Figure 5.11 and Figure 5.12. The Suite's Web-based drag and drop capabilities, which show how to construct a report by dragging rows/columns for analysis, are depicted in Figure 5.11. The Performance Suite reporting with OLAP capabilities is depicted in Figure 5.12. Note the mixture of graphs and tables.

Raden (1997) discusses approaches that may be used in selecting the appropriate OLAP technology for an organization. Menninger (1997) discusses how an organization should go about developing an object-oriented OLAP application. For more on

FIGURE 5.8 COGNOS IMPROMPTU SAMPLE OUTPUT

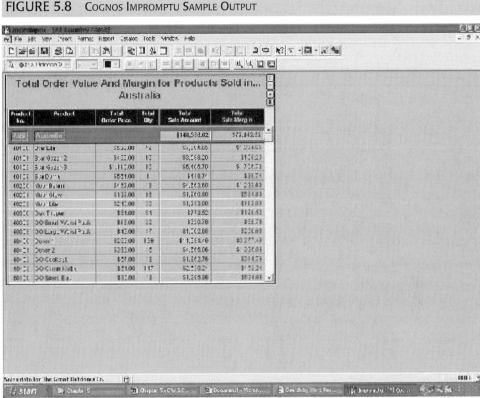

Courtesy of Cognos, Inc.

FIGURE 5.9 TEMTEC EXECUTIVE VIEWER ADVANCED MAP DATA DISPLAY

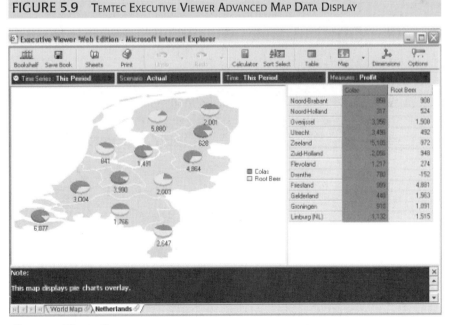

Courtesy of Temtec Inc.

FIGURE 5.10 TEMTEC EXECUTIVE VIEWER TRAFFIC LIGHT DISPLAY

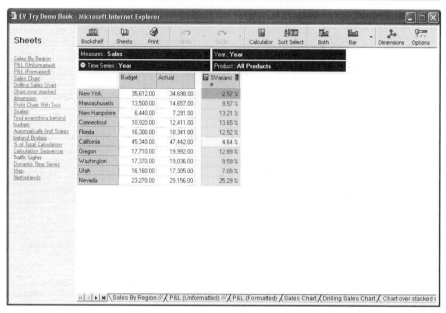

Courtesy of Temtec Inc.

FIGURE 5.11 BRIO PERFORMANCE SUITE SCREEN SHOT OF WEB-BASED DRAG-AND-DROP QUERY

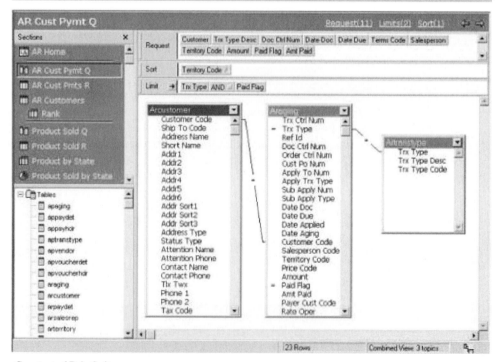

Courtesy of Brio Software

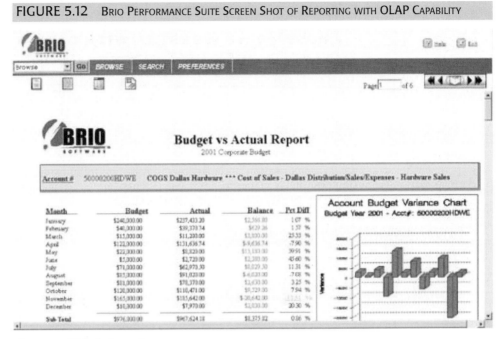

FIGURE 5.12   BRIO PERFORMANCE SUITE SCREEN SHOT OF REPORTING WITH OLAP CAPABILITY

Courtesy of Brio Software Inc.

OLAP, see Barquin and Edelstein (1997a, 1997b), Dash (2001), Kudyba (2002), Ledman (2003), Menninger (1997), Gonzales and Robinson (2003), Havenstein (2003a), and Raden (1997).

5.11 DATA MINING

Traditional data analysis is done by inserting data into standards or customized models. In either case, it is assumed that the relationships among various system variables are well known and can be expressed mathematically. However, in many cases, relationships may not be known. In such situations, modeling is not possible and a data mining approach may be attempted.

Data mining (DM) is a term used to describe knowledge discovery in databases. Data mining is a process that uses statistical, mathematical, artificial intelligence and machine-learning techniques to extract and identify useful information and subsequent knowledge from large databases. Formerly the term was used to describe the process through which undiscovered patterns in data were identified. However, over time, the original definition has been modified to include most types of (automated) data analysis. According to the Gartner Group, data mining is the process of engineering mathematical patterns from usually large sets of data. These patterns can be rules, affinities, correlations, trends, or prediction models (see Nemati and Barko, 2001; Linden, 1999).

Data mining is on the interface of computer science and statistics, utilizing advances in both disciplines to make progress in extracting information from large databases. It is an emerging field that has attracted much attention in a very short time.

EMPOWERING WORKERS WITH DATA MINING AT ROCKWELL INTERNATIONAL

Rockwell International's air transport division (Cedar Rapids, Iowa) needed to access the corporate database frequently. For many years, only a few MIS personnel had the technical know-how to dig corporate data out of the mainframe. However, executives and managers increasingly demanded access to information stored in the mainframe. Frustration and delays in providing information were common. The MIS department operated under a heavy workload. Furthermore, because of the priority given to top management, other employees had to wait days or even months to get the information they needed. Today, managers can easily and quickly get most of the data they need by themselves.

The solution was provided by creating a special database on a server in a client/server environment. Managers can develop their own applications with LightShip (from Pilot Software, pilotsw.com). Managers can go right after the information they need without having to be programmers, resulting in less frustration and backlog, and happy employees at Rockwell.

Source: Condensed from public information provided by Pilot Software Inc., pilotsw.com.

Glymour et al. (1997) discuss statistical themes and lessons directly relevant to data mining, and some opportunities for synergy between the computational and statistical communities for further advances in data analysis.

Data mining includes tasks known as knowledge extraction, data archaeology, data exploration, data pattern processing, data dredging, and information harvesting. All these activities are conducted automatically and allow quick discovery even by non-programmers (see DSS in Action 5.32). The following are the major characteristics and objectives of data mining:

- Data are often buried deep within very large databases, which sometimes contain data from several years. In many cases, the data are cleaned and consolidated in a data warehouse.
- The data mining environment is usually a client/server architecture or a Web-based architecture.
- Sophisticated new tools, including advanced visualization tools, help to remove the information *ore* buried in corporate files or archival public records. Finding it involves massaging and synchronizing these data to get the right results. Cutting-edge data miners are also exploring the usefulness of *soft* data (unstructured text stored in such places as Lotus Notes databases, text files on the Internet, or a corporate-wide intranet).
- The miner is often an end-user, empowered by data drills and other power query tools to ask ad hoc questions and obtain answers quickly with little or no programming skill.
- *Striking it rich* often involves finding an unexpected result and requires end-users to think creatively.
- Data mining tools are readily combined with spreadsheets and other software development tools. Thus, the mined data can be analyzed and processed quickly and easily.
- Because of the large amounts of data and massive search efforts, it is sometimes necessary to use parallel processing for data mining.

Effectively leveraging data mining tools and technologies can lead to acquiring and maintaining a strategic competitive advantage. Data mining offers organizations an indispensable decision-enhancing environment to exploit new opportunities by transforming data into a strategic weapon. See Nemati and Barko (2001). Many authors have written on the practical and theoretical approaches of data mining, including Web, text, search, and organizational transformation issues. Among them are Anthes (2002), Barquin and Edelstein (1997a, 1997b), Barth (1997), Berry (2000, 2002, 2003a, 2003b), Bhandari et al. (1997), Bigus (1996), Bolen (2001), Boyd (2001), Buck (2000), Copeland (2001), Dunham (2003), Fayyad (2003), Finlay (2001), Gimes (2001), Glymour et al. (1997), Haskett (2000a, 2000b), Hudnell and Kitayama (2000), Lamont (2000), Linden (1999), Linoff and Berry (2002), Nemati and Barko (2001), Palshikar (2001), Saarenvirta (2001), Swartz (2003), Skalak (2001), Small and Edelstein (1997), Swift (2001), Tillett (2000), Walker (2002), and Zaima (2003). Also see the Kdnuggets Web site (www.kdnuggets.com). See Groth (1998), Haskett (2000a, 2000b), and Nemati and Barko (2001) for excellent introductions to the topic.

HOW DATA MINING WORKS

Intelligent data mining, according to Dunham (2003), discovers information within data warehouses that queries and reports cannot effectively reveal. Data mining tools find patterns in data and may even infer rules from them. Three types of methods are used to identify patterns in data (Nemati and Barko, 2001):

- Simple models (SQL-based query, OLAP, human judgment)
- Intermediate models (regression, decision trees, clustering)
- Complex models (neural networks, other rule induction)

These patterns and rules can be used to guide decision-making and forecast the effect of decisions. Data mining can speed analysis by focusing attention on the most important variables. The dramatic drop in the cost/performance ratio of computer systems has enabled many organizations to start applying the complex algorithms of data mining techniques. Each *data mining application class* is supported by a set of algorithmic approaches to extract the relevant relationships in the data. These approaches differ in the classes of problems they are able to solve (see Haskett, 2000b). The classes are:

- ***Classification:*** infers the defining characteristics of a certain group (e.g., customers who have been lost to competitors). These methods involve seeding a set of data with a known set of classes (perhaps found by clustering), and mapping all other items (customers) into these sets. Decision trees and neural networks are useful techniques.
- ***Clustering:*** identifies groups of items that share a certain characteristic (clustering differs from classification in that no predefining characteristic is given). Clustering approaches address segmentation problems. Clustering algorithms can be used to identify classes of customers with certain needs to be met.
- ***Association:*** identifies relationships between events that occur at one time. Association approaches address a class of problems typified by market basket analysis. In retailing, there is an attempt to identify what products sell with what other ones, and to what degree. Statistical methods are typically used.

- *Sequencing:* similar to association, except that the relationship occurs over a period of time (e.g., repeat visits to a supermarket, use of a financial planning product). Purchases can be tracked because the purchaser can be identified by an account number or some other means.
- *Regression:* used to map data to a prediction value. Linear and nonlinear techniques are used. This is a form of *estimation*. It often involves identifying metrics and evaluating an item (customer) along the metrics by assigning scores. Sales predictions may be accomplished as well.
- *Forecasting:* estimates future values based on patterns within large sets of data (e.g., demand forecasting). This is another form of *estimation*. There is an attempt to utilize statistical time-series methods to predict future sales.
- *Other techniques:* these are typically based on advanced artificial intelligence methods. They include case-based reasoning, fuzzy logic, genetic algorithms, and fractal-based transforms.

In Table 5.7, we show these data mining functions along with representative algorithms and application examples. Also see Groth (1998).

Firms often effectively use their data mining systems to perform market segmentation by *cluster analysis*. Cluster analysis is a means of identifying classes of items so that items in a cluster have more in common with each other than with items in other clusters. We provide a detailed description of cluster analysis and an excellent example in the banking field in Case Application 5.3. Similarly, JCB Co., Ltd. (Japan) has effectively used cluster analysis as part of its data mining effort in segmenting customers and directing appropriate marketing products to the segments at the right time in the right format at the right price (see the *revenue management* subsection in Chapter 4). See DSS in Action 5.33 for a description. Tillett (2000) describes how another bank effectively mines customer data via cluster analysis using Web-based tools. In DSS in Action 5.31, we discussed how OLAP tools were used for a similar purpose.

Data mining can be either *hypothesis driven* or *discovery driven*. **Hypothesis-driven data mining** begins with a proposition by the user, who then seeks to validate the truthfulness of the proposition. For example, a marketing manager may begin with the proposition, "Are DVD players sales related to sales of television sets?" **Discovery-**

TABLE 5.7   Data Mining Functions, Algorithms, and Application Examples.

Data Mining Function	*Algorithm*	*Application Examples*
Associates	Statistics, set theory	Market basket analysis
Classification	Decision trees, neural networks	Target marketing, quality control, risk assessment
Clustering	Neural networks, statistics, optimization, discriminant analysis	Market segmentation design reuse
Modeling	Linear and nonlinear regression, curve fitting, neural networks	Sales forecasting, interest rate prediction, inventory control
Sequential patterns	Statistics, set theory	Market basket analysis over time, customer life cycle analysis

Source: Adapted from J. P. Bigus, *Data Mining with Neural Networks,* New York: McGraw-Hill, 1996.

DSS IN ACTION 5.33

DATA MINING AT JCB CO., LTD.

As the largest credit card issuer in Japan, JCB Co., Ltd. has established itself as an international brand. The company, with 34 million cardholders, offers 200 services and 600 card types. In July 1999, JCB's sales department started to develop a data mining project to track increasingly diverse and complex customer needs. The system was completed in three months with SAS Enterprise Miner. (Enterprise Miner contains many integrated models and algorithms, including decision trees, neural networks, regression, memory-based reasoning, bagging and boosting ensembles, two-stage models, clustering, time series, and associations. See www.sas.com for details.) The JCB system includes customer profiling and customer relationship management.

JCB segments its customers (cluster analysis) to increase the response rate of its marketing campaigns, which in turn increases revenue. Then, through customer profiling technology, it devises customer-focused sales strategies. The system analyzes how members use their cards, helping JCB identify and retain its most profitable customers. JCB plans to serve its customers for several decades by offering different services for various life stages.

"By clustering and making associations with the data, we are trying to figure out what customers need. And we would like to polish our business models by repeating the process of planning, doing, checking and practicing," says Makoto Nakaoka, manager of JCB's business administration department. In a short time, JCB quadrupled the rate of customer responses to direct-mail solicitations and initiated a successful campaign to retain current cardholders, at a success rate six to ten times greater than ever before.

Source: Marla Hudnell and Hajime Kitayama, "Transforming Business with Data Mining," *SAS com*, November/December 2000, pp. 22–23.

driven data mining finds patterns, associations, and relationships among the data. It can uncover facts that were previously unknown or not even contemplated by an organization.

Buck (2000) organized the classes of data mining tools and techniques as they relate to information and business intelligence technologies. Her taxonomy is

- Mathematical and statistical analysis packages
- Personalization tools for Web-based marketing
- Analytics built into marketing platforms
- Advanced CRM tools
- Analytics added to other vertical industry-specific platforms
- Analytics added to database tools (e.g., OLAP)
- Standalone data mining tools

In data mining (and OLAP), the scalability of the methods and of the data warehouse (or database) are critical issues. This is so because of the amount of data and searching required. See Small and Edelstein (1997) and Section 5.7 for more on these issues and how they can be handled.

Edelstein (2001) describes the seven steps necessary for successful data mining. See DSS in Focus 5.34. If these are followed, and business practices are right, then the data mining effort should succeed. Acting on the results is critical, because discovering relationships in the data has no impact unless the relationships are utilized.

A number of misconceptions have developed about data mining. We describe these in DSS in Focus 5.35. Many of these reflect the way that data mining is utilized in practice. For example, data mining methods are typically used mainly by IT staff and management, and by consultants/analysts because it is too hard for nontechnical per-

DSS IN FOCUS 5.34

THE SEVEN STEPS OF DATA MINING

Data mining uses a variety of data analysis tools to discover patterns and relationships in data that may be used to make accurate predictions. Data mining helps organizations develop the most accurate models of their customers and prospective customers. The seven steps of data mining are:

1. Define the business problem.
2. Build (find or acquire) the data-mining database.

3. Explore the data.
4. Prepare the data for modeling.
5. Build (or find) the models.
6. Evaluate the models.
7. Act on the results.

Source: Adapted from Herbert Edelstein, "Pan for Gold in the Clickstream," *InformationWeek*, March 12, 2001, pp. 77–91.

DSS IN FOCUS 5.35

DATA MINING MYTHS

Data mining is a powerful analytic tool that enables business executives to advance from describing historical customer behavior to predicting the future. It finds patterns that unlock the mysteries of customer behavior. The results of data mining can be used to increase revenue, reduce expenses, identify fraud, and identify business opportunities, offering new competitive advantage. There are a number of myths about data mining, listed below. Data mining visionaries have gained enormous competitive advantage by understanding that these myths are just that—myths.

- *Data mining provides instant, crystal-ball predictions.* Data mining is a multi-step process that requires deliberate, proactive design and use.
- *Data mining is not yet viable for business applications.* The current state-of-the-art is ready to go for almost any business.

- *Data mining requires a separate, dedicated database.* Because of advances in database technology, a dedicated database is not required, even though it may be desirable.
- *Only Ph.D.s can do data mining.* Newer Web-based tools make data mining by managers possible.
- *Data mining is only for large firms with lots of customer data.* If the data accurately reflect the business or its customers, a company can utilize data mining.

Source: Adapted partly from Arlene Zaima, "The Five Myths of Data Mining," *What Works: Best Practices in Business Intelligence and Data Warehousing*, Vol. 15, The Data Warehousing Institute, Chatsworth, CA, June, 2003, pp. 42–43.

---

sonnel to interpret results. But this is changing as the tools become easier to use. In 2001, only around 35 percent of corporate management and staff directly used data-mining tools (see Nemati and Barko, 2001). These results are comparable to those for data warehouses and OLAP.

Data mining is iterative because data miners make mistakes. Actually, it is the process of discovery that is iterative. Thomas A. Edison quipped that he *failed* to invent the light bulb 100 times before he succeeded. So, just like the famous inventor's work process, data mining is a process of discovery. It is an experimental process that requires sound experimental design. See DSS in Focus 5.36 for specific "errors" that data miners typically make in practice because they often do not understand the process but do understand the expected results.

DSS IN FOCUS 5.36

DATA MINING BLUNDERS

Here are ten data mining mistakes that are often made in practice. Try to avoid them:

- Select the wrong problem for data mining.
- Ignore what your sponsor thinks data mining is, and what it really can and cannot do.
- Leave insufficient time for data preparation. This takes more effort than is generally understood.
- Look only at aggregated results, never at individual records. IBM's DB2 Intelligent Miner Scoring can highlight individual records of interest.
- Be sloppy about keeping track of the mining procedure and results.
- Ignore suspicious findings and quickly move on.

- Run mining algorithms repeatedly and blindly. Don't think hard enough about the next stage of data analysis. Data mining is a very hands-on activity.
- Believe everything you are told about the data.
- Believe everything you are told about your own data mining analysis.
- Measure your results differently from the way your sponsor measures them.

Source: Adapted from David Skalak, "Data Mining Blunders Exposed!" *DB2 Magazine*, Quarter 2, 2001, pp. 10–13.

DATA MINING TOOLS AND TECHNIQUES

There are many methods for performing data mining. Data-mining software may utilize one or more of these techniques; this is one of the distinguishing characteristics of data-mining software. Data mining tools and techniques can be classified based upon the structure of the data and the algorithms used. The main ones are:

- ***Statistical methods.*** These include linear and nonlinear regression, point estimation, Bayes's theorem (probability distribution), correlations, and cluster analysis.
- ***Decision trees.*** Decision trees are used in classification and clustering methods. Decision trees break problems down into increasingly discrete subsets, by working from generalizations to increasingly more specific information. A decision tree can be defined as a root followed by internal nodes. Each node (including the root) is labeled with a question. The arcs associated with each node cover all possible responses. Each response represents a probable outcome (see Dunham, 2003).
- ***Case-based reasoning.*** Using historical cases, the case-based reasoning approach can be used to recognize patterns. For example, customers of Cognitive Systems Inc. use such an approach for help desk applications. One customer has a 50,000-query case library. New cases can be matched quickly against the 50,000 samples in the library, providing automatic answers to queries with more than 90 percent accuracy. For more on case-based reasoning, see Chapter 12.

- ***Neural computing.*** Neural networks utilize many connected nodes (which operate in a manner similar to how the neurons of the human brain function). This approach examines a massive amount of historical data for patterns. Thus, one can go through large databases and, for example, identify potential customers for a new product (see DSS in Action 5.37) or companies whose profiles suggest that they are heading for bankruptcy. Many applications are in financial services (Fadlalla and Lind, 2001) and in manufacturing. A comprehensive description of neural networks is covered later in the text.

DATA MINING AT MARRIOTT

Marriott Club International (www.marriot.com), America's largest seller of vacation time-share condos, had a problem. The company has a database with millions of names. It used to send advertisements to all of them at great expense, but the response was minimal. The company decided to identify the customers on their list who were more likely to respond. Marriott uses neural computing technology in its data mining; the objective is to detect patterns by combing through the digitized customer lists.

Marriott started with names, mostly of hotel guests. Digging into a trove of motor vehicle records, property records, warranty cards, and lists of people who have bought by mail or on the Web, a computer program enriches the prospect list. It adds such facts as the cus-

tomers' ages, their children's ages, their estimated income, what cars they drive, and whether they play golf. The Marriott system then identifies who is most likely to respond to a mailed flier.

With these factors, Marriott is able to cast its net a little more narrowly and catch more fish. Data mining has increased the response rate to Marriott's direct mail time-share pitches by 33 percent. In addition, the company has reported significant savings on its mail costs. The same approach can be applied to Internet advertising, as was done by Site59.com Inc.

Source: Condensed from J. Novack, "The Data Miners," *Forbes,* February 12, 1996, and www.marriotclub.com.

- *Intelligent agents.* One of the most promising approaches to retrieving information from databases, especially external ones, is the use of intelligent agents. With the availability of a vast and growing amount of information through the Internet, finding the right information is becoming more difficult. Web-based data mining applications are typically enabled by intelligent software agents. This topic is discussed in a later chapter.
- *Genetic algorithms.* Genetic algorithms work on the principle of expansion of possible outcomes. Given a fixed number of possible outcomes, genetic algorithms seek to define new and better solutions. Genetic algorithms are used for clustering and association rules.
- *Other tools.* Several other tools can be used. These include rule induction and data visualization. The best source of new tool development is vendor Web sites.

The case-based reasoning, neural computing, intelligent agent, and genetic algorithm methods have their foundations in artificial intelligence.

Data mining algorithms are important (see Dasu and Johnson, 2003). When dealing with customer behavioral data, which can encompass a hundred dimensions or more, algorithms should be capable of dealing effectively with high-dimensional data. These algorithms must also be able to work with business constraints and rules. Simple statistics do not work. Knowledge of the business constraints, of the relations between products, and of the various behavioral segments of customers is a must.

Since the terrorist attacks on September 11, 2001, there have been numerous advances in the utilization of data mining methods by law-enforcement agencies to track terrorism and crime in general. See DSS in Action 5.38 for details and an example.

TEXT MINING

Text mining is the application of data mining to nonstructured or less structured text files. Data mining takes advantage of the infrastructure of stored data to extract additional useful information. For example, by data mining a customer database, an analyst

DSS IN ACTION 5.38

DHS DATA MINING SPINOFFS AND ADVANCES IN LAW ENFORCEMENT

In late 2002, John Poindexter, former head of the National Security Council, caused a flap with his proposal for a new Information Awareness Office within the Pentagon. Critics blasted Poindexter's plans for data mining numerous credit, banking, and retail purchase records of U.S. citizens, in the name of detecting possible terrorist patterns of behavior.

In reality, agencies like the National Reconnaissance Office and the National Security Agency have been doing this for years, and in mid-2003 the Northern Command did so as well. In fact, data-mining tools used by national intelligence agencies are already being utilized by domestic law-enforcement agencies in the United States. The tools transferred from the U.S. Space Command to Northern Command, and from there to the Department of Homeland Security, show both the common technology base for all environments and the possible civil-liberties concerns inherent in such tech transfers. All agencies are concerned about respect for civil liberties. Better intelligence coordination with state and local police forces is a chief goal.

The NRO and NSA use large-scale commercial database tools and specialized pattern-recognition tools. Defense contractors are responsible for integrating tools together in software suites that would prove useful to intelligence agencies. Many were working with the Department of Homeland Security's constituent agencies before DHS formed at the end of 2002. They deploy the tools for domestic drug enforcement and counterterrorism duties through the channels of the Northern Command and DHS.

For example, Northrop-Grumman's Web-enabled Temporal Analysis System (WebTAS) was developed in conjunction with the Air Force Research Labs and used during the Iraq campaign. It is available to regional police intelligence coalitions through the DHS. WebTAS displays maps and shows links corresponding to relations among targets. Clicking on a link calls up related databases that can tell an analyst, for example, all of the calls that the target has made in the last few days. To pick up patterns that might be buried in the noise of too much information, an embedded behavioral-correlation engine predicts possible trends for developing situations and flags circumstances that identify problems for gathering further intelligence.

New cooperation among Homeland Security investigators, especially in mining data, is producing major breakthroughs in nonterrorist cases, including the deaths of 19 illegal aliens found stuffed into a trailer in Victoria, Texas, on May 14, 2003. Detected via data mining techniques, money transfers and phone calls made by victims and more than 50 witnesses who survived the incident led authorities to a legal U.S. resident, who they believe led a smuggling ring that took aliens across the Mexican border to U.S. cities for a substantial fee. Coconspirators around the United States were also identified. After the suspect fled the country, she was lured by a sting operation to Honduras, where she was arrested and extradited to the United States.

Sources: Adapted from Loring Wirbel, "Data Mining Comes Down to Earth," *Electronic Engineering Times,* No. 1270, May 19, 2003, pp. 18, 22; Mark Hosenball, "Crime Breakthrough," *NewsWeek,* June 20, 2003, p. 9.

---

might discover that everyone who buys product A also buys products B and C, but six months later. Text mining operates with less structured information. Documents rarely have a strong internal infrastructure, and when they do, it is frequently focused on document format rather than document content. Text mining helps organizations to

- Find the "hidden" content of documents, including additional useful relationships.
- Relate documents across previous unnoticed divisions; for example, discover that customers in two different product divisions have the same characteristics.
- Group documents by common themes; for example, all the customers of an insurance firm who have similar complaints and cancel their policies.

Ellingsworth and Sullivan (2003) describe the process of text mining (see DSS in Focus 5.39). They also describe how the Fireman's Fund Insurance Company utilizes

DSS IN FOCUS 5.39

HOW TO MINE TEXT

Term extraction is the most basic form of text mining. Like all text mining techniques, it maps information from unstructured data into a structured format. The simplest data structure in text mining is the feature vector, or weighted list of words. The most important words in a text are listed, along with a measure of their relative importance. Text reduces to a list of terms and weights. The entire semantics of the text may not be present, but the key concepts are identified. To do this, text mining performs the following:

1. Eliminate commonly used words (the, and, other).

2. Replace words with their stems or roots (e.g., eliminate plurals, and various conjugations and declensions). Thus the terms "phoned," "phoning," and "phones" are mapped to "phone."

3. Calculate the weights of the remaining terms. The most common method is to calculate the frequency with which the word appears. There are two common measures: the term frequency, or *tf factor*, measures the actual number of times a word appears in a document, while the inverse document frequency, or *idf factor*, indicates the number of times the word appears in all documents in a set. The reasoning is that a large *tf factor* increases the weight, while a large *idf factor* decreases it, because terms that occur frequently in all documents would be common words to the industry and not be considered important.

For example, consider the first paragraph of this DSS in Focus box up to the colon. There were some 20 terms with 28 occurrences once we factored out common words. Here is a list of terms that appeared more than once, along with their relative frequencies (tf factors) out of a total of 28:

Term	Term Factor
data	.0714
structure	.0714
term	.0714
text	.0714
text mining	.1429
weight	.0714

When you consider all the important words in the paragraph, they comprise one-half of its total importance and could be used to identify its semantics. Clearly the paragraph is about text mining (weight = 0.1429) and involves text and data with structure and weight.

Source: Adapted partly from Martin Ellingsworth and Dan Sullivan, "Text Mining Improves Business Intelligence and Predictive Modeling in Insurance," *DM Review*, Vol. 13, No. 7, July 2003, pp. 42–44.

text mining to help predict expected claims and understand why outcomes deviate from the predictions. Text mining is used to extract entities and objects for frequency analysis, identify files with certain attributes for further statistical analysis, and create entirely new data features for predictive modeling. The first of these three was used in dealing with the court cases involving Firestone tires on Ford SUVs. Bolen (2001) describes a pharmaceutical application of effective text mining. See DSS in Action 5.40 for details. In DSS in Action 5.41, we describe details of another effective pharmaceutical text-mining application.

Here is a list of some popular text mining tools and vendors:

- SAS Text Miner (www.sas.com)
- IBM Intelligent Miner for Text (www.ibm.com)
- SPSSLexiquest (www.spss.com)
- Insightful Miner for Text (www.insightful.com)
- Megaputer Intelligence TextAnalyst (www.megaputer.com)

DSS IN ACTION 5.40

TEXT MINING

Text mining is a very effective approach to automatically performing analysis on standard and Web documents. For example, an international pharmaceutical firm used text mining to evaluate 500 text-based responses from patients participating in a clinical study of a new allergy medication. Text mining software detected a cluster of 50 patients who used specific words that described negative side effects. Further examination indicated that these patients all received a high dosage of the drug, and that women older than 40 were especially sensitive to the high dosage. Consequently, dosage levels are adjusted, and warnings to women over 40 are included with the medicine.

Source: Adapted from A. Bolen, "Data Mining for Text," *SAS com*, November/December 2001.

DSS IN ACTION 5.41

DATA MINING AT PFIZER

Pfizer, a large pharmaceutical company, uses text mining to look for parallels in pharmaceutical testing in the extremely large database that the National Institutes of Health uses to catalog medical research. The text mining project targets biomedical documents extracted from various external sources, such as MedLine, a medical research literature service provided by the National Institutes of Health.

The Pfizer system searches the database of documents and extracts a set of documents characterized by simple search criteria based on a combination of keywords. Next, the set of documents is further segmented into topics. Topics are characterized by lists of keywords extracted from the free-format text contained in the documents. The scientists choose topics of interest by examining keyword lists. Pfizer has realized several benefits. First, the company has discovered that text mining is not only a technology for the categorization of information. The results of text mining also permit the building of new applications for further navigation of data and decision support. These new applications can take a prototype to complete development much faster than ever before. It is now possible to rapidly assemble powerful, easy-to-use analytical applications that address the full gamut of requirements.

Source: Adapted from Lawrence Bell, "For Pfizer, AlphaBlox Is Just What the Doctor Ordered." *What Works: Best Practices in Business Intelligence and Data Warehousing*, Vol. 10, The Data Warehousing Institute, Chatsworth, CA, June, 2003, p. 31.

SAMPLER OF DATA MINING APPLICATIONS

Data mining can be very helpful, as shown by the following representative examples. Note that the intent of most of these examples is to identify a business opportunity to create a sustainable competitive advantage.

- *Marketing:* predicting which customers will respond to Internet banners or buy a particular product; segmenting customer demographics.
- *Banking:* forecasting levels of bad loans and fraudulent credit card usage, credit card spending by new customers, and which kinds of customers will best respond to new loan offers or other products and services.
- *Retailing and sales:* predicting sales and determining correct inventory levels and distribution schedules among outlets.
- *Manufacturing and production:* predicting when to expect machinery failures, finding key factors that control the optimization of manufacturing capacity.

- **Brokerage and securities trading:** predicting when bond prices will change, forecasting the range of stock fluctuation for particular issues and the overall market; determining when to trade stocks.
- **Insurance:** forecasting claim amounts and medical coverage costs, classifying the most important elements that affect medical coverage, predicting which customers will buy new policies with special features.
- **Computer hardware and software:** predicting disk drive failure, forecasting how long it will take to create new chips, predicting potential security violations.
- **Government and defense:** forecasting the cost of moving military equipment, testing strategies for military engagements, predicting resource consumption.
- **Airlines:** capturing data not only on where customers are flying but also the ultimate destination of passengers who change carriers in mid-flight. With this information airlines can identify popular locations they are not currently serving so as to add routes and capture lost business.
- **Health care:** correlating demographics of patients with critical illnesses; using data mining, doctors can develop better insights on symptoms and how to provide proper treatments.
- **Broadcasting:** predicting what programs are best shown during prime time and how to maximize returns by inserting advertisements.
- **Police:** tracking crime patterns, locations, criminal behavior, and attributes to help solve criminal cases (see DSS in Action 5.55 in Section 5.13).

Palshikar (2001) provides several examples of effective data mining in practice. See DSS in Focus 5.42 for information about data-mining and analysis efforts at DHS. Census data can be combined with other market data when segmenting customers (see Gimes, 2001). For the capabilities of data mining and a comparison of data mining tools, see Dunham (2003), Roiger and Geatz (2003).

Wal-Mart continues to pioneer data mining efforts. In fact, Wal-Mart even notices blips in data due to ethnic holidays and plans for them. See DSS in Action 5.43. Data mining is critical when utilized in a customer relationship (resource) management (CRM) system, as is described in DSS in Focus 5.44. See Berry (2000, 2002, 2003a, 2003b), Fayyad (2003), Linoff and Berry (2000), and Swift (2001).

A less typical application of data mining was applied to improving the performance of National Basketball Association (NBA) teams in the United States. The NBA developed *Advanced Scout*, a PC-based data mining application used by coaching staffs to discover interesting patterns in basketball game data. The process of pattern interpretation is facilitated by allowing the user to relate patterns to videotape. See Bhandari et al. (1997) for details.

KDD AND DATA MINING

Data mining and knowledge discovery in databases (KDD) are frequently used as synonyms. Fayyad et al. (1996) define **knowledge discovery in databases (KDD)** as a process of using data mining methods to find useful information and patterns in the data, whereas data mining is the use of algorithms to identify patterns in data derived by the KDD process. KDD is a comprehensive process that encompasses data mining. The input to the KDD process consists of organizational data. The enterprise data warehouse enables KDD to be implemented efficiently because it provides a single source for data to be mined. Dunham (2003) summarizes the KDD process as consisting of the following steps:

- **Selection:** Identification of the data that will be considered within the data mining process.

DSS IN FOCUS 5.42

HOMELAND SECURITY DATA MINING AND ANALYSIS

The U.S. government's Total Information Awareness (TIA) project, spearheaded by the Defense Advanced Research Projects Agency (DARPA), has been called "the mother of all data-mining projects." The research and development program, headed by John Poindexter, aims to identify, track, and prevent individuals from planning and organizing terrorist activities. Much of the effort focuses on unifying and probing databases that carry information on financial transactions. The program will also create large databases that sift through the purchases, travel, immigration status, income, and other data of millions of Americans. There are three parts to the TIA project:

- *Voice recognition.* Sifting through electronically recorded transmissions and providing rapid translations of foreign languages
- *A tool* to find connections between transactions, such as passports, airline tickets, rental cars, gun or chemical purchases, arrests, and other suspicious activities
- *Collaboration.* A mechanism to enable information and analysis sharing among agencies

Experts say it may only take the government a year to get this technology up and running. The key to success will be facilitating information sharing among departments. The technology to mine these data sources is there today, but developing systems to talk to each other may be a challenge for some time to come.

Even the National Science Foundation (NSF) is getting involved in developing and promoting data mining methods for the DHS. In 2002, the government intelligence community provided $6 million to supplement existing NSF research on data mining, with comparable funding likely for two more years. Many data-mining projects are summarized on the NSF Web site.

Sources: Adapted from Todd Datz, "Integrating America." *CIO*, December 1, 2002, p. 44–51; Nikki Swartz, "Data Mining Initiatives," *Information Management Journal*, Vol. 37, No. 2, March/April 2003, p. 17; NSF, "Fact Sheet: Data Mining and Homeland Security Applications," Office of Legislative and Public Affairs, www.nsf.gov/od/lpa/news/03/fact030124.htm January 24, 2003.

- *Preprocessing:* Erroneous and missing data must be dealt with. This involves correction and/or utilizing predicted values.
- *Transformation:* The data must be converted into a single common format for processing; this may involve encoding data or reducing the number of variables with which to deal.
- *Data mining:* Algorithms are applied to the transformed data in order to produce output.
- *Interpretation/evaluation:* To be useful, the results must be presented in a manner that is meaningful to the user.

DSS IN ACTION 5.43

WAL-MART: A PIONEER OF DATA MINING

Wal-Mart has pioneered massive data mining efforts to transform its supplier relationships. Wal-Mart captures point-of-sale transactions from over 2,900 stores in six countries and continuously transmits these data to its massive Teradata data warehouse. Wal-Mart allows more than 3,500 suppliers to access data on their products and perform data analyses. The suppliers use these data to identify customer buying patterns at the store-

display level. They use this information to manage local store inventory and identify new merchandising opportunities. In 1995, Wal-Mart computers processed over 1 million complex data queries.

Source: Adapted from P. Westerman, *Data Warehousing: Using the Wal-Mart Model*, San Francisco: Morgan Kaufmann, 2000; and public sources.

DSS IN FOCUS 5.44

DATA MINING TO IDENTIFY CUSTOMER BEHAVIOR

Understanding customer behavior is important to adjusting business strategies, increasing revenues, and identifying new opportunities. Many organizations have a massive amount and impressive variety of data and information resources that promise to reveal much more about customer behavior than was ever thought possible. Many firms have reached a point of rich data and poor utilization. For most retail environments, three sources of customer data are most critical to data mining efforts toward better understanding of behavior:

- Demographic data
- Transaction data
- Online interaction data

Clickstream analytics can identify who did and did not buy your product, why, and when.
Retail uses of data mining evolve as:

Step 1: *Web analytics.* Gather Web site statistics that track customers' online behavior: hits, pages, sales volume, etc. This helps adjust a Web site to meet customer needs.

Step 2: *Customer analytics.* These add depth to understanding customer interactions. Firms gather data from multiple sources, including Web site interactions, transaction data from offline purchases, and demographic data. This is critical in CRM and revenue management in that a better understanding allows an organization to cluster customers into groupings.

Step 3: *Optimization.* This promises the largest payoff. Subtle patterns can be detected and utilized to optimize customer interactions. This is the goal of CRM (Chapter 8) and revenue management (Chapter 4).

Consider J. Crew, a major online and catalog retailer of men's and women's apparel, shoes, and accessories. J. Crew has had immense success with optimization analytics. The company previously used a cumbersome manual procedure to recommend similar and complementary styles to online purchasers. In the fall of 2002, J. Crew deployed optimization analytics. The analytic engine recommendations, done automatically, generate twice as many sales as the older, manual system.

Source: Adapted from Usama Fayyad, "Optimizing Customer Insight," *Intelligent Enterprise*, May 2003.

INTELLIGENT DATA MINING AND TEXT MINING

New intelligent data and text mining methods, often based on artificial intelligence methods like artificial neural networks and intelligent agents, continue to be developed and applied in practice. These methods often prove to be very effective on specific kinds of problems and sets of data and text. Many are applied to identifying information and knowledge on Web pages scattered around the world. We describe some new intelligent-based methods for data mining in DSS in Focus 5.45. Also see Anthes (2002). See the Kdnuggets Web site (www.kdnuggets.com) for some additional information on intelligent methods for data mining.

When organizations are plagued by fraud, especially in financial transactions, as in e-commerce, they turn to specialized data-mining tools to detect patterns in the data. Generally these methods use neural networks in addition to clustering and statistical methods. SAS Anti-Money Laundering software is one example of how this is implemented in practice. See DSS in Action 5.46 for an example.

A team of Norwegian biologists have developed intelligent methods to *search and mine* the Web for genetic studies that contain information relevant to their endeavors. Since every three years we double the amount of information that we generate and store on earth (see Pallatto, 2002a), methods like these become increasingly important for scientific researchers as well as for smoothly running businesses. See DSS in Action 5.47 and Copeland (2001) for how this is done. Other methods, such as intelligent agents, may also be utilized in intelligent mining. Lamont (2000) describes how intelligent agents can

---

DSS IN FOCUS 5.45

NEW INTELLIGENT METHODS TO MINE DATA

Here are some new intelligence-based methods for searching, sifting, and analyzing huge data sets and Web documents:

Non-Obvious Relationship Awareness (NORA) (Systems Research & Development). NORA can take information from disparate sources about people and their activities and find obscure, nonobvious relationships. Useful for reaching further into the world of criminals and terrorists (see the Opening Vignette and DSS in Action 5.38).

Outbreak detection (Tom Mitchell at Carnegie Mellon University). This is distributed data mining. Tracks millions to trillions of items looking for disease outbreaks in real-time.

Upside Down (Streamlogic Inc.). Instead of archiving data and running search queries, Upside Down archives search queries and runs data through them. The focus is on identifying what people are looking for rather than what is found. This is some 6,000 times faster than the conventional approach.

What's the Answer? (Verity Inc.). The smart software puts human learning (rules) into the search

software, enabling it to learn through logistic-regression classification. For example, instead of responding with a list of Web sites, a search engine could simply scan through several of them and answer the question that is posed (e.g., "What is the population of the world?").

Web Fountain (IBM). This software is based on Andrew Tomkin's research results. In teaching computers to read for comprehension and recognize patterns in text documents, he set the software up to *read everything on the Web*. Web Fountain developed from this. Now trends in public opinion and popular culture can be identified as they emerge, and tracked as they migrate quickly around the world. If you ask the Web Fountain the right kinds of questions, market research results can almost instantaneously appear. Web Fountain went online in late 2003 with a few pilot customers.

Sources: Adapted from Gary H. Anthes, "The Search Is On," *ComputerWorld*, April 15, 2002; Brent Schlender, "How Big Blue is Turning Geeks into Gold," *Fortune*, June 9, 2003, pp. 133–140.

---

be used to identify knowledge on the Web. Boyd (2001) describes how the BizWorks software package provides intelligent agents for internal and Web searches.

DATA MINING SOFTWARE

Data-mining software features more complicated algorithms for neural networking, clustering, segmentation, and classifications that are generally more sophisticated that OLAP methods (see Finlay, 2001). Many software vendors provide powerful data-

---

DSS IN ACTION 5.46

UNITY TRUST BANK FIGHTS FRAUD WITH SAS ANTI-MONEY LAUNDERING

Unity Trust Bank attempts to detect suspicious transactions, as is required by British law. However, small charitable organization transactions look very similar to those of money launderers. Using SAS Anti-Money Laundering software, the bank focuses on suspicious behavior instead of transactions. Using the software, Unity Trust is able to successfully identify most fraudu-

lent and suspicious transactions, which can be further examined to determine their validity and turned over to law-enforcement officials.

Source: Adapted partly from E. Walker, "Innovation and Social Responsibility in Financial Services," *SAS com*, November/December 2002.

Biologists in Norway *automatically* search and mine data from the vast collection of biological literature on the Internet. This approach is the first step toward developing an intelligent application to read and correlate the enormous catalog of scientific literature to help derive genetic interaction. Researchers at the Norwegian Radium Hospital created a Web-based search and extraction method to sift through this gold mine of biomedical knowledge. The PubGene data/text mining software reads scientific literature and automat-ically catalogs it. PubGene has analyzed over 10 million gene and text databases from Medline (a service of the National Library of Medicine) to identify 3712 named human genes and identify correlations among them. Eventually, PubGene may acquire genomic data more quickly and apply the knowledge with a higher level of accuracy than human researchers can.

Source: Adapted from Ron Copeland, "Innovation: Genetic Gold Mine," *InformationWeek*, May 21, 2001, p. 77.

mining tools. These include Angoss Knowledge Engineering (KnowledgeServer/ KnowledgeSeeker), Cognos (a variety of tools), Cytel Statistical Software (XL Miner, performs data mining in Excel), DataMind Corporation (DataMind), IBM (DB2 Intelligent Miner Scoring, IMS), PolyAnalyst (Megaputer Intelligence Inc.), and SAS (a variety of tools). Angoss KnowledgeSeeker even induces rules from data. These rules can be utilized in expert systems. IBM's DB2 Intelligent Miner Scoring (IMS) provides real-time relational data mining analyses and scoring. It utilizes the Predictive Model Markup Language (PMML) from the data mining group. This software brings the data mining process one step closer to automation. PolyAnalyst includes both intelligent data mining and text mining methods. See Buck (2000) for a list of data mining software. Some software firms may make their data mining and OLAP tools available to university scholars for free or at greatly discounted prices. Check individual vendors' Web sites and directly with them.

5.12 DATA VISUALIZATION, MULTIDIMENSIONALITY, AND REAL-TIME ANALYTICS

Online analytical processing includes not only obtaining and analyzing data and information but also presenting it to the user and interpreting it. Doing so involves data visualization, multidimensionality, and real-time analytics.

DATA VISUALIZATION

Visual technologies make pictures worth a thousand numbers, and decision support applications more attractive and understandable to users. **Data visualization** refers to technologies that support visualization and sometimes interpretation of data and information at several points along the data processing chain (Figure 5.6; see Fayyad, Grinstein, and Wierse, 2002). It includes digital images, geographic information systems, graphical user interfaces, multidimensions, tables and graphs, virtual reality, three-dimensional presentations, and animation. Visual tools can help identify relationships directly. The ability to identify important trends in corporate and market data provides enormous advantages. More accurate predictive models provide significant business advantages in applications that drive content, transactions, or processes. Confident action, based on superior methods of visual data analysis, helps companies improve income and avoid costly mistakes (see Hallett, 2001). For example, network monitoring systems continue to become increasingly complicated and sophisticated. Visualization simplifies the reporting of test results. Consonus (Salt Lake City, Utah) designs, builds, and operates data centers, IT networks, and Web-enabled application delivery systems. Consonus uses the HP OpenView Management Suite to help manage these data centers. OpenView helps manage customers' Web systems and provides them with an understanding of how customers view their sites' performance and availability. See McCarthy (2002) for details.

Data visualization enables OLAP and data mining, especially utilizing Web-based tools. Rather than having to wait for reports or compare sterile columns of numbers, a manager can utilize a browser interface in real-time to look at vital organizational performance data. By using visual analysis technologies, managers, engineers, and other professionals have spotted problems that for years went undetected by standard analysis methods.

Visualization software packages offer users capabilities for self-guided exploration and visual analysis of large amounts of data. For example, see the ILOG Visualization Suite (www.ilog.com). Some examples of OLAP systems with excellent visualization include Visual Insights (Cognos) and nVizn (SPSS Inc.). Cognos Visualizer, among other features, utilizes traffic light displays in tables and graphs. Numerical results are displayed in red/yellow/green indicating their status. SPSS's nVizn is a Java-based developer's tool kit for creating visualization applications. See Ulfelder (2000b) for details. See DSS in Focus 5.48 for ideas on visualization in Finance, and DSS in Action 5.49 for how it is quickly evolving. Visualization technologies can be integrated to cre-

---

DSS IN FOCUS 5.48

FINANCIAL DATA VISUALIZATION

To prevent systems from automatically identifying meaningless patterns in data, chief financial officers (CFOs) want to make sure that the processing power of a computer is always tempered with the insight of a human being. One way to do this is through data visualization, which uses color, form, motion, and depth to present masses of data in a comprehensible way. Andrew W. Lo, director of the Laboratory for Financial Engineering at Massachusetts Institute of Technology's Sloan School of Management, developed a program in which a CFO can use a mouse to "fly" over a three-dimensional landscape representing the risk, return, and liquidity of a company's assets. With practice, the CFO can begin to zero in on the choicest spot on the three-dimensional landscape: the one where the trade-

off among risk, return, and liquidity is most beneficial. Lo says, "The video-game generation just loves these 3-D tools."

So far, very few CFOs have cruised three-dimensional cyberspace, but this continues to change. Most still spend the bulk of their time on routine matters, such as generating reports for the Securities and Exchange Commission. In 1996, Glassco Park president Robert J. Park said, "What we have in financial risk management today is like what we had in computer typesetting in 1981, before desktop publishing." See DSS in Action 5.49 for how this change is occurring.

Source: Condensed from P. Coy, "Higher Math and Savvy Software are Crucial," *Business Week,* October 28, 1996.

DSS IN ACTION 5.49

FINANCIAL DATA VISUALIZATION: PART 2

Visualization, if done properly, is an incredibly powerful paradigm. SmartMoney.com's Web-based Maps gives Merrill Lynch analysts an easy-to-examine visual representation of financial information and customized three-dimensional pictures of the ever-changing financial markets. Beyond the cutting-edge financial services providers like Merrill Lynch, visualization is becoming ubiquitous in other enterprises as well. And developers are extending its use to serve increasingly diverse audiences. From the financial services markets to highly technical quality engineering companies that create testing tools to service providers using powerful network monitoring tools, visualization is becoming an in-demand, value-added tool. Future uses are on the drawing boards as research scientists discover applications for tomorrow's business.

The financial services industry is a robust adopter, given the increasing sophistication of the market and the high level of competition. To respond to some of this data complexity, Merrill Lynch uses Maps for its internal, proprietary data products to access real-time updates on stocks and mutual funds.

Merrill Lynch brokers can track client holdings individually or in aggregate, giving them an investment snapshot into their portfolio and their client's portfolio. The mapping technology can present data with size, value (through colors), and hierarchy, and allows users to click on and call up specific data sets from the map. Users can build dynamic, interactive, three-dimensional treetops from hierarchical company financial reports, share them with users via the Internet, and integrate them into existing applications.

Source: Adapted from Jack McCarthy, "Envisioning Enterprise Data," *InfoWorld*, Vol. 24, No. 46, November 18, 2002, pp. 53–54.

---

ate different information presentations, especially with virtual reality (VR) methods. In Chapter 4, we discussed visual spreadsheets and visual interactive simulation. Data visualization enables these problem-solving methods in addition to providing graphic features to OLAP and data-mining tools.

Data visualization is easier to implement when the necessary data are in a data warehouse, or better yet in a multidimensional server. Harrah's does exactly this in managing its casinos. See DSS in Action 5.50. Our discussion focuses mainly on the concept of multidimensionality. In the next section, we present geographic information systems, a topic closely related to data visualization.

DSS IN ACTION 5.50

HARRAH'S VISUAL HURRAH!

In 2002, Harrah's Entertainment, which runs 21 casinos in the United States, installed Compudigm International's visualization technology at its Las Vegas headquarters with plans to expand to more casinos. The visualization environment presents data in a form that allows decision-makers to see depth and worth in real-time and effect performance. Harrah's decision-makers can now view the flow of traffic across the casino floor in real-time. They can identify which slot machines are popular with the customers and which are most profitable by the minute. They can install more of the better ones when needed. The data-visualization software also enables managers to determine casino layout on-the-fly. They can examine their *Rewards* program visually. Compudigm initially developed this product for the gaming industry, but since has extended its technology into financial services and telecommunications. See the Chapter 1 Opening Vignette for more details on how Harrah's utilizes business intelligence tools.

Source: Adapted from Brian Ploskina, "The Gestalt of Data," *InteractiveWeek*, June 18, 2001.

NEW DIRECTIONS IN DATA VISUALIZATION

Since the late 1990s data visualization has moved both into mainstream computing, where it is integrated with decision support tools and applications, and into intelligent visualization which includes data (information) interpretation. The following are some interesting areas:

- Interactive graphs and models that let users drill down into the underlying data to reorganize and compare data so that their meaning is clearer. Visualization tools can be useful in three areas: (1) statistical analysis, (2) graphical presentation tools, and (3) analytic applications.
- WatchMark Corporation, a subsidiary of Lucent Technologies uses a sophisticated data-visualization tool for wireless network operators. WatchMark Pilot Release 1.3 incorporates an innovative video replay engine with VCR-like controls, which enables network operators to quickly review the events that preceded a network problem, much like viewing an instant replay of a televised sporting event.
- Comshare Inc. provides OpenViz so that users can interact with images and data in meaningful ways. This reaffirms the notion that sophisticated visualization solutions now belong on the desktops of business professionals. OpenViz is a suite of components—supporting both Microsoft Common Object Model (COM) and JavaBean models—that enable IT developers to extend commercial and custom-developed business intelligence solutions to encompass business-class data visualization.
- Identitech Inc. has developed Graphical Interface for Information Cognition, a data-visualization tool designed to support business decision-making. This software can be programmed to map data to sets of rectangles whose colors symbolize different levels of conditions, such as normal, high, and low.
- Analogous to a *visual spreadsheet* (Chapter 4), Visual Insights ADVIZOR allows users to find and understand patterns and trends hidden in complex data. It combines ease of use, industry-standard data access, and the power of interactive data visualization to create the next-generation user interface for business decision-making.
- There is an emerging new category of enterprise data visualization applications, termed on-line visualization for an enterprise (OLIVE). OLIVE systems are chart-centric applications that deliver visual business intelligence to the enterprise. There are 12 attributes that an enterprise charting application tool should have to qualify as an OLIVE tool, including (1) chart definition language and (2) a lifecycle process (see Craig, 1998).
- Visual software to reduce fraud and mitigate risk, especially in law enforcement, is an area of major developments. ChoicePoint (Alpharetta, Georgia, www.choicepoint.net) provides such software and services. Many organizations developing tools for the Department of Homeland Security are producing business intelligence spin-offs in law enforcement. See DSS in Action 5.38.
- Developments in virtual reality (VR) have wide-ranging impacts in business as well as other fields. See DSS in Action 5.51 for some applications and a Web software sampler. In addition, ChoicePoint's age-progression software, a form of predictive visualization, helps find missing children. By early 2003, ChoicePoint had assisted in recovering 782 missing children. See its Web site to see the results of age progression software.
- On the hardware side, there are continually new developments in visualization. Some involve special headgear or eyeglasses, others utilize holographic projec-

DSS IN ACTION 5.51

VIRTUAL REALITY VISUALIZATION

Visual applications include the latest developments in virtual reality (VR), which of course include more than just seeing images. Virtual reality representations have enabled advances in medicine, especially in training. VR-simulations provide a way to train doctors and dentists on the look-and-feel of real surgical procedures. Three-dimensional images of organs (gall bladders, hearts, etc.) have enabled robotic surgery. VR can be used to treat phobias (fear of flying, thunderstorms, etc.). Haptics (virtual-touch technology) in conjunction with VR is accelerating applications. The Harvard School of Dental Medicine is working on a facility to enable dental training via haptics. Surgical applications are under development to accurately provide the texture, weight, and fragility of real body parts. Ortho Biotech Inc. has developed a mobile virtual reality simulator to help doctors understand how chemotherapy patients feel physically. Most doctors who try the simulator change how they talk about and treat cancer-related fatigue.

In Calgary, Alberta, the Cave Automated Virtual Environment is housed in a 3 by 3 meter room (possibly a forerunner of the holodeck of *Star Trek* fame). The Cave Project runs single cell simulations, cancer cell simulations, and a model human in a Java-based 3-D language. The project is at the forefront of bioinformatics. Eventually, Cave plans to develop 3-D models of diseases progressing through the human body.

VR has been used for flight training for years. Pilots can learn their manual and technical skills through virtual reality–based simulations before assuming real flight responsibilities. Automobile manufacturers use virtual reality with simulations to help solve design problems and reduce costs. MathWorks, Inc. provides a Virtual Reality Toolbox as part of its MATLAB and Simulink products. The Toolbox gives engineers an in-depth animated look at dynamic models.

Finally, VR is making major headway through Web applications, especially through the Virtual Reality Markup Language (VRML). For example, Land's End uses Web 3-D technology (My Virtual Model by Public Technologies Multimedia, Montréal, Quebéc) to help shoppers evaluate garments on lifelike models. Three-D Web technology includes products like MetaCreations' MetaStream 3-D streaming format, Flatland Online's 3DML (markup language), Play Inc.'s Amorphium graphics engine, Oz.Com's Fluid3D plug-in for RealNetworks' RealPlayer G2; and Cycore's Cult3D modeling application.

Sources: Adapted from C.T. Heun, "Virtual Landscape: A Fantastic Human Voyage," *InformationWeek*, April 15, 2002; K. McMasters, "Almost There," *PC Magazine*, November 13, 2001; Business Wire, "Virtual Reality Doctors Empathize with Cancer Patients," *Business Wire*, November 1998; J. Edwards, "3-D Finally Gets Serious," *CIO*, March 1, 2000.

tion. Typically, these involve virtual reality representations of data as landscapes. Others are television-based. For example, Actuality Systems, Burlington, Massachusetts (www.actuality-systems.com), has developed a three-dimensional display for television. The Perspecta display is a 20-inch (51-cm) sphere in which 3-D images float. By mid 2003, ten displays had been sold (at $40,000 each). NASA uses it to view star clusters, while the U.S. Army displays battlefield simulations. Experts are experimenting with the display in other areas, including medicine, energy, and software research. Eventually the company plans to develop a display system that eliminates the globe and is reasonably priced for general consumers. See the firm's Web site for sample images. Also see Copeland (2003).

Major OLAP vendors provide three-dimensional visualization tools with their decision support tools. For example, Forest Tree 6.0 is a Web-enabled development tool with a three-dimensional visualization version that enables users to visualize and easily manage multiple dimensions of data in a single view. New visual tools are continually being developed to analyze Web site performance. EBizinsights XL is one such tool. See Section 5.14 for more.

MULTIDIMENSIONALITY

Spreadsheet tables have two dimensions. Information with three or more dimensions can be presented by using a set of two-dimensional tables or a fairly complex table. In decision support, an attempt is made to simplify information presentation and allow the user to easily and quickly change the structure of tables to make them more meaningful (e.g., by flipping columns and rows, aggregating several rows and columns-rollup, or disaggregating a set of row or columns—drill down).

MULTIDIMENSIONAL PRESENTATION

Summary data can be organized in different ways for analysis and presentation. An efficient way to do this is called **multidimensionality**. The major advantage of multidimensionality is that data can be organized the way managers rather than system analysts like to see them. Different presentations of the same data can be arranged easily and quickly.

Underlying every OLAP (and data mining) system is a conceptual data model often referred to as the multidimensional data model or multidimensional modeling (MDM). This technique helps conceptualize business models as a set of measures described by ordinary facets of business. The method is particularly useful for sifting, summarizing, and arranging data to facilitate analysis. In contrast to the techniques for designing on-line transaction processing systems, which rely on entities, relationships, functional decomposition, and state transition analysis, MDM utilizes the constructs of facts, dimensions, hierarchies, and sparsity. Choosing an appropriate tool requires examining the criteria of functionality, fit, performance, scalability, and future use. See Raden (1997).

Three factors are considered in multidimensionality: dimensions, measures, and time. Here are some examples:

- *Dimensions:* products, salespeople, market segments, business units, geographic locations, distribution channels, countries, industries
- *Measures:* money, sales volume, head count, inventory profit, actual vs. forecasted
- *Time:* daily, weekly, monthly, quarterly, yearly.

A manager may want to know the sales of a product in a certain geographic area, by a specific salesperson, during a specified month, or in terms of units. The answer to such a question can be provided regardless of the database structure, but it can be provided much faster, and by the user, if the data are organized in multidimensional databases or if the query or related software products are designed for multidimensionality. In either case, users can navigate through the many dimensions and levels of data via tables or graphs and are able to make quick interpretations, such as uncovering significant deviations or important trends.

Multidimensionality has some limitations, according to a Gartner Group research report (Gray and Watson, 1998):

- The multidimensional database can take up significantly more computer storage room than a summarized relational database.
- Multidimensional products cost significantly more, percentage-wise, than standard relational products.
- Database loading consumes system resources and time, depending on data volume and number of dimensions.
- Interfaces and maintenance are more complex than in relational databases.

Multidimensionality is available in different degrees of sophistication. Thus there are several types of software from which multidimensional systems can be constructed at different price levels. Multidimensionality is especially important in DSS/BI/BA systems, including *enterprise information systems* (e.g., Decision Web from Comshare Inc., www.comshare.com, and Pilot Analysis Server from Pilot Software Inc., www.pilotsw.com).

Tools with multidimensional capabilities often work in conjunction with database query systems and other OLAP tools. For example, IBM's Cube Views automates the creation of OLAP metadata at the database level so that metadata can be shared among applications that access the database. Cube Views aggregates data into multidimensional charts, allowing users to access the data from different perspectives, and returns answers to queries as XML-based Web services. Cube Views is supported by many business intelligence vendors, including Brio Software Inc., Crystal Decisions Inc., Cognos Inc., MicroStrategy Inc., Informatica Corp., InterNetivity, and BusinessObjects S.A. See Callaghan (2003b). Seagate Software's (part of Seagate Technology LLC) Crystal Reports builds reports that extract and analyze data from relational databases. This is part of the Crystal Enterprise software for distributing reports based on that information. Crystal Analysis Professional builds reports that extract and analyze multidimensional data from online analytical processing systems, such as Hyperion Essbase and Seagate Holos, as well as from mainstream databases, such as Microsoft SQL Server 2000, and IBM DB2 with built-in OLAP technology. See Whiting (2001). Other tools include Brio Enterprise (www.brio.com), PowerPlay (www.cognos.com), and InterNetivity Databeacon (www.internetivity.com), and Business Objects (www.businessobjects.com).

For examples of business intelligence software that readily handles multidimensionality, see Callaghan (2003b), Whiting (2001), and the "Annual Product Review" issue of *DM Review* every July (www.dmreview.com).

REAL-TIME ANALYTICS

A recent research study indicates that humans will record more information in the next three years than since the dawn of civilization. We need specialized methods to store our information in many formats, and to quickly retrieve and exploit it (see Pallatto, 2002a). Business users increasingly demand access to real-time, unstructured, or remote data, integrated with the contents of their data warehouse (see Devlin, 2003). For example, the buses in Houston, Texas, have been more reliable and efficient ever since they were equipped with instantaneous data gathering devices giving the drivers the ability to access information and modify traffic light changes (see "Houston Buses Due for 'Intellectual Overhaul,' " *ORMS Today*, June 2003, p. 19). In many cases, real-time data updates and access are critical for the organization's success. See DSS in Action 5.52 for an example of real-time data collection and analysis, where they must be performed as a matter of life and death.

Data warehousing and business intelligence tools traditionally focus on assisting managers in making strategic and tactical decisions. In 2003, with the advent of real-time data warehousing, there was the start of a shift toward utilizing these technologies for operational decisions. This "active" use of data warehouses is just beginning to change the focus of these tools (see Coffee, 2003). See DSS in Focus 5.53 for some details of how the real-time concept evolved. Hewlett-Packard is moving toward an *Adaptive Enterprise* strategy for delivering on-demand computing (see Follett, 2003).

The trend to business intelligence software producing real-time data updates for real-time analysis and real-time decision-making is growing rapidly (see Baer, 2002; CIO Insight, 2003; Coffee, 2003; Devlin, 2003; Gates, 2002; Langseth and Vivatrat, 2002; Madsen, 2003; Pallatto, 2002a; Peterson, 2003; Raden, 2003a, 2003b; Barquin, Paller,

DSS IN ACTION 5.52

WHEN REAL-TIME DATA COLLECTION AND ANALYSIS MAKE RESPONSE TIMES REAL

The City of Richmond, British Columbia, uses real-time data collection and analysis. Richmond is on a coastal island and has an average elevation of only 3 feet (1 meter) above sea level. It is important for city officials to know instantly whether its network of flood-control pumps is operating, how well, and why. Clearly, this is important in other parts of the world, as in The Netherlands. Other excellent examples of the need for real-time data collection and analysis are in the source reference.

Source: Adapted from Tony Baer, "Analyzing Data in Real Time," *Application Development Trends*, April 2002, pp. 50–52.

DSS IN FOCUS 5.53

ACTIVE DATA WAREHOUSING: REAL-TIME REALITIES

In 2003, an expansion of the role of data warehousing in practice was under way. Real-time systems were abuzz, along with all the usual complications of making data and information instantaneously available to those who need them. Peter Coffee believes that real-time systems must feed a real-time decision-making process. Consequently, he was extremely interested in the remarks of Stephen Brobst, CTO of the Teradata division of NCR, speaking at a Chicago conference, "Creating the Real-Time Enterprise." Here is a summary of some comments:

Active data warehousing is a process of evolution in how an enterprise uses data. "Active" implies that the data warehouse becomes much more of an operational tool and represents much more of an opportunity to change the way the enterprise makes tactical decisions that dramatically increase its value to all its partners. Brobst provides a five-stage model that fits Coffee's experience of how organizations "grow" in their data utilization. The stages are reporting, analysis, prediction, operationalizing, and active warehousing:

Reporting.   What happened?

Analysis.   Why did it happen?

Prediction.   What will happen?

Operationalizing.   What is happening?

Active warehousing.   What do I want to happen?

"As the trend toward externalization escalates, the demand for near real-time decision support on organizationally consistent data is forcing IT groups to evaluate data management infrastructure agility. Organizations are enhancing centralized data warehouses to serve both operational and strategic decision-making." Anthony Bradley, META Group. Here is a comparison between traditional and active data warehousing environments.

Traditional Data Warehouse Environment	*Active Data Warehouse Environment*
Strategic decisions only	Strategic and tactical decisions
Results sometimes hard to measure	Results measured with operations
Daily, weekly, monthly data currency acceptable; summaries often appropriate	Only comprehensive detailed data available within minutes is acceptable
Moderate user concurrency	High number (1000 or more) users accessing and querying the system simultaneously
Highly restrictive reporting used to confirm or check existing processes and patterns. Often uses pre-developed summary tables or data marts	Flexible ad hoc reporting, as well as machine assisted modeling (e.g., data mining) to discover new hypotheses and relationships
Power users, knowledge workers, internal users	Operational staffs, call centers, external users

Source: Adapted from P. Coffee, " 'Active' Warehousing." *eWeek*, June 23, 2003; "Active Data Warehousing." Teradata Corp., www.teradata.com.

and Edelstein, 1997). Part of this push involves getting the right information to operational and tactical personnel so that they can utilize new business intelligence tools and up-to-the-minute results on which to base their decisions, since these employees generally deal with the short-term aspects of running an organization (see Chapter 2 for a discussion of Anthony's model).

Analytic systems continue to get faster, and many customers demand very current data. More and more IT managers are facing the expensive question of whether to take analytic systems real-time (see Baer, 2002). More and more *real-time* data warehousing/ analytics projects are under development and being deployed. The demand for real-time applications continues to grow. The proliferation of rules engines (business rules management), for example, creates pressure to implement more automated business processes that can best be implemented in a real-time data warehouse. When processes that require instantaneous updates are necessary for answering analytical questions, a real-time response is necessary. Query, OLAP, and data mining response times must be close to zero (see Raden, 2003a).

Real-time data warehouses are updated on a regular basis, not just weekly or monthly. In 2003, daily updating was expected; and the interval continued to shrink. In addition to real-time queries, business analytic applications are being deployed. The latter can instantaneously identify customer buying patterns based on store displays, and recommend immediate changes to placement or the display itself. Other applications include call-center support, fraud detection, revenue management, transportation, and many financial transactions. Obviously airlines, hotel chains, auto rental agencies, and even retail organizations in their *revenue management* efforts can update supply-and-demand elasticity curves to dynamically price their products and services (see Chapters 2 and 4).

On the other hand, an important issue in real-time computing is that not all data should be updated continuously. This may certainly cause problems when reports are generated in real-time, because one person's results may not match another person's. A company using BusinessObjects WebIntelligence noticed a significant problem with real-time intelligence. Real-time reports are all different when produced at slightly different times (see Peterson, 2003). Also, it may not be necessary to update certain data continuously, like course grades from three or more years ago.

Real-time requirements change the way we view the design of databases, data warehouses, OLAP, and data mining tools, since they are literally updated concurrently

---

DSS IN FOCUS 5.54

DATA WAREHOUSE ARCHITECTURES FOR REAL-TIME ANALYTICS

The primary schema for a data warehouse is either a star schema or a "normalized" schema. The latter is a term so loosely defined that it is hard to describe, but a normalized schema typically resembles a third (or higher) normal form (3NF) schema that is not dimensional. These 3NF designs do not support query and analysis. Their only purpose is to act as a staging area, an upstream data repository for a series of star schemas, OLAP cubes, and other structures that are directly queried by analysts. Teradata implementations are the exception to the rule. Because of the unique characteristics of the massively parallel architecture and database optimizer, Teradata can process analytical SQL against a 3NF schema with acceptable performance.

Source: Adapted from Neil Raden, "Real Time: Get Real, Part II," *Intelligent Enterprise,* June 30, 2003, p. 16.

while queries are active. On the other hand, the substantial business value in doing so has been demonstrated, so it is crucial that organizations adopt these methods in their business processes. See DSS in Focus 5.54.

Examples of Web-based, real-time business intelligence software include BusinessObjects WebIntelligence, Cognos Supply Chain Analytics and BI Series 7, DataMirror Livebusiness, IBM DB2 Intelligent Miner Scoring (IMS), Informatica Analytics Delivery Platform, Informatica PowerAnalyzer, InterNetivity Databeacon, KnowNow LiveSheet for Excel, NetIQ Corp. WebTrends, PeopleSoft Enterprise Performance Management, SAS Supply Chain Intelligence Suite (SAS), and Sonic Software SonicMQ. For reviews, see Havenstein (2003b), Lindquist (2003), and Wallace (2000).

5.13 GEOGRAPHIC INFORMATION SYSTEMS

A **geographic information system (GIS)** is a computer-based system for capturing, storing, checking, integrating, manipulating, and displaying data with digitized maps. Its most distinguishing characteristic is that every record or digital object has an identified geographic location. By integrating maps with spatially oriented (geographic location) databases (called *geocoding*) and other databases, users can generate information for planning, problem-solving, and decision-making, thereby increasing their productivity and the quality of their decisions, as many banks and large retailers have done. Areas as diverse as retailing, banking, grocery, agriculture, natural resource management, public administration, NASA, the military, emergency preparedness, and urban planning have all successfully used GIS since the beginning of the 1970s.

Spatial data have become very important to many organizations. They are a new basis on which to manage infrastructures. As GIS tools and data sources become increasingly sophisticated and affordable, they help more companies and governments to understand precisely where their trucks, workers, and resources are, where they need to go to service a customer, and the best way to get from here to there. The areas of targeted marketing are growing rapidly. Organizations can easily segment a population. For example, the Credit Union of Texas (Dallas, Texas) utilizes a GIS to help decide where to place billboard and ATMs, and to help identify the areas most responsive to direct mailing. The typical response rates for the credit union is from 5 to 10 percent, much better than the average of 1 to 2 percent. Customers also enjoy receiving less mail from the credit union. They receive only relevant mailings. See Franklin (2002) for details. See DSS in Action 5.55 for some important examples.

Banks use GIS for displays that support

- Determining branch and ATM locations
- Analyzing customer demographics (e.g., residence, age, income level) for each of the bank's products
- Analyzing volume and traffic patterns of business activities
- Analyzing the geographic area served by each branch
- Finding the market potential for banking activities
- Evaluating strengths and weaknesses against those of the competition
- Evaluating branch performance.

A GIS is used as a geographic spreadsheet that allows managers to model business activities and perform what-if analyses (e.g., What if we close a branch or merge

DSS IN ACTION 5.55

GIS AND GPS TRACK WHERE YOU ARE
AND HELP YOU WITH WHAT YOU DO

Here are some examples of how GIS, in conjunction with GPS, helps firms and governments keep track of and improve their efforts. GIS helps companies differentiate their delivery services and meet demand for ever-shrinking delivery windows.

UltraEx, a West Coast company that specializes in same-day deliveries (of items like emergency blood supplies and computer parts), equips all of its vehicles with @Road's GPS receivers and wireless modems. In addition to giving dispatchers a big-picture view of the entire fleet, @Road helps UltraEx keep clients happy by letting *them* track the location and speed of their shipments on the Web in real-time. This Delivery 411 service, which UltraEx codeveloped with @Road, shows customers a map of the last place the satellite detected the delivery vehicle and how fast it was traveling. Dispatchers can choose the closest driver for each job, and drivers who own their vehicles are unable to falsify mileage sheets because @Road reports exact mileage for each vehicle. UltraEx spends roughly $2 a day per vehicle to have @Road, "but if the driver can make one more pickup per day, we're way ahead," says Michael Oakes, vice president of business development at UltraEx.

Publix Direct, the online grocery service of Publix Supermarkets, uses GIS-enabled logistics software from Descartes to optimize delivery routes. When a customer places an order, the software does an on-the-fly analysis to determine the most profitable delivery windows given the customer's location, order size, other scheduled deliveries in that zone, and estimates of driving and service times based on data from Navigation Technologies. Within five to 15 seconds, the customer sees delivery-time options that would be most cost-effective for Publix. Customers choose a 90-minute window, and then get a confirmation e-mail giving a 60-minute estimated time of arrival on the day of the delivery. The software is so accurate that Publix Direct handles more than 7,000 orders a week—and delivers 97 percent of them on time. "The economics of delivery are a make-or-break facet of this business," says Jim Cossin, director of fulfillment operations for Publix Direct. "This allows us to balance the convenience factor with the customer, offering them as many possible windows as we can, while at the same time creating economically feasible routes in the background."

Location is germane to virtually every government function, and many municipalities are at the forefront of applying GIS. New York City pioneered CompStat, which uses GIS to map criminal activity and police deployment by date, time, and location. By making precinct commanders accountable for their own policing strategies, it has been a major factor in reducing the city's violent crime rate by nearly *70 percent* in the past decade, says Lawrence Knafo, deputy commissioner of New York City's Department of IT and Telecom (DOITT). In March 2003, New York expanded its use of GIS to launch a 311 (telephone) service to handle nonemergency service requests. (In most of the United States, dialing 911 on the telephone will connect you directly to the police.) Calls are entered into a CRM system that taps into GIS databases to verify callers' addresses and cross-streets before city workers are dispatched. Operators can access location-based information, such as garbage pickup times, and contact information for local elected officials. Beyond enabling efficient responses to service requests, the system allows the city to aggregate—and map, spatially and temporally—311 data across service sectors. *Geocoding* the calls makes it possible to analyze how well (or poorly) the city is providing services, helping policy-makers decide *how best to allocate scarce resources*. Knafo thinks that analysis of geocoded 311 and 911 data *could reveal previously unnoticed patterns in quality-of-life complaints that tend to precede violent crimes*. He says, "We might be able to actually stop crime before it happens."

Some police departments, neighborhood activists, and concerned citizens in other cities are utilizing GIS to fight crime. Geographical information about neighborhoods is integrated with crime reports to analyze crime patterns. By identifying trends and providing information to citizens, police are better able to set up surveillance activities, and citizens can modify behaviors, leading to lower crime in these areas.

Source: Adapted partly from A. Dragoon, "Putting IT on the Map," *CIO*, May 15, 2003.

branches? What if a competitor opens a branch?). Each map consolidates pages of analysis. Some pioneering banks are First Florida Banks (Tampa, Florida) and NJB Financial (Princeton, New Jersey).

For many companies, the intelligent organization of data within a GIS can provide a framework to support the process of decision-making and of designing alternative strategies. Some examples of successful GIS applications are summarized in Table 5.8. Leading companies incorporate geographical information systems into their business intelligence systems. GIS *ideally* incorporate census data (see www.census.gov) as a source of demographic data for effective decision-making (see Gimes, 2001). For many organizations, GIS and related spatial analysis are a top priority. Sears invested several million dollars in GIS technology for logistics leading to a savings of $52 million per year (see Gonzales, 2003). The U.S. Defense Department has invested some $21 billion in the satellite system that feeds *Geophysical positional systems (GPS)*. GPS devices detect their position on earth within a reasonable precision to couple these devices with mapping software. GPS in conjunction with GIS are making major inroads in business intelligence applications. Commercial and government uses are endless, since detection devices are relatively inexpensive. See DSS in Action 5.55 and DSS in Action 5.56 for examples of how these technologies have been used and potentially could be used.

TABLE 5.8   GIS Applications

Organization	*GIS Application*
Pepsi Cola Inc., Super Value, Acordia Inc.	Used in site selection for new Taco Bell and Pizza Hut restaurants; combining demographic data and traffic patterns
CIGNA (health insurance)	Uses GIS to answer such questions as, How many CIGNA-affiliated physicians are available within an 8-mile radius of a business?
Western Auto (a subsidiary of Sears)	Integrates data with GIS to create a detailed demographic profile of store's neighborhood to determine the best product mix to offer at the store
Sears, Roebuck & Co.	Uses GIS to support planning of truck routes
Health maintenance organizations	Tracks cancer rate and that of other diseases to determine expansion strategy and allocation of expensive equipment in their facilities
Wood Personnel Services (employment agencies)	Maps neighborhoods where temporary workers live to locate marketing and recruiting cities
Wilkening & Co. (consulting services)	Designs optimal sales territories and routes for their clients, reducing travel costs by 15 percent
CellularOne Corporation	Maps its entire cellular network to identify clusters of call disconnects and to dispatch technicians accordingly
Sun Microsystems	Manages leased property in dozens of places worldwide
Consolidated Rail Corporation	Monitors the condition of 20,000 miles of railroad track and thousands of parcels of adjoining land
Federal Emergency Management Agency	Assesses the damage of hurricanes, floods, and other natural disasters by relating videotapes of the damage to digitized maps of properties
	Combines GIS and GPS as a navigation tool
Toyota (and other car manufacturers)	Directs drivers to destinations via the best route

DSS IN ACTION 5.56

GIS + GPS HELPS RAILROAD COMPANIES FIND THEIR CARS, AND MAYBE EVEN DRIVE TRAINS

CSX Transportation Inc. has equipped 3100 locomotives with a Global Positioning System. Union Pacific Railroad has installed satellite-based monitoring devices on 100 of its freight cars (out of 155,308) to test car tracking. By combining GIS with a GPS, a freight company can identify the position of a railroad car or truck within 100 meters. Railroad companies can readily identify locomotives that have left their route, and the specific cars that have been left behind or sent with the wrong locomotive. Further benefits include the ability to prevent accidents. In the future, it may be possible to drive trains and other vehicles by using such systems in conjunction with artificial intelligence methods (as NASA uses in the Mars Rovers). For example, at The University of Georgia's National Environmentally Sound Production Agriculture Laboratory, scientists are developing a farm tractor that is controlled by a gyroscope and GPS. Bad weather and visibility issues are not a problem in that the tractor knows where it is. Scientists have not yet developed devices that would let the system detect small obstacles. This could readily be accomplished with a robotic vision system and artificial intelligence methods to interpret what it sees.

Sources: Adapted partly from L. Rosencrance, "Railroads Hot for Satellite Monitoring," *ComputerWorld*, April, 2000; E. Minor, "Look Ma, No Hands!" *Athens Daily News* (AP), 2001, March, 2001.

GIS AND THE WEB/INTERNET/INTRANET

Most major GIS software vendors provide Web access, such as embedded browsers, or a Web/Internet/intranet server that hooks directly to their software. Thus, users can access dynamic maps and data via the Internet or a corporate intranet. GIS Web services are proliferating. These geographical systems form a an information-rich global infrastructure that adds a new dimension to the GIS industry by integrating multiple and disparate application services. GIS Web services is revolutionizing how companies use and interact with geospatial information. For example, GIS can help the manager of a retail operation determine where to open a store located on a major city intersection, within a 15-minute drive of a freeway exit ramp, surrounded by middle-class neighborhoods with professional families. See Gonzales (2003). Big Horn Computer Services (Buffalo, New York) uses a Web-adapted GIS to develop a custom application for a national television network that wants its affiliate stations to be able to access an intranet containing demographic information about their viewers. Using a Web browser, employees at each station can view thematically shaded maps analyzing their market.

A number of firms are deploying GIS on the Internet for internal use or for use by their customers. For example, Visa Plus, which operates a network of automated teller machines, has developed a GIS application that lets Internet users call up a map to locate any of the company's 257,000 ATM machines worldwide. As GIS Web server software is deployed by vendors, more applications will be developed. Maps, GIS data, and information about GIS are available over the Web through a number of vendors and public agencies. Related to this is the inclusion of spatial data in data warehouses, for later use with Web technology.

Some important GIS software are ArcView and ArcInfo (ESRI), AGISMap (AGIS), GeoMedia (Intergraph), and MapInfo Professional (MapInfo). ArcInfo's (www.esri.com/arcinfo8/) data model provides tools to model complex spatial systems with no programming. Culpepper (2002) describes how the CommunityViz (www.communityviz.com) software integrates city-planning simulation and modeling functionality to ESRI's ArcView GIS software. The user can set up and run different scenarios, based on user-specified variables and constraints, to determine relationships among municipal projects and social, environmental, or economic indictors. Entire sets of policies may be tested.

Current trends for GIS as a decision support/business intelligence tool involve continuing the combination or integration of GIS with other, especially Web-based, decision support/business intelligence tools, such as data warehouses, ERP, collaboration tools, and personal productivity applications. GIS data can integrate into other systems via XML through the Geography Markup Language (GML) (see Lais, 2000). One critical area that GIS have been successfully integrated into is CRM (see Dragoon, 2003a; Winslow and Lea, 2002; Sonnen, 1999; and DSS in Action 5.55). For further details on GIS, GPS, and the Web, see Dragoon (2003a), Duffy (2002), Hapgood (2001), Korte (2001), Kowal (2002), Lais (2000, 2001), Leatham (2000), Price and Schweitzer (2002), and Winslow and Lea (2002).

5.14 BUSINESS INTELLIGENCE AND THE WEB: WEB INTELLIGENCE/WEB ANALYTICS

BUSINESS INTELLIGENCE

Business intelligence activities—from data acquisition, through warehousing, to mining—can be performed with Web tools or are interrelated with Web technologies and electronic commerce. Specifically, business intelligence tools can be used to analyze Web site performance in real-time. Users with browsers can log onto a system, make inquiries, get reports, and so on, in a real-time setting. This is done through intranets, and for outsiders via extranets (see www.informationadvantage.com; also, for a comprehensive discussion of business intelligence on the Web, see the white paper at businessobjects.com).

A 2001 IDC survey of 500 IT managers indicated that 20 percent of organizations having 500 or more employees are linking their business intelligence activities to the Internet (see Kudyba, 2002; Dash, 2001). Users definitely want to improve the application of business intelligence on and to the Web. The number of organizations that recognize the importance of doing so is steadily growing.

Electronic commerce software vendors are providing Web tools that connect the data warehouse with the e-commerce ordering and cataloging systems. One example is Tradelink, a product of Hitachi (www.hitachi.com). Hitachi's e-commerce tool suite combines e-commerce activities, such as catalog management, payment applications, mass customization, and order management, with data warehouses (marts) and ERP systems. Case Application 5.2 indicates how a firm provided a Web-based self-service system so that end user customers could handle their own benefits accounts.

Data warehousing and decision support vendors are integrating their products with Web technologies and e-commerce, or creating new ones for the same purpose. Examples are Comshare's DecisionWeb, Brio's eWarehouse (www.brio.com), Web Intelligence from Business Objects, Cognos's DataMerchant, and Hyperion's Appsource "wired for OLAP" product, which integrates OLAP with Web tools. Pilot's Internet Publisher incorporates Internet capabilities within the Pilot Decision Support Suite. IBM's Decision Edge and MicroStrategy's DSS Web are other tools that offer OLAP capabilities on the Intranet from anywhere in the corporation, using browsers, search engines, and other Web technologies. MicroStrategy offers DSS Agent and DSS Web for help in drilling down for detailed information, providing graphical views, pushing information to users' desktops, and more. Bringing interactive querying, reporting, and other OLAP tasks to many users (company employees and business partners) via the Web can also be facilitated by using Oracle's Financial Analyzer and Sales Analyzer, Hummingbird BI/Web and BI/Broker, and several of the products cited above.

Data marts continue to become much more popular in the Web environment. For example, Bell Canada uses its intranet extensively for fast data access to its multiple data marts (over 300 analysts; see *PCWeek*, July 28, 1997), and at Nabisco, the large food company, financial analysts track the profits and losses of 8000 products using Web browsers, saving millions of dollars (*InfoWorld*, Sept. 28, 1998).

WEB ANALYTICS/WEB INTELLIGENCE

Web analytics and **Web intelligence** are the terms used to describe the application of business analytics/business intelligence to Web sites. The tools and methods are highly visual in nature (see Section 5.12). Schlegel (2003) describes the basics of Web analytics, and even provides a proposed clickstream analysis architecture. As clickstream operations increase, the amount of data to process will grow exponentially, and scalability issues will become critical for Web intelligence/Web analytics. See DSS in Focus 5.57 and Section 5.7. Werner and Abramson (2001) describe a method (based on sorting and aggregation) to process a billion records a day for a Web data warehouse. See also Hayes (2001) and Ruber (2003) for information about Web clickstream analysis. Langseth and Vivatrat (2002) discuss why proactive, Web-based business intelligence is a hallmark of the real-time enterprise. Sodhi and Aichlmayr (2001) discuss how and why we should embed specific analytical models in Web-based data mining tools. See DSS in Action 5.58 for information, with an example, about how Web analytics are used in practice.

Informatica Corp. has focused closely on using the Web to enable organizations to track business performance. Using the Informatica Enterprise business intelligence platform, organizations gather business performance metrics via voice systems, the Web, and wireless transmission. The Informatica Analytics Delivery Platform is an Internet-based system that provides real-time business performance results.

NetIQ Corp.'s WebTrends business intelligence tool focuses on real-time analysis of Web traffic and online transactions. WebTrends enables organizations to track con-

---

DSS IN FOCUS 5.57

THE CHALLENGES OF CLICKSTREAM ANALYSIS

There are many complications when dealing with Web intelligence/Web analytics. Here is a list of things to look out for when preparing to perform clickstream analysis:

- Data preparation can consume 80 percent of the project resources.

- Raw clickstream data must be obtained from multiple servers.

- Individual customer data are usually buried in a mass of other data about pages served, hosts, referring pages, and browser types.

- A single page request can generate multiple entries into server logs.

- Taking a sequence of log records and creating a session of page views involves lots of data cleansing to eliminate superfluous data.

- Identifying the sessions in the data stream is complex. It requires cookies or other session identification numbers in URLs.

- Proxy servers (where customer requests do not come from the home server) confuse the identity of a session and why it ended.

Source: Adapted from Edelstein, 2001, p. 80.

DSS IN ACTION 5.58

WEB ANALYTICS IMPROVES PERFORMANCE FOR ONLINE MERCHANTS

Online merchants anxious to improve the return of their Web site investment must learn their visitors' actions in real-time. This goes well beyond performing clickstream analysis and collecting the transaction reports with separate tools.

Online sales grew 52 percent to $78 billion in 2002, according to a Forrester Research report issued on January 28, 2003. E-commerce sales were fueled by growth in new product categories and retailer mastery of digital marketing, Web analytics, and multichannel marketing. Companies with traditional catalog businesses advanced online sales to reduce the burden on call center operations and to lower order-processing costs.

It is critical to understand customers' online behavior to determine how and what to market to them. Understanding and properly using the operating metrics of an e-commerce site can make or break a business. For example, special product promotions can be put online in a matter of days, versus the months required for expensive catalog revisions and nationwide mailings.

Web analytics can boost the bottom line. Yun-Hui Chong, Internet director for Newport News, says that the data her company receives about the activities of its 1.6 million monthly Web visitors enables it to look at the return on investment of all online marketing campaigns. "Based on that, we optimize our banners and the presentation of merchandise," she says. "We also use it to do clickstream analysis to understand how customers are reacting to our site." It has become particularly important to identify customers who abandon the site or just browse certain categories. The firm sends them very customized e-mail promotions about these categories. Since it began doing so, there have been significant increases in conversion and revenue per e-mail sent. Targeting browsers and abandoners via e-mail on three product categories experiencing the worst conversion rates resulted in a better than sixfold increase in revenue per e-mail sent, while the cost per order dropped some 83 percent. Web analytics clearly pays off!

Source: Adapted from Peter Ruber, "Analytics Improve Merchandising." *InternetWorld*, June 2003, pp. 11–12.

DSS IN FOCUS 5.59

WEB SERVICES BUSINESS INTELLIGENCE TOOLS

Here is a sample of business intelligence tools that support Web services, especially through XML integration:

Actuate Corp. (www.actuate.com): Actuate 6

Business Objects (www.businessobjects.com): Business Objects, WebIntelligence, BusinessObjects Developer Suite

ClearForest Corp. (www.clearforest.com): ClearResearch, ClearEvents, ClearSight

Cognos, Inc. (www.cognos.com): Cognos Series 7, Cognos Web Services SDK

Crystal Decisions (www.crystaldecisions.com): Crystal Enterprise, Crystal Reports, Crystal Analysis Professional

Dimensional Insight, Inc. (www.dimins.com): DI-Diver, DI-ProDiver, DI-WebDiver, DI-ReportDiver, DI-Broadcast

Hummingbird Ltd. (www.humingbird.com): Hummingbird BI

Information Builders Inc. (www.informationbuilders.com): WebFocus

Insight Corp. (www.insight.com): StatServer, Analytics Server

Microstrategy Inc. (www.microstrategy.com): Microstrategy Web Universal, Microstrategy SDK

SQL Power Group Inc. (www.sqlpower.ca): Power*Dashboard

Targit (www.targit.com): Targit Analysis 2K2

Source: Adapted from Jack Vaughan, "XML Meets the Data Warehouse," *Application Development Trends*, January 2003, pp. 27–30.

sumer purchasing trends, revenue, and the effectiveness of ad campaigns or sales promotions, through millions of site visits daily. Site59.com Inc., a travel site that specializes in last-minute getaway packages, discovered through WebTrends Live analyses that visitors could not easily find all the available travel packages on the site. The analysis indicated how to streamline and improve the design. Since then, Site59.com has experienced an increase in the number of visitors and the proportion of those who make online purchases (see Pallatto, 2002a, 2002b).

EBizinsights XL from Visual Insights (www.visualinsights.com) enables visual Web site performance analysis. Graphic in nature, and implemented on an OLAP system, EBizinsights includes a Visual Portal to enable the user to select and tailor views of about 200 graphical reports ("insights"). Visual Path Analysis graphically displays the paths that users have followed through a Web site. EBizinsights and similar tools are essential in evaluating Web site effectiveness and design. See www.visualinsights .com and Anonymous (2002) for details. Angoss KnowledgeWeb is another example of a Web mining/analytic tool. See Hallett (2001) for more on Web analytics visualization tools. See DSS in Focus 5.59 for examples of software packages that support Web analytics. See Figure 5.13 for a sample screenshot.

FIGURE 5.13   SCREEN SHOT FROM EBIZINSIGHTS VISUAL PORTAL ANALYSIS OF WEB PERFORMANCE

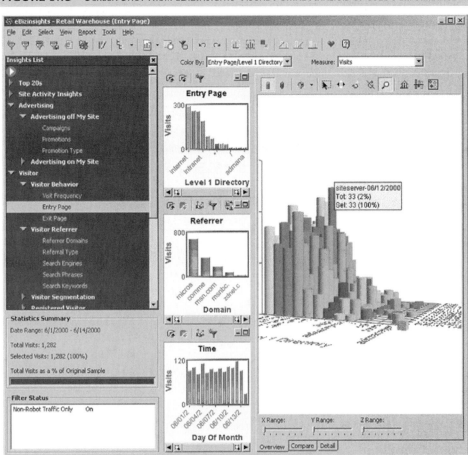

Courtesy of Visual Insights

❖ CHAPTER HIGHLIGHTS

- Data exist in internal, external, and personal sources.
- External data are available on thousands of online Web sites, commercial databases, directories, reports, and so on.
- Data for MSS must be collected frequently in the field using one or several methods.
- MSS may have data problems, such as incorrect data, nontimely data, poorly measured and indexed data, too many data, or no data.
- Commercial online databases, such as CompuServe and Dow Jones Information Service, can be major sources of MSS/BI data.
- The Internet has become a major external data source for MSS/BI.
- Intranets are providing internal data for MSS/BI.
- Most major databases have Web links to enable direct query via Web browsers on client workstations.
- Data are usually organized in relational, hierarchical, or network architectures. For many MSS/BI/BA, the relational database type is preferable.
- Structured query language (SQL) is a standard means of access for querying relational databases.
- Multimedia databases have become increasingly more important for decision-making applications.
- Object-oriented databases are easy to use and can be accessed very quickly. They are especially useful in distributed MSS and complex DSS.
- One of the most critical objectives is to make databases intelligent so that users can find information quickly by themselves.

- A data warehouse is a specially constructed data repository where data are organized so that they can be easily accessed by end users for several applications.
- Data marts contain data on one topic (e.g., marketing). They can be a replication of a subset of data in the data warehouse. They are a less expensive solution that can be replaced by or can supplement a data warehouse.
- Data marts can be independent of or dependent on a data warehouse.
- Data multidimensionality enables people to view data quickly in different dimensions, even if the data are in different files and databases.
- Business intelligence is moving toward real-time capabilities.
- Visualization is an important business intelligence capability.
- Business intelligence methods include OLAP and data mining.
- Online analytical processing (OLAP) is a set of tools for timely data analysis. It is extremely important in MSS/BI/BA applications.
- Data mining is the discovery of knowledge in databases. It is often done on data in data warehouses.
- Data mining can be hypothesis-driven or discovery-driven.
- The Web continues to impact dramatically on how database management systems are developed and operate.

❖ KEY WORDS

- business analytics
- business intelligence
- client/server architecture
- content-management system (CMS)
- data
- data mart
- data integrity
- data mining
- data quality (DQ)
- data visualization
- data warehouse
- database management systems (DBMS)

- dependent data mart
- development technology
- discovery-driven data mining
- document management systems (DMS)
- hypothesis-driven data mining
- independent data mart
- information
- intelligent database
- Internet
- knowledge
- metadata
- multidimensionality

- object-oriented database management system (OODBMS)
- online analytical processing (OLAP)
- online (commercial) databases
- query tools
- relational database
- source systems
- structured query language (SQL)
- user participation
- Web analytics
- Web intelligence

❖ QUESTIONS FOR REVIEW

1. Define data, information, and knowledge. Identify two examples of each.

2. Describe the role of the Internet in MSS data management and business intelligence.

3. What is SQL? Why is it important?
4. List the major categories of data sources for an MSS/BI.
5. Why are data quality and data integrity so important?
6. Describe the benefits of commercial databases.
7. Define object-oriented database management.
8. Define document management.
9. Define a star schema.
10. What are intelligent databases, and why are they so popular?
11. How can an expert system provide a good interface to commercial databases?
12. Define data multidimensionality and a multidimensional database.
13. Describe why visualization is so important in business intelligence.

14. Define a data warehouse, and list some of its characteristics.
15. What is the difference between a database and a data warehouse?
16. Describe the role that a data warehouse can play in MSS. List its benefits.
17. Define a data mart and explain why they are important.
18. Describe OLAP.
19. Define data mining and list its major technologies.
20. What is meant by real-time business analytics?
21. Differentiate data mining, text mining, and Web mining.
22. Distinguish between KDD and data mining.
    Explain how the Web is impacting business intelligence/business analytic methods and technologies.

❖ QUESTIONS FOR DISCUSSION

1. Relate data warehousing to OLAP and data visualization.
2. Discuss the relationship between multiple sources of data, including external data, and the data warehouse.
3. Explain the relationship between SQL and a DBMS.
4. Compare OLTP to OLAP.
5. Define and describe a commercial database (online) service. Name one or two with which you are familiar.
6. Explain the relationship between OLAP and data mining.
7. Describe multidimensionality and explain its potential benefits for MSS.
8. Identify a commercial DBMS provider. Prepare a short report that describes the services offered, the fees, and the process for obtaining the service.
9. It is said that a relational database is the best for DSS (as compared to hierarchical and network structures). Explain why.

10. Explain the issue of data quality and some of the measures one can take to improve it.
11. It is said that object-oriented DBMS are the best solutions to a complex (especially distributed) DSS. Explain.
12. What is a data warehouse, and what are its benefits? Why is Web accessibility important?
13. Describe the major dimensions of data quality.
14. Why is data quality such an important issue to an organization?
15. Discuss the benefits of DMS.
16. Discuss what an organization should consider before making a decision to purchase data-mining software.
17. Distinguish data mining from other analytic tools.
18. Explain the process of text mining.
19. Describe the concepts underlying Web intelligence and Web analytics.

❖ EXERCISES

1. A university is installing a DSS for budget preparation, expense monitoring, and financial planning. There are four schools at the university and 18 departments. In addition, there are two research institutions and many administrative services. Prepare a diagram that shows how the DSS will be distributed to all users. Comment on the data and its sources for such a DSS. Suggest what decisions could be supported at each managerial level. Explain how OLAP can be utilized effectively by the university.

2. Typically, data on a university campus are stored in different physical locations for different purposes. For example, the registrar's office, the housing office, the individual departmental offices, the personnel office, the staff benefits office, and the fund-raising and development office may maintain separate unintegrated databases with student (and faculty) records.
   a. Explain what problems can occur in obtaining data to support complex decisions.

b. Explain how a data warehouse might help solve these problems.

c. Discuss some of the behavioral (political) and technical problems that can occur in developing and implementing a data warehouse in such an environment.

d. Visit or call several offices and departments at your university (or at your place of business) and determine how basic data on students and faculty (or customers and employees) are stored, maintained, and manipulated. Find out whether they have multiple databases and what chronic problems they encounter.

3. Review the list of data problems in Table 5.1. Provide additional suggestions for each category.

4. The U.S. government spends millions of dollars gathering data on its population every 10 years (plus some mid-decade adjustments). Census data are critical in determining the representation of each state in the House of Representatives and the number of Electoral College votes to which each state is entitled in presidential elections. More important, census data provide information about U.S. markets. The demographics indicate family and gender makeup, income, educational level, and other information for states, metropolitan statistical areas (MSAs), and counties. Such data are available from various sources, including books, disks, CD-ROMs, and the World Wide Web (see Internet Exercise 6). In this exercise, we take a real-world view of external but readily available data.

a. Find an electronic source of standard census data files for states and MSAs.

b. Access the data and examine the file structures. Do the contents and organization of each make sense? Why or why not? If not, suggest improvements.

c. Load the state P1 data population table into a spreadsheet file (Excel if possible) and into a database file (Access if possible). How difficult was this? How could it have been made easier? Don't forget to delete the comments and U.S. totals (if present) at the top, for later use. Note that Washington, D.C., is listed as well. Print the table.

d. Using the state P1 population data, sort the data based on population size. What are the five most populous states and the five least populous states? Which five states have the greatest and least population densities? Which state has the most males, and which state has the most females? Which three states have the most people living on farms, and which state has the fewest lonely people? Which file type (spreadsheet or database) did you use, and why? What features made it easy to do these analyses?

e. Load the state basic Table P6 (household income) into a spreadsheet or database file. Which five states have the most people earning $100,000 or more per year? Which five states have the highest percentages of people earning $100,000 or more per year? Combine these data with data from Table P1 to determine which five states have the most people per square mile earning $100,000 or more per year? Which file type (spreadsheet or database) did you use, and why? What features made it easy to do these analyses?

f. Data warehousing and data mining are used to combine data and identify patterns. Use data (load and save them in spreadsheet or database files) from the following files: P1: Population; P3: Persons by Age; P4: Households by Size; P6: Household Income; P8: Other Income Measures; and P9: Level of Education. Synthesize these tables into a usable set and determine whether there are any relationships at the state level between

  i. Population per square mile and education
  ii. Income and age
  iii. Household size and education. Can you think of any other relationships to explore? If you can, do so. What made this task difficult or easy? Explain.

g. Examine the MSA data tables and see whether any of the relationships found for the state data above hold.

h. How does the profile of your MSA (or the one closest to where you live) compare with your state's census profile and with that of the entire United States? How did you determine this?

5. Given the following list of employees in a manufacturing company, use DBMS software or a spreadsheet to

a. Sort the employees by department

b. Sort the employees by salary in ascending order

c. Sort the employees by department and sort the employees of each department by age in ascending order

d. Calculate the average salary

e. Calculate the average salary of female employees

f. Calculate the average age in Department A

g. List the names of females who were hired after December 31, 1995

h. Show the age distribution graphically (use a 5-year grouping) as a pie chart

i. Compute the linear regression relationship of salary vs. age for all employees

j. Compute the relationship for females and males independently. Is there a significant difference?

Name	Gender	Age	Date Hired	Dept.	Salary
Martin Dean	M	28	06 Jan. 88	A	$22,000
Jane Hanson	F	35	15 Mar. 96	D	$33,200
Daniel Smith	M	19	06 Dec. 90	C	$18,500
Emily Brosmer	F	26	10 Jan. 88	B	$27,000
Jessica Stone	F	45	26 May 83	A	$38,900
Tom Obudzinski	M	38	01 Dec. 98	B	$29,800
Kathleen Braun	F	32	18 Apr. 92	B	$35,600
Lisa Gregory	F	48	03 Sept. 91	C	$32,400
Timothy Parker	M	29	03 Aug. 93	A	$21,200
Jessica Hibscher	F	53	30 July 94	D	$38,900
Adam Handel	M	62	29 Nov. 97	A	$40,250
Melissa Black	F	42	01 Dec. 89	B	$26,400
Ray Ernster	M	29	02 July 87	C	$23,200
Daniel Baim	M	38	26 Feb. 88	C	$31,000
Amy Melnikov	F	45	30 Apr. 86	A	$36,400
Adrienne Cammizzo	F	30	15 June 86	A	$25,400
Steven Knowless	M	48	22 Oct. 85	D	$33,200
Patricia Salisbury	F	56	26 Feb. 84	B	$42,600
Matthew Broekhuizen	M	44	01 Jan. 88	C	$45,400
Sarah Parent	F	64	01 Jan. 99	A	$38,200

6. Investigate the integration of data warehouse and GIS. Start with www.mapinfo.com.
7. Take a test drive of demos of DecisionWeb (Comshare) and of business intelligence from sterling.com, Temtec, Brio, and Cognos. Do not miss Sybase's free interactive CD on business intelligence (hosted by soccer star Alexi Lalas). Prepare a report.
8. Examine how new data capture devices such as RFID tags (see DSS in Action 5.3) help organizations to accurately identify and segment their customers for activities such as targeted marketing. Scan the literature and the Web, and develop five potential new applications (not in this text) of RFID technology. What issues could arise if a country's laws required such devices to be embedded in everyone's body for a national identification system?
9. Consider the problem facing the city of London (U.K.). Since February 17, 2003, the city has instituted a fee for automobiles and trucks in the central city district. There are 816 cameras digitally photographing the license plate of every vehicle passing by. Computers read the plate numbers and match them against records in a database of cars for which the fee has been paid for that day. If a match is not found (and the system was initially only 90 percent accurate), the car owner receives a citation by mail. The citations range from about $128 to $192 depending upon when they are paid. Examine the issues pertaining to how this is done, the mistakes that are made, and the size of the databases involved, including that of the images from the license plates. Also examine how well the system is working by investigating press reports. (This exercise was inspired by Ray Hutton, "London on $8 a Day!" *Car and Driver*, August 2003, pp. 130–131.)

❖ INTERNET EXERCISES

1. Surf the Internet to find information about data warehousing. Identify some newsgroups that have an interest in this concept. Explore ABI/Inform in your library, e-library, and Yahoo for recent articles on the topic, including the areas of data mining, multidimensionality, and OLAP. Begin with www.dw-institute.org and the major vendors: sas.com, oracle.com, and ncr.com. Also check cio.com, dmreview.com, dssresources.com, and pwp.starnetic.com.
2. Survey some data-mining tools and vendors. Start with fairisaac.com, and www.egain.com. Also consult dmreview.com.
3. Contact some DBMS vendors and obtain information about their products. Special attention should be given to vendors that provide tools for multiple purposes, such as Cognos, Software A&G, SAS Institute, and Oracle. Free demos are available from some of these vendors over the Web (e.g., brio.com).

Download a demo or two and try them. Write a report describing your experience.

4. America Online, stock brokerages, and portals provide a free service that shows the status of investors' stock market portfolios, including profits (losses) and prices (with a 15-minute delay or even in real-time). How is such individualized information retrieved so quickly? Why must such data be updated so quickly?

5. What economic data are available from government agencies? Who provides what types of data? How easy are these data to access, download, and use? (Provide 10 examples.)

6. Search the Internet to identify sources of U.S. government census data files. Download and examine some of the files. Are they flat ASCII text data files, spreadsheet files, or database files (and what are their formats)? Were they compressed or archived? If so,

how easy was it to extract the data? Which tables (files) would be useful, and what kinds of analyses could be performed with such data (e.g., for a consumer product marketing firm, a financial services firm, an insurance company, and a real estate developer)?

7. Find recent cases of successful business intelligence applications. Try business intelligence vendors and look for cases or success stories.

8. Visit teradatauniversitynetwork.com. Identify cases on business intelligence, data warehousing, and data mining. Describe recent developments in the field.

9. Go to Web sites (especially, SAS, SPSS, Cognos, TemTec, Business Objects) and look at success stories for business intelligence (OLAP and data mining) tools. What do you find in common among the various success stories? How do they differ?

❖ GROUP EXERCISES

1. Each group member will check a major DBMS vendor (Oracle, Sybase, Informix, and so on). Examine their major Web-related products. Explain the connection of the databases to data mining and to electronic commerce.

2. Data visualization is offered by all major data warehouse vendors, as well as by other companies, such as www.ilog.com. Students are assigned one to each vendor to find the products and their capabilities. (For a list of vendors, see www.dw-institute.org.) Each group summarizes the products and their capabilities.

3. Interview administrators in your college or executives in your organization to determine how data warehousing, data mining, OLAP, and visualization business intelligence/DSS tools could assist them in their work. Write up a proposal describing your findings. Include cost estimates and benefits in your report.

4. Go through the list of data warehousing risks in DSS in Action 5.19 and find three examples of each in practice.

DATA WAREHOUSING
AND OLAP AT CABELA'S

Cabela's, "the world's foremost outfitter," (Sidney, Nebraska) is the world's largest mail order distributor of products for outdoor enthusiasts. Cabela's has 6,000 employees. Every year Cabela's mails more than 60 million catalogs in 60 editions to customers across the entire United States and in 135 other countries. Cabela's also owns eight stores, an e-commerce Web site, and four tele-marketing centers in the United States

In the mid-1990s, executives needed to develop a greater understanding of their customers' behaviors, individual tastes, and purchase preferences. They needed to characterize the different segments of the company's customer base. Essentially they needed a way to *cluster* or group their customers to understand them, and to target market specific products to the members of each cluster (segment)

At the time, Cabela's relied on outsourced business intelligence and in-house packaged solutions to build separate mailing lists for every single catalog and promotion. This process was costly and slow. In addition, the data's integrity was called into question.

Cabela's adopted IBM's DB2 Universal Data Enterprise Edition and IBM DB2 Warehouse Manager as its platform. Query response times are now 80 percent faster than before; maintenance time and costs have been cut in half. The knowledge gleaned from the data warehouse has enabled the firm's marketing team to improve catalog hit rates and has led to far-reaching improvements to printed catalogs and the e-commerce Web site, enhancing the customer experience and boosting customer loyalty.

About 30 users (including four full-time statisticians and their staff, and senior managers) access the data warehouse with BRIO Explorer as the front-end querying and reporting tool, and SAS as the statistical analysis tool (both are OLAP tools). The warehouse contains 11 years of information stored in about 700 gigabytes.

Within a few months of deployment, sales in most market segments rose significantly. Since it has succeeded, improvements are already underway on the OLAP side to help better understand the crucial relationships among customers, markets, products, prices, and geography—the key factors that drive the business.

By leveraging data assets with additional data management and business intelligence technologies, Cabela's will achieve deeper and more powerful insights that will bring added value to its customers; and to the bottom line.

CASE QUESTIONS

1. Describe how Cabela's ran its marketing process before the system was developed.
2. Why is it important for a firm like Cabela's to segment its customers? What benefits can the firm obtain? Are there any disadvantages? Explain.
3. Why was it important for Cabela's to have kept 11 years of sales data on hand? Could the firm have used more?
4. How have OLAP tools helped Cabela's improve the performance of the business?
5. Describe how OLAP tools could help Cabela's do even better than it is doing with the system described.
6. Describe how data mining tools could help Cabela's do even better than it is with the system described.
7. Go to the Web sites of the vendors mentioned in the case and examine the current OLAP, data mining, and data warehousing features and capabilities of each. Describe in detail how Cabela's could use each one.
8. Describe the competitive nature of the system.

Adapted from Jerry Rivkind, "Cabela's Data Warehouse Satisfies Hunt for Business Insight." *What Works: Best Practices in Business Intelligence and Data Warehousing*, Vol. 15, The Data Warehousing Institute, Chatsworth, CA, June, 2003, pp. 8–9.

CASE APPLICATION 5.2

BLUE CROSS AND BLUE SHIELD OF MINNESOTA'S PAIN-FREE CRM SAVES THE DAY THROUGH DATA INTEGRATION AND PLANNING

By taking the time to integrate data for its online CRM system, a regional health plan has succeeded where other large insurers have not. In 2001, John Ounjian, senior vice president and CIO of Blue Cross and Blue Shield (BCBS) of Minnesota, convinced General Mills, an $8 billion consumer goods firm, to join his regional health plan on the promise that he would install a Web-based customer service system so that subscribers could manage their health benefits online. Subscribers could select health plans tailored to their individual needs and budgets, calculate their own contributions to their coverage, research information on prescription drugs and other treatments, locate participating physicians, and check the status of claims.

To implement this system, he needed to install a brand-new infrastructure to integrate his Web and call center operation and provide timely, accurate information to customers. He also had to migrate megabytes of data stored in back-end, legacy databases to the Web front end—massaging and reformatting the data so consumers could understand them.

The online customer self-service system (deployed in January 2002) not only met the specifications of General Mills, but also managed to beat national providers Aetna, Cigna, and Humana out of several very large accounts, such as 3M, Northwest Airlines and Target.

Ounjian says that his company's membership grew by 10 percent, or 200,000 new members, in 2002, largely because of its online customer self-service system, when several national insurers lost millions of members. In addition to offering a viable solution to customer problems, Web self-service also provides the necessary foundation for delivering health plans tailored to the needs of individual consumers—a direction in which the industry is moving to decrease managed care costs.

Ounjian realized that the plan needed to lay down a whole new infrastructure, or *chassis*. It would also need a sound data management strategy to overcome problems when it tried to move raw data from back-end systems to the Web front end. Ounjian uses Oracle databases on the front end to reassemble and synchronize back-end data so that consumers find consistent, timely information regardless of whether they use the Web channel or the call center channel. Ounjian indicates that he uses different vendors for the several components of the Web self-service architecture because there was no single vendor that could supply everything for an integrated CRM system. He wanted the flexibility to layer different applications and functionality from different vendors on top of his infrastructure.

Ounjian's biggest problem was to devise a tactical strategy for moving data and transactions from the front end to the back end, and vice versa. Making megabytes of back-end data available and understandable to users on the front end is one of the biggest challenges for any successful CRM project, regardless of industry. If you cannot get accurate information to customers in a format they understand, they will not use the system. The millions of records that had to be migrated made the task even more daunting.

Ounjian believes the reason why so many CRM projects—not just in health care but across industries—run into problems or fail altogether is because they aren't grounded by an underlying plan for transferring data that originates in one system and in one form to another system in a different form.

In early 2003, the system was being used by 61 employers with 450,000 individual employees. BCBS plans to increase that number throughout 2004.

CASE QUESTIONS

1. Describe how the BCBS system works.
2. Why was it so important to develop the infrastructure in advance of deploying the systems?
3. How did the BCBS system integrate various data sources?
4. How can users utilize the system as a decision-making/business intelligence system?
5. Describe how managers at BCBS could use the system in an OLAP and in a data mining framework.
6. Describe the competitive nature of the system.

Adapted from Meredith Levinson, "Pain-free CRM," *CIO*, May 15, 2003, pp. 79–80.

CLUSTER ANALYSIS FOR DATA MINING

INTRODUCTION

Cluster analysis is a very important set of methods for classifying items into common groupings called *clusters*. The methods are common in biology, medicine, genetics, the social sciences, anthropology, archaeology, astronomy, character recognition, and even in MIS development. As data mining has increased in popularity, the methods have been applied to business, especially to marketing. Cluster analysis has been used extensively for fraud detection, both credit card and e-commerce fraud, and market segmentation of customers in CRM systems. More applications in business continue to be developed as the strength of cluster analysis is understood and utilized.

CLUSTER ANALYSIS FOR DATA ANALYSIS

Cluster analysis is an exploratory data analysis tool for solving classification problems. The object is to sort cases (people, things, events, etc.) into groups, or clusters, so that the degree of association is strong between members of the same cluster and weak between members of different clusters. Each cluster describes the class to which its members belong. An obvious one-dimensional example of cluster analysis is to establish score ranges into which to assign class grades for a college class. This is similar to the cluster analysis problem that the U.S. Treasury Department faced when establishing new tax brackets in the 1980s. A fictional example of clustering occurs in J .K. Rowling's *Harry Potter* books. The *Sorting Hat* determines which House (e.g., dormitory) to which to assign first-year students at the Hogwarts School. Another example involves how to seat guests at a wedding. As far as data mining goes, the importance of cluster analysis is that it may reveal associations and structures in data that were not previously apparent but are sensible and useful once found.

Cluster analysis results may be used to

- Help identify a classification scheme (e.g., types of customers)
- Suggest statistical models to describe populations
- Indicate rules for assigning new cases to classes for identification, targeting, and diagnostic purposes
- Provide measures of definition, size, and change in what were previously broad concepts
- Find typical cases to represent classes

CLUSTER ANALYSIS METHODS

Cluster analysis may be based on one or more of the following, general methods:

- Statistical (including both hierarchical and nonhierarchical)
- Optimal
- Neural networks
- Fuzzy logic
- Genetic algorithms

Each of these methods generally work with one of the following two general method classes:

- *Divisive:* all items start in one cluster and are broken apart.
- *Agglomerative:* all items start in individual clusters, and the clusters are joined together.

Most cluster analysis methods involve the use of a *distance* between pairs of items. That is, there is a measure of similarity between every pair of items to be clustered. Often they are based on true distances that are measured, but this need not be so, as is typically the case in IS development. Weighted averages may be used to establish these distances. For example, in an IS development project, individual modules of the system may be related by the similarity between their inputs, outputs, processes, and the specific data used. These factors are then aggregated, pairwise by item, into a single distance measure.

CLUSTERING EXAMPLE

Consider the similarity (distance) matrix that represents the similarities among eight items shown in Table 5.9. Items 4 and 5 have a lot in common, as do items 1 and 3, and 3 and 10; though 1 and 10 are moderately related, and 1 and 5 have little in common. To evaluate a solution, we add the pairwise values of all the items in each cluster. If we want three balanced clusters (between 2 and 3 items per cluster), the solution of clusters {1, 3, 6}, {2,8}, and {4, 5, 7} have a value of (9 + 6 + 10) + 8 + (10 + 8 + 9) = 60. Can we do better? Try it!

Now that we have a data set, some critical issues to address are

TABLE 5.9   Similarity (Distance) Matrix

The values below the diagonal equal the values above; that is, the distance from 1 to 2 is the same as from 2 to 1. Diagonal values do not exist.

Item	1	2	3	4	5	6	7	8
1	–	3	9	2	1	6	4	5
2		–	4	5	6	2	3	8
3			–	5	7	10	4	2
4				–	10	2	8	1
5					–	4	9	3
6						–	3	3
7							–	5
8								–

- How many clusters are to be found (when do we stop)?
- Should all the clusters have an approximately equal number of items?
- How do we handle dimensional scaling when different measures are used in establishing the distance value?
- Can distance really be measured?

HIERARCHICAL CLUSTERING METHOD AND EXAMPLE

We start with a set of items, each within its own cluster. We determine the maximum number of clusters we want to have. The basic method is to

1. Decide which data to record from your items (measures of similarity).

2. Calculate the distance between all initial clusters. Store the results in a distance matrix.

3. Search through the distance matrix and find the two most similar clusters.

4. Fuse these two clusters together to produce a cluster that now has at least two items.

5. Calculate the distances between this new cluster and all the other clusters (some of which may contain one item).

6. Repeat steps 3 to 5 until you have reached the prespecified maximum number of clusters.

Note that some methods go all the way to a single cluster of all items. To identify the solution you want, identify where you have obtained the desired number of clusters, and stop.

Applying the hierarchical method to our matrix above with a goal of three balanced clusters, the initial solution is

$\{1, 2, 3, 4, 5, 6, 7, 8\}$ at a value of 134. Though this is an excellent value, we want three clusters.

We first combine items 4 and 5 (value = 10) to get

$\{4, 5\} \{1, 2, 3, 6, 7, 8\}$ at 10 + 74 = 94, which is pretty good.

We next combine 3 and 6 (value = 10) to get

$\{3, 6\} \{4, 5\} \{1, 2, 7, 8\}$ at 10 + 10 + 28 = 48.

Next, we combine 7 into the cluster with 4 and 5 to get

$\{3, 6\} \{4, 5, 7\} \{1, 2, 8\}$ at = 53.

We stop because we have three clusters as balanced as can be with these data (two groups of three items, one group of two items).

The above example may actually be formulated as an optimization problem and solved with an efficient algorithm (see Aronson and Klein, 1991).

CLUSTER ANALYSIS SOFTWARE

Aside from data mining methods in which cluster analysis methods are embedded, there are several specialized packages for cluster analysis. These include:

- ClustanGraphics (Clustan)
- DecisionWORKS Suite (Advanced Software Applications)
- SPSS (SPSS)
- PolyAnalyst Cluster Engine (Megaputer)
- Sokal code (see Hand, 1981)

There are also many free codes available from academic sites. Do a Web search to find them.

EFFECTIVE CLUSTER ANALYSIS/ DATA MINING APPLICATIONS

Goulet and Wishart (1996) provide an excellent example of how a bank was able to classify its customers to dramatically improve their financial services. The Co-opérative Desjardin's Movement is the largest banking institution in Québec (Canada). When this analysis was done, there were 1,329 branches and 4.2 million members. The organization had combined assets in excess of (Canada) $80 billion. It was in the process of reducing teller services, increasing ATM use and other IT methods, and reducing staff. The organization, in addition to banking, offered products and services that included life and property insurance, and several others. Since each branch is independent, the Confédération needed to market its products to both its branches and its members. At the start of the study, the bank executives realized that they needed a typology of its members not only to retain customer loyalty, but also to capture more market share by identifying profitable services to satisfy members' needs and improve market penetration.

The bank performed a *cluster analysis* of a sample of 16,000 members. By doing so, it identified 16 variables that reflected the characteristics of financial transaction patterns. Thirty *member types* were identified. Next, all 4.2 million members were classified with best fits of the 16 measures, which were used to place them into *one or more* of the 30 member type clusters.

Now financial managers and analysts can identify members whose financial transactions fall into one or more of the 30 clusters. Given a particular member's cluster, the profitability of each transaction cluster and individual customer accounts can be measured. Each branch manager can view his or her customers as investments in a portfolio, and particular market segments for the branch's products and services are readily identified.

The results are impressive. The bank can identify members with large transaction volumes in one account by matching them to their other loan or insurance accounts. The managers can then suggest more economical consolidations of members' investments and loans, thus leading to a higher level of customer satisfaction. Additionally, managers can suggest better diversification of members' investments. But the most impressive results are in the bank's marketing efforts. The bank can focus on products and services that have the best financial performance and target them to appropriate customers. This reduces mailing and other contact costs. Response rates have been improved by targeting product promotions achieving better branding and customer retention. In fact, more profitable customers are retained at lower costs.

FURTHER READING

For more details on cluster analysis, algorithms, and software, see Aldenderfer and Blashfield (1984), Aronson and Iyer (2001), Goulet and Wishart (1996), Hand (1981), Klein and Aronson (1991), Romesburg (1984), and Zupan (1982). Also, since Web sites change almost daily, we recommend that you perform a Web search on *cluster*, *cluster analysis*, and *cluster methods*. There are excellent academic sites, many of which include free computer codes.

A BETTER SOLUTION TO THE EXAMPLE

Though not balanced, the cluster solution {1, 3, 4}, {3, 5, 6}, and {5} has a value of 72, better than the solutions described earlier.

Cluster Analysis References

Aldenderfer, M.S., and R.K. Blashfield. (1984). *Cluster Analysis*. Thousand Oaks, CA: Sage.

Aronson, J.E., and L.S. Iyer. (2001). "Cluster Analysis." In *Encyclopedia of Operations Research & Management Science*, Norwell, MA: Kluwer.

Goulet, M., and D. Wishart. (1996, June). "Classifying a Bank's Customers to Improve Their Financial Services." In *Proceedings of the Conference of the Classification Society of North America (CSNA)*, Amherst, MA.

Hand, D. (1981). *Discrimination and Classification*. New York: Wiley.

Klein, G., and J.E. Aronson. (1991). "Optimal Clustering: A Model and Method." *Naval Research Logistics*, Vol. 38, No. 1.

Romesburg, H. (1984). *Cluster Analysis for Researchers*. Belmont, CA: Lifetime Learning.

Zupan, J. (1982). *Clustering of Large Data Sets*. New York: Research Studies Press.

CASE QUESTIONS

1. Explain why cluster analysis is important for data mining.
2. Identify the different methods of performing cluster analysis. Study the literature and Web sites to determine the kinds of problems to which each method can appropriately be applied.
3. Explain how cluster analysis works.
4. Search the Web for free and cheap cluster analysis software. Download one and describe how it works and the types of problems it solves.
5. Describe how the Co-opérative Desjardin's Movement performed its cluster analysis.
6. Describe the benefits obtained from cluster analysis by the Co-opérative Desjardin's Movement.

CHAPTER 6

DECISION SUPPORT SYSTEM DEVELOPMENT

LEARNING OBJECTIVES

❖ Understand the basic concepts of systems development

❖ Describe the four phases of the (PADI) system development life cycle: planning, analysis, development, and implementation

❖ Understand prototyping and throwaway prototyping and why DSS are typically developed using these methods

❖ Describe the factors that lead to DSS success or failure

❖ Discuss the importance of project management and the necessary skills of a good project manager

❖ Describe the three technology levels of DSS: DSS primary tools, DSS integrated tools (generators), and specific DSS

❖ Understand the learning process that occurs during DSS development

Up until now, we have presented the basic concepts and components of decision-making and decision support. Now we must learn how to implement a decision support system. Unfortunately, acquiring a DSS is not as simple as obtaining productivity software like a word processor. DSS are usually designed to handle complex situations, and few are available right off the shelf. Though OLAP software has facilitated DSS development, most DSS require some custom-design, development, and implementation for each specific application. We present the DSS development process in the following sections:

6.1 Opening Vignette: Osram Sylvania Thinks Small, Strategizes Big—Develops the InfoNet HR Portal System

6.2 Introduction to DSS Development

6.3 The Traditional System Development Life Cycle

6.4 Alternative Development Methodologies

6.5 Prototyping: The DSS Development Methodology

6.6 Change Management

6.7 DSS Technology Levels and Tools

6.8 DSS Development Platforms

6.9 DSS Development Tool Selection

6.1 OPENING VIGNETTE: OSRAM SYLVANIA THINKS SMALL, STRATEGIZES BIG—DEVELOPS THE INFONET HR PORTAL SYSTEM[1]

A *business portal* is a central aggregation point for corporate data, tools, and links accessed through a browser interface. Portals appeal to organizations whose information and business processes are scattered across many different reports, applications, systems, and geography. Thinking small when building a first portal makes sense.

Rather than trying to create a mega-enterprise portal for everyone and everything, companies focus on first building a small, specialized portal that solves a *pressing problem* in a particular department or business function—a prototype. That is the way the small, motivated team of IT and business staff at Osram Sylvania approached HR InfoNet, a portal focused on *human resources*. The North American division of Osram GmbH (Germany), has $3.7 billion in sales and 12,500 employees in 30 locations. Osram Sylvania manufactures and markets lighting, precision materials, and component products.

The lighting industry is highly competitive. *HR is strategic to Osram Sylvania.* Finding, recruiting, and hiring specialized scientists, engineers, and hourly staff is a major challenge. Employee benefits administration was accomplished with an expensive outsourcing solution. The recruitment problem needed a faster solution than the existing, slow, tedious paper-based system. With the existing system, employees could not do what-if comparisons or even see the cost of the programs they chose (it was voice-actuated). Another problem was that the system did not perform routine life status changes (e.g., adding a child to a family's benefits). These requests were handled manually. Improvement was clearly necessary. An interactive Web portal for employee self-service benefits would improve employee service.

Bringing job requisitions and benefits enrollment online was the initial goal of HR InfoNet. While the IT requirements were relatively straightforward, there were two internal issues. The first was that only about one-third of the employees had computers. The second was that the head of the project, Roger Rudenstein, had been hired in 1995 to head up the PeopleSoft system group to maintain and extend the PeopleSoft HR system and the interface with the new payroll system. The group was so busy with the payroll conversion that it could not start the HR portal until early 1996. There was a sense from earlier projects that an intranet (an internal Internet) was the appropriate technology platform for the HR system. This first decision, to build an intranet, was adopted.

Roger championed the project from the IT side, and Geoff Hunt, vice president of human resources, and Nancy Dobrusin and Julie Thibodeau, his counterparts in the HR department, championed it from the business side. They also had ongoing support

---

[1]Adapted from Rudenstein (2000).

from Michelle Marshall and the corporate communications department throughout the process.

The team adopted the strategy *think small, strategize big*. Resources were minimal for developing HR InfoNet. There were no dedicated staff, no funds to hire consultants, and *no budget*, despite the fact that this was a crucially strategic project. Roger targeted a solution that they could make workable. *Think small* meant that it was necessary to conserve both money and precious time. *Strategize big* meant that the development platform and solution architecture would have to handle future applications as well as current solutions as the portal grew in capability (scalable). It was almost a given that in-house technology was to be used. This cut down on IT staff training and licensing.

After a few suggestions from several coworkers, and some evaluation of potential systems, the team adopted the Lotus Notes/Domino Server. They developed their experience by *just doing it*. Within three months, they had successfully deployed a portal application for posting job requisitions in LotusScript and Notes/Domino databases with agents. This validated the technology, and so they continued with the next application, allowing employees to examine and correct their benefits online. For employees without computers, they developed kiosks that used standard browsers with special security features. Hourly employees were given network IDs and training.

The next step of the job requisition application process was to create an intranet-based workflow to allow managers to describe job openings and route them to the correct HR person using online forms. These postings can now be submitted directly to the corporate Web site. After successfully creating the initial HR InfoNet portal, they expanded it to include more HR benefits and compensation information.

In early 2000, the portal allowed employees to view their benefits, compare the costs of different programs, access information to help make their benefits decisions, change benefits enrollment, and perform many HR management duties, such as developing plans for salary reviews, management bonus programs, head count reports, and retirement packages. By then, the portal served as the focal point for the firm's job postings, requisitions, and hiring workflow, as well as the interface with HR benefits for all employees.

Employee feedback on the new HR capabilities has been extremely positive. Recruiting cycle time has improved, and HR productivity is higher. HR benefits administration is much more user-friendly, and even kiosk users have embraced the system. By taking benefits administration in-house, the company saves $500,000 annually—an excellent return on the project.

Instead of thinking big and trying to solve every problem at once, which is how traditional systems analysis works, the team used a focused approach, tackling the *key problem* first and then moving on to the next one. This evolutionary development (iterative development) is known formally as prototyping. Thinking big can lead to million-dollar budgets, hiring staff, preparing thousands of pages of specifications, and so on. And a large project is much less likely to succeed than a small project. Instead, they *strategized big* by developing a plan and technology strategy to achieve some quick successes, while offering a solid foundation on which to build the future. The *think small, strategize big* prototyping approach led to a major success for the HR InfoNet portal at Osram Sylvania. We present their practical insights into applying this philosophy in DSS in Focus 6.1.

Success leads to success, and so the team is developing more applications within and like HR InfoNet. HR InfoNet proved the validity of the portal concept. The team will continue to develop new applications in succession planning, performance management process (PMP), and time and attendance. Over three years, Osram Sylvania estimates a 251 percent return on investment (ROI) and a savings of $1.5 million.

❖ QUESTIONS FOR THE OPENING VIGNETTE

1. What was the strategic business need? What were the benefits of the completed HR InfoNet system? Explain.

2. Why was it important to have an IT champion, a functional business (HR) champion, and an executive champion involved in the project?

3. Who were the users? What decisions did the system assist the users in making?

4. How were the users involved in the system development? How was management involved?

5. Do you feel that if the development team had "thought big," that is, tried to design and develop a total solution over a long period of time, they would have

---

DSS IN FOCUS 6.1

GUIDELINES FOR A "THINK SMALL, STRATEGIZE BIG" IMPLEMENTATION

Here are some practical insights for applying the *think small, strategize big* philosophy, as outlined in the Osram Sylvania HR InfoNet development described in the Opening Vignette.

- *Draw on "hidden" talent.* Osram Sylvania used a small group of staff involved in another project at virtually no cost. Management gave them a challenge and interesting, exciting extra work. They also had the strong support of the IT infrastructure staff, which was critical to their success.

- *Partner with the business staff.* Roger Rudenstein was already working with his functional counterparts in HR business systems, benefits, and compensation. He had an office near them and helped in joint planning and collaboration. He worked hard to determine their needs and make suggestions on how IT could meet these needs. *Successful IT projects involve the users throughout the entire development process.*

- *Use an iterative process.* Prototyping was critical. The team members did not have all the details before starting development but were able to refine on the fly. They used an iterative process, where they sat down with the business staff and worked out an agreement that described what they were trying to do. Then they developed a prototype, and the many ongoing iterations evolved into the application, quickly moving the project along. Employee feedback via focus groups and other

means helped them stay on track and kept the users involved, which helped lead to success.

- *Choose the right technology tools.* Notes/Domino was chosen because the company was already using it, and so it was free. After becoming familiar with it, the team members realized it would meet their current and future needs. The fact that all its applications are integrated was also a critical factor. Cementing the system together was relatively easy, and there was a common interface—a Web browser.

We add the following:

- *Enlist a champion in higher management.* The full support of an executive sponsor leads to resources for a project. The HR InfoNet had several champions.

- *Build a user training program into the system release.* This leads to better adoption and satisfaction. It also leads to fewer problems with non–computer specialists using the system when it is released. Users must be appropriately trained, else they may become noncooperative.

- *Align the project with business needs.* Without this, it is difficult to get an executive sponsor. The benefits of the project were clear at the outset. New benefits unfolded as the project evolved. There was a critical need for the project.

Source: Partly adapted from Rudenstein (2000).

succeeded? What could have gone wrong? Do you think they knew this in advance?

6. What technology issues, behavioral issues, and implementation issues had to be worked through in developing the HR InfoNet system?

7. What implementation approach was adopted? Why?

8. Comment on how success breeds success in DSS development.

6.2 INTRODUCTION TO DSS DEVELOPMENT

The HR InfoNet system illustrates a number of important DSS/BI development and implementation issues. It was built with an important DSS development approach called *prototyping* (see DSS in Action 6.2). Prototyping is one adaptation of the traditional **system development life cycle (SDLC).** The development team started small and expanded the system over time. They developed the system sequentially in modules. As each module was completed, it was refined and deployed to users. Then the next module was developed, refined, and added to the system; then the next; and so on. The system evolved as more and more subsystems could be feasibly developed within the budget and on time. And, as the team and managers learned more about business problems by working with users and managers throughout the development process, they were able to refine the way the older subsystems worked and use their newfound knowledge in developing the new modules. The IMERYS Case Application 6.1 was developed in a similar manner. As more was learned about the structure of the real system from DSS users and experts, the new knowledge was incorporated into the newer modules and the older ones were either updated or scheduled to be updated.

The large-scale HR InfoNet system was developed quickly by using a common in-house technology platform. HR InfoNet was created by a team consisting of IS specialists and HR specialists. This was an institutional DSS designed to be used on a recurring basis by many employees, some of whom were not computer literate. Finally, the system continues to evolve because its success led managers and the team to see new ways to apply the ideas developed to other decision-making situations.

Development of a DSS, especially a large one, is a complicated process. It involves issues ranging from technical (e.g., hardware selection and networking) to behavioral (e.g., user interfaces and the potential impact of DSS on individuals, groups, and the entire organization). This chapter concentrates mainly on DSS software development issues.

Because there are several types and categories of DSS, there is no single best approach to DSS development. There are many variations because of the differences in organizations, decision-makers, and the DSS problem area. Some DSS are designed to support a one-time decision, like the Scott Housing decision (Web Chapter), whereas the IMERYS DSS in Case Application 6.1 was developed for recurrent use. Some systems can be developed in a few days in an OLAP package, spreadsheet, or another tool, while others, like the Osram Sylvania HR InfoNet, took several months and will continue to evolve over the next several years. We now explore issues involving DSS development time, managerial aspects, change management, and more.

DSS IN ACTION 6.2

USER INTERFACE PROTOTYPING
LEADS TO DSS SUCCESS

Some years ago, I worked for an international consulting firm in Pittsburgh, Pennsylvania. I visited a large midwestern (U.S.) tractor manufacturer to determine its needs for an assembly line balancing method and to propose a decision support system. If the company accepted the proposal, I would implement it. Though there are many methods for solving assembly line balancing problems, this situation was different. Even though I was familiar with published work on line balancing, I discovered that the company's industrial engineers had developed a unique, remarkable, effective approach that utilized information from their manufacturing methods database. I did not push existing methods on them. Instead, I developed specifications for a unique system and included, as a major portion of the proposal, a *prototype of the user interface*—a set of menus, displays, and reports—so that the industrial engineering chief could see how the system would look and work (many users view the user interface as the entire system).

With the interface prototype, the client saw what he was going to get. The prototype enhanced user and managerial involvement, and guided their expectations. It was a focal point that led users and managers to feel that the proposed system would be exactly what they had needed for several years. The proposal was accepted, and the project was initiated and successfully completed on time and under budget. The user-interface prototype also was very useful to me as a system development guide.

_____

Source: Jay E. Aronson.

6.3 THE TRADITIONAL SYSTEM DEVELOPMENT LIFE CYCLE

Development is a very deliberate and orderly approach to making a system a reality. A methodology is needed to provide structure to system development. There are many "traditional" system development life cycles (SDLCs) for information systems, including DSS. Every computer-aided software engineering (CASE) tool has adopted a variation. Further complicating matters, each organization that develops a system can create in-house variations to suit its specific needs. Each methodology emphasizes different steps in different ways. But all SDLCs that make intuitive and practical sense must follow certain guidelines and processes.

Ideally, a need of some kind starts the process, and a completed system is its result. A traditional SDLC consists of four fundamental phases—planning, analysis, design, and implementation (PADI)—which lead to a deployed system (Figure 6.1). The system is a cycle because it is possible to return to any phase from any other, though an ideal progression is to follow each phase in order. All projects must go through these phases. Each phase consists of a series of steps, which rely on techniques that produce deliverables. We have adopted the SDLC described by Dennis and Wixom (2003). In Table 6.1, we show the fundamental phases, the steps, and the deliverables for each step. The SDLC presentation seems to be linear, but at any time the project can be halted or can return to an earlier step in any phase. This applies to Web system development as well, though there are some specific issues which we discuss later. We now discuss the phases and steps (see Table 6.1). In Table 6.2, we show the system development phases and Web impacts.

Ideally, the project "flows" down and to the right. The upward arrows indicate that changes while developing a system can return the process to an earlier stage.

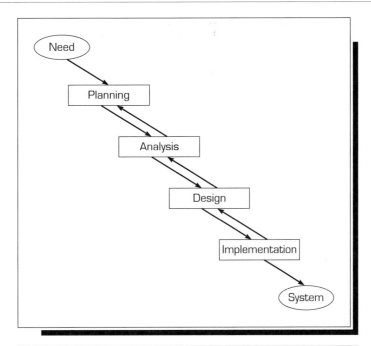

FIGURE 6.1   THE TRADITIONAL SYSTEM DEVELOPMENT LIFE CYCLE (SDLC)

Ideally, the project "flows" down and to the right. The upward arrows indicate that changes while developing a system can return the process to an earlier stage. This is also known as *waterfall development.*

1. *Planning.* The *planning* phase starts with a business need not being met. This includes possible opportunities identified through environmental scanning. Is there a problem that needs to be solved? Project initiation involves a system request that is decided on. If it appears worthwhile, a **feasibility study** (analysis) is conducted. The feasibility study considers whether the idea is viable. Questions concerning technical feasibility, cost feasibility, and organizational feasibility are answered here. If the project is approved, a project manager is assigned, and he or she creates a work plan, staffs the project, and adopts methods for managing it.

2. *Analysis.* The *analysis phase* is like a journalist's interview. It asks and answers such important questions as who the users will be, what the system will accomplish, and where and when it will run. This phase starts with the development of an analysis strategy or a plan to guide the project. If there is an existing system, it is analyzed, along with ways of moving to the new system. This leads to further information gathering, leading up to the development of a process model and a data model.

3. *Design.* The *design phase* indicates how the system will work, considering all the details of the hardware, software, network infrastructure, user interface, and so on. In this phase, the user interface, forms, displays, reports and programs, databases, and files are specified. In the design strategy, the amount of the system to be purchased or contracted (vs. built in-house) is decided on. This leads to the architecture design, which leads to the database and file design, which in turn leads to the program design. Collectively, these are the system specifications.

4. *Implementation.* The *implementation* phase brings it all together. This is where the system is built or purchased. Construction involves not only building the system

TABLE 6.1	The Traditional System Development Life Cycle	
Major Phase	*Minor Step*	*Deliverable*
Planning: Why build the system?	1. Identify business value	System request
	2. Analyze feasibility	Feasibility study
	3. Develop work plan	Work plan
	4. Staff project	Staffing plan
		Project charter
	5. Control and direct project	Project management tools
		CASE tool
		Standards list
		Project "binders" or files
		Risk assessment
Analysis: Who, what, when, and where will the system be?	6. Analyze problem	Analysis plan
	7. Gather information	Information
	8. Model process(es)	Process model
	9. Model data	Data model
Design: How will the system work?	10. Design physical system	Design plan
	11. Design architecture	Architecture design
		Infrastructure design
	12. Design interface	Interface design
	13. Design database and files	Data storage design
	14. Design program(s)	Program design
Implementation: System delivery	15. Construction	Test plan
		Programs
		Documentation
	16. Installation	Conversion plan
		Training plan

Source: Based on Dennis and Wixom (2000).

but also testing it to verify that it works. Better planning can lead to systems with fewer bugs. Installation is the last step and involves actually getting the system up and running.

In Figure 6.1, we illustrate the four steps in the structure of an SDLC, which are sometimes referred to as the *waterfall model* (Swanson et al., 1999). Water and everything in it have a tendency to move downward, but if there is a need to return to an earlier step, it is possible to hop up the waterfall against the effects of gravity.

The process of system analysis, design, and implementation creates *organizational change*, which must be managed (Section 6.6). DSS development and implementation involve implementing change—change in an organization or in an individual's work. Throughout the development process, there are a number of factors that must go right (previewed in DSS in Focus 6.3) or the system will fail (there may be other, often overlooked factors as well). User expectations must be managed, users and managers must be involved, executive and IT sponsors must be established, and communication with them all must be open. We list a number of common implementation headaches in DSS in Focus 6.4. A critical issue in project management is to determine whether or not a project is truly failing, and when to kill it. Worthen (2001) describes how to identify when your project is in trouble. We indicate this in DSS in Focus 6.5.

TABLE 6.2   System Development Phases and Web Impacts

System Development Phase	Web Impacts	Impacts on the Web
Planning	Access to high-quality, Web-based, graphics-oriented tools Access to information Collaboration with the software development team via Web-based collaboration tools Consistent user-friendly interface for tools	Required for all Web-based implementations/sites
Analysis	All of the above Access to models and data	Required for all Web-based implementations/sites
Design	All of the above Project management software Repository management software Collaborative computing (GSS) software	Required for all Web-based implementations/pages/sites Improved site management Improved tools for monitoring and improving Web performance
Implementation	All of the above Higher quality systems Web-based software systems and languages improve continually. They readily lead to e-commerce applications	E-commerce applications Higher-quality systems

---

DSS IN FOCUS 6.3

SUCCESSFUL SYSTEMS DEVELOPMENT: WHAT WORKS!

Over the last half-century of system implementation, several, consistent themes leading to success have emerged. Here are the top ten items that have a positive impact on productivity in software development, based on a recent survey:

- Reuse of high-quality deliverables
- High management experience
- High staff experience
- Effective methods/process
- Effective management tools and skills
- Effective CASE tools
- High-level programming languages
- Quality estimating tools
- Specialist occupations
- Effective client participation (communication)
- Strong communication skills among team members

In organizations with productivity rates in the top 5 percent of clients polled, there is a very strong tendency for most of these factors to be better than average: project management tools and methods, quality control tools and methods, maintenance tools and methods, and development tools and methods. Companies at the bottom had these typically ranked as poor. *Note that the most important factors tend not to be technical.* Available and effective technology is a given. Solid managerial, organizational, and communication skills are necessary for project success.

Source: Adapted and expanded from C. Jones (2000a, 2000b).

DSS IN FOCUS 6.4

SYSTEM IMPLEMENTATION HEADACHES AND HOW TO SPOT THEM

Sources of implementation headaches include management expectations, customization and process issues, resource shortages, and technology integrations. The following is a list of some warning signs of a troubled implementation and what can go right:

1. No project team or management support (or, no players, no game). But a strong project team of empowered managers and technical staff helps ensure realistic objectives, a sound project plan, the right resources, and the necessary buy-in.

2. *Hazy purpose, no defined schedule, a ballooning scope.* The project needs a clear understanding at the start. A phased development approach (prototyping) on a schedule can keep a project going, provide feedback, and because of the lessons learned while developing the system, keep the scope of the project within reasonable bounds.

3. *Unclear aspects of make-vs.-buy decisions.* The team must determine how much of the project should be developed, how much should be purchased, and how much of the purchased part should be modified. The scope of the project impacts on these factors, as well as the development team's capabilities and available time.

4. *Few product integrations are functional right out of the box.* Set realistic expectations for standardized software, and plan to modify it.

5. *Qualitative benefits, some benefits (and costs) are fuzzy.* Not all benefits can be measured in dollars. Some involve "feeling good" about a decision. Gather data about them and use them to justify your work.

6. *No user buy-in.* Users must be part of the development process from the start. Include them and get them excited.

7. *Poor project management skills.* The project manager must have good project-management skills to complete the project successfully.

8. *No accountability and no responsibility.* The development team is neither accountable nor responsible for what it does or doesn't do. Use good management skills to enforce accountability and responsibility.

Source: Partly adapted from A. R. Starck, "How to Implement Like a Pro," *Support Management,* May/June 1998; D. Slater, "Business Line Backers," *CIO Enterprise,* March 15, 1998.

CASE TOOLS

For complex projects, the SDLC should be managed with computer-aided software engineering (CASE) tools. These tools are essentially information systems for systems analysts and can help manage every aspect of developing a system.

CASE tools that assist in the analysis phase in creating system diagrams are called *upper* CASE, CASE tools that manage the diagrams and generate code for the database tables are called *lower* CASE, and *integrated* CASE (I-CASE) tools do both. Some CASE tools are designed to handle strictly object-oriented systems by supporting the constructs of the universal modeling language (UML) (see Dennis, Wixom, and Tegarden (2002); Krutchteen, 1998; Jacobson and Griss, 2001; Satzinger and Orvik, 2002). CASE tools are critical for the new agile system development methods and reusable code objects, both discussed later. For details on how well object-oriented analysis and its performance levels are accepted by systems analysts, as compared to traditional methods, see Fedorowicz and Villeneuve (1999) and Morris et al. (1999).

Though CASE tools may seem to impose many restrictions on the creative aspect of system development, they handle a lot of the system checking as the system is being built. For example, an analyst may try to use a specific data field, but if it is not defined in advance in the CASE tool framework, the tool will not allow its use. These data and others are stored in the CASE *repository*, which helps to ensure *logical consistency*

DSS IN FOCUS 6.5

RECOGNIZE WHEN YOUR PROJECT IS FAILING

Your (DSS/BI or enterprise) project is in trouble when you experience one or more of the following:

1. Your gut is rumbling. You feel nervous.

2. Your project manager starts smoking cigarettes. Changes in employees' behavior indicate problems. If they stop talking, there is a problem. If they aren't excited, there is a problem.

3. The rumor mill is churning overtime.

4. Every day you learn something new about the software.

If some or all of the warning signs are there, it is time for action. Here's what you can do:

• Take responsibility for everything that has gone wrong (tough to do, but important—problem ownership).

• Do an analysis of the project to date. Even find an outsider to audit the project so far.

• Kill the project on a Wednesday, so that your employees have the rest of the week to wrap up loose ends and salvage what they can, and then can come back to work next week for a fresh start.

• Don't take too long winding down.

• Don't sue the vendor. It takes too long. Spill your guts to them. They hate bad publicity.

• Finally, update your resume (backup plan).

Source: Adapted from Worthen (2001).

---

within the new system and maintain the system's *documentation*. Some versions of CASE tools can even be considered groupware because of the way system developers can collaborate while developing the system.

CASE, AND OTHER ANALYSIS AND DESIGN TOOLS

Some well-known CASE tools are Oracle/9i Developer Suite, Rational Rose and Rational Suite Analyst Studio (IBM Corp.), Paradigm Plus (Platinum Technology), Visible Enterprise Workbench (includes Visible Analyst and Visible Developer 3.0) (Visible System Corporation), Logic Works Suite, the AxiomSys Systems Analysis CASE Tool, and AxiomDsn (Structured Technology Group Inc.), V32, C32, X32 and O32 (object-oriented environment including UML) (Blue River Software), and Visual Studio and Visual Studio .NET (for rapidly building XML Web services, Windows-based applications, and Web solutions) (Microsoft Corp.). Figure 6.2 is a screenshot of a diagram from Visible Analyst.

New analysis and design software provides analysis, reporting, and collaboration tools. Sybase PowerDesigner, a RAD design tool, supports physical relational data models and provides UML modeling capabilities. It includes an enterprise-class repository and collaboration tools for application developers, database designers, and data analysts. Multiple users can simultaneously store and share design information at the same time, collaborating on multiple application design projects. Oracle Internet Development Suite includes a Java tool, reporting tools, application development tools, business intelligence tools, and enterprise portal building tools in an integrated framework. Rational RequisitePro helps identify requirements. Rational ClearQuest provides reliable and efficient project metrics. It includes reports, charts, and a Web interface.

The Internet has affected analysis and design tools. In the past, a development project might take three to six months. This is too long for e-commerce applications. Analysis and design are extremely important and complicated in Web-based develop-

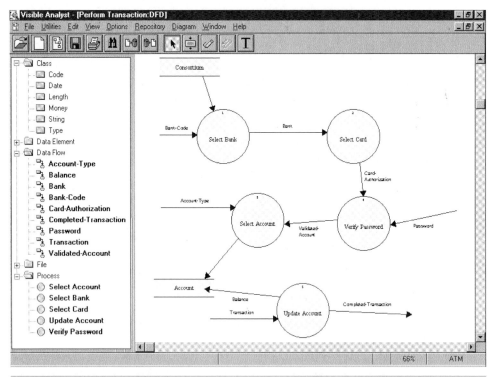

FIGURE 6.2 SCREENSHOT FROM VISIBLE ANALYST

Courtesy Visible System Corporation.

ment, due to the diversity and distributed nature of the players, and because customers interact directly with your business online. The following factors must be carefully considered in systems analysis and design (see Gates, 2001):

1. *Communication.* This is a given.
2. *Requirements.* Requirements become more critical in a Web-based application because of the need to communicate their functions and requirements, and the impact of changing requirements.
3. *Integration.* Different components must function seamlessly.
4. *Business modeling.* Form must follow function.

Integration is a major complication of systems implementation. This is especially critical for e-commerce applications. Microsoft XDocs can smooth out the process of integrating data from multiple servers. It also allows individual users to integrate their data with new or existing servers. Office XML can then integrate directly. See Scannell and Moore (2002) for details.

CODE DEBUGGING AND TESTING

Debugging and testing constitute an often overlooked aspect of systems implementation. Humphrey (2002) indicates that even experienced software engineers inject one defect in about every 10 lines of code. It is easier and cheaper to detect errors early. Xerox Corp. estimated how long it takes to find and fix a bug at each stage: code reviews by the programmer (3 minutes); code inspections by other programmers (25 minutes); small module testing (32 minutes); and complete system testing

DSS IN ACTION 6.6

ZAP BUGS EARLY

The Sustainable Computing Consortium, a collaboration of major corporate IT users, university researchers, and government agencies, estimates that buggy or flawed software cost businesses some $175 billion worldwide in 2001. In the United States, software bugs cost companies nearly $60 billion per year, according to the Commerce Department's National Institute of Standards and Technology (NIST). One-third of these costs could be eliminated with improved testing that catches errors earlier in the software development process, NIST says. Gartner Inc. analyst Theresa Lanowitz indicates that a software defect left unfixed until late in the development cycle costs 80 to 1,000 times more to fix than if it was dealt with earlier. Experts indicate that if 1 percent of software bugs can be found and corrected, then 90 percent of system problems disappear. One way to avoid many system bugs is to educate and communicate with users. They must understand that specifications do not change once testing begins (see Agans, 2002). And of course, a debugging strategy must include the programmers.

Source: Adapted from Horowitz (2003).

(1,400 minutes). It is better to adopt methods that help identify problems early in the development process. Agile methods tend to do this. See DSS in Action 6.6 for an indication of the cost of sloppy coding.

Testing and quality-assurance tools and services are being modified to meet more generalized quality requirements, as well as to deliver much more potent and versatile results than testing alone. Automated testing is being transformed into automated code inspection. The idea is to enable a deeper understanding of an application's properties at the code level, and reveal the impact of any changes made to the code itself. This is very important for interactive Web site deployment, where such code can make or break an organization. See Connors (1999).

In the Internet-driven age, tools and applications must integrate and work well together. Testing is an often-overlooked part of software development. Testing must be well thought out and done correctly. Testing software for server applications has been developed. Products that test load, performance, stress, and reliability of servers include (see Gates, 2000):

- RadView's WebLoad
- LoadRunner from Mercury Interactive Corp.
- SilkPerformer from Segue Software
- QARun, QADirector, QALoad, TrackRecord, FileAID from Compuware
- RequisitePro (robot test recording tool) from Rational Software Corp.

Rational Suite TestStudio is designed for functional, performance, and reliability testing.

Finally, sophisticated methods are being developed to assist with debugging. For example, Gerard Holzman of Bell Labs is using Omega Automata theory, a branch of mathematical logic, to automatically generate models needed for error checking of codes. Holzman expects that by 2008, methods like his will be standard in software development tools (see Leon, 2001).

PROJECT MANAGEMENT

Many DSS development projects are large-scale systems. Such systems are developed by teams, and the team leader must have good project management skills. Standish Group International Inc. (www.standishgroup.com; see Johnson, 1999) indicates some surprising facts about IS/IT projects. Though IT project success rates are up, and cost and time overruns are down, in 1998 only 26 percent of all projects surveyed (out of 23,000 application projects at large, medium, and small U.S. companies) succeeded outright (28 percent failed outright, while 46 percent were challenged, i.e., did not do well because of major cost or time overruns or major changes in scope). From another source, the *Wall Street Journal* estimates that 50 percent of all corporate technology projects don't meet expectations, and that 42 percent of software projects are abandoned before even getting off the ground (Abbott, 2000).

Large companies have lower success rates (24 percent) than medium (28 percent) and small (32 percent) companies. But the success rates in 1994 were much worse (only 9 percent for large, 16 percent for medium, and 28 percent for small). The dollars wasted on IT projects declined from $150 billion in 1994 to a mere $97 billion in 1998. (Projects costing less than $750,000 succeed 55 percent of the time. In the range $1–2 million, 18 percent succeed; for $5–10 million, 7 percent do; Abbott, 2000.) Thus larger projects fail more frequently than smaller ones. This is especially true with ERP and data warehousing systems, which are designed to streamline organizations' overall information systems, including DSS. Improvements in successes have been more dramatic since 1994 in large firms, probably due in part to better project management and better standards (see Johnson, 1999). Basically, IT projects are doing better but could improve.

The smaller the team and the shorter the duration of the project, the greater is the likelihood of success. Certain industries have higher success rates. For example, success rates vary for the retail industry (59%), financial sector (32%), manufacturing (27%), and government (18%). Retail also had the fewest challenged projects and failed projects (see Johnson, 1999).

Johnson (1999) further reports that corporations in America spend more than $275 billion every year on approximately 200,000 application software development projects, most of which will fail for lack of skilled project management. The cornerstone tenets of project management are planning, execution, and control of all resources, tasks, and activities necessary to complete a project. It is a team activity, and deals with people. The four P's of project management are "People Performing Perfect Process." Typically, organizational factors lead to project failures.

Downs (2001) indicates that big projects always take a long time to become profitable. It took the Suez Canal nearly a century to break even. This is similar to where we are with the digital infrastructure that supports e-commerce. The Suez Canal is representative of all great infrastructure projects. They attempt to do what has never been done before, so their design and construction have many unknowns. Setbacks, accidents, and exasperating changes in strategy occur frequently (see Downes, 2001).

As in the construction industry (see the *failures* in the next subsection), a major issue is that the software industry rationalizes its failures. It continues to make the same planning, programming, and managerial mistakes (Abbott, 2000). Project management is a critical area that needs major improvement (in DSS in Focus 6.7, we describe a project management primer). Johnson (1999) reports that chief information officers (CIOs) desire the following skills in a project manager: technology and business knowledge, judgment, negotiation, communication, and organization (also see DSS in Focus 6.8, with reasons for project success in DSS in Focus 6.9). They emphasize the business side rather than the technical side, and softer skills like diplomacy and time management seem to be valued most. Many firms are making project-management skills a core competency. They view them as the future of IT. For example, FMI Corporation was able to reduce its IS staff by 20 percent with a rise in productivity of 30 percent because of a new project management focus (and an SAP implementation)

DSS IN FOCUS 6.7

A PROJECT MANAGEMENT PRIMER

Trepper (2000a) provides a project management primer. Few companies seem to be proficient at project management—and most fail to follow any kind of best-practice approach. As the primer points out, most organizations fail to spend enough time on:

1. Defining requirements.
2. Managing change.
3. Obtaining executive-level buy-in.
4. Setting project timelines based on realistic goals and priorities.
5. Solving project management problems with a technology silver bullet or training (software may help use it).

In addition, there are five things that many firms do not do at all, which ultimately leads to failure (Trepper, 2000a):

- Establish or define baselines.
- Have defined project control functions.
- Offer formal training.
- Take the time to define repeatable processes.
- Correctly estimate how difficult or complex a program is.

Source: Adapted from Charles H. Trepper, "A Project Management Primer." *Application Development Trends*, August 2000, pp. 51–56.

---

that helped the IT people develop a broader skills set and understood how the software was related to the business (Fryer, 1997). For more on project management, see Lientz and Rea (2000).

Yourdon (2000) indicates that developers often do not fully understand the status of their project deliverables, even as they near project completion. One possible reason the status and deliverables are unknown is that the developers' processes are hidden from the project manager and end users. Developers sometimes feel that they are working in the dark. Again, communication among developers, project manager, end users, and managers is critical for implementation success. The entire software process should be completely visible to the users.

A good team is extremely important for the success of business intelligence (BI) projects. Good DSS/BI projects, by their nature, are designed to meet strategic business goals and therefore require much more involvement and input from people on the business side of the organization. Finding the right people for your development team is critical for business intelligence project success. Technical skills are important, but

---

DSS IN FOCUS 6.8

PROJECT MANAGEMENT SKILLS

Developing the following managerial skills and qualities will definitely help a project manager (technological competency is assumed):

- Leadership
- Communication
- Conflict resolution
- Negotiation
- Team building
- Listening skills
- Relationship management

Source: Adapted from Jill Vitiello, "Fast Track into Management." *ComputerWorld*, July 16, 2001, pp. 42–43.

DSS IN FOCUS 6.9

PROJECT SUCCESS FACTORS

The top 10 reasons for project success are:

1. Executive support
2. End-user involvement
3. Experienced project manager
4. Clear business objectives
5. Minimized scope
6. Standard infrastructure

7. Firm basic requirements (know where you are going)
8. Formal methodology
9. Reliable estimates
10. Skilled staff

Source: Adapted from Julia King, "Back to Basics." *ComputerWorld*, April 22, 2002, pp. 36–37.

---

soft skills are necessary to handle the business and technical aspects of the project, else it will fail (see Bunker, 2002).

These teams must collaborate and communicate. Sometimes the members are in different locations. Consequently, new project management software includes collaboration capabilities. Such software not only provides a repository for all work performed, but also provides online collaboration capabilities. Communication is crucial to project success (Kemp, 2000). The project manager must *enable* the team's communication.

EXPERTISE

Software development teams are typically formed de novo for each new project, depending on project requirements and who is available (Faraj and Sproull, 2000). The most critical resource for knowledge teams is expertise, but by itself this is not sufficient to produce high-quality work. Expertise must be managed and coordinated. Faraj and Sproull (2000) investigated the importance of expertise coordination in practice in software development teams. They found that expertise coordination shows a strong relationship with team performance that remains significant over and above team input characteristics, presence of expertise, and administrative coordination. Expertise can lead to success, but the team still needs good communication and project-management skills along with a committed sponsor.

E-COMMERCE AND WEB PROJECTS

Developing an e-commerce or Web project has exasperated the need for project management skills and teamwork. Trepper (2000b) describes some key factors that specifically lead to successful e-commerce development. They are essentially identical to those required for any IT project:

- Collaboration among IT, users, business partners, and customers
- Concern for customer usability
- Building systems to tightly fit the company's business model
- Standard, reusable components
- Performance monitoring

See DSS in Action 6.10 for what can happen when an e-commerce implementation is not planned, but is rushed into implementation. Project management skills are crucial

DSS IN ACTION 6.10

SIGMA-ALDRICH LEARNS: IT IS BETTER TO PLAN AN E-COMMERCE APPLICATION THAN TO SEE WHAT HAPPENS

Sigma-Aldrich, a supplier of chemicals to research laboratories, set up an experimental e-commerce site, Pipeline, in late 1998, not expecting much. The Web site was not connected to core inventory and order-processing systems in SAP. Orders were keyed into the company's order-processing application manually, from information in flat files produced by Pipeline. A typical Web order took 50 percent longer to process than a standard telephone order (12 minutes vs. 8). Customer service agents could handle some 45 Web orders, as opposed to 60 telephone orders daily. They did not think this would be a problem, because they did not expect many Web orders.

When online sales took off, the problems began. Within six months of operations, the Web site brought in an unexpected volume of sales: $1 million. Since a typical order is between $200 and $300, this meant a lot of orders to process. Within two months of operations,

Sigma executives realized that they needed to upgrade Pipeline to eliminate the extra handling of orders.

After a detailed search, they chose Haht Commerce (Raleigh, North Carolina) for the upgrade. They eliminated the original Domino Web Server in favor of the Haht Web server software. The integration project cost $1.9 million and took six months. Over the following three years, the effort resulted in benefits worth $4.7 million. The system not only processed orders faster, but it also involved less work than telephone orders and, most important, a dramatic increase in business. By the end of 1999, the entire Pipeline effort cost a total of about $25 million ($5 million per year over five years). Functional silos were broken down as several different groups began to cooperate.

Source: Adapted from Kim S. Nash. (2002, July). "Chemical Reaction." *Baseline*, pp. 58–60

---

to the success of any DSS/BI project (see Trepper, 2000b). For more on project success factors, project management, and skills, see Fraser (2002), Frye and Mason (2001), and King (2002).

PROJECT IMPLEMENTATION FAILURE

Since DSS/BI/IS development projects fail or are challenged more often than they succeed, we felt it prudent to examine the causes of failures and some examples. Managers of most organizations are reluctant to discuss system failures. However, one can learn much by examining failures in addition to successes. A number of IS academic and trade journals regularly report failures, recognizing their importance. The only benefit to having bad project experiences is that they can help shape better project managers (Melymuka, 2000). Sometimes it is time to pull the plug on a troubled project. Kapur (2001) describes a flowchart that indicates when to kill a troubled project. Essentially, there are milestones in the development process that are go/no-go points in time. At these times, the project's viability and ability to deliver should be carefully evaluated.

Earlier, we discussed the factors that lead to project success. When some or even one of them are not present, project failure may result (see Fonseca, 2003). For example, a dedicated champion in upper management is considered necessary, but not sufficient to lead to success. But when the champion leaves the organization, the resource base of the project may be jeopardized, leading to failure.

The Standish organization reports (see Melymuka, 2002b) that projects typically fail because of:

- Lack of stakeholder involvement
- Incomplete requirements

- Lack of sponsor support
- Unrealistic expectations.
- Lack of commitment from your business customers

In October 2000, *ComputerWorld* put together a list of botched IT projects. Their *Top 10* disaster list consisted of large and very complex projects. Many were the toughest IT projects the organizations had ever attempted. Five were hideously difficult enterprise resources planning (ERP) implementations (see Nash, 2000). As others have suggested, the root causes of IT failure in this list have not changed a bit over the years. They include: miscommunication, hazy goals, scope creep, inept leadership, and pitiful project management. See Nash (2000) for details.

Briggs and Arnott (2002) identified the factors that led to the failure of a DSS at a medium-size, national manufacturing company in Sydney, Australia. They called these factors *evolutionary disruptors*. During development, the external consultants lost the support of top management. Briggs and Arnott (2002) identified the following development environment disruptors: many organizational culture factors, top management support, user attitude, analyst attitude, user experience, and development team capabilities. Their development process disruptors included: user education, support, involvement, evaluation, training, and more. Knowledge of these disruptors may give DSS developers an early alert to the likelihood of project failure. We describe important software project risks in DSS in Focus 6.11.

Only one-third of enterprise software projects can be classified as successful, according to a survey of business users done by the Boston Consulting Group's Information Technology practice (see Booker, 2000). Only 33 percent of the enterprise application initiatives studied (100 users responsible for an enterprise initiative over the past three years) could be considered positive or successful when analyzed in terms of value creation, cost effectiveness, tangible financial impact, and goal attainment. When more up-front time and effort are spent in systems analysis, the likelihood of success increases (56 percent vs. 8 percent). Clearly, analysis is critical for success.

DSS IN FOCUS 6.11

SOFTWARE PROJECT RISKS

Software project risk is the product of the uncertainty associated with project risk factors and the magnitude of potential loss due to project failure. In a multinational study, 25 percent of all software development projects were cancelled, and 80 percent ran over budget, with the average exceeding budget by 50 percent. Of those systems deployed into production, more than 75 percent were considered operational failures because they are either not used or do not meet user specifications. A total of 53 risk factors were identified. The top 10 risks identified were:

- Lack of top management commitment to the project
- Failure to gain user commitment
- Misunderstanding the requirements

- Lack of adequate user involvement
- Lack of required knowledge/skills in the project personnel
- Lack of frozen requirements (final systems were a moving target)
- Changing scope/objectives
- Introduction to new technology
- Failure to manage end user expectations
- Insufficient/inappropriate staffing

Source: Adapted from Schmidt, R., K. Lyytinen, M. Keil, and P. Cule, "Identifying Software Project Risks: An International Delphi Study," *Journal of Management Information Systems*, Vol. 17, Spring 2001.

Large-scale projects have always proved troublesome. The same problems that plague DSS and IS/IT development impact all kinds of projects. Earlier in this chapter, we mentioned the Suez Canal project as troublesome. Consider the failure of *The Big Dig* described in DSS in Action 6.12. As with many failures, communication and other managerial issues were the critical problems. On the IT/DSS/BI side, Wheatley (2000) describes how the British government has created major crises through inept, large-scale IT systems development and deployment. Most of the problems are related to project management factors and unrealistic expectations (see DSS in Action 6.13).

As is true for many enterprise IS projects, data warehouse projects often fail to meet expectations. They tend to be high-risk projects. The Cutter Consortium surveyed about 150 companies that had developed data warehouses (see Whitting, 2003). The study indicated that technology is indeed part of the problem, but management and organizational factors also contribute to failure. In the study, 20 percent indicated that their data warehouses contributed no value, while 15 percent call them a complete success. Some 39 percent indicated that their systems were moderate successes, while 26 percent indicate that the data warehouse contributes limited value. Even though project success rates are improving over time because of better data warehousing development tools and methods, there is much work to be done to overcome these appalling success rates.

We call the reader's attention to a data warehouse implementation failure in DSS in Focus 6.14. The most important factors leading to failure were no user involvement, no clear objectives stated early, and no real executive sponsorship. These were a few of the key indicators that the project was in trouble from the start. See DSS in Focus 6.14 for more details.

Carr (2002) describes the Hershey's Chocolate failure that resulted from implementing a large-scale enterprise resource management system just before the busy 1999 holiday season. The ERP almost bankrupted the company (see DSS in Action 6.15). Fortunately, on the second try, Hershey seemed to get it right.

Jiang et al. (1998, 1999) describe ways to help identify some causes of failure at the inception of a project. Their approach is based on the "orientations" of the systems analysts and their perceptions of failure. This may indeed be at the heart of communications problems among the development team and between team members and users.

DSS IN ACTION 6.12

DIGGING FOR ANSWERS IN PROJECT MANAGEMENT

An excellent example of a project failure is *The Big Dig* (officially known as the Central Artery/Tunnel Project), a public works project in Boston. Essentially, the main automobile commuter route through Boston is moving underground. This project is more difficult to execute than the Panama Canal and Hoover Dam. The initial cost estimate of the project was $2.2 billion (to ensure federal funding). As of 2002, the project may cost $14.1 billion or more, most to come directly from taxpayers' wallets. The Big Dig illustrates the problems that DSS projects frequently face. The initial problems were based on unrealistic cost estimates and inadequate managerial oversight in tunnel design. Subcontractors failed to provide complete information on problems

and delays to other subcontractors, which had a domino effect in delaying the whole project. The sheer size of the project indicated that IT systems could have been utilized for effective management, that is, to track costs. But they were not effectively used. Once management straightened out the finances, it improved communication and reporting procedures. The critical lesson from The Big Dig is to maintain communication among all stakeholders. Problems must be reported accurately and truthfully as they occur.

Source: Adapted from M. Levinson, "The Money Pit." *CIO*, December 1, 2000.

DSS IN ACTION 6.13

UK IT PROJECTS ARE NOT OK!

The British government has attempted several initiatives in upgrading its governmental procedures and regulations into the e-government age. Many of these large-scale initiatives have failed. A notable failure was the new Passport Agency software ($180 million) released in the summer of 1999. Passport processing times went from 10 days to 8 weeks overnight. (British law required release of the system whether it was ready or not.) This debacle was yet another in a long string of IT failures. There was a similar problem a few months earlier with the computerization of the Home Office's Immigration and Nationality Directorate. The system was supposed to process more applications, faster and with fewer people. The reality was that it took longer and required more people to process fewer applications. Other problems with the new Social Security system, the national air traffic control computer system (cost overruns over 200 percent), the National Health Service system, and the cancellation of a large-scale post office system.

Problems in government agency IT development seem to be comparable to those in industries that develop large-scale projects. Finally, the House of Commons Select Committee on Public Accounts examined 25 government IT projects that failed. In the January 2000 report, some very typical problems were described. For example, the committee found that there was often

- a failure to set clear objectives
- a lack of senior management support
- taking on projects that were technically overambitious

In addition, there are many public sector challenges, including politics; staffing and skill-level problems (people earn less money in the public sector); and government organizational structures are more conservative and less flexible than those in the private sector.

The project-management lessons learned are:

- Planners need to have clear project objectives and milestones.
- Projects that are part of an overall strategy must clearly fit together, and the personnel implementing the separate projects must understand this clearly.
- Carefully examine the full implications of introducing changes to IT systems, including the impact of any policy changes (like passport laws) that may affect demand for services.
- Contingency plans are essential to cover the risk that the system won't be delivered on time.
- Planners should consider whether programs with sweeping goals might be too ambitious to attempt in one project.
- Arrangements with subcontractors should include terms with incentives to reach project goals and penalties if they don't.
- Delays in implementing projects place them at risk of being overtaken by technological developments.

Source: Adapted from Malcolm Wheatley, "Her Majesty's Flying I.T. Circus." *CIO*, August 1, 2000, pp. 113–124.

With the growing strategic importance of systems in organizations, firms are encouraging even more active participation by business managers on IS projects (see Kirsch, Sambamurthy, Ko, and Purvis, 2002).

PROJECT MANAGEMENT SOFTWARE

Along with the managerially oriented project skills set, there are excellent software tools to assist project managers. These include Microsoft Project, PlanView (PlanView Inc.), and ActiveProject (Framework Technologies Corporation). Many of these tools are Web-enabled to allow collaborative teamwork online over time and distance. Microsoft Project 2000 with Microsoft Project Central software includes a friendly Web-based collaboration tool. PlanView Web Software is designed to handle project and workforce management (PlanView, Inc., Austin, Texas). PlanView is a dynamic, multidimensional tool for resource and program management. It includes the

DSS IN FOCUS 6.14

ANATOMY OF A DATA WAREHOUSE IMPLEMENTATION FAILURE

Here are several important red flags that popped up early in a real-world data warehouse implementation project. They were leading indicators predicting that the project was headed for failure. To their credit, when the pilot project failed, executives cut their losses and canceled the project.

- No prelaunch objectives or metrics
- Many major systems projects underway simultaneously
- The CEO set budgets and deadlines before the project team was on board (they were not involved)
- No insider presence on the data warehouse project team
- Overburdened project manager
- Source data availability unconfirmed at the outset
- No user demand for sophisticated data analysis
- No routine meetings of executive sponsors and project manager
- No initial involvement of business managers
- Failure of the pilot project.

Some lessons learned from the failure include the following:

- Executive sponsorship and partnership with IS are the most critical success factors for developing a data warehouse. If possible, establish dual leadership by business and IS executives for the project or pick a project manager from the business side.
- Don't let the project proceed without a clear understanding of the business objectives and how they will be measured.
- Do an incremental pilot project to determine whether you can obtain the projected benefit.
- Expect to make a major investment in ongoing management of the data warehouse.
- When all else fails, cut and run.

Source: Adapted from L. G. Paul, "Anatomy of a Failure," *CIO Enterprise*, November 15, 1997, pp. 55–60.

HomeView Portal. Most project management tools are Web-based, including onProjects opEnterprise, PlanView, Rational Software's Rational Unified Process (RUP), Business Engine's BEN, and Microsoft Project.

Gates (2003) describes how many vendors of project management tools have added portfolio management tools into project management systems. For example, WorkLenz, from Metier Ltd., aggregates and analyzes project data across the enterprise to identify inefficiencies, predict future work, and improve processes. Microsoft Project includes a centralized repository of projects and resources. OptEnterprise, from onProject, Inc., allows users to view all projects, tasks, resources, issues, files, events, and notices. This helps an organization to see how all projects fit together and how they affect each other and various departments in the organization. See Gates (2003) for details.

Still another aspect new project management tools are addressing is collaboration among disparate development teams. Project managers are using GSS software and systems like Groove and WebEx directly. In addition, project management software systems are incorporating GSS capabilities. For example, Georgia (2001) describes Inovie Software's TeamCenter and Primaverea Systems' TeamPlay, which provide collaboration features and Web functionality. Metier's WorkLenz product includes document attachment sharing, threaded notes discussions, and e-mail alerts features to aid in collaboration. In addition, the product is Web-enabled so it can be accessed from anywhere.

DSS IN ACTION 6.15

THE ELUSIVE SWEET TASTE OF SUCCESS

In late 1996, Hershey's management approved what came to be known as the Enterprise 21 project. The goal was to replace legacy mainframe systems with new enterprise client/server software. Part of Enterprise 21 was a Year 2000 project. More important, the new systems were supposed to allow Hershey to change and streamline its business processes.

Hershey selected SAP to provide the heart of the system, which would be complemented by planning and transportation management software from Manugistics, and new sales software from Siebel Systems. Siebel doesn't seem to have had much to do with what went wrong, but, by adding a third major systems-implementation project concurrently, it certainly aggravated the problems.

The complete systems overhaul of the SAP implementation was rushed to completion. And *it failed*. Basic order-management and fulfillment processes broke down, causing the company not to meet many retailers' orders. The immediate impact was about $150 million in lost sales for the year. The damage to sales and retailer confidence lingered into early 2000. Accenture helped with the mySAP implementation. Here's what went wrong and how it could have been better handled:

The Big Bang. Hershey was attempting too much at once. Hershey's rushed an ERP into action because of the potential Y2K problems. It did not perform thorough testing. Better planning and a slower implementation would have helped.

Unentered Data. Hershey was very good at crisis management. It stored candy everywhere informally. Unfortunately, the formal ERP did not know about these locations, so data on inventory on hand could not be entered, and consequently the ERP was unaware of how to fill orders. Employees were not used to inputting this information into formal computer systems.

No Leadership. Management did not understand how much effort in systems development and organizational change would be required for success. Managerial buy-in and oversight are important.

Fortunately, the second ERP attempt has moved in the right direction. And customer confidence is building.

Source: Adapted from David F. Carr, "Sweet Victory." *Baseline 2.0,* December 2002, pp. 68–73

DSS IN ACTION 6.16

GM NORTH AMERICA'S DIGITAL PROJECT DASHBOARD

A project tracking dashboard helps keep GM North America projects on the road. The system color-codes all of the company's IT projects: green when one is on plan, yellow when at least one key target has been missed, and red when the project is significantly (even if temporarily) behind. Essentially, the dashboard reports information with a traffic light approach like an OLAP (Chapter 5) or an executive information system (Chapter 8).

For each IT project, four criteria are tracked and rated: performance to budget, performance to schedule, delivery of business results, and risk. The information is updated monthly and displayed in Excel and

PowerPoint. Red means that a project needs *help*. The project may need more money, people, or better business buy-in, or a business champion, or help with a vendor. The dashboard provides an early warning system to alert project managers of problems. Intervention is automatic if a project is in the red for three or more months. For critical projects, one red is sufficient. More details are available in a *4-up Report* that provides a detailed synopsis of a project's status by financial, deliverables, milestones, and risk activities.

Source: Adapted from Tracy Mayor, "Red Light, Green Light." *CIO,* October 1, 2000, pp. 108–112

One approach to project portfolio management is to create a digital dashboard to track projects' progress. This is essentially an executive information systems-see Chapter 8. General Motors has developed such an approach. See DSS in Action 6.16 for details.

Project management software and methods are surveyed on a regular basis. For example, see Trepper (2000a, 200b), who provides a list of representative project/process management products.

6.4 ALTERNATIVE DEVELOPMENT METHODOLOGIES

PARALLEL DEVELOPMENT: A TRADITIONAL METHODOLOGY

There are several alternative development methodologies, all of which are based on the traditional SDLC. The one most closely resembling the SDLC is *parallel development*. In parallel development, the design and implementation phases split into multiple copies following the analysis phase. Each of these copies involves development of a separate subsystem or subproject. They all come together in a single implementation phase in which a systems integrator puts the pieces together in a cohesive system. Part of DSS implementation is handled in this manner; the four components, database, model base, user interface, and knowledge, can essentially be developed in parallel.

RAPID APPLICATION DEVELOPMENT METHODOLOGIES

Rapid application development (RAD) methodologies adjust the SDLC so that parts of a system can be developed quickly and users can obtain some functionality as soon as possible. These include methods of *phased development, prototyping*, and *throwaway prototyping*. All of these are useful in developing Web systems via Web programming tools. Because Web sites, especially e-commerce sites, evolve quickly and continually, these methods are critical for their development.

The **phased development** methodology involves breaking a system up into a series of versions that are developed sequentially. Each version has more functionality than the previous one, and they evolve into a final system. The advantage is that users gain functionality quickly; the disadvantage is that the systems with which users start to work are incomplete by design. We now turn to the major methodology under which DSS and Web systems are developed: prototyping.

Prototyping involves performing the analysis, design, and implementation phases concurrently and repeatedly (Figure 6.3). System prototypes are quickly developed and demonstrated to users, whose input is used to refine them. The main advantage is that systems are quickly provided to users even if not yet ready for institutional use. Feedback is obtained, and the system can be modified on moving to the next prototype. Further analysis may be needed as well. One disadvantage is that changes are introduced quickly and there is no attempt to correct design decisions early on. Instead they are repaired as the system evolves (this concept is important in agile system development, which we discuss in the next subsection). This is like the development of the Chevrolet Monza (automobile), which initially required that the engine be dropped out in order to change two of the spark plugs during a tune-up. Customers bought the car, and eventually, in later designs, the problem was fixed by inserting panels so the plugs could be reached. On the other hand, if done carefully with good design practices, prototyping is very effective (see

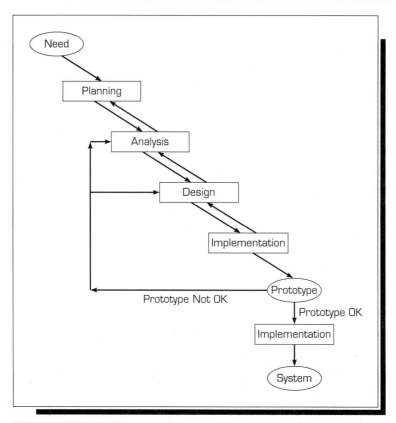

FIGURE 6.3   PROTOTYPING DEVELOPMENT PROCESS: A RAPID APPLICATION
DEVELOPMENT (RAD) METHOD

DSS in Focus 6.17). For example, the IMERYS Case Application 6.1 model was developed by starting with a small plant to gain understanding. More complex plants and more functionality were added to the system over time.

Throwaway prototyping is similar to both prototyping and the traditional SDLC (Figure 6.4). As in the SDLC, the analysis phase is thorough, but design prototypes are developed to assist in understanding more about the system being developed, especially when it is not clearly understood. Often throwaway prototypes are developed as pilot tests on simpler development platforms to learn about user requirements and the final system to be deployed. For example, it is possible to work out calculation methods in Excel so as to map out the functionality of a program before committing to the formal development in a programming language. (If you do not fully understand what you are trying to develop, we encourage this approach.) Once the pilot test is successful, the prototype is discarded and a preliminary design of the real system takes place. After that, the DSS is completed using the SDLC or prototyping approach. The design prototype helps the team work out details used in the system that is developed.

AGILE DEVELOPMENT AND EXTREME PROGRAMMING (XP)

Agile development is a relatively new form of rapid prototyping, a rapid application development (RAD) method. There are a number of these *lightweight* programming methodologies: Extreme Programming (XP), Scrum, and Crystal. Extreme

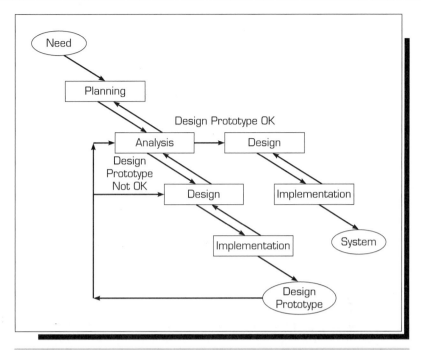

FIGURE 6.4   THROWAWAY PROTOTYPING DEVELOPMENT PROCESS: ANOTHER RAPID APPLICATION DEVELOPMENT METHOD

The design prototype helps the team work out details used in the system that is developed.

Programming are probably the most popular examples of agile processes (Hudson, 2002). These methods attempt to bypass much of the formalism inherent in the system-development life cycle, and even that of prototyping.

Two-thirds of all corporate IT organizations were using some form of *agile* software development process by 2003. Agile methods are ideally suited for projects that have unclear or rapidly changing requirements (see Sliwa, 2002). For example, Daimler

---

DSS IN FOCUS 6.17

PROTOTYPING WORKS BECAUSE . . .

Here are some ways to ensure success using a prototyping approach to DSS development.

- *Gain the unshakable support of the company's top business executive* to obtain the proper visibility and resources committed to the project.

- *Align new systems across several business processes, not just one.* This yields a broader level of support for the project.

- *Slice up a project into pieces.* This allows you to manage the project better by staying on track.

- *Deliver results in phases, not at the end.* Early deliverables allow managers and users to see the benefits without having to wait for the big bang (especially if it doesn't do what is needed; this *prototyping process* encourages user input for correction and refinement).

Source: Based on B. Caldwell, "Taming the Beast," *InformationWeek*, March 10, 1997.

Chrysler AG's ITM Financial Organization uses these new methods to speed development of its new Java applications (Joukhadar, 2001). Motorola Inc. has used elements of Extreme Programming in some of its development organization, but found that it was not useful for global development projects. Such projects require large teams. Some developers feel that using Extreme Programming will drive higher-quality and rapid application development (Copeland, 2001).

Characteristics of the tools include: heavy user input, self-organizing teams that do not rely on management to direct them, and incremental delivery. Agile methodologies typically eliminate the extensive documentation process that can bog down a development project. Projects are broken down into pieces based on requirements. Functional code for each piece is delivered in short time frames (14 to 90 days), and is subject to frequent testing. Despite the benefits, there may be problems with integrating agile-based projects into other ones. Companies should at least consider supplementing old processes with some of the agile approaches (see Sliwa, 2002).

Berinato (2001) describes how to utilize agile development methods to succeed in software development. Essentially, the agile development methods indicate that you should test the code frequently, take ownership of the process, have a business sponsor, and monitor developments to be alert to potential problems that can be fixed as they arise. And you should be willing to kill the project if it looks hopeless. He adds that small budgets force developers to focus on the essential. Small budgets also make it easier to kill failing projects. Requirements should be kept to a minimum. One should build on success, not hope. Keep development teams small, and assign non-IT executives to software projects.

Extreme Programming was created to facilitate the fast, streamlined development of high-quality applications. As enumerated by Joukhadar, (2001), its features include:

- User *stories* or needs that determine software features are usually written on index cards and are the basis of requirements for a project.
- Simple functionality tests are written by users before coding begins.
- Coding is broken down into very small segments of functionality that can be completely coded in two or three days.
- Programmers work in pairs; projects rotate frequently among teams, giving all programmers an understanding of the entire project.
- Code is frequently refactored and revised to improve quality and performance.

According to Copeland (2001), Extreme Programming advocates 12 core development practices that include:

- Application development teams put small code releases into production early.
- Pair programming: two developers work together.
- On-site customer required to aid in project development (solves the problem of user involvement by *requiring* it).
- All programmers are given collective ownership of code and the ability to change it.

Copeland (2001) notes that agile modeling includes certain general concepts:

- Creating simple content
- Testing code often
- Using several design models

The critical weakness of agile processes is the lack of documentation and design. The clear advantage is that they focus a lot of attention on testing. See the Agile Alliance

Web site (agilealliance.com) and the extreme programming Web site (www.extreme-programming.org) for further information about these methods.

DEBUGGING AND TESTING IN AGILE SYSTEMS DEVELOPMENT

As we described earlier, the processes of debugging and testing, though critical, are often overlooked in systems development. The agile system development methods (RAD) build the debugging and testing in so that they become a way of life.

6.5 PROTOTYPING: THE DSS DEVELOPMENT METHODOLOGY

Because of the semistructured or unstructured nature of problems addressed by decision support systems, it is quite unlikely that managers and DSS developers have a complete understanding of the decision-making problem. They may not understand the scope of the problem, the types of appropriate models or technologies to apply, and/or the information needs. So most DSS are developed through the prototyping process. Prototyping is also known as **iterative design** or **evolutionary development**. (Other names are *middle-out process*, *adaptive design*, and *incremental design*.)

The prototyping development methodology aims at building a DSS in a series of short steps with immediate feedback from users to ensure that development is proceeding correctly. Therefore, DSS tools must be flexible to permit changes quickly and easily.

We show the details of the prototyping methodology in Figure 6.3. Prototyping is a process of building a "quick and dirty" version of a system. The evolutionary approach starts with overall DSS planning and some analysis. Users and managers, as well as an executive sponsor, must be involved. Other factors, critical for success or leading to failure are mentioned in the Opening Vignette and several of the DSS in Action and DSS in Focus boxes.

Next, the analysis, design, and prototype implementation phases are iteratively performed until a small prototype is sufficiently developed (decided on jointly by the developers, managers, and users). Then the final implementation of this part of the system takes place. Simultaneously, further iterations occur in the loop of analysis-design-implementation-system prototype as other subsystems or capabilities are added to the deployed system until a fairly stable, comprehensive system evolves. This is how the systems in the Opening Vignette and in Case Application 6.1 were developed.

The first major decision involves which subproblem to build first. The user and the developer jointly identify a subproblem for which the initial DSS prototype is to be implemented. This early joint effort sets up initial working relationships between the participants and opens the lines of communication. The subproblem should be small enough that the nature of the problem, the need for computer-based support, and the nature of this support are clear or quickly established. It should be of high interest value to the decision-maker. In the Opening Vignette, it was the employee benefits subsystem that provided intense visibility for the system because *everyone* used it. For Case Application 6.1, it was the small calcine plant and mocked up versions of several reports (See DSS in Action 6.2). This approach helps to excite managers and users about the potential of the system they want.

A prototype is ideally a small but usable system for the decision-maker. No major system analysis or feasibility study is involved. In fact, the developer and the user go through all the steps of the system-development process quickly, though on a small scale. The system should, of necessity, be simple. As the system evolves, it must be evaluated continuously. At the end of each cycle it is evaluated by both the user and the developer.

The interaction of user, developer, and technology is extremely important in this process. There is a balance of effort and cooperation between user and developer: The user takes the lead in the use and evaluation activities, and the developer is stronger in the design and implementation phases. The user plays an active role, in contrast to the situation in conventional system development, where the user often operates in a reactive or passive role. Note that the specification of needed data or information evolves as the prototype evolves along with user and developer experience.

As was described in Chapter 2, decision-makers must share a common frame in order to make intelligent decisions. McCarthy and McCarthy (2002) advocate that managing a technology development group requires setting such a shared vision of a project and setting the rules for how team members are to work together. Malhotra et al. (2001) describe how a flexible group support system was continuously modified to support an engineering product design team. The GSS development team was eventually required to attend the technical sessions of the product design group so that its members could gain first-hand knowledge of how the system was being used, and how the design group wanted it to be modified—that is, to share the vision with the users. System development teams are often scattered around the globe, sometimes working for other companies. The need for enhanced collaboration and teamwork is paramount. The vision is not only to build better teams by leveraging the best minds and common tools, but also to potentially bring customers into development. Project management engagements are moving to a higher level of interactivity, requiring collaboration management (see Johnson, 2001). GSS can assist software developers. New CASE tools include collaborative software; for example, CollabNet SourceCast (Web-based), VA Software, and Quovix. These Web-based systems track software versions, provide online collaboration, and a repository (see Fry, 2002).

Evaluation is an integral part of the development process and is the control mechanism for the entire iterative design process. The evaluation mechanism is what keeps the cost and effort of developing a DSS consistent with its value. At the end of the evolution, a decision is made on whether to further refine the DSS or to stop.

If the prototype is OK, we move to formal implementation of the DSS, which could include all the user training, and so on. Subsequent cycles expand and improve the original version of the DSS. All the analysis, design, construction, implementation, and evaluation steps are repeated in each successive refinement.

Years ago, under the traditional SDLC, the analyst obtained information requirements and other data from the user and went away for a long period of time to develop a system. Over time, the business environment, the organization, the users' needs, and even the users might change. When the system was delivered, it might not meet anyone's needs, or the champion may have left the organization (for an excellent example of this situation, see Vedder, Van Dyke, and Prybutok, 2002). In prototyping, looping back to early stages implies that the initial analysis was incomplete, as is expected.

The iterative design approach produces a specific DSS application. The process is fairly straightforward for a DSS designed for personal support. The process becomes more complicated, although not invalid, for a DSS that provides group support or organizational support. Specifically, there is a greater need for mechanisms to support communication among users and developers. There is also a need for mechanisms to accommodate personal variations while maintaining a common core system that is standard for all users.

Most DSS and Web sites are developed with the prototyping methodology. One reason is that prototyping allows the developers to get a usable (perhaps partial) system up and running relatively fast. And if one views DSS and Web sites as never complete, but always in a state of evolution, prototyping is an ideal methodology (see DSS in Focus 6.18). Some prototyping of non-DSS is performed with the same software packages with which the DSS is developed, including DSS generators and DSS tools like report generators, GUI generators, and spreadsheets. An application generator is often nothing more than a collection of prototyping tools that enables a full range of system development activities and is very similar to a DSS generator.

Specifically, DSS development is done through prototyping for the following reasons:

- *Users and managers are involved in every phase and iteration.* The iterative nature allows users to be involved in system design, which is important for DSS. This approach stems from a need for user expertise in the design and recognizes that successful implementation is more easily achieved with active involvement. Sometimes this involvement is called the *joint application development (JAD) method*.
- *Learning is explicitly integrated into the design process.* Since the users are involved in system design, both users and system developers learn about the decision-making, the ill-structured, complex problem, and the technologies that can potentially be applied to it.
- *Prototyping essentially bypasses the formal life-cycle substep 7*—information requirement definition (see Table 6.1). Requirements evolve as experience is gained. This strategy assumes that the requirements are only partially known at the beginning of system development, and it attempts to clarify users' needs by actively involving them in a low-cost, fast-feedback development process.
- *A key criterion associated with prototyping is the short interval between iterations.* The feedback must be fast. This criterion results from the required learning process: Accurate and timely feedback is a prerequisite to effective learning.
- *The initial prototype must be low-cost.* It must fall below the minimum threshold of capital outlays requiring formal justification. The development of a prototype may be a risky decision, particularly for a DSS. However, because the benefits of a DSS are often intangible, relating to such issues as improved decision-making or better understanding, a high initial investment may result in a decision not to proceed (see DSS in Focus 6.14).

DSS IN FOCUS 6.18

HOW COMPANIES SPEED IT DEPLOYMENT

Here are some concepts that can move a project from impulse drive to warp drive. Many of them involve aspects of the prototyping development methodology.

1. Target small, tactical applications
2. Make application deployment iterative and open to customization
3. Use commodity hardware
4. Use object technology
5. Devolve big projects already under way
6. Break major projects into manageable deliverable chunks
7. Use packaged applications
8. Employ IT service providers

Source: J. Hibbard, "Time Crunch," *InformationWeek,* July 13, 1998, pp. 42–52.

ADVANTAGES OF PROTOTYPING

Some of the major advantages of prototyping are

- Short development time
- Short user reaction time (feedback from user)
- Improved user understanding of the system, its information needs, and its capabilities
- Low cost.

DISADVANTAGES AND LIMITATIONS OF PROTOTYPING

When such an approach is used, the gains obtained from cautiously stepping through each of the system's life-cycle stages might be lost. These gains include a thorough understanding of the information system's benefits and costs, a detailed description of the business's information needs, an easy-to-maintain information system design, a well-tested information system, and well-prepared users. However, this could be avoided by using a CASE tool to enforce consistency.

DATA WAREHOUSE DEVELOPMENT

Data warehouses are developed with prototyping in practice, as are most enterprise-wide information systems. There are four common data warehousing development methodologies:

- The NCR Data Warehousing Methodology
- The SAS Institute Rapid Data Warehousing Method
- Microsoft Data Warehousing
- The Kimball Method

O'Donnell, Arnott, and Gibson (2002) have analyzed and compared these methods. While each is successful in its own way, some spend more effort on planning (e.g., NCR), while others do not. In most cases, when a project fails, it is due to a lack of experience on the part of the designers and implementers, and that the organization attempted to develop projects that are too large.

6.6 CHANGE MANAGEMENT

The implementation or modification of a DSS, or, for that matter, any information system or technology, introduces change into an organization. The people-intensive job of developing software has had essentially the same problems for over 40 years, because people do not handle change well (Humphrey, 2002). One of the most difficult and rewarding tasks that managers must perform is change management. It is a remarkably subtle process that has plagued leaders for millennia (see Machiavelli's *The Prince*). Change management is crucial for DSS, where the users are trying to solve problems, not just obtain data or information from an information system. There are many ways to manage a change process (see Dupuy, 2002). Employees must become accustomed to new systems as they are implemented (see Trepper, 2000b). Generally, change must be fully supported by top management (see Xu and Kaye, 2002) and involve everyone who is affected in any way by the change (see Chiasson and Lovato, 2001; and again, *The Prince*). Proper training is important, but the involvement of all stakeholders is

DSS IN ACTION 6.19

USER INVOLVEMENT IS CRITICAL
IN SYSTEMS IMPLEMENTATION

Managers at Frito-Lay made a critical blunder when they developed a pilot knowledge management system portal but neglected to involve the sales team in the design of the tool. This directly undermined user acceptance of the system. Later, it was necessary to backtrack, plug in missing features, and *win back the support* of the sales force, who suspected that even a revised tool would be a waste of time. For four months, the project team worked closely with the salespeople. Better

collaboration (involvement) helped to significantly reduce turnover. Early involvement of users is essential for buy-in. If they have input in the design, it becomes *their* tool. It is important for a development team to listen to their needs, in order to develop something to help the company's business processes.

Source: Modified from Melymuka (2001a).

important at all stages of development (see DSS in Action 6.19). The project manager must have good communication skills when dealing with users and managers. Melymuka (2001a) recommends 10 seemingly simple steps to get users involved in systems development (see DSS in Focus 6.20).

Project success certainly may depend upon politics to keep all stakeholders involved. Politics may be necessary to maintain project support (see Levinson, 2002; Kemp, 2000). Trust must be developed and maintained (Gonzales, 2001). Such trust is sometimes difficult to obtain if outside consultants are used. Sometimes outsiders are viewed not simply as change agents, but as people who are attempting to make cuts rather than bring about true change.

Difficult situations may be managed by accurately identifying and prioritizing project iterations. One approach is that of the Dysfunction, Impact, and Feasibility (DIF) Matrix (Gonzales, 2001). It may prove useful in defining interrelated, overlapping requirements, prioritizing iterations, and providing for nonbiased decision-making.

A trend to maintain existing legacy systems by enhancing them with a Web-based front-end has developed. While this is often a good quick fix, it is like installing a jet engine in a car—eventually the car will break down. Legacy systems may not support the current set of business processes. It is important to determine the right time to

DSS IN FOCUS 6.20

HOW TO ENGAGE USERS
IN SOFTWARE DEVELOPMENT

Often users do not know what they want or need. A good project manager communicates well and often with managers and users. He or she will put users' priorities ahead of those of the IT group. Here are 10 steps to getting users engaged in system development:

1. Get management buy-in
2. Understand the users' business
3. Consider the users' priorities
4. Assign good communicators
5. Talk with users all along the business process
6. Don't meet at their offices
7. Turn off cell phones
8. Focus on users' problems, not on IT
9. Listen well; explain things back
10. Use prototypes

Source: Adapted from Melymuka (2001b).

DSS IN ACTION 6.21

PEOPLE FEAR LOSING JOBS
TO TECHNOLOGY (IN THE 1700s)

Jacquard developed what can be described as the world's first successful computational device, the *Jacquard Loom*, in Lyon, France, in the mid-1700s. It was a silk weaving device that used punched cards to control the patterns (you can see demonstrations of these looms at La Maison des Canuts in Lyon). After he introduced the technology, the silk weavers burned his factory down. They felt that their livelihood was threatened. The lesson is that people who are not involved in a change process will resist change. Ultimately, the Jacquard Loom became an industry standard that gave French silk manufacturers a competitive edge over much of the world.

replace the entire legacy system—basically, to face the question of when the system *must* be replaced (see Champy, 2001).

Often a shift in organizational culture is required. When badly managed, new systems are often doomed from the start. User expectations must be managed. They must buy into the new system and any new work methods. Most DSS success factors rely on top management truly supporting the change, proper involvement of all stakeholders affected by change, and open communication about the change (see Guimaraes, Igbaria, and Lu, 1992). Organizational and management factors are the critical ones in change management. Resistance to change should be expected and managed. An excellent example of resistance to change occurred in the mid-1700s in France (see DSS in Action 6.21). Some systems implementers have likened migration to a new system to the grieving and mourning process (see DSS in Action 6.22).

It is important to manage user expectations of new systems. For example, Klein and Jiang (2001) describe how consonance can be used in systems development. Consonance indicates the harmony between what a user expects and what he or she

DSS IN ACTION 6.22

RESISTANCE TO CHANGE: GOOD GRIEF!

When a technology user at a Fortune 100 Company heard about plans for a new customer relationship management system, he refused to believe it. He identified every problem that would derail the system and concluded that it was not meant to be. As the project team began to resolve the issues, he started to get angry, according to a project manager. Later, as the system was clearly going to become a reality, the user attempted to bargain. He wanted to get new people to use the new system, while the existing staff would continue to use the old system. When it was close to the switchover date, he withdrew and became depressed. Eventually, he converted over to the new system. Project managers did not understand his resistance. Later on, they realized that the user was acting as if he were grieving. He handled the death of the old system as he would have handled the death of a loved one. This may explain why people resist change. Users facing the loss of a system often go through the same stages of grief: denial, anger, bargaining, depression, and acceptance. Every time there is a change, whether for worse or better, some level of grieving may occur. This may be the way humans react to change out of their control. The best way to get users past their grief is to focus on the positive aspects of the new system. User involvement in a positive way is important. Additional education and proper training also can help.

Source: Partly based on Kathleen Melymuka, "Mourning an Old System." *ComputerWorld*, May 29, 2000, pp. 50–51.

gets. When there is a match, because expectations are managed, the user is most satisfied with the system.

The Lewin-Schein change theory (Lewin, 1947; Schein, 1956) is a truly elegant and infinitely practical guide to considering the many complex and sometimes baffling issues inherent in the dynamic change process (Levasseur, 2001). The three basic steps are:

- *Unfreezing.* Create an awareness of the need for change and a climate receptive to change.
- *Moving.* Change the magnitude and/or direction of the forces defining the initial need for change by developing new methods and learning new attitudes and behaviors.
- *Refreezing.* Reinforce the desired changes that have occurred and establish a maintainable and stable new equilibrium.

The Lewin-Schein change theory very concisely describes how to introduce change into an organization, while it very flexibly allows for varying changes, magnitudes of change, and environments of change. Levasseur (2001) indicates that it is important to examine the cause of the change. Sometimes a crisis can motivate the change. Other times, a desire to improve motivates the change. DSS are implemented, typically, to provide more information and models to a decision-maker who needs access to these tools. A fundamental principle of effective change management is that people will support what they help to create. Active participation by the stakeholders is the most important element of effective change. Most failures occur because of ineffective communication at the beginning and a failure to involve individuals affected by the change. We describe these issues throughout this chapter.

Implementation success depends on continuing to develop a sense of teamwork and active communication among users and other stakeholders. Change agents—especially managers, project team members, and consultants—must provide visionary leadership to enable the process, rather than top-down, command-and-control micromanagement that inhibits it. Then the leaders of the change effort can create and maintain the momentum crucial to success.

The final, or refreezing, step of the model calls for the change agents to work actively with people in the organization to install, test, debug, use, measure, and enhance the new system. They cannot simply deliver a report to senior management and leave the implementation to the people affected by it. This would be like performing open-heart surgery and asking the patient to take responsibility for his or her care from that point on. Successful refreezing requires a commitment to remain actively involved until required new behaviors have replaced behaviors dating from before the change. This obviously does not happen immediately or without ongoing support when institutionalizing the change (see Levasseur, 2001 for details).

Levasseur (2002) describes a method called *ideal state analysis* (ISA), which is a tool for tracking systems implementation. An ideal state is a description of what someone wants, completely independent of what he or she thinks is possible-a vision. The ISA process essentially follows the Lewin-Schein change process in the following three steps:

Step 1:   Create the ideal future state.
Step 2:   Perform an honest assessment of the current state.
Step 3:   Develop a number of creative alternatives to bridge the gap between the current state and the ideal state.

Zand and Sorensen (1975) studied a large sample of management science implementation projects at many organizations. They found that the overall success of a project was directly related to how successful the issues of each step in the change process were handled. We describe the favorable and unfavorable forces encountered by their subjects in Table 6.3.

TABLE 6.3 Favorable and Unfavorable Forces During Stages of Lewin-Schein Change Model

Stage of Change	Favorable Forces	Unfavorable Forces
Unfreezing	• Top managers felt the problem was important to the company. • Top management became involved. • Unit management recognized a need to change. • Top management initiated the project. • Both top management and unit management were open and candid during discussion • Unit managers were willing to revise some of their initial assumptions.	• Unit managers were unable to state their problems clearly. • Top management felt the overall problem was too big. • Unit management felt threatened by the project. • Some unit management resented the project. • Unit management lacked confidence in the analysis. • Unit managers felt they were capable of handling the project alone.
Moving	• Unit management and analysts gathered data jointly. • All relevant data were accessible and available. • New alternations were devised. • Unit management reviewed and evaluated all alternatives. • Top management was advised of options. • Top management participated in the development of a solution. • All proposals for solutions were improved sequentially.	• Analysts were often not effective in educating unit management. • Unit management did not participate in the development of new solutions. • Unit management often did not fully understand the proposed solution of the analysts. • Analysts felt the project was concluded too quickly.
Refreezing	• Unit management tried the solution. • Frequency of utilization demonstrated the superiority of the new solution. • Analysts initiated positive feedback after early adoption and use. • Final solution was widely accepted after initial success. • Unit management expressed satisfaction with the new solution.	• Analysts did not try to support new managerial behavior after the solution was used. • Analysts did not try to reestablish stability after the solution was used. • Results were often difficult to quantify or measure.

Source: Reprinted from "Theory of Change & Effective Use of Management Science," by Zand, Dale E., and Sorenson, Richard E., published in *Administrative Science Quarterly,* Vol. 20, no. 4, by permission of *Administrative Science Quarterly.*

6.7 DSS TECHNOLOGY LEVELS AND TOOLS

The classification of **technology levels** is important not only for understanding the development of DSS (and ES) but also for developing a framework for their use. Sprague and Carlson (1982) describe a framework that defines the classes of development platforms. There are three **DSS technology levels:** DSS primary tools, DSS integrated tools (generators), and specific DSS. We indicate some of the impacts between the DSS Technology Levels and the Web in Table 6.4.

DSS PRIMARY TOOLS

At the lowest level of DSS technology are the primary tools. These fundamental elements facilitate the development of either a DSS generator or a specific DSS. Examples of **DSS tools** are programming languages, graphics, editors, query systems, and random-number generators. Also included in this category are new Web programming systems (e.g., Java, .Net, PHP) that contain objects that enhance the development of Web-based DSS/BI.

DSS INTEGRATED TOOLS

A **DSS integrated tool** or **DSS generator (engine)** is an integrated development software package that provides a set of capabilities for building a specific DSS quickly, inexpensively, and easily. A generator has diverse capabilities ranging from modeling, report generation, and graphical display to performing risk analysis. These capabilities are integrated into an easy-to-use package. A popular PC-based generator is Excel. Fourth-generation languages, such as Cognos PowerHouse 4GL and PowerHouse Web (for developing Web-based OLAP applications), are also integrated tools capable of

TABLE 6.4 DSS Technology Levels/Tools and Web Impacts

DSS Technology Level/Tool	Web Impacts	Impacts on the Web
DSS primary tools	Improved programming languages that are readily deployed on Web application servers and clients	Used to write programs that affect Web infrastructure and message passing protocols and mechanisms; and e-commerce
DSS integrated tools (generators)	Improved generators (higher-level programming languages and systems) that are readily deployed on Web application servers	Same as above
Specific DSS	Can be deployed directly on the Web with access to data and models on several application servers via a friendly, graphics-based user interface	Same as above These are specifically e-commerce applications Impacts e-commerce directly because they link customers to organizations Analysis of Web-based commerce

accessing and manipulating data in a modeling framework. OLAP systems should certainly be viewed as DSS integrated tools. Even a linear programming modeling language like Lingo should be considered an integrated tool. Lingo was used by IMERYS (Case Application 6.1). In a highly data intensive environment, most integrated tools can be accessed via standard Web browser technology, as is outlined in the typical DSS architecture in Figure 3.1.

SPECIFIC DSS (DSS APPLICATIONS)

The final product—the DSS application that actually accomplishes the work—is called a **specific DSS (SDSS)**. Two examples are the HR InfoNet system (Opening Vignette) and the IMERYS POP DSS (Case Application 6.1). There are many examples of DSS/BI deployed on the Web. For example, see the Web sites of Decision Support Inc. (www.decisionsupport.com) and Yankelovich Partners (secure.yankelovich.com/info/decision_support_system.html).

RELATIONSHIPS AMONG THE THREE LEVELS

The relationships among the three levels are illustrated in Figure 6.5. **DSS primary tools** are used to construct integrated tools, which in turn are used to construct specific DSS. However, primary tools can also be used to directly construct specific DSS. In addition (not shown), there may be simpler tools for constructing more complicated tools.

DSS generators or integrated suites are extremely helpful in constructing specific DSS and in providing flexibility to adapt quickly to changes. Using generators can save a significant amount of time and money, thus making a DSS financially feasible. Developing DSS only with primary tools can be very time-consuming and expensive, especially if the primary tools must be developed. Most early DSS were developed without generators, but new ones are almost exclusively developed with Web-based generators.

FIGURE 6.5   DSS TECHNOLOGY LEVELS

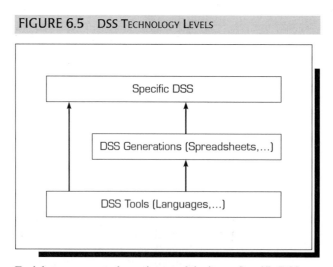

Each box represents the entire set of the items. Specific DSS
may be developed using either DSS tools, or DSS generators;
while DSS generators may only be developed in DSS tools.

6.8 DSS DEVELOPMENT PLATFORMS

Based on the technology levels described in the preceding section, there are several basic DSS development software platforms. The most important ones are the following:

- *Write a customized DSS in a general-purpose programming language such as Visual Basic or COBOL.* This strategy was viable in the 1980s and throughout the 1990s, but very few organizations do it any longer. Sometimes, though, ultra-large-scale DSS, with many interfaces to other CBIS, are constructed this way.
- *Use a fourth-generation language (4GL).* There are several classes of 4GL, such as data-oriented languages, spreadsheets, and financial-oriented languages. These tools can boost programmers' productivity by a magnitude of 10 or even more over general-purpose languages. Even the new OLAP systems have embedded 4GLs; for example, Cognos PowerHouse 4GL and PowerHouse Web. For the most part, these languages have been replaced by direct OLAP use on multidimensional data cubes and spreadsheets.
- *Use OLAP with a data warehouse or a large database.* Online analytical processing engines not only create multidimensional data cubes but also provide analysis tools that effectively function as "decision support suites." If a manager wants to establish relationships in his or her data but prefers not to know how it is done, data mining methods can hide the methods while producing reasonably effective results.
- *Use a DSS integrated development tool (generator or engine).* An integrated package eliminates the need to use multiple 4GLs. The best-known are Excel and Lotus 1-2-3. Generators are more efficient than a collection of individual 4GLs, but they are subject to more limitations.
- *Use a domain-specific DSS generator.* Domain-specific DSS generators are designed to build a highly structured system, usually in a functional area. They include OLAP systems specifically designed for analysis in retailing, manufacturing, and other areas.
- *Develop the DSS using CASE methodology.* As explained in Section 6.3, systems are developed by following a traditional life cycle, and CASE tools can assist in developing large, complex systems. So CASE tools can be used in developing DSS. CASE tools enforce consistency so that a prototype cannot use nonexistent data (see DSS in Action 6.23).
- *Develop a complex DSS by integrating several of the above approaches.* This approach is especially suitable for complex DSS. For example, prototypes can be developed with programming languages and generators while the project is managed with a CASE tool.

Most of these platforms have integrated links to the Web, and many use Web browser interfaces.

6.9 DSS DEVELOPMENT TOOL SELECTION

There are many commercially available DSS tools and generators at a wide variety of prices. Some of the software runs only on large mainframes, while other software runs only on PCs. Most of the software runs on the Web. Programming language surveys

---

DSS IN ACTION 6.23

SOUTHWESTERN BELL MAKES A CASE

Southwestern Bell provides telephone services to 15.7 million land subscribers and 5.2 million wireless telephone subscribers, each with dozens of options, in Texas, Arkansas, Kansas, Missouri, and Oklahoma. Southwestern Bell needed to construct a large-scale, complex sales negotiation tool to make the process of data organization for customer services more efficient. The company needed clear documentation of both the process and the benefits of object-oriented design. It adopted the Rational Rose CASE tool to build this large-scale, complex application framework.

The company also needed the ability to convey complex design information to people with little technological experience. Rose was effective because of its graphical depictions of objects, which are easy to

manipulate. Furthermore, Rose is enhanced through the use of team-enabling features (for collaboration—a GSS). The company also used Rose's code generation capabilities so that changes in design would immediately be reflected in the final product. Through the Rose CASE tool, analysis moves directly into design and into implementation via code, while maintaining system documentation.

The features of this CASE tool helped make abstract concepts communicable both to team members and to interested external parties.

Source: Adapted from "Southwestern Bell Makes a Rational Call," Rational Software Corporation, www.rational.com, February 2000.

---

appear on a regular basis. For example, Kay (2000) presents a description of current programming languages, features, and a linguistic sampler. This guide may prove useful in selecting a programming language for a particular application. Several interdependent questions must be addressed by an organization intending to use DSS tools, including which tools to use, which hardware to run them on, which operating system to use, and which networks to run them on.

HARDWARE SELECTION

DSS run on platforms ranging from an individual PC (a simple Excel application) to the largest multiprocessor computers like the ones that the National Oceanic and Atmospheric Administration (NOAA) uses to run national U.S. weather forecasts. Some run on networks of Unix workstations (including grid computing networks), while others use PCs as Web clients attached to a Web server. Usually the existing hardware architecture of an organization and its availability to the users (see the Opening Vignette) govern the choice of hardware.

SOFTWARE SELECTION

Selecting the DSS tools or generator is a complex process because

- At the time when selection must be made, DSS information requirements and outputs are not completely known.
- There are hundreds of software packages on the market.
- Software packages are updated very rapidly.
- Price changes are frequent.
- Several people may be involved in the evaluation team.
- One language can be used in the construction of several DSS. Thus, the required capabilities of the tools may change from one application to another.
- Portions of a large DSS may have to be developed with different tools.

- The selection decision involves dozens of criteria against which competing packages are compared. Several criteria are intangible; others are in direct conflict with one other.
- Technical, functional, end-user, and managerial issues are all considered.
- Commercially available evaluations conducted by companies such as Data Decisions, Data Pro, and Software Digest Inc., and the buyer's guides in trade journals such as *eWeek* and *InfoSystems*, are subjective and often superficial, especially for tools that are also used for non-DSS applications.
- The desirability of staying with a few vendors and the nonavailability of client/server open system environments that allow mixing and matching of products from multiple vendors must be considered.

THE SELECTION OF A DSS GENERATOR

When an organization has a DSS generator in-house, it is generally the most likely one to be selected for DSS applications (e.g., Lotus Notes at Osram Sylvania in the Opening Vignette). However, firms do not necessarily use only one generator. Some DSS generators are better than others for certain types of applications. Thus, organizations typically use several generators and may at times need to purchase a new DSS generator. Since there are many criteria, some of which are qualitative, and often many alternatives, a decision aid such as Expert Choice (Expert Choice Inc.) can greatly improve the selection process (Chapter 4). See DSS in Action 6.24 for an example involving software selection.

COMPONENT REUSE

Software selection can be simpler if an organization utilizes one or just a few development platforms/languages. With a limited number, components can be reused *if they are designed and implemented in such a way that reuse is relatively easy*. Den Haan (2001), Hudson (2001), Williams (2000), and Zellen (2001) indicate that component reusability makes good sense. Reusability is one of the basic premises of knowledge management, but for code development, it is at a micro level. There is no point in reinventing the wheel. If you can design components to do fairly standard tasks, then reuse them. On the other hand, managing and documenting components can be very complex processes. The development of the Reusable Asset Specification (RAS) may help. The open standard of the RAS provides guidelines on how to describe, develop, and apply a library of reusable software assets. It uses the unified modeling language (UML) for design models and Rational Unified Process (RUP) for workflow descriptions. The basic concepts of component reuse are part of UML (see Booch and Rumbaugh, 1998; Jacobson and Griss, 2001; Jacobson, Griss, and Jonsson, 1998; Kruchten, 1998). In 2001, the RAS was still in its infancy, but it has the potential to have major financial impacts on code development.

Packaged and homegrown components must integrate tightly for component-based development to meet its potential. This is especially critical for e-commerce applications. This is now easier than ever, but tough challenges persist. Expectations are that a large percentage of all new applications will be assembled primarily from components (see Williams, 2000). Den Haan (2001) describes issues in applications integration. This is a critical problem because there is no universal development language. Today's complex integration problems include:

- Application-to-application (A2A)
- Business-to-business (B2B)

DSS IN ACTION 6.24

HOW I CHOSE HELP DESK SOFTWARE

When Leonard Lopez obtained funding to purchase new software for his help desk, he developed a logical, rational, reasonable approach. He decided that he needed (1) a logical process for help desk software selection that would include gathering requirements, analyzing data, and making a decision; (2) an implementation of this process that would work with a limited budget within a limited time frame; and (3) a good final decision. Along the way, he defused many political and behavioral issues, including staff members forming camps in favor of one product over another, aggressive vendor salespersons, and outsourcing part of the process to a knowledgeable consultant.

His aggressive 16-week selection process plan was as follows:

Week(s)	Function(s)
1	Determine and contact key participants
2	Establish a process for requirements-gathering sessions
3 and 4	Conduct requirements-gathering sessions
4 and 5	Compose requirements in RFP format
6 and 7	Distribute RFPs to potential vendors (allow at least 2–3 weeks for a reply)
8 and 9	Gather revisions for requirements; publish and communicate requirements
10 and 11	Collect and summarize RFP data
12	Select RFP short list; advise participants
13	Set short list interviews and demonstrations
14	Accumulate interview findings; make selection of primary and secondary choices
15	Negotiate contract details with primary selection
16	Finalize selection contracts; set implementation plan in place

Lopez developed a decision-making model as part of this process to develop and weight criteria. He concluded that some of the important issues that must be dealt with in software selection are the following:

- The software selection affects future use. You are investing in future upgrades not yet created.
- Conduct negotiations with vendors with a partnership in mind to get the support or flexibility you'll need further down the road.

- To ensure full participation in your selection efforts, budget for participants from other departments.
- The architecture you purchase must be technically compatible with your environment. Make sure you select a compatible product.

Source: Modified from L. Lopez, "How I Chose Help Desk Software," *Support Management*, March 1998, pp. 16–28.

- Business-to-consumer (B2C)
- Web-to-host
- Wireless-to-host
- Window-to-host

Organizations are attempting to connect their strategic e-business applications with the back-office and with industry portals and electronic communities, opening the enterprise to business partners, customers, suppliers, and new markets. The scope of component integration and code reuse is broadening, too. Component reuse may be the key to integration, especially if the components have been integrated in other applications (den Haan, 2001).

OUTSOURCING

When selecting software, one must consider whether to develop it in-house or outsource the work. A major complication with outsourcing is that the organization that wanted the software developed, and not the outsider firm that developed it, has responsibility for the finished product. Since the organization is ultimately responsible for the system, members of the organization (users, managers, executive sponsors) must be involved as if the system were developed in-house. When Daimler Chrysler Capital outsourced financial applications (e-commerce operations) to an ASP (application service provider), its managers learned that they had to be clear about what they wanted the system to do and how it interfaced into the organization. Outsourcing will not necessarily improve an inefficient operation. It is also important to recognize that the firm owns the project and is ultimately responsible for it. See Cone (2001) for details and tips.

Yourdon (2001) indicates that almost every IT project today includes some element of outsourcing for application development, data center operations, Web hosting, end-user training, and so on. When outsourcing, it is wise to consider a number of important aspects. For example, long-term projects require long-term commitments from vendors (for a price). Since vendor purchases account for more than 60 percent of a typical IT budget after personnel costs, it is important to know how to choose an IT vendor (Melymuka, 2002a). See DSS in Focus 6.25 for details.

There are mixed reviews in industry on outsourcing DSS and IT projects versus internal development (see DSS in Focus 6.26; Morris, 2000). On average, there is a slightly higher investment (15%) in DSS projects when they are outsourced, but the payoff is substantially higher (ROIs of 140% vs. 104%). On the other hand, as this book went to press, there was a general trend to move large-scale projects back in-house because of dissatisfaction with major consulting firms. See DSS in Focus 6.27, Koch (2003), and Overby (2003) for details.

DSS IN FOCUS 6.25

SELECTING A VENDOR

1. Establish the need as it relates to the business.

2. Select a team that includes both technical and management members.

3. Choose a strategy. Attempt to standardize.

4. Write a request for proposals (RFP). This forces the team to consider what is important.

5. Focus on the total cost of ownership, not just the initial cost.

6. Develop your negotiation strategy in parallel with your RFP.

7. Consider the value of relationships as you evaluate bids.

8. Keep your options open.

9. Be a good customer.

10. If possible, split the contract between two vendors.

11. Anticipate the future.

12. Stay pragmatic. Do not let technology distract you.

Source: Adapted from K. Melymuka (2002a), pp. 32–33.

IN-HOUSE VS. OUTSOURCING DSS DEVELOPMENT

Morris (2003) reports on a recent IDC study on the financial impact of business analytics (e.g., DSS/BI). IDC investigated information on costs and returns through on-site interviews with end users, IT managers, and financial executives at 43 organizations. The analytic application ranged from marketing campaign analysis to fraud detection to portfolio management, spanning a variety of industries. Overall, analytics implementations generate a mean five-year return on investment (ROI) of 112 percent with a median five-year investment of just over $2 million. Returns ranged from 17 percent to over 2000 percent.

For 46 percent of the organizations, the ROIs were less than 100 percent; 34 percent were between 101 and 1000 percent; while 20 percent reported ROIs of over 1000 percent. Although business analytics (DSS) imple-

mentations are substantial investments for organizations, they can deliver substantial benefits. DSS applications clearly pay off. Interestingly enough, the median total five-year investment for organizations that developed the applications in house was $2,088,660, with a median return of 104 percent. On the other hand, for organizations that outsourced their applications, the median total five-year investment for organizations was $1,807,656 (15% less), with a substantially higher median return of 140 percent. Of course, whether one builds or buys depends on the problem being addressed, the level of skill within the organization, and the availability of packaged (ready-made) solutions.

Source: Adapted from Morris (2003).

6.10 TEAM-DEVELOPED DSS

A **team-developed DSS** requires a substantial effort, though the team may consist of only a few people, like the team that developed the HR InfoNet in the Opening Vignette. Team-developed DSS need extensive planning and organization. The planning and organization depend on the specific DSS, the organization in which it will be used, and so on. Certain activities are generic and can be performed by any team.

A complex DSS requires a group of people to build and manage it. The number of people in the group depends on such factors as the size of the effort and the tools used.

CONSULTANTS: CAN'T LIVE WITH THEM, CAN'T LIVE WITHOUT THEM (AND CAN'T ELIMINATE THEM!)

CIOs are using fewer consultants for enterprise projects. Just as in the project-management success studies, many organizations are not achieving their goals in enterprise projects. In a Conference Board survey of ERP project managers released in 2001, 40 percent of the respondents indicated that they had failed to achieve their original business case, even after a year or more of operations. More than 20 percent shut down the projects before completion. For all the companies, even the ones claiming success, on average costs were 25 percent over budget, and annual support costs went up

by an average of some 20 percent over the legacy systems they replaced. In mid-2002, companies were seeing the same occur with CRM. Companies are dissatisfied with the pricing and delivery models of consulting firms. In a survey of IT and business leaders by Peerstone Research, none of the Big Five rated better than a C in terms of the respondents' willingness to recommend them.

Source: Modified from Christopher Koch, "It's Time to Take Control." *CIO*, July 15, 2002, pp 46–52.

Some companies have initiated a DSS effort with as few as two or three people; others have employed as many as twelve to fifteen.

The organizational placement of the DSS development group varies. Some typical locations are within the IS department, as a highly placed executive staff group, or within a functional group such as finance, accounting, or marketing.

The process that a DSS team follows depends on the specific application. The group may be temporary, created for a specific DSS, or it may be permanent, in which case the group members are assigned to specific DSS projects.

Many of the DSS developed from the 1980s to the mid-1990s were large-scale, complex systems designed primarily to provide organizational support. Such systems are still under development for complex problems and for company-wide applications. These systems are constructed by a team composed of users, intermediaries, DSS developers, technical support experts, and IS personnel. Because there can be several people in each category, the teams can be large and their composition may change over time. Developing a DSS with a team is a complex, lengthy, costly process. Since the early 2000s, tools and generators have improved, which means that smaller teams can handle complex DSS development.

6.11 END USER DEVELOPED DSS

PCs have diffused throughout organizations, communication with data servers (mainframes and others) has improved, and software tools have improved in capability, quality, price, and user-friendliness. Consequently, users now have the necessary tools to develop their own DSS/BI, even Web-based systems.

Broadly defined, **end user computing** (also known as **end user development**) is the development and use of computer-based information systems by people outside the formal information-system area. This includes *all* users in all functional areas at all skill levels at all levels in an organization: managers, executives, staff, secretaries, and others.

User-developed DSS has a more narrow definition. It includes decision-makers and professionals (knowledge workers, like financial or tax analysts and engineers) who build or use computers to solve problems or enhance their productivity (see DSS in Action 6.28). OLAP tools for multidimensional data cube analysis fall into this category.

We next turn to the advantages and risks of user-developed DSS.

USER-DEVELOPED DSS: ADVANTAGES AND RISKS

There are several important advantages that explain why users want to develop their own DSS:

- *Delivery time is short.* There is no wait for an IS development team to schedule and carry out development.
- *The prerequisites of extensive and formal user requirements specifications are eliminated.* These specifications are often incomplete or incorrect in DSS because of such issues as users' inability to specify the requirements or communication issues between analysts and users. It sometimes takes a long time to develop these specifications.
- *Some DSS implementation problems are reduced.*
- *The cost is usually very low.*

OLAP GIVES SERVICE MERCHANDISE END USER DSS

In the late 1980s discount stores forced most catalog showrooms under. Companies like Service Merchandise Company knew nothing about their customers' buying habits or how to target marketing campaigns precisely so as to react quickly enough to reverse the downward slide. Sales and profits declined over six or seven years. Because Service Merchandise already had deployed a 500-gigabyte data warehouse, managers could use the data to analyze their customers' purchasing habits.

They used DecisionMaster (Intrepid Systems Inc.), a relational OLAP tool, to analyze the data to find patterns in sales and inventory by region, store, and individual items. Individual managers can now track marketing campaigns to determine what works and what doesn't. They can adjust the campaigns for each market. And, if necessary, the OLAP helps target underperforming stores as candidates to be closed.

"When we recognize trends we can act much faster," said Michael Presley, Service Merchandise's director of buying and inventory management. "Before we had this in place, we had to do it all by ad hoc (database) requests, which were limited and slow." Presley now transfers chunks of data to his own spreadsheets and manipulates them directly. Whole new analytic worlds have opened for Presley with the ability to slice and dice and analyze data for individual stores, items, product classes, and supply vendors. "I have more data now than I ever imagined," Presley said.

Postscript. Service Merchandise went into involuntary Chapter 11 bankruptcy in early 1999. Service Merchandise closed 134 underperforming stores in early 1999 as part of its out-of-court restructuring. The retailer had a successful 1999 retail holiday season, in part due to the DSS. In 2002, after three years of bankruptcy, Service Merchandise eliminated its stores. It currently maintains only a Web presence (www.service-merchandise.com).

Source: Adapted from Stewart Deck, "Analysis May Help Retailer End Slump," *Computerworld,* Vol. 32, No. 38, September 21, 1998, pp. 57–58; Anonymous, "Service Merchandise Announces Intention to Close Up to 134 Stores," *BusinessWire,* February 9, 1999.

Some serious end user–developed DSS risks include the following:

- User-developed DSS can be of poor quality. Lack of formal DSS design experience and the tendency of end users to ignore conventional controls, testing procedures, and documentation standards can lead to low-quality systems (see DSS in Focus 6.29).
- There are three categories of potential quality risks: substandard or inappropriate tools and facilities used in DSS development; risks associated with the development process (e.g., the inability to develop workable systems or the development of systems that generate erroneous results); and data management risks (e.g., loss of data or use of stale, inappropriate, or incorrect data).
- Security risks may increase because of users' unfamiliarity with security measures.
- Lack of documentation and maintenance procedures may cause problems, especially if the developer leaves the organization.

REDUCING THE RISKS OF END-USER COMPUTING

Because most *personal DSS* and many *organizational DSS* are developed by end users, it is important to manage and reduce the risk associated with end user–developed DSS. Experienced development teams use a variety of tools and languages to build DSS. However, end users typically use a **DSS integrated tool** like Excel. They usually follow the "I only own a hammer" approach to problem-solving: "When all you own is a hammer, every problem you have looks like a nail."

UH-OH: USER DEVELOPED DSS RISK

An oil and gas company in Dallas, Texas, lost millions of dollars in an acquisition deal, and several executives were fired because of an error in a spreadsheet model. The executives had made their decisions based on inaccurate spreadsheet data.

Such errors are common. Few spreadsheet disasters have been published, but consultants and independent audits have found errors in as many as 30 percent of the spreadsheet models created with off-the-shelf spreadsheet systems. A company might have tens of thousands of spreadsheet models in use. What would the impact be if even only 1 percent of them have errors? Decision-makers rely on spreadsheet analyses, many of which have never been checked for errors.

Source: Adapted from R. Panko, "Finding Spreadsheet Errors—Most Spreadsheet Models Have Design Flaws That May Lead to Long-term Miscalculations," *CommunicationsWeek*, May 29, 1995, p. 100.

Many spreadsheet applications pose considerable risk to an organization because they support important tasks like financial analysis, budgeting, and forecasting applications. If logical errors or poor documentation create misinformation or make the spreadsheet difficult to interpret, the risk of using incorrect data for financial decisions is great. The cost of an erroneous business decision based on poor data can be enormous (see DSS in Focus 6.29). Quality issues are the most troublesome. How can the work of an end user be validated when the end user develops and uses his or her own system?

Several studies address the issue of risks and controls in end-user development. Some factors contributing to spreadsheet errors include developer inexperience, poor design approaches, application types, problem complexity, time pressure, and the presence or absence of review procedures (Janvrin and Morrison, 2000). Other factors, including gender, application expertise, and work group configuration, can influence spreadsheet error rates. Janvrin and Morrison (2000) propose applying a structured design approach to developing systems in spreadsheets. This development approach reduced errors significantly in two experiments. Schultheis and Sumner (1994) determined that a number of controls are applied in practice to spreadsheet applications. Developers use more controls in high-risk spreadsheet applications. Also see Panko (1998; 1999).

Survey data show that spreadsheet errors are common. Freeman (1996) reports in a survey that about 90 percent of spreadsheets with over 150 rows contained at least one significant formula mistake. Overconfidence is perhaps the most serious aspect of spreadsheet errors because it reduces the extent to which end users validate their models before using them to make important decisions. These errors can cost companies millions of dollars in new projects and other business decisions (Berglas and Hoare, 1999).

Whittaker (1999) suggests two simple, obvious, often-skipped approaches to minimizing spreadsheet errors: (1) understand the nature and dynamics of the problem being modeled; and (2) spend time reviewing the spreadsheet model. He also mentions that there are spreadsheet audit tools (Spreadsheet Professional, Operis Analysis Kit, Spreadsheet Detective) available to help identify formula assumptions.

The structure that CASE tools enforce on system analysts, designers, and implementers can force an end user to adhere to methods that create logical consistency in a specific DSS. Also, the issue of level of experience with the development platform and the decision-making problem can influence the quality of a DSS. The upshot is that an organizational unit must take the responsibility to ensure that end user–developed DSS meet rigid quality standards. The data must be accurate, timely, and appropriate, and the system must get the right answers. The system must be documented and maintained. The unit that ensures these risk factors might be part of an IS center or even a DSS team.

One approach that works well in practice is to *license* end user–developed applications. When a new end-user DSS application is to be created, the user can develop it with an organizationally approved methodology (say, structured design). At the inception, the basic features must be outlined in a one-page report to the DSS licensing group—call it the DLG. A member of the DLG assists the developer by providing appropriate tools and data, as well as methods to access data if they reside on other systems. In this way, security is preserved. When the DSS is completed, it must be documented, and the DLG must approve its use. The documentation must be good enough so that if the developer leaves the organization, the system can be maintained by the DLG. The DSS is then approved for the individual to use. A copy of all the material is stored with the DLG, and the information about the DSS is cataloged in a knowledge base available to all members of the organization. This practice promotes software reuse. Employees in other departments can search for DSS related to their own work and can ask to use or expand someone else's system on an experimental basis. DSS can be licensed for individual use, several individuals' use, work group use, departmental use, organizational use, or interorganizational use. Each level up requires even tighter restrictions on quality and documentation to ensure that the risks in DSS use are minimized.

6.12 PUTTING THE DSS TOGETHER

In Chapter 3, we described a typical Web-based DSS architecture (Figure 3.1). The structure consisted of several Web servers and a client, all integrated to help decision-makers in business intelligence work. Integration is still a difficult issue, and more critical now that DSS/BI tools have migrated to the Web and also readily provide collaboration and communication tools to decision-makers. These and other considerations must be handled as new DSS are developed and legacy systems migrate to the Web.

Development tools increase the productivity of developers and help them construct a DSS responsive to users' needs. The philosophy of development tools and generators is based on two simple yet very important concepts: the use of highly automated tools throughout the development process, and the use of prefabricated pieces in the manufacturing of a whole system whenever possible (e.g., component reuse) (Yongbeom and Stohr, 1998). The first concept increases the productivity of the developer in the same way that an electric saw improves the productivity of a carpenter who formerly used a hand saw. The second concept increases productivity analogously to the way a prefabricated wall increases the productivity of a carpenter building a house. Fortunately, a component is not "consumed" when it is used, in the sense that the wall is. It can be used again and again. As the components of a DSS are developed, care must be taken to make them fit together (like the components of a house—the plumbing must fit inside the walls but must link the outside water supply to the sinks and tubs, and so on).

A DSS is more than just the DBMS, MBMS, user interface, and knowledge component. There are interfaces among the components and with external systems.

Typically, DSS databases must be refreshed regularly from other source databases. There may be special tools for necessary functions like report generation. There may be several databases and models, each of which is developed and used differently; and there may be many people involved in the development in terms of data gathering (refer to the Web Chapter on P&G's supply chain redesign). Not only do the components have to be constructed, but the specific tools and generators for development also must be selected, installed, and managed.

The system core includes a development language or a DSS generator. Some of the necessary capabilities mentioned above are integrated into DSS generators. Others can be added as needed. These components can be used to build a new DSS or update an existing one. The construction involves the combining of software modules. Fortunately, the newer object-oriented operating systems provide a consistent, user-friendly environment for DSS development. Tools and generators that run in them can easily share results and data. Since a consistent, user-friendly interface can be developed quickly (say, in Microsoft .NET), component interfacing problems are generally minimal. In fact, Web browser GUI interfaces are commonly used to front-end legacy DSS and databases instead of rewriting the whole system (see DSS in Action 3.4). Alternatively, legacy systems have been moved to Web servers along with creating the Web-browser front end.

TRENDS IN DSS/BI IMPLEMENTATION

In Chapters 2 and 3, we described some recent developments in DSS/BI. There are several trends that continue to impact DSS/BI applications. They include:

- Managers are more readily accepting DSS/BI tools, techniques, and methods.
- Artificial intelligence tools and methods (expert systems, neural networks, genetic algorithms, fuzzy logic, etc.) are being embedded in DSS/BI.
- Web technologies continue to enable new developments in DSS/BI from data, information, and knowledge access to direct communication and collaboration.
- GSS continues to proliferate through collaborative computing.
- Computer technology continues its fast-paced evolution. Capabilities are increasing dramatically, and costs are decreasing. This leads to greater capabilities being embedded in DSS/BI.
- Enterprise resource management/enterprise resource planning (ERM/ERP) systems, though extremely expensive, are proliferating. These often provide and incorporate DSS methods for improved decision-making. One future development of the IMERYS model (Case Application 6.1) will be to use its results to drive a new ERP.

❖ CHAPTER HIGHLIGHTS

- The traditional system development life cycle (SDLC) is a structured approach for managing the development of information systems.
- The four fundamental phases of the traditional SDLC are planning, analysis, design, and implementation.
- Each phase of the SDLC has several small steps, each with its own techniques and deliverables.
- Computer-aided software engineering (CASE) tools are useful for managing large information-system development.

- There is a need for good project management skills in system development team leaders.
- In practice most information systems do not succeed. It is important to understand the factors that lead to failure so that they can be recognized early.
- DSS are usually developed by prototyping (iterative design, evolutionary development) development methodology.
- Prototyping is a rapid application development (RAD) methodology.

- Prototyping consists of rapid cycles through the fundamental phases of the SDLC, with user feedback guiding system modifications. This is a form of joint application development (JAD) and rapid application development (RAD). Typically DSS developed with prototyping continue to evolve following deployment.
- Iterative prototyping methodology is most common in DSS development because information requirements are not precisely known at the beginning of the process.
- Prototyping helps the user understand the decision-making situation as the system evolves.
- New agile development and extreme programming methods are formal prototyping methods that are useful for developing small- to medium-sized systems quickly.
- Change management is difficult; a number of organizational factors must be present if it is to occur successfully.
- The deceptively simple Lewin-Schein model of change management (unfreeze, move, refreeze) elegantly describes how change can be managed.
- DSS technology levels are DSS primary tools, DSS integrated tools (generators, engines), and specific DSS.
- DSS are typically constructed with a DSS generator consisting of an integrated set of development tools.

- Selecting DSS software and hardware is difficult because it involves both quantitative and qualitative factors.
- There are many Web-based DSS tools and generators on the market. The appropriate ones for building a specific DSS must be selected carefully.
- DSS can be built by teams or by individuals.
- A team building a DSS must follow a structured process.
- Most end-user DSS developed with an integrated tool like an Excel spreadsheet are used for personal support.
- The major benefits of end users developing their own DSS are short delivery time, users' familiarity with their needs, low cost, and easier implementation.
- End user–developed DSS can be of poor quality. Appropriate controls based on system-development methods can improve quality. The two primary ones are (1) to understand the model of the problem, and (2) to review the model carefully.
- Assembling a DSS can involve many components and their interfaces.
- New DSS/BI software are incorporating artificial intelligence methods and better collaboration systems (GSS), and exploit Web technologies.

❖ KEY WORDS

- DSS generator (engine)
- DSS integrated tool
- DSS primary tools
- DSS technology levels
- DSS tools
- end-user computing
- end-user development

- evolutionary development
- feasibility study
- iterative design
- phased development
- prototyping
- rapid application development (RAD)

- specific DSS (application)
- system development life cycle (SDLC)
- team-developed DSS
- technology levels (of DSS)
- throwaway prototyping
- user-developed DSS

❖ QUESTIONS FOR REVIEW

1. List and describe the fundamental phases and minor steps of the traditional system development life cycle (SDLC).
2. Define computer-aided software engineering (CASE). Why is it important?
3. List the reasons why good project management skills are needed by DSS development team leaders.
4. Define change management.
5. List the reasons why information systems fail in practice.
6. Define prototyping.
7. Describe how the phases of prototyping relate to those of the traditional SDLC.
8. Compare a throwaway (design) prototype to a system prototype.
9. List the reasons why prototyping is the method of choice for developing most DSS.

10. List the three technology levels of DSS.
11. Define DSS integrated tools (generators) and discuss their objectives.
12. List the DSS development platforms.
13. List some of the difficulties in selecting DSS software.
14. List the differences between team-developed DSS and end user–developed DSS.
15. Define end user and *end-user computing*.
16. List the major advantages of end user–developed DSS.
17. List the potential quality risk areas in end user–developed DSS.
18. List methods for improving the quality of DSS developed in spreadsheets.
19. List all the different components that a DSS might have. Explain why it is sometimes hard to cement them together.
20. List the major trends in DSS.

❖ QUESTIONS FOR DISCUSSION

1. Describe how the fundamental phases of the SDLC match Simon's four phases of decision-making. Compare Simon's definition of implementation to the SDLC definition.
2. Explain how CASE tools can enforce standards in system development.
3. Why is the traditional SDLC an inappropriate methodology for developing most DSS?
4. Explain why prototyping is also known as evolutionary development.
5. Describe the similarities between prototyping and the traditional SDLC. Describe how they are different.
6. Compare prototyping software to prototyping consumer products (say, automobiles). What is similar, and what is different?
7. Explain the reasoning behind prototyping a user interface (see DSS in Action 6.2).
8. How does the iterative process secure more user input than conventional development approaches?
9. Describe agile development and extreme programming methods.
10. How does the user develop a better understanding of the decision-making problem through the iterative process?
11. What are the disadvantages of not having complete specifications for a DSS but instead letting it evolve from a small prototype?
12. How can a CASE tool be used in DSS development through prototyping?
13. Explain the methods of agile development and extreme programming.
14. What is the importance of component reuse. What are the advantages and disadvantages?
15. Describe the organizational issues and solutions in change management.
16. Describe how the three DSS technology levels interact.
17. Explain how the classification of technology levels can improve understanding of the DSS development process.
18. Give two examples each of specific DSS, DSS generators, and DSS primary tools not mentioned in this text.
19. Explain how an OLAP package can be a DSS generator.
20. Discuss how to select DSS software. What makes it so difficult?
21. Explain how OLAP running on multidimensional data cubes is an end user–developed DSS.
22. Discuss the reasons why end user–developed DSS can be of poor quality. What can be done to improve the situation?
23. Comment on the statement "When all you own is a hammer, every problem you have looks like a nail" as it relates to end user–developed DSS. Investigate some ways that this issue can be managed properly.
24. How has the World Wide Web changed our views of cementing the components of a DSS together?

❖ EXERCISES

1. Identify the latest developments in CASE tools and methods in the academic and trade literature. Explain how these improvements can impact DSS development.
2. Identify critical issues in the academic and trade literature on information system project management. Describe the five most important issues and what industry is doing to solve them.
3. You have been assigned the task of redesigning the interface for the automatic teller machine at your bank. Describe how you will approach this problem.[2]
4. *Throwaway prototype.* It is possible to use a spreadsheet package like Excel to map out the functionality of a program before committing to a formal development in a programming language. Do this for a problem that your instructor gives you.
5. Identify three OLAP systems specifically designed for analysis in functional business areas such as retailing and manufacturing. Describe their basic features and recommended uses.
6. *Situation evaluation.* Many hours and much expense were involved in developing a DSS to assist a manager in making an important decision. The prototyping approach was used, and so the decision-maker and the system developers worked together (and were paid). When it came time for the manager to make the decision, she queried the system, discarded the advice, and made a different decision. How could this happen? Could the system still have been beneficial to the manager? Why or why not? If so, how? Could the system still be beneficial to the organization? Why or why not?

---

[2]Adapted from Dennis and Wixom (2003).

❖ INTERNET EXERCISES

1. Explore CASE tools on vendors' Web sites. Select a single CASE tool, download the demo, and try it. Make a list of the important features of the tool. Is this CASE tool upper CASE, lower CASE, or I-CASE? Why? Report your findings to the class.
2. Explore project management software on vendors' Web sites. Select a single project-management package, download the demo, and try it. Make a list of the important features of the package. Be sure to investigate its Web, repository, and collaboration features. Report your findings to the class.

3. Search the Web and recent literature for information on object-oriented database and model base development software. (*Hint*: UML.) For a reasonable sample of 10 sites, answer the following questions: What vendors are there, and what products do they offer? How do these products differ from the traditional packages? How can they be used for DSS development? How do they incorporate component reuse?

❖ GROUP EXERCISES

1. *Software selection.* Build an Expert Choice (AHP) model to help you evaluate and select a DSS generator package (integrated tool, OLAP) to solve a specific problem (see Chapters 2 and 5 for appropriate software examples). Develop criteria, and so on, in terms of a particular decision-making application. Explain which package you would choose and why.
2. Thomasett (2002) has developed paper-based exercises designed to engage project stakeholders. These

exercises involve developing a common vision of a success, determining project scope, developing a stakeholder agreement (contract) to govern the project, and developing a quality agreement to determine what is most to least important. These exercises have proven successful in practice. Obtain the reference and use the exercises for your major project in this class or another class under the direction of your instructor.

❖ GROUP PROJECT

Continue developing the DSS Term Project from Chapter 4. Focus on the system development issues. What major problems is your group encountering?

How are you resolving them? Finish the project and report your results to the class.

CLAY PROCESS PLANNING AT IMERYS: A CLASSICAL CASE OF DECISION-MAKING

Part 4: Development and Implementation of the Process OPtimization DSS

INTRODUCTION

In Case Applications 2.1, 2.2, and 4.1, we presented some of the decision-making processes, the decisions, the linear programming model, and the database requirements of the Process OPtimization (POP) DSS. In this case application we discuss the process by which the entire system was developed and implemented.

THE POP DSS APPROACH

In November 1998, an analyst/consultant attended a one-day meeting in which the feasibility of the approach was discussed. It was determined that a decision support system could be built, and that it would be wise to spend some time canvassing the market for an appropriate mathematical programming language (a DSS generator) that could solve problems on the order of magnitude expected (very large because of the complexity of the operations), would be relatively easy to understand (close to English), and could link to standard database systems such as Access (for an easy-to-use interface and data storage). In December the team held a workshop to cover the basic and advanced features of linear programming (the model type) and to discuss how optimization modeling languages work, as well as the strengths and weaknesses of the leading systems. Several commercial packages were evaluated at that time, and from these the team selected Lingo (Lindo Systems Inc., lindo.com) because of its fairly natural problem statements, its automatic linking to databases, its ability to solve problems of unlimited size, and some familiarity with Lindo, its predecessor. Embedded in Lingo is a set of robust solvers (Lindo for linear programming problems, Gino for nonlinear programming problems), problem size is limited only by real system memory, the language runs on a variety of platforms from PC to RISC workstation to mainframe, and it links to Access and other database systems directly through the Windows

object database control (@ODBC) method. The PC platform was selected based on its uniform availability throughout the organization, and specific managers (mine managers, plant managers, and the sales forecasting manager) were contacted and informed about the project to gain support and because they would be contacted later for information and their knowledge about the clay processes being modeled.

By the end of December, a small DSS POP team was formed. It consisted of the manager of the project, the manager of the small calcine plant selected for initial modeling, two IS specialists, an accounting specialist, and a mathematical programming analyst/consultant.

At this point, much was unknown about the project, but it was felt to be worth investigating. The idea seemed viable, and the payoff in terms of better planning and scheduling was worth the risk.

SYSTEM DEVELOPMENT–PROTOTYPING: A LEARNING EXPERIENCE

The prototyping approach had proven very successful in the past and was deemed appropriate for this project. Over time, as the team members learned more and more about clay processing, the structure of the model became more complex, the size became quite large, and the model itself became more accurate. Simple models that grew in complexity were in turn examined and discarded until a workable approach evolved. As the model evolved, with the help of users and managers, new potential uses of the system were developed, leading to model refinements and new system queries and reports.

PROJECT INITIATION

In January 1999, the team began to analyze process flowcharts of the small calcine (dry clay processing) plant and developed a very unstructured, direct model that did not utilize database interaction. At that time, IMATEL tendered an offer for ECCI, which led to the team leader's temporarily leaving the team and making the manager of the small plant the team leader. This potential buyout led

---

Contributed by the initial POP development team: Jay E. Aronson, Chris Hutchings, Teresa A. Rhodes, C. Allen Orr, John Brooker, and Trish Layton. Additional material contributed by Tammy Brack.

directly to changes in the priorities of the plants to be modeled because different company plants (specific plants were not known but were projected) would not be part of the new, yet to be formed company (per U.S. Justice Department approval), while plants would be brought in from other companies. Some of these plants were part of the Dry Branch Kaolin Company, which was already owned by IMATEL. As a consequence, work on some processing plants that initially were to be modeled was put on hold, while other model segments required completion fairly quickly.

There were several factors that complicated the progress of the project. The mathematical programming analyst/consultant was available for only two or three days per week. Members of the team had other, full-time responsibilities. For example, the new team manager still ran her plant, one IS analyst was developing the firm's demand-forecasting system, the other was still working on quality-issue projects, and the accounting specialist still continued his other full-time activities. Not knowing how the plants would be divided up and sold off, the team proceeded as planned with the small plant and developed mock-up prototypes of proposed interfaces (screens and reports) with which it felt managers would be the most comfortable. The team also worked closely with several users to get a sense of the kinds of screens and reports that would be useful. An annual time period would be modeled, but the ability to create versions of the model for various time horizons would be designed into the system. The POP DSS was developed and deployed on an IBM PC-compatible notebook computer.

THE FIRST MODEL—THE SMALL CALCINE PLANT

By late March, the team had developed a fairly accurate, but not database-linked, model of the small calcine plant. Its accuracy was demonstrated to the larger, continuous improvement initiative team, and the POP team was directed to continue its efforts because management and users could see large potential benefits in assisting decision-making and in profitability. At each step of the way, the team apprised the managers and potential users of its progress to keep communication lines open and to seek advice. At this time, one IS analyst determined a way to link the database to the model, and a new, simpler modeling approach was considered and developed. The multicommodity, near-network model is described in Case Application 4.1.

MODEL AND DATABASE INTERFACING

The new model structure could be readily stored directly in an Access database, and Lingo, through the Windows @ODBC interface mechanism, could link the two together. Lingo models can be defined by sets, both primi-

tive (e.g., clay, plant) and derived (e.g., link, linksum) (Chapter 4). Each set can be represented by a table in a relational database, while each entry in the set maps into a column. These sets include model data to be fed directly from the database into the Lingo model, as well as the values of the decision variables found by the Lingo optimizer, which are automatically fed back into the database. The Lingo model itself appears as a series of statements indicating its mathematical definition and the data definitions and their source. Using the set concept, coupled with Lingo's ability to manipulate data, the mathematical programming analyst quickly developed a new structure for the model. The basic design of the database was quickly worked out once the multicommodity, near-network model was developed. The team quickly converted the small model to the new structure and validated it.

SYSTEM DEVELOPMENT BEGINS

From this point onward, it was relatively easy to modify the Lingo model because of the general set structure, and so the team was able to focus on the data, screens, and reports.

Given input parameters and solution entries in the POP database tables, a menu system was created to manage the generation of cases, queries, and solution reports, which could be solved and stored in the tables of the POP database. Early in this part of the process, a process utilization report was prepared which included a bar graph showing all the clay processes and their utilization. The equipment running at 100 percent capacity could be examined more closely in the model to verify that the plants were running as efficiently as possible. This report was instrumental in making it possible for the managers to visualize how the summarized results could be used in practice. This one report was key in obtaining a buy-in by management teams and analysts in the organization.

Over the next several months, the IS specialists worked with users and the mathematical programming analyst to develop a prototype of a complete menu system (along with methods for demand management) and useful queries and reports. The analyst continued to gain an understanding of the clay processing steps so that any structural changes made to the Lingo model (e.g., shared processing equipment and capacities) were immediately communicated to the IS specialists.

START OF THE MINING MODEL

The idea of developing a mining model either independently or as part of the POP model was suggested in May 1999. Much brainstorming took place so that the team could conceptualize how to do this. However, modeling of this portion of the operation was not quite clear this early in the project. Thus, it was put on hold, as was modeling of the more complicated plants that soon might be sold.

THE SECOND PLANT:
THE LARGE CALCINE (DRY) PLANT

In June 1999, the team completed the small calcine plant model and started work on the next plant, a calcine (dry) plant. The front-end operation of this plant involved several steps that took clay from crude sheds (where it was piled up after extraction from the mines) and purified it. It then followed a series of initial steps and blends before it went through one of five separate calcine procedures that paralleled the process steps for the small calcine plant. In fact, the small calcine plant was fed from this larger one and functioned as a sixth calcine unit. The complexity of the model increased in that several different clays were fed into the plant to blend into a number of different products, while other clays left to be processed elsewhere. In some cases, clays left to return later in a different form. And some co-products (by-products) of production were recycled back into the system at various stages). All these aspects were handled over time, as the team examined flow sheets and interviewed the plant manager and assistant manager. As the complexity of the processes grew, the team wanted a graphical representation of the entire clay processing operation, which they viewed as a precursor of the LP model. This was relatively easy to develop because the POP model is essentially a network flow problem. It was easier to focus on this picture of the plants than to look at 40 or more clay flow sheets. Many of the clays in a family usually follow a common set of processing steps, but the variations were hard to follow until the graphical representation was created. In some cases, the flow sheets were out of date, but so as soon as updated information was learned, it was added to the graphical model and the DSS model.

In late June, the team met with the mining manager to learn a bit more about mining operations. The plant's operations were modeled, and the model merged with the model of the small plant's operations in mid-July. Testing indicated interesting features about which sets of equipment the model recommended using. Also, some new final clay products and intermediate processing of clays from other plants were identified, which led to a data and model update. The objective at this stage was to incorporate as much as possible about clay production. This portion of the model handled on the order of hundreds of thousands of tons of calcine clay annually.

MODEL DEVELOPMENT CONTINUES—
INFEASIBILITY IS NOT AN OPTION

As the model was validated thus far, the modeling team noticed that occasionally it *went infeasible* when demands in excess of production capacity were needed. When a linear programming model becomes infeasible, few of the solution results are useful to a manager. In fact, normally an analyst must debug the model to determine the cause of the problem. Since the users were managers, not analysts, the model was updated to allow for *feasible infeasibility*. For a penalty cost per ton, the demand for almost any clay could be met from an external source that really did not exist. This set of dummy clay sources supplied the unmet demand. This allowed the model to obtain a solution, put a cost on not meeting demand, and let a manager determine what could be done to correct the situation (perhaps defer some demand) by setting up a new scenario (a what-if case) and running it. This form of multicriteria decision-making has an objective that imposes a cost for not meeting demand targets and another for maximizing net profit. The role of open market purchases was expanded as well.

MODEL DEVELOPMENT CONTINUES—
JUSTICE PREVAILS

Once this portion of the model was running, the Justice Department ruled that the amount of calcine capacity that had to be sold summed up to that of one of the five calcine units and the small calcine plant. The hydrous (wet clay) portion of this plant (which was to be modeled next) was also to be sold. Given this development, the model's demands were adjusted, the capacities of the soon-to-be-sold portions of the plants were zeroed out in the model, and some of the demand was moved to the other plant. The model was restructured to break the demand out of the plant so that any plant could be used to meet the demand if it produced that clay. The ability to restrict demand to a plant remained in the model because some customers prefer this.

THE THIRD PLANT: THE HYDROUS PLANT

Since the hydrous portion of the first major plant that was modeled (the calcine portion) was to be sold, the team skipped creating its model and moved to the complete hydrous plant in the Sandersville area. This plant can produce over 1 million tons of finished clay annually. It is much more complex than the previously modeled calcine plants because six different classes of clay are processed and each follows a different path through the process. Some processes are skipped by some clays. There are several hundred blends that include finished calcine clays (from the second plant) and clays from other plants not yet modeled. Different recipes for crude clays from the mines are used for each clay class, some of the clays have coarse and fine components blended from crude clays, and even different recipes of crude clays and intermediate clays can be used to produce finished products with identical properties. Different chemicals mixed in different blends can also produce clays with identical properties. Each finished clay had a unique flow sheet and a few blends that were recommended. Some had alternative final processing steps.

At the start of the hydrous plant modeling, the team worked out the details for an accurate, integrated mining model. This model portion would prove invaluable by determining which crude clays to mine, and from where, in addition to how to blend and process the clays. The mining model portion required no new modeling structures.

Toward the end of this phase, access to the open market, in terms of purchasing finished clay products, was modeled to give the DSS flexibility in terms of what it recommended—processing or purchasing. This contributed to keeping the solution feasible. Transfer operations were modeled as clays are transported from plant to plant in several stages of processing. Transfers can be by truck, rail, or pipeline.

THE POP DSS IS "FINISHED"

The graphical model made it possible to work through the complex details of the hydrous plant and mines. Through the fall of 1999, the team poured over flow sheets and worked with the plant manager, the mining manager, and several very knowledgeable specialists. In October, the manager of the small calcine plant left the team (her plant was no longer part of the company) and the two IS specialists worked part-time to complete the last of phase 1 of the POP development. Another IS specialist was brought on board as the POP administrator. In early November

1999, the POP system was validated and deployed. It was immediately used to determine which clays were to be substituted for the ones that were becoming depleted at this point in time. It also identified the appropriate substitute equipment to be used when a major piece of equipment was to be down for a major overhaul. POP was used to prepare the next year's production plan and budget. All in all, POP was a dramatic success.

CONCLUSION—NOT!

Two well-known sayings in DSS development circles are: (1) There is no such thing as a finished DSS; and (2) Success breeds success. Successful DSS are continually evolving. Another clay family was added to the POP DSS in late November 1999. In the winter of 2000, we expanded the POP DSS to include another major hydrous plant along with its blends (linking them to products made at the other plants), additional crude clay quality factors, and more access to the open market. More clays were added in 2002, as their production was moved from a plant not in the model to one that was. About every three to six months, the data in POP are refined to reflect reality. And as new equipment is added, as old equipment is removed, and as new final products, blends, and crude clays are added to the plants, POP is updated to represent them.

CASE QUESTIONS

1. Compare the steps (fundamental phases and minor steps) of prototyping described in the chapter to the development approach used for POP. How similar are they?
2. Comment on how prototyping helped the team and the users develop a solid understanding of the processes being modeled.

3. Identify the POP DSS components: the model base, the database, and the user interface.
4. What capabilities of Lingo and Access made the POP DSS a success?
5. Comment on the statements "DSS continuously evolve" and "Success breeds success" in terms of the POP DSS.

COLLABORATION, COMMUNICATION, ENTERPRISE DECISION SUPPORT SYSTEMS, AND KNOWLEDGE MANAGEMENT

LEARNING OBJECTIVES FOR PART III

❖ Understand how the Web enables collaboration and communication

❖ Understand the fundamental principles and capabilities of group support systems

❖ Understand the fundamental principles and capabilities of enterprise information systems, including data warehousing, enterprise resource planning/management systems, and supply chain management

❖ Describe the fundamental principles and capabilities of knowledge management

The DSS concepts outlined in Chapters 1–6 are used by millions of people and thousands of organizations worldwide to successfully support their decision-making. Individuals do not work in a vacuum. Typically, groups of people work together. Very effective computerized methods have evolved to support the complex situations and settings of work groups. Part III describes collaborative computing in several key frameworks: group support systems (Chapter 7), enterprise-wide DSS (Chapter 8), and knowledge management (Chapter 9). These frameworks are more methodologies than DSS classifications.

Group support systems (GSS) were the first true form of collaborative computing in practice. GSS enabled the concept of the *electronic meeting* (*e-meeting*). They are now used routinely by many organizations in asynchronous modes (different times and different places) over the Web for a variety of purposes, including distance learning. Expensive new large-scale, enterprise-wide support systems, enterprise resource planning (ERP), also known as enterprise resource management (ERM) systems, are changing the landscape of modern organizations by bringing many complex business functions together under a single umbrella. And knowledge management, a relatively new form of enterprise-wide collaborative computing, makes any needed knowledge of an organization available in a meaningful form to anyone, anyplace, and anytime. Knowledge management provides an exciting new paradigm with the potential to revolutionize the way we view and use computing. The Internet (World Wide Web) is impacted by and impacts these collaborative computing methodologies. The Internet is the platform that enables collaborative computing: sharing data, information, and knowledge.

CHAPTER 7

COLLABORATIVE COMPUTING TECHNOLOGIES: GROUP SUPPORT SYSTEMS

LEARNING OBJECTIVES

❖ Understand the basic concepts of groupwork, communication, and collaboration

❖ Describe how computers and computer systems enhance communication and collaboration in an enterprise

❖ Explain the underlying principles and capabilities of collaborative computing/group support systems (GSS)

❖ Explain the concepts and importance of the time/place framework

❖ Understand the concepts of process gain, process loss, task gain, and task loss, and explain exactly how GSS introduces, increases, or decreases each of them

❖ Describe specifically how a GSS utilizes parallelism and anonymity, and how they lead to process/task gains/losses

❖ Describe how to structure an electronic meeting

❖ Understand the three technologies of GSS

❖ Understand how the Web enables collaborative computing/group support systems/electronic meetings

❖ Explain how GSS software enables distance learning

❖ Define creativity and how GSS can enhance it.

Groups make most of the complex decisions in organizations. People work together. The increase in organizational decision-making complexity increases the need for meetings and for groupwork. Supporting groupwork where team members may be in different locations and working at different times emphasizes important aspects of communications, computer technologies, and work methodologies. Group support is a critical aspect of this century's decision support systems. Effective computer-supported cooperative work (CSCW) systems have evolved to provide gains (and losses) in task performance and processes. CSCW includes group support systems (GSS), electronic meeting systems, and electronic conferencing systems. Many readers may currently use distance learning, an important form of collaborative computing. Finally, we discuss creativity and how collaborative computing can enhance it. The sections of this chapter are as follows:

7.1 OPENING VIGNETTE: CHRYSLER SCORES WITH GROUPWARE[1]

THE CHRYSLER SCORE PROGRAM

Chrysler Corporation has met the challenge of reducing supply costs while improving suppliers' profitability through its supplier cost-reduction effort (SCORE) initiative. SCORE challenges suppliers in Chrysler's extended enterprise to continuously seek out and identify opportunities to reduce costs. SCORE is Chrysler's way of documenting cost reductions and quality enhancements in a variety of areas, including design, manufacturing, logistics, sourcing, and administrative transactions.

The cost-cutting program was originally paper-based. It began in 1989 when Chrysler took the unprecedented step of offering its suppliers a cut of whatever cost savings they could achieve. In 1994 Chrysler moved the program online. Three years after going online, Chrysler went from an overall net loss of $2.6 billion to a net gain of $3.5 billion in 1996. The SCORE program, a precursor of electronic commerce, has had a remarkable return on investment.

Chrysler pursues efficiency, quality, and affordability while enhancing its suppliers' profit margins. Chrysler works with its suppliers as partners, not adversaries, with the goal of finding ways to improve efficiency and mutually reduce costs. A supplier's incentive is significant; it can be half of the total savings. In a recent independent report, automotive suppliers ranked Chrysler number one in terms of their business relationships with them. The feeling is mutual. In 1997 Chrysler presented 13 of its suppliers with its highest honor, the Platinum Pentastar Award for outstanding overall

---

[1]Adapted from J. L. Hartley, B. M. Greer, and S. Park, "Chrysler Leverages Its Suppliers' Improvement Suggestions." *Interfaces*, Vol. 32, No. 4, July/August 2002, pp. 20–27; D. Walker, "Supply Chain Collaboration Saves Chrysler $2.5 Billion and Counting," *Automatic I.D. News*, Vol. 14, No. 9, August 1998, p. 60; J. Fontana, "Chrysler's $2B Score," *InternetWeek*, March 9, 1998, pp. 1, 90; J. Fontana, "Chrysler Saves Big Online," *CommunicationsWeek*, April 28, 1997, pp. 1, 84–85; J. T. Landry, "Supply Chain Management: The Case for Alliances," *Harvard Business Review*, Vol. 76, No. 6, November/December 1998, pp. 24–25; Konicki (2002a, 2002b); K. M. Carrillo, "Tools Address Different Ends of the Supply Chain," *InformationWeek*, No. 699, September 7, 1998, p. 26; also see Covisint, covisint.com, 2003; and Lotus Development Corporation, lotus.com, 2003.

performance. Chrysler wants to be its suppliers' best customer because the best customers always get the best service.

THE SCORE SYSTEM

In 1989 paper-based SCORE business processes were developed and deployed. The goal was to identify waste in the value chain and eliminate it. The paper-based system was moderately successful. To enhance communication and collaboration and speed up the process, Chrysler moved from a paper-based system to a groupware environment.

The business process was already in place, and by 1994 appropriate technology had evolved to support it. The first online SCORE was a single, pure Lotus Notes application database with hundreds of Notes clients. Suppliers had access to the Chrysler SCORE system via the Internet or via a modem. They used an online Notes form in which they described the cost savings. With a push of a button, this cost savings/quality improvement proposal was submitted to Chrysler. The information about a proposed savings is collected, reviewed by a buyer, and if it has merit, is sent to all team members (finance, purchasing, engineering), who then collaborate on it. About 70 percent of all suggestions have been adopted. The second-generation online system, SCORE2, supported automated procurement functions and e-mail. SCORE2 also contained user profiles, system intelligence enablers, database reports, and bilingual support. SCORE2 involved reengineering the successful business process for smoother operation.

By 1998 SCORE had become a company standard for dealing with suppliers, adding all procurement to the previous focus on goods used only in the production of automobiles. With the latest release, SCORE3, there were 1,000 suppliers online. The Web-based SCORE3 allows users to access the program through Covisint (covisint. com), an *extranet* that is a collaborative effort among the major U.S. automakers and hundreds of their suppliers. Covisint became operational in 1998, and Chrysler required its top three tiers of suppliers to connect to it by mid-1999.

SCORE BENEFITS

Chrysler's benefits are enhanced relationships with suppliers and better-quality purchasing practices, which yield a better-quality product. SCORE lets Chrysler use its suppliers' expertise to become a better company. The initiative has yielded substantial dollar savings: $2.5 billion through 1998, including more than $1 billion in 1997 and $1.2 billion in 1998. The benefits to suppliers include identifying quality methods and reaping identical cost benefits from shared cost savings. The main benefit to customers is simple and obvious: a higher-quality product at an equal or lower price.

In 2000, Chrysler saved $2 billion, and *all* of its suppliers were online.

COMMENTS

Paul Lawrence, at the Harvard Business School, and Ranjay Gulati, at Northwestern University, studied the supply relationships at two of the largest U.S. manufacturers, Chrysler and Ford. They interviewed executives and surveyed the purchasing experts for each of the major components of an automobile.

Their work indicates that to build more flexible and efficient supply chains, manufacturers need to forge close, long-term ties with their suppliers. They need to work together to refine products and components, respond to shifts in demand, and unclog bottlenecks, while sharing sensitive information. High-trust relationships can be achieved through alliances with outside suppliers—if both sides take certain steps to foster a collaborative environment.

"Manufacturers often get the best of two worlds when they form strong supplier alliances," says Gulati. "They get to work with independent, flexible companies able to specialize in a given component, and they also achieve the close integration thought to be possible only with in-house divisions." Building a high-trust alliance requires a great deal of time and effort. "For managers willing to invest in relationships," comments Lawrence, "the real choice is not the old 'make versus buy' but 'make, buy, or ally.' "

Chrysler's extended enterprise system demonstrates that managing a company's supply chain is just as important as managing its plants or distribution system. If it is done well in collaboration with its suppliers, the company gains a major strategic advantage over its competitors.

Chrysler's SCORE system has become a showcase example of the Lotus groupware platform. "It clearly is one of the best quantifications of value the industry has seen this starkly," says Jeff Papows, president and CEO at Lotus.

"Chrysler is giving us a sense of what's to come when you combine groupware, standards and interenterprise communication," comments Gary Rowe, a principal with Rapport Communication. "This is the value of having organizations invest in that type of infrastructure."

According to Tom Stallkamp, executive vice president of procurement and supply, "What we're doing is pursuing efficiency, quality and affordability without eroding our suppliers' profit margin."

"I've never had negative feedback from a supplier about SCORE. They all love it," says Bernie Bedard, manager of the supplier continuous improvement team, "It's basically a win-win, a way to work together in partnership and demonstrate that you're committed to see them grow as well as see Chrysler grow."

Four elements in Chrysler and its suppliers' organizations that clearly were observed to contribute to SCORE's success were: (1) a process champion, (2) suppliers in the process, (3) employees, and (4) evaluation and implementation. Companies designing such a supplier-suggestion process should definitely consider ways to reduce delays during evaluation, minimize the number of low-value suggestions, and involve the entire supply chain.

❖ QUESTIONS FOR THE OPENING VIGNETTE

1. What prompted Chrysler to investigate development of a collaborative business process with its suppliers?

2. Explain how the supply chain works and how Chrysler uses technology to enhance communication between itself and suppliers within the supply chain construct.

3. Explain why Chrysler migrated from a paper application to a groupware application.

4. Describe the collaboration that SCORE allows between the suppliers and the company, and within the company.

5. Describe the benefits for suppliers and for Chrysler.

6. How would you improve on SCORE?

7. Check the literature and the Web to see how SCORE has evolved since this opening vignette was written. What additional features does it have? What are the annual savings?

7.2 GROUP DECISION-MAKING, COMMUNICATION, AND COLLABORATION

The Opening Vignette illustrates how computerized support can be provided to people who work effectively in groups for the benefit of their organizations. The SCORE system involves collaboration between groups at Chrysler and their vendors and also between groups within Chrysler. Other firms are using this model successfully. For example, Johnson Controls has cut production costs by $20 million with a collaboration portal that integrates supplier applications (see Hall, 2002). The London insurance market, through collaboration, has cut office costs by 10 percent, and paper processes by over 30 percent; Timex has cut production-development cycles by up to 40 percent (Konzer, 2002); and Lockheed Martin won a $19 billion contract on the basis of its collaboration capabilities (Konicki, 2001). People make decisions, they design and manufacture products, they develop policies and strategies, they design software, and so on. They collaborate and communicate—people perform **groupwork**. Some characteristics of groupwork are listed below:

- A group performs a task, sometimes decision-making, sometimes not.
- Group members may be located in different places.
- Group members may work at different times.
- Group members may work for the same or for different organizations.
- The group can be permanent or temporary.
- The group can be at any managerial level or can span levels.
- There can be synergy (process and task gains) or conflict in groupwork.
- There can be gains and/or losses in productivity from groupwork.
- The task may have to be accomplished very quickly.
- It may be impossible or too expensive for all the team members to meet in one place.
- Some of the needed data, information, or knowledge may be located in many sources, several of which are external to the organization.
- The expertise of non–team members may be needed.

When people work in teams, especially when the members are in different locations and may be working at different times, they need to communicate, collaborate, and access a diverse set of information sources in multiple formats.

For groups to collaborate effectively, appropriate communication methods and technologies are needed. The Internet and its derivatives, intranets and extranets, are the platforms on which most communications for collaboration occur. The **Internet (World Wide Web** or **Web)**, a network of computer networks, supports interorganizational decision-making through collaboration tools and access to data, information, and knowledge from inside and outside the organization. Intraorganizational networked decision support can be effectively supported by an **intranet**, basically an internal Internet. People within an organization can work with Internet tools and procedures through enterprise information portals. Specific applications can include important internal documents and procedures, corporate address lists, e-mail, tool access, and software distribution. An intranet operates safely behind a company's **firewall**, which typically isolates it from inappropriate external access. A good example of an intranet application is the Osram Sylvania HR InfoNet (a portal) described in the Chapter 6 Opening Vignette. An **extranet** links a work group, functioning like an intranet for group members from several different organizations. Several automobile manufacturers have involved their suppliers and dealers in extranets to help them deal with customer complaints about their products. Other extranets are used to link teams together to design products, where several different suppliers must collaborate on design and manufacturing techniques. And extranets like the Covisint are used by entire industries to link companies and suppliers (see the Opening Vignette; Kemp, 2001).

There have been many advances in Web-based collaborative design, as is described in the opening vignette. New tools are continually under development (see Anthes, 2000). Autodesk's Architectural Studio and CoCreate's OneSpace allow several designers to work simultaneously. Most major auto manufacturers are moving in this direction because it substantially reduces the cost and time of bringing new models to market (see Konicki, 2002b, Gladwin, 2001). This market should be worth well over $100 billion by 2007 (see Konicki, 2002a, 2000b). For details on how GSS can enhance systems analysis and design, see Lowry and Wilson (2000), and Maybury (2001).

Even in hierarchical organizations, decision-making is usually a shared process. A group may be involved in a decision or in a decision-related task, such as creating a short list of acceptable alternatives or choosing criteria for evaluating an alternative. The following activities and processes characterize meetings:

- A meeting is a joint activity engaged in by a group of people typically of equal or near-equal status.
- The outcome of the meeting depends partly on the knowledge, opinions, and judgments of its participants.
- The outcome of the meeting also depends on the composition of the group and on the decision-making process used by the group.
- Differences in opinion are settled either by the ranking person present or, more often, by negotiation or arbitration.

Many computerized tools have been developed to provide group support. These tools are called **groupware** because their primary objective is to support groupwork. The work itself may be known as **computer-supported cooperative work (CSCW)**. (The literature uses the word *cooperative*, and we adhere to it, though *collaborative* might be a more accurate term. For example, consider two or more groups involved in negotiations.) Groupware tools can be readily found via a Web search. Some notable ones include GroupSystems OnLine and MeetingRoom, Groove, NetMeeting, WebEx, and PlaceWare. Some e-mail, chatroom, and instant messenger software exhibit groupware features.

Telecommuting, teleconferencing, supply chain management, and electronic commerce are *all* enabled through communication and collaboration technologies. It is almost impossible to be away from the office (home, dormitory, etc.) and not be connected. Distance learning is a fast-developing area of **collaborative computing**. And groupware can enhance creativity in the decision-making process.

Groups and groupwork (teams and teamwork) in organizations are proliferating. Consequently, groupware continues to evolve to support effective groupwork. For examples of effective groupware use in industry, see McGee and Murphy (2001), who describe the leading innovators in collaboration.

7.3 COMMUNICATION SUPPORT

Communication is a vital element for decision support. *Without communication, there is no collaboration.* Individual decision-makers must communicate with colleagues, experts, government agencies, customers, vendors, business partners, and other interested parties. They also need data and information (and *knowledge*) from many locations around the globe. Groups of decision-makers must communicate, collaborate, and negotiate in their work. Most organizations would quickly become nonfunctional without their communication systems. Virtual teams, especially those performing design work, require fast communication technology for success in their efforts (see Chapter 6). Effective e-commerce is possible only via modern Web-based communication technologies.

Modern information technologies, especially via the Web, provide *inexpensive, fast, capable, reliable* means of supporting communications. (See DSS in Focus 7.1 for some unsupported aspects of communication.) Networked computer systems, like the Internet, intranets, and extranets, are the enabling platforms that support communication. Historically, these systems began with the telegraph, the telephone, radio, and television. Technologies that followed built upon them. Within about 100 years, we have developed fax machines, electronic mail (e-mail), chat programs, newsgroups, listservs (electronic mailing lists), electronic bulletin boards, and inexpensive, effective desktop videoconferencing systems (see DSS in Action 7.2, and Donston (2002) for effective uses and the benefits of videoconferencing). The use of desktop videoconferencing systems has grown dramatically in the wake of the events of September 11, 2001 (see Cope, 2002; Goodridge, 2001b). Even three-dimensional television systems have entered the market (Connolly, 2001). Most of these technologies operate on the Web/Internet. Because they are so widely used in modern enterprises and even at home, we will not discuss the details here. We next turn to collaborative technologies that include the latest communication developments of **electronic meeting systems (EMS)** and electronic conferencing systems and services, generally using the Internet for connecting decision-makers.

As Davids (1999) comments in reference to videoconferencing, the following advantages apply to all improved communications methods in organizations: (1) improving employee productivity, (2) involving more people in key decision-making, (3) blurring geographic boundaries, (4) creating a consistent corporate culture, and (5) improving employees' quality of life.

Communication may be considered a social matter in which negotiating differences in understanding among and between communicators is a primary business priority. It is important to understand how individuals interact in the decision-making process. Smoliar and Sprague (2002) consider communication along three dimensions—meaning, authority, and trust—based on the work of Anthony Giddens. These notions may soon open up a rich understanding of how we communicate when working together.

COMMUNICATION PROBLEMS

Communication can be problematic in general, but computerized communication methods do not transmit most of our nonverbal cues, which are important in establishing the richer meaning of a message by adding context. A large part of what we mean (perhaps exceeding 50 percent) is conveyed via nonverbal cues. Facial expressions, body language, voice tone, expression, inflection, touching, and distance are but a few. (For example, it is possible to accurately determine who will win a U.S. presidential election by measuring the average rate of each candidate's eye blinking. The one who blinks the least has won every election from the Kennedy–Nixon contest in 1960 through 2000. Jay Aronson used this method in the third debate of the 2000 election to predict the winner accurately.) There are cross-cultural aspects and language subtleties that are not easily transmitted through computer-mediated communication channels.

Emoticons were a first attempt to include nonverbal cues in text-based e-mail. For example, in the emoticon system, the characters :) are a happy face called a "smiley," and writing your message in all capital letters means you are SHOUTING! These have been updated into icons in instant messenger software.

Some aspects of communication, such as the frequency of touching and the interpersonal distance between participants, are difficult to capture through technology. However, video technology can show facial expressions and some body language. Researchers are attempting to develop collaborative systems that capture more of this imprecise nature of human communication that makes the meaning of the message received more precise. They are also developing output devices, like robot faces that can reflect mood, to do the same (e.g., see Dan Ferber, "The Man Who Mistook His Girlfriend for a Robot," *Popular Science,* September 2003; available at www.popsci .com/popsci/archives, search on "face").

VIDEOCONFERENCING IS READY FOR PRIME TIME

Videoconferencing technology can cut travel expenses and increase a company's productivity. Dan Denardo, manager of global videoconferencing at Dow Chemical Company (an $18 billion per year firm), says that videoconferencing vastly improves customer service and helps Dow deliver products to the market faster. "We know it can decrease cycle time, since we can hold more meetings in the same amount of time," Denardo says. Dow has about 160 video cameras at its headquarters in Midland, Michigan, and has achieved an estimated annual travel cost savings of more than $7 million. At Dow, the technology is advancing from in-house conference rooms to customer sites. "It is fairly cheap hardware, the customers really like it and it sets us apart," Denardo comments. By July 1999, Dow had linked six customers.

Quantum Corporation (a $4.9 billion per year storage vendor) saves about $500,000 per month in travel expenses, lost time, and productivity, according to Albert Villarde, a network analyst. Quantum has over 20 video-equipped conference rooms around the globe. The primary business advantage is the speed-up in information sharing.

Estimates vary, but Pat Conway, product marketing manager at videoconferencing vendor VTEL Corporation, estimates that videoconferencing should reduce a firm's travel budget by about 15 percent. The most significant savings come from the increased speed of information delivery because of more frequent, impromptu meetings.

Technology varies from PC desktop video to stand-alone conference rooms. Most companies use DSL or cable television Internet connections, or ISDN lines because of the higher bandwidth. Videoconferencing is an economical way to cut travel costs and boost productivity. Since September 11, 2001, these technologies have become critical, because air travel is not as convenient as previously.

Source: Partly adapted from L. Wood, "Videoconferencing Shows It's Ready for Prime Time," *InternetWeek,* July 12, 1999, p. 26.

7.4 COLLABORATION SUPPORT: COMPUTER-SUPPORTED COOPERATIVE WORK

In modern organizations, people collaborate. Groups make most major decisions in organizations. Solving complex problems requires that people work together, necessitating the formation of workgroups.

Communication primarily transmits information from a sender to a receiver, but collaboration is much deeper. Collaboration conveys meaning or knowledge among group members. Material is actively worked on during collaboration. Collaboration includes sharing documents, information, and knowledge, as well as such activities as brainstorming and voting. Collaboration implies people actively *working together* and requires collaborative computing support tools that build on communication methods. Computer-supported cooperative work (CSCW) systems are known as group support systems (GSS) or groupware. They include electronic meeting systems and electronic conferencing systems.

TIME/PLACE FRAMEWORK

The effectiveness of a collaborative computing technology depends on the location of the group members and on the time that shared information is sent and received. A framework for classifying IT communication support technologies was proposed by DeSanctis and Gallupe (1985, 1987). Communication is divided into four cells, which are shown together with representative computerized support technologies in Figure 7.1. The four cells are organized along the two dimensions of *time* and *place*.

FIGURE 7.1   TIME/PLACE COMMUNICATION FRAMEWORK AND SOME COLLABORATIVE COMPUTING SUPPORT TECHNOLOGIES

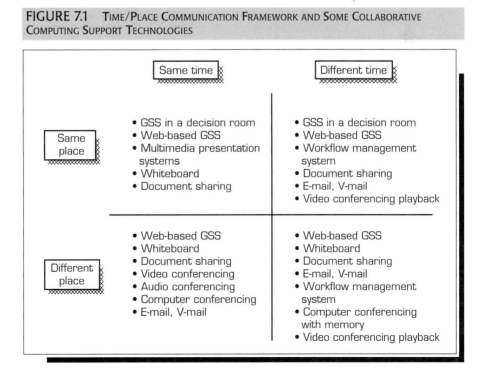

- *Time.* When information is sent and received almost simultaneously, the communication is **synchronous**. Telephones, televisions, and face-to-face meetings are examples. **Asynchronous** communication occurs when the receiver receives the information at a different time than it was sent.
- *Place.* The senders and the receivers can be in the same room or not.

The four cells of the framework are as follows:

- *Same time/same place.* Participants meet face-to-face in one place at the same time, as in a traditional meeting or decision room. This is still an important way to meet, even when Web-based, because it is sometimes critical for participants to leave the office to eliminate distractions (if so, turn off your cell telephone ringer).
- *Same time/same place.* Participants are in different places, but they communicate at the same time, for example, with videoconferencing.
- *Same time/same place.* People work in shifts. One shift leaves information for the next shift.
- *Same time/same place.* Participants are in different places. They send and receive information at different times. This occurs when team members are traveling, have conflicting schedules, or work in different time zones. Meetings such as these require some special handling. For example, when brainstorming, it is important not to barrage group members who enter the meeting later with all the ideas that have been generated. That makes them feel excluded. The previously generated ideas should be fed slowly to them.

GROUPWARE

The term *groupware* refers to software products that provide collaborative support to groups. Groupware provides a mechanism for teams to share opinions, data, information, knowledge, and other resources. Different collaborative computing technologies support groupwork in different ways, depending on the time/place category in which the work occurs, the purpose of the group, and the task. New tools are evolving to support *anytime/anyplace* meetings.

There are thousands of packages that contain some elements of groupware. Some have only rudimentary collaboration capabilities (e.g., voting; see DSS in Action 7.3), whereas others provide support for every aspect of collaboration (full **electronic meetings** with videoconferencing). Almost all utilize Internet technology for the consistent Web browser-style user interface and communication protocols.

Groupware typically contains capabilities for at least one of the following: **electronic brainstorming**, electronic conferencing or meeting, group scheduling, calendaring, planning, conflict resolution, model building, videoconferencing, electronic document sharing (e.g., screen sharing, whiteboards, or liveboards), voting, organizational memory. There are electronic meeting services like WebEx Meeting Center (webex.com), PlaceWare Conference Center (placeware.com), and MCI Conferencing (e-meetings.mci.com), where anyone can hold a meeting for a fee. Some groupware, such as Lotus Notes/Domino (lotus.com), Microsoft NetMeeting (microsoft.com), Groove (groove.net), and GroupSystems OnLine (groupsystems. com), support a fairly comprehensive range of activities. Each vendor provides success stories about its GSS product or service, as well as demos, trial versions, or video presentations on its Web site. We next briefly describe some popular groupware systems.

LOTUS NOTES/DOMINO

Lotus Notes/Domino was the first widely used groupware. Lotus Notes/Domino enables collaboration by letting users access and create shared information through

DSS IN ACTION 7.3

INTERNET VOTING

Collaborative technologies that include voting mechanisms operating over the Internet have enhanced groupwork. Voting for public office may be the ultimate form of groupware use. A hot topic in the United States in early 2000 was whether or when states will permit public elections over the Internet. Texas was the first state to permit voting over the Internet, but it was tightly regulated. The resident had to be in orbit in the space shuttle. In 2000 Alaska permitted straw polling via the Internet for residents living in isolated regions. Straw polling is a formal part of the Alaska presidential primary process. The state of Washington allowed any registered voter to use the Internet in the 2000 presidential primary. California and Arizona also tested Intenet voting. There are problems with anonymity and with voter validation, but they seem to be no worse than paper-based polling practices (such as those known to have occurred in Chicago some years ago). Internet voting can cut costs on mailing and processing paper ballots, as well as reduce human error in counting. After the problems of the 2000 U.S. presidential election, several states adopted electronic voting machines which effectively utilize Web-based technology at polling places. Georgia deployed them in the next state and local election, and eventually will move to Web polling. In 2000, several states were investigating how to establish accurate Web-based polling. For more on online voting, see Harrison (2000) and Tillett (2000).

specially programmed Notes documents. For example, Chrysler's SCORE system in the Opening Vignette and the Osram Sylvania HR InfoNet enterprise portal in the Chapter 6 Opening Vignette were programmed in Lotus Notes/Domino. Notes provides online collaboration capabilities through Web Conferencing on Demand, workgroup e-mail, distributed databases, bulletin whiteboards, text editing, (electronic) document management, workflow capabilities, consensus building, voting, ranking, and various application development tools, all integrated into one environment with a graphical menu-based user interface. Notes fosters a virtual corporation and creates interorganizational alliances. Though increased competition is cutting into its market share, there are millions of Notes users in thousands of organizations. Many applications have been programmed directly in Lotus Notes. This includes Learning Space, a **courseware** package that supports distance learning.

MICROSOFT NETMEETING

Microsoft NetMeeting is a real-time collaboration package that includes whiteboarding (relatively free-form graphics to which all participants can contribute simultaneously), application sharing (any Microsoft Windows application document), remote desktop sharing, file transfer, text chat, data conferencing, and desktop audio- and videoconferencing. This application sharing is a vast improvement over what was simply called *whiteboarding* a decade ago. The NetMeeting client is included in the Windows operating system. See DSS in Action 7.4 for an example of the successful use of NetMeeting. Also see the NetMeeting in Action stories at microsoft.com.

GROOVE

Groove Workspace is the Groove end-user application for secure discussions, file-sharing, projects, and meetings. Used alone or with Groove Enterprise Servers and Hosted Services, Groove Workspace enables spontaneous, online-offline collaboration that reduces project costs and speeds time-to-market for products and services. The Groove Outliner tool is an open-ended brainstorming tool that allows shared space members to build structured hierarchical lists. The Groove peer-collaboration platform works

---

NETMEETING PROVIDES A REAL-TIME ADVANTAGE

Jack O'Donnell is CEO of O'Donnell & Partners, a corporate interior contracting firm in Manhattan with branch offices in Chicago, London, and Milan. Until recently, O'Donnell felt the need to be on-site when any project was in its crucial stages. "Phone calls weren't enough, nor was e-mail—especially when you're dealing with a team of architects, designers, and contractors who speak different languages and all have their own professional jargon," he says. "Add to that the need for working on plans, sketches, and blueprints together at meetings, and my partners and I found we were spending most of our time at airports."

Microsoft NetMeeting provides collaborative computing support for groupwork, including application sharing through its Remote Desktop Sharing feature. It also provides real-time video. Now O'Donnell and his team members meet online. "Everyone can prepare a presentation that shows and doesn't just tell the progress of their part of the project," says O'Donnell. "We can work on files together, as if we were sitting across from each other at a conference table. And we can see each other's expressions, so it feels more like a real meeting." (See DSS in Focus 7.2.)

O'Donnell estimates that Web conferencing saved his company at least a half-million dollars in travel costs in 1999. And that did not include the benefit of having fewer people out sick with whatever virus they picked up on their last plane trip.

Source: Adapted from M. Delio, "Power Meetings in Cyberspace, *Knowledge Management*, Vol. 2, No. 12, Dec. 1999, pp. 77–78.

---

across corporate firewalls and requires no special configuration or IT administration (see groove.net). A very functional demo version is available for download (no video-conferencing). Though it takes a while to structure a first meeting and download all files to users, it is definitely an inexpensive, useful, peer-to-peer package. A screenshot of a Groove Outliner session is shown in Figure 7.2.

GROUPSYSTEMS MEETINGROOM AND ONLINE

GroupSystems MeetingRoom and OnLine (groupsystems.com) was one of the first comprehensive same time/same place electronic meeting packages and set the pace for the industry. GroupSystems OnLine (originally called Groupsystems) runs in asynchronous mode (anytime/anyplace) over the Web, while MeetingRoom runs over a local area network. GroupSystems OnLine was a response to the needs of the marketplace, and was used in many academic studies to establish needed tools and how they should operate. These packages set the pace for the rest of the marketplace; their capabilities are described in a later section.

WEBEX MEETING CENTER AND PLACEWARE CONFERENCE CENTER

WebEx Meeting Center (WebEx.com) is pay-per-use groupware. It provides a low-cost, simplified way to hold electronic meetings over the Web. Meeting time and space are rented and accessed over the Web. WebEx contains all the features you need to run a meeting. WebEx Meeting Center integrates data, voice, and video within a standard Web browser for real-time meetings over the Internet from any desktop, laptop, or wireless handheld device. WebEx contains all the tools needed to share documents or opinions. WebEx Meeting Center is a fully hosted solution, initiating online meetings that require no IT staff involvement, and has very low start-up costs. The WebEx

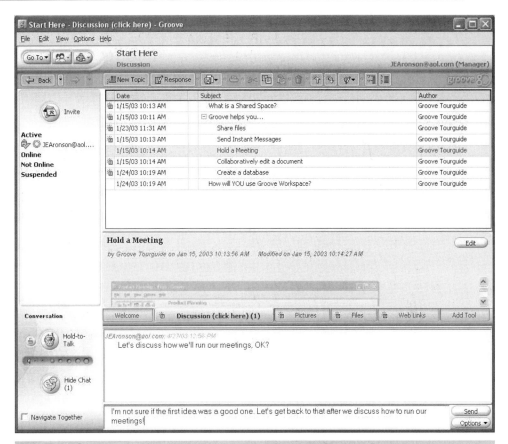

FIGURE 7.2   EXAMPLE OF ELECTRONIC BRAINSTORMING IN THE GROOVE WORKSPACE

The participant types his/her ideas in the small box at the bottom. Then, he/she clicks the send button. The idea is then added to the threaded discussion and appears above the box.

MediaTone Network provides fast communication for videoconferencing. The PlaceWare Conference Center (placeware.com) provides essentially the same services, along with the Placeware Virtual Classroom, a distance learning environment.

REMARKS

Successful **enterprise-wide collaboration systems** like Lotus Notes/Domino can be expensive to develop and operate. To obtain the full benefits of such groupware, a well-trained, full-time support staff is required to develop applications and operate the system. On the other hand, Groove is relatively cheap and provides easy to use and set up collaboration for an organization.

Industry reports estimate that all forms of groupware (audio-conferencing, video-conferencing, data conferencing, Web-based conferencing, etc.) have become a more established part of the corporate decision-making process. In 2001, the total collaboration market totaled $4.4 billion, up 20 percent over the previous year. By 2005, spending should reach about $8.8 billion. This growth is driven by time and money savings through less travel, and by organizational decentralization and globalization. See Anonymous (2002d).

7.5 GROUP SUPPORT SYSTEMS

Most groupwork takes place in meetings. Despite the many criticisms of the effectiveness and efficiency of meetings, people still get together in groups to discuss issues and to work. Meetings can be effective despite the fact that up to 80 percent of what is discussed in a meeting is either forgotten or remembered incorrectly.[2] See DSS in Focus 7.5 for a description of what does and does not work in meetings. 3M Corporation's 3M Meeting Network (www.3m.com/meetingnetwork/) and technography.com have information, surveys, and tips about how to run more effective meetings. The goal of groupware, as it was specifically developed as group support systems (GSS), is to support the work of groups throughout every work activity—including meetings.

Despite the inefficiency of meetings, groupwork can and does provide some benefits, and some dysfunctions. In DSS in Focus 7.6, we identify a set of potential benefits, or **process gains**, of collaborative work. Even so, collaborative work can often be plagued with dysfunctions called **process losses** (see DSS in Focus 7.7).

The goal of GSS is to increase some of the benefits of collaboration and eliminate or reduce some of the losses. Researchers have developed methods for improving the *processes* of groupwork, and some of these methods are group dynamics. Two representative methods are the **nominal group technique (NGT)** and the **Delphi method**. These methods are manual approaches to supporting groupwork. See Lindstone and Turroff (1975) and the Web Chapter on these topics for details.

The limited success of such methods as NGT and the Delphi method led to attempts to use information technology to support group meetings. The major technology is called a **group support system (GSS)**. At the start of the 1990s, this term was coined to replace *group decision support system* (GDSS) because researchers recognized that collaborative computing technologies were doing more than supporting decision-making.

A group support system (GSS) is any combination of hardware and software that enhances groupwork. GSS is a generic term that includes all forms of collaborative computing. GSS evolved after information technology researchers recognized that technology could be developed to support the many activities normally occurring at face-to-face meetings (idea generation, consensus building, anonymous ranking, voting, etc.).

A complete GSS is still considered a specially designed information system, but since the mid-1990s many of the special capabilities of GSS have been embedded in productivity tools. For example, Microsoft NetMeeting Client is part of Windows. Most GSS are easy to use because they have a Windows GUI or a Web browser interface. Most GSS are fairly general and provide support for activities like idea generation, conflict resolution, and voting.

An **electronic meeting system (EMS)** is a form of groupware that supports anytime/anyplace meetings. Group tasks include, but are not limited to, communication, planning, idea generation, problem-solving, issue discussion, negotiation, conflict resolution, system analysis and design, and collaborative group activities such as document preparation and sharing (Dennis et al., 1988, p. 593). Typically EMS include desktop videoconferencing, whereas in the past GSS did not. However, there is a blurring between these two concepts, so today they should be considered synonymous.

GSS settings range from a group meeting at a single location for solving a specific problem (e.g., building design; see DSS in Action 7.4) to multiple locations held via

---

[2]This makes one wonder about the effectiveness of the traditional classroom setting.

DSS IN FOCUS 7.5

THE SEVEN SINS OF DEADLY MEETINGS AND SEVEN STEPS TO SALVATION

Since meetings can be ineffective, unproductive, and unending (to say the least), it helps to understand what can go wrong and what can go right. Bad meetings can be a source of negative messages about an organization and its members. Because more work is becoming groupwork, the number of meetings will likely increase. There are a variety of tools and techniques that, along with common sense, can make meetings less painful, more productive, and maybe even fun. The following is a summary of the "seven sins" of deadly meetings and seven approaches to making meetings more productive.

Sin 1: People don't take meetings seriously. They arrive late, leave early, and spend most of their time doodling.

Salvation: Adopt a mind-set that meetings are real work. Disciplined meetings are about mind-set—a shared conviction among all the participants that meetings are real work.

Sin 2: Meetings are too long. They should accomplish twice as much in half the time.

Salvation: Time is money. Track the cost of meetings and use computer-enabled simultaneity to make them more productive. Meetings should last no longer than 90 minutes. Often people don't appreciate how expensive meetings really are. Bernard DeKoven (Technography.com, Katy, Texas) developed the Meeting Meter. It is a taxi-like meter that tallies the meeting's total cost (excluding travel time and illness; a Web search will identify several that run directly on the Web). One quick look at the numbers, and it's back to work, quickly. Groupware can provide parallelism, especially in brainstorming, cutting meeting time down.

Sin 3: People wander off the topic. Participants spend more time digressing than discussing.

Salvation: Get serious about agendas and store distractions in a "parking lot." Make sure you have an agenda. This involves *planning the meeting*.

Sin 4: Nothing happens once the meeting ends. People don't convert decisions to action.

Salvation: Convert from "meeting" to "doing," and focus on common documents. When people leave meetings, they may or may not remember what happened or what is supposed to happen next. The capacity for misunderstanding is unlimited. Group memory is needed. Shared documents must be created. This is the most powerful role for technology: people should leave with real-time minutes.

Sin 5: People don't tell the truth. There's plenty of conversation but not much candor.

Salvation: Embrace anonymity. People may not feel secure enough to say what they really think. GSS that provide anonymity can help.

Sin 6: Meetings are always missing important information, and so they postpone critical decisions.

Salvation: Get data, not just furniture, into meeting rooms. Again, GSS can help in providing a means for capturing and maintaining data.

Sin 7: Meetings never get better. People make the same mistakes over and over again.

Salvation: Practice makes perfect. Monitor what works and what doesn't, and hold people accountable. At Charles Schwab & Company, someone serves as an "observer" and creates a Plus/Delta list for virtually every meeting. This list records what went right and what went wrong, and it becomes part of the minutes. Over time, both for specific meeting groups and for the company as a whole, these lists create an agenda for change. These lists form an *organizational memory*.

How much can meetings improve? Bernard DeKoven says, "People don't have good meetings because they don't know what good meetings are like. Good meetings aren't just about work. They're about fun—keeping people charged up. It's more than collaboration, it's 'coliberation'—people freeing each other up to think more creatively."

Source: Adapted from E. Matson, "The Seven Sins of Deadly Meetings," *Fast Company*, No. 2, April 1996, p. 122.

telecommunication channels for the purpose of considering a variety of problems (e.g., a class over distance learning; see the WELCOM Web Chapter, and the situation faced by rocket engine designers at Boeing-Rocketdyne, described by Malhotra et al. (2001). Also see Burke (2002). Using effective new collaboration methods that continue to evolve, GSS can operate in asynchronous mode (different times).

SOME BENEFITS OF GROUPWORK (PROCESS GAINS)

- It provides *learning*. Groups are better than individuals at understanding problems.
- People readily take ownership of problems and their solutions. They take responsibility.
- Group members have their egos embedded in the decision, and so they will be committed to the solution.
- Groups are better than individuals at catching errors.
- A group has more *information* (knowledge) than any one member. Groups can combine this knowledge to create new knowledge. More and more creative alternatives for problem-solving can be generated, and better solutions can be derived (through *stimulation*).
- A group may produce *synergy* during problem-solving.
- Working in a group may stimulate the creativity of the participants and the process.
- A group may have better and more precise communication working together.
- Risk propensity is balanced. Groups moderate high-risk takers and encourage conservatives.

GSS can be considered in terms of the common group activities that can benefit from computer-based support: *information retrieval*, including access of data values from an existing database and retrieval of information from other group members; *information sharing*, the display of data for the whole group on a common screen or at group members' workstations for viewing; and *information use*, the application of software technology (e.g., modeling packages or specific application programs; see DSS in Focus 7.8; Andrienko et al., 2002; Dias and Climaco, 2002), procedures, and group problem-solving techniques for reaching a group decision. Creativity in problem-solving can be enhanced via GSS (discussed later in this chapter).

The goal of GSS is to provide support to meeting participants to improve the productivity and effectiveness of meetings by speeding up the decision-making process (efficiency) or by improving the quality of the results (effectiveness). GSS attempts to increase process and task gains and decrease process and task losses (see Reinig and Shin, 2002). Specific GSS process gains are listed in DSS in Focus 7.9. Overall, GSS has been successful in practice (see Holt, 2002); however, some process and task gains may decrease, while some process and task losses may increase.

Improvement is achieved by providing support to group members for the exchange of ideas, opinions, and preferences. Specific features such as **parallelism** and **anonymity** produce this improvement. Many experiments, field studies, and surveys have been done to determine the effectiveness of GSS (e.g., Fjermestad, 2000/2001; Fjermestad and Hiltz, 1998; Dennis, Wixom, and Vandenberg, 2001). After a few decades of GSS experience, it is clear that GSS is a winner. Saved travel time (especially when using the Web) and parallelism have led to decreased costs, while anonymity leads to the generation of more ideas and more creative ideas. For examples, see Case Application 7.1, the WELCOM Web Chapter, DSS in Action 7.10, and the success stories on GSS vendor Web sites, where collaborative computing led to dramatic speed-ups in process and cost savings.

DSS IN FOCUS 7.7

POTENTIAL DYSFUNCTIONS OF GROUPWORK (PROCESS LOSSES)

- Social pressures of conformity may result in **groupthink** (people begin to think alike and not tolerate new ideas—yielding to *conformance pressure*).

- It is a time-consuming, slow process (only one member can speak at a time).

- Lack of coordination of the meeting work and poor meeting planning.

- Inappropriate influences (domination of time, topic, opinion by one or few individuals; *fear of contributing* because of the possibility of *flaming*, and so on).

- Tendency of group members to rely on others to do most of the work (free-riding).

- Tendency to produce compromised solutions of poor quality.

- Nonproductive time (socializing, preparing, waiting for late-comers—*air-time fragmentation*).

- Tendency to repeat what was already said (because of failure to remember or process).

- High cost of meeting (travel, participation, etc.).

- Tendency of groups to make riskier decisions than they should.

- Incomplete or inappropriate use of information.

- Too much information (*information overload*).

- Few information cues.

- Incomplete or incorrect task analysis.

- Inappropriate or incomplete representation in the group.

- Attention blocking.

- Attenuation blocking.

- Concentration blocking.

- Slow feedback.

DSS IN FOCUS 7.8

MODELS IN GROUP DECISION-MAKING—EC 2000 2ND EDITION FOR GROUPS

Based on the Analytic Hierarchy Process (AHP) decision-making methodology implemented as Expert Choice (Chapter 4), EC 2000 2nd Edition for Groups helps group members define objectives, goals, criteria, and alternatives and then organize them into a hierarchical structure. Using PCs, participants compare and prioritize the relative importance of the decision variables. EC 2000 for Groups then synthesizes the group's judgments to arrive at a conclusion and allows individuals to examine how changing the weighting of their criteria affects the outcome.

EC 2000 for groups imitates the way people naturally make decisions: gathering information, structuring the decision, weighing the variables and alternatives, and reaching a conclusion (Chapters 2 and 4). It supports the decision process. The group structures an AHP decision hierarchy for the problem as members perceive it; members provide the judgments, and members make the decision.

Source: Partly adapted from Expert Choice Inc., Pittsburgh, PA, expertchoice.com, May 2003. Used by permission.

DSS IN FOCUS 7.9

GSS PROCESS GAINS

- Supports parallel processing of information and idea generation.

- Enables the participation of larger groups with more complete information, knowledge, and skills.

- Permits the group to use structured or unstructured techniques and methods.

- Offers rapid, easy access to external information.

- Allows parallel computer discussions.

- Helps participants frame the big picture.

- Anonymity allows shy people to contribute to the meeting (*get up and do what needs to be done*).

- Anonymity helps prevent aggressive individuals from driving the meeting.

- Provides for multiple ways to participate in instant, anonymous voting.

- Provides structure for the planning process to keep the group on track.

- Enables several users to interact simultaneously (conferencing).

- Records all information presented at the meeting (organizational memory).

DSS IN ACTION 7.10

EASTMAN CHEMICAL BOOSTS CREATIVE PROCESSES AND SAVES $500,000 WITH GROUPWARE

THE PROBLEM

Eastman Chemical wanted to use creative problem-solving sessions to process ideas. Customers would present any number of problems, and they would use flip charts and Post-it notes to come up with better solutions. But organizing and studying the notes took far too long. The company needed more ideas and better methods to meet customers' needs. Traditional methods were not effective. The process was extremely unproductive and time-consuming.

THE SOLUTION

Eastman Chemical chose GroupSystems to support its problem-solving and dramatically improved its meetings. Here's how the meetings work now. First, participants define the problem and frame it. Then participants brainstorm ideas to develop potential solutions to the problem, trying for "outside-the-box" thinking using creativity techniques. Recently, some 400 ideas were generated by nine people in a two-hour session (through parallelism). After categorizing similar items, the team establishes common decision criteria to pick

the top three ideas using the Alternative Analysis tool. Results are then copied into an Excel spreadsheet to develop an action plan.

In addition, Eastman ran 100 R&D managers through sessions to determine top strategies. They defined eight opportunities, with an action plan to establish the top three—after generating 2,200 ideas!

THE RESULTS

Henry Gonzales, manager of the polymer technology core competency group at Eastman, states, "We found that with GroupSystems, we had more unusual ideas, a richer pool to choose from, and we got to the point a lot faster. I did a study and calculated that the software saved 50 percent of people's time, and projected a cost savings of over $500,000 for the 12 people during a year's time." Consequently, Eastman Chemical bought a second license and upgraded to another facility so that more people could use the groupware.

Source: Adapted from "GroupSystems Case Studies," GroupSystems.com, groupsystems.com, June 2003.

7.6 GROUP SUPPORT SYSTEMS TECHNOLOGIES

There are three options for deploying GSS technology: (1) in a special-purpose **decision room**, (2) at a multiple-use facility, and (3) as Web-based groupware with clients running wherever the group members are.

The earliest GSS were installed in expensive, customized, special-purpose decision rooms (electronic meeting rooms) with PCs with sunken displays hidden under desks and a large public screen at the front of the room. The original idea was that only executives and high-level managers would use the facility. The software in a special-purpose electronic meeting room usually runs over a local area network (LAN), and these rooms are fairly plush in their furnishings. Electronic meeting rooms can be constructed in different shapes and sizes. A common design includes a room equipped with 12–30 networked personal computers, usually recessed into the desktop (for better participant viewing). A server PC is attached to a large-screen projection system and connected to the network to display the work at individual workstations and aggregated information from the facilitator's workstation. Adjacent to the decision room there sometimes are break-out rooms equipped with PCs connected to the server where small subgroups can consult. The output from the subgroups can also be displayed on the large public screen.

Organizations still use electronic decision rooms, and these rooms very ably support same time/same place meetings (at many universities, companies, and government agencies). One Ohio school district even built a portable facility in a bus (the driver's seat turns around to become the facilitator's seat). There is still a need and a desire for groups to meet face to face even when supported by collaborative technology. A facility like this can conveniently provide videoconferencing and distance education, and may even function as a fairly expensive computer lab.

A second option is to construct a multiple-use facility, sometimes a general-purpose computer lab or computer classroom that also is a less elegant but equally useful GSS room. For example, at the Terry College of Business of The University of Georgia, Sanford Hall has a 48-seat lab/computer classroom with GroupSystems MeetingRoom installed. This room also "triples" as a distance learning classroom because it contains the latest academic videoconferencing software and hardware. Since a decision room might not be used 100 percent of the time for groupwork, this is an effective way to lower or share costs.

For the first and second options, a trained facilitator is necessary to coordinate the meetings. The group leader works with the facilitator to structure the meeting. The success of a GSS session depends largely on the quality, activities, and support of the facilitator (Miranda and Bostrom, 1997). For details on facilitator support, an important but often neglected aspect of GSS, see Ngwenyama et al. (1996).

Since the late 1990s, the most common approach has been the third option: using Web-based or LAN-based groupware that allows group members to work from any location at any time (e.g., Lotus Notes, Groove, WebEx, PlaceWare, GroupSystems, NetMeeting). This groupware often includes audioconferencing and videoconferencing. The availability of relatively inexpensive groupware (for purchase or for rent) combined with the power and low cost of capable PCs makes this type of system viable. Some groupware, notably Groove, runs in a peer-to-peer mode, where each person works on a copy of the entire conference so that only differences among the files need be transmitted. Thus standard telephone connections work relatively well (without video or audio modes). Also, the high cost of constructing a facility and finding an experienced facilitator, and the need to have participants connect from other locations

TABLE 7.1   Collaborative Computing/GSS and Web Impacts

Collaborative Computing/GSS	Web Impacts	Impacts on the Web
Collaboration	Consistent, friendly, graphical user interface for client units	Improvements in management, hardware, software, and infra-structure due mainly to collaboration in (Web-based) CASE and other systems analysis and design tools
	Convenient, fast access to team members	
	Improved collaboration tools	
	Access to data/information/knowledge on servers	
	Enables document sharing	
	Enables anywhere/anytime collaboration	Improvements in site design and development methods
	Enables collaboration between companies, customers and vendors	Simultaneous Web surfing (e.g., Groove)
Communication	Improved, fast communication among group members and links to data/information/knowledge sources	Same as above
	Makes audio and video conferencing a reality, especially for individuals not using a LAN	
Decision Rooms	Consistent, friendly, graphical user interface for clients	Same as above
	Communication support	
	Access to Web-based tools	
	Room design teams can collaborate to provide dramatic improvements in facilities	
Mixed-mode Facilities	Same as above	Same as above
Colocated Team Facilities (members in different locations)	Provides fast connections to enable real-time collaboration	Same as above

at any time, led to less need for the first two approaches. The Web provides flexibility in running meetings, and it creates interesting issues about how to facilitate such meetings. Time deadlines are generally imposed for each phase of an anytime/anyplace meeting. The deadlines are set to allow for time zones and travel. Another issue for non-face-to-face meetings is that participants want to see the people with whom they are working. Some systems have access to still pictures, while videoconferencing enhances some meeting aspects by showing some body language. We described some major groupware packages earlier in this chapter. In Table 7.1, we provide collaborative computing/GSS and Web impacts. Next, we describe some of the features and structure of a comprehensive GSS through GroupSystems.

7.7 GROUPSYSTEMS MEETINGROOM AND ONLINE

GroupSystems MeetingRoom and OnLine are comprehensive groupware that support a wide variety of group processes. MeetingRoom is the LAN version, while OnLine is the Web-enabled version. Both provide the same set of tools and capabilities. We will refer to the software simply as GroupSystems. An overview of the tools and their relationship to the major GSS activities is shown in Figure 7.3. Agenda is the control panel for scheduling and running GroupSystems activities, that is, the meeting manager. The tools in GroupSystems are divided into standard tools and advanced tools.

GroupSystems *standard tools* support group processes, including brainstorming, list building, information gathering, voting, organizing, prioritizing, and consensus building:

- ***Electronic Brainstorming*** gathers ideas and comments in an unstructured manner. Groups work rapidly in generating a free flow of ideas. Participants contribute simultaneously (parallelism) and anonymously.
- ***Group Outliner*** allows the group to create and comment on a multilevel list of topics in a tree or outline structure. Participants can attach comments at every level of the outline. Comments are integrated and collaborative.
- ***Topic Commenter*** allows participants to comment on a list of topics. This idea generation is more structured than that of Electronic Brainstorming but less structured than that of Group Outliner.

FIGURE 7.3   STRUCTURE OF GROUPSYSTEMS FOR WINDOWS

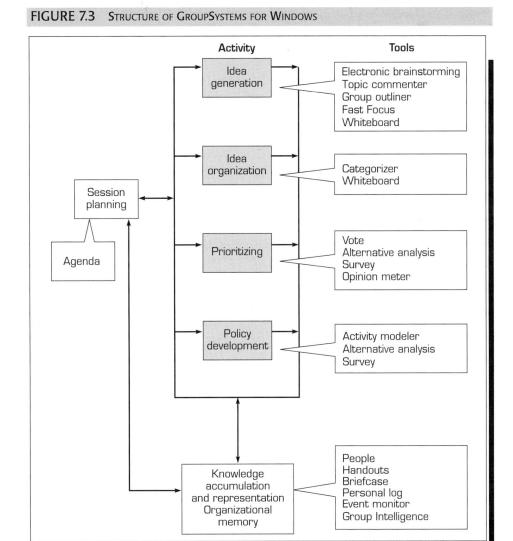

- *Categorizer* allows the group to generate a list of ideas and supporting comments. Categories are created for the ideas, and participants can drag the ideas into the desired category.
- *Vote* supports consensus development through group evaluation of issues. Several voting methods are provided. Results are tabulated electronically and displayed statistically or graphically.

GroupSystems *advanced tools* include add-ins for analysis, surveys, and modeling:

- *Alternative Analysis* allows the group to weight or rate a list of alternatives against a list of criteria because collaborative decisions require the evaluation of multiple perspectives and ideas. The group can test what-if assumptions by adjusting the weighting of the criteria.
- *Survey* allows the creation, administration, and analysis of an online questionnaire.
- *Activity Modeler* provides user-friendly group support for simultaneous business process reengineering modeling.

In addition, the *GroupIntelligence* module enables teams to capture and incorporate the organizational memory from previous group sessions and combine, publish, and apply them to a new session.

Agenda (the control panel) supports the facilitator. Through Agenda, the facilitator plans and runs the meeting and captures and saves session reports and data.

GroupSystems includes several other group resources:

- *People* contains a list of participants with background information.
- *Whiteboard* is a group-enabled drawing and annotation tool.
- *Handouts* are reference materials for group viewing.
- *Opinion Meter* is a fast, simple version of the vote tool for gauging opinions.

The following *individual resources* improve individual productivity:

- *Briefcase* allows access to commonly used applications (word processing, calculators, e-mail).
- *Personal Log* allows personal note taking.
- *Event Monitor* informs members of new activities and information.

7.8 THE GSS MEETING PROCESS

Face-to-face, same time/same place electronic meetings generally follow a common progression. First, the group leader meets with the facilitator to plan the meeting (this is critically important), select the software tools, and develop an agenda. Second, the participants meet in the decision room, and the leader poses a question or problem to the group. Third, the participants type their ideas or comments (brainstorm), and the results are displayed publicly. Because the participants can see what others are typing on their own monitors, they can provide comments or generate new ideas. Fourth, the facilitator, using idea organization software, searches for common themes, topics, and ideas, and organizes them into rough categories (key ideas) with appropriate comments (new research is attempting to automate this part of the electronic meeting). The results are publicly displayed. Fifth, the leader starts a discussion, either verbal or electronic. The participants next prioritize the ideas. Sixth, the top five or ten topics are sent to idea-generation software following a discussion. The process (idea generation, idea organization, prioritization) can be repeated or a final vote can be taken.

The major activities of a typical GSS session are listed in DSS in Focus 7.11. For examples of GSS use in practice, see DSS in Action 7.10 and the GroupSystems.com Web site (groupsystems.com).

Anytime/any place meetings have become a standard approach because of the proliferation of Web-based GSS. Some differences are that participants want to know about the other participants (if they are not using videoconferencing concurrently or have never met the other participants), task completion times must be assigned (especially if the meeting spans multiple time zones), and the facilitator's task becomes more difficult, especially when the meeting runs around the clock (McQuaid et al., 2000). Deadlines are imposed so that the group can move on to the next phase of the meeting. The same issues affect distance learning environments.

It is very important to remind participants of where they are in the group meeting process and to keep them focused on long-term tasks. Other issues include security (to protect valuable information from theft), universal access (from home or other sites), folder invitations and information (participants must be invited to participate in meeting segments), information about the participants (on virtual business cards), indicating who is on the system (to alleviate feelings of loneliness), and facilitator controls (to start and stop sessions, and restrict access to activities). *Planning the session* is the most critical issue. Facilitators must provide incentives and develop investment in the out-

---

DSS IN FOCUS 7.11

THE STANDARD GSS PROCESS

1. **Idea generation.** This exploratory step looks at the problem and attempts to develop creative ideas about its important features. The ideas can have anything to do with the problem, from potential solutions to criteria to mitigating factors. An electronic brainstorming tool is appropriate; its output is a list of ideas. Typical time is 30–45 minutes.

2. **Idea organization.** An idea-organizing tool places the many ideas generated on a list of key issues. The output of this stage is a list of a few key ideas (about one for every 20 original ideas) with the supporting details. Typical time is 45–90 minutes.

3. **Prioritization.** At this stage, the key ideas are prioritized. A voting tool is appropriate; its output is a prioritized list of ideas and details. Typical time is 10–20 minutes.

4. **Idea generation.** New ideas are generated based on the prioritization of the key ideas. A brain-

storming tool that provides structure, such as Topic Commentator, is appropriate here. The ideas generated are typically focused on solutions. This stage's output may consist of about 20 ideas for each of the original key ideas.

The process continues until a final idea is selected as a solution to the problem that prompted the meeting, or a few solutions are identified to be investigated in more depth. Some meetings are oriented to decision-making. Others are exploratory in nature and are focused simply on generating ideas to pursue in follow-up meetings or individual work. Often a GSS meeting takes longer than a nonsupported one, but participants are generally more thorough in their brainstorming and analysis, and they "feel" that they have made a better decision using the system. See Nunamaker et al. (1991) for more details.

come, communicate often and explicitly, assign roles and tasks with accountability, and be explicit in goal and activity communication.

GSS SUCCESS

The success of a GSS is based mostly on its effectiveness. A system succeeds if it cuts costs (especially travel costs, see DSS in Action 7.13), supports participants in making better decisions, and/or increases productivity substantially (see the Opening Vignette, Case Application 7.1, the WELCOM Web Chapter, DSS in Action 7.4 and 7.10). In order to succeed, a GSS needs many of the usual information system success factors: an organizational commitment, an executive sponsor, an operating sponsor, user involvement and training, a user-seductive interface, and so on. The executive sponsor and organizational commitment through him or her are critical for success. If the organizational culture does not readily support face-to-face collaboration, then it must be *changed* to do so before introducing GSS (see DSS in Focus 7.12). Otherwise, the system will not be used, and it will be deemed a failure. This is the critical issue in knowledge management (see Chapter 9), which involves collaboration at the enterprise level. Having a dedicated, well-trained, personable facilitator is critical. Finally, the GSS must have the correct tools to support the organization's groupwork and must include *parallelism* and *anonymity* to provide process and task gains. *Good planning* is the key to running successful meetings, and this also applies to electronic meetings (see DSS in Focus 7.5). If anything, bad planning might make a group believe that the GSS is to blame for its poor performance. Finally, GSS must demonstrate cost savings, either through a more effective and efficient meeting process or through reduced travel costs.

DSS IN FOCUS 7.12

CRAFTING A COLLABORATIVE CULTURE

Collaboration is about people; and if you want people to collaborate, the collaboration tool will not change their attitudes. Technology provides around 20 percent of the solution. The rest involves how to motivate the users to really use the system. The managers must create a workplace that supports collaboration. This involves three simple steps:

1. **Know what you want.** Get team members to articulate their definition of *success*. This is part of the team-building process. At Boeing-Rocketdyne, the team created a formal contract indicating goals and how the team would function (an excellent idea for class groups).

2. **Determine resource constraints.** These include everything from the geographic distribution of team members to reporting relationships to motivations. Each constraint limits the possible tools the team can use.

3. **Determine what technologies can be used to overcome resource constraints.** Keep in mind business needs rather than fun, new, or convenient technologies. For example, videoconferencing and detailed product and code design work require high-bandwidth connections.

Once all this is determined, one must still set up group sessions with good facilitation to guide and train the participants in tool use. A learning environment is ideally created in the process.

Source: Partly adapted from Agrew (2000).

7.9 DISTANCE LEARNING

According to SRI Consulting, the online learning and institutional training market will grow to exceed $20 billion by 2005 (see Sistek-Chandler, 2001). Developments in distance learning technologies continue to change the way courses are delivered—and received. Traditional courses also benefit from the new technologies. In this section, we describe background and advances in distance learning, and how they relate to GSS.

LEARNING, COLLABORATIVE COMPUTING, AND GSS

The classroom is a natural setting in which to enhance learning by providing computerized support, either as a supplement or through complete *courseware*. Learning is the basic process of incorporating new knowledge into one's own set of knowledge. It typically involves the sequence of predetermined steps outlined in DSS in Focus 7.13. The learning process generally requires *communication* and *collaboration*. Collaborative computing (GSS) can improve the classroom experience. GSS features like brainstorming (a form of discussion or chat) and voting can support class members performing groupwork. GSS use in the classroom increases observed learning, self-reported learning, on-task participation, and satisfaction. On the other hand, anonymity and other GSS features can introduce some process losses into the education process, such as flaming and buffoonery, which must be planned for by the instructor and thoughtfully managed (see Schweizer, 1999). The instructor must control flaming and buffoonery, and run discussions in an electronic medium in much the same way as in a traditional classroom (see DSS in Focus 7.14).

The Web is an effective vehicle for distributing course materials, including lecture notes. Even with the availability of detailed course materials, class attendance does not seem to drop off. (Not attending class is ill-advised. Educational research indicates that class attendance is the most significant factor in course success.) Textbooks feature Web sites with separate areas for students and faculty. Even simple collaborative computing technologies like e-mail and listservs can enhance the educational experience,

---

DSS IN FOCUS 7.13

WHAT IS LEARNING?

A learning process normally incorporates

1. Establishing the objectives of the learning process.
2. Finding and revising (or creating) instructional material.
3. Assessing students' levels of knowledge.
4. Assigning appropriate material to students.
5. Defining the form of access students have to components or modules.
6. Revising and following up students' progress and intervening when necessary.

7. Providing and managing communication between students and instructors and between students.
8. Assessing the learning process.
9. Preparing reports on the learning process results.

Source: Adapted from UCAID, "The Internet2 Project," internet2.edu, May, 2003. Also see "Exploring the Future of Learning—The Internet2 K20 Initiative" at k20.internet2.edu/projects/mu_thinkquestlive2002.html.

DSS IN FOCUS 7.14

HOW TO RUN ONLINE DISCUSSIONS

According to Schweizer (1999), professorial roles in online discussions are very much the same as in face-to-face discussions. She recommends the following ways for the professor to fit into the discussion:

- Use online discussions to build a community. Be informal about your tone in the discussion.
- Relate online discussions to current class material. Refer in class to issues raised in the discussions. In class, if a student want to pursue a point (and you have no time), move it to the online discussion.
- Structure the discussion topic; focus it around a problem to be solved. Assign one student the task of providing an intial solution. Everyone else must refine it.
- Define roles for various discussants. They might include: original proposer, idea extender, constructive critic, responder to critic, consolidator, etc.

- Clarify the reward for participation. This could involve grades or even enhancing knowledge for the exam. Exam questions may even be derived directly from discussions.
- Outlaw "just opinions." Insist that points must be backed by specific references to readings, other discussants, other source materials, or analysis that the student has performed.
- Keep a discussion board as a "for fun" place where students can post anything they wish as a means of letting other students know them better. The professor may or may not subscribe to this discussion list.

Source: Expanded from David G. Brown, "The Role You Play in Online Discussions." *Syllabus*, December 2002.

---

as the text authors can attest. A critical success factor is that class members and instructors be properly trained in technology use.

WHY USE COLLABORATIVE COMPUTING IN LEARNING?

Tyran and Shepherd (2000) describe an interesting research framework for collaborative technology use (GSS) in the traditional classroom. There are factors related to the context of the group learning situation, the group learning process, and the outcomes of the learning process. Alavi et al. (1995) showed that students in a distant collaborative environment exhibited a higher level of critical thinking and were more committed to and cohesive with their teams. It seems to be a worthwhile effort to move courses online.

Collaborative computing technologies are directly applicable to distance learning environments. By the end of the 1990s, technology had advanced to the point where computer-supported traditional classes could move to online, Web-based distance-learning environments. There is a definite need to enhance existing classrooms with collaborative support and to make education available outside the confines of the classroom. See Lau (2000), and Tschang and Senta (2001).

DISTANCE LEARNING

Distance learning (DL) takes place when learning involves tools or technologies designed to overcome the restrictions of same time/same place learning. The history of distance learning in the United States dates back to 1728, when an advertisement in

The Boston Globe offered shorthand lessons through the mail. Bunker (1999) and Matthews (1999) provide the history of DL.

Distance learning is exciting and has unlimited potential to revolutionize learning at universities and colleges, at public and private schools, and in corporate on-the-job training. But distance learning is not a new concept! When television was invented in the 1920s, it was heralded as a device that would revolutionize education. Radio was used in the 1920s and 1930s for distance learning programs (it is still so used in the Australian Outback), and video distance learning systems have been in operation for decades (see DSS in Action 7.15 for the "early" experiences of one author). Now that technology has evolved, television, or rather videoconferencing and collaborative computing through the Internet, is finally fulfilling its destiny by providing support tools to enable distance learning.

Internet and videoconferencing and collaborative computing tools customized to the classroom environment allow inexpensive and widespread distance learning. Distance learning has developed into a substantive sector of higher education around the world over the last few decades. It is becoming an increasingly popular alternative to traditional degree programs and workshops. DL is a nontraditional way of deliver-

---

DSS IN ACTION 7.15

DISTANCE LEARNING–DÉJÀ VU? AGAIN?

In 1980 I accepted a position as an assistant professor at Southern Methodist University (SMU). During my interview, I discovered that about half my teaching would be "education at a distance" through the TAGER Network (the Association of Graduate Education and Research Network—now the Green Education Network), a closed-circuit television system over which almost all of the master's-level programs in engineering were offered (see engr.smu.edu). TAGER, operational since 1964, is a consortium of five colleges and universities and many companies in the Dallas–Fort Worth Metroplex. TAGER broadcasts courses from the colleges and universities to the firms. The video and audio signal is sent via closed-circuit microwave, while the talk-back from students off campus is by way of leased phone lines (audio only). The firm is obligated to provide a media classroom for the course and allow students to attend. On campus there are four classroom studios, each equipped with two cameras (one in the rear and one overhead).

Students saved driving time (up to three days per week—possibly 80 miles (130 km) each way—and in many cases this was the only way they could pursue a graduate degree), while the universities were able to increase class sizes without requiring additional space and, more important, to attract high-level, highly motivated students who enriched the classroom experience for all. In 1978 the program was expanded to include

videotape that could be mailed anywhere in the world. In the mid-1980s, SMU joined the National Technological University (NTU) as a member school. NTU offers its own degree programs, but students attend classes from any member school, generally beamed by satellite to their workplace. This enhanced career portability for part-time students.

It did not take me long to figure out that telephone office hours would be necessary and that the class would require a lot of extra preparation time. Even so, the preparation paid off when the course was offered a second time. There were a few other benefits: A faculty member who had to miss class (which rarely happened, of course) could record the lecture in advance; I got really good at identifying students by their voices, to the point that when they came to my office I could recognize them as soon as they spoke; and the evidence of a very occasional academic honesty issue could be recorded on videotape.

Even though this technology seems quite passé now, it was remarkably robust and challenging then, and a good experience for the students and the faculty. Many of the lessons, tips, and research topics I now see in distance learning articles are the same ones that I experienced, learned, or developed on the fly in the early 1980s.

Source: Jay E. Aronson.

ing education and focuses on working professionals whose primary requirement is the element of convenience. Student profiles have changed dramatically over the last two decades. As the economics of education and socioeconomic trends evolve, students are completing their college educations in nontraditional ways. Thousands of educational institutions worldwide offer courses through DL, not including the comparable if not larger number of independent companies offering remote education courses. Continuing Education, required of many professional fields from medicine to engineering, is readily offered via distance-learning systems (Morris, 2003). In early 2003, there were an estimated 350,000 students enrolled in fully online degree programs (Dunham, 2003), and the numbers continue to grow daily.

A scan of the literature in 2004 indicates that distance learning has gone global. It is especially important in Third World countries that can use Internet, telephone, satellite, radio, and television links to span great distances to deliver education, especially in the primary and secondary grades. And in more developed countries, governments are setting up digital curricula, both to provide inexpensive education resources to their citizens (see Ashling, 2003; Telecomworldwire, 2003), and to alleviate public school teacher shortages, as in Texas (Raghunathan, 2002). Even Latin is being taught online (for a personal experience, see Shelton, 2000).

Most major colleges and universities utilize technology to offer a variety of sophisticated distance learning programs. Hundreds of fully accredited colleges and universities in the United States offer DL-delivered degrees in thousands of fields. Almost all offer bachelor's degrees, and most offer master's degrees. Many offer certificate programs as well. There are over a hundred distance learning MBAs (see Dearlove and Crainer, 2001) and doctorate programs. Programs ranged from those delivered by traditional institutions to those sponsored by Jones International University—a virtual campus only. See Petersons.com, ECollege.com, www-icdl.open.ac.uk/icdl/, and usdla.org for information about specific distance learning programs. See Moloney and Tello (2003) and Riffee (2003) to learn how to create successful online education. Also see Brooks et al. (2001), Buck (2001), and Gilbert (2001).

For an example of an executive MBA program offered as a blend of on-campus experience and distance learning technology at the University of Georgia, see DSS in Action 7.16. For experiences involving moving courses and blended courses to online environments, see Dollar (2000), Schell (2000), Stith (2000), and Warnock et al. (2000). There is a trend for organizations to partner with universities in structuring degree programs and courses. The UGA/IBM program described in DSS in Action 7.16 is a good example. Goodridge (2002) additionally describes how IBM and Microsoft have structured successful master's degrees with several leading universities. General Motors has partnered with Cardean University in an online MBA program (see Goodridge, 2001a). DL programs have many advantages, but also, unfortunately, some disadvantages.

ADVANTAGES OF DL PROGRAMS[3]

- Learning can be as effective as by traditional means, or even more so.
- The flexible time frame provides educational opportunities for many, including senior managers and executives.
- Students need not quit their jobs.
- Students can travel as part of their existing jobs.
- Access is available anywhere and anytime.

---

[3]Partly adapted from Jana (2000) and Schell (2000).

DSS IN ACTION 7.16

THE BLENDED-LEARNING MBA

The University of Georgia and Pricewaterhouse-Coopers (PWC) (now part of IBM) have partnered to pioneer a new kind of MBA program. The two-year program blends distance, classroom, and team learning with technical and business courses.

The program begins with all enrolled students visiting the campus for two weeks to meet the faculty and get to know each other. After the first week, students split into teams of about five people, and they work within these teams for the rest of the school year.

The teams write a contract to define their responsibilities and commitments, such as the amount of time to be spent on conference calls and how to handle collaborative research. The contract can also include consequences for people who don't live up to their responsibilities. After the two-week stint, consultants return to work. Each week, they log on to Blackboard (courseware) via the Web to listen to prerecorded lectures and complete weekly reading assignments. The teams participate in conference calls as needed. Each semester students regroup at The University of Georgia for on-site learning for a week.

This program readily handles logistical and content problems with traditional full-time programs (difficult because of the one- to two-year commitment away from work) and typical part-time programs (the employees travel in their consulting). At the time when the program began, pure distance learning MBA programs were still evolving. This blended-learning program provides students with many of the benefits of both an on-campus experience and a distance learning environment. An additional benefit is that since the spring 2003 semester, Blackboard has become standard courseware for all Terry College of Business courses. Traditional courses can exploit many of the features of courseware to enhance the learning environment.

Source: Adapted from J. Mateyaschuk, "An MBA on the Go," *InformationWeek,* No. 744, July 19, 1999; also see J. Reingold, and M. Schneider, "The Executive MBA Your Way," *BusinessWeek,* No. 3651, October 18, 1999, and The University of Georgia, MBA Program Documentation, 2004; also see Bostrom, Kadlec, and Thomas (2002).

- New technology can be presented to a large audience cheaply.
- Online classes can teach specific skills.
- Online classes cost less.
- More information can be made available to students, adding breadth and depth to a course.
- It is possible to have more one-on-one interaction with an instructor (through e-mail).
- Student/faculty contact time increases.
- DL meets the need for continuous learning.
- The course materials are consistent.
- Attendance is not required and can be handled flexibly (a plus and a minus).
- The technology can handle "discussion-style" courses as well as technical courses.
- Students' attitudes evolve and improve as familiarity with the technology increases.
- Students show positive gains in learning.
- Impacts (higher learning levels, higher test scores) have been observed to be greater in online courses (Dollar, 2000; Reid, 1999).

DISADVANTAGES OF DL PROGRAMS[4]

- There are fewer (or very different) social interactions (lack of face-to-face meetings).
- There is less or no on-campus interaction.

_____

[4]Partly adapted from Jana (2000) and Schell (2000).

- There can be communication problems (especially with video).
- Students must be highly self-motivated and tightly focused.
- Students must be highly disciplined and organized.
- Students must have effective time management skills.
- Students must be extremely dedicated.
- Online classes require major administrative support.
- Online classes require major technical support.
- Faculty preparation and delivery time is significantly higher than for a traditional course (up to three times the time and effort is needed).
- Courses must be redesigned to utilize the best presentation mechanisms for topic delivery.
- Extra rewards for faculty are recommended because of the extra effort (could be a plus).
- Faculty need special training in effective instruction methods and in the technology.
- Students need special training in the technology.
- The course requires a *very reliable* technological infrastructure, including hardware, software, and a *trained* staff.
- The learner must assume much more responsibility.
- Mastery of the material establishes the grade, though collaborative methods allow an instructor to identify contributors.
- Students must work hard—these are real courses, not correspondence courses.

DISTANCE LEARNING COURSEWARE

There are hundreds of courseware packages that enable distance learning. These range from more general collaboration tools like Lotus Notes, Microsoft NetMeeting, Interwise, Groove, PlaceWare, WebEx, and GroupSystems to specialized courseware from the popular Blackboard (Figure 7.4) and WebCT Vista to Lotus Notes Learning Space and the PlaceWare Virtual Classroom.

Blackboard (www.blackboard.com) is powerful courseware that handles all aspects of online learning in a Web environment. The University of Georgia program described in DSS in Action 7.16 uses Blackboard for student interaction through establishment of groups, discussion lists and virtual classrooms (both among group members and among all class members), document sharing, e-mail between students and between students and faculty, submission of assignments, and feedback. Lectures, lecture notes, PowerPoint (or other) presentations, the syllabus, and all course handouts and materials are available on Blackboard. Online exams and quizzes are established directly and managed automatically. Question types include true/false, multiple choice short word, matching, and paragraph answer. Student exam and quiz results are automatically recorded. The Online Gradebook allows an instructor to enter all grades, with weights; grades are automatically (and privately) reported to students when they log into their accounts (no more posting grades on the door). Finally, a course may be copied into another, so that the documents need not all be reposted manually. Jay Aronson uses it for *all* his classes. See the sample screenshot in Figure 7.4.

LearnLinc Virtual Classroom (EDT Learning) and InterWise allow online instructors to control class presentations using synchronized multimedia and content over the Web. It also offers application sharing, electronic hand raising, and a "glimpse" feature that allows instructors to acquire a screen capture of any student's desktop. One-way streaming video and audio or prerecorded communications, as well as two-way audio

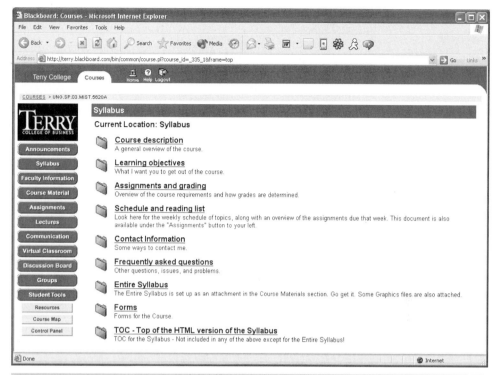

FIGURE 7.4   BLACKBOARD COURSEWARE SCREEN SHOT

Source: Screen Capture (©2003) Blackboard.com. Used with permission of Blackboard.com.

in multicast audioconferencing, can be used. TestLinc provides comprehensive testing capabilities. There are many online and journal Buyer's Guides of tools and software for conferences, meetings, and distance learning.

ONLINE CORPORATE TRAINING

More and more organizations are training their employees online, not just in the latest technologies but also in policies, sales, and other areas. Professionals are increasingly pressed for time. Web-based learning technologies allow organizations to keep their staff members up-to-date with the latest innovations, policies, and methods. In 1999 private industry spent $58 billion annually on employee training. Driven by the demand for cheaper, more interactive courses, online learning is fast becoming the standard operating procedure. Classroom use has dramatically dropped in the first few years of the millennium. Computer-based training costs about 50 percent less than the traditional classroom setting and does not involve travel costs or have class size restrictions. Web-based or online courses accounted for more than half of all training by 2002 (up from 17 percent in 1998). Training via the Web can run 24 hours per day every day (24/7). Web-based training (WBT) can be faster and cheaper than classroom training. IBM estimates a savings of $500,000 for every 1,000 hours of training outside the traditional classroom. International Data Corporation (IDC) predicts that revenue from

Internet-based training program sales will have grown at a compound annual rate of 64.5 percent through 2003. Advanced electronic learning requires real-time, two-way communication, via either audio- or videoconferencing tools, allowing students and instructors to interact and providing feedback. For most Web training, students view a live or recorded class and participation is limited to posting on bulletin boards and e-mail discussions (see Boisvert, 2000; Kiser, 1999; Markel, 1999; Mottl, 2000).

As outlined by Hickey (2002), the top five reasons for online training are:

1. Slash costs
2. Shorten the learning process
3. Extend your reach
4. Train more, more often
5. Make money (sell your courseware)

In Case Application 7.2, we describe how Dow Chemical utilized online learning to save millions in costs, and to generate opportunities and build trust and commitment among its employees. Charles Schwab & Co. deployed an online training system for its 5,000 call-center representatives (see Swanson, 2000). Distance learning (also called e-learning) has moved out of the office. Even sports teams and emergency workers are utilizing technology to learn new skills and stay proficient in their areas (see Shachtman, 2000).

DISTANCE LEARNING RESOURCES

The following is a sample of organizations and journals involved in promoting and supporting distance learning:

- *Center for Distance Learning at Texas A&M University (cdlr.tamu.edu).* This resource center has a model classroom that can be viewed on the Web.
- *Lucent Foundation Learning and Development Programs at Lucent Technologies (www.lucent.com/news/foundation/learning.html).* Resources include research abstracts, published articles, case studies, and brochures with tips on how to set up a distance learning course or program.
- *American Council on Education ACENET (acenet.edu).* This organization stays current on many important issues in education. It publishes a checklist on how to evaluate the quality of an organization's distance learning program.
- *Online Certification, Education and Distance Learning (www.ocedl.com).* Keeps tabs on the future of distance learning, certification, education, and distance education.
- *U.S. Distance Learning Association (www.usdla.org).* Lists many articles, and links to relevant resources.
- *Distance Education Clearinghouse (www.uwex.edu/disted/home.html).* Lists many articles, and links to relevant resources.
- *American Journal of Distance Education (www.ajde.com).* A current journal on the issues and practice of distance learning.
- *CADE: Journal of Distance Education (www.cade-aced.ca).* A current journal on the issues and practice of distance learning.

EVALUATION OF DISTANCE LEARNING

Although initially slow to gain acceptance, many corporations are taking advantage of distance learning via Web-based streaming and through private company intranets (Stamberg, 2002). The top e-learning providers are discussed by Hickey (2002). Organizations are taking a serious look at the return on investment of distance learning (see Harris, 2003; Belange and Deannett, 2000). While the jury is still out, academia and industry are attempting to determine the true *value* of distance learning. Clearly, though, corporate training pays off (see DSS in Action 7.17).

Distance learning is a form of collaboration and knowledge management and can be done in a 24/7 framework. It is critical to assess the impact of Web-based courses in terms of benefits and costs. Most student experiences are positive (see Dollar, 2000; Schell, 2000). Students tend to learn more using groupware, especially when learning spans a distance. Students in distance learning environments tend to perform better than those in traditional classrooms (Dollar, 2000). Several factors are important in distance learning situations. A high level of student motivation, a strong work ethic, and intensive student support measures typically result in success for distance learners. The most important factor for achieving success in distance learning is the degree to which instructors and support staff are able to encourage students to undertake responsibility for their own learning. Clearly, collaborative technology can enhance learning performance and increase affective experiences in the context of cooperative learning (Chuang, Bernard, and Shahid, 2002).

Both students and faculty must understand how collaborative technology impacts on how they perform course work. Some issues revolve around training, determining which technology to use and how, what to distribute and when, and what standards to use for files that students submit.

Distance learning is radically changing education, and socioeconomic, technological, and economic changes must be examined as the learning behaviors and expectations of learners change. There is a sharply growing demand for flexible, adaptive, time- and geography-independent learning environments (Meso and Liegle, 2000). Despite its disadvantages, distance learning continues to grow dramatically because of the increased demand.

DSS IN ACTION 7.17

EMPLOYEE TRAINING PAYS OFF

Employee training pays off. Companies tend to lose their value if they cut training programs. If they invest in training, they increase their value. According to the American Society of Training and Development, publicly traded firms that invest in training and development increase their total shareholder return in the following year by between 19.8 percent and 36.9 percent. An increase of $680 per employee in a company's training expenditures generates, on average, a 6 percent improvement in total shareholder return in the following year. As a specific example, consider the First National Bank of Colorado. CEO Dave Gilman invested heavily in training. As a result, the bank's assets have grown from $228 million to $650 million. Training also significantly lowered its employee turnover rate.

Source: Adapted from Nancy Nachman-Hunt, "Employee Training Pays Back Big, First National CEO Believes." *Boulder County Business Report*, Vol. 22, No. 2, January 24, 2003.

7.10 CREATIVITY AND IDEA GENERATION

CREATIVITY

Creativity is complex. It can be considered a fundamental human trait and a level of achievement (see DSS in Focus 7.18 for a formal description of creativity). Personality-related creativity traits (inventiveness, independence, individuality, enthusiasm, flexibility) can be assessed through a 36-item scale called Personal Barriers to Creative Thought and Innovative Action (Hellriegel and Slocum, 1992, pp. 237–238) and the widely used Torrance Tests of Creative Thinking (TTCT) (Cramond, 1995; Torrance, 1988). However, researchers have established that creativity can be learned and improved and is not as strongly dependent on individual traits as originally thought. Innovative companies recognize that creativity may not necessarily be the result of genius as much as the result of being in an idea-nurturing work environment (e.g., see Gatignon et al., 2002; Schmitt and Brown, 2001; Sebell et al., 2001; Leifer et al., 2000). It is also important for a manager to remember that creative individuals tend to have creative lives even outside of the office (see White and Wright, 2002; Williams, 2002).

Once a problem is formulated, potential criteria and alternatives must be identified. Idea generation is an ideal approach. Creative ideas generally lead to better solutions. In brainstorming, there are some specific creativity measures: the quantitative (number of ideas) and qualitative (quality of ideas) components. Both can be positively impacted by the use of a **creativity support system (CSS)** (essentially a GSS) (Wierenga and van Bruggen, 1998; Massetti, 1996).

Many organizations recognize the value of creativity and innovation (see Bean and Radford, 2001). They are aware of the collaborative nature of creativity and the kinds of environments that foster it (e.g., one critical aspect required for creativity is permission to fail: the Post-it Notes adhesive from 3M Corporation was a dismal failure as a superglue but became remarkably successful once a purpose was discovered for a weak adhesive). Organizations that are remarkably creative tend to have failure as a way of life (see Sutton, 2001; Murphy and Khiralla, 2000; Nelson and Wawiorka, 1999). Creativity and innovation go hand in hand. Quite often what seems like a bad idea at first becomes the source of a creative innovation many years later. For example, the limiting factor in building a mile-high skyscraper (designed in 1956 by Frank Lloyd Wright) was the fact that cabled elevators could not ascend that far. About 40 years later, Otis Elevator Company unveiled a viable prototype (that could even transport people sideways). Fundamental innovations can take 15–25 years to reach fruition (Port and Carey, 1997).

Schrage and Peters (1999) believe that collaboration, serious play, and prototyping (serious trial and error—mostly error) are necessary to foster creativity. The workplace should be a fun place for the innovative knowledge worker. Play involves improvising with the unanticipated in ways that create new value. Creative processes cannot be managed the same way that conventional incremental improvements are. "Innovation can be nurtured and guided by setting soft goals, by evaluating progress with a shrewd eye toward long-range strategy and changes in the outside world, and by creating a climate that encourages bold thinking" (Port and Carey, 1997). The "creative class" must be managed in such a way that the nature of the job and the structure of the work environment meet the members' inner needs and desires (see Florida, 2002a, 2002b). A manager fostering creativity should "allow and enable" rather than structure and control, according to John Kao, founder and CEO of the Idea Factory (Silverstone, 1999). Vance and Deacon (1997, 1999) claim that to encourage creativity it is important to be "outrageous" in our attitudes and activities (also see Kaneshige, 2000). Thinking outside the box unleashes creative energy. It is important to develop many simulations (prototypes) that eventually (hopefully) will lead to a success (possibly after many failures; Thomas Edison had over 1,800 failures before he developed a sustainable light bulb). Schrage and Peters (1999) advise: "Be willing to fail early and often; know when the costs outweigh the benefits; know who wins and who loses from an innovation; build a prototype that engages customers, vendors, and colleagues; create markets around prototypes; and simulate the customer experience." Once creativity is unleashed, it can dramatically enhance the bottom line in the long run. Creativity is important in problem-solving (see Handzic and Cule, 2002), and thus it is critical to develop computerized support systems for it.

Creativity and innovation can be stimulated by a number of environmental factors. An environment that meets the "serious play" criterion is part of the process. Stimulation by other creative people in the environment can push a group forward. How? Some stimulation can come directly from exciting ideas developed as a consequence of association (or synergy) among creative people. This can be done formally by presenting a person with a string of related (even distantly related) concepts. And, some stimulation comes from friction among employees. Some research suggests that some dissatisfaction and discomfort is a must to spark innovation. One should not hire people like oneself. The differences cause stimulation; for example, in brainstorming they broaden the viewpoints (see Sutton, 2001). These differences were capitalized at Boeing-Rocketdyne in using a GSS, as Malhotra et al. (2001) describe: "Innovation, most often, comes from the collaboration of individuals from a cross-section of disciplines, inside and outside of an organization."

A number of association methods have been proposed and empirically proven to be effective in stimulating creativity. And viewing ideas in a different frame (again outside the box, from different angles, etc.) can stimulate creativity (see von Oech, 1998, 2002, and Creative Think at creativethink.com). Next we discuss creativity and innovation in the context of idea generation and electronic brainstorming.

DSS IN FOCUS 7.18

WHAT IS CREATIVITY?

Creativity is fairly complex to define formally but very easy to recognize when you see it. Formally, *creativity* can be defined as either a trait or an achievement (Eysenck, 1994). As a trait, creativity is a dispositional variable characteristic of a person leading to the production of acts, items, and instances of novelty. As an achievement, we refer to the creative product—for example, the output of a process, such as the "quality" of the ideas generated in an electronic brainstorming session. Creative achievement may depend on the trait of creativity but also on much more. Formal research has found that the following variables affect creativity as achievement: cognitive variables (intelligence, knowl-

edge, skills, etc.), environmental variables (cultural and socioeconomic factors), and personality variables (motivation, confidence, and creativity as a trait) (Eysenck, 1994, p. 209). Studies of factors affecting the creativity of marketing programs describe three classes of influencing factors: problem-solving inputs, situational factors, and motivational factors (Andrews and Smith, 1996). These factors are very similar to Eysenck's variables. All in all, experts know when they see creative traits and achievements.

Source: Partly adapted from Wierenga and van Bruggen (1998).

IDEA GENERATION THROUGH ELECTRONIC BRAINSTORMING

Idea generation methods and techniques have been adopted to enhance the creativity of both individuals and groups. **Idea generation** software (**electronic brainstorming**) helps to stimulate the free flow of turbulent creative thinking: ideas, words, pictures, and concepts set loose with fearless enthusiasm, based on the principle of synergy (association). Some packages are designed to enhance the creative thought process of the human mind and can be used to create new product ideas, marketing strategies, promotional campaigns, names, titles, slogans, or stories, or just for brainstorming.

Bombarding the user with many ideas is a key feature of idea generating software. This is critical because it helps the user move away from an analytic mode and into a creative mode. Psychological research indicates that people tend to anchor their thoughts early on, using their first ideas as springboards for other ideas. Therefore, subsequent ideas may not be significantly new, but simply minor variations of the original idea. Because brainstorming software is free of human subjectivity, it can help broaden the thinking platform and encourage truly unique ideas to emerge. Recent studies have characterized creativity and how it can be enhanced by software tools.

By definition, idea generation in GSS is a collaborative effort. One person's idea triggers another's ideas, which trigger even more ideas (in *idea chains* developed by association). With collaborative computing-support tools (e.g., GSS), the individuals do all the thinking while the software system encourages them to move along. The technology is an anonymous, safe way to encourage participants to voice opinions that they might be reluctant to express in a more conventional setting. By building on each other's ideas, people can obtain creative insights they did not have before, based on associations with existing ideas and with their memories. There is a percolation effect as ideas work their way through the process. Associations trigger memories that can activate creativity. The exchange of information (learning) can lead to increases in output and creativity (Dennis, 1996; Dennis et al., 1997/1998; Rees and Koehler, 1999). There are many relatively inexpensive idea generation packages on the market.

Under the right electronic brainstorming conditions, more ideas and ideas that are more creative overall can be generated. A number of different conditions have been explored. Aronson et al. (2000) investigated time-pressure impacts on idea generation and quality. Time pressure matters. Dennis et al. (1997) studied single versus multiple dialogues in brainstorming, and Dennis et al. (1999) examined the impact of decomposing a problem by time periods or by task. Massetti (1996) investigated the impact of different brainstorming tools on creativity, and Hilmer and Dennis (2000) studied categorization impacts.

Generally, if the right approach is used in electronic brainstorming, more ideas and more creative ideas are generated. But a word of caution is in order. Sometimes a group may experience a process gain in the number of ideas and the number of creative ideas but also experience a process loss resulting from *information overload*. The results of each idea generation session can be stored (GSS provides organizational memory) so that they can be carried over from one meeting to another to enhance the creativity of more people.

What if an individual needs to brainstorm alone? There are methods for enhancing individual brainstorming. Satzinger et al. (1999) developed simulated brainstorming to help individuals trigger more creative responses when brainstorming alone. They compared the impact of a simulator that randomly generates ideas to an individual decision-maker, versus an individual decision-maker not using a simulator in brainstorming. The participants using the simulator generated more ideas and more creative ideas than the others.

Research on how a group should organize itself to generate ideas shows that, in contrast to findings on non-computer-mediated idea generation, a single GSS-supported group generates more ideas of higher quality than the same number of participants working as individuals or in several smaller groups (Bostrom et al., 1993). Web-based systems for idea generation (all the groupware mentioned earlier in this chapter) are readily available.

Loosely related to brainstorming, cognitive maps (e.g., Banxia Decision Explorer) can help an individual or group understand a *messy* (wicked) problem, develop a common frame, and enhance creativity. A cognitive map shows how concepts relate to each other, thus helping users organize their thoughts and ideas. In this way they can visualize the problem they are trying to solve (Lipp and Carver, 2000; Sheetz et al., 2000).

CREATIVITY-ENHANCING SOFTWARE

Though electronic brainstorming enhances creativity, it is primarily human beings who produce the results. In the next two subsections we describe software and methods that enhance human creativity by actually performing some of the creative tasks of a human being. Some of these systems actually exhibit creative behavior.

COMPUTER PROGRAMS THAT EXHIBIT CREATIVE BEHAVIOR

For several decades people have attempted to write computer programs that exhibit intelligent behavior. A major characteristic of intelligent behavior is creativity. Can computers be creative?

Intelligent agents (smartbots) can function as facilitators in GSS. Chen et al. (1995) describe an experiment in which an intelligent agent assisted in idea convergence. The agent's performance was comparable to that of a human facilitator in identifying important meeting concepts, but inferior in generating precise and relevant concepts. But the agent was able to complete its task faster than its human counterparts. This concept is in its infancy but has potential for supporting Web-based GSS, where the facilitator cannot be available on a 24/7 basis.

Rasmus (1995) describes three creativity tools. The first one is called Copycat, a program that seeks analogies in patterns of letters. Identifying patterns is the essence of intelligence. Copycat, consisting of several intelligent agents, can find analogies to strings of letters (e.g., find an analogy for transforming *aabc* to *aabd*). This ability can be generalized to other problems that require conceptual understanding and the manipulation of objects. The ability of the program to anticipate the meaning of the transformation and find analogous fits provides evidence that computers can mimic a human being's ability to create analogies. The second system, Tabletop, is also capable of finding analogies. A third system, AARON, is a sophisticated art drawing program and the result of 15 years of research. Its developer, Harold Cohen, created a comprehensive knowledge base to support AARON. Similar computer programs have been developed to write poems and music and create works in other media. The increased knowledge base, processing speed, and storage now available enable such programs to create artwork of good quality.

CREATIVITY SOFTWARE ALTERNATIVES TO IDEA GENERATION

Goldfire (Invention Machine Corporation, Cambridge, MA, invention-machine.com) is an intelligent partner that accelerates technical innovation. Goldfire's semantic processing technology reads, understands, and extracts key concepts from company databases, intranets, and the Internet. The software reads the content, creates a problem solution tree (knowledge index), and delivers an abstract listing of the technical content in relevant documents. Goldfire uses scientific and engineering knowledge as the foundation for its semantic algorithms to accelerate new product and process design innovations.

Goldfire is based on the theory of inventive problem-solving (TRIZ—a Russian acronym). TRIZ was first developed by Genrich Altshuller and his colleagues in Russia in 1946. Over 2 million patents were examined, classified by level of inventiveness, and analyzed to look for the following innovation principles:

1. Problems and solutions repeated across industries and sciences.
2. Patterns of technical evolution repeated across industries and sciences.
3. Innovations using scientific effects outside the field where they were developed.

The TRIZ creative process is described on the Web sites of the *TRIZ Journal* (triz-journal.com) and Ideation International (ideationtriz.com).

SOFTWARE THAT FACILITATES HUMAN CREATIVITY

There are several good software packages that can help stimulate creativity. Some have very specific functions, and others use word associations or questions to prompt users to take new, unexplored directions in their thought patterns. This activity can help users break cyclic thinking patterns, get past mental blocks, or overcome procrastination. Such software can use several different approaches to release the user's flow of ideas. ThoughtPath, Creative WhackPack, and IdeaFisher are just a few of these packages.

ThoughtPath (Synectics Company, www.thoughtpath.com) enhances creativity by walking a user through a series of steps that have demonstrated success in practice. ThoughtPath guides the user through problems and opportunities toward a creative, workable solution. It helps users gain insights into their problems and issues. ThoughtPath is designed to promote outside-the-box thinking. A tour is available on the Web.

Creative Think (creativethink.com) provides the Creative WhackPack (based on von Oech, 1998), a deck of 64 cards that will "whack" you out of habitual thought patterns and let you look at your problem in a new way. The cards ("a physical package") are designed to stimulate the imagination. Fortunately, all 64 illustrated cards are up and running on the Web site (as software); you can select the Give Me Another Creative Whack button to select one at random.

IdeaFisher has an associative lexicon of the English language that cross-references words and phrases. The associative links make it easy for the computer to provide the user with words related to a given theme on some level, based on analogies and metaphors. Many such nonlinear associations can be outrageous, but as mentioned earlier, outrageousness can often trigger new, useful (and profitable) ideas. Personal associations can also be added to the database to broaden its creative application base. IdeaFisher has been described as "a thesaurus on steroids." IdeaFisher has many add-

DSS IN ACTION 7.19

FISHING FOR IDEAS WITH IDEAFISHER

IdeaFisher (ideafisher.com) has three components: QBank, IdeaBank, and Notepad. QBank's questions are organized to assist in formulating an exact problem more accurately; a series of modification questions encourage the user to branch into different lines of thought, and a series of evaluation questions help the user to test and compare the quality of creative ideas to the original objective. This list of central ideas can then be used to decide what to pursue in IdeaBank.

IdeaBank is a massive database of idea words, concepts, and associations with the cross-referencing power of a huge number of direct idea associations and a very large number of secondary (linked) associations. The inclusion of polar opposites stimulates an even larger group of associations.

For example, using the word *car*, the set of Topical Categories includes

- Varieties/Examples (cars)
- Varieties/Examples (named automobiles)

- Varieties/Examples (trailers)
- Varieties/Examples (trucks/buses/vans).

Under the heading Varieties/Examples (car), we find a long list that includes

- Abandoned vehicle
- American muscle car
- Antique car
- Clown's funny car
- Gas guzzler
- Fleet of vehicles.

IdeaBank also lets the user add personal associations and phrases to Topical Categories or to create their own customized Topical Categories.

The third component of the system, Notepad, allows the two databases to work together efficiently. The user can then focus on productive efforts in selecting alternative lines of thought, maximizing the number of high-quality ideas, and selecting the best ones.

on modules designed for specific creative problem-solving situations. Modules include Strategic Planning, Speech and Presentation, Public Relations, General Problem-solving, and more. Writers can use IdeaFisher's Creative Writing Module to help generate analogies to get past writer's block. In DSS in Action 7.19, we describe IdeaFisher's components and list of some of the Varieties/Examples IdeaFisher presents for the Topical Category *car*.

❖ CHAPTER HIGHLIGHTS

- People collaborate in their work. Groupware (collaborative computing software) supports group-work.
- Group members may be in the same organization or may span organizations; they may be in the same or in different locations; they may work at the same or at different times.
- When people work in teams, especially when the members are in different locations and may be working at different times, they need to communicate, collaborate, and access a diverse set of information sources in multiple formats.
- Collaborative computing is known by a number of terms, including groupware, group support systems (GSS), and computer-supported cooperative work (CSCW).

- The Internet (Web), intranets, and extranets support decision-making through collaboration tools and access to data, information, and knowledge.
- Internet and Web technology has had a major impact on how we communicate and work.
- An intranet is an internal Internet.
- An extranet links a workgroup, such as an intranet for group members from several different organizations. A common use is for groupware applied to a supply chain involving several organizations using Internet technology.
- Groups and groupwork (teams and teamwork) in organizations are proliferating. Consequently, groupware continues to evolve to support effective groupwork.

- Communication technologies are the foundation on which groupware rests.
- Collaboration is much deeper than communication; it conveys meaning or knowledge; material is actively worked on during collaboration.
- The time/place framework is a convenient way to describe the communication and collaboration patterns of groupwork. Different technologies can support different frameworks.
- People may work together at the same time or at different times, in the same place or in different places.
- Groupware refers to software products that provide collaborative support to groups (including meetings).
- Though meetings can be inefficient and ineffective, most groupwork occurs in meetings.
- Groupware typically contains capabilities for electronic brainstorming, electronic conferencing or meeting, group scheduling, calendaring, planning, conflict resolution, model building, videoconferencing, electronic document sharing, voting, and so on.
- Groupware can support anytime/anyplace groupwork.
- Most groupware allows group members to communicate over the Internet with a Web browser interface.
- There are many benefits (process and task gains) to groupwork, but there are also many dysfunctions (process and task losses).
- A group support system (GSS) is any combination of hardware and software that enhances groupwork.
- Group support systems (GSS) are also known as electronic meeting systems (EMS), computer-supported cooperative work (CSCW) systems, collaborative computing, and groupware.
- GSS attempts to increase process and task gains and reduce process and task losses of groupwork.
- Parallelism and anonymity provide many GSS gains.
- GSS may be considered in terms of the common group activities of information retrieval, information sharing, and information use.

- GSS can be deployed in an electronic decision room environment, in a multipurpose computer lab, or over the Web.
- Web-based groupware is the norm for anytime/anyplace collaboration.
- GSS software may include modules for idea generation (via outlining or brainstorming), idea organization, stakeholder identification, topic commentator, voting, policy formulation, and enterprise analysis.
- GSS same time/same place meetings generally follow a fixed pattern: (1) planning, (2) question posing, (3) brainstorming, (4) idea organization, (5) discussion and idea prioritization, and (6) more idea generation.
- The classroom is a natural setting in which to enhance learning by providing computerized support.
- Distance learning (DL) takes place when learning is performed with tools or technologies designed to overcome the restrictions of same time/same place learning.
- As the economics of education and socioeconomic trends evolve, students are completing their college educations in nontraditional ways.
- Both students and faculty must understand how collaborative technology impacts on how they perform course work.
- Creativity is a complex concept.
- Creativity can be learned and fostered with good managerial techniques and a supportive environment.
- Idea generation (electronic brainstorming) allows participants to generate and share ideas simultaneously and anonymously.
- Creativity-support systems (CSS), essentially GSS, can provide computer support to the creative process.
- Human creativity can be supported with idea generation (electronic brainstorming) systems.
- Creativity software programs use association and "thinking outside the box" to trigger new concepts.

❖ KEY WORDS

- anonymity
- asynchronous
- collaborative computing
- computer-supported cooperative work (CSCW)
- courseware
- creativity
- creativity support system (CSS)
- decision room
- Delphi method
- distance learning (DL)

- electronic brainstorming
- electronic meeting systems (EMS)
- electronic meeting (e-meeting)
- enterprise-wide collaboration systems
- extranet
- firewall
- group support systems (GSS)
- groupthink
- groupware
- groupwork

- idea generation
- Internet
- intranet
- nominal group technique (NGT)
- parallelism
- process gain
- process loss
- synchronous
- virtual corporation
- World Wide Web (Web)

❖ QUESTIONS FOR REVIEW

1. List the characteristics of groupwork.
2. List the activities of meetings.
3. What is the primary objective of groupware?
4. List the reasons why communication is so important for collaborative computing.
5. List the differences between collaboration and communication.
6. List the frames and collaborative technologies in the time/place framework of IT communication support.
7. List the reasons why meetings can be ineffective and inefficient. Also, list ways to solve the problems.
8. Define groupware. List its goals.
9. List the benefits (gains) of groupwork.
10. List the dysfunctions (losses) of groupwork.
11. Define a group support system (GSS). List its potential capabilities.
12. Define an electronic meeting system (EMS).
13. What is parallelism? What is anonymity?
14. List the three options for deploying GSS technology and their advantages and disadvantages.
15. List the factors that lead to GSS success.
16. List the important issues involving anytime/anyplace meetings.
17. What is learning?
18. List the features of collaborative computing that can enhance the traditional classroom environment.
19. List the reasons why distance learning is becoming more popular.
20. List the advantages and disadvantages of distance learning.
21. Define creativity and list the ways that GSS (CSS) can enhance creativity.

❖ QUESTIONS FOR DISCUSSION

1. Explain the differences and similarities among features of the Internet, intranets, and extranets.
2. Explain how a group might be noncooperative but need to collaborate.
3. How does groupware attain its primary objective?
4. Describe in detail why communication is so important for collaborative computing.
5. What is nonverbal communication? Explain why it is important in human-to-human interaction. What methods are currently being used to incorporate nonverbal communication into collaborative computing?
6. Explain why collaboration is deeper than communication.
7. Explain why it is useful to describe groupwork in terms of the time/place framework.
8. Describe the kinds of support that groupware can provide.
9. Explain why most groupware is deployed over the Web.
10. Describe and compare each of the groupware packages mentioned in this chapter.
11. Describe the advantages of deploying groupware over the Web.
12. Compare GSS to noncomputerized group decision-making.
13. Explain why meetings can be so inefficient. Given this, explain how effective meetings can be run.
14. Discuss the details of process gains (benefits) of groupwork.
15. Discuss the details of process losses (dysfunctions) of groupwork.
16. Explain how GSS can increase some of the benefits of collaboration and eliminate or reduce some of the losses.
17. Explain how some of the features of GSS have become embedded in computerized productivity tools.
18. The original term for group support system was group decision support system (GDSS). Why was the word "decision" dropped? Does this make sense? Why or why not?
19. Discuss how parallelism and anonymity can produce improvements in group processes.
20. Describe the three technologies through which GSS is deployed. What are the advantages and disadvantages of each?
21. Why are deadlines important for anytime/anyplace meetings? What can happen if they are not set?
22. Explain what factors lead to GSS success.
23. In terms of the advantages and disadvantages of distance learning, explain why some students prefer a distance learning environment and others prefer a traditional learning environment.
24. How have GSS, the Web, and videoconferencing enabled effective distance learning?

25. Explain in detail why companies are moving toward online training.
26. Explain in detail what creativity is.
27. Explain how GSS can support creativity.
28. Explain how idea generation (electronic brainstorming) works.
29. Can computers be creative? Why or why not?

❖ EXERCISES

1. Make a list of all the communications methods you use during your day (work and personal). Which are the most effective? Which are the least effective? What kind of work or activity does each communications method enable?
2. Investigate the impact of turning off every communication system in a firm (telephone, fax, television, radio, and all computer systems). How effective and efficient would the following types of firms be: airline, bank, insurance company, travel agency, department store, grocery store? What would happen? Do customers expect 100 percent uptime? (When was the last time a major airline's reservation system was down?) How long would it be before each type of firm would not be functioning at all? Investigate what organizations are doing to prevent this situation from occurring.
3. In many nations telephone systems are inadequate, inefficient, or nonexistent, despite the widespread availability of computer systems. What do firms operating in countries under these conditions do to bypass these crippling effects on communication?
4. Investigate body language and report your findings. If possible, use this subject as a presentation topic, actively using body language. How does body language affect the meaning of the message being conveyed? Include in your report how researchers are attempting to incorporate the nonverbal cues of body language into collaborative computing. Also explain how an MIS or CS specialist could incorporate what may be learned from a theater/drama class into his or her professional life.
5. Investigate how researchers are trying to develop collaborative computer systems that portray or display nonverbal communication factors.
6. For each of the following software packages, check the trade literature and the Web for details and explain how computerized collaborative support system capabilities are included: Groove, GroupSystems Online, NetMeeting, WebEx.
7. Investigate methods for improving the effectiveness and efficiency of meetings.
8. From your own experience or from the vendor's information, list all the major capabilities of Lotus Notes and explain how they can be used to support decision-making.
9. Compare Simon's four-phase decision-making model to the GSS-use sequence described in DSS in Focus 7.11.
10. How would you feel about taking a distance learning course that uses courseware (e.g., WebCT Vista or Blackboard) to enhance groupwork and communication with the instructor? Find three (or more) articles in the literature that describe the experiences of students and faculty in a distance learning course and compare your thoughts with their experiences. What advantages and disadvantages does such an approach have?

❖ GROUP EXERCISES

1. Access the Web Chapter (prenhall.com/turban) on Group Brainstorming and do the exercises.
2. Access the Groove Web site (groove.net). Download the demo software to each group member's computer and use it to brainstorm and vote on a specific problem or issue (note, as of press time, the demo version was fully functional but did not support addins or video). When brainstorming, think broadly. Did you feel comfortable with the software? Why or why not?
3. Access the Web site of a for-lease Web-based groupware service (e.g., WebEx). Describe what features it offers and how they could help the members of a group work together. If the site offers a free trial, have your group try it out and report your experience to the class.
4. Identify colleges and universities that provide courses via distance learning (use both traditional library sources and Web sources). Find at least four articles on the topic. What types of courseware do these institutions use? Are the courseware tools effective when compared with standard teaching methods?
5. Case Study. As part of some recent fieldwork (Dennis and Garfield, 1999), several groups at a hospital met to discuss issues of and develop ideas for strategic planning. Some groups used GSS-supported electronic meetings (reluctantly), while other groups used the traditional meeting approach. Most of the

members who started with the GSS discarded it, realized how much better off they were with it, and went back to it. When the central administration examined suggestions from both sets of groups (traditional meetings and GSS-supported meetings), it pursued the ideas of the GSS-supported groups almost exclusively. Why do you think this happened? Explain.

❖ INTERNET EXERCISES

1. How are decisions supported by groupware? Identify software products on the Web that help groups work and make decisions. Download a package, install it, and try it (or if it runs on the Web, just run it). Report your findings to the class.
2. Search the Internet to identify sites that describe methods for improving meetings. Investigate ways that meetings can be made more effective and efficient.
3. Access the Web site of GroupSystems.com (groupsystems.com) and identify its current GSS products.
4. Access the Expert Choice Inc. Web site (expertchoice.com).
   a. Find information about their group support products.
   b. Team Expert Choice is related to the concept of the AHP described in Chapter 4. Evaluate this product in terms of decision support. Do you think that keypad use provides process gains or process losses? How and why?
5. Identify five real-world GSS success stories at vendor Web sites (use at least three different vendors). Describe them. How did GSS software and methods contribute to the success? What common features do they share? What different features do individual successes have?
6. Access a demo version of a GSS (e.g., Groove, WebEx, or even NetMeeting) on the Web. Use the system for a meeting of your group to solve another group assignment for any of your courses (check with your instructor). Explain why you did or did not feel comfortable with the software.
7. Identify three Web-based courseware systems. Compare and contrast their features. If a "test drive" or demo is available, try it out. Which one do you prefer and why? Report your findings to the class.
8. Go the Creative Think Web site (creativethink.com) with a problem in mind that you are trying to solve (e.g., selecting a graduate school, an undergraduate school, a job). Use the Give Me Another Whack button to enhance your thinking. Try a few of their Whacks to see if they can help you. Did they?
9. For one of the creativity software packages described in the text, go to the company's Web site, download and try out a demo, and describe your experience in a report. Include what you liked and didn't like, and what you found useful and didn't find useful.

❖ TERM PAPERS

1. Describe the latest developments in collaborative computing/GSS in a term paper.
2. The activities and competence of a group facilitator are critical to the success of a GSS session. Identify recent articles and Web sites on GSS facilitation and write a term paper describing what makes a good facilitator for GSS and how GSS can support the facilitator.
3. Some GSS researchers are concerned with the cross-cultural effects of computer system use. This is especially important in GSS, where opinions are usually entered and synthesized by meeting participants at different places around the globe. Examine the literature and write a term paper on the major issues of how GSS provides either process gains or processes losses in a multicultural electronic meeting setting.

PFIZER'S EFFECTIVE AND SAFE COLLABORATIVE COMPUTING PILL

INTRODUCTION

In the United States, the long, difficult research and development involved in getting a new drug to market often requires an immense collaborative effort. Drug companies must conduct broad, expensive trials before their products even reach the Food and Drug Administration (FDA) for approval. Out of the tens of thousands of compounds discovered each year, only 7 percent make it to market. After an extensive development phase, pharmaceutical companies must back up their drug efficacy claims with mountains of paper (typically more than 1 million pages—equivalent to a tractor trailer full of paper) sent to the FDA, the federal agency that evaluates pharmaceutical products before they are placed on the market. The FDA's approval process is also a long, detailed one.

In addition, drug companies also face added pressure because of a congressionally mandated restructuring of the FDA's review process. The FDA is required to shorten its review process to 12 months from its typical 18–24 months to get drugs to market faster without compromising safety.

To move documentation more swiftly through the FDA's approval procedure, Pfizer developed an electronically based drug submission process. Pfizer's Electronic Submission Navigator (ESUB) is a vast improvement over its old paper-based method of submitting documentation to the FDA. Pfizer's award-winning system cost $3.2 million to develop and netted the company at least $142 million in revenues through the start of 2000 because of shorter cycle times. But ESUB has also changed the way that research clinicians and the IT staff collaborate.

"Esub has had enormous impact in that it has transformed the way we do things internally," says George Milne, president of research and development for Pfizer's central research division in Groton, Connecticut. "Our ability to execute new drug filings has been brought to an unprecedented scale," he claims. "It's much more than just an interesting computer system. The tools that Esub gives us will stimulate insight. We expect it to lead to a cascading effect of innovation." Esub has directly impacted the industry and serves as a benchmark for the FDA submission process.

TRUCKLOADS OF PAPER

In mid-1995 Pfizer's researchers were developing Trovan, a new antibiotic drug being readied for FDA approval. The potential new product would be the largest anti-infective submission ever received by the FDA.

Typically, researchers and support staff produced separate sections of a paper document reporting the results of drug trials. Each section was eventually assembled into a master document called a *new drug application* (NDA). Once compiled, the NDA was edited, copied, and sent to the FDA to start the approval process.

The FDA distributed portions of the report to reviewers who wrote their own analyses. Document management, revision control, and cross-reference accuracy were a major challenge. Individual reviewers worked with 20,000-page sections, each a stack 5 or 6 feet high. Cross-referencing caused major headaches. A reviewer who needed to check something on a page outside his or her section had to wait for the FDA to send a runner to copy it from the master version in the library warehouse. The reviewers needed access to the latest version of every section of the document.

To solve this problem, Pfizer's staff used computer-aided NDAs (CANDAs) to build sections of the document electronically. Though they didn't provide all the data and performance was slow, it was the best that current technology could provide in 1995.

At that time the Web was beginning to take off, and Walter Hauck (an associate director in charge of clinical applications development and now director of clinical systems) suggested that the time had come to experiment with it. In April 1996 Hauck and his IT team showed a crude prototype to one of the Trovan clinicians, who in turn showed it to Scott Hopkins, executive director of anti-infectives. Hopkins instantly saw the benefit of the project and gave it the go-ahead.

Pfizer's IT team created about one Esub prototype per week, rewriting the code nearly 40 times until it became easier to manage. During Esub's development, the size of the NDA for Trovan was grossly underestimated. The submission grew to almost 50,000 documents,

Adapted from M. Blodgett, "Prescription Strength," *CIO*, February 1, 2000, pp. 94–98.

close to 180 gigabytes. As the project grew, the prototyping process created excitement among members of the IT team and the clinical team.

ESUB EMERGES

On December 28, 1996, nine months after its conception, Esub was delivered. Because Trovan was so complex in terms of its trials and use, the teams identified and solved tough problems first. In March 1997, Esub handled the submission of Viagra with ease. Now the clinical team can collaborate on new drug applications, with the FDA and its reviewers using Esub to coordinate their work.

ESUB BENEFITS

The benefits of Esub go far beyond a typical return on investment. Esub has become a company-wide collaborative data-sharing system that is also being considered by the FDA as a benchmark for other drug company submissions. Pfizer maintains a competitive advantage in building quality dossiers in real time. Esub has also created a heightened role for IT within the Pfizer organization.

By working collaboratively with its business partners, Pfizer's IT team constructed a system that

- Provides a global view of the status of a trial or application process.
- Enhances Pfizer's competitive advantage by linking drug researchers around the world; Esub has attracted business partners, including other drug manufacturers seeking to forge strategic alliances with Pfizer to help market and distribute their drugs.
- Enables Pfizer to penetrate world markets much more quickly by filing concurrent submissions in different countries.
- Gives the company the ability to deliver five new drugs every 12 months—the fastest rate in the industry.
- Features an electronic table of contents to negotiate the forms of an NDA.
- Allows portable review with a full-featured system— important because the FDA frequently uses outside consultants.

By 2000, the number of users of the system had increased to 2,000 worldwide at both Pfizer and government regulatory agencies. The Esub repository has grown to 5 terabytes, with roughly 1 terabyte of new data added each quarter. The most important Esub benefit is intangible: new, safe, effective drugs that can be offered to patients quickly.

CASE QUESTIONS

1. What kind of collaboration does Pfizer's Esub support?
2. Who are the collaborators?
3. How does Esub support collaboration?
4. What are the benefits of Esub? What possible disadvantages might Esub have?

5. What specific benefits does the FDA obtain from collaborating with Pfizer through Esub?
6. How could Esub function as the heart of an extranet with Pfizer, its regulatory agency (FDA), salespersons, pharmacies, medical researchers, and doctors treating patients?

CASE APPLICATION 7.2

DOW CHEMICAL CREATES THE WORLD'S LARGEST CLASSROOM

THE PROBLEM

In 2000, Dow Chemical fired 61 employees and took lesser disciplinary measures against another 540 for sending offensive e-mail over company servers. Not convinced that simply monitoring future employee e-mail was an appropriate response to the situation, CEO Bill Stavropoulos (now chairman) decided that all 40,000 Dow employees across 70 countries would take six hours of training on workplace respect and responsibility. This comprehensive response to a pervasive workplace problem would be prohibitively expensive for most global organizations. But Dow could deliver the training through a Web-based training system, Learn@dow.now.

THE SOLUTION

Between October 2000 and February 2001, more than 40,000 employees took and passed the course—a two-hour overview and a four-hour class in their native language. Dow saved about $2.7 million by doing so. Savings included $162,000 on manual record-keeping of class completions, $300,000 on classroom facilities and trainers, $1 million on course handouts, and $1.2 million in salary savings. Most of these savings were due to shorter training time.

IMPLEMENTATION OF THE SOLUTION AND RESULTS

The learning system also delivered a tremendous payback in mergers and acquisitions. The rapid assimilation of new employees is key to unlocking the value in acquisitions. Manufacturing-site employees joining Dow must complete a three-part operations discipline course. So far, 11,000 employees have completed their course work online in 30 percent of the time normally required in traditional classroom settings. Dow has saved $2 million in training costs. Learn@dow.now was also the method that 27,000 employees used to complete the environmental health and safety work processes courses, saving $6 mil-

lion. Safety incidents have declined as a result, even though the Dow workforce has grown by 25 percent.

Dow spent $1.3 million on the e-learning system. In the first full year of operation, the company estimates the total cost benefits of Learn@dow.now at $30 million—$844,279 saved on manual record-keeping, $3.1 million on training delivery costs, $5.2 million in reduced class materials, and $20.8 million on salaries (Web-based training requires 40 percent to 60 percent less time than a traditional classroom environment.)

When launched, Learn@dow.now offered 15 course titles. By the end of its first year, the system delivered 98 course titles and recorded 24,492 course completions. In 2000, the system offered 426 course options with 208,464 completions.

A GLOBAL CLASSROOM

Learn@dow.now has grown quickly and is now one of the most comprehensive Web-based learning tools around. Current courses range from cost accounting and business ethics to chemistry and hazardous materials handling—each one offered in Dutch, English, French, German, Italian, Portuguese, and Spanish (with some available in Chinese, Indonesian, Japanese, and Thai). Most classes require a post-test to determine whether the employee has mastered the subject matter for certification. When an employee finishes a class, a record of completion is automatically transferred to his or her permanent training file in PeopleSoft 7 HRMS.

As for the online respect and responsibility class, the value has gone beyond the several million dollars saved by delivering the information through Learn@dow.now. Senior leadership demonstrated a strong commitment to protect the company's values of respect for people and to take swift and decisive action where those values are compromised. Dow used the best available technology to design and deliver this important information globally.

Adapted from Stephanie Overby, "The Dow Chemical Co.: The World's Biggest Classroom," *CIO*, February 1, 2002, pp. 56–60.

CASE QUESTIONS

1. Why was it important for senior managers to commit to sensitivity training?

2. Why was an online learning mechanism selected?

3. What other benefits were obtained through the learning system?

4. What benefits did Dow obtain through the learning system?

CHAPTER
8

ENTERPRISE INFORMATION SYSTEMS

LEARNING OBJECTIVES

❖ Describe the concepts, definitions, and issues in enterprise information systems.

❖ Determine how to extract information needs from executives and managers.

❖ Compare the features and capabilities of enterprise information systems and DSS/BI.

❖ See the relationships among enterprise information systems, data warehouses, online analytical processing, data mining, and other forms of business intelligence/DSS.

❖ Discuss the capabilities and characteristics of (Web-based) enterprise information portals.

❖ Describe supply chain management issues and how enterprise information systems handle them.

❖ Discuss customer relationship management concepts and issues.

❖ Describe how the Web impacts enterprise information systems, and vice versa.

❖ Describe how enterprise information systems have improved frontline decision-making by providing access to real-time data.

❖ Describe emerging enterprise information systems, including product life-cycle management, business process management, and business activity monitoring.

Support systems optimize their effectiveness when they are easily accessible by all users. Web Portal technologies using the Internet, intranets, and extranets have emerged as efficient means to deliver a vast array of information to quickly and effectively support individual decision-makers making specific decisions (Chapters 3–6, and 9), and the processes of individuals collaborating from a distance, as well as group work (Chapters 7 and 9). In this chapter, we shift our attention to systems that deal with enterprise-wide support. First, attention is given to top executives, especially to their role in discovering problems, or trends that may create problems, and in identifying opportunities. The work of executives has been transformed by the vast amounts of information made readily accessible by computer technology. Second, attention is given to decisional situations involving decision-makers in different locations. Next we describe enterprise resource planning (ERP)/enterprise resource management (ERM) systems that integrate all the routine transaction processing in the organization and in the customer and supply chain management systems that integrate business processes throughout the organization. Then we turn to customer relationship (resource) management (CRM) systems that directly enhance the organization's customer service and bottom line. We also discuss frontline systems that use real-time data capture and access to provide decision-making assistance at the tactical and operational levels. Finally, we introduce some emerging enterprise information systems. Many of these technologies have a data warehouse as their foundation, and utilize the Web for data access from servers and for communication and collaboration.

8.1 OPENING VIGNETTE: THE UNITED STATES MILITARY TURNS TO PORTALS[1]

The U.S. Army, Air Force, and Navy have each implemented Web-based portals as a method to enhance communications, improve quality-of-life issues, and rapidly share front-line combat intelligence, as was demonstrated in the recent war with Iraq. AKO (*Army Knowledge Online*) was built using Art Technology Group Inc's. Dynamo software to serve a community estimated at 1.2 million users. This allows information to be pushed out to users based upon rank, division, location, and duties. The portal can be accessed through the Internet and the Army's proprietary SIPRnet (Secret IP Router Network) to enable logistics services, personnel and operations applications, e-mail, and instant messaging to be accessed from virtually anywhere in the world. It is comprehensive in scope, ranging from supporting combat readiness to handling issues such as informing noncommissioned officers about what they need to do to earn promotion, since the portal is linked to the Army's personnel files.

---

[1]Adapted from Dennis Callaghan, "Armed Services Turn to Portals," *eWeek*, November 19, 2001; Jade Boyd, "Navy to Add Web to Its Battle Plan," *InternetWeek*, No. 881, October 8, 2001, p. 11.

The Navy's portal, part of a $6.9 billion intranet consolidation project, links land-based logistics and support operations with onboard ship systems. This provides commanders with enhanced strategic and tactical information to improve their decision-making ability. This is not just a battle-support system. There are many daily activities that must be supported for a ship to remain at sea for months. The system handles everything from payroll and benefits to providing up-to-date technical manuals. One of the main goals of the portal was to link disparate legacy systems and databases, providing a single easy-to-use interface. This integration was critical to the system's use and success.

Portals are used not only to provide a bridge to connect support applications with tactical applications, but also to link systems and technologies which, up until now, have been separately developed, maintained, and accessed.

❖ QUESTIONS FOR THE OPENING VIGNETTE

1. How can timely access to information be used by the military to support its operations?
2. What capabilities should a military portal support?
3. How does portal technology support an overall information systems architecture?
4. Identify issues of concern when developing a portal.
5. The vignette does not mention a data warehouse. In your opinion, is one needed? Why or why not?
6. Identify the supply chain activities that military portals might need to support.

8.2 ENTERPRISE INFORMATION SYSTEMS: CONCEPTS AND DEFINITIONS

The Opening Vignette introduces us to systems that support tactical and strategic decision-making at all levels of an organization. In many organizations, a variety of decisions are made on a daily basis by middle and top managers, marketing analysts, and other knowledge workers in many locations, even in different countries. In the 1980s and through most of the 1990s, systems serving the needs of top executives were designed as independent (standalone) systems and were called **executive information systems (EIS).** This approach made such systems affordable mostly to large corporations. Today, executives are supported by systems that support other employees as well. They are called **enterprise information systems (EIS)**. The Opening Vignette demonstrates that these systems serve many users, and therefore are very cost-effective. Well-built enterprise information systems provide executives with the same capabilities that were provided by EIS. In addition, as a result of improved system integration and delivery methods, they serve many other users throughout the enterprise.

Enterprise information systems projects were a high priority among CIOs for the next several years. See DSS in Focus 8.1 for a breakdown from two surveys.

In this chapter, we cover several types of enterprise information systems. We will start with a discussion of the information needs of executives and what IT capabilities are available to meet these needs across the enterprise. Then we relate enterprise

CIO SPENDING PLANS: NOW AND LATER

The Gartner Group surveyed 620 CIOs in January 2003 to determine what priorities they had for the new year, and Merrill Lynch & Co. surveyed 50 U.S. CIOs in February 2003 for their priorities when the economy improved. Most of these spending plans involved developing enterprise information systems.

The top 10 priorities for 2003 included:

1. Security enhancement tools
2. Application integration/middleware/messaging
3. Enterprise (information) portal deployment
4. Network infrastructure/management tools
5. Internal e-enabling infrastructure
6. Web design, development, and content management tools
7. Storage management
8. Customer relationship management (CRM)
9. Web services (internal and external)
10. XML-based processes/messaging

The most important first software projects to be funded once the economy improved were

- Customer relationship management (CRM) (20%)
- Security (20%)
- Enterprise resource planning (ERP) (16%)
- Storage (16%)
- Application integration (14%)
- Corporate (enterprise information) portals (14%)
- Supply chain management (SCM) (14%)
- Business intelligence/data warehousing (DSS/BI) (12%)
- Analytic applications (DSS/BA) (10%)

Source: Adapted from Kathleen Melymuka, "Ready, Set . . ." *ComputerWorld*, July 21, 2003, pp. 37–38.

information systems to the data-warehousing concepts presented in Chapter 5. Following that, we discuss organizational decision support systems, which leads to the concept of the supply chain and its management. We finish the chapter by covering several high-impact, emerging enterprise information systems: process life-cycle management (PLM), business process management (BPM), and business activity monitoring (BAM) systems. In Table 8.1, we describe the impacts of the Web on each of these enterprise information systems, and vice versa.

8.3 THE EVOLUTION OF EXECUTIVE AND ENTERPRISE INFORMATION SYSTEMS

During the 1980s it was felt that the then-existing information technologies, including DSS, were not adequate for executive use (Rockart and Delong, 1988). The published information about DSS showed that most personal DSS supported the work of professionals and middle-level managers. Organizational DSS provided support primarily to planners, analysts, and researchers. Rarely did top executives directly use a DSS. The situation was in contrast to the fact that the most important job of top executives is to make decisions. What was needed was a tool that could handle executives' special needs for timely and accurate information in a meaningful format.

Executive information systems (EIS), also known as **executive support systems (ESS)** (Watson et al., 1997), are a technology that emerged in response to the situa-

TABLE 8.1   Enterprise Information Systems Technologies, and Web Impacts

Enterprise Information System Technology	Web Impacts	Impacts on the Web
Executive Information Systems (EIS)	Consistent, friendly, graphical user interface Convenient, fast, and direct access to (hard and soft) data on servers and data warehouses Web graphics have improved the reporting of information Drill down and rollup capabilities are enabled by automatic hyperlinks Enhanced communication and collaboration Improved decision-making	Better management and use of Web resources at the strategic level Data captured are utilized in improving Web site design and performance
Executive Support Systems (ESS)	Same as above Access to analytical models (business intelligence)	Same as above
Enterprise Information Systems (EIS: as evolved from Executive Information Systems)	Same as above	Same as above Plus better management and use of Web resources at the tactical and operational levels (improved frontline decision-making)
Supply Chain Management Systems	Same as above Quick and ready access to needed information Simplifies and enables effective collaboration and communication along the supply chain Can provide access to analytical tools with which to use to *optimize* the supply chain Links customers' and vendors' value and supply chains to your organization's Improved performance of the supply chain	Same as above Specifically, improved performance of Web-enabled businesses and e-commerce sites Enables logistics tools for Web-based operations
Enterprise Resource Planning/Enterprise Resource Management (ERP/ERM) Systems	Same as for executive information systems Provides an architecture for data access and use Improved decision-making throughout the organization, and especially in human resources, accounting, finance, marketing, and production and service delivery	Provides a need for more Web servers and other infrastructure, including integrating suppliers and customers into an organization's operations
Customer Relationship (Resource) Management (CRM) Systems	Same as for executive support systems, with a focus on the customers' needs Provides access to data mining, OLAP, and other business analytic and business intelligence tools to improve sales and customer service Increased sales	Helps target specific customer segments so that the Web site is more effective and useful
Product Life-cycle Management (PLM) Systems	Browser technology provides a convenient GUI interface Access to real-time data Access to product documentation for items in every stage of development Access to collaboration and communication technologies by all individuals involved in product development, including those outside the organization	For organizations developing Web infrastructure and software: improvements in the Web itself and e-commerce
Business Process Management (BPM) Systems	User interface Data Access Communication and collaboration tools Increased need due to e-commerce	Same as above
Business Activity Monitoring (BAM) Systems	Same as above	Same as above

tion just described (see also DSS in Focus 8.2). In a survey conducted by the Center for Information Systems Research (CISR) at MIT, it was found that people with the title of chief executive officer (CEO), chief financial officer (CFO), or chief operations officer (COO) were the major users of EIS. Nord and Nord (1996) found that the most popular uses of EIS were for decision support by providing data and information (50%), for scheduling (50%), to set agendas and schedule meetings (43.8%), for electronic briefing (31.5%), and for browsing data and monitoring situations (31.3%).

In the mid-1990s, with advances in data warehousing (Chapter 5) and in Web technologies, the independent EIS concept was replaced by the more cost-effective enterprise system. The current trend is toward increased integration of vast amounts of decision support information by Web-enabling legacy databases. Web portals enable organizations to reach their constituents (e.g., customers, vendors, employees) providing large amounts of information that can be personalized to the needs of the individual. They have also had an impact on organizational business processes, providing a forum for such activities as virtual meetings and remote training.

DEFINITIONS

The terms *executive information system* and *executive support system* mean different things to different people. Often the terms are used interchangeably. The following definitions, based on Rockart and DeLong (1988), distinguish between EIS and ESS.

DSS IN FOCUS 8.2

WHY EIS?

The most common benefits of an EIS are improvement in the quality and quantity of information available to executives. The following factors were identified by Watson et al. (1996, 1997).

INFORMATION NEEDS (INTERNAL AND EXTERNAL)

- More timely information
- Greater access to operational data
- Greater access to corporate databases
- More concise, relevant information
- New or additional information
- More information about the external environment
- More competitive information
- Faster access to external databases
- Faster access to information
- Reduced paper costs.

EIS IMPROVEMENTS IN EXECUTIVE JOB PERFORMANCE ABILITY

- Enhanced communications
- Greater ability to identify historical trends
- Improved executive effectiveness
- Improved executive efficiency
- Fewer meetings and less time spent in meetings
- Enhanced executive mental models
- Improved executive planning, organizing, and control
- More focused executive attention
- Greater support for executive decision-making
- Increased span of control.

- *Executive information system (EIS).* An EIS is a computer-based system that serves the information needs of top executives. It provides rapid access to timely information and direct access to management reports. EIS is very user-friendly, is supported by graphics, and provides exceptions reporting and drill-down capabilities. It is also connected to the Internet, intranets, and extranets.
- *Executive support system (ESS).* An ESS is a comprehensive support system that goes beyond EIS to include communication, office automation, analysis support, and business intelligence.
- *Enterprise information system (EIS).* This is a corporate-wide system that provides holistic information from a corporate point of view. Different users across the enterprise can use the system for different purposes. These systems serve the needs of top executives as well. Enterprise systems are an important part of the *enterprise resources management* (ERP) concept, which we present later in this chapter.

For an example of an EIS, consider the executive information system of Health Management Systems, Inc. (www.hmstn.com), which is customized to increase productivity and management effectiveness in the health-care industry. Srivihok (1999) also investigates EIS success factors, while Hung (1999) investigated ESS usage patterns between experts and novices.

ENTERPRISE SUPPORT SYSTEMS

The most important goal of enterprise support systems (ESS) is providing a tool for *enterprise support*. For this reason, one can distinguish two types of EIS: one designed especially to support top executives, and the other intended to serve a wider community of users.

An executive-only EIS can be modified to be part of an enterprise-wide information system. As such, executive systems have become less strictly defined, and EIS applications are embracing a range of products targeted to support professional decision-makers throughout the enterprise (see DSS in Action 8.3). EIS are already providing some of the needed capabilities. In addition, there are an increasing number of tools designed to help functional managers (finance, marketing, etc.). These tools are integrated with EIS.

Enterprise support systems have even been found to help developing countries. They have had impact in Malaysia, China (PRC), Uzbekistan, South Africa, Egypt, and Ukraine (see Lalkaka and Albetti, 1999). Lalkaka and Albetti (1999) describe how ESS can lead to better use of agricultural resources and skills, higher value added in light chemical engineering, and garment goods for both export and domestic consumption. Rouse (1993) indicates that ESS contribute to the creation of plans for new products and services, as well as new ventures that accelerate job creation. These lead to important contributions to economic development.

Enterprise information systems continue to diffuse into lower organizational levels. They have definitely moved down the organization to the management level (see Xianzhong and Kaye, 2002). Capabilities once provided exclusively to executives are now provided at the operational level for frontline support (see Section 8.15). Nord and Nord (1995), in their study of all *Fortune 500* companies using EIS, discovered that 50 percent of all CEOs, 31.3 percent of all presidents, 93.8 percent of all vice presidents, and 87.5 percent of all middle managers used EIS on a regular basis. For this reason,

DSS IN ACTION 8.3

GENERAL MOTORS EMPLOYEE-CENTRIC PORTAL SHIFTS INTO HIGH GEAR

Employee benefits, such as the 401K plan, affect all 180,000 U.S. employees of General Motors Corporation. In light of the Enron scandal, many employees pay much closer attention to where their retirement funds are invested, and as a result, they change their investment options much more frequently. Employees at General Motors Corp. have been given immediate access to all benefits-related information, including forms, FAQs, and policies and procedures.

GM's chief technology officer, Tony Scott, reported that one of the company's primary goals was to provide access to all employees regardless of location, even for employees who work at home. The portal was built on the Sun Microsytems Solaris platform and iPlanets

application server. It is a self-service application that provides HR and benefits services *immediately* to each employee. The development of the portal did not undergo a formal cost/benefit analysis, but should greatly reduce administrative costs and simplify the communication of benefits-related changes. The new portal has greatly enhanced communcation to employees delivering personalized information on a real-time basis.

Source: Adapted from Elisabeth Goodridge, "Portal Gives Workers Cruise Control," *InformationWeek*, No. 864, November 19, 2001, p. 73.

the acronym EIS is now interpreted to mean *enterprise information system* or *everybody's information system.* As a matter of fact, most vendors do not use the term *executive information systems* at all in the names of their products. Instead, the term **business intelligence (BI)** or *enterprise systems* is used to describe the new role of EIS, especially now that data warehouses can provide data in easy-to-use, graphics-intensive query systems capable of slicing-and-dicing data and providing active multi-dimensional analysis (see Chapter 5). As an example, Crystal Enterprise provides a default interface called e-Portfolio that allows users to view, schedule, and export reports in a Web-browser. It includes alerts, so an executive or enterprise information system can be developed in this system. See McAmis (2003) for details.

In 2003, MasterCard completed a $160 million overhaul of its IT system at the enterprise level. The System Enhancement Strategy (SES) was completed by rewriting *all* of the system's applications internally. The system includes a massive data warehouse and includes all of its enterprise applications. MasterCard has not reported on the payoff, but it appears to be substantial. See Gibson (2003). On the other hand, the high level of complexity that plagues enterprise information systems often leads to failure, as was the case with McDonald's, described in Case Application 8.2.

8.4 EXECUTIVES' ROLES AND INFORMATION NEEDS

In Chapter 2 we discussed the roles of managers, including decision-making. Even though providing executive information is no longer the focus of EIS, the process for identifying information needs is exactly the same as for enterprise information systems. The executive decisional role is a major one, and so we divide it into two phases. Phase I involves the identification of problems and opportunities. Phase II involves decisions on what to do about them. Figure 8.1 provides a flowchart of this process. This division can be used to understand executives' information needs and consequently the capabilities of an enterprise information system.

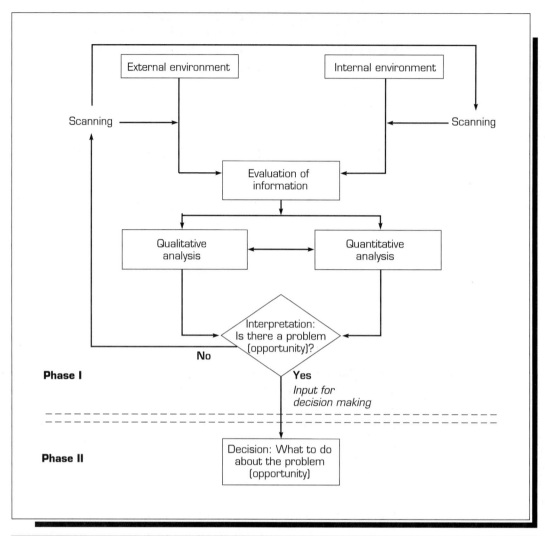

FIGURE 8.1   THE DECISION-MAKING PROCESS OF EXECUTIVES (DECISIONAL ROLE)

As shown in Figure 8.1, information flows to the system from the external and internal environments. Internal information is generated from the functional units (finance, marketing, production, accounting, personnel, etc.). External information comes from the Internet and other online databases, newspapers, Internet news services, industry publications, government reports, and personal contacts. Web-enabled data warehouses have provided a repository of external information that was not readily available as recently as 10 years ago. Clearly the combined information is an extremely valuable organizational resource needed for successful competition and survival. However, because of the large amount of information available, **environmental scanning** is needed to identify and determine what is relevant. Some scanning of news stories, internal reports, and Web information can be performed by intelligent software agents (see Liu et al., 2000). The collected information is evaluated and channeled to quantitative and qualitative analyses (carried out by experts and/or expert systems when needed). Then an executive or a team decides whether a problem or opportunity exists. If it is decided that there is a problem, this interpretation becomes an input to the next phase: making a decision on what to do about the problem. Not shown in the figure is the extensive communication that may take place among executives, managers, and staff. The basic purpose of EIS is to support Phase I of the process as shown in Figure 8.1. Phase II can be supported by specific DSS/business intelligence (BI)/business analytics (BA) applications.

METHODS FOR FINDING INFORMATION NEEDS

There are several methods for determining executives' information needs (Watson et al., 1997) (also see the Web Chapter on this book's Web site, prenhall.com/turban/).

One major complication in ascertaining the information needs of executives is that *needs change as tasks and responsibilities change.* To respond to this challenge, organizations have emphasized flexibility in meeting their EIS needs through the use of business intelligence tools (Chapter 5). Because of this, many organizations see EIS as constantly evolving and thus never completely finished (unlike most DSS/BI/BA applications; see Chapter 6).

8.5 CHARACTERISTICS AND CAPABILITIES OF EXECUTIVE SUPPORT SYSTEMS

The desired characteristics of an EIS and some of its capabilities are presented in Table 8.2. Most vendors provide these capabilities in their business intelligence enterprise systems. The important ones are described next in some detail.

DRILL DOWN

One of the most useful capabilities of an EIS is to provide details of any summarized information. For example, an executive may notice a decline in corporate sales from a daily (or weekly) report. To discover the reason, he or she may want to see the sales for each region. If a problematic region is identified, the executive may want to see further details (e.g., by product or by salesperson). In certain cases, this **drill-down** process may continue into several levels of detail.

Drill-down paths that are manually constructed and maintained typically use hypertext-style connections rather than menus in systems with a GUI (i.e., the button for requesting a drill-down path is typically defined as a *hot spot* directly over the high-level data to be explained). This frees up screen space for delivering information and can speed access to drill-down information by eliminating the additional mouse movements typically required by pull-down or pop-up menus. Similarly, Web tools and hyperlinks can be used for an intranet-based drill down. Songini (2003f) describes how Boehringer developed an integrated enterprise information system that successfully blended an ERP with business intelligence/business analytic tools. One critical feature of the EIS is its drill-down capabilities. See DSS in Action 8.4.

Menu-driven drill down is generally a characteristic of ad hoc query applications, and the menus in these applications are almost always automatically generated by the

TABLE 8.2   The Characteristics and Benefits of EIS

Quality of information
- Is flexible
- Produces correct information
- Produces timely information
- Produces relevant information
- Produces complete information
- Produces validated information

User interface
- Includes a sophisticated graphical user interface (GUI)
- Includes a user-friendly interface
- Allows secure and confidential access to information
- Has a short response time (timely information)
- Is accessible from many places
- Includes a reliable access procedure
- Minimizes keyboard use by including infrared controllers, a mouse, touch pads, and a touch screen
- Provides quick retrieval of desired information
- Is tailored to the management styles of individual executives
- Contains a self-help menu

Technical capability provided
- Access to aggregate (global) information
- Access to electronic mail
- Extensive use of external data
- Written interpretations
- Highlighting of problem indicators
- Hypertext and hypermedia
- Ad hoc analysis
- Multidimensional presentation and analysis
- Information presented in hierarchical form
- Incorporation of graphics and text in the same display
- Management-by-exception reports are provided
- Trends, ratios, and deviations are shown
- Access to historical and most current data is provided
- Organization around critical success factors
- Provides forecasting
- Information produced at various levels of detail (drill down)
- Filtering, compressing, and tracking of critical data
- Support of open-ended problem explanation

Benefits
- Facilitates the attainment of organizational objectives
- Facilitates access to information
- Allows the user to be more productive
- Increases the quality of decision making
- Provides a competitive advantage
- Saves time for the user
- Increases communication capacity
- Increases communication quality
- Provides better control in the organization
- Allows the anticipation of problems and opportunities
- Allows planning
- Allows a search for the cause of a problem
- Meets the needs of executives

software based on the user's logical position in the database and knowledge of the structure of the database. This knowledge of the database structure may have been specified in advance, or it may have been obtained dynamically by the application directly querying the database dictionary. Conceivably, a query application could generate several hundred menus and submenus covering all possible combinations of logical positions and valid drill-down paths.

Drill-down paths, supported by star schemas or snowflake schemas within the enterprise data warehouse, enable the executive or other key decision-maker to formulate an area for further investigation, then easily transfer between highly summarized to detailed information. Online analytic processing (OLAP) tools (see Chapter 5) include drill-down where, at a mouse click, a user can disaggregate a summary row or column in a tabular report. In contrast, rows and columns can be "reaggregated" through a process called *roll up*. Try this out in the Temtec Executive Viewer OLAP package (www.temtec.com).

DSS IN ACTION 8.4

BOEHRINGER CURES SLOW REPORTING WITH AN ERP/BI COMBINATION

The pharmaceutical giant Boehringer turned to an SAS/Cognos integrated system to speed up financial reporting. Boehringer Ingelheim GMBH is a massive company, with $7.6 billion in revenue, and 32,000 employees in 60 countries. Web-enabled reporting and financial applications are keeping the company very, very competitive.

The firm uses a Web-enabled version of SAP AG's Financials software, allowing it to *drill down* and draw conclusions based on the latest financial and operational data. The financial status of the firm is known on a daily basis by top executives. With the new applications, it takes the firm just two hours after the close of business at the end of each month to close its books. This can be done daily, if need be. (It formerly took three days or more). The system contains three years of SAP data in its Oracle data warehouse. The data are used to spot sales trends and track expenses.

In addition to the SAS software, the system utilizes a Manugistics production and planning application, and Cognos Impromptu (see Chapter 5) to report financial results from the Oracle data warehouse. Impromptu creates standard income statements, cost-center reporting, and account-level analysis. The firm also uses the Cognos PowerPlay analysis tool for multidimensional views of and *drill down* through profit-and-loss data. Cognos UpFront provides reporting to executives over the Web.

Currently there is a one day lag in getting results through the system. This is very close to the real-time analytics and active warehousing described in Chapter 5.

Source: Adapted from Mark L. Songini, "Boehringer Cures Slow Reporting," *ComputerWorld*, July 21, 2003, p. 30.

CRITICAL SUCCESS FACTORS

Factors that must be considered in attaining an organization's goals are called **critical success factors (CSFs)**. Such factors can be strategic, managerial, or operational and are derived mainly from three sources: organizational, industrial, and environmental. Success factors exist at the corporate level as well as at the industry, division, plant, department, level, and individual levels. The strategic planning process involves identifying CSFs at all levels.

Once identified, critical success factors can be monitored according to five types of information: key problem narratives, highlight charts, top-level financials, key factors, and detailed responsibility reports (Kogan, 1986). The monitoring can be done by intelligent agents. A brief description of each of the five types follows:

- *Key problem narratives.* These reports highlight overall performance, key problems, and possible reasons for the problems within an organization. Explanations are often combined with tables, graphs, or tabular information.
- *Highlight charts.* These summary displays show high-level information based on the user's own judgment or preference. Because they are designed from the user's perspective, these displays quickly highlight areas of concern, visually signaling the state of organizational performance against CSFs.
- *Top-level financials.* These displays provide information on the overall financial health of the company in the form of absolute numbers and comparative performance ratios.
- *Key factors.* These factors provide specific measures of CSFs, called **key performance indicators (KPIs)**, at the corporate level. The displays are often used on an exception basis to examine specific measures of CSFs flagged as problems on highlight charts (see DSS in Focus 8.5).

DSS IN FOCUS 8.5

TYPICAL KEY PERFORMANCE INDICATORS

Profitability	Profitability measures for each department, product, region, and so on; comparisons of departments and products and with competitors	Human resources	Turnover rate, level of job satisfaction
Financial	Financial ratios, balance sheet analysis, cash reserve position, rate of return on investment	Planning	Corporate partnership ventures, sales growth and market share analysis
Marketing	Market share, advertisement analysis, product pricing, weekly (daily) sales results, customer sales potential	Economic analysis	Market trends, foreign trade and exchange rates, industry trends, labor cost trends
		Consumer trends	Consumer confidence level, purchasing habits, demographic data

- *Detailed KPI responsibility reports.* These reports indicate the detailed performance of individuals or business units in areas critical to the success of the company.

STATUS ACCESS

In this mode, the *latest data* or reports on the status of key indicators can be accessed at any time via networks. The *relevance* of information is important, and emphasis is placed on current data. This may require daily (as in the Pizzeria Uno situation described in a Web Chapter) or even hourly operational tracking and reporting. In extreme cases, real-time reporting may be required. See Chapter 5 for a detailed discussion of *real-time (business) analytics* and *active warehousing.*

ANALYSIS

Analytic capabilities are available in executive information systems. Instead of merely having access to the data, executives can use the EIS to do analyses on their own. Analyses, generally handled by BI/BA software systems embedded in EIS, can be performed in the following ways:

- *Using built-in functions.* Several EIS products include built-in analytic functions similar to those available in DSS/BI/BA integrated tools (generators). For example, Comshare's DecisionWeb features ad hoc analysis capabilities that allow executives to easily compute trends and variances. It is also possible to perform multidimensional analyses on data and convert tables to graphics. Most recent software packages include an integrated analysis capability as part of their online analytical processing (OLAP) engine. These include Pilot Software's Decision Support Suite, Informix's MetaCube Product Suite, Cognos's PowerPlay and Impromptu Data Access (see Figure 5.8), and Temtec's Executive Viewer (see Figures 5.9 and 5.10, and DSS in Action 5.29).
- *Integration with DSS products.* Several EIS products have easy interfaces to DSS tools. For example, Comshare's DecisionWeb includes an open scripting language that allows it to integrate easily with many mainframe, server, or workstation DSS tools, such as Excel. Others export multidimensional data cubes for further analy-

sis by OLAP engines. Tools like Cognos Powerplay and Impromptu generate the SQL code required to access data from an enterprise data warehouse or other data source, thereby freeing up a user from having a requisite skill in understanding and utilizing the DBMS. Some fourth-generation (natural) languages have evolved to enable analysis while directly accessing a database or data warehouse.

- ***Analysis by intelligent agents.*** Simple comparisons, trends, or ratios can be calculated automatically and an alert issued if there are significant deviations from standards.

Liu et al. (2000) provide an example of the use of intelligent agents for strategic management in the pulp and paper industry in Finland. The agent scans the environment by monitoring certain Web sites, looking for relevant news and price information. Findings are customized into reports for each executive and can be sent as e-mail alerts. Alerts are very important to executives because often they do not read routine reports. See DSS in Focus 5.20.

Analysis can be done as follows. First, executives identify information that they want to analyze in more depth. Then they either directly request the analysis action from an EIS menu (e.g., to compute a trend line), using a Web-based drag-and-drop operation (see Figure 5.11 for how Brio's OLAP does this), or they export the data shown in the current display to a separate product that offers the desired analysis capability. Depending on the EIS, the process of exporting to and starting up another tool may simply be a menu choice within the EIS or can require the executive to save the display to a file, exit the EIS, launch the other tool, and read the file written by the EIS. Once the executive accesses the other tool (often a spreadsheet), analysis features are typically selected from menus. Whether the analysis is performed within the EIS or by an external tool, the results of the analysis are displayed in a default format, and the executive then has options to modify the display to improve its understandability. See Figures 5.9 through 5.12.

EXCEPTION REPORTING

Exception reporting is based on the concept of *management by exception*. Accordingly, the executive should give attention to exceptions to standards. Thus, exception reporting calls the executive's attention only to cases with a very bad (or very good) performance. For example, the EIS can compute variances and highlight them if they exceed a certain threshold. This approach saves considerable time in sifting through data for exception conditions.

USE OF COLORS AND AUDIO

Typically, critical items are reported not only numerically but also in traffic light colors: green for OK, yellow for a warning, and red for performance outside the preset boundaries of the plan (danger) (see Figure 5.10 for how Temtec's Executive Viewer does this). The colors (or shading, for the color-blind) alert the user to problems requiring immediate attention. Some systems are equipped with audio signals to alert the user to arriving information.

NAVIGATION OF INFORMATION

Navigation of information is a capability that allows large amounts of data to be explored easily and quickly. This capability can be enhanced with hypermedia tools

(Frolick and Ramarapu, 1993) and intelligent agents (Lamont, 2003). The drill-down and roll up capabilities of EIS (OLAP/BI/BA) enables information navigation. Multidimensional data cubes (see Chapter 5) can also be easily navigated via a variety of visualization tools, including those based on virtual reality (see DSS in Action 5.51).

COMMUNICATION

Executives need to communicate with one another. Communication can be verbal, by e-mail, a transfer of a report addressed to someone's attention, a call for a meeting, a comment made to a news group on the Internet, or the interface of a voice mail to a PDA. Additional communication can be provided through collaborative computing technologies such as those provided by GSS (e.g., Lotus Notes/Domino, Groove.net, Microsoft's NetMeeting; see Chapter 7). Executive chat rooms, bulletin boards, and other Web-support tools are popular, as are integrated personal electronic communication devices, such as cell phones that support Web browsing and PDA's.

8.6 COMPARING AND INTEGRATING EIS AND DSS

The characteristics and capabilities described above are unique primarily because an EIS is designed to support top executives, helping them to discover problems and opportunities. A DSS, on the other hand, supports analyses that attempt to answer the question of what to do with a specific problem or opportunity (*what-if*). Tables 8.3 and 8.4 compare the two systems. Table 8.3 contains portions of typical DSS definitions related to EIS. Table 8.4 compares EIS and DSS along several dimensions derived from the characteristics and capabilities of EIS.

Examination of the two tables shows that in a general sense, EIS is definitely part of the decision support field. That is, EIS is designed to support some tasks of the top management decision-making process. However, in a functional sense EIS and DSS are two different but complementary applications. The differences are simple but profound. Fundamentally, EIS is a structured, automated tracking system that operates continuously to keep management abreast of what is happening in all important areas both inside and outside the corporation. EIS has been described as being similar to a pilot's cockpit in an airplane. The gauges and indicators tell the pilot the current status and the direction in which the airplane is heading. The pilot knows that there are prob-

TABLE 8.3   Definitions of DSS as They Relate to EIS

Relevant Portion of DSS Definition	Author	Comparison to EIS
CBIS consisting of three subsystems: a problem-solving subsystem . . .	Bonczek et al. (1980)	No problem-solving subsystem exists in an EIS.
DSS can be developed only through an adaptive process . . .	Keen (1980)	EIS may or may not be developed through an adaptive process.
Model-based set of procedures . . .	Little (1970)	EIS is not model-based.
Extendible system supporting decision modeling used at irregular intervals	Moore and Chang (1980)	EIS is not extendible, might not have modeling capabilities, and is used at regular intervals.
Utilizes data and models . . .	Morton (1971)	EIS does not use models.

TABLE 8.4   Comparison of EIS and DSS

Dimension	EIS	DSS
Focus	Status access, drill down	Analysis, decision support
Typical users	Senior executives	Analysts, professionals, managers (via intermediaries)
Impetus	Expediency	Effectiveness
Application	Environmental scanning, performance evaluation, identification of problems and opportunities	Diversified areas where managerial decisions are made
Decision support	Indirect support, mainly high-level and unstructured decisions and policies	Supports semistructured and unstructured decision making, ad hoc decisions, and some repetitive decisions
Type of information	News items, external information on customers, competitors, and the environment; scheduled and demand reports on internal operations	Information supporting specific situations
Principal use	Tracking and control, opportunity identification	Planning, organizing, staffing, and controlling
Adaptability to individual users	Tailored to the decision-making style of each individual executive, offers several options of outputs	Permits individual judgments, what-if capabilities, some choice of dialog style
Graphics	A must	Important part of many DSS
User-friendliness	A must	A must if no intermediaries are used
Processing of information	Filters and compresses information, tracks critical data and information	EIS triggers questions, answers worked out by using the DSS and fed back into the EIS
Supporting detailed information	Instant access to the supporting details of any summary (drill down)	Can be programmed into the DSS but usually is not
Model base	Limited built-in functions	The core of the DSS
Construction	By vendors or IS specialists	By users, either alone or with specialists from the information center or IS department
Hardware	Mainframe, RISC workstations, Web, LANs, or distributed systems	Mainframe, RISC workstations, Web, PCs, or distributed systems
Nature of software packages	Interactive, easy access to multiple databases, online access, sophisticated DBMS capabilities, complex linkages	Large computational capabilities, modeling languages and simulation, application and DSS generators
Nature of information	Displays pregenerated information about the past and present, creates new information about the past, present, and future	Creates new information about the past, present, and future

lems if certain indicators are out of the safe range, colored lights flash, or a siren sounds. The automobile dashboard provides another analogy. In fact, digital dashboards (portals) in enterprise information systems have evolved from this notion. See Section 5.9 and Figure 5.7 for some details.

EIS delivers information that managers need in their day-to-day jobs. The information is typically presented in a structured, easy-to-access manner with only limited capability for direct ad hoc analysis. If there are analytic capabilities in EIS, they tend to be of a repetitive nature (e.g., trend analysis), as opposed to the unique ad hoc analysis of DSS, which can be provided through OLAP systems. Although this is the usual case, both DSS and EIS may center on the investigation and understanding of problems that are not necessarily predictable, structured, or repetitive.

EIS is designed very differently from DSS. For example, a good EIS must offer a high-speed, nontechnical way for managers to investigate business dynamics (i.e., to understand where and why things are happening so that tactical changes and course corrections can be made). This is also a major area that distinguishes EIS from a standard MIS reporting system. Any summary appearing on an EIS screen must offer instant access to the supporting detail; otherwise, it is just a glorified briefing book (slide show) showing dynamically refreshed data. In addition, the supporting details must be meaningful (e.g., time-series orientation with graphical and numerical content, written narratives from knowledgeable staff, or artificial intelligence (AI)-provided explanations).

INTEGRATING EIS AND DSS: AN EXECUTIVE SUPPORT SYSTEM

We have just concluded that EIS differs from DSS. Indeed, they are treated as independent system applications in many organizations. However, in some cases there are major benefits in integrating the two technologies. For example, at a large drug company, product managers download the previous day's orders of their products from an EIS to their PCs. Then they run a spreadsheet DSS model with the data to predict their end-of-month status. The results of this model are then uploaded to the EIS. By 11:00 a.m. every day, senior managers can check their EIS to see each brand manager's end-of-month status prediction.

The integration of EIS and DSS can be accomplished in several ways. One alternative is to use the EIS output to launch the DSS application. For instance, if executives at General Electric's major appliance division decide that an immediate marketing response is needed to a competitor's action reported by the EIS, exactly what that response should be is determined by DSS models and simulation tools. The DSS is fed from the same reservoir of raw data that feeds the EIS (e.g., the data warehouse), but the DSS action is triggered by the EIS. More sophisticated systems include feedback from the DSS to the EIS, and even an explanation capability. If an intelligent module with explanation and interpretation capabilities is added, then the system can be defined as an intelligent ESS.

The user's role is another dimension along which EIS and DSS can be integrated. Executive roles differ substantially from the roles of typical DSS users, namely, middle-line and functional supervisory levels and functional analysts, such as financial and marketing analysts. Lower-level managers focus much of their time on pursuing predetermined strategies, but executives are faced with developing these strategies. Ambiguity and uncertainty characterize an executive's environment, resulting in a need for the what-if and goal-seeking analyses provided by most DSS. Studies have shown, however, that many senior executives leave this technical analysis to lower-level functional managers and staff analysts.

Most business intelligence and enterprise software vendors (e.g., Business Objects, Cognos, Pilot, Microstrategy, TemTec) provide software products for EIS and DSS applications, such as sales reporting and analysis, product profitability reporting, profit/loss analysis and reporting, enterprise budget reporting, critical success factor and key performance indicator reporting, and performance analysis and reporting. Such software transforms existing corporate data into usable performance information for management decision-making. In addition, such products often include productivity tools (e.g., a personal calendar) and communication tools designed to meet the divergent information needs of executives.

Integration is a key issue. As executives have become increasingly technologically savvy and mobile, the need to provide EIS in mobile computing devices such as cell telephones and PDA's (e.g., the Blackberry devices at blackberry.com) continues to increase.

INTEGRATING EIS AND GROUP SUPPORT/COLLABORATION

As shown in Figure 8.1, the information generated in Phase I flows to Phase II, where a decision is made on what to do about the problem. A DSS supports the quantitative analysis of Phase I and can support Phase II as well. In Phase II, however, the decision can be made by a group. EIS include collaboration tools (see Chapter 7), sometimes through enterprise information portals (see Lipschutz, 2003), and sometimes through the products that database vendors provide (see Callaghan, 2003c). Several EIS vendors have developed direct interfaces to GSS. For example, IMRS has enhanced its On Track product with a Lotus Notes/Domino application called Executive Forum. Several enterprise software vendors have Lotus Notes/Domino–based enhancements and Web links in their major products. Others use products by Microsoft, Groove.net, and other GSS vendors. This is especially crucial in supply chain management systems, a very specific kind of enterprise information system that requires collaboration to function properly.

8.7 EIS, DATA ACCESS, DATA WAREHOUSING, OLAP, MULTIDIMENSIONAL ANALYSIS, PRESENTATION, AND THE WEB

In Chapter 5 we discussed the data warehouse: a repository of cleansed and filtered enterprise-wide data for read-only access and use by executives, managers, and analysts. The issue of data access in an enterprise was also discussed in Chapter 5. Rather than designing and implementing an EIS to access several disparate databases in a variety of formats on different computing platforms, data warehouses are increasingly being used as the sole data sources for EIS. When a data warehouse is front-ended by an SQL query code generator (e.g., PowerBuilder), natural language query system, or automatic form builder, it enhances the ability of any user (not just executives) to access needed data. In the mid-1990s, developers and researchers started to explore advanced data-visualization methods (Chapter 5) and multimedia use within EIS. Multimedia can be provided over an intranet. Storage and network capacities have increased to the point where vasts amounts of audio and video data are stored and easily disseminated.

Once data are accessed and provided, analysis and display become important. The combination of **multidimensional analysis** with online analytical processing (OLAP) tools allows the display of data in both spreadsheet and graphical formats, along with the ability to slice-and-dice the multidimensional data cube that the user requests from the data warehouse. OLAP methods provide analysis tools (see DSS in Action 8.6 and 8.7). Many of these tools are being developed to be Web-ready so that OLAP of the data from the data warehouse can be directly tapped into via the corporate intranet. Some representative packages include

- BrioQuery (Brio Technology Inc).
- Business Objects (Business Objects Inc).

DSS IN ACTION 8.6

NEIMAN MARCUS USES NATURAL LANGUAGE SEARCH TO BOOST ONLINE SALES

The online portion of Neiman Marcus (www. neiman-marcus.com), one of the industry leaders in luxury retail, determined that more than 50 percent of its customers had abandoned its Web site because they could not find what they were looking for. The problem was not a lack of inventory. In fact in most cases Neiman Marcus had the product, but the search engine worked so poorly that it was frequently not found. To overcome this problem, Neiman Marcus implemented an iPhrase Technologies One Step natural language search engine.

This allows customers to input queries in English-language sentences. The search language improves search capabilities by removing ambiguities and often suggests other products, thereby improving the sales experience, and *increasing sales*.

Source: Adapted from Martin Scheiner, "Nieman Marcus Uses Natural Language Search to Boost Online Sales," *Customer Relationship Management*, January 1, 2003, p. 57.

DSS IN ACTION 8.7

ALLIED SIGNAL SAYS YES TO EIS

Allied Signal is a $12 billion worldwide manufacturer of aerospace and automotive components and specialty materials, such as fibers, chemicals, plastics, and circuit board laminates. Aerospace president Dan Burnham was the catalyst for the EIS. The project started in January 1993 because he wanted faster reports and better-organized information, and to get it all on his desktop. The biggest hurdle was distribution. Dozens of division executives at remote sites needed to contribute information that could be collated quickly into a single system. Comshare's Commander OLAP was used to develop a prototype of the information Burnham requested. In a month, expansive drill-down capabilities with charts and graphs were demonstrated to financial executives. Then they ironed out what data they were going to collect to report.

Three months later, Dan Newsum, manager of distributed applications, installed the first EIS on Dan Burnham's desktop. Then, after a month of training sessions and fine-tuning based on user reactions, Newsum rolled out the system to the desktops of more than 150 people at 15 different sites. Commander's ability to accommodate rapid application updates made it possi-

ble to use rapid prototyping to provide updates to users in a couple of hours without user involvement.

In the first 18 months, system use spread to 500 users, and when new applications were completed, it reached 750. "People are working with information they never could access before in ways they had never thought possible," Newsum remarks. When the EIS was getting started, Newsum's group tracked 29 general metrics on the company's performance. After months of user feedback, many of these abstract numbers have been fleshed out into full-blown applications using Comshare's Execu-View and Prism. Many of the applications are running on client/server platforms using Comshare's OLAP Server, which includes a multidimensional data store. This OLAP Server has greatly improved users' ability to analyze data. Now Comshare's OLAP is being employed for new budgeting applications and a financial data warehouse. These applications have raised the level of knowledge in the company about how to work with information.

Source: Adapted from Comshare Brochure 718282, 1995, and www.comshare.com, 2003.

- DecisionWeb (Comshare Inc).
- DataFountain (Dimensional Insight Inc).
- DSS Web (MicroStrategy Inc).
- Focus Fusion (Information Builders Inc).
- InfoBeaconWeb (Platinum Technology Inc).
- Oracle Express Server (Oracle Corporation).
- Pilot Internet Publisher (Pilot Software Inc).

BusinessQuery for Excel from Business Objects is an example of an OLAP tool that uses Excel as its front end. It lets Excel users easily define their queries in the spreadsheet and add information extracted from corporate databases directly to the spreadsheet for further analysis. This Excel interface enables users who are familiar with spreadsheets to instantly access and manipulate data from a variety of sources. On the data mining side, XL Miner (Cytel Statistical Software) is a handy system that works within the Excel spreadsheet package.

Of special interest is Pilot Software's Decision Support Suite. With Decision Support Suite, an end user can extract data from various sources and turn them into intuitive, screen-based information. The on-screen data view allows the user to drill down into deeper levels of information.

Pilot Decision Support Suite's interface is based on objects, such as documents, menus, images, charts, and text. These items can have data or actions (e.g., an SQL query) associated with them. Building an interface includes selecting an object, pasting it in the workspace, sizing it, and then tying a desired action or predefined function to it. Generally, various objects combine to produce a particular result. This is an easy-to-use form of object-oriented programming.

We briefly describe the system developed at Sara Lee Corporation in DSS in Action 8.8. The Sara Lee system combines an integrated set of executive information and decision support applications to perform multidimensional OLAP dynamically with a three-tier architecture (see Figure 5.3) data warehouse in an open environment. For further information, see Barquin and Edelstein (1997a), the five articles entitled "Data Warehousing: The Essential Guide," *CIO*, October 1, 1998 (you can find current articles at www.cio.com), dmreview.com, and the Data Warehousing Institute Web site, www.dw-institute.org.

ENTERPRISE INFORMATION PORTALS AND EIS

Earlier, we described the cockpit analogy of an executive or enterprise information system. Enterprise portals (also known as dashboards, see Chapter 5 and Bochner, 2003) via the Internet or company intranets have evolved into the main platform that integrates all systems across an organization. See the Opening Vignette and DSS in Action 8.3.

An **enterprise (information) portal** integrates internal applications, such as database management, document management, and e-mail, with external applications, such as news services and customer Web sites. It is a Web-based interface that gives users access to all these applications through their PCs. Enterprise portals bring both external and internal information to all employees' desktops, much as an EIS does.

The most important reasons for deploying an enterprise information portal (sometimes called a **corporate portal**) include distributing information more effectively, encouraging collaborative work, managing content and information, integrating with enterprise applications, supporting customers, supporting suppliers and partners, improving Internet administration, and reducing training costs (see Fry, 2002). Portals provide internal collaboration (see Lipschutz, 2003) leading to effective and fast decision-making. Virtual communities (Chapter 9) can thrive utilizing enterprise infor-

DSS IN ACTION 8.8

SARA LEE UPGRADES SALES ANALYSIS WITH A DSS/EIS SUITE

As a consumer products manufacturer, Sara Lee Corporation depends on its ability to analyze the sales of the retailers it serves. In 1993, however, the meat division of Sara Lee, which represents about $4 billion of the company's $16 billion in annual sales, was having a tough time performing sales analyses for the brands it supports. The division's DSS was running in an older-generation proprietary IBM legacy mainframe environment that could not be easily upgraded or expanded to accommodate the growing number of users. The solution, which began to be installed in late 1993 and went live in May 1994, was a three-tier client/server system now known as the IA Decision Support Suite from Information Advantage. The suite is an integrated set of executive information and decision support applications designed to perform multidimensional online ana-

lytical processing dynamically against a data warehouse in an open environment. Users can drill down, drill up, skip multiple hierarchy levels, and create personal sets and calculations without having the IS department predefine drill paths or write stored procedures. In doing so, they can identify trends and exceptions, draw comparisons, perform calculations, and obtain fast answers. Users also benefit from the intuitivity and flexibility of a customizable GUI. The data warehouse is based on a high-speed relational database sorting and indexing engine from Red Brick Systems.

Source: Condensed from *Chain Store Age*, Vol. 71, No. 9 (Sec. 3), September 1995, pp. 22B–22C. Also see "How Sara Lee Replaced a Mainframe Decision Support System with Client/Server-based Analysis Tools," *I/S Analyzer Case Studies*, Vol. 34, No. 4, April 1995, pp. 7–11.

mation portal collaboration features, especially when members are scattered around the globe (see Grodner, 2003).

The main goal of an enterprise portal is to give each user a personalized and integrated view of business information, applications, and services. Portal users may be internal or external to an organization (see White, 2002). Enterprise portals have diverse capabilities and therefore employ several layers of multiple technologies, such as the following:

- *Groupware/collaboration technologies:* discussions, chat sessions, and library projects
- *Presentation:* data visualization tools, such as Web OLAP, JavaScript, and VBScript for Web display
- *Personalization and customization:* software agents that customize information for individual users using push technology
- *Publishing and distribution:* storehouses of documents in portable formats, as well as publish and subscribe engines; content management systems are accessed via enterprise information portals
- *Search:* both full-text search engines and those that search descriptions of documents and other content
- *Categorization:* tools for creating and maintaining different categories of information for different audiences, such as multidimensionality tools
- *Integration:* tools for accessing disparate back-end data sources, such as ERP packages, relational databases, and external data, such as stock price quotations.

The enterprise information portal has become the de facto standard Web interface for delivering content to business users. In many organizations, personalized portals are rapidly replacing generalized Web-browser interfaces to corporate intranets and e-commerce applications (White, 2002).

Portals are often integrated with enterprise applications such as ERP, CRM, and supplier relationship management/electronic procurement. Consequently, organizations are deploying portals to support strategic business initiatives and using them as tools for managing enterprise applications (Varon, 2002). Portals provide the much-needed ability to integrate and unify access to a firm's applications, back-end systems, data sources, and content repositories. Unlike many other enterprise applications, portals have an excellent return on investment. By mid-2003, the major portal vendors had migrated their products completely to a Java server technology foundation, and XML for their data structures. Consequently, they all support the creation of Web services. Here are seven excellent enterprise information portal products: Art Technology Group Inc.'s ATG, BEA Systems Inc.'s WebLogic Portal, Computer Associates International Inc.'s Cleverpath Portal, IBM WebSphere Portal, Plumtree Software Inc.'s Corporate Portal, SybaseInc.'s Enterprise Portal, and Vignette Corp.'s Application Portal. In addition, many specific EIS vendors have developed portals that are tightly aligned with their main products. Notably, these include SAP AG's MySAP. In the past, detailed knowledge of a portal's programming structure was necessary for applications development. Now, expertise in Java and XML are sufficient background for anyone to develop a portal application in most vendor portal products. See Rapoza (2003) for details. Covisint, the North American automobile industry exchange extranet, utilizes a portal and functions directly with an XML-based data representation in its hub-based portal (*Portals Magazine*, 2003).

Cap Gemini Ernst & Young (www.cgey.com) has developed a set of questions to help organizations determine the value they can derive from implementing a portal. These questions follow along the scales of intent, usage, user experience, technology, support, learning, Web- content management, and Search. We provide a sample in DSS in Focus 8.9

The Delphi Group studied 600 companies considering developing portals. The breakdown of the types of portals that the companies were considering was: enterprise information (62%), customer (55%), employee (54%), supplier partner (30%), and other (8%) (see Copeland, 2001).

All of the major DSS/business intelligence/business analytics vendors provide enterprise information portals as top layers to their products. Look at Hummingbird's

---

DSS IN FOCUS 8.9

ENTERPRISE INFORMATION PORTAL EFFECTIVENESS

Here is a sample of Cap Gemini Ernst & Young's portal effectiveness questions, to be answered on a 1 to 7 scale (see www.cgey.com for more on this survey and how to use it):

Intent:

- Portals are being positioned/used for Web-enabling routine business transactions.

- Portals are being positioned/used for community enablement and knowledge sharing.

- Portals are being positioned/used for collaborative decision-making among functional areas.

Analytics/Collaboration:

- Transactions on the portal are supported by quantitative analytics and history.

- Transactions are supported by qualitative Web data.

Source: Adapted from Jim Rapoza, "EIPs More Compelling Than Ever," *eWeek*, July 21, 2003, pp. 51–58.

Enterprise Information Portal as a representative of the set. See the annual "Portals Buyers Guide" in the July issue of *Portals Magazine* for more on specific products.

The cost of a portal depends on its purpose. Highly customized portals that integrate many applications can cost millions of dollars to develop. On the other hand, a simple portal with minimal integration effort can cost as little as $50,000, especially if it is developed on top of existing platforms (see Konicki, 2000). Even though spending on e-business projects fell in 2002, more than a third of executives planned to purchase portal software (Varon, 2002). The enterprise portal market was $80 million in 2002. It is expected to grow to $2 billion in 2005 (see Fry, 2002). Gartner Dataquest forecast in the summer 2002 that portal sales would grow an average of 24 percent per year from 2001 to 2006. In DSS in Focus 8.10, we discuss the growth of the enterprise information market. See McDonnough (2003b) for more details.

ENTERPRISE INFORMATION PORTAL EXAMPLES

Hewitt Associates in Lincolnshire, Illinois, a human resources outsourcing company, saves $8 million per year and provides 75 percent faster responses to client requests for benefits information through its enterprise information portal. Clients from various companies enter a personalized portal environment and obtain their pension information updated from a personal profile. Hewitt expects a 100 percent return on its portal investment within two years. The portal is the primary desktop for 500 employees, and the company is investigating how to expand it to 11,000 employees worldwide (see Copeland, 2001; Konicki, 2000).

DSS IN FOCUS 8.10

THE ENTERPRISE INFORMATION PORTAL MARKET

The enterprise portal software market is expected to continue double-digit growth. Several factors that will contribute to its growth through 2007 are:

Software vendors that have recently added enterprise portals to their product portfolio will penetrate their installed base at a rapid rate.

Demand for portals will increase as more companies begin to understand the technology and benefits associated with them.

More direct and measurable benefits will be marketable as portals are deployed to improve specific business processes.

Benefits will become more widely understood as larger software vendors invest significant marketing dollars in educating the prospect base.

Broader adoption and deployment of enterprise portals will increase sales among organizations that initially deployed a portal to focus on the needs of a single department or employee.

The areas in which the organizations surveyed have targeted their first portal are

- Corporate (23.7%)
- HR (20.7%)
- Marketing (20.5%)
- Sales (20.2%)
- Customer services (19.8%)
- IS (19.7%)
- Line of business employees (19.3%)
- Finance (16.6%)
- Research & development (10.3%)
- Other (4.2%)

Source: Adapted from Brian McDonnough, "The State of Enterprise Portal Initiatives: Portal Adoption Trends 2003," Special IDC Report, *Portals Magazine*, Vol. 33, No. 22, July 2003, pp. 23–25.

Cigna's portal (MyCigna.com) integrates data from multiple health-care and retirement benefit plans in an effort to increase sagging market share. With the economy in decline, Maysteel could not afford a new ERP system, so it developed a portal application that would allow executives and quality control staff to access the data they need (Varon, 2002). At Maysteel, portals link legacy systems to new systems. The structure of this portal matches that of the executive information system. One of Pratt & Whitney's 100 portal-supported applications (for 4,000 users) helped the firm to reduce jet aircraft engine overhaul time by 30 percent. The portal provides detailed information about the use of the engine's 28,000 parts, so engineers can predict potential failures and replace the part in advance. Consequently, Pratt is expanding its engine repair business, a $37.9 billion market in 2002. And engineers on the road can access the portal from anywhere (Varon, 2002).

Clarian Health Partners, an integrated health-care company (Indianapolis, Indiana) has developed an enterprise information portal for its three hospitals. It directly assists doctors, administrators, and consumers (see Ericson, 2002). Bank One Corp. developed a foreign currency exchange portal to let its customers examine exchange rates, execute trades of foreign currency, confirm settlement, make cross-currency payments, and view account status (see Boyd, 2001). We described how the U.S. military has successfully adopted enterprise information portals in the Opening Vignette. In DSS in Action 8.3, we described the General Motors enterprise information portal (also see Goodridge, 2001). General Electric, Staples, and DuPont have all developed successful portals as well.

Even governments and other state agencies and universities are developing enterprise portals that save time and money for their constituents. See DSS in Action 8.11 for details on the state of New Jersey's home-grown e-government portal (www.nj.gov; Yamada, 2003). Other government agencies that have developed portals include the U.S. federal government (FirstGov.com; Kaneshige, 2002), the U.S. Internal Revenue Service (www.irs.gov; *Portals Magazine*, 2002), and the states of New Mexico (Rapoza, 2002) and Rhode Island (Vaas, 2003a). Rapoza (2002) provides a list of Web resources for government XML and Web services. Companies like ezgov.com specialize in developing Web-based solutions for governments and their agencies. Many colleges and universities have turned to enterprise information portals to enable information resources and tools for students, staff, and faculty. Vaas (2003b) describes Texas Tech University's portal efforts.

Portals deliver almost immediate productivity gains to workers, customers, and business partners (see DSS in Action 8.11). They add context to business data, and executives like having a single, personalized window into the health and well-being of their organizations (see Copeland, 2001). Portals leave data in their original format and provide users with a window into them. Portals are relatively inexpensive and scalable, in that new users and applications are literally added daily (as in the State of New Jersey portal).

Another application area for portals is knowledge management, another type of enterprise information system (see Kim, 2002). The collaboration features of portals enable the creation and sustainability of virtual communities (*of practice*), which is very important to the smooth functioning of knowledge management systems. See DSS in Action 8.12 and Maybury (2001). Other capabilities of portals enable knowledge management systems. For example, Orbital Software Group's Organik provides a question-and-answer infrastructure for portals. Users can ask questions, find experts, and share knowledge (see Copeland, 2001). For more on how portals are used in knowledge management systems, see Chapter 9 and McDonough (2003a).

DSS IN ACTION 8.11

NEW JERSEY GETS AGGRESSIVE ABOUT ITS E-GOVERNMENT PORTAL

New Jersey's state government has developed a portal (www.nj.gov) that has hundreds of Web services, 100 online communities, massive amounts of important information, financial transactions, a kids' section, an extranet, and an intranet, and attracts 3,000 newly registered users every month. The $2.5 million portal, built from scratch over two years, was developed and is maintained by state employees with no outsourcing. Though it is difficult to determine a direct savings, the portal provides many new services and options. By way of example, one group of 500 users saves the state about $1 million annually by using the portal instead of a customized dial-up system.

The successful New Jersey portal allows state residents to register cars, pay for fishing licenses, and buy gifts from the state museum's gift shop. Lottery agents can check on ticket orders, merchants can register business names, and corporations can pay state taxes. Each member has a set of individual, customized services and information.

In July 2003, there were 33,000 users, including 22,500 residents, 4,000 state employees, 4,000 business owners, and 2,500 local government officials. The features and services offered over the portal continue to grow over time.

Source: Adapted from Ken Yamada, "Jersey Online," *Portals Magazine*, Vol. 33, No. 22, July, 2003, pp. 27–29.

DSS IN ACTION 8.12

THE MYHONEYWELL PORTAL ENABLES KNOWLEDGE MANAGEMENT: BREAKS DOWN KNOWLEDGE BARRIERS

Honeywell developed its MyHoneywell Portal to break down its silos of knowledge in deploying a knowledge management initiative. Honeywell faced and managed the standard organizational culture issue of developing an information- and knowledge sharing culture. Empirical research indicates that knowledge-sharing capabilities and tools are the most important features required for employee portals. The typical breakdown of the most important portal characteristics is knowledge management and search (32%), integration (25%), collaboration (22%), application development/deployment (13%), and expertise location (8%). See Kaneshige (2003) for details.

8.8 SOFT INFORMATION IN ENTERPRISE SYSTEMS

Watson et al. (1996) recognized that decision-makers require soft information, often provided informally, for making decisions. They performed an in-depth study of how and to what extent soft information is included in EIS. **Soft information** is "fuzzy, unofficial, intuitive, subjective, nebulous, implied, and vague." They found that soft information was used in most EIS, broken down into the following categories:

- Predictions, speculations, forecasts, and estimates (78.1%)
- Explanations, justifications, assessments, and interpretations (65.6%)
- News reports, industry trends, and external survey data (62.5%)
- Schedules and formal plans (50.0%)
- Opinions, feelings, and ideas (15.6%)
- Rumors, gossip, and hearsay (9.4%).

SERFIN FINANCIAL GROUP IN MEXICO CITY USES EIS

Because of the critical economic situation in 1994, Mexican banks found themselves burdened with a large amount of loan obligations. Serfin Financial Bank, the third-largest bank in Mexico, survived by implementing an EIS and a data warehouse to enable its top managers to review and continue tracking outstanding loans and to monitor the daily growth of liabilities on a branch-by-branch basis.

Serfin realized that it was technologically behind the times because its decision-makers had been using simple graphical spreadsheet software to view daily customer data. To update its capabilities, the bank instituted an EIS that allowed users to perform more complex tasks, such as monitoring daily performance, budgeting, and forecasting activities. The system was linked to a Sybase database and collected data from disparate operating systems at the three primary data centers in Mexico City, Guadalajara, and Monterey. The data warehouse took more time to complete than the EIS development.

In the beginning, the SAS EIS served only the top 12 executive officers. By using the new system, Serfin reduced its response time for performing a forecast from 2 hours to 30 seconds, leading to better performance. The system helped the bank get through the financial crisis.

Source: Condensed from Thomas Hoffman, "Mexican Bank Finds Crisis Control," *ComputerWorld*, Vol. 29, No. 25, June 1995, p. 79.

The widespread use of soft information in the form of predictions, speculations, forecasts, and estimates is important for planning purposes. Other research documents the use of these types of soft information. Generally the EIS support staff can enter this information, but sometimes the EIS may generate the information automatically based on historical data (by data mining) or by **intelligent agents (IA)** scanning news sources and internal reports. Explanations, justifications, assessments, and interpretations help executives make sense of what is happening inside and outside the firm. Many enterprise systems allow users to clip explanations onto screens or e-mail before providing the information to other users. News reports are gaining popularity as **news feeds**, both textual and video, and have become widely available, especially via the Web. As intelligent agents filter news (internal and external), we expect more news feeds to be provided through enterprise systems. On an individual basis, CNN.com provides free access to news feeds in a similar manner.

The inclusion of soft information enhances the value of enterprise systems for executive users (see DSS in Action 8.13). Most of the participants in the Watson et al. (1996) study indicate that with respect to soft information they plan to concentrate efforts on external news services, competitor information, and the ease of process entering soft information. A few firms are focusing on making it easier for users to add soft information themselves.

8.9 ORGANIZATIONAL DSS

Organizational decision support was first defined by Hackathorn and Keen (1981), who distinguished three types of decision support: individual, group, and organizational. They maintain that computer-based systems can be developed to provide decision support for each of these levels. They perceive organizational decision support as focusing on an organizational task or activity involving a sequence of operations and actors (e.g., developing a divisional marketing plan or corporate capital budgeting). Furthermore, they believe, each individual's activities must mesh closely with other people's work. Computer support was seen primarily as a vehicle for improving communication, coordination, and problem-solving. A visualization of an organizational decision support system from a research dimension is provided by Konsynski and Stohr (1992).

There are several definitions of **organizational decision support system (ODSS)**:

- Watson (1990) defined an ODSS as "a combination of computer and communication technology designed to coordinate and disseminate decision-making across functional areas and hierarchical layers in order that decisions are congruent with organizational goals and management's shared interpretation of the competitive environment."
- Carter et al. (1992) defined ODSS as "a DSS that is used by individuals or groups at several workstations in more than one organizational unit who make varied (interrelated but autonomous) decisions using a common set of tools."
- Swanson (Swanson and Zmud, 1990) called ODSS a distributed decision support system (DDSS). He stated that an organizational DSS should not be thought of as a manager's DSS. Rather, it should be viewed as supporting the organization's division of labor in decision-making. He defined a DDSS as a DSS that supports distributed decision-making.
- King and Star (1990) provided a different perspective. They believe that the concept of ODSS is fundamentally simple: Apply the technologies of computers and communications to enhance the organizational decision-making process. In principle, ODSS takes the vision of technological support for group processes to the higher level of organizations in much the same way that group DSS extends the vision of technological support for individual action to the group process. This is done today on an intranet (see Ba et al., 1997).

Based on the above definitions, George (1991/1992) found that all ODSS have certain common characteristics:

- The focus of an ODSS is an organizational task, activity, or decision that affects several organizational units or corporate problems.
- An ODSS cuts across organizational functions or hierarchical layers.
- An ODSS almost necessarily involves computer-based technologies and may also involve communication technologies.

For implementation issues of ODSS, see Kivijarvi (1997).

RELATIONSHIP OF ODSS TO GSS AND ENTERPRISE INFORMATION SYSTEMS

Because of its complexity, and the need for internal communication and collaboration, an ODSS can be integrated directly with a group support system (GSS), an executive information system, or any enterprise information system. For example, the Egyptian cabinet ODSS (see DSS in Action 8.14) includes an executive information system. Within such a system, GSS could help prioritize items and resolve conflicts by providing direct collaboration capabilities. Clearly, ODSS are a type of enterprise information system that directly provides decision support (business intelligence/business analytics). Even though such systems were deployed as independent systems in the past, they are now typically integrated with intranet support infrastructures, obtaining data from data warehouses and including OLAP and other business intelligence/business analytic capabilities. In fact, such ODSS are often integrated directly with ERP systems, which we describe next.

ODSS IN THE EGYPTIAN CABINET

INTRODUCTION

The Egyptian cabinet is composed of 32 ministers, each responsible for one department (e.g., labor, energy, or education). The cabinet is headed by the prime minister and deals with countrywide policies and strategic issues. The cabinet also includes four sectored ministerial committees assisted by staff. The cabinet makes extremely important decisions in areas such as national socioeconomics and infrastructure. Many of the issues are complex and require considerable preparation and analysis. Because of conflicting interests, there is sometimes considerable disagreement among the ministries.

The cabinet must work with the parliament and with many government agencies. In addition, there are many links between the cabinet and external agencies, ranging from universities to international bodies. Information is essential for effective decision-making. Decisions are made by many people (individually or in groups) at many locations and levels, and the composition of the decision-makers changes frequently. All this makes the decision-making process very complex.

THE CABINET'S INFORMATION AND DECISION SUPPORT CENTER

To properly support the information needs of the cabinet, a special center was developed—the information and decision support center (IDSC). Dozens of specific DSS were developed; since the center's inception in 1985, several of them have been highly interrelated and interconnected. Examples of specific DSS are the following:

- *Customs tariff policy formulation DSS.* This problem area involved six ministries, so coordination was difficult and the diversity of opinions played a major role in decisions. The DSS helped to achieve a consistent tariff structure and increased government revenue (yet minimized the burden on low-income families).

- *Debt management DSS.* Egypt relies on foreign debt (about 5,000 loans amounting to more than $40 billion in the mid-1990s). The purpose of the DSS was to manage the debt (e.g., to schedule payments, decide on appropriate refinancing, simulate projections of the debt structure).

CONCLUSION

The use of ODSS has significantly leveraged the strategic decision-making process in Egypt. However, the system supported by the ODSS was very complex. It provided for ODSS analysis throughout a complex organization and was used by many people in several organizational units. This large-scale ODSS was highly integrated with an extensive data-management system.

Source: Based on material from H. El Sherif, "Managing Institutionalization of Strategic Decision Making for the Egyptian Cabinet," *Interfaces*, Vol. 20, No. 1, 1990; H. El Sherif and O. A. El Sawy, "Issue-Based Decision Support Systems for the Egyptian Cabinet," *MIS Quarterly*, Vol. 12, No. 4, December 1988.

8.10 SUPPLY AND VALUE CHAINS AND DECISION SUPPORT

Enterprise systems related to the supply chain and its management constitute a special class. In this section we present some basic information on supply chains and their management.

DEFINITIONS AND BENEFITS

The concept of a supply chain originally referred to the flow of materials from its sources (suppliers) to a company and then inside the company to areas where it was needed. Concomitantly there was recognition of a **demand chain** that described order generation, taking, and fulfillment. Soon it was realized that these two concepts are interrelated, and so they have been integrated under the name *supply chain*.

DEFINITIONS

A **supply chain** refers to the flow of materials, information, and services from raw material suppliers through factories and warehouses to the end customers. A supply chain also includes the *organizations* and *processes* that create and deliver products, information, and services to the end-customers. It involves many activities, such as purchasing, materials handling, production planning and control, logistics and warehousing inventory control, and distribution and delivery.

The function of **supply chain management (SCM)** is to deliver an effective supply chain and do it in an effective manner, namely, to plan, organize, and coordinate the supply chain's activities. Good supply chain management practices generally lead to increased revenue, as we describe in DSS in Action 8.15. For an overview of SCM, see Hugos (2003), Sheikh (2003), and Handfield and Nichols (1999).

BENEFITS

The goals of modern SCM are to reduce uncertainty and risks in the supply chain, thereby positively affecting inventory levels, cycle time, processes, and customer service. All these contribute to increased profitability and competitiveness.

The benefits of supply chain management were recognized long ago not only in business but also in the military. In today's competitive environment, efficient and effective supply chains are critical for the survival of most organizations and are greatly dependent on the supporting information systems.

THE COMPONENTS OF THE SUPPLY CHAIN

The term *supply chain* comes from a picture of how partnering organizations in a specific supply chain are linked together. As shown in Figure 8.2, a simple supply chain links a company that manufactures or assembles a product (in the middle of the chain) with its suppliers (on the left) and its distributors and customers (on the right). The upper part of the picture shows a generic supply chain, while the bottom part shows the specific example of making wine.

Note that the supply chain has three parts:

1. **Upstream.** This part includes the suppliers (they can be manufacturers and/or assemblers) and their suppliers. Such relationships can be extended to the left in several tiers, all the way to the origin of the material (e.g., mining ores or growing crops).
2. **Internal supply chain.** This part includes all the processes used in transforming the inputs from suppliers to outputs, from the time materials enter an organization to the time the product(s) goes to distribution outside the organization.

DSS IN ACTION 8.15

SCM IS STRAIGHT AS AN ARROW

Arrow Electronics utilizes good supply chain management practices and systems to produce new revenue to help insulate the firm during the sharp downturns in the electronics industry. It includes Arrow Collaborator, an interactive Web application (part of the suite of SCM tools of Arrow's Connectivity Dashboard) that helps customers monitor and control their own supply chains.

Source: Adapted from H. Green and P. Katz, "Arrow Takes Aim at Supply Chain," *Optimize,* September 2002.

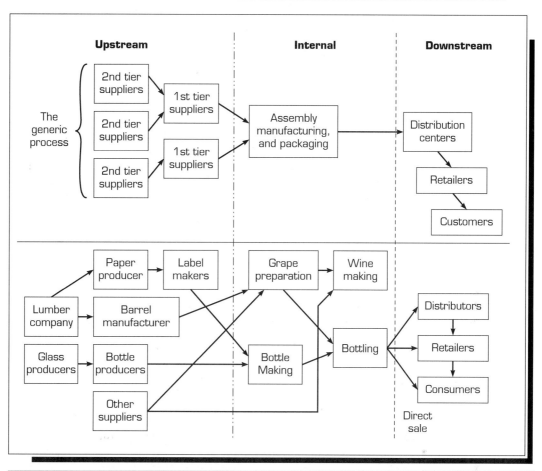

FIGURE 8.2   SUPPLY CHAINS OF WINE MAKING

3. Downstream. This part includes all the processes involved in delivering the product to the final customers. The supply chain actually ends when the product reaches its after-use disposal—presumably back to Mother Earth somewhere.

A supply chain involves activities that take place during a **product life cycle**, from "dirt to dust" (see Section 8.14 for details on product life-cycle management systems) However, a supply chain is more than that, because it also involves the movement of information and money and the procedures that support the movement of a product or a service. The organizations and individuals involved are part of the chain as well (see Poirier, 1999).

Supply chains come in all shapes and sizes and can be fairly complex, as shown in Figure 8.3. As the figure demonstrates, the supply chain for a car manufacturer includes hundreds of suppliers, dozens of manufacturing plants (parts) and assembly plants (cars), dealers, direct business customers (fleets), wholesalers (some of which are virtual, e.g., www.cardirect.com), customers, and support functions such as product engineering and purchasing. The automobile industry is an extremely interesting case in point. The automobile industry in North America has developed the Covisint extranet to coordinate the supply chains of its members, from all the many parts and raw materials vendors to the dealers who sell the cars (*Portals Magazine*, 2003). Auto

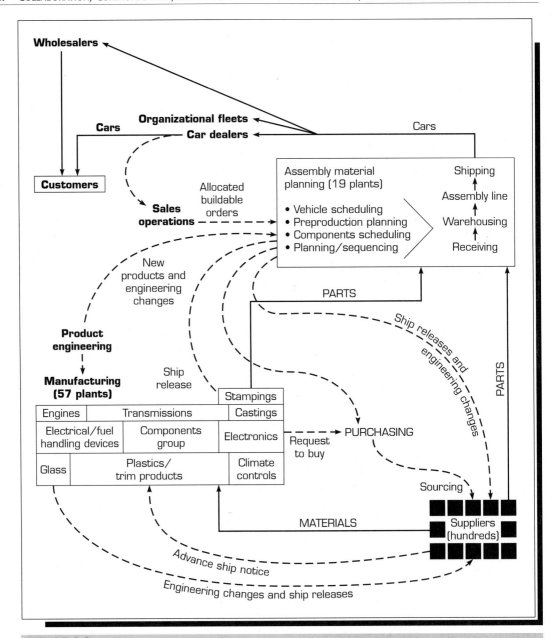

FIGURE 8.3   AN AUTOMOTIVE SUPPLY CHAIN

Source: Modified from Introduction to Supply Chain Management by Handfield/Nichols, ©1998. Reprinted by permission of Prentice-Hall, Inc., Upper Saddle River, NJ. Handfield, R.B., and E.L. Nichols, Jr. (1999). *Introduction to Supply Chain Management.* Upper Saddle River, NJ: Prentice Hall.

manufacturers can link seamlessly with their suppliers in total security, offering more services, and making more and better decisions faster and at a lower cost. (Because of U.S. antitrust laws, an auto manufacturer may only collaborate and communicate with its own vendors and dealers, but not with other manufacturers.) See Evans (2003) and Koch (2002) for more on Covisint.

Note that in this case the chain is not strictly linear, as in Figure 8.2. Here there are some loops in the process. Sometimes the flow of information and even of goods can be bidirectional. For example, not shown in this figure is the *return* of cars to dealers, known as **reverse logistics**, in the case of defects, a recall by the manufacturer or trade-ins.

Also note that a supply chain is much more than physical. It includes information and financial flows. The Chapter 2 Opening Vignette describes a situation where information flow was just as critical for the success of the work teams as moving products out the door. As a matter of fact, a supply chain of a digitizable product or service may not include any physical material.

The flow of goods, services, information, and so on, is usually designed not only to effectively transform raw items to finished products and services but to do so in an efficient manner. Specifically, the flow must end with the delivery of a product or service to the customer whenever it is needed, and it must be followed with an increase in value that can be determined by value-chain analysis, in which business analtyics methods are applied directly to SCM. As an example, Diageo plc implemented a supply chain planning system that significantly reduced inventory levels, resulting in a massive savings. See DSS in Action 8.16.

THE SUPPLY CHAIN AND THE VALUE CHAIN

The concept of the supply chain is related to the concepts of **value chain** and value system. According to the **value chain model** (Porter, 1985), the activities conducted in any organization can be divided into primary activities and support activities. The five *primary activities* are (1) inbound logistics (inputs), (2) operations (manufacturing and testing in a manufacturing firm), (3) outbound logistics (storage and distribution), (4) marketing and sales, and (5) service.

These activities are linked together. The output of the first is the input to the second, and so on. A value is added each time an input changes to an output. The primary activities are sequenced and work progressively in the manner shown below, and value is added at each activity.

Incoming materials are processed (in receiving, storage, etc.), and value is added to them in what is called inbound logistics. Then the materials are used in operations, where more value is added in making products. The products need to be prepared for delivery packaging, storing, and shipping, and so more value is added. Then marketing and sales deliver the products to customers. Finally, after-sales service is performed for the customer. All the value-adding activities result in profit (it is hoped). They are supported by the following *support activities*: (1) the firm's infrastructure (accounting, finance, management), (2) human resources management, (3) technology development

---

DSS IN ACTION 8.16

SCM PROVIDES INVENTORY REDUCTION

Diageo plc, a global beer (Guinness) and alcohol manufacturer (Johnnie Walker, Cuervo) has implemented Manugistics supply chain planning software to support its U.S. collaborative planning, forecasting, and replenishment processes. Ultimately, the software will be deployed to support its global manufacturing facilities. Diageo plans to save $1.1 million in inventory reduction

and some $600,000 in logistics benefits over the next few years through more accurate forecasts. Sales should grow by 1 percent, or $3.3 million.

Source: Adapted from B. Bacheldor, "Keep Supply Chains Flowing," *InformationWeek*, April 14, 2003.

(R&D), and (4) procurement. Each support activity can support any or all of the primary activities, which can also support each other.

Firms try to *optimize the total value* along the entire chain. There are many ways to increase the value, and many decisions need to be made for this purpose. It is important to note that *true* supply chain optimization must involve some of the models described in Chapter 4 along with methods for their solution and analysis. Very often, in this age of Web-based commerce, a manager will claim that a problem is far too complex to be modeled. Managers who make such claims do not understand their job and should be fired. Supply chain optimization is often interpreted simply as making some improvement in communication and collaboration along the supply chain. While such improvements are certainly good practice and often reduce overall costs, they do not mean that an organization is applying normative and/or descriptive models to the problem of managing the supply chain. True supply chain optimization is very effective. Consider the IMERYS Case Applications in Chapters 2, 4, and 6. By modeling and optimizing a portion of the supply chain, the firm increased its net profit by around 10 percent without utilizing additional resources.

Experts estimate that if the auto supply chain were optimized, vehicle makers and their suppliers could save somewhere between $1,700 and $3,000 per car. There is approximately $700 billion of inventory in the auto supply chain. Technology can easily cut this amount by one-third through supply chain optimization. See Wallace (2000). Keskinocak and Tayur (2001), Sodhi (2001), Quinn (2003), and Wallace (2000) describe how optimization efforts can impact the supply chain. Quinn (2003) describes how John Deere optimizes inventory throughout the supply chain, which is tricky because of its seasonal nature. See DSS in Action 8.17.

DSS IN ACTION 8.17

JOHN DEERE TRULY OPTIMIZES INVENTORY THROUGH SUPPLY CHAIN MANAGEMENT

One of the first scientific applications to business was the development of a calculus approach to optimizing inventory (economic order quantity or EOQ). John Deere, a 166-year-old lawn mowing, tractor, and other vehicle firm, with annual sales of about $3 billion, has taken its distribution supply chain to a new level of efficiency, utilizing specialized software from SmartOps Corp. In 2001, management wanted to reduce the finished-goods inventory both in company warehouses and at dealers. But customer service was not to suffer. The critical question asked how low inventory could go before it affected customer sales. Excess inventory and sales losses due to stockouts are expensive. Balance is important. Many of Deere's products are seasonal; demand forecasting is complicated by the fact that they are often impulse purchases,.

To maintain a leading position in the industry, John Deere adopted three basic supply chain goals: (1) improve service levels from dealers to customers; (2) reduce finished-goods inventory to target levels by 2005; and (3) improve factory and supplier flexibility to accommodate seasonal demand. However, some managers felt that inventory would have to increase for many products.

Fortunately, SmartOps Multistage Inventory Planning & Optimization (MIPO) software determines optimal inventory placement plans for the customer's supply chain by product, location, and time. It helps identify the optimal mix of inventories throughout the supply chain from raw materials to finished products. After a successful five-month pilot test, the software was adjusted, tested for seasonality in a second pilot test, and then deployed to cover all 2,500 dealers. The system has significantly reduced finished-product inventories without negatively impacting customer service.

Source: Adapted from Paul Quinn, "Inventory Optimization: Lean But Not Mean." *SCS Magazine*, May 2003, pp. 32–34.

Seasonal demand is also faced by Just Born, which manufactures 600 million Peeps (gooey pink and yellow marshmallow chicks) annually. Eighty percent are sold during the Easter season. Uncertain seasonal demand, though difficult to model, can be handled by the firm's optimizing SCM and forecasting efforts. This should save it millions in excess inventory of Peeps and raw materials. See Kaplan (2001) for details.

A firm's value chain is part of a larger stream of activities that Porter calls a value system. A **value system** consists of the suppliers that provide the inputs necessary to the firm and, as well, their value chains, which include suppliers to the suppliers (possibly in several tiers). Once the firm creates products, they pass through the value chains of distributors (who also have their own value chains), all the way to the buyers (customers), who also have their own value chains. Gaining and sustaining a competitive advantage and supporting this advantage by means of IT require an understanding of the entire value system. The concepts of value chain and value system concepts apply both to products and services and to any organization, private or public.

A close examination of the value chain and value system concepts shows that they are closely related to the supply chain. The primary activities of the value chain correspond to the generic model in Figure 8.2. Some of the support activities of value chains can be identified in Figure 8.3. Note, too, that the value system concept corresponds to the concept of an **extended supply chain**, which includes suppliers and other business partners. Wal-Mart Corporation is extremely effective at using information technology to integrate its supply chain heavily with the supply chains of their vendors and customers.

One of the major goals of SCM is to maximize the value added along the supply chain, and this is where computerized decision support enters the picture. The Web/Internet has extended the ability of organizations to implement supply chain management systems. For example, it has simplified the ability to exchange purchase orders, track shipments, and determine inventory levels.

DECISION-MAKING AND THE SUPPLY CHAIN

To maximize the value added along the supply chain, it is necessary to make decisions and evaluate their potential impact. For example, in inbound logistics one must decide where, when, and how much to buy. Inbound materials can be transported in various ways; the question is which one to select. In each link of the chain, decisions must be made on how to move material, information, and money so as to most increase the value.

Supply chain management methods are even affecting nonmanufacturing operations. For example, the Public Broadcasting Service in the United States has adapted SCM concepts to reinvent the way it distributes its programming. See DSS in Action 8.18 for how this is done. And see Anthes (2003) for some details and a diagram of the PBS supply chain.

Supply chain management software is available for decision support for both primary and secondary activities, including optimization of manufacturing processes (see www.manugistics.com), scheduling, inventory management, and procurement. These activities and others are described in Section 8.12.

Special DSS/BI/BA models can determine the costs and benefits of investing in information technologies in an attempt to create value along the supply chain. The implementation of DSS in the supply chain environment is complex because of the difficulties and uncertainties along the way. Let us explain.

DSS IN ACTION 8.18

PBS TELEVISION'S BRAVE NEW SCM

The U.S. Public Broadcasting Service (PBS) is leading the television industry in adapting supply chain management methods in how it manages and distributes programs. By 2006, its overhaul will fundamentally change the dynamics and economics of TV broadcasting. In 2003, PBS distributed programs to its 177 member stations as real-time video streams from satellites. A single show might be sent a dozen times depending upon time zones, scheduling, and weather conditions. Someone at the receiving end generally had to be there to *catch* the transmission. This programming *chain* was fraught with labor-intensive activities that created problems. And the equipment needed to make it work could cost more than $10 million. PBS's new approach involves PCs, store-and-forward IP-based file transmis-

sions, no videotape, and software (including metadata) to replace the manual operations.

The new system allows member stations to pull content into their schedules, as opposed to PBS pushing the content to them. Pilot testing took place in 2003, and by mid-2004 the first production operations were online.

The new system has increased broadcast reliability and will save member stations more than $100 million annually. The industry will probably adopt these concepts worldwide because of the savings and quality improvements.

Source: Adapted from Gary H. Anthes, "TV for the 21st Century," *ComputerWorld,* July 21, 2003, p. 32.

8.11 SUPPLY CHAIN PROBLEMS AND SOLUTIONS

INTRODUCTION

Adding value along the supply chain is essential for competitiveness or even survival. Unfortunately, such additions are limited by many problems along the chain.

Supply chain problems have been recognized both in the military and in business operations for generations. Some of them have caused armies to lose wars and companies to go out of business. These problems are most evident in a complex or long supply chain and in cases where many business partners are involved.

There are hundreds of examples of companies that were unable to meet demands or had inventories too large and too expensive to maintain. Several other problems are typical in a supply chain; for example, lack of overall supply chain strategy and failure to recognize the full range of organizational implications. Many companies erroneously think that good SCM can be attained only through an ERP (ERM is also used for ERP) system.

Companies that experience such problems sometimes pay substantial penalties or even end up going out of business. On the other hand, some world-class companies, such as Wal-Mart, Federal Express, and Dell, have superb supply chains with innovative applications.

An interesting supply chain decision-making problem involved the difficulty of fulfilling orders received electronically for toys during the holiday season of 1999–2000. During the last months of 1999, online toy retailers, including eToys, Amazon.com, and Toys'R'Us, conducted a massive advertising campaign for Internet orders featuring $20- to $30-discount vouchers. Customer response was overwhelming, but some retailers had underestimated the demand and as a result made incorrect ordering, inventory, and shipment decisions. In consequence they were unable to obtain the necessary toys from manufacturing plants and warehouses and deliver them to customers by Christmas Eve. Hershey's Chocolate experienced a similar problem

AVIALL'S WEB-BASED LOGISTICS SCM HITS THE SPOT

Aviall Inc. was saved from financial disaster by a controversial $40 million IT project that included developing a marketing Web site as a key element. This transformed Aviall from a catalog business into a full-scale logistics business (SCM) that hundreds of aviation parts manufacturers and airlines depend on for ordering, inventory control, and demand forecasting. Aviall is now the logistics back-end for the aviation firms. The Aviall systems-integration work took place despite the shrinking of the airline industry.

The $3 million Web logistics system has reduced the cost of ordering from $9 per order to $0.39. The Web site generates $60 million (7.5%) of the company's $800 million annual revenue. Over three to five years, the firm expects this to rise to 30 percent of total revenue.

Source: Adapted from Steve Alexander, "Web Site Adds Inventory Control and Forecasting," *ComputerWorld*, February 24, 2003, p. 45.

when the foundation of its ERP for SCM was built on low data quality and accuracy (see DSS in Action 6.15 and Carr, 2002). This almost bankrupted the firm. Hershey's finally got it right through a new ERP implementation. On the other hand, proper implementation of an SCM systems, along with accurate and timely data, can streamline operations and lead to business opportunities. Aviall invested heavily in a Web-based SCM system that saved it from going under and created new business opportunities, including a major contract from Rolls-Royce PLC (see DSS in Action 8.19 and DSS in Action 5.11).

In the remaining portion of this section we will look closely at some specific problems in managing the supply chain and some proposed solutions, many of which are supported by information systems.

TYPICAL PROBLEMS ALONG THE SUPPLY CHAIN

Problems along the supply chain stem mainly from *uncertainties* and the need to coordinate several activities and/or internal units and business partners.

The major source of uncertainties is the *demand forecast*, which can be influenced by several factors, such as competition, prices, weather conditions, and technological developments. Similar problems occur in forecasting the costs of marketing, raw materials which may be commodities, and transportation. Other uncertainties exist in *delivery times*, which depend on many factors ranging from machine failures to road conditions. Quality problems with materials and parts can also create production time delays, and traffic jams can interfere with shipments. Worthen (2003) describes some major issues in demand forecasting and how such systems must be integrated with SCM. Also see DSS in Action 8.20.

Many other factors can cause supply chain problems (for details, see Jacobs and Whybark, 2000). A major symptom of poor SCM is poor customer service—meaning that people do not get the product or service when and where it is needed, or that they get poor-quality goods and services. Other symptoms are high inventory costs, loss of revenue, and extra costs for special shipments and for expediting shipments.

Other problems in SCM involve obtaining and maintaining accurate real-time data on the supply-chain status, and integrating supply chain information into other enterprise information systems. Access to accurate SCM data is critical for the system

---

DSS IN ACTION 8.20

NIKE'S FORECASTING SYSTEM RUNS INTO OBLIVION

Nike, the sneaker giant, spent some $400 million in developing state-of-the-art forecasting software. Nike deployed its i2 forecasting system in June 2000, and nine months later Nike executives acknowledged that they would be taking a major inventory write-off because the forecasts from the automated system were very inaccurate. With this announcement in February 2001, Nike's stock value plummeted, along with its reputation as an innovative user of technology. Court documents from shareholder lawsuits indicate some of the inherent limitations of demand-forecasting software. The i2 forecasting system did not communicate with Nike's existing

systems, impairing its ability to analyze large amounts of product information. Some data were entered manually, greatly increasing the likelihood of mistakes. Most important, the forecasts were very inaccurate. Relying exclusively on the automated projections, Nike ordered $90 million worth of shoes, such as the Air Garnett II, that became very poor sellers. The company also had a shortfall of $80 million to $100 million on popular models like the Air Force One.

Source: Adapted from Ben Worthen, "Future Results Not Guaranteed," *CIO*, July 15, 2003.

---

to succeed. Although many firms claim they now have a better view into their supply chains, a more realistic picture has emerged. Supply chains are often poorly understood, filled with data that are poorly or inadequately mined or used, and create opportunities for competitors. According to the Bain and Company survey "Why Companies Flunk Supply Chain 101," 85 percent of 162 senior executives placed a top priority on improving supply chain performance, but only 10 percent of them properly tracked it, while only 7 percent collected the right information to report correct metrics on their progress. Only one-third of them tracked performance beyond their own enterprise (see Zipperer, 2002). Part of the problem is cultural, and part derives from not being able to track the data. It is crucial to *gather* accurate and timely data throughout the supply chain to enable better decision-making. This presents an opportunity for software vendors, and especially for organizations using SCM tools to obtain real-time supply chain information. Vendors like i2 Technologies, Manugistics Group, Oracle, SAP, and PeopleSoft are rising to the occasion (see Bacheldor, 2003a; Zimmermann, 2003). RFID (radio-frequency identification tag) technology promises to improve SCM efficiency by more accurately tracking pallet and other cargo movement. For more on RFID technology and its potential impacts in SCM, see Bacheldor (2003a), Edwards (2003), Kimball (2003), Ewalt (2002, 2003), and Chapter 5.

There are a number of ways to integrate SCM systems into other enterprise information systems. Database vendors (e.g., IBM, Oracle) that sell large data warehouse technology, and other business intelligence vendors (e.g., Cognos, Hyperion) provide integrated SCM (see Songini, 2003a). The most typical blends are with ERP, EIS, and CRM. The critical issue is getting accurate data shared among the applications. Even artificial intelligence approaches can be integrated (see Nissen, 2001).

SOLUTIONS TO SUPPLY CHAIN PROBLEMS

Over the years organizations have developed many solutions to supply chain problems. One of the earliest was vertical integration. For example, Henry Ford purchased rubber plantations in South America in order to control tire production. Undoubtedly, the most common solution used by companies is building *inventories* as insurance against uncertainties. With this approach,, products and parts flow smoothly. The main problem is that it is very difficult to determine inventory levels correctly, which must be done for each product and part. When inventory levels are set too high, the cost of keeping the inventory is very high. When the inventory is too low, there is no insurance against high demand or slow delivery (lead) times, and revenues (and customers) may be lost. In either event, the total penalty cost, including opportunities lost and bad reputation gained, can be very high. Thus, major attempts are made to properly control inventory, as shown in DSS in Action 8.21.

Proper SCM and inventory management require making decisions and coordinating the different activities and links of the supply chain so that goods can move smoothly and on time from suppliers to customers. This practice keeps inventories low and costs down. Coordination is needed because companies depend on each other but do not always work together toward the same goal.

Effective SCM requires that suppliers and customers work together in a coordinated manner by sharing and communicating the information necessary for decision-making. For example, Wal-Mart allows its major suppliers to enter its intranet and retrieve sales data on a daily basis. Thus, the suppliers can make better production-

---

DSS IN ACTION 8.21

HOW LITTLEWOODS STORES IMPROVED ITS SCM

Littlewoods Stores is one of Britain's largest retailers of high-quality clothing, with 136 stores throughout the United Kingdom. The retail clothing business is very competitive, and so in the late 1990s the company embarked on an IT-supported initiative to improve its supply chain efficiency. A serious SCM problem was overstocking.

In order to get better SCM, the company reengineered its supply chain processes. It first introduced a Web-based performance-reporting system. Using DSS models, the system analyzes marketing and finance data, space planning, merchandizing, and purchasing data on a daily basis. For example, merchandizing can now perform sophisticated sales, stock, and supplier analyses to make key operational decisions on pricing and inventory.

Using the Web, analysts can view sales and stock data in veritably any grouping of levels and categories, even at SKU (merchandise part number) and day levels. Furthermore, users can easily drill down to detailed sales and other data. The system uses a data warehouse, DSS/BI/BA, and other end-user-oriented software to make better decisions. Here are some other examples of decisions made and their results:

- The ability to strategically price merchandise differently in different stores saved $1.2 million in 1997 alone.

- Better inventory management eliminated $17 million of overstocked inventory and saved a margin of roughly $4 million.

- Better inventory management reduced the need for stock liquidations saving $1.4 million a year in inventory operating costs.

- The average stock-to-store lead time of 48 days was reduced to five days, improving overall responsiveness to customer demand.

- Marketing distribution expenses were cut by $7 million a year.

- Strategically pricing merchandise differently according to location, accounting for regional variation, and encouraging sales saves $1.2 million per year.

- Reduction in logistic employees from 84 to 49 people saves about $1 million annually.

- Reducing backup inventory expenses by about $4 million a year. For example, because of quick replenishment, stock levels went down by 80 percent.

Within a year there were more than 600 Web-based users, and the data warehouse grew to over 1 gigabyte.

Source: Adapted from "Customers' Success Stories," and press releases at the MicroStrategy Corporation's Web site, www.microstrategy.com, January 2000.

scheduling decisions. Wal-Mart Stores Inc. built an intelligence-sharing inventory and supply chain management system that changed the face of business. See Johnson (2002) for a history of the Wal-Mart experience; some details appear in Chapter 5. A rapid flow of information along the supply chain makes suppliers very efficient. Therefore, suppliers and buyers must participate together in the design of supply chains to achieve their shared goals. In fact, Wal-Mart does not officially take ownership of certain classes of merchandise until sold.

Collaboration along the supply chain is critical, but not sufficient for SCM success. Though optimization is also necessary (see the preceding section). Konicki (2002) describes how better collaboration along the retailing supply chain could save the industry $40 billion annually. In 2002, Sears, Roebuck ran supply chain collaboration tests with Michelin North America tires. Sears successfully avoided a catastrophe by opening up its supply chain data to Michelin, which boosted production to avoid a forecasted shortfall due to a major sale. See Konicki (2002) for details. See Lee-Young and Barnett (2001) for details on the need for real-time collaboration and communication along the retail-fashion supply chain.

To properly control the uncertainties mentioned earlier, it is necessary to understand what causes the uncertainties, determine how the uncertainties will affect other activities up and down the supply chain, and formulate ways to reduce or eliminate the uncertainties. The problem is exacerbated by insufficient utilization of optimization and descriptive (typically simulation) models in SCM. Combined with these issues is the need for an effective, efficient communication environment for all business partners. For example, computerized POS information can be transmitted once a day, or even in real-time, to distribution centers, suppliers, and shippers. This enables optimal inventory levels.

The following are some other solutions to SCM problems:

- Use outsourcing rather than do it yourself during demand peaks.
- Similarly, "buy" rather than "make" whenever appropriate.
- Configure optimal shipping plans.
- Optimize purchasing.
- Create strategic partnerships with suppliers.
- Use a just-in-time approach to purchasing so that suppliers quickly deliver small quantities whenever supplies, materials, and parts are needed.
- Reduce the number of intermediaries, which usually add to supply chain costs, by using electronic commerce for direct marketing.
- Reduce the lead time for buying and/or selling by automatic processing using EDI or extranets.
- Use fewer suppliers.
- Improve the supplier–buyer relationship.
- Manufacture only after orders are in, as Dell does with its custom-made computers.
- Achieve accurate demand by working closely with suppliers.
- Apply true optimization and descriptive models to SCM.

Most of the above solutions are enhanced by IT support, especially in the form of enterprise resource planning (ERP) systems. But it is important to note that even in the e-commerce arena, products and services *must be delivered*. Aksoy and Derbez (2003) present a supply chain management systems product review. Check the *OR/MS Today* Web site for updates.

8.12 MATERIALS REQUIREMENT PLANNING (MRP), ENTERPRISE RESOURCE PLANNING/ENTERPRISE RESOURCE MANAGEMENT (ERP/ERM), AND SUPPLY CHAIN MANAGEMENT (SCM) SYSTEMS

The concept of the supply chain is interrelated with the computerization of its activities as they have evolved over the last 50 years. See Hugos (2003) and Sheikh (2003) for background details.

THE EVOLUTION OF COMPUTERIZED SUPPLY CHAIN AIDS

Historically, many supply chain activities were managed with inefficient and ineffective paper transactions. Since the early business utilization of computers, attention has been given to the automation of processes along the supply chain. The first software programs appeared in the 1950s and the early 1960s and supported short segments along the supply chain. Typical examples are inventory-management systems, scheduling, and billing. The major objective was to reduce costs, expedite processing, and decrease errors. Such applications were developed in the functional areas independently of each other.

It soon became clear that there were interdependencies between some supply chain activities. Early on, for instance, it was realized that production schedules are directly related to inventory management and purchasing plans. The material requirements planning (MRP) model was devised in the 1960s. Since this model often required daily updating, the need for computer support was obvious. This resulted in commercial MRP software packages.

MRP systems involve inventory models with lead times, a master production schedule of all final products (which may be demand forecast-driven), and bills of materials for every assembly. The bills of materials are a list of all the components of an assembly or final product. They form a tree structure of interrelated parts from the tiniest parts to the major assemblies that form each final product. The MRP system takes a proposed production schedule of final products and, using lead times and existing inventory records, backtracks through the records to create a parts explosion, which is a list of batches of parts that must be produced, and when, to meet the lead-time requirements of the parts and final products. Ideally a smooth production plan is generated, utilizing a factory's overall capacity at as close to 100 per cent as possible. Capacity requirements planning (CRP) was developed to smooth out the MRP plan based on a factory's specific and overall machine center capacities.

While MRP packages were useful in many cases, helping to drive inventory levels down and streamlining portions of the supply chain, they often failed. One of the major reasons for their failure was the realization that schedule/inventory/purchasing operations are closely related to both financial and labor resources. This realization resulted in an enhanced MRP methodology and software called manufacturing requirements planning, or MRP II.

During this evolution, information systems became more and more integrated. This led to the concept of enterprise resource planning (ERP), which concentrated on integrating enterprise transaction-processing activities. Later, ERP was expanded to include internal suppliers and customers, and then external suppliers and customers, in what is known as extended ERP/SCM software.

WHY INTEGRATION?

Creating a twenty-first-century enterprise cannot be done effectively with functionally oriented twentieth-century computer technology. Different departments using functional systems may be unable to communicate with each other in the same language. Worse yet, crucial sales, inventory, and production data often have to be painstakingly entered manually into separate computer systems each time a person who is not a member of a specific department needs ad hoc information related to the specific department. In many cases employees simply do not get the information they need, or they get it when it is too late.

Sandoe and Saharia (2001) list the following major benefits of integration (in order of importance):

- **_Tangible benefits:_** inventory reduction, personnel reduction, productivity improvement, order-management improvement, financial close-cycle improvements, IT cost reduction, procurement-cost reduction, cash-management improvements, revenue and profit increases, transportation logistics-cost reduction, maintenance reduction, and on-time delivery improvement.
- **_Intangible benefits:_** information visibility, new and/or improved processes, customer responsiveness, standardization, flexibility, globalization, and business performance.

Note that in both types of benefits, many items are directly related to improved SCM. For a further discussion of the improvements integration has provided to SCM, see the white paper "Competition's New Battleground: The Integrated Value Chain" at www.cambridgetechnology.com.

INTEGRATING THE SUPPLY CHAIN

For generations the various links of company supply chains were managed independently of each other. However, since the 1950s, and thanks to the introduction of computer-based information systems, companies have started to integrate these links. Integration was facilitated by the need to streamline operations in order to meet customer demands in the areas of product and service costs, quality, delivery, technology, and cycle time brought about by increased global competition. Furthermore, the new forms of organizational relationships and the information revolution, especially the Internet and electronic commerce, brought SCM to the forefront of attention. See DSS in Action 8.22.

ENTERPRISE RESOURCE PLANNING/ENTERPRISE RESOURCE MANAGEMENT (ERP/ERM)

With the advance of enterprise-wide client/server computing comes a new challenge: how to control all major business processes with a single software architecture in real-time. The integration solution, known as **enterprise resource planning (ERP)** (sometimes called enterprise resource management, ERM), promises benefits from increased efficiency to improved quality, productivity, and profitability (for details, see Umble and Umble, 2002). The name ERP is somewhat misleading because the software does not concentrate on either planning or resources. A major objective of ERP is to _integrate_ all departments and functions across a company into a single computer system that can serve the entire enterprise's needs. For example, improved order entry allows immediate access to inventory, product data, customer credit history, and prior order information. This raises productivity and increases customer satisfaction. One

DSS IN ACTION 8.22

HOW WARNER-LAMBERT APPLIES AN INTEGRATED SUPPLY CHAIN

It all begins on eucalyptus farms in Australia, where the fast-growing trees produce some of the materials used in Listerine antiseptic mouthwash, one of the major products of Warner-Lambert (WL). The materials collected from eucalyptus trees are shipped from Australia to the WL manufacturing plant in the United States. WL's major problem is to determine how much Listerine to produce. Listerine is purchased by thousands of retail stores, some of which are giants, such as Wal-Mart, and many of which are small. The problem that the manufacturing plant faces is how to forecast the overall demand. A wrong forecast will confront WL either with excessive inventories or with shortages. Maintaining inventories is expensive, and shortages may result in loss of business and reputation.

WL forecasts demand with the help of Manugistic's Demand Planning DSS. (Manugistics is an SCM software vendor). Used with other products in the Manugistics Supply Chain Planning Suite, the system analyzes manufacturing, distribution, and sales data against expected demand and business-climate information to help WL decide how much Listerine (and other products) to make and distribute, and how much of each raw ingredient is needed. For example, the model can anticipate the impact of promotions or of a production line being down. The sales and marketing groups at WL meet monthly with employees in finance, procurement, and other departments. The groups enter the expected demand for Listerine into a Marcam Corporation Prism Capacity Planning DSS that schedules the production of Listerine in the amounts needed and generates electronic purchase orders for WL's suppliers.

WL's supply chain excellence stems from its innovative collaborative planning, forecasting, and replenishment (CPFR) program. WL launched CPFR a few years ago when it started sharing strategic plans, performance data, and market insight with Wal-Mart Inc. over private networks. The company realized that it could benefit from WL's market knowledge just as Wal-Mart could benefit from its product knowledge. During the CPFR pilot, WL increased its products' shelf-fill rate—the extent to which a store's shelves are fully stocked—from 87 percent to 98 percent, earning the company about $8 million a year in additional sales, or the equivalent of a new-product launch. WL now uses the Internet to expand the CPFR program to all its suppliers and retail partners.

Source: Compiled and adapted from *Store*, June 15, 1998; *CIO*, August 15, 1998; Manugistics' Logistics Management and Distribution Reports, November 1999.

option is to self-develop an integrated system by using existing best-of-the-breed functional commercial packages or by programming your own systems. The other option is to use commercially available integrated software known as ERP. The leading software for ERP is SAP R/3. Oracle, J. D. Edwards, Computer Associates, PeopleSoft, and Baan Company provide similar products. All include Web modules designed to be easily accessible from a company's enterprise portal. (SAP AG includes J2EE compliance in its application server; see Taft, 2003.) These software packages have been widely adopted and have been extended to include decision support tools designed to increase their integration with organizational EIS systems. Several takeovers and mergers of major ERP and CRM providers were in progress in 2003 (see Ferguson and Vaas, 2003). This obviously leads to consolidation of products and services, and the creation of software with, hopefully, the best features of each. For details, see Ferguson and Vaas (2003), McCright (2003a), and Songini (2003d, 2003e), among others.

ERP systems are based on a value-chain view of the organization in which functional departments coordinate their work. ERP systems integrate an organization's business activities by storing data about those activities in a centralized database. Enterprise resource planning systems are designed to enhance competitiveness by upgrading an organization's ability to generate timely, accurate information throughout the enterprise and its supply chain. Commercially available software packages promise seamless integration of all information flows: financial and accounting, human resource, operations, supply chain, and customer information, providing a unified view of the business, encompassing all functions and departments by establishing a single enterprise-wide database in which all business transactions are entered, recorded, processed, monitored, and reported (see Umble and Umble, 2002).

A successful ERP implementation can shorten production cycles, increase the accuracy of demand forecasts, improve customer service, and trim excess operating expenses; it may lead to a reduction in overall information technology costs by eliminating redundant information and computer systems (see Umble and Umble, 2002). It may also lead to better inventory control and use. Flextronics International, a $1.1 billion Singapore-based firm, deployed an ERP to its 26 locations worldwide. The company improved its inventory turnover immediately. Its own managers shop online in their internal store. The consolidated supply inventory helps Flextronics purchasing managers negotiate better terms with suppliers (see Legare, 2002).

See Koch (2002) for an ERP primer and the "ERP Life Cycle Focus Guide: Planning, Execution and Post-Implementation" (available from www.cio.com), which examines best practices and decision-making needed to successfully harness ERP during its life cycle. For additional background on ERP, see Buchanan, Daunais, and Micelli (2000), Langenwalter (2000), and Ptak and Schragenheim (2000).

ERP software crosses functional departments and can be extended along the supply chain to suppliers and customers. Companies have successfully integrated hundreds of applications using ERP software, saving millions of dollars and significantly increasing customer satisfaction. For example, Mobil Oil consolidated 300 different information systems by implementing SAP R/3 in its U.S. petrochemical operations. ERP forces discipline and organization around business processes, making the alignment of IT and business goals more likely. Moreover, by using ERP a company discovers all the "dusty corners" of its business. Hershey's Chocolates learned this lesson (DSS in Action 6.15) when, in its first ERP implementation, it neglected to indicate to the ERP where its inventory was stored (this was always done informally in anticipation of a major demand spike). The ERP was unaware of the inventory, and consequently the firm was unable to meet demand during its busiest season (see Carr, 2002). Mobile Oil also experienced a major failure in implementing an ERP for SCM.

An ERP suite provides a single interface for managing all the routine activities performed in manufacturing—from entering sales orders to coordinating shipping, as well as after-sales customer service. This collaboration is extremely important in manufacturing. For example, Dow Corning extended its ERP (SAP R/3) with some of the best collaboration and electronic document management (EDM) tools available. The EDM manages critical content that includes over 2 million active materials-based data sheets for developers, customers, and partners. The collaboration tools provide e-mail services and Web collaboration tools (see Ericson, 2003). And Herman Miller extended the capabilities of its ERP system to include real-time communication and decision-making for all users in its MySIGN portal. Along with 150 internal users are 400 supplier users. More recently, ERP systems have begun to incorporate functionality for customer interaction and managing relationships with suppliers and vendors, making the systems less inward-looking.

ERP has played a critical role in getting small- and medium-sized manufacturers focused, which facilitates business-process changes across the enterprise. Vendors continue to create products to meet their needs. These include the SAP Business One Suite, the PowerEasy Corp. ERP suite for the Mac OS X, and ERP systems from Best Software and Microsoft (see Ferguson, 2003; Vizard and Darrow, 2003). Integrating multiple plants and distribution facilities results in better supply chain management.

The cost of a modest ERP implementation can range from $2 million to $4 million, depending on the size of the organization and the specific products and services purchased from vendors. The cost of a full-blown implementation in a large organization can easily exceed $100 million. A recent survey of 63 companies with annual revenues ranging from $12 million to $63 billion indicated that the average implementation cost $10.6 million and took 23 months to complete (see Umble and Umble, 2002). An important financial issue is when and how much to spend to upgrade an ERP. According to AMR Research (see Low and Goldberg, 2002), most companies that are upgrading their ERP systems spend their money in the following categories: professional services (23–28%), hardware (20–24%), employee labor and training (16–23%), software for upgrades (8–15%), additional software (9–15%), and networks (7–10%).

Despite the expense, the returns can be staggering when ERP succeeds. Owens Corning saved $50 million in logistics, materials management, and sourcing through its ERP. The system also led to inventory reductions because material planners had access to more up-to-date and accurate data that improved the company's ability to track and control system-wide inventory and forecast future demand (see Umble and Umble, 2002). For a comprehensive treatment of the costs, implementation problems, and payback of ERP, see Koch et al. (2002).

SECOND-GENERATION ERP

First-generation ERP aimed at automating key business office processes. During the 1990s, it provided an additional benefit. Companies that were using home-grown ERP systems were faced with the expensive task of expanding to support a four-digit year as a result of the then upcoming year 2000. ERP package system implementation provided the additional benefit of compliance (a benefit now taken for granted). And indeed, ERP projects saved companies millions of dollars. By the late 1990s the major benefits of ERP had been exploited, but the ERP movement was far from over. A second, more powerful generation of ERP development started with the objective of leveraging existing systems to increase efficiency in handling transactions, improve decision-making, and further transform ways of doing business.

As you may recall, in Chapter 5 OLTP and OLAP were treated as two different but complementary activities. First-generation ERP basically supported OLTP and other routine transactional activities. For example, an ERP system has the functionality of electronic ordering, or the best way to bill the customer—all it does is automate the transactions.

The reports generated by ERP systems provided planners with statistics about what happened in the company, costs, and financial performance. However, with ERP the planning systems were rudimentary. Reports from ERP systems provided a snapshot of time, but they did not support the continuous planning activities central to supply chain planning, a system that continues to refine and enhance the plan as changes and events occur, up to the very last minute before the plan is executed.

This deficiency created a need for decision-making-oriented systems, and this is what SCM and business intelligence software vendors provided. These products offer DSS/BI/BA capabilities in short segments of the supply chain. As an illustration, we look at the ERP and SCM approaches to the planning problem. There is a fundamental difference between the two; in SCM the question becomes, "Should I take your order?" instead of the ERP approach, "How can I best take or fulfill your order?"

Thus, SCM systems have emerged as a *complement* to ERP systems to provide intelligent decision support capabilities. An SCM system can be designed to overlay existing ERP systems and to extract data from every step of the supply chain, providing a clear global picture of where the enterprise is heading. Creating a plan from an SCM system allows companies to quickly assess the impact of their actions on the entire supply chain, including customer demand. Therefore, it makes sense to integrate ERP and SCM. ERP implementations are also integrating with capacity planning, CRM, and real-time performance analysis systems (see Ferris, 1999). ERP integration with e-commerce efforts is also important (see Siau and Messersmith, 2002).

HOW IS SUCH INTEGRATION DONE?

One approach to achieving such integration is to work with different software from different vendors for example, using SAP as an ERP, and adding Manugistics manufacturing-oriented software, as shown earlier in the Warner-Lambert case. Such an approach calls for integrating and fitting together different software, which may be a complex issue unless special interfaces exist. A suboption is to use **advanced planning and scheduling (APS)** packages, which are modules that can be integrated with ERP or total SCM. APS helps in optimizing production and ensuring that the right materials are in the right warehouse at the right time to meet customers' demands.

The second approach is for ERP vendors to add decision support and business intelligence capabilities, which solves the integration problem. But, as in the integration of DBMS and spreadsheets in Excel or Lotus 1-2-3, you get a product with some weaker functionalities. Most ERP vendors add such functionalities for another reason: because it is cheaper and easier for the customer. The added functionalities, which create the second-generation ERP, include not only decision support but also CRM, electronic commerce, and data warehousing and mining. Companies were eager to use post-ERP systems, as shown in DSS in Action 8.23.

The third option is to rent applications rather than build systems. When applications are rented, the ERP vendor (or other rentee) takes care of the functionalities and the integration problems. This relatively new approach is known as the ASP alternative.

APPLICATION SERVICE PROVIDERS AND ERP OUTSOURCING

An **application service provider (ASP)** is a software vendor who leases ERP-based applications, including those with DSS capabilities, to organizations. The basic concept is the same as old-fashioned time-sharing. The outsourcers set up the systems and run them for you. Use of ASP is considered a risk management strategy and it best fits small- to middle-sized companies.

The ASP concept is especially useful in ERP projects that are expensive to install, take a long time to implement, and are hard to staff. However, an ASP offering is also evident in ERP-added functions such as DSS/BI/BA, EC, CRM, data marts, desktop productivity, and other supply chain-related applications.

The use of an ASP has some downsides. First, ERP vendors demand a five-year commitment, but in five years ERP software may change drastically and purchase prices may fall dramatically. Second, flexibility is lost. Rented systems are fairly standard and may not fit your needs. Transition from a rented system can be expensive and time-consuming.

ERP PROBLEMS AND FAILURES

An ERP can help organize and manage a firm's supply chain, thereby leading to dramatic overall savings in production and management costs. Despite their strategic importance, ERP implementations report an unusually high failure rate, sometimes jeopardizing the core operations of the implementing organization (Hong and Kim,

DSS IN ACTION 8.23

HOW U.S. COMPANIES ARE SUCCEEDING WITH ERP

Here is how several U.S. companies are succeeding with ERP installations.

- **Owens Corning,** a maker of building materials, changed its business model and corporate thinking in 1999. For example, instead of selling shingles and roofing vents separately, it started to sell complete roofing systems that include parts, installation, delivery, and other services. To do this economically, the company uses business intelligence (data warehouse and mining) to analyze the data generated by the ERP system (from SAP). The data warehouse provides valuable information on customer profitability, product line profitability, sales performance, and SCM activities. The ERP is also integrated with shop-floor process control that uses SCM software.

- **General Instruments,** a telecommunications equipment maker, and SCM software vendor, pushes parts data into Metaphase's product management tool. From there data enter Oracle's ERP system. Previously product data were entered manually into each system, resulting in high costs and many errors. The company also uses product con-

figuration tools that assist the sales force and manufacturing department to ensure that certain product configurations are possible before orders are placed on the ERP. More than 3,000 component suppliers have direct access to product data over the Web using Metaphase's technology.

- **Rollerblade Inc.,** an in-line skate maker, uses an ERP (from J. D. Edward) as the platform for the company's forecasting, sales-force automation, and data warehousing systems. With the ERP integrated platform, decision support activities were ineffective. Now a profitability and sales analysis by product, region, and time is done regularly and effectively.

- **Mott's North America** installed ERP and found that it did not address its marketing and customer service problems properly. Using SAP's advanced features, the company added production planning and shipment scheduling optimization. Integration with electronic commerce was also achieved. Now, for example, distributors can use the Web to check their order status by themselves with the R/3 system.

2002). There have been many dramatic and expensive ERP failures (see DSS in Action 8.24). We have mentioned the Hershey Chocolates ERP failure several times. Hershey rushed to deploy the system without carefully considering what it actually did. Data inaccuracies plagued the system and created massive disruptions in operations. See DSS in Action 8.25.

In 1998, the city of Atlanta, Georgia, implemented a PeopleSoft ERP system that cost over $10 million. The system worked so poorly that the city eventually had to discard it. The intention of the deployment was to handle Y2K issues in a rush. Instead of evaluating and improving existing business processes, the city pushed its consultants to modify the program to handle the existing ones. Paper methods were not abandoned, and there was a serious lack of training and skill in the IS group responsible for the ERP. See Bennett (2002). Also see Case Application 8.2 on McDonald's major disaster when implementing a major enterprise information system.

A successful ERP can be the backbone of business intelligence for an organization, giving management a unified view of its processes. But in June 2000, Frank Gillett, then a senior analyst with Forrester Research, Inc., stated, "It's been our experience that most of the ERP [vendors] don't understand decision support and when they try to implement it, don't do it well" (Menezes, 2000). When used appropriately, ERP software integrates information used by the accounting, manufacturing, distribution, and human resources departments into a seamless computing system. However, there are challenges that come with implementing an ERP system. ERP implementations fail more often than not (Legare, 2002). When ERP implementation fails, it is usually

---

DSS IN ACTION 8.24

NOTABLE ERP IMPLEMENTATION FAILURES

In the September 30, 2002 issue of *ComputerWorld* (Anonymous, 2002) appears a list of the top 10 corporate IT failures in the 1990s. Several of them were major ERP implementations. These include the

- SAP ERP system for drug distributor FoxMeyer Corp. The system's deficiencies allegedly helped drive the firm into bankruptcy.
- SAP ERP system for W.W. Grainger, Inc. Grainger spent at least $9 million on SAP software and services in 1998 and 1999. During the worst six months, Grainger lost $19 million in sales and $23 million in profits.

- IBM-led installation and integration of SAP for Hershey Foods Corp. Hershey lost 12 percent of sales in its busiest 1999 Halloween and Christmas candy season.
- Oracle ERP and application integration for the agricultural cooperative Tri Valley Growers. Tri Valley bought over $6 million in ERP software and services in 1996. It eventually stopped using the software and stopped paying the vendor. Oracle denied all claims. The case was settled in January 2002.

---

because the organization did not dedicate enough time or money to training, and to managing culture-change issues. See Gale (2002). In fact, training is often last-minute and weak (Gale, 2002).

The successful implementation of an enterprise resource planning (ERP) system is a massive task. For an organization to reap the benefits of ERP, it must first develop a plan for success. But the organization must be prepared to be reengineered, with its staff disrupted and a drop in productivity, before the payoff is realized (see Umble and Umble, 2002).

ERP systems take a lot of time and money to implement. ERP system implementations disrupt a company's culture, create extensive training requirements, and lead to

---

DSS IN ACTION 8.25

HERSHEY'S EVENTUAL SWEET SUCCESS IN ERP

Hershey Foods Corp. ran into major problems when it deployed SAP AG's R/3 ERP software and other business applications in 1999. In September 1999, Hershey's former CEO and chairman, Kenneth L. Wolfe, announced that problems with the ERP were going to prevent the company from delivering $100 million worth of Kisses and Jolly Ranchers for Halloween that year. Hershey's stock price fell more than 8 percent that day. Analysts did not fully trust Hershey's ability to deliver candy until the following fall, when things had long gone back to normal. Hershey's experience is pretty average. Studies have shown that most companies that install enterprise software are late, their business processes suffer temporarily, and their revenue can take a hit for as long as six months. One ERP expert has quipped that implementing ERP is like pouring cement on your business processes.

Fortunately, the candy maker had better luck with its upgrade to the Web-based version of R/3, started in July 2001 and completed in May 2002. The cost of the upgrade was 20 percent below budget, with none of the order-processing and product-shipment disruptions caused by the $112 million system in 1999. In addition, Hershey's made more than 30 improvements to its core business processes within 60 days of deploying the new system. Costs have been reduced, as have processing times. The system has achieved a near-zero defect production environment and, using SAP's business analysis tools, can measure the impact of sales and marketing programs instantaneously.

Source: Adapted from Lave Low and Michael Goldberg, "Hershey's Bittersweet Lesson," *CIO*, November 15, 2002, pp. 22–24; Todd R. Weiss, "Hershey Upgrades R/3 ERP System Without Hitches," *ComputerWorld*, September 9, 2002, p. 25.

productivity dips and mishandled customer orders that can temporarily damage the bottom line. Between 50 percent and 75 percent of U.S. firms have experienced some level of failure when implementing advanced manufacturing or information technology (see Umble and Umble, 2002).

ERP implementation is a transformation in the way an organization does business, and should be viewed as such by top management. There are a number of reasons why an ERP fails. Many failures are predictable, but overzealous CEOs and/or CIOs push the system to perform in ways for which it is not designed. Often data are simply unavailable, or cost excessive amounts to obtain. ERP definitely forces a *formalization* of business processes, which some firms are reluctant to do. Enterprise software is difficult to work with and expensive. Implementations take a long time. It is hard to get people to change the ways they work so that the system will function correctly. But they eventually adapt. And there will be problems at first because enterprise software is not just software. It requires changing the way business is done.

Some of the biggest ERP system implementation failures occur because the new software's capabilities and needs are mismatched with the organization's existing business processes and procedures. An ERP system that is not designed to meet the specific business needs of the company can cause major problems. A significant mismatch between the technological capabilities of the system and the existing structure, processes, or business needs of the organization will generate major disruptions. Less severe mismatches between business processes and software requirements will create significant problems for implementers and users (see Umble and Umble, 2002). In DSS in Focus 8.26, we describe some ways to avoid ERP implementation failure and critical success factors. Also see Umble, Haft, and Umble (2003), who investigate critical success factors, software selection steps, and implementation procedures critical to a successful ERP implementation, and Akkermans and van Helden (2002), who look into how ERP critical success factors interrelate. Hong and Kim (2002) investigate the organizational *fit* of ERP. Their results, from a field survey of 34 organizations, show that ERP implementation success significantly depends on the organizational fit of ERP and certain implementation contingencies.

Probably the *most critical factor* in ERP failure is that *the organization's business processes do not match those modeled in the ERP*. For example, early ERP systems were designed for the discrete parts industry. Many flow process firms (chemical, pharmaceutical, mining, etc.) met with dismal and very expensive failures when they attempted to get an ERP package to work. If the actual business processes do not match those modeled in the ERP, one or both of two things must be done for the implementation to proceed: (1) the actual business processes must be changed to match the model of the ERP system; and/or (2) additional, generally expensive software must be written, by the organization or its consultants, to accommodate the differences. Typically, some of each must be done. Regardless, there will be problems. The former generally hits organizational culture roadblocks and creates ill-will toward the system. And the ERP modeled processes may be inappropriate for the organization. The latter creates the usual set of problems that accompany the development of any new software. However, if the ERP software is upgraded by the vendor, there is no guarantee that the additional software will work. So the millions of dollars spent in developing add-on software may go to waste, as the home-grown software must be modified or completely rewritten. Consequently, there have been many problems and additional expenses in ERP deployment. For example, a large manufacturer of earth-moving equipment (each piece of equipment sells for several million dollars) "successfully" installed an ERP to handle its operations. When a client wanted to make a change in one of the options in the five tractors it ordered (e.g., a CD player instead of

---

DSS IN FOCUS 8.26

AVOIDING ERP IMPLEMENTATION FAILURE

The three primary reasons for the failure of all IT-related projects (see Chapter 6) are

- Poor planning or poor management (77%)
- Change in business goals during the project (75%)
- Lack of business management support (73%).

Specifically, ERP implementation failures fall into 10 categories:

- Poor leadership from top management.
- Automating existing redundant or non-value-added processes in the new system.
- Unrealistic expectations. ERP implementations are expensive, require a lot of time to implement, and often lose money while being fine tuned.
- Poor project management.
- Inadequate user education and training.
- Trying to maintain the status quo.
- A bad match between the ERP business model and actual business processes.
- Inaccurate data. As in any enterprise system, inaccurate data can lead to disaster.
- ERP implementation is viewed as an IT project. It is a set of business processes, not a project. It continues to evolve as the organization's environment and business processes change.
- Significant technical difficulties.

The following six basic building blocks are required to implement an ERP system successfully:

- Organizational commitment. This is true for all large-scale, enterprise information systems. ERP affects all business processes.
- Clear communication of strategic goals.

- View ERP as an enterprise-wide venture.
- Select a compatible ERP system.
- Ensure data accuracy.
- Resolve multi-site issues (e.g., whether to standardize across the enterprise or not; whether to implement all sites simultaneously or phase in).

In light of all this, we can establish the following critical success factors for ERP implementations:

- Strong leadership provided by an executive management planning committee.
- The implementation is viewed as an ongoing process.
- Implementation teams are composed of the company's best workers representing all functions.
- Mid-level management is totally involved in the implementation.
- Excellent project management techniques are used.
- The old systems, including all informal systems, are eliminated.
- Proper measurements are implemented and closely monitored.
- An aggressive but achievable implementation schedule is established.
- Successful change management techniques are applied.
- Extensive education and training is provided.

Source: Adapted and condensed from Elisabeth J. Umble and Michael M. Umble, "Avoiding ERP Implementation Failure," *Industrial Management*, Vol. 44, No. 1, January/February 2002, pp. 25–34.

---

a cassette deck in the cabs), the production manager indicated that it could not be done. A multimillion dollar contract was in jeopardy because, in order to make the change, the company had to cancel the order for the tractors and create a new one. For the client, the problem was solved by the CEO walking out and bringing the CD player directly to the plant foreman and telling him to override the production requirements. Then additional software costing several million dollars was written to allow changes in the production order while the tractor was being built. Clearly, the ERP system was inflexible in that it did not anticipate long construction times in its internal model. Such ERP problems can cripple or even bankrupt an organization.

In addition, ERP generally does not include normative or descriptive models. It is great at processing data into usable information, but typically does so at the transaction level. A good dose of optimization and/or simulation models, depending on the situation, could definitely improve its performance.

8.13 CUSTOMER RELATIONSHIP (RESOURCE) MANAGEMENT (CRM) SYSTEMS

INTRODUCTION

Customer relationship management (CRM) is an enterprise approach to understanding and influencing customer behavior through meaningful communications in order to improve customer acquisition, customer retention, customer loyalty, and customer profitability (Swift, 2001). A **customer relationship management (CRM) system** (also known as a customer resource management system) provides the technology to do so. Corporations that achieve high customer retention and high customer profitability aim for *the right product (or service), to the right customer, at the right price, at the right time, through the right channel, to satisfy the customer's need or desire* (Swift, 2001). This is the main goal of CRM. Though it has the same goal as revenue management (see Chapter 4), CRM generally puts a major focus on the selling side. A broader definition of CRM includes all activities that turn casual (seemingly one-time) consumers into loyal customers by satisfying or exceeding their requirements so that they will buy again. E-commerce influence impacts the need for quality and accurate CRM (see Berkowitz, 2001; Kohli, 2001).

CRM is an interactive process that turns customer information into positive customer relationships. It empowers many more customer contact personnel, information workers, marketing and sales functions, and management employees with significantly better and more informative business intelligence about their customers. CRM should be integrated into everything a company does, everyone it employs, and everywhere it transacts. When a firm states that excellent customer service is its goal, this means that it is the goal of the *entire* organization, not just the people who connect directly with customers (see Swift, 2001). CRM is fundamentally an enterprise-level DSS. And CRM efforts are not restricted to companies. Government agencies use it to improve customer service (Scalet, 2000), and nonprofit organizations for fund-raising efforts (see Cohen, 2002).

Customer loyalty is important. In competitive markets, if you do not maintain customers' loyalty, another firm will take them away. In the mobile phone industry, between 20 and 30 percent of customers change their provider every year. Identifying who is likely to *churn* and maintaining even a small percentage can generate millions of dollars in maintained revenue (Swift, 2001). Loyal customers are typically more profitable customers. If an organization can accurately predict future sales based on customer behavior, it will lead to cross selling. CRM enables customer retention and higher profits by knowing the customer and using cross selling. It enables accurate target marketing by helping identify customers and their needs via customer segmentation.

For decades, airlines have recognized the importance of retention. They recognized early that incentives generate further purchases and positive contacts with customers, leading to long-term growth and customer retention. Airlines pioneered customer retention programs and revenue management (sometimes called yield management) efforts to provide the right product to the right customer at the right price in the right manner, and utilized technology to apply optimization methods to manage price, supply, and demand. Superior and personalized customer service to their best customers and special privileges (free flights) have created brand loyalty. Hotels, rental car agencies, passenger railroads, and other travel industry firms soon adopted these methods. Now they are being adopted by the mainstream, including industry segments such as retail, insurance, and service.

CRM gathers data on and tracks customers. The point is to use data better to manage relationships with customers. The Chicago White Sox, a U.S. major league baseball team, uses CRM to increase fan loyalty (winning is better for building loyalty, but winning better with technology is even better) and increases sales. See DSS in Action 8.27.

MARKETING

Marketing has moved through the phases of (1) mass marketing, (2) target marketing, (3) customer marketing, and (4) 1-to-1 marketing. Each phase has used technology to boost sales. Now CRM is enabling the concept of 1-to-1 marketing. In 1-to-1 market-

---

DSS IN ACTION 8.27

THE CHICAGO WHITE SOX BAT 1000 WITH CRM

In 1997, the White Sox organization realized that getting a better handle on its fan base, particularly season ticket holders and those looking for group tickets, would lead to more sales and better customer retention. The team draws millions of fans every year and already had a prospecting base of hundreds of thousands of potential ticket buyers, but was still using paper and file folders to manage the information. Each account executive was responsible for nearly 600 accounts and 600 seats in group accounts. Tom Sheridan, manager of ticket sales for the Chicago White Sox, says that it was hard to keep on top of all the information, especially since the team was receiving 50 to 75 calls per day from season ticket holders.

The White Sox deployed a GoldMine (FrontRange Solutions) CRM. Its databases track people who have called and expressed interest in purchasing tickets, purchased leads and names obtained from contests (for telemarketing), and customers who have purchased tickets. In 2003, there were more than 30,000 records in the main ticket sales database, and more than 100,000 in the direct mail database. The Sox's inbound- and outbound call teams use these databases to solicit season tickets, group sales, company outings, suites, and events for the party areas.

The Sox use GoldMine to do more than just track leads. The CRM is used for marketing, suite-holder relations, and community relations. The team tracks season ticket holders' seat locations, create dates (to locate people by the year they purchased tickets), and records birthdays (to send out birthday cards). It also tracks whether ticket holders have purchased memberships to the Stadium Club. In addition, the Sox keep track of demographic information like the number of customers who take the Chicago Transit Authority instead of driving cars. This information was critical in helping the Sox in its efforts to track traffic. The CRM has also been instrumental in improving returning lost articles to their owners (by around 50%), since the software maintains data on customer seat locations.

GoldMine gives the Sox the ability to be more service-oriented toward season ticket holders instead of sending them impersonal mass mailings. The Sox are better able to target customers' needs, since every conversation with every season ticket holder is tracked. Account executives can focus on new sales and better customer service.

Source: Adapted from Lisa Picarille, "Batting 1,000." *Customer Relationship Management*, May 2003.

ing, there is a shift from product focus to customer focus. Customer loyalty is critical for success (see Reichheld et al., 1997).

COMMUNICATION WITH THE CUSTOMER

Part of CRM's goal is to increase opportunities by improving the process so as to communicate with the *right customer*, providing the *right offer* (product and price), through the *right channel*, and at the *right time* (Swift, 2001). CRM attempts to identify, or segment, existing and potential customers, so that the right products and services reach them at the right price in the right way at the right time. How a firm communicates is an issue. Cass and Lauer (2002) evaluated the use of language specifically appropriate to personal relationships to describe what transpires in an information-mediated CRM.

Companies that understand the importance of customer contacts and can provide solutions for multichannel contact centers as well as voice-only call centers will improve customer service and increase profitability. These seven powerful strategies work (Aspect Communications, 2003):

1. Make self-service an attractive option.
2. Conduct interactions in real-time.
3. Exploit the value of voice over IP.
4. Integrate the Web into your contacts.
5. Keep your best agents on board.
6. Make extraordinary service ordinary.
7. Integrate everything.

THE VALUE OF A CUSTOMER

The high-value, loyal, returning, satisfied, profitable customer is the key focal point for profitable and growth organizations globally. So it is important for organizations to *know their customers*. See DSS in Focus 8.28. The Hard Rock Café learned how to *know* its customers, leading to greater revenue. See DSS in Action 8.29. Also see Deck (2001).

DSS IN FOCUS 8.28

KNOW YOUR CUSTOMER

To increase a firm's return on investment, the right culture, information, and relationship technologies are critical for effective CRM. With CRM, it is possible to

1. Know who your customers are, and who your best customers are.
2. Stimulate what your customers buy, know what they won't buy, and why.
3. Time when and how your customers buy.
4. Learn customers' preferences and make them loyal.

5. Define the characteristics of your best/profitable customers.
6. Identify and model channels that best meet the needs of specific customer classes.
7. Predict what customers may or will buy in the future.
8. Retain your best customers for many years.

_____

Source: Adapted partly from Swift (2001).

DSS IN ACTION 8.29

BETWEEN A ROCK AND A HARD PLACE

Worthen (2001) describes how the Hard Rock Café has used its Web e-commerce initiative to capture demographic data about its customers. The Hard Rock utilizes CRM to target promotions accurately to its customers. It knows that the system is working because promotions are yielding return visits in "substantial" double-digits as compared to the standard 2 to 3 percent response rate of direct mail promotions. Second, 70 percent of the people who get their picture taken at the café claim their photos online. Finally, sales were over $200 million for the first half of 2000, whereas the total sales for 1999 were $388 million. And this was so with an initial decline in sales before the CRM Web effort began. The Hard Rock is building a *community* of its customers.

No company can afford to offer the highest level of service to all its customers. Only by calculating your customers' value to your firm can you properly allocate your valuable resources (see Gupta and Lehmann, 2002). And being a truly customer-centric organization requires that the information be shared firm-wide and used effectively (LoFrumento, 2003). The customers must be segmented into classes, and each class approached with appropriate products at appropriate prices (see Swift, 2001; Levinson, 2000).

In fact, there may be several classes of customers that your organization simply cannot afford to meet. For example, no automobile manufacturer has developed a car that sells for under $1,000 new. If a product is not profitable, then every customer who buys one reduces overall profitability. A firm should know when to *fire a customer*. Certain groups of customers are not profitable. They should be identified, and carefully examined before dropping them (because there may be ties to other family members who are profitable customers; for an excellent example, see Swift, 2001).

LoFrumento (2003) describes how a bank identified its most profitable customers—surprisingly, small businesses, not the large businesses and college students. The impact to the bottom line was staggering. The bank turned an $18 million loss into a $4 million profit. This is similar to what Harrah's (Chapter 1 Opening Vignette) and Mohegan Sun (Case Application 8.2) learned. Their most profitable customers were not the casino high-rollers, but the low-rollers. The Royal Bank of Canada (Toronto) has just 17 percent of its customers providing 93 percent of its profits (Selden and Colvin, 2002).

For e-commerce, the best authority for what customers want may be the customers themselves. Using clickstream analysis, though, cross selling opportunities can be identified. See Fickel (2000).

Some studies show that the average customer retention rate in the United States is about 80 percent. Thus 20 percent of a firm's customers *leak out* every year, which means that the firm must replenish them with profitable customers or lose them all in five years (Gupta and Lehmann, 2002). It is important to recognize that keeping existing customers is generally easier and more profitable than finding new ones. It can cost up to 10 times as much to sell to a new customer than to an existing one. Loyalty is important. Companies can boost profits by 100 percent by retaining just 5 percent more of their customers. And an organization should be able to determine the value to its bottom line of increasing customer satisfaction 1 percent (Gupta and Lehmann, 2002).

Determining the lifetime value of a customer, including influence on attracting new customers is critical. For example, the estimated life-time value (LTV) for a supermarket/grocery store of a customer with a family of four is about $250,000. And this amount appears to be only half of the expenditures that the family will make on food-related purchases (Swift, 2001). Every CRM initiative should include a determination of the lifetime value of a customer, including his or her influence on the family, and other factors.

CRM TECHNOLOGIES

Early CRM efforts were simply sales-force automation tools. They included contact information in a database, along with some personal information to be used by salespeople. Relationship technologies now include massive, active data warehouses, which are the foundation of modern CRM (see Chapter 5). Today CRM includes business intelligence/business analytics through *data mining* and *OLAP* (see Cippola, 2001). These integrate CRM with other tools, such as ERP and other EIS.

Once data are gathered in a data warehouse for a CRM effort, data mining and OLAP/BI/BA tools (Chapter 5) are utilized to analyze them. These powerful tools can derive the relationships among customer behavior, demographics, products, and other factors. The term *predictive analytics* is sometimes used to describe these activities. Compton (2003) identifies the best things you can do with your data. These are almost all customer-oriented, and thus apply to CRM. See DSS in Focus 8.30. Customer segmentation is often handled by data mining (see Case Application 5.3). Many classes of customers can be readily identified by data mining tools (see the examples in Chapter 5, and Levinson, 2000).

CRM systems are being integrated with other enterprise information systems, including ERP, EIS, SCM, PLM, BPM, and BAM. Though the integration often leads to problems, the benefits of doing so can be enormous. See Maselli (2002) and Targowski (2001) for some details.

The potential for mining revenue-generating and cost-saving relationships from data is increasing as companies build bigger data warehouses, applications become more integrated, computers become more powerful, and vendors of analytic software introduce products that are easier to use. It is important to be able to predict which customers are likely to leave, which ones will probably respond to the next promotion,

---

DSS IN FOCUS 8.30

THE 10 BEST THINGS YOU CAN DO WITH YOUR DATA

Follow these 10 steps and you will have information that really means something:

1. Ensure data quality.

2. Measure success on metrics that matter.

3. Enable users to get the insight they need.

4. Unify data across channels. Eliminate stovepipes.

5. Establish meaningful customer segments.

6. Encourage customer growth.

7. Take the bad with the good. Study customer losses and bad experiences.

8. Model and predict profitable loyalty and motivations. Understand your customers.

9. Make the right call. Contact each customer, potential customer, and lost customer in appropriate ways.

10. Keep the data secure from harm, misuse, and theft.

Source: Adapted from Jason Compton, "The 10 Best Things to Do With Your Data," *Customer Relationship Management,* April 2003, pp. 44–47.

which ones are ripe for cross selling and what will happen if prices change. Predictive modeling can identify the range of products and services that best suit particular customers (Sabri, 2003). Data mining methods (Chapter 5) are often used (see Anthes, 2003; Betts, 2003). Of course, real-time data analysis and reporting applications require accurate data (see Reimers, 2003).

BankFinancial Corp. (Chicago) uses the SPSS Clementine data mining *workbench* to predict customer behavior so as to accurately target promotions to existing and potential customers. Analytical frameworks are discussed by Anthes (2003). Also see Betts (2003).

Using data mining tools integrated with GIS, one can establish customers' geographical preferences. For example, Betts (2003) describes how Cognos business intelligence tools identified national preferences for chicken burgers versus beef burgers at Red Robin Gourmet Burgers franchises in the United States.

Revenue (management) optimization software automates the process of calculating the prices businesses need to charge to maximize profits. It adjusts prices using optimization algorithms (see Chapter 4) that factor in variables like demand forecasts, inventory, and the economic elasticity of supply and demand. Harrah's uses a Manugistics revenue management application to adjust room prices in its casino hotels (see Songini, 2003c).

CRM SOFTWARE

On average, firms spend 2.5 percent of their annual revenue on customer technologies, half of their overall IT spending (see Guptill, 2003). Myron (2003) indicates that the CRM software and services market share in 2003 was a $6.7 billion global market. Siebel, SAP, and Oracle are the big three, capturing 59 percent of the global market. Customer relationship management systems are proliferating around the world. Global market estimates range from about $10 billion to $30 billion by 2006, with compound annual growths of up to 9 percent. The largest market penetration is in the United States, which will continue to lead the global CRM market in overall revenue and market size. Analysts expect other regions to have higher percentage growth rates than the United States. See Picarille (2003) for details.

The three major CRM software vendors are Siebel Systems Inc., SAP AG, and Oracle. Others include ACCPAC International, Inc., Amdocs, Broadvision, Aspect Communications, E.piphany, GoldMine Software Corp., i2 Technologies, Interact Commerce, Kana Software, Microsoft Corp., Nortel Networks, Onyx, PeopleSoft Inc., Pivotal Corp., Salesforce.com Inc., Salesnet Inc., and SupportWizard Inc. CRM tools for small- to medium-sized businesses are provided by Pivotal Corp., Salesnet Inc., and SupportWizard Inc. (see Callaghan, 2003a). For information about specific products, see the CRM Buyers Guide at www.destinationcrm.com, and CRMguru.com (2002a). See Dyche (2002) for methods of choosing appropriate CRM technologies for an organization. Some firms, rather than make major modifications to vendors' products, have opted to develop their CRM systems in-house. See Pender (2000) for details.

CRM BENEFITS

CRM has always been easy for small organizations. Representatives of a small organization can readily apply the personal touch. But now large companies are attempting to succeed at CRM. CRM benefits include (Swift, 2001):

1. Lower cost of recruiting customers.
2. No need to recruit so many customers to maintain a steady business volume.
3. Reduced sales costs. Existing customers are generally more responsive.
4. Higher customer profitability through segmentation and targeting products and services.
5. Increased customer retention and loyalty. Customers stay longer, buy more, and contact you more.
6. Improved customer service.
7. Evaluation of customer profitability leads to identifying the most profitable classes of customers and how to create new profitable classes.
8. Migration from a product focus to a *customer focus*.

Here are some details that underlie the benefits. Mass mailings are wasteful. Some 98 percent of promotional coupons are discarded. It costs up to 10 times more to generate revenue from a new customer than from an existing one. A 5 percent increase in the retention rate can increase company profits by 60 to 100 percent. Servicing a customer through a call center is six times more expensive than via the Internet. Loyal customers who refer another one generate business at little or no cost. Referred customers generally stay longer, use more products, and become profitable customers faster.

CRM PROBLEMS AND ISSUES

Most problems and issues with CRM are due to organizational factors. They crop up during an attempted implementation. One-third of all CRM projects generate great results, one-third create minor improvements, and the final third produce nothing (CRMguru.com, 2002b). According to a study by Gartner Inc., 42 percent of the CRM end-user licenses bought in 2002 were not being used (see Songini, 2003d). Levinson (2002) indicates that a failure to rethink business processes, not technology trouble, kills most CRM implementations. Most salespeople view the technology that was "imposed" on them in 2001 as a failure. Many firms did not involve the users in the selection or development of the CRM. CRM experts believe that 80 percent of the benefits of CRM come from new business processes, while only 20 percent are due to technology. See Close (2002) for details.

According to an *InfoWorld*–CTO Network Survey (see April and Harreld, 2002), CRM problems are due to difficult integration (39%), high cost/low ROI (27), resistance from staff or customers (24), other (5), and solutions do not meet needs (5).

Integration presents a whole new set of problems. The problem is acute in that many organizations have legacy systems that work perfectly but just do not readily integrate with new tools. For example, the Minnesota Department of Vehicle Services (DVS) had a two-week delay in renewing a driver's license. There was a month delay in obtaining a car title. Moving to the Web was difficult because most of the data were only available on paper via fax. The major difficulty organizations face is integrating the CRM into the data sources (see April and Harreld, 2002). Further difficulties occur in integrating CRM with other enterprise systems.

A CRM solution aimed at sales force productivity improvements must consider the overall aspects of sales management, especially the organizational culture and user involvement (see Thoreson, 2003).

CRM projects are big and costly. Like most large-scale IT projects, they often do not meet their objectives (see Boslet, 2001). CRM is hard work. Corporations often rush into CRM projects, spending millions without making the necessary preparations.

CRM efforts are plagued by all the problems involved in large-scale IT developments (see Boslet, 2001):

- Necessary preparations include allocating enough time and money, establishing realistic goals, and getting firm commitments from top managers
- Adapting business processes
- Retraining employees
- Finding the right system integrators

Cigna HealthCare's failure, illustrated in DSS in Action 8.31, identifies many factors to consider when developing a large-scale CRM system.

There is a *dark side* to CRM due to people and society issues. A key issue is that CRM can make an organization seem impersonal (see Scofield, 2002). Customers like the *personal touch*, and many organizations, from Marriott International (DSS in Action 8.32) to the Chicago White Sox (DSS in Action 8.27), recognize and capitalize on this. It is important to use the CRM to capture customer knowledge to improve the personal touch. If the personal touch is lost, an organization can cease to be a positive force in the community, which leads to lost revenue. Hollowell and Verma (2002) indicate that the goals of personalization are simple: learn and understand what the customer really wants, then ensure that the customer gets the same look-and-feel, and message across any channel. The businesses that have the most successful CRM strategies learn to create solutions for their customers instead of finding customers for their products. Waltner describes how Art Technology Group Inc. provides CRM software that drives the automated personalization of Web site content for individual shoppers. IExplore Inc., a Chicago-based travel company, uses ATG's Dynamo Suite to target online information for individuals. This is an extremely important issue, because Web sites are growing to unwieldy size and customers often cannot find what they want. It also enables cross selling, an important CRM feature, by providing items that its projections show a customer may want.

DSS IN ACTION 8.31

CIGNA HEALTHCARE INSURES FAILURE

Cigna HealthCare attempted a $1 billion IT overhaul that included a CRM initiative. It failed. Disruptions produced major problems in customer service. The firm went from 13.3 million members to 12.5 million. Its stock plunged 40 percent in value. Cigna's transformation was hobbled not only by the insurance giant's haste to get its new systems up and running, but by its eagerness to cash in on technology's promise of reduced costs and increased productivity. As soon as the new system went online, the company eliminated its customer service reps. The lessons Cigna learned include (also see Chapter 6):

1. Keep the project management in-house, even if using consultants.
2. Test in a real environment and end-to-end before going live. Migrate in stages.
3. Make sure your back-end data are cleansed and filtered.
4. Bring in a focus group of customers (involve them) after testing the system. Then use their comments to redesign the front end for them.
5. Train and retrain the customer service reps on the new systems.
6. Do not expect productivity gains for months after going live, and do not make business decisions based on anticipated projected savings or gains. Wait until they occur.

Source: Adapted from A. Bass, "Cigna's Self-Inflicted Wounds," *CIO*, March 15, 2003.

MEASURING CRM SUCCESS

A critical issue when developing a CRM is determining appropriate metrics by which to measure success. Specific bottom line measurements are difficult but not impossible to obtain. In a recent study of CIOs (see Patton, 2002), they were asked how their organization would measure the ROI or value of its CRM implementation. They responded with reduced reporting cycle (53%), reduced expenses/costs of doing business (44%), improved external customer satisfaction (36%), improved internal customer satisfaction (35%), reduced sales cycle (32%), increased productivity (25%), increased sales (18%), and other (6%).

Strategic benefits are intangible and often difficult to measure. CRM capabilities can impact other value-added activities (along the value chain), thereby enhancing customer experience and *gaining competitive advantage* (Swift, 2001). The financial contribution CRM makes often comes from new business practices without clear precedents. CRM depends on changing the behavior of customers whose purchasing patterns are motivated by many external factors (see Swift, 2001). For example, DSS in Action 8.32 describes how Marriott International utilizes a CRM and how it plans to evaluate the results. The Marriott experience led to a set of keys to success, outlined in DSS in Focus 8.33. Also see Case Application 8.3.

Signs of CRM system success include: (1) companies use the system to meet *key* customer needs; (2) they derive in-depth analysis of customer costs and potential profit; (3) they link information from disparate business units or eliminate information silos; and (4) they redesign organizational incentives and structure to empower those employees who are closest to the customers (see Sviokla and Wong, 2003).

Swift (2001) provides a set of many questions to ask, issues, and rules to estimate your likelihood of CRM success. These questions are broken down into the following categories: (1) rules for discussions with CRM solution providers; (2) business (internal) questions and issues; (3) information technology questions; (4) business users' questions; and (5) red flags. Each should be considered carefully in determining an organization's readiness for CRM. See Swift (2001) for details.

For additional information about CRM, see Swift (2001), Berkowitz (2001), Berson (2000), Cippola (2001), CRMguru.com (2002a, 2002b), Dyché (2001, 2002), Fayyad (2003), Hayes (2001), Linoff and Berry (2002), Newman (2002), Stackpole (2001), Tillett (2000), and Tourniaire (2003).

8.14 EMERGING ENTERPRISE INFORMATION SYSTEMS: PRODUCT LIFECYCLE MANAGEMENT (PLM), BUSINESS-PROCESS MANAGEMENT (BPM) AND BUSINESS ACTIVITY MONITORING (BAM)

In this section, we describe several, relatively new enterprise information systems that have begun to have major impacts on organizations. These include product lifecycle management (PLM), business process management (BPM), and business activity monitoring (BAM). Each *system* is really a methodology that affects the entire enterprise. Each one has essentially become a Web-based *enterprise information portal* (dashboard) that gathers information from many disparate sources, integrates them, and provides them to the user for a specific purpose. Product lifecycle management systems have grown from the manufacturing and design engineering disciplines, while business process management and business activity monitoring systems have evolved from

DSS IN ACTION 8.32

MARRIOTT'S SUITE RETURNS

Traditionally, hotels measure performance by how much money is made from each room. But Marriott International has started to account for itself differently, using customer relationship management (CRM) systems to assemble an income stream based on how much each guest spends, not just on one room in a single stay, but over time, in different cities, at a wide range of hotels, resorts, and conference centers. Though Marriott will not be able to measure the bottom line on the efforts for some time, it has deployed the mechanisms to do so. Marriott executives believe that these changes will ultimately lead to greater profitability.

There is not much growth potential in the lodging industry from building and renting more rooms. Consequently, hotels must find ways to get customers to spend more when they visit. Non-room income accounted for 34 percent of hotel company revenues across the industry in 1999. Income from these sources, which include restaurants, grew faster than revenue from room rentals. This is critical for Marriott, because there are not many markets left where there is not an existing Marriott hotel.

Marriott uses CRM data from its loyalty program for cross selling to guests and meeting planners and smoothing transactions with the franchisees that run its hotels. It also personalizes service to both its corporate and individual clients. These efforts should increase revenue from happier, and more loyal, customers.

Marriott tracks how much more money guests spend at its resorts if they participate in a new vacation-planning program called Personal Planning Service. Marriott executives believe that the Personal Planning Service, which helps generate more revenues from each guest's visit, will also result in repeat business because guests have better vacations. The program's database helps hotel employees set up golf tee times, dinner reservations, or other activities for guests before they start their vacations. Guests who sign up for the program work with a concierge who arranges an itinerary for the trip and records it in the database. The next time a traveler vacations at a Marriott resort, concierges there can use the information to set up a similar set of activities, if the guest wants them. *Guests who participate in the program spend an average of $100 more per day at hotel golf courses, restaurants, and activities like guided tours for which Marriott gets commissions.* These efforts create *brand loyalty* leading to repeat business. The new sales-force database also provides salespeople with a companywide view of customer accounts to help better understand what each customer wants to buy, right down to what they like to serve for breakfast meetings.

The system has made a difference because Marriott captured $55 million in cross-chain sales last year, a measurement it could not to track before. Overall, Marriott earned $8.7 billion in sales in 1999, beating its top rivals Hilton, Hyatt, and Starwood.

Source: Adapted from Elena Varon, "Suite Returns," *CIO*, August 15, 2000.

DSS IN FOCUS 8.33

THE KEYS TO CRM SUCCESS

Here are some quick guidelines to help you in creating a successful CRM implementation.

Do:

- Look for ways to measure how customer behavior should change once CRM systems are deployed.

- Take the long view. It may take up to a year before a firm starts accruing benefits.

- Focus on which of the problems CRM is supposed to fix.

Don't:

- Rely on cost savings to deliver value. Like revenue management, the focus is on revenue generation, not cost containment.

- Equate past customer satisfaction with future customer value.

Source: Partially adapted from Elena Varon, "Suite Returns." *CIO*, August 15, 2000, p. 122.

executive and enterprise information management systems concepts. All of the functionality of these systems was previously provided by sets of separate software tools, but now they are available as application suites that integrate the tools directly. They can be viewed as sitting on top of the tool set that comprises them. All of them are becoming integrated with the systems that provide data to them, as well as some capabilities. They include executive and enterprise information systems (EIS), CRM, ERP, and SCM. We discuss these in detail next.

PRODUCT LIFECYCLE MANAGEMENT SYSTEMS

Product lifecycle management (PLM) is an integrated, information-driven approach to all aspects of a product's life, from its design through manufacture, deployment, and maintenance, culminating in the product's removal from service and final disposal. PLM software suites enable accessing, updating, manipulating, and reasoning about product information produced in a fragmented and distributed environment. Another definition of PLM is the integration of business systems to manage a product's life cycle. (University of Michigan PLM; Stackpole, 2003).

PLM's goal is to streamline product development and boost innovation in manufacturing. PLM has the potential to vastly improve a company's ability to innovate, get products to market, and reduce errors. PLM applications hold the promise of seamlessly flowing *all* of the information produced throughout *all* phases of a product's life cycle to *everyone* in an organization, along with key suppliers and customers. An automotive company or aerospace manufacturer, for example, can shrink the time it takes to introduce new models in a number of ways. Product engineers can dramatically shorten the cycle of implementing and approving engineering changes across an extended design chain. Purchasing agents can work more effectively with suppliers to reuse parts. And executives can take a high-level view of all important product information, from details of the manufacturing line to parts failure rates culled from warranty data and information collected in the field (Stackpole, 2003).

Unlike ERP packages, PLM requires integrating many independent databases and getting people from different business functions to work together better. PLM is more a strategy than a system. It is a strategy to integrate and share information about products between applications and among different constituencies, such as engineering, purchasing, manufacturing, marketing, sales, and after-market support (Stackpole, 2003).

The goal of PLM software is to help corporations track and share product data inside and outside of the enterprise. Information contained in these systems often includes hefty CAD files on products ranging from computer parts to aircraft engines (Jones, 2001).

PLM evolved out of product design engineering software. Typically, PLM is utilized in manufacturing. PLM is even being applied to the retail fashion industry to improve sales and reduce inventory. It has also been applied to the construction industry.

A PLM system tracks all the electronic information about the life of a product. A PLM system links together all of the processes required to design, build, deploy, and maintain the product (Gallagher, 2003). As with the other enterprise information systems described in this section, there are many tools that perform most of the main functions of PLM. PLM integrates them into one application suite. Through the suite, PLM enhances communication and collaboration in product design and manufacturing.

By digitizing not just the design of a product but also the processes that go into creating it, companies have been able to avoid mistakes in engineering and conflicts in different versions of product information, saving millions, sometimes over than 30 percent of operational costs (see Gallagher, 2003).

Like ERP, PLM is a set of interconnected modules, each of which addresses a specific function. But whereas ERP is designed to handle primarily transactional data, PLM manages all the unstructured data associated with product design and manufacture (Bartholomew, 2003).

Product data is the central component of an enterprise PLM system. PLM can be broken down into six distinct segments: innovation and portfolio management, project and program management, collaborative design, product data management, manufacturing process planning, and services and support management (D'Amico, 2003). Improving each leads directly to improvements in different aspects of design and manufacturing. See DSS in Action 8.34 for how Lear has improved its design and manufacturing processes.

PLM AND KNOWLEDGE MANAGEMENT SYSTEMS

PLM can be viewed in terms of a knowledge management system (Chapter 9) for manufacturing and product-version control. PLM is concerned with integrating requirement specifications, design documents, manufacturing plans, and post-release product support and evolution documents into a common *repository*. Making these critical documents available in all phases of the project to all of the stakeholders should enhance collaboration, reduce communication costs and delays, reduce redundant reengineering time, and improve how early-stage designers and engineers understand the real-world performance and challenges of the products they create. This should result in the development of more generalized, reusable assembly platforms, shorter development cycles, more frugal component counts, and possibly lower warranty-service charges. (Compton, 2002).

PLM BENEFITS

PLM offers many benefits when properly implemented. These include:

- Flexibility in engineering job roles
- Reduced engineering change order (ECO) times and quantities because PLM requires completeness
- More interchangeable parts because changes are correct and consistent

---

DSS IN ACTION 8.34

PLM FLIES AT LEAR

Lear, a $14.4 billion automotive supplier, has invested heavily in PLM because executives see it as a way to manage Lear's product-development efforts more effectively for its customers, leading car manufacturers. Previously, project information was conveyed in an ad hoc manner through spreadsheets and e-mail. The information was typically inconsistent. Using EDS PLM Solutions, Lear built the foundation of a system to give car-makers a constant flow of information about their projects, from engineering schedules to parts changes to quality statistics.

- Improved product designs
- Faster product development times
- Better and faster design and manufacturing decisions (like standardized vs. customized parts)
- Greater overall design and manufacturing efficiency
- Reduced time-to-market of products
- Improved quality control
- Integrated manufacturing and design systems
- Enhanced collaboration in design and engineering, and with suppliers, partners, and customers
- A centralized product repository with content management capabilities for all product-design information, accessed via a portal

Efficiencies in design reduce the time it takes to get a product to market. For example, through a PLM system, Flextronics reduced week-long ECO delays to less than a day. Overall, PLM reduces costs and improve efficiencies. For example, PLM has enabled Air International Group Ltd. to source components more competitively from a larger pool of suppliers, making the firm more competitive. It passes along a 5 to 10 percent savings when it puts its own projects out to bid (see Trommer, 2003). GEIS experienced many benefits from its PLM implementation, as is described in DSS in Action 8.35.

PLM ISSUES

PLM systems exhibit many of the common problems of enterprise information systems.

A successful implementation requires a focus on business need. It must deliver business value. PLM requires the requisite senior executive champion, and appropriate user involvement and training. Developing a complete PLM solution can be nearly as complex as developing a complete ERP (Vijayan, 2003a).

PLM systems must integrate with existing MRP, ERP, and SCM software to be effective. They typically exhibit few immediate benefits and are very difficult to implement. Like ERP, a PLM system can fail, but when it succeeds, the payoff can be very high.

PLM requires a corporate strategy. It must be supported at the highest level in the organization, and change must be managed as it affects many manufacturing and design processes. PLM should be viewed as a change management issue, not an engineering drawing control issue (Stackpole, 2003). It involves changes in organizational

---

DSS IN ACTION 8.35

THE GEIS PLM SYSTEM

GE Industrial Systems (GEIS), a $5 billion subsidiary of General Electric Co., is implementing a major product life-cycle management (PLM) project to reduce product-development time, improve supply chain efficiency, and reduce costs. GEIS is developing the PLM to create a collaborative environment for planning, development, sourcing, and program management. GEIS is migrating nearly 15 million product-related documents into the new system. By 2005, there will be more than 10,000 employees accessing the completed system (see Vijayan, 2003a).

DSS IN ACTION 8.36

GENERAL MOTORS DRIVES FAST WITH PLM

Kirk Gutman, global product development officer at General Motors, offered a compelling real-world example of an aggressive and successful PLM strategy. GM has been working since 1996 to create and use a global PLM environment that comprises a common geometry foundation—the "math highway," as GM calls it—and a massively collaborative PDM layer built on the EDS PLM that supports 18,000 users and 1,800 supplier Teamcenter connections across North America, Europe, and Asia. The business results to date are compelling: System simplification—1,500 product develop-

ment applications alive in 1995 have been reduced to 500, with systems savings of $1 billion. GM obtained a 35 percent reduction in its overall global product development budget while expanding from 19 to 30 development programs. GM was able to reduce the cycle time from styling freeze to production from 60 months in the early 1990s to 18 months in 2002.

Source: Adapted from Kevin O'Marah, "The Roadmap to PLM Starts with Corporate Strategy." *CIO,* December 4, 2002.

---

culture because it affects many business processes. General Motors recognized this, and through its PLM obtained substantial savings. See DSS in Action 8.36.

PLM VENDORS

Manufacturing companies spent $2.3 billion on PLM application suites in just the first half of 2003 (Stackpole, 2003). The market for product life-cycle management (PLM) software is expected to reach some $7.5 billion in 2006, and $14 billion in 2008. Growth drivers include the software's ability to help manufacturers lower product development and support costs, and to protect a company's intellectual capital. Key drivers include a major push from technology vendors, which offer PLM software that runs in conjunction with ERP systems or manufacturing management software (D'Amico, 2003). Based on 2001 revenue, the leading PLM vendors are EDS, SAP, Parametric Technology Corp, IBM/Dassault, Telelogic, MatrixOne, Aspen Technology, and Agile Software. They command 69 percent of the market. EDS commands only 13 percent of the market. There are a lot of smaller players commanding the remaining 31 percent of the market. They include Agile Software, Arena Solutions Inc., PeopleSoft, Baan, CoCreate Software Inc., Omnify Software Inc., Oracle, OSI Software Inc., and Optiva (for details, see D'Amico, 2003; Weinberger, 2003).

BUSINESS PROCESS MANAGEMENT (BPM) SYSTEMS

A **business process management (BPM) system** integrates data, applications and people together through a common business process. It aims to streamline and automate business processes thus offsetting the administrative burden of the organization and creating an environment where processes can be leveraged for strategic value (see Datz, 2002; and CKB, 2003).

BPM software can graphically map business processes, such as issuing or collecting a bill; transform that visual map into an application or set of applications; and manage the electronic workflow to monitor that the work gets done and allow changes and improvements to the workflow (see Scheier, 2003).

BPM provides a comprehensive framework for automating people-intensive processes, and integrating legacy and packaged applications into everyday operations. Most importantly, BPM institutes process control and policies that allow organizations to manage risk and comply with external mandates and regulations. BPM systems allow businesses to take full ownership of their processes and make adjustments in real-time as conditions change (CKB, 2003).

Essentially BPM is an enterprise information portal into all business processes. It integrates ERP, EIS, CRM and SCM systems to let managers see every relevant factor to the organization's health and progress. BPM enables the real-time access of relevant information about business processes. Essentially, BPM delivers the promise of executive information systems in real-time. BPM attempts to capture and monitor best practices that lead to productivity improvements as is evident by the iUniverse situation in DSS in Action 8.37.

Business performance management unifies methodologies, processes, rules, and collaboration workflows among all managers, at all levels, across the enterprise. The attributes of the management process, a unified approach, and collaboration support are essential to proactively managing and improving financial and operational performance (Hyperion, 2003). These improvements can lead to new opportunities. See DSS in Action 8.38.

Business intelligence (BI) provides managers with information that enables them to understand their business for a given moment in time. Business performance management, in contrast, provides managers with applications that support a process for managing their business as well as information from BI applications (Hyperion, 2003).

DSS IN ACTION 8.37

IUNIVERSE AUTOMATES WITH BPM

Book-publisher iUniverse deployed Intalio's BPM software in part to automate catalog delivery to its dealers and other partners. Before the BPM was implemented, only one partner had an automated system in place to receive catalogs; the other partners' deliveries had to be entered manually into the system by an iUniverse employee, which took about 120 hours per month. The BPM system has enabled that employee to be diverted to another segment of the company and has permitted other iUniverse partners to automate their own catalog delivery systems.

Source: Condensed from Amy Rogers, "Intalio Banks on Business Processes," *CRN*, April 2003, No. 1040.

DSS IN ACTION 8.38

IJET TRAVEL'S BPM FLIES HIGH

iJet Travel Intelligence provides online, open-source intelligence information and crisis-management services to individuals and corporations. Initially, iJet knew that using some process-change management technology would be important in achieving its business objectives. After deploying a BPM system in 2001, iJet could create, optimize, change, and manage its business processes quickly, without costly and time-consuming intervention by the IT department. Analytics are utilized to perform impact analysis on various customer-travel scenarios, helping companies assess the legal liabilities of sending workers abroad. The system lets analysts create job requirements, tap the appropriate intelligence sources, and review existing information residing in iJet's repositories. The BPM environment provides continuous value, letting iJet quickly generate accurate and objective alerts. Most significant, iJet has grown by revamping business models and processes to adapt to new market conditions and strategies.

Source: Adapted from Greg Meyer, "Case Study: Jet-Fueled," *Optimize*, February 2003, p. 32.

However, vendors routinely include BI/BA capabilities in BPM to enhance their products' capabilities. For example, Hyperion's business performance management software includes business intelligence and business analytics features. As with PLM, the software tools for BPM have existed for some time, but now vendors are packaging them together.

BPM BENEFITS

Business process management (BPM) software can pay for itself within a year or two by linking expensive legacy applications to new, more streamlined workflows. Trimac Corp., a trucking company in Calgary, Alberta, expects a return on its $500,000 BPM investment within two years. This will come about through reduced paperwork and additional business from customers who find Trimac's BPM-based ordering system easier to use than those of competitors (Scheier, 2003). BPM results in improved workflow through redesign as it is automated. Firms should measure their returns from BPM efforts not only on cost reduction but also on process improvement.

The Wiltshire Constabulary (a police force in the U.K.) has adopted a BPM for its e-policing project. Officers feel that it should help reduce the time spent on nonoperational matters and administrative work. This will enable them to spend more time on primary duties, such as patrolling their beats.

Process improvements indicating that a BPM implementation is underway can lead to dramatic cost savings. Shell Oil experienced this. See DSS in Action 8.39.

BPM ISSUES

BPM forces an organization to look carefully at its processes. If they are to be managed carefully, then they should be correct. So, like PLM and other enterprise information systems, notably ERP and SCM, BPM implementations require a careful look at business processes. Organizational culture change issues must be managed because processes will change as the implementation moves forward. As with any enterprise

---

DSS IN ACTION 8.39

SHELL OIL QUICKLY DEPLOYS A BPM SYSTEM AND SAVES A MILLION CLAMS

Shell Oil's U.S. Tax Organization (Houston, Texas) was given a mandate to cut its monthly financial reporting time in half and provide a clear trail in case of audits. The core problem, which is common to large enterprises, was the heterogeneity of the systems involved, including geographically dispersed divisions running primarily SAP R/3 but also J.D. Edwards and Oracle Financials.

Shell adopted TeamWorks, Lombardi Software's BPM software, to handle the enterprise application integration. Fortunately, TeamWorks did not require extensive coding. It took only three months to deploy the application. Because the team could quickly prototype business processes with the tool, financial analysts

and IT people focused more on evaluating how they worked, instead of on the technology. The key focus was the business process. It was important for Shell to decide which area of the business process to automate and identify bottlenecks that had the greatest challenges.

Shell recouped its $1 million investment in less than six months and derived more value from its $1 billion SAP investment. Now the company plans to develop BPM applications in other operations, including exploration, refineries, and financial services.

Source: Adapted from M. LaMonica, "Process Power," *CIO*, January 1, 2003.

system, it is important not to track what exists, but to determine whether the process is the right one, or even if it should be done at all. As with CRM and PLM, integration problems occur during implementation (Scheier, 2003). BPM systems are large-scale, so they exhibit the same problems as other enterprise systems. They require a senior champion, user involvement, and have a high probability of failure. Essentially, the McDonald's enterprise system failure (Case Application 8.2) was a BPM effort.

BPM VENDORS

BPM vendors include Apriso Corp., BEA Systems, Business Objects SA, Computer Sciences Corp./Metastorm, FileNET, Fuego Inc., Fujitsu Software, HandySoft Corp., Hyperion Solutions Corp, IBM, IDS Scheer AG, Intalio Inc., J.D. Edwards & Co., Lombardi Software Inc., Metastorm, Microsoft Corp., Nobilis Software, Pegasystems Inc., PeopleSoft Inc., Q-Link Technologies, SAP AG, Savvion, SeeBeyond Technology Corp., Siebel Systems, Silas Technologies/Ultimus, Staffware PLC, Tibco Software, Unisys Corp., Vitria Technology Inc., and WebMethods. Scheier (2003) provides a BPM vendor list with product descriptions. Vendors continue to integrate business intelligence/business analytics into BPM software, as well as integrate their BPM systems into others.

For further details on BPM, see CKB (2003), LaMonica (2003), Leahy (2003), Smith and Fingar (2003), and the BPM vendor sites.

BUSINESS ACTIVITY MONITORING (BAM) SYSTEMS

Business activity monitoring (BAM) systems consist of real-time systems that alert managers to potential opportunities, impending problems, and threats, and then empower them to react through models and collaboration. Situations are detected in real-time, quickly analyzed, and solved.

Business activity monitoring (BAM) software monitors the activities of a specific facility, such as a factory or a call center, or a specific business process, such as logistics or sales. BAM integrates data from different processes within the company and from outside partners, unstructured (soft) information, and provides collaboration capabilities for teams to make decisions (see Keating, 2003). Its two activities include detecting a developing situation as quickly as possible, and formulating a speedy response. Information technology can collect data from a variety of internal and external sources in real-time, analyze them to detect unexpected patterns that indicate an emerging situation, and then deliver the results to those responsible for reacting. This technically agile aspect of the *real-time enterprise* is often labeled business activity monitoring (see Keating, 2003).

As a technology layer, BAM sits on top of a BPM solution to capture and analyze business process data in real-time. Events are displayed in an enterprise information portal (dashboard). The display offers instant insight into business metrics like CRM call center success rates or supply chain inventory levels. Real-time alerting to breakdowns in processes such as shipping schedules lets users react to problems in real-time. BAM applications gather data from many disparate sources and present them as a unified whole (see April, 2003).

BAM evolved from the basic ideas of executive information systems. But now, mature integration and business-intelligence tools, real standards such as XML, and improved software development methods and tools make such real-time technology feasible (see Keating, 2003).

Monitoring an activity depends on the ability to recognize significant events that occur within the activity and respond appropriately based on the application of business rules. The rules may be either predetermined or, in a more sophisticated BAM system, learned by the system over time via artificial intelligence methods like intelligent agents (McKie, 2003). BAM reports the business process flow directly. Filters can indicate when any important parameter is off, and an alert (as in an executive information system) tells the manager to look into why. Essentially, BAM systems deliver real-time executive information system capabilities to all decision-makers. General Electric uses its *CXO dashboards* to give executives their real-time organization's status (see Keating, 2003). A simple BAM can send e-mail alerts.

BAM BENEFITS

BAM helps not just in recognizing and responding to events, but also in enabling managers to resolve event occurrences quickly and review their impacts to make more timely and informed decisions (see McKie, 2003). Essentially the two most important benefits are real-time data access in a usable format, and access to tools to collaborate and model the problem, leading to a quick solution. So faster and presumably better decisions will be made.

A business activity has to be intelligently automated in order to be monitored. The monitoring must be intelligent, and the results must be easy to access, visualize, or act upon to derive value. Activity modeling is the first step in creating a successful BAM system. This involves finding activities worth monitoring, defining their steps and events, and tying those events to performance metrics to be monitored (see McKie, 2003). Analyzing activities leads to improved processes.

BAM ISSUES

BAM systems suffer from many of the shortcomings of all enterprise information systems. Often executives fail to consider the readiness of technology or of the business processes that they want to monitor. This was one reason for the failure of the McDonald's enterprise system (Case Application 8.2). Enterprise systems require a senior management champion, and proper involvement and training of users. Integration issues can plague a BAM effort. Data must be extracted from many different sources and provided to many users.

Change management issues are paramount. As with most EIS, adopting the model and method requires not only technology, but also a *change in business processes*, that is, change management. In the case of BAM, delays built into information flows to allow lower-level managers to respond to them are eliminated. This has caused problems in executive information systems, and higher-level managers must learn to leave some problems in the hands of those responsible, at least for a time, to allow them the opportunity to respond. Executives must not undermine the authority of their employees.

As with any EIS, effective BAM requires working closely with the business units to identify the key indicators (critical success factors) and analytical techniques that provide reliable early warnings of impending issues (*alerts*). Also, again as for any EIS, a good way to start with real-time BAM is to focus on a well-defined business problem with a demonstrable return (Keating, 2003).

BAM has the capacity to get the right information to the people who need it faster. Simultaneously, the information is reported higher in management. Executives must let the responsible managers on the front lines deal with their problems and issues in a timely manner before reacting (see the next section). The key to success is to provide those closest to the situation with the information they need for decision-making, and at the same time help higher levels of management to more effectively monitor the effects of the decisions (see Keating, 2003).

DSS IN FOCUS 8.40

ANATOMY OF CELEQUEST'S BAM SOFTWARE

The Celequest 2.0 BAM software monitors business events, relates them to historical or contextual information from data warehouses or operational systems, and then alerts users to exception conditions as they occur.

Celequest 2.0 has four integrated components. Among them is the Activity Server, that provides streaming database technology to cache temporal views of events and integrate historical context data. The Activity Server utilizes an Adaptive Modeling Engine that executes business rules, manages exception conditions, and enables dynamic event modeling, including time-series analysis.

With the Scenario Modeler component, users model complex analytical scenarios and evaluate them as they happen within a spreadsheet-type interface. Alerts are presented through the Activity Dashboard,

while the Application Workbench component creates baseline business views and data models to represent ongoing business activity. This information is correlated with contextual information to provide a meaningful picture of the activity.

The BAM software can monitor business events like an increase in call volume in a call center, changes in investment positions, inventory levels falling below a certain threshold, a demand forecast drop, and an increase in product returns. The target markets are financial services, retail, manufacturing and Homeland Security contractors.

Source: Adapted from Dennis Callaghan, "Celequest Releases BAM Application," *eWeek*, June 30, 2003.

BAM VENDORS

BAM vendors continue to improve their products by increasing functionality and by integrating them with other enterprise information systems and business intelligence/business analytics products (see Havenstein, 2003). Integrated BAM suites help configure, track, and analyze performance metrics (Bednarz, 2003), sometimes called *business optimization*. Cognos, Information Builders, and some other firms have developed monitor and alert features into their business intelligence systems. (Cognos executive information systems had these capabilities in the 1990s.) Others, like Actimize Ltd. and SeeRun Corp., have developed predictive analytics for customer relationship management into their systems (see Smith, 2003).

BAM vendors include Actimize Ltd., Celequest Inc., Cognos, FirstRain Inc., Information Builders, Iteration Software, Microsoft, Quantive LLC, Savvion Inc., SeeBeyond, SeeRun Corp., Sybase, Tibco Software, Vitria Technology Inc., and WebMethods.

In DSS in Focus 8.40, we describe the capabilities of the Celequest BAM application, which contains extensive modeling capabilities, as a representative example. Also see Callaghan (2003b). See DSS in Action 8.41 to see how the software works in practice.

8.15 FRONTLINE DECISION SUPPORT SYSTEMS

Decisions at all levels in an organization contribute to its success. But decisions that maximize a sales opportunity or minimize the cost of customer service requests are made on the front lines by those closest to situations that arise during the course of daily business. Whether it is an order exception, an upselling opportunity, or a contract that hangs on a decision, a decision-maker must be able to make effective decisions rapidly based on context and according to strategies and guidelines set forth by senior management.

DSS IN ACTION 8.41

BROCADE'S CELESTE BAM SYSTEM

Brocade is testing the Celequest BAM application suite to build business models to analyze data in the familiar spreadsheet format. Formulas can be added, just like in Excel.

Brocade is using the Celequest BAM system to look at data from the manufacturing process. Managers need to know when the data fall outside acceptable limits. Managers can monitor everything from constantly changing prices to the quality of the components manufactured for Brocade by suppliers. They can then access static data from the data warehouse, compare them against historical trends, and automatically get results.

Source: Adapted from Ephraim Schwartz, "Is BAM a Scam or Score?" *InfoWorld*, July 3, 2003.

Frontline decision-making is the process by which companies automate decision processes and push them down into the organization and sometimes out to partners. It includes **empowering employees** by letting them devise strategies, evaluate metrics, analyze impacts, and make operational changes.

Frontline decision-making serves business users, such as line managers, sales executives, and call center representatives, by incorporating decision-making into their daily work. These workers need applications to help them make good operational decisions that meet overall corporate objectives. Frontline decision-making provides users with the right questions to ask, the location of needed data, and metrics (e.g., for customer and product profitability) that translate data into corporate objectives and suggest actions that can improve performance. Some aspects of CRM function as frontline systems. For example, the Chicago White Sox CRM (DSS in Action 8.27) helps salespeople interact directly with their existing and potential customers. Real-time analytic application products have emerged to support these actions (see Section 5.12 for more on real-time analytics).

Today's transactional applications and decision support tools do not by themselves readily enable frontline users to make better decisions. Systems like those from SAP AG and Siebel Systems do not implement simple decision processes or present data in a way that can be analyzed in complex situations. Executives may obtain context from reports and systems created from them (e.g., financial or executive information systems), but these do not provide frontline workers with guidance on daily problems. At the same time, traditional decision support from vendors like Pilot Software, Cognos, and Business Objects SA is intended for experts who can access data, slice-and-dice it, and give it business meaning, but are unlikely to be at the front lines. So organizations need a new generation of enterprise analytic applications to implement frontline decision-making.

FRONTLINE SYSTEMS

In frontline decision-making, every operational process has a corresponding decision process for evaluating choices and improving execution. For example, order management has cross sellcross selling suggestions, and a customer service representative can offer additional items to customers based on their specific needs.

Frontline decision-making automates simple decisions—like freezing the account of a customer who has failed to make payments—by predefining business rules and the events that trigger them. At more complex decision points, such as inventory allocation, frontline decision-making gives managers the necessary context—available alternatives, business impacts, and success measurements—to make the right decision. In order for business users to take advantage of ordinary decision support, they have to know what questions to ask, where the information resides, and the components of any metric.

The frontline software that began to appear on the market in late 1999 can help solve standard problems, such as what to do if a specific bank customer withdraws 100 percent more than the average withdrawal, by packaging a self-service solution that requires business logic (including rules, algorithms, intelligent systems, etc.) in a single browser. Also provided are metrics such as lifecycle expectancy, decision workflow, and so on. Finally, to be successful, such systems must work hand in hand with transactional systems.

Real-time frontline systems are under development as executive information system capabilities have moved to the operational level of the organization. Look for new developments in conjunction with real-time analytics and active warehousing. According to Forrester Research Inc., such systems are essential for the survival of many companies, but it will take five years for the technology to mature. The major current vendors are Hyperion Solutions Corporation, NCR Corporation, SAS Institute Inc., and i2 Technology. However, almost all the SCM, ERP, and business intelligence vendors mentioned in this chapter may deploy such systems. For further details, see McCullough (1999) and Sheth and Sisodia (1999).

8.16 THE FUTURE OF EXECUTIVE AND ENTERPRISE INFORMATION SYSTEMS[2]

Executives and other managers place substantial requirements on computerized support. *First*, they often ask questions that require complex, real-time analyses for the answers. This is why many of today's EIS/ESS are linked to data warehouses and are developed with real-time OLAP in separate multidimensional databases along with organizational DSS, which provide the necessary analytical tools. But sometimes even these systems lack the ability to respond in real-time. Delay in the delivery of information can mean loss of competitive position, loss of sales, and loss of profits. This is changing as real-time (active) data warehousing and analytics are deployed. Various types of enterprise information systems and frontline systems are moving these capabilities to all decision-makers who need up-to-date information and analytic capabilities. *Second*, like other infrequent, untrained, or uncooperative users, executives (along with most users today) require systems that are easy to use, easy to learn, and easy to navigate. Current support systems generally possess these qualities through Web-based interfaces. However, ease of use can also mean that the system has enough intelligence to automatically determine which tasks need to be performed and either performs these tasks directly or guides the user through them. Although current systems enable executives to monitor the present state of affairs, they typically cannot automate the processes of interpreting or explaining information. Automation of these tasks requires integration of current executive support system capabilities with those of an intelligent

---

[2]Part of this section was condensed from unpublished work by D. King, Comshare Inc., 2000 (Courtesy of D. King).

system. *Third*, executives tend to have highly individualized work styles. Although the current generation of enterprise systems can be molded to the needs of an executive, it is very difficult to alter the look-and-feel of the system or to change the basic way in which the user interacts with it. Intelligent agents can learn how any user utilizes a system and create a "path" through the information that the user can automatically follow. *Finally*, any information system is essentially a social system. One of the key elements of an enterprise system is the communication and collaboration capabilities it provides for members of the (executive) team. Therefore, visualization, including multimedia documents, is becoming critical, as is the integration of collaborative computing tools into enterprise information systems.

The enterprise systems of the future will look substantially different from today's systems. Developers of decision support/business intelligence technology for executives must be alert to the needs of top executives. And developers of enterprise information systems must be alert to the needs of all decision-makers in the organization. Like most other systems, enterprise and standalone EIS/ESS have migrated to the networked world of the technical workstation (advanced PC clients with Web browser GUI interfaces) and intranets. Computing capacity continues to grow at almost astronomical rates, and memory, DASD, and network bandwidth cease to be impediments to highly complex decision support applications. In mid-2003, it was announced that research on magnetics will result in a thousand-fold increase in the capacity of PC hard drives for about the same cost as existing drives. (This will have a dramatic impact on data warehouse sizes, as well as on the amount of information available directly in portable devices.) Mobility, wireless connectivity, and the need to support multimedia integrated EIS on a variety of devices are just some of the challenges to be overcome in the next few years. Nobel (2003) indicates how some PDAs can already access enterprise information systems directly. Also see Brewin and Hablem (2001).

Enterprise information systems continue to evolve. New types of enterprise systems are continually developed and utilized, as is evident from the creation of CRM, PLM, BPM, and BAM. In summary, here are some major developments we expect to see in the next few years:

- *Hardware and software advances.* As hardware shrinks and speeds up, and software becomes more capable, more information can be made available to decision-makers anytime, anyplace. There will continue to be increased use of portable devices for information access and display. These include mobile PCs, PDAs, and cell telephones. Though scalability is an issue, data warehouses are at the petabyte range and will continue to increase in size.
- *Virtual reality and three-dimensional image displays.* The development of virtual reality standards (virtual reality mark-up language, VRML), the ability to examine terabytes of data in map form or on a landscape (Chapter 5) via three-dimensional visualization, and higher-quality display units are beginning to affect enterprise systems. There will be an increase in the utilization of spatial data, as supplied from geographic information systems and used in geophysical satellite systems (see Chapter 5). As these tools are deployed for general use, executives and managers are adopting them in data visualization for information evaluation and decision-making.
- *Increased utilization of multimedia data.* Many organizations thrive on soft information. Much of this can be textual, audio, or visual. Decision-makers, especially executives, typically use such information more frequently than hard infor-

mation in their work. As the capabilities of computing hardware and software increase, these types of information can be made readily available.

- ***Increased collaboration and communication throughout the enterprise.*** As collaborative computing technologies become integrated into the many types of EIS, the walls of the silos break down so that information flows to where it is needed. Although organizational culture issues must be dealt with, strong leadership at the highest levels will enable the use of such tools when the benefits are made clear. Knowledge-management systems (see Chapter 9) succeed because of increased collaboration and communication at the enterprise level.

- ***Automated support and intelligent assistance.*** Expert systems and other AI technologies (e.g., natural language) are currently being embedded in or integrated with existing enterprise and decision support systems. This clearly adds more automated support and assistance to the analytic engines underlying enterprise systems. However, we are also likely to see other forms of intelligent or automated assistance. One such form is the intelligent agent. Another example of currently deployed agent technology is news filtering. Thus, instead of thinking of an executive support system as a single system, we can think of it as a society of cooperating agents whose actions need to be coordinated. For example, Comshare's Detect and Alert agent, which is embedded in Decision Web, provides automatic surveillance of large databases and external news sources, with delivery of immediate personal alerts to users' desktops. Comshare's Decision Web uses intelligent component expansion (ICE) to identify the drill-down paths of exceptions (see DSS in Focus 8.4). Another agent tracks users' actions, learns how users use the system, and adopts appropriate screens in the user's preferred order. Other agents can be deployed in Web-enabled EIS. Expert systems, artificial neural networks, genetic algorithms, and fuzzy logic can play an active role in the decision-making process. These tools are utilized to provide advice and identify relationships in data. They can also be utilized to scan through large amounts of text and data to retrieve nuggets of information as part of data-mining efforts in seeking opportunities for or identifying threats to the organization.

❖ CHAPTER HIGHLIGHTS

- Enterprise systems serve the whole organization and frequently business partners as well.
- The major enterprise systems are (1) for executive support, (2) for organizational decision support, and (3) for support along the supply chain.
- Executives' work can be divided into two major phases: finding problems (opportunities) and deciding what to do about them.
- EIS serves the information needs of top executives. It used to be an independent system, but today its capabilities are generally provided as part of a business intelligence/enterprise system.
- EIS provides rapid access to timely information at various levels of detail. It is very user-friendly.
- Drill-down and rollup are important EIS capabilities. They allow an executive to look at details (and details of details), and to reaggregate the details.

- EIS uses a management-by-exception approach. It centers on CSFs, key performance indicators, and highlighted charts.
- Data warehouses and client/server front-end environments make an EIS a useful tool.
- Organizational DSS (ODSS) deals with decision-making across functional areas and hierarchical organizational layers.
- ODSS is used by individuals and groups, and operates in a distributed environment.
- The effectiveness and efficiency of the supply chain are critical to the survival of organizations.
- The major components of the supply chain are upstream (suppliers), internal, and downstream (customers).
- The value chain is a concept that attempts to maximize the value added when moving along the supply chain.

- Enterprise systems are becoming part of corporate portals for communication, collaboration, access, and dissimilation of information.
- Customer relationship management (CRM) systems enable customer loyalty, retention, and cross selling.
- Product life-cycle management (PLM) systems improve manufacturing processes by integrating design and manufacturing systems, essentially providing knowledge management capabilities.
- Business performance management (BPM) systems integrate information from many sources to improve an organization's workflow performance
- Business activities monitoring (BAM) provides managers with real-time information and models and collaboration capabilities in order to respond to situations and make timely decisions.
- Frontline systems automate or facilitate decisions at the place where customers interface with organizations.

❖ KEY WORDS

- advanced planning and scheduling (APS)
- application service provider (ASP)
- business activity monitoring (BAM) systems
- business intelligence (BI)
- business process management (BPM) systems
- critical success factor (CSF)
- corporate (enterprise) portal
- customer relationship management (CRM) system
- demand chain
- drill down

- empowering employees
- enterprise information systems (EIS)
- enterprise (information) portal
- enterprise resource planning (ERP)
- environmental scanning
- exception reporting
- executive information system (EIS)
- executive support system (ESS)
- extended supply chain
- frontline decision-making
- intelligent agent (IA)
- key performance indicators (KPI)
- multidimensional analysis

- navigation of information
- news feeds
- organizational decision support system (ODSS)
- product life cycle
- product life-cycle management (PLM) system
- reverse logistics
- soft information (in EIS)
- supply chain
- supply chain management (SCM)
- value chain
- value chain model
- value system

❖ QUESTIONS FOR REVIEW

1. Define executive information system (EIS).
2. Define executive support system (ESS).
3. What are the key differences between an EIS and an ESS?
4. List the pressures for the creation of an EIS.
5. Define enterprise support system.
6. List the major benefits of an EIS.
7. Define drill down and roll up, and list their advantages.
8. Define status access.
9. Define exception reporting.
10. List the major differences between EIS and DSS.
11. Describe how soft information can help an executive in decision-making.
12. Define ODSS (give at least two definitions).
13. Define supply chain and list its major components.
14. Discuss supply chain management (SCM) and its benefits.
15. Define enterprise resource planning/enterprise resource management (ERP)/(ERM).

16. List the major characteristics of ERP.
17. List the major tangible and intangible benefits of system (and software) integration.
18. Describe an ASP.
19. Define a corporate (enterprise information) portal (dashboard).
20. Describe the benefits of customer relationship (resource) management (CRM) systems.
21. Define PLM. Describe how it enhances SCM and ERP.
22. Describe BPM. Explain how it integrates with enterprise information systems and data warehouses.
23. Describe BAM. How can an effective BAM interact with other decision support/business intelligence/business analytic systems.
24. Explain how the Web has impacted all of the enterprise systems described in the chapter.
25. Describe frontline decision-making.

❖ **QUESTIONS FOR DISCUSSION**

1. If a DSS is used to find answers to management questions, what is an EIS used for?
2. Discuss how CSFs can be monitored and why they should be.
3. What are the major benefits of integrating EIS and DSS? What problems can occur?
4. It is said that drill down will be fully automated someday. What advantage will such automation give the executive? How can an intelligent agent be used to automate drill down in EIS?
5. What is soft information? Give four examples. Why is it important for an EIS to provide soft information?
6. Data mining (Chapter 5) is critical for enterprise information systems. Explain why.
7. Describe how multidimensional analysis, visualization, and OLAP are influencing EIS design and use.
8. Compare and contrast a value chain and a supply chain.

9. How can cooperation between a company and its suppliers reduce inventory costs?
10. Discuss the reasons for ERP's inability to support decision-making directly.
11. Discuss the major problems that could develop along the supply chain.
12. ERP software vendors have Web-based products. Discuss the benefits of Web-based ERP.
13. Discuss why EIS has moved toward the enterprise information (corporate) portal.
14. Business intelligence and ERP software as we know them today cannot support frontline decisions. Why not?
15. Describe in detail how a customer relationship management (CRM) system is an enterprise information system.
16. Compare and contrast the capabilities of PLM, BPM, BAM, SCM, and ERP.

❖ **EXERCISES**

1. Prepare a diagram showing the supply chains of (a) a toy manufacturer, (b) a PC manufacturer, and (c) a university. Clearly show the major components.
2. A. Paller described an EIS as being like the displays in an airplane cockpit. Because most of us are not airplane pilots, we can use the analogy of the gauges and indicator lights on a car dashboard. Explain the analogy between an airplane cockpit or an automobile dashboard and EIS or OLAP in terms of its use and effect on an organization.
3. Three surprising benefits ensue as an organization develops an enterprise system: the organization settles on a common terminology for its information, a common format is used, and a common depository of data is developed (now called a data warehouse). How might this happen otherwise? Consider several organizations with which you are affiliated. How might common terminology and a data warehouse be helpful to you? What disadvantages might there be? Explain.
4. Choose a real-world information scanning and reporting problem for which Temtec Executive Viewer might be appropriate. Develop a prototype EIS in Executive Viewer.
5. Choose a real-world information scanning and reporting problem for which Pilot Decision Support

Suite might be appropriate. Develop a prototype EIS in Pilot Decision Support Suite.
6. There are documented cases in the literature of EIS development strictly in spreadsheet packages. Develop a small EIS in Excel (or another spreadsheet). Use publicly available Cencus data.
7. Why are EIS diffusing down to lower levels of management? How does this affect an organization's ability to provide the same level of support to all levels of management using an EIS? Explain.
8. Consider the supply chain for a textbook. Explain how ERP could help Prentice Hall, the publisher of this book. Identify some major decisions that need to be made with respect to textbook production and distribution, and explain what type of DSS could be useful and how it could be integrated with an ERP.
9. Investigate ways that CRM can be used to optimize the relationship between an organization and its customers. Describe how this can be done at your organization or, if you are not working, at your college or university. Write up your findings in a five-page report.
10. Describe in detail how PLM, BPM, and BAM relate to other enterprise information systems.

❖ GROUP EXERCISES

1. Develop an EIS in a Windows-based database system (e.g., Access) to access critical census data (assume that it changes regularly). Highlight exceptional cases in color. Use regression and forecasting models. Link the data to a spreadsheet (e.g., Excel) containing the models. Describe the system in a report and highlight the difficulties encountered.

2. Divide the class into groups and assign each group to an ERP vendor (Oracle, SAP, Peoplesoft, etc.). Each group will investigate what business intelligence capabilities, including EIS, are incorporated into the core ERP (e.g., SAP R/3). Have the groups compare results and prepare a unified report.

❖ INTERNET EXERCISES

1. Access the Web sites of sap.com, oracle.com, baan.com, and www.peoplesoft.com, and find out how they incorporate business intelligence and EIS in their offerings.

2. EIS is tightly related to data warehousing and OLAP. Find recent articles on this relationship (try cio.com for the search). Also, check vendor Web sites, such as sas.com. Contact the SAS Institute and identify its product strategy regarding EIS, data warehousing, and OLAP. Access the Cognos Web site (cognos.com), download a demo of one of its EIS products, and try it. Report your experience to the class.

3. Access the Data Warehousing Institute's Web site (dw-institute.org) and identify current database trends, data warehousing, data mining, multitiered architectures, client/server architecture, and OLAP specifically as they relate to EIS. Report your findings.

4. Repeat Internet Exercise 3 for the Teradata University Network Web site. (teradatauniversitynetwork.com)

5. Access the Web sites of several EIS software vendors. Compare their products. What are their latest product offerings? What hardware platforms do they promote for their products? Which companies provide products that are Web-ready? Describe their capabilities. Which companies provide collaborative computing (GSS) capabilities?

6. Access the BusinessObjects Web site (businessobjects.com) and download and try BusinessQuery for Excel. Describe your experience. Do the same for the currently available downloadable demo version of BusinessObjects.

7. Access www.supply chain.com, cio.com, and other sources, and find the recent developments that relate to SCM and decision-making.

8. Prepare a presentation of state-of-the-art corporate portals. Start with www.microstrategy.com and www.oracle.com, and point out the capabilities and benefits.

9. Access the Web sites of several CRM software vendors. Compare their products. What are their latest product offerings? What hardware platforms do they promote for their products? Describe their capabilities. Which companies provide collaborative computing (GSS) capabilities?

10. Access the Web sites of several PLM (e.g., ptc.com), BPM, and BAM software vendors. Compare their products. What are their latest product offerings? What hardware platforms do they promote for their products? Describe their capabilities. How do they integrate into other enterprise information systems? Which companies provide collaborative computing (GSS) capabilities?

11. Access acxiom.com, epiphany.com, ncr.com, hyperion.com, and ptc.com. Identify their frontline system initiatives.

HOW LEVI'S GOT ITS JEANS INTO WAL-MART

Years ago, Levi's and blue jeans were synonymous. By the mid-1990s, Levi's had missed the baggy pants craze that had overtaken American high schools. In 1996, Levi's sales peaked at $7.1 billion. In 2002, they fell to $4.1 billion, a six-year low. Levi's jeans market share fell to about 12 percent from 18.7 percent in 1997. To survive, Levi's had to begin selling to mass-channel retailers such as Wal-Mart, which meant transforming the company's IT.

Wal-Mart, the world's largest retailer, is where moms go to stock up on jeans for their kids. So if you want to sell to the kids and their families, you must sell at Wal-Mart. Levi's introduced a new, less expensive Signature jeans line specifically for this market. And Wal-Mart, the largest clothing retailer in the world, wanted more affluent customers, so it needed major name brands. By partnering with Wal-Mart, Levi's expected to get the volume it needed to survive.

To a large extent, the success of the Levi's strategy depended on the performance of its technology. Wal-Mart requires its major vendors to utilize technology in their supply chains. The technology must link to Wal-Mart's systems. Selling to the mass market requires supply chain improvements. Globalization demands standardized enterprise systems.

CIO David Bergen joined Levi Strauss to get Levi's ready for Wal-Mart. Bergen had to rethink the supply chain, which included every detail of how Levi's jeans, jackets, and shirts would get from factories to new regional warehouses to Wal-Mart's 3,422 U.S. stores when they were needed, not before and certainly not after. This was much more complex than the demands placed on Levi's by smaller department store chains, such as Macy's (243 stores) or even J.C. Penney (1,049 stores). Complicating this challenge was the fact that Bergen would be going live with a completely upgraded supply chain system during the back-to-school rush, the worst time for a retailer to roll out a new technology.

In 2000, Bergen began working to make Levi's technology fit for the "mass channel," the big discount stores where 31 percent of all the jeans in the country are sold. When Bergen arrived, the company was in tentative discussions with Kmart, Target, Wal-Mart, and others. Bergen knew that without a technology overhaul, Levi's would

fail. He was most concerned that the company's national distribution strategy did not match Wal-Mart's business processes. Levi's had a poor on-time delivery record, the result of manufacturing and logistics problems dating from its move to largely overseas manufacturing in the late 1990s.

During exploratory meetings, Bergen knew that, the Levi's supply chain would initially be unable to deliver the services Wal-Mart expected. Being a supplier to Wal-Mart demands a certain level of performance and cost control. Wal-Mart drives you to work with your supply chain to put the same requirements on your suppliers that Wal-Mart puts on you. If you can't make your supply chain work, you do not benefit from being a supplier. At Levi's, executives could not track where its product was moving in the pipeline: how many pairs of jeans were being manufactured in which factories, and how many were sitting in trucks or in distribution centers. That was unacceptable to Wal-Mart, a supply chain pioneer that moves products off its shelves faster than any retailer and expects replenishment on time to keep costs down. Levi's needed to both get a handle on how its products were doing in stores and accelerate the speed at which those products moved from import dock to warehouse to retail shelf.

The lack of information available to Levi's executives translated into poor performance even without Wal-Mart. Beforehand, Levi's was delivering 65 percent of its product on time to customers, a poor performance. After its supply chain management improved, the rate was 95 percent, which could improve sales by 10 percent to 15 percent. Much of the benefit was due to improved demand-replenishment systems and forecasting technology. Additions included a dashboard that executives use to shows how each line of jeans is doing with each store on a weekly, monthly, or annual basis. Executives can also click on a specific product to track how it moves from the factory to the distribution centers to the stores. It shows how many pairs of jeans are available at a given time, what the demand is from the stores, and whether the company is meeting that demand. Executives can drill down to the product level.

The new system connects employees working within the supply chain to salespeople all the way up to the com-

---

Adapted from Kim Girard, "How Levi's Got Its Jeans into Wal-Mart," *CIO*, July 15, 2003.

pany's financial office. Executives use the dashboard to track trends and prevent problems. For example, during the third quarter of 2002, when the company started shipping Dockers Stain Defender pants, it expected to sell about 2 million pairs. The dashboard, however, alerted Levi's to that fact that the pants were flying off the shelves and another 500,000 more would be needed to meet demand. Having this information at its fingertips helped the company plan in advance and meet the demand. The same sort of information would be crucial to replenish Wal-Mart's shelves during the back-to-school season.

As part of this network of facilities, Levi's also developed a scanning tool for its manufacturers to check the accuracy of cartons ready to ship. The company implemented technology to exchange information with Wal-Mart EDI transactions that support collaborative

forecasting. And a set of Manugistics applications allows the company to collaborate with Wal-Mart on demand forecasting, product modifications, and order planning. Levi's can plan, define, and ship prepackaged orders to the retailer.

By 2003, there were encouraging signs that Levi's was turning around. Sales for the company's third and fourth quarters grew for the first time since 1996. During the spring and fall of 2002, for the first time in a long time, Levi's started appearing on NPD Fashionworld's top-10 list of brands preferred by young women. Levi's plans to upgrade its business processes and its improved replenishment system had helped the company get the right sizes to the right stores. The next phase is to develop a global ERP for between $1 million and $5 million, plus consulting fees.

CASE QUESTIONS

1. Why was it so important to overhaul the Levi Strauss supply chain system?
2. What SCM features do you think the system utilized (hint: see the chapter)?
3. What benefits did the new system deliver?
4. How can analytics help Levi Strauss?

5. What advantages could Levi Strauss obtain by implementing an ERP system to integrate with this SCM system?

CASE APPLICATION 8.2

MCDONALD'S ENTERPRISE INFORMATION EFFORT: MCBUSTED!

McDonald's planned to spend $1 billion over five years to tie all its operations in to a real-time digital network (enterprise information system). Eventually, executives at company headquarters would have been able to see every performance detail in every store, at any time, through this massive enterprise information system. After just two years, McDonald's cancelled the expensive program.

In early May 2003, McDonald's announced that it would write off a $170 million loss for the discontinuation in December 2002 of the global, real-time digital Innovate network, which represented the most expensive and extensive information technology project in the company's history. The $170 million was just part of the $1 billion that McDonald's planned to spend on Innovate start-

ing in January 2001. Innovate was designed to let McDonald's management see how many billions of burger patties, buns, and chicken nuggets were being consumed at any or all stores at any time of the day. Every detail of every property was to be available in *real-time*. The billion-dollar project failed before it even got off the ground because of the difficulty of transforming even a simple business into a real-time enterprise.

Fast growth led McDonald's to want to create a means to control the key quality that makes a fast-food chain successful: *consistency*. McDonald's opened more than 1,700 new restaurants a year over 10 years, taxing its outdated data-collection systems. A Web-based network that sent information instantly around the world was needed so that executives could monitor, and possibly

---

Adapted from Larry Barrett and Sean Gallagher, "McBusted," *Baseline*, No. 20, July 2003.

affect on a minute-by-minute basis, the company's ability to get a consistent product to customers quickly. If connected to every key piece of equipment in every store, the real-time digital network would have allowed McDonald's to better serve customers by using information and communications technologies to monitor the quality of the oil used to make french fries, or to ensure that each bun was toasted to the proper level of crispiness. It would have given McDonald's executives a detailed view of the entire system in real-time. Sales, service time, staffing, supply chain data, vendor locations, equipment repair orders, and every other datum that McDonald's currently tracks with its aging internally developed system, which typically made the data available to decision-makers in a week or more, could be pulled up in seconds through a Web browser. In theory, by working closely with suppliers and store managers, the company could improve the consistency of the product.

Innovate was also supposed to streamline the delivery of employee training and benefit data. Using the Internet to convey training information, like how to clean fryers or use the point-of-sale system, McDonald's hoped to leverage its training system across this platform.

By instantaneously collecting and sending data to stores from the corporate office, executives could monitor performance and fix it on the fly. For example, if a particular store was not moving people through the lines or drive-through up to the standards, executives could ask the local manager to add another employee or two to improve service time. If certain products were not moving, executives could investigate whether the in-store advertising was in place.

The supply chain would also be monitored. Every item from warehouse to store could be tracked to the second. If there was a run on Big Mac's in a particular store, supplies could be diverted en-route. McDonald's could react to customer demand quickly, and draw substantial financial rewards from the resulting efficiency. On the other hand, monitored remotely and, eventually, managed remotely, the system would take a lot of responsibility away from individual store managers.

Eventually, the Internet-based network would have linked all of the company's 30,000-plus restaurants and 300-plus approved vendors 24 hours a day, seven days a week, to the back-office system at its corporate office in

Oak Brook. This would have given McDonald's executives a complete, instant picture of the company's operations around the world, and, in theory, the ability to act quickly when necessary to adjust the deployment of promotions and supplies to meet demand.

Some $170 million was spent on the "research and development" of Innovate. McDonald's claims that the decision to terminate Innovate was based on the company's recent financial difficulties. On the other hand, had McDonald's made the $1 billion investment in Innovate to streamline its supply chain and improve its day-to-day operations, it would have needed to achieve at least a 1.5 percent improvement in sales, or roughly $231 million a year, to pay for the initial rollout. That is an additional 1.5 percent above the 3 to 5 percent in annual sales McDonald's was already projecting.

McDonald's first attempt at a large-scale, real-time enterprise data systems failed. This was no shock to some experts. McDonald's has a relative lack of experience in this area, spent too much money, and has little to show for it. McDonald's is not known for being at the cutting edge of technology or the executive-level appreciation and understanding of technology. Peter Abell, an analyst at AMR Research, says that "a real-time global network would tax even the most ambitious information technology organization. Configuring and integrating the software necessary to communicate back to Oak Brook from 30,000-plus locations including some in third-world locations where broadband connectivity is still just a dream—was more fantasy than reality." Abell continues, "The real challenge is determining whether or not there are enough cost benefits to make it worthwhile in the first place."

"The biggest problem a company like McDonald's would have is getting high-speed bandwidth in every location," Abell says. "Some parts of the U.S. still don't have reliable high-speed connectivity. And they're international. So that could definitely be problematic."

Though the company had shown little to no excitement or expertise in large-scale information systems implementations when Innovate was initiated, its executives thought they could do a Wal-Mart-like makeover of their core technology infrastructure. What they found out was that their expertise in developing and mass-producing fast food had little relevance to software integration and implementation.

CASE QUESTIONS

1. Investigate and describe the McDonald's supply chain. How do information flows follow it?
2. Why was the McDonald's enterprise information "McSystem" cancelled?
3. Would the system have been cost-effective had it survived?
4. What problems would the McDonald's enterprise information system have encountered?

5. Examine the ERP situation at Hershey's Chocolate described in this chapter and Chapter 6. Compare and contrast Hershey's ERP experiences to McDonald's. What lessons could McDonald's learn from Hershey's?

CASE APPLICATION 8.3

MOHEGAN SUN'S CRM HITS THE JACKPOT

The Mohegan Sun Casino tracks the habits of its customers (gamblers), even low rollers, to build loyalty and get them to return. Mohegan Sun has 6,200 slot machines, 260 table games, and 36 poker tables.

Sue Vanwiggeren, 76, has for the past year taken a two-hour bus ride from Fall River, Massachusetts, to Uncasville, Connecticut, to visit the Mohegan Sun Casino. She usually comes three or four times a week, for the day, and has gotten to know many other senior citizens who do the same. Vanwiggeren likes slot machines, but especially likes blackjack. She does not just come for the gambling, but also for the "freebies." The $15 bus fare was paid in points earned through her frequent-gamer Player's Club card. Mohegan Sun also mailed her a coupon for a chance to spin a giant prize wheel and one for a free buffet dinner. Most people think about high rollers playing high-stakes games and dropping thousands of dollars a night when they think about gamblers. Even though there are such players, they are *not the core* of the casino business. People like Ms. Vanwiggeren are.

At Mohegan Sun, cardholders collect points like a checking account and can use them any way they want: to eat, drink, buy gifts or clothes, pay for hotel rooms or massages, or for hourly childcare services while gambling, or for gassing up the car on the way out.

Mohegan Sun works to get repeat business with a customer-loyalty program mixed with outside demographic data, surrounded by data mining and analysis software. Information technology helps marketing identify exactly who, in a six-state radius, it should try to attract. Mohegan Sun spent $77 million on promotional programs last year, up from $71 million in 2001. In 2003, the casino had the first full year of operating its expanded gaming floors and luxury hotel.

Promotions are definitely geared to certain age groups. For example, the casino targets senior citizens with coupons for bus rides and weekday meals. Other programs are broader, intended to appeal to as many Northeastern gamblers as possible. For example, with Swipe & Win, customers run a magnetic-striped Player's Club card that they got in the mail through a kiosk to try to win cash. There are five other major promotions that the casino rotates monthly to bring in customers, who can play once per day. In the summer of 2002, it gave away $500,000 to 25,000 people. Prizes ranged from $25 to $50,000.

But more important, Mohegan Sun can identify the gambling history of each of the casino's 2 million Player's Club members (as well as of anyone using a credit card, but not cash just yet). Using collected data, a customer relationship management (CRM) system is used to analyze gaming patterns with demographics to identify profitable customer segments. The casino can determine how popular each contest is and with whom. The casino also tracks when patrons use Player's Club cards on the property to play slot machines or table games, or to redeem points at stores or restaurants. This helps determine how much additional revenue the casino got from those customers after luring them in with promotions.

Direct mail campaigns across industries, on average, draw a 3 to 5 percent response rate. But 75 to 80 percent of the people who get Swipe & Win mail promotions visit the casino. When analysts noticed that Tuesdays were slow days on the gaming floors, marketing staff created *double-swipe Tuesdays*, which brought more people in.

An electronic item-tracking system inside the mini-bar monitors what has been taken so that housekeepers know what to cart to each room the next day. The system automatically charges room accounts for items pulled out for longer than a half minute.

Overall, the system is a success. It increases demand and enhances profitability.

CASE QUESTIONS

1. Why is it important for an organization to use CRM to segment customers? What do organizations do with the information?
2. Examine data mining in Chapter 5. How can data mining be used to identify profitable customers?
3. How could credit card and Player's Club data be used to track additional spending on the property? Determine at least three categories of spending and explain how could this be effective in developing further comps for customers.
4. Identify similarities and differences between the Mohegan Sun case and the Harrah's situation in the Chapter 1 Opening Vignette.

Adapted from Kim S. Nash, "Mohegan Sun: Play for Keeps," *Baseline*, No. 20, July 2003.

KNOWLEDGE MANAGEMENT[1]

LEARNING OBJECTIVES

❖ Define knowledge and describe the different types of knowledge.

❖ Describe the characteristics of knowledge management.

❖ Describe organizational learning and its relationship to knowledge management.

❖ Describe the knowledge management cycle.

❖ Describe the technologies that can be utilized in a knowledge management system.

❖ Describe different approaches to knowledge management.

❖ Describe the activities of the chief knowledge officer and others involved in knowledge management.

❖ Describe the role of knowledge management in organizational activities.

❖ Describe ways of evaluating intellectual capital in an organization.

❖ Describe how knowledge management systems are implemented.

❖ Describe the roles of technology, people, and management in knowledge management.

❖ Describe the benefits and drawbacks of knowledge management initiatives.

❖ Describe how knowledge mangement can revolutionize the way an organization functions.

In this chapter we describe the characteristics and concepts of knowledge management. In addition, we will explain how firms use information technology to implement knowledge management systems and how these systems are transforming modern organizations. Knowledge management, while conceptually ancient, is a relatively new form of collaborative computing. The goal of knowledge management is to capture, store, maintain, and deliver useful knowledge in a meaningful form to anyone who needs it anyplace and anytime within an organization. Knowledge management is *collaboration at the organization level*. Knowledge management has the potential to revolutionize the way we collaborate and use computing, as will be discussed in the following sections:

9.1 Opening Vignette: Siemens Knows What It Knows Through Knowledge Management

9.2 Introduction to Knowledge Management

---

[1]Portions of this chapter were contributed by Babita Gupta, California State University—Monterey Bay; Lakshmi S. Iyer, University of North Carolina—Greensboro; Dorothy E. Leidner—Baylor University; Richard McCarthy, Quinnipiac University; and Patrick Simpkins, NASA.

9.1 OPENING VIGNETTE: SIEMENS KNOWS WHAT IT KNOWS THROUGH KNOWLEDGE MANAGEMENT[2]

THE PROBLEM

Siemens AG, a $73 billion electronics and electrical-engineering conglomerate, produces everything from light bulbs to X-ray machines, from power generation equipment to high-speed trains. During its 156-year history, Siemens has developed into one of the world's largest and most successful corporations. Siemens is well known for the technical brilliance of its engineers, but much of their knowledge was locked and unavailable to other employees. Facing the pressure to maximize the benefits of corporate membership of each business unit, Siemens AG needed to learn to leverage the knowledge and expertise of its 460,000 employees worldwide.

THE SOLUTION

The roots of knowledge management at Siemens go back to 1996, when a number of people within the corporation with an interest in knowledge management (KM) formed a *community of interest*. They researched the subject, learned what was being done by other companies, and determined how KM could benefit Siemens. Without suggestion or encouragement from senior executives, mid-level employees in Siemens business units began creating repositories, communities of practice, and informal techniques of sharing knowledge. By 1999, the central board of Siemens AG confirmed the importance of knowledge management to the entire company by creating an organizational unit that would be responsible for the worldwide deployment of KM.

The movement toward knowledge management by Siemens has presented several challenges to the company, the most notable of which are technological and cultural. At the heart of Siemens's technical solution to knowledge management is a Web site called ShareNet, which combines elements of a database repository, a chat room, and a search engine. Online entry forms allow employees to store information they think might be useful to colleagues. Other Siemens employees are able to search the repository or browse by topic, and then contact the authors for more information using one of the available communication channels. In addition, the system lets employees post an alert when they have an urgent question. Although KM implementation at Siemens

[2]*Sources*: Adapted from Gary S. Vasilash, "447,000 Heads Are Better Than One," *Automotive Design & Production*, June 2002; "Business: Electronic Glue," *The Economist*, June 2, 2001; Simon Williams, "The Intranet Content Management Strategy Conference," *Management Services*, September 2001; Megan Santosus, "How Siemens Keeps KM Blooming," In the Know at cio.com, February 2003; Kim Ann Zimmermann, "Happy Together: Knowledge Management and Collaboration Work Hand-in-Hand to Satisfy the Thirst for Information," *KMWorld*, May 2003.

involved establishing a network to collect, categorize, and share information using databases and intranets, Siemens realized that IT was only the tool that enabled knowledge management. Randall Sellers, director of knowledge management for the Americas Region of Siemens, states: "In my opinion, the technology or IT role is a small one. I think it's 20 percent IT and 80 percent change management—dealing with cultural change and human interfaces."

Siemens used a three-pronged effort to convince employees that it is important to participate in the exchange of ideas and experiences and to share what they know. The challenge is managing the people who manage the knowledge. You have to make it easy for them to share, or they won't. Siemens has assigned 100 internal evangelists around the world to be responsible for training, answering questions, and monitoring the system. Siemens's top management has shown its full support for the knowledge management projects. And the company is providing incentives to overcome employees' resistance to change. When employees post documents to the system or use the knowledge, Siemens rewards them with "shares" (like frequent-flyer miles). An employee's accumulation of shares can be exchanged for things like consumer electronics or discounted trips to other countries. However, the real incentive of the system is much more basic. Commission-driven salespeople have already learned that the knowledge and expertise of their colleagues available through ShareNet can be indispensable in winning lucrative contracts. Employees in marketing, service, R&D, and other departments are also willing to participate and contribute once they realize that the system provides them with useful information in a convenient way.

The ShareNet has undergone tremendous growth, which resulted in several challenges for Siemens. The company strives to maintain a balance between global and local knowledge initiatives as well as between knowledge management efforts that support the entire company and those that help individual business units. Furthermore, Siemens works to prevent ShareNet from becoming so overloaded with knowledge that it becomes useless. A group is assigned to monitor the system and remove trivial and irrelevant content.

RESULTS

ShareNet has evolved into a state-of-the-art Web-based knowledge management system that stores and catalogs volumes of valuable knowledge, makes it available to every employee, and enhances global collaboration. Numerous companies, including Intel, Philips, and Volkswagen, studied ShareNet before setting up their own knowledge management systems. Teleos, an independent knowledge management research company, has acknowledged Siemens as one of the Most Admired Knowledge Enterprises worldwide for five years in a row.

Siemens has realized a variety of quantifiable benefits afforded by knowledge management. For example, in April 1999, the company developed a portion of ShareNet to support the Information & Communications Networks Group at the cost of $7.8 million. Within two years, the tool helped to generate $122 million in additional sales.

Ultimately, knowledge management may be one of the major tools that will help Siemens prove that large diversified conglomerates can work and that being big might even be an advantage in the Information Age.

❖ QUESTIONS FOR THE OPENING VIGNETTE

1. How did the Siemens knowledge management system evolve?
2. How does Siemens view knowledge (intellectual) assets?

3. What does leveraging expertise mean? How did Siemens do this? Explain how this relates to the high return on investment.

4. Describe the benefits of the Siemens ShareNet knowledge management system.

5. Explain the meaning of culture transformation as it occurred at Siemens. Include how the various constituencies bought into the system in your answer.

6. Explain how Internet and Web technologies enabled the knowledge management system.

9.2 INTRODUCTION TO KNOWLEDGE MANAGEMENT

CONCEPTS AND DEFINITIONS

The Opening Vignette illustrates the importance and value of identifying an organization's knowledge and sharing it throughout the organization. In a major initiative, Siemens AG developed ShareNet and other knowledge management systems to leverage its **intellectual assets** (also called *intellectual capital*), the valuable knowledge of its employees. Siemens transformed its culture as the knowledge management system was deployed, leading to significantly lower operating costs and more collaboration throughout the global enterprise. Though it is hard to measure, organizations recognize the value of their intellectual assets. Fierce global competition drives companies to better utilize their intellectual assets by transforming themselves into organizations that foster the development and sharing of knowledge. Mitre Corporation (see the Web Chapter) had similar experiences with knowledge management.

With roots in organizational learning, and innovation, the idea of knowledge management is not new (see Cahill, 1996; Gupta et al., 2000). However, the application of information technology tools to facilitate the creation, storage, transfer, and application of previously uncodifiable organizational knowledge is a new and major initiative in organizations. Successful managers have always used intellectual assets and recognized their value. But these efforts were not systematic, nor did they ensure that knowledge gained was shared and dispersed appropriately for maximum organizational benefit. **Knowledge management (KM)** is a process that helps organizations identify, select, organize, disseminate, and transfer important information and expertise that are part of the organization's memory and that typically reside within the organization in an unstructured manner. The structuring of knowledge enables effective and efficient problem-solving, dynamic learning, strategic planning, and decision-making. Knowledge management initiatives focus on identifying knowledge, explicating it in such a way that it can be shared in a formal manner, and leveraging its value through reuse. The information technologies that together make knowledge management available throughout an organization are referred to as a knowledge management system (KMS). (See Santosus and Surmacz, 2001; Gamble and Blackwell, 2002; Holsapple, 2003a, 2003b; Probst, Raub, and Romhardt, 2002; Rumizen, 2002; Smith and McKeen, 2003.)

Through a supportive organizational climate and modern information technology, an organization can bring its entire organizational memory and knowledge to bear upon any problem anywhere in the world and at any time. For organizational success, *knowledge, as a form of capital, must be exchangeable among persons, and it must be able to grow.* Knowledge about how problems are solved can be captured, so that knowledge management can promote organizational learning, leading to further knowledge creation.

KNOWLEDGE

Knowledge is very distinct from data and information in the information technology context (see Figure 9.1). Whereas *data* are a collection of facts, measurements, and statistics, *information* is organized or processed data that are timely (i.e., inferences from the data are drawn within the time frame of applicability) and accurate (i.e., with regard to the original data) (Hoffer, Prescott and McFadden, 2002; Watson, 2001). **Knowledge** is information that is *contextual, relevant,* and *actionable.* For example, a map giving detailed driving directions from one location to another could be considered data. An up-to-the-minute traffic bulletin along the freeway that indicates a traffic slowdown due to construction several miles ahead could be considered information. Awareness of an alternative, back-roads route could be considered knowledge. In this case, the map is considered data because it does not contain current relevant information that affects the driving time and conditions from one location to the other. However, having the current conditions as information is only useful if you have knowledge that will enable you to avert the construction zone. *The implication is that knowledge has strong experiential and reflective elements that distinguish it from information in a given context.* Having knowledge implies that it can be exercised to solve a problem, whereas having information does not carry the same connotation. An *ability to act* is an integral part of being knowledgeable. For example, two people in the same context with the same information may not have the same ability to use the information to the same degree of success. Hence there is a difference in the human capability to add value. The differences in ability may be due to different experiences, different training, different perspectives, and other factors. While data, information, and knowledge may all be viewed as assets of an organization, knowledge provides a higher level of meaning about data and information. It conveys *meaning,* and hence tends to be much more valuable, yet more ephemeral.

Unlike other assets, knowledge has the following characteristics (Gray, 1999):

- *Extraordinary leverage and increasing returns.* Knowledge is not subject to diminishing returns. When it is used, it is not consumed. Its consumers can add to it, thus increasing its value.
- *Fragmentation, leakage, and the need to refresh.* As knowledge grows, it branches and fragments. Knowledge is dynamic; it is information in action. Thus,

---

FIGURE 9.1   DATA, INFORMATION, AND KNOWLEDGE.

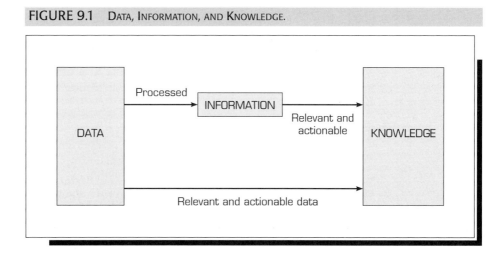

an organization must continually refresh its knowledge base to maintain it as a source of competitive advantage.

- *Uncertain value.* It is difficult to estimate the impact of an investment in knowledge. There are too many intangible aspects.
- *Uncertain value of sharing.* Similarly, it is difficult to estimate the value of sharing the knowledge, or even who will benefit most.

Over the last few decades, the industrialized economy has been going through a transformation from being based on natural resources to being based on intellectual assets (Hansen et al., 1999; Alavi, 2000; von Krogh et al., 2000). The **knowledge-based economy** is a reality (see Bennet and Bennet, 2003a; Kurtzman, 2003). Rapid changes in the business environment cannot be handled in traditional ways. Firms are much larger, and in some areas turnover is extremely high, fueling the need for better tools for collaboration, communication, and knowledge sharing. Firms *must* develop strategies to sustain competitive advantage by leveraging their intellectual assets for optimal performance (e.g., in the National Basketball Association; see Berman et al., 2002). To compete in the globalized economy and markets requires quick response to customer needs and problems.

To provide service, managing knowledge is critical for consulting firms spread out over wide geographical areas, and for virtual organizations, as is demonstrated in the Web Chapter on Sigma, a virtually structured German consulting firm.

There is a vast amount of literature about what knowledge and knowing mean in epistemology (the study of the nature of knowledge), the social sciences, philosophy, and psychology (Polanyi, 1958, 1966). Though there is no single definition of what knowledge and knowledge management specifically mean, the business perspective on them is fairly pragmatic. Information as a resource is not always valuable (i.e., information overload can distract from what is important); knowledge as a resource is valuable because it focuses attention back toward what is important (Hoffer, Prescott and McFadden, 2002). Knowledge implies an implicit understanding and experience that can discriminate between its use and misuse. Over time, information accumulates and decays, whereas knowledge evolves. *Knowledge is dynamic in nature.* This implies, though, that today's knowledge may well become tomorrow's ignorance if an individual or organization fails to update knowledge as environmental conditions change. For more on the potential drawbacks of managing and reusing knowledge, see Section 9.9.

The term **intellectual capital**, often used as a synonym for "knowledge," implies that there is a financial value to knowledge. Though intellectual capital is difficult to measure, some industries have tried. For example, in 2000 the value of the intellectual capital of the property-casualty insurance industry has been estimated to be between $270 billion to $330 billion (Mooney, 2000).

Knowledge evolves over time with experience, which puts connections among new situations and events in context. Given the breadth of the types and applications of knowledge, we adopt the simple and elegant definition that *knowledge is information in action* (O'Dell et al., 1998).

TACIT AND EXPLICIT KNOWLEDGE

Polanyi (1958) first conceptualized the difference between an organization's tacit and explicit knowledge. **Explicit knowledge** deals with more objective, rational, and technical knowledge (data, policies, procedures, software, documents, etc.). **Tacit knowledge** is usually in the domain of subjective, cognitive, and experiential learning; it is highly personal and difficult to formalize (Nonaka and Takeuchi, 1995).

Explicit knowledge comprises the policies, procedural guides, white papers, reports, designs, products, strategies, goals, mission, and core competencies of the enterprise and the information technology infrastructure. It is the knowledge that has been codified (documented) in a form that can be distributed to others or transformed into a process or strategy without requiring interpersonal interaction. For example, a description of how to process a job application would be documented in a firm's human resources policy manual. Explicit knowledge has also been called **leaky knowledge** because of the ease with which it can leave an individual, document, or the organization, since it can be readily and accurately documented (Alavi, 2000).

Tacit knowledge is the cumulative store of the experiences, mental maps, insights, acumen, expertise, know-how, trade secrets, skill sets, understanding, and learning that an organization has, as well as the organizational culture that has embedded in it the past and present experiences of the organization's people, processes, and values. Tacit knowledge, also referred to as *embedded knowledge* (Madhaven and Grover, 1998), is usually either localized within the brain of an individual or embedded in the group interactions within a department or a branch office. Tacit knowledge typically involves expertise or high skill levels.

Sometimes tacit knowledge is easily documentable but has remained tacit simply because the individual housing the knowledge does not recognize its potential value to other individuals. Other times, tacit knowledge is unstructured, without tangible form, and therefore difficult to codify. Polanyi (1966) suggests that it is difficult to put some tacit knowledge into words. For example, an explanation of how to ride a bicycle would be difficult to document explicitly, and thus is tacit. Successful transfer or sharing of tacit knowledge usually takes place through associations, internships, apprenticeship, conversations, other means of social and interpersonal interactions, or even through simulations (see Robin, 2000). Nonaka and Takeuchi (1995) claim that intangibles like insights, intuitions, hunches, gut feelings, values, images, metaphors, and analogies are the often overlooked assets of organizations. Harvesting this intangible asset can be critical to a firm's bottom line and its ability to meet its goals. Tacit knowledge has been called **sticky knowledge** because it is relatively difficult to pull it away from its source.

Historically, MIS has focused on capturing, storing, managing, and reporting explicit knowledge. Organizations now recognize the need to integrate both types of knowledge in formal information systems. **Knowledge management** is the systematic and active managing of ideas, information, and knowledge residing in an organization's employees. For centuries, the mentor-apprentice relationship, because of its experiential nature, has been a slow but reliable means of transferring tacit knowledge from individual to individual. When people leave an organization, they take their knowledge with them. One critical goal of knowledge management is to retain the valuable know-how that can so easily and quickly leave an organization. **Knowledge management systems (KMS)** refer to the use of modern information technologies (e.g. the Internet, intranets, extranets, LotusNotes, Software filters, Agents, Data Warehouses) to systematize, enhance, and expedite intra- and inter-firm knowledge management (Alavi and Leidner, 1998). KMS are intended to help an organization cope with turnover, rapid change, and downsizing by making the expertise of the organization's human capital widely accessible. They are being built in part because of the increasing pressure to maintain a well-informed, productive workforce. Moreover, they are built to help large organizations provide a consistent level of customer service, as illustrated in DSS in Action 9.1. For more on the basics of knowledge and the economy, see Kurtzman (2003), Holsapple (2003), and Teece (2003).

DSS IN ACTION 9.1

CINGULAR CALLS ON KNOWLEDGE

How do you make sure that each of your customer service agents at 22 call centers nationwide can answer virtually any question asked by one of your 22 million clients? That was the challenge faced by Cingular Wireless (www.cingular.com), a major mobile communications provider based in Atlanta, Georgia.

Cingular Wireless turned to knowledge management to accomplish this massive task. Cingular benchmarked knowledge management solutions of technology-oriented companies, such as Dell and Microsoft. Steve Mullins, vice president of customer experience for Cingular Wireless, and Monica Browning, Cingular's director of knowledge management, met with several knowledge management software vendors to learn how their tools operate. "We thought about how [the KM software] would integrate with what we envisioned the future desktop to look like," says Mullins. "This system would be the foundation for what we use throughout all of our departments."

Following a review of KM solutions used by other companies, Cingular chose eService Suite by ServiceWare of Edison, New Jersey. ServiceWare's decision integrity department helped Cingular put together a basis for proving the software's return on investment (ROI).

To ensure successful implementation of the system, Cingular embarked on a campaign to obtain the support of everyone involved, from senior executives to each call center agent who would use the system. A pilot program was initiated at technical support departments at three call centers.

To help manage the organizational changes that accompany a shift to knowledge management, Cingular enlisted the help of leading consulting firms Cap Gemini Ernst & Young and Innovative Management Solutions.

A major issue in developing the knowledge management system involved capturing knowledge and storing it in the system. Cingular accomplished it by combining the efforts of its employees and an external authoring group from Innovative Management Solutions. Cingular divided the process into phases. This made it possible to populate the knowledge base with technical support information, common topics, information on rate plans, and so on. Browning estimates that it

was about four months before the knowledge repository was ready for the first group of users.

The KM system uses complex (artificial intelligence-based) algorithms to process natural language queries and provide customer service agents with lists of most likely answers to their questions. The software also determines the relevance of possible answers by ranking them partly on exact text and phrase matching. In addition, the system can match synonyms and assign additional weight to certain expressions. The system attempts to provide even more focused solutions by retrieving answers from the pool of knowledge that is relevant to a particular user and his or her profile.

Understanding that knowledge must grow and evolve, Cingular encourages users to contribute their expertise to the system. The software can automatically record a sequence of steps that an agent took to find a correct solution to a certain problem and give the agent an option to provide additional feedback.

Cingular realized that ensuring validity and integrity of the knowledge stored and distributed by the knowledge management system is one of the key factors of the system's success. To that end, the company employs a KM team that is responsible for monitoring, maintaining, and expanding the system. The team consists of about 25 full-time employees based in Cingular's Atlanta headquarters. The KM team works closely with various departments of the company and subject-matter experts to ensure that the knowledge base has the right answers in a user-friendly format at the right time. In addition, the team reviews contributions to the knowledge base made by the agents and makes appropriate changes or additions to the knowledge base.

Cingular's clients are often the ultimate beneficiaries of the company's knowledge. That is why Cingular plans to bring its knowledge closer to its customers by extending the knowledge management system online and to retail stores. Customers will be able to access instructions on using wireless services and features, handsets, and other devices that Cingular carries, as well as troubleshooting tips.

Source: Adapted from Jennifer O'Herron, "Building the Bases of Knowledge," *Call Center Magazine,* January 2003.

9.3 ORGANIZATIONAL LEARNING AND TRANSFORMATION

Knowledge management is rooted in the concepts of organizational learning and organizational memory. When members of an organization collaborate and communicate ideas, teach, and learn, knowledge is transformed and transferred from individual to individual (see Bennet and Bennet, 2003a).

THE LEARNING ORGANIZATION

The term **learning organization** refers to an organization's capability of learning from its past experience (DiBella, 1995). Before a company can improve, it must first *learn*. Learning involves an interaction between experience and competence. In communities of practice, these are tightly related. Communities of practice provide not only a context for newcomers to learn, but also a context for new insights to be transformed into knowledge (see Wenger, 2002a). We discuss communities of practice later in this chapter. To build a learning organization, three critical issues must be tackled: (1) meaning (determining a vision of what the learning organization is to be), (2) management (determining how the firm is to work), and (3) measurement (assessing the rate and level of learning). A learning organization as one that performs five main activities well: systematic problem-solving, creative experimentation, learning from past experience, learning from the best practices of others, and transferring knowledge quickly and efficiently throughout the organization (Garvin, 1993). Best Buy deliberately and successfully structured its knowledge management efforts around creating a learning organization where it captured best practices (see Barth, 2001). Also see Brown and Duguid (2002).

ORGANIZATIONAL MEMORY

A learning organization must have an **organizational memory** and a means to save, represent, and share its organizational knowledge. Estimates vary, but it is generally believed that only 10–20 percent of business data are actually used. Organizations "remember" the past in their policies and procedures. Individuals ideally tap into this memory for both explicit and tacit knowledge when faced with issues or problems to be solved. Human intelligence draws from the organizational memory and adds value by creating new knowledge. A knowledge management system can capture the new knowledge and make it available in its enhanced form. See Jennex and Olfman (2003) and Cross and Baird (2000).

ORGANIZATIONAL LEARNING

Organizational learning is the development of new knowledge and insights that have the potential to influence an organization's behavior. It occurs when associations, cognitive systems, and memories are shared by members of an organization (see Schulz, 2001; and Croasdell et al., 1997). Learning skills include (Garvin, 2000a, 2000b):

- Openness to new perspectives
- Awareness of personal biases

- Exposure to unfiltered data
- A sense of humility

Establishing a corporate memory is critical for success (Brooking 1999; Cross and Baird, 2000; Hackbarth and Grover, 1999; Hinds and Aronson, 2002). Information technology plays a critical role in organizational learning, and management must place emphasis on this area to foster it (see Andreu and Ciborra, 1996; Davenport and Sena, 2003); Gray and Tehrani, 2003; O'Leary, 2003).

Since organizations are becoming more virtual in nature (see the Web Chapter on Sigma), they must develop methods for effective organizational learning. Modern collaborative technologies can help in knowledge management initiatives. Organizational learning and memory depend less on technology than on the people issues, as we describe next.

ORGANIZATIONAL CULTURE

The ability of an organization to learn, develop memory, and share knowledge is dependent on its culture. *Culture* is a pattern of shared basic assumptions (Kayworth and Leidner, 2003; Schein, 1997, 1999). Over time organizations learn what works and what doesn't work. As the lessons become second nature, they become part of the **organizational culture**. New employees learn the culture from their mentors along with know-how.

The impact of corporate culture on an organization is difficult to measure. However, strong culture generally produces strong, measurable bottom-line results: net income, return on invested capital, and yearly increases in stock price (Hibbard, 1998). For example, Buckman Laboratories, a pharmaceutical firm, measures culture impact by sales of new products. Buckman undertook to change its organizational culture by making knowledge-sharing part of the company's core values. After instituting a knowledge-sharing initiative, sales of products less than five years old rose to 33 percent of total sales, up from 22 percent (Hibbard, 1998; also see Martin, 2000). Sharing initiatives and proper motivation are critical for knowledge management success. This is even trickier in the public sector (see Chiem, 2001b). On the other hand, an organizational culture that does not foster sharing can severely cripple a KM effort (see De Long and Fahey, 2000; Hinds and Aronson, 2002).

Encouraging employees to use a knowledge management system, both for contributing knowledge and for seeking knowledge can be difficult. The reasons *people do not like to share knowledge* are as follows (Vaas, 1999):

- Willing to share, but not enough time to do so.
- No skill in knowledge management techniques.
- Don't understand knowledge management and benefits.
- Lack of appropriate technology.
- No commitment from senior managers.
- No funding for knowledge management.
- Culture does not encourage knowledge sharing.

Sometimes a technology project fails because the technology does not match the organization's culture. (This is a much deeper issue than having a low fit between the technology and the task and hand; see McCarthy, Mazouz, and Aronson, 2001.) This is especially true for knowledge management systems, because they rely so heavily on individuals contributing their knowledge. Most KM systems that fail in practice do so because of organizational culture issues (see Drucker, 2001).

9.4 KNOWLEDGE MANAGEMENT INITIATIVES

When asked why the organization was building a worldwide knowledge management system, the chief knowledge officer of a large multinational consulting firm replied, "We have 80,000 people scattered around the world that need information to do their jobs effectively. The information they needed was too difficult to find and, even if they did find it, often inaccurate. Our Intranet is meant to solve this problem" (Leidner, 1998). A survey of European firms by KPMG Peat Marwick in 1998 found that almost half of the companies reported having suffered a significant setback from losing key staff. Similarly, a survey conducted in the same year by Cranfield University found that the majority of responding firms believed that much of the knowledge they needed existed inside the organization, but that finding and leveraging it were ongoing challenges. Finally, in some highly skilled professions like medicine, retaining and utilizing knowledge of the best practices is critical for life and death situations (see Lamont, 2003a). It is precisely these types of difficulties that have led to the systematic attempt to manage knowledge (see Compton, 2001; Holsapple, 2003a, 2003b). Between early 2001 and early 2003, American firms laid off 3.6 million workers (not including retirements). Nineteen percent of baby boomers in executive, administrative, or managerial positions are expected to retire by 2008. When people leave an organization, their knowledge assets leave with them ("Intellectual capital has legs;" see Taylor, 2001). In an era of uncertainty, shrinking budgets, and staff reductions, knowledge is at risk. The most knowledgeable employees typically leave first. Critical social networks are damaged. Trust decays. And the time required for knowledge transfer is compressed and compromised. In fact, knowledge transfer is affected by all the factors that encourage or inhibit interpersonal communications (see Roberts, 2000). Knowledge management systems attempt to capture knowledge before people leave (see Beazley, Boenisch and Harden, 2002; Horgan, 2003; Kurtzman, 2003; Lesser and Prusak, 2001).

Most KM initiatives have one of three aims: (1) to make knowledge visible mainly through maps, yellow pages, and hypertext, (2) to develop a knowledge-intensive culture, or (3) to build a knowledge infrastructure (Davenport and Prusak, 1998). These aims are not mutually exclusive, and, indeed, firms may attempt all three as part of a knowledge management initiative.

There are several activities or processes that surround the management of knowledge. These include the creation of knowledge, the sharing of knowledge, and the seeking and use of knowledge. Various terms have been used to describe these processes. What is important is an understanding of how knowledge flows through an organization, rather than any particular label assigned to a knowledge activity (see Lesser, Fontaine, and Slusher, 2000; Wenger, 2002b).

KNOWLEDGE CREATION

Knowledge creation is the generation of new insights, ideas, or routines. Nonaka (1994) describes knowledge creation as an interplay between tacit and explicit knowledge and as a growing spiral as knowledge moves among the individual, group, and organizational levels. There are four modes of knowledge creation: socialization, externalization, internalization, and combination. The socialization mode refers to the conversion of tacit knowledge to new tacit knowledge through social interactions and shared experience among organizational members (e.g., mentoring). The combination mode refers to the creation of new explicit knowledge by merging, categorizing, reclassifying, and synthesizing existing explicit knowledge (e.g., statistical analyses of market data). The other two modes involve interactions and conversion between tacit and explicit knowledge. Externalization refers to converting tacit knowledge to new explicit knowledge (e.g., producing a written document describing the procedures used in solving a particular client's problem). Internalization refers to the creation of new tacit knowledge from explicit knowledge (e.g., obtaining a novel insight through reading a document). For further information see Von Krogh, Ichijo, and Nonaka (2000); Soo et al. (2002).

KNOWLEDGE SHARING

Knowledge sharing is the willful explication of one's ideas, insights, solutions, experiences (i.e., knowledge) to another individual either via an intermediary, such as a computer-based system, or directly. However, in many organizations, information and knowledge are not considered organizational resources to be shared, but individual competitive weapons to be kept private (Davenport, 1997b). Organizational members may share personal knowledge with a certain trepidation—the perceived threat that they are of less value if their knowledge is part of the organizational public domain. Research in organizational learning and knowledge management suggests that some facilitating conditions include trust, interest, and shared language (Hanssen-Bauer and Snow, 1996), fostering access to knowledgeable members (Brown and Duguin, 1991), and a culture marked by autonomy, redundancy, requisite variety, intention, and fluctuation (Nonaka, 1994). Also see Santosus (2001) and Chiem (2001a).

KNOWLEDGE SEEKING

Knowledge seeking, also referred to as knowledge sourcing (see Gray and Meisters, 2003) is the search for and use of internal organizational knowledge. While lack of time or lack of reward may hinder the sharing of knowledge, the same can be said of knowledge seeking. Individuals may sometimes prefer to not reuse knowledge if they feel that their own performance review is based on the originality or creativity of their ideas. Such was the case for marketing employees in a global consumer goods organization described in Alavi, Kayworth and Leidner (2003).

Individuals may engage in knowledge creation, sharing, and seeking with or without the use of information technology tools. For example, storytelling (described in Chapter 2 as a decision-making technique) is an ancient approach to transmitting and gathering knowledge. Nuances of how the story is told cue the gatherer as to importance and detail. Storytelling may be considered a form of verbal best practices. See Angus (2001), Eisenhart (2001), Gamble and Blackwell (2002), Gill (2001), Reamy (2002a, 2002b), and Swap et al. (2001) for details on how storytelling is used in knowledge management. We next describe two common approaches to knowledge management.

9.5 APPROACHES TO KNOWLEDGE MANAGEMENT

THE PROCESS APPROACH

There are two fundamental approaches to knowledge management: the process approach and the practice approach (see Table 9.1). The **process approach** attempts to codify organizational knowledge through formalized controls, processes, and technologies (Hansen et al, 1999). Organizations adopting the process approach may

TABLE 9.1   Process and Practice Approaches to Knowledge Management.

	Process Approach	*Practice Approach*
Type of Knowledge Supported	Explicit knowledge—codified in rules, tools, and processes (DeLong and Fahey, 2000)	Mostly tacit knowledge—unarticulated knowledge not easily captured or codified (Leonard and Sensiper, 1998)
Means of Transmission	Formal controls, procedures, and standard operating procedures with heavy emphasis on information technologies to support knowledge creation, codification, and transfer of knowledge (Ruggles, 1998)	Informal social groups that engage in storytelling and improvisation (Wenger and Snyder, 2000)
Benefits	Provides structure to harness generated ideas and knowledge (Brown and Duguid, 2000) Achieves scale in knowledge reuse (Hansen et al., 1999)	Provides an environment to generate and transfer high-value tacit knowledge (Brown and Duguid, 2000; Wenger and Snyder, 2000) Provides spark for fresh ideas and responsiveness to changing environment (Brown and Duguid, 2000)
Disadvantages	Fails to tap into tacit knowledge. May limit innovation and forces participants into fixed patterns of thinking	Can result in inefficiency. Abundance of ideas with no structure to implement them.
Role of Information Technology	Heavy investment in IT to connect people with reusable codified knowledge (Hansen et al., 1999)	Moderate investment in IT to facilitate conversations and transfer of tacit knowledge (Hansen et al., 1999)

Source: Adapted from Alavi, Kayworth, and Leidner (2003).

implement explicit policies governing how knowledge is to be collected, stored, and disseminated throughout the organization. The process approach frequently involves the use of information technologies, such as intranets, data warehousing, knowledge repositories, decision support tools, and groupware (Ruggles, 1998), to enhance the quality and speed of knowledge creation and distribution in the organizations. The main criticisms of the process approach are that it fails to capture much of the tacit knowledge embedded in firms and forces individuals into fixed patterns of thinking (Brown and Duguid, 2000; DeLong and Fahey, 2000; Von Grogh, 2000). This approach is favored by firms that sell relatively standardized products that fill common needs. Most of the valuable knowledge in these firms is fairly explicit because of the standardized nature of the products and services. For example, a kazoo manufacturer has minimal product changes or service needs over the years, and yet there is steady demand and a need to produce the item. In these cases, the knowledge is typically static in nature.

Even large firms that utilize tacit knowledge, such as Cap Gemini Ernst & Young, have invested heavily to ensure that the process approach works efficiently. The 250 people at Cap Gemini Ernst & Young's Center for Business Knowledge manage an electronic repository and help consultants find and use information. Specialists write reports and analyses that many teams can use. And each of Cap Gemini Ernst & Young's more than 40 practice areas has a staff member who helps codify and store documents. The resulting area databases are linked through a network (Hansen et al., 1999). Naturally, people-to-documents is not the only way consultants in firms like Cap Gemini Ernst & Young and Accenture share knowledge; they talk with one another as well. But they do place a high degree of emphasis on the codification strategy (Hansen et al., 1999).

THE PRACTICE APPROACH

In contrast, the **practice approach** to knowledge management assumes that a great deal of organizational knowledge is tacit in nature, and that formal controls, processes, and technologies are not suitable for transmitting this type of understanding. Rather than building formal systems to manage knowledge, the focus of this approach is to build the social environments or communities of practice necessary to facilitate the sharing of tacit understanding (Brown and Duguid, 2000; DeLong and Fahey, 2000; Gupta and Govindarajan, 2000; Hansen et al, 1999; Wenger and Snyder, 2000). These communities are informal social groups that meet regularly to share ideas, insights, and best practices. This approach is typically adopted by companies that provide highly customized solutions to unique problems. For these firms, knowledge is shared mostly through person-to-person contacts. Collaborative computing methods (e.g., GSS or e-mail) help people communicate. The valuable knowledge for these firms is tacit in nature, which is difficult to express, capture, and manage. In this case, the environment and the nature of the problems being encountered are extremely dynamic. Because tacit knowledge is difficult to extract, store, and manage, the explicit knowledge that points to how to find the appropriate tacit knowledge (people contacts, consulting reports) is made available to an appropriate set of individuals who might need it. Consulting firms generally fall into this category. Firms adopting the codification strategy implicitly adopt the network storage model in their initial knowledge management systems (Alavi, 2000).

The challenge to firms that adopt the personalization strategy, and hence the network storage model, is to develop methods to make the valuable tacit knowledge explicit, capture it, and contribute it to and transfer it from a knowledge repository in a knowledge management system. Several major consulting firms are developing methods to do so. They store pointers to experts within the KMS, but they also store the tips, procedures, and best practices as well as the context in which they work. To make their personalization strategies work, firms like Bain invest heavily in building networks of people and communications technology, such as telephone, e-mail, and videoconferencing. They also commonly have face-to-face meetings (Hansen et al., 1999).

In reality, a knowledge management initiative can, and probably will, involve both approaches. Process and practice are not mutually exclusive. Alavi, Kayworth, and Leidner (2003) describe the case of an organization that began its KM effort with a large repository but evolved the knowledge management initiative into a community-of-practice approach that existed side by side with the repository. In fact, community members would pass information from the community forum to the organizational repository when they felt that the knowledge was valuable outside their community. DSS in Action 9.2 illustrates how Texaco successfully manages its knowledge using the practice approach.

HYBRID APPROACHES

Many organizations use a hybrid of the process and practice approaches. Early in the development process, when it may not be clear how to extract tacit knowledge from its sources, the practice approach is used so that a repository stores only explicit knowledge that is relatively easy to document. The tacit knowledge initially stored in the repository is contact information about experts and their areas of expertise. Such information is listed so that people in the organization can find sources of expertise (e.g., the process approach). From this start, best practices can eventually be captured and managed, so the knowledge repository will contain an increasing amount of tacit knowledge over time. Eventually, a true process approach may be attained. But if the environment changes rapidly, only some of the best practices will prove useful.

DSS IN ACTION 9.2

TEXACO DRILLS FOR KNOWLEDGE

Texaco (www.texaco.com), a company that pumps over a million barrels of oil a day, has discovered a new source of power—the collective knowledge and expertise of its 18,000 employees in 150 countries around the world. Texaco believes that connecting people who have questions with people who have answers gives it the power to work faster and more efficiently.

At Texaco, managing knowledge is a critical business challenge. John Old, Texaco's knowledge guru, approaches this challenge with a strategy that leverages human connections. Old states that knowledge, by its nature, is contextual; thus, systems that simply allow people to record what they know are ineffective. He strongly believes that a successful knowledge management solution must recognize the importance of human connections.

Texaco uses technology to help people build personal relationships and share knowledge. One of the systems at work at Texaco is PeopleNet, a search engine for employees on the company's intranet. Employees who have questions can use PeopleNet to review profiles of their colleagues who might have the right answers. Texaco discovered that having biographies and pictures of its employees online makes it possible to establish credibility and trust between people who have not met each other. And it is trust that makes effective knowledge transfer possible.

Another tool that Texaco uses to connect its employees is a software system called Knowledge Mail from Tacit Knowledge Systems. This software analyzes e-mail sent and received by employees to help them make good contacts with colleagues who work on the same issues.

John Old speaks of several important lessons that Texaco has learned while managing knowledge. He points out that people are more eager to share knowledge when they are united by a clear, specific, and measurable business purpose. Knowledge sharing becomes even more successful when they trust each other and see direct benefits that can be derived from the knowledge exchange. In addition, it is important to give people enough time to reflect on what they know and what they need to learn.

Texaco's approach to knowledge management has provided many positive results. The knowledge management efforts help Texaco's employees successfully resolve numerous issues that range from adjusting oil well pumps to deciding whether or not to enter into new lines of business.

Source: Adapted from Fara Warner, "He Drills for Knowledge," *Fast Company*, September 2001.

Regardless of the type of knowledge management system developed, a storage location for the knowledge—a knowledge repository—of some kind is needed.

The J.D. Edwards intranet-based Knowledge Garden helps its consultants share best practices (practice approach) and find subject experts (process approach) who can help them solve problems faster and more consistently. The application codifies the company's knowledge base using Site Server taxonomies and delivers personalized updates automatically based on user needs (Microsoft Corporation, 2001).

Hansen et al. (1999) indicate that firms that attempted to straddle the two strategies (i.e., to use about half of each) in their knowledge management efforts *generally have failed*. Management consulting firms run into serious trouble when they straddle the strategies. When firms use either strategy exclusively, they also run into trouble. The most successful efforts involve about an 80/20 percent split in the strategies. With the practice approach, there is a need to provide some codified knowledge in a repository so that people can access it on an as-needed basis. With the process approach, it is necessary to provide access to knowledge contributors, as additional advice and explanations might prove useful or even necessary.

On the other hand, certain, highly skilled, research-oriented industries may exhibit traits that require about equal efforts with both approaches. For example, Koenig (2001) argues that the pharmaceutical firms in which he has worked indeed require

about a 50/50 split. We suspect that industries that require both a lot of engineering effort (how to create products) and heavy-duty research effort (where a large percentage of research is unusable) would fit the 50/50 hybrid category. Ultimately, any knowledge that is stored in a knowledge repository must be reevaluated, else the repository will become a *knowledge landfill*.

For many examples of these strategies in practice, see Gamble and Blackwell (2002) and Martin (2000).

BEST PRACTICES

Best practices are the activities and methods that the most effective organizations use to operate and manage various functions. Chevron, for example, recognizes four levels of best practices (O'Dell et al., 1998). They include:

1. A good idea that is not yet proven but makes intuitive sense.
2. A good practice, an implemented technique, methodology, a procedure, or process that has improved business results.
3. A local best practice, a best approach for all or a large part of the organization based on analyzing hard data. In other words, the scope within the organization of the best practice is identified: Can it be used in a single department or geographical region, or can it be used across the organization, or anywhere in between?
4. An industry best practice, similar to the third level but using hard data from industry.

Historically, the first knowledge repositories simply listed best practices and made them available within the firm. Now that knowledge repositories are electronic and Web-accessible, they can have wide-ranging impact on the use of knowledge throughout a firm. Raytheon successfully uses best practices to merge three distinct corporate cultures (see Swissler, 2001). See O'Dell and Grayson (2003) and O'Dell et al. (2003), and O'Dell and Grayson (1998) for more on best practices.

THE KNOWLEDGE REPOSITORY

A **knowledge repository** is neither a database nor a knowledge base in the strictest sense of the terms. Rather, a knowledge repository stores *knowledge*, which is often text-based and has very different characteristics. Do not confuse a knowledge repository with the knowledge base of an expert system. They are *very* different mechanisms.

Capturing knowledge is the objective of the knowledge repository. The structure of the repository is highly dependent upon the types of knowledge stored. The repository can range from simply a list of frequently asked (and obscure) questions and solutions, to a listing of individuals with their expertise and contact information, to detailed best practices for a large organization.

DEVELOPING THE KNOWLEDGE REPOSITORY

Most knowledge repositories are developed using several different storage mechanisms, depending upon the types and amount of knowledge to be maintained and used. Each has its strengths and weaknesses to be utilized for different purposes within a KM system. Developing a knowledge repository is not an easy task. The most important aspects and difficult issues are making the contribution of knowledge relatively easy for the contributor, and determining a good method for cataloging the knowledge. "One of the biggest hurdles in putting a formalized knowledge management structure . . . is making the structure as seamless as possible," according to Terry Jordan, VP of marketing for Hyperwave (hyperwave.com). "You really have to make the process painless, or you lose all of the knowledge that you are trying to capture because people don't want to have to go through an enormous number of steps" (Zimmermann, 2003b). The users should *not* be involved in running the storage and retrieval mechanisms of the knowledge repository. Typical development approaches include developing a large-scale Internet-based system, or purchasing a formal electronic document management system or a knowledge management suite. The structure and development of the knowledge repository are a function of the specific technology used for the knowledge management system.

9.6 INFORMATION TECHNOLOGY IN KNOWLEDGE MANAGEMENT

KNOWLEDGE MANAGEMENT SYSTEM CYCLE

A functioning knowledge management system follows six steps in a cycle (Figure 9.2). The reason for the cycle is that knowledge is dynamically refined over time. The knowledge in a good KM system is never finished because the environment changes over time, and the knowledge must be updated to reflect the changes. The cycle works as follows:

1. Create knowledge. Knowledge is created as people determine new ways of doing things or develop know-how. Sometimes external knowledge is brought in. Some of these new ways may become best practices.

FIGURE 9.2   THE KNOWLEDGE MANAGEMENT CYCLE

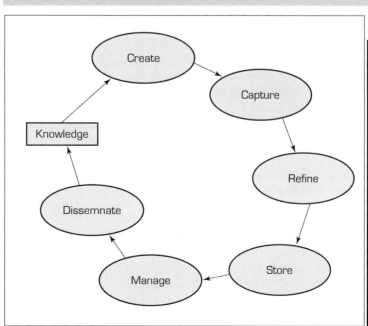

2. Capture knowledge. New knowledge must be identified as valuable and be represented in a reasonable way.
3. Refine knowledge. New knowledge must be placed in context so that it is actionable. This is where human insights (tacit qualities) must be captured along with explicit facts.
4. Store knowledge. Useful knowledge must then be stored in a reasonable format in a knowledge repository so that others in the organization can access it.
5. Manage knowledge. Like a library, the knowledge must be kept current. It must be reviewed to verify that it is relevant and accurate.
6. Disseminate knowledge. Knowledge must be made available in a useful format to anyone in the organization who needs it, anywhere and anytime.

As knowledge is disseminated, individuals develop, create, and identify new knowledge or update old knowledge which they replenish into the system (see Allard, 2003; Gaines, 2003).

Knowledge is a resource that is not consumed when used, though it can age. (For example, driving a car in 1900 was different from driving one now, but many of the basic principles still apply.) Knowledge must be updated. Thus, the amount of knowledge grows over time.

COMPONENTS OF KNOWLEDGE MANAGEMENT SYSTEMS

Knowledge management is more a methodology applied to business practices than a technology or a product. Nevertheless, information technology is *crucial* to the success of every knowledge management system. Information technology enables KM by providing the enterprise architecture upon which it is built. Knowledge management systems are developed using three sets of technologies: *communication, collaboration,* and *storage and retrieval.*

Communication technologies allow users to access needed knowledge, and to communicate with each other—especially with experts. E-mail, the Internet, corporate intranets, and other Web-based tools provide communication capabilities. Even fax machines and the telephone are used for communication, especially when the practice approach to knowledge management is adopted.

Collaboration technologies provide the means to perform group work. Groups can work together on common documents at the same time (synchronous) or at different times (asynchronous); in the same place, or in different places. This is especially important for members of a community of practice working on knowledge contributions. Other collaborative computing capabilities, such as electronic brainstorming, enhance group work, especially for knowledge contribution. Additional forms of group work involve experts working with individuals trying to apply their knowledge. This requires collaboration at a fairly high level. Other collaborative computing systems allow an organization to create a virtual space so that individuals can work online anywhere and at any time.

Storage and retrieval technologies originally meant using a database management system to store and manage knowledge. This worked reasonably well in the early days for storing and managing most explicit knowledge, and even explicit knowledge about tacit knowledge. However, capturing, storing, and managing tacit knowledge usually requires a different set of tools. Electronic document-management systems and specialized storage systems that are part of collaborative computing systems fill this void. These storage systems have come to be known as knowledge repositories.

We describe the relationship between these knowledge management technologies and the Web in Table 9.2.

TABLE 9.2   Knowledge Management Technologies and Web Impacts

Knowledge Management	*Web Impacts*	*Impacts on the Web*
Communication	Consistent, friendly, graphical user interface for client units Improved communication tools Convenient, fast access to knowledge and knowledgeable individuals Direct access to knowledge on servers	Knowledge captured and shared is utilized in improving communication, communication management, and communication technologies
Collaboration	Improved collaboration tools Enables anywhere/anytime collaboration Enables collaboration between companies, customers, and vendors Enables document sharing Improved, fast collaboration and links to knowledge sources Makes audio and video conferencing a reality, especially for individuals not using a LAN	Knowledge captured and shared is utilized in improving collaboration, collaboration management, and collaboration technologies (GSS)
Storage and Retrieval	Consistent, friendly, graphical user interface for clients Servers provide for efficient and effective storage and retrieval of knowledge	Knowledge captured and shared is utilized in improving data storage and retrieval systems, database management/ knowledge repository management, and database and knowledge repository technologies

TECHNOLOGIES SUPPORTING KNOWLEDGE MANAGEMENT

Several technologies have contributed to significant advances in knowledge management tools. Artificial intelligence, intelligent agents, knowledge discovery in databases, and Extensible Markup Language (XML) are examples of technologies that enable advanced functionality of modern knowledge management systems and form the base for future innovations in the KM field. See Davenport and Sena (2003), Gray and Tehrani (2003), Malafsky (2003), and O'Leary (2003) for descriptions of how many of these technologies are utilized in knowledge management systems.

ARTIFICIAL INTELLIGENCE

In the definition of knowledge management, *artificial intelligence* is rarely mentioned. However, practically speaking, AI methods and tools are embedded in a number of knowledge management systems, either by vendors or by system developers. AI methods can assist in identifying expertise, eliciting knowledge automatically and semiautomatically, interfacing through natural language processing, and intelligent search through intelligent agents. AI methods, notably expert systems, neural networks, fuzzy logic, and intelligent agents, are used in knowledge management systems to do the following:

- Assist in and enhance searching knowledge (e.g., intelligent agents in Web searches).
- Help establish knowledge profiles of individuals and groups.
- Help determine the relative importance of knowledge when it is contributed to and accessed from the knowledge repository.
- Scan e-mail, documents, and databases to perform knowledge discovery, determine meaningful relationships, glean knowledge, or induce rules for expert systems.
- Identify patterns in data (usually through neural networks).
- Forecast future results using existing knowledge.

- Provide advice directly from knowledge by using neural networks or expert systems.
- Provide a natural language or voice command–driven user interface for a knowledge management system.

INTELLIGENT AGENTS

Intelligent agents are software systems that learn how users work and provide assistance in their daily tasks. There are other kinds of intelligent agents as well (see Chapter 13). There are a number of ways that intelligent agents can help in knowledge management systems. Typically they are used to elicit and identify knowledge. Examples are:

- IBM (ibm.com) offers an intelligent data mining family, including Intelligent Decision Server (IDS), for finding and analyzing massive amounts of enterprise data.
- Gentia (Planning Sciences International, gentia.com) uses intelligent agents to facilitate data mining with Web access and data warehouse facilities.
- Convectis (HNC Software Inc., hnc.com, www.fairisacc.com/fairisaac/) uses neural networks to search text data and images to discern the meaning of documents for an intelligent agent. This tool is used by InfoSeek, an Internet search engine, to speed up the creation of hierarchical directories of Web topics.

Combining intelligent agents with enterprise knowledge portals is a powerful technique that can deliver to users exactly what they need to perform their tasks. The intelligent agent learns what the user prefers to see, and how the user organizes it. Then the intelligent agent takes over to provide it at the desktop, just as a good administrative assistant would.

KNOWLEDGE DISCOVERY IN DATABASES

Knowledge discovery in databases is a process used to search for and extract useful information from volumes of documents and data. It includes tasks known as knowledge extraction, data archaeology, data exploration, data pattern processing, data dredging, and information harvesting. All of these activities are conducted automatically and allow quick discovery even by nonprogrammers. Data and document mining is ideal for eliciting knowledge from databases, documents, e-mail, and so on. Data are often buried deep within very large databases, data warehouses, text documents, or knowledge repositories, all of which may contain data, information, and knowledge gathered over many years. (For more on data mining, see Chapter 5.)

AI methods are useful data mining tools that include automated knowledge elicitation from other sources. Intelligent data mining discovers information within databases, data warehouses, and knowledge repositories that queries and reports cannot effectively reveal. **Data mining** tools find patterns in data and may even (automatically) infer rules from them. Patterns and rules can be used to guide decision-making and forecast the effect of these decisions. KDD can also be used to identify the meaning of data or text, using KM tools that scan documents and e-mail to build an expertise profile of a firm's employees. Data mining can speed up analysis by providing needed knowledge.

Extending the role of data mining and knowledge discovery techniques for knowledge externalization, Bolloju et al. (2002) propose a framework for integrating knowledge management into enterprise environments for next-generation decision support

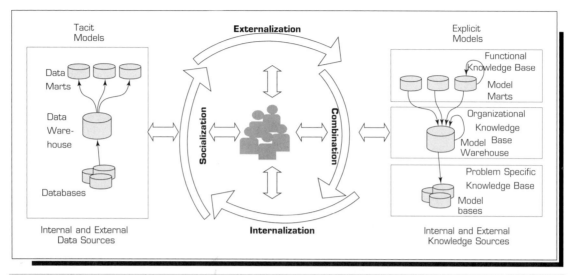

FIGURE 9.3   FRAMEWORK FOR INTEGRATING DECISION-SUPPORT AND KNOWLEDGE MANAGEMENT SYSTEMS.

Source: N. Bolloju, M. Khalifa, and E. Turban, "Integrating Knowledge Management into Enterprise Environments for the Next Generation of Decision Support," *Decision Support Systems,* Vol. 33, June 2002.

systems. Their framework, shown in Figure 9.3, includes **model marts** and **model warehouses**. Model marts and model warehouses are analogous for models to data marts and data warehouses (Chapter 5). They act as repositories of knowledge created by employing knowledge-discovery techniques on past decision instances stored in data marts and data warehouses. The model marts and model warehouses capture operational and historical decision models, similar to the data in data marts and data warehouses. For example, a model mart can store decision rules corresponding to problem-solving knowledge of different decision-makers in a particular domain, such as loan approvals in a banking environment.

This integrated framework accommodates different types of knowledge transformations proposed by Nonaka (1995). Systems built around this framework are expected to enhance the quality of support provided to decision-makers, support knowledge management functions such as acquisition, creation, exploitation, and accumulation, facilitate discovery of trends and patterns in the accumulated knowledge, and provide means for building up organizational memory.

EXTENSIBLE MARKUP LANGUAGE (XML)

Extensible Markup Language (XML) enables standardized representations of data structures so that data can be processed appropriately by heterogeneous systems without case-by-case programming. This method suits e-commerce applications and supply chain management systems that operate across enterprise boundaries. XML not only can automate processes and reduce paperwork, but also can unite business partners and supply chains for better collaboration and knowledge transfer. XML-based messages can be taken from back-end repositories and fed out through the portal interface and back again. A portal that uses XML allows the company to communicate better with its customers, linking them in a virtual demand chain where changes in customer requirements are immediately reflected in production plans. Wide adoption of XML can pretty much solve the problem of integrating data from disparate sources. Due to its potential to tremendously simplify systems integration, XML may become the universal language that all portal vendors embrace (see Ruber, 2001; Wallach, 2001).

Vendors are quickly moving to integrate the advantages offered by XML standards. For example, Interwoven's content management software, Teamsite, now fully supports XML, enabling organizations to provide content available in any format across the enterprise. Sequoia Software's XML Portal Server (XPS) and Hummingbird's Enterprise Portal Suite also support the XML standard for data exchange.

9.7 KNOWLEDGE MANAGEMENT SYSTEMS IMPLEMENTATION

The KMS challenge is to identify and integrate the three essential components (communication technologies, collaboration technologies, and storage and retrieval technologies) to meet the knowledge management needs of an organization. The earliest knowledge management systems were developed with networked technology (intranets), collaborative computing tools (groupware), and databases (for the knowledge repository). They were constructed from a variety of off-the-shelf IT components (see Ruggles, 1998). Many organizations, especially large management consulting firms like Accenture and J.D. Edwards, developed their knowledge architecture with a set of tools that provided the three technology types. Collaborative computing suites such as Lotus Notes/Domino and GroupSystems OnLine provide many KMS capabilities. Other systems were developed by integrating a set of tools from a single or multiple vendors. For example, J.D. Edwards used a set of loosely integrated Microsoft tools and products to implement its Knowledge Garden KMS, as did KPMG. In the early 2000s, KMS technology has evolved to integrate the three components into a single package. These include enterprise knowledge portals and knowledge management suites

KNOWLEDGE MANAGEMENT PRODUCTS AND VENDORS

Technology tools that support knowledge management are called **knowware**. Most knowledge management software packages include one or more of the following tools: collaborative computing tools, knowledge servers, enterprise knowledge portals, electronic document management systems, knowledge harvesting tools, search engines, and knowledge management suites. Many packages provide several tools because they are necessary in an effective knowledge management system. For example, most electronic document management systems also include collaborative computing capabilities.

Knowledge management systems can be purchased in whole or in part from one of numerous software development companies and enterprise information systems vendors, they can be acquired through major consulting firms, or can be outsourced to the application service providers (ASPs). All three alternatives will be discussed in the later part of this chapter. *KMWorld* publishes a "Buyers' Guide" in every April edition.

SOFTWARE DEVELOPMENT COMPANIES AND ENTERPRISE INFORMATION SYSTEMS VENDORS

Software development companies and enterprise information systems vendors offer numerous knowledge management packages: from individual tools to comprehensive knowledge management suites. The variety of knowware that is readily available on the market allows companies to find the tools that will meet their unique knowledge management needs. We next review some software packages and their vendors in each of the seven knowware categories that we identified earlier.

Collaborative Computing Tools.   Collaboration tools, or groupware, were the first used to enhance tacit knowledge transfer within an organization. One of the earliest collaborative computing systems, GroupSystems, provides many of the tools that support group work, including electronic brainstorming and idea categorization. Lotus Notes/Domino provides an enterprisewide collaborative environment. Other collaboration tools include MeetingPlace (Latitude), QuickPlace (Lotus Development Corp.), eRoom (eRoom Technology Inc.), Groove Networks (groove.net), and PlaceWare (PlaceWare Inc.).

Knowledge Servers.   A knowledge server contains the main knowledge management software, including the knowledge repository, and provides access to other knowledge, information, and data. Examples of knowledge servers include the Hummingbird Knowledge Server, the Intraspect Software Knowledge Server, the Hyperwave Information Server, the Sequoia Software XML Portal Server, and Autonomy's Intelligent Data Operating Layer (IDOL) Server. Autonomy's IDOL Server connects people to content, content to content, and people to people through modules that enable organizations to integrate various personalization, collaboration, and retrieval features. The server provides a knowledge repository, a central location for searching and accessing information from many sources, such as the Internet, corporate intranets, databases, and file systems, thereby enabling the efficient distribution of time-sensitive information. The server seamlessly extends and integrates with the company's e-business suite, allowing rapid deployment applications that span the enterprise and can even leverage AI-assisted technology to harvest knowledge assets.

Enterprise Knowledge Portals.   **Enterprise knowledge portals (EKP)** are the doorways into many knowledge management systems. They have evolved from the concepts underlying executive information systems, group-support systems, Web browsers, and database management systems. They are an ideal way to configure a knowledge management system. Most combine data integration, reporting mechanisms, and collaboration, while document and knowledge management is handled by a server. An enterprise information portal is a virtual place on a network of online users. The portal aggregates each user's total information needs: data and documents, e-mail, Web links and queries, dynamic feeds from the network, and shared calendars and task lists. The personal information portal has evolved into an enterprise knowledge portal (Silver, 2000).

When enterprise information portals first entered the market, they did not contain knowledge management features. Now most do. Leading portal vendors include Autonomy, Brio, Corechange, DataChannel, Dataware, Epicentric, Glyphica, Intraspect, Hummingbird, InXight, KnowledgeTrack, IBM/Lotus, Knowmadic, OpenText, Plumtree, Portera, Sequoia Software, Verity, and Viador. Database vendors such as Microsoft, Oracle, and Sybase also sell knowledge portals.

The KnowledgeTrack Knowledge Center offers integrated business-to-business (B2B) functions and can scale from dot-coms to large enterprises. Knowledge Center can be built into the enterprise architecture instead of simply sitting on top, the way most intranet portals do. The Knowledge Center integrates with external data sources, including ERP, online analytical processing (OLAP), and CRM systems. Knowledge Center supports communities of practice and enables them for large-project management, allowing information to be shared among all of the extended enterprise value chains.

Hyperwave's Hyperwave Information Portal (HIP) aggregates information from disparate sources and features dynamic link management, which verifies the quality of the link and hides links to unauthorized content. HIP manages connections between information sources and makes structured and unstructured corporate information searchable via a standard browser. In DSS in Action 9.3, we describe how Smith Lyons, a Canadian law firm, developed a successful enterprise knowledge portal. See Levinson (2002) for an example of how a university used a portal to connect students, faculty, staff, alumni, and businesses to share services, research, and applications. For more on portals, see Bhatt and Fenner (2001), Collins (2001), Firestone (2003), Levinson (2002), Liautaud and Hammond (2000), Mack et al. (2001), Roberts-Witt (2000), Wallach (2001), Zimmermann (2002), and *InfoWorld* (2000).

Electronic Document Management (EDM).   Electronic document management systems focus on the document in electronic form as the collaborative focus of work. EDM systems allow users to access needed documents, generally via a Web browser

---

DSS IN ACTION 9.3

PORTAL OPENS THE DOOR TO LEGAL KNOWLEDGE

Richard Van Dyk, CIO of Smith Lyons (www.smithlyons.com), a Toronto-based international law firm, knew exactly what kind of system he was looking for to manage the firm's documents and knowledge. He had spent a year defining his requirements and had composed a complex flowchart on his whiteboard. Smith Lyons wanted to take thousands of pieces of information, give people different views into that information, and have a high level of link management. Van Dyk considered document management tools to be too inflexible for the way lawyers practice law. "We needed a flexible environment that we could massage and manipulate and that would allow people to continue working as they have," says Van Dyk.

"Lawyers are basically document generators," he says. "Due to time constraints, they spend more time collecting documents than organizing them." Because the firm's 550 attorneys and support specialists each had a distinct working methodology, often reflecting the requirements of a specific area of practice, Van Dyk knew they would resent having a rigid system they could not easily personalize.

The profusion of document management, knowledge management, and portal systems makes finding the right product difficult. Each has its strengths and weaknesses. Organizations coming from a document-centric perspective, like Smith Lyons, need to organize and manage content at the back end while developing highly customized individual user interfaces at the front end.

The solution that best met Van Dyk's criteria was the Hyperwave Information Portal from Hyperwave

Information Management of Westford, Massachusetts. "What I liked about Hyperwave's portal environment was that as soon as we installed it, we had a framework to begin knowledge mapping—tagging and indexing documents by subject and key words and phrases—and for building the database structures in our repositories," says Van Dyk. The firm had definite ideas on how to structure templates and specific pieces of information that are unique to a legal practice. These issues included myriad legal forms and documents generated by the proprietary software applications used for different practice areas.

Once the portal was set up, Smith Lyons's developers began to customize the views for each desktop PC by creating wizards that connect users to their own secure information areas and to intranet pages containing company activity information. In development, too, is an extranet on which lawyers will be able to post status reports to clients and deliver confidential documents and contracts.

"That flexibility in building our DM portal allows our lawyers and specialists to be incredibly specific in their searches," says Van Dyk. Lawyers also can share their accumulated knowledge more easily with colleagues in the same practice areas, by referencing legal citations, court decisions, and winning strategies that have worked in the past.

Source: Adapted from P. Ruber, "Finding the Right Balance: A Canadian Law Firm Interrogated Its Requirements Before Selecting a Portal Solution," *Knowledge Management,* September 2000.

over a corporate intranet. EDM systems enable organizations to better manage documents and workflow for smoother operations. They also allow collaboration on document creation and revision.

Many knowledge management systems use an EDM system as the knowledge repository (see Case Application 9.2). There is a natural fit in terms of the purpose and benefits of the two. Pfizer uses a large-scale document management system to handle the equivalent of truckloads of paper documents of drug approval applications passed between Pfizer and the FDA, its regulating agency. This EDM system dramatically cut the time required for FDA submission and review, making Pfizer more competitive in getting new and effective drugs to market (Blodgett, 2000).

Systems like DocuShare (Xerox Corporation) and Lotus Notes (Lotus Development Corporation) allow direct collaboration on a common document. Some other EDM systems include EDMS (Documentum Inc.), Enterprise Work Management (Eastman Software Inc.), FYI (Identitech), The Discovery Suite (FileNet Corporation), Livelink (Open Text Corporation), PageKeeper Pro (Caere Corporation), Pagis Pro (ScanSoft Inc.), Xpedio (IntraNet Solutions), and CaseCentral.com (Document Repository Inc.).

A new approach to electronic document management, called **content management systems (CMS)**, are changing the way documents and their content are managed. A content management system produces dynamic versions of documents, and automatically maintains the "current" set for use at the enterprise level. With the explosion of Web-based materials, organizations need a mechanism to provide content that is consistent and accurate across the enterprise. EDM systems, enterprise information portals, and other CMS fill that need. The goal is to provide large numbers of knowledge workers with access to large amounts of unstructured text (Sullivan, 2001). An IDC survey of attendees at the KMWorld 2001 Conference and Exposition in October indicated that 63 percent of all respondents have or planned to implement a CMS, while 59 percent rated CMS as very to critically important (Feldman, 2002). Also see Bankes (2003), Clyman, 2002; Jia (2002), and Lamont (2003b).

A subset of CMS is *business rules management*. New software tools and systems, such as Ilog JRules and Blaze Advisor, have been developed to handle these smaller chunks of content.

Knowledge Harvesting Tools.   Tools for capturing knowledge unobtrusively are helpful because they allow a knowledge contributor to be minimally (or not at all) involved in the knowledge-harvesting efforts. Embedding this type of tool in a KMS is an ideal approach to knowledge capture. Tacit Knowledge Systems's KnowledgeMail is an expertise-location software package that analyzes users' outgoing e-mail to parse subject expertise. It maintains a directory of expertise and offers ways to contact experts while maintaining privacy controls for them. Autonomy's ActiveKnowledge performs a similar analysis on e-mail and other standard document types. Intraspect Software's Knowledge Server monitors an organization's group memory, captures the context of its use, such as who used it, when, for what, how it was combined with other information, and what people said about it, and then makes the information available for sharing and reuse. KnowledgeX by KnowledgeX, Inc. and a number of other products provide similar functionality.

Search Engines.   Search engines perform one of the essential functions of knowledge management—locating and retrieving necessary documents from vast collections accumulated in corporate repositories. Companies like Google, Verity, and Inktomi offer a wide selection of search engines capable of indexing and cataloging files in various formats as well as of retrieving and prioritizing relevant documents in response to user queries.

Knowledge Management Suites. Knowledge management suites are complete knowledge management solutions out-of-the-box. They integrate the communications, collaboration, and storage technologies into a single convenient package. A knowledge management suite must still access internal databases and other external knowledge sources, so some integration is required to make the software truly functional. IBM/Lotus offers an extensive range of knowledge management products: the Domino platform, QuickPlace and Sametime, Discovery Server and Learning Space, as well as the WebSphere portal. See DSS in Action 9.4 to learn how Commerce Bank implemented a knowledge management system based on the IBM/Lotus platform. Several vendors also provide fairly comprehensive sets of tools for KM initiatives, which include Dataware Knowledge Management Suite, KnowledgeX by KnowledgeX, Inc., and many others. Autonomy Knowledge Management Suite offers document categorization and workflow integration. Microsoft provides central components of knowledge management solutions, and is working on developing an encompassing KM framework. Some enterprise information systems vendors, such as SAP, PeopleSoft, and Oracle, are developing knowledge management-related technologies as a platform for business applications. Siebel Systems is repositioning itself as a business-to-employee knowledge management platform. Knowledge management suites are powerful approaches to developing a KMS because they offer one user interface, one data repository, and one vendor.

CONSULTING FIRMS

All of the major consulting firms (Accenture, Cap Gemini Ernst & Young, etc.) have massive internal knowledge management initiatives. Usually these become products after they succeed internally and provide assistance in establishing knowledge management systems and measuring their effectiveness. Consulting firms also provide some direct, out-of-the-box proprietary systems for vertical markets. Most of the major management consulting firms define their knowledge management offerings as a *service*. For more on consulting firm activities and products, see McDonald and Shand (2000).

KNOWLEDGE MANAGEMENT APPLICATION SERVICE PROVIDERS (ASPs)

Application service providers (ASPs) have evolved as a form of KMS outsourcing on the Web. There are many ASPs for e-commerce on the market. For example, Communispace is a high-level ASP collaboration system that focuses on connecting people to people (not just people to documents) to achieve specific objectives, regardless of geographic, time, and organizational barriers. As a hosted ASP solution, it is easy to rapidly deploy within organizations. Unlike conventional KM systems that organize data and documents, or chat rooms where people simply swap information, Communispace contains a rich assortment of interactions, activities, and tools that connect people to the colleagues who can best help them make decisions, solve problems, and learn quickly. Communispace is designed to build trust online. It attempts to make a community self-conscious about taking responsibility for its actions and knowledge. Its Climate component helps participants to measure and understand how people are feeling about the community. The Virtual Café gives dispersed employees a way to meet and learn about each other through pictures and profiles.

DSS IN ACTION 9.4

KNOWLEDGE MANAGEMENT: YOU CAN BANK ON IT

Commerce Bank is a $15.4 billion financial institution that is quickly growing to become a dominant player in the financial services market of Philadelphia and southern New Jersey. During its 30 years of existence, it has developed a network of 214 branches and made ambitious plans for continuous growth. Commerce Bank names itself "America's Most Convenient Bank. It lives up to that name by maintaining a strong banking network and by empowering each branch to make business decisions in an effort to better meet the needs of its customers.

While undergoing explosive growth, Commerce Bank encouraged its associates to learn all about its customers and the right ways to service them. However, the company realized that its most important asset, knowledge, was locked away in the file cabinets and in the heads of its associates. To support this initiative, Commerce Bank needed to tap into that knowledge and find a way to train employees consistently and conveniently across the entire branch network.

The first step for new employees is Commerce University, a boot camp where they are instilled with the fundamentals of customer service. But the program covers only a few of the range of issues that an associate might encounter.

The need for knowledge management at Commerce Bank was apparent. Jack Allison, VP of systems development says: "We had folks in administration that could spend 70 percent of their time answering calls and clarifying answers for branches. At times, we could wait weeks or months for the right answer to certain questions. Knowing that training may not give answers for every scenario, we needed to give associates a tool that could help them find any answer to any topic at any time. We have so many regulations and products, we needed a way to give our employees all the knowledge to process these."

Commerce bank envisioned a solution—a workflow-based knowledge management system that could provide instant answers to questions for the bank's employees and online customers. To make this vision a reality, Commerce chose to develop a system based on IBM's Lotus Notes, which the bank has been using since 1995. Using IBM's Domino server, the Lotus Notes client, and an application development tool kit,

Commerce Bank created a full-fledged knowledge management system, called Wow Answer Guide.

Introduced in 2000, Wow Answer Guide provides a central repository of knowledge about all bank transactions, helps employees learn a process and respond to customer inquiries, and stores information electronically. In addition, the system allows employees to register for the bank's continuing education courses.

The complete Wow Answer Guide contains more than 400 applications, and Commerce plans to add even more, such as a customer-relationship management system. The flexibility of the platform simplifies the application-development process and allows adding new features and expanding functionality with minimal investments of time and effort.

"[The Wow Answer Guide] is especially good for the green associate or veteran who is still learning how to process a new product," says Allison. "We don't want our associates on a scavenger hunt to get the correct information."

Commerce Bank realized that knowledge management would be beneficial not only to the bank's employees, but also to its clients. "We wanted to put information in our customers' hands so they could conduct [online] transactions with confidence," said Allison. In the summer of 2000, Commerce Bank deployed a new version of Wow Answer Guide that empowered the bank's online customers.

Knowledge management at Commerce Bank proved to be an effective investment. According to Allison, the application has saved the bank $20,000 per week, or approximately $1 million a year. In fact, the bank achieved a return on investment within a month of launching Wow Answer Guide.

By drawing on the power of the Domino platform, Commerce Bank created workflow-based applications that streamline internal knowledge sharing and route data and information to the appropriate employees within the organization. This dramatically reduces the completion time for approval-intensive transactions, improves the bank's capacity, and minimizes labor costs.

Source: Adapted from Deena Amato-McCoy, "Commerce Bank Manages Knowledge Profitably," *Bank Systems & Technology*, January 2003.

A recent trend among application service providers is to offer a complete knowledge management solution, including a KM suite and the consulting to set it up as CommuniSpace does.

INTEGRATION OF KM SYSTEMS WITH OTHER BUSINESS INFORMATION SYSTEMS

Since a knowledge management system is an enterprise system, it must be integrated with other enterprise and information systems in an organization. Obviously, when it is designed and developed, it cannot be perceived as an add-on application. It must be truly integrated into other systems. Through the structure of the organizational culture (changed if necessary), a knowledge management system and its activities can be directly integrated into a firm's business processes. For example, a group involved in customer support can capture its knowledge to provide help on customers' difficult problems. In this case, help-desk software would be one type of package to integrate into a KMS, especially into the knowledge repository.

Since a KMS can be developed on a knowledge platform/server consisting of communication, collaboration, and storage technologies, and most firms already have many such tools and technologies in place, it is often possible to develop a KMS in the organization's existing tools (e.g., Lotus Notes/Domino). Or an enterprise knowledge portal can provide universal access and an interface into all of an individual's relevant corporate information and knowledge. In this case, the KMS effort would provide the linkage for everyone into the entire enterprise information system.

INTEGRATION WITH DECISION SUPPORT SYSTEMS (DSS) / BUSINESS INTELLIGENCE (BI) SYSTEMS

Knowledge management systems typically do not involve running models to solve problems. This is typically done in decision support systems/business intelligence systems. However, since a knowledge management system provides help in solving problems by applying knowledge, part of the solution may involve running models. A KMS can integrate into a set of models and data, and can activate them if a specific problem calls for it. Also, the know how and best practice application of models can be stored in a knowledge management system.

INTEGRATION WITH ARTIFICIAL INTELLIGENCE

Knowledge management has a natural relationship with artificial intelligence (AI) methods and software, though knowledge management, strictly speaking, is not an artificial intelligence method. There are a number of ways in which knowledge management and artificial intelligence can integrate. For example, if the knowledge stored in a KMS is to be represented and used as a sequence of if-then-else rules, then an expert system becomes part of the KMS (see Rasmus, 2000). An expert system could also assist a user in identifying how to apply a chunk of knowledge in the KMS. Natural language processing assists the computer in understanding what a user is searching for. Artificial neural networks help to *understand* text to determine the applicability of a specific chunk of knowledge as it applies to a particular problem. They are also used to enhance search engines. The most common integration of artificial intelligence and knowledge management is in identifying and classifying expertise by examining e-mail messages and documents. These include artificial intelligence-based tools, such as Tacit Knowledge Systems Inc. (tacit.com) ActiveNet and KnowledgeMail, and Inxight Software (inxight.com) Categorizer.

Much work is being done in the field of artificial intelligence relating to knowledge engineering, tacit-to-explicit knowledge transfer, and knowledge identification, understanding, and dissemination. Companies are attempting to realign these technologies and the resultant products with knowledge management. The AI technologies most often integrated with knowledge management are intelligent agents, expert systems, neural networks, and fuzzy logic. Several specific methods and tools were described earlier.

INTEGRATION WITH DATABASES AND INFORMATION SYSTEMS

Since a KMS utilizes a knowledge repository, sometimes constructed out of a database system or an electronic document management system, it can automatically integrate to this part of the firm's information system. As data and information updates are made, the KMS can utilize them. As was described earlier, knowledge management systems also attempt to glean knowledge from documents and databases through artificial intelligence methods, a process known as **knowledge discovery in databases (KDD)**. This knowledge is then represented textually within the knowledge repository described earlier.

INTEGRATION WITH CUSTOMER RELATIONSHIP MANAGEMENT SYSTEMS

Customer relationship management (CRM) systems help users in dealing with customers (see Chapter 8). One aspect is the help-desk notion described earlier. But CRM goes much deeper. It can develop usable profiles of customers and predict their needs, so that an organization can increase sales and better serve its clients. A KMS can certainly provide tacit knowledge to people who use CRM directly in working with customers.

INTEGRATION WITH SUPPLY CHAIN MANAGEMENT SYSTEMS

The supply chain is often considered to be the logistics end of the business. If products do not move through the organization and go out the door, the firm will fail. So it is important to optimize the supply chain and manage it properly. A new set of software called supply chain management (SCM) systems attempts to do so (see Chapter 8). SCM can benefit through integration with KMS because there are many issues and problems in the supply chain that require the company to combine both tacit and explicit knowledge. Accessing such knowledge will directly improve supply chain performance.

INTEGRATION WITH CORPORATE INTRANETS AND EXTRANETS

Communication and collaboration tools and technologies are necessary for KMS to function. KMS is not simply integrated with the technology of intranets and extranets, but is typically developed on them as the communications platform. Extranets are specifically designed to enhance the collaboration of a firm with its suppliers and sometimes with customers (see Chapter 7). If a firm can integrate its KMS into its intranets and extranets, not only will knowledge flow more freely, both from a contributor and to a user (either directly or through a knowledge repository), the firm can also capture knowledge directly with little user involvement, and can deliver it when the system "thinks" that a user needs knowledge.

9.8 ROLES OF PEOPLE IN KNOWLEDGE MANAGEMENT

Managing a knowledge management system requires great effort. Like any other information technology, getting it started, implemented, and deployed requires a champion's effort. Many issues of management, people, and culture must be considered to make a knowledge management system a success. In this section, we address those issues. Managing the knowledge repository typically requires a full-time staff (similar to a reference library staff). This staff examines, structures, filters, catalogs, and stores knowledge so that it is meaningful and can be accessed by the people who need it. The staff assists individuals in searching for knowledge, and performs "environmental scanning:" If they identify specific knowledge that an employee or client might need, they send it directly to whoever needs it, thus adding value to the organization. (This is standard procedure for Accenture knowledge management personnel.) Finally, the knowledge repository staff may create communities of practice (see Case Application 9.1) to gather individuals with common knowledge areas to identify, filter, extract, and contribute knowledge to a knowledge repository.

Most of the issues concerning the success, implementation, and effective use of a knowledge management system are people issues. And since a knowledge management system is an enterprisewide effort, many people are involved. They include the chief knowledge officer (CKO), the CEO, the other officers and managers of the organization, members and leaders of communities of practice, KMS developers, and KMS staff. Each person or group has an important role in either the development, management, or use of a KMS. By far, the CKO has the most visible role in a KMS effort, but the system cannot succeed unless the roles of all the players are established and understood. And the team must consist of the right people, possessing the appropriate level of experience, to take on the various roles (see Robb, 2001).

THE CHIEF KNOWLEDGE OFFICER

Knowledge management projects that involve establishing a knowledge environment conducive to the transfer, creation, or use of knowledge attempt to build *cultural receptivity*. These attempts are centered on changing the behavior of the firm to embrace the use of knowledge management. Behavioral-centric projects require a high degree of support and participation from the senior management of the organization to facilitate their implementation. Most firms developing knowledge management systems have created a knowledge management officer, a *chief knowledge officer (CKO)*, at the senior level. The objectives of the CKO's role are to maximize the firm's knowledge assets, design and implement knowledge management strategies, effectively exchange knowledge assets internally and externally, and promote system use. He or she is responsible for developing processes that facilitate knowledge transfer (Adams, 2001).

A chief knowledge officer must do the following (adapted from Duffy, 1998):

- Set knowledge management strategic priorities.
- Establish a knowledge repository of best practices.
- Gain a commitment from senior executives to support a learning environment.
- Teach information seekers how to ask better and smarter questions.
- Establish a process for managing intellectual assets.
- Obtain customer satisfaction information in near real-time.
- Globalize knowledge management.

The CKO is responsible for defining the area of knowledge within the firm that will be the focal point, based on the mission and objectives of the firm (Davis, 1998). The CKO is responsible for standardizing the enterprisewide vocabulary and controlling the knowledge directory. This is critical in areas that must share knowledge across departments, to ensure uniformity. CKOs must get a handle on the company's repositories of research, resources, and expertise, including where they are stored and who manages and accesses them (e.g, perform a knowledge audit). Then the CKO must encourage pollination among disparate workgroups with complementary resources (see McKeen and Staples, 2003).

The CKO is responsible for creating an infrastructure and cultural environment for knowledge sharing. He or she must assign or identify (and encourage/motivate) the *knowledge champions* within the business units. The CKO's job is to manage the content their groups produce (e.g., the Chrysler Tech Clubs; see Case Application 9.1), continually add to the knowledge base, and encourage colleagues to do the same. Successful CKOs should have the full and enthusiastic support of their managers and of top management. Ultimately, the CKO is responsible for the entire knowledge management project while it is under development, and then for management of the system and the knowledge once it is deployed.

A CKO needs a range of skills to make KM initiatives succeed. These attributes are indispensable according to CKOs and consultants (see Flash, 2001a):

- Interpersonal communication skills to convince employees to adopt cultural changes.
- Leadership skills to convey the KM vision and passion for it.
- Business acumen to relate KM efforts to efficiency and profitability.
- Strategic thinking skills to relate KM efforts to larger goals.
- Collaboration skills to work with various departments and persuade them to work together.
- Ability to institute effective educational programs.
- Understanding of information technology and its role in advancing KM.

CEO, OFFICERS, AND MANAGERS OF THE ORGANIZATION

Briefly, the CEO is responsible for championing the KM effort. He or she must ensure that a competent and capable CKO is found and that the CKO can obtain all the resources (including access to people with knowledge sources) needed to make the project a success. The CEO must also gain organization-wide support for contributions to and use of the KMS. The CEO must also prepare the organization for the cultural changes that are about to occur. Support is the critical responsibility of the CEO. The CEO is the primary change agent of the organization (see Flash, 2001b).

The officers—the CFO, COO, CIO and others—generally must make available to the CKO the resources needed to get the job done. The chief financial officer (CFO) must ensure that the financial resources are available. The chief operating officer (COO) must ensure that people begin to embed knowledge management practices into their daily work processes. There is a special relationship between the CKO and chief information officer (CIO). Usually the CIO is responsible for the IT vision of the organization and for the IT architecture, including databases and other potential knowledge sources. The CIO must cooperate with the CKO in making these resources available. Knowledge management systems are expensive propositions, and it is wise to use existing systems if they are available and capable.

Managers must also support the KM effort and provide access to sources of knowledge. In many KMS, managers are an integral part of the communities of practice.

COMMUNITIES OF PRACTICE

The success of many KM systems has been attributed to the active involvement of the people who contribute to and benefit from using the knowledge. Consequently, communities of practice have appeared within organizations that are serious about their knowledge management efforts. As discussed earlier, a **community of practice (COP)** is a group of people in an organization with a common professional interest. Ideally, all the KMS users should each be in at least one COP. Creating and nurturing COPs properly is one key to KMS success (see Lesser, Fontaine, and Slusher, 2000; Liedtka, 2002; Wenger, 2002a, 2002b)

COPs are where the organizational culture shift really happens when developing and deploying KMS. A supportive culture must be developed for a KMS to succeed (see Lesser, Fontaine, and Slusher, 2000; Wenger, 2002a, 2002b). In DSS in Action 9.5, we describe how Xerox Corp. successfully generated improved practices and cost savings through communities of practice.

In a sense, a community of practice owns the knowledge that it contributes because it manages the knowledge on its way into the system and must approve modifications to it. The community is responsible for the accuracy and timeliness of the knowledge it contributes, and for identifying its potential use. A number of researchers have investigated how successful COPs form and function. In Table 9.3, we illustrate the many ways that communities of practice add value to the organization through knowledge management efforts. Basically, COP make organizations run smoothly because they enable knowledge flow. Informed people make better decisions. People who are involved are happier at work.

Wenger, McDermott, and Snyder (2002a, 2002b) recommend seven design principles for successful communities of practice. Each of these facilitate knowledge creation and use. We describe these in DSS in Focus 9.6.

Storck and Hill (2000) investigated one of the earliest communities of practice at Xerox. When established at Xerox, the COP was a new organizational form. The word

---

DSS IN ACTION 9.5

KNOWLEDGE MANAGEMENT PREVENTS COPYING ERRORS OF THE PAST THROUGH COMMUNITIES

In the past, Xerox Corporation shared stories among service technicians, but only in small groups, and its service manuals were very out of date. Technicians generally improvised in the field, and there was no mechanism for sharing solutions throughout the entire organization.

To better manage its corporate knowledge, Xerox Corp. developed Eureka. This knowledge management system for copier service technicians captures best practices and especially solutions to problems. Now similar situations can be dealt with efficiently and effectively anywhere in the world. Eureka's effectiveness was demonstrated when Xerox had a situation with a leading copier that developed intermittent failures all over the world. Xerox was unable to identify the source of the problem and had already replaced six machines. The problem was occurring again in Rio de Janeiro, where Xerox estimated it would cost about $40,000 to replace machines, not to mention the cost of customer goodwill. Gilles Robert, a service technician at Xerox Canada in Montreal, had traced the problem to a 50-cent fuse

holder that had a tendency to oxidize and needed to be swabbed with alcohol every so often. He had posted the tip on Eureka. When the copiers were failing in Rio, Eureka was just coming online in Brazil in Portuguese. The engineers there mentioned the problem, and Eureka provided the solution.

Personal recognition motivates technicians to submit tips to Eureka. Each tip has the author's name published with it. By early 2000, Eureka contained nearly 5,000 tips. Xerox has deployed it to over 44,000 technicians worldwide. One of Eureka's guiding principles is, "We should never create the same solution twice. If a solution already exists, it should be used rather than recreating a new solution. In addition, we should focus on continuously improving existing solutions." Eureka! It works!

Sources: Adapted from S. Barth, "Knowledge as a Function of X," *Knowledge Management,* February 2000; C. Moore, "Eureka! Xerox Discovers Way to Grow Community Knowledge," *KMWorld,* October 1999.

TABLE 9.3   How Communities of Practice Add Value to the Organization

Name of Added Value	*Attributes That Create Value*
Creation of higher-quality knowledge	• Diversity in membership and less emphasis on hierarchical status reduce the likelihood of groupthink • Limited requirements for formal reporting allows people to perform riskier brainstorming • Reflection process occurring at the end of meetings consolidates learning
Fewer surprises and plan revisions	• Broad participation diffuses knowledge across business units • Openness of interaction format results in effective conflict resolution
Greater capacity in dealing with unstructured problems	• Work occurs under a set of superordinate goals; not task goals • The sponsoring organization accepts self-evolving community role • Knowledge leaders can emerge based on issues instead of by assignment to a team or roles within a team
More effective knowledge sharing among business and corporate staff units	• Voluntary participation implies higher motivation leading to faster, deeper learning internalization • Trust increases due to indeterminate life span and long-term relationships
Improved likelihood of implementing joint goal	• The community yields greater external validity because it exists external to the formal organizational structure • The community has more influence than an individual, given the organizational level of the community members
More effective individual development and learning	• Group learning is more effective than learning alone • The community's development process embodies learning opportunities through practice

Source: Adapted from Table 5.2 "Strategic Community: Adding Value to the Organization," in Lesser, Fontaine, and Slusher (2000), p. 77.

community captured the sense of responsible, independent action that characterized the group, which continued to function within the standard boundaries of the large organization. Management sponsored the community, but did not mandate it. Community members were volunteers. We list and describe the six key principles that support communities of practice at Xerox in Table 9.4. Brailsford (2001) described how Hallmark Cards built its communities of practice. Similar discoveries were made. For more on communities of practice, see Barth (2000a), Brown and Duguid (2002), Cothrel and Williams (1999a, 1999b), Eisenhart (2000), Lesser, Fontaine, and Slusher (2000) Lesser and Prusak (2002), Liedtka (2002), McDermott (2002), Smith and McKeen (2003), Storck and Hill (2000, 2002), and Wenger (2002a, 2002b).

KMS DEVELOPERS

These are the team members who actually develop the system. They work for the CKO. Some are organizational experts who develop strategies to promote and manage the organizational culture shift. Others are involved in system software and hardware selec-

---

DSS IN FOCUS 9.6

SEVEN PRINCIPLES FOR DESIGNING SUCCESSFUL COMMUNITIES OF PRACTICE

Here are seven ways to encourage vibrant communities of practice in an organization:

1. **Design for evolution.** Communities of practice are organic, and many organizational factors influence their direction. Plan carefully. One does not so much manage a community as shepherd it.

2. **Open a dialog between inside and outside.** Good community design requires an understanding of the community's potential to develop and steward knowledge, but it often takes an outside perspective to help members see possibilities. The COP should not close in on itself.

3. **Invite different levels of participation.** There are typically three main levels of community participation. The first is a small core of people who actively participate in discussions. As the COP matures, this group evolves into the leadership. The next level is the active group. These members attend meetings regularly and participate occasionally in the community forums, but not regularly or as intensely as the core group. A large portion of the COP is peripheral and rarely participates. Do not exclude these people. They often utilize the knowledge generated. The key to good community participation, and a healthy degree of movement between levels, is to design community activities that allow participants at all levels to feel like full members.

4. **Develop public and private spaces.** The heart of a community is the web of relationships among community members, and private space is necessary to get the relationships to grow.

5. **Focus on Value.** Since participation is generally voluntary, the COP must provide value. Communities must create events, activities, and relationships that help their potential value emerge and enable them to discover new ways to harvest it rather than determine expected value in advance.

6. **Combine familiarity and excitement.** Vibrant communities supply divergent thinking and activity. Routine activities provide stability for relationship building.

7. **Create a rhythm for the community.** There is a tempo associated with the members' interactions. This rhythm is the strongest indicator of its aliveness and potential. The COP should contain a balance between large and small group sessions, and between idea-sharing forums and tool-building projects. The rhythm will evolve with the community, but it is important to find the right one at each stage.

Source: Adapted from Wenger, McDermott, and Snyder, 2002a, 2002b.

---

tion, programming, testing, deploying, and maintaining the system. Still others initially are involved in training users. Eventually the training function moves to the KMS staff.

KMS STAFF

Enterprisewide KM systems require a full-time staff to catalog and manage the knowledge. This staff is either located at the firm's headquarters or dispersed in knowledge centers throughout the organization. Most large consulting firms have more than one knowledge center.

Earlier we described the function of the staff as similar to that of reference librarians. They actually do much more. Some members are functional area experts who are now cataloging and approving knowledge contributions, and pushing the knowledge out to clients and employees who they believe can use the knowledge. These functional experts may also work in a liaison role with the functional areas of the communities of practice. Others work with users to train them on the system or help them with their

TABLE 9.4   The Six Key Principles Supporting Communities of Practice at Xerox

Community Characteristic	Actions
Interaction format	Consists of meetings, collaborative computing, interaction structure, e-mail, etc.
Organizational culture	Leverages common training, experience, and vocabulary.
	Facilitates working around constraints.
Mutual interest	Builds commitment and promotes continuous improvement of processes.
Individual and collective learning	Recognizes and rewards knowledge contribution and use; leverages knowledge; provides a culture of knowledge sharing.
Knowledge sharing	Embeds knowledge sharing into work practices.
	Reinforces with immediate feedback the value of knowledge sharing.
Community processes and norms	Builds trust and identity.
	Minimizes linkage to the formal control structure.
	Motivates the community to establish its own governance processes.

Source: Adapted from J. Storck and P. A. Hill, "Knowledge Diffusion Through Strategic Communities," *Sloan Management Review*, Vol. 41, No. 2, Winter 2000.

searches. Still others work on improving the system's performance by identifying better methods with which to manage knowledge. For example, Cap Gemini Ernst & Young has 250 people managing the knowledge repository and assisting people in finding knowledge at its Center for Business Knowledge. Some staff members disseminate knowledge, while others are liaisons with the 40 practice areas. They codify and store documents in their areas of expertise (see Hansen et al., 1999).

9.9 ENSURING SUCCESS OF KNOWLEDGE MANAGEMENT

Organizations can gain several benefits from implementing a knowledge management strategy. Tactically, they can accomplish some or all of the following: reduce loss of intellectual capital due to people leaving the company; reduce costs by decreasing the number of times the company must repeatedly solve the same problem, and by achieving economies of scale in obtaining information from external providers; reduce redundancy of knowledge-based activities; increase productivity by making knowledge available more quickly and easily; and increase employee satisfaction by enabling greater personal development and empowerment. The best reason of all may be a strategic need to gain a competitive advantage in the marketplace (Knapp, 1998). There are many factors necessary for knowledge management to succeed. For example, Gold, Malhotra and Segars (2001) describe how a knowledge infrastructure consisting of technology, structure, and culture along with a knowledge process architecture of acquisition, conversion, application, and protection are essential "preconditions" for effective knowledge management. The situation in an organization must be "right" in order for a knowledge management effort to succeed. See DSS in Action 9.7 for an example of a knowledge management success in law enforcement.

DSS IN FOCUS 9.7

SCOTLAND YARD COULD CAPTURE JACK THE RIPPER NOW!

Scotland Yard (www.met.police.uk) could not capture Jack the Ripper, who terrorized London from 1888 to 1891. Now Scotland Yard could use its new knowledge management system to track him down. The new Scotland Yard (Metropolitan Police Service) has 25,000 police officers and 11,000 civilian staff. The Service polices 788 square miles of Greater London. To improve its capabilities, the Service has implemented a collaborative, Web-based knowledge management system to improve access to and management of case files. Now police can access over 600,000 case files online, of which the hard copy occupies over nine miles of shelf space in a West London repository. The new system pro-vides officers and support staff with a much faster, more efficient method of tracking down case papers, which can often contain information that will help in new investigations. The system enables more precise search results, ultimately enabling officers to investigate crimes more effectively. And the complete records are available 24/7. Expected savings at the onset of the project were estimated to be $2.4 million. Sherlock Holmes, who worked with officers in the Yard (fictionally), would have been proud.

Source: Adapted from Haimila, 2000.

See O'Dell, Elliot, and Hubert (2003), Smith and McKeen (2003), and Tobin (2003) for more on KM success.

KNOWLEDGE MANAGEMENT VALUATION

In general, companies take either an asset-based approach to knowledge management valuation or one that links knowledge to its applications and business benefits (Skyrme and Amidon, 1998). The former approach starts by identifying intellectual assets and then focuses management's attention on increasing their value. The second uses variants of a *balanced scorecard,* where financial measures are balanced against customer, process, and innovation measures. Among the best-developed measurement methods in use are the balanced scorecard approach (see Berkman, 2002; Kestelyn, 2002; Lunt, 2001; Miyake, 2002; Roberts, 2001; Schroek, 2001; Zimmermann, 2003a), Skandia's Navigator, Stern Stewart's economic value added (EVA), M'Pherson's inclusive valuation methodology, the return on management ratio, and Levin's knowledge-capital measure. Lunt (2001) describes how Duke Children's Hospital, Hilton, and Borden have improved performance across their enterprises through the balanced scorecard approach, leading to better customer service. See Skyrme and Amidon (1998) for details on how these measures work in practice.

Another method of measuring the value of knowledge is to estimate its price if it were offered for sale. Most firms are reluctant to sell knowledge unless they are expressly in the business of doing so. Generally a firm's knowledge is an asset that has competitive value, and if it leaves the organization, the firm loses its competitive advantage can repeat sell. However, the knowledge and access to the knowledge can be priced at a value making it worth a firm's while to sell. For example, American Airlines' Decision Technologies Corp. grew from a small internal analysis team in the 1970s. Initially the team was created to solve problems and provide decision support only to American Airlines. As it grew, it became an independent corporation within AMR Corp., and it began to provide consulting and systems to other airlines, including American's competitors. The major consulting firms are in the business of selling expertise. Therefore their knowledge management efforts, which began as internal systems, evolved into quite valuable systems that their clients use on a regular basis. Clearly the same knowledge can be repeatedly sold.

Success indicators with respect to knowledge management are similar to those for assessing the effectiveness of other business-change projects. They include growth in the resources attached to the project, growth in the volume of knowledge content and usage, the likelihood that the project will survive without the support of a particular individual or individuals, and some evidence of financial return either for the knowledge management activity itself or for the entire organization (Davenport et al., 1998).

FINANCIAL METRICS

Even though traditional accounting measures are incomplete for measuring KM, they are often used as a quick justification for a knowledge management initiative. Returns on investment (ROIs) are reported to range from 20:1 for chemical firms to 4:1 for transportation firms, with an average of 12:1, based on the knowledge management projects assisted on by one consulting firm (Abramson, 1998).

In order to measure the impact of knowledge management, experts recommend focusing KM projects on specific business problems that can be easily quantified. When the problems are solved, the value and benefits of the system become apparent (MacSweeney, 2002).

At Royal Dutch/Shell group, the return on investment was explicitly documented: the company had invested $6 million in a knowledge management system in 1999 and within two years obtained $235 million in reduced costs and new revenues (King, 2001). Hewlett-Packard offers another example of documented financial returns. Within six months of launching its @HP company-wide portal in October of 2000, Hewlett-Packard realized a $50 million return on its initial investment of $20 million. This was largely due to a reduction in volume of calls to internal call centers and to the new paperless processes (Roberts-Witt, 2002). Also see the Web Chapter on Mitre Corp, which invested less than $8 million for an estimated $60 million return in two years.

The financial benefit might be perceptual, rather than absolute, but it need not be documented in order for the KM system to be considered a success.

NON-FINANCIAL METRICS

Traditional methods of financial measurement may fall short when measuring the value of a KMS, because *they do not consider intellectual capital an asset*. Therefore it is necessary to develop procedures for valuing the *intangible* assets of an organization, as well as to incorporate models of intellectual capital that in some way quantify innovation and the development and implementation of core competencies.

When evaluating intangibles, there are a number of new ways to view capital. In the past, only customer goodwill was valued as an asset. Now the following are included (adapted from Allee, 1999):

- *External relationship capital:* how an organization links with its partners, suppliers, customers, and regulators.
- *Structural capital:* systems and work processes that leverage competitiveness, such as information systems.
- *Human capital:* the individual capabilities, knowledge, skills, and so on, that people have.
- *Social capital:* the quality and value of relationships with the larger society.
- *Environmental capital:* the value of relationships with the environment.

For example, a knowledge management initiative undertaken by Partners HealthCare System, Inc. has not resulted in quantifiable financial benefits, but has greatly increased the social capital of the company. The knowledge management system for physicians implemented by Partners reduced the number of serious medication errors by 55 percent at some of Boston's most prestigious teaching hospitals. Calculating return on investment for such a system turns out to be an extremely difficult proposition, which is why only a small fraction of hospitals use similar systems. While the company is unable to determine how the system affects its bottom line, it is willing to justify the costs based on the system's benefits to the society (Melymuka, 2002). For more on KM valuation, see Conway (2003), Hanley and Malafsky (2003), Housel and Bell (2001), Smith and McKeen (2003), Stone and Warsone (2003), Strassmann (2001), and Zimmermann (2003a).

CAUSES OF KM FAILURE

No system is infallible. There are many cases of knowledge management failing. Estimates of KM failure rates range from 50 percent to 70 percent, where a failure is interpreted to mean that *all* of the major objectives were not met by the effort (Ambrosio, 2000). Failures typically happen when the knowledge management effort mainly relies on technology and does not address whether the proposed system will meet the needs and objectives of the organization and its individuals (Swan et al., 2000; also see the Opening Vignette, Barth, 2000b; Berkman, 2001; Malhotra, 2003; McDermott, 2002; Roberts-Witt, 2000; and Sviokla, 2001). Other issues include lack of commitment (this occurred at a large Washington, DC, constituent lobbying organization), and not providing reasonable incentive for people to use the system (as occurred at Pillsbury Co.; see Barth, 2000b; Silver, 2000). DSS in Action 6.19 illustrates how Frito-Lay narrowly avoided failure of its KMS. Unfortunately, Ford and Firestone were not as lucky when the tires started blowing out on the Ford Explorer. See DSS in Action 9.8 for details. In this case, the knowledge was available, just not integrated in a way that allowed stakeholders to access and analyze it. Similarly, the disasters of September 11, 2001 might have been avoided or lessened. In the United States, the Department of Homeland Security is making a massive effort to integrate its sources of knowledge (see Datz, 2002; Matthews, 2002; Moore, 2002; the Chapter 5 Opening Vignette and several DSS in Actions). Soo et al. (2002) outline several knowledge "traps" that can lead to failure. We describe these in DSS in Focus 9.9. Barth (2000b) describes several important knowledge management initiatives that miserably. Finally, Roberts-Witt (2002) outlines how enterprises implementing portals can and do fail.

FACTORS LEADING TO KM SUCCESS

To increase the probability of success of knowledge management projects, companies must assess whether there is a strategic need for knowledge management in the first place. The next step is to determine whether the current process of dealing with organizational knowledge is adequate and whether the organization's culture is ready for procedural changes. Only when these issues are resolved should the company consider technology infrastructure and decide whether a new system is needed. When the right technological solution is chosen, it becomes necessary to properly introduce it to the entire organization and gain the participation of every employee (Kaplan, 2002). One should not rely too heavily on technology to succeed (see the Opening Vignette, the online cases in Web Chapters, and Jacob and Ebrahimpur, 2001). Typically a knowledge management effort is only about 10 to 20 percent technology. The rest of the effort is organizational.

Major factors that lead to knowledge management project success (adapted from Davenport et al., 1998) include:

DSS IN ACTION 9.8

FORD AND FIRESTONE SKID AND SPIN WHEN KNOWLEDGE MANAGEMENT FAILS

The Ford Explorer was one of the most successful SUV automobiles in history, until a failure to share related knowledge scattered throughout Ford and Firestone prevented both companies from discovering a major problem with the Explorer's tires in time to recall them in 2000. (See news reports from 2000 for more details on the tire problem and the recall.)

In 1995, well before the tire problem occurred, Ford had initiated a knowledge management system, the Best Practices Replication Process, that has produced $1 billion in benefits. The system began as a manual process, and, as it succeeded, evolved into an online Web-based **knowledge repository model** system on an intranet. Ford's knowledge management system has three simple procedural rules:

The process is managed, with distinct roles and responsibilities. Simple organisms don't need central nervous systems; complex ones can't live without them.

No practice would get into the system unless proven.

Every improvement would be described in the both the technical language of the work group involved and its country's language(s): time, head count, gallons, quality. That way Mexican and French employees could easily compare *manzanas* with *pommes*, as well as pesos with euros.

Ford structures *communities of practice* around how vehicles are made. Each group has a companywide community administrator, selected by the director of manufacturing. At each plant, each community chooses an individual as the focal point. The focal point spends one to two hours a week working on knowledge management as part of his or her job.

From 1995 through 2000, about 3,000 proven best practices were shared across Ford's manufacturing

operations. The documented value of the shared knowledge in 2000 totaled $850 million, with another $400 million expected in the following year from new ideas. The system is so successful that Royal Dutch/Shell and Nabisco have licensed the process and parts of it have been patented.

Even though Ford shares knowledge extremely well, no one knew about the tremendous problem with the Explorer tires. This disaster happened because:

> Knowledge is best shared *within* communities. People with something in common talk more than strangers do. Neither Ford's nor Firestone's social network was rich enough to support the kind of communication that might have uncovered the problem. They were outside the loop in this matter—or rather, there was not even a loop.

The more widely dispersed knowledge is, the more powerful a force is needed to extract and share it. At Ford, managers are given improvement goals to meet, and they first look at the Best Practices Replication System for ideas that they know worked at least somewhere. The particular task pulls knowledge from wherever it is. Unfortunately, the knowledge at Ford and Firestone indicating a potential problem was buried too deeply, and was spread far and wide throughout organizations.

One lesson to be learned from the Firestone/Ford KM failure is this: Organizations should extract as much important knowledge as they can because they just never know what might prove truly important, or when.

Source: Adapted from T. A. Stewart, "Knowledge Worth $1.25 Billion," *Fortune*, Vol. 142, No. 13, November 27, 2000.

- A link to a firm's economic value, to demonstrate financial viability and maintain executive sponsorship.
- A technical and organizational infrastructure on which to build.
- A standard, flexible knowledge structure to match the way the organization performs work and uses knowledge. Usually, the organizational culture must change to effectively create a knowledge-sharing environment.
- A knowledge-friendly culture leading directly to user support.
- A clear purpose and language, to encourage users to buy into the system. Sometimes simple, useful knowledge applications need to be implemented first.
- A change in motivational practices, to create a culture of sharing.

KNOWLEDGE MANAGEMENT TRAPS

A recent study of the knowledge management practices of six firms identified several knowledge "traps" into which even the best firms fell. These can help show the way to avoid failure in KM efforts. The lessons include:

1. Formal databases must be treated as strategic tools rather than mere storage facilities. Sometimes database systems are perceived as too complicated to utilize, and so they are underutilized. Strategic information is overlooked because it is too hard to get to. The organization must make it possible to get to the information, and to really capture and codify knowledge.

2. Managing formal database systems per se does not equate to knowledge management. Databases are important for capturing information, but a strong, informal network is necessary for good access. Also, databases are only one component of a knowledge management system. When textual data are stored, we really consider this a knowledge repository, not a database.

3. Informal networking is an important source of knowledge, but over-reliance on it can be detrimental. Even though informal channels often contain critical information, there is an inherent risk that informal interactions may be too dependent on chance. Lack of structure can lead to knowledge loss.

4. To ensure that informal networking is less susceptible to randomness, it should be made more structured. See above. Structure helps

5. Senior management may not know the true state of their firm's knowledge systems. There is a distinct difference between the perceptions of senior managers and junior managers in their view of the effectiveness of their knowledge management systems. This is mainly because the senior managers do not actively use the system, while junior managers do. The attitudes of senior managers may not be the best measure of the success of a KMS.

6. You can't teach an old dog new tricks. Basically, older managers do not absorb new training well.

7. Unless carefully managed, knowledge is a dark power. It is difficult to determine how to generate knowledge that is truly useful for an organization. Organizational factors may hinder the capture and free distribution of knowledge. Trust is critical.

8. Creativity in problem-solving is the main driver of new knowledge creation and innovation. But creativity must be supported by appropriate mechanisms. Resources must be provided to help employees be creative. Often lack of time hinders individuals. They may be expected to contribute and use knowledge in a KMS, while not diminishing any other aspect of their jobs.

Source: Adapted from C. Soo et al., "Knowledge Management: Philosophy, Processes, and Pitfalls, *California Management Review*, Vol. 44, No. 4, Summer 2002, pp. 129–150.

- Multiple channels for knowledge transfer—because individuals have different ways of working and expressing themselves. The multiple channels should reinforce one another. Knowledge transfer should be easily accomplished and as unobtrusive as possible.
- A level of process orientation to make a knowledge management effort worthwhile. In other words, new, improved work methods can be developed.
- Nontrivial motivational methods, such as rewards and recognition, to encourage users to contribute and use knowledge.
- Senior management support. This is critical to initiate the project, provide resources, help identify important knowledge on which the success of the organization relies, and market the project.

Effective knowledge sharing and learning require cultural change within the organization, new managerial practices, senior management commitment, and technological support. The organizational culture must shift to a culture of sharing. This should be handled through strong leadership at the top, and by providing knowledge management tools that truly make people's jobs better. As for encouraging system use and knowledge sharing goes, people must be *properly* motivated to contribute knowledge. The mechanism for doing so should be part of their jobs, and their salaries should reflect this. People must also be motivated to utilize the knowledge in the KMS. Again, this should be part of their jobs and their reward structures.

As more companies develop knowledge management capabilities, some of the ground rules are becoming apparent. Success depends on a clear strategic logic for knowledge sharing, the choice of appropriate infrastructure (technical or non-technical), and an implementation approach that addresses the typical barriers: motivation to share knowledge, resources to capture and synthesize organizational learning, and ability to navigate the knowledge network to find the right people and data.

POTENTIAL DRAWBACKS TO KNOWLEDGE MANAGEMENT SYSTEMS

While managing knowledge has many positive outcomes, as discussed in examples throughout this chapter, it would be short sighted to not consider the potential negative outcomes associated with reusing knowledge. Henfridsson and Söderholm (2000) analyze the situation that faced Mrs. Fields cookies. Mrs. Fields grew remarkably fast and successfully during the early 1980s. A key aspect of the company's strategy was to provide expertise directly from the headquarters to every store. As the number of stores increased, the only feasible way to achieve direct control was through the use of information systems designed to mimic the decision-making of the real Debbi Fields. Systems placed in each store would input data (e.g., temperature, day of the week, date); the system would process them and output instructions telling the store manager, say, how many cookies of each type to bake each hour. In essence, the software provided each store manager with explicit directions for planning each day's production, sales, and labor scheduling, along with inventory control and ordering. Because of the well-functioning computer systems, which in principle were systems designed to make the company's tacit knowledge available to all stores, Mrs. Fields was able to successfully function with few managerial levels. However, Mrs. Fields was very slow to respond as the market began to change and consumers became more health conscious. By embedding so much knowledge into systems incapable of adaptation, the organization tied itself to a certain way of doing things and failed to engage in knowledge creation (i.e., failed to pick up the signals in the environment that might have suggested a change in strategy or product focus). By the early 1990s, the company had fallen into bankruptcy. Mrs. Fields's situation illustrates that *while organizations may achieve significant short-term gains through knowledge management systems, they must not neglect the creative process of new knowledge creation, less they find themselves applying yesterday's solutions to tomorrow's problems.*

CLOSING REMARKS

For millennia we have known about the effective use of knowledge and how to store and reuse it. Intelligent organizations recognize that knowledge is an intellectual asset, perhaps the only one that grows over time, and, when harnessed effectively, can sustain competition and innovation. Organizations can use information technology to perform true knowledge management. Leveraging an entire organization's intellectual resources can have tremendous financial impact.

With knowledge management, the definition is clear, the concepts are clear, the methodology is clear, the challenges are clear and surmountable, the benefits are clear and can be substantial, and the tools and technology—though incomplete and somewhat expensive—are viable. Key issues are organizational culture, executive sponsorship, and measuring success. Technological issues are minimal compared to these. Knowledge management is not just another expensive management fad. Knowledge management is a new paradigm for how we work.

❖ CHAPTER HIGHLIGHTS

- Knowledge is different from information and data. Knowledge is information that is contextual, relevant, and actionable. It is dynamic in nature.
- Tacit (unstructured, sticky) knowledge is usually in the domain of subjective, cognitive, and experiential learning; explicit (structured, leaky) knowledge deals with more objective, rational, and technical knowledge, and is highly personal and hard to formalize.
- A learning organization has an organizational memory and a means to save, represent, and share it.
- Organizational learning is the development of new knowledge and insights that have the potential to influence behavior.
- The ability of an organization to learn, develop memory, and share knowledge is dependent on its culture. Culture is a pattern of shared basic assumptions.
- Knowledge management is a process that helps organizations identify, select, organize, disseminate, and transfer important information and expertise that typically reside within the organization in an unstructured manner.
- The fastest, most effective and powerful way to manage knowledge assets is through the systematic transfer of best practices.
- Knowledge management requires a major transformation in organizational culture to create a desire to share (give and receive) knowledge, and a commitment to KM at all levels of a firm.
- The knowledge management model involves the following cyclical steps: create, capture, refine, store, manage, and disseminate knowledge.
- The chief knowledge office (CKO) is primarily responsible for changing the behavior of the firm to embrace the use of knowledge management and then managing the development operation of a knowledge management system.
- Communities of practice (COPs) provide pressure to break down the cultural barriers that hinder knowledge management efforts.
- Knowledge management is an effective way for an organization to leverage its intellectual assets.
- It is difficult to measure the success of a KMS. Traditional methods of financial measurement fall short because they do not consider intellectual capital an asset.
- The two knowledge management approaches are the process approach and the practice approach.
- The two strategies used for knowledge management initiatives are the personalization strategy and the codification strategy.
- The two storage models used for knowledge management projects are the repository storage model and the network storage model.
- Standard knowledge management initiatives involve the creation of knowledge bases, active process management, knowledge centers, collaborative technologies, and knowledge webs.
- A knowledge management system is generally developed using three sets of technologies: communication, collaboration, and storage.
- A variety of technologies can make up a knowledge management system: the Internet, intranets, data warehousing, decision support tools, groupware, and so on. Intranets are the primary means of displaying and distributing knowledge in organizations.
- Knowledge management is not just another expensive management fad. It is a new paradigm for the way we work.

❖ KEY WORDS

- best practices
- chief knowledge officer (CKO)
- content management system (CMS)
- community of practice (COP)
- data mining
- electronic document management (EDM)
- enterprise Knowledge Portal (EKP)
- explicit knowledge
- intellectual asset
- intellectual capital
- knowledge
- knowledge audit
- knowledge-based economy

- knowledge discovery in databases (KDD)
- knowledge harvesting
- knowledge management (KM)
- knowledge management suites
- knowledge management system (KMS)

- knowledge repository
- knowledge repository model
- knowware
- leaky knowledge
- learning organization
- model marts
- model warehouses

- organizational culture
- organizational learning
- organizational memory
- practice approach
- process approach
- sticky knowledge
- tacit knowledge

❖ QUESTIONS FOR REVIEW

1. Describe what is meant by an intellectual asset.
2. Define knowledge and knowledge management.
3. Define explicit knowledge. Why is it also called leaky knowledge?
4. Define tacit knowledge. Why is it also called sticky knowledge?
5. How can tacit knowledge be transferred or shared?
6. Define organizational learning and relate it to knowledge management.
7. Define organizational memory and relate it to the idea of a knowledge repository.
8. Define organizational culture.
9. List the ways that organizational culture can impact on a knowledge management effort.
10. What is the primary goal of knowledge management?
11. Describe the process approach to knowledge management.
12. Describe the practice approach to knowledge management.
13. Describe the roles and responsibilities of the people involved in a knowledge management system, especially the CKO.
14. What is a community of practice?
15. List the steps in the cyclic model of knowledge management. Why is it a cycle?
16. List the steps of knowledge management implementation.
17. List the major knowledge management success factors.
18. Describe the role of IT in knowledge management.

❖ QUESTIONS FOR DISCUSSION

1. Why is the term "knowledge" so hard to define?
2. Describe and relate the different characteristics of knowledge.
3. Explain why it is important to capture and manage knowledge.
4. Compare and contrast tacit knowledge and explicit knowledge.
5. Explain why organizational culture must sometimes change before knowledge management is introduced.
6. How does knowledge management attain its primary objective?
7. How can employees be motivated to contribute to and use knowledge management systems?
8. What is the role of a knowledge repository in knowledge management?
9. Explain the importance of communication and collaboration technologies to the processes of knowledge management.
10. Explain why firms adopt knowledge management initiatives.
11. Explain how the wrong organizational culture can reduce the effectiveness of knowledge management.
12. Explain the role of the CKO in developing a knowledge management system. What major responsibilities does he or she have?
13. What is meant by a culture of knowledge sharing?
14. Discuss the knowledge management success factors.
15. Why is it so hard to evaluate the impacts of knowledge management?
16. Explain how the Internet and related technologies (Web browsers, intranets, etc.) enable knowledge management.
17. List three top technologies most frequently used for implementing knowledge management systems and explain their importance.
18. Explain the roles of a community of practice.
19. Describe an enterprise knowledge portal and explain its significance.

❖ EXERCISES

1. Make a list of all the knowledge management methods you use during your day (work and personal). Which are the most effective? Which are the least effective? What kinds of work or activities does each knowledge management method enable?
2. Read the Sigma Case Application in the Web Chapter and answer the two Case Questions.
3. Investigate the literature for information on the position of CKO. Find out what percentage of firms with KM initiatives have CKOs and what their responsibilities are.
4. Investigate the literature for new measures of success (metrics) for knowledge management and intellectual capital. Write a report on your findings.
5. Describe how each of the key elements of a knowledge management infrastructure can contribute to its success.
6. Based on your own experience or on the vendor's information, list the major capabilities of a particular knowledge management product, and explain how it can be used in practice.
7. Describe how to ride a bicycle, drive a car, or make a peanut butter and jelly sandwich. Now have someone else try to do it based solely on your explanation. How can you best convert this knowledge from tacit to explicit (or can't you)?
8. Examine the top five reasons that firms initiate knowledge management systems, and investigate why these are important in a modern enterprise.
9. Read the article by E. Berkman titled "Don't Lose Your Mind Share," available at *cio.com*. Describe the major problems that Hill and Knowlton faced in February 1999, and what Ted Graham did to solve them.
10. Read the book by Thomas Cahill, *How the Irish Saved Civilization* (New York: Anchor, 1996), and describe how Ireland became a knowledge repository for Western Europe just before the fall of the Roman Empire. Explain in detail why this was important for Western civilization and history.
11. Examine your university, college, school, etc., and describe the roles that the faculty, administration, support staff, and students have in the creation, storage, and dissemination of knowledge. Explain how the process works. Explain how technology is currently used and how it potentially could be used.

❖ GROUP EXERCISES

1. Compare and contrast the capabilities and features of electronic document management with those of collaborative computing and of knowledge management systems. Each team represents one type of system.
2. Search the Internet for knowledge management products and systems, and create categories for them. Assign one vendor to each team. Describe the categories you created and justify them.
3. If you are working on a decision-making project in industry for this course as part of the project (if not, use one from another class or from work), examine some typical decisions in the related project. How would you extract the knowledge you need? Can you use that knowledge in practice? Why or why not?
4. Read the article by A. Genusa titled "Rx for Learning," available at *cio.com* (February 1, 2001), which describes Tufts University Medical School's experience with knowledge management. Determine how these concepts and such a system could be implemented and used at your college or university. Explain how each aspect would work, or if not, explain why not.

❖ INTERNET EXERCISES

1. How does knowledge management support decision-making? Identify products or systems on the Web that help organizations accomplish knowledge management. Start with *brint.com, decision–support.net,* and *knowledge.com*. Try one out and report your findings to the class.
2. Try the KPMG Knowledge Management Framework Assessment Exercise at *kmsurvey.londonweb.net* and assess how well your organization (company or university) is doing with knowledge management. Are the results accurate? Why or why not?
3. Search the Internet to identify sites dealing with knowledge management. Start with *google.com,* *kmworld.com, kmmag.com*, and *km-forum.org*. How many did you find? Categorize the sites based on whether they are academic, consulting firms, vendors, and so on. Sample one of each and describe the main focus of the site.
4. Identify five real-world knowledge management success stories by searching vendor Web sites (use at least three different vendors). Describe them. How did knowledge management systems and methods contribute to their success? What features do they share? What different features do individual successes have?

5. Search the Internet for vendors of knowledge management suites, enterprise knowledge portals, and out-of-the-box knowledge management solutions. Identify the major features of each product (use three from each), and compare and contrast their capabilities.

6. J.D. Edwards (*jdedwards.com*) developed a knowledge management intranet initiative called the *Knowledge Garden.* Access both the J.D. Edwards and Microsoft Web sites and investigate its current capabilities.

DAIMLERCHRYSLER EBOKS WITH KNOWLEDGE MANAGEMENT

In 1980 Chrysler Corporation (www.daimlerchrysler. com) came back from near bankruptcy with innovative designs and a view of a shared culture in design, development, and manufacturing. The company began new ways of looking at its business, its suppliers, and its workers. After the acquisition of American Motors Corporation (AMC) in 1987, executives developed and deployed advanced, dedicated platform design and production methods, which showed enormous potential. Jack Thompson, the technology center development director, worked closely with Chairman Lee Iacocca on the development of a modern new engineering and design facility. Thompson designed the center around knowledge-sharing and productivity principles: open air, natural light, and escalators (because people don't talk on elevators/lifts).

In 1994 the tech center opened, providing a home for a transformed engineering culture. Two years later, the corporate headquarters was moved next to the tech center so executives could be nearby. By 2000, over 11,000 people were working at the Auburn Hills, Michigan, center. In November 1998, Daimler-Benz became the majority owner of Chrysler Corporation, renaming the company DaimlerChrysler. Chrysler's fast, efficient, and innovative nature, as a result of the extremely successful platform approach to design and engineering, led to the buy-in—the largest merger in manufacturing history.

Platform production at DaimlerChrysler has teams of engineers focused on a single type of car platform (small car, minivan, etc.), working on new models as a system from concept to production. Cars are designed by a single team considering customer needs and preferences, as opposed to the standard practice of organizing the new designs by organizational functions (silos). Platform teams of employees work and learn together focused on the product, with a payoff in market responsiveness, reduced cost, and increased quality. The Chrysler LH, the first model developed with the platform approach, took 39 months to produce; typically the time to market exceeds 50 months. Since then, major automobile manufacturers have greatly reduced these times.

While the benefits were clear, Chrysler executives noticed that unexplained errors were popping up in the new platforms (like leaving a moisture barrier out of car doors). *There was an organizational memory problem:* Mentoring and peer support became limited. Informal and formal professional collaboration had stopped. The same mistakes were being made, corrected, and repeated. People were not learning about new developments in their core areas. The typical collaboration found among groups doing similar work was sharply reduced, and so problems and solutions were not being documented or shared.

Collaboration and communication needed to be reestablished within groups with common training, interests, and responsibilities (design, engineering, body, engine, manufacturing, etc.). The goal was to reestablish these links while becoming more competitive with even faster product-cycle times. Chrysler needed to institutionalize knowledge sharing and collaboration. In 1996 Chrysler Corporation made *knowledge management* a vital condition for design and engineering, leading to dramatic improvements in productivity.

First, engineers mapped out where the knowledge was within the organization (a **knowledge audit**, see Rapport, 2001). There were many categories, or "buckets of knowledge," ranging from product databases to CAD/CAM systems to manufacturing, procurement, and supply vehicle test data. Within each category, details were identified and codified. Sharing knowledge meant integrating these knowledge buckets, while resolving cultural issues that impeded sharing across platform boundaries. Chrysler created informal cross-platform *Tech Clubs,* functionally organized communities of practice to reunite designers and engineers with peers from other platform groups. Each community would then codify its knowledge and provide mentoring and apprenticing opportunities for learning.

The *Engineering Book of Knowledge (EBOK)* is Chrysler's intranet supporting a knowledge repository of

Adapted from W. Karlenzig, "Chrysler's New Know-Mobiles," *Knowledge Management,* May 1999, pp. 58–66; M. Rapport, "Unfolding Knowledge." *Knowledge Management Magazine,* July, 2001; and other sources.

process *best practices* and technical know-how to be shared and maintained. It was initially developed by two engineering managers but continues through encouraged employee participation in grassroots (i.e., supported at the lower levels of the organization) Tech Clubs. EBOK is written in GrapeVine (GrapeVine Technologies), running as a Lotus Notes application, and is accessed with the Netscape browser and NewsEdge.

Knowledge is explored and entered into the EBOK through an iterative team approach: the Tech Clubs. Best practices are identified, refined, confirmed, and finally entered into the EBOK in a secure interactive electronic repository. When an author proposes a best practice, users in the Tech Club responsible for that area of knowledge react by commenting on the knowledge through a discussion list. One manager, the *Book Owner,* is ultimately responsible for approving new entries and changes to the book. The Book Owner joins the conversation. The author can respond to the comments by either building a better case or going along with the discussion. Ultimately the Tech Club decides, and the Book Owner enters the new knowledge. The Book Owner is the individual who is ultimately responsible for the accuracy of the book, and therefore approves entries to, modifications to, and deletions from the book.

The EBOK is DaimlerChrysler's official design review process. The EBOK even contains best-practices information about DaimlerChrysler's competitors. DaimlerChrysler has determined that EBOK is both a best practices tool (the codification strategy with a repository storage model) and a collaboration tool (the personalization strategy with a network storage model). DaimlerChrysler officials recognize that because the environment changes and new methods are being continually developed, the EBOK will never be fully complete. The EBOK is a *living book.* The EBOK *leverages* technology knowledge.

The EBOK is central to DaimlerChrysler's new way of working. The plan is to have more than 5,000 users with access to 3,800 chapters, of which just over half were completed by early 1999. Through the EBOK, DaimlerChrysler reconciled its platform problems and developed a technical memory while tracking competitive information, quality information, and outside standards. Even though there is no central budget for books of knowledge and associated processes, DaimlerChrysler is deploying knowledge in other departments, such as manufacturing, finance, and sales and marketing.

CASE APPLICATION QUESTIONS

1. Platform design at DaimlerChrysler led directly to a reduction in the time to market and in costs for new vehicles. Explain how it caused new problems.

2. What is meant by a community of practice? How did DaimlerChrysler leverage the knowledge within such a community?

3. Describe the Engineering Book of Knowledge (EBOK). Explain how it is updated by adding new knowledge of practice.

4. It has been said that "the proper role for all knowledge management tools is to leverage technology in service to human thinking." Explain this statement.

5. How successful was the knowledge management initiative at DaimlerChrysler?

6. Consider how a book of knowledge could impact another organization, ideally one with which you are affiliated (e.g., your university, job, part-time job, family business). Describe the potential impacts, and list the benefits. Would there be any organizational culture issues to deal with? Why or why not?

CASE APPLICATION 9.2

CHEVRON'S KNOWLEDGE MANAGEMENT INITIATIVES COOK WITH GAS

Chevron (www.chevron.com) wanted to explore, develop, adapt, and adopt knowledge management methods to leverage its expertise throughout the enterprise to maintain a competitive position in the marketplace. The improvements gained from identifying, sharing, and managing intellectual assets can impact positively on drilling, office work, safety, and refineries. Improvements were generated by focusing on process, culture, best practices, and technology, including Internet technology.

Chevron uses knowledge management in drilling, refinery maintenance and safety management, capital project management, and other areas. The electronic document management system impacts on several different areas at Chevron.

Drilling. Chevron adopted an *organizational learning system (OLS)* that improves drilling performance by sharing information globally. The system uses a simple software tool to capture lessons from the first wells in a new area, and then uses that knowledge to drill the rest of the wells faster and cheaper. Well costs have dropped by 12 to 20 percent, and cycle time has been reduced as much as 40 percent in some cases (offshore drilling vessels can cost up to $250,000 a day). Oil & Gas Consultants International developed the OLS for Amoco. Chevron found it through a best-practices survey.

Refineries. The company uses knowledge management is to maintain six refineries. Sam Preckett, reliability-focused maintenance-system manager, is developing a process to improve information and knowledge sharing. Preckett and others realized that they were not effectively using the data and information already stored in Chevron's enterprise information systems. Preckett has been developing an informal best practices methodology for maintenance by "trying to learn how we do things."

Getting knowledge to users is only part of the system; another part captures the tacit knowledge and experiences of workers. Chevron is trying to motivate workers to participate. Preckett said that at Chevron creative thinking is promoted from the executive level, which "allows

him to do interesting things" to achieve efficiency gains through knowledge sharing.

Electronic Document Management. Another specific need under the knowledge management umbrella was addressed by the DocMan system, initiated in December 1994 to improve the timeliness of document access, management, and integration, and sharing of information among individual divisions to meet regulatory compliances. A long-standing application, DocMan works for the Warren Petroleum Limited Partnership Mont Belvieu complex in Texas (of which Chevron is a joint owner). To handle cultural resistance to change, management emphasized the benefits of the DocMan system: faster access to documents, elimination of wasted effort searching for documents, and assets protection. DocMan delivered a 95 percent return on investment over its 5-year project life. The investment payout period was 1.1 years based on an annual savings of $480,000.

Capital Project Management. Through knowledge management, Chevron implemented a new standard methodology for capital project management. In one case, 60 companies shared data and practices, and so it was possible to compare performance to determine which companies were best and why.

What have been the overall results? Improved management of knowledge was instrumental in reducing operating costs from $9.4 billion to $7.4 billion from 1992 to 1998 and in reducing energy costs by *$200 million a year*. During the 1990s, efforts like this were essential in reducing costs, achieving productivity gains of over 50 percent (in barrels of output per employee), and improving employee safety performance more than 50 percent. Chevron now calls itself a *learning organization*. Some gains from knowledge management at Chevron are qualitative: Employees' work is more interesting and challenging when it involves finding and applying new knowledge. Jobs are potentially more fulfilling and more personally rewarding.

Adapted from L. Velker, "Knowledge the Chevron Way," *KMWorld,* Vol. 8, No. 2, February 1, 1999, pp. 20–21; "The Means to an Edge: Knowledge Management: Key to Innovation," *CIO,* September 15, 1999; M. Santosus, "ChevronTexaco's Soft Sell," *In the Know* at cio.com, March 2003.

CASE APPLICATION QUESTIONS

1. Explain how Chevron is a learning organization?
2. Describe the gains that Chevron experienced through its knowledge management programs.
3. To what different areas did Chevron apply knowledge management, and how successful were they?
4. Why is it important to document cost savings of knowledge management systems?
5. If dramatic payoffs can be achieved through knowledge management (as with the DocMan system), why don't more companies do so?

INTELLIGENT DECISION SUPPORT SYSTEMS

LEARNING OBJECTIVES FOR PART IV

❖ Understand the foundations, definitions and capabilities of artificial intelligence and expert systems

❖ Understand the process of knowledge engineering, particularly, knowledge acquisition and inference mechanisms

❖ Understand how the artificial neural networks are used to develop intelligent DSS

❖ Understand how genetic algorithms are used to develop intelligent systems

❖ Understand how fuzzy logic can be used to develop intelligent systems

❖ Understand state-of-the art applications of intelligent agents and recommendation systems on the Internet

In addition to traditional decision support systems, techniques developed in artificial intelligence have been adopted to build systems that provide intelligent support. These systems include rule-based expert systems and second-generation advanced intelligent systems that use artificial neural networks, genetic algorithms, case-based reasoning, and intelligent agent techniques.

In this part, we first present an overview of artificial intelligence and rule-based expert systems (Chapter 10). These systems are constructed through a process of knowledge engineering, which involves several tasks. First, knowledge is collected from people or documented sources by a process called knowledge acquisition. The acquired knowledge is organized into a knowledge base that can then be used by the Inference engine to solve new problems. Chapter 11 describes the process of knowledge acquisition, representation, inference mechanisms, knowledge validation, and uncertainty processing. Chapter 12 describes advanced technologies that are commonly used in the world of commerce. They include artificial neural networks, genetic algorithms, and fuzzy logic applications. Chapter 13 provides the most cutting-edge decision support technologies over the Internet, with a focus on intelligent agents and recommendation systems that have gained much attention recently.

CHAPTER 10

ARTIFICIAL INTELLIGENCE AND EXPERT SYSTEMS: KNOWLEDGE-BASED SYSTEMS

LEARNING OBJECTIVES

❖ Describe the concept and evolution of artificial intelligence

❖ Understand the importance of knowledge in decision support

❖ Describe the concept and evolution of rule-based expert systems

❖ Understand the architecture of rule-based expert systems

❖ Explain the benefits and limitations of rule-based systems for decision support

❖ Identify proper applications of expert systems

Some managerial decisions are qualitative in nature and need judgmental knowledge that resides in human experts. Thus, it is necessary to incorporate this knowledge in developing decision support systems. The system that integrates knowledge from experts is called a *knowledge-based decision support system* (KBDSS) or *intelligent decision support systems* (IDSS). A KBDSS can enhance the capabilities of decision support not only by supplying a tool that directly supports decision-makers but also by enhancing various computerized decision support systems. The foundation for building such systems consists of the techniques and tools that have been developed in the area of artificial intelligence, expert systems being the primary one. This chapter introduces the essentials of artificial intelligence and expert systems in the following sections:

10.1 OPENING VIGNETTE: INTELLIGENT SYSTEMS IN KPN TELECOM AND LOGITECH[1]

THE PROBLEM

KPN Telecom is a major telecommunication company that offers fix-line networks in the Netherlands, data/IP services in Western Europe, and mobile services in the Netherlands, Germany, and Belgium. It has more than 38,000 employees serving 7.9 million fix-line customers, 13.4 million mobile customers, and 1.4 million Internet subscribers. It is listed on the Amsterdam, New York, London, and Frankfurt stock exchanges. For a company of this size, a major problem is to maintain its efficient operation with minimum costs.

One problem that has caused trouble in the company's information systems department is how to maintain its more than 35,000 computer workstations to work properly. Since these workstations were ordered at different times and have different hardware and software configurations, it is extremely time-consuming and sometimes frustrating to fix endless service calls from users. Even worse, a substantial portion of maintenance knowledge is lost due to employee turnover or retirement.

THE SOLUTION

A rule-based system called Archimedes was developed to capture, manage, and automate the installation and maintenance of the 35,000 workstations. The system uses a tool called Authorete (www.haley.com/1688884221315072/Authorete.html) to capture the knowledge about installation problems and their solutions embodied in KPN documents, processes, procedures, and the IT staff's collective experience.

The core of Archimedes is its *knowledge base* and a friendly user interface. Instead of using a complicated structure, knowledge is represented in plain sentences. This makes it much easier to build and maintain the knowledge base. These sentences specify how IT specialists currently analyze software installations and how they fix the problems. The system guides users through a series of meaningful statements within pull-down menus to help KPN developers and refine knowledge.

The *knowledge management* module has a natural-language processing unit that enables user friendly communications with the system. The IT professionals in the company can dictate sentences through a speech-recognition component. The natural-language processing unit can then analyze the sentences to understand the precise meaning and store the parsed structure and logic in the knowledge base.

THE RESULTS

Successful implementation has resulted in a substantial decrease in maintenance manpower, a reduction from 30 to five employees. The quality of services and ability to maintain a consistent computing environment are also improved.

❖ QUESTIONS FOR THE OPENING VIGNETTE

1. Describe the common characteristics in these two cases.
2. Describe the motivation for developing these intelligent systems.

---

[1]Adapted from "Rule-Based Systems Maintains Software on 35,000 workstation," *Expert Systems*, November 2001.

3. Explain the role of the intelligent systems and their potential benefits

4. What are the major difficulties in developing these systems?

5. How are these systems different from traditional DSS described in previous chapters?

6. What managerial lessons can be learned from these systems?

10.2 CONCEPTS AND DEFINITIONS OF ARTIFICIAL INTELLIGENCE

The Opening Vignette illustrates that in some decision situations the support offered by data and model management alone may not be sufficient. Additional support was provided by expert systems (ES) to substitute for human expertise by supplying the necessary knowledge. However, several other intelligent technologies can be used to support decision situations that require expertise. All these technologies use qualitative **knowledge**, rather than mathematical models, to provide the needed supports referred to as **knowledge-based systems**. The major technology underlying these applications is *artificial intelligence*.

ARTIFICIAL INTELLIGENCE DEFINITIONS

Artificial intelligence (AI) is an area in computer science. The term encompasses many definitions (Jackson, 1999; Raynor, 1996), but most experts agree that AI is concerned with two basic ideas. First, it involves studying the thought processes of humans (to understand what intelligence is); second, it deals with representing and duplicating these processes via machines (e.g., computers and robots).

One well-publicized definition of AI is as follows: Artificial intelligence is behavior by a machine that, if performed by a human being, would be called intelligent. A thought-provoking definition is provided by Rich and Knight (1991): "Artificial intelligence is the study of how to make computers do things at which, at the moment, people are better."

A well-known application of artificial intelligence is Deep Blue, the chess program developed by a research team at IBM (see AIS in Action 10.1). It beats the world champion, Garry Kasparov, in a game that usually only smart people can win.

To understand what artificial intelligence is, we need first to look at the abilities that are considered signs of intelligence:

- Learning or understanding from experience
- Making sense out of ambiguous or contradictory messages
- Responding quickly and successfully to a new situation (different responses, flexibility)
- Using reasoning in solving problems and directing conduct effectively
- Dealing with perplexing situations
- Understanding and inferring in ordinary rational ways
- Applying knowledge to manipulate the environment
- Thinking and reasoning
- Recognizing the relative importance of different elements in a situation.

An interesting test designed to determine whether a computer exhibits intelligent behavior was designed by Alan Turing and is called the **Turing test**. According to this

AIS IN ACTION 10.1

INTELLIGENT COMPUTER BEATS CHESS GRAND MASTER

In 1997, Deep Blue, a computer system armed with artificial intelligence, beat the Russian world chess champion, Garry Kasparov, who is considered by many the best chess player who ever lived, in a six-game match. This was the first time that a computer demonstrated intelligence in an area that requires human intelligence. The system ran on an IBM RS/6000 SP machine capable of examining 200 million moves per second—or 50 billion positions—in the three minutes allocated for a single move in a chess game. The RS/6000 machine was the same type of system used in hundreds of commercial and technological applications. The first match between Deep Blue and Kasparov actually took place in 1996. Deep Blue also won that match.

A six-person design team led by Chung-Jen Tan designed a hybrid heuristic and brute-force search model to assess the value of different moves. Although the victory of the computer does not imply that computer intelligence will prevail, it does indicate the potential of artificial intelligence, particularly in the area of intelligent decision support. Computers armed with intelligent reasoning capabilities will help managers to minimize risks and maximize performance.

In February 2003, another man-computer match between Garry Kasparov and Deep Junior, the three-time computer chess champion programmed by Amir Ban and Shay Bushinsky in Israel, ended in a 3–3 tie. This further confirmed that the knowledge captured in the computer chess program can be as powerful as that of the best human player. More information about these matches can be found at www.research.ibm.com/ deep-blue/ and www.uschess.org/news/press/ uspr0307.html.

test, a computer can be considered smart only when a human interviewer cannot identify the computer while conversing with both an unseen human being and an unseen computer.

CHARACTERISTICS OF ARTIFICIAL INTELLIGENCE

Although AI's ultimate goal is to build machines that mimic human intelligence, the capabilities of current commercial AI products are far from exhibiting any significant success in the abilities just listed. Nevertheless, AI programs are continually improving, and they increase productivity and quality by automating several tasks that require some human intelligence. Artificial intelligence techniques usually have the features described below.

SYMBOLIC PROCESSING

Symbolic processing is an essential characteristic of artificial intelligence, as reflected in the following definition: Artificial intelligence is the branch of computer science dealing primarily with symbolic, non-algorithmic methods of problem-solving. This definition focuses on two characteristics:

- *Numeric versus symbolic.* Computers were originally designed specifically to process numbers (**numeric processing**). However, people tend to think symbolically; our intelligence seems to be based in part on our mental ability to manipulate **symbols** rather than just numbers. Although symbolic processing is at the core of AI, this does not mean that AI does not involve math; rather, the emphasis in AI is on the manipulation of symbols.

- *Algorithmic versus heuristic.* An **algorithm** is a step-by-step procedure that has well-defined starting and ending points and is guaranteed to find a solution to a specific problem. Most computer architectures readily lend themselves to this step-by-step approach. Many human reasoning processes tend to be non-algorithmic; in other words, our mental activities consist of more than just following logical, step-by-step procedures. Rather, human thinking relies more on rules learned from previous experience and on gut feelings.

HEURISTICS

Heuristics consists of intuitive knowledge, or rules of thumb, learned from experience. Its role in AI is seen in the following definition: Artificial intelligence is the branch of computer science that deals with ways of representing knowledge using symbols with rule-of-thumb, or heuristic, methods for processing information (*Encyclopaedia Britannica*). By using heuristics, one does not have to rethink completely what to do every time a similar problem is encountered. For example, when a salesperson plans to visit clients in different cities, a popular heuristic is to visit the nearest next one (called the nearest-neighbor heuristic). Many AI methods employ some kind of heuristics to reduce the complexity of problem-solving.

INFERENCING

As an alternative to heuristics, artificial intelligence also builds reasoning capabilities that can build higher-level knowledge from existing heuristics. This reasoning consists of **inferencing** from facts and rules using heuristics or other search approaches.

MACHINE LEARNING

Learning is an important capability for human beings. Artificial intelligent systems do not have the same learning capabilities that humans have, but they do have mechanical learning capabilities, called machine learning, that allow the system to adjust its behavior and react to changes in outside environment. There are many machine-learning methods for developing intelligent systems, including inductive learning, artificial neural networks, and genetic algorithms.

10.3 EVOLUTION OF ARTIFICIAL INTELLIGENCE

The development of artificial intelligence includes four major stages. Figure 10.1 shows the evolution from 1960 to now. First, in 1956, a group of computer scientists gathered at Dartmouth College to discuss the great potential of computer applications. They were confident that computers, given enormous computing power, would be able to solve many complex problems and outperform human beings in many areas. At that time, scientists had little understanding of the complexity of human intelligence and were overly optimistic about what the computer could achieve. Many solutions created at that time were primitive, and hence the stage is called the *naive solution stage*.

After several years of trial and error, scientists started focusing on developing more effective problem-solving methods, such as knowledge-representation schemes, reasoning strategies, and effective search heuristics. Since the feature of this stage is the development of general purpose methods, it is named the *general method stage*.

After building enough general purpose methods, people started applying them to real-world applications. The application at this stage is different from the first one in that we already knew that solving common sense problems is difficult. Therefore, most applications were targeted at a narrowly defined **domain** with specialized knowledge. Systems of this kind are called **expert systems (ES)**. The feature is that acquisition of expert knowledge plays a key role in development such systems. We call it the *domain knowledge stage*.

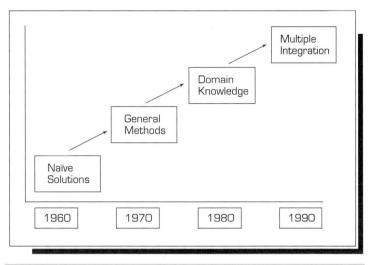

FIGURE 10.1   FOUR STAGES OF AI EVOLUTION

AIS IN FOCUS 10.2

ARTIFICIAL INTELLIGENCE VERSUS NATURAL INTELLIGENCE

The potential value of artificial intelligence can be better understood by contrasting it with natural, or human, intelligence. AI has several important advantages:

- *AI is more permanent.* Natural intelligence is perishable from a commercial standpoint in that workers can change their place of employment or forget information. However, AI is permanent as long as the computer systems and programs remain unchanged.

- *AI offers ease of duplication and dissemination.* Transferring a body of knowledge from one person to another usually requires a lengthy process of apprenticeship; even so, expertise can seldom be duplicated completely. However, knowledge embodied in a computer system can be easily transferred from that computer to any computer on the Internet or on an intranet.

- *AI can be less expensive than natural intelligence.* There are many circumstances in which buying computer services costs less than having corresponding human power carry out the same tasks. This is especially true when knowledge is disseminated over the Web.

- *AI, as a computer technology, is consistent and thorough.* Natural intelligence is erratic because people are erratic; they do not always perform consistently.

- *AI can be documented.* Decisions made by a computer can be easily documented by tracing the activities of the system. Natural intelligence is difficult to document. For example, a person may reach a conclusion but at some later date may be unable to re-create the reasoning process that led to it, or to even recall the assumptions that were part of the decision.

- *AI can execute certain tasks much faster than a human.*

- *AI can perform certain tasks better than many or even most people.*

Natural intelligence does have several advantages over AI, such as:

- Natural intelligence is *creative*, whereas AI is rather *uninspired.* The ability to acquire knowledge is inherent in human beings, but with AI, tailored knowledge must be built into a carefully constructed system.

- Natural intelligence enables people to benefit from and use *sensory experience* directly, whereas most AI systems must work with symbolic input and representations.

Since 1990, more advanced problem-solving methods have been developed. There is a strong need to integrate multiple techniques and solve problems in multiple domains. Hybrid systems such as integrating rule-based and case-based systems, or integrating artificial neural networks and genetic algorithms, become necessary. We call it the *integration stage*.

The use of artificial intelligence in decision support systems has advantages and limitations. See AIS in Focus 10.2 for a comparison of artificial and natural intelligence.

10.4 THE ARTIFICIAL INTELLIGENCE FIELD

Artificial intelligence is a collection of concepts and ideas related to the development of an intelligent systems. These concepts and ideas may be developed in different areas and be applied to different domains. In order to understand the scope of AI, therefore, we need to see a group of areas that may be called the AI family. Figure 10.2 shows the major branches of AI studies. They are briefly described below.

EXPERT SYSTEMS

The name **expert system** was derived from the term knowledge-based expert system. An expert system (ES) is a system that uses human knowledge captured in a computer to solve problems that ordinarily require human expertise. Later sections of this chapter have detailed explanations.

NATURAL LANGUAGE PROCESSING

Natural language processing (NLP) technology gives computer users the ability to communicate with a computer in their native language. This technology allows for a conversational type of interface, in contrast to using a programming language consisting of computer jargon, syntax, and commands. It includes two subfields: Natural language understanding investigates methods of enabling computers to comprehend instructions given in ordinary English so that they can understand people more easily. Natural language generation strives to have computers produce ordinary English language so that people can understand them more easily. The limited success in this area is typified by current systems that can recognize and interpret written sentences. Details on these topics are discussed in Appendix 10-B and in Reiter and Dale (2000) and McRoy et al. (2001).

SPEECH (VOICE) UNDERSTANDING

Speech understanding is the recognition and understanding of spoken language by a computer. More information about spoken-language processing can be found in Balentine et al. (1999) and Huang et al. (2001). Applications of the technology have become more and more popular. For instance, many companies have adopted the technology in their call centers. See AIS in Action 10.3 for a description.

ROBOTICS AND SENSORY SYSTEMS

Sensory systems, such as vision systems, tactile systems, and signal-processing systems, when combined with AI, define a broad category of systems generally called **robotics**. A robot is an electromechanical device that can be programmed to perform manual

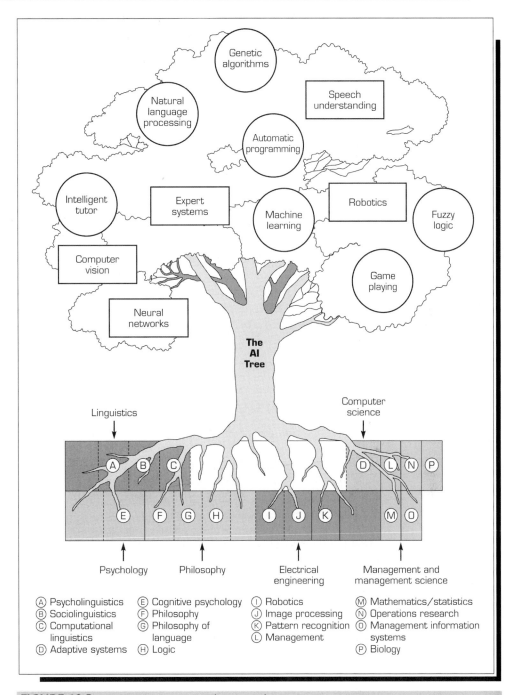

FIGURE 10.2   THE DISCIPLINES OF AI (THE ROOTS) AND THE APPLICATIONS

tasks. The Robotics Institute of America formally defines a robot as "a reprogramma-ble multifunctional manipulator designed to move materials, parts, tools, or specialized devices through variable programmed motions for the performance of a variety of tasks."

An "intelligent" robot has a sensory apparatus of some kind, such as a camera, that collects information about the robot's operations and environment. The intelligent

---

AIS IN ACTION 10.3

AUTOMATIC SPEECH RECOGNITION POPULAR IN CALL CENTERS

Speech recognition is no longer a wishful technology. More and more companies are using it for interacting with customers. In the United States alone, there are more than 50,000 call centers which spend more than $90 billion dealing with customers' requests. With human operators costing around $1 per minute, speech recognition offers companies an opportunity to lower their overheads.

Charles Schwab, an American discount stockbroker, introduced the first speech system for retail broking in 1996. That year, the number of new accounts with the company increased by 41 percent, and the call-centers took 97 million calls. The automated attendant can understand the names of 15,000 individual equities and funds; takes up to 100,000 calls a day; and is 93 percent accurate in identifying queries the first time they are made. Costs have been cut from $4–5 per call to $1.

AT&T, the leading long-distance phone company in the United States, has also deployed a natural language processing system in its customer-care centers. It uses it to process more than 2 million calls a month.

Source: Adapted from "Just Talk To Me," *Economist Technology Quarterly*, December 8, 2001.

---

part of the robot allows it to interpret the collected information and to respond and adapt to changes in its environment rather than just follow instructions. See Wise (1999) and Cook (2002) for more on robots.

COMPUTER VISION AND SCENE RECOGNITION

Visual recognition has been defined as the addition of some form of computer intelligence and decision-making to digitized visual information received from a machine sensor such as a camera. The combined information is then used to perform or control such operations as robotic movement, conveyor speed, and production-line quality. The basic objective of computer vision is to interpret scenarios rather than generate pictures. Interpreting scenarios is defined in different ways depending on the application. For example, in interpreting pictures taken by a satellite, it may be sufficient to roughly identify regions of crop damage. On the other hand, robot vision systems can be designed to precisely identify assembly components and correctly affix them to the item being assembled. For details, see Sonka et al. (1998) and Forsyth and Ponce (2002).

INTELLIGENT COMPUTER-AIDED INSTRUCTION

Intelligent computer-aided instruction (ICAI) refers to machines that can tutor humans. To a certain extent, such a machine can be viewed as an expert system. However, the major objective of an expert system is to render advice, whereas the purpose of an ICAI is to teach.

Computer-assisted instruction, which has been in use for many years, brings the power of a computer to bear on the educational process. AI methods are now being applied to the development of intelligent computer-assisted instruction systems in an attempt to create computerized tutors that shape their teaching techniques to fit the learning patterns of individual students. These are known as **intelligent tutoring systems (ITS)**, and many more have been implemented on the Web (see AIS in Focus 10.4).

AIS IN FOCUS 10.4

INTERNET-BASED INTELLIGENT TUTORING SYSTEMS

Intelligent tutoring systems are computer-based systems that can help the user to learn knowledge in a particular domain in a more flexible way. Key intelligence that affects the success of such systems is the ability to analyze the learner's behavior and adjust the learning path accordingly. Many companies are introducing Internet-based intelligent tutoring systems (ITS) as a cost-effective approach to deliver training wherever the trainees may be. This is especially beneficial in complex domains where students must master a variety of concepts and apply them in unique situations. For such cases, regular training over the Internet is not enough. With ITS, programs can be customized and instructors can monitor students' progress from a distance. Course developers can easily maintain and update training materials, and the instructor's productivity is enhanced by ITS. These systems also provide for customized training and remediation, similar to one-to-one "private" tutoring. ITS use different intelligent systems, ranging from expert systems to case-based reasoning (Chapter 12), which contains realistic problem-solving situations and solutions.

The case base of examples and exercises captures realistic problem-solving situations and presents them to the student as virtual simulations. Each example or exercise includes the following:

- A multimedia description of the problem, which may evolve over time (e.g., in a tactical scenario)

- A description of the correct actions to take, including order-independent, optional, and alternative steps

- A multimedia explanation of why these steps are correct

- A list of methods for determining whether students have correctly performed the steps

- A list of principles that must be learned to take the correct action.

Students solve the problems interactively, which gives them an opportunity to practice the necessary skills and also reveals any knowledge deficiencies. ITS monitors students as they perform these simulations, diagnosing the strengths and weaknesses of their performance, and tailors instruction to correct weaknesses.

This is a new paradigm for ITS education. An example is the ITS Authoring Tool from Stottler Henke Associates (www.shai.com), which helps in building enterprise training programs that can be delivered on intranets and corporate portals. An application of intelligent tutoring systems for turbine startup training in an electronic power plant is reported by Lopez et al. (2003).

Source: Condensed from *PC AI*, July/Aug. 1999.

NEURAL COMPUTING

A **neural (computing) network** is a set of mathematical models that simulate the way a human brain functions. Such models have been implemented in flexible, easy-to-use PC-based neural network packages such as BrainMaker (www.calsci.com/) and NeuroShell (www.wardsystems.com/). Its applications in business are abundant. For examples, see Ainscough et al. (1997), Fadlalla and Lin (2001), and Haykin (1998). We discuss neural computing in depth in Chapter 12.

GAME PLAYING

Game playing is one of the first areas that AI researchers studied. It is a perfect area for investigating new strategies and heuristics, and one in which it measures the results. Deep Blue (described in AIS in Action 10.1) is a good example of successful development.

LANGUAGE TRANSLATION

Automated translation uses computer programs to translate words and sentences from one language to another without much interruption from humans. For example, the LOGOS Group (Modena, Italy, www. logos.it) has created a software package for multiple language translations. Globalink Inc. has a Language Assistant Series that runs under Windows. Several programs translate Web pages to foreign languages (see www.worldpoint.com, www.babelfish.altavista.com, and www.free.translation .com).

Korea Telecom offers Koreans an opportunity to access Web sites in Japanese and read an abstract of their content (www.idetect.com). Once a Web site is selected for a detailed view, an automatic translation is provided. A description of using onto- logical learning in automated terminlogy translation is available in Navigli et al. (2003).

FUZZY LOGIC

Fuzzy logic (fuzzy sets) is a technique for processing linguistic terms. It extends the notion of logic beyond a simple true/false to allow for partial (or even continuous) truths. Inexact knowledge and imprecise reasoning are important aspects of expertise in applying common sense to decision-making situations. In fuzzy logic, the value of true or false is replaced by the degree of set membership. For example, in the tradi- tional boolean logic, a person's credit record is either good or bad. In fuzzy logic, the credit record may be assessed as both good and bad, but each to a different degree. See Chapter 12, and Nguyen and Walker (1999) for more details.

GENETIC ALGORITHMS

Genetic algorithms are intelligent methods that use computers to simulate the process of natural evolution to find patterns from a set of data. For a specific problem, the solu- tion is represented as a "chromosome" that generally contains a sequence of 0s and 1s indicating the values of decision variables. A genetic method starts with a randomly

---

AIS IN ACTION 10.5

AGENTS FOR TRAVEL PLANNING AT USC

Planning business trips is a tedious task that includes selecting a flight, reserving a hotel room, and possibly reserving a car. Once a schedule is set, many other deci- sions must be made, based on past experience, such as whether to drive to the airport or take a taxi. The time and effort required to make informed decisions usually outweighs the cost. Schedules can change, prices can decrease after a ticket is purchased, flight delays can result in missed connections, and hotel rooms and rental cars can be given away because of late arrivals. All these contigencies add more stress for the traveler.

To address these issues, an integrated travel plan- ning and monitoring system, called Travel Assistant, was developed at the University of Southern California. The system provides information necessary to make an informed travel plan. It uses information agents to pro- vide information for planning and monitoring agents to

trace any changes in the original plan. The information agent takes a particular information request, navigates to the appropriate Web site, extracts information from the Web site, and then returns it as an XML document for processing.

Monitoring agents are built on top of the informa- tion agents and keep track of the status of the schedule. If any information that may cause schedule changes is found (e.g., cancellation or delay of the flight), the agents will sent the message to the user. They peform their tasks at regular intervals. Major messages sent by agents include: flight delayed, flight cancelled, fax to a hotel, airfare drop, and availability of earlier flights.

Source: Abriged from C. Knoblock, "Agents for Gathering, Integrating, and Monitoring Information for Travel Planning," *IEEE Intelligent Systems*, Vol. 17, No. 6, 2003.

generated population of solutions and randomly combines portions of chromosomes to form new solutions with multiple generations of duplication and an occasional mutation. The evolution continues until a satisfactory solution is reached. See Goldberg (1994) for an excellent introduction, the Java implementation in Ghanea-Hercock, and Ghanea-Hercock (2003), and Chapter 12 for more descriptions.

INTELLIGENT AGENTS

Intelligent agents are small programs that reside on computers to conduct certain tasks automatically. A virus detection program is a good example. It resides on your computer, scans all incoming data, and removes found viruses automatically. An intelligent agent runs in the background, monitors the environment, and reacts to certain trigger conditions. Intelligent agents are finding applications in personal assistant devices, electronic mail and news filtering and distribution, appointment handling, and Web applets for electronic commerce and information gathering (see AIS in Action 10.5 for an example and Chapter 13 for more details).

10.5 BASIC CONCEPTS OF EXPERT SYSTEMS

Expert systems are computer-based information systems that use expert knowledge to attain high-level decision performance in a narrow problem domain. MYCIN, developed at Stanford University in the early 1980s for medical diagnosis, is generally considered to be the most well known expert system. Other applications in taxation, credit analysis, equipment maintenance, and fault diagnosis have also been popular in most large- and medium-sized organizations as a major tool for improving productivity and quality (Nedovic and Devedzic, 2002; Nurminen et al., 2003).

The basic concepts of expert systems include several fundamental issues, including what is expertise, who are experts, how expertise can be transferred, and how the system works. We shall describe them in this and the following sections.

EXPERTS

An **expert** is a person who has special knowledge, judgment, experience, and methods, along with the ability to apply these talents to give advice and solve problems. It is the expert's job to provide knowledge about how to perform the task that the knowledge-based system will perform. The expert knows which facts are important and understands the meaning of the relationships among them. In diagnosing a problem with an automobile's electrical system, for example, an expert mechanic knows that fan belts can break and cause the battery to discharge.

So far, there is no standard definition of expert, but decision performance and the level of knowledge a person has are typical criteria used in determining whether someone is an expert. Typical experts have a few general concepts. First, they must be able to solve the problem and achieve a performance level significantly better than the average. Second, experts are relative. An expert at one time or in one region may not be an expert in another time or region. For example, an attorney in New York may not be a legal expert in Beijing, China. A medical student may be an expert on illness compared to a layperson, but is no expert in a top-tier hospital. Experts have expertise that can solve problems and explain certain phenomenon in the problem domain. Typically, human experts are capable of doing the following:

- Recognizing and formulating the problem
- Solving the problem quickly and correctly
- Explaining the solution
- Learning from experience
- Restructuring knowledge
- Breaking rules if necessary
- Determining relevance
- Degrading gracefully (being aware of one's limitations).

EXPERTISE

Expertise is the extensive task-specific knowledge possessed by experts. The level of expertise determines the performance of a decision. Expertise is often acquired from training, reading, and experience in practice. It includes explicit knowledge, such as theories learned in a textbook or a classroom, and implicit knowledge gained from experience. The following is a list of possible knowledge types:

- Theories about the problem domain
- Rules and procedures regarding the general problem domain
- Rules (heuristics) about what to do in a given problem situation
- Global strategies for solving these types of problems
- Metaknowledge (knowledge about knowledge)
- Facts about the problem area.

Experts who have the types of knowledge outlined above are able to make better and faster decisions than non-experts in solving complex problems. Expertise often has the following characteristics:

- Expertise is usually associated with a high degree of intelligence, but not necessarily with the smartest person.
- Expertise is usually associated with a vast quantity of knowledge.
- Experts learn from past successes and mistakes.
- Expert knowledge is well-stored, organized, and quickly retrievable from an expert.
- Experts can call up patterns from their experience (excellent recall).

FEATURES OF EXPERT SYSTEMS

Expert systems must have the following features:

- **Expertise:** As described above, experts are differentiated by their levels of expertise. Expert systems must possess the expertise that will enable the system to make expert-level decisions. The system must exhibit expert performance and adequate robustness.
- **Symbolic reasoning:** The basic rationale of artificial intelligence is to use symbolic reasoning rather than mathematical calculation. This is also true for expert systems. That is, knowledge must be represented symbolically, and the primary reasoning mechanism must also be symbolic. Typical symbolic reasoning mechanisms include backward chaining and forward chaining, which will be described in later sections.
- **Deep knowledge:** This concerns the level of expertise in a knowledge base. The knowledge base must contain complex knowledge not easily found among non-experts.

- *Self-knowledge:* Expert systems must be able to examine their own reasoning and explain why a particular conclusion was reached. Most experts have very strong learning capabilities that enable them to constantly update their knowledge. Expert systems also need to be able to learn from their successes and failures and from other knowledge sources.

The development of expert systems is divided into two generations. Most first-generation expert systems use if-then rules to represent and store their knowledge. Second-generation expert systems are more flexible in adopting multiple knowledge representations and reasoning methods. They may integrate neural networks with rule-based inferences to pursue a higher decision performance. Table 10.1 provides a comparison between conventional systems and expert systems.

WHY DO WE NEED EXPERT SYSTEMS?

There are several reasons for a company to adopt an expert system. First, experts in the company may retire or leave. Expert systems are an excellent tool for preserving the professional knowledge crucial to competitiveness. Second, certain knowledge needs to be documented or examined. Expert systems are an excellent tool for documenting professional knowledge for examination or improvement. Third, education and training are important but difficult tasks. Expert systems are a good tool for training new employees and disseminating knowledge in an organization. Finally, experts are often

TABLE 10.1   Comparison of Conventional Systems and Expert Systems

Conventional Systems	Expert Systems
Information and its processing are usually combined in one sequential program.	Knowledge base is clearly separated from the processing (inference) mechanism (i.e., knowledge rules are separated from the control).
Program does not make mistakes (programmers or users do).	Program may make mistakes.
Do not (usually) explain why input data are needed or how conclusions are drawn.	Explanation is a part of most ES.
Require *all* input data. May not function properly with missing data unless planned for.	Do not require all initial facts. Typically can arrive at reasonable conclusions with missing facts.
Changes in the program are tedious (except in DSS).	Changes in the rules are easy to make.
The system operates only when it is completed.	The system can operate with only a few rules (as the first prototype).
Execution is done on a step-by-step (algorithmic) basis.	Execution is done by using heuristics and logic.
Effective manipulation of large databases.	Effective manipulation of large knowledge bases.
Representation and use of data.	Representation and use of knowledge.
Efficiency is usually a major goal.	Effectiveness is the major goal.
Effectiveness is important only for DSS.	
Easily deal with quantitative data.	Easily deal with qualitative data.
Use numerical data representations.	Use symbolic and numerical knowledge representations.
Capture, magnify, and distribute access to numeric data or information.	Capture, magnify, and distribute access to judgment and knowledge.

TABLE 10.2   Difference Between Human Experts And Expert Systems

Features	Human experts	Expert systems
Mortality	Yes	No
Knowledge transfer	Hard	Easy
Knowledge documentation	Hard	Easy
Decision consistency	Low	High
Unit usage cost	High	Low
Creativity	High	Low
Adaptability	High	Low
Knowledge scope	Broad	Narrow
Knowledge type	Common sense and technical	Technical
Knowledge content	Experience	Symbols

rare and expensive. Expert systems allow knowledge to be transferred more easily at a lower cost.

Of course, expert systems are not real experts. They have advantages but also shortcomings. Table 10.2 shows the comparison between human experts and expert systems.

10.6 APPLICATIONS OF EXPERT SYSTEMS

Expert systems have been applied in many business and technological areas to support decision-making. A scenario of using expert systems is shown in AIS in Action 10.6. AIS in Action 10.7 shows a few recent sample applications. Early applications, such as DENDRAL for molecular-structure identification, and MYCIN for medical diagnosis, were primarily in the field of science. XCON, or configuration of the VAX computer system in the Digital Equipment Corporation, was a successful example in business. More recent applications in risk management and pension fund advising are also interesting. Table 10.3 shows some representative expert systems and their application domains. The following are some classic applications that we should know:

DENDRAL
The DENDRAL project was initiated by Edward Feigenbaum in 1965. It used a set of knowledge- or rule-based reasoning commands to deduce the likely molecular structure of organic chemical compounds from known chemical analyses and mass spectrometry data. DENDRAL proved to be fundamentally important in demonstrating how rule-based reasoning could be developed into powerful knowledge-engineering tools and led to the development of other rule-based reasoning programs at the Stanford Artificial Intelligence Laboratory (SAIL), the most important of which was MYCIN.

MYCIN
MYCIN is a rule-based expert system that diagnoses bacterial infections of the blood. It was developed by a group of researchers at Stanford University in the 1970s. By asking questions and backward-chaining through a rule base of about 500 rules, MYCIN can recognize about 100 causes of bacterial infections. This allows MYCIN to recommend effective drug prescriptions. In a controlled test, its performance was rated to be equal to human specialists. The reasoning and uncertainty processing methods are pioneers in the area and have generated long-term impact in expert systems development.

AIS IN ACTION 10.6

SAMPLE SESSIONS OF A RULE-BASED EXPERT SYSTEM

A rule-based expert system contains rules in its knowledge base. The rules are used to generate questions for the user and to provide recommendations. Suppose you have an expert system that recommends notebook computers based on a customer's needs. The following is a possible consultation session:

☐ What is your primary task to be performed on the notebook computer?
  ☐ Word processing
  ☐ Communications
  ☐ Multimedia applications
Answer: 1 (click the first check box)

☐ Where are you going to use the notebook more often?
  ☐ Office
  ☐ Travel
Answer: 2 (click the second check box)

☐ What is your budget range?
  ☐ below 10K,
  ☐ between 10–12K,
  ☐ above 12K
Answer: 2 (click the third check box)

☐ System recommendation
You should consider buying an IBM X24

Reasons: it is light and more suitable for your word-processing and travel needs, it also fits your budget.

More description may be found at www.computing.surrey.ac.uk/research/ai/ PROFILE/mycin.html.

XCON

XCON is a rule-based system developed at the Digital Equipment Corporation, a big mini-computer manufacturer merged with Compaq Computers in 2000. The system uses rules to help determine the optimal system configuration that fits customer require-

AIS IN ACTION 10.7

SAMPLE APPLICATIONS

Customer Support at Logitech. LogiTech is one of the world's largest vendors of mouses and Web cameras. Because it offers many different models of mouses and Web cameras, customer support is a major challenge. To take advantage of the Internet and technologies in intelligent systems, the company deploys an interactive knowledge portal to provide Web-based self-help customer support to its QuickCam customer in North America. The noHold Knowledge Platform emulates the way a human would interact with a customer, allows the user to ask questions or describe problems in natural language, and carries on an intelligent conversation with the user until it has enough information to provide

an accurate answer. (Source: "Logitech Deploys Online Customer Support," *Expert Systems*, November 2001.)

China's freight train system. An expert system was developed in China to allocate freight cars and determine what and how much to load on each car. The ES is integrated with the existing MIS, and the system is distributed to many users. For details see Geng et al. (1999).

Electricity market forecaster. EnvaPower developed an electricity market forecasting system, called MarketMonitor, that uses artificial intelligence techniques to gather, synthesize, and analyze a large amount of factors that may affect the consumption of electricity. (*Source: Expert Systems*, May 2002, Vol. 19, No. 2.)

TABLE 10.3 Sample Applications Of Expert Systems

Expert Systems	Organization	Application Domain
MYCIN	Stanford University	Medical diagnosis
XCOM	DEC	System configuration
Expert Tax	Coopers & Lybrand	Tax planning
Loan Probe	Peat Marwick	Loan evaluation
La-Courtier	Cognitive Systems	Financial planning
LMOS	Pacific Bell	Network management
Fish-Expert	North China	Disease diagnosis

ments. The system can handle in one minute a customer request that typically took the sales team 20–30 minutes. With the expert system, service accuracy increased to 98 percent from a manual approach of 65 percent, thereby saving millions of dollars every year.

CREDIT ANALYSIS

Expert systems have been developed to support the needs of commercial lending institutions. They can help analyze the credit record of a customer and assess a proper credit line. Rules in the knowledge base can also help assess the risk and risk-management policies. This kind of system is employed in over one-third of the top 100 commercial banks in the United States and Canada.

PENSION FUND ADVISER

Nestle Foods Corporation has developed an expert system that provides information on employee pension fund status. The system maintains an up-to-date knowledge base to give participants advice concerning the impact of regulation changes and conformance with new standards. A system offered on the Internet at the Pingtung Teacher's College in southern Taiwan has functions that allow the participants to plan their retirement through a what-if analysis that calculates their pension benefits under different scenarios.

AREAS FOR APPLICATIONS

Expert systems have been applied commercially in the following areas.

1. *Finance:* insurance evaluation, credit analysis, tax planning, financial report analysis, financial planning, performance evaluation.
2. *Data processing:* system planning, equipment selection, equipment maintenance, vendor evaluation, network management.
3. *Marketing:* customer-relationship management, market analysis, product planning, market planning.
4. *Human resources:* human resource planning, performance evaluation, staff scheduling, pension management, legal advising.
5. *Manufacturing:* production planning, quality management, product design, plant-site selection, equipment maintenance and repair.

10.7 STRUCTURE OF EXPERT SYSTEMS

Expert systems can be viewed as having two environments: the **development environment** and the **consultation (runtime) environment** (Figure 10.3). The development environment is used by an ES builder to build the components and put knowledge into

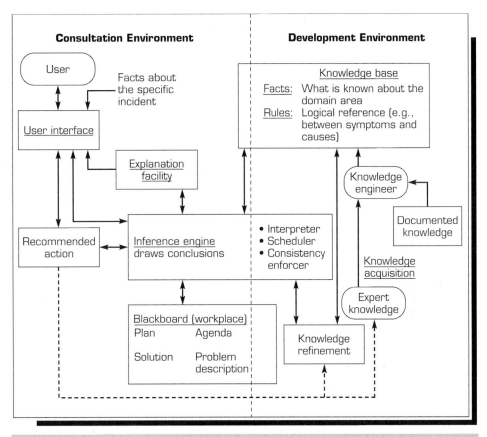

FIGURE 10.3 STRUCTURE OF AN EXPERT SYSTEM

the knowledge base. The consultation environment is used by a non-expert to obtain expert knowledge and advice. These environments can be separated once a system is completed.

The three major components that appear in virtually every expert system are the **knowledge base**, **inference engine**, and user interface. An expert system that interacts with users may also contain the following additional components:

- **Knowledge acquisition** subsystem
- **Blackboard** (workplace)
- **Explanation subsystem** (justifier)
- **Knowledge-refining system**

Most expert systems do not at present contain the knowledge-refinement component. A brief description of each component follows.

KNOWLEDGE ACQUISITION SUBSYSTEM

Knowledge acquisition is the accumulation, transfer, and transformation of problem-solving expertise from experts or documented knowledge sources to a computer program for constructing or expanding the knowledge base. Potential sources of knowledge include human experts, textbooks, multimedia documents, databases (public and private), special research reports, and information available on the Web.

Acquiring knowledge from experts is a complex task that often creates a bottleneck in ES construction. In building large systems one needs a **knowledge engineer** or knowledge elicitation expert to interact with one or more human experts in building the knowledge base. Typically the knowledge engineer helps the expert structure the problem area by interpreting and integrating human answers to questions, drawing analogies, posing counterexamples, and bringing conceptual difficulties to light.

KNOWLEDGE BASE

The **knowledge base** contains the relevant knowledge necessary for understanding, formulating, and solving problems. It includes two basic elements: (1) facts, such as the problem situation and the theory of the problem area, and (2) special heuristics or rules that direct the use of knowledge to solve specific problems in a particular domain. (In addition, the inference engine can include general purpose problem-solving and decision-making rules.) The heuristics express the informal judgmental knowledge in an application area. Knowledge, not mere facts, is the primary raw material of expert systems.

INFERENCE ENGINE

The "brain" of the ES is the **inference engine**, also known as the control structure or the rule interpreter (in rule-based ES). This component is essentially a computer program that provides a methodology for reasoning about information in the knowledge base and on the blackboard, and for formulating conclusions. This component provides directions about how to use the system's knowledge by developing the agenda that organizes and controls the steps taken to solve problems whenever consultation takes place. It will be further elaborated in Section 10.8.

USER INTERFACE

Expert systems contain a language processor for friendly, problem-oriented communication between the user and the computer. This communication can best be carried out in a natural language. Due to technological constraints, most existing systems use the question-and-answer approach to interact with the user. Sometimes it is supplemented by menus, electronic forms, and graphics.

BLACKBOARD (WORKPLACE)

The **blackboard** is an area of working memory set aside as a database for the description of a current problem as specified by the input data; it is also used for recording intermediate hypotheses and decisions. Three types of decisions can be recorded on the blackboard: a plan (how to attack the problem), an agenda (potential actions awaiting execution), and a solution (candidate hypotheses and alternative courses of action that the system has generated thus far).

Consider an example. When your car fails, you enter the symptoms of the failure into the computer for storage in the blackboard. As the result of an intermediate hypothesis developed in the blackboard, the computer may then suggest that you do some additional checks (e.g., see whether your battery is connected properly) and report the results. This information is recorded in the blackboard.

EXPLANATION SUBSYSTEM (JUSTIFIER)

The ability to trace responsibility for conclusions to their sources is crucial both in the transfer of expertise and in problem-solving. The **explanation subsystem** (also called **Justifier**) can trace such responsibility and explain the ES behavior by interactively answering questions like the following:

- Why was a certain question asked by the expert system?
- How was a certain conclusion reached?
- Why was a certain alternative rejected?
- What is the plan to reach the solution? For example, what remains to be established before a final diagnosis can be determined?

In simple ES, the explanation shows the rules used to derive the specific recommendations.

KNOWLEDGE REFINING SYSTEM

Human experts have a **knowledge-refining system**; that is, they can analyze their own knowledge and its use, learn from it, and improve on it for future consultations. Similarly, such evaluation is necessary in computerized learning so that the program can analyze the reasons for its success or failure. This could lead to improvements that result in a more accurate knowledge base and more effective reasoning. Such a component is not available in commercial expert systems at the moment but is being developed in experimental ES at several universities and research institutions.

10.8 HOW EXPERT SYSTEMS WORK

Among the components in Figure 10.3, the knowledge base and inference engine are the most critical modules for an expert system to function properly. Knowledge must be represented and organized properly in the knowledge base. The inference engine can then use the knowledge to infer new conclusions from existing facts and rules. In this section, we introduce the knowledge base structure and inference engine of rule-based systems.

KNOWLEDGE REPRESENTATION AND ORGANIZATION

Expert knowledge must be represented in a computer-understandable format and organized properly in the knowledge base of an expert system. There are many different ways of representing human knowledge, including **production rules**, **semantic networks**, and **logic** statements (all described in detail in Chapter 11). In rule-based systems, knowledge in the knowledge base is represented in *IF-THEN rules* that combine the *condition* and the *conclusion* for handling a specific situation. The IF part indicates the condition for the rule to be activated, and the THEN part shows the action or the conclusion if all IF conditions are satisfied.

In the example of selecting a notebook computer, several rules may be defined for choosing between Acer 320 and IBM X30:

Rule 1:

IF the primary task = word processing
AND primary usage = travel
THEN weight requirement = light

Rule 2:

IF the primary task = word processing
AND primary usage = office
THEN weight requirement = don't care

Rule 3:

IF budget <=12,000
AND budget >10,000
AND weight requirement = light
Then NB model = IBM X30

Rule 4:

IF budget < 10,000
AND weight requirement = don't care
THEN NB model = Acer 320.

The advantage of using production rules is that they are easy to understand and new rules can easily be added into the knowledge base without affecting existing rules. The uncertainty associated with each rule may be added to enhance its accuracy. **Uncertainty processing** is another topic that will be discussed in Chapter 11.

A major task of expert system development is to acquire the knowledge from human experts and convert it into production rules that can be handled by an inference engine. The inference engine chooses applicable rules from the knowledge base, integrates them, and reasons to find the conclusion.

THE INFERENCE ENGINE

In complex decisions, expert knowledge often cannot be represented in single rules. Instead, rules may be chained together dynamically to cover numerous conditions. The process of chaining multiple rules together based on available data is called inference. The component conducting inference in an expert system is called the inference engine. Two popular approaches for inferencing are forward chaining and backward chaining. More reasoning strategies, such as case-based reasoning, and advanced techniques are discussed in Chapters 11 and 12.

FORWARD CHAINING

Forward chaining looks for the IF part of a rule first. Once all the IF conditions are met, the rule is chosen for deriving the conclusion. If the conclusion derived from the first state is not final, then it is used as new fact to match with the IF condition of other rules to find a more useful conclusion. This process continues until a final conclusion is reached.

Using the notebook-selection rule base described earlier as an example, forward chaining would check two IF conditions associated with Rules 1 and 2: whether the primary task is word processing, and whether the primary usage is in office or travel. If the task is word processing and usage is travel, then Rule 1 applies and the weight requirement is set to light. Since the weight requirement is not the final goal, the inference engine further searches the knowledge base and finds that one IF condition of Rule 3 matches the conclusion from Rule 1. Because Rule 3 has more IF conditions to be checked, the inference engine triggers Rule 3 and checks to see whether the price condition is satisfied. If the price condition is also satisfied, then Rule 3 will be activated and the system recommends IBM X30 to the user. The sequence of activating rules in the rule base is Rule 1 → Rule 2 → Rules 3 or 4 (depending upon the result in the preceding step). Table 10.4 shows the sessions interacting with the user.

BACKWARD CHAINING

Backward chaining is the reverse of forward chaining. It *starts from the conclusion* and hypothesizes that the conclusion is true. The inference engine then identifies the IF conditions necessary for making the conclusion true and locates facts to test whether the IF conditions are true. If all IF conditions are true, then the rule is chosen and the conclusion is reached. If some conditions are false, then the rule is discarded and the next rule is picked as the second hypothesis. If no facts prove that all the IF conditions are true or false, the inference engine continues to seek for rules whose conclusion would match the undecided IF condition to move a step further for checking the conditions. Similarly, this chaining process continues until a set of rules is found to reach a conclusion or to prove unable to reach a conclusion.

Using the same example, the inference process of backward chaining starts from Rule 3. The inference engine assumes that IBM X30 is a product for recommendation and checks the IF conditions of "weight requirement" and "budget." Since weight requirement is the conclusion of Rules 1 and 2, the engine chains these two rules with Rule 3. The new IF conditions become "primary task" and "primary usage." The sequence of activating rules in this case is Rule 3 → Rule 1 → Rule 2. Table 10.4 shows the sessions with the user.

TABLE 10.4   Consultation Sessions Using Different Inference Strategies

Forward Chaining	*Backward Chaining*

☐ What is your primary task to be performed on the notebook computer?
  ■ Word processing
  ☐ Communications
  ☐ Multimedia applications
☐ Where are you going to use the notebook more often?
  ☐ Office
  ■ Travel
☐ What is your budget range?
  ☐ below 10K,
  ■ between 10–12K,
  ☐ above 12K
☐ System recommendation
  You should consider buying an IBM X24
	☐ What is your budget range?
	  ☐ below 10K,
	  ■ between 10–12K,
	  ☐ above 12K
	☐ What is your primary task to be performed on the notebook computer?
	  ■ Word processing
	  ☐ Communications
	  ☐ Multimedia applications
	☐ Where are you going to use the notebook more often?
	  ☐ Office
	  ■ Travel
	☐ System recommendation
	  You should consider buying an IBM X24

Reasons: it is light and more suitable for your word-processing and travel needs, it also fits your budget.	Reasons: it is light and more suitable for your word-processing and travel needs, it also fits your budget.

DEVELOPMENT PROCESS OF EXPERT SYSTEMS

Expert systems development is a process for eliciting knowledge from experts and storing it in the knowledge base. Since human experts may be unwilling or unable to articulate their knowledge, knowledge acquisition is a critical and tough task.

A typical process for developing expert systems includes knowledge acquisition, knowledge representation, selection of development tools, system prototyping, evaluation, and improvement. Since the inference engine is common to different systems, **expert system shells** are useful tools that can implement a rule-based system in a very short time. An expert system shell is an expert system without the knowledge in the knowledge base. The system runs once the knowledge is stored in the knowledge base. More details are available in Chapter 11.

10.9 PROBLEM AREAS SUITABLE FOR EXPERT SYSTEMS

Expert systems can be classified in several ways. One way is by the general problem areas they address. For example, diagnosis can be defined as "inferring system malfunctions from observations." Diagnosis is a generic activity performed in medicine, organizational studies, computer operations, and other fields. The generic categories of expert systems are listed in Table 10.5. Some ES belong to two or more of these categories. A brief description of each category follows:

Interpretation systems infer situation descriptions from observations. This category includes surveillance, speech understanding, image analysis, signal interpretation, and many kinds of intelligence analyses. An interpretation system explains observed data by assigning them symbolic meanings describing the situation.

Prediction systems include weather forecasting, demographic predictions, economic forecasting, traffic predictions, crop estimates, and military, marketing, and financial forecasting.

Diagnostic systems include medical, electronic, mechanical, and software diagnoses. Diagnostic systems typically relate observed behavioral irregularities to underlying causes.

Design systems develop configurations of objects that satisfy the constraints of the design problem. Such problems include circuit layout, building design, and plant

TABLE 10.5   Generic Categories of Expert Systems

Category	Problem Addressed
Interpretation	Inferring situation descriptions from observations
Prediction	Inferring likely consequences of given situations
Diagnosis	Inferring system malfunctions from observations
Design	Configuring objects under constraints
Planning	Developing plans to achieve goals
Monitoring	Comparing observations to plans, flagging exceptions
Debugging	Prescribing remedies for malfunctions
Repair	Executing a plan to administer a prescribed remedy
Instruction	Diagnosing, debugging, and correcting student performance
Control	Interpreting, predicting, repairing, and monitoring system behaviors

layout. Design systems construct descriptions of objects in various relationships with one another and verify that these configurations conform to stated constraints.

Planning systems   specialize in planning problems, such as automatic programming. They also deal with short- and long-term planning in areas such as project management, routing, communications, product development, military applications, and financial planning.

Monitoring systems   compare observations of system behavior with standards that seem crucial for successful goal attainment. These crucial features correspond to potential flaws in the plan. There are many computer-aided monitoring systems for topics ranging from air traffic control to fiscal management tasks.

Debugging systems   rely on planning, design, and prediction capabilities for creating specifications or recommendations to correct a diagnosed problem.

Repair systems   develop and execute plans to administer a remedy for certain diagnosed problems. Such systems incorporate debugging, planning, and execution capabilities.

Instruction systems   incorporate diagnosis and debugging subsystems that specifically address the student's needs. Typically, these systems begin by constructing a hypothetical description of the student's knowledge that interprets her or his behavior. They then diagnose weaknesses in the student's knowledge and identify appropriate remedies to overcome the deficiencies. Finally, they plan a tutorial interaction intended to deliver remedial knowledge to the student.

Control systems   adaptively govern the overall behavior of a system. To do this, the control system must repeatedly interpret the current situation, predict the future, diagnose the causes of anticipated problems, formulate a remedial plan, and monitor its execution to ensure success.

Not all the tasks usually found in each of these categories are suitable for expert systems. However, there are thousands of decisions that do fit into these categories.

10.10 BENEFITS AND CAPABILITIES OF EXPERT SYSTEMS

Thousands of expert systems are in use today in almost every industry and in every functional area. Wong and Monaco (1995) provide a comprehensive review and literature analysis of expert systems in business. Eom (1996) made a comprehensive survey of about 440 operational expert systems in business. His survey revealed that many ES have a profound impact, shrinking the time for tasks from days to hours, minutes, or seconds, and that the nonquantifiable benefits of the systems include improved customer satisfaction, improved quality of products and services, and accurate and consistent decision-making. Expert systems in finance and in engineering applications are discussed in Nedovic and Devedzic (2002) and Nurminen et al. (2003). For many firms, ES have become indispensable tools for effective management. The major potential ES benefits are discussed next.

INCREASED OUTPUT AND PRODUCTIVITY

ES can work faster than humans. For example, XCON (see this book's Web site) has enabled DEC to increase the throughput of VAX configuring orders fourfold.

DECREASED DECISION-MAKING TIME

Using recommendations provided by an ES, a human can make decisions much faster. For example, American Express representatives make charge-approval decisions in less than five seconds, compared to about three minutes before implementation of an ES. This property is important in supporting frontline decision-makers (Chapter 8) who must make quick decisions while interacting with customers.

INCREASED PROCESS AND PRODUCT QUALITY

ES can increase quality by providing consistent advice and reducing the size and rate of errors. For example, XCON reduced the error rate of configuring computer orders from 35 percent to 2 percent (initially—even less in later releases), thus improving the quality of the minicomputers.

REDUCED DOWNTIME

Many operational ES are used for diagnosing malfunctions and prescribing repairs. By using ES it is possible to reduce machine downtime significantly. For example, on an oil rig one day of lost time can cost as much as $250,000. A system called Drilling Advisor was developed to detect malfunctions in oil rigs. This system saved a considerable amount of money for the company by significantly reducing downtime.

CAPTURE OF SCARCE EXPERTISE

The scarcity of expertise becomes evident in situations where there are not enough experts for a task, the expert is about to retire or leave the job, or expertise is required over a broad geographic area. The example described in the Opening Vignette is a good example.

FLEXIBILITY

ES can offer flexibility in both the service and manufacturing industries.

EASIER EQUIPMENT OPERATION

Expert systems make complex equipment easier to operate. STEAMER was an early ES intended to train inexperienced workers to operate complex ship engines. Another example is the ES developed for Shell Oil Company to train people to use complex computer program routines.

ELIMINATION OF THE NEED
FOR EXPENSIVE EQUIPMENT

Often a human must rely on expensive instruments for monitoring and control. ES can perform the same tasks with lower-cost instruments because of their ability to investigate the information provided by instruments faster and more thoroughly.

OPERATION IN HAZARDOUS ENVIRONMENTS

Many tasks must be performed in hazardous environments. An ES can allow humans to avoid such environments. It enables workers to avoid hot, humid, or toxic environments, such as a nuclear power plant that has malfunctioned. This feature is extremely important in military conflicts.

ACCESSIBILITY TO KNOWLEDGE AND HELP DESKS

Expert systems make knowledge accessible, thus freeing experts from routine work. People can query systems and receive useful advice. One area of applicability is the support of help desks (Dryden, 1996). See the Exsys Corporation (www.exsys.com), www.inference.com, and Ginesys Corporation (www.ginesys.com) Web sites. Another is the support of call centers that now use Web-based intelligent systems (Thomas et al., 1997; Orzech, 1998) (see www.clarify.com).

ABILITY TO WORK WITH INCOMPLETE OR UNCERTAIN INFORMATION

In contrast to conventional computer systems, expert systems, like human experts, can work with incomplete, imprecise, uncertain data, information, or knowledge. The user can respond with "don't know" or "not sure" to one or more of the system's questions during a consultation, and the ES will still be able to produce an answer, although it may not be a certain one.

PROVISION OF TRAINING

ES can provide training. Novices who work with ES become more and more experienced. The explanation facility can also serve as a teaching device, and so can notes and explanations inserted into the knowledge base.

ENHANCEMENT OF PROBLEM-SOLVING AND DECISION-MAKING

ES enhance problem-solving by allowing the integration of the judgments of top experts into the analysis. For example, an ES called Statistical Navigator was developed to help novices use statistically complex computer packages.

IMPROVED DECISION-MAKING PROCESSES

ES provide rapid feedback on decision consequences, facilitate communication among decision-makers on a team, and allow rapid response to unforeseen changes in the environment, thus providing a better understanding of the decision-making situation.

IMPROVED DECISION QUALITY

ES are reliable. They do not become tired or bored, call in sick, or go on strike, and they do not talk back to the boss. ES consistently pay attention to details and do not overlook relevant information and potential solutions, thereby making fewer errors. Also, ES provide the same recommendations to repeated problems.

ABILITY TO SOLVE COMPLEX PROBLEMS

One day ES may explain complex problems whose solution is beyond human ability. Some ES are already able to solve problems in which the required scope of knowledge exceeds that of any one individual. This allows decision-makers to gain control over complicated situations and improve the operation of complex systems.

KNOWLEDGE TRANSFER TO REMOTE LOCATIONS

One of the greatest potential benefits of ES is its ease of transfer across international boundaries. An example of such a transfer is an eye-care ES (for diagnosis and recommended treatment) developed at Rutgers University in conjunction with the World Health Organization. The program has been implemented in Egypt and Algeria, where serious eye diseases are prevalent but eye specialists are rare. The PC program is rule-based and can be operated by a nurse, a physician's assistant, or a general practitioner. The Web is used extensively to disseminate information to users in remote locations. The U.S. government, for example, places advisory systems on safety and other topics on its Web sites (www.osha-slc.gov/dts/osta/oshasoft).

ENHANCEMENT OF OTHER INFORMATION SYSTEMS

Expert systems often provide intelligent capabilities to other information systems.

Many of these benefits lead to improved decision-making, improved products and customer service, and a sustainable strategic advantage. Some may even enhance the organization's image. Basden (1994) provides a model of three levels of benefits from ES: feature benefits, task benefits, and role benefits. This model can be used to predict ES success (Section 10.12).

10.11 PROBLEMS AND LIMITATIONS OF EXPERT SYSTEMS

Available ES methodologies may not be straightforward and effective, even for many applications in the generic categories. The following problems have slowed down the commercial spread of ES:

- Knowledge is not always readily available.
- It can be difficult to extract expertise from humans.
- The approach of each expert to a situation assessment may be different yet correct.
- It is hard, even for a highly skilled expert, to abstract good situational assessments when under time pressure.
- Users of expert systems have natural cognitive limits.
- ES work well only within a narrow domain of knowledge.
- Most experts have no independent means of checking whether their conclusions are reasonable.
- The vocabulary, or jargon, that experts use to express facts and relations is often limited and not understood by others.
- Help is often required from knowledge engineers who are rare and expensive, a fact that could make ES construction costly.
- Lack of trust on the part of end-users may be a barrier to ES use.
- Knowledge transfer is subject to a host of perceptual and judgmental biases.

Last, but not least, expert systems may not be able to arrive at conclusions. For example, the fully developed XCON could not initially fulfill about 2 percent of the orders presented to it. Moreover, expert systems, like human experts, sometimes produce incorrect recommendations.

The Web is the major facilitator of ES that overcomes several of these limitations. The ability to disseminate ES to the masses makes them more cost-effective. Consequently, more money can be spent on better systems.

Gill (1995) studied the longevity of commercial expert systems. He discovered that only about one-third of all commercial ES studied survived over a five-year period. The short-lived nature of so many systems was generally not attributable to failure to meet technical performance or economic objectives. Instead, managerial issues, such as lack of system acceptance by users, inability to retain developers, problems in transitioning from development to maintenance, and shifts in organizational priorities, appeared to be the most significant factors resulting in long-term ES disuse. Proper management of ES development and deployment can resolve most of these issues in practice.

These limitations clearly indicate that today's ES fall short of generally intelligent human behavior. However, several of these limitations will diminish or disappear with technological improvements over time.

10.12 EXPERT SYSTEM SUCCESS FACTORS

Several researchers have investigated the reasons why expert systems succeed and fail in practice. This work includes studies by Eom (1996), Guimaraes et al. (1996), Kunnathur et al. (1996), Tsai et al. (1994a), and Yoon et al. (1995). As with many management information systems, two of the most critical factors are a champion in management, user involvement, and training. Management must support the project, and users must feel ownership. Many studies have shown that the level of managerial and user involvement directly affects the success level of MIS, specifically ES. However, these factors alone are not sufficient to guarantee success, and the following issues should also be considered:

- The level of knowledge must be sufficiently high.
- Expertise must be available from at least one cooperative expert.
- The problem to be solved must be mostly qualitative (fuzzy), not purely quantitative (otherwise, a numerical approach should be used).
- The problem must be sufficiently narrow in scope.
- ES shell characteristics are important. The shell must be of high quality and naturally store and manipulate the knowledge.
- The user interface must be friendly for novice users.
- The problem must be important and difficult enough to warrant development of an ES (but it need not be a core function).
- Knowledgeable system developers with good people skills are needed.
- The impact of ES as a source of end-user job improvement must be considered. The impact should be favorable. End-user attitudes and expectations must be considered.
- Management support must be cultivated.

Managers attempting to introduce ES technology should establish end-user training programs that demonstrate its potential as a business tool (Guimaraes et al., 1996). As part of the managerial support effort, the organizational environment should favor the adoption of new technology (Kunnathur et al., 1996). Finally, Tsai et al. (1994a) present the following conclusions:

- Business applications for expert systems are often justified by their strategic impact in terms of gaining a competitive advantage rather than their cost-effectiveness. The major value of expert systems stems from capturing and disseminating expert-type skills and knowledge to improve the quality and consistency of business operations.

- The most popular and successful expert systems are those that deal with well-defined, structured applications, or where no more than several hundred rules are needed, such as in the production area. Expert systems have been less successful when applications require instincts and experienced judgments, as in the human resources management area, or where there are thousands of rules and exceptions.

Gill (1996b) conducted a survey of 52 successful expert systems and found that ES that persist over time change the nature of the users' tasks and jobs in a manner that motivates continued use of the system. These tools offer users a greater sense of control, increase work-related variety or decrease work-related drudgery, enable users to perform tasks at much higher proficiency levels or to assess their own task performance, and so on. Gill cautioned expert systems developers and their managers to recognize that design features providing such intrinsic motivation must be built into the technology. As soon as the idea for an expert system (or, in fact, an IT-based application) has been conceived, it is time to start assessing its impact on user motivation. And if the outcome of such assessments is that motivational impacts will most likely be negative, the viability of the development effort should be reconsidered—expert systems whose "motivation for use" is negative just do not last very long. An interesting study of a failing system at a large consumer product company is reported by Vedder et al. (1999).

10.13 TYPES OF EXPERT SYSTEMS

Expert systems appear in many varieties. The following classifications of ES are not exclusive; that is, one ES can appear in several categories.

EXPERT SYSTEMS VERSUS KNOWLEDGE-BASED SYSTEMS

According to this classification, an expert system is a system whose behavior is so sophisticated that we would call a person who performed in a similar manner an expert. MYCIN and XCON are good examples. Highly trained professionals diagnose blood diseases (MYCIN) and configure complex computing equipment (XCON). These systems truly attempt to emulate the best human experts.

In the commercial world, however, there are systems that can effectively and efficiently perform tasks that do not really need an expert. Such systems are called knowledge-based systems (also known as advisory systems, knowledge systems, intelligent job-aid systems, or operational systems). As an example, let us look at a system that gives advice on the immunizations recommended for travel abroad. This advice depends on many attributes, such as the age, gender, and health of the traveler and the country of destination. One needs to be knowledgeable to give such advice, but one need not be an expert. In this case, practically all the relevant knowledge is documented in a manual available from most public health departments (in only 1 or 2 percent of the cases is it necessary to consult a physician). Another example is automated help desks (see AIS in Action 10.8).

The distinction between the two types of ES systems may not be so sharp in reality. Many systems involve both documented knowledge and undocumented expertise.

AIS IN ACTION 10.8

AUTOMATING THE HELP DESK

Millions of employees work in organizations as providers of information and are in direct contact with customers. Often customers are frustrated because all the lines are busy when they call an information center. ("All agents are busy. You are important to us; please stay on the line. Someone will be with you as soon as possible.") Also, the information provided may not be accurate. The solution is to automate the help desk by using expert systems.

An example is Color Tile Company, which uses Expert Advisor (from Software Artistry Inc.) to support queries from its own employees. Formerly, operators had to search through numerous manuals to pro-vide advice on how to fix problems in the point-of-sale terminals at the many Color Tile stores. Using the ES, operators can now determine the solution to the problem much faster and more accurately. Such systems are now available for employees on intranets and for customers on extranets. Peppers et al. (1999) provide the example of Canadian Tire Acceptance Ltd., which serves 4 million credit card holders. By employing Web technology the intelligent center integrated all incoming inquiries (fax, telephone, Web). Using an ES, the system analyzes customers' profiles and recognizes needs so that better service can be provided.

Basically it is a matter of how much expertise is included in systems that classifies them in one category or the other. Knowledge systems can be constructed more quickly and cheaply than expert systems.

RULE-BASED EXPERT SYSTEMS

Many commercial expert systems are **rule-based systems** because the technology of rule-based systems is well developed and the development tools can be used by end-users. In such systems, knowledge is represented as a series of rules.

FRAME-BASED SYSTEMS

In **frame-based systems**, knowledge is represented as frames, a representation of the object-oriented programming approach (see the discussion of knowledge representation in Chapter 11).

HYBRID SYSTEMS

Hybrid systems include several knowledge-representation approaches; at a minimum they typically involve frames and rules. Advanced techniques such as artificial neural networks and fuzzy logic are sometimes integrated with rules to provide better advices.

MODEL-BASED SYSTEMS

Model-based systems are structured around a model that simulates the structure and function of the system under study. The model is used to compute values that are compared to observed values. The comparison triggers action (if needed) or further diagnosis (Chapter 12).

READY-MADE (OFF-THE-SHELF) SYSTEMS

Expert systems can be custom-made to meet the needs of a specific user or purchased as ready-made packages for general use. **Ready-made systems** are similar to such application packages as accounting general ledgers or project management in operations management. Ready-made systems enjoy the economy of mass production and therefore are considerably less expensive than customized systems. They can be used as soon as they are purchased (several are available on the Web). Unfortunately, ready-made systems are very general in nature, and the advice they render may not be of value to a user involved in a complex situation. However, their popularity has been increasing as their prices decrease and their capabilities increase. There are two types of ready-made system: those for general use, and those that are industry-, country-, or product-specific.

REAL-TIME EXPERT SYSTEMS

In **real-time Expert Systems**, a strict limit is set on the system's response time, which must be fast enough to control the process being computerized. In other words, the system always produces a response by the time it is needed.

10.14 EXPERT SYSTEMS ON THE WEB

The relationship between ES and the Internet (the Net) and intranets can be divided into two categories. The first is the use of ES on the Net. In this case the Net supports ES (and other AI) applications. The second is the support ES (and other AI methods) give to the Net.

USING ES ON THE NET

One of the early reasons for ES development was its potential to provide knowledge and advice to large numbers of users. Because knowledge is disseminated to many people, the cost per user becomes small, making ES very attractive. However, according to Eriksson (1996), attaining this goal has proven to be very difficult. Because advisory systems are used infrequently, they need a large number of users to justify their construction. As a result, very few ES disseminate knowledge to many users.

The widespread availability and use of the Internet and intranets provide the opportunity to disseminate expertise and knowledge to mass audiences. By implementing expert systems (and other intelligent systems) as knowledge servers, it becomes economically feasible and profitable to publish expertise on the Net. ES running on servers can support a large group of users who communicate with the system over the Net. In this way user interfaces based on Web protocols and the use of browsers provide access to the knowledge servers. This implementation approach is described in Eriksson (1996). At the Exsys Web site you can try *Banner with Brains*, which integrates expert system capabilities into a Web banner (see AIS in Action 10.9).

ES can be transferred over the Net not only to human users but to other computerized systems, including DSS, robotics, and databases. Other ES Net-support possibilities include system construction. Here, collaboration between builders, experts, and knowledge engineers can be facilitated by Internet-based groupware. This can reduce the cost of building ES. Knowledge-acquisition costs can be reduced, for example, in cases where there are several experts or where the expert is in a different location from the knowledge engineer. Knowledge maintenance can also facilitate the use of the Net, which is also helpful to users.

Finally, the Web can greatly support the spread of multimedia-based expert systems. Such systems, called intelimedia systems, support the integration of extensive multimedia applications and ES. Such systems can be very helpful for remote users,

AIS IN ACTION 10.9

BANNER WITH BRAINS: WEB-BASED EXPERT SYSTEMS FOR RESTAURANT SELECTION

Selecting a restaurant for dating or business in a foreign city has never been easier thanks to the availability of services over the Web and support from expert systems. On the Web site of Exsys (www.exsys.com), you can try a demo system that integrates an expert system with a banner. All interactions are through the banner.

The expert system is familiar with restaurants in Albuquerque, New Mexico. When you need to find a restaurant, the system asks about the occasion and the type of food you desire. Your preference data are then fed to a spreadsheet of information on the various restaurants. The system creates a probabilistic ranking of the restaurants that meet your needs. It then weights various factors based on the specified occasion and displays up to five restaurants. It also explains why these restaurants are recommended. This kind of application will become increasingly popular in the future.

Note: site accessed in June 2003.

such as those in the tourism industry (see _IEEE Intelligent Systems_, November/December 2002), and in remote equipment-failure diagnosis.

The other aspect of the ES–Internet relationship is the support ES and other AI technologies can provide to the Internet and intranets. The major contributions of AI to the Internet and intranets are summarized in Table 10.6.

Information about the relationships between expert systems, intelligent agents and other AI, and the Internet is readily available on the Internet. For example, the Web

TABLE 10.6	Ai/Es And Web Impacts	
Aspects	**Impacts From The Web**	**Impacts On The Web**
Knowledge acquisition	Experts in different areas may collaborate over the Internet Knowledge acquisition can be done at different times to fit the schedules of different experts Knowledge acquired from different experts may be shared on the Internet to stimulate discussion for enhancement	Knowledge of Web operations and activities may be acquired and managed for sharing and use
Expert systems development	Collaborative design of expert systems by a geographically distributed team becomes possible Outsourcing of the design effort becomes feasible ES evaluation can be done remotely Web provides a unified multimedia user interface for easy system integration Web services provide a better platform for designing ES	ES can be designed to support Web activities, automatic services, and better performance
Expert systems consultation	Users in remote areas can use the system to solve problems Expertise is easily disseminated to a large body of users	Application of ES for Web browsing and monitoring

sites of PC AI (a magazine) (www.pcai.com) and the American Association for Artificial Intelligence (www.aaai.org) provide a good set of hyperlinks to related Web sites. UMBC (agents.umbc.edu) provides a good collection of resources on intelligent agents.

❖ CHAPTER HIGHLIGHTS

- Artificial intelligence is a discipline that investigates how to build computer systems to perform tasks that can be characterized as intelligent.
- The major characteristics of AI are symbolic processing, the use of heuristics instead of algorithms, and the application of inference techniques.
- AI has several major advantages over human intelligence—it is permanent, easily duplicated and disseminated, cheaper, consistent and thorough, and it can be documented.
- Natural (human) intelligence has advantages over AI—it is creative, uses sensory experiences directly, and reasons from a wide context of experiences.
- Knowledge rather than data or information is the major focus of AI.
- Major areas of AI include expert systems, natural language processing, speech understanding, intelligent robotics, computer vision, fuzzy logic, intelligent agents, intelligent computer-aided instruction, and neural computing.
- Expert systems are the most widely applied AI technology. Such systems attempt to imitate the work of experts. They capture human expertise and apply it to problem-solving.
- To be effective, an expert system must be applied to a narrow domain and the knowledge must include qualitative factors.
- Natural language processing investigates techniques that allow users to communicate with computers in a natural language. It include textual-based and voice-based natural language user interfaces.
- An intelligent robot is a computer-based program or machine that can respond to changes in its environment. Most of today's robots do not have this capability.
- Intelligent tutoring systems use AI technology to help the user learn knowledge. Artificial intelligence can improve the performance of training and teaching.
- The power of an ES is derived from the specific knowledge it possesses, not from the knowledge-representation and inference schemes it uses.
- Expertise is task-specific knowledge acquired from training, reading, and experience.
- Experts can make good, fast decisions in complex situations.

- Most knowledge in organizations is possessed by a few experts.
- Knowledge can be declarative (facts) or procedural.
- Expert system technology can transfer knowledge from experts and documented sources to the computer and make it available for use by non-experts.
- Major components of an ES are the knowledge-acquisition subsystem, knowledge base, inference engine, blackboard, user interface, and explanation subsystem.
- The inference engine provides reasoning capability for expert systems.
- Inferences of ES can be done by forward chaining or backward chaining.
- Knowledge engineers are professionals who know how to capture knowledge from the expert and structure it in a form that can be processed by the computer-based expert systems.
- Expert systems are popular in 10 generic categories: interpretation, prediction, diagnosis, design, planning, monitoring, debugging, repair, instruction, and control.
- The expert system shell is an expert system development tool that has the inference engine and building blocks for the knowledge base and the user interface. Knowledge engineers can easily develop a prototype system by entering rules in the knowledge base.
- Expert systems have many benefits. The most important are improved productivity or quality, preservation of scarce expertise, enhancement of other systems, coping with incomplete information, and providing training.
- Many ES failures are caused by nontechnical problems, such as lack of managerial support and poor end-user training.
- Although there are several technical limitations to the use of expert systems, some of them will disappear with improved technology.
- Some ES are available as ready-made systems; they render advice for standard situations. A trend is developing toward disseminating such advice on the Internet, intranets, and extranets.
- Some expert systems provide advice in a real-time mode.
- ES and AI provide support to the Internet and intranets as well.

❖ KEY WORDS

- algorithm
- artificial intelligence (AI)
- automated translation
- backward chaining
- blackboard
- consultation environment
- development environment
- domain
- expert
- expert system (ES)
- expert system shell
- expertise
- explanation subsystem
- forward chaining
- frame-based system
- fuzzy logic
- game playing

- genetic algorithms
- heuristics
- hybrid system
- inference engine
- inferencing
- intelligent agent (IA)
- intelligent computer-aided instruction (ICAI)
- intelligent tutoring system (ITS)
- justifier
- knowledge
- knowledge acquisition
- knowledge base
- knowledge engineer
- knowledge-refining system
- knowledge-based system
- logic

- model-based system
- natural language processing (NLP)
- neural computing (networks)
- numeric processing
- production rules
- ready-made system
- real-time ES
- robotics
- rule-based system
- semantic networks
- sensory system
- speech understanding
- symbol
- symbolic processing
- Turing test
- uncertainty processing
- visual recognition

❖ QUESTIONS FOR REVIEW

1. What is artificial intelligence?
2. What is the Turing test?
3. What do we mean by inferencing?
4. List the major advantages of artificial intelligence over natural intelligence.
5. List the major disadvantages of artificial intelligence as compared to natural intelligence.
6. Describe the difference between a knowledge base for an application and an organizational knowledge base.
7. List the major AI technologies.
8. Define an expert system.
9. Define natural language processing.
10. Define speech recognition and understanding. Why is it useful?
11. Define an intelligent agent. Why is it useful?
12. List the major benefits of intelligent computer-aided instruction.
13. List the types of knowledge that constitute expertise.
14. Define the ES development environment and contrast it with the consultation environment.
15. List and define the major components of an ES.
16. What is the role of a knowledge engineer?
17. Describe how expert systems perform inference?
18. What are the major activities performed in the ES blackboard (workplace)?
19. Describe generic categories of ES applications.
20. Describe some of the limitations of ES.
21. Describe the success factors of ES.
22. What is a ready-made (off-the-shelf) ES?
23. What is a real-time ES?
24. What are the benefits of deploying an ES on the Web?
25. How can an ES help a decision-maker in Web use?

❖ QUESTIONS FOR DISCUSSION

1. Compare numeric and symbolic processing techniques.
2. Do you agree that using speech communication as the user interface could increase willingness to use expert systems. Why or why not?
3. It is said that powerful computers, inference capabilities, and problem-solving heuristics are necessary but not sufficient for solving real problems. Why?
4. Explain how the Web improves the benefit/cost ratio of ES and enables systems that otherwise are not justifiable.
5. Explain the relationship between the development environment and the consultation (run-time) environment.
6. Explain the difference between forward chaining and backward chaining, and the situations where each one is more appropriate.

7. What kinds of mistakes might ES make and why? Why is it easier to correct mistakes in ES than in conventional programs?
8. We list 10 categories of ES applications in the chapter. Find 20 sample applications, two in each category, from the various functional areas in an organization (accounting, finance, production, marketing, HR).
9. Review the limitations of ES discussed in this chapter. From what you know, which of these limitations are the most likely to still be limitations in the year 2100? Why?

10. A ready-made ES is selling for $5,000. Developing one will cost you $50,000. A ready-made suit will cost you $100, and a tailored one will cost you $500. Develop an analogy between the two situations and describe the markets for the ready-made and customized products. Why does a ready-made ES cost only 1 percent of the cost of developed one, while a ready-made suit costs 20 percent of the cost of a tailored one?
11. Given the current status of the Web, discuss how it is changing the availability of ES and how it is being used to embed expertise in other systems.

❖ EXERCISES

1. Interview an information system manager. Determine the extent to which the company is using AI-based technologies. Ask what the company plans for the next three to five years. Are there any problems? (List and discuss.) Prepare a two-page report on your visit.
2. Explore the literature to identify the major problems in getting AI applications accepted. What is required on the part of management?

3. Find five applied expert systems in the recent literature (within one year) in one or several business functional areas in which you have a strong interest. Compare their purposes, complexity, knowledge representation, and the tools with which they were constructed (shells or programming languages).

❖ GROUP EXERCISES

1. In-class knowledge exercise: Make a peanut butter and jelly sandwich. Describe all the details of what you do as you make it and have someone in the class write down all the steps. How long is the list? Did you leave anything out? Next, have a classmate attempt to make a sandwich by following the instructions explicitly as written (someone else should read the instructions aloud). Did it work? Add the missing steps to the original list. How much longer is the new list than the old one? Would you follow the same sequence of steps if you were making 100 sandwiches instead of one? Explain why or why not. If you were selling sandwiches, what would you do differently?
2. Internet games have become very popular. Designing a good computer game needs to use 3D graphics and artificial intelligence technologies. Search the literature to specify what AI techniques are able to make computer entertainment more exciting and challenging.
3. Consider the decision-making situation defined by the following rules:
   - If it is a nice day and it is summer, then I go to the golf course.
   - If it is a nice day and it is winter, then I go to the ski resort.
   - If it is not a nice day and it is summer, then I go to work.

   - If it is not a nice day and it is winter, then I go to class.
   - If I go to the golf course, then I play golf.
   - If I go to the ski resort, then I go skiing.
   - If I go skiing or I play golf, then I have fun.
   - If I go to work, then I make money.
   - If I go to class, then I learn something.
   a. Follow the rules for the following situations (what do you conclude for each one?):
      - It is a nice day and it is summer.
      - It is not a nice day and it is winter.
      - It is a nice day and it is winter.
      - It is not a nice day and it is summer.
   b. Are there any other combinations that are valid? Explain.
   c. What needs to happen for you to "learn something" in this knowledge universe? Start with the conclusion "learn something" and identify the rules used (backward) to get to the needed facts.
   d. Encode the knowledge into a graphical diagram (like an influence diagram). Use a circle to represent a fact such as
      The day is nice
      or
      The day is not nice
      and an arrow to indicate influence.

e. Write a basic (or other third-generation language) program to execute this knowledge. Use IF-THEN-(ELSE) statements in your implementation. How many lines long is it? How hard would it be to modify the program to insert new facts and a rule such as
  - If it is cloudy and it is warm
  - and it is not raining
  - and it is summer
  - then I go play golf.

f. Implement the knowledge in a spreadsheet or database package on a PC.

g. Advanced exercise. In an implementation similar to the one in part (d), write a new implementation but store the knowledge in variables. Let the program search the arrays to make decisions.

❖ INTERNET EXERCISES

1. In 1995 there were about 2,000 Web sites related to AI (Hengl, 1995). Today there are substantially more. Do a search and describe how many Web sites you find. Categorize the first 20 into groups, or if you used a search engine that grouped them, what groups did you find?

2. Identify some news groups that have an interest in applied AI. Post a question regarding the use of AI technologies for decision support.

3. Link yourself to several demonstrations on the Web site of Exsys (www.exsys.com/). Go over the tutorials and the "try me" demos. Choose one example to describe its advantage and limitations, and comment on how to develop a better one if you are going to develop one.

4. Access the Web site of the American Association for Artificial Intelligence (www. aaai.org). Examine the workshops it has offered over the last year and list the major topics related to intelligent systems.

❖ DEBATES

1. Computers are programmed to play chess, scrabble, and even crossword puzzles (American Scientist, September/October 1999). They are getting better and better; in fact, a computer beat the world's number-one chess grand master, Garry Kasparov. Do you agree that such computer systems exhibit intelligence? Why or why not?

2. Prepare a table showing all the arrangements you can think of that justify the position that computers cannot think. Then prepare arguments that show the opposite.

3. Bourbaki (1990) describes Searle's argument against use of the Turing test. Summarize all the important issues in this debate.

4. Proponents of AI claim that we will never have machines that truly think because they cannot, by definition, have a soul. Supporters claim a soul is unnecessary. They argue that humanity originally set out to create an artificial bird for flight. Instead it eventually created the airplane, which is not a bird, but functionally acts as one. Debate the issue.

❖ GROUP TERM PROJECT

1. Find applications of artificial intelligence and expert systems. Identify an organization with which at least one member of your group has a good contact who has a decision-making problem that requires some expertise (but is not too complicated). Understand the nature of its business and identify the problems that have been supported or can potentially be supported by intelligent systems. Some examples include selection of suppliers, selection of a new employee, job assignments computer selection, market-contact method selection, and determining admission to graduate school.

GATE ASSIGNMENT DISPLAY SYSTEM

PROBLEM

Gate assignment, the responsibility of gate controllers and their assistants, is a complex and demanding task at any airport. At O'Hare Airport in Chicago, for example, two gate controllers typically plan berthing for about 500 flights a day at about 50 gates. Flights arrive in clusters for the convenience of customers who must transfer to connecting flights, and so controllers must sometimes accommodate a cluster of 30 or 40 planes in 20 to 30 minutes. To complicate the matter, each flight is scheduled to remain at its gate a different length of time, depending on the schedules of connecting flights and the amount of servicing needed. Mix these problems with the need to juggle gates constantly because of flight delays caused by weather and other factors and you get some idea of the challenges. The problem is even more complex because of its interrelationship with remote parking and constraints related to ground-equipment availability and customs requirements.

SOLUTION

Many airports are introducing expert systems to solve these problems. The pioneering work was done at Chicago O'Hare in 1987–1988. The Korean Air system at Kimpo Airport, Korea, won the 1999 innovative application award from the American Association of Artificial Intelligence (www.aaai.org). The two systems have several common features and similar architectures.

SYSTEM CAPABILITIES

An intelligent gate assignment system can be set up and quickly rescheduled and contains far more information than a manual system. Its superb graphical display shows times and gate numbers. The aircraft are symbolized as colored bars; each bar's position indicates the gate assigned, and its length indicates the length of time the plane is expected to occupy the gate. Bars with pointed ends identify arrival–departure flights; square ends are used for originator–terminator flights. The system also shows, in words and numbers near each bar, the flight number, arrival and departure times, plane number, present fuel load, flight status, ground status, and more.

Each participating aircraft carries a small radio transmitter that automatically reports to the mainframe system when the nose wheel touches down on the field. The system immediately changes that plane's bar from "off," meaning off the field, to "on," meaning on the field. When the plane is stopped at its gate, the code changes to "in." So gate controllers have access to an up-to-the-second ground status for every flight in their display.

The system also has a number of built-in reminders. For instance, it won't permit an aircraft to be assigned to the wrong kind of gate and explains why it can't. The controller can manually override such a decision to meet an unusual situation. The system also keeps its eye on the clock—when an incoming plane is on the field and its gate hasn't been assigned yet, flashing red lines bracket the time to alert the controller.

BENEFITS OF THE SYSTEM

Three major benefits have been identified. First, the assistant gate controller can start scheduling the next day's operations four or five hours earlier than was possible before. The Korean system, for example, produces a schedule in 20 seconds instead of in five manually worked hours. Second, the ES is also used by zone controllers and other ground operations (towing, cleaning, resupply). At O'Hare, for example, each of the 10 zone controllers is responsible for all activities at a number of gates (funneling, baggage handling, catering service, crew assignment, etc.). Third, superreliability is built into these systems.

CASE QUESTIONS

1. Why is the gate assignment task so complex?
2. Why is the system considered a real-time ES?
3. What are the major benefits of the ES compared to the manual system?

Source: Based on press releases from the American Association of Artificial Intelligence (1999) and Texas Instruments Data System Group (1988).

CHAPTER 11

KNOWLEDGE ACQUISITION, REPRESENTATION, AND REASONING

LEARNING OBJECTIVES

❖ Understand the nature of knowledge

❖ Understand the knowledge-engineering process

❖ Different approaches for knowledge acquisition

❖ Explain the pros and cons of different knowledge acquisition approaches

❖ Illustrate methods for knowledge verification and validation

❖ Understand inference strategies in rule-based intelligent systems

❖ Explain uncertainties and uncertainty processing in expert systems

We have learned the concepts and structure of the rule-based expert systems (ES). For such systems to be useful, it is critical to have powerful knowledge in the knowledge base and a good inference engine that can derive valid conclusions from the knowledge base. In this chapter, we describe the process for acquiring knowledge from human experts, knowledge representation, inference mechanisms, knowledge validation, and uncertainty processing. The chapter is divided into the following sections:

11.1 OPENING VIGNETTE: DEVELOPMENT OF A REAL-TIME KNOWLEDGE-BASED SYSTEM AT ELI LILLY

THE PROBLEM

Eli Lilly (lilly.com) is a large US-based, global pharmaceutical company (41,000 employees worldwide and marketing in 158 countries).

Production of medicines requires a special process called fermentation. A typical fermentation process operates as a series of stirred vessels in which a culture of microorganisms is grown and transferred to progressively larger tanks. In order to have quality products, the fermentation process must be monitored carefully and controlled consistently. Unfortunately, some key quality parameters are difficult to control using traditional statistical process control. For example, it is difficult to quantify the state of a fermentation seed, but without this information predictions of the behavior of a production vessel may be imprecise. Furthermore, Lilly operates many plants that use the same process but are operated by different employees. The quality of the product may vary substantially when different operators use their experience to control the process. The turnover of experienced operators also causes a problem for some plants.

THE SOLUTION

Eli Lilly is using expert systems to overcome this problem. Its motivation for adopting this approach was to make the expertise of key technical employees available to the process operators 24 hours a day. In addition, it was felt that an expert system would allow relevant portions of the knowledge base to be cloned and made available to all of the company's plants. Eli Lilly installed Gensym's G2 (gensym.com/manufacturing/g2_overview.shtml) at its Speke site to construct an intelligent quality-alert system that would provide consistent real-time advice to the operators.

DEVELOPMENT PROCESS

The system focuses on the seed stage of the fermentation process. Four knowledge engineers were involved in the system development, three for knowledge elicitation and one for coding knowledge into G2 rules and procedures. The knowledge engineers had domain knowledge, but they were asked to simply record the knowledge of the experts and not pre-empt or optimize it with personal attitudes toward the domain, and in particular not to rationalize the knowledge into a framework with which the interviewer was familiar. They were also asked not to intimidate the experts by virtue of their domain expertise. The entire development process took six months to complete. Its development includes the following major steps:

1. *Knowledge elicitation.* The knowledge engineers interviewed ten experienced experts to acquire their knowledge. The knowledge acquisition tool, KAT, was used to facilitate the knowledge acquisition.
2. *Knowledge fusion.* The interview resulted in ten different knowledge bases represented in graphs. A joint session integrated the project owner, the knowledge base owner, and the knowledge engineers.

Source: Adapted from A. Ranjan et al., "From Process Experts to a Real-Time Knowledge-Based System," *Expert Systems*, Vol. 19, No. 2, 2002, pp. 69–79.

3. *Coding the knowledge base.* The resulting knowledge graph was then converted into rules acceptable to G2. A total of 60 rules were produced.

4. *Testing and evaluation.* The system was tested using values that simulated anomalies for the variables and output verification.

❖ QUESTIONS FOR THE OPENING VIGNETTE:

1. Why did Eli Lilly need to develop an intelligent system for providing advice to process operators?

2. Why was the coding knowledge engineer asked not to use his/her own knowledge framework but to record only knowledge from the experts?

3. Why do we need knowledge engineers to develop expert systems? Can we ask experts to develop the system by themselves?

4. What do you think of their approach, which developed ten separate knowledge bases and then put them together through knowledge fusion? What are the pros and cons of this approach?

5. For system testing and evaluation, they used simulated data rather than real data. Why is this acceptable for real-time expert systems? Can you think of a better approach for system testing and evaluation?

6. What are the benefits of using knowledge-acquisition tools?

11.2 CONCEPTS OF KNOWLEDGE ENGINEERING

The Opening Vignette illustrates the process of acquiring knowledge and deploying it in a real-time monitoring system. It also illustrates the use of computer-aided knowledge acquisition tools to make the job easier and integrate knowledge from multiple experts. The process of acquiring knowledge from experts and building a knowledge base is called **knowledge engineering**. The activity of knowledge engineering (KE) is defined in the pioneer work by Feigenbaum and McCorduck (1983):

> The art of bringing the principles and tools of AI research to bear on difficult applications problems requiring experts' knowledge for their solutions. Knowledge engineering involves the cooperation of human experts in the domain who work with the knowledge engineer to codify and make explicit the rules (or other procedures) that a human expert uses to solve real problems.

Knowledge engineering can be viewed from two perspectives: narrow and broad. According to the narrow perspective, knowledge engineering deals with knowledge acquisition, representation, validation, inferencing, explanation, and maintenance. Alternatively; according to the broad perspective, the term describes the entire process of developing and maintaining intelligent systems. In this book, we use the narrow definition.

The knowledge possessed by human experts is often unstructured and not explicitly expressed. A major goal of knowledge engineering is to help experts articulate what they know and document the knowledge in a reusable form.

THE KNOWLEDGE-ENGINEERING PROCESS

The knowledge-engineering process includes five major activities:

- ***Knowledge acquisition.*** Knowledge acquisition involves the acquisition of knowledge from human experts, books, documents, sensors, or computer files. The knowledge may be specific to the problem domain or to the problem-solving procedures, it may be general knowledge (e.g., knowledge about business), or it may be **metaknowledge** (knowledge about knowledge). By the latter, we mean information about how experts use their knowledge to solve problems and about problem-solving procedures in general. Byrd (1995) formally verified that knowledge acquisition is the bottleneck in expert system development. Thus, much theoretical and applied research is still being conducted in this area. An analysis of more than 90 expert system applications and their knowledge-acquisition techniques and methods is available in Wagner et al. (2003).
- ***Knowledge representation.*** The acquired knowledge is organized in an activity called knowledge representation. This activity involves preparation of a knowledge map and encoding the knowledge in the knowledge base.
- ***Knowledge validation.*** The knowledge is validated and verified (e.g., by using test cases) until its quality is acceptable. Test case results are usually shown to the expert to verify the accuracy of the ES.
- ***Inferencing.*** This activity involves the design of software to enable the computer to make inferences based on the knowledge and specifics of a problem. Then the system can provide advice to a nonexpert user.
- ***Explanation and justification.*** This involves the design and programming of an explanation capability—for example, programming the ability to answer questions such as why a specific piece of information is needed by the computer or how a certain conclusion was derived by the computer.

Figure 11.1 shows the process of knowledge engineering and the relationships among these activities. Knowledge engineers interact with human experts or solicit known knowledge from other sources in the knowledge-acquisition stage. The acquired

FIGURE 11.1   Process of Knowledge Engineering

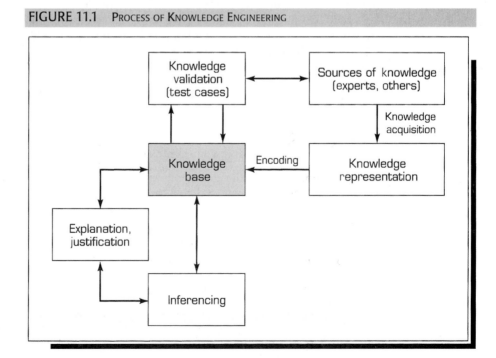

AIS IN ACTION 11.1

DEVELOPMENT OF TIRE-DEFECT DIAGNOSIS EXPERT SYSTEMS IN EGYPT

A tire is composed of complex formulations of fibers, textiles, and steel cords. Truck tires are normally made up of special raw materials. The manufacturing process includes five steps and more than 80 raw materials. Unless well controlled, many factors may cause the product to be defective.

TIREDDX (Tire Defect Diagnosis Expert System) is an integrated intelligent system developed in one of the leading truck-tire production companies in Egypt. It is capable of diagnosing the probable cause(s) of a defect by tracing the acquired quality and production information at various steps of the tire-manufacturing process.

The system was developed in three major steps:

1. *Acquiring and formulating the related knowledge.* This step included collecting relevant items of knowledge and information from experts. The knowledge-acquisition step has two major stages. The first stage built a global picture of the knowledge base. The second stage allowed more rules to be added after building a prototype from the first stage.

2. *Design and development of different knowledge bases.* Knowledge is represented in the form of rules and stored in knowledge bases.

3. *Testing the knowledge base for validation.* Using historical cases to evaluate the system. The performance of the system is comparable with human experts.

The results show that the system has the following advantages:

1. Reduces the time required to reach diagnostic decision.

2. Formulates more consistent diagnostic decisions.

3. Better utilizes the company's information systems.

Source: Adapted from M. G. Abou-Ali and M. Khamis, "TIREDDX: An Integrated Intelligent Defects Diagnostic System for Tire Production and Service," *Expert Systems With Applications*, 24, 2003, pp. 247–259.

knowledge is then coded into a representation scheme to build a knowledge base. The knowledge engineer can collaborate with human experts or use test cases to verify and validate the knowledge base. The valid knowledge can be used in a knowledge-based system to solve new problems via machine inference and to explain the provided recommendation. Details of these activities are discussed in the following sections. AIS in Action 11.1 illustrates the development of a tire-defect expert system in Egypt.

11.3 SCOPE AND TYPES OF KNOWLEDGE

The most important factor in knowledge acquisition is the extraction of knowledge from sources of expertise and its transfer to the knowledge base and sometimes to the inference engine. Acquisition is actually done throughout the entire development process.

Knowledge is a collection of specialized facts, procedures, and judgment rules. Some types of knowledge used in AI are shown in Figure 11.2. These types of knowledge may come from one source or from several sources.

SOURCES OF KNOWLEDGE

Knowledge can be collected from many sources, such as books, films, computer databases, pictures, maps, flow diagrams, stories, sensors, songs, or even observed behavior. Sources are of two types: **documented** and **undocumented**. The latter resides in peo-

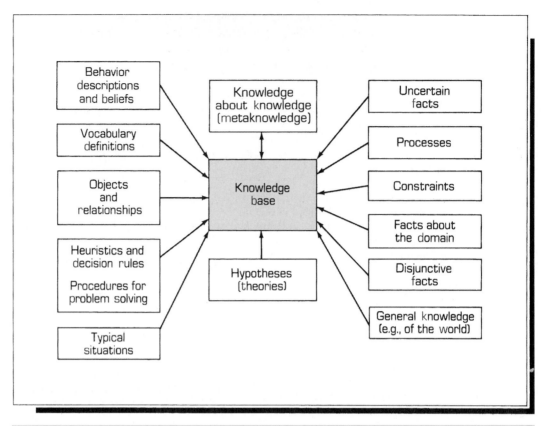

FIGURE 11.2   TYPES OF KNOWLEDGE TO BE REPRESENTED IN THE KNOWLEDGE BASE

Source: Adapted from R. Fikes and T. Kehler, "The Role of Frame-based Representation in Reasoning," *Communications of ACM,* Sept. 1985. Copyright 1985, Association for Computing Machinery Inc. Reprinted by permission.

ple's minds. Knowledge can be identified and collected by using one or several of the human senses. It can also be identified and collected by machines (sensors, scanners, pattern matchers, intelligent agents, etc.).

The multiplicity of sources and types of knowledge contributes to the complexity of knowledge acquisition. This complexity is only one reason why it is difficult to acquire knowledge. Other reasons are discussed in Section 11.4.

ACQUISITION FROM DATABASES

Many expert systems are constructed from knowledge extracted in whole or in part from databases. With the increased amount of knowledge stored in databases, the acquisition of such knowledge becomes more difficult. For discussion and recent developments, see ACM SIGKDD (acm.org/sigkdd/), the *Data Mining and Knowledge Discovery Journal* (kluweronline.com/issn/1384-5810), and the Microsoft Web site (research.microsoft.com). Roiger and Geatz (2002) give a very good practical description of techniques for mining knowledge from data and their applications. Some techniques, such as neural networks and genetic algorithms, will be described in Chapter 12.

ACQUISITION VIA THE INTERNET

With the increased use of the Internet, it is possible to access vast amounts of knowledge. The acquisition, availability, and management of knowledge via the Internet are becoming critical issues for the construction and maintenance of knowledge-based systems, particularly because they allow the acquisition and dissemination of large quantities of knowledge in a short time across organizational and physical boundaries. Methods and standards were first established in 1996. For details of mining knowledge from the World Wide Web, see Charkrabarti (2002). The Internet community provides an "expert system" with a scope far greater than is possible with standard computer-based systems. Benjamins et al. (1999) describe ontologies for building acquisition tools utilizing intranet/Internet tools available within organizations. Adopting such tools as HTML browsers allows users to quickly become familiar with acquisition systems. Additions to standard HTML can be applied to include metadata information, allowing explicit information to be stored and retrieved. The detailed case studies given by Benjamins et al. (1999) highlight the difficulties in adopting this approach and address differences between ontology-based and key-word-based knowledge retrieval. Also worth noticing is the development of the semantic Web, which incorporates semantic knowledge into the Web representation (Davies, 2003). See Chapter 13 for a detailed description.

LEVELS OF KNOWLEDGE

Knowledge can be represented at different levels. The two extremes are shallow knowledge (surface knowledge) and deep knowledge.

SHALLOW KNOWLEDGE

Shallow knowledge is the representation of surface-level information that can be used to deal with very specific situations. For example, if you don't have gasoline in your car, the car won't start. This knowledge can be shown as a rule:

> **If** gasoline tank is empty, **then** car will not start.

The shallow version basically represents the input–output relationship of a system. As such, it can be ideally presented in terms of IF-THEN rules. Shallow representation is limited. A set of rules by itself may have little meaning for the user. It may have little to do with the manner in which experts view the domain and solve problems. This may limit the ability of the system to provide appropriate explanations to the user. Shallow knowledge may also be insufficient in describing complex situations. Therefore, a deeper presentation is often required.

DEEP KNOWLEDGE

Human problem-solving is based on deep knowledge of a situation. **Deep knowledge** is the internal and causal structure of a system and involves the interactions between the system's components. Deep knowledge can be applied to different tasks and different situations. It is based on a completely integrated, cohesive body of human consciousness that includes emotions, common sense, intuition, and so on. This type of knowledge is difficult to computerize. The system builder must have a perfect understanding of the basic elements and their interactions as produced by nature. To date, such a task has been found to be impossible. However, it is possible to implement a computerized representation that is deeper than shallow knowledge. To explain how this is done, let us return to the gasoline example. If we want to investigate at a deeper level the relationship between lack of gasoline and a car that won't start, we need to know the various components of the gas system (e.g., pipes, pump, filters, and a starter). Such a system is shown schematically in Figure 11.3.

To represent this system and knowledge of its operation, we use special knowledge-representation methods such as semantic networks and frames (Section 11.8). These

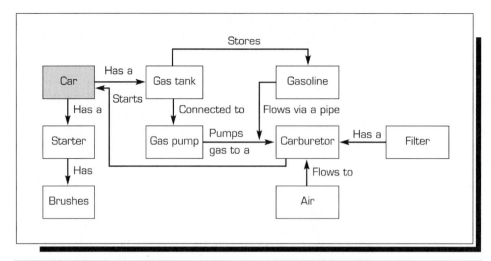

FIGURE 11.3 SCHEMATIC REPRESENTATION OF DEEP KNOWLEDGE: AUTOMOBILE GAS SYSTEM

allow the implementation of deeper-level reasoning such as abstraction and analogy, an important expert activity. We can also represent the objects and processes of the domain of expertise at this level; the relationships between objects are important.

Tutoring is an important type of expertise that has been represented with a deep-level approach. The goal of tutoring is to convey to students a domain knowledge that is best represented at the deep level: concepts, abstractions, analogies, and problem-solving strategies.

Deep knowledge is much more difficult to collect and validate. For a discussion, see DeFanti et al. (1997) and Bergeron (2003).

MAJOR CATEGORIES OF KNOWLEDGE

Knowledge can be categorized as declarative knowledge, procedural knowledge, or metaknowledge.

DECLARATIVE KNOWLEDGE

Declarative knowledge is a descriptive representation of knowledge. It tells us facts: what things are. It is expressed in a factual statement "There is a positive association between smoking and cancer." Domain experts tell us about truths and associations. This type of knowledge is considered shallow or surface-level information that experts can verbalize. Declarative knowledge is especially important in the initial stage of knowledge acquisition.

PROCEDURAL KNOWLEDGE

Procedural knowledge considers the manner in which things work under different sets of circumstances. The following is an example: "Compute the ratio between the price of a share and the earnings per share. If the ratio is larger than 12, stop your investigation. Your investment is too risky. If the ratio is less than 12, check the balance sheet." Thus, procedural knowledge includes step-by-step sequences and how-to types of instructions; it may also include explanations. Procedural knowledge involves automatic responses to stimuli. It may also tell us how to use declarative knowledge and how to make inferences.

Declarative knowledge relates to a specific object. It includes information about the meaning, roles, environment, resources, activities, associations, and outcomes of the object. Procedural knowledge relates to the procedures used in the problem-solving process (e.g., information about problem definition, data gathering, the solution process, evaluation criteria).

METAKNOWLEDGE

Metaknowledge is knowledge about knowledge. In ES, metaknowledge is knowledge about the operation of knowledge-based systems, that is, about their reasoning capabilities.

11.4 METHODS OF KNOWLEDGE ACQUISITION FROM EXPERTS

Knowledge acquisition is not an easy task. It includes identifying the knowledge, representing the knowledge in a proper format, structuring the knowledge, and transfering the knowledge to a machine. Some difficulties are described in AIS in Focus 11.2. The process of knowledge acquisition can be greatly influenced by the roles of the three major participants: the knowledge engineer, the expert, and the end-user.

A unique approach to the interrelationships of these participants is offered by Sandahl (1994). Sandahl indicates that experts should take a very active role in the creation of the knowledge base. The knowledge engineer should act more like a teacher of knowledge structuring, a tool designer, and a catalyst at the interface between the expert and the end-users. The requirements for a qualified knowledge engineer are listed in AIS in Focus 11.3. This approach could minimize such problems as interhuman conflicts, knowledge-engineering filtering, and end-user acceptance of the system. Also, knowledge-maintenance problems can be reduced. Wagner and Holsapple (1997) have analyzed the roles the participants play in knowledge acquisition. They suggest that it is more appropriate to think of the participants as playing one or more roles, including acting as knowledge sources, agents, and targets for knowledge-acquisition

---

AIS IN FOCUS 11.2

DIFFICULTIES IN KNOWLEDGE ENGINEERING

Acquiring knowledge from experts is not an easy task. The following are some factors that add to the complexity of knowledge transfer:

- Experts may not know how to articulate their knowledge or may be unable to do so.
- Experts may lack time or may be unwilling to cooperate.
- Testing and refining knowledge is complicated.
- Methods for knowledge elicitation may be poorly defined.
- System builders tend to collect knowledge from one source, but the relevant knowledge may be scattered across several sources.

- Builders may attempt to collect documented knowledge rather than use experts. The knowledge collected may be incomplete.
- It is difficult to recognize specific knowledge when it is mixed up with irrelevant data.
- Experts may change their behavior when they are observed or interviewed.
- Problematic interpersonal communication factors may affect the knowledge engineer and the expert.

processes. They further develop a participant model to explain participant interactions in a metaview of knowledge acquisition. This view allows for a more flexible consideration of the many possible combinations that can and do occur in reality.

ROLES OF KNOWLEDGE ENGINEERS

The ability and personality of the knowledge engineer directly influence the expert. Part of successful knowledge acquisition involves developing a positive relationship with the expert. The **knowledge engineer** is responsible for creating the right impression, positively communicating information about the project, understanding the expert's style, preparing the sessions, and so on. The skills required by knowledge engineers are shown in AIS in Focus 11.3.

The basic model of knowledge engineering portrays teamwork in which a knowledge engineer mediates between the expert and the knowledge base. Figure 11.4 shows the following tasks performed by knowledge engineers at different stages of knowledge acquisition:

- Advise the expert on the process of interactive knowledge elicitation.
- Set up and appropriately manage the interactive knowledge-acquisition tools.
- Edit the unencoded and coded knowledge base in collaboration with the expert.
- Set up and appropriately manage the knowledge-encoding tools.
- Validate application of the knowledge base in collaboration with the expert.
- Train clients in effective use of the knowledge base in collaboration with the expert by developing operational and training procedures.

The **elicitation of knowledge** from the expert can be seen as a process of modeling (see AIS in Focus 11.4) and be done manually or with the aid of computers. Most manual elicitation techniques have been borrowed (often with modifications) from psychology or from system analysis. These elicitation methods are classified in different ways and appear under different names; for a discussion, see Moody et al. (1999).

AIS IN FOCUS 11.3

REQUIRED SKILLS OF KNOWLEDGE ENGINEERS

Knowledge engineers are human professionals who are able to communicate with experts and consolidate knowledge from various sources to build a valid knowledge base. They can use computers and special methods to overcome difficulties in knowledge engineering. Listed here are some of the skills and characteristics that are desirable in knowledge engineers:

- Computer skills (hardware, programming, software)
- Tolerance and ambivalence
- Effective communication abilities (sensitivity, tact, diplomacy)
- Broad educational background
- Advanced, socially sophisticated verbal skills

- Fast-learning capabilities (of different domains)
- Understanding of organizations and individuals
- Wide experience in knowledge engineering
- Empathy and patience
- Persistence
- Logical thinking
- Versatility and inventiveness
- Self-confidence.

Because of these requirements knowledge engineers are in short supply (and they are costly as well because of high salaries). Some of the automation developments described later attempt to overcome the short-supply problem.

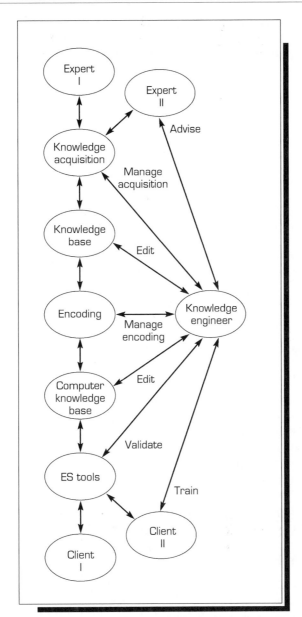

FIGURE 11.4   KNOWLEDGE ENGINEERS' ROLES IN INTERACTIVE KNOWLEDGE ACQUISITION

Source: Adapted from B. R. Gaines, University of Calgary, with permission.

The methods can be classified into three categories: manual, semiautomatic, and automatic. **Manual methods** are basically structured around an interview of some kind. The knowledge engineer elicits knowledge from the expert or other sources and then codes it in the knowledge base. The three major manual methods are interviewing (structured, semistructured, unstructured), tracking the reasoning process, and observing. Manual methods are slow, expensive, and sometimes inaccurate. Therefore, there is a trend toward automating the process as much as possible.

Semiautomatic methods are divided into two categories: those intended to support the experts by allowing them to build knowledge bases with little or no help from

AIS IN FOCUS 11.4

KNOWLEDGE MODELING

Several key contributions made during the 1980s—Allen Newell's notion of knowledge level, William Clancey's critical analyses, and the broader wave of second-generation expert system research have shaped our current perception of the knowledge-acquisition problem. Central to the current perception is the knowledge model, which views knowledge acquisition as the construction of a model of problem-solving behavior—that is, a model in terms of knowledge instead of representations.

The concept of knowledge-level modeling has matured considerably. The practical knowledge-level models incorporated in today's methodologies do not simply reflect the knowledge content of a system; they also make explicit the structures within which the knowledge operates in solving various classes of problems. This enables the reuse of models across applications.

The structures provide a framework for knowledge acquisition and a decomposition of the overall acquisition task. Identified parts of knowledge-level models—domain models or problem-solving methods—can serve in different systems or in different roles in the same system. The main advantage remains: The knowledge level focuses attention on the knowledge that makes systems work rather than on the symbol-level, computational-design decisions that provide the operational framework. The topic of knowledge modeling is described in a series of articles in *IEEE Expert* (February–August 1996). Musen et al. (1999) report the use of a domain model to drive an interactive knowledge-editing tool, allowing expertise to be entered regardless of the representation requirements of the target expert system. More recent work includes knowledge modeling on the Web. For details, see Davies et al. (2003).

knowledge engineers and those intended to help knowledge engineers by allowing them to execute the necessary tasks in a more efficient or effective manner (sometimes with only minimal participation by an expert).

In **automatic methods**, the roles of both the expert and the knowledge engineer are minimized or even eliminated. For example, the induction method, which generates rules from a set of known cases, can be applied to build a knowledge base. The roles of the expert and knowledge engineers are minimal. The term "automatic" may be misleading, but it indicates that, compared with other methods, the contributions from a knowledge engineer and an expert are relatively small.

MANUAL METHODS

INTERVIEWS

The most commonly used form of knowledge acquisition is face-to-face **interview analysis**. This is an explicit technique that appears in several variations. It involves a direct dialog between the expert and the knowledge engineer. Information is collected with the aid of conventional instruments (e.g., tape recorders or questionnaires) and is subsequently transcribed, analyzed, and coded.

In the interview, the expert is presented with a simulated case or, if possible, with an actual problem of the type that the ES will be expected to solve. The expert is asked to talk the knowledge engineer through the solution. Sometimes this method is called the **walk-through** method. One variant of the interview approach begins with no information at all being given to the expert. Any facts the expert requires must be asked for explicitly. This variant makes the expert's path through the domain more evident, especially in terms of defining the input an ES would require.

The interview process can be tedious. It places great demands on the domain expert, who must be able not only to demonstrate expertise but also to express it. On the other hand, it requires little equipment, is highly flexible and portable, and can yield a considerable amount of information. There are two basic types of interviews: unstructured (informal) interviews and structured interviews.

UNSTRUCTURED INTERVIEWS

Many knowledge-acquisition interview sessions are conducted informally, usually as a starting point. Starting informally saves time; it helps to move quickly to the basic structure of the domain. Usually it is followed by a formal technique. Contrary to what many people believe, **unstructured interviews** are not simple. In fact, they may present the knowledge engineer with some very problematic after-effects.

Unstructured interviewing, according to McGraw and Harbison-Briggs (1989), seldom provides complete or well-organized descriptions of cognitive processes. There are several reasons for this: the domains are generally complex; the experts usually find it very difficult to express some of the more important elements of their knowledge; domain experts may interpret the lack of structure as implying that they need not prepare for the interview; data acquired from an unstructured interview are often unrelated, exist at varying levels of complexity, and are difficult for the knowledge engineer to review, interpret, and integrate; and finally, few knowledge engineers have the training and experience to efficiently conduct an unstructured interview.

EXAMPLE

Here is a simple, hypothetical example of acquisition of knowledge about site selection for a hospital extension clinic. The dialog between the expert (E) and the knowledge engineer (KE) might look like the following:

> E: I understand that you are somehow going to try to capture my knowledge about site selection of clinics so that hospital administrators in our system in other cities can use it.
> KE: Yes, indeed! And thank you for spending time with me, Kathleen. We've noticed that you have a special knack for identifying the right locations. So far, you've picked very successful operations.
> E: Well, thanks.
> KE: So, tell me, what's the most important factor in determining where to put a new facility?
> E: Really, it's demographics. We need to locate it close to our potential customers.
> KE: So, is it also important that it not be too close to another agency's operation?
> E: Not necessarily. It is important that it not be located too close to our main hospital or our other facilities, but if the population density is high enough, we can locate it close to a competitor.
> KE: Tell me, then, what kind of demographics are you looking for?
> E: Well, in a large city, if there are at least 2,000 people per square mile over about four square miles, generally they can support a profitable clinic.
> KE: What about competitors' locations?
> E: If a competitor is within two miles, the density has to exceed 3,500 people per square mile. And if there are two competitors within two miles of each other already, there's no point in even trying to break into the market, except for certain special services.
> KE: What about income? Is that important?
> E: We must limit our indigent cases to no more than 2 percent of our clients, and so we generally look for an average family income greater than $30,000 per year.
> KE: Is being near public transportation important? And so on.

By interviewing the expert, the knowledge engineer slowly learns what is going on. Then he or she builds a representation of the knowledge in the expert's terms.

The process of knowledge acquisition involves uncovering the attributes of the problem and making explicit the thought process (usually expressed as rules) that the expert uses to interpret them.

The unstructured interview is most common and appears in several variations. In addition to the talk-through, one can ask the expert to teach through or read through. In a teach-through the expert acts as an instructor and the knowledge engineer as a student. The expert not only tells what he or she does but also explains why and instructs the knowledge engineer in the skills and strategies needed to perform the task. In a read-through approach the expert is asked to instruct the knowledge engineer how to read and interpret the documents used for the task. More detailed descriptions of unstructured interviews can be found in Burns (2000).

STRUCTURED INTERVIEWS

A structured interview is a systematic goal-oriented process. It forces organized communication between the knowledge engineer and the expert. The structure reduces the interpretation problems inherent in unstructured interviews and allows the knowledge engineer to prevent the distortion caused by the subjectivity of the domain expert. Structuring an interview requires attention to a number of procedural issues, which are summarized in Table 11.1.

Because every interview is different in very specific ways, it is difficult to provide comprehensive guidelines for the entire interview process. Therefore, interpersonal communication and analytic skills are important. However, there are several guidelines, checklists, and instruments that are fairly generic in nature (McGraw and Harbison-Briggs, 1989).

There are many structured interview methods. Some are based on psychology, others are based on disciplines such as anthropology. Interviewing techniques, though very popular, have many disadvantages. They range from inaccuracy in collecting information to bias introduced by the interviewers (Kuhn and Zohar, 1995).

In summary, interviews are important techniques, but they must be planned carefully, and the interview results must be subjected to thorough verification and validation methodologies. Interviews are sometimes replaced by tracking methods. Alternatively, they can be used to supplement tracking or other knowledge-acquisition methods.

TABLE 11.1   Procedures for Structured Interviews

- The knowledge engineer studies available material on the domain to identify major demarcations of the relevant knowledge.
- The knowledge engineer reviews the planned expert system capabilities. He or she identifies targets for the questions to be asked during the knowledge acquisition session.
- The knowledge engineer formally schedules and plans the structured interviews (using a form). Planning includes attending to physical arrangements, defining knowledge acquisition session goals and agendas, and identifying or refining major areas of questioning.
- The knowledge engineer may write sample questions, focusing on question type, level, and questioning techniques.
- The knowledge engineer ensures that the domain expert understands the purpose and goals of the session and encourages the expert to prepare before the interview.
- During the interview the knowledge engineer follows guidelines for conducting interviews.
- During the interview the knowledge engineer uses directional control to retain the interview's structure.

Source: Condensed from K. L. McGraw and B. K. Harbison-Briggs, *Knowledge Acquisition, Principles and Guidelines.* Englewood Cliffs, NJ: Prentice Hall, 1989.

We recommend that before interviewing the main experts, the knowledge engineer should interview a less knowledgeable or minor expert using the interviewing approaches outlined above. This may help the knowledge engineer learn about the problem, its significance, the experts, and the users. The interviewer will also be able to better understand the basic terminology and (if a novice in the area) identify archived sources about the problem first. The knowledge engineer should next read about the problem. Then the main experts can be interviewed much more effectively.

PROCESS TRACKING AND PROTOCOL ANALYSIS

Process tracking is a set of techniques that attempt to track the reasoning process of an expert. It is a popular approach among cognitive psychologists who are interested in discovering the expert's train of thought in reaching a conclusion. The knowledge engineer can use the tracking process to find what information is being used and how it is being used. Tracking methods can be informal or formal. The most common formal method is protocol analysis.

Protocol analysis, particularly the set of techniques known as verbal protocol analysis, is a method by which the knowledge engineer acquires detailed knowledge from the expert. A protocol is a record or documentation of the expert's step-by-step information processing and decision-making behavior. In this method, which is similar to interviewing but more formal and systematic, the expert is asked to perform a real task and to verbalize his or her thought processes. The expert is asked to think aloud while performing the task or solving the problem under observation. Usually, a recording is made as the expert thinks aloud; it describes every aspect of the information-processing and decision-making behavior. The recording then becomes a record, or protocol, of the expert's ongoing behavior. Later, the recording is transcribed for further analysis (e.g., to deduce the decision process) and coded by the knowledge engineer. (For further details, see Ericsson and Simon, 1984, and Wolfgram et al., 1987.)

In contrast with interactive interview methods, a protocol analysis mainly involves one-way communication. The knowledge engineer prepares the scenario and plans the process. During the session the expert does most of the talking while interacting with data to solve the problem. Concurrently, the knowledge engineer listens and records the process. Later, the knowledge engineer must be able to analyze, interpret, and structure the protocol into knowledge representation for review by the expert.

The process of protocol analysis is summarized in Table 11.2, and its advantages and limitations are presented in Table 11.3.

OBSERVATIONS

Sometimes it is possible to observe an expert at work. In many ways, this is the most obvious and straightforward approach to knowledge acquisition. However, the

---

TABLE 11.2 Procedure of Protocol Analysis

- Provide the expert with a full range of information normally associated with a task.
- Ask the expert to verbalize the task in the same manner as would be done normally while verbalizing his or her decision process and record the verbalization on tape.
- Make statements by transcribing the verbal protocols.
- Gather the statements that seem to have high information content.
- Simplify and rewrite the collected statements and construct a table of production rules from the collected statements.
- Produce a series of models by using the production rules.

Source: Organized from J. Kim and J. F. Courtney, "A Survey of Knowledge Acquisition Techniques and Their Relevance to Managerial Problem Domains," Decision Support Systems, Vol. 4, Oct. 1988, p. 273.

TABLE 11.3	Advantages and Limitations of Protocol Analysis

Advantages

The expert consciously considers decision-making heuristics.

The expert consciously considers decision alternatives, attributes, values.

The knowledge engineer can observe and analyze decision-making behavior.

The knowledge engineer can record, and later analyze with the expert, key decision points.

Limitations

The expert must be aware of why he or she makes a decision.

The expert must be able to categorize major decision alternatives.

The expert must be able to verbalize the attributes and values of a decision alternative.

The expert must be able to reason about the selection of a given alternative.

View of decision making is subjective. Explanations may not track with reasoning.

Source: K. L. McGraw and B. K. Harbison-Briggs, *Knowledge Acquisition, Principles and Guidelines,* Englewood Cliffs, NJ: Prentice Hall, 1989, p. 217. © 1989. Reprinted by permission of Prentice-Hall, Inc., Upper Saddle River, NJ.

difficulties involved should not be underestimated. For example, most experts advise several people and may work in several domains simultaneously. If so, the knowledge engineer's observations will cover all the other activities as well. Therefore, large quantities of knowledge are being collected, of which only a little is useful. In particular, if recordings or videotapes are made, the cost of transcribing large amounts of knowledge should be carefully considered.

Observations, which can be viewed as a special case of protocols, are of two types: motor movements and eye movements. In the first type, the expert's physical performance of the task (e.g., walking, reaching, talking) is documented. In the second type, a record is made of where the expert fixes his or her gaze. Observations are used primarily as a way of supporting verbal protocols. They are generally expensive and time-consuming.

OTHER MANUAL METHODS

Many other manual methods can be used to elicit knowledge from experts. A representative list is given here; for a complete discussion, see the classic books by Hart (1992) and Scott et al. (1991).

- *Case analysis.* Experts are asked how they handled specific cases in the past. Usually this method involves analyzing documentation. In addition to the experts, other people (e.g., managers and users) may be questioned.
- *Critical incident analysis.* In this approach only selected cases are investigated, usually those that are memorable, difficult, or of special interest. Both experts and nonexperts may be questioned.
- *Discussions with the users.* Even though users are not experts, they can be quite knowledgeable about some aspects of the problem. They can also indicate areas where they need help. The expert may be unaware of some of their needs.
- *Commentaries.* With this method, the knowledge engineer asks experts to give a running commentary on what they are doing. This method can be supported by videotaping the experts in action or by asking an observer to do the commentary.
- *Conceptual graphs and models.* Diagrams and other graphical methods can be instrumental in supporting other acquisition methods. A conceptual model can be used to describe how and when the expert's knowledge will come into play as the expert system performs its task.

- *Brainstorming.* These methods can be used to solicit the opinions of multiple experts and can help generate ideas. Electronic brainstorming can also be used, including blackboarding, which has been implemented as electronic whiteboards. The recently available software, such as Microsoft Netmeeting, MSN Messenger (msn.com), and the home meeting program developed at the University of Washington (engr.washington.edu/edge/homemeeting.html), are powerful tools for holding remote knowledge-acquisition sessions.
- *Prototyping.* Working with a prototype of the system is a powerful approach to induce experts to contribute their knowledge. Experts like to criticize systems, and changes can be made instantly.
- *Multidimensional scaling.* The complex technique of **multidimensional scaling** identifies various dimensions of knowledge and then places the knowledge in a form of a distance matrix. With the use of least-squares fitting regression, the various dimensions are analyzed, interpreted, and integrated.
- *Johnson's hierarchical clustering.* This is another scaling method, but it is much simpler to implement and therefore is used more often. It combines related knowledge elements into clusters (two elements at a time).
- *Performance review.* Because expert system development is an ongoing process, all of the above can be applied iteratively as the system evolves.

SEMIAUTOMATIC METHODS

Knowledge acquisition can also be supported by computer-based tools. These provide an environment in which knowledge engineers or experts can identify knowledge through an interactive process. Repertory grid analysis (RGA) is a typical method.

REPERTORY GRID ANALYSIS

RGA is based on Kelly's model of human thinking called **personal construct theory** (Hart, 1992; Stewart and Mayes, 2000). More information about the theory can be found at the BizTech research archives (brint.com/PCT.htm/) and the personal construct psychology Web site (repgrid.com/pcp/). According to this theory, each person is viewed as a personal scientist who seeks to predict and control events by forming theories, testing hypotheses, and analyzing results of experiments. Knowledge and perceptions about the world (or about a domain or a problem) are classified and categorized by each individual as a personal, perceptual model. Based on the model developed, each individual is able to anticipate and then act on the basis of these anticipations.

This personal model matches our view of an expert at work; it is a description of the development and use of the expert's knowledge, and so it is suitable for expert systems as suggested by Hart (1992). RGA is a method of investigating such a model.

How RGA Works. RGA uses several processes. First, the expert identifies the important objects in the domain of expertise. For example, computer languages (LISP, C11, COBOL) are objects in the situation of needing to select a computer language. This identification is done in an interview.

Second, the expert identifies the important attributes considered in making decisions in the domain. For example, the availability of commercial packages and ease of programming are important factors in selecting a computer language.

Third, for each attribute, the expert is asked to establish a bipolar scale with distinguishable characteristics (traits) and their opposites. For example, in selecting a computer language, the information shown in Table 11.4 can be included.

Fourth, the interviewer picks any three of the objects and asks, "What attributes and traits distinguish any two of these objects from the third?" For example, if a set

---

TABLE 11.4   RGA Input for Selecting a Computer Language

Attribute	*Trait*	*Opposite*
Availability	Widely available	Not available
Ease of programming	High	Low
Training time	Low	High
Orientation	Symbolic	Numeric

---

includes LISP, PROLOG, and COBOL, the expert may point to orientation. Then the expert will say that LISP and PROLOG are symbolic in nature, whereas COBOL is numeric. These answers are translated to points on a scale of 1 to 3 (or 1 to 5). This step continues for several triplets of objects. The answers are recorded in a grid, as shown in Table 11.5. The numbers in the grid designate the points assigned to each attribute for each object.

Once the grid is completed, the expert may change the ratings in the boxes. The grid can be used afterward to make recommendations in situations where the importance of the attributes is known. For example, in a simplistic sense, it can be said that if numeric orientation is very important, then COBOL will be the recommended language. For an interesting application, see Hunter and Becker (2000).

Use of RGA in Expert Systems.   A number of knowledge-acquisition tools have been developed based on RGA. These tools are aimed at helping in the conceptualization of the domain. Three representative tools are ETS, AQUINAS, and KRITON.

Expertise transfer system (ETS) is a computer program that interviews experts and helps them build expert systems. ETS interviews experts to uncover vocabulary conclusions, problem-solving traits, trait structures, trait weights, and inconsistencies. It has been used to construct prototypes rapidly (often in less than two hours for very small ES), to aid the expert in determining whether there is sufficient knowledge to solve a problem, and to create knowledge bases for a variety of different ES shells from its own internal representation. An improved version of ETS, called NeoETS, has been developed to expand the capabilities of ETS. The method is limited to classification-type problems (for details, see Boose and Gaines, 1990). ETS is now part of AQUINAS.

AQUINAS is a very complex tool (Boose and Bradshaw, 1993, 1999) that extends the problem-solving and knowledge representation of ETS by allowing experts to structure knowledge in hierarchies. A set of heuristics has been defined and incorporated in Dialog Manager, a subsystem of AQUINAS, to provide guidance in the knowledge-acquisition process to domain experts and knowledge engineers.

TABLE 11.5   Example of a Grid

Attribute	*Orientation*	*Ease of Programming*	*Training Time*	*Availability*
Trait *Opposite*	*Symbolic (3)* *Numeric (1)*	*High (3)* *Low (1)*	*High(1)* *Low (3)*	*High (3)* *Low (1)*
LISP	3	3	1	1
PROLOG	3	2	2	2
C++	3	2	2	3
COBOL	1	2	1	3

Enquire Within (EnquireWithin.co.nz) is an online interactive software tool that charts and clarifies thoughts and perceptions based on repertory grid interview techniques. Users are taken through compare and contrast processes, resulting in a graphical representation indicating how one has evaluated and described the subject matter for a particular session. Its uses include analyzing personal relationships or opportunities, decision-making support, and development of expert systems, and as a computer-based school study aid.

A few PC-based repertory grid analysis tools are available (e.g., PCGRID from April Metzler at Lehigh University). One of the first Web-based tools for knowledge acquisition, *WebGrid*, enhances collaborative knowledge acquisition (see also tiger.cpsc.ucalgary.ca/WebGrid/WebGrid.html). Also, there are software packages such as *Circumgrids* (W. Chambers, University of South Florida) for analyzing repertory grids via methods such as cluster analysis and factor analysis or principal component analysis.

OTHER COMPUTER-AIDED TOOLS

A smart knowledge-acquisition tool must be able to add knowledge to the knowledge base incrementally and refine or even correct existing knowledge. Sleeman and Mitchell (1996) describe two systems, REFINER1 and TIGON, that allow a domain expert to perform knowledge acquisition directly. These systems have been used, respectively, for patient management and for the diagnosis of turbine errors. REFINER is a case-based system that infers a prototypical description for each class, which is labeled by the domain expert. REFINER1 uses existing cases directly from databases. It then allows the expert to work with proposed modifications that would remove particular inconsistencies. TIGON was developed to detect and diagnose faults in a gas turbine engine. It incorporates background material from which it produces analogous rule bases automatically. See Sleeman and Mitchell (1996) for details.

The KAVAS-2 project is a knowledge acquisition, visualization, and assessment system that addresses the requirement to manage data and information flow in medicine (see Medical Informatics Laboratory ApS, ehto.be/aim/volume2/kavas.html). Protocols and procedures are provided to increase data and information generation, improve the quality of patient management, and reduce costs in health care service. A toolbox (KAVIAR) is provided to define modeling-process goals, identify suitable tools to address these goals, apply selected tools to the problem, measure the quality of the proposed solution, and validate the results.

Visual modeling techniques are often used to construct the initial domain model. The objective of the visual modeling approach is to give the user the ability to visualize real-world problems and manipulate elements of them through the use of graphics (Demetriads et al., 1999; Humphrey, 1999; Lee et al., 1995). Kearney (1990) indicates that diagrams and drawings are useful in representing problems; they serve as a set of external memory aids and can reveal inconsistencies in an individual's knowledge (Lockwood and Chen, 1994). Machine learning methods can induce decision trees and rules (see Chapter 12). A tool available for download via the Internet is XpertRule from Attar Software (attar.com). It provides a graphical development environment, allowing specification of decision trees based on business-process logic. Deployment of developed applications can be via standalone machines, networks, or Internet/intranets via the XpertRun run-time environment. Figure 11.5 shows a screenshot of its Knowledge Builder.

TEIRESIAS (Davis, 1993) is a classic program that was developed to assist knowledge engineers in the creation (or revision) of rules for a specific ES while working with the EMYCIN shell. The program uses a natural language interface to help the knowledge engineer test and debug new knowledge, and it provides an expanded

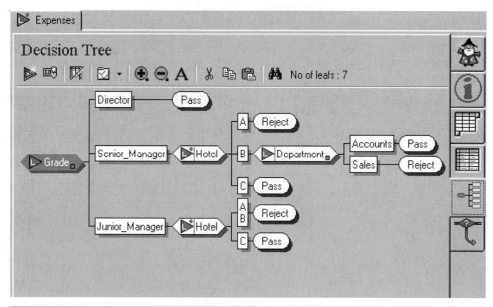

FIGURE 11.5 DECISION TREE FOR KNOWLEDGE BUILDING

Source: Adapted from attar.com/pages/info_kb.htm.

explanation capability. For example, if system builders find that a set of knowledge rules lead to an inadequate conclusion, they can have TEIRESIAS show all the rules used to reach that conclusion. With the rule editor, adjustments can easily be made. To expedite the process, TEIRESIAS translates each new rule, which is entered in natural language, into LISP. Then it retranslates the rule into natural language. The program can thus point out inconsistencies, rule conflicts, and inadequacies (for acquisition aids from databases, see the *International Journal of Intelligent Systems*, September 1992). A more recent use of TEIRESIAS has been in assisting in the tracking of computer system hackers. TEIRESIAS is used to monitor systems during normal operation and analyzes the information flow, looking for repeating strings of information. These strings represent an individual computer system; an attempt to break into the computer system would modify them, allowing a computer to monitor its own operation (see *Wired*, October 29, 1998, wired.com/news/technology/story/0,1282,15905,00.html). For further information and actual applied use, refer to the IBM Web site (research. ibm.com/topics/serious/bio).

Most of the preceding tools and many others were designed as standalone tools based on the assumption that they would be used by a specific ES participant (e.g., an expert) for the execution of a specific task. In reality, however, participants can play multiple roles or even exchange roles. Therefore, there is a trend toward integrating the acquisition aids. For an overview of such integration tools, see Boose and Gaines (1990) and Diamantidis and Giakoumakis (1999). Examples of such tools are PROTÉGÉ-II (Musen et al., 1995; Gennari et al., 2003), KSM (Cuena and Molina, 1996), and KADS (commonkads.uva.nl and van Harmelen, 1996).

AUTOMATIC KNOWLEDGE-DISCOVERY METHODS

In addition to semiautomatic methods that use computers to support the knowledge-acquisition process, there are situations where knowledge can be discovered from existing data. The process of using computers to extract knowledge from data is called knowledge discovery. In early 1990s, the process was also called machine learning, but knowledge discovery and data mining (KDD) are now more popular.

The difference between machine learning and knowledge discovery is vague. Some people tend to define machine learning as inductive learning, and knowledge discovery as including more techniques (e.g., clustering, neural networks).

XpertRule from Attar Software (attar.com) is a software tool that extracts information from graphical decision trees. Excel add-on products for data mining, such as XLMiner (resample.com/xlminer/index.shtml), are also handy in discovering knowledge from data. A glossary of terms related to knowledge discovery can be found in *Machine Learning* (1998, vol. 30, pp. 271–274). More software tools and information about knowledge discovery and data mining may be found on KDNuggets (kdnuggets.com). The following are a few useful machine-learning Web sites:

- Austrian Research Institute for AI–Machine Learning Group, ai.univie.ac.at/ oefai/ml/ml.html
- Machine Learning Network at UCI, ics.uci.edu/ai/ml/machine-learning.html
- MINEit Software Limited, kdnuggets.com/software.html
- Machine Learning Network–Online Information Service, mlnet.org
- Machine Learning Applied to Information Retrieval, National Research Council, Canada, iit.nrc.ca/bibliographies/ml-applied-to-ir.html

According to Roiger and Geatz (2002), typical methods for knowledge discovery include the following:

- ***Inductive learning.*** Rules are induced from existing cases with known results. The induced rules can then be stored in a knowledge base for consultation. This method will be described in Section 11.6.
- ***Neural computing.*** Neural computing is another problem-solving approach in which historical cases are used for deriving solutions to new problems. It mimics the human brain by building artificial neurons and storing knowledge in the connection of neurons.
- ***Genetic algorithms.*** Genetic algorithms use the principle of natural selection to gradually find the best combination of knowledge from known cases. As in the natural process of evolution, the basic operations for discovering knowledge are reproduction, crossover, and mutation.

In Chapter 12, we shall describe how inductive learning and other methods work. Techniques are also available for discovering knowledge from documents and the Internet. See AIS in Focus 11.5 for a description.

11.5 KNOWLEDGE ACQUISITION FROM MULTIPLE EXPERTS

An important element in the development of an ES is the identification of experts. This is a complicated task, perhaps because practitioners use so many support mechanisms for certain tasks (e.g., questionnaires, informal and formal consultations, texts). These support mechanisms contribute to the high quality of professional output, but they may also make it difficult to identify a "knowledge czar" whose estimates, processes, or knowledge are clearly superior to what the system and mix of staff, support tools, and consulting skills produce in the rendering of normal client service.

TABLE 11.6   Benefits of and Problems with Participation of Multiple Experts

Benefits	Problems
On the average, fewer mistakes by a group of experts than by a single expert	Groupthink phenomena
Several experts in a group eliminate the need for using a world-class expert (who is difficult to get and expensive)	Fear on the part of some domain experts of senior experts or a supervisor (lack of confidentiality)
Wider domain than a single expert's	Compromising solutions generated by a group with conflicting opinions
Synthesis of expertise	Wasted time in group meetings
Enhanced quality from synergy among experts	Difficulties in scheduling the experts
	Dominating experts (controlling, not letting others speak)

The usual approach to this problem is to build ES for a very narrow domain in which expertise is clearly defined; then it is easy to find one expert. However, even though many ES have been constructed with one expert—an approach advocated as a good strategy for ES construction—there could be a need for **multiple experts**, especially when more serious systems are being constructed or when expertise is not particularly well defined. The case described in the Opening Vignette (Ranjan et al., 2002) is a good example of using multiple experts.

Table 11.6 lists the benefits and problems of multiple experts. The major purposes of using multiple experts are

- To better understand the knowledge domain.
- To improve knowledge-base validity, consistency, completeness, accuracy, and relevancy.
- To provide better productivity.
- To identify incorrect results more easily.
- To address broader domains.
- To be able to handle more complex problems and combine the strengths of different reasoning approaches.

When multiple experts are used, there are often differences of opinion and conflicts that must be resolved. This is especially true when knowledge bases are being developed from multiple sources where these systems address problems that involve the use of subjective reasoning and heuristics.

Other related issues are identifying the various aspects of the problem and matching them to the appropriate experts, integrating knowledge from different experts, assimilating conflicting strategies, personalizing community knowledge bases, and developing programming technologies to support these issues.

MULTIPLE-EXPERT SCENARIOS

There are four possible scenarios, or configurations, for using multiple experts (McGraw and Harbison-Briggs, 1989; O'Leary, 1993; Rayham and Fairhurst, 1999; Scott et al., 1991): individual experts, primary and secondary experts, small groups, and panels.

INDIVIDUAL EXPERTS

In this case, several experts contribute knowledge individually. Using multiple experts in this manner relieves the knowledge engineer of the stress associated with multiple-expert teams. However, this approach requires that the knowledge engineer have a means of resolving conflicts and handling multiple lines of reasoning. An example of a Delphi process performed with questionnaires for acquiring knowledge about hospital operating-room scheduling is provided by Hamilton (1996a). Once acquired, the knowledge was deployed in an expert system at multiple sites.

PRIMARY AND SECONDARY EXPERTS

In this case, a primary expert is responsible for validating information retrieved from other domain experts. Knowledge engineers may initially consult the primary expert for guidance in domain familiarization, refinement of knowledge acquisition plans, and identification of potential secondary experts.

SMALL GROUPS

In this case, several experts are consulted together and asked to provide agreed-upon information. Working with small groups of experts allows the knowledge engineer to observe alternative approaches to the solution of a problem and the key points made in solution-oriented discussions among experts.

PANELS

To meet goals for verification and validation of ongoing development efforts, some programs establish a council of experts. The members of the council typically meet together at times scheduled by the developer for the purpose of reviewing knowledge base development efforts, content, and plans. In many cases, the functionality of the expert system is tested against the expertise of such a panel.

These scenarios determine in part the method to be used for handling multiple experts.

METHODS OF HANDLING MULTIPLE EXPERTISE

The expert judgments of multiple experts may differ. Several major approaches to the issue of integrating expert opinions have been defined by Medsker et al. (1995), O'Leary (1993), and Scott et al. (1991).

- Blend several lines of reasoning through consensus methods such as Delphi, NGT, and GSS.
- Use an analytic approach, such as group probability (O'Leary, 1993), or an analytic hierarchy process (Hurley and Lior, 2002).
- Keep the lines of reasoning distinct and select a specific line of reasoning based on the situation (Scott et al., 1991).
- Automate the process, using software (ACACIA Web site, sop.inria.fr/acacia/) or a blackboard approach (Englemore and Morgan, 1989).
- Decompose the knowledge acquired into specialized knowledge sources (blackboard systems).

11.6 AUTOMATED KNOWLEDGE ACQUISITION FROM DATA AND DOCUMENTS

As described in Section 11.4, knowledge may also be discovered from existing cases or documents using computer software. The reasons for using automated knowledge acquisition are summarized in AIS in Focus 11.5. For rule-based expert systems, a classic method is to use rule inductive methods in machine learning. Knowledge may also

---

AIS IN FOCUS 11.5

REASONS FOR AUTOMATED KNOWLEDGE ACQUISITION

There are two major reasons for the use of automated knowledge acquisition: good knowledge engineers are highly paid and difficult to find, and domain experts are usually busy and sometimes uncooperative. As a result, manual and even semiautomatic elicitation methods are slow and expensive. In addition, they have some other deficiencies:

- The correlation between verbal reports and mental behavior is often weak.

- In certain situations, experts are unable to provide an overall account of how they make decisions.

- The quality of the system depends too much on the quality of the expert and the knowledge engineer.

- The expert does not understand the ES technology.

- The knowledge engineer may not understand the business problem.

- It is difficult to validate the acquired knowledge.

---

be discovered from documents, this is often called text mining. Details are outlined in AIS in Focus 11.6. In this section, we describe rule induction in detail.

The objectives of using automated knowledge acquisition are:

- To increase the productivity of knowledge engineering (reduce the cost).
- To reduce the skill level required from the knowledge engineer.

AIS IN FOCUS 11.6

ACQUISITION OF DOCUMENTED KNOWLEDGE

Knowlege can often be acquired from other sources in addition to, or instead of, human experts. This approach has the major advantage of eliminating the need to use an expert. It is employed in knowledge-based systems where handling a large or complex amount of information rather than world-class expertise is the main concern. Searching through corporate policy manuals or catalogs is an example.

At present, very few methodologies deal with knowledge acquisition from documented sources. It may be difficult to find the necessary knowledge in a database. One way to improve such searches is the use of domain knowledge to guide the search (Owrang and Groupe, 1996). Another is the use of intelligent agents (Chapter 13). Acquisition from documented sources has a great potential for automation. Documented knowledge of almost any type can be easily and inexpensively scanned and transferred to a computer's database. The knowledge can then be analyzed manually or with the use of AI technologies (a combination of natural language processing, intelligent agents, and expert systems). Thus, expert systems can be used to build other expert systems.

Hahn et al. (1996) are developing a methodology for knowledge acquisition and concept learning from texts (in German). The method relies on a quality-based model of terminological reasoning (using concepts from natural language processing). The goal is to be able to scan two kinds of documents: test reports on information-technology products (about 100 documents with 100,000 words) and medical-findings reports (about 120,000 documents with 10 million words).

Another approach, based on explicit relation markers, is proposed by Bowden et al. (1996). Initial tests with their implementation, KEP, are encouraging.

The capability of constructing an ES that can scan databases, digitized books, journals, and magazines is increasing. Data stored in another computer system can be retrieved electronically to create or update the knowledge base of the expert system, all without the intervention of a knowledge engineer or an expert. The field is basically at the stage of developing new methods that interpret meanings in order to determine rules and other forms of knowledge, such as frames for case-based reasoning. A number of new methods are being developed and implemented. More details about text mining and Web mining can be found in Sullivan (2001), Chakrabarti (2002), and Berry (2003).

- To eliminate (or drastically reduce) the need for an expert.
- To eliminate (or drastically reduce) the need for a knowledge engineer.
- To increase the quality of the acquired knowledge.

AUTOMATED RULE INDUCTION

Induction is the process of reasoning from the specific to the general. In ES terminology it is the process by which a computer program generates rules from example cases. A rule induction system is given examples of a problem (called a **training set**) for which the outcome is known. After it has been given enough examples, the rule induction system can create rules that fit the example cases. The rules can then be used to assess new cases for which the outcome is not known. The heart of a rule induction system is an algorithm used to induce the rules from the examples (see AIS in Focus 11.7). An application of rule induction for retaining-wall selection is described in AIS in Action 11.8.

An example of a simplified rule induction can be seen in the work of a loan officer in a bank. Requests for loans include information about the applicants, such as income level, assets, age, and number of dependents. These are the attributes, or characteristics, of the applicants. If we log several example cases, each with its final decision, we will find a situation that resembles the data in Table 11.7.

AIS IN FOCUS 11.7

INDUCTION ALGORITHMS

Induction methods use a variety of algorithms to convert a knowledge matrix of attributes, values, and selections to rules. Such algorithms vary from statistical methods to neural computing.

ID3 is a popular induction algorithm. It begins by converting the knowledge matrix into a decision tree. The algorithm uses entropy to assess the relative contribution of different attributes to classify the training cases and then chooses the most important one to be the root. The training sample is then divided into several groups according to the choosen attribute. The above procedure is repeated for each group until the training subsets cannot be further decomposed. The decision tree resulting from the induction can be further converted into rules. A very good description of the ID3 algorithm is available in Quinaln (1986) and A. Colin, "Building Decision Trees with the ID3 Algorithm" (*Dr. Dobbs's Journal Software Tools Professional Program*, Vol. 21, No. 6, 1996). Many rule induction programs are available from data-mining vendors. More information can be found at Kdnuggets (kdnuggets.com).

Extensions to include uncertain reasoning (probabilistic knowledge) in ID3 were devised by P. E. Maher and D. St. Clair ("Uncertain Reasoning in an ID3 Machine Learning Framework," *Second IEEE*

International Conference on Fuzzy Systems, IEEE, Piscataway, NJ, 1993). Inclusion of fuzzy logic (another type of probabilistic knowledge) in decision trees and further applications are given by Umano et al. (1994). Integrating Baysian statistics and rule induction was first presented by Liang (1992). More recently, the rough-fuzzy approach has reportedly been used to reduce the resulting rule set (Shen and Chouchoulas, 2002).

An inductive learning algorithm, as defined by Tolun and Abu-Soud (1998), further addresses problems with symbolic learning algorithms such as ID3 when working on unseen training examples (small-junctions problem). In this instance the ID3 is unable to classify unknown examples because the decision tree is too specific. ILA selects features after considering all the examples for a given decision, therefore providing more general rules, which do not contain unnecessary and irrelevant conditions. Further developments include the method for automated extraction of hierarchical decision rules (Tsumoto, 2003) and combining rule induction with other methods, such as neural networks (e.g., Jerez et al 2003). More information on the integrated method is available in Chapter 12.

AIS IN ACTION 11.8

INDUCTION-BASED SYSTEM
FOR RETAINING-WALL SELECTION

Retaining walls are used in building construction projects for excavating the foundation. Design engineers often encounter the problem of choosing the most suitable of various different alternatives, such as a slurry wall, steel-rail pile, and H-section pile. Making the best decision requires professional knowledge and experience in order to reduce the risk.

This selection task has been automated by the development of a system combining rules and cases. The system stores cases in the case base and induce rules from them. The rules are used to make decisions when a new case is encountered. The system has the following major components:

1. *Case base.* The case base serves as an organizational memory that stores all previous designs.

2. *Rule base.* The rule base stores all rules induced from the case base.

3. *Rule induction mechanism.* The module uses XpertRule to generate rules.

4. *Rule reasoning mechanism.* The module derives new conclusion from existing rules.

5. *User interface.* The interface allows the system to interact with the user.

A preliminary performance test recorded 71 percent accuracy on 48 test cases. The result was considered acceptable.

Source: Abridged from J. B. Yang, "A Rule Induction–Based Knowledge System for Retaining Wall Selection," *Expert Systems with Applications*, Vol. 23, 2002, pp. 273–279.

From these cases, it is easy to infer the following three rules:

- If income is $70,000 or more, approve the loan.
- If income is $30,000 or more, age is at least 40, assets are above $249,000, and there are no dependents, approve the loan.
- If income is between $30,000 and $50,000 and assets are at least $100,000, approve the loan.

ADVANTAGES OF RULE INDUCTION

One of the leading researchers in the field, Donald Michie, has pointed out that only certain types of knowledge can be properly acquired using manual knowledge-acquisition methods such as interviews and observations. These are cases in which the domain of knowledge is certain, small, loosely coupled, or modular. As the domain gets larger or uncertain, and more complex, experts become unable to explain how they perform. Nonetheless, they can still supply the knowledge engineer with suitable examples of problems and their solutions. Using rule induction allows ES to be used in more complicated and more commercially rewarding fields.

Another advantage is that the builder does not have to be a knowledge engineer. He or she can be the expert or a system analyst. This not only saves time and money

TABLE 11.7 Case for Induction: A Knowledge Map (Induction Table)

Applicant	Annual Income ($)	Assets ($)	Age (years)	Number of Dependents	Decision
Mr. White	50,000	100,000	30	3	Yes
Ms. Green	70,000	None	35	1	Yes
Mr. Smith	40,000	None	33	2	No
Ms. Rich	30,000	250,000	42	0	Yes

but also solves the difficulties in dealing with a knowledge engineer who may be an outsider unfamiliar with the business.

Machine induction also offers the possibility of deducing new knowledge. Once rules are generated, they are reviewed by an expert and modified if necessary. A big advantage of rule induction is that it enhances the thinking process of the reviewing expert.

DIFFICULTIES IN IMPLEMENTATION

Despite the advantages, there are several difficulties with the implementation of rule induction:

- Some induction programs may generate rules that are not easy for a human to understand because the way the program classifies a problem's attributes and properties may not be the way a human would do it.
- Rule induction programs do not select the attributes. An expert must still be available to specify which attributes are significant (e.g., important factors in approving a loan).
- The search process in rule induction is based on special algorithms that generate efficient decision trees, which reduce the number of questions that must be asked before a conclusion is reached. Several alternative algorithms are available. They vary in their processes and capabilities.
- The method is only good for rule-based classification problems, especially of the yes/no type. (However, many problems can be rephrased or split so that they fall into the classification category.)
- The number of attributes must be fairly small. The upper limit on the number of attributes is approached very quickly.
- The number of examples necessary can be very large.
- The set of examples must be "sanitized"; for example, cases that are exceptions to rules must be removed. (Such exceptions can be determined by observing inconsistent rules.)
- The method is limited to situations under certainty.
- A major problem with the method is that the builder does not know in advance whether the number of examples is sufficient and whether the algorithm is good enough. To be sure of this would presuppose that the builder had some idea of the solution, but the reason for using induction is that the builder does not know the solution, and wants to discover it by using the rules.

Because of these limitations, the rule induction method is generally used to provide a first prototype; then it is translated into something more robust and crafted into an improved system through an evolutionary design and development method.

SOFTWARE PACKAGES

Many software packages for induction are available. Some of them are free, while some are commercial products. A list of selected software can be found at kdnuggets.com/software/classification-tree-rules.html. Some of them are standalone, and others are add-on products of Excel. In fact, popular statistical packages like SAS and SPSS are adding the induction method as a standard module for data analysis. Popular ones include CART 5.0 (incorporating classification costs into consideration, salford-systems.com/) and C4.5 (a revised version of ID3 from Ross Quinlan, cse.unsw.edu.au/~quinlan/).

Most of these programs not only generate rules but also check them for possible logical conflict. All of the programs are ES shells; that is, they can be used to generate the rules and then to construct an ES that uses this knowledge. K-Vision even allows incorporation of an entire induction table into a set of rules represented as a single node. For further details, see Reynolds and Zannon (2000). A good introduction to the method can be found in Roiger and Geatz (2002).

INTERACTIVE INDUCTION

Instead of inducing rules from cases in a batch mode, knowledge can be induced by interacting with experts incrementally. This is called **interactive induction** (Jeng et al., 1996). Interactive induction needs an expert supported by computer software. One interesting tool that combines induction and interactive acquisition is ACQUIRE from Acquired Intelligence Inc. (aiinc.ca).

ACQUIRE captures the knowledge of an expert through interactive interviews, distills it, and automatically generates a rule-based knowledge base. ACQUIRE provides a variety of ways of capturing human knowledge, all of them focused on a qualitative representation of knowledge, and uses specific patterns of information to describe the situations experts can observe or contemplate. Thus, ACQUIRE can capture both explicit and implicit knowledge.

ACQUIRE guides an expert through successive steps of knowledge structuring, yielding models of domain knowledge at varying levels of generality. The most general of these models is the Object Network. An object is anything that occurs, is considered, or is concluded by the expert. The domain expert attributes a set of values or meanings to each object and organizes them into a network. The details of the individual rules are completed by a number of methods, including action tables (induction tables) and IF-THEN-ELSE rules. Finally, the reasoning path is created and conflicts among reasoning paths are resolved. Contexts in which a rule is applied are also specified.

ACQUIRE interacts with experts (without knowledge engineers); it helps them bypass their cognitive defenses and biases and identify the important criteria and constructs used in decision-making. For details and demo systems, see aiinc.ca.

11.7 KNOWLEDGE VERIFICATION AND VALIDATION

Knowledge acquired from experts needs to be evaluated for quality, including evaluation, validation, and verification. These terms are often used interchangeably. We use the definitions provided by O'Keefe et al. (1987).

- **Evaluation** is a broad concept. Its objective is to assess an expert system's overall value. In addition to assessing acceptable performance levels, it analyzes whether the system would be usable, efficient, and cost-effective.
- **Validation** is the part of evaluation that deals with the performance of the system (e.g., as it compares to the expert's). Simply stated, validation is building the right system, that is, substantiating that a system performs with an acceptable level of accuracy.
- **Verification** is building the system right or substantiating that the system is correctly implemented to its specifications.

In the realm of expert systems, these activities are dynamic because they must be repeated each time the prototype is changed. In terms of the knowledge base, it is necessary to ensure that we have the right knowledge base (i.e., that the knowledge is valid). It is also essential to ensure that the knowledge base was constructed properly (verification). For each IF statement, more than 30 criteria can be used in verification (see *PC AI*, March/April 2002, p. 59).

In performing these quality-control tasks, we deal with several activities and concepts, as listed in Table 11.8. The process can be very difficult if one considers the many sociotechnical issues involved (Sharma and Conrath, 1992).

A method for validating ES, based on validation approaches from psychology, was developed by Sturman and Milkovich (1995). The approach tests the extent to which the system and the expert decisions agree, the inputs and processes used by an expert compared to the machine, and the difference between expert and novice decisions. Validation and verification techniques on specific ES are described by Ram and Ram (1996) for innovative management. Avritzer et al. (1996) provide an algorithm for reliability testing of expert systems designed to operate in industrial settings, particularly to monitor and control large real-time systems.

Automated verification of knowledge is offered in the ACQUIRE product described earlier. Verification is conducted by measuring the system's performance and is limited to classification cases with probabilities. It works as follows: When an ES is presented with a new case to classify, it assigns a confidence factor to each selection. By comparing these confidence factors with those provided by an expert, one can measure the accuracy of the ES for each case. By performing comparisons on many cases, one can derive an overall measure of ES performance (O'Keefe and O'Leary, 1993).

TABLE 11.8   Measures of Validation

Measure or Criterion	Description
Accuracy	How well the system reflects reality, how correct the knowledge is in the knowledge base
Adaptability	Possibilities for future development, changes
Adequacy (or completeness)	Portion of the necessary knowledge included in the knowledge base
Appeal	How well the knowledge base matches intuition and stimulates thought and practicability
Breadth	How well the domain is covered
Depth	Degree of detailed knowledge
Face validity	Credibility of knowledge
Generality	Capability of a knowledge base to be used with a broad range of similar problems
Precision	Capability of the system to replicate particular system parameters, consistency of advice, coverage of variables in knowledge base
Realism	Accounting for relevant variables and relations, similarity to reality
Reliability	Fraction of the ES predictions that are empirically correct
Robustness	Sensitivity of conclusions to model structure
Sensitivity	Impact of changes in the knowledge base on quality of outputs
Technical and operational validity	Quality of the assumed assumptions, context, constraints, and conditions, and their impact on other measures
Turing test	Ability of a human evaluator to identify whether a given conclusion is made by an ES or by a human expert
Usefulness	How adequate the knowledge is (in terms of parameters and relationships) for solving correctly
Validity	Knowledge base's capability of producing empirically correct predictions

Source: Adapted from B. Marcot, "Testing Your Knowledge Base," AI Expert, Aug. 1987.

Rosenwald and Liu (1997) have developed a validation procedure that uses the rule base's knowledge and structure to generate test cases that efficiently cover the entire input space of the rule base. Thus, the entire set of cases need not be examined. A symbolic execution of a model of the ES is used to determine all conditions under which the fundamental knowledge can be used. For an extensive bibliography on validation and verification, see Grogono et al. (1991) and Juan et al. (1999). An easy approach to automating verification of a large rule base can be found in Goldstein (2002).

11.8 REPRESENTATION OF KNOWLEDGE

The knowledge acquired from experts or induced from a set of data must be represented in a format that is both understandable by humans and executable on computers. There are many different methods for knowledge representation. The most popular is the production rule. Frames, decision trees, objects, and logics are also useful in some cases. They are described in this section.

PRODUCTION RULES

Production rules are the most popular form of knowledge representation for expert systems. Knowledge is represented in the form of condition–action pairs: IF this condition (or premise or antecedent) occurs, THEN some action (or result or conclusion or consequence) will (or should) occur. Consider these two examples:

- If the stop light is red AND you have stopped, THEN a right turn is okay.
- If the client uses purchase requisition forms AND the purchase orders are approved and purchasing is separate from receiving AND accounts payable AND inventory records, THEN there is strongly suggestive evidence (90 percent probability) that controls to prevent unauthorized purchases are adequate. (This example from an internal control procedure includes a probability.)

Each production rule in a knowledge base implements an autonomous chunk of expertise that can be developed and modified independently of other rules. When combined and fed to the inference engine, the set of rules behaves synergistically, yielding better results than the sum of the results of the individual rules. In reality, knowledge-based rules are not independent. They quickly become highly interdependent. For example, adding a new rule may conflict with an existing rule, or it may require a revision of attributes or rules.

Rules can be viewed, in some sense, as a simulation of the cognitive behavior of human experts. According to this view, rules are not just a neat formalism to represent knowledge in a computer, rather, they represent a model of actual human behavior.

Rules can appear in different forms. Some examples follow:

- ***IF premise, THEN conclusion.*** If your income is high, THEN your chance of being audited by the IRS is high.
- ***Conclusion, IF premise.*** Your chance of being audited is high, IF your income is high.
- ***Inclusion of ELSE.*** If your income is high OR your deductions are unusual, THEN your chance of being audited by the IRS is high, OR ELSE your chance of being audited is low.

> • ***More complex rules.*** IF the credit rating is high AND the salary is more than $30,000 OR assets are more than $75,000 AND pay history is not "poor," THEN approve a loan up to $10,000 and list the loan in category B. The action part may include additional information: THEN approve the loan and refer the applicant to an agent.

The IF side of a rule can include dozens of IFs. The THEN side can include several parts as well.

For further discussion of the use of production rules in active and deductive databases, see Palopoli and Torlone (1997). For an example of the use of production rules in an expert system used in production environments, see Stack (1997) and Guth (1999).

KNOWLEDGE AND INFERENCE RULES

Two types of rules are common in AI: knowledge and inference. Knowledge rules, or **declarative rules**, state all the facts and relationships about a problem. **Inference rules**, or procedural rules, on the other hand, advise on how to solve a problem given that certain facts are known. The knowledge engineer separates the two types of rules: Knowledge rules go to the knowledge base, whereas inference rules become part of the inference engine.

For example, assume you are in the business of buying and selling gold. The knowledge rules might look like the following:

* ***RULE 1:*** IF an international conflict begins THEN the price of gold goes up.
* ***RULE 2:*** IF the inflation rate declines THEN the price of gold goes down.
* ***RULE 3:*** IF the international conflict lasts more than seven days and IF it is in the Middle East THEN buy gold.

Inference rules contain rules about rules and thus are also called **metarules**. They pertain to other rules (or even to themselves). Inference (procedural) rules may look like the following:

* ***RULE 1:*** IF the data needed are not in the system THEN request them from the user.
* ***RULE 2:*** IF more than one rule applies THEN deactivate any rules that add no new data.

ADVANTAGES AND LIMITATIONS OF RULES

Rule representation is especially applicable when there is a need to recommend a course of action based on observable events (see AIS in Action 11.9). It has several major advantages:

> * Rules are easy to understand. They are communicable because they are a natural form of knowledge.
> * Inference and explanations are easily derived.
> * Modifications and maintenance are relatively easy.
> * Uncertainty is easily combined with rules.
> * Each rule is often independent of all others.

AIS IN ACTION 11.9

RULE-BASED SYSTEMS TACKLE EMPLOYEE SHRINK

Innovative computer-based technologies are taking the battle against employee-related shrink (theft) to a higher level. Several new applications are aimed at identifying dishonest personnel, who account for an estimated 38 percent of retail shrink, as well as those who may simply be making errors at the point of sale.

PLATINUM Solutions offers a rule-based system that targets employee theft at the retailer's point of sale. "The rules are interrelated statements or business policies governing what is allowed and what is not allowed," explains Carl Fijat, a management consultant with PLATINUM Solutions.

Rule-based software can help retailers find fraud patterns by collecting and storing information about incidents occurring at the point of sale and classifying them according to the policies expressed as knowledge in the program. For example, it can be programmed to post "self-ringing employee" alerts when employees ring up returns for themselves. "Excessive credit to purchases" is posted when a staff member processes purchases whose value exceeds a certain limit and the account being credited is labeled "in-house."

One of the products of PLATINUM Technologies (the parent company) is AionDS, which models and encapsulates retailers' business policy logic into rules, Fijat explains. Each rule defines a premise and one or more resulting actions. Rules can be expressed in easy-to-understand, English-like language; this makes it easier for loss-prevention executives to communicate system requirements to those developing rule-based software, thus leading to more effective knowledge representation and acquisition.

AionDS, and rule-based software in general, is particularly valuable in isolating patterns not discernible from reading exception reports. For example, if an employee authorizes a legitimate cash sale, signs off, then signs on under someone else's identification number to refund the immediate sale, and then signs back on again as himself or herself, the system can use a rule to track such fraudulent activity.

Source: Modified and condensed from J. R. Ross, "New Rule-Based Systems Tackle Employee Shrink," *Stores*, Vol. 78, No. 8, August 1996, pp. 71–72.

The major limitations of rule representation are as follows:

- Complex knowledge requires thousands of rules, which may create difficulties in using and maintaining the system.
- Builders like rules, so they try to force all knowledge into rules rather than look for more appropriate representations.
- Systems with many rules may have a search limitation in the control program. Some programs have difficulty in evaluating rule-based systems and making inferences.

Table 11.8 lists the major characteristics of rules.

SEMANTIC NETWORKS

Semantic networks focus on the relationships between different concepts. They are graphical depictions of knowledge composed of nodes and links that show hierarchical relationships between objects; see Sowa (1997), Cox (2001), and Russel and Norvig (2002).

A simple semantic network is shown in Figure 11.6. It is made up of a number of circles, or nodes, that represent objects and descriptive information about the objects. Objects can be any physical item, such as a book, a car, a desk, or even a person. Nodes can also be concepts, events, or actions. A concept might be the relationship between supply and demand in economics, an event such as a picnic or an election, or an action such as building a house or writing a book. Attributes of an object can also be used as

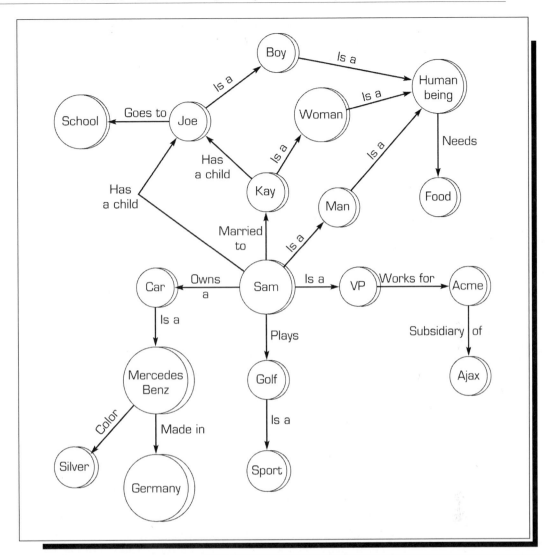

FIGURE 11.6 REPRESENTATION OF KNOWLEDGE IN A SEMANTIC NETWORK

nodes. These might represent size, color, class, age, origin, or other characteristics. In this way, detailed information about objects can be presented.

Nodes are interconnected by links, or arcs, that show the relationships between the various objects and descriptive factors. Some of the most common arcs are of the is-a or has-a type. Is-a is used to show a class relationship, that is, that an object belongs to a larger class or category of objects. Has-a links are used to identify characteristics or attributes of object nodes. Other arcs are used for definitional purposes.

Now refer to the example in Figure 11.6. As you can see, the central figure in the domain of knowledge is a person called Sam. One link shows that Sam is a man, and that a man is a human being, or is part of a class called humans. Another arc from Sam shows that he is married to Kay. Additional arcs show that Kay is a woman, and that a woman is in turn a human being. Other links show that Sam and Kay have a child, Joe, who is a boy and goes to school.

Some nodes and arcs show other characteristics about Sam. For example, he is a vice president of Acme, a company that is a subsidiary of Ajax. We also see that Sam plays golf, which is a sport. Furthermore, Sam owns a Mercedes-Benz whose color is silver. We also see that Mercedes-Benz is a type of car that is made in Germany.

One of the most interesting and useful facts about a semantic network is that it can show **inheritance**. Because a semantic network is basically a hierarchy, the various characteristics of some nodes actually inherit the characteristics of others. As an example, consider the links showing that Sam is a man and that a man is in turn a human being. Here, Sam inherits all the properties of human being. We can ask the question, Does Sam need food? Because of the inheritance links, we can say that he needs food if human beings need food. See Mili and Pachet (1995) for details on a hierarchical semantic network concept called regularity that subsumes inheritance. They present novel ways in which semantic networks can support hypertext functionality with a specific interest in generating argumentative documents (documents that develop a thesis or prove an assertion).

Semantic nets are used basically as a visual representation of relationships and can be combined with other representation methods.

FRAMES

If we need to focus on the properties of certain objects, then using frames and objects is a good choice. A **frame** is a data structure that includes all the knowledge about a particular object. This knowledge is organized in a special hierarchical structure that permits a diagnosis of knowledge independence. Frames are basically an application of **object-oriented programming** for AI and ES. They are used extensively in ES. See Fensel et al. (1998) for a discussion of the frame-based Knowledge Acquisition and Representation Language (KARL), Jackson (1999) for a more detailed description of frames and their uses, and Chaudhri and Lowrance (1998) for details of the frame representation system and graphical browsing tool GKB-Editor.

Frames, as in frames of reference, provide a concise structural representation of knowledge in a natural manner. In contrast to other representation methods, the values that describe one object are grouped together into a single unit called a frame. Thus, a frame encompasses complex objects, entire situations, or a managerial problem as a single entity. The knowledge in a frame is partitioned into slots. A slot can describe declarative knowledge (e.g., the color of a car) or procedural knowledge (e.g., "activate a certain rule if a value exceeds a given level"). The major capabilities of frames are summarized in Table 11.9.

A frame provides a means of organizing knowledge in slots that contain characteristics and attributes. In physical form, a frame is somewhat like an outline with categories and subcategories. A typical frame describing an automobile is shown in Figure

---

TABLE 11.9   Capabilities of Frames

- Ability to clearly document information about a domain model (e.g., a plant's machines and their associated attributes)
- Related ability to constrain the allowable values that an attribute can take on
- Modularity of information, permitting ease of system expansion and maintenance
- More readable and consistent
- Syntax for referencing domain objects in the rules
- Platform for building a graphic interface with object graphics
- Mechanism that allows the scope of facts considered during forward or backward chaining to be restricted
- Access to a mechanism that supports the inheritance of information down a class hierarchy

Automobile Frame

Class of: Transportation
Name of manufacturer: Audi
Origin of manufacturer: Germany
Model: 5000 Turbo
Type of car: Sedan
Weight: 3300 lb.
Wheelbase: 105.8 inches
Number of doors: 4 (default)
Transmission: 3-speed automatic
Number of wheels: 4 (default)
Engine: (Reference Engine Frame)
  • Type: In-line, overhead cam
  • Number of cylinders: 5
Acceleration (procedural attachment)
  • 0–60: 10.4 seconds
  • Quarter mile: 17.1 seconds, 85 mph
Gas mileage: 22 mpg average (procedural attachment)

Engine Frame

Cylinder bore: 3.19 inches
Cylinder stroke: 3.4 inches
Compression ratio: 7.8 to 1
Fuel system: Injection with turbocharger
Horsepower: 140 hp
Torque: 160 ft/LB

FIGURE 11.7   FRAME DESCRIBING AN AUTOMOBILE

11.7. Note that the slots describe attributes such as name of manufacturer, model, origin of manufacturer, type of car, number of doors, engine, and other characteristics.

CONTENT OF A FRAME

A frame includes two basic elements: slots and facets. A **slot** is a set of attributes that describe the object represented by the frame. For example, in the automobile frame, there are weight and engine slots. Each slot contains one or more facets. The **facets** (sometimes called subslots) describe some knowledge or procedural information about the attribute in the slot. Facets can take many forms:

  • *Values.* These describe attributes such as blue, red, and yellow for a color slot.
  • *Default.* This facet is used if the slot is empty, that is, without any description. For example, in the car frame one default value is that the number of wheels on the car is 4. It means that we can assume the car has four wheels unless otherwise indicated.
  • *Range.* Range indicates what kind of information can appear in a slot (e.g., integer numbers only, two decimal points, 0 to 100).
  • *If added.* This facet contains procedural information or attachments. It specifies an action to be taken when a value in the slot is added (or modified). Such procedural attachments are called demons.

- ***If needed.*** This facet is used in a case when no slot value is given. Much like the if-added situation, it triggers a procedure that goes out and gets or computes a value.
- ***Other.*** Slots can contain frames, rules, semantic networks, or any type of information.

Certain procedures can be attached to slots and used to derive slot values. For example, slot-specific heuristics are procedures for deriving slot values in a particular context. An important aspect of such procedures is that they can be used to direct the reasoning process. In addition to filling slots, they can be triggered when a slot is filled.

In Figure 11.7, both acceleration and gas mileage are procedural attachments. They refer to a step-by-step procedure that defines how to acquire this information. For example, to determine acceleration, time needed to go from 0 to 60 mph and quarter-mile elapsed time would be described. A procedural attachment to determine gas mileage would state a procedure for filling the gas tank, driving a certain number of miles, determining the amount of gasoline used, and computing the gas mileage in terms of miles per gallon.

HIERARCHY AND INHERITANCE OF FRAMES

Most AI systems use a collection of frames linked together in a certain manner to show their relationship. This is called a hierarchy of frames. For example, Figure 11.8 illustrates a hierarchy of frames describing different kinds of automobiles.

The hierarchical arrangement of frames permits inheritance frames. In Figure 11.8, the root of the tree is at the top, where the highest level of abstraction is represented. Frames at the bottom are called leaves of the tree. The hierarchy permits inheritance of

FIGURE 11.8   HIERARCHY OF FRAMES DESCRIBING VEHICLES

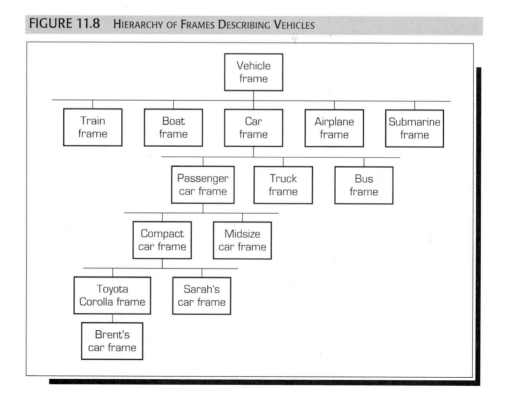

characteristics. Each frame usually inherits the characteristics of all related frames of higher levels. For example, a passenger car has the general properties of a car (e.g., an engine and carburetor). These characteristics are expressed in the internal structure of the frame. **Inheritance** is the mechanism for passing such knowledge, which is provided in the value of the slots, from frame to frame.

Parent frames provide a more general description of the entities. More general descriptions are higher in the hierarchy. Parent frames contain the attribute definitions. When we describe actual physical objects, we **instantiate** the child's frame. The instances (child frames) contain actual values of the attributes. An example is shown in Figure 11.9.

Note that every parent is a child of a higher-level parent. In building a frame it is possible to have a frame in which different slots are related to different parents. The only frame without a parent is the one at the top of the hierarchy. This frame is called a master frame. It is the root frame, and has the most general characteristics. The use of frame-based tools to build expert systems is demonstrated in tools such as CORVID (exsys.com).

OBJECT-ORIENTED KNOWLEDGE REPRESENTATIONS

The frame-based approach for knowledge representation has not been very popular in expert systems design, but the follow-up approach that adopts many concepts from frames, known as the object-oriented approach, has become a norm in system analysis and design. Clearly, hypermedia, especially over the Web, can exploit the object-oriented approach. In this approach, different kinds of knowledge can be encapsulated in objects, and these objects can communicate actions directly. Devedzic et al. (1996) describe how knowledge can be represented as objects in ES, along with the reasoning process. Their model, Reasoning Objects for Building Inference Engines (ROBBIE), is

FIGURE 11.9 PARENT AND CHILD FRAMES

Name: Toyota Corolla		Name: Brent's car Instance of: Toyota Corolla frame	
Slots	Facets	Slots	Facets
Owner	Check registration list	Owner	Brent
Color	List, per manufacturer		
No. of cylinders		Color	Blue
Range	4 or 6		
If needed	Ask owner	No. of cylinders	6
Model	Sedan sport	Model	4D sedan
Range	2–4 doors		
If needed	Ask owner		
Vintage (year)		Vintage (year)	1994
Range	1970–1995		
If needed	Ask owner		
(a) Parent frame		(b) Child frame	

based on a hierarchy in which each level is more detailed. At the highest level is a blackboard and agents for interaction. As we move down the hierarchy, first the system is defined, then its blocks, then its components, and finally the primitives that form the pattern matching, conflict resolution, and so on.

Production rules and frames comprise a successful combination of knowledge-representation methods. By themselves, production rules do not provide a totally effective representation facility for many ES applications. In particular, their expressive power is inadequate for defining terms and for describing domain objects and static relationships among objects. In essence, frames are objects and fit the paradigm of an object-oriented approach to ES development rather well. Objects encapsulate properties and actions, just as frames store knowledge. Furthermore, frames are organized into classes, which are organized into hierarchies. Each frame inherits its properties from its parent frame, just as an object inherits properties. Rules can either guide the frames' behaviors or be embedded in the frame (some accounting applications using frames and rules adopt the latter approach).

The object-oriented paradigm fits the hybrid ES structure well in working with frames and rules. Bogarin and Ebecken (1996) describe an object-oriented approach of combining objects and rules for flexible pipe evaluation and design in the petroleum industry. The objects select which sets of rules to apply to a given situation. The ES runs numerical heuristics as well. For a detailed overview of frames and rule integration, see Thuraisingham (1989). CORVID and many other development tools have adopted the integrated approach. For applications using CORVID as the development tool, check out the Web site at exsys.com. An earlier application is described in AIS in Action 11.10.

AIS IN ACTION 11.10

PACE: AN ES PLANNING ADVISOR ON CURRICULUM AND ENROLLMENT

The National University of Singapore is developing an advising system for students studying for the BBA degree. The system uses a combination object-oriented knowledge-based paradigm, which provides efficient and flexible knowledge representation, improved performance, and ease of software development and maintenance. The idea of the ES is not to provide wise and sympathetic counsel but to focus students more clearly on issues to consider and let them simulate different scenarios before seeking advice, cutting down the effort required from the advising staff. The planning advisor on curriculum and enrollment (PACE) simplifies the process of ensuring consistency and schedulability by combining object-oriented and knowledge-based system methodologies. Object hierarchies (trees) represent data and knowledge structures (e.g., courses and curriculum requirements). Localized knowledge is embedded as methods within objects, and global knowledge is stored in a rule base. The inference engine uses both forward and backward chaining on global and relevant local rules to generate advice and guide students in course selection and scheduling.

Production rules are stored as methods within objects. Separate concepts are stored as separate objects and linked dynamically (e.g., relationships among curriculum, courses, and staff). By embedding the rules within objects, performance improves because the search time is less. Curriculum objects have properties (much like a frame) and are structured in a curriculum tree. A student chooses courses from the course tree. Then a long-term schedule is generated. There are also links to the university's databases.

Source: Adapted from H. Gunadhi, K. -H. Lim, and W. -Y. Yeong, "PACE: A Planning Advisor on Curriculum and Enrollment," *Proceedings of the 28th Annual Hawaii International Conference on Systems Sciences*, Hawaii, 1995.

DECISION TABLES

Knowledge of relations may also be represented in **decision tables** and decision trees. In a decision table, knowledge is organized in a spreadsheet format using columns and rows. The table is divided into two parts. First, a list of attributes is developed, and for each attribute all possible values are listed. Then a list of conclusions is developed. Finally, the different configurations of attributes are matched against the conclusion.

Knowledge for the table is collected in knowledge-acquisition sessions. Once constructed, the knowledge in the table can be used as input to other knowledge-representation methods. It is not possible to make inferences with the domain tables by themselves except when rule induction is used. Some ES shells can incorporate an entire decision table into a single rule (e.g., K-Vision from Ginesys Corporation, ginesys.com). Decision tables are easy to understand and program.

DECISION TREES

Decision trees are related to tables and are popular in many places. These trees are similar to the decision trees used in decision theory. They are composed of nodes representing goals and links representing decisions.

The major advantage of decision trees is that they can simplify the knowledge-acquisition process. Knowledge diagramming is often more natural to experts than formal representation methods (e.g., rules or frames). For further discussion, see Gruber and Cohen (1987) and Jackson (1999).

Decision trees can easily be converted to rules. The conversion can be performed automatically by a computer program. In fact, machine-learning methods are capable of extracting decision trees automatically from textual sources and converting them to rule bases.

In the example shown in Figure 11.10, the decision tree renders the knowledge used to help diagnose the reasons behind an automobile not starting. This problem can be described as a number of knowledge rules, for example:

- *RULE 1:* IF the car does not start THEN check if the starter motor turns
- *RULE 2:* IF the starter motor turns THEN check if there is fuel in the tank ELSE check that the headlights work
- *RULE 3:* IF headlights do not work THEN battery is flat ELSE there is a starter motor problem

PREDICATE CALCULUS

Another form that is useful for showing logic relationships and their reasoning is **predicate logic**. Facts and observations in a problem domain are defined as premises, which are used by the logical process to derive new facts and conclusions.

For a computer to perform reasoning using logic, some method must be used to convert statements and the reasoning process into a form suitable for manipulation by a computer. The result is what is known as symbolic logic—a system of rules and procedures that permit the drawing of inferences from premises using logical techniques.

The two basic forms of computational logic are **propositional logic** (or **propositional calculus**) and **predicate logic** (or **predicate calculus**). A proposition is nothing more than a statement that is either true or false. Once we know what it is, it becomes a premise that can be used to derive new propositions or inferences. Rules are used to determine the truth (T) or falsity (F) of the new proposition.

In propositional logic we use symbols, such as letters of the alphabet, to represent propositions, premises, or conclusions. For example, consider the propositions used in this simple deductive process:

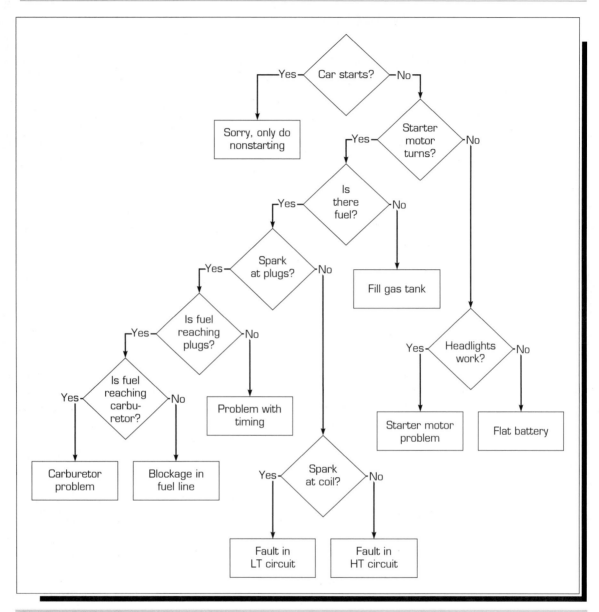

FIGURE 11.10   A DECISION TREE FOR A DIAGNOSIS OF CAR MALFUNCTION

Statement: A—The mail carrier comes Monday through Friday.
Statement: B—Today is Sunday.
Conclusion: C—The mail carrier will not come today.

Simple single propositions of this kind are not very interesting or useful. Real-world problems involve many interrelated propositions. To form more complex premises, two or more propositions can be combined using logical connectives. These connectives or operators are designated as AND, OR, NOT, IMPLIES, and EQUIVALENT. The resulting symbolic expression looks very much like a math formula. It can be manipulated using the rules of propositional logic to infer new conclusions.

Because propositional logic deals primarily with complete statements and whether they are true or false, its ability to represent real-world knowledge is limited. Consequently, AI uses predicate logic instead.

Predicate logic permits you to break a statement down into its component parts, namely, an object, a characteristic of the object, or some assertion about the object. In addition, predicate calculus lets you use variables and functions of variables in a symbolic logic statement. Predicate logic (calculus) is the basis for the AI language called **PROLOG (programming in logic)**. (Note: Predicate refers to the verb part of a sentence. In PROLOG, the action or relationship between objects is stated first.) For example, in PROLOG we represent the fact that the mail carrier will arrive on Monday as *arrive(mailcarrier, monday),* and the rule "If the mail arrives on Monday, the case is acceptable," is represented as [accept :- arrive(mailcarrier, Monday)]. Please note that the symbol ":-" stands for "is derived from." It is the same as in production rules, except that the conclusion is stated first. In fact, predicate logic provides the theoretical foundation for rule-based expert systems. Facts such as this one, along with rules expressed within the language, form the basis for inferencing. For further details, refer to Bratko (2000) and Puls (2002).

SELECTION OF REPRESENTATION METHODS

Different representation methods have their advantages and limitations (see Table 11.10). Production rules are popular in the design of first-generation expert systems. The object-oriented method has become very popular in recent years. Predicate logic provides a theoretical foundation for rule-based inferences.

Knowledge representation should support the tasks of acquiring and retrieving knowledge as well as subsequent reasoning. Several factors must be taken into account in evaluating knowledge representation for the above three tasks:

TABLE 11.10 Advantages and Disadvantages of Different Knowledge Representations

Scheme	Advantages	Disadvantages
Production rules	Simple syntax, easy to understand, simple interpreter, highly modular, flexible (easy to add to or modify).	Hard to follow hierarchies, inefficient for large systems, not all knowledge can be expressed as rules, poor at representing structured descriptive knowledge.
Semantic networks	Easy to follow hierarchy, easy to trace associations, flexible.	Meaning attached to nodes might be ambiguous, exception handling is difficult, difficult to program.
Frames	Expressive power, easy to set up slots for new properties and relations, easy to create specialized procedures, easy to include default information and detect missing values.	Difficult to program, difficult for inference, lack of inexpensive software.
Formal logic	Facts asserted independently of use, assurance that only valid consequences are asserted (precision), completeness.	Separation of representation and processing, inefficient with large data sets, very slow with large knowledge bases.

- Naturalness, uniformity, and understandability of the representation
- Degree to which knowledge is explicit (declarative) or embedded in procedural code. For further information on implicit/explicit knowledge, see Krogh, et al (2000).
- Modularity and flexibility of the knowledge base.
- Efficiency of knowledge retrieval and the heuristic power of the inference procedure. (Heuristic power is the reduction of the search space achieved by a heuristic mechanism.)

Sometimes, no single knowledge-representation method is by itself ideally suited for all tasks. When several sources of knowledge are used simultaneously, the goal of uniformity may have to be sacrificed in favor of exploiting the benefits of multiple knowledge representations, each tailored to a different subtask. The necessity of translating among knowledge representations becomes a problem in these cases. Nevertheless, some recent ES shells use two or more knowledge-representation schemes (e.g., the CORVID system, exsys.com/).

11.9 REASONING IN RULE-BASED SYSTEMS

Once the knowledge representation in the knowledge base is completed, or is at least at a sufficiently high level of accuracy, it is ready to be used. A computer program is needed to access the knowledge for making inferences. This program is an algorithm that controls a reasoning process and is usually called the **inference engine** or the control program. In rule-based systems, it is also called the **rule interpreter**.

The inference engine directs the search through the knowledge base, a process that may involve the application of inference rules in what is called pattern matching. The control program decides which rule to investigate, which alternative to eliminate, and which attribute to match. The most popular control programs for rule-based systems, forward and backward chaining, are described in the next section.

Before we investigate the specific inferencing techniques used in expert systems, it is interesting to examine how people reason, which is what AI attempts to mimic. There are several ways people reason and solve problems. An interesting view of the problem-solving process is one in which they draw on "sources of power." Lenat (1982) identified nine such sources:

1. Formal reasoning methods (e.g., logical deduction)
2. Heuristic reasoning, or IF-THEN rules
3. Focus, or common sense applied to specific goals
4. Divide and conquer, or dividing complex problems into subproblems (sometimes called **chunking**)
5. Parallelism—neural processors (perhaps a million) operating in parallel
6. Representation, or ways of organizing pieces of information
7. Analogy, or the ability to associate and relate concepts
8. Synergy, in which the whole is greater than the sum of its parts
9. Serendipity, or fortuitous accidents.

These sources of power range from the purely deductive reasoning best handled by computer systems to inductive reasoning, which is more difficult to computerize. Lenat (1982) believes that the future of AI lies in finding ways to tap sources that have

TABLE 11.11	Reasoning Methods
Method	**Description**
Deductive reasoning	Move from a general principle to a specific inference. A general principle is composed of two or more premises.
Inductive reasoning	Move from some established facts to draw general conclusions.
Analogical reasoning	Derive an answer to a question by known analogy. It is a verbalization of internalized learning process (Owen, 1990). Use of similar past experiences.
Formal reasoning	Syntactic manipulation of a data structure to deduce new facts following prescribed rules of inferences (such as predicate calculus).
Procedural (numeric) reasoning	Use of mathematical models or simulation (such as model-based reasoning, qualitative reasoning, and **temporal reasoning,** or the ability to reason about the time relationships between events).
Metalevel reasoning	Knowledge about what is known (e.g., about the importance and relevance of certain facts and rules).

only begun to be exploited. These sources of power are translated to specific reasoning or inference methods as summarized in Table 11.11.

Inferencing with rules involves the implementation of modus ponens, which is reflected in the search mechanism. Consider the following example:

Rule 1: IF an international conflict begins,
        THEN the price of gold will go up.

Let us assume that the ES knows that an international conflict has just started. This information is stored as a fact in the database (or assertion base), which means that the premise (the IF part) of the rule is true. With modus ponens, the conclusion is then accepted as true. We say that Rule 1 fires. Firing a rule occurs only when all the rule's hypotheses (conditions in the IF part) are satisfied (evaluated to be true). Then the conclusion drawn is stored in the assertion base. In our case, the conclusion (the price of gold will go up) is added to the assertion base and can be used to satisfy the premise of other rules. The true (or false) values for either portion of the rules can be obtained by querying the user or by checking other rules. Testing a rule premise or conclusion can be as simple as matching a symbolic pattern in the rule to a similar pattern in the assertion base. This activity is called pattern matching.

Every rule in the knowledge base can be checked to see whether its premise or conclusion can be satisfied by previously made assertions. This process can be done in one of two directions, forward or backward, and continues until no more rules can fire or until a goal is achieved.

There are two methods for controlling inference in rule-based ES: **forward chaining** and **backward chaining** (each of which has several variations). First, we provide an intuitive description of the two methods; then we discuss them in detail.

EXAMPLE 1

Suppose you want to fly from Denver to Tokyo and there are no direct fights between the two cities. Therefore, you try to find a chain of connecting flights starting from Denver and ending in Tokyo. There are two basic ways you can search for this chain of flights:

- Start with all the flights that arrive in Tokyo and find the city where each flight originated. Then look up all the flights arriving at these cities and determine where they originated. Continue the process until you find Denver. Because you are working backward from your goal (Tokyo), this search process is called backward chaining (or goal-driven).
- List all the flights leaving Denver and note their destination cities. Then look up all the flights leaving these cities and find where they land; continue this process until you find Tokyo. In this case, you are working forward from Denver toward your goal, and so this search process is called forward chaining (or data-driven).

This example also demonstrates the importance of heuristics in expediting the search process. Going either backward or forward, you can use heuristics to make the search more efficient. For example, in the backward approach you can look only at flights that go westward. Depending on the goals of your trip (e.g., minimize cost, minimize travel time, or maximize stopovers), you can develop additional rules to expedite the search even further.

Example 2

Suppose your car does not start. Is it because you are out of gas? Or is it because the starter is broken? Or is it because of some other reason? Your task is to find out why the car won't start. From what you already know (the consequence—the car won't start), you go backward and try to find the condition that caused it. This is a typical application of ES in the area of diagnosis (i.e., the conclusion is known, and one or more of the causes are sought).

A good example of forward chaining is a situation in which a water system is overheating. Here the goal is to predict the most likely reason. After reviewing the rules and checking additional evidence, you can finally find the answer. In forward chaining, you start with a condition or a symptom that is given as a fact.

As we show later, the search process in both cases involves a set of knowledge rules. After determining which rules are true and which are false, the search ends with a finding. The word chaining signifies the linking of a set of pertinent rules.

The search process is directed by what is sometimes called a **rule interpreter**, which works as follows:

- In forward chaining, if the premise clauses match the situation, then the process attempts to assert the conclusion.
- In backward chaining, if the current goal is to determine the correct conclusion, then the process attempts to determine whether the premise clauses (facts) match the situation.

BACKWARD CHAINING

Backward chaining is a goal-driven approach in which you start from an expectation of what is going to happen (hypothesis) and then seek evidence that supports (or contradicts) your expectation. Often this entails formulating and testing intermediate hypotheses (or subhypotheses).

On a computer the program starts with a goal to be verified as either true or false. Then it looks for a rule that has this goal in its conclusion. It then checks the premise of the rule in an attempt to satisfy the rule. It examines the assertion base first. If the search fails there, the program looks for another rule that has the same conclusion as the first rule. An attempt is then made to satisfy the second rule. The process continues until all the possibilities that apply are checked or until the rule initially checked (with the goal) is satisfied. If the goal is proven false, then the next goal is tried. (In some inferencing, the rest of the goals can be tried in succession even if the goal is proven true.)

EXAMPLE 3

Here is an example involving an investment decision: whether to invest in IBM stock. The following variables are used:

A = Have $10,000
B = Younger than 30
C = Education at college level
D = Annual income of at least $40,000
E = Invest in securities
F = Invest in growth stocks
G = Invest in IBM stock (the potential goal)

Each of these variables can be answered as true (yes) or false (no).

The facts: We assume that an investor has $10,000 (i.e., that A is true) and that she is 25 years old (B is true). She would like advice on investing in IBM stock (yes or no for the goal).

The rules: Our knowledge base includes these five rules:

R1: IF a person has $10,000 to invest and she has a college degree
     THEN she should invest in securities.
R2: IF a person's annual income is at least $40,000 and she has a college degree
     THEN she should invest in growth stocks.
R3: IF a person is younger than 30 and she is investing in securities
     THEN she should invest in growth stocks.
R4: IF a person is younger than 30 and older than 22
     THEN she has a college degree
R5: IF a person wants to invest in a growth stock
     THEN the stock should be IBM.
These rules can be written as:
R1: IF A and C, THEN E.   R4: IF B, THEN C.
R2: IF D and C, THEN F.   R5: IF F, THEN G.
R3: IF B and E, THEN F.

Our goal is to determine whether to invest in IBM stock.

Start.   In backward chaining we start by looking for a rule that includes the goal (G) in its conclusion (THEN) part. Because rule R5 is the only one that qualifies, we start with it. If several rules contain G, then the inference engine will dictate a procedure for handling the situation.

Step 1:   Try to accept or reject G. The ES goes to the assertion base to see whether G is there. At present, all we have in the assertion base is

A is true.   B is true.

Therefore, the ES proceeds to step 2.

Step 2:   R5 says that if it is true that we invest in growth stocks (F), then we should invest in IBM (G). If we can conclude that the premise of R5 is either true or false, then we have solved the problem. However, we do not know whether F is true. What shall we do now? Note that F, which is the premise of R5, is also the conclusion of R2 and R3. Therefore, to find out whether F is true, we must check either of these two rules.

Step 3: We try R2 first (arbitrarily); if both D and C are true, then F is true. Now we have a problem. D is not a conclusion of any rule, nor is it a fact. The computer can either move to another rule or try to find out whether D is true by asking the investor for whom the consultation is given if her annual income is above $40,000.

What the ES does depends on the search procedures used by the inference engine. Usually a user is asked for additional information only if the information is not available or cannot be deduced. We abandon R2 and return to the other rule, R3. This action is called **backtracking** (i.e., knowing that we are at a dead end, we try something else. The computer must be preprogrammed to handle backtracking).

Step 4: Go to R3; test B and E. We know that B is true because it is a given fact. To prove E, we go to R1, where E is the conclusion.

Step 5: Examine R1. It is necessary to determine whether A and C are true.

Step 6: A is true because it is a given fact. To test C, it is necessary to test R4 (where C is the conclusion).

Step 7: R4 tells us that C is true (because B is true). Therefore, C becomes a fact (and is added to the assertion base). Now E is true, which validates F, which validates our goal (i.e., the advice is to invest in IBM). A negative response to any of the preceding statements would result in a "Do not invest in IBM stock" response. Then another investment decision (conclusion) would have to be considered, but this time all the facts derived from the previous tries would be used.

Note that during the search the ES moved from the THEN part to the IF part to the THEN part, and so on (Figure 11.11). This is a typical search pattern in backward chaining. As we show next, forward chaining starts with the IF part, moves to the THEN part, then to another IF part, and so on. Some systems allow a change in

FIGURE 11.11   BACKWARD CHAINING

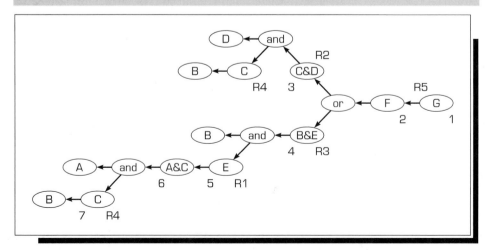

the direction of the search midstream; that is, they can go from THEN to THEN (or from IF to IF) as needed.

FORWARD CHAINING

Forward chaining is a data-driven approach. We start from available information as it becomes available or from a basic idea, and then we try to draw conclusions.

The ES analyzes the problem by looking for the facts that match the IF part of its IF-THEN rules. For example, if a certain machine is not working, the computer checks the electricity flow to the machine. As each rule is tested, the program works its way toward one or more conclusions.

EXAMPLE 4

Let us use the same example we introduced in backward chaining. Here we reproduce the rules:

R1: IF A and C, THEN E.   R4: IF B, THEN C.
R2: IF D and C, THEN F.   R5: IF F, THEN G.
R3: IF B and E, THEN F.

and the facts:
A is true (the investor has $10,000). B is true (the investor is younger than 30).

Start: In forward chaining (Figure 11.12), we start with known facts and derive new facts using rules having known facts on the IF side.

Step 1: Because it is known that A and B are true, the ES starts deriving new facts using rules having A and B on the IF side. Using R4, the ES derives a new fact C and adds it to the assertion base as true.

Step 2: Now R1 fires (because A and C are true) and asserts E as true in the assertion base.

Step 3: Because B and E are both known to be true (they are in the assertion base), R3 fires and establishes F as true in the assertion base.

Step 4: Now R5 fires (because F is on its IF side), which establishes G as true. So the expert system recommends an investment in IBM stock. If there is

FIGURE 11.12   FORWARD CHAINING

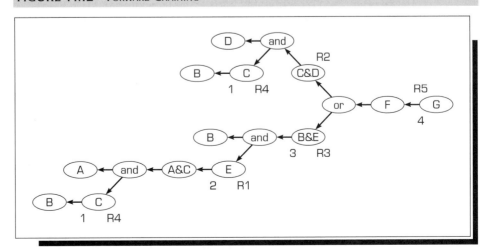

more than one conclusion, more rules may fire, depending on the inferencing procedure.

We have seen that an antecedent–consequence rule system can run forward or backward, but which direction is better? The answer depends on the purpose of the reasoning and the shape of the search space. For example, if the goal is to discover everything that can be deduced from a given set of facts, the system should run forward, as in accounting audit applications, because most facts are initially available in documents and forms. In some cases, the two strategies can be mixed (the process is bidirectional).

The execution of forward or backward chaining is accomplished with the aid of a rule interpreter. Its function is to examine production rules to determine which are capable of being fired and then to fire them. The control strategy of the rule interpreter (e.g., backward chaining) determines how the appropriate rules are found and when to apply them.

Inferencing with rules (as well as with logic) can be very effective, but there are some obvious limitations to these techniques. One reason for this is summarized by the familiar axiom that there is an exception to every rule. For example, consider the following argument:

Proposition 1: Birds can fly.
Proposition 2: An ostrich is a bird.
Conclusion: An ostrich can fly.

The conclusion is perfectly valid but is false for this limited-knowledge universe; ostriches simply do not cooperate with the facts. For this reason, as well as for a more efficient search, we sometimes use other inferencing methods.

THE INFERENCE TREE

An **inference tree** (also called a goal tree or logical tree) provides a schematic view of the inference process. It is similar to a decision tree and an influence diagram (Russell and Norvig, 2002). Note that each rule is composed of a premise and a conclusion. In building an inference tree, the premises and conclusions are shown as nodes. The branches connect the premises and the conclusions. The operators AND and OR are used to reflect the structures of the rules. There is no deep significance to the construction of such trees—they just provide better insight into the structure of the rules. Inference trees map the knowledge in a convenient manner. In fact, the current generation of Windows-based ES shells use a kind of inference tree to display the knowledge base on the screen (e.g., G2, and CORVID).

Figure 11.13 presents an inference tree for Example 3. Using the tree, we can visualize the process of inference and movement along its branches. This is called tree traversal. To traverse an AND node, we must traverse all the nodes below it. To traverse an OR node, it is sufficient to traverse just one of the nodes below. The inference tree is constructed upside-down: The root is at the top (end), and the branches point downward. The tree starts with "leaves" at the bottom. (It can also be constructed from left to right, much like a decision tree.) Inference trees are composed basically of clusters of goals. Each goal can have subgoals (children) and a supergoal (parent).

Single inference trees are always a mixture of AND nodes and OR nodes; they are often called AND/OR trees (note that the NOT operation is allowed). The AND node signifies a situation in which a goal is satisfied only when all its immediate subgoals are satisfied. The OR node signifies a situation in which a goal is satisfied when any of its immediate goals are satisfied. When enough subgoals are satisfied to achieve the pri-

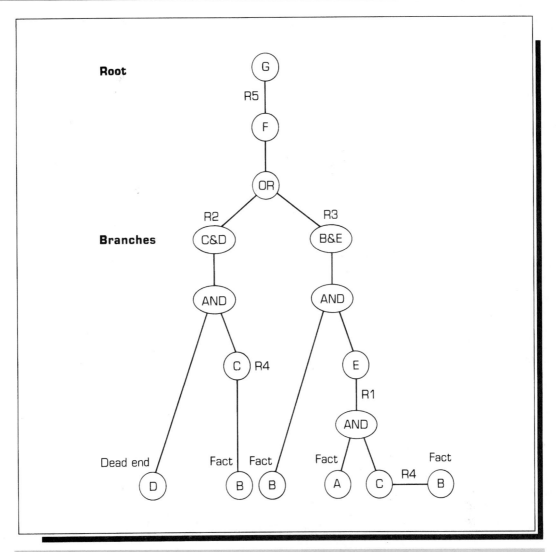

FIGURE 11.13   INFERENCE TREE

mary goal, the tree is said to be satisfied. The inference engine contains procedures for expressing this process as backward or forward chaining. These procedures are organized as a set of instructions involving inference rules. They aim at satisfying the inference tree and collectively contribute to the process of goal (problem) reduction. For further discussion, see Russell and Norvig (2002).

The inference tree has another big advantage: it provides a guide for answering the why and how questions in the explanation process. The how question is asked by users when they want to know how a certain conclusion has been reached. The computer follows the logic in the inference tree, identifies the goal (conclusion) involved in it and the AND/OR branches, and reports the immediate subgoals. The *why* question is asked by users when they want to know why the computer requests certain information as input (in backward chaining). To deal with why questions, the computer identifies the goal involved with the computer-generated query and reports the immediate subgoals.

11.10 EXPLANATION AND METAKNOWLEDGE

EXPLANATION

Human experts are often asked to explain their views, recommendations, or decisions. If expert systems are to mimic humans in performing highly specialized tasks, they too need to justify and explain their actions. An explanation is an attempt by an ES to clarify its reasoning, recommendations, or other actions (e.g., asking a question). The part of an ES that provides explanations is called an **explanation facility** (or **justifier**). The explanation facility has several purposes:

- Make the system more intelligible to the user.
- Uncover the shortcomings of the rules and knowledge base (debugging of the systems by the knowledge engineer).
- Explain situations that were unanticipated by the user.
- Satisfy psychological and social needs by helping the user feel more assured about the actions of the ES.
- Clarify the assumptions underlying the system's operations to both the user and the builder.
- Conduct sensitivity analyses (using the explanation facility as a guide, the user can predict and test the effects of changes on the system).

Explanation in rule-based ES is usually associated with a way of tracing the rules that are fired during the course of a problem-solving session. This is about the closest to a real explanation that today's systems come, given that their knowledge is usually represented almost exclusively as rules that do not include basic principles necessary for a human-type explanation.

Programs such as MYCIN replay the exact rule used when asked for an explanation. DIGITAL ADVISOR is a slight improvement over this. Instead of feeding back the rule verbatim, ADVISOR determines the generic principle on which the rule is based (at that point in the consultation) and displays it. CORVID provides the rules in the chain of reasoning leading to the conclusion that is hypothesized as the current goal.

In developing large ES, a good explanation facility is essential. Large ES always include more facts and rules than one can easily remember. Often, a new rule added during ES development interacts with other rules and data in unanticipated ways and can make the ES display strange explanations.

Explanation is an extremely important function because understanding depends on explanation, thus making implementation of proposed solutions easier. For example, an experiment conducted with auditors by Ye and Johnson (1995) indicated that ES explanation facilities can make a system's advice more acceptable to users. They also found that justification is the most effective type of ES explanation for bringing about a change in users' attitudes toward the system. Also, explanation is essential in ES used for training purposes.

To understand an event or a situation, you have to explain to yourself exactly what is going on, the role of every participant, and their actions. You need to know the goals of the participants, their intentions, and their potential behavior. Thus, constructing explanations can become a very complex task, especially when it is done by machines. For this reason, many of the explanation facilities available in development tools provide only two basic types of explanation: the why and the how.

WHY EXPLANATIONS

A typical *why* question is posed by the user to the computer after the computer asks the user to provide some information. For example, in an investment example, we might have the following dialog:

COMPUTER: What is your annual income?
CLIENT: Why? (Why do you need to know?)

The computer displays Rule 2 as a response. However, ideally we would like to see a reply like this:

COMPUTER: In checking R2, I need to know whether your income is above $40,000. If this is true, I will conclude that because you have a college degree, you should invest in growth stocks.

The ES asks for this input when it is unable to find income information in the conclusion part of any rule. In the example cited, the computer actually backtracked to R3 and successfully arrived at a final conclusion.

HOW EXPLANATIONS

A typical *how* question is posed by users when they would like to know how a certain conclusion or recommendation was reached. Simple systems are limited to the final conclusion. More complex systems can handle intermediate conclusions as well. The system can explain why a certain rule was fired; that is, it shows the chain of rules used to reach the conclusion. In the investment problem, the how explanation might look like this:

COMPUTER: Invest in IBM stocks.
CLIENT: How? (How was the conclusion reached?)
COMPUTER: (Displays the rules R5–R3–R7–R4 in the sequence that they were fired.)
IDEAL COMPUTER: Given that you have $10,000 to invest and you are younger than 30, then according to R4 you have a college degree. If this is the case, then according to R1 you should invest in securities. For a young investor like you, according to R3, you should invest in growth stocks if you are going to invest at all. Finally, according to R5, if you need to invest in growth stocks, then IBM is your best bet.

The *why* and *how* explanations often show the rules as they were programmed and not in a natural language. However, some systems have the ability to present these rules in a natural language.

OTHER EXPLANATIONS

Wick and Slagle (1989) expanded on the two basic questions by proposing a "journalistic" explanation facility. They view the user–system interaction as an event to be reported much like a news story, which ideally includes the six elements who, what, where, when, why, and how. When an explanation facility is designed along these lines, all bases are covered.

Some sophisticated ES do supply other explanations. For example, some systems provide a limited *why not* capability. Let us assume that the system selects IBM as a growth stock. The user may ask, "Why not GE?" and the system may answer, "Because the annual growth rate of GE is only 7 percent, whereas that of IBM is 11 percent, using Rule 78." Then Rule 78 might be displayed. This example illustrates a possible connection between the ES and a regular database. The computer may need to access a database to provide explanations.

There are special problems in explaining the reasoning process when rules are (automatically) induced. Most such systems only display the rules and leave the real explanation up to the user. Kim and Park (1996) developed a system that produces detailed explanations.

Explanation is much more difficult in non-rule-based systems than in rule-based ones because the inference procedures are more complex. For an overview of the topic of explanation, see Cawsey (1995). For recent advances, see *Expert Systems with Applications* and the special issue of *Explanation: The Way Forward*, Vol. 8., No. 4, 1995.

METAKNOWLEDGE

There are different methods for generating explanations. One easy way is to preinsert pieces of English text (scripts) into the system. For example, each question that can be asked by the user can have an answer text associated with it. This is called a **static explanation**. Several problems are associated with static explanations. For example, all questions and answers must be anticipated in advance, and for large systems this is very difficult. Also, the system essentially has no idea about what it is saying. In the long run, the program might be modified without changing the text, thus causing inconsistency.

A better form of explanation is a **dynamic explanation**, which is reconstructed according to the execution pattern of the rules. With this method, the system reconstructs the reasons for its actions as it evaluates rules.

Most current explanation facilities fail to meet some of the objectives and requirements listed earlier. Most ES explanation facilities consist of printing out a trace of the rules being used. Explanation is not treated as a task that requires intelligence in itself. If ES are to provide satisfactory explanations, future systems must include not only knowledge of how to solve problems in their respective domains but also knowledge of how to effectively communicate to users their understanding of this problem-solving process. Obviously, the balance between these two types of knowledge varies according to the primary function of the system. Constructing such knowledge bases involves formalizing the heuristics used in providing good explanations.

With current ES, much of the knowledge vital to providing a good explanation (e.g., knowledge about the system's problem-solving strategy) is not expressed explicitly in the rules. Therefore, the purely rule-based representation may be difficult to grasp, especially when the relationships between the rules are not made explicit in the explanation. Kidd and Cooper (1985) have developed an explanation facility that can show the inference tree and the parts of it that are relevant to specific queries, thus overcoming some of the deficiencies cited earlier.

In keeping with Kidd's concepts of explanation, Ye and Johnson (1995) provide a categorization of the explanation methods. Their typology of ES explanations includes the following:

- *Trace or line of reasoning.* A record of the inferential steps taken by an ES to reach a conclusion.
- *Justification.* An explicit description of the causal argument or rationale behind each inferential step taken by the ES (based on empirical associations involving the encoding of large chunks of knowledge).
- *Strategy.* A high-level goal structure that determines how the ES uses its domain knowledge to accomplish a task (or metaknowledge).

Justification requires a deeper understanding of the domain than the trace method does. By demonstrating that the conclusions developed by the system are based on sound reasoning, it increases the confidence of ES users in the problem-solving ability of the system and hence the acceptability of the conclusions. Since ES can achieve high performance levels only within narrow problem areas, justification enables users to make more informed decisions on whether to follow the advice. Strategy involves knowledge about the problem-solving procedure. Generally, the last two explanation types are more difficult to incorporate in an ES because strategic knowledge tends to be buried implicitly in the knowledge base and an ES does not need an explicit representation of justification knowledge to execute (Ye and Johnson, 1995). Future ES may provide these advanced explanation capabilities.

A system's knowledge about how it reasons is called **metaknowledge**, or knowledge about knowledge. The inference rules presented earlier are a special case of metaknowledge. Metaknowledge allows the system to examine the operation of the declarative and procedural knowledge in the knowledge base.

Explanation can be viewed as another aspect of metaknowledge. Over time, metaknowledge will allow expert systems to do even more. They will be able to create the rationale behind individual rules by reasoning from first principles. They will tailor their explanations to fit the requirements of their audience. And they will be able to change their own internal structure through rule correction, reorganization of the knowledge base, and system reconfiguration.

11.11 INFERENCING WITH UNCERTAINTY

Uncertainty is an important component in expert systems. According to Parsaye and Chignell (1988), uncertainty is treated as a three-step process in artificial intelligence, as shown in Figure 11.14. In Step 1, an expert provides inexact knowledge in terms of rules with likelihood values. These rules can be numeric (e.g., a probability value), graphical, or symbolic ("It is most likely that").

In Step 2, the inexact knowledge of the basic set of events can be directly used to draw inferences in simple cases (Step 3). However, in many cases the various events are interrelated. Therefore, it is necessary to combine the information provided in Step 1 into a global value for the system. Several methods can be used for such integration.

FIGURE 11.14   THREE-STEP PROCESS FOR DEALING WITH UNCERTAINTY IN AI

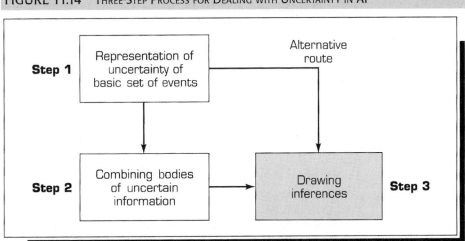

The major methods are Bayesian probabilities, theory of evidence, certainty factors, and fuzzy sets.

In Step 3, the purpose of the knowledge-based system is to draw inferences. These are derived from the inexact knowledge of Steps 1 and 2, and they are usually implemented with the inference engine. Working with the inference engine, experts can adjust the input they give in Step 1 after viewing the results in Steps 2 and 3.

THE IMPORTANCE OF UNCERTAINTY

Although uncertainty is widespread in the real world, its treatment in the practical world of AI is very limited. As a matter of fact, many real-world knowledge-based systems completely avoid the issue of uncertainty. People feel that it is not necessary to represent uncertainty in dealing with uncertain knowledge. Why is this so?

The answer given by practitioners is very simple. Even though they recognize the problem of uncertainty, they feel that none of the methods available are accurate or consistent enough to handle the situation. In fact, knowledge engineers who have experimented with proposed methods for dealing with uncertainty have found either no significant difference from treating the situation as being under assumed certainty or large differences between the results when they used different methods. Does this mean that uncertainty avoidance is the best approach and therefore that this material should be deleted from the book? Certainly not!

Uncertainty is a serious problem. Avoiding it may not be the best strategy. Instead, we need to improve the methods for dealing with uncertainty. Theoreticians must realize that many of the concepts presented in this chapter are foreign to many practitioners. Even structured methods, such as the Bayesian formula, seem extremely strange and complex to many people.

REPRESENTING UNCERTAINTY

The three basic methods of representing uncertainty are numeric, graphical, and symbolic.

NUMERIC

The most common method of representing uncertainty is numeric, using a scale with two extreme numbers. For example, 0 can be used to represent complete uncertainty, while 1 or 100 represents complete certainty. Although such representation seems trivial to some people (maybe because it is similar to the representation of probabilities), it is very difficult for others.

In addition to the difficulties of using numbers, there are problems with cognitive bias. For example, experts figure the numbers based on their own experience and are influenced by their own perceptions. For a discussion of these biases, see Parsaye and Chignell (1988). Finally, people may inconsistently provide different numeric values at different times.

GRAPHICAL

Although many experts are able to describe uncertainty in terms of numbers, such as "It is 85 percent certain that," some find this difficult. The use of horizontal bars may help experts to express their confidence in certain events. Such a bar is shown in Figure 11.15. Experts are asked to place markers somewhere on the scale. Thus, expert A expresses very little confidence in the likelihood of inflation, whereas expert B is more confident that inflation is coming.

Even though graphical presentation is preferred by some experts, graphs are not as accurate as numbers. Another problem is that most experts do not have experience

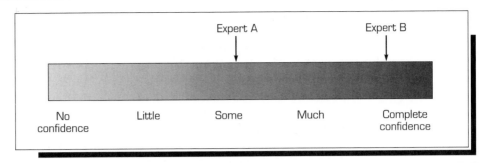

FIGURE 11.15   CONFIDENCE SCALE ABOUT THE OCCURRENCE OF INFLATION

in marking graphical scales (or setting numbers on the scale). Many experts, especially managers, prefer ranking (which is symbolic) over either graphical or numeric methods.

SYMBOLIC

There are several ways to represent uncertainty by using symbols. Many experts use a Likert scale to express their opinion. For example, an expert may be asked to assess the likelihood of inflation on a five-point scale: very unlikely, unlikely, neutral, likely, and very likely. Ranking is a very popular approach among experts with nonquantitative preferences. Ranking can be either ordinal (i.e., listing of items in order of importance) or cardinal (ranking complemented by numeric values). Managers are especially comfortable with ordinal ranking.

When the number of items to be ranked is large, people may have a problem with ranking and may tend to be inconsistent. A method that can be used to alleviate this problem is a pairwise comparison combined with a consistency checker; that is, rank the items two at a time and check for consistencies. One methodology for such ranking, the Analytical Hierarchy Process, was described in Chapter 5. For further discussion of ranking, see Parsaye and Chignell (1988). The method of fuzzy logic, presented in Chapter 12, includes a special symbolic representation combined with numbers.

Symbolic representation methods are often combined with numbers or converted to numeric values. For example, it is customary to give a weight of 1 to 5 to the five options on a Likert-like scale.

PROBABILITIES AND RELATED APPROACHES

THE PROBABILITY RATIO

The degree of confidence in a premise or a conclusion can be expressed as a probability. *Probability* is the chance that a particular event will occur (or not occur). It is a ratio computed as follows. The probability of X occurring, stated as $P(X)$, is the ratio of the number of times X occurs, $N(X)$ to the total number of events that take place $\Sigma N(X)$.

Multiple probability values occur in many systems. For example, a rule can have an antecedent with three parts, each with a probability value. The overall probability of the rule can be computed as the product of the individual probabilities if the parts of the antecedent are independent of one another. In a three-part antecedent, the probabilities may be .9, .7, and .65, and the overall probability is

$$P = (.9)(.7)(.65) = .4095$$

The combined probability is about 41 percent. But this is true only if the individual parts of the antecedent do not affect or interrelate with one another.

Sometimes one rule references another. Here, the individual rule probabilities can propagate from one to another, and so we must evaluate the total probability of a sequence of rules or a path through the search tree to determine whether a specific rule fires. Or we may be able to use the combined probabilities to predict the best path through the search tree.

In knowledge-based systems, there are several methods for combining probabilities. For example, they can be multiplied (i.e., joint probabilities) or averaged (using a simple or a weighted average); in other instances, only the highest or lowest values are considered. In all such cases, rules and events are considered independently of each other. If there are dependencies in the system, the Bayesian extension theorem can be used.

THE BAYESIAN EXTENSION

Bayes' theorem is a mechanism for combining new and existent evidence, usually given as subjective probabilities. It is used to revise existing prior probabilities based on new information.

The Bayesian approach is based on subjective probabilities; a **subjective probability** is provided for each proposition. If E is the evidence (sum of all information available to the system), then each proposition P has associated with it a value representing the probability that P holds in light of all the evidence E, derived by using Bayesian inference. Bayes' theorem provides a way of computing the probability of a particular event given some set of observations we have already made. The main point here is not how this value is derived but that what we know or infer about a proposition is represented by a single value for its likelihood.

This approach has two major deficiencies. The first is that the single value does not tell us much about its precision, which may be very low when the value is derived from uncertain evidence. To say that the probability of a proposition being true in a given situation is .5 (in a range of 0–1) usually refers to an *average* figure that is true within a given range. For example, .5 plus or minus .001 is completely different from .5 plus or minus .3, yet both can be reported as .5. The second deficiency is that the single value combines the evidence for and against a proposition without indicating the individual value of each.

The subjective probability expresses the degree of belief, or how strongly a value or a situation is believed to be true. The Bayesian approach, with or without new evidence, can be diagrammed as a network.

DEMPSTER–SHAFER THEORY OF EVIDENCE

The Dempster–Shafer theory of evidence is a well-known procedure for reasoning with uncertainty in artificial intelligence. For details see Shafer (1976) and Yager et al. (1994). It can be considered an extension of the Bayesian approach.

The Dempster–Shafer approach distinguishes between uncertainty and ignorance by creating **belief functions**. Belief functions allow us to use our knowledge to bound the assignment of probabilities when the boundaries are unavailable.

The Dempster–Shafer approach is especially appropriate for combining expert opinions because experts differ in their opinions with a certain degree of ignorance and, in many situations, at least some epistemic information (i.e., information constructed from vague perceptions). The Dempster–Shafer theory can be used to handle epistemic information as well as ignorance or lack of information. Unfortunately, it assumes that the sources of information to be combined are statistically independent of each other. In reality, there are many situations in which the knowledge of experts overlaps; that is, there are dependencies among sources of information. For such cases, extensions such as those proposed by Ling and Rudd (1989) are necessary.

THEORY OF CERTAINTY FACTORS

CERTAINTY FACTORS AND BELIEFS

Standard statistical methods are based on the assumption that an uncertainty is the probability that an event (or fact) is true or false. In **certainty theory**, as well as in fuzzy logic, uncertainty is represented as a degree of belief. There are two steps in using every nonprobabilistic method of uncertainty. First, it is necessary to be able to express the degree of belief. Second, it is necessary to manipulate (e.g., combine) degrees of belief when using knowledge-based systems.

Certainty theory relies on the use of certainty factors. **Certainty factors** (CFs) express belief in an event (or fact or hypothesis) based on evidence (or on the expert's assessment). There are several methods of using certainty factors to handle uncertainty in knowledge-based systems. One way is to use 1.0 or 100 for absolute truth (complete confidence) and 0 for certain falsehood. Certainty factors are not probabilities. For example, when we say there is a 90 percent chance of rain, then there is either rain (90 percent) or no rain (10 percent). In a nonprobabilistic approach, we can say that a certainty factor of 90 for rain means that it is very likely to rain. It does not necessarily mean that we express any opinion about our argument of no rain (which is not necessarily 10). Thus, certainty factors do not have to sum up to 100.

Certainty theory introduces the concepts of **belief** and **disbelief**. These concepts are independent of each other and so cannot be combined in the same way as probabilities, but they can be combined according to the following formula:

$$CF(P,E) = MB(P,E) - MD(P,E)$$

Where:

CF = certainty factor
MB = measure of belief
MD = measure of disbelief
P = probability
E = evidence or event

Another assumption of certainty theory is that the knowledge content of rules is much more important than the algebra of confidences that holds the system together. Confidence measures correspond to the information evaluations that human experts attach to their conclusions; for example, "It is probably true" or "It is highly unlikely."

COMBINING CERTAINTY FACTORS

Certainty factors can be used to combine estimates by different experts in several ways. Before using any ES shell, make sure that you understand how certainty factors are combined; for an overview see Kopcso et al. (1988). The most acceptable way of combining them in rule-based systems is the method used in EMYCIN. In this approach, we distinguish between two cases, described next.

Combining Several Certainty Factors in One Rule. Consider this rule with an AND operator:

> IF inflation is high, CF = 50 percent (A) AND
> unemployment rate is above 7 percent, CF = 70 percent (B)
> AND
> bond prices decline, CF = 100 percent (C)
> THEN stock prices decline.

For this type of rule, all IFs must be true for the conclusion to be true, but in some cases there is uncertainty as to what is happening. Then the CF of the conclusion is the minimum CF on the IF side:

$$CF(A, B, C) = \text{minimum}[CF(A), CF(B), CF(C)]$$

Thus, in our case, the CF for stock prices to decline is 50 percent. In other words, the chain is as strong as its weakest link.

Now look at this rule with an OR operator:

> IF inflation is low, CF = 70 percent; OR
> bond prices are high, CF = 85 percent;
> THEN stock prices will be high.

In this case it is sufficient that only one of the IFs is true for the conclusion to be true. Thus, if both IFs are believed to be true (at their certainty factor), then the conclusion will have a CF with the maximum of the two:

$$CF \ (A \text{ or } B) = \text{maximum} \ [CF \ (A), CF \ (B)]$$

In our case, CF = 85 percent for stock prices to be high. Note that both cases hold for any number of IFs.

Combining Two or More Rules.   Why might rules be combined? There may be several ways to reach the same goal, each with different CFs for a given set of facts. When we have a knowledge-based system with several interrelated rules, each of which makes the same conclusion but with a different certainty factor, then each rule can be viewed as a piece of evidence that supports the joint conclusion. To calculate the certainty factor (or the confidence) of the conclusion, it is necessary to combine the evidence, which is done as follows:

Let us assume that there are two rules:

R1:   IF the inflation rate is less than 5 percent
       THEN stock market prices go up (CF = 0.7)

R2:   IF the unemployment level is less than 7 percent
       THEN stock market prices go up (CF = 0.6).

Now let us assume a prediction that during the next year the inflation rate will be 4 percent and the unemployment level will be 6.5 percent (i.e., we assume that the premises of the two rules are true). The combined effect is computed as

$$
\begin{aligned}
CF(R1,R2) &= CF(R1) + [CF(R2)] \times [1 - CF(R1)] \\
&= CF(R1) + CF(R2) - [CF(R1)] \times [CF(R2)]
\end{aligned}
$$

In probabilistic terms, when we combine two dependent probabilities (joint probabilities), we get

$$CF(R1,R2) = [CF(R1)] \times [CF(R2)]$$

Here we have deleted this value from the sum of the two certainty factors, assuming an independent relationship between the rules. For example,

$$\text{Given } CF(R1) = 0.7 \text{ AND } CF(R2) = 0.6,$$

$$CF(R1,R2) = 0.7 + 0.6 - (0.7)(0.6) = 0.88$$

That is, the ES tells us that there is an 88 percent chance that stock prices will increase.

Note: If we just added the CFs of R1 and R2, their combined certainty would be larger than 1. We modify the amount of certainty added by the second certainty factor by multiplying it by (1 minus the first certainty factor). Thus, the greater the first CF, the less the certainty added by the second. But additional factors always add some certainty.

For a third rule to be added, the following formula can be used:

$$CF(R1,R2,R3) = CF(R1,R2) + [CF(R3)] [1 - CF(R1,R2)]$$
$$= CF(R1,R2) + CF(R3) - [CF(R1,R2)][CF(R3)]$$

Assume that a third rule is added:

R3:   IF bond price increases,
       THEN stock prices go up (CF = 0.85).

Now, assuming all the rules are true in their IF part, the chance that stock prices will go up is

$$CF(R1,R2,R3) = 0.88 + 0.85 - (0.88)(0.85) = 0.982$$

That is, there is a 98.2 percent chance that stock prices will go up. Note that CF(R1,R2) was computed earlier as 0.88. For a situation with more rules, we can apply the same formula incrementally. See Russell and Norvig (2002) for more information on uncertainty and probabilistic ES.

11.12 EXPERT SYSTEMS DEVELOPMENT

An expert system is basically computer software—an information system; so its development follows a software development process. The goal of a development process is to maximize the probability of developing viable, sustainable software within cost limitations and on schedule, while managing change (because introducing a new, computerized approach or even implementing software to perform an existing method of working involves change). The availability of expert system shells and other development tools has enabled rapid prototyping in system development (see Chapter 6). The idea of rapid prototyping, which involves performing the analysis, design, and implementation phases concurrently and repeatedly in short cycles, ultimately leading to deployment of the system, is feasible. Prototyping is also known as iterative design or evolutionary development. It is the most commonly used DSS development methodology. One of its advantages is that decision-maker(s) and user(s) learn more about the problem they are trying to solve while performing the prototyping process, as occurred in the Opening Vignette and in the case applications.

Using the prototyping approach to developing ES includes the following six major phases (as illustrated in Figure 11.16).

- *Phase I:* project initialization
- *Phase II:* system analysis and design
- *Phase III:* rapid prototyping and a demonstration prototype
- *Phase IV:* system development
- *Phase V:* implementation
- *Phase VI:* postimplementation.

PHASE I: PROJECT INITIATION

Project initialization is the first step in developing expert systems. Its main goal is to identify problems and prepare for further actions. Major tasks that must be done in this phase include:

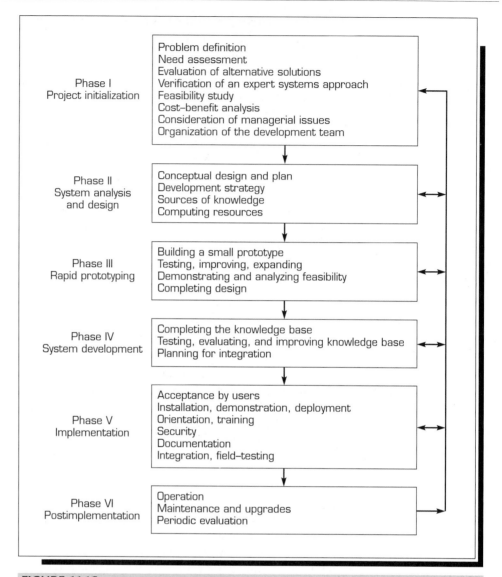

FIGURE 11.16 SCHEMATIC VIEW OF THE ES DEVELOPMENT LIFE CYCLE

- *Problem definition.* Identify problems that are suitable for systems development.
- *Need assessment.* Determine the functional requirements of the system.
- *Evaluation of alternative solutions.* Examine the availability of experts, education and training, packaged knowledge, conventional software.
- *Verification of an expert system approach.* Futher verify the requirements, justify the needs, and assess the appropriateness of developing such a system.
- *Feasilibity study.* Evaluate whether the project is technologically feasible, managerially feasible, and change can be initiated and sustained.
- *Cost-benefit analysis.* This last part of the feasibility study involves determining economic feasibility: formally identifying and estimating the potential costs and benefits of the system. Many criteria including internal rate of return (IRR) or net present value (NPV) can be used for evaluating ES projects. For details, see Chapter 6 and Web material.

- *Managerial consideration.* Examine managerial issues, including project initiator, financing, resources, legal and other constraints, selling the project, identifying a champion, potential of gaining access to users and user support.
- *Organizing the development team.* The team must be assembled and commitment established before starting formal development because of the nature of the prototyping process.
- *Ending milestone.* Approval of the project in principle.

PHASE II: SYSTEM ANALYSIS AND DESIGN

Once the concept of the project has been approved, a detailed system analysis must be conducted to estimate system functionality. The major tasks in this phase are explained below.

CONCEPTUAL DESIGN

A conceptual design of an ES is similar to an architectural sketch of a house. It provides a general idea of what the system will look like and how it will solve the problem. The design shows the general capabilities of the system, the interfaces with other computer-based information systems, the areas of risk, the required resources, the anticipated cash flow, the final composition of the team, including identification of the expert(s) and an estimate of their commitment, and any other information that will be necessary for detailed design later. Once the conceptual design is completed, it is necessary to determine the development strategy.

DEVELOPMENT STRATEGY AND METHODLOGY

There are three **AI development strategies**: develop in-house, outsource, and a blended approach in which external consultants (possibly even from software vendors) join in-house teams. The needs of the particular project and expected development costs and benefits or the organization's policies dictate which approach should be chosen.

- *In-house development.* This strategy is attractive for organizations that already have the needed skills and resources. It is also appropriate if the expert system will contain propriatory or sensitive knowledge. In-house development can be done by the end-users (called *end-user computing*) or a professional team with experts in different areas.
- *Outsourcing.* An organization may hire an outside firm to do the development. There are many different ways, including *hiring a consulting firm, partner with a university, join an industry consortium,* and *buying into an AI firm.*
- *Blended approach.* The development may be done by a team consisting of internal and external members. This allows expertise outside the organization to be incorporated in systems development.

SOURCE OF KNOWLEDGE

Expert systems use both human experts and documented sources for knowledge. The greater the need for human expertise, the longer and more complicated the acquisition process becomes. Several issues may surface in selecting experts.

- Who selects the experts?
- Who is an expert (possessing what characteristics)?
- How can several experts be managed if need be?
- How can the expert be motivated to cooperate?

Experts are relatively easy to identify, especially when recommended by others. They solve problems quickly, find high-quality appropriate solutions, and focus on what is important. The issue of managing several experts can be difficult, particularly if they disagree. Generally it is wise to use a single expert (especially in dealing with economics-based systems) if his or her point of view has been helpful in problem-solving in the past. Knowledge from other experts can be incorporated into the system later.

Expert cooperation is another issue. Experts may ask, "What's in it for me?" "Why should I contribute my wisdom and risk my job?" and so on. Before building an ES that requires the cooperation of experts, management should be clear on the following points:

- Should experts be compensated for their contributions (royalties, special rewards, payment)?
- Are experts truthful in describing how they solve problems?
- How can experts be assured that they will not lose their jobs or that their jobs will not be deemphasized once the ES is fully operational?
- What about the other people in the organization whose jobs may change or be eliminated because of the ES?

SELECTION OF DEVELOPMENT ENVIRONMENT

After obtaining expert cooperation, the development environment must be chosen. Three alternatives are available: ES shells, development languages, and hybrid environment.

- ***ES shells.*** **Expert system shells** are software that has most of the necessary mechanisms, including a built-in inference engine and diversified user-interface functions, but is provided by the vendor with an empty knowledge base. Once the knowledge is entered into the knowledge base, the system is operational. A good example is EXSYS's CORVID. Once you enter the facts and rules, the system can operate. Figure 11.17 shows the basic shell concept.
- ***Programming languages.*** Expert systems can be developed in higher-level computer languages, particularly the so-called **fifth-generation languages (5GLs),** such

---

FIGURE 11.17   SHELL CONCEPT FOR BUILDING EXPERT SYSTEMS

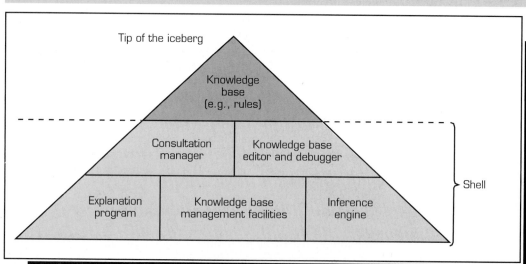

Source: B. G. Buchanan, in Texas Instruments' first satellite program.

as **LISP** and **PROLOG**. PROLOG, for instance, has built-in logic inference capabilities, which makes the design of the inference engine much easier.

- *Hybrid environment.* Expert systems may be developed in a hybrid environment that combines various supporting tools. The hybrid system is also called a **toolkit**, from which the knowledge can select appropriate tools for appropriate tasks.

Shells are probably the most common tool. They can be categorized as *general* or *domain-specific*. In selecting a shell, make sure that it can handle the specific nature of the application properly, including explanation and interfacing with databases and other systems.

Shells have limitations and disadvantages. Because they are inflexible, it can be difficult to fit them to nonstandard problems and tasks. As a result, a builder may use several shells, as well as environments and other tools, in a single application. This may cause problems as each software package is upgraded and in training and maintenance. Shells are end-user tools (similar to DSS generators), and their use is subject to all the problems of end-user computing (poor documentation, security, development of inappropriate methods, use of stale data or knowledge, improper maintenance, etc.).

Despite their limitations, shells are extremely useful and are used extensively by many organizations. In some cases, they are employed primarily in training or as the initial tool in the prototyping cycle (which makes a shell that can produce code quite useful).

Domain-specific tools are designed to be used only in the development of an ES for a specific application area. For example, there are shells for diagnostic systems, configuration, financial applications, help desks (Knowledge Library at *Ask.Me OnLine* for computer software support, amol.com, and *PlanWrite* for developing a business plan, brs-inc.com), and scheduling. *Firepond* offers *SalesPerformer* and *e-ServicePerformer* (firepond.com).

Domain-specific tools may include some rule-based tools, an inductive mechanism, or a knowledge-verification component. Domain-specific tools enhance the use of more standard tools by providing special development support and a user interface. These features permit faster application development. Some include embedded knowledge (e.g., Knowledge Library at Ask.Me OnLine, amol.com). There are only a few commercial domain-specific shells and tools.

PHASE III: RAPID PROTOTYPING AND A DEMONSTRATION PROTOTYPE

The prototyping process is actually less a phase and more a cycle of phases. Because of the way that knowledge is acquired and incorporated into an ES, we describe it as a phase. Prototyping has been crucial to the development and success of many systems. A prototype in ES starts as a small-scale system. It includes representation of the knowledge captured in a manner that enables quick inferencing and creation of the major components of an ES on a rudimentary basis. For example, in a rule-based system the first prototype, the **demonstration prototype**, may include only 10–50 rules and be built with a shell. A small number of rules is sufficient to produce limited consultations and test the proof of concept of the ES.

A prototype helps the builder decide on the structure of the knowledge base before spending time on acquiring and implementing more rules. Developing a prototype has other advantages. Rapid prototyping is essential in developing large systems because the cost of a poorly structured and/or discarded ES can be quite high.

The process of rapid prototyping starts with the design of a small system. The designer determines what aspect (or segment) to prototype, how many rules to use in the first iteration, and so on. The knowledge is acquired for the first iteration and represented in the ES. Next, a test is conducted. The test can be done using historical or hypothetical cases, and the expert is asked to judge the results. The knowledge-representation methods and the software and hardware effectiveness are also examined. A potential user should also test the system. The results are then analyzed by the knowledge engineer, and if improvement is needed, the system is redesigned. Usually the system goes through several iterations with refinements, and the process continues until it is ready for a formal demonstration. Once the system has been demonstrated, it is tested again and improved. This process continues until the final (complete) prototype is ready.

The prototyping phase can be short and simple, or it can take several months and be fairly complex. Some early ES, such as the famous Campbell Soup Company's Soup Cooker diagnostic ES, took a little more than a year to develop. The lessons learned during rapid prototyping are automatically incorporated into the final design as the process iterates. After the demonstration prototype is shown, another go/no-go decision is made.

PHASE IV: SYSTEM DEVELOPMENT

Once the initial prototype is ready and management is satisfied, system development begins. Plans must be made for how to continue. At this stage, the development strategy may be changed (e.g., a consultant may be hired). The detailed design is also likely to be changed, and so are other elements of the plan. If the prototype built in a shell is useful, redesigning in a programming language such as C++ or PROLOG for execution speed is also acceptable.

Depending on the nature of the system—its size, the amount and type of required interfaces with other systems, the dynamics of the knowledge, the development strategy—one or both of the following approaches is used for system development:

- Continue with prototyping (common)
- Use the traditional SDLC (rare).

System development can be a lengthy and complex process. In this phase, the knowledge base is developed, and continuous testing, reviews, and improvements are performed. Other activities include the creation of interfaces (e.g., with databases, documents, multimedia objects, hypermedia, and the Web), creating and testing the user's interface, and so on. In the Opening Vignette, a user interface was created so that facts could be entered at once rather than screen by screen, and another interface was developed for database interaction. In this phase, prototyping continues, but needs are handled as they arise. The two major tasks are to develop the knowledge base and to evaluate and improve the system.

A detailed description of the tasks in this phase is available on the Web site of the book.

PHASE V: IMPLEMENTATION

Finishing system development is not the end of system development. The process of implementing an ES can be long and complex. Major tasks in this phase include the following:

- *Acceptance by the user.* A proper strategy must be adopted to ensure that the user accepts the system in their daily operations. Demonstration of the system and user orientation and training are very important to reduce possible resistance.
- *Installation approaches and timing.* When the system is ready for on-line operations, it must be integrated into the current business process. A parallel process that combines existing procedures and the new procedure with the system may help. It is also important to choose the right timing for starting the deployment of the system.
- *Documentation and security.* The system must be fully documented to ensure maintainability. Since the system contains sensitive knowledge belonging to the organization, it is very important to have a good security mechanism.
- *Integration and field testing.* If the expert system stands alone, it can be field-tested. Otherwise, it must be integrated with or embedded in another information system before field-testing can commence. Field testing is extremely important because conditions in the field may differ from those in cases provided by experts.

PHASE VI: POSTIMPLEMENTATION

Several activities are performed once the system is deployed to users. The most important of these activities are system operation, maintenance, upgrading and expansion, and evaluation.

OPERATION

According to Prerau (1990), if the expert system is to be delivered as a service, a system operations group (or several groups if there are several sites) should be formed and trained. If the system is to be a product run by users, an operator-training group may need to be formed, and consideration should be given to providing help for user-operators with problems. If the system is embedded into another system, the operators of the other system should be trained in any new operating procedures required.

MAINTENANCE

Because an expert system evolves over time, it is never really finished. Thus, it is important to plan maintenance. It must be revised on a regular basis with regard to the applicability of the rules, the integrity and quality of the data feeds, the use of the interlinked databases, and so on (Beerel, 1993). Because experts are constantly training themselves on new situations or reorganizing their knowledge in accounting for unencountered situations, an ES must be adjusted for these cases. In addition, software and hardware bugs must be fixed as found, and the system must be upgraded to run on new software releases and hardware platforms. Just as in the traditional system-development life cycle, there is a maintenance cycle, and a long-term maintenance team must be formed and trained to perform these tasks.

   If the expert system is embedded in another system, some thought should be given to whether one maintenance group will serve the overall system or whether the expert system will be maintained separately. For separate maintenance, procedures for coordinating the two maintenance groups must be developed. For further discussions of maintenance and upgrading, see McCaffrey (1992) and Karimi and Briggs (1996).

EXPANSION (UPGRADING)

Expert systems evolve continuously and therefore expand continuously. All new knowledge must be added, and new features and capabilities must be included as they become available. Upgrading tasks generally fall under the jurisdiction of the maintenance team. However, some expansion can also be performed by the original developer(s) or even by a vendor.

EVALUATION

Expert systems need to be evaluated periodically (e.g., every 6 or 12 months, depending on the volatility of their environment). When evaluating an ES, questions like the following should be answered:

- What is the actual cost of maintaining the system as compared to the actual benefits?
- Is the maintenance provided sufficient to keep the knowledge up to date so that system accuracy remains high?
- Is the system accessible to all users?
- Is acceptance of the system by users increasing?

If the users have been encouraged to comment on the ES and the feedback process is easy, it is much easier to maintain a system under continuous feedback. This also reduces the effort of the periodic evaluation.

11.13 KNOWLEDGE ACQUISITION AND THE INTERNET

The rapid growth of Internet use opens an opportunity for knowledge acquisition over the Internet. The traditional reasons for the poor productivity of manual knowledge-acquisition methods were addressed earlier in this chapter. The availability of the Internet can alleviate many of these problems. In general, the Internet provides a very convenient channel to access knowledge which would otherwise be costly to obtain if not impossible. This can be viewed from two perspectives: the Internet as a communication medium, and the World Wide Web (the Web) as an open source of knowledge.

INTERNET AS A COMMUNICATION MEDIUM

Knowledge acquisition relies heavily on communication between experts and the knowledge engineer. Traditionally, this communication process occurs in a place where they get together. That is to say, they are usually in the same place at the same time. This restriction is now removed by the Internet-based knowledge-acquisition tool. The knowledge engineer can communicate with the expert even though they are far away from each other, as long as they have access to the Internet.

The Internet or an intranet can be used to facilitate knowledge acquisition. For example, electronic interviewing can be conducted if the knowledge engineer and the experts are in different locations. Experts can validate and maintain knowledge bases from a distance. Documented knowledge can be reached via the Internet. The problem is to identify the relevant knowledge, a task that can be facilitated by intelligent agents.

Tochtermann and Fathi (1994) observe that interviewing methods attempt to map the unstructured, nonlinear knowledge of an expert into a linear structure (rules) by which knowledge losses occur. The linear structure is mapped back onto a nonlinear structure when implemented, leading to more inconsistencies. Support of hypermedia on the Web can be used to represent the expertise in a more natural way. Natural links can be created in the knowledge (Tochtermann and Zink, 1995; Tung et al., 1999). HypEs (Tung et al., 1999) is a proposed architecture for the development of media-rich expert systems. It is designed to employ multiple media (text, sound, image, graphics, animation, video) for knowledge acquisition, storage, and user-interface activities.

Ralha (1996) addresses issues pertaining to the problem of automatically structuring informal knowledge available on the Internet through a distributed hypermedia system: the Web. Hypermedia technology via the Web provides an ideal approach to the development of knowledge-based systems by enlarging the human–machine communication channel. This new approach to integrating hypermedia technology with knowledge acquisition deals with knowledge before formalizing it. A twofold, qualitative spatial reasoning approach is adopted: First, dynamic linking takes place; second, the topology of the hyperspace, with qualitative spatial relations based on a primitive concept of connections between spatial regions (called a hypermap), is developed.

INTERNET AS AN OPEN KNOWLEDGE SOURCE

With ever more Web pages built on it, the Internet has also become a valuable source of knowledge. The value of this knowledge source is further empowered by many portals and powerful search engines.

Many Web search engines incorporate intelligent agents to identify and deliver the information an individual wants. Smeaton and Crimmins (1996) developed a data-fusion agent to conduct multiple Web searches and organize them for the user. Yahoo provides recommended Web sites from a search using automated collaborative filtering (ACF) technology. ACF is a technique that provides recommendations based on statistical matches of people's evaluations of a set of objects in some given domain (movies, books, Web pages, etc.). The agent contacts other people's agents to determine the likelihood that a given object will match your needs. Descriptions of these and other Web-related intelligent agents are provided in Chapter 13. AnswerChase from MODiCO Inc. (answerchase.com) provides an Internet search robot that supplies search results based on query strings entered in the form of paragraphs. Another example of this type of robot in action can be seen on the Ask Jeeves Web site (ask.com).

The tools described above provide intelligent search capabilities through documents or the Web. One key to using the Web is to provide a method for eliciting knowledge from experts via an anyplace/anytime collaborative-computing environment. It is valuable when experts are unavailable or the knowledge engineer cannot find a qualified expert in a domain. WebGrid-II is one of the first Web-based knowledge-elicitation approaches. Shaw and Gaines (1996) describe the features of WebGrid-II, an Internet implementation grounded in personal-construct theory. WebGrid-II allows a group of people to collaborate through the Internet to develop knowledge in a different place/different time environment while adhering to the constructs from the repertory grid techniques to elicit personal constructs about a set of elements relevant to the domain of interest. It is available at Webgrid.co.uk.

Finally, because the amount of information provided over the Web is growing exponentially, scientists are developing methods for structuring information in distributed hypermedia systems. Knowledge acquisition from the Web becomes an appealing approach to developing knowledge-based systems. The use of Web mining will be very useful in the future (Berry, 2003; Chakrabarti, 2002; Sullivan, 2001).

❖ CHAPTER HIGHLIGHTS

- Knowledge engineering involves acquisition, representation, reasoning (inference), and explanation of knowledge.
- Knowledge is available from many sources, some of which are documented, and others undocumented (experts).
- Knowledge can be shallow, describing a narrow input-output relationship, or deep, describing complex interactions and a system's operation.
- Knowledge acquisition, especially from human experts, is difficult because of several communication and information-processing problems.
- The methods of knowledge acquisition can be divided into manual, semiautomated, and automated.
- The primary manual approach is interviewing. Interviewing methods range from completely unstructured to highly structured.
- The reasoning process of experts can be tracked by several methods. Protocol analysis is the primary method used in AI.
- Repertory grid analysis (RGA) is the most common technique for semiautomated interviews used in AI. Several software packages that use RGA improve the knowledge-acquisition process.
- Rule induction examines historical cases and generates the rules used to arrive at certain recommendations.
- There are benefits as well as limitations and problems in using several experts to build a knowledge base.
- The major methods of dealing with multiple experts are consensus methods, analytic approaches, selection of an appropriate line of reasoning, automation of the process, and a blackboard system.
- Validation and verification of the knowledge base are critical success factors in ES implementation.
- Case-based reasoning, neural computing, intelligent agents, and other machine-learning tools can enhance the task of knowledge acquisition.
- To build a knowledge base, a variety of knowledge-representation schemes are used, including production rules, logic, semantic networks, and frames.
- Production rules are the most popular way of representing knowledge. They take the form of an IF-THEN statement such as, "IF you drink too much, THEN you should not drive."
- There are two types of rules: declarative (describing facts) and procedural (inference).
- Propositional logic is a system of using symbols to represent and manipulate premises, prove or disprove propositions, and draw conclusions.
- Predicate calculus is a type of logic used to represent knowledge in the form of statements that assert information about objects or events and apply them in reasoning.

- Semantic networks are graphical depictions of knowledge that show relationships (arcs) between objects (nodes); common relationships are is-a, has-a, owns, and made from.
- A major property of networks is the inheritance of properties through the hierarchy.
- Decision trees and tables are often used in conjunction with other representation methods. They help organize the knowledge acquired before it is coded.
- A frame is a holistic data structure based on object-oriented programming technology.
- Frames are composed of slots that may contain different types of knowledge representation (e.g., rules, scripts, formulas).
- Frames can show complex relationships, graphical information, and inheritance in a concise manner. Their modular structure helps in inference and maintenance.
- Integrating several knowledge-representation methods is gaining popularity because of decreasing software costs and increasing capabilities.
- The kernel of an inference engine is the mechanism for searching and reasoning. The major ones are rule chaining (backward and forward) and case-based reasoning.
- In backward chaining, the search starts from a specific goal. You seek evidence that supports (or contradicts) the acceptance of your goal. Then, depending on your application of the rules, whether your goal is contradicted or accepted, you can try another goal.
- In forward chaining, the search starts from the facts (evidence), and you try to arrive at one or more conclusions.
- The chaining process can be described graphically by an inference tree.
- Inferencing with frames often involves the use of rules.
- Case-based reasoning is based on experience with similar situations.
- In case-based reasoning, the attributes of an existing case are compared with critical attributes derived from cases stored in the case library.
- An explanation can be static, in which case a canned response is available for a specific configuration; it can also be dynamic, in which case the explanation is reconstructed according to the execution pattern of the rules.
- Processing uncertainty is important because knowledge may be inexact, and experts may be uncertain at any given time.
- Uncertainty processing methods include probabilities, Bayesian statistics, and the certainty factor approach.
- Three basic methods can be used to represent uncertainty: numeric (probability-like), graphical, and qualitative.

- Disbelief expresses a feeling about what is not going to occur.
- Certainty theory combines evidence available in one rule by seeking the lowest certainty factor when several certainty factors are added, and the highest certainty factor when any one of several factors is used to establish evidence.
- Building an expert system is a complex process with six major phases: system initialization, system analysis and design, rapid prototyping, system development, implementation, and postimplementation.
- A feasibility study and a cost-benefit analysis help to justify the development of an ES.
- A feasibility study is essential for the success of any medium- to large-sized ES.
- The potential system users must be involved in the ES development.
- The conceptual design of an ES contains a general idea of what the system will look like and how it will solve the problem.

- Expert systems can be developed in-house, by outsourcing, or through a blend of the two. There are several variations of each approach.
- Shells are integrated packages in which the major components of an expert system (except for the knowledge base) are preprogrammed.
- Although ES can be developed with several tools, the trend is toward developing the initial prototype with a simple (and inexpensive) integrated tool (either a shell or a hybrid environment).
- Many ES are built by creating a small-scale demonstration prototype, testing it, and improving and expanding it. This process, which is repeated many times, has many advantages.
- Validation is determining whether the right system was built or whether the system does what it was meant to do and at an acceptable level of accuracy. Verification confirms that an ES has been built correctly according to specifications.

❖ KEY WORDS

- AI development strategy
- Automatic methods
- Backtracking
- Backward chaining
- Belief functions
- Certainty factors
- Certainty theory
- Chunking
- Decision Tables
- Declarative knowledge
- Declarative rules
- Deep knowledge
- Demonstration prototype
- Disbelief
- Documented knowledge
- Domain-specific tools
- Dynamic explanation
- Elicitation of knowledge
- Expert system shells
- Expert transfer system
- Explanation
- Explanation facility
- Facets
- Fifth-generation languages (5GL)

- Forward chaining
- Frame
- Induction
- Inference engine
- Inference rules
- Inference tree
- Inferencing
- Inheritance
- Interactive induction
- Interview analysis
- Instantiate
- Justifier
- Knowledge engineer
- Knowledge engineering
- Knowledge evaluation
- Knowledge representation
- Knowledge validation
- Knowledge verification
- LISP
- Manual methods
- Metaknowledge
- Metarules
- Multidimensional scaling
- Multiple experts

- Object-oriented programming
- Personal construct theory
- Predicate logic/calculus
- Procedural knowledge
- Process tracking
- Production rule
- PROLOG (programming in logic)
- Propositional calculus
- Propositional logic
- Protocol analysis
- Rule interpreter
- Semantic networks
- Semiautomatic methods
- Shallow knowledge
- Slot
- Static explanation
- Structured interview
- Subjective probability
- Toolkits
- Training set
- Undocumented knowledge
- Unstructured interview
- Walk-through

❖ QUESTIONS FOR REVIEW

1. What are the steps in the knowledge-engineering process?
2. What is the difference between documented knowledge and undocumented knowledge?
3. Compare declarative knowledge and procedural knowledge.
4. Define and contrast shallow knowledge and deep knowledge.

5. Give four reasons why knowledge acquisition is difficult.

6. What are the desired major skills of a knowledge engineer?

7. Name three techniques of automated knowledge acquisition.

8. What is repertory grid analysis?

9. What is the major advantage of using documented knowledge?

10. List the major difficulties of knowledge acquisition from multiple experts.

11. Briefly discuss the five major approaches to knowledge acquisition from multiple experts.

12. Define evaluation, validation, and verification of knowledge.

13. List the major knowledge-representation methods.

14. Describe the concept of semantic networks and list its major advantages and limitations.

15. What is a production rule? What are the basic parts of a production rule?

16. What are the major advantages and disadvantages of rule representation?

17. Define a frame, and give an example of a frame for a sailboat or a kitchen.

18. Describe the difference between forward chaining and backward chaining, and explain why backward chaining is considered goal-driven, whereas forward chaining is considered data-driven.

19. What is an inference tree? What is its major purpose?

20. What is metaknowledge? How is it related to the explanation facility?

21. Describe the general process of dealing with uncertainty.

22. What is the role of belief functions in the theory of evidence?

23. Describe the major phases in the ES development life cycle.

24. Describe the activities of project initialization.

25. What is included in a conceptual design of ES?

26. What are the major guidelines for selecting experts?

27. What is the difference between a shell and a programming environment?

28. What are the major components of a shell and the advantages and drawbacks of using a shell?

29. What are the differences between domain-specific tools and general-purpose tools?

30. What is the purpose of rapid prototyping?

31. List all the activities conducted in implementation.

❖ QUESTIONS FOR DISCUSSION

1. Assume that you are to collect knowledge for one of the following systems:
   a. An advisory system on equal opportunity hiring situations in your organization
   b. An advisory system on investment in residential real estate
   c. An advisory system on how to prepare your federal tax return (form 1040)
   What sources of knowledge would you consider? (Consult Figure 11.2.)

2. Discuss the major advantages of rule induction. Give an example that illustrates the method, and indicate a situation where you think it would be most appropriate.

3. Transfer of knowledge from a human to a machine is said to be more difficult than transfer from a human to a human. Why?

4. What are the major advantages and disadvantages of working with a prototype system for knowledge acquisition?

5. Discuss some of the problems of knowledge acquisition through the use of expert reports.

6. Review the functions of ACQUIRE from the Web site. What are the major benefits of ACQUIRE (or similar products) compared to a conventional rule-induction package?

7. Why is it important to have knowledge analyzed, coded, and documented in a systematic way? How is this related to the knowledge-management systems and e-learning systems that many organizations are adopting?

8. Machine-learning methods develop knowledge models automatically by a computer. Explain why or why not machine-learning techniques such as rule induction and neural computing can enhance knowledge acquisition.

9. Why is frame representation considered more complex than production rule representation? What are the advantages of the former over the latter?

10. Provide an example that shows how a semantic network can depict inheritance.

11. Class scheduling is a domain that needs a certain expertise. The scheduler needs to consider the professor's preferences, student course conflicts, equipment available in different classrooms, equipment requirement of different courses, and so on. Identify a knowledge rule with a procedural rule that is useful for class scheduling.

12. Certainty factors are popular in rule-based systems. Why? What unique features does the theory of uncertainty provide?

13. If you had a dialog with a human expert, what questions besides "why?" and "how?" would you be likely to ask? Give examples.

14. Describe the relationship between metaknowledge and explanations.

15. What can happen if the wrong knowledge representation of a problem domain or an inappropriate ES shell or tool is selected?

❖ EXERCISES

1. Fill in Table E11.1 with regard to the type of communication between the expert and the knowledge engineer. Use the following symbols: Y, yes; N, no; H, high; M, medium; L, low.

TABLE E11.1 Communication between Expert and Knowledge Engineer

Method	Type of Communication				
	Face-to-Face Contact	Written Communication	Continuing for a Long Time	Time Spent by Expert	Time Spent by Knowledge Engineer
Interview analysis					
Observations of experts					
Questionnaires and expert report					
Analysis of documented knowledge					

2. Read the accompanying knowledge-acquisition session involving a knowledge engineer (KE) and an expert (E), and complete the following:
   a. List the heuristics cited in this interview.
   b. List the algorithms mentioned.

   KE: Michael, you have the reputation for finding the best real estate properties for your clients. How do you do it?

   E: Well, Marla, first I learn about the client's objectives.

   KE: What do you mean by that?

   E: Some people are interested in income, others in price appreciation. There are some speculators, too.

   KE: Assume that somebody is interested in price appreciation. What would your advice be?

   E: Well, I first find out how much money the investor can put down and to what degree he or she can subsidize the property.

   KE: Why?

   E: The more cash you use as a down payment, the less subsidy you will need. Properties with high potential for price

appreciation need to be subsidized for about two years.

   KE: What else?

   E: Location is very important. As a general rule, I recommend looking for the lowest-priced property in an expensive area.

   KE: What else?

   E: I compute the cash flow and consider the tax impact by using built-in formulas in my calculator.

3. The authors of this book are coming to town and would like to know where to go for lunch. Unfortunately, you will be out of town, and you don't know specifically what they like to eat or the kind of atmosphere they like. But you do know how to encode your knowledge in an induction table like the one shown in Table E11.2. Using specific restaurants as the decisions (not yes/no but the restaurants themselves), construct an induction table reflecting your knowledge about local restaurants. To make this problem a good learning experience, work with a classmate, with one of you playing the part of the knowledge engineer, and the other the expert. Now switch roles, and for a second advisory problem rec-

TABLE E11.2   Comparisons of Automated Rule Induction and Interactive Methods

Method or Tool	Time of Expert	Time of Knowledge Engineer	Skill of Knowledge Engineer
Rule induction			
Autointelligence			
Smart editors			
ETS			

ommend a local hotel. (Note that because these are not yes/no decision problems, the advice can conclude with more than one choice.)

4. Construct a semantic network for the following situation: Mini is a robin; it lives in a nest on a pine tree in Ms. Wang's backyard. Robins are birds; they can fly and they have wings. They are an endangered species, and they are protected by government regulations.

5. Prepare a set of frames of an organization given the following information:
   - Company: 1,050 employees, $130 million annual sales, Mary Sunny is the president
   - Departments: accounting, finance, marketing, production, personnel
   - Production department: five lines of production
   - Product: computers
   - Annual budget: $50,000 + $12,000 × number of computers produced
   - Materials: $6,000 per unit produced
   - Working days: 250 per year
   - Number of supervisors: 1 for every 12 employees
   - Range of number of employees: 400–500 per shift (two shifts per day). Overtime or part-time on a third shift is possible.

6. The following is a typical instruction set found in the manuals in most car shops (this one is based on Nissan's shop manual):
   - Topic: starter system troubles.
   - Procedures: Try to crank the starter. If it is dead or cranks slowly, turn on the headlights. If the headlights are bright (or dim only slightly), the trouble is in the starter itself, the solenoid, or the wiring. To find the trouble, short the two large solenoid terminals together (not to ground). If the starter cranks normally, the problem is in the wiring or in the solenoid; check them up to the ignition switch. If the starter does not work normally, check the bushings. If the bushings are good, send the starter to a test station or replace it. If the headlights are out or are very dim, check the battery. If the battery is okay, check the wiring for breaks, shorts, and dirty connections. If the battery and connecting wires

are not at fault, turn the headlights on and try to crank the starter. If the lights dim drastically, it is probably because the starter is shorted to ground. Have the starter tested or replace it. (Based on Carrico et al., 1989.) Now translate the information into rules. (Can you do it in only six rules?)

7. You are given a set of rules for this question: Should we buy a house or not?
   R1: IF inflation is low,
       THEN interest rates are low,
       ELSE interest rates are high.
   R2: IF interest rates are high,
       THEN housing prices are high.
   R3: IF housing prices are high,
       THEN do not buy a house,
       ELSE buy a house.
       a. Run backward chaining with a high inflation rate as given.
       b. Run forward chaining with a low inflation rate as given.
       c. Prepare an inference tree for the backward-chaining case.

8. You are given an ES with the following rules:
   R1: IF interest rates fall,
       THEN bond prices will increase.
   R2: IF interest rates increase,
       THEN bond prices will decline.
   R3: IF interest rates are unchanged,
       THEN bond prices will remain unchanged.
   R4: IF the dollar rises (against other currencies),
       THEN interest rates will decline.
   R5: IF the dollar falls,
       THEN interest rates will increase.
   R6: IF bond prices decline,
       THEN buy bonds.
       a. A client has just observed that the dollar exchange rate is falling. He wants to know whether to buy bonds. Run a forward chaining and a backward chaining, and submit a report to him.
       b. Prepare an inference tree for the backward chaining you did.

c. A second client observed that interest rates are unchanged. She asks for advice on investing in bonds. What will the ES tell her? Use forward chaining.

9. You are given an expert system with seven rules pertaining to the interpersonal skills of a job applicant:

R1: IF the applicant answers questions in a straightforward manner,
THEN she is easy to converse with.

R2: IF the applicant seems honest,
THEN she answers in a straightforward manner.

R3: IF the applicant has items on her resume that are found to be untrue,
THEN she does not seem honest,
ELSE she seems honest.

R4: IF the applicant is able to arrange an appointment with the executive assistant,
THEN she is able to strike up a conversation with the executive assistant.

R5: IF the applicant strikes up a conversation with the executive assistant and the applicant is easy to converse with,
THEN she is amiable.

R6: IF the applicant is amiable,
THEN she has adequate interpersonal skills.

R7: IF the applicant has adequate interpersonal skills,
THEN we will offer her the job.

Solve the following three independent cases:

a. Assume that the applicant does not have any items on her resume that are found to be untrue and that she is able to arrange an appointment with the executive assistant. Run a forward-chaining analysis to find out whether we will offer her the job.

b. It is known that the applicant answers questions in a straightforward manner. Run a backward-chaining analysis to find out whether we will offer the applicant the job.

c. We have just discovered that the applicant was able to arrange an appointment with the executive assistant. It is also known that she is honest. Does she have interpersonal skills?

❖ GROUP EXERCISES

1. Have everyone in the group consider the fairly easy task of doing laundry. Individually, write down all the motions you use in sorting clothes, loading the washer and dryer, and folding the clothes. Compare notes. Are any members of the group better at the task than others? For simplicity, leave out details such as "go to the laundromat." Code the doing-laundry facts in a rule base. How many exceptions to the rules did you find?

2. For the group ES project, determine how it could provide benefits for the company for which you built it. Formally estimate potential benefits and costs. Are there any disadvantages? How serious are they? Demonstrate the project to the client and gauge his or her reaction. Will he or she be likely to adopt ES technology in the near future? Why or why not? Include with your final report a letter from your contact in the company.

❖ INTERNET EXERCISES

1. Access the Web site of CORVID at exsys.com and try the demo systems available. Summarize the characteristics of the demo systems and any new knowledge acquired there.

2. Search the Internet to find a knowledge-acquisition tool that was not introduced in this chapter and summarize its major functional features.

3. Search the Internet to find an intelligent system application used in a video rental store. Describe the possible rules included in the knowledge base and summarize the requirements specific to the development of Web-based expert systems. How are Web-based systems different from traditional systems?

❖ GROUP PROJECT

Development a Small Rule-Based Expert System for Wine Selection

Building a small knowledge base with an expert system shell is fairly easy. Here is an example. Selecting an appropriate wine for a certain type of food is not so simple. Many qualitative factors influence the choice. Delegating the decision to a waiter can be risky in some restaurants and even riskier at home if you are trying to impress someone. So it may be useful for a restaurant to develop an expert system to advise the customer. Using the CORVID expert system shell for this student project, follow the steps specified below to develop your ES for wine selection:

1. Specify the problem (pairing wine and food at a restaurant).
2. Name the system (Sommelier).
3. Write the starting text ("Sommelier will help you select a wine . . .").
4. Decide on an appropriate coding for an uncertainty situation (e.g., 0/1, 0 to 10, or 2100 to 100: we will use 0 to 10).
5. Decide on any other inferencing parameters as required by the shell (e.g., use all the rules or only some of the rules; set the threshold levels).
6. Prepare any concluding note that you want the user to see at the end of the consultation ("Thank you for using Sommelier. Bon appetit!").
7. Work with an expert to list the potential choices. There are 12 possible wines, including aged cabernet sauvignon blanc, crisp chardonnay, gerwürztraminer, merlot, pinot noir, zinfandel, and so on.
8. Develop a working knowledge of food and wine (this is the best part for the knowledge engineers who must gain some familiarity with the problem domain).
9. Develop a knowledge map with an expert (OK, maybe we did some testing on our own) in tabular form. This helps us focus on the knowledge.
10. Build the initial set of rules, the knowledge base, in the shell, and debug them. In Exsys, this involves developing qualifiers, which are the questions to be posed to derive facts, and the answer set of possible fact values for each one. Qualifiers are explained below.
11. Demonstrate the system to the expert, refine the rules, and collect additional cases and rules. Repeat steps 9–11 until the recommendation given by the expert(s) and the system are the same.
12. Deploy the system (Bon appetit!).

Write the rules in the standard format required by the shell. CORVID uses the concept of qualifiers. For exam-ple, it is known that the wine depends on the menu selection: You might have meat, fish, poultry, or pasta, and you may have an appetizer as well. Each fact-gathering statement is called a qualifier. For example, qualifier 1 is the meat menu selection. Literally its text is the phrase "The meat menu selection is." Qualifier text generally ends in a verb. The qualifier can assume the following values: (1) prime ribs, (2) grilled steak, and (3) filet mignon. These are called the values of the qualifier.

Now the first rule might be constructed as

IF the meat menu selection is prime ribs
THEN pinot noir, confidence 9/10
AND merlot, confidence 8/10
AND aged cabernet sauvignon, confidence 6/10.

This means that each of the three choices is appro-priate, but pinot noir is the best choice (9), followed by merlot (8), and then by aged cabernet sauvignon (6).

To build this rule, create a new qualifier and then select the number of the qualifier (1) and the appropriate value (1 for prime ribs). This forms the IF part of the rule. Click to the THEN part of the rule and call up the choices (step 7) and select the appropriate values for the THEN part with the appropriate confidence level (don't forget the confidence level or the system will recommend no wine, leading to a rather dour evening). In this case the three wines are appropriate, but pinot noir is the best recommendation.

When all the rules are applied to the particular meal, the system might not recommend pinot noir overall. As other rules are consulted, the certainty in the choice may decrease. For example, the appetizer and the cost of the wine may influence the recommendation. Another con-sideration is the universe of the system's knowledge. If your menu selection is not on the considered list, the sys-tem will not know what to recommend because the main course is not part of its knowledge universe.

Construct the knowledge base and implement the prototype to show some sample sessions.

Source: Lisa Sandoval, a graduate student at California State University, Long Beach, developed this ES student project: "Your Sommelier."

CHAPTER
12

ADVANCED INTELLIGENT SYSTEMS

LEARNING OBJECTIVES

❖ Understand second-generation intelligent systems

❖ Learn the concept and application of case-based systems

❖ Understand the concept and different types of artificial neural networks

❖ Learn the advantages and limitations of artificial neural networks

❖ Understand the concepts and applications of genetic algorithms

❖ Understand fuzzy set theories and their applications in designing intelligent systems

In addition to rule-based systems, a few advanced techniques are available for designing intelligent systems that can learn by themselves. These include case-based systems, artificial neural networks, genetic algorithms, and fuzzy reasoning systems. The case-based system contains a case base that maintains unique expert experience. Artificial neural networks use artificial neurons executable on computers to mimic the human brain. Genetic algorithms modify the natural-selection process to find useful knowledge. Fuzzy systems convert between symbolic reasoning and mathematical calculation to improve decision performance in certain problem domains. The chapter is organized in the following sections:

12.1 OPENING VIGNETTE: HOUSEHOLD FINANCIAL'S VISION SPEEDS LOAN APPROVALS WITH NEURAL NETWORKS

INTRODUCTION

Household Financial Corporation (HFC) sells and services auto loans and credit cards, including private label cards. In mid-1998, Household acquired Beneficial Corporation, creating the HFC and Beneficial divisions with 1,400 branch offices in 46 states. Its largest revenue-generating business unit is the consumer finance division, which underwrites equity loans. The keys to competitiveness are efficiency and customer intimacy.

A problem experienced by consumer finance companies investing in technology is that loan products are complicated and subject to heavy regulatory restrictions. Laws vary by state and sometimes by county. The loan approval decision process uses many variables (consumer's income, employment history, credit history, outstanding debts, etc.). Capturing them in a software application is difficult.

Around 1994 the head of consumer finance, Bob Elliot, determined that Household should offer faster underwriting decisions than its rivals to compete effectively. Household could use technology to obtain central loan approval while a customer was still in the office, rather than ship the hard copy of the application and wait for days. This vision was the start of the Vision system.

SYSTEM DEVELOPMENT

System development began in late 1994. An object-oriented approach was taken so that multiple versions (more than 59) could be easily maintained and quickly updated. Pilot testing began in mid-1996, and the entire system was completely deployed in early 1997. At the heart of Vision is a neural network. The network has been trained to recognize patterns of successful and unsuccessful loans based on past company history. Given a set of data representing an online loan application, the neural network can quickly recommend approval or denial of a loan. It can quickly be rerun with new information, dramatically speeding up the approval process, and creating a competitive advantage.

THE VISION SYSTEM

Household's Vision system integrates all phases of the process from lead to loan and connects to an intelligent underwriting engine. Vision contains seven integrated modules:

1. *Training* for account executives (AE),
2. *Lead Management Actions and Inquiries* to better manage customers,
3. *Solicitation* to handle contact management and create loan proposals,
4. *Underwriting* to model financial solutions using the customer's financial information,
5. *Closing* to generate all the necessary documents,
6. *Perfected Product* to bar-code documents to be sent to a central loan processing facility for scanning, and
7. *Service* to handle all aspects of customer service.

THE NEURAL NETWORK

In the Underwriting module, a neural network is fed risk, the interest rate, and other variables along with customer data for evaluation to determine loan terms. Typical underwriting requests are performed in minutes rather than in hours or days, the standard for the industry. The neural network engine for underwriting decisions is based on technology from HNC Software and Fair, Isaacs & Company. The HNC neural network performs fraud detection. Strategyware (Fair, Isaacs & Company) is at the heart of the system's suggestive selling component. The networks are trained with data patterns for good and bad customers so that they can identify these cases when deployed. Once the neural networks have been trained, they can estimate credit worthiness and potential fraud, even for cases unlike those they have seen before.

BENEFITS AND COSTS

The cost of the entire system over three years came to $83 million. Two key benefits of Vision are the reduced training time for new account executives (AEs) and the reduced AE administrative overhead. The AEs spend almost all their time servicing customers, directly leading to increased sales. When this was demonstrated in pilot testing, minimal resistance among the AEs disappeared, thus ensuring their cooperation. By mid-1999, Vision was handling an average of 11,000 new loan applications per day, totaling 3 million transactions per day.

Household's branches now sell at least 10 percent more loans than before, and branches added to Household's network through acquisition show gains as high as 18 percent. Another key measure of corporate performance in consumer finance is the managed basis efficiency ratio, expenses divided by revenue, minus policyholders' benefits. Household has lowered this ratio from more than 40 percent to less than 35 percent (lower is better). Household achieved a 40 percent total return on investment over Vision's first few years and expects a five-year return on investment of 129 percent. Household continues to tweak the system as regulations change and as AEs generate ideas for new functionality (leading to regular retraining of the neural networks).

UNEXPECTED BENEFITS

The Vision system's neural network has already produced several unexpected benefits. As Vision learns, it helps the company make smarter decisions about customers by recognizing patterns and how they can be successfully used. Suppose an irate credit card holder calls about a late fee. He is not yet a profitable customer for the company. He has a single card with little or no balance and has rejected Household offers for credit insurance products and equity loans. Vision considers the potential lifetime value of the customer and cancels the late fee.

Vision recognizes patterns in the customer's history, including the fact that this is the first late payment and that the customer fits the profile of a person who will most likely be in the market for significant new loans the following year. Vision authorizes waiving the fee. Then the system can prompt the rep with suggestive selling for this now-happy customer. The system will also be upgraded to the Web-based architecture for a more friendly user interface.

Source: Adapted from D. Salter, "Loan Star," *CIO*, Vol. 13, No. 8, February 1, 2000, pp. 100–106, www.cio.com; Fadlalla and Lin (2001).

CONCLUSION

The system ties the company more closely to existing and prospective customers. Loan approvals are faster, sales proposals more targeted, and customer service more responsive. The Vision system dramatically cuts down the approval waiting time and creates more opportunities. Household has developed a customer intimacy that translates to higher profits.

❖ QUESTIONS FOR THE OPENING VIGNETTE

1. Describe why neural networks were used in Vision.
2. Describe how neural networks were used in Vision.
3. Describe some benefits of integrating the neural network systems into the Vision system. Explain what could have happened otherwise.
4. What is the benefit of retraining the system regularly?
5. Describe any other techniques that could replace the neural network for building such a system.
6. Explain how the top-management champion supported the development of Vision and how the users ultimately bought into the system.
7. Describe how such a system can be converted to a Web-based system and the advantages and drawbacks of converting it to a Web-based system.

12.2 MACHINE-LEARNING TECHNIQUES

Many organizations use neural networks to automate complex decision-making. Neural networks can readily identify patterns from which they generate a recommended course of action. Since such networks learn from past experience to improve their own performance, they are members of a technology family called machine learning. **Machine learning** is different in several ways from the conventional knowledge-acquisition methods described in Chapter 11. Knowledge acquisition from human experts often suffers from the expert's unwillingness or inability to provide accurate knowledge, whereas machine learning is an attempt to implicitly induce expert knowledge from historical decisions. In other words, instead of asking the experts to articulate their decision knowledge, the learning module of the system is able to identify patterns and rules from the historical data available in the database or organizational files.

Attempts at discovering problem-solving knowledge have been made for generations, starting long before the computer age. Consider the following: statistical models such as regression or forecasting, management science models such as inventory-level determination and resource allocation, and financial models such as make-versus-buy decisions and equipment-replacement methods. Unfortunately, such methods are often limited to processing quantifiable factors. When problems are complex and factors are qualitative, standard models cannot solve them; additional, deeper, richer knowledge is needed.

Machine learning is a family of methods that attempt to allow machines to acquire knowledge for problem-solving by showing them historical cases. Machine learning is nontrivial. One problem is that there are many models of learning. Sometimes it is difficult to match the learning model with the problem type (e.g., scheduling). Machine learning is considered an artificial intelligence method even though some of its technologies do not formally exhibit intelligence. However, it is definitely useful for designing an intelligent decision-support system.

LEARNING

Learning is a process of self-improvement and thus an important feature of intelligent behaviors. Understanding learning is a critical area of AI because it is an investigation into the basic principles that underlie intelligence rather than an application itself. Machine learning is also essential to providing intelligent DSS with self-enhancement capabilities.

Human learning is a combination of many complicated cognitive processes, including induction, deduction, analogy, and other special procedures on observing or analyzing examples. Machine-learning techniques are no different; most of them adopt similar ideas and have them implemented on computers. The following are relevant observations on how learning relates to intelligent systems:

- Learning systems demonstrate interesting learning behaviors, some of which (like chess- and checkers-playing programs) actually challenge the performance of humans (see Chapter 10).

- Although AI sometimes matches human-level learning capabilities, it is not able to learn as well as humans or in the same way that humans do (e.g., checkers-playing programs learn quite differently from humans).

- There is no claim that machine learning can be applied in a creative way, though such systems can handle cases to which they have never been exposed. Simulated creativity is an intensely studied AI topic (see the Imagination Engines Inc. Web site at www.imagination-engines.com).

- Learning systems are not anchored in any formal bedrock; thus their implications are not well understood. Many systems have been exhaustively tested, but exactly why they succeed or fail is not precisely clear.

- A common thread running through most AI approaches to learning (distinguishing them from non-AI approaches to learning) is the manipulation of symbols rather than numeric information.

MACHINE-LEARNING METHODS

Machine learning has two major categories: **supervised learning** and **unsupervised learning**. Supervised learning is a process of inducing knowledge from a set of observations whose outcomes are known. For example, we induce a set of rules from historical loan-evaluation data. Since the decisions on these loan cases are known, we can test how the induced model performs when it is applied to these cases. Unsupervised learning is used to discover knowledge from a set of data whose outcomes are unknown. A typical application is to classify customers into several different lifestyles. Before the classification, we do not know how many different kinds of lifestyles are available, nor which customer belongs to a particular lifestyle. Figure 12.1 shows the machine-learning methods in each category. Following are several examples of machine-learning methods and algorithms:

- *Inductive learning.* This method is used in knowledge acquisition, as in rule induction. It was discussed in Chapter 11.
- *Case-based reasoning* and **analogical reasoning**. This approach is employed in knowledge acquisition and inferencing.
- *Neural computing.* This approach can be used for knowledge acquisition, and thus can be used for decision support.
- *Genetic algorithms.* These algorithms attempt to follow the evolutionary processes of biological systems in which the fittest survive and so are excellent learners.

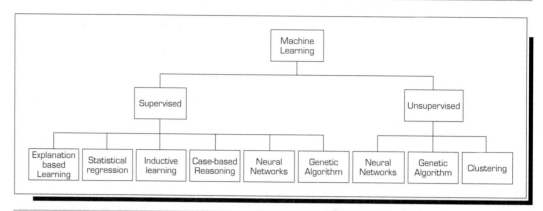

FIGURE 12.1 TAXONOMY OF LEARNING METHODS

- ***Cluster analysis.*** This approach is used to put data into several groups based on their similarity. The groups can then be used for marketing or other purposes.
- ***Statistical methods.*** Some statistical methods, such as multiple discriminant analysis, are suitable for analyzing knowledge that is quantitative in nature and have been applied to knowledge acquisition, forecasting, and problem-solving.
- ***Explanation-based learning.*** This approach combines existing theories and new cases, using the new cases to modify existing theories, and using theories to explain why one instance is or is not a prototypical member of a class (Mitchell et al., 1986).

12.3 CASE-BASED REASONING

The basic premise of machine learning is that data preserving previous decision experience exist. These experience-based records are called cases. They may be used either as direct references to support similar decisions in the future or to induce rules or decision patterns. The former, called **case-based reasoning** (CBR), adapts solutions used to solve old problems for use in solving new problems. The latter, called **inductive learning**, allows the computer to examine historical cases and generates rules that can be chained (forward or backward) to solve problems. In this section, we describe the concept of CBR and its application in intelligent DSS. Inductive learning was introduced in Chapter 11. This section describes how case-based reasoning works.

The foundation of case-based reasoning is a case base containing a number of previous cases for decision-making. Case-based reasoning has proved to be an extremely effective approach for problems in which the rules are inadequate (Kolonder, 1993). In fact, since experience is an important ingredient in human expertise, case-based reasoning is thought to be a more psychologically plausible model of the reasoning of an expert than a rule-based model. A theoretical comparison of the two is summarized in Table 12.1. According to Riesbeck and Schank (1989), the use of this approach is justified by the fact that human thinking does not use logic (or reasoning from first principles) but is basically a processing of the right information retrieved at the right time. So the central problem is the identification of pertinent information whenever needed.

TABLE 12.1	Comparison of Case-based and Rule-based Reasoning	
Criterion	**Rule-based Reasoning**	**Case-based Reasoning**
Knowledge unit	Rule	Case
Granularity	Fine	Coarse
Knowledge acquisition units	Rules, hierarchies	Cases, hierarchies
Explanation mechanism	Backtrack of rule firings	Precedent cases
Characteristic output	Answer and confidence measure	Answer and precedent cases
Knowledge transfer across problems	High if backtracking; low if deterministic	Low
Speed as a function of knowledge base size	Exponential if backtracking; linear if deterministic	Logarithmic if index tree is balanced
Domain requirements	Domain vocabulary	Domain vocabulary
	Good set of inference rules	Database of example cases
	Either few rules or rules apply sequentially	Stability (a modified good solution is probably still good)
	Domain mostly obeys rules	Many exceptions to rules
Advantages	Flexible use of knowledge	Rapid response
	Potentially optimal answers	Rapid knowledge acquisition
		Explanation by examples
Disadvantages	Computationally expensive	Suboptimal solutions
	Long development time	Redundant knowledge base
	Black-box answers	

Source: Based on M. Goodman, "PRISM: A Case-based Telex Classifier," in A. Rappaport and R. Smith (eds.), *Innovative Applications of Artificial Intelligence,* Vol. 2. Cambridge, MA: MIT Press, 1990. Courtesy of Marc Goodman, Cognitive Systems Inc.

CASE DEFINITION

A case is the primary knowledge element in a case-based reasoning application. It is a combination of the problem features and proper business actions associated with each situation. These features and actions may be represented in natural language or in a specific structured format (e.g., objects).

Kolodner (1989) classified cases into three categories, **ossified cases**, **paradigmatic cases**, and **stories**, based on their different characteristics and the different ways of handling them. Ossified cases appear very often and are quite standard. They may be generalized into rules or other forms of knowledge through inductive learning. Paradigmatic cases contain certain unique features that cannnot be generalized. They need to be stored and indexed in the case base for future reference. Stories are special cases that contain rich contents and special features of deep implications. Figure 12.2 shows the way the three types of cases may be handled. Case-based reasoning is particularly designed for processing paradigmatic cases that cannot be properly handled by rule-based reasoning.

The following is a possible scenario of CBR in loan evaluation. When a new case is received, the system builds a set of features to represent it. Let us assume that the applicant is a 40-year-old married man, with a $50,000 annual-income job in a mid-size manufacturing company. The set of features is [age=40, marriage = yes, salary = 50,000, employer = mid-size, industry= manufacturing]. The system goes to the case base to find similar cases. Suppose the system finds the following three similar cases:

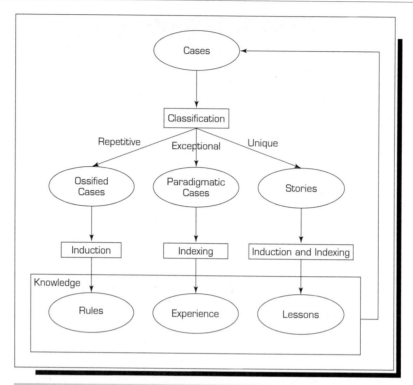

FIGURE 12.2   DERIVING KNOWLEDGE FROM DIFFERENT TYPES OF CASES

John = [age=40, marriage = yes, salary = 50,000, employer = mid-size, industry= bank]

Ted = [age=40, marriage = yes, salary = 45,000, employer = mid-size, industry= manufacturing]

Larry = [age=40, marriage = yes, salary = 50,000, employer = small, industry= retailing]

If John and Ted performed well in their loans, and Larry was unable to pay back due to company bankruptcy, then the system can recommend that the loan be approved, because John and Ted, who are more similar to the new applicant (four of the five attributes are the same), were able to pay back without problems. Larry is considered less similar to the new applicant (only three of the five attributes are the same) and hence is less useful for reference.

CBR makes learning much easier and the recommendation more sensible. Many applications of case-based reasoning have been implemented. For example, Shin and Han (2001) reported an application of CBR to corporate bond rating. Hastings, Branting, and Lockwood (2002) applied CBR to rangeland management. Humphrey et al. (2003) describe an application of CBR to evaluate supplier environment-management performance. Park and Han (2002) applied CBR to bankruptcy prediction. Khan and Hoffman (2003) reported the development of a case-based recommendation system without the involvement of human knowledge engineers. Pham and Setchi (2003) applied case-based reasoning to design adaptive product manuals. An application to automate a help desk is described in AIS in Action 12.1. Table 12.2 shows the advantages of using CBR.

TABLE 12.2   Advantages of Case-based Reasoning

- Knowledge acquisition is improved: easier to build, simpler to maintain, less expensive to develop and support.
- System development time is faster.
- Existing data and knowledge are leveraged.
- Complete formalized domain knowledge (as is required with rules) is not required.
- Experts feel better discussing concrete cases (not general rules).
- Explanation becomes easier. Rather than showing many rules, a logical sequence can be shown.
- Acquisition of new cases is easy [can be automated; for an example of knowledge acquisition of cases, see diPiazza and Helsabeck (1990)].
- Learning can occur from both successes and failures.

AIS IN ACTION 12.1

KONICA AUTOMATES A HELP DESK WITH CASE-BASED REASONING

Konica Business Machines (Windsor, Connecticut) wanted to fully automate its help desk for internal and external support (both for its commercial products and for in-house applications and systems). This need arose from its desire to be a $1 billion operation by the next millennium and because the company had received past awards for superior tech support for office products.

Case-based reasoning (CBR) was chosen as the most promising approach. After Konica evaluated several case-based reasoning tools, Ty Butler, the director of domestic tech support, selected Software Artistry's Expert Advisor. The most unusual feature of Expert Advisor is its multiple problem-resolution modes. It also uses decision trees and has adaptive learning, tech search, and other useful features.

The case-based reasoning approach has been demonstrated to be an effective means of automating help desks. In CBR, the situation to be diagnosed is entered into the system verbatim. Then the text is analyzed by a natural language processor which interprets the situation and makes a first attempt at structuring the information to compare it to existing cases stored in a (knowledge) case base. Once the cases are examined, the most likely situations are presented, and the user can either go with the recommended course of action or refine the wording to tighten up the description of the problem. The cases must be written very carefully so that the system can apply AI technology in solving real problems. In the early prototypes, Konica knowledge

engineers started building cases for five products using technical documentation as a source document. At a certain point, actual calls to the help desk were used to generate cases. Moving to real cases brought the hit rate up.

Konica's implementation, Expert Advisor, runs on IBM Pentium servers. It is used by both the internal tech support people and by customers directly. Konica's 750 technicians and 6,000 dealer technicians generate 90 percent of the support calls for copiers, 20 percent of those for fax machines, and 30 percent of those for multifunction products. The rest of the calls come from end-users. There are 20 help desk technicians plus six knowledge engineers. Knowledge engineers build decision trees rather than case bases and focus on clearing the bulk of the calls instead of developing highly specialized structures. The tech support people still handle unusual cases, but the system is also incorporating digitized photos of components and procedures, which are especially useful to the help-desk agents.

In the early stages of development, Expert Advisor produced a 65 percent hit rate for problem resolution. The adaptive-learning features will be incorporated next to improve the hit rate.

Note: This case was updated by Narasimha Bolloju of the City University of Hong Kong. It was prepared based on the material publisehd in *Datamation*, Vol. 42, No. 2, January 15, 1996.

PROCESS OF CASE-BASED REASONING

The process of case-based reasoning is shown graphically in Figure 12.3. Boxes represent processes, and ovals represent knowledge structure. The major steps in the process are described in the following list, reprinted from Slade (1991).

1. *Assign indexes.* Features of the new event are assigned as indexes characterizing the event. For example, our first air shuttle flight might be characterized as an airplane flight.

2. *Retrieve.* The indexes are used to retrieve a similar past case from memory. The past case contains the prior solution. In our example, we might be reminded of a previous airplane trip.

3. *Modify.* The old solution is modified to conform to the new situation, resulting in a proposed solution. For our airplane case, we would make appropriate modifications to account for changes in various features, such as destination, price, purpose of the trip, departure and arrival times, and weather.

4. *Test.* The proposed solution is tried out. It either succeeds or fails. Our airplane reminder generates certain expectations.

5. *Assign and store.* If the solution succeeds, then assign indexes and store a working solution. The successful plan is then incorporated into the case memory. For a typical airplane trip there will be few expectation failures and, therefore, little to make this new trip memorable. It will be just one more instance of the airplane script.

6. *Explain, repair, and test.* If the solution fails, explain the failure, repair the working solution, and test again. The explanation process identifies the source of the problem. The predictive features of the problem are incorporated into the indexing rules to anticipate this problem in the future. The failed plan is repaired to fix the problem, and the revised solution is then tested. For our air shuttle example, we realize that certain expectations fail. We learn that we do not get an assigned seat and do not have to pay ahead of time. We might decide that taking the air shuttle is more like riding on a train. We can then create a new case in memory to handle this new situation and identify predictive features so that we will be reminded of this episode the next time we take the shuttle. In support of this process are the following types of knowledge structures, represented by ovals in the figure:

   - *Indexing rules.* Indexing rules identify the predictive features in the input that provide appropriate indexes in the case memory. Determining the significant input features is a persistent problem.

   - *Case memory.* Case memory is the episodic memory that comprises the database of experience.

   - *Similarity metrics.* If more than one case is retrieved from episodic memory, the similarity metrics can be used to decide which case is more like the current situation. For example, in the air shuttle case, we might be reminded of both airplane rides and train rides. The similarity rules might initially suggest that we rely on the airplane case.

   - *Modification rules.* No old case is going to be an exact match for a new situation. The old case must be modified to fit. We require knowledge about what kinds of factors can be changed and how to change them. For the airplane ride, it is acceptable to ride in a different seat, but it is usually not advisable to change roles from passenger to pilot.

   - *Repair rules.* Once we identify and explain an expectation failure, we must try to alter our plan to fit the new situation. Again, we have rules for what kinds of changes are permissible. For the air shuttle, we recognize that paying for the ticket on the plane is an acceptable change. We can generate an explanation that recognizes an airplane ride as a type of commercial transaction and suggests that there are alternative, acceptable means of paying for services.

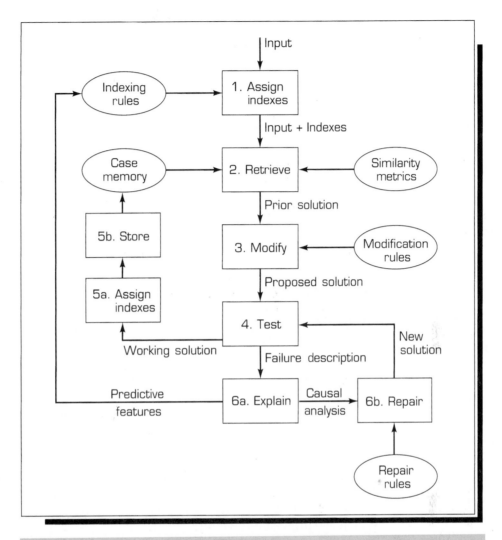

FIGURE 12.3 CASE-BASED REASONING FLOWCHART

Source: AI Magazine, Spring 1991, p. 46; based on C.K. Riesback and R.L. Schank, *Inside Case-based Reasoning,* Hillsdale, NJ: Lawrence Erlbaum Associates, 1989, p. 32. Copyright © 1989, American Association for Artificial Intelligence. All rights reserved.

A detailed description of the reasoning process and recent applications can be found in Chou (2001), Finnie and Sun (2003), and Humphreys et al. (2003). An examination of case libraries in problem-solving is in Hernandez-Serrano and Jonassen (2003).

USES, ISSUES, AND APPLICATIONS

Case-based reasoning can be used on its own or can be combined with other reasoning paradigms. Several implementations of CBR systems combine rule-based reasoning (RBR) in order to address limitations such as accuracy in case indexing and adaptation (Golding and Rosenboom, 1996; Stefanoski and Wilk, 2001). Table 12.3 provides some guidelines for the selection of CBR applications.

TABLE 12.3   When to Use Case-based Reasoning

Domain cannot be formalized with rules because

- Domain has a weak or unknown causal model.
- Domain has undefined terms.
- Contradictory rules apply in different situations.
- Application requires complex output (such as battle plans).
- Domain is already precedent-based (e.g., in fields such as law, medical diagnosis, and claim settlement).
- Domain formalization requires too many rules.
- Domain is dynamic, requiring rapid generation of solutions to new problem types.
- Domain task benefits from records of past solutions to reuse successful ones and avoid bad ones.

Source: Based on M. Goodman, "PRISM: A Case-based Telex Classifier," in Rappaport and Smith (1990). Courtesy of Marc Goodman, Cognitive Systems Inc.

Table 12.4 provides CBR applications in different fields. For a good CBR Web site, see www.cbr-web.org, maintained by the University of Kaiserslautern in Germany. It contains applications, demos, and research material.

For successful applications, the following issues and questions regarding case-based implementation require careful thought by designers:

- What makes up a case? How can we represent case memory?
- Automatic case-adaptation rules can be very complex.
- How is memory organized? What are the indexing rules?
- The quality of the results is heavily dependent on the indexes used.
- How does memory function in relevant information retrieval?
- How can we perform efficient search (knowledge navigation) of the cases?
- How can we organize (cluster) the cases?
- How can we design the distributed storage of cases?
- How can we adapt old solutions to new problems? Can we simply adapt the memory for efficient query, depending on context? What are the similarity metrics and the modification rules?

TABLE 12.4   Case-based Reasoning Application Categories and Examples

- CBR in electronic commerce—intelligent product catalog search, intelligent customer support and sales support.
- WWW and information search—browsing advisor, retrieving tour packages from travel catalog, case-based information retrieval in construction, and skill profiling in electronic recruitment.
- Planning and control—conflict resolution in air traffic control and planning of bioprocess recipes in brewing industry.
- Design—conceptual building design aid, conceptual design aid for electromechanical devices, and VLSI design.
- Reuse—reuse of structural design calculation documents, reuse of object-oriented software, and reuse assistant for engineering designs.
- Diagnosis—predicting blood alcohol content, online troubleshooting and customer support, and medical diagnosis.
- Reasoning—heuristic retrieval of legal knowledge, reasoning in legal domains, and computer-supported conflict resolution through negotiation or mediation.

Source: www.cbr-web.org.

- How can we factor errors out of the original cases?
- How can we learn from mistakes? That is, how can we repair and update the case base?
- The case base may need to be expanded as the domain model evolves, yet much analysis of the domain may be postponed.
- How can we integrate CBR with other knowledge representations and inferencing mechanisms?
- Are there better pattern-matching methods than the ones we currently use?
- Are there alternative retrieval systems that match the CBR schema?

Since 1995, increasing evidence has shown positive results for the use of case-based reasoning in solving practical problems (Althoff, 1995; Azuaje et al., 1999; Cercone et al., 1999; Grupe et al., 1998; Kim et al., 2002; Lee and Kim, 2002; Lawton, 1999; Lenz et al., 1996; Luu, 2003; Pal and Palmer, 2000). AIS in Action 12.2 summarizes a successful application in jet engine maintenance.

SUCCESS FACTORS FOR A CASE-BASED REASONING SYSTEM

Case-based reasoning systems exhibit some unique properties that, if properly managed and implemented, can lead to very successful systems. Klahr (1997) describes seven principles for a successful CBR strategy. They are as follows:

- ***Determine specific business objectives.*** Every software project should have a business focus. Call-center and help-desk environments have great potential for CBR methods.

DSS IN ACTION 12.2

CASE-BASED REASONING IMPROVES JET ENGINE MAINTENANCE, REDUCES COSTS

Snecma is the leading French manufacturer of aircraft engines, ranking fourth in the world. One of Snecma's goals is to improve engine maintenance technology to reduce the cost of ownership for its customers. The CASSIOPÉE project was designed to perform engine troubleshooting using CBR. It performs technical maintenance of the Cfm 56-3 aircraft engines on all Boeing 737s.

Troubleshooting accounts for 50 percent of the average engine's downtime. The 16,000 cases were culled from an eight-year history of all Cfm 56-3 engines sold. Error cases were removed from the set, and the model was supplemented with technical parameters of the engines. A decision tree is used to organize the cases and drive the questioning. On average, a case is described by 40 attributes out of a total of 80 (not all are used simultaneously).

The demonstrated benefits of CASSIOPÉE are the following:

- Reduced downtime for the engines, avoiding delays for the airlines.
- Minimized diagnosis costs.
- Reduced diagnostic errors.
- Development of a record and documentation of the expertise of the most skilled maintenance specialists to build a corporate memory and help transfer know-how to the novice.

The CASSIOPÉE system is in use in the aftersale division at Cfm-International, a subsidiary of Snecma and General Electric. It is fully integrated in the end-user environment. CASSIOPÉE assists Cfm engineers in offering quicker and better advice to airline maintenance crews when airplanes are at the departure gate.

Source: Abstracted and modified from Lenz et al. (1996). Also see Manago and Auriol (1995).

- *Understand your end-users and customers.* A successful case base directly supports the end-user. The case base (knowledge) must be at the level of expertise of the end-users. Shortcuts should be provided for more knowledgeable end-users.
- *Design the system appropriately.* This includes understanding the problem domain and types of information the case base will provide and recognizing system and integration requirements.
- *Plan an ongoing knowledge management process.* The knowledge in the case base must be updated as new cases arise (to avoid gaps in the case base) or as new products or services are delivered (new content is added).
- *Establish achievable returns on investment (ROI) and measurable metrics.* Develop a level of acceptable ROI (5–13 percent is being achieved in the field) and a means to measure it (20 fewer phone calls with a 13 percent larger customer base handled; or the ability to handle four times more questions than under the manual system).
- *Plan and execute customer-access strategy.* The strength of CBR is that it can be put into the hands of customers, even over the Web, thus providing service 24 hours every day (e.g., Broderbund Software's Gizmo Trapper). This empowers customers to obtain the assistance they need when they need it. It also further broadens the use of the system, which helps in identifying exceptions and updating the case base. This is a key success component.
- *Expand knowledge generation and access across the enterprise.* Just as knowledge is made available to customers, internal customers who are in direct contact with external customers may be able to provide helpful feedback and knowledge.

Tools available for developing CBR systems can be found in AIS in Focus 12.3.

AIS IN FOCUS 12.3

TOOLS FOR DEVELOPING CBR SYSTEMS

Case-Based reasoning systems are usually built with the help of special tools. Some representative tools are listed in the following table. The home page of AI-CBR (www.ai-cbr.org) and the University of Kaiserslautern's case-based reasoning Web site (www.cbr-web.org) provide details and pointers to numerous CBR tools and applications.

Source: AI-CBR, www.ai-cbr.org (searched in July 2003 and checked in Jan 2004).

Vendor and Product(s)	*URL*
AcknoSoft—KATE	www.acknosoft.com
Case Bank Support Systems Inc.—Spotlight	www.casebank.com
Inductive Solutions Inc.—Induce-It	www.inductive.com
Inference Corporation—k-commerce (formerly called CBR3)	www.inference.com or CBR Express, CasePoint, Generator, and WebServer
Intellix—Knowledge Server	www.intellix.com
ServiceSoft—Knowledge Builder and Web Adviser	www.servicesoft.com
TreeTools—HELPDESK-3	www.treetools.com.br

12.4 BASIC CONCEPT OF NEURAL COMPUTING

Neural computing is a problem-solving methodology that attempts to mimic how our brains function. It is one of several successful approaches to machine learning. The resulting model from neural computing is often called an **artificial neural network (ANN)** or a **neural network (NN)**.

The study of neural networks began from a single neuron, called a **perceptron**, which is capable of converting a set of inputs to its outputs. After some initial success, the perceptron model fell into disfavor because it was unable to solve the simple XOR problem. A dramatic resurgence came in the late 1980s, when the multiple-layer architecture was proposed and proved powerful in solving complex problems. This renewed interest developed because of the need for brainlike information processing, advances in computer technology, and progress in neuroscience toward better understanding of the mechanisms of the brain. Potential commercial and military applications with large payoffs also motivated (and funded) this research.

BIOLOGICAL AND ARTIFICIAL NEURAL NETWORKS

The human brain is composed of special cells called **neurons**. These cells do not die when a human is injured (all other cells reproduce to replace themselves and then die). This phenomenon may explain why we retain information. Information storage spans sets of neurons. The estimated number of neurons in a human brain is 50 billion to 150 billion, of which there are more than 100 different kinds. Neurons are partitioned into groups called networks. Each network contains several thousand highly interconnected neurons. Thus, the brain can be viewed as a collection of neural networks.

The ability to learn and react to changes in our environment requires intelligence. Thinking and intelligent behavior are controlled by the brain and the central nervous system. People who suffer brain damage have difficulty learning and reacting to changing environments. Even so, undamaged parts of the brain can often compensate with new learning.

A portion of a network composed of two cells is shown in Figure 12.4. The cell itself includes a **nucleus** (at the center). To the left of cell 1, the **dendrites** provide input signals to the cell. To the right, the **axon** sends output signals to cell 2 via the axon terminals. These axon terminals merge with the dendrites of cell 2. Signals can be transmitted unchanged, or they can be altered by synapses. A **synapse** is able to increase or decrease the strength of the connection from neuron to neuron and cause excitation or inhibition of a subsequent neuron. This is where information is stored.

An artificial neural network model emulates a biological neural network. Neural computing actually uses a very limited set of concepts from biological neural systems (see AIS in Focus 12.4). It is more of an analogy to the human brain than an accurate model of it. Neural concepts are usually implemented as software simulations of the massively parallel processes that involve processing elements (also called *artificial neurons* or *neurodes*) interconnected in a network architecture. The artificial neuron receives inputs analogous to the electrochemical impulses the dendrites of biological neurons receive from other neurons. The output of the artificial neuron corresponds to signals sent out from a biological neuron over its axon. These artificial signals can be changed by weights in a manner similar to the physical changes that occur in the synapses (see Figure 12.5).

It is important to recognize that artificial neural networks were originally proposed to model the human brain's activities. The human brain has much more complexity than the model can capture, so neural computing models are not very accurate

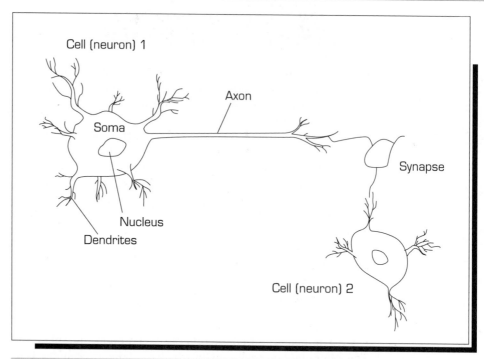

FIGURE 12.4   PORTION OF A NETWORK: TWO INTERCONNECTED BIOLOGICAL CELLS

representations of real biological systems. Despite extensive research in neurobiology and psychology, important questions remain about how the brain and the mind work. Research and development on ANNs continue to produce interesting and useful results that inspire systems that borrow features from biological systems.

ELEMENTS OF ARTIFICIAL NEURAL NETWORKS

A neural network is composed of processing elements organized in different ways to form the network's structure. The basic processing unit is the neuron. A number of neurons are organized into a network. There are many ways to organize neurons, and these are referred to as **topologies**. One popular approach, known as the **feedforward-**

FIGURE 12.5   PROCESSING INFORMATION IN AN ARTIFICIAL NEURON

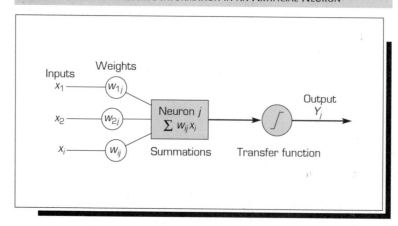

AIS IN FOCUS 12.4

THE RELATIONSHIP BETWEEN BIOLOGICAL AND ARTIFICIAL NEURAL NETWORKS

The list below (Medsker and Liebowitz, 1994, p. 163) shows some of the relationships between biological and artificial networks.

Biological	*Artificial*
Soma	Node
Dendrites	Input
Axon	Output
Synapse	Weight
Slow speed	Fast speed
Many neurons (10^9)	Few neurons (a dozen to hundreds of thousands)

Zahedi (1993) sees a dual role for artificial neural networks (ANNs). We borrow concepts from the biological world to improve the design of computers. ANN technology is used for complex information processing and machine intelligence. And it can also be used as simple biological models to test hypotheses about biological neuronal information processing.

---

backpropagation paradigm (or simply **backpropagation**), allows all neurons to link the output in one layer to the input of the next layer, but does not allow any feedback linkage. This is the most commonly used paradigm (Haykin, 1999, p. 21).

PROCESSING ELEMENTS

The **processing elements (PEs)** of an ANN are artificial neurons. Each of the neurons receives inputs, processes them, and delivers a single output, as shown in Figure 12.5. The input can be raw input data or the output of other processing elements. The output can be the final result (e.g., 1 means yes, 0 means no), or it can be inputs to other neurons.

NETWORK STRUCTURE

Each ANN is composed of a collection of neurons grouped in layers. A typical structure is shown in Figure 12.6. Note the three layers: input, intermediate (called the **hidden layer**), and output. Several hidden layers can be placed between the input and output layers.

Like a biological network, an ANN can be organized in several different ways (topologies or architectures); that is, the neurons can be interconnected in different ways. Therefore, ANNs appear in many configurations called architectures. When information is processed, many of the processing elements perform their computations at the same time. This **parallel processing** resembles the way the brain works, and it differs from the serial processing of conventional computing.

NETWORK INFORMATION PROCESSING

Once the structure of a network is determined, information can be processed. We now present the major concepts related to the processing.

Inputs   Each input corresponds to a single attribute. For example, if the problem is to decide on approval or disapproval of a loan, some attributes could be the applicant's income level, age, and home ownership. The numeric value, or representation, of an attribute is the input to the network. Several types of data, such as text, pictures, and voice, can be used as inputs. Preprocessing may be needed to convert the data to meaningful inputs from symbolic data or to scale the data.

Outputs   The outputs of the network contain the solution to a problem. For example, in the case of a loan application it can be yes or no. The ANN assigns numeric values,

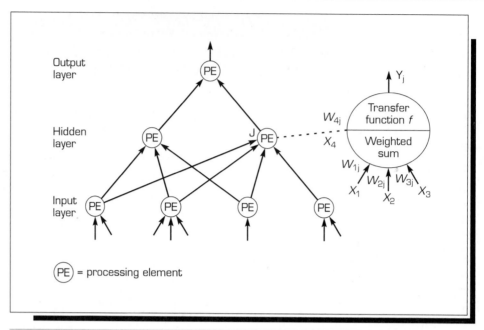

FIGURE 12.6   NEURAL NETWORK WITH ONE HIDDEN LAYER

like 1 for yes and 0 for no. The purpose of the network is to compute the values of the output. When the resulting value is not exactly 0 or 1, postprocessing of the outputs is required.

Connection Weights   **Connection weights** are the key elements in an ANN. They express the relative strength (or mathematical value) of the input data or the many connections that transfer data from layer to layer. In other words, weights express the relative importance of each input to a processing element and ultimately the outputs. Weights are crucial in that they store learned patterns of information. It is through repeated adjustments of weights that the network learns.

Summation Function   The **summation function** computes the weighted sums of all the input elements entering each processing element. A summation function multiplies each input value by its weight and totals the values for a weighted sum Y. The formula for n inputs in one processing element (Figure 12.7a) is

$$Y = \sum_{i=1}^{n} X_i W_i$$

For the jth neuron of several processing neurons in a layer (Figure 12.7b), the formula is

$$Y_j = \sum_{i=1}^{n} X_i W_i$$

Transformation (Transfer) Function   The summation function computes the internal stimulation, or activation level, of the neuron. Based on this level, the neuron may or may not produce an output. The relationship between the internal activation level and the output can be linear or nonlinear. The relationship is expressed by one of several

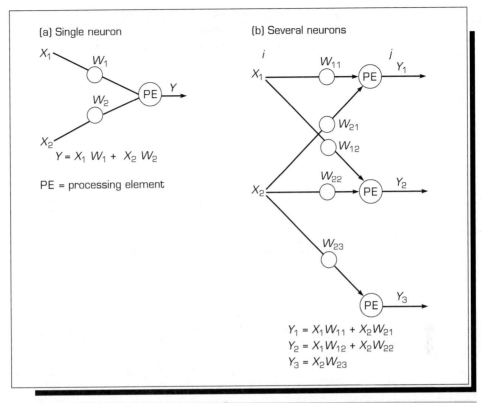

(a) Single neuron

(b) Several neurons

$Y = X_1 W_1 + X_2 W_2$

PE = processing element

$Y_1 = X_1 W_{11} + X_2 W_{21}$
$Y_2 = X_1 W_{12} + X_2 W_{22}$
$Y_3 = X_2 W_{23}$

FIGURE 12.7   SUMMATION FUNCTION FOR SINGLE NEURON (A) AND SEVERAL NEURONS (B)

types of **transformation (transfer) functions**. Selection of the specific function impacts the network's operation. The **sigmoid (logical activation)** function (or **transfer function**) is a popular and useful nonlinear transfer function:

$$Y_T = 1/(1 + e^{-Y})$$

where Y_T is the transformed (normalized) value of Y (see AIS in Focus 12.5).

The transformation modifies the output levels to reasonable values (typically between 0 and 1). This transformation is performed before the output reaches the next level. Without such a transformation, the value of the output becomes very large, especially when there are several layers of neurons. Sometimes, instead of a transformation function, a **threshold value** is used. For example, any value of 0.5 or less becomes 0, and any value above 0.5 becomes 1. A transformation can occur at the output of each processing element, or it can be performed only at the final output nodes.

NEURAL NETWORK ARCHITECTURE

There are several effective neural network models and algorithms (Haykin, 1999). The most popular ones are backpropagation, associative memory, and the recurrent network. The backpropagation architecture is shown in Figure 12.6. The other two architectures are shown in Figures 12.8 and 12.9, respectively.

ASSOCIATIVE MEMORY SYSTEMS

Associative memory is the ability to recall complete situations from partial information. These systems correlate input data with information stored in memory.

AIS IN FOCUS 12.5

EXAMPLE OF ANN FUNCTIONS

Summation function: $Y = 3(0.2) + 1(0.4) + 2(0.1) = 1.2$

Transformation (transfer) function: $Y_T = 1/(1 + e^{-1.2}) = 0.77$

$X_1 = 3$ $W_1 = 0.2$

$X_2 = 1$ $W_2 = 0.4$ Processing element $Y = 1.2$

$X_3 = 2$ $W_3 = 0.1$

Information can be recalled even from incomplete or noisy input. Associative memory systems can detect similarities between new input and stored patterns (Haykin, 1999).

One type of unsupervised learning, **competitive filter associative memory**, can learn by changing its weights in recognition of categories of input data without being given examples in advance. A leading example of such a single-layer, self-organizing system for a fixed number of classes in the inputs is the Kohonen network (Haykin, 1999).

HIDDEN LAYER

Complex practical applications require one or more (hidden) layers between the input and output neurons and a correspondingly large number of weights. Many commercial

---

FIGURE 12.8   NEURAL NETWORK STRUCTURES: FEEDFORWARD FLOW

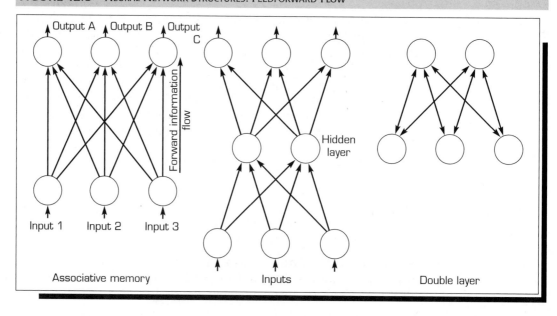

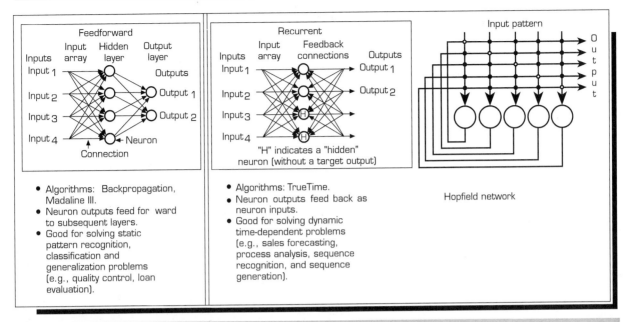

FIGURE 12.9 RECURRENT STRUCTURE COMPARED WITH FEEDFORWARD SOURCE

Source: Based on *PC AI,* May/June 1992, p. 35.

ANNs include three and sometimes up to five layers, with each containing 10–1,000 processing elements. Some experimental ANNs employ millions of processing elements. Since each layer increases the training effort exponentially, the use of more than three hidden layers is rare in most commercial systems because of the amount of computation required.

RECURRENT STRUCTURE

A **recurrent network** (double layer) is one in which an activity must go through the network more than once before the output response is produced. A recurrent structure does not require the knowledge of a precise number of classes in the training data. Instead, it uses a feedforward and feedbackward approach to adjust parameters as data are analyzed to establish arbitrary numbers of categories that represent the data presented to the system.

A well-known simple recurrent network is that of Hopfield, shown in Figure 12.8. Also shown in the figure is a recurrent network that includes neurons without output and a comparison of recurrent and feedforward systems.

12.5 LEARNING IN ARTIFICIAL NEURAL NETWORKS

An important consideration in an artificial neural network is the use of an appropriate learning algorithm (or training algorithm). There are hundreds of them. **Learning algorithms** in ANN can also be classified as supervised learning and unsupervised learning (Figure 12.10).

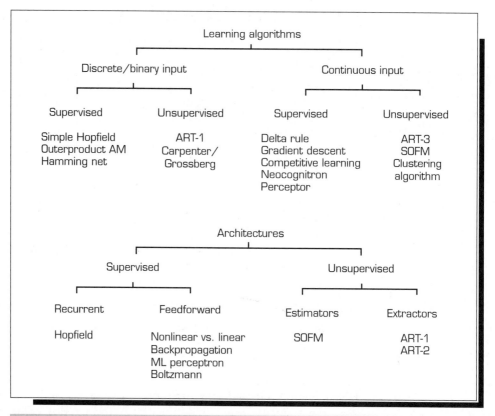

FIGURE 12.10   TAXONOMY OF ANN ARCHITECTURES AND LEARNING ALGORITHMS

Source: Based on L. Medsker and J. Liebowitz, *Design and Development of Expert Systems and Neural Computing,* New York: Macmillan, 1994, p. 166.

Supervised learning uses a set of inputs for which the appropriate (desired) outputs are known. For example, a historical set of loan applications with the success or failure of the individual to repay the loan has a set of input parameters and presumed known outputs. In one type, the difference between the desired and actual outputs is used to calculate corrections to the weights of the neural network. A variation of this approach simply acknowledges for each input trial whether the output is correct as the network adjusts weights in an attempt to achieve correct results. Examples of this type of learning are backpropagation and the Hopfield network.

In **unsupervised learning**, only input stimuli are shown to the network. The network is **self-organizing**; that is, it organizes itself internally so that each hidden processing element responds strategically to a different set of input stimuli (or groups of stimuli). No knowledge is supplied about which classifications (outputs) are correct, and those that the network derives may or may not be meaningful to the network developer (this is useful for cluster analysis).

However, setting model parameters can control the number of categories into which the network classifies the inputs. Regardless, a human must examine the final categories to assign meaning and determine the usefulness of the results. Examples of this type of learning are **adaptive resonance theory (ART)** and **Kohonen self-organizing feature maps**.

GENERAL LEARNING PROCESS

In supervised learning, the learning process is inductive; that is, connection weights are derived from existing cases. The usual process of learning involves three tasks (Figure 12.11):

1. Compute temporary outputs.
2. Compare outputs with desired targets.
3. Adjust the weights and repeat the process.

When existing outputs are available for comparison, the learning process starts by setting the connection weights, either by rules or randomly. The difference between the actual output (Y or Y_T) and the desired output (Z) for a given set of inputs is an error called delta (in calculus, the Greek symbol delta means "difference").

The objective is to minimize the delta (reduce it to 0 if possible), and this is done by adjusting the network's weights. The key is to change the weights in the right direction, making changes that reduce the delta (error). We will show how this is done later.

Information processing with an ANN consists of an attempt to recognize patterns of activities (**pattern recognition**). During the learning stages, the interconnection weights change in response to training data presented to the system.

Different ANNs compute the delta in different ways, depending on the **learning algorithm** being used. There are hundreds of learning algorithms for various situations and configurations, some of which are discussed later.

HOW A NETWORK LEARNS

Consider a single neuron that learns the inclusive OR operation—a classic problem in symbolic logic. There are two input elements, X_1 and X_2. If either or both of them have a positive value, then the result is also positive. This can be shown as

FIGURE 12.11   LEARNING PROCESS OF AN ARTIFICIAL NEURAL NETWORK

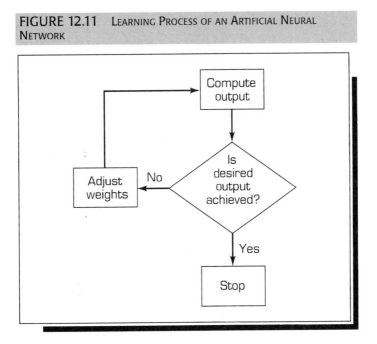

	Inputs		
Case	*X₁*	*X₂*	*Desired Results*
1	0	0	0
2	0	1	1 (positive)
3	1	0	1 (positive)
4	1	1	1 (positive)

The neuron must be trained to recognize the input patterns and classify them to give the corresponding outputs. The procedure is to present to the neuron the sequence of the four input patterns so that the weights are adjusted after each iteration (using feedback of the error found by comparing the estimate to the desired result). This step is repeated until the weights converge to a uniform set of values that allow the neuron to classify each of the four inputs correctly. The results shown in Table 12.5 were produced in Excel. In this simple example, a threshold function is used to evaluate the summation of input values. After calculating outputs, a measure of the error (delta) between the output and the desired values is used to update the weights, subsequently reinforcing the correct results. At any step in the process for a neuron j we have

$$\text{Delta} = Z_j - Y_j$$

where Z and Y are the desired and actual outputs, respectively. Then, the updated weights are

$$W_i(\text{final}) = W_i(\text{initial}) + \text{alpha} \times \text{delta} \times X_1$$

where alpha is a parameter that controls how fast the learning takes place.

As shown in Table 12.5, each calculation uses one of the X_1 and X_2 pairs and the corresponding value for the OR operation along with initial values W_1 and W_2 of the

TABLE 12.5   Example of Supervised Learning

				Initial				*Final*	
Step	*X₁*	*X₂*	*Z*	*W₁*	*W₂*	*Y*	*Delta*	*W₁*	*W₂*
1	0	0	0	0.1	0.3	0	0.0	0.1	0.3
	0	1	1	0.1	0.3	0	1.0	0.1	0.3
	1	0	1	0.1	0.5	0	1.0	0.1	0.5
	1	1	1	0.3	0.5	1	0.0	0.3	0.5
2	0	0	0	0.3	0.5	0	0.0	0.3	0.5
	0	1	1	0.3	0.5	0	0.0	0.3	0.5
	1	0	1	0.3	0.7	0	1.0	0.5	0.7
	1	1	1	0.5	0.7	1	0.0	0.5	0.7
3	0	0	0	0.5	0.7	0	0.0	0.5	0.7
	0	1	1	0.5	0.7	1	0.0	0.5	0.7
	1	0	1	0.5	0.7	0	1.0	0.7	0.7
	1	1	1	0.7	0.7	1	0.0	0.7	0.7
4	0	0	0	0.7	0.7	0	0.0	0.7	0.7
	0	1	1	0.7	0.7	1	0.0	0.7	0.7
	1	0	1	0.7	0.7	1	0.0	0.7	0.7
	1	1	1	0.7	0.7	1	0.0	0.7	0.7

Parameters: alpha = 0.2; threshold = 0.5.

neuron's weights. Initially, the weights are assigned random values, and the learning rate, alpha, is set low. Delta is used to derive the final weights, which then become the initial weights in the next iteration (row).

The initial values of weights for each input are transformed using the above equation to assign the values that are used with the next input (row). The threshold value (0.5) sets the output Y to 1 in the next row if the weighted sum of inputs is greater than 0.5; otherwise, Y is set to 0. In the first step, two of the four outputs are incorrect (delta = 1) and a consistent set of weights has not been found. In subsequent steps, the learning algorithm improves the results until it finally produces a set of weights that give the correct results ($W_1 = W_2 = 0.7$ in step 4 of Table 12.5). Once determined, a neuron with these weight values can quickly perform the OR operation.

In developing an ANN, an attempt is made to fit the problem characteristic to one of the known learning algorithms. There are software programs for all the different algorithms, but it is best to use a well-known and well-characterized one, such as backpropagation, which we describe next.

BACKPROPAGATION

Backpropagation (short for *back error propagation*) is the most widely used supervised learning algorithm in neural computing (Principe et al., 2000). It is very easy to implement. A backpropagation network includes one or more hidden layers. This type of network is considered feedforward because there are no interconnections between the output of a processing element and the input of a node in the same layer or in a preceding layer. Externally provided correct patterns are compared with the neural network's output during (supervised) training, and feedback is used to adjust the weights until all the training patterns are categorized as correctly as possible by the network (the error tolerance is set in advance).

Starting with the output layer, errors between the actual and desired outputs are used to correct the weights for the connections to the previous layer (Figure 12.12). For any output neuron j, the error (delta) = $(Z_j - Y_j)$ (df/dx), where Z and Y are the desired and actual outputs, respectively. The sigmoid function, $f = [1 + \exp(-x)]^{-1}$, is an effective way to compute the output of a neuron in practice, where x is proportional to the sum of the weighted inputs to the neuron. With this function, the derivative of the sigmoid function $df/dx = f(1 - f)$ and the error is a simple function of the desired and actual outputs. The factor $f(1 - f)$ is the *logistic function*, which serves to keep the error

FIGURE 12.12   BACKPROPAGATION OF ERRORS FOR A SINGLE NEURON

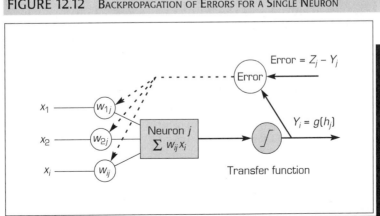

correction well bounded. The weights of each input to the *j*th neuron are then changed in proportion to this calculated error. A more complicated expression can be derived to work backward in a similar way from the output neurons through the hidden layers to calculate the corrections to the associated weights of the inner neurons. This complicated method is an iterative approach to solving a nonlinear optimization problem that is very similar in meaning to the one characterizing multiple linear regression.

The procedures of the learning algorithm are as follows:

> 1. Initialize weights with random values and set other parameters.
> 2. Read in the input vector and the desired output.
> 3. Compute the actual output via the calculations working forward through the layers.
> 4. Compute the error.
> 5. Change the weights by working backward from the output layer through the hidden layers.

The procedure is repeated for the entire set of input vectors until the desired output and the actual output agree within some predetermined tolerance. Given the calculation requirements for one iteration, a large network can take a very long time to train (and thus in one variation, a set of cases are run through and an aggregated error is fed backward to speed up learning). Sometimes, depending on the initial random weights and network parameters, the network does not converge to a satisfactory performance level. If so, new random weights must be generated, and the network parameters or even its structure may have to be modified before another attempt is made. Current research is aimed at developing algorithms and using parallel computers to improve this process. For example, genetic algorithms (described later in this chapter) can be used to guide the selection of the network structure.

12.6 DEVELOPING NEURAL NETWORK–BASED SYSTEMS

Although the development process of ANNs is similar to the structured design methodologies of traditional computer-based information systems, some phases are unique or have some unique aspects. In the process described here, we assume that the preliminary steps of system development, such as determining information requirements, conducting a feasibility analysis, and gaining a champion in top management for the project, have been completed successfully. Such steps are generic to any information system.

As shown in Figure 12.13, the development process for an ANN application includes nine steps. In Step 1, the data to be used for training and testing of the network are collected. Important considerations are that the particular problem is amenable to neural network solution and that adequate data exist and can be obtained. In Step 2 training data must be identified, and a plan must be made for testing the performance of the network.

In Steps 3 and 4, a network architecture and a learning method are selected. The availability of a particular development tool or the capabilities of the development personnel may determine the type of neural network to be constructed. Also, certain problem types have demonstrated high success rates with certain configurations (e.g., multilayer feedforward neural networks for loan application and fraud detection, as in

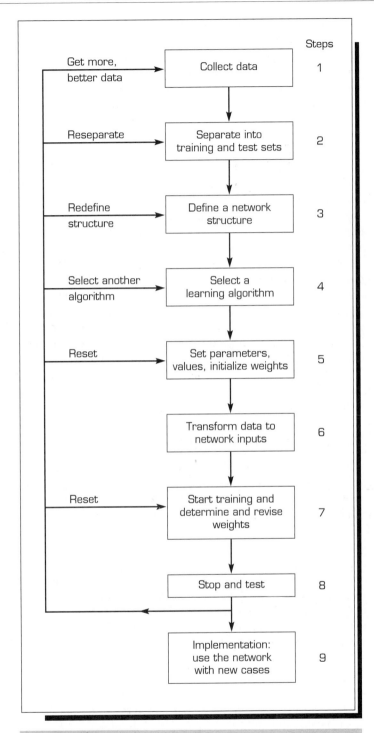

FIGURE 12.13   FLOW DIAGRAM OF THE DEVELOPMENT PROCESS OF AN ARTIFICIAL NEURAL NETWORK

the Opening Vignette). Important considerations are the exact number of neurons and the number of layers (some packages use genetic algorithms to select the network design; see Section 12.10 for details).

There are parameters for tuning the network to the desired learning-performance level. Part of the process in Step 5 is initialization of the network weights and parameters, followed by modification of the parameters as training-performance feedback is received. Often, the initial values are important in determining the efficiency and length of training. Some methods change the parameters during training to enhance performance.

Step 6 transforms the application data into the type and format required by the neural network. This may mean writing software to preprocess the data or performing these operations directly in an ANN package. Data storage and manipulation techniques and processes must be designed for conveniently and efficiently retraining the neural network when needed. The application data representation and ordering often influence the efficiency and possibly the accuracy of the results.

In Steps 7 and 8, training and testing are conducted iteratively by presenting input and desired or known output data to the network. The network computes the outputs and adjusts the weights until the computed outputs are within an acceptable tolerance of the known outputs for the input cases. The desired outputs and their relationships to input data are derived from historical data (a portion of the data collected in Step 1).

In Step 9, a stable set of weights is obtained. Now the network can reproduce the desired outputs, given inputs like those in the training set. The network is ready for use as a standalone system or as part of another software system where new input data will be presented to it and its output will be a recommended decision.

Now let us examine these nine steps in some detail.

DATA COLLECTION AND PREPARATION

The first two steps in the ANN development process involve collecting data and separating them into a training set and a testing set. The training cases are used to adjust the weights, and the testing cases are used for network validation. The data used for training and testing must include all the attributes that are useful for solving the problem. The system can only learn as much the data can tell. Therefore, collection and preparation of data is the most critical step in building a good system.

In general, the more data used, the better. Larger data sets increase processing time during training but improve the accuracy of the training and often lead to faster convergence to a good set of weights. For a moderately sized data set, typically 80 percent of the data are randomly selected for training, 20 percent for testing; for small data sets, typically all the data are used for training and testing; and for large data sets, a sufficiently large sample is taken and treated like a moderately sized data set.

For example, if a bank wants to build a neural network–based system for assessing from clients' financial data whether they may go bankrupt, then it needs to first identify what financial data may be used as inputs and how to obtain them. The following five attributes may be useful inputs: (1) working capital/total assets, (2) retained earnings/total assets, (3) earnings before interest and taxes/total assets, (4) market value of equity/total debt, and (5) sales/total sales. The output is a binary variable: bankruptcy or not.

SELECTION OF NETWORK STRUCTURE

Once the training and testing data sets are identified, the next step is to design the structure of the neural networks. This includes the selection of a topology and determination of (1) input nodes, (2) output nodes, (3) number of hidden layers, and (4) number of hidden nodes. Unless in special situations, the multilayer feedforward topology is often used in business applications.

Design of input nodes must be based on the attributes of the data set. In the example of predicting bankruptcy, we may choose a three-layer structure that includes one input layer, one output layer, and one hidden layer. The input layer contains five nodes, each of which is a variable, and the output layer contains a node with 0 for bankrupt and 1 for safe. Determining the number of hidden nodes is tricky. A few heuristics have been proposed, but none of them is questionably the best. A typical approach is to choose the average number of input and output nodes. In the previous case, the hidden node may be set to (5+1)/2 = 3. Figure 12.14 shows a possible structure for the bankruptcy-prediction problem.

CHOOSING A LEARNING ALGORITHM

Once the network structure is chosen, we need to find a learning algorithm to identify a set of connection weights that best cover the training data and have the best predictive accuracy. For the feedforward topology we chose for the bankruptcy-prediction problem, a typical approach is to use the backpropagation algorithm. Since many commercial packages are available on the market, there is no need to implement the learning algorithm by ourselves. Instead, we choose a suitable commercial package and analyze the data.

NETWORK TRAINING

Training of artificial neural networks is an iterative process that starts from a random set of weights and gradually enhances the fitness of the network model and the known data set. The iteration continues until the error sum is converged to below a preset acceptable level. In the backpropagation algorithm, two parameters, **learning rate** and **momentum**, may be adjusted to control the speed of reaching a solution. These determine the ratio of the difference between the calculated value and actual value of the

FIGURE 12.14   ARCHITECTURE OF THE BANKRUPTCY PREDICTION NEURAL NETWORK

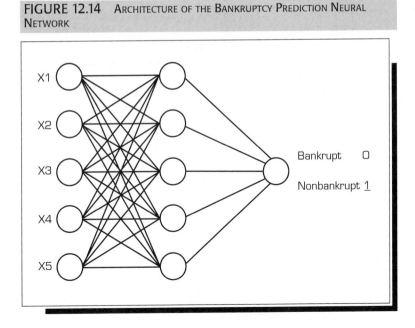

AIS IN FOCUS 12.6

ANN SOFTWARE

There are many tools for developing neural networks (see this book's Web site and the periodic resource lists in *PC AI*, www.pcai.com). Some of these tools function like expert-system shells. They provide a set of standard architectures, learning algorithms, and parameters along with the ability to manipulate the data. Some development tools can support up to several dozen network paradigms and learning algorithms. In addition to the standard products, there are many specialized products (e.g., Database Mining Marksman, HNC Software Inc.; NeuroShell Professional by the Ward Systems Group).

Some ANN development tools are spreadsheet add-ins. Most can read spreadsheet, database, and text files. Some are freeware or shareware. Some ANN systems have been developed in Java to run directly on the Web, accessible through a Web browser interface. Other ANN products are designed to interface with expert systems as hybrid development products.

The use of ANN tools is constrained by their configuration. Developers may instead prefer to use more general programming languages, such as C++, or a spreadsheet to program the model and perform the calculations. A variation on this is to use a library of ANN routines. hav.Software (www.hav.com) provides a library of C++ classes for implementing standalone or embedded feedforward, simple recurrent, and random-order recurrent neural networks.

A number of neural network shells can generate code, usually C++, that can be embedded in another system that can access source data or is called directly by a GUI for deployment independent of the development system. Or, after training an ANN in a development tool, given the weights, network structure, and transfer function, one can easily develop one's own implementation in a third-generation programming language such as C++. Some of the more popular or useful ANN development packages are BrainMaker, NeuroShell Easy, SPSS Neural Connection, NeuroSolutions, and NeuralWare.

---

training cases. Some software packages may have their own parameters in their learning heuristics to speed up the learning process. You need to read carefully when using these software.

Some data conversion may be necessary in the training process. This includes (1) changing the data format to meet the requirements of the software, (2) normalization of the data scale to make them more comparable, and (3) removing problematic data. Once the training data set is ready, it is loaded into the package and the learning procedure is executed. Depending upon the number of nodes and the size of the training data set, reaching a solution may take from a few thousands to millions of iterations.

TESTING

Recall that in Step 2 of the development process (Figure 12.14) the available data are divided into training and testing data sets. Once the training has been completed, it is necessary to test the network. The testing (Step 8) examines the performance of the derived network model by measuring its ability to classify the testing data correctly. **Black-box testing** (comparing test results to historical results) is the primary approach for verifying that inputs produce the appropriate outputs. Error terms can be used to compare results against known benchmark methods.

The network is generally not expected to perform perfectly (zero error is difficult, if not impossible, to attain), and only a certain level of accuracy is really required. For example, if 1 means non-bankrupt and 0 means bankrupt, then any output between 0.1 and 1 might indicate a certain likelihood of non-bankrupt. The neural network application is usually an alternative to another method that can be used as a benchmark with which to compare accuracy. For example, a statistical technique such as multiple regression or another quantitative method may be known to classify inputs correctly 50 percent of the time.

The neural network implementation often improves on this. For example, Liang (1992) reported that ANN performance was superior to the performance of multiple discriminant analysis and rule induction. Ainscough and Aronson (1999) investigated the application of neural network models in predicting retail sales given a set of several inputs (regular price, various promotions, etc.). They compared their results to those of multiple regression and improved the adjusted R^2 (correlation coefficient) from .5 to .7. If the neural network is replacing manual operations, performance levels and speed of human processing can be the standard for deciding whether the testing phase is successful.

The test plan should include routine cases as well as potentially problematic situations. If the testing reveals large deviations, the training set must be reexamined and the training process may have to be repeated (some "bad" data may have to be omitted from the input set). Note that one cannot equate neural network results exactly with those found by statistical methods. For example, in stepwise linear regression, input variables are sometimes determined to be insignificant, but because of the nature of neural computing, a neural network uses them to attain higher levels of accuracy. When they are omitted from a neural network model, its performance typically suffers.

IMPLEMENTATION

Implementation of an ANN (Step 9) often requires interfaces with other computer-based information systems and user training. Ongoing monitoring and feedback to the developers are recommended for system improvements and long-term success. It is also important to gain the confidence of users and management early in the deployment to ensure that the system is accepted and used properly.

APPLICATIONS OF ANN

Artificial neural networks have been applied in many domains. A survey of their applications in finance can be found in Fadlalla and Lin (2001). Recent reports include live intrusion tracking (Thaler, 2002), Web-content filtering (Lee et al., 2002), exchange-rate prediction (Davis et al., 2001), and hospital-bed allocation (Walczak, 2002).

In general, ANNs are suitable for problems whose inputs are both categorical and numerical and the relationships between inputs and outputs are not linear, or the input data are not normally distributed. In such cases, general statistical methods are not reliable. Since ANNs do not make any assumptions about the data distribution, their power is less affected than traditional statistical methods when data are not properly distributed.

12.7 GENETIC ALGORITHM FUNDAMENTALS

Genetic algorithms are sets of computational procedures that conceptually follow steps inspired by the biological processes of evolution. Better and better solutions evolve from previous generations until an optimal or near-optimal solution is obtained.

Genetic algorithms (also known as *evolutionary algorithms*) demonstrate *self-organization* and *adaptation* in much the same way that the fittest biological organisms survive and reproduce. The method *learns* by producing offspring that are better and better as measured by a fitness (to survive) function. Algorithms of this type have been applied to problems like vehicle routing (Baker and Syechew, 2003), bankruptcy prediction (Shin and Lee, 2000), and Web search (Nick and Themis, 2001).

EXAMPLE 1: THE VECTOR GAME

To illustrate how genetic algorithms work, we describe the Vector game (Walbridge, 1989). This game is similar to MasterMind. As your opponent gives you clues about how good your guess is (a fitness function), you create a new solution using knowledge of the current solutions and their quality.

DESCRIPTION

Vector is played against an opponent who secretly writes down a string of six digits (in a genetic algorithm, this string consists of chromosomes). Each digit can be either 0 or 1. For this example, the secret number is 001010. You must try to guess this number as quickly as possible. You present a number (a guess) to your opponent, and he or she tells you how many of the digits (but not which ones) you guessed are correct (the fitness function or quality of your guess). For example, the guess 110101 has no correct digits (score = 0). The guess 111101 has only one correct digit (the third one). Thus, the score (the fitness, or value, of the solution) = 1.

RANDOM TRIAL AND ERROR

There are 64 possible six-digit strings of numbers. If you pick numbers at random, it will take, on average, 32 guesses to obtain the right answer. Can you do it faster? Yes, if you can interpret the feedback provided to you by your opponent (a measure of the goodness or fitness of your guess). This is how a genetic algorithm works.

GENETIC ALGORITHM SOLUTION

Step 1:   Present to your opponent four strings selected at random. (Select four arbitrarily. Through experimentation, you may find that five or six would be better.) Assume that you have selected these four:

> (A)   110100; for a score = 1 (one digit correctly guessed)
> (B)   111101; score = 1
> (C)   011011; score = 4
> (D)   101100; score = 3

Because none of the strings is entirely correct, continue.

Step 2:   Delete (A) and (B) because of their low scores. Call (C) and (D) parents.
Step 3:   "Mate" the parents by splitting each number as shown between the second and third digits (the position of the split is randomly selected):

> (C)   01:1011
> (D)   10:1100

Now combine the first two digits of (C) with the last four of (D) (this is called *crossover*). The result is (E), the first offspring:

> (E)   011100; score = 3

Similarly, combine the first two digits of (D) with the last four of (C). The result is (F), the second offspring:

(F)   101011; score = 4

It looks as though the offspring are not doing much better than the parents.

Step 4:   Now copy the original (C) and (D).

Step 5:   Mate and crossover the new parents, but use a different split. Now you have two new offspring, (G) and (H):

(C)   0110:11
(D)   1011:00
(G)   0110:00; score = 4
(H)   1011:11; score = 3

Next, repeat Step 2: Select the best "couple" from all the previous solutions to reproduce. You have several options, such as (G) and (C). Select (G) and (F). Now duplicate and crossover. Here are the results:

(F)   1:01011
(G)   0:11000
(I)   111000; score = 3
(J)   001011; score = 5

You can also generate more offspring:

(F)   101:011
(G)   011:000
(K)   101000; score = 4
(L)   011011; score = 4

Now repeat the processes with (J) and (K) as parents, and duplicate the crossover:

(J)   00101:1
(K)   10100:0
(M)   001010; score = 6

This is it! You have reached the solution after 13 guesses. Not bad when compared to the average of 32 for a random guess out of 64 possibilities.

Note: Using common sense and logic, this problem can be solved faster. However, the example is easy to follow; if the problem is complex, the logical solution is not as obvious. We outline the general genetic algorithm process in Figure 12.15.

GENETIC ALGORITHM DEFINITION AND PROCESS

A genetic algorithm is an iterative procedure that represents its candidate solutions as strings of genes called **chromosomes** and measures their viability with a fitness function. The *fitness function* is a measure of the objective to be obtained (maximum or minimum). As in biological systems, candidate solutions combine to produce offspring in each algorithmic iteration called a *generation*. The offspring themselves can become candidate solutions. From the generation of parents and children, a set of the fittest survive to become parents that produce offspring in the next generation. Offspring are produced by specific genetic operators that include reproduction, crossover, and mutation:

- *Reproduction.* Through **reproduction**, genetic algorithms produce new generations of improved solutions by selecting parents with higher fitness ratings or by giving such parents a greater probability of being contributors and by using random selection.

- *Crossover.* Many genetic algorithms use strings of binary symbols for chromosomes, as in our Vector game, to represent solutions. **Crossover** means choosing a random position in the string (e.g., after two digits) and exchanging the segments either to the right or the left of this point with another string partitioned similarly to produce two new offspring.

- *Mutation.* This genetic operator was not shown in the game. **Mutation** is an arbitrary change in a situation. Sometimes it is used to prevent the algorithm from getting stuck. The procedure changes a 1 to a 0 or a 0 to a 1 instead of duplicating them. This change occurs with a very low probability (say, 1 in 1,000).

FIGURE 12.15   FLOW DIAGRAM OF THE GENETIC ALGORITHM PROCESS

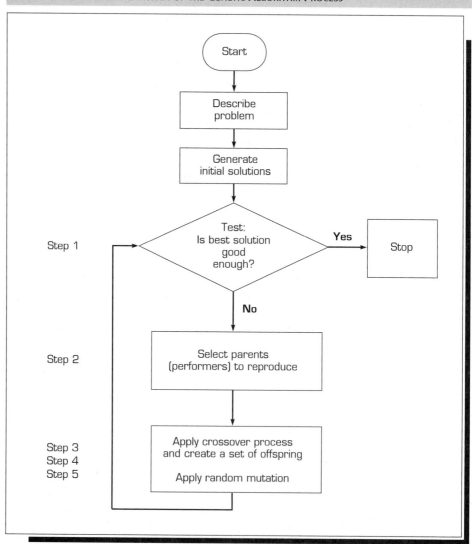

HOW A GENETIC ALGORITHM WORKS

Figure 12.15 is a flow diagram of a typical genetic algorithm process. The problem to be solved must be described in a manner amenable to solution by a genetic algorithm. Typically, this means that a string of 1s and 0s can represent a solution, and that an easily computed fitness function, which we assume is to be maximized, can be established. (In the general case, integers or continuous variables can be used; minimization presents no conceptual problem.) An initial set of solutions is generated, and their fitness functions are computed. The sum of the fitness functions is computed, and each solution's probability of being selected to generate a pair of offspring is equal to its fitness function divided by the sum.

A set of new offspring is generated through crossover and a small random amount of mutation. Parents are selected based on the probability distribution described above. The next generation consists of a set of the best new offspring and parents. The process continues until a good enough solution is obtained, an optimum is guaranteed, or no improvement occurs over several generations.

A few parameters must be set for the genetic algorithm. Their values are dependent on the problem being solved and are usually determined by trial and error.

- Number of initial solutions to generate.
- Number of offspring to generate.
- Number of parents and offspring to keep for the next generation.
- Mutation probability (very low).
- Probability distribution of crossover point occurrence (generally equally weighted).

Sometimes these parameters can be varied for better performance while the algorithm is running. For more information on the methodology, see Goldberg (1989, 1994), Mitchell (1999), Niettinen (1999), and Reed and Marks (1999).

EXAMPLE 2: THE KNAPSACK PROBLEM

The knapsack problem is a conceptually simple optimization problem that can be solved directly with analytical methods. Even so, it is ideal for illustrating a genetic algorithm approach. You are going on an overnight hike and have a number of items that you could take along. Each item has a weight (in pounds) and a benefit or value to you on the hike (say, in U.S. dollars), and you can take one, at most, of each item (sorry, no partial items allowed—it's all or nothing). There is a capacity limit on the weight you can carry (only one constraint, but there can be several measures and capacities including volume, time, etc.). The knapsack problem has many important applications, including determining what items to carry on a space shuttle mission. For our example, there are seven items, numbered 1 through 7, with respective benefits and weights as follows:

Item	1	2	3	4	5	6	7
Benefit	5	8	3	2	7	9	4
Weight	7	8	4	10	4	6	4

The knapsack holds a maximum of 22 pounds. The string 1010100, with a total benefit or fitness of 7 + 4 + 4 = 15, can represent a solution of items 1, 3, and 5.

We set up the problem in an Excel worksheet, where we represent a solution as a string of seven 1s and 0s, and the fitness function as the total benefit, which is the sum of the gene values in a string solution times their respective benefit coefficients. The method generates a set of random solutions (initial parents), uses the objective functions (total benefit) for the fitness function, and selects parents ran-

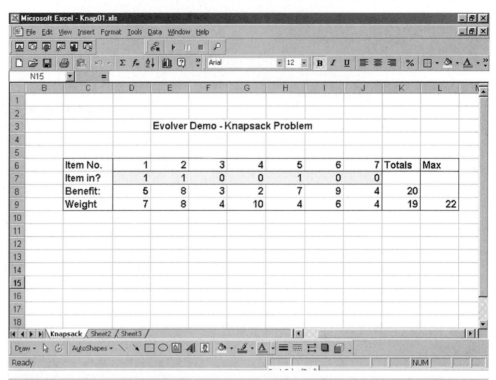

FIGURE 12.16 EVOLVER SOLUTION TO THE KNAPSACK PROBLEM EXAMPLE

domly to create generations of offspring by crossover and mutation operations. Selection is statistically based on the parents' fitness values. Higher values are more likely to be selected than lower ones. In Figure 12.16, we show the best solution found by Evolver, an easy-to-use Excel add-in genetic algorithm package (Palisade Software, www.palisade.com; demo available online).

12.8 DEVELOPING GENETIC ALGORITHM APPLICATIONS

Genetic algorithms are a type of machine learning for representing and solving complex problems. They provide a set of efficient, domain-independent search heuristics for a broad spectrum of applications, including:

- Dynamic process control
- Induction of optimization of rules
- Discovering new connectivity topologies (e.g., neural computing connections, i.e., neural network design)
- Simulating biological models of behavior and evolution
- Complex design of engineering structures
- Pattern recognition
- Scheduling
- Transportation and routing
- Layout and circuit design

- Telecommunication
- Graph-based problems

A genetic algorithm interprets information that enables it to reject inferior solutions and accumulate good ones, and thus it learns about its universe. Genetic algorithms are also suitable for parallel processing (Mitchell, 1999).

Over the last decade, the number of successful business applications of genetic algorithms has been increasing. For example, since 1993 Channel 4 television (England) has been using a genetic algorithm (embedded in an ES) to schedule its commercials to maximize revenues (see the Attar Software Ltd. Web site, www.attar.com, and *ComputerWorld*, December 20, 1993). And a team of researchers at the Electrotechnical Laboratory (ETL) in Japan has developed a hardware-implemented genetic algorithm on a central processing unit (CPU) chip that minimizes the impact of imperfect clock cycles in integrated-circuit fabrication variations. They have demonstrated that increasing the chip yield rate from 2.9 percent to 51.1 percent clears the path toward inexpensive gigahertz clock rate CPUs for PCs (Johnson, 1999).

Examples of genetic algorithms applied to real problems include assembly-line balancing (Kim et al., 1998; Rao, 1998) (see AIS In Action 12.7), facility layout (Tavakkoli-Moghaddain and Shayan, 1998), machine and job shop scheduling (Cheng et al., 1999; Liu and Tang, 1999; Norman and Bean, 2000), production planning (Hung et al., 1999), industrial packing and cutting (Hopper and Turton, 1999), assigning tasks to earth-observing satellites (Wolfe and Sorensen, 2000), construction scheduling with limited resources (Leu and Chung, 1999), utility pricing (Wu, 1999), personnel planning (Easton and Nashat, 1999), sawmill board-cut selection (Ferrar and King, 1999), scheduling ship maintenance for a large fleet (Deris et al., 1999), solving routing problems based on the traveling salesperson problem (Baker and Syechow, 2003; Hwang et al., 1999; Schmitt and Amini, 1998), design and improvement of water-distribution systems and similar networks (Castillo and Gonzalez, 1998; Roe, 1998), and determining creditworthiness and aircraft design (Rao, 1998). Several applications are listed in Goldberg (1994), Koza (1992), and Kumar and Gupta (1995). These include driver scheduling for a public transportation system, job shop scheduling, vehicle routing (Baker and Syechew, 2003), and Web searching (Ncik and Themis, 2001). AIS in Action 12.7 describes a real-world application. Genetic algorithms are often used to improve the performance of other AI methods such as expert systems or neural networks. A role genetic algorithms play in neural networks is to dynamically adjust to find the optimal network weights (Kuo and Chen, 2004). The integration of multiple methods is discussed in Section 12.10.

Since the kernel of genetic algorithms is pretty simple, it is not difficult to write computer codes to implement them. For better performance, there are software packages available on the market. A brief description is provided in AIS in Focus 12.8.

12.9 FUZZY LOGIC FUNDAMENTALS

Fuzzy logic deals with the kind of uncertainty that is inherently human in nature. This technique, which uses the mathematical theory of **fuzzy sets** (Jamshidi et al., 1997; Klir and Yuan, 1995; McNeill and Freiberger, 1993; Nguyen and Walker, 1999), simulates the process of normal human reasoning by allowing the computer to behave less precisely and logically than conventional computer methods require.

The thinking behind this approach is that decision-making is not always a matter of black and white or true or false; it often involves gray areas, that is, maybe. In

AIS IN ACTION 12.7

GENETIC ALGORITHMS SCHEDULE ASSEMBLY LINES AT VOLVO TRUCKS NORTH AMERICA

The buyer of a Volvo 770 trailer cab has dozens of choices: engine size, paint color, fabric, wood-grain finish, stereo, type of suspension, axles, bumpers, pneumatic systems, transmissions, and so on. When the cost is more than $100,000 and the time to be spent in the cab is about 2,000 hours a year, the buyer should have plenty of options. This leads to millions of configurations in which Volvo can build a truck. When a specific truck is to be built, all the tools and parts must be available, but this is difficult to schedule with so many possible combinations.

Gus N. Riley is responsible for scheduling the assembly line in Volvo's million-square-foot factory in Dublin, Virginia. He must cope with hundreds of constraints. Until 1995 Riley solved this operations research problem by eyeballing the production requirements for each week (average output is 550 trucks) and sorting color-coded punch cards, each representing one truck and its characteristics that might affect scheduling. It took four days to construct a week's schedule, and there were always bottlenecks as conditions changed on the factory floor.

In August 1996 Volvo installed OptiFlex (I2 Technologies), which uses genetic algorithms to evolve a good schedule from a sequence of so-so schedules. Jeffrey Herrmann, a vice president at I2 Technologies, explains, "You tell it what the production at the end of a

period should be and then you go have a cup of coffee." The program randomly devises 100 feasible solutions and ranks them according to cost, labor constraints, materials availability, and productivity. Then the program connects parts of good schedules to parts of other ones in an effort to find even better solutions. The process is similar to cattle breeding (but much faster).

The offspring of these genetic pairings are thrown into the pool, which is evaluated and ranked again. The pool is always kept at 100 by deleting poorer solutions. Running through roughly five iterations a second, it comes up with maybe not the best possible schedule, but a good one, in minutes.

Each Wednesday Riley feeds in data to make the weekly schedule five weeks out. He eyeballs it and tinkers with it by tightening some constraints and loosening others. He catches errors in data entry. OptiFlex, running on a Pentium PC connected to the factory network, accepts corrections and quickly generates new solutions. Creating a schedule takes only one day instead of four. And reworking the schedule because of unforeseen events, such as customers changing their minds about features or broken equipment, takes only minutes.

Source: Adapted from S. S. Rao, "Evolution at Warp Speed," *Forbes*, Vol. 161, No. 1, January 12, 1998, pp. 82–83.

---

fact, creative decision-making processes are unstructured, playful, contentious, and rambling.

Fuzzy logic can be useful because it is an effective and accurate way to describe human perceptions of decision-making problems. Most situations are not 100 percent true or false. There are many control and decision-making problems that do not easily fit into the strict true–false situation required by mathematical models; or if they can be described this way, it is not the best way to do so. A recent introduction to fuzzy logic can be found in Dwinnell (2002).

Let's look at an example of a fuzzy set that describes a tall person. If we survey people to define the minimum height a person must attain before being considered tall, the answers could range from 5 to 7 feet (1 foot is about 30 cm., 1 inch is 2.54 cm.). The distribution of answers may look like this:

Height	Proportion Voted for
5'10"	0.05
5'11"	0.10
6'	0.60
6'1"	0.15
6'2"	0.10

AIS IN FOCUS 12.8

GENETIC ALGORITHM SOFTWARE

Many genetic algorithm codes are available for free (search the Web for research and commercial sites), and there are, as well, a number of commercial packages with online demos. Representative commercial packages include Evolver, an Excel spreadsheet add-in (Palisade Software, www.palisade.com) and XpertRule GenAsys, an ES shell with an embedded genetic algorithm (Attar Software, www.attar.com). Genetic algorithms are also related to artificial life scenarios, such as John Conway's Game of Life (e.g., Stephen Stuart's Java implementation at www.tech.org/stuart/life/). Figure 12.17 shows a sample screen of Evolver.

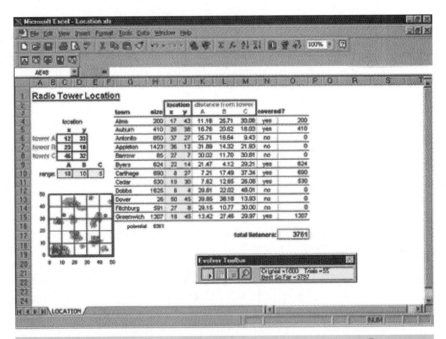

FIGURE 12.17   A SCREENSHOT OF GENETIC ALGORITHM APPLICATIONS IN EVOLVER

Suppose that Jack is 6 feet tall. From probability theory, we can use the cumulative probability distribution and say there is a 75 percent chance that Jack is tall.

In fuzzy logic, we say that Jack's degree of membership in the set of tall people is 0.75. The difference is that in probability terms Jack is perceived as either tall or not tall, and we are not completely sure whether he is tall. In contrast, in fuzzy logic we agree that Jack is more or less tall. Then we can assign a membership function to show the relationship of Jack to the set of tall people (the fuzzy logic set):

$$<Jack, 0.75 \equiv Tall>$$

This can be expressed in a knowledge-based system as "Jack is tall" (CF = 0.75). An important difference from probability theory is that related memberships do not have to total 1. For example, the statement "Jack is short" (CF = 0.15) indicates that the combination is only 0.90. In probability theory, if the probability that Jack is tall is .75, then the probability that he is not tall (i.e., that he is short, assuming only two events) must be .25.

In contrast to certainty factors that include two values (e.g., the degrees of belief and disbelief), fuzzy sets use a spectrum of possible values called belief functions. We

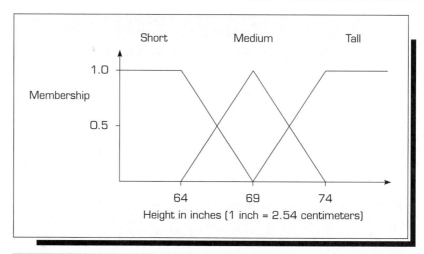

FIGURE 12.18   MEMBERSHIP FUNCTIONS IN FUZZY SETS

express our belief that a particular item belongs to a set through a membership function, as shown in Figure 12.18. At a height of 69 inches, a person starts to be considered tall, and at 74 inches he or she is definitely tall. Between 69 and 74 inches, the person's membership function value varies from 0 to 1. Likewise, a person has a membership function value in the set of short people and medium-height people, depending on his or her height. The medium range spans both the short and tall ranges, and so a person has a belief of potentially being a member of more than one fuzzy set at a time. This is a critical strength of fuzzy sets; they lack crispness, yet they are consistent in their logic.

The application of fuzzy logic to managerial decision support has recently been gaining momentum despite the fact that it is complex to develop, requires considerable computing power, and is difficult to explain to users. However, with increasing computational power and software, the situation has been changing since the 1990s.

FUZZY LOGIC APPLICATIONS

Fuzzy logic is difficult to apply when people supply the membership information. The problems range from linguistic vagueness to difficulty in supplying the definitions needed. Fuzzy logic is being used extensively in the area of consumer products where the input is provided by sensors rather than by people. Some examples are air-conditioners, antilock brakes, toasters, video camcorders, dishwashers, and microwaves (see AIS in Focus 12.9). Fuzzy logic in consumer products is sometimes called *continuous logic* (after all, who wants a fuzzy camcorder?). Fuzzy logic provides smooth motion in consumer products. This is appropriate for subway control systems and for other motor controls and navigation (Bartos, 1999; Hengl, 2002; McFetridge and Ibrahim, 1998).

Many fuzzy logic applications in the area of controls have been reported. For example. James (2000) describes the application of fuzzy logic to paper mill automation. Machacha and Bhattacharya (2000) apply fuzzy logic to project selection. Fuzzy logic has also proven accurate in predicting accident risk (Anonymous, 2000) and software risk assessment (Xu et al., 2003). We next describe three fuzzy logic applications.

AIS IN FOCUS 12.9

FUZZY LOGIC APPLICATIONS

Fuzzy logic has been applied to the following areas:

- Selecting stocks to purchase (e.g., the Japanese Nikkei stock exchange)
- Retrieving data (fuzzy logic can find data quickly)
- Regulating antilock braking systems in cars
- Autofocusing in cameras
- Automating the operation of laundry machines
- Building environmental controls
- Controlling the image position in video cameras
- Controlling the motion of trains
- Identifying the dialect of orca whales

- Inspecting beverage cans for printing defects
- Keeping space shuttle vehicles in steady orbit
- Matching golf clubs to customers' swings
- Regulating water temperature in showerheads
- Controlling the amount of oxygen in cement kilns
- Increasing accuracy and speed in industrial quality-control applications
- Sorting problems in multidimensional spaces
- Enhancing models involving queuing (waiting lines)
- Decision-making

EXAMPLE 3: FUZZY STRATEGIC PLANNING

Hall (1987) developed STRATASSIST, a fuzzy expert system that helps small- to medium-sized firms plan strategically for a single product. During a consultation, STRATASSIST asks questions in five areas that a firm should consider in evaluating its own strengths and weaknesses:

- Threat of substitutes
- Threat of new entries
- Buyer group power
- Supplier group power
- Rivalry within the industry.

Each question asks the user to rate the firm along these dimensions. STRATASSIST feeds the answers into its fuzzy knowledge base, which consists of rules such as

IF the importance of personal service in the distribution of your product is at least more or less high,

THEN strategic action should be to distribute the firm's product or service through small, flexible, local units.

Hall used uncommonly rigorous experimental design procedures to test STRATASSIST's effectiveness. He asked MBA students to develop strategic plans for a fictional company. One-third of the students used STRATASSIST output in their planning, one-third used answers to the questions in the five strength/weakness areas, and one-third worked without STRATASSIST. Twelve expert judges from academia and industry rated the students' plans. The students who used STRATASSIST were judged to have formulated significantly better strategies than the others. See Hutchinson (1998) and Dwinnell (2002) for additional applications of fuzzy logic in decision-making.

EXAMPLE 4: FUZZINESS IN REAL ESTATE

In conducting property appraisals it is necessary to use judgment to generate estimates. Experience and intuition are essential factors. Some of the needed estimates are land value, value of buildings, building replacement costs, and the amount the building has appreciated. Then it is necessary to review sales of comparable properties, decide what is relevant, and finally estimate the net income.

Most of the above data are fuzzy. Using a program called FuziCalc, a spreadsheet program modeled on Excel, Dilmore (1995) facilitated the appraisal process, making it faster and more accurate. See Bagnoli and Smith (1998) for additional fuzzy logic applications in real estate.

EXAMPLE 5: A FUZZY BOND-EVALUATION SYSTEM

The value of bonds depends on such factors as company profitability, assets and liability, market volatility, and even foreign exchange risk (for foreign bonds). There is considerable fuzziness in factors like foreign exchange risk. Chorafas (1994) constructed a fuzzy logic system that helps in making decisions about investing in bonds. The results indicate superior values over an average noncomputerized bond evaluation.

New applications of fuzzy logic are continually being developed because of its effectiveness. For example, a fuzzy logic system was proposed for terrorist detection (Cox, 2001). For other applications, see Derra (1999), Gungor and Arikan (2000), Liao (2003), Xu et al. (2003), Yuan et al. (2002).

12.10 DEVELOPING INTEGRATED ADVANCED SYSTEMS

Neural computing, expert systems, genetic algorithms, and fuzzy logic are effective ways to deal with complex problems efficiently. Each method handles uncertainty and ambiguity differently, and these technologies can often be blended to utilize the best features of each, achieving impressive results. For example, a combination of neural computing and fuzzy logic can result in synergy that improves speed, fault tolerance, and adaptiveness.

There are many real-world applications of intelligent systems integration. These include the United Technologies Carrier product-reliability system, which integrates a rule-based system and a neural network (Deng and Tsacle, 2000; Moon et al., 1998), plastic molding control—integrating neural networks and fuzzy logic (Mapleston, 1999), construction price estimation—integrating expert system and neural network (Li and Love, 1999), forecasting—integrating genetic algorithms and fuzzy logic (Cox, 1999; Li and Kwan, 2003), motor control—integrating neural networks, expert systems, and fuzzy logic (Bartos, 1999), and the prediction and optimization of a ceramic casting process—integrating neural networks and fuzzy logic (Kuo and Chen, 2004; Lam et al., 2000). The sections that follow show a few alternatives for integration of multiple methods.

FUZZY NEURAL NETWORKS

Fuzzy neural networks combine fuzzy logic with artificial neural networks. The integration can be either way. The input and output variables can be processed by the fuzzy logic before entering the neural networks for learning. This step is called **fuzzification**. The neural network takes the fuzzified input and output to derive a model. The model is then converted back to the original input and output scales. This step is called **defuzzification**. The output of the "defuzzified" fuzzy system can further become the input to another intelligent system. This kind of integration can also be applied to fuzzy decision trees and fuzzy expert systems. Combining fuzzy logic with rule induction produces fuzzy rules (Dubois et al., 2003; Jeng et al., 1996). We describe an example of combining fuzzy logic with ANNs next.

EXAMPLE 6: INTERNATIONAL STOCK SELECTION

An international investment company uses a combination of fuzzy logic and artificial neural networks (called FuzzyNet) to forecast the expected returns from stocks, cash, bonds, and other assets to determine the optimal allocation of assets. Because the company invests in global markets, it is first necessary to determine the creditworthiness of various countries, based on past and estimated performances of key socioeconomic ratios, and then select specific stocks based on company, industry, and economic data. The final stock portfolio must be adjusted according to the forecast of foreign exchange rates, interest rates, and so forth, which are handled by a currency exposure analysis. The integrated network architecture of the system is shown in Figure 12.19. The integrated system includes the following technologies:

- *Expert system.* The system provides the necessary knowledge for both country and stock selection (rule-based system).
- *Neural network.* The neural network conducts forecasting based on the data included in the database.

FIGURE 12.19 FuzzyNet Architecture

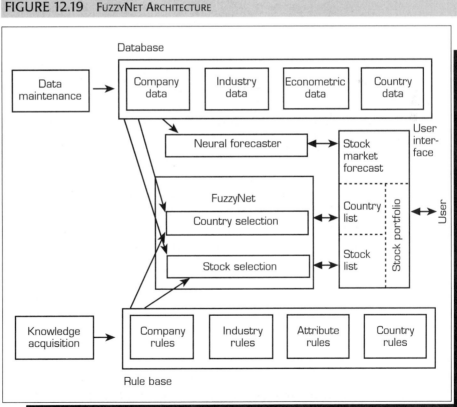

Source: F. Wong et al., "Neural Networks, Genetic Algorithms, and Fuzzy Logic for Forecasting," *Proceedings, International Conference on Advanced Trading Technologies,* New York, July 1992, p. 48. Adapted, with permission, from *Financial Analysts Journal,* Jan./Feb. 1992. Copyright 1992, Association for Investment Management and Research, Charlottesville, VA. All rights reserved.

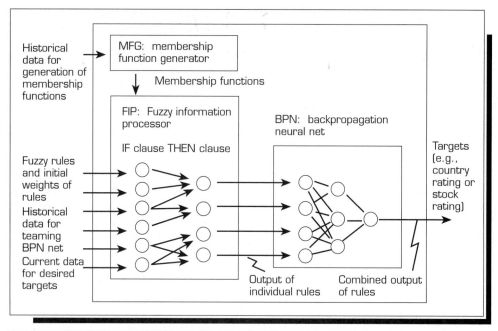

FIGURE 12.20   INFORMATION FLOW IN FUZZYNET

Source: Adapted, with permission, from *Financial Analysts Journal,* Jan./Feb. 1992. Copyright 1992, Association for Investment Management and Research, Charlottesville, VA. All rights reserved.

- *Fuzzy logic.* The fuzzy logic component supports the assessment of factors for which there are no reliable data. For example, the credibility of rules in the rule base is given only as a probability. Therefore, the conclusion of the rule can be expressed either as a probability or as a fuzzy membership degree.

The rule base feeds into FuzzyNet (Figure 12.20) along with data from the database. FuzzyNet is composed of three modules: a membership function generator (MFG), a fuzzy information processor (FIP), and a backpropagation neural network (BPN). The modules are interconnected, and each performs a different task in the decision process.

GENETIC ALGORITHMS AND NEURAL NETWORKS

The genetic learning method can perform rule discovery in large databases, with the rules fed into the conventional expert system or some other intelligent system. A typical way to integrate genetic algorithms with neural network models is to use a genetic algorithm to search for potential weights associated with network connections. A good genetic learning method can significantly reduce the time and effort necessary to find the optimal neural network model. Kim and Han (2002) developed a hybrid system to conduct activity-based costing. Wang (2003) presents a hybrid intelligent method for modeling EDM process. Integration of rules and case-based reasoning is also a good way of improving rule-based systems (Marling et al., 2002).

By using several advanced technologies it is possible to handle a broader range of information and solve more complex problems (see AIS in Action 12.10). This concept is valid not only in cutting-edge technologies but also in any integration of decision models.

HYBRID EXPERT AND FUZZY LOGIC SYSTEM DISPATCHES TRAINS

The Carajás line is one of the busiest railway routes and leading carriers of iron ore in the world. The 892-kilometer-long single-track line connects São Luís harbor with the Carajás iron ore mine in the state of Pará in the Amazon (Brazil). The line has become even busier because a unique real-time knowledge-based system is increasing its productivity and reducing its operating costs, without compromising safety.

Train dispatchers try to keep the trains running safely all day and all night while attempting to maximize the amount of iron ore transported per day, economize on fuel consumption, and minimize train delays. For over 10 years, paper and pencil were used to solve this difficult task.

An innovative, rule-based expert system that uses fuzzy logic has transformed the culture of train operations. Operational rules are directly used in the ES. Fuzzy logic techniques analyze train movements and help the operators make the best possible decisions (priorities of trains, etc.). The module that generates the initial train-movement plans has helped increase the volume of iron ore transported by about 15 percent while saving about 1.6 liters of fuel per 1,000 metric tons of ore transported. With system improvements, further gains are expected.

_____

Source: Modified from Vieira and Gomide (1996), pp. 51–53.

❖ CHAPTER HIGHLIGHTS

- Machine learning is a family of methods that allow machines to acquire knowledge for problem-solving by showing them historical cases.
- Machine-learning methods can be classified into supervised and unsupervised learning. Supervised learning methods derive knowledge from cases whose outcomes are known, while unsupervised learning methods derive knowledge from cases whose outcomes are unknown.
- Popular machine-learning methods include inductive learning, case-based reasoning, neural networks, genetic algorithms, cluster analysis, and fuzzy logic.
- Case-based reasoning is based on experience with similar situations.
- In case-based reasoning, the attributes of an existing case are compared with critical attributes derived from cases stored in the case library.
- Cases include ossified cases, paradigmatic cases, and stories. Different types of cases must be handled differently to maximize the effect of learning.
- Case-based reasoning has advantages over rule-based reasoning in that it can capture expert knowledge, better explain decisions, and build up incremental learning capabilities.
- Neural computing is a set of methods that emulates the way the human brain works. The basic processing unit is a neuron. Multiple neurons are grouped into layers and linked together. The knowledge is stored in the weight associated with each connection between two neurons.

- Backpropagation is the most popular paradigm in neural networks. Most business applications are handled by this algorithm. A backpropagation-based neural network consists of an input layer, an output layer, and a certain number of hidden layers (usually one). The nodes in one layer are fully connected to the nodes in the next layer. Learning is done through a trial-and-error process of adjusting the connection weights.
- Genetic algorithms are a set of learning methods that emulate the natural evolution process. They include three basic operations: reproduction, crossover, and mutation.
- Reproduction is a process that creates the next-generation population based on the performance of different cases in the current population.
- Crossover is a process that allows elements in different cases to be exchanged to search for a better solution.
- Mutation is a process that changes an element in a case to search for a better solution.
- Fuzzy logic deals with the kind of uncertainty that is inherently human in nature. It allows numerical data to be converted into linguistic terms, such as young or good, for symbolic processing.
- Fuzzy logic can be combined with other techniques, such as rule induction and neural networks, to achieve better performance.
- Fuzzy logic-based systems include two steps. The first, called fuzzification, converts numerical data into fuzzy terms. The second, called defuzzification, converts the fuzzy description back to the original scale.

❖ Key Words

- adaptive resonance theory (ART)
- analogical reasoning
- artificial neural networks (ANNs)
- associative memory
- axon
- backpropagation
- black-box testing
- case base
- case-based reasoning (CBR)
- chromosome
- competitive filter associative memory
- crossover
- defuzzification
- dendrites
- explanation-based learning
- feedforward-backpropagation
- fuzzification

- fuzzy logic
- fuzzy sets
- genetic algorithms
- hidden layer
- inductive learning
- Kohonen self-organizing feature maps
- learning algorithm
- learning rate
- machine learning
- massive parallel processing
- momentum
- mutation
- neural computing
- neural networks
- neurons
- ossified cases
- paradigmatic cases

- parallel processing
- pattern recognition
- processing elements (PEs)
- recurrent network
- reproduction
- self-organizing
- sigmoid (logical activation) function
- stories
- summation function
- supervised learning
- synapse
- threshhold value
- topologies
- transfer function
- transformation (transfer) function
- unsupervised learning
- weights

❖ Questions for Review

1. What is machine learning? What are the differences between supervised learning and unsupervised learning?
2. List different techniques for supervised learning and unsupervised learning.
3. Define case-based reasoning.
4. List five advantages of case-based reasoning.
5. Review the case-based reasoning process. Briefly discuss each step.
6. What is an artificial neural network?
7. Explain the following terms: neuron, axon, dendrite, synapse.
8. Describe biological and artificial neural networks.
9. What is a hidden layer?
10. How do weights function in an artificial neural network?
11. Describe the role of the summation function.
12. Describe the role of the transformation function.
13. What is a threshold value?

14. Why are learning algorithms important to ANN?
15. Define associative memory.
16. Briefly describe backpropagation.
17. List the major benefits of neural computing.
18. List the major limitations of neural computing.
19. Describe the learning process in genetic algorithms. Why is it similar to a biological process?
20. Describe the major genetic algorithm operators.
21. List three applications of genetic algorithms.
22. What are the basic premises on which the fuzzy logic approach is based?
23. What are the major advantages of fuzzy logic? What are the major disadvantages?
24. What is a fuzzy neural network? Give a sample application of a fuzzy neural network.
25. Describe how genetic algorithms can be integrated with other intelligent methods, and give a sample application.

❖ Questions for Discussion

1. Machine learning is a discipline that investigates how computers can learn from existing data. Scholars disagree about whether machines can really learn. Some insist that computers do not learn, and are only taught by humans. Do you agree? Please comment.
2. Case-based reasoning produces new decisions based on past cases. Advocates claim that it can capture the

experience of experts and alleviate problems of rule-based systems. Do you agree, and why?
3. Compare artificial and biological neural networks. What aspects of biological networks are not mimicked by artificial ones? What aspects are similar?
4. The performance of ANN relies heavily on the summation and transformation functions. Explain the

combined effects of the summation and transformation functions, and how they differ from statistical regression analysis.

5. ANNs can be used for both supervised and unsupervised learning. Explain how they learn in a supervised mode and in an unsupervised mode.

6. Review the ANN development process. Compare it to the development process of expert systems. Use an example to show both processes, and list their similarities and differences.

7. Explain the difference between a training set and a testing set. Why do we need to differentiate them? Can the same set be used for both purposes? Why or why not?

8. Real-world scenario: A neural network has been constructed to predict the creditworthiness of applicants. There are two output nodes, one for yes (1, yes; 0, no) and one for no (1, no; 0, yes). An applicant received a score of 0.83 for the "yes" output node and a 0.44 for the "no" output node. Discuss what may have happened and whether the applicant is a good credit risk.

9. Everyone would like to make a great deal of money in the stock market. Only a few are very successful. Why is an ANN a promising approach? What can it do that other decision-support technologies cannot do? How could it fail?

10. Similarly, describe how an investor can use genetic algorithms to make a fortune on the stock market? Can a GA-based system perform better than an NN-based system? Why or why not?

11. Describe three advantages of fuzzy reasoning and provide an example to support each. If you disagree in any of the three cases, explain why.

12. Describe the advantages and disadvantages of integrating multiple methods for developing intelligent systems. Describe all the possible integrations between CBR, ANN, GA, fuzzy logic, and rule-based systems, and assess their feasibility.

❖ EXERCISES

1. Access the University of Kaiserslauten's case-based reasoning Web site (www.agr.informatik.uni-kl.de/Isa/cbr/cbr-homepage.html). Examine the latest CBR research and demo software. How is CBR different from rule-based concepts? Try some reasoning software, compare the method to rule-based inferencing, and write up your experience in a report.

2. Identify a news group that is interested in case-based reasoning. Post a question regarding recent successful applications and see what feedback you get. What are the latest concerns and questions?

3. For each of the following applications, would it be better to use a neural network or an expert system? Explain your answers, including possible exceptions or special conditions.
   a. Diagnosis of a well-established but complex disease
   b. Price-lookup subsystem for a high-volume merchandise sale
   c. Automated voice-inquiry processing system
   d. Training new employees
   e. Handwriting recognition

4. Review this neural network and compute Z.
   where $X_1 = 15$, $X_2 = 8$, $X_3 = 14$, $W_1 = 0.6$, $W_2 = 0.3$, $W_3 = 0.1$, weight for $Y_1 = 0.6$, weight for $Y_2 = 0.45$.
   a. Compute the value of Z without a transfer function.
   b. Compute the value of Z with a threshold function. If the value is 5 or less, call it 0; otherwise call it 1.

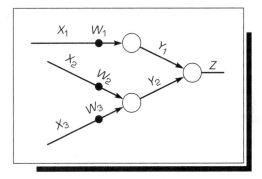

c. Compute the value of Z with the sigmoid transfer function used at all neurons.

5. Using the Braincel neural network package (download a demo from the Web, www.promland.com) or another, build, train, and test a neural network to solve the following simple regression formula that predicts Y as a function of X (for this simple case, train the network on the entire set of data):

X	Y
0	0
.1	.05
.2	.11
.3	.25
.4	.4
.5	.66
.6	.89
.7	1.0

In a spreadsheet, plot the data, and solve the simple linear regression formula $Y = a + bX$. Compare the estimates made by the neural network and by the regression. Calculate the sum-of-the-squares error and R^2 for each. Which one is better?

6. Develop a deployable neural network code for a credit approval system. There are three neurons in the input layer, four in the hidden layer, and one in the output layer. Three input factors were considered for a potential client: credit rating, debt to income ratio, and net income. They have already been scaled so that the lowest value for any potential customer is 0 and the highest value is 1. These are the inputs. The output represents credit approval. If the output is 1, then credit is approved. If the output is 0, then credit is denied. The transfer function is a threshold function. If the total flow arriving in a hidden layer neuron is 0.5 (one-half) or greater, then, the *flow out* is set to 1, otherwise it is set to 0. The weights from the three inputs to the hidden layer are (rows = from inputs, columns = to hidden nodes)

		Hidden Node		
from ^{to}	1	2	3	4
Input 1	0.1,	0.3,	0.4,	0.6
Node 2	0.2,	0.1,	0.6,	0.3
3	0.1,	0.6,	0.4,	0.15

The weights from the hidden layer neurons to the output node are

$$0.3, 0.4, 0.2, 0.2.$$

7. Express the following statements in terms of fuzzy sets:
   a. The chance for rain today is 80 percent. (Rain? No rain?)
   b. Mr. Smith is 60 years old. (Young?)
   c. The salary of the President of the United States is $250,000 per year. (Low? High? Very high?)
   d. The latest survey of economists indicates that they believe that the recession will bottom out in April (20 percent), in May (30 percent), or in June (22 percent).
8. Compare the effectiveness of genetic algorithms versus standard methods for problem solving as described in the literature. How effective are genetic algorithms?
9. Investigate custom online newspaper systems on the Web (e.g., CRAYON) and evaluate how effective they are at filtering the news so that you get only the material you really want. Which ones worked best?
10. Investigate at least two Web sites of computer systems that exhibit creative behavior (e.g., GenJam, www.it.rit.edu/~jab/genjam.html). What types of creative behavior do they exhibit? Explain how they work.

❖ **GROUP EXERCISES**

1. Identify a real-world application problem suitable for case-based reasoning and develop a plan for developing an intelligent system that integrates the case-based and rule-based approaches.
2. Consider the set of data that relates daily electricity usage as a function of outside high temperature (for the day).

Temperature, X	*Kilowatts, Y*
46.8	12,530
52.1	10,800
55.1	10,180
59.2	9,730
61.9	9,750
66.2	10,230
69.9	11,160
76.8	13,910
79.7	15,110
79.3	15,690
80.2	17,020
83.3	17,880

   a. Plot the raw data. What pattern do you see? What do you think is really affecting electricity usage?
   b. Solve this problem with linear regression $Y = a + bX$ (in a spreadsheet). How well did this work? Plot your results. What is wrong? Calculate a sum-of-the-squares error and R^2.
   c. Solve this problem with nonlinear regression. We recommend a quadratic function, $Y = a + b_1X + b_2X_2$. Again, how well did this work? Plot your results. Is anything wrong? Calculate a sum of the squares error and R^2.
   d. Break up the problem into three sections (look at the plot) and solve it with three linear regression models, one for each section. How well did this work? Plot your results. Calculate a sum of the squares error and R^2. Is this modeling approach appropriate? Why or why not?
   e. Build a neural network to solve the original problem. (You may have to scale the X and Y values to be between 0 and 1.) Train it (on the entire set of data) and solve the problem (make predictions for

each of the original data items). How well did this work? Plot your results. Calculate a sum of the squares error and R^2.

f. Which method worked best and why?

3. Build a real-world neural network. Using demo software downloaded from the Web (Braincel at www.promland.com or another), identify real-world data (e.g., start searching on the Web at www.research.ed.asu.edu or use data from an organization with which someone in your group has a contact) and build a neural network to make predictions. Topics might include sales forecasts, predicting success in an academic program (predict GPA from high school rating and SAT scores—see ftp://psych .colorado.edu/pub/stat/gpa.txt, being careful to look out for "bad" data, e.g., GPAs of 0.0), housing prices, or even survey the class for weight, gender, and height and try to predict height based on the other two. (*Hint:* Use U.S. Census data, on this book's Web site or at www.census.gov, by state to identify a relationship between education level and income.) How good are your predictions? Compare the results to predictions generated by standard statistical methods (regression). Which method was better? How could your system be embedded in a DSS for real decision making?

4. *Fuzzy logic.* Survey your class by having everyone write down a height representing tall, medium, and short for men and for women. Tally the results and determine what is meant by tall, medium, and short in a fuzzy way. Create the membership functions in these sets and examine the results.

❖ INTERNET EXERCISES

1. Case-based reasoning has been used lately for data mining. Explore the Web to find vendors and research literature about this topic.

2. Explore the Web sites of several neural network vendors, such as California Scientific Software (www.calsci.com), NeuralWare Inc. (www.neuralware .com), and Ward Systems Group (www.wardsystems .com), and review some of their products. Download at least two demos and install, run, and compare them.

3. Explore the Web to identify the current status of neural network research.

4. Examine genetic algorithm vendor Web sites and investigate their business applications. What kinds of applications are most prevalent?

5. Examine fuzzy logic vendor Web sites and identify the kinds of problems to which fuzzy logic is currently being applied. Find a demo version of a system and try it out. Report your findings to the class.

6. Use the Internet to find information about neuro-fuzzy logic systems.

7. Access the Web and e-journal in your library to find at least three reports on the use of integrated methods for intelligent decision support. Evaluate whether the applications are feasible in the real world.

KONICA AUTOMATES A HELP DESK WITH CASE-BASED REASONING

Konica Business Machines (Windsor, Connecticut) wanted to fully automate its help desk for internal and external support (both for its commercial products and for in-house applications and systems). This need arose from its desire to be a $1 billion operation by the next millennium and because the company had received past awards for superior tech support for office products.

Case-based reasoning (CBR) was chosen as the most promising approach. After Konica evaluated several case-based reasoning tools, Ty Butler, the director of domestic tech support, selected Software Artistry's Expert Advisor. The most unusual feature of Expert Advisor is its multiple problem-resolution modes. It also uses decision trees and has adaptive learning, tech search, and other useful features.

The case-based reasoning approach has been demonstrated to be an effective means of automating help desks. In CBR, the situation to be diagnosed is entered into the system verbatim. Then the text is analyzed by a natural language processor which interprets the situation and makes a first attempt at structuring the information to compare it to existing cases stored in a (knowledge) case base. Once the cases are examined, the most likely situations are presented and the user can either go with the recommended course of action or refine the wording to tighten up the description of the problem. Clearly, the

cases must be written very carefully so that the system can apply AI technology in solving real problems. In the early prototypes, Konica's knowledge engineers started building cases for five products using technical documentation as a source document. At a certain point, actual calls to the help desk were used to generate cases. Moving to real cases brought the hit rate up.

Konica's implementation, Expert Advisor, runs on IBM Pentium servers. It is used by both the internal tech support people and by customers directly. Konica's 750 technicians and 6,000 dealer technicians generate 90 percent of the support calls for copiers, 20 percent of those for fax machines, and 30 percent of those for multifunction products. The rest of the calls come from end-users. There are 20 help-desk technicians plus six knowledge engineers. Knowledge engineers build decision trees rather than case bases and focus on clearing the bulk of the calls instead of developing highly specialized structures. The tech support people still handle unusual cases, but the system is also incorporating digitized photos of components and procedures, which are especially useful to the help desk agents.

In the early stages of development, Expert Advisor produced a 65 percent hit rate for problem resolution. The adaptive-learning features will be incorporated next to improve the hit rate.

CASE QUESTIONS

1. Why did Konica want to automate its help desk?
2. Why was CBR selected as the technology of choice?
3. Who are the Expert Advisor end-users? Does this present any challenges for the implementation team?
4. Why did the hit rate go up when the knowledge engineers dropped the technical manuals in favor of real cases?
5. What will the adaptive-learning feature of Expert Advisor do for the effectiveness of the system?

Source: Based on L. The, "AI Automates a Help Desk," *Datamation*, Vol. 42, No. 2, January 15, 1996, pp. 54–64. Also see L. The, "Morph Your Help Desk in Customer Support," *Datamation*, Vol. 42, No. 2, January 15, 1996, pp. 52–54 and the accompanying "Feature Summary on Help Desk Software," pp. 56–57.

MAXIMIZING THE VALUE OF THE JOHN DEERE & COMPANY PENSION FUND

Managing the pension fund of John Deere & Company, a large manufacturer of earthmoving machines, agricultural machines, and other heavy equipment, is not simple. About $1 billion of the more than $5 billion is managed internally by the corporate finance department. To achieve a better return on the investment, this department has been using neural computing since 1993. Initially, the company allocated $100 million on an experimental basis to be invested in high-technology, large capitalization stocks (such as IBM). Later, another $100 million was allocated to mid-sized stocks.

Using historical data, an individual artificial neural network has been built for each of the 1,000 largest U.S. corporations. The data include 40 input fundamental and technical variables, such as growth rate, financial ratios, historical price movements, market share, and earning per share. Once a week, the current data of each company are fed into a neural network model that predicts the future performance of each stock. The model then ranks the 1,000 stocks based on their anticipated performance in the stock market. From this list, a portfolio of the top 100 stocks is selected and the fund is allocated proportionally to the predicted return. The neural network models are frequently retrained because of changing conditions in the marketplace.

Although the internal structure of the model and its performance level (success) are trade secrets of the company, the returns are well ahead of industry benchmarks.

CASE QUESTIONS

1. Explain why neural networks are used.
2. Why is historical data used?
3. Is the neural network really learning? Why or why not?
4. How could the neural network possibly outperform a human?
5. Describe at least two related applications of neural computing.

Based on M. G. Star, "Deere Pension Fund Uses Neural Network." *Pensions and Investments,* Vol. 22, No. 22, Oct. 31, 1994, pp. 1, 42.

INTELLIGENT SYSTEMS OVER THE INTERNET

LEARNING OBJECTIVES

- ❖ Understand the cutting-edge intelligent systems that run over the Internet
- ❖ Understand the concept and power of intelligent agents
- ❖ Learn various applications of intelligent agents
- ❖ Learn the concept of representing semantic knowledge over the Web
- ❖ Learn the concept of recommendation systems over the Internet
- ❖ Understand methods for designing recommendation systems

The second-generation intelligent systems are armed with powerful learning algorithms, as described in Chapter 12. Since the mid-1990s, the dramatic increase in the number of Internet users has driven the application of intelligent systems to a new platform, the World Wide Web (WWW, or simply put, the Web). In this chapter, we focus on important new technologies that have been implemented on the Web, including intelligent agents, recommendation systems, and semantic Web. The chapter is organized as follows:

13.1 OPENING VIGNETTE: SPARTAN USES INTELLIGENT SYSTEMS TO FIND THE RIGHT PERSON AND REDUCE TURNOVER

Spartan Stores is a retailing chain with 115 supermarkets and deep-discount drugstores in Michigan and other Midwestern states. It is also a primary distributor for 330 independent supermarkets and over 6,000 convenience stores.

Spartan holds a brand position as the neighborhood market, and its management recognized that one of the most critical factors in support of this was the quality and consistency of the people it hires. Spread across two large states and without centralized hiring standards, the chain's 100+ store managers were making hiring decisions with criteria that were not always consistent across the retail organization. They spent an inordinate amount of time screening candidates and often did not give enough attention to the crucial qualities of the applicants.

A supermarket manager's day is unbelievably long and stressful. Industry turnover in staff is high, over 100 percent. It costs, on average, $3,000 to replace an employee. Spartan's director of human resources, Linda Esparza, put it this way, "We just want to operate our stores better. Customer service is what we're going to use to differentiate ourselves." Some national chains are moving into the market, and Spartan is in a good position to distinguish itself as the neighborly alternative. "It's not the sheer applicant numbers we're looking for," says Esparza, "it's more the efficiency of finding people who are the right cultural fit."

Front-end positions in a supermarket tend to be critical in terms of a customer-service strategy. These positions include cashiers, department managers, and bagger—the employees in direct contact with customers who remember their names, go out of their way to help them, and make them feel welcome. These employees are the key element in building customer loyalty, so knowing how to hire the right people for front-end positions is vital to the success of the business.

THE SOLUTION

Spartan acted quickly to address this need, deciding to take advantage of the latest in automated hiring systems. Such systems can analyze the profile of an applicant to assess the match between the applicant's characteristics and the requirement of the position. They play the role of recommending proper candidates from a huge pool of applicants and can save a substantial amount of time and money.

After surveying the solutions available on the market, Spartan adopted Unicru's Hiring Management System. Unicru integrated Spartan's prescreening criteria into its automated application process. It also installed a psychological screening test designed to find the most dependable, friendly, and helpful employees. The system provides Web-based assessments for friendly use. All applicants are asked to use the system. Those recommended by the system will be further interviewed and hired. Those assessed to be inappropriate are told that no position fits them. A hiring manger can receive a screened job application within 30 seconds to four minutes after an application is complete, along with suggested interview questions targeted to the candidate. In some cases, managers will be automatically paged in order to meet a strong candidate before he or she leaves the store.

BENEFITS

Despite a deep economic recession and increased competition from huge chains like Wal-Mart, Spartan survived its first quarter (2002) of net loss in its history. By taking smart, swift action to enhance its operational efficiency, the company quickly returned to profitability in the spring and summer of the same year. Major benefits from deploying the automated hiring system include the following:

- **Reduced turnover rate.** The turnover rate is down from over 100 percent to 59 percent. While this may be partly due to the economic recession, hiring more dependable people more consistently has a major effect.
- **Increased operational efficiency.** The system also provides information about the efficiency of its hiring. The HR manager can now look in detail at each store, region, or the entire enterprise, and spot immediate needs as well as long-term trends in human resource needs.
- **Higher functional integration.** The system can use the collected application data to evaluate the company's WOTC (Work Opportunity Tax Credit) eligibility. In 19 stores, Spartan was able to apply for enough WOTC tax credit so that the system could pay by itself.

Overall, the system uses intelligent technology to help store managers use less time to achieve more accuracy in picking the right fit. Similar applications can be found in the Brooks Group in Greensboro, North Carolina, and Finish Line, Inc., a leading athletic retailer based in Indianapolis, Indiana.

❖ QUESTIONS FOR THE OPENING VINGNETTE

1. Describe the nature of the hiring management decision and the reasons why an intelligent system is suitable.
2. List the benefits of the system at Spartan. Can you foresee any other benefits that are not described above?
3. What kind of knowledge structure seems appropriate for the development and operation of an intelligent hiring system? Review the techniques that you learned in Chapters 10, 11, and 12, and explain why you picked a particular technique and think it is appropriate.
4. How do you feel about being selected or rejected by a system instead of through an interview with a human manager? What issues do you see in adopting the system at Spartan?

13.2 WEB-BASED INTELLIGENT SYSTEMS

The Opening Vignette illustrates an application of autonomous computer systems, also often called *intelligent agents*. These programs can perform certain tasks automatically according to the rules and inference mechanisms given by the designer. Since the introduction of the Internet and the World Wide Web (WWW), these systems have been armed with a Web-based architecture and friendly user interface. Given the explosion

---

Source: Abridged from Maher, K., "Web-based Tools Help Find The Right Persons for the Job," *Wall Street Journal*, November 26, 2002; "Intelligent Employment Agent," *Expert Systems*, Vol. 18, No. 3, 2001, p. 161; "Finish Line Introduces Consistency and Reduce Turnover," www.unicru.com.

of information on the Web, autonomous agents will become very popular. In fact, many Internet services are already using them to provide better service. For example, a retailing store may use an agent to automatically answer frequently asked questions or to reply to e-mails. An auction Web site may use software agents to monitor the auctioning process.

A major feature of Web-based intelligent systems is that they use the Web as a platform to deliver services. Their user interfaces are Web-enabled. Moreover, they are able to communicate with each other through a Web-based protocol. For example, when a Web-based system has to reply to a client's e-mail, it must be able to retrieve key words from the e-mail, determine the theme of the message, and choose a proper answer from its knowledge base. Figure 13.1 shows an example of how a Web-based system works over the Internet. The user enters the request in the box and clicks the "find it" button. The system interprets the query and converts it into a set of machine-understandable codes for execution. The system then outputs the findings at the bottom. The Web-based user interface is a friendly channel through which the user interacts with the system. The kernel of the system (including the knowledge base and the interpreting and reasoning mechanisms) is hidden behind the Web. Most users will not be aware of their existence.

Web-based intelligent systems can be used for many purposes and can have different forms. There are small systems, often called *agents*, that perform very specific tasks.

FIGURE 13.1   A SIMPLIFIED MECHANISM FOR PRODUCT SEARCH IN A WEB-BASED INTELLIGENT SYSTEM

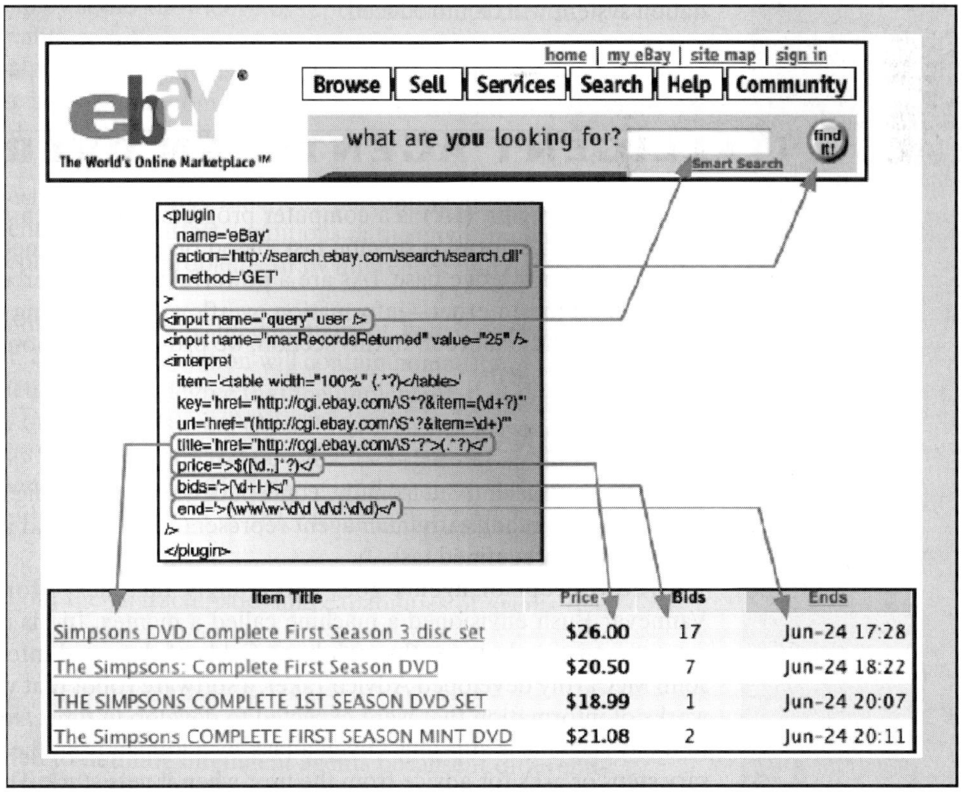

Source: Adapted from Menczer, et al. (2002).

- **Reactivity.** Intelligent agents are able to perceive their environment and respond in a timely fashion to changes that occur in it in order to satisfy their design objectives.
- **Proactiveness.** Intelligent agents are able to exhibit goal-directed behavior by taking the initiative in order to satisfy their design objectives.
- **Social ability.** Intelligent agents are capable of interacting with other agents (and possibly humans) in order to satisfy their design objectives.

Lee et al. (1997) identified four different levels of agent intelligence, as follows:

- **Level 0 (the lowest).** These agents retrieve documents for a user under straight orders. Popular Web browsers fall into this category. The user must specify the URLs where the documents are. These agents help in navigating the Web.
- **Level 1.** These agents provide a user-initiated searching facility for finding relevant Web pages. Internet search agents such as Google, Alta Vista, and Infoseek are examples. Information about pages, titles, and word frequency is stored and indexed. When the user provides key words, the search engine matches them against the indexed information. These agents are referred to as search engines.
- **Level 2.** These agents maintain user profiles. Then they monitor Internet information and notify the users whenever relevant information is found. An example of such agents is WebWatcher, the tour-guide agent for the Web developed at Carnegie Mellon University (www.cs.cmu.edu). Agents at this level are frequently referred to as semi-intelligent or software agents.
- **Level 3.** Agents at this level have a learning and deductive component of user profiles to help a user who cannot formalize a query or specify a target for a search. DiffAgent (Carnegie Mellon University) and Letizia (MIT) are examples. Agents at this level are referred to as learning agents or truly intelligent agents.

COMPONENTS OF AN AGENT

Intelligent agents are computer programs that contain the following components:

- **Owner.** User name, parent process name, or master agent name. Intelligent agents can have several owners. Humans can spawn agents, processes can spawn agents (e.g., stock brokerage processes using agents to monitor prices), or other intelligent agents can spawn their own supporting agents.
- **Author.** Development owner, service, or master agent name. Intelligent agents can be created by people or processes and then supplied as templates for users to personalize.
- **Account.** Intelligent agents must have an anchor to an owner's account and an electronic address for billing purposes or as a pointer to their origin.
- **Goal.** Clear statements of successful agent task completion are necessary, as well as metrics for determining the task's point of completion and the value of the results. Measures of success can include simple completion of a transaction within the boundaries of the stated goal or a more complex measure.
- **Subject description.** The subject description details the goal's attributes. These attributes provide the boundaries of the agent, task, possible resources to call on, and class of need (e.g., stock purchase, airline ticket price).
- **Creation and duration.** The request and response dates requested.
- **Background.** Supporting information.
- **Intelligent subsystem.** An intelligent subsystem, such as a rule-based expert system or a neural computing system, provides several of the characteristics described above.

13.3 INT

13.4 CHARACTERISTICS OF AGENTS

In most cases an agent is designed to accomplish a single task. The task could be searching the Internet to find where and when certain items are auctioned. Or it might be filtering electronic mail. More advanced agents are capable of doing multiple tasks, but in all probability many future agent systems will really be multi-agents, combinations of different agents that each handles a separate simple task (Wooldridge, 2002). Although there is no commonly accepted definition of intelligent agent, several traits or abilities that many people think of when discussing intelligent agents can be considered their major characteristics.

AUTONOMY OR EMPOWERMENT

An agent is autonomous; that is, it is capable of acting on its own or of being empowered. Since an agent is goal-oriented, collaborative, and flexible, it must be able to make some decisions on its own. When it meets an obstacle, it must be able to alter its course or behavior and find ways around the impediment. Maes (1995) points out that regular computers respond only to direct manipulation, but with the advent of agents, users are able to give open-ended commands to their electronic agents to get work done. For example, an agent should be able to accept a high-level request and decide on its own where and how to carry it out. In the process, the agent should be able to ask clarification questions and modify requests instead of blindly obeying commands.

Autonomy implies that an agent takes initiative and exercises control over its own actions in the following ways:

- **Goal-oriented.** Accepts high-level requests indicating what a human wants and is responsible for deciding how and where to satisfy the requests. These are referred to by Hess et al. (2000) as homeostatic goal(s).
- **Collaborative.** Does not blindly obey commands but can modify requests, ask clarification questions, or even refuse to satisfy certain requests.
- **Flexible.** Actions are not scripted; able to dynamically choose which actions to invoke, and in what sequence, in response to the state of its external environment.
- **Self-starting.** Unlike standard programs directly invoked by a user, an agent can sense changes in its environment and decide when to act.

The autonomy capability is also a consequence of the agent's intelligence, mobility, and interactivity attributes, which will be described later.

COMMUNICATION (INTERACTIVITY)

Many agents are designed to interact with other agents, humans, or software programs. This is a critical ability in view of the narrow repertoire of any given agent. Instead of making a single agent conduct several tasks, additional agents can be created to handle undelegated tasks. Thus, there is need for communication. Agents communicate by following certain communication languages and standards such as ACL and KQML (Bradshaw, 1997; Jennings et al., 1998).

AUTOMATES REPETITIVE TASKS

An agent is designed to perform narrowly defined tasks, which it can do over and over without getting bored or sick or going on strike.

REACTIVITY

Agents perceive their environment (which may be the physical world, a user via a graphical user interface, a collection of other agents, the Internet, or perhaps all of these combined) and respond in a timely fashion to changes that occur in it. This means that agents can recognize changes in their environment.

PROACTIVENESS (OR PERSISTENCE)

Agents do not simply act in response to their environment. They are able to exhibit goal-directed behavior by taking an initiative.

TEMPORAL CONTINUITY

The agent should be a continuously running process, not a one-shot deal that terminates after completing a series of commands. The program can, however, be temporarily inactive while waiting for something to occur.

PERSONALITY

For an agent to be effective, it must be believable and able to interact with human users.

OPERATING IN THE BACKGROUND: MOBILITY

An agent must be able to work out of sight, in the realm of cyberspace or in other computer systems, without the constant attention of its user (or "master"). Some developers use the terms remote execution or mobile agent in referring to this attribute.

MOBILITY

In the Internet environment, an agent may need mobility to work on different machines. An agent with this capability is called a **mobile agent**; it can transport itself across different system architectures and platforms, and is far more flexible than those that cannot. Many electronic commerce agents are mobile.

INTELLIGENCE AND LEARNING

At present, most agents cannot learn and thus are not truly intelligent. Only some agents can learn. This goes beyond mere rule-based reasoning because the agent is expected to use learning to behave autonomously. Many members of the AI community argue that there is little demand for agents that learn by "spying" on their users. Nonetheless, the ability to learn often begins with the ability to observe users and predict their behavior. One of the most common examples of a learning agent is the software assistant found in many commercial software programs (e.g., in Microsoft Office applications). These agents offer hints to the user, based on patterns the program detects in the user's activities. Some of the newer Internet search engines boast intelligent agents that can learn from previous requests by the user. An agent that makes recommendations based on detected behavior is called a recommender. We shall discuss the concept of recommendation in later sections. For a comprehensive discussion of the concepts described above and some additional characteristics, see Hess et al. (2000).

Agents are sometimes confused with objects and expert systems. A summary of the differences between them is provided in AIS in Focus 13.1.

AIS IN FOCUS 13.1

INTELLIGENT AGENTS, OBJECTS, AND EXPERT SYSTEMS

Objects and agents are similar in some ways in that they are both designed for independent operation. They are also different in some ways. Objects are defined as computational entities that encapsulate some state, are able to perform actions or methods on this state, and communicate by message passing. The major difference is that agents have a clear intention and goal. In other words, when an object in a computer program receives a message, it has to react. An agent, in contrast, may choose not to react if the request is not consistent to its goal. The distinction is nicely encapsulated in the following slogan:

Objects do it for free; agents do it because they want to.

To summarize, the differences include:

- Agents embody a stronger notion of autonomy than objects, and, in particular, they decide for themselves whether or not to perform an action on request from another agent.
- Agents are capable of flexible (reactive, proactive, social) behavior, but the standard model of objects has nothing to say about this type of behavior.

- A multi-agent system is inherently multithreaded, in that each agent is assumed to have at least one thread of control.

Agents are often considered to be a realization of small expert systems over the Internet. Although agents and ES have similarities in that both intend to incorporate domain knowledge to automate decision-making, they are also different in the following respects:

- Classic expert systems are not coupled to any environment and act through a user as a middleman; agents can actively search information from the environment where they reside.
- Expert systems are not generally capable of reactive and proactive behavior.
- Expert systems are not generally equipped with social ability in the sense of cooperation, coordination, and negotiation.

Source: Wooldridge (2002).

13.5 WHY INTELLIGENT AGENTS?

Alvin Toffler, in *Future Shock* (1970), warned of an impending flood, not of water but of information. He predicted that we would eventually be so inundated with data that we would be paralyzed and unable to choose between options. His prediction is becoming a reality.

Information overload is one of the unintended by-products of the information age. Managers and other decision-makers cannot be expected to read every document that crosses their desks, every relevant datum available in databases, every article in the magazines and journals to which they subscribe, or even all the e-mail that hits their computer mailboxes. The Gartner Group believes that

- The amount of data collected by large enterprises doubles every year.
- Knowledge workers can analyze only about 5 percent of this data.
- Most of their efforts are spent in trying to discover important patterns in the data (60% or more), a much smaller percentage is spent determining what these patterns mean (20% or more), and very little time (10% or less) is spent actually doing something about the patterns.
- Information overload reduces our decision-making capabilities by 50 percent.

However, the real crisis began to develop with the emergence of the Internet. The Internet contains a collection of information-generating and -replicating machines.

Thousands of new systems and even more new users bring new sources of data onto the Net every minute. It can be an overwhelming experience to log onto the Net for the first time, because so many resources are immediately available. Experienced users look for ways to filter the data so that they can make sense out of the streams of information found online. Search engines and directories help with the winnowing process, but even they bring up volumes of data, much of which is only loosely tied to the immediate concerns of the decision-maker. In addition, search engines rarely discriminate between copies of the same information offered through different sources, and as a result replication adds to the pile of useless information.

In spite of all of this, managers are expected to take account of key business information and make good decisions.

A major value of intelligent agents is that they are able to assist in searching through all the data. They save time by making decisions about what is relevant to the user. With these agents at work, the competent user's decision-making ability is enhanced with information rather than paralyzed by too much input. Agents are artificial intelligence's answer to a need created by computers (Nwana and Ndumu, 1999).

Information access and navigation are today's major applications of intelligent agents, but there are several other reasons why this technology is expected to grow rapidly. For example, intelligent agents can improve computer network management and security, support e-commerce, empower employees, and increase productivity and quality (Papazoglou, 2001; Vlahavas et al., 2002). The advantage of agents can be even greater when a wireless computing environment is involved. Agents can handle many routine activities that need to be done quickly. The cost of non-agent-based wireless systems for information discovery is very high. The reasons for the success of agents are listed below:

- **Decision support.** There is a need for increased support for tasks performed by knowledge workers, especially in the decision-making area. Professionals who can make timely and knowledgeable decisions greatly increase their effectiveness and the success of their businesses in the marketplace.
- **Frontline customer support.** As indicated in Chapter 8, there is a need to empower employees interacting with customers at the frontline. Such empowerment can be achieved by using intelligent agents.
- **Repetitive office activities.** There is a pressing need to automate tasks performed by administrative and clerical personnel in functions such as sales or customer support, so as to reduce labor costs and increase office productivity.
- **Mundane personal activity.** In a fast-paced society, time-strapped people need new ways to minimize the time spent on routine personal tasks, such as booking airline tickets, so that they can devote more time to professional activities.
- **Search and retrieval.** It is not possible to directly manipulate a distributed database system in an e-commerce setting with millions of data objects. Users will have to relegate the tasks of searching, costing, and other comparisons to agents. These agents perform the tedious, time-consuming, repetitive tasks of searching databases, retrieving and filtering information, and delivering it to users.
- **Domain experts.** It is advisable to model costly expertise and make it widely available. For example, expert software agents could be models of real-world agents, such as translators, lawyers, diplomats, union negotiators, stockbrokers, and even clergy.

Here are some management-oriented tasks that an agent can perform: advise, alert, broadcast, browse, critique, distribute, enlist, empower, explain, filter, guide, identify, match, monitor, navigate, negotiate, organize, present, query, remind, report, retrieve, schedule, search, secure, solicit, sort, store, suggest, summarize, teach, translate, and watch.

In short, software agents can improve the productivity of the end-user by performing a variety of tasks. The most important of these are *gathering information, filtering it,* and *using it for decision support.*

13.6 CLASSIFICATION AND TYPES OF AGENTS

Agents can be classified in different ways. The most popular classifications are by application type and by characteristics. Other classifications are according to control structure, computational environment, and programming language.

CLASSIFICATION BY APPLICATION TYPE

Franklin and Graesser (1996) use a taxonomic tree to classify autonomous agents (Figure 13.2). Relevant to managerial decision-making are *computational* agents, *software* agents, and *task-specific* agents.

ORGANIZATIONAL AND PERSONAL AGENTS

Organizational agents execute tasks on behalf of a business process or computer application. **Personal agents** perform tasks on behalf of individual users.

For example, corporate use of agent monitoring software is becoming a key component in the drive to cut support costs and increase computer productivity. Intelligent agents can search through e-mail messages for certain key words. Depending on what key words are contained in a message, the agent automatically sends out answers based on frequently asked questions (FAQs) files. A company can use such an agent to help customers obtain answers to their questions quickly (e.g., www.egain.com and www.brightware.com).

Another example of an organizational intelligent agent is an automatic e-mail sorting system. When a new message comes in, it is automatically routed to the right file and folder.

Personal agents are very powerful. They allow users to go directly to the information they want on the Internet. Busy people do not have the time or desire for extended browsing through the Internet, and so the agent can help in browsing.

FIGURE 13.2   CLASSIFICATION OF INTELLIGENT AGENTS

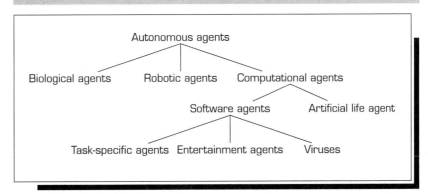

Source: S. Franklin and A. Graesser, Institute for Intelligent Systems, University of Memphis, TN.

PRIVATE AND PUBLIC AGENTS

A **private agent** (personal) works for only one user and is created by that user. **Public agents** are created by a designer for the use of anybody who has access to the application, network, or database.

SOFTWARE AGENTS AND INTELLIGENT AGENTS

According to Lee et al. (1997), truly intelligent agents (level 3 of intelligence) must be able to learn and exhibit autonomy. However, most Internet and electronic commerce agents do not exhibit these characteristics yet. Therefore, they are often called software agents (level 2 of intelligence). The second generation of Internet and electronic commerce now under development includes some learning capabilities (see media.mit .edu/research/softwareagents/projects).

Another classification by Wooldridge (2002) includes the following different applications:

- Agents for workflow and business process management
- Agents for distributed sensing
- Agents for retrieval and management
- Agents for electronic commerce
- Agents for human-computer interaction
- Agents for virtual environments
- Agents for social simulation

CLASSIFICATION BY CHARACTERISTICS

Of the various characteristics of agents, three are of special importance: *agency*, *intelligence*, and *mobility*. According to IBM (1995), agents can be classified in terms of a space defined by these three dimensions.

Agency is the degree of autonomy and authority vested in the agent, and can be measured, at least qualitatively, by the nature of the interaction between the agent and other entities in the system. At a minimum, an agent must run asynchronously. The degree of agency is enhanced if an agent represents a user in some way. A more advanced agent can interact with other entities, such as data, applications, or services. Even more advanced agents collaborate and negotiate with other agents.

Intelligence is the degree of reasoning and learned behavior—the agent's ability to accept the user's statement of goals and carry out the tasks delegated to it. At a minimum, there can be some statements of preferences, perhaps in the form of rules, with an inference engine or some other reasoning mechanism to act on the preferences. Higher levels of intelligence include a user model or some other form of understanding and reasoning about what a user wants done and planning the means to achieve this goal. Farther out on the intelligence scale are systems that learn and adapt to their environment, both in terms of the user's objectives and in terms of the resources available to the agent. Such a system, like a human assistant, might discover new relationships, connections, or concepts independently of the human user and exploit these in anticipating and satisfying user needs.

Mobility is the degree to which the agents themselves travel through the network. Some agents may be static, either residing on the client machine (to manage a user interface, for instance) or initiated at the server. Mobile scripts can be composed on one machine and shipped to another for execution in a suitably secure environment; in this case, the program travels before execution, and thus no state data need be attached. Finally, agents can be mobile with state, transporting from machine to machine in the middle of execution and carrying accumulated state data with them. Such agents can be viewed as mobile objects, which travel to agencies where they can present their credentials and obtain access to services and data managed by the agencies. Agencies can also serve as brokers or matchmakers, bringing together agents with similar interests and compatible goals, and providing a meeting point where they can interact safely.

Mobile agents can move from one Internet site to another, and can send data to and retrieve data from the user, who can focus on other work in the meantime. This can be very helpful to a user. For example, if users want to continuously monitor an electronic auction that takes a few days (e.g., at www.onsale.com), they essentially would have to be online continuously for the whole period of the auction. Software applications that automatically watch auctions and stocks are readily available. For example, a mobile agent travels from site to site, looking for information on a certain stock as instructed by the user. If the stock price hits a certain level, or if there is news about the stock, the agent alerts the user. What is unique about a mobile agent is that it is a software application that moves on its own to different computers to execute (Murch and Johnson, 1999).

Nonmobile agents can be defined by two dimensions (Figure 13.3a), and mobile agents are defined in a three-dimensional space (Figure 13.3b). For example, in Figure 13.3a we see that expert systems, which are not agents, may fall below the threshold line and so are regular software agents. True intelligent agents are listed above the threshold line.

OTHER CLASSIFICATIONS

King (1995) classifies agents into interface, tutors, scheduling assistants, search agents, report agents, presentation agents, navigation agents, and role-playing agents. Murch and Johnson (1999) use the following categories: personal use, network management, information and Internet access, mobility management, e-commerce, user interface, application development, and military applications. Gilbert and Janca (1997) classify Internet agents into nine categories based on the area of application. These will be presented in the next section.

FIGURE 13.3   INTELLIGENT AGENTS SCOPE IN TWO DIMENSIONS (A) AND IN THREE DIMENSIONS (B)

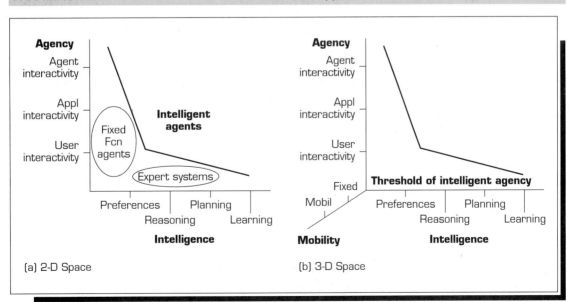

Source: Based on IBM (1995) and Gilbert and Janca (1997).

13.7 INTERNET-BASED SOFTWARE AGENTS

The use of network- and Internet-based software agents is growing rapidly. New and improved applications seem to appear almost every week (see agents.umbc.edu).

According to IBM's white paper (Gilbert and Janca, 1997), there are nine major application areas that relate to Internet agents:

- Assistance in workflow and administrative management
- Collaboration with other agents and people
- Support of electronic commerce
- Support of desktop applications
- Assisting in information access and management, including searching and FAQs
- Processing e-mail and messages
- Controlling and managing network access
- Managing systems and networks
- Creating user interfaces, including navigation (browsing)

Many examples of agents in each of the nine categories are available in Gilbert and Janca (1997) and Wooldridge (2002). The following are sample applications in the network- and Internet-related areas.

E-MAIL AGENTS (MAILBOTS)

These agents assist the user with e-mail (Figure 13.4). For example, Maxims (Maes, 1994) monitors what the user does routinely with e-mail and memorizes the user's situation–action pairs. These pairs are stored in a memory of examples. The situations are described in terms of a set of features, including the names of those who send messages to the user and receive messages from the user. When a new situation occurs, the agent analyzes the features of the situation and suggests an action to the user (e.g., read, delete, forward, or archive). The process is similar to case-based reasoning. The agent communicates with Eudora, a Windows-based e-mail software system.

The agent measures the confidence (or fit) of a suggested action to a situation. If the confidence is high, the agent executes the suggestion with the approval of the user. Otherwise, the agent waits for instructions on what to do. The agent's performance improves with time as the memory of examples increases. Several commercial e-mail agents are available (e.g., Beyond Mail for intelligent messaging from Banyan Inc., www.banyan.com).

Several other e-mail agents help the user to handle large numbers of messages. For example, Motiwalla (1995) developed an intelligent agent for prioritizing e-mail messages based on the user's preferences or knowledge.

According to Murch and Johnson (1999), e-mail agents can

- Control any unwanted, unsolicited e-mail.
- Alert users by voice if a designated message arrives.
- Automatically forward mail messages to designated destinations.
- Consolidate mail from several sources, the way the user wants it.
- Search the Internet for certain sources and deliver them to the user by e-mail.
- Distinguish business-related e-mail from private or personal mail. Automatically answer mail and respond according to conditions, for example, "I am on vacation until. . . . My agent will automatically make an appointment for you."

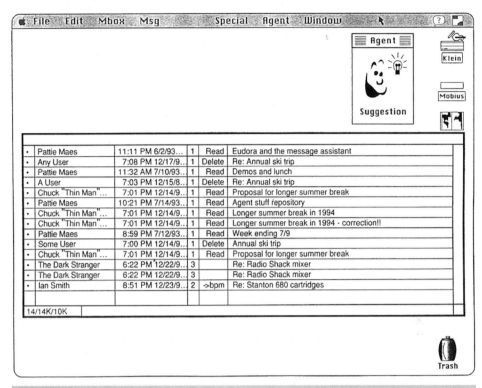

FIGURE 13.4   E-MAIL AGENT

The e-mail agent makes recommendations to the user (middle column). It predicts what actions the user will take on messages, such as which messages will be read and in which order and which messages will be deleted, forwarded, archived, and so on.

Source: Maes (1994), p. 34. Maes, P. (1994, July). "Agents That Reduce Work and Information Overload," *Communication of the ACM,* Vol. 37, No. 7.

- Perform regular administrative tasks involving desktop e-mail (e.g., backing up files, archiving, indexing).

WEB BROWSING ASSISTING AGENTS

Some agents can facilitate browsing by offering the user a tour of the Internet. Such an agent, known as a tour guide, works while the user browses. For example, WebWatcher (www.cmu.edu) helps in finding pages related to the current page, adding hyperlinks to meet the user's search goal and giving advice on the basis of user preferences.

Another example is Letizia (www.media.mit.edu/research/softwareagents). This agent monitors the user's activities with a browser and collects information about the user's behavior. Using various heuristics, the agent tries to anticipate additional items that might be of interest to the user. A similar agent is Netcomber Activist from IBM (activist.gpl.ibm.com). This agent monitors a user surfing through the Yahoo catalog. The user can build an interest profile, customize newspapers for daily reading, and so on.

FREQUENTLY ASKED QUESTIONS AGENTS

These agents guide people to the answers to FAQs. People tend to ask the same or similar questions, and in response news groups, support staffs, and vendors have developed files of FAQs and the most appropriate answers. The problem is that people use natural language, thus asking the same question in several different ways. The agent addresses the problem by indexing large numbers of FAQ files and providing an interface where people can pose their questions in a natural language. The agent uses the text of a question to locate the answer. Because of the limited number of FAQs and the semistructuredness of the questions, the reliability of FAQ agents is very high. GTE Laboratories has developed a FAQ agent that accepts questions from users of Usenet news groups in natural language and answers them by matching question–answer pairs (Whitehead, 1995). FAQFinder can deal with complex FAQs that change over time. The agent can also deal with multiple FAQs in the same domain. For details see O'Leary (1996). Both www.askjeeves.com and agents.umbc.edu are available to the public (see Internet Exercise 10).

INTELLIGENT SEARCH (OR INDEXING) AGENTS

Web information seeking and retrieval are increasingly important and suitable for software agents (Detlor and Arsenault, 2002). *Web robot*, *spider*, *wanderer*, and similar names describe agents that traverse the Web and perform such tasks as information retrieval and discovery, validating links or HTML, and generating statistics. These **search engines** (or *indexing agents*) are very popular, and thousands of them, many of which are very specialized, are available (www.searchengineguide.com). Representative names are InfoSeek, Lycos, Excite, and Hotbot. To achieve better results there are metasearch engines that combine several search engines and other methods of search. **Metasearch engines** (e.g., Spider, Savvy Search, Metacrawler, All-in-One, Web Compass) integrate the findings of the various search engines to answer queries posted by the user.

Indexing agents carry out massive autonomous searches of the Web. First, they scan millions of documents and store an index of key words and words from document titles and texts. The user can then query the agent by asking it to find documents containing certain key words. For details, see Etzioni and Weld (1995) and Wooldridge (2002). Indexing agents were developed for knowledge sharing and acquisition in large databases and documents. For example, see Jones et al. (1995).

INTERNET SOFTBOT FOR FINDING INFORMATION

The search agents described above suggest locations on the Web to the user. Their suggestions are based on a weak model of what the user wants and what information is available at the suggested location. An **Internet softbot** attempts to determine what the user wants and to understand the contents of information services. Etzioni and Weld (1994) discuss the pioneering work on these at the University of Washington. Early softbot agents were able to work only with structured information, such as stock quotes and weather maps or the Federal Express package-tracking service. Therefore, early agents relied on a simple model of the information service for the precise semantics associated with information provided by the service, increasing the reliability of the search. Also see Chen et al. (1997). Recently, Internet softbots such as google.com and www.askjeeves.com have become more powerful.

NETWORK MANAGEMENT AND MONITORING

A slew of intelligent agents were developed to monitor, diagnose problems, conduct security, or manage Internet (or other network) resources (e.g., Bhutani and Khan, 2003; Vlahavas et al., 2002). Some representative agents are described next:

- ***Patrol Application Management.*** This is a family of products that uses intelligent agents to perform such tasks as monitoring and managing applications, databases, middleware, and underlying network resources. It also automates administrative action by pinpointing and correcting potential problems before they affect user productivity. Similar software is AgentWorks (Legent Corporation), which also has the ability to work with other intelligent agents, and Optivity Planning network monitoring (Nortel Networks Inc.).

- ***WatchGuard*** (Seattle Software Labs, www.watchguard.com) is an intelligent Internet and intranet firewall which includes a built-in intelligent agent designed to simplify the configuration, management, and security of networks. The intelligence of the system provides automatic alerts to system administrators whenever questionable configurations or outside attacks are detected.

- ***AlertView*** (Intel Corporation) uses agents to monitor network resources, databases, and e-mail systems for threshold violations. It has about 100 predefined threshold templates to make programming these responses easier.

- ***InterAp.*** InterAp (California Software) is a suite of Internet applications for Windows that uses agent technology to search the Web and automate file transfer.

- ***Mercury Center's NewsHound*** (www.sjmercury.com/hound.html) is a watcher agent that enables information to automatically come back to you based on your query. It can save a lot of time and effort if you structure your query correctly, thus allowing you to automatically scan a variety of national newspapers without having to look at each of them. You just have to construct a good query. Newshound allows you to create a mini Nexis eclipse or a mini Dialog alert. For a small businessperson or investor, it is great. Granted, you are not searching the megavolume of data that you can on Dialog, Nexis, Newsnet, or Datatimes, but you can't beat the price.

- ***Infosage*** (www.infosage.ibm.com) allows users to set up their own simple topical trees as alerts. The user sends IBM an interest profile; IBM uses the profile to filter various news feeds and then sends the filtered information back to the user via e-mail. Related to this is the concept of **Webcasting**, a form of customized broadcasting in which information appears on the user's screen in a ticker-tape format as it becomes available (push technology).

ELECTRONIC COMMERCE AGENTS

Intelligent agents are playing an ever-greater role in e-commerce. See Wang (1999), Jacso (1999), Murch and John (1999), Lee et al. (2002), and Wooldridge (2002). Hundreds of commercial agents perform several major e-commerce activities on the Web. Here we classify these agents by major type of activity, based on Maes et al. (1999). The six classes parallel a customer's six steps in purchasing decision-making and are shown in Figure 13.5 together with a brief explanation. Note that the process is cyclic and the steps may overlap each other.

The classification in Figure 13.5 can help in identifying where agent technologies can be of assistance; for example, see the CASBA system in Kraff et al. (2000). The characteristics of agents described earlier make them well-suited for mediating consumer behaviors involving information filtering and retrieval, personalized evaluations, complex coordination, and time-based interactions. Here are some details and examples.

- ***Need identification.*** Agents can assist the buyer with need identification by providing product information and stimuli. For example, Amazon.com provides its customers with an agent that continuously monitors a set of data (e.g., the arrival of new books) and notifies customers when a book in their area of interest arrives. Similar agents watch for stocks to go below or above a certain level, sending out

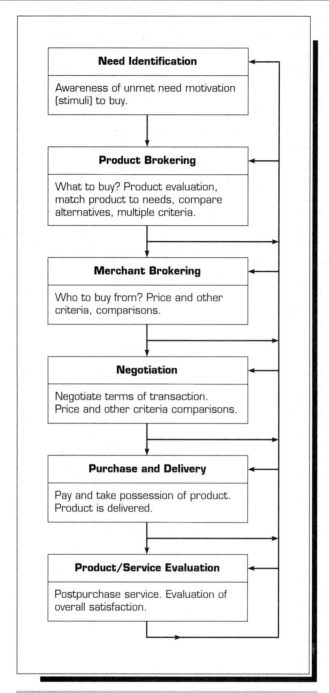

FIGURE 13.5   THE PURCHASING DECISION-MAKING PROCESS

e-mails when that level is reached. Expedia.com notifies customers about low-priced airline tickets for a desired destination whenever they become available.

- ***Product brokering.*** Once a need is established, customers search for a product (or service) that will satisfy it. Several agents are available to assist customers with this task. The pioneering agent in this category, Firefly, was purchased by Microsoft and is no longer available. Based on people's likes (favorite movies, music, interests), Firefly helped marketers predict what customers were likely to want next, and the means to reach them with a customized pitch could be much cheaper yet more effective than mass advertising. Agents that monitor what items are on auction and when are also available (e.g., www.vendio.com).

- *Merchant brokering.* Once a customer knows what product he or she wants, it is necessary to find the best buy. Bargain Finder (Andersen Consulting) was the pioneering agent in this category. Used in online CD shopping, it queried the price of a specific CD at a number of online vendors and returned a list of prices. The Web site BestWebBuys.com helps users to search more than a dozen online stores to find the lowest prices for books or CDs. The agent used in job Web sites for matching recruiters and applicants is another example.

- *Negotiation.* In some markets, price negotiation is common. The benefit of dynamically negotiating a price is that there is a better chance to reach a deal. One type of negotiating agent is used in electronic auctions that last several hours or days (e.g., www.ebay.com). An agent can save valuable time for the bidder by monitoring the process and informing the bidder based on certain criteria. For example, auctionBot (built at the University of Michigan, but retired in 2001) allows users to create auction agents by specifying a number of parameters that vary depending on the type of auction selected. Then it is up to the agent to manage the auction until a final price is met or the deadline for the offer is reached. Another agent bargains on behalf of the seller with the client. The buyer can negotiate with the agent to reach a more acceptable price (Liang and Doong, 2000). Agents can negotiate in pairs, or one agent can negotiate for a buyer with several sellers' agents. In such a case the contact is made with each seller's agent individually, but the buyer's agent can conduct comparisons (Yan et al., 2000).

- *Purchase and delivery.* Agents are used extensively during the actual purchase, including arranging payment and delivery with the customer. For example, if you make a mistake while filling out an electronic order form, an agent will point it out immediately. In buying stocks, the agent tells you when a stock you want to buy on margin is not marginable or when you do not have sufficient funds.

- *Product service and evaluation.* Agents can be used to facilitate after-sale service. For example, the automatic answering agents for e-mail cited earlier are usually productive in answering customer queries. Agents can monitor usage and notify you that it is time to take your car in for periodic maintenance. Agents that facilitate feedback from customers are also useful. For example, Answer Agent and Advice Agent (www.brightsare.com) deal with e-mail from customers, providing replies to queries and advice.

- *Other e-commerce agents.* A large number of agents support many e-commerce activities ranging from advertisement to payment support. See the lists provided periodically by www.botspot.com and www.agents.umbc.edu (see the Agents 101 tutorial). For example, bullsEye2 (www.intelliseek.com) is an intelligent desktop portal. Intelligent agents offer you a productive way to find and manage products, news, and even research. This is a free service that delivers personalized content to users. Mysimon.com tries to imitate human navigational behavior on the Net. Simon shops in real time, and so you find the product at the right place and at the best price.

- *Fraud-detection agents.* Fraud is a big problem in e-commerce because buyers cannot see the products or the sellers. Several vendors offer agent-based fraud-detecting systems.

- *Learning agents.* Several learning agents are used in e-commerce. For example, Learn Sesame (Open Sesame) uses learning theory in monitoring customers' interactions and preferences. Then the agent delivers customized advertisements. Netperceptions Corporation uses a similar approach to personalize content and create customer-loyalty programs. Finally, Plangent (Toshiba) "moves around and thinks." It performs tasks relying on a knowledge base of auctions.

An application of agents in target marketing is described in AIS in Action 13.2.

OTHER AGENTS

Other applications of agents include, but are not limited to, the following areas:

- *User interface agents.* As user populations grow and diversify, computer interfaces will need to learn user habits and preferences and adapt to individuals. Intelligent agents can help with both these problems. Intelligent agent technology allows systems to monitor the user's actions, develop models of user abilities, and automatically help out when problems arise (Conway and Koehler, 2000).
- *Learning and tutoring.* Agents can be built into an e-learning or intelligent tutoring system to facilitate students. A recent study indicates that a speech-driven anthropomorphic agent embodied in the interface of an intelligent tutoring system (ITS) can enhance students' learning experience (Moundridou and Virvou, 2002).
- *Supply-chain management.* Several companies develop agents that support different activities along the supply chain. An example of such an application is described in *Intelligent Systems Report*, January 1999. Lockheed Martin Aircraft uses several agents to monitor the entire supply chain to provide comprehensive decision-support information. More information will be found in Villa (2002).
- *Workflow and administrative management.* Administrative management includes both workflow management and areas such as computer–telephone integration,

---

AIS IN ACTION 13.2

FUJITSU (JAPAN) USES AGENTS FOR TARGETED ADVERTISING

With the increasing popularity of e-commerce, a large body of customer information can be readily acquired on-line. Customer preference ratings for the products offered by a company are an important application that can be utilized in direct marketing campaigns to provide automatic product recommendations.

Since 1996 Fujitsu has been using an agent-based technology called Interactive Marketing Interface (iMi) that allows advertisers to interact directly with targeted customers, providing valuable services and information. The system enhances the customers' Internet experience.

The iMi service provides advertisers with the ability to interact directly with specific segments of the consumer market through the use of software agents, while ensuring that consumers remain anonymous to advertisers. Consumers submit a profile to iMi indicating per-

sonal characteristics, such as product categories of interest, hobbies, travel habits, and the maximum number of e-mail messages per week they want to receive from the iMi service. In turn customers electronically receive product announcements, advertisements, and marketing surveys from advertisers based on their personal-profile information. By answering marketing surveys or acknowledging the receipt of advertisements, consumers earn iMi points redeemable for gift certificates and telephone cards.

The system demonstrates practical commercial applications of agent technology and closely maps the concept of mobile, active agents.

Source: Condensed from Cheung et al. (2003) and a news release from General Magic Corporation, September 1996.

where processes are defined and then automated. In these areas, users need not only to make processes more efficient but also to reduce the cost of human agents. Intelligent agents can be used to ascertain and then automate user wishes or business processes. An example is FlowMark (IBM Corporation), which provides an environment for direct manipulation of graphical objects that define and capture the activity steps of any business process (e.g., handling a claim, approving a line of credit, registering a patent). An activity can be automated (carried out by the execution of a program) or performed by a person. The user defines the process by drawing connectors between the activities and specifying the rules for when each is to be carried out. FlowMark supports both parallel and sequential activities, where the output of one activity step is the input to the next activity step. Once defined, the model can be verified for completeness and correctness. For a more complex system, see Fakes and Karakostas (1999). Agents are also useful in enhancing workflow management in small and medium enterprises (Montaldo et al., 2003).

- *Web mining.* The information discovered and extracted from Web sites must be generalized based on the user's experience. Intelligent agents can learn about their user's interests (Chau et al., 2002; Etzioni, 1996; Menczer, 2003).
- *Monitoring and alerting.* An interesting example of a monitoring and alerting agent is NewsAlert, developed by King and Jones (1995). NewsAlert ensures that the data that reach the manager's desktop are of paramount importance. Liu et al. (2000) implemented a similar agent in the pulp and paper industry in Finland. The agent monitors a few dozen Web sites and provides the user with news on specific topics, prices, and any other needed information. The information is delivered as an electronic newsletter customized for the user. Agents can help monitor the auction process (Lee et al., 2003).
- *Collaboration.* Because an agent typically represents an individual user's interests, collaboration is a natural area for agent-to-agent interaction and communication (e.g., Karacapilidis et al., 2003). IBM, for example, is exploring multi-agent interaction through several research efforts. Agents operate in the background to automatically perform routine tasks for the user, such as filing documents, sending e-mail, looking for particular topics, or archiving older documents. These agents can be created by designers as part of an application for automating routine tasks, such as progress tracking or serving as reminders of overdue items, or for performing more powerful functions, such as manipulating field values and bringing data in from other applications.
- *Mobile commerce.* Agents play a critical role in mobile commerce. For example, Matskin and Tveit (2001) describe the application of mobile commerce agents in WAP-based services. Recommendation systems can also be applied in mobile advertising (Yuan and Tsao, 2003).

13.8 DSS AGENTS AND MULTI-AGENTS

DSS AGENTS

Some of the agents described earlier can be classified as problem-solving or DSS agents (see Kvarroov.com). A framework for DSS agents has been proposed by Hess et al. (2000), who distinguish five types: data monitoring, data gathering, modeling, domain managing, and preference learning. Table 13.1 maps these categories against

TABLE 13.1 Example Agents Utilized in the Extension of the Holsapple and Whinston (1996) Manufacturing Firm DSS.

	Agent Essential Characteristics			Reference Point		
Autonomous Agent	Homeostatic Goal	Persistence	Reactivity	Employer/ Client	Task	Domain
Data monitoring	Report when any price change crosses given threshold values	Stay at supplier's site "forever" or as long as the vendor supplies parts	Capable of detecting vendor price changes	User	Monitor the current rates of the three types of resources and report on them	Vendor site on an extranet
Data gathering	Report discovery of potential suppliers of manufactured parts at reasonable prices	Lifetime of the DSS	Capable of examining directory sites and understanding language used there	User	Look for alternate vendors of specific part; if found, send message back with name and location of source	Travel to directory
Modeling	Maintain "optimal" price and resource policies; report significant dollar consequences	Lifetime of the DSS	Capable of receiving inputs from the domain manager agent (DMA) and passing results back to the DMA	Domain manager agent (DMA)	When notified by DMA, formulate an LP model, solve it using Excel's solver, and report solution to DMA	Model base management system (MBMS) of DSS
Domain managing (say, in the DBMS)	Monitor location and tasks of both local and remote agents functioning on behalf of domain activities; respond to all messages.	Lifetime of the DSS	Capable of communicating with agents (even at a distance) and keeping track of their whereabouts	User	Monitor all other agents (both local and remote) acting on behalf of the domain; trigger appropriate actions on hearing from them	Database management system (DBMS) of DSS (similar agents exist in the MBMS and DGMS)
Preference learning	Learn a specific user's preferences based on the actual history of user/DSS interactions	"Lifetime" of a user of the DSS, even across different sessions	Capable of observing user actions and storing them	User	Record whether specific user takes modeling agent's advice or proceeds on own	Dialog generation and management system (DGMS) of DSS

three major characteristics and three reference points. This table, based on the work of Holsapple and Whinston (1996), presents examples from a manufacturing firm DSS.

Furthermore, Hess et al. have proposed a general framework in which they map the five types of agents against the three major components of DSS (data, modeling, user interface). This framework is shown in Figure 13.6, and it can be used as a guide in agent development and research.

MULTI-AGENTS

Multi-agent systems are a computer-based environment that contains multiple software agents to perform certain tasks. The theoretical basis for multiple agents started with research in a field called **distributed artificial intelligence (DAI)**, which basically represents the intelligent part of distributed problem-solving. DAI is the study of distributed but centrally designed AI systems (Avouris and Gasser, 1992) and involves the design of a multiple-agent distributed system with a problem to solve or a task to accomplish. The issue is how to perform in an effective and efficient manner.

FIGURE 13.6   THE AGENT-ENHANCED GENERAL DSS FRAMEWORK

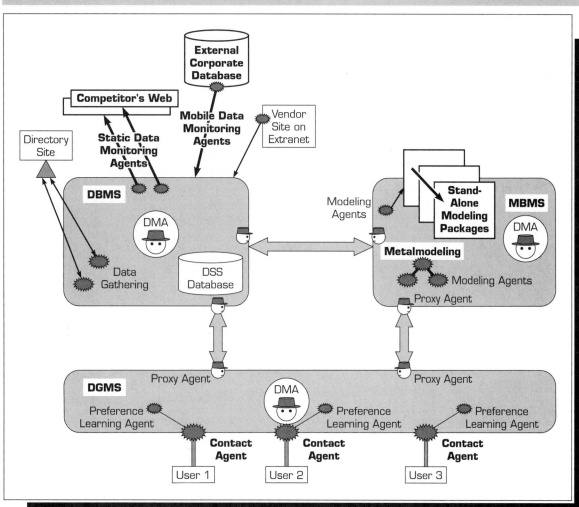

The DAI approach decomposes the task into subtasks, each of which is addressed by an agent. Therefore, in distributed problem-solving it is assumed that there is a single body that is able, at design time, to directly influence the preferences of all the agents in the system (O'Hare and Jennings, 1996). The infrastructure of DAI can be constructed with an architecture known as a blackboard (Avouris and Gasser, 1992). Nute et al. (1995) provide an example of how to perform forest management with a blackboard architecture written in PROLOG. Shih and Srihari (1995) describe DAI in manufacturing-system control.

However, distributed artificial intelligence systems differ from multi-agent systems. There is no single designer standing behind all of the agents in a multi-agent system. The agents can be working toward different goals, even contradictory goals, and sometimes in parallel; they can cooperate or compete with each other (Decker et al., 1999). In a DAI system, an agent acting in a particular way is good for the system as a whole, which is not necessarily the case in a multi-agent system. However, by using incentives, it is possible to influence the agents in a multi-agent system. For example, Chi and Turban (1995) proposed a DAI system for an EIS. Wang et al. (1996) define a model of an autonomous agent in a multi-agent environment, focusing on belief-state models of the agents and the changes that communication forces on their belief states. Chau et al. (2002) used the multi-agent approach to Web mining. O'Hare and O'Grady (2003) proposed a multi-agent system for intelligent content delivery. This should lead to better communication so that the agents can solve a problem cooperatively in a distributed open system. The agent environment is called a multi-agent processing environment (MAPE). Figure 13.7 shows an example of a multi-agent system architecture called Genie, in which the identification agent identifies proper user, the calendar agent schedules events, and the Web agent interacts with the user through Web-based user interfaces (Riekki et al., 2003).

In a multi-agent system, for example, a customer may want to place a long-distance call. Once this information is known, agents representing the carriers submit bids simultaneously. The bids are collected, and the best bid wins. In a complex system, the customer's agent may take the process one step further by showing all bidders the offers, allowing them to rebid or negotiate. This process is currently accomplished manually by increasing the number of companies that place projects and subassemblies up for bids in business-to-business electronic commerce (Turban et al., 2000).

FIGURE 13.7   GENIE THE NET: A SAMPLE MULTI-AGENT SYSTEM

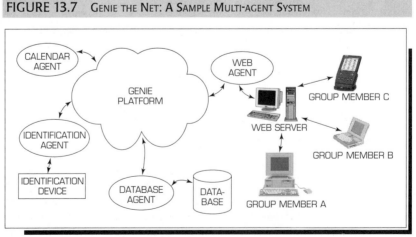

Source: Adapted from Riekki et al. (2003).

A complex solution is decomposed into subproblems, each of which is assigned to an agent that works on the problem independently of others and is supported by a knowledge base. Information is acquired and interpreted by knowledge-processing agents that use deductive and inductive methods as well as computations. The data are refined, interpreted, and sent to the coordinator, who transfers to the user interface whatever is relevant to the user's specific inquiry or need. Multimedia agents can organize the presentation to fit individual executives. If no existing knowledge is available to answer an inquiry, knowledge creating and collecting agents of various types are triggered.

13.9 SEMANTIC WEB: REPRESENTING KNOWLEDGE FOR INTELLIGENT AGENTS

Intelligent agents need to be able to communicate in a flexible way. A key issue in the development of intelligent agents on the Internet is that most information on the Web is not designed for use by other software programs. Traditionally, knowledge over the Web is represented in a format called HTML (Hyper Text Markup Language). It is designed for humans and is based on the concept that information consists of pages of text and graphics containing links. HTML exercises powerful control over the appearance of a Web page.

Unfortunately, HTML does not present the content in a way that another software can easily understand and use. Furthermore, some data may be hidden in the database, and this makes it very difficult for a software agent to acquire them. For example, if a travel agent needs to find a flight from New York to Tokyo on Wednesday afternoon, it would not be able to do so on an HTML-based Web page, because the Web page does not contain information that allows the agent to locate the flight schedule (unless the agent has the permission to use a query language to access the data base). It is also difficult for a software agent to find a product item from a Web page containing many products. Software agents do not care about the page's appearance; they are only concerned with the content.

The semantic Web is a solution to this problem. It provides a content presentation and organization standard so that content can be shared safely among different software applications. With mutually understandable semantic constructs, knowledge on the Web is easier for computer agents to access, understand, and share. Figure 13.8 shows an example of how semantic Web can enhance the power of software agents. When Alex receives an e-mail invitation and needs to make travel arrangements to a conference, software agents can integrate his personal preferences with data from different airlines, hotels, and rental car agencies to make the best arrangements.

DEFINITION OF THE SEMANTIC WEB

The semantic Web is part of the effort to incorporate the meanings and interrelationships of concepts into Web information. As described by Berbers-Lee (2001), the semantic Web is *an extension of the current Web, in which information is given well-defined meanings, better enabling computers and people to work in cooperation*. The semantic Web is meant to enable an environment in which independent, Internet-connected information systems can exchange knowledge and action specifications, resulting in the execution of an activity acceptable to all the systems involved (Schwartz, 2003).

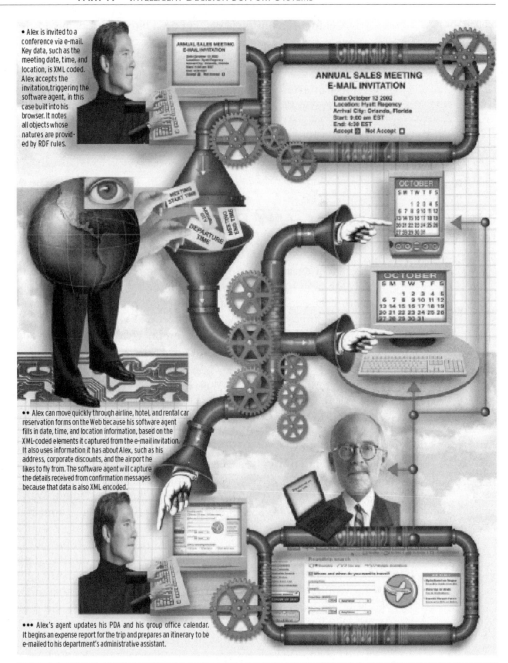

FIGURE 13.8   SAMPLE APPLICATION OF SOFTWARE AGENTS ON A SEMANTIC WEB

Note: Adapted from Cherry (2002).

In practice, the semantic Web is a collaborative effort led by the World Wide Web Consortium (W3C) with the participation of a large number of researchers and industrial partners. W3C defines the **semantic Web** as *the representation of data on the World Wide Web. It is based on the Resource Description Framework (RDF), which integrates a variety of applications using XML* (extensible markup language) *for syntax and URIs for naming* (www.w3c.org). It is built on two existing technologies: XML and *Web services.* The concepts of RDF, XML, and URI will be described later in this section.

XML AND WEB SERVICES

XML is an extension of HTML that represents the meaning of concepts through user-defined tags. It is the foundation of both Web services and semantic Web. In an HTML document, typical information includes definitions like "title" and "fonts." These are called tags. XML allows more tags to be defined to include semantic information. For instance, we can define a tag called "product" or "account receivable" to reveal that the data content is a product or an account receivable. The following is a sample representation of the concept "birds" in XML.

```
<?xml version = "1.0">
<birds>
  Animals that fly:
  <bird>
    <name>Tweety<name?
    <color>Blue</color>
    <location>Mike'Home</loction>
    <eats>birdseeds</eats>
  </bird>
</birds>
```

As you can see, the above representation contains certain attributes of birds that may be used by other applications.

Web services are an XML-based technology that has gained the support of most major software companies, such as IBM, Microsoft and Sun Microsystems. It is central to the envisioned semantic Web.

More and more businesses are using XML in their systems. A typical example is the Galileo system, which connects more than 42,000 travel agency locations to 37 car rental companies, 47,000 hotels, and 350 tour operators. Without the technology, the operation of such a complicated heterogeneous system would not have been possible (Staab, 2003). Amazon.com has also taken advantage of the technology to create an XML version of its database for partners to integrate its service. The concept of Web services is quite simple: it defines standards for connection, communication, description, and discovery among Web-based modules.

Figure 13.9 shows the major building blocks of Web services. As can be seen, Web services include four layers: transport, messaging, service description, and publication and integration (Huhns, 2002).

- *Transport layer.* This layer is responsible for data transmission. It is built on the existing data-transport foundation (including HTTP, SMTP, and FTP mechanisms).
- *XML messaging layer.* The kernel of this layer is XML. The simple object-access protocol (SOAP) provides the protocol that Web-based systems use to communicate with each other when they need to request services, such as finding a product or a flight schedule.
- *Service description layer.* In order for a Web service to be known to other services, a description language is necessary. Web Services Description Language (WSDL) allows services to be described in a machine-readable form that can specify the names of functions, their required parameters, and their results.
- *Publication and integration layer.* This top layer publishes available services for application. The Universal Description, Discovery, and Integration (UDDI) gives users and businesses a "yellow page" of services so that they can easily find needed services. See www.uddi.org for detail.

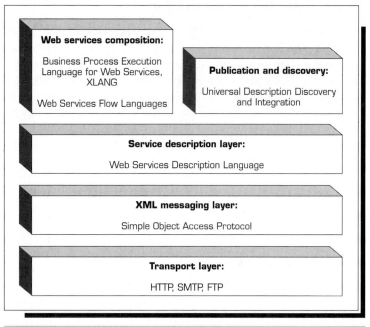

FIGURE 13.9 ARCHITECTURE OF WEB SERVICES

LAYER CAKE OF THE SEMANTIC WEB

The semantic Web extends the layers defined in Web services to further enhance the organization of knowledge and the interoperability of different agents. Ontology definition is a critical factor for presenting knowledge in an interchangeable way. Key components of the semantic Web technology include the following (Preece and Decker, 2002):

- A unifying data model such as RDF (Resource Description Framework). See www.w3.org/rdf.
- Language with defined semantics built on RDF, such as DAML + OIL (DARPA Agent Markup Language plus Ontology Inference Layer). See www.daml.org for more detail.
- Ontologies of standardized terminology for marking up Web resources, used by semantically rich service-level descriptions and support tools that assist the generation and processing of semantic markup.

Tim Berners-Lee presented a "layer cake" of the semantic Web at the 2000 XML conference. The layer cake, as shown in Figure 13.10, includes the major elements of the semantic Web. The foundation consists of the basic machine-readable form of data representation in Unicode and Universal Resource Indicator (URI). XML is then used to render the data. On top of XML are RDF and a four-layer architecture to support information exchange among agents: ontology, logic, proof, and trust.

UNIVERSAL RESOURCE IDENTIFIERS

Universal Resource Identifiers (URIs) are similar to URLs (Universal Resource Locators) in the Internet, but are more general. A URL points to a particular Web site, while an URI points to any available Web resource. Therefore, all URLs are also URIs, but not vice versa. Resources can further be broadened to include objects not available on the Internet. Figure 13.11 shows an example of the semantic Web.

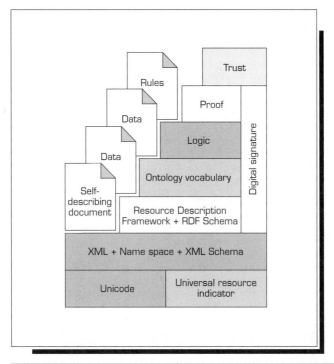

FIGURE 13.10   *"Layer Cake" of Semantic Web by Tim Berners-Lee*

Source: Adapted from Hendler, 2001.

RESOURCE DESCRIPTION FRAMEWORK

Resource Description Framework (RDF) is designed to relate one URI to another. It provides a data model that supports fast integration of data sources by bridging semantic differences. RDF is a sort of statement about resources and their relationships. It can, for instance, express the relationship that Mary is John's sister or that a new auc-

FIGURE 13.11   Weather Service Class and Its Properties on the Semantic Web

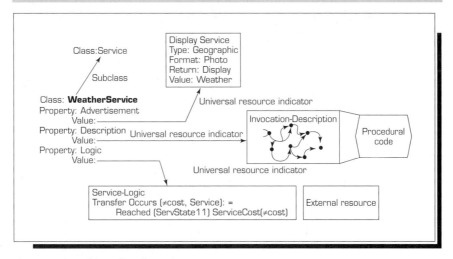

Source: Adapted from Hendler, 2001.

tion bid is higher than the current highest bid. Therefore, RDF is often used to represent metadata about other Web resources such as XML files, and may be called a *resource metadata*. More detail can be found in Decker et al. (2000) or McBride (2002).

ONTOLOGY

Ontology is defined in the *Oxford English Dictionary* as "the science or study of being." In artificial intelligence, we usually attribute the notion of ontology to the specification of a conceptualization—that is, defined terms and the relationships between them. Or, simply put, ontology is a set of terms related to a knowledge domain, including the vocabulary, the semantic interconnections, and some simple rules of inference and logic for particular topics. For example, the ontology of cooking and cookbooks may include ingredients, procedures for processing the ingredients, and the differences between various cooking styles. For the semantic Web, an ontology is a collection of related RDF statements that together specify a variety of relationships among data elements and ways of making logical inferences among them.

LOGIC

Service logic states the rules governing the use of ontological statements. For example, if a transaction rule requires that a certain amount of money must be transferred after a service invocation is reached (e.g., ServState11), then the rule may be represented as:

```
TransferOccurs(#cost, Service):=
   Reached(ServState11), ServiceCost(#cost).
```

PROOF AND TRUST

Proof and trust are high-level functions in the semantic Web. Agents negotiating the execution of certain functions need to check complex logic, exchange proofs, and build trust before they can collaborate. For example, when a bidding agent submits a high bid, the auction agent needs to see proof that the bidding agent is legitimate before accepting its offer.

ADVANTAGES AND LIMITATIONS OF THE SEMANTIC WEB

Using the semantic Web to design intelligent agents has the following advantages:

- *Easy to understand.* The semantic Web demonstrates objects and their relationships as graphic templates for easy understanding.
- *Easy resource integration.* It is easier to integrate systems and modules designed in the semantic Web. This also makes it easier to do system analysis and maintenance.
- *Saving development time and costs.* The semantic Web allows incremental ontology creation, which can more rapidly produce a usable system. The ability to use other resources more easily can save development time and costs.
- *Automatic updating of content.* Since agents can easily locate specific knowledge on the semantic Web, they can have functions to automatically update or import contents. This adds the level of intelligence to the software agents.
- *Easy resource reuse.* Ontology-based annotations can turn briefings into reusable resources.

The limitations of the semantic Web include the following:

- The graphical representation may be oversimplified. For example, an arrow is used to represent a relation between two instances, but this method is unable to show more complicated multiple-party relations.
- The semantic Web needs more tools for searching content and building references to pre-existing instances.

- The ontology may not be correctly defined. In some cases, the outcome may be severe. It is still hard to prove the completeness or correctness of a defined ontology.
- Agents dealing with a semantic Web containing information that is inconsistent, incorrect, or lacks reliable sources may be contaminated or misled to a wrong decision.
- Since the semantic Web allows agents from different systems to communicate and share information, security and related issues are a key concern. This is always a problem for an open system.

APPLICATION OF SEMANTIC WEB SERVICES

Semantic Web services combine the semantic Web with Web services. One of the first applications of semantic Web services is the MusicBrainz (www.musicbrainz.org), which provides a large database of music metadata for sharing (Swartz, 2002). By 2002, it already had more than 300,000 tracks. In fact, the idea of MusicBrainz can be traced back to the Internet Compact Disc Database (CDDB) project started in 1996. After CDDB was acquired by a content-delivery company and no longer open for free use, several projects were created to replace it. One of them, the CDIndex, later became MusicBrainz.

The major function of MusicBrainz is to provide semantic information over the Web for other systems to use. When you purchases a new CD and insert it into your computer, your audio player will probably come up with a generic name (e.g., *Audio CD23*), complete with *track 1*, *track 2*, and so on. If you were using MusicBrainz, the audio player would have attempted to connect to the MusicBrainz server, to see if that CD's metadata were available. If it were, your CD player would have renamed the CD and the tracks. If the metadata were not available and you had filled the names for your own use, then MusicBrainz would ask you whether you wanted to share the information. If you did, the information would be sent to MusicBrainz to share with other users. MusicBrainz provides the metadata in RDF. Figure 13.12 shows a graphical representation of MusicBrainz RDF data.

FIGURE 13.12   GRAPHICAL REPRESENTATION OF MUSICBRAINZ DATA

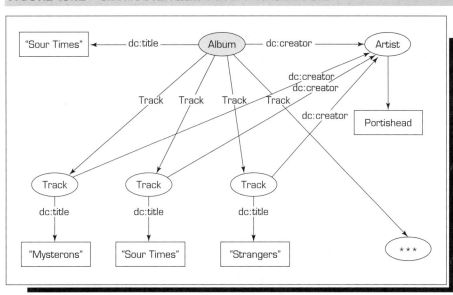

Source: Adapted from Swartz (2002).

Because MusicBrainz's data format is open (in the RDF format), it can be repurposed for numerous applications. For example, file-sharing systems (e.g., Napster, Freenet, Audio Galaxy) can use the metadata to provide more information about the MP3s that are available for download or to make it easier to search for a song. Artists can provide links so that appreciative fans can donate money if they like the music.

13.10 WEB-BASED RECOMMENDATION SYSTEMS

A major e-commerce application of intelligent systems uses them to recommend appropriate products to customers. A typical example is the book recommendation agent adopted by online bookstores. The "people who bought this book also bought" area in Figure 13.13 is the output of the recommendation agent at Barnes and Noble.

The major motivation for using recommendation agents is that personalization is a major trend in marketing and customer services. Each person must be treated as a unique customer so that products/services can be offered according to the customer's unique interests. In order to support such a marketing effort, it is essential to collect and analyze contextual information related to a user's interests and information needs. For example, once you have visited an online bookstore, such as Amazon.com, the store keeps track of what you have viewed and purchased, and uses the data as a basis for recommending new items for your consideration (see AIS in Action 13.3). Intelligent

FIGURE 13.13   BOOK RECOMMENDATIONS AT BN.COM

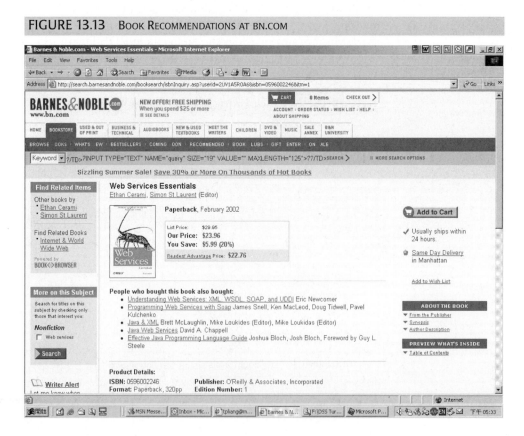

AMAZON.COM USES COLLABORATIVE FILTERING TO RECOMMEND PRODUCTS

Online bookstore Amazon.com has more than 29 million customers and several million catalog items. In order to enhance its marketing and customer services, Amazon.com uses recommendation algorithms extensively to personalize its Web service for each customer's unique shopping needs. Clicking on the "Your Recommendations" link leads customers to an area where they can filter their recommendations by product line and subject area, rate the recommended products, rate their previous purchases, and see why items are recommended. It also has an interesting function, called *shopping cart recommendation*, which offer customers product suggestions based on the items in their shopping cart.

The recommendation algorithm is a modified version of collaborative filtering called *item-to-item collaborative filtering*, which scales to massive data sets to accommodate enormous numbers of users and product offerings and produces real-time recommendations to customers. The major difference is that, instead of matching similar customers together, the algorithm matches each of the user's purchased and rated items to similar items, and subsequently recommends those similar items to the user.

Mechanism for generating recommendations
The key concept of the algorithm is to process item similarity offline in order to improve computing efficiency. Rather than matching the user to similar customers, the Amazon algorithm matches each of the user's purchased and rated items to similar items, then combines them into a recommendation list.

To determine the most similar match for a given item, the algorithm calculates the similarity between a single product and all related products to build a similar-items table by finding similar items that customers tend to purchase together. The degree of correlation between different items is constructed. Based on the similar-items table and the particular items ordered by a customer, the system is able to identify items similar to each product that the user purchased or rated. Finally, the system compiles these items into a recommendation list that includes the most correlated or popular items as recommendations to the user.

Source: Linden et al. (2003).

---

systems that provide the service are called **recommendation systems** (or **agents**) or **recommender systems (or agents)**. A recommendation system is an intelligent system that can identify a customer's interests from existing usage data and accordingly make suggestions to enhance customer loyalty and achieve higher conversion/retention rates.

TAXONOMY OF RECOMMENDATION MECHANISMS

The user profile is the foundation around which most of the functions of a recommendation system are designed. Many recommendation methods have been developed in a relatively short time. A comprehensive survey by Montaner et al. (2003) divided their functions into two major categories: *profile generation and maintenance* and *profile exploitation and recommendation*. The system needs to build and maintain a user profile and then extract useful information from it for making recommendations. Each category includes several dimensions, as shown in Table 13.2.

PROFILE GENERATION AND MAINTENANCE

A recommendation system needs to generate and maintain a user profile in order to know the user. Unfortunately, users often do not want to spend time indicating their interests to create a profile. Moreover, a user's interests may change over time, making profiles difficult to maintain. The following aspects are important for generating and maintaining profiles:

TABLE 13.2   Dimensions in Recommendation Functions

Profile Generation and Maintenance	*Profile Exploitation and Recommendation*
User profile representation	Information filtering method
Initial profile generation	User profile-item matching technique
Profile learning technique	User profile matching technique
Relevance feedback	Profile adaptation technique

Source: Montaner et al. (2003).

- *User profile representation.* Several approaches have been taken to represent user profiles, such as a history of the user's purchases, Web navigation or e-mails, or demographic features (e.g., gender, age, occupation).
- *Initial profile generation.* Once the structure of the profile is determined, an initial set of user profile data must be created. The initial user profiles may be created manually or automatically from existing data or predefined stereotypes.
- *Profile-learning technique.* User profile data must be processed to find useful patterns for recommendations. The most typical approaches for profile learning are *clustering* and *classifiers*. Clustering techniques allow users to be clustered into many similar clusters. Recommendations can be made based on their similarity. Classifiers use information about an item and the user profile as inputs and have the output category represent how strongly to recommend an item to a user. The discovery of association rules by inductive learning is a good example of classifiers.
- *Relevance feedback.* Human interests change over as time passes. Therefore, the system needs to collect relevant feedback information. The feedback may be *explicit* or *implicit*. The explicit approach asks users to explicitly evaluate items to indicate their preference (e.g., ranking items after browsing). The implicit approach has an embedded module in the system to infer user preferences by monitoring certain evidences, such as the browsed Web pages, browsing time, or keystroke sequences.
- *Profile-adaptation technique.* Since the user's interests may change over time, the information gathered from relevance feedback must be analyzed to modify the user's profile. The adaptation includes adding new information and gradually forgetting old information. A typical forgetting approach is to define a time window for analysis. Data moving out of the window will be forgotten.

PROFILE EXPLOITATION AND RECOMMENDATION

A recommendation system relies on the available information (e.g., items and user profile) to make decisions. Three main tasks are important for performing the job: information-filtering methods, item-profile matching (for content-based filtering), and user-profile matching (for collaborative filtering).

- *Information-filtering method.* Information filtering means identifying useful items from a large number of candidates. Three methods are popular: demographic filtering, collaborative filtering, and content-based filtering. Demographic filtering uses the user's demographic data to determine which item may be appropriate for recommendation. Content-based filtering recommends items for the user based on the description of previously evaluated items and information available from the content (e.g., keywords). Collaborative filtering matches people with similar interests and make recommendations accordingly. Hybrid approaches that use more than one method are also available. Content-based and collaborative filtering will be described later.

- *User profile–item matching.* Content-based filtering systems use direct comparisons between the user profile and new items. Thus, a user profile–item matching is necessary. Several methods exist. Popular ones include keyword matching and nearest-neighbor algorithms.
- *User-profile matching.* Collaborative filtering needs to find similar users before making a recommendation. In general, the process of computing includes three steps: find similar users, create a neighborhood, and compute a prediction based on the selected neighbors. Clustering and classification techniques are useful in this stage.

COLLABORATIVE FILTERING

Collaborative filtering uses the concept of market segmentation (dividing customers into peer groups with similar needs) in predicting user preferences. In essence, it compares the current user's profile (e.g., purchase history, browsing behavior) to the profiles of users in the rest of the population to identify users in the database who may be similar to the current user. Interests found from similar users are used to infer the interest of the current user, and recommendations are made accordingly. Collaborative recommendation systems have been used by the *Los Angeles Times*, the *London Times*, CRAYON, and Tango to provide customized online newspapers (Goldberg & colleagues, 1992). Figure 13.14 shows the architecture of a collaborative recommender system.

Data collected in a collaborative filtering system typically comprise a two-dimensional user-product matrix where the rows feature the users and the columns feature the products (e.g., books or videos). User preference for each of the products is represented by the value in the cell in the matrix. Unfortunately, this sort of data orga-

FIGURE 13.14   AN ARCHITECTURE OF COLLABORATIVE AND USAGE-BASED WEB RECOMMENDER

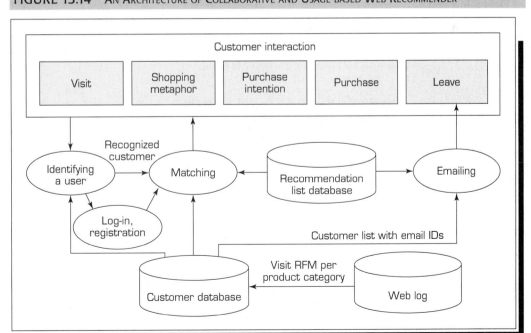

Source: Ha (2002).

nization often leads to severe scaling and performance problems when data sets become very large—for example, when millions of users and products are represented in the user-product matrix. Besides, as most users refuse to provide product evaluations or tend to purchase only a small number of items in the product catalog, the user-product matrix tends to be very spare and becomes inefficient when applied on a large scale. These problems may be partially resolved by using dimensionality-reduction techniques, such as clustering and principal-component analysis. Yet it is not at all possible to achieve a reduction in data size without a tradeoff in recommendation quality.

Similarity between customers can be measured in a number of ways. Similarity index is a measurement frequently used for assessing similarity between individuals. Commonly used similarity metrics include Jaccard's coefficient, distance measure, and the Pearson product-moment correlation coefficient (Herlocker et al., 1999). After user similarity is computed, clustering models are applied to group customers into peer groups. Cluster analysis is the most useful statistical tool for aggregating discrete units (e.g., consumers) into groups (i.e., segments) based on their similarities (Iacobucci et al., 2000). Cluster-analysis tools typically begin with a set of segments, each of which contains a randomly sampled user. The algorithm then matches the rest of the users against those already assigned into the segments, while simultaneously tracking emerging communities of interest and weeding out unpopular segments. The process is repeated until all the users in the database are assigned into one of the segments in the model.

In general, a collaborative filtering system generates recommendations by predicting a person's preferences as the weighted sum of other people's preference in his/her subset, with the weights being proportional to the strength of correlation between two individuals.

It should be noted that this approach has several limitations. Since the algorithm works by grouping customers into subsets, poor recommendations may be given to those users whose tastes are unusual compared to the rest of the population. The system also fails to provide users with reasons for a recommendation. In addition, since the algorithm can only be used when the database contains the preference data for a particular item, it cannot generate recommendations for a new product that nobody has used or rated. For example, most collaborative filtering algorithms cannot advise a user on whether a new book is good.

CONTENT-BASED FILTERING

Unlike collaborative filtering algorithms, content-based filtering does not consider similarities between users in making recommendations. Instead, it offers recommendations solely on the basis of similarities between products or information packets. Content-based filtering uses attributes associated with the object (e.g., keywords in a document) and their matches with known user rankings on previously purchased items in predicting user preferences. It seeks to identify idiosyncratic features of the items the user had bought and recommends items with similar features. For instance, most classes of products can be segregated into a set of distinct categories (e.g., music can be classified by artists or by type, such as pop, jazz, and classical). A person who purchased a classical CD by Beethoven is more likely to be interested in a classical CD by Mozart than another user who mostly purchases jazz. Hence, a list of items related to the user's previous purchases may provide a reasonable recommendation to meet the user's shopping needs.

The algorithm typically starts by analyzing the morphology of the texts or product descriptions of various documents/products to identify their idiosyncratic features and

AIS IN ACTION 13.4

CONTENT-BASED FILTERING IN EUROVACATION.COM

Recommendation systems are increasingly used by travel and tourism Web sites to help travelers make faster, more informed decisions about their vacations. EuroVacations.com, one of the most successful travel-counseling Web sites, employs Triplehop Technologies's TripMatcher to provide customized recommendations on destinations and travel products according to the site visitors' stated or implied preferences.

The software, called Destination Wizard on the EuroVacations site, works primarily on a content-based approach in generating recommendations. Users are asked to indicate their needs and constraints (e.g., activities interested in, budget, duration) by ticking the options available under a list of questions. The system then compares the user inputs with the attributes of a list of available travel products and destinations in the database.

To reduce user effort, the system simultaneously builds an attribute-based behavioral profile of the user based on the user's interactions with the system on each visit to the Web site, and from this extracts implicit information about the users' interests. It then predicts the user's preference by combining statistics on past queries and a weighted average of the importance of different attributes assigned by similar users. Hence, users only need to answer a limited number of questions to obtain personalized recommendations targeted to their interests. The system presents the output to the user in order of relevance. By exploiting content-based recommendation technology, EuroVacation.com has achieved a higher browser-to-buyer conversion rate.

express their characteristics as a string of keywords or associated words. It then compares the content (characteristics) of various items in the catalog against a user profile built up by analyzing the content of items the user has rated or bought in the past. The algorithm usually applies formulas that give higher weights to certain indexing words or attributes to compute the similarity of the products. It then recommends goods in order of their similarity to the user's previous purchases.

In contrast to collaborative filtering, content-based filtering scales and performs well even if the user has few purchases or ratings. However, the algorithm suffers from a number of shortcomings. First, the characteristics of certain classes of goods (e.g., food, drawings) cannot be comprehensively or wholesomely captured by a few discriminating words. Thus the recommendations generated by the algorithm tend to neglect aesthetic aspects of the product, such as layout, images, diagrams, and other important qualities, such as loading time (for Web offerings). Also, the user may not be given novel information because the recommendations only involve a search for items similar to previous purchases. An example of content-based filtering used in Eurovacation.com is illustrated in AIS in Action 13.4.

13.11 MANAGERIAL ISSUES OF INTELLIGENT AGENTS

Intelligent agents provide an innovative way to process routine tasks automatically. Certain managerial issues are important because they are given a certain degree of autonomy and authorization. This is especially true for mobile agents (Schoder and Eymann, 2000).

COST JUSTIFICATION

With technology rapidly changing and intelligent agents still evolving, it may be hard to justify spending lots of money on something that may be obsolete tomorrow. Simple software agents, such as the wizards found in software products, are fairly easy to justify because they are usually included as one of the features of the software product (e.g., Excel).

Standalone agents that perform complex tasks, on the other hand, can be quite expensive. Most of the cost of these agents derives from the tremendous amount of R&D that goes into creating them. In addition, they may be custom programs that require extensive programming time. Justifying agents is like justifying other decision-support systems. The benefits are often intangible and the results are hard to quantify, but if you do not invest in the technology, your competitor will, and you may be left behind (see Hendler, 1999).

SECURITY

Agents are a technology with many unknown ramifications. In light of the great concern about the security of systems, does it make sense for a company to knowingly send out agents that could come back laden with a virus or hiding a Trojan horse? Will other companies even allow unfamiliar agents to visit their systems? Firewalls and other available security software and hardware make it possible to forbid entry to an unknown agent, but it is difficult to stop impostors.

PRIVACY

There are cases in which agents have intruded on people's privacy. For example, some Microsoft users have been informed that the software giant has built cookies into some of its packages that capture information about new owners and Web users. If the user does not object, this information is delivered back to Microsoft by its agents when the user logs onto the Internet.

INDUSTRIAL INTELLIGENCE AND ETHICS

Legitimate industrial intelligence gathering is usually expensive and time-consuming. Illegitimate business practices, such as cyber-spying, can be all the more tempting because they are hard to detect and there are no clear-cut rules or laws governing many of these activities. If a competitor is not satisfied with just getting information about a firm, it can also arm its agents with assault capabilities. Given the borderless nature of the Internet, the risk that an unethical firm will compete unfairly by stealing another's costly research and development becomes even more frightening. What is to keep seemingly friendly programs from doing untold damage? Perhaps it will be possible to build an intelligent agent that can discriminate friendly or neutral agents from belligerent outside agents and take appropriate defensive action (Mandry et al., 1999).

OTHER ETHICAL ISSUES

Agents represent a significant new way of interacting with the world. Just as a unique etiquette ("netiquette") has evolved on the Internet, there will need to be new definitions of acceptable and unacceptable uses for agents. Who will establish the definitions and the ethical philosophy for how agents are to be used?

New technology is accompanied by new opportunities for those who have access to it. Who will have access to agents? Will all companies have agents? Will those with early access to agents be able to build insurmountable barriers to competition? Will agents displace people from jobs in research and strategic planning?

AGENT LEARNING

The theory behind agents is that the more you use them, the more they learn, and, therefore, the more effective they are. Agents can learn from one of three sources. The first is the defined rules established in the agent's programming. The second is the user interface; in other words, the agent learns the Net activities and preferences of the user. The third source is exterior databases or a knowledge base. The managerial issue pertains to justifying the cost (determining which method is most cost-effective) and making sure the agent learns what you want it to learn.

AGENT ACCURACY

Along with agent learning comes agent accuracy. Assuming that the agent develops the ability to learn, the next issue facing managers is the accuracy of the data submitted to and returned by the agent. The inherent desire is to blindly accept recommendations from an agent that has cost so much, both in time and money. But is this wise? Managers must be comfortable with the source from which agents draw data. There must be some control over the quality of this information, or the agent's results will not be believable. Even worse is the possibility that strategic decisions will be made using incorrect information.

HEIGHTENED EXPECTATIONS

With any new technology or product come high expectations. This is especially true in regard to intelligent agents. It sounds wonderful to have an agent to carry out tasks in only a few minutes that would normally take hours or days to accomplish. But the reality is that many agents are not yet a cure-all in the expanding world of information. Because the development of intelligent agents is far from complete, their cost-effectiveness may be small. This will result in disappointment and rejection by people who are not prepared for what they get. Managers pushing for the use of intelligent agents must communicate with everyone involved to ensure that their expectations are realistic.

SYSTEM ACCEPTANCE

Like the introduction of any new technology, the addition of intelligent agents to an existing system can sometimes create problems. Systems have different architectures and operating systems. This, along with the presence of a whole host of different software packages that maintain databases, can make agents less effective or even nonfunctional. Methods are being developed to provide standards for interagent and agent-to-system interoperability (Finin et al., 1997; Genesereth, 1997).

SYSTEM TECHNOLOGY

As intelligent agents become more powerful, the systems required to run them must also be more powerful. Many companies have obsolete computer systems that are only a few years old. Managers must ensure, before investing in agent technology, that their system can provide the resources required by the agents. In addition, agent technology is rapidly expanding, and so system technology flexibility is a must.

❖ Chapter Highlights

- There are several definitions of intelligent agents (IA). Basically, they are software that execute tasks with some degree of autonomy.
- Intelligent agents can save time and are consistent. Some agents have a considerable amount of autonomy. Others have very little.
- Major characteristics of IA are autonomy, background operation, communication capabilities, and reactivity. Some are mobile, mainly if they are Web-related.
- The major purpose of IA is to deal with information overload. However, agents can improve productivity, quality, and speed.
- Agents can be classified in several ways, depending on their mission.
- Mobile agents can perform tasks in different locations. Other agents work in one place (e.g., a server or a workstation).
- Agents can be classified into three major application types: Internet, e-commerce, and others.

- Multi-agent systems can be used to perform tasks more complex than those performed by single agents, but they have not yet matured.
- Intelligent agents play a major role in data mining, helping to find unnoticeable relationships, and quickly providing answers to queries.
- Semantic Web is a new form of representing knowledge on the Web. It enables intelligent agents to exchange knowledge based on a standard protocol.
- Product recommendation is a very important application of intelligent systems. It analyzes user profiles and makes recommendations based on predicted user interests.
- Recommendation mechanisms may be collaborative, content-based, or demographical filtering. Each method has its advantages and limitations.
- Applications of intelligent agents must take security, privacy, and other managerial issues into consideration.

❖ Key Words

- agency
- agent
- bots
- collaborative filtering
- content-based filtering
- demographic filtering
- distributed artificial intelligence (DAI)
- intelligent agent (IA)
- Internet softbot

- knowbots
- metasearch engines
- mobile agents
- mobility
- multi-agent systems
- multi-agents
- organizational agents
- personal agents
- private agents
- public agents

- search engines
- semantic Web
- semantic Web services
- softbots (intelligent software robots)
- software agents
- software demon
- Webcasting
- Web mining
- wizards

❖ Questions for Review

1. Define intelligent agent (IA). What does it mean?
2. List the major components of IA.
3. Define the autonomy of IA.
4. List the major characteristics of IA.
5. Define mobile agents, and describe the difference between mobile agents and multi-agents.
6. List the major advantages of IA.
7. List and describe the types of agents according to the classification by IBM.
8. Describe the work of an FAQ agent.
9. Describe how agents that compare prices, and similar information, work.
10. Define distributed artificial intelligence (DAI).
11. List and describe the six steps in electronic shopping.

12. Describe the semantic Web, and explain the differences between the semantic Web and XML.
13. Define the recommendation agent and its role in e-commerce.
14. Briefly illustrate the mechanism for product recommendations.
15. Describe why a recommendation system needs a user profile and how a user profile can be built and maintained.
16. Describe content-based filtering and collaborative filtering, and compare their advantages and limitations.
17. List and describe major managerial issues related to the use of IA.

❖ QUESTIONS FOR DISCUSSION

1. What are the major characteristics of the information-overload problem?
2. Relate the Internet to the information-overload problem and discuss how IA can be used to solve the information-overload problem.
3. Discuss the tasks that an e-mail agent can carry out.
4. Distinguish between a search engine and a meta-search engine. What roles can intelligent agents play in improving search performance?
5. What is the difference between a browsing agent and a search (indexing) agent?
6. Personalogic and similar agents attempt to learn about people's preferences. Explain how such information can be used in marketing and advertising.
7. What role can IA play in electronic commerce?
8. Explain the benefits of NewsAlert and similar agents in reducing information overload.
9. Distinguish between DAI and multi-agents. What are the advantages and limitations of multi-agent systems?
10. Why is negotiation so important in electronic commerce? What is the advantage of IA negotiation?
11. Review the four levels of IA intelligence. Provide a sample application of intelligent agents at each level.
12. Review IBM's IA model: agency, intelligence, mobility. Can you compare a search engine to Personalogic in this model?
13. Why is semantic Web useful for developing a more friendly environment for intelligent agents? What is the difference between semantic Web and semantic networks, or other mechanisms for representing information over the Internet?
14. Recommendation systems are gaining more popularity in e-commerce. Discuss the pros and cons of using the recommendation mechanism in an electronic shop. Do you like the recommendation mechanism of Amazon.com? Why or why not?

❖ EXERCISES

1. Read the paper by Maes et al. (1999) regarding the use of IA in electronic commerce. Examine the categories of applications and find commercial examples of each.
2. Find the relationship between fuzzy logic and DAI (or intelligent agents). Prepare a report. Explain the importance of fuzzy logic systems in this situation.
3. How are IA actually constructed? Investigate the literature and write a report. Visit www.robocup.org and examine its annual competition. Explain how IA can be used there.
4. What mundane tasks would you like an intelligent agent to perform for you? List them (you may want to include some tasks that are now being handled for you by other people), and describe how an IA could help. Compare your results to those of other class members.
5. Find an article reporting the application of intelligent agents to movie recommendation, and design a collaborative filtering mechanism for user profile generation and maintenance. What features must be included in the user profile? What mechanism may be used to match the user profile and item features?
6. Find an article reporting the application of intelligent agents to music recommendation, and design a content-based filtering mechanism for this purpose.

❖ GROUP EXERCISES

1. Visit the Web site of Microsoft or contact its resellers. Find out what IA wizards do to improve the use of operating systems, spreadsheets, and other software products. Prepare a report to compare the use of software agents in Microsoft products before and after the year 2000.
2. Investigate the use of intelligent agents in electronic commerce. You may begin with http://www.botspot.com/, and find recent work by searching www.media.mit.edu, www.agents.umbc.edu, and other Web sites. Prepare a report on developments since 2000.
3. Prepare a report about the use of collaborative filtering and content-based filtering approaches in online stores and services.
4. Visit www.w3.org and other Web sites related to the development of semantic Web. Please summarize the rationale for its development and what tools are available for developing semantic Web–based intelligent systems.

❖ Internet Exercises

1. Access www.compare.net. Ask the agent to price a specific CD for you. Do you think that you can get the CD cheaper at a local store?
2. RINGO (jolomo.net/ringo.html) is based on social information filtering. Visit the Web site, explain the social information filtering and its possibilities in the use of the service to obtain suggestions for music and movies you may like.
3. Access Autonomy Inc.'s Web site (www.autonomy.com). Examine the various products and services provided. Identify where intelligent systems and agents might be used. Examine products for KM, e-commerce, i-WAP, and new media.
4. Access the IBM Web site (www.almaden.ibm.com/almaden/projects.html) to find the IBM strategies on IA. Can you find IA projects that were completed or supported by IBM? Explain why or why not.
5. Investigate the latest research on DAI systems and multi-agent systems (start with www.agentlink.org).
6. Post several queries to www.google.com and www.ask.com. Compare the top 10 answers from them. What is the major difference between the two sites? Prepare a report to explain the difference.

IMPLEMENTING MSS IN THE E-BUSINESS ERA

As seen throughout the book, supporting decision making today is highly inter-related with Web technologies. The concluding part of this book is divided into two chapters. In Chapter 14 we describe the field on e-commerce (EC) as it is related to MSS. Special attention is given to the relationships between EC tools and decision making. Also, the support provided by MSS tools to EC is described.

The MSS technologies described in this text can be implemented as stand-alone systems, but they can also be integrated with other computer-based systems and among themselves. Chapter 15 provides a coverage of the major implementation issues related to such integration. Also described in this chapter are the major impacts of MSSs on individuals, organizations, and society. The book is closed at the end of Chapter 15 with a brief discussion of the future MSS.

CHAPTER 14

ELECTRONIC COMMERCE

LEARNING OBJECTIVES

❖ Describe electronic commerce: its scope, benefits, limitations, and types

❖ Understand auctions and portals mechanisms

❖ Describe the major applications of business-to-consumer e-commerce, including service industries and electronic auctions

❖ Discuss the importance and activities of B2C market research, eCRM, and online advertising

❖ Describe business-to-business and collaborative commerce applications

❖ Describe emerging e-commerce applications, such as intrabusiness and B2E commerce, and e-learning

❖ Describe e-government activities

❖ Describe mobile commerce and pervasive computing

❖ Describe the e-commerce infrastructure and support services, including payments and logistics

❖ Discuss some ethical and legal e-commerce issues

The impact of electronic commerce (e-commerce, or EC) on decision-making regarding procurement, shopping, business collaboration, and customer services as well as on delivery of various services is so dramatic that almost every organization is affected. E-commerce is changing all business functional areas and their important tasks, ranging from advertising to paying bills (see Drucker, 2002). It is also changing the face of IT in general and decision support in particular (see Earl and Khan, 2001). The nature of competition is also changing drastically, due to new online companies, new business models, and the diversity of EC-related products and services. E-commerce provides unparalleled opportunities for companies to expand worldwide at a small cost, increase market share, and reduce costs. Finally, traditional DSS can facilitate the use of certain EC activities as well as integrate with it. Therefore, EC is highly correlated with managerial decision-making, as will be seen throughout this chapter.

14.1 Opening Vignette: EC Provides Decision Support to Hi-Life Corporation
14.2 Overview of E-Commerce
14.3 EC Mechanisms: Electronic Auctions and Portals

14.1 OPENING VIGNETTE: E-COMMERCE PROVIDES DECISION SUPPORT TO HI-LIFE CORP.

THE PROBLEM

Hi-Life Corporation owns and operates 720 convenience retail stores in Taiwan, where it sells over 3,000 different products. A major problem is keeping a proper level of inventory of each product in each store. Overstocking is expensive because of storage costs and tying money up to buy and maintain the inventory. Understocking reduces sales and could result in unhappy customers who may go to a competitor. To calculate the appropriate level of inventory, it is necessary to know exactly how many units of each product are in stock at any given time. This is known as *stock count*. Periodic stock count is needed since the actual amount in stock frequently differs from the theoretical one (inventory = previous inventory – sales + arrivals). The difference is due to "shrinkage" (theft, misplaced items, etc.). Until 2002, stock count was done manually using data-collection sheets on which the product names were preprinted. Employees counted the quantity of each product and recorded it on a data-collection sheet. Then the data were painstakingly keyed into each store's PC. The process took over 21 person-hours in each store each week. Moreover, the process was expensive and frequently was delayed, causing problems along the entire supply chain due to delayed counts and errors. Suppliers, customers, and employees were unhappy.

THE SOLUTION

The first phase of improvement was introduced in the spring of 2002. Management introduced Pocket PC from HP (Jornada), which runs on Microsoft Windows (Chinese version). Pocket PC (a handheld device) enables employees to enter inventory tallies directly on forms on the screen by hand, using Chinese characters for additional notes. Jornada Pocket PC has a synchronized cradle called Activesync. Once a Pocket PC is placed in the cradle, inventory information can be relayed instantly to Hi-Life's headquarters. The main menu of Pocket PC contains an order-placing program, product information, and even weather reports in addition to the inventory module.

In the second phase, in 2003, a compact bar code scanner was added on in the Pocket PC's expansion slot. The employees scan the product bar codes and enter the quantity found on the shelf. This expedites data entry and minimizes errors in product

Sources: Compiled from hp.com/jornada and microsoft.com/asia/mobile (May 2002).

identification. The up-to-the-second information enables headquarters, using DSS formulas, to compute appropriate inventory levels, shipment schedules, and purchasing strategies, all in just a few minutes. The stores use the Internet (with a secured VPN) to upload data to the headquarters intranet.

THE RESULTS

The results were astonishing. Inventory-taking was reduced to less than four hours per store. Errors were down by more than 90 percent, order placing was simple and quick, and administrative paperwork was eliminated. Furthermore, quicker and more precise inventory count resulted in lower inventory levels and shorter response times for changes in demand. Actually, the entire product-management process became more efficient, including purchasing, stocking, selling, shelf-price audit and price checks, re-ticketing, discontinuance, and customer inquiries. The new e-commerce-based system provides a total merchandise solution. The employees like the solution too. It is very user-friendly, both to learn and to operate, and the battery provides at least 24 hours of power, so charging can be done after hours. Finally, Hi-Life's employees now have more time to plan, manage, and chat with customers. More important, faster and better decisions are enabled at headquarters, contributing to greater competitiveness and profitability for Hi-Life.

❖ QUESTIONS FOR THE OPENING VIGNETTE

1. How was the decision-making improved? Relate your answer to the generic DSS components and flow of information.
2. Summarize the benefits to the customers, suppliers, store management, and employees.
3. The data collected at Activesys can be uploaded to a PC and transmitted to the corporate intranet via the Internet. It is suggested that transmission be done using a wireless system. Comment on the proposal.

WHAT WE CAN LEARN FROM THE VIGNETTE

The output of a decision-support system is only as good as the input data. When the data are inaccurate and/or delayed, the decisions are not good enough. This was the case with the old system, and Hi-Life paid for it by having high inventories and low customer satisfaction. The solution described in this vignette was provided by an electronic commerce system which expedited and improved the flow of information to the corporate DSSs. **Electronic commerce (EC)**, which is the subject of this chapter, describes the process of buying, selling, transmitting, or exchanging products, services, and information via computerized networks, primarily by the Internet. (See Turban et al., 2004). The application illustrated in this vignette is referred to as business-to-employees (B2E) e-commerce because it is in the area of *intrabusiness transaction* where employees are involved. EC tools like the one in the vignette support decision-making and therefore qualifies EC as a DSS tool in the opinion of some researchers. In addition to these, DSS tools like modeling and intelligent agents can facilitate the process of EC (see Shim et al., 2002). We will illustrate both approaches later in this chapter. We also provide here an overview of the e-commerce field and comment on its relationship to decision support. Let us begin with an overview of EC.

14.2 OVERVIEW OF E-COMMERCE

DEFINITIONS AND CONCEPTS

There are several definitions of EC and the related term e-business.

DEFINITIONS

E-Commerce. Electronic commerce (EC) describes the process of buying, selling, transferring, or exchanging products, services, and/or information via computer networks, including the Internet.

E-Business. Some people view the term *commerce* only as describing transactions conducted between business partners. When this definition of commerce is used, some people find the term *electronic commerce* to be fairly narrow. Thus, many use the term **e-business** instead. E-business refers to a broader definition of EC, not just the buying and selling of goods and services, but also servicing customers, collaborating with business partners, conducting e-learning, and conducting electronic transactions within an organization. Others view e-business as the "other than buying and selling" activities on the Internet, such as collaboration and intrabusiness activities.

In this book we use the broadest meaning of electronic commerce, which is basically equivalent to e-business. The two terms will be used interchangeably throughout the text.

PURE VS. PARTIAL EC

Electronic commerce can take several forms depending on the *degree of digitization* (the transformation from physical to digital) of (1) the *product* (service) sold, (2) the *process*, and (3) the *delivery agent* (or intermediary). Choi et al. (1997) created a framework that explains the possible configurations of these three dimensions. A product can be physical or digital, the process can be physical or digital, and the delivery agent can be physical or digital. In traditional commerce all three dimensions are physical, and in *pure EC* all dimensions are digital. All other combinations include a mix of digital and physical dimensions. If there is at least one digital dimension, the situation is EC, but only *partial EC*. For example, buying a shirt at Wal-Mart Online, or a book from Amazon.com is partial EC because the merchandise is physically delivered by FedEx. However, buying an e-book from Amazon.com or a software product from buy.com is *pure EC*, because the ordering, delivery, payment, and transfer are all done online.

EC Organizations.   Purely physical organizations (corporations) are referred to as **brick-and-mortar** (or old-economy) **organizations**, whereas companies engaged only in EC are **virtual organizations** or **pure play companies. Click-and-mortar** (or **click-and-brick**) **organizations** conduct some e-commerce activities, but their primary business is done in the physical world. Many brick-and-mortar companies are gradually changing to click-and-mortar ones (e.g., Wal-Mart Online).

INTERNET VS. NON-INTERNET EC

Most EC is done over the Internet. But EC can also be conducted on private networks, such as *value-added networks* (VANs) that add communication services to existing common carriers, on *local area networks* (LANs), or even on a single computerized machine. For example, buying food from a vending machine and paying with a smart card or a cell phone can be viewed as an EC activity.

Here are more examples of non-Internet EC:

- You can buy software for your PDA that will assist you to choose the right wine while shopping (e.g., Pocket Quicken from Landware, Pocket Vineyard from Amy Reiley, PDA Sommelier).
- You do not need to stop and pay the toll on many roads and bridges, or put a coin in the meter when you park your car. Your car is equipped with an ID device that is recognized by a wireless reader. The fees are charged against your pre-established account.

TYPES OF E-COMMERCE TRANSACTIONS

The Opening Vignette shows an example of business-to-employees EC (B2E), in which a businesses collaborates electronically with its employees. E-commerce transactions can be done between other parties as follows:

- ***Business-to-business (B2B).*** Both the seller and the buyer are organizations. The vast majority of EC volume is of this type.
- ***Collaborative commerce (c-commerce).*** Business partners collaborate electronically. Collaboration of this type frequently occurs between and among business partners along the supply chain.
- ***Business-to-consumer (B2C).*** The sellers are organizations, the buyers are individuals.
- ***Consumer to business (C2B).*** The consumer makes known a need for a particular product or service, and suppliers compete to provide the product or service. (An example would be Priceline.com, where the customer names a desired price and Priceline tries to find a supplier to fulfill it.)
- ***Consumer-to-consumer (C2C).*** An individual sells products (or services) to other individuals.
- ***Intrabusiness (intraorganizational) commerce.*** An organization uses EC internally to improve its operations. A special case of this known as B2E (business-to-employee) was illustrated in the Opening Vignette.
- ***Government-to-citizens (G2C) and to others.*** The government provides services to its citizens via EC technologies. Governments can do business with other governments (G2G), as well as with businesses (G2B).
- ***Mobile commerce (m-commerce).*** E-commerce done in a wireless environment, such as using cell phones to access the Internet.

EC BUSINESS MODELS

Each of the above types of electronic commerce is executed in one or more business models. For example, in B2B one can sell from catalogs or in auctions. The major business models of EC are summarized in Table 14.1 (for details see Turban et al., 2004).

BRIEF HISTORY AND SCOPE OF EC

E-commerce applications began in the early 1970s with such innovations as electronic transfer of funds. However, the applications were limited to large corporations and a few daring small businesses. Then came electronic data interchange (EDI), which automated routine transaction processing and extended EC to all industries. Since the commercialization of the Internet and the introduction of the Web in the early 1990s, EC applications have expanded rapidly. By 2000 there was a major shakeout in the EC industry, with hundreds of dot-com companies going out of business (Kaplan, 2002). However, by 2003 the rapid growth resumed. Today most medium-sized and large organizations and many small ones are practicing some EC.

TABLE 14.1   E-Commerce Business Models

EC Model	*Description*
Online direct marketing	Manufacturers or retailers sell directly to customers. Very efficient for digital products (services). Allows for customization.
Electronic tendering systems	Businesses conduct online tendering, requesting quotes from suppliers. Uses B2B reverse-auction mechanism.
Name-your-own-price	Customers decide how much they are willing to pay. An intermediary (e.g., priceline.com) tries to match a provider.
Find the best price	Customers specify a need. An intermediary (e.g., hotwire.com) compares providers and shows the lowest price. Customer must accept in a specified time or lose the deal.
Affiliate marketing	Vendors ask partners to place logos (or banners) on partners' site. If customers click, come to vendors, and buy, vendors pay commission to partners.
Viral marketing	Spread your brand on the Net by word-of-mouth. Receivers send your information to their friends (watch for real viruses).
Group purchasing (e-coops)	Aggregating the demands of small buyers to get a large volume. Then conduct tendering, or negotiate a low price.
Online auctions	Placing auctions of various types on the Internet. Very popular in C2C, but gaining ground in other types of EC.
Product customization	Using the Internet to self configure products or services, price them, and then fulfill them quickly (build-to-order).
Electronic marketplaces and exchanges	Create virtual marketplaces (private or public) where transactions can be conducted in an efficient way (more information to buyers and sellers, less transaction cost).
Value-chain integrators	Aggregates information and packages it for customers, vendors, or others in the supply chain.
Value-chain service providers	Specialized services in supply-chain operations, such as logistics or payment services.
Information brokers	Providing services related to EC information, such as trust, content, matching buyers and sellers, evaluating vendors and products.
Bartering online	Exchanging surplus products and/or services that is completely administered online. Company receives "points" for its contribution that can be used to purchase what it needs (intermediary manages the process).
Dip discounters	Gain marketshare via dip discounts (e.g., half.com) for customers that only consider price in their purchasing decisions.
Membership model	Only members can use the services provided, including access to certain information, conducting trades, etc. (e.g., egreetings.com).
Supply-chain improvers	Restructuring supply chains to hubs, or other configuration. Increases collaboration, reduces delays, and smooths flows.

THE SCOPE OF EC

The field of e-commerce is broad, and we use Figure 14.1 to describe it. As can be seen in the figure, there are many EC applications (top of the figure), some of which were illustrated in the Opening Vignette about Hi-Life Corp.; others will be shown throughout the book. (Also see Huff et al., 2001; Farhoomand and Lovelock, 2001.) To execute these applications, companies need the right information, infrastructure, and support services. Figure 14.1 shows that EC applications are supported by infrastructure and by five support areas (shown as supporting pillars) defined below: people, public policy, marketing and advertisement, support services, and business partnerships.

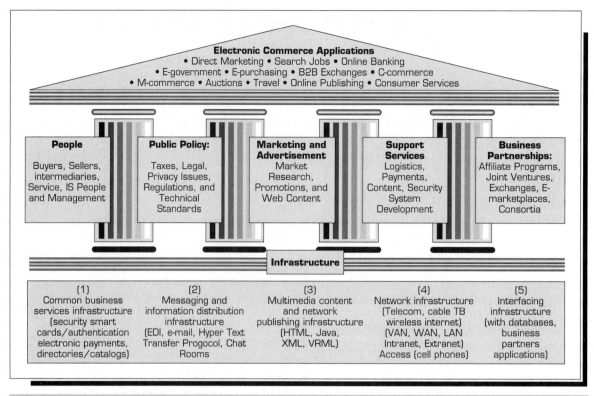

FIGURE 14.1   THE FIELD OF E-COMMERCE

- **People.** Sellers, buyers, intermediaries, information systems specialists and other employees, and any other participants.
- **Public Policy.** Legal and other policy and regulating issues, such as privacy protection and taxation, that are determined by the government.
- **Marketing and Advertisement.** Like any other business, EC usually requires the support of marketing and advertising. This is especially important in B2C online transactions, where the buyers and sellers usually do not know each other.
- **Support Services.** A large number of services is needed to support EC. These range from payments to order delivery and content creation.
- **Business Partnerships.** Joint ventures, e-marketplaces, and business partnerships of various sorts are common in EC. These occur frequently throughout the *supply chain* (i.e., the interactions between a company and its suppliers, customers, and other partners).

The supporting infrastructure includes hardware, software, and networks, ranging from browsers to multimedia.

All of these EC components require good *management practices*. This means that companies need to plan, organize, motivate, devise strategy, and reengineer processes as needed.

BENEFITS OF E-COMMERCE

Few innovations in human history have encompassed as many benefits to organizations, individuals, and society as does e-commerce. The benefits have just begun to

TABLE 14.2   Benefits of E-Commerce

To Organizations

- Expands a company's marketplace to national and international markets. With minimal capital outlay, a company can quickly locate more customers, the best suppliers, and the most suitable business partners worldwide.
- Enables companies to procure material and services from other companies, rapidly and at less cost.
- Shortens or even eliminates marketing-distribution channels, making products cheaper and vendors' profits higher.
- Decreases (by as much as 90 percent) the cost of creating, processing, distributing, storing, and retrieving information by digitizing the process.
- Allows lower inventories by facilitating pull-type supply-chain management. This allows product customization and reduces inventory costs.
- Lowers telecommunications costs because the Internet is much cheaper than value-added networks (VANs).
- Helps some small businesses compete against large companies.
- Enables very specialized niche markets.

To Customers

- Frequently provides less expensive products and services by allowing consumers to conduct quick online searches and comparisons.
- Gives consumers more choices in selecting products and vendors.
- Enables customers to shop or make other transactions 24 hours a day, from almost any location.
- Delivers relevant and detailed information in seconds.
- Enables consumers to get customized products, from PCs to cars, at competitive prices.
- Makes it possible for people to work and study at home.
- Makes possible electronic auctions that benefit buyers and sellers (see Section 14.3).
- Allows consumers to interact in electronic communities and to exchange ideas and compare experiences.

To Society

- Enables individuals to work at home and do less traveling, resulting in less road traffic and lower air pollution.
- Allows some merchandise to be sold at lower prices, thereby increasing people's standard of living.
- Enables people in developing countries and rural areas to enjoy products and services that are otherwise are not available. This includes opportunities to learn professions and earn college degrees, or to receive better medical care.
- Facilitates delivery of public services, such as government entitlements, reducing the cost of distribution and chance of fraud, and increasing the quality of social services, police work, health care, and education.

materialize, but they will increase significantly as EC expands. The major benefits are summarized in Table 14.2.

LIMITATIONS AND FAILURES OF E-COMMERCE

Counterbalancing its many benefits, EC has some limitations, both technical and non-technical, that have slowed its growth and acceptance. These limitations and inhibitors are listed in Table 14.3; some have been contributing factors in the failures of many EC projects and dot-com companies in recent years. As time passes, the limitations, especially the technical ones, will lessen or be overcome. In addition, appropriate planning can minimize the negative impact of some of them.

TABLE 14.3   Limitations of E-commerce

Technical Limitations	*Nontechnical Limitations*
1. Lack of universally accepted standards.	1. Unresolved legal issues (for quality, security, and reliability. See Section 14.12.)
2. Insufficient telecommunications bandwidth.	2. Lack of national and international government regulations and industry standards.
3. Still-evolving software-development tools.	3. Lack of mature methodologies for measuring benefits of and justifying EC.
4. Difficulties in integrating the Internet and EC applications and software with some existing (especially legacy) applications and databases.	4. Many sellers and buyers waiting for EC to stabilize before they take part.
5. Need for special Web servers in addition to the network servers.	5. Customer resistance to changing from a real to a virtual store. People do not yet sufficiently trust paperless, faceless transactions.
6. Expensive and/or inconvenient Internet accessibility for many would-be users.	6. Perception that EC is expensive and unsecured.
	7. An insufficient number (critical mass) of sellers and/or buyers for profitable EC operations.

Despite its limitations and failures, e-commerce has made very rapid progress. B2B activities, e-auctions, e-government, e-learning, and some B2C activities are ballooning. As experience accumulates and technology improves, the ratio of EC benefits to cost will increase, resulting in an even greater rate of EC adoption.

THE DSS-EC CONNECTION

DSS and EC are connected in three major ways: DSS supports EC activities, EC facilitates decision support, and EC and DSS work together (see Geoffrion and Krishnan, 2001; Power, 2002). Let us elaborate.

DSS SUPPORTS EC ACTIVITIES

Several e-commerce activities require making a choice. Here are some examples, but more will be provided in the remainder of this chapter.

- Fulfilling EC orders involves scheduling and transporting goods to many customers. DSS models can optimize this activity (e.g., see Lummus and Vokurka, 2002).
- Matching buyers and sellers can be done by a DSS, based on criteria and constraints.
- Improving Internet marketing operations is frequently done with DSS models (e.g., see Wierenga and Bruggen, 2001).
- Conducting a risk analysis (e.g., starting a dot.com business, or EC initiative), see Westland, 2002 for details.
- Optimal selection of transportation routes in a B2B exchange is provided by Trajecka.com (Geoffrion and Krishnan, 2001).
- DSS can assist in running B2C operations (Wierenga and Bruggen, 2001).
- The tools of data warehouse and data mining are essential to analysis of EC data, such as data collected on consumers' activities on the Internet and statistical data on consumer purchasing activities. (e.g., see Huang et al., 2002, Chen 2003b).

- Using business intelligence and DSS tools, e-Commerce Solution Ltd. (U. K.) optimizes online promotions and makes better, more profitable decisions, yielding benefits to both the company's merchants and clients (microstrategy.com, ECS story, 2002).

EC FACILITATES DECISION SUPPORT

Decision support can be facilitated in many ways. We mention some of them here; others were discussed in previous chapters or will be treated later in this chapter.

- EC provides efficient and effective transfer of information needed for decision support.
- EC enhances the decision-support process (Cohen et al., 2001).
- Data collected and stored using an EC infrastructure drive airline scheduling and yield management. Airlines use DSS to build optimal scheduling and pricing (Smith et al., 2001).

EC AND DSS WORKING TOGETHER

Many of the activities that bring about improvements in the supply chain involve a joint EC/DSS approach. For example, EC is used to restructure a liner supply chain into a hub. At the same time DSS is used in supply-chain management (SCM) models for optimizing scheduling (see Geoffrion and Krishnan, 2001). Other examples are:

- Inventory management.
- A strategic change in a call center was done by integrating simulation decision support with the call center's operations (Saltzman and Mehrotra, 2001).
- Planning of airline marketing and distribution is done by combining EC with DSS models (Smith et al., 2001).
- A great many DSS applications facilitated by Web-enabled software are reported by Cohen et al., 2001.
- Streaming financial reporting promises time savings, greater efficiency, and better decision-making capability. "Virtual closing," or closing the company's books in one day (McClenahen, 2002), is used in companies like Cisco (a promoter of "virtual close"). Extensive use of extranets and intranets enabled Cisco to reduce transaction time and cost, and increase value-added activities.
- Yuan (2003) describes a DSS/EC comparison-shopping engine.
- By using DSS predictive models and EC segmentation approaches, Verhoef et al. (2003) constructed a marketing database application.
- By collecting data from POS terminals in their 360 stores, transferring the data over an extranet, and storing them in the corporate data warehouse, Best Buy is able to conduct extensive business-intelligence analysis using a Microstrategy DSS engine (see BPM at microstrategy.com).

14.3 E-COMMERCE MECHANISMS: AUCTIONS AND PORTALS

In order to better understand how e-commerce works, let us look at two common support mechanisms: electronic auctions and portals.

ELECTRONIC AUCTIONS

Selling on the Internet can be done from electronic catalogs at their fixed prices. In some stores you can negotiate catalog prices electronically. Alternatively, you can use auctions where prices are determined dynamically by competitive bidding.

An **auction** is a market mechanism whereby sellers place offers and buyers make sequential bids. Auctions are characterized by the competitive nature of reaching a final price. They have been an established method of commerce for generations, and are especially suited to deal with products and services for which conventional marketing channels are ineffective or inefficient. Auctions can expedite the disposal of items that need liquidation or a quick sale.

The Internet provides an eficient infrastructure for executing auctions at lower administrative cost, and with many more involved sellers and buyers. Individual consumers and corporations alike can participate in this rapidly growing form of e-commerce. There are several types of auctions, each with its own motives and procedures. Auctions are divided here into two major types: *forward* auctions, and *reverse* auctions.

Forward Auctions.   **Forward auctions** are used mainly as a selling channel from one seller to many potential buyers. Usually, items are placed at sites, such as *eBay.com*. Buyers bid continously, and the highest bidder wins the items. Sellers and buyers can be individuals or businesses.

Reverse Auctions.   In **reverse auctions**, there is one buyer, usually an organization, that wants to buy a product or a service. Suppliers are invited to submit bids. Online bidding is much faster than conventional bidding and usually attracts many more bidders. Normally, the lowest bid wins.

BENEFITS OF AUCTIONS

Auctions are used in B2C, B2B, C2B, e-government, and C2C commerce, and they are becoming popular in many countries. The benefits for sellers, buyers, and auctioneers are:

- *Benefits to Sellers*
  - Increased revenues from broadening customer base and shortening cycle time.
  - Optimal price setting, determined by the market (more buyers).
  - Saves on the commission to intermediaries (fees at physical auction are very high compared to e-auctions).
  - Can liquidate large quantities quickly.
  - Improved customer relationship and loyalty (in the case of specialized B2B auction sites and electronic exchanges).
  - Save on administrative expenses.

- *Benefits to Buyers*
  - Increased opportunities to find unique items and collectibles.
  - Chance to bargain instead of buying at a fixed price.
  - Entertainment. Participation in e-auctions can be entertaining and exciting.
  - Anonymity. With the help of a third party, buyers can remain anonymous.
  - Convenience. Buyers can bid from anywhere, even with a cell phone; they do not have to travel to an auction place.
  - Administrative costs are much lower.
  - Procurement time can be shortened dramatically.

- *Benefits to Auctioneers*
  - High "stickness" of the Web site; customers just keep returning to the auction site.
  - Expansion of the auction business and more revenue for the auctioneer.

Electronic auctions began in the 1980s on private networks, but their use was limited. The Internet has opened many new opportunities for e-auctions, and millions of sellers and buyers now participate. Auctions can be conducted from the seller's site or from a third-party site. For example, eBay, the best-known third-party site, offers hundreds of thousands of different items in several types of auctions. Over 300 other major companies, including Amazon.com and dellauction.com, also offer online auctions.

BARTERING

Related to auctions is electronic bartering, the exchange of goods or services without a monetary transaction. In addition to the individual-to-individual bartering ads that appear in some newsgroups, bulletin boards, and chat rooms, there are several intermediaries that arrange for corporate bartering (e.g., barterbrokers.com). These intermediaries try to match partners to a barter.

Auctions in B2B are frequently done through a third-party intermediary. A well-known one is FreeMarkets.com. In DSS in Action 14.1 we show how this company facilitates both forward and reverse auctions.

DSS IN ACTION 14.1

FREEMARKETS.COM

FreeMarkets is a leader in creating B2B online auctions for buyers of industrial parts, raw materials, commodities, and services around the globe. The company has created auctions for goods and services in hundreds of industrial product categories. FreeMarkets auctions more than $5 billion worth of purchase orders a year and saves buyers an estimated 2 to 25 percent of total expenses (administrative and items).

FreeMarkets operates two types of marketplaces. First, the company helps customers purchase goods and services through its B2B global marketplace, where *reverse auctions* usually take place. Second, FreeMarkets helps companies improve their asset-recovery results by getting timely market prices for surplus assets through the FreeMarkets AssetExchange, employing *forward auctions* process, as well as other selling models.

FreeMarkets Onsite Auctions provide the following:

- *Asset-disposal analysis.* Market makers work with sellers to determine the best strategy to meet asset-recovery goals.
- *Detailed sales offering.* The company collects and consolidates asset information into a printed or online sales offering for buyers.
- *Targeted market outreach.* FreeMarkets conducts targeted advertisement to a global database of 500,000 buyers and suppliers.
- *Event coordination.* The company prepares the site, provides qualified personnel, and enforces auction rules.

- *Sales implementation.* FreeMarkets summarizes auction results and assists in closing sales.

ASSET-RECOVERY SUCCESS STORIES

- *New Line Cinema* (newline.com) had unique memorabilia that been in storage for years. In 2001 it decided to auction these via the FreeMarket auction marketplace. An experimental case was the release of a sequel titled *Austin Powers: The Spy Who Shagged Me.* Items from the original production included a 1965 Corvette driven by Felicity Shagwell (sold in the auction for $121,000) and one of Austin's suits (sold for $7,500). In addition to freeing storage space and generating income, the auction was covered in newspapers and TV, providing publicity for the sequel. An additional benefit is that the auctions are linked to the company's online store. If you cannot afford the 1965 Corvette, you can buy a T-shirt or a poster of a new movie. Finally, the auction created a dedicated community of users and is now conducted on a regular basis.

- *American Power Conversion Corp.* (apcc.com) needed a channel for end-of-life (old models) and refurbished power-protection products. These were difficult to sell in the regular distribution channels. Before using auctions, the company used special liquidation sales, which were not very successful. FreeMarkets deployed the auction site (using AuctionPlace technology, but customizing the applications). It also helped the company determine the auction strategies (e.g., starting bid price and auction running length) which is facilitated by DSS modeling. The site became an immediate success. The company is considering selling regular products there, but only merchandise for which there is no conflict with the company's regular distributors.

E-PROCUREMENT SUCCESS CASE

The contribution of FreeMarkets here is that it allows you to conduct a reverse auction either from your own site, providing you with all the necessary expertise, or from the FreeMarkets' site. The process and benefit of this service are demonstrated in the following success story.

- *Singapore Technologies Engineering (STE)*, a large, integrated global engineering group specializing in the fields of aerospace, electronics, land systems, and marine, had the following goals when it decided to use e-sourcing with the help of FreeMarkets:
  1. Minimize the cost of products it needed to buy, such as board parts.
  2. Identify a new global supply base for its multi-sourcing strategy.
  3. Ensure maximized efficiency in the procurement process.
  4. Find new, quality suppliers for reliability and support.
  5. Consolidate existing suppliers.

These are typical goals of business purchasers. FreeMarkets started by training STE's corporate buyers, and other staff. Then it designed an improved process that replicated the traditional negotiations with suppliers. Finally, it took a test item and prepared a live RFQ, placing it for bid in the FreeMarkets Web site. FreeMarkets is using a five-step process that starts with the RFQ and ends with supplier management (which includes suppliers' verification and training). STE saved 35 percent on the cost of printed circuit board assemblies.

QUESTIONS FOR THE CASE

1. Enter FreeMarkets.com and explore the current activities of the company.
2. Look at six customer success stories (three for sourcing, three for supplying and asset recovery). What common elements can you find?
3. Identify additional services provided by the company to support sourcing (e-procurement).
4. If you work in a business, register with FreeMarkets.com and examine the process as a buyer and as a seller.
5. How does surplus asset recovery become more efficient with FreeMarkets?
6. Compare auctioning at FreeMarkets to auctioning with eBay.

Sources: Compiled from FreeMarkets.com, success stories. Site accessed December 15, 2002 and March 28, 2003.

E-COMMERCE PORTALS

The use of portals is becoming very popular in the business community. There are several different types of portals.

INFORMATION PORTALS

With the growing use of intranets and the Internet, many organizations encounter information overload at a number of different levels. Information is scattered across numerous documents, e-mail messages, and databases in different locations and systems. Finding relevant and accurate information is often time-consuming and requires access to multiple systems.

As a consequence, organizations lose a lot of productive employee time. One solution to this problem is to use portals. A **portal** is an information gateway. It attempts to address information overload through an intranet-based environment to search and access relevant information from disparate IT systems and the Internet, using advanced search and indexing techniques. An *information portal* is a single point of access through a Web browser to critical business information located inside and outside of an organization, and it can be personalized.

TYPES OF PORTALS

Portals appear under many descriptions and shapes. One way to differentiate them is to look at their content, which can vary from narrow to broad, and their community or audience, which can also vary. We distinguish six types of portals:

1. *Commercial (public) portals* offer content for diverse communities and are the most popular portals on the Internet. Although they offer customization of the user interface, they are intended for broad audiences and offer fairly routine content, some of it in real-time (e.g., a stock ticker, news on a few preselected items). Examples are Yahoo.com, lycos.com, and msn.com.

2. *Publishing portals* are intended for communities with specific interests. These portals involve relatively little customization of content, but they provide extensive online search and some interactive capabilities. Examples are techweb.com and zdnet.com.

3. *Personal portals* target specific filtered information for individuals. They offer relatively narrow content but are typically much more personalized, effectively having an audience of one.

4. *Mobile portals* are portals that are accessible from mobile devices. Although most of the other portals mentioned here are PC-based, increasing numbers of portals are accessible via mobile devices. One example of a **mobile portal** is i-mode from DoCoMo in Japan.

5. *Voice portals* are Web sites, usually portals, with audio interfaces. This means that they can be accessed by a standard phone or a cell phone. AOLbyPhone is an example of a service that allows you to retrieve e-mail, news, and other content. It uses both speech-recognition and text-to-speech technologies. Companies like tellme.com and i3mobile.com offer appropriate software.

6. *Corporate portals* coordinate rich content within relatively narrow corporate and partners communities. They are also known as *enterprise portals* or *enterprise information portals*.

CORPORATE PORTALS

Kounadis (2000) more formally defines a corporate portal as a personalized, single point of access through a Web browser to critical business information located inside and outside of an organization. In contrast with publishing and commercial portals such as Yahoo!, which are only gateways to general information on the Internet, corporate portals provide single-point access to specific enterprise information and applications available on the Internet, intranets, and extranets.

Corporate portals offer employees, business partners, and customers an organized focal point for their interactions with the firm. Through the portal, all of them can have structured and personalized access to information across large, multiple, and disparate enterprise information systems, as well as the Internet. A schematic view of a corporate portal is provided in Figure 14.2.

Many large organizations are already implementing corporate portals to cut costs, free up time for busy executives and managers, and add to their bottom line (see the ROI white papers and reports at plumtree.com). There are several types of corporate portals, as shown in DSS in Focus 14.2.

Functionalities of Portals.   The functionalities of portals vary from the simple information portal that stores data and enables users to navigate and query them, to the sophisticated collaborative portal that allows collaboration. An example of the capabilities of portals is provided by Imhoff (2001), who divides portal functionalities into toolbox, library, and workbench (see top of page 758):

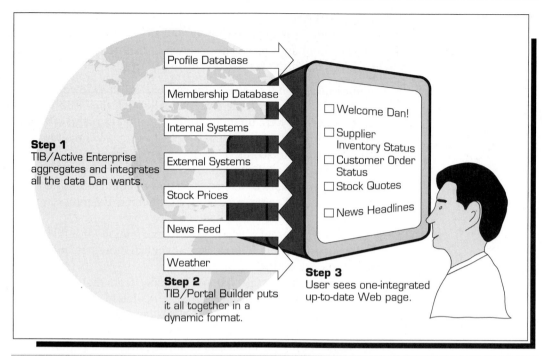

FIGURE 14.2   SCHEMATIC VIEW OF A CORPORATE PORTAL

Source: Courtesy of Tibco Software, Inc.

DSS IN FOCUS 14.2

TYPES OF CORPORATE PORTALS

The following types of portals can be found in organizations:

- *A portal for suppliers.* Using such portals, suppliers can manage their own inventories online. They can view what they sold to the portal owner and for how much. They can see the inventory levels of products at the portal-owner organization, and they can send material and supplies when they see that a reorder level is reached. Supplier can also collaborate with corporate buyers and other staff via the portal.

- *A portal for customers.* Customers can use a customer-facing portal for viewing products and services and placing orders that they can later self-track. They can view their own accounts and see what is going on there in almost real-time. Thus, customers personalize their views of the portal. They can configure products (services), place orders, pay, and arrange warranty and delivery. They can see their outstanding invoices as well.

- *A portal for employees.* Such portals are used for training, dissemination of news and information, discussion groups, and more. They are used for self-service activities, mainly in the personnel area (e.g., change your address, fill in expense report, register for classes, get reimbursed for tuition). Employees' portals are sometimes bundled with supervisors' portals in what is also known as workforce portals (e.g., EWM from Timera.com).

- *Supervisor portals.* These portals enable managers and supervisors to control the entire workforce-management process—from budgeting to scheduling workforce.

  Other types. Several other types exist: business intelligence portals (Imhoff, 2001; Ferguson, 2001), intranet portals (Ferguson, 2001), and knowledge portals (see Kesner, 2003).

Toolbox. This encompasses profitability analysis, pattern recognition, customer view, capacity planning, and resource management, all of which are basically DSS tools.

Library. This includes all the necessary resources. It is a kind of encyclopedia with a dictionary, metrics, cases reports, and news.

Workbench. This is the place where a user can work with the toolbox and/or the library. It is organized by application, such as marketing, planning, customer care, or inventory management.

A comprehensive list of portal functionalities is also described by Ferguson (2001). Several other mechanisms are used in e-commerce (see Turban et al., 2004, for the details). These mechanisms enable the applications described in Sections 14.4–14.10.

14.4 BUSINESS-TO-CONSUMER APPLICATIONS

Forrester Research Institute, the Gartner Group, and others predict that online B2C will be in the range of $300 to $800 billion in the year 2004, up from $515 million in 1996 (see cyberatlas.com and emarketer.com). For 2004 the total of B2C and B2B is estimated to be in the range of $3.5 billion to $8 billion, depending on the estimators and their definition of what they measure. Here we will look at some of the major categories of B2C applications.

ELECTRONIC RETAILING: STOREFRONTS AND MALLS

For generations, home shopping from catalogs has flourished, and television shopping channels have been attracting millions of shoppers for more than two decades. However, these methods have drawbacks. Both can be expensive. Also, paper catalogs are sometimes not up-to-date, and many people are troubled by the waste of paper in catalogs that just get tossed out. Television shopping is limited to what is shown on the screen at any given time.

Like any mail-order shopping experience, e-commerce enables you to buy from home, and do it 24 hours a day, seven days a week. However, EC overcomes some of the limitations of the other forms of home shopping. It offers a wide variety of products and services, including the most unique items, usually at lower prices. Furthermore, within seconds shoppers can get very detailed information on products, and can easily search for and compare competitors' products and prices. Finally, while in the traditional mail order business there are only few sellers, using the Internet buyers can find hundreds of thousands of sellers. **Electronic retailing (e-tailing)** is the direct sale of products through electronic storefronts or electronic malls, usually designed around an electronic catalog format and/or auctions.

ELECTRONIC STOREFRONTS

Hundreds of thousands of solo storefronts can be found on the Internet, each with its own Internet name and EC portal. **Electronic storefronts** may be *extensions* of physical stores such as Home Depot, The Sharper Image, or Wal-Mart. Others are new businesses started by entrepreneurs who saw a niche on the Web. Examples of these are Amazon.com, CDNow, Uvine.com, and Alloy.com.

There are two types of storefronts, general and specialized. The specialized store sells one or a few products (e.g., flowers, wines, dog toys). The general storefronts sell many products. The goods bought most often are computers and computer-related items, office supplies, books and magazines, CDs, cassettes, movies and videos, clothing and shoes, toys, and food. The services bought most often online include entertainment, travel services, stock and bond trading, electronic banking, insurance, and job matching. (Services will be presented as a separate topic later in this section.) Directories and hyperlinks from other Web sites and intelligent search agents help buyers find the best stores and products to match their needs. Storefronts are used by manufacturers (e.g., dell.com) and by retailers (e.g., Officedepot.com, Walmart.com). Both types may sell to individuals and/or to organizations. Storefronts may or may not be affiliated with electronic malls.

ELECTRONIC MALLS

An electronic mall, also known as a cybermall or e-mall, is a collection of individual shops under one Internet address. The basic idea of an electronic mall is the same as that of a regular shopping mall—to provide a one-stop shopping place that offers many products and services. Representative cybermalls are Downtown Anywhere (da.awa.com), Cactus Hill HandCrafters Mall (cactushill.com), America's Choice Mall (mall.choicemall.com), and Shopping 2000 (shopping2000.com). Some malls specialize in certain products and services. For example, 2bsure.com mostly provides services.

There are two types of malls. In the first type, *referrals malls* (e.g., hawaii.com), you cannot make a purchase but are transferred to a participating storefront. In the second type (e.g., store.yahoo.com, amazon.com) you can consummate a purchase.

As is true for vendors located in a physical shopping mall, a vendor located in an e-mall gives up a certain amount of independence. Its success depends on the popularity of the mall in addition to its own marketing efforts. On the other hand, malls generate streams of prospective customers who otherwise might never stop by the store.

A cybermall may include thousands of vendors. For example, shopping.yahoo.com and eshop.msn.com include tens of thousands of products from thousands of vendors.

E-TAILING: THE ESSENTIALS

A *retailer* is a sales *intermediary* that operates between manufacturers and customers. However, many manufacturers sell directly to consumers, supplementing their sales through wholesalers and retailers (multichannel approach). In the physical world, retailing is done in stores (or factory outlets) that customers must visit in order to make a purchase. Companies that produce a large number of products, such as Procter & Gamble, must use retailers for efficient distribution. However, even if you sell only relatively few products (e.g., Kodak), you still may need retailers to reach a large number of customers.

Paper catalog sales free a retailer from the need for a physical store from which to distribute products. Customers can browse catalogs on their own time instead of shopping in a physical store. With the ubiquity of the Internet, the next logical step was for retailing to move online. Online retail sales are called electronic retailing, or e-tailing, and those who conduct retail business online are called e-tailers. E-tailing can also be conducted through auctions. E-tailing also makes it easier for a manufacturer to sell directly to the customer, cutting out the intermediary. In this chapter we will deal with the various types of e-tailing and related issues.

The concept of retailing and e-tailing implies sales of goods and/or services to individual customers. However, the distinction between B2C and B2B e-commerce is not always clear-cut. For example, Amazon.com sells books mostly to individuals (B2C), but it also sells to corporations (B2B). Amazon.com's chief rival, Barnes & Noble, has a special division that caters only to business customers. Walmart.com sells to both individuals and businesses (via Sam's Club). Dell sells its computers to both consumers and businesses from dell.com, and similarly staples.com, and insurance sites sell to both individuals and corporations.

There are several models of B2C (see Turban et al., 2004). One of the most interesting properties of some of these models is their ability to offer customized products at a reasonable price and do it fairly quickly (e.g., Dell computers). Many sites offer self-configuration from their B2C portals (e.g, nike.com). For more on build-to-order in EC, see the online appendix to this chapter.

The most well known B2C site is Amazon.com, whose story is presented in Case Application 14.1 at the end of the chapter.

DECISION SUPPORT IN E-TAILING

The following are the major decisions faced by e-tailers that may be supported by DSS:

- *Resolving channel conflict.* If a seller is a click-and-mortar company such as Levi's or GM, it may face a conflict with its regular distributors when it sells directly online. Known as **channel conflict**, this situation can alienate the regular distributors and has forced some companies (e.g., lego.com) to limit their B2C efforts; others (e.g., some automotive companies) have decided not to sell direct online. However, a better approach is to try to collaborate in some way with the existing distributors, who may decide to restructure their services. For example, you can configure a car online but pick it up from a dealer, where you arrange financing, warranties, and other matters. DSS can facilitate conflict resolution, for example, through the use of group DSS (GDSS) tools.

- *Resolving conflicts inside click-and-mortar organizations.* When an established company decides to sell direct online on a large scale, it may create a conflict within its existing operation. Conflicts may arise in areas such as pricing of products and services, allocation of resources (e.g., advertising budget), and offline logistics services necessitated by the online activities (e.g., handling of returned items). As a result of these conflicts, some companies have completely separated the "clicks" or "bricks" (the online portion of the organization) from the "mortar" (the traditional brick-and-mortar part of the organization). This may increase expenses and reduce the synergy between the two operations. Deciding how to organize online and offline operations and whether or not to separate them can be facilitated by DSS models. GDSS can also be used to resolve conflicts.

- *Determining order fulfillment and logistics.* E-tailers face the problem of how to ship very small quantities to a large number of buyers. This can be a difficult decision, especially when returned items need to be handled. DSS can help with scheduling, routing, shipments, inventory management, and other logistics-related decisions (see Keskinocak and Tayur, 2001).

- *Determining viability of online e-tailers.* Many pure online e-tailers (excluding service industries) were unable to survive and folded in 2000–2002 (see Kaplan, 2002). Companies had problems with customer acquisition, order fulfillment, and forecasting demand. Online competition, especially in commodity-type products such as CDs, toys, books, and groceries, became very fierce, due to the ease of entry to the marketplace. DSS models can be used to foster the EC strategy.

- *Identifying appropriate revenue models.* Many dot-com companies were selling at or below cost with the objective of attracting customers and advertisers to their sites. The idea was to generate enough revenue from selling advertising. This model did not work. Too many dot-com companies were competing on too few advertising dollars, which went mainly to a small number of well-known sites such as AOL and Yahoo. To succeed in EC, it is necessary to identify appropriate revenue models. A DSS can be constructed to examine alternative revenue sources and predict their viability over time.

- ***Risk analysis.*** In deciding on new EC initiatives or on a dot.com company, a risk analysis is needed. A DSS modeling can be a help in such cases (see Westland, 2002).

SERVICE INDUSTRIES ONLINE

Selling books, toys, computers, and most other products on the Internet may reduce vendors' selling costs by 20 to 40 percent. Further reduction is difficult to achieve because the products must be delivered physically. Only a few products (e.g., software or music) can be digitized to be delivered online for additional savings. On the other hand, delivery of services (e.g., buying an airline ticket, stocks, or insurance online) can be done 100 percent electronically, with considerable cost reduction potential. Therefore, delivering services online is growing very rapidly, with millions of new customers added annually. The online services to be discussed here are banking, trading of securities (stocks, bonds), job matching, travel, and real estate. For applications of DSS and knowledge management in health care service, see Pederson and Larsen, 2001.

CYBERBANKING

Electronic banking, also known as **cyberbanking** and online banking, includes various banking activities conducted from home, a business, or on the road instead of at a physical bank location. Electronic banking has capabilities ranging from paying bills to applying for a loan. It saves time and is convenient for customers. For banks, it offers an inexpensive alternative to branch banking (e.g., about 2 cents cost per transaction vs. $1.07 at a physical branch) and a chance to enlist remote customers. Many banks are beginning to offer home banking, and some use EC as a major competitive strategy.

Electronic banking offers several of the benefits listed in Section 14.2, such as expanding the customer base and saving the cost of paper transactions. In addition to regular banks with added online services, we are seeing the emergence of **virtual banks** dedicated solely to Internet transactions, such as netbank.com and ingdirect.com.

International and Multiple-Currency Banking.   International banking and the ability to handle trading in multiple currencies are critical for international trade. Although some international retail purchasing can be done by giving a credit card number, other transactions may require cross-border banking support. Transfers of electronic funds and electronic letters of credit are other important services in international banking. For example, Hong Kong and Shanghai Bank (hsbc.com.hk) has developed a special system (called HEXAGON) to provide electronic banking in 60 countries. Using this system, the bank has leveraged its reputation and infrastructure in the developing economies of Asia to rapidly become a major international bank without developing an extensive new branch network (Peffers and Tunnainen, 1998). The system is now in active use. An example of support for EC global trade is provided at tradecard.com, which operates in conjunction with MasterCard.

Supporting Foreign Currency Trading.   Banks and companies such as Oanda provide currency conversion of over 150 currencies. International traders can be assisted by many other online services (see financialsupermarket.com and foreign-trade.com).

ONLINE SECURITIES TRADING

About 35 million people in the United States are now using computers to trade stocks, bonds, and other financial instruments. In Korea, more than half of the stock traders are using the Internet. Why? Because it makes lots of dollars and "sense." An online trade typically costs a trader between $3 and $15, compared to an average fee of $100 from a full-service broker and $25 from a discount broker. There is no waiting on busy telephone lines. Furthermore, the chance of making mistakes is small because there is no oral communication with a securities broker in a frequently very noisy physical environment. Orders can be placed from anywhere, any time, even from your cell phone, and you can find on the Web, by yourself, a considerable amount of information regarding investing in a specific company or in a mutual fund (e.g., money.cnn.com; bloomberg.com).

How does online trading work? Let's say you have an account with Charles Schwab. You access Schwab's Web site (schwab.com), from your PC or your Internet-enabled mobile device, enter your account number and password to access your personalized Web page, and then click on "stock trading." Using a menu, you enter the details of your order (buy or sell, margin or cash, price limit, market order, etc.). The computer tells you the current "ask" and "bid" prices, much as a broker would do on the telephone, and you can approve or reject the transaction. Some well-known companies that offer only online trading are E*Trade, Ameritrade, Brownco, and Suretrade.

Both online banking and securities trading require tight security. Otherwise, your money may be at risk.

THE ONLINE JOB MARKET

The Internet offers a perfect environment for job seekers and for companies searching for hard-to-find employees. The online job market is especially effective for technology-oriented jobs. Thousands of companies and government agencies use the Internet to advertise available positions for all types of jobs, accept resumes, and take applications. The online job market is used by:

1. *Job seekers.* Job seekers can reply to employment ads online. Or they can take the initiative and place resumes on their own home pages or on appropriate Web sites, send messages to members of newsgroups asking for referrals, and use recruiting firms such as Career Mosaic (careermosaic.com), Job Center (jobcenter.com), and Monster Board (monster.com). For entry-level jobs and internships for newly minted graduates, job seekers can use jobdirect.com. Need help writing your resume? Try resume-link.com or jobweb.com. Finally, if you want to know if you are underpaid or how much you can get if you relocate to another city, use Wageweb.com.

2. *Job offerers.* Many organizations advertise openings on their Web sites. Others use sites ranging from Yahoo! to the bulletin boards of recruiting firms. In many countries the government must advertise openings on the Internet.

3. *Recruiting firms.* Hundreds of job-placement brokers and related services are active on the Web. They use their own Web pages to post available job descriptions and advertise their services in electronic malls and in others' Web sites. Recruiters use newsgroups, online forums, bulletin boards, and chat rooms. Job-finding brokers help candidates write their resumes and get the most exposure. Matching of candidates and jobs is done by companies such as peopleclick.com.

Due to the large number of resumes available on the Internet, it is too expensive to evaluate them manually. Resumix (see AIS in Action 14.3) can help.

TRAVEL

The Internet is an ideal place to plan, explore, and economically arrange almost any trip. Potential savings are available through special sales, comparisons, use of auctions,

---

AIS IN ACTION 14.3

RESUMIX.COM

From the time a position becomes available or a resume is received, Yahoo! Resumix (enterprise.yahoo.com/resumix) gives the recruiter the control while dispersing the work. Hiring managers can view job applications; operators can scan resumes; and a recruiter can search for a candidate or identify existing employees for training programs, redeployment opportunities, or new initiatives.

The core of this powerful system is Resumix's knowledge base. As a computerized intelligent system, it goes beyond simply matching words. The knowledge base interprets a candidate's resume, determining skills based on context and matching them to the position criteria. For example, you might be looking for a product manager. Being a member of the AMA (American Marketing Association) might be one of the desirable properties for the job. However, with a basic keyword search, you might get candidates who have listed AMA but are really members of the American Medical Association or the American Meatpackers Association. This information is not relevant to your search. The Resumix knowledge base would select only the candidates with relevant skills.

Resumix offers a best-of-breed and comprehensive recruiting and hiring solution that delivers:

- Top-quality, comprehensive resume screening to identify talented candidates with relevant qualifications.

- The ability to hire the right candidate quickly—before your competition does.

- Tools to save valuable time and money at every stage of the hiring process.

- Collaboration functionality to enable the human resource team, hiring managers, and company executives to conveniently work together.

Opportunities to develop deep relationships with candidates and employees

QUESTIONS FOR THE CASE

1. What kind of support is described here: EC to DSS, DSS to EC, or Joint?

2. What is the role of the knowledge base?

3. Relate this case to e-commerce.

Source: Compiled from enterprise.yahoo.com/resumix, March 2003.

---

and the elimination of travel agents. Examples of comprehensive travel online services are Expedia.com, Travelocity.com, and Orbitz.com. Services are also provided online by all major airline vacation services, large conventional travel agencies, car rental agencies, hotels, and tour companies. Online travel services allow you to purchase airline tickets, reserve hotel rooms, and rent cars. Most sites also support an itinerary-based interface, including a fare-tracker feature that sends you e-mail messages about low-cost flights to your favorite destinations or from your home city. Finally, Priceline.com allows you to set a price you are willing to pay for an airline ticket or hotel accommodations, and then attempts to find a vendor that will match your price. A similar service is offered by hotwire.com, which tries to find the lowest available price for you.

REAL ESTATE

Real estate transactions are an ideal area for e-commerce. You can view many properties on the screen, saving time for you and the broker. You can sort and organize properties according to your preferences and decision criteria, and preview the exterior and interior designs of the properties, shortening the search process. Finally, you can find detailed information about the properties and frequently get even more detail than brokers will provide. In some locations brokers allow the use of such databases only from their offices, but considerable information is now available on the Internet. For example, Realtor.com allows you to search a database of over 1.2 million homes across the United States. The database is composed of local "multiple listings" of all available properties and properties just sold in hundreds of locations.

In another application, homebuilders now provide three-dimensional floor plans on their Web sites for potential home buyers. They use "virtual home models" that enable buyers to "walk through" mockups of homes.

Successful implementations of B2C frequently require market research, which can be facilitated by DSS models.

14.5 MARKET RESEARCH, E-CRM, AND ONLINE ADVERTISING

To successfully conduct B2C it is important to find out who the actual and potential customers are and what motivates them to buy. Several research institutions collect Internet usage statistics (e.g., acnielsen.com, emarketer.com). They also look at factors that inhibit shopping. Merchants can then prepare marketing and advertising strategies based on this information.

Online purchasing constitutes a fundamental change for most customers. However, if the customer has previously used mail-order catalogs or television shopping, the change will not be so drastic. But moving away from a physical shopping mall to an electronic mall may not be simple. Furthermore, shopping habits keep changing as a result of innovative marketing strategies. Finding out what specific groups of consumers (e.g., teenagers or residents of certain geographical zones) want is done via **segmentation**, dividing customers into specific segments, like age or gender. However, even if we know what groups of consumers want in general, each individual consumer is very likely to want something different. Some like classical music, whereas others like jazz. Some like brand names, but price is more important to many others. Learning about customers is extremely important for any successful business, especially in cyberspace. Such learning is facilitated by *market research*.

A MODEL OF CONSUMER BEHAVIOR ONLINE

For decades, market researchers have tried to understand consumer behavior, and they have summarized their findings in various models of consumer behavior. The purpose of a consumer-behavior model is to help vendors understand how a consumer makes a purchasing decision. A vendor who understands the process may be able to influence the buyer's decision by advertising or special promotions.

Figure 14.3 shows the basics of a consumer-behavior model adjusted to fit the e-commerce environment. The EC model is composed of the following parts:

- *Independent* (or uncontrollable) *variables* are shown at the top of Figure 14.3. They can be categorized as personal characteristics and environmental characteristics.
- Vendors' *controlled variables* (*intervening* or *moderating* variables) are divided into market stimuli, on the left, and EC systems at the bottom. Here DSS models can be useful for the vendor.
- The *decision-making process*, shown in the center of the figure, is influenced by the independent and intervening variable. This process ends with the buyers' decisions, shown on the right, resulting from the decision-making process.
- The *dependent variables* describe the decisions made.

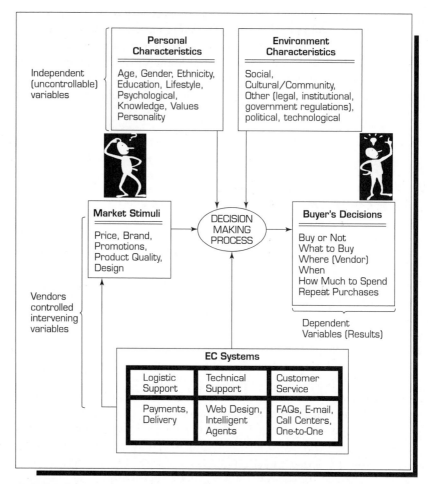

FIGURE 14.3   CONSUMER-BEHAVIOR MODEL ADJUSTED TO FIT THE E-COMMERCE ENVIRONMENT

Figure 14.3 identifies some of the variables in each category. In this chapter, we deal briefly with only some of the variables. Discussions of other variables can be found in Internet marketing books, such as Strauss et al. (2003) or Sterne (2002).

Before we discuss some of the model's variables, let us examine who EC consumers are. Online consumers can be divided into two types: individual consumers, who get much of the media attention, and organizational buyers, who do most of the actual shopping in cyberspace. Organizational buyers include governments, private corporations, resellers, and public organizations. Purchases by organizational buyers are generally used to create products (services) by adding value to raw material or components. Organizational buyers may also purchase products for resale without any further modifications (e.g., retailers, resellers).

INDEPENDENT VARIABLES OF THE MODEL

There are two types of independent variables:

Personal Characteristics.   Personal characteristics, shown in the top-left portion of Figure 14.3, include age, gender, and other demographic variables. Several Web sites provide information on customer buying habits online (e.g., emarketer.com, jmm.com). The major demographics that such sites track are gender, age, marital status, educational level, ethnicity, occupation, and household income.

Psychological variables are another personal characteristic studied by marketers. These include personality and lifestyle characteristics. Those interested in the details of psychological variables should see Solomon (2002).

Environmental Variables.   As shown in the box in the top-right portion of Figure 14.3, the *environmental variables* can be grouped into the following categories:

- *Social variables.* These play an important role in EC purchasing. People are influenced by family members, friends, coworkers, and "what's in fashion this year." Of special importance are Internet communities (covered in Chapter 15) and discussion groups, which communicate via chat rooms, electronic bulletin boards, and newsgroups. These topics are discussed in various places in the text.
- *Cultural/community variables.* It makes a big difference whether a consumer lives near Silicon Valley in California or in the mountains in Nepal. Chinese shoppers differ from French shoppers, and rural shoppers differ from urban ones.
- *Other environmental variables.* These include the available information, government regulations, legal constraints, and situational factors.

INTERVENING (MODERATING) VARIABLES

Some intervening variables can be controlled by vendors. Others are determined by the marketplace. In the offline environment, intervening variables include pricing, advertisement, promotions, and branding. Also important are the physical environment (e.g., displays in stores), logistic support, and customer services. All of the foregoing are described in marketing textbooks.

TECHNOLOGY AND WEB-SITE VARIABLES (EC SYSTEMS IN FIG. 14.3)

Vendors can control the following technology variables: logistics and payment support, which must be secured, easy to use, and inexpensive; technical support, which includes appropriate site design and availability of intelligent shopping aids (intelligent agents); and customer service, which includes all CRM tools.

BUYING DECISIONS (DEPENDENT VARIABLES) OF THE MODEL

The customer has to make several decisions: to buy or not to buy; what to buy; where, when, and how much to buy. These decisions depend on the independent and intervening variables. The objective of learning about customers and conducting market research to enable the vendors who control e-commerce systems and provide market stimuli to know enough make decisions on the intervening variables.

The model in Figure 14.3 is simplified. In reality it can be more complicated, especially when new products or procedures need to be purchased. For example, for online buying, a customer may go through the following five adoption stages: awareness, interest, evaluation, trial, and adoption. For details see McDaniel and Gates (2001) and Solomon (2002), and this is the area where DSS can play a major role. Understanding the structure of the model in Figure 14.3 is necessary, but in order to really make use of it, we need to learn about the decision-making process itself, as presented next.

THE CONSUMER DECISION-MAKING PROCESS AND MODELS

Let us return to the central part of Figure 14.3, where consumers are shown making purchase decisions. Several models have been developed in an effort to describe the details of the decision-making process that leads up to and culminates in a purchase. These models provide a framework for learning about the process in order to predict, improve, or influence consumer decisions. Here we introduce three relevant models.

A GENERIC PURCHASING-DECISION MODEL

A general purchasing-decision model consists of five major phases. In each phase we can distinguish several activities, and in some of them, one or more decisions. The five phases are: (1) need identification, (2) information search, (3) evaluation of alternatives, (4) purchase and delivery, and (5) after-purchase evaluation. Although these phases offer a general guide to the consumer decision-making process, do not assume that all consumer decision-making will necessarily proceed in this order. In fact, some consumers may proceed to a certain point and then revert back to an earlier phase or skip a phase. For details, see Strauss et al. (2003).

A CUSTOMER DECISION MODEL IN WEB PURCHASING

The above purchasing-decision model was used by O'Keefe and McEachern (1998) to build a framework for a Web-purchasing model, called the Consumer Decision-Support System (CDSS). According to their framework, shown in Figure 14.4, each of the phases of the purchasing model can be supported by both CDSS facilities and Internet and Web facilities. The CDSS facilities support the specific decisions in the process. Generic EC technologies provide the necessary mechanisms and enhance communication and collaboration. Specific implementation of this framework is demonstrated throughout the text.

ONLINE BUYER DECISION-SUPPORT MODEL

Silverman et al. (2001) developed a model for a Web site that supports buyer decision-making and search. This model aims at correcting the existing situation by describing an appropriate purchasing framework. Another model was developed by Chaudhury et al. (2001). The planner of B2C marketing needs to consider such Web purchasing models in order to better influence the customer decision-making (e.g., by effective one-to-one advertising and marketing).

FIGURE 14.4 CONSUMER DECISION-SUPPORT SYSTEM (CDSS)

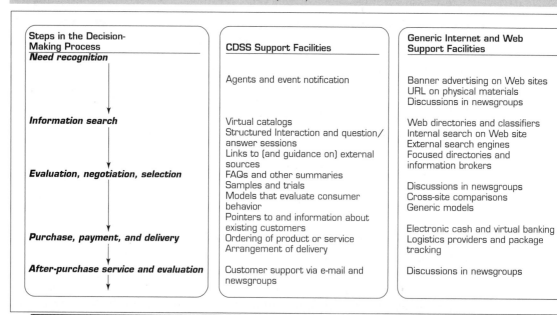

Source: O'Keefe and McEachern (1998).

HOW MARKET RESEARCHERS FIND OUT WHAT CUSTOMERS WANT

There are basically two ways to find out what customers want. The first is to ask them, and the second is to infer what they want by observing what they do in cyberspace.

USING SOFTWARE AGENTS TO ENHANCE MARKET RESEARCH

Software agents are computer programs that conduct routine tasks, search and retrieve information, support decision-making, and act as domain experts. They sense the environment and act autonomously without human intervention. This results in a significant savings of users' time (up to 99 percent in some cases). There are various types of agents that can be used in EC, ranging from *software agents*, which are agents with no intelligence, to *learning agents* that exhibit some intelligent behavior.

Agents are used to support many tasks in electronic commerce. But first, it will be beneficial to distinguish between search engines and the more intelligent type of agents. A **search engine** (usually a mobile software agent) is a computer program that can automatically contact other network resources on the Internet, search for specific information or key words, and report the results. Unlike search engines, an **intelligent agent** uses expert knowledge (knowledge-based) capabilities to do more than just "search and match." For example, it can monitor movements on a Web site to check whether a customer seems lost or is venturing into areas that may not fit his or her profile, and if so, the agent can notify the customer and even provide corrective assistance. Depending on their level of intelligence, agents can do many other things. In this section we will concentrate on intelligent agents for assisting shoppers (see Yuan, 2003).

ASKING CUSTOMERS WHAT THEY WANT

The Internet provides easy, fast, and relatively inexpensive ways for vendors to find out what customers want by interacting directly with them. The simplest way is to ask potential customers to fill in electronic questionnaires. To get them to do so, vendors need to provide some inducements. For example, in order to play a free electronic game or participate in a sweepstakes, you are asked to fill in an online form and answer some questions about yourself (e.g., see bizrate.com). Marketers not only learn what you want from the direct answers, but also try to infer from your preferences of music, for example, what types of books, clothes, or movies you may be likely to prefer. This inference is done by using DSS behavioral models.

In some cases, asking customers what they want may not be feasible. Moreover, some customers may refuse to answer questionnaires or may provide false information (as is done in about 40 percent of the cases, according to studies done at Georgia Tech University). Also, questionnaires can be lengthy and costly to administer. Therefore, a different approach may be needed—observing what customers do in cyberspace.

TRACKING CUSTOMER ACTIVITIES ON THE WEB

Today it is possible to learn about customers by observing their behavior on the Internet. Many companies offer *site-tracking* services, based on cookies, Web bugs, or spyware programs. For example, Nettracker (from sane.com) collects data from client/server logs and provides periodic reports that include demographic data, such as where customers come from or how many customers have gone straight from the home page to ordering. The company also translates Internet domain names into real-company names and includes general and financial corporate information.

The Web is an incredibly rich source of business intelligence, and many enterprises are scrambling to build data warehouses that capture the knowledge contained in the clickstream data from their Web sites. By analyzing the user behavior patterns contained in these clickstream data warehouses, savvy businesses can expand their markets, improve customer relationships, reduce costs, streamline operations, strengthen their Web sites, and plot their business strategies. This is an example of DSS/EC synergy. For details see Sweiger et al.(2002).

SEARCH AND FILTERING AGENTS

Intelligent agents can help customers to determine what to buy to satisfy a specific need. This is achieved by looking for specific product information and critically evaluating it. An agent helps consumers decide what product best fits their profile and requirements.

COLLABORATIVE FILTERING AGENTS

Once a company knows a consumer's preferences (e.g., what music he or she likes), it would be useful to infer, without asking, what other products or services this consumer might enjoy. One way to do this is through **collaborative filtering**, which uses customer data to infer customer interest in other products or services. Such predictions are based on statistical DSS-type formulas derived from behavioral sciences (for details, see sins.berkeley.edu/resources.collab/). There are several methods and formulas to execute collaborative filtering, all using software agents. For details see Ridell et al. (2002). The predictions can also be based on what we know about other customers with similar profiles. One of the pioneering filtering agents was Firefly (now embedded in Microsoft's Passport System). Many personalization systems are based on collaborative filtering (e.g., backflip.com, c5corp.com, and blink.com).

BRAND- AND VENDOR-FINDING AGENTS

Once the consumer has decided what to buy, a comparison agent will help in doing comparisons, usually of prices from different vendors. A pioneering intelligent agent for online price comparison was *Bargainfinder* from Andersen Consulting. This agent was used only in online shopping for CDs. The agent queried the price of a specific CD from a number of online vendors and returned the list of vendors and prices. Today much more sophisticated agents, such as Mysimon.com and dealtime.com, help comparisons. Some of these look at multiple criteria, not just price, and even let you prioritize the criteria. The latter include a built-in DSS for such prioritization.

The information collected by market research is used for customer-relationship management (CRM) and for advertising, the topics we discuss next.

CRM AND SHOPPING AIDS

Whether an organization is selling to organizations or to individuals, it can often gain a competitive edge by providing superb customer service. In e-commerce, customer-relationship management is even more critical because customers and merchants do not meet face-to-face (see Greenberg, 2002).

SERVICE DURING A PRODUCT (SERVICE) LIFE CYCLE

CRM should be provided during the four phases of a product life cycle outlined below:

Phase 1: Requirements. Assist the customer to determine his or her needs by providing photographs of a product, video presentations, textual descriptions, articles or reviews, sound bites on a CD, and downloadable demonstration files. Use intelligent agents to make requirement suggestions.

Phase 2: Acquisition. Help the customer to acquire a product or service (online order entry, negotiations, closing of sale, delivery).

Phase 3: Ownership. Support the customer on an ongoing basis while he or she owns the product (interactive online user groups, online technical support, FAQs and answers, resource libraries, newsletters, online renewal of subscriptions).

Phase 4: Retirement. Help the customer to dispose of the product (online resale, classified ads, auctions).

Many activities can be conducted in each of these phases. For example, when an airline offers information such as flight schedules and fare quotes on its Web site, it is supporting Phases 1 and 2. Similarly, when computer vendors provide electronic help desks for their customers, they are supporting Phase 3. Dell will help you to auction your obsolete computer, and Amazon.com will help you to sell used books; activities that support Phase 4.

FACILITATING CRM

When CRM is supported electronically, we refer to it as **eCRM**. Several tools are available for facilitating eCRM. For example:

- *FAQs.* Companies provide online answers to the questions customers ask most.
- *E-mail.* Companies can send confirmations, product information, and instructions to customers. They can also take orders, complaints, and other inquiries. To save on expenses, customers' e-mails are answered by intelligent agents called **autoresponders**. Only if a human answer is really needed will a human agent follow up.
- *Tracking capabilities.* Customers can track the status of their orders, services (e.g., FedEx shipments, banking or stock-trading activities), or job applications.
- *Personalized Web pages.* Customers build individualized pages at the vendor's site; customized information can be provided there.
- *Chat rooms.* Customers can interact with each other and with the vendor's personnel who monitor the chat room.
- *Web-based call centers.* A comprehensive communication center takes customers' inquiries in any form they come (fax, telephone, walk-ins, e-mail, letters), routes them to the appropriate person, and answers them quickly, whenever possible. Customers can also interact with the vendor and get quick problem resolution. An application of Web-based call centers is becoming very popular, and it frequently incorporate a DSS (see Saltzman and Mehrotra, 2001). For more on DSS/CRM connection and applications, see Kohli et al., 2001, KPMG Consulting, 2002, and McClenahen, 2002.

ADVERTISING ONLINE

Advertising is an attempt to disseminate information in order to influence a buyer–seller transaction. Traditional advertisements on TV or in newspapers are impersonal, one-way mass communication. Direct-response marketing (telemarketing) contacts individuals by means of direct mail or by telephone calls and requires them to respond in order to make a purchase. The direct-response approach personalizes advertising and marketing, but it can be expensive, slow, and ineffective.

Internet advertising redefines the process of advertising, making it media-rich, dynamic, and interactive. It improves on traditional forms of advertising in a number of ways: Internet ads can be updated at any time at minimal cost, and therefore can always be timely. Internet ads can reach very large numbers of potential buyers all over the world and are sometimes cheaper in comparison to print (newspaper and magazine), radio, or television ads. Ads in these other media are expensive because they are determined by space occupied (print ads), by how many days (times) they are run, and on the number of local and national stations and print media that run them. Internet ads can be interactive and targeted to specific interest groups and/or to individuals. Finally, the use of the Internet itself is growing very rapidly, and it makes sense to move advertising to the Internet, where the number of viewers is growing. Nevertheless, the Internet has some shortcomings as an advertising medium, most of which relate to the difficulty of measuring advertisement effectiveness and justifying its cost. For example, it is difficult to measure the actual results of placing a banner ad or an e-mail, and the audience is still relatively small (compared to television, for example).

ADVERTISING METHODS AND STRATEGIES

The most common forms of advertisement online are banners, pop-ups, and e-mails. The essentials of these and some other methods are briefly presented next.

Banners.   **Banners** are electronic billboards, and banner advertising is the most commonly used form of advertising on the Internet. Typically, a banner contains a short text or graphical message to promote a product or a vendor. It may even contain video clips and sound. When customers click on a banner, they are transferred to the advertiser's home page or storefront. Advertisers go to great lengths to design banners that catch consumers' attention.

There are two types of banners. **Keyword banners** appear when a predetermined word is queried from a search engine. They are effective for companies that want to narrow their target to consumers interested in particular topics. **Random banners** appear randomly and might be used to introduce new products to the widest possible audience, or for brand recognition.

A major advantage of using banners is the ability to customize them to the target audience. Keyword banners can be customized to a market segment or even to an individual user. If the computer system knows who you are, or what your profile is, you may be sent a banner that is supposed to *match* your interests. However, one of the major drawbacks of using banners is that limited information is allowed due to their small size. Hence advertisers need to think of creative but short messages to attract viewers. Another drawback is that banners, which were a novelty in the late 1990s and so were noticed by viewers, are ignored by many viewers today. A new generation of banner-like ads are the pop-ups.

Pop-Ups, Pop-Unders, and Similar Ads.   One of the most annoying phenomena in Web surfing is the increased use of pop-ups, pop-unders, and similar ads. A **pop-up ad** is the automatic launching of new browser windows with an ad, when entering or exiting a site, on delay, or on other triggers. It focuses either in front of or behind the active window (Martin and Ryan, 2002). A **pop-under ad** is an ad that appears underneath the current browser window. When users close the active window, they see the ad. These methods are controversial: Many users strongly object to these ads, which they consider intrusive. For further details and how to fight pop-ups, see DSS Online 14.1.

E-mail Advertising.   E-mail is emerging as an Internet advertising and marketing channel that affords cost-effective implementation and a better and quicker response rate than other advertising channels (e.g., print ads). Marketers develop or purchase a list of e-mail addresses, place them in a customer database, and then send advertisements via e-mail. A list of e-mail addresses can be a very powerful tool because the marketer can target a group of people or even individuals. However, there is a potential for misuse of e-mail advertisements, and as with pop-ups there is the problem of a flood of unsolicited mail (see DSS Online 14.1).

Electronic Catalogs and Brochures.   Printed catalogs have been a medium of advertising for a long time. Recently electronic catalogs and CD-ROMs have been gaining popularity. The merchant's objective in using online catalogs is to advertise and promote products and services. From the customer's perspective, online catalogs offer a source of information that can be searched quickly with the help of special search engines. Comparisons involving catalog products can be made very effectively.

A customized catalog is a catalog assembled specifically for a particular company or even an individual, usually a regular customer of the catalog owner.

Other Forms of Internet Advertising.   Online advertising can be done in several other forms, including posting advertisements in chat rooms, to newsgroups, and in classified ads (see infospace.com). Advertising on Internet radio is just beginning, and soon advertising on Internet television will commence. Of special interest is advertising to members of Internet communities. Community sites are gathering places for people of similar interests and are therefore a logical place to promote products related to those interests. Advertising at a community site (e.g., at geocities.com) is targeted to people with similar interests, giving them a chance to buy the advertised products at a discount.

SOME ADVERTISING ISSUES AND APPROACHES

There are many issues related to the implementation of Internet advertising: how to design ads for the Internet, where and when to advertise, and how to integrate online and offline ads. Most such decisions require the input of marketing and advertising experts. We present several illustrative issues below.

Unsolicited Advertisements: Spamming and More.   A major issue related to pop-ups and e-mail advertising is **spamming**, the practice of indiscriminate distribution of electronic ads without permission of the receiver. For discussion, see DSS Online 14.1.

E-Mail Spamming.   E-mail spamming, also known as unsolicited commercial e-mail or UCE, has been part of the Internet era for years. Unfortunately, the situation is getting worse. The drivers of spamming and some of the potential solutions are described in DSS Online 14.1.

Permission Marketing.   This approach is one answer to e-mail spamming. It offers consumers incentives to accept advertising and e-mail voluntarily. How to do this? Ask people what they are interested in, ask permission to send them marketing information, and then do it in an entertaining, educational, or other interesting manner.

Permission marketing is the basis of several Internet marketing strategies. For example, millions of users receive e-mails periodically from airlines such as American and Southwest. Users of this marketing service can ask for notification of low fares from their hometown or to their favorite destinations. In addition, users can easily unsubscribe at any time. Permission marketing is also extremely important for market research (see mediametrix.com).

In one particularly interesting form of permission marketing, companies such as Clickdough.com, Getpaid4.com, and CashSurfers.com have built customer lists of millions of people who are happy to receive advertising messages whenever they are on the Web. These customers are paid 25–50 cents an hour to view messages while they do their normal surfing. They may also be paid 10 cents an hour for the surfing time of any friends they *refer* to the above sites.

Viral marketing.   **Viral Marketing** refers to online word-of-mouth marketing (see alladvantage.com). The main idea in viral marketing is to have people forward messages to friends, asking them, for example, to "check this out." A marketer can distribute a small game program, for example, which comes embedded with a sponsor's e-mail that is easy to forward. By releasing a few thousand copies, vendors hope to reach many more thousands. Word-of-mouth marketing has been used for generations, but its speed and reach are greatly multiplied by the Internet. Viral marketing is one of the new models being used to build brand awareness at a minimal cost. It has long been a favorite strategy of online advertisers pushing youth-oriented products.

Unfortunately, though, several e-mail hoaxes have spread via viral marketing. Also, a danger of viral marketing is that a destructive computer virus can be added to an innocent advertisement, related game, or message. However, when used properly, viral marketing can be both effective and efficient.

Interactive Advertising and Marketing.   Conventional advertising is passive, targeted to mass audiences, and for that reason may be ineffective. Therefore, all advertisers, whether online or not, attempt to customize their ads to special groups and, if possible, to individuals. A good salesperson is trained to interact with sales prospects, asking questions about the features they are looking for and handling possible objections as they come up. Online advertising comes closer to supporting this one-to-one selling process than more traditional advertising media possibly can.

Ideally, in interactive marketing, advertisers present customized, one-on-one ads. The term interactive points to the ability to address an individual, gather and remember that person's responses, and serve that customer based on his or her unique responses. When the Internet is combined with database marketing, interactive marketing becomes a very effective and affordable competitive strategy.

Online Promotions: Attracting Visitors to a Site.   The following are examples of ways to attract visitors to a Web site.

- *Making the top list of a search engine.* Web sites submit their URLs to search engines. The search engine's intelligent program (called a spider) crawls through the submitted site, indexing all related content and links. Some lists generated by search engines includes hundreds or thousands of items. Users who view the results submitted by a search engine typically start by clicking on the first 10 or so items, and soon get tired. So, for best exposure, advertisers like to make the top of the list. How to do it? A company can get to the top of a search engine's list merely by adding, removing, or changing a few sentences on its Web pages. By doing so, the Web designer may alter the way a search engine's program ranks its findings.
- *Online events, promotions, and attractions.* People generally like the idea of something funny or something free, or both. Contests, quizzes, coupons, and free samples are an integral part of e-commerce as much as, or even more than, in offline commerce. Running promotions on the Internet is similar to running offline promotions. These mechanisms are designed to attract visitors and keep their attention. For innovative ideas about promotions and attractions used by companies online, see Sterne (2002) and Strauss et al.(2003).

14.6 B2B APPLICATIONS

In **business to business (B2B)** applications, the buyers, sellers, and transactions involve only organizations. Business-to-business comprises about 85 percent of the total e-commerce volume. It covers a broad spectrum of applications that enable an enterprise to form electronic relationships with its distributors, resellers, suppliers, customers, and other partners. By using B2B, organizations can restructure their supply chain and partnership relationships (see Warkentin, 2001).

There are several business models for B2B applications. The major ones are sell-side marketplaces, buy-side marketplaces, and electronic exchanges.

SELL-SIDE MARKETPLACES

In the sell-side marketplace model, organizations attempt to sell their products or services to other organizations electronically from their own marketplace (private e-marketplace). This model is similar to the B2C model in which the buyer is expected to come to the seller's site, view catalogs, and place an order. In this case, however, the buyer is an organization.

The key mechanisms in the sell-side model are: (1) electronic catalogs that can be customized for each large buyer, and (2) forward auctions. Sellers such as Dell Computer (dellauction.com) use this method extensively. In addition to auctions from their Web site, organizations can use third-party auction sites, such as eBay, to liquidate items. Companies such as freemarkets.com are helping organizations to auction obsolete and old assets and inventories (asset-recovery programs).

The sell-side model is used by thousands of companies and is especially powerful for companies with superb reputations. Examples are major computer companies such as Cisco, IBM, and Intel. The seller in this model can be either a manufacturer, a distributor (e.g., bigboxx.com, avnet.com), or a retailer. In this model, EC is used to increase sales, reduce selling and advertising expenditures, increase delivery speed, and reduce administrative costs. This model is especially suitable to customization. Customers can configure their orders online at cisco.com, dell.com, and so on. This results in fewer misunderstandings about what customers want, and in much faster order fulfillment.

BUY-SIDE MARKETPLACES

The **buy-side marketplace** is a procurement model in which EC technology is used to streamline the purchasing process in order to reduce the cost of items purchased, the administrative cost of procurement, and the purchasing-cycle time. It is usually conducted on the buyer's private e-marketplace. A major method of such **e-procurement** is the reverse-auction. Here, a company that wants to buy items places a request for quotation (RFQ) on its Web site, or in a third-party bidding marketplace. Once RFQs are posted, suppliers (usually preapproved ones) submit bids electronically. The bids are routed via the buyer's intranet to the engineering and finance departments for evaluation. Clarifications are made via e-mails, and the winner is notified electronically. Such auctions attract larger pools of willing suppliers. General Electric, for example, saves 10 to 15 percent on the cost of the items placed for bid and up to 85 percent on the administrative cost (Turban et al., 2004); in addition, cycle time is reduced by about 50 percent. The seller in the buy-side model can be either a manufacturer, a distributor, or a retailer. Procurements using a third-party buy-side marketplace model are especially popular for medium-sized and small organizations.

E-PROCUREMENT

Purchasing by using electronic support is referred to as e-procurement. In addition to reverse auctions, e-procurement uses other mechanisms. Two popular ones are:

Group Purchasing.   In **group purchasing**, the requirements of many buyers are aggregated so that they total to a large volume. Once buyers' orders are aggregated, they can be placed on a reverse auction, or a volume discount can be negotiated. The orders of small buyers usually are aggregated by a third-party vendor, such as consorta.com or shop2gether.com. Group puruchasing is especially popular in the health care industry (all-health.com).

Desktop Purchasing.   In the variation of e-procurement known as **desktop purchasing**, suppliers' catalogs are aggregated in an internal master catalog on the buyer's server, so that the company's purchasing agents or even end-users can shop more conveniently. It is mostly suitable for maintenance, replacement, and operations (MRO) indirect items, such as office supplies. In the desktop-purchasing model, a company has many suppliers, but the quantities purchased from each are relatively small. This model is most appropriate for large companies and for governmental entities.

ELECTRONIC EXCHANGES

E-marketplaces in which there are many sellers and many buyers are called **public exchanges** (in short, exchanges). They are open to all and frequently are owned and operated by a third party. According to Kaplan and Sawhney (2000), there are basically four types of exchanges:

- *Vertical distributors for direct material.* These are B2B marketplaces where *direct materials* (materials that are inputs to manufacturing) are traded in an environment of long-term relationship, known as **systematic sourcing**. Examples are plasticsnet.com and papersite.com. Both fixed and negotiated prices are common in this type of exchange.
- *Vertical exchanges for indirect material.* Here indirect materials in one industry are purchased on an "as-needed" basis (spot sourcing). Buyers and sellers may not even know each other. ChemConnect.com and isteelasia.com are examples. In such vertical exchanges, prices are continually changing, based on the matching of supply and demand. This is called dynamic pricing. Auctions are typically used in this kind of B2B marketplace, sometimes done in private trading rooms, which are available in exchanges like ChemConnect.com (see DSS in Action 14.4).
- *Horizontal distributors.* These are "many-to-many" e-marketplaces for indirect (MRO) materials, such as office supplies, used by any industry. Prices are fixed or negotiated in this systematic sourcing type exchange. Examples are EcEurope.com, globalsources.com, and alibaba.com.
- *Horizontal exchanges.* Here, needed services, such as temporary help or extra space, are traded on an "as-needed" basis (spot sourcing). For example, employease.com matches temporary labor with employees. Prices are dynamic and vary depending on supply and demand.

All four types of exchanges offer diversified support services, ranging from payments to logistics. Vertical exchanges are frequently owned and managed by a group of big players in an industry (referred to as a consortium). For example, Marriott and Hyatt own a procurement consortium for the hotel industry, and Chevron Texaco and Chevron own an energy e-marketplace. The vertical e-marketplaces offer services particularly suited to the e-community they serve.

Since B2B activities involve many companies, specialized network infrastructure is needed. Such infrastructure works either as an Internet/EDI or as an extranet.

THE DSS-B2B CONNECTION

DSS/B2B relationships are probably the strongest in DSS/EC. The reason is that B2B concentrates on supply-chain relationships, where it is necessary to make decisions

CHEMICAL COMPANIES "BOND" AT CHEMCONNECT

Buyers and sellers of chemicals and plastics can meet electronically in a large vertical exchange called ChemConnect (chemconnect.com). Using this exchange, global industry leaders such as British Petroleum, Dow Chemical, BASF, Hyundai, Sumitomo, and many more can reduce trading-cycle time and cost, and can find new markets and trading partners around the globe.

ChemConnect provides a public trading marketplace and an information portal to more than 9,000 members in 150 countries. In 2003, over 60,000 products were traded in this public e-marketplace. This is an unbiased, third-party-managed market that offers three trading places:

- *A public exchange floor.* Here members can post items for sale or bid anonymously for all types of products, at market prices. A large catalog displays, by category, offers to sell and requests to buy, including starting prices and shipping terms. If the prices are not established, buyers can bid by changing the starting prices.

- *The commodities floor.* This space allows the more than 200 top producers, intermediaries, and buyers to buy, sell, and exchange commodity products online, in real-time, through regional trading hubs.

- *Corporate trading rooms.* In these ChemConnect-managed private online virtual rooms, members can conduct private auctions and negotiate long-term contracts or spot deals (one-time, as-needed purchases) in real-time. The trading room allows

companies to make money-saving deals in 30 minutes that might take weeks or months with a manual method. Companies can host a private auction in a trading room as they negotiate simultaneously online with suppliers or buyers on the public exchange floor.

In all three of the trading mechanisms, up-to-the-minute market information is available and can be translated into 30 different languages. Members pay transaction fees only for successfully completed transactions. Business partners provide several support services, such as financial services for the market members.

The marketplace works with certain rules and guidelines that ensure an unbiased approach to the trades. There is full disclosure of all legal requirements, payments, trading rules, and other relevant information (click on "Legal info and privacy issues" at the Web site). ChemConnect is growing rapidly, adding members, and trading volume.

QUESTIONS FOR THE CASE

1. What are the advantages of such an exchange?
2. Why are there three trading places?
3. Why does the exchange provide information-portal services?
4. Why are the rules needed?

Source: compiled from chemconnect.com.

regarding inventory management, shipments and logistics, supply-chain synchronization, warehousing, production scheduling, and more (see Kohli et al., 2001). DSS applications are traditionally concentrated in these areas.

Another area of interface is collaborative planning, collaborative design, and other types of B2B collaboration in which workflow systems, groupware, and GDSS plays a major role. Such systems are described in the next section.

14.7 COLLABORATIVE COMMERCE

Collaborative commerce (c-commerce) refers to non-selling/buying EC transactions between and among organizations, such as joint product design, joint forecasted demand, and other joint decision-making activities. An example would be a company that collaborates electronically with a vendor that is designing a product or part for it. C-commerce implies communication, information sharing, joint decision-making, and collaboration, supported electronically by tools such as groupware and specially designed EC collaboration tools. DSS models may also be involved. Let us look at some areas of collaboration.

- *Retailer-suppliers.* Large retailers, such as Wal-Mart, collaborate with their major suppliers to conduct production and inventory planning and forecasting of demand. Such collaboration enables the suppliers to improve their production planning as well.
- *Vendor-managed inventory.* This is a service provided by large suppliers, such as Procter & Gamble, to large retailers, such as Wal-Mart, in which the vendor monitors and replenishes the inventory for the retailer. In some cases, vendor-managed inventory programs are now available to small retailers as well. DSS models are used to determine under quantity.
- *Product design.* All the parties involved in a specific product design share data and use special tools. One such tool is *screen sharing*, in which several people can work on the same screen while in different locations. This enables suppliers to provide quick feedback when they see the drawings of a product the customer wants. Changes made in one place are visible to others instantly. Documents that can be processed through collaborative product design include blueprints, bills of material, accounting and billing documents, and joint reports and statements (for details, see Ragusa et al., 2001).
- *Collaborative manufacturing.* Manufacturers can create dynamic collaborative networks. For example, Original Equipment Manufacturers (OEM) outsource components and subassemblies to suppliers, which in the past often created problems in coordination, work flows, and communication. Collaborative tools have improved the outsourcing process, and are especially useful during changes, which may be initiated by any partner of the supply chain.

Many business activities and functions lend themselves to collaborative processes: (1) planning and scheduling: material positioning, visibility forecasts, advanced planning, forecasting, and capacity management; (2) design: mechanical, electrical, test, and others, as well as component selection and design of and for the supply chain; (3) new product information: design validation, bill-of-material management, prototyping, production validation, and testing; (4) product-content management: generating changes, change-impact assessment, phase-in of changes; (5) order management: order capture and configuration, order tracking, and delivery arrangements; (6) sourcing and procurement: approving vendors, reverse auctions (tendering), supplier selection, strategic sourcing, component selection. A major tool for such collaboration is **collaborative workflow management** for production.

The major benefits of c-commerce are smoothing the flow in the supply chain, reducing inventories along the supply chain, reducing operating costs, increasing customer satisfaction, and increasing a company's competitive edge. The challenges faced by the collaborators are software-integration issues, technology selection, trust and security, and resistance to change and collaboration. Specialized tools for c-commerce applications are provided by vendors such as glyphica.com, allegis.com, lotus.com, and ca.com. According to Maybury (2001), creating a collaborative environment requires a delicate balance of technology, knowledge, and trust. For details, see Turban et al. (2004) and the discussion of people-to-people EC in the next section.

14.8 INTRABUSINESS, BUSINESS-TO-EMPLOYEES, AND PEOPLE-TO-PEOPLE EC

E-commerce can be done not only between business partners, but also within organizations. Such activity is referred to as *intrabusiness* EC or in short, **intrabusiness**. Intrabusiness can be done between a business and its employees (B2E), among units within the business (usually done as c-commerce), and among employees in the same business.

BUSINESS-TO-ITS-EMPLOYEES (B2E) COMMERCE

Companies are finding many ways to do business with their own employees electronically. They disseminate information to employees over the intranet, for example. They also allow employees to manage their fringe benefits and take training classes electronically. In addition, employees can buy discounted insurance, travel packages, and tickets to events on the corporate intranet, and they can electronically order supplies and material needed for their work. And many companies have electronic corporate stores that sell the company's products to its employees, usually at a discount. Of the many types of employees that benefit from B2E, we have elected to describe the salespeople in the field.

SALES FORCE AUTOMATION

Sales Force Automation (SFA) is a technique of using software to automate the business tasks of sales, including order processing, contact management, information sharing, inventory monitoring and control, order tracking, customer management, sales forecast analysis, and employee performance evaluation. Of special interest is the support provided to sales employees when they are in the field. Recently SFA become interrelated with CRM, since the salespeople constitute the contact point with customers. One area related to DSS is the *empowerment* of salespeople and other customer-facing employees to make quick decisions when they are in the customer's office, frequently while talking to the customer. Advancements in wireless technologies have created opportunities to provide salespeople with new capabilities, as shown in the case of PAVECA Corp. (DSS in Action 14.5). Many other companies, ranging from Maybelline (see Microsoft Corp., 2002) to Kodak have equipped their sales forces with similar mobile devices.

E-COMMERCE BETWEEN UNITS WITHIN THE BUSINESS

Large corporations frequently consist of independent units, or strategic business units (SBUs), which "sell" or "buy" materials, products, and services from each other. Transactions of this type are easily automated and performed over the intranet. An SBU can be considered as either a seller or a buyer. An example would be company-owned dealerships. This type of EC helps in improving internal supply-chain operations, as Dell Computers does when it repairs computers (see AIS in Action 14.6, p. 780).

E-COMMERCE BETWEEN CORPORATE EMPLOYEES

Many large organizations allow their employees to post classified ads on the company intranet, through which employees can buy and sell products and services from each other. This service is especially popular in universities, where it has been conducted since even before the commercialization of the Internet. This is an example of C2C e-commerce.

DSS IN ACTION 14.5

PAVECA OF VENEZUELA USES WIRELESS IN SALES FORCE AUTOMATION

PAVECA, Venezuela's largest paper-goods manufacturer and exporter, manufactures toilet paper, paper towels, tissues, and other paper products. The company enjoys a significant amount of market share and seeks to maintain that position. It chose to use some interesting e-commerce technologies to cut operating costs and improve customer service at the same time.

PAVECA was able to shave two days off its order-processing time, which not only led to faster order approval, but also increased the number of daily shipments out of its warehouse. Part of the solution revolved around a wireless implementation that allowed sales reps to use their wireless PDAs to connect to the Internet while in the field. The salespeople can log directly into the intranet to get all the information they need in real-time. Orders can then be entered into the system in real-time. The time from taking the order to entering it into the ERP system was reduced from about three days (using a manual process) to about 20 seconds (using the wireless solution).

The system revolved around two pieces of software from iWork Software (iworksoftware.com): an automatic data-collection system and a workflow-integration solution. The combination allowed salespeople to automatically register sales transactions into the ERP system as they occurred. Each salesperson had a PDA

connected directly to the company's ERP system in real-time. When an order is entered into the PDA, it goes into the ERP system, and follows a predefined automated workflow.

While the main goal was to improve workflow, there's another benefit here: better customer service. Because of the direct links and integration, customers can get their orders faster, and there's less chance of errors occurring. Customers are happier and more loyal, and so indirectly, the bottom line increases yet again because customers are more likely to place additional orders in the future. Finally, the transmitted data enter directly into the corporate DSS models, enabling quick decisions in response to the field reports filed by the salespersons.

QUESTIONS FOR THE CASE

1. How does the DSS benefit from EC?

2. What are the advantages of using wireless systems?

3. What segments of the supply chain are supported?

Sources: Compiled from paveca.com.ve and Blacharski, 2002.

14.9 E-GOVERNMENT, E-LEARNING, AND CUSTOMER-TO-CUSTOMER EC

E-GOVERNMENT

As e-commerce matures and its tools and applications improve, greater attention is being given to its use to improve the business of public institutions and governments (country, state, county, city, etc.).

E-government is the use of Internet technology in general, and of e-commerce in particular, to deliver information and public services to citizens, business partners and suppliers, and workers in the public sector. It is also an efficient way of conducting business transactions with citizens and businesses and within governments. The potential benefits of e-government are:

- Improves the efficiency and effectiveness of the functions of government, including the delivery of public services.
- Enables governments to be more transparent to citizens and businesses by giving access to more of the information generated by government.

AIS IN ACTION 14.6

HOW DELL COMPUTER FULFILLS CUSTOMER REPAIR ORDERS

One of Dell Inc.'s success factors is its superb logistics and order-fulfillment systems. Customer orders, which are received mostly online, are automatically transferred to the production area, where configuration is done to determine which components and parts are needed to create the customized computer that the customer wants. Once configuration is done, the problem becomes how to get all the needed components so that a computer can be ready for shipment in two to three days. As part of the solution, Dell created a network of dedicated suppliers for just-in-time deliveries, as well as a sophisticated computerized global network of components and parts inventories. The global network is also used for *product services* (e.g., repairs upgrades, demanufacturing).

Let's examine how Dell provides service when a computer in the customer's possession needs to be repaired. Dell is trying to achieve for repairs, upgrades, and other services the two- or three-day shipment target it uses for new computers. For repair activities, Dell needs parts and subassemblies to be delivered to hundreds of repair stations, worldwide, from internal warehouses or external vendors. The search for the parts and their delivery must be done very quickly. To facilitate this, Dell is using an online *intelligent inventory optimization system* from LPA software (xelus.com). The system can reconcile the demand for parts with the action needed (e.g., repair, upgrade, transfer, or demanufacture). For example, the intelligent system allows Dell to factor the yield on reusable parts into its supply projection. This allows Dell to use repairable parts to compress time and reduce costs, enabling a team of

about 10 employees to successfully process more than 6,000 service orders every day.

The online system generates timely information about demand forecast, the cost of needed inventory, and "days of supply of inventory." It compares actual to forecasted demand. This enables Dell to communicate critical information to external and internal customers, reducing order-fulfillment delays.

Producing or acquiring the required parts through component substitution, upgrades, and engineering change orders must be effective in order to provide superb customer service at a low inventory cost. The system also provides an online standard body of knowledge about parts and planning strategies.

QUESTIONS FOR THE CASE

1. What types of EC transactions and models can you identify in the system?

2. Enter xelus.com and find information about its inventory optimization and other SCM-related products. List the major capabilities of the products it offers.

3. Enter dell.com and find information about how Dell conducts repair (warranty) customer service.

4. What competitive advantage is provided by this Dell system?

Sources: Compiled from an advertising supplement in *CIO Magazine* (October 1, 1999), xelus.com (June 2000), and dell.com (2002).

- Facilitates fundamental changes in the relationships between citizens and governments.
- Offers greater opportunities for citizens to provide feedback to government agencies and to participate in democratic institutions and processes.

E-government applications can be divided into three major categories: *government-to-citizens (G2C), government-to-business (G2B),* and *government-to-government (G2G).* Government agencies are increasingly using the Internet to provide services to citizens. An example would be **electronic benefits transfer (EBT)**, in which government transfers Social Security, pension, and other benefits directly to recipients' bank accounts or to smart cards. Governments also are using the Internet to conduct business with businesses (sell to or buy from). For example, electronic tendering systems, using reverse auctions, are becoming mandatory. Many governments are moving public services online. Chen (2003a) presents several DSS-related issues in e-government initiatives. For another example, see DSS in Action 14.7.

According to microstrategy.com (a government success story), the state of Ohio is using intelligent e-business technology and software to improve the delivery of education.

E-LEARNING AND TRAINING

The topic of e-learning is becoming a major e-business activity, especially since world-class universities such as MIT, Harvard, and Stanford in the United States and Oxford in the United Kingdom have begun to implement it.

DSS IN ACTION 14.7

CONTRACT MANAGEMENT IN AUSTRALIA

The focus of Contract and Management Services (CAMS), an agency of the Western Australia (WA) government, is to develop online contract-management solutions for the public sector. CAMS Online allows government agencies to search existing contracts to discover how to access the commonly used contracts across government. It also assists suppliers wanting to sell to the government. Suppliers can view the current tenders (bids) on the Western Australia Government Contracting Information Bulletin Board, and download tender documents from this site.

CAMS Online also provides government departments and agencies with unbiased expert advice on e-commerce, Internet, and satellite services, and how-to's on building a bridge between the technological needs of the public sector and the expertise of the private sector. The center offers various types of support for government procurement activities.

SUPPORT OF E-COMMERCE ACTIVITIES

WA's e-commerce activities include electronic markets for government buying. Government clients can purchase goods and services on the *CAMS Internet Marketplace,* which provides services ranging from sending a purchase order to receiving an invoice and paying for an item. The *WA government electronic market* provides online supplier catalogs, electronic purchase orders, and electronic invoicing, EFT, and check and credit card payments. Other e-commerce functions are *ProcureLink*, an established CAMS service that sends electronic purchase orders to suppliers for EDI, EDI Post (an online hybrid mail service), facsimile, and the Internet; *SalesNet*, by which the government secures credit card payments for the sale of government goods and services across the Internet; and *DataLink*, which enables the transfer of data using a secure and con-trolled environment for message management. DataLink is an ideal solution for government agencies needing to exchange large volumes of operational information.

For example, the Victoria government and the new South Wales government in Western Australia are spending over $500 million (U.S.) on e-procurement systems under the Government Electronic Market System (ecc.online.wa.gov.au/news,19, September 2002).

TRAINING ONLINE

In addition to G2B functions, the site also offers citizens online training. A service called *Westlink* delivers adult training and educational programs to remote areas and schools, including rural and regional communities. A video-conferencing service offers two-way video and audio links, enabling government employees to meet together electronically from up to eight sites at any one time.

Access to the Online Services Centre is given to government employees and businesses that deal with the government via the CAMS Web site at business.wa.gov.au.

QUESTIONS FOR THE CASE

1. How is contract management facilitated by e-commerce tools?

2. What other e-commerce activities does the government perform?

3. Describe the WA online training program and the role in e-learning promotion the government should assume.

Source: business.wa.gov.au, February, 2001, ecc.online.wa.gov.au/news (June–November 2002).

DEFINITION

E-learning is the online delivery of information for purposes of education, training, or knowledge management. It is a Web-enabled system that makes knowledge accessible to those who need it, when they need it, anytime, anywhere. E-learning is useful both as an environment for facilitating learning at schools and as an environment for efficient and effective corporate training. Liaw and Huang (2002) describe how Web technologies can facilitate learning. For an overview and research issues of e-learning, see Piccoli et al. (2001), who also provide a comparison with traditional classroom teaching.

THE BENEFITS AND DRAWBACKS

In theory, there are many benefits to e-learning. However, it has also many drawbacks, and thus is a controversial topic.

Benefits of E-Learning. E-learning is the great equalizer. It can eliminate barriers of time, distance, and socioeconomic status, and thus enable individuals to take charge of their own lifelong learning. In the information age, learning opportunities truly span a lifetime—from childhood through adulthood. Skills and knowledge need to be continually updated and refreshed to keep up with today's fast-paced culture. New content, technologies, and trends in e-learning will help countries and organizations adapt to the demands of the Internet economy by educating their citizens and training their workers. In short, e-learning can save money, reduce travel time, increase access to experts, enable large number of students to take classes simultaneously, provide on-demand education, enable self-paced learning, and make learning less frustrating (see Liaw and Huang, 2002).

Other benefits of e-learning are summarized in Table 14.4.

Drawbacks of E-Learning. E-learning has few drawbacks. For example, it requires special training for instructors, equipment, and support services (higher cost). The lack of face-to-face interaction may be a negative for many learners. Assessment may be difficult, and maintenance and updating are costly. There is an issue of protecting intellectual property as well as student retention. Weaver (2002) provides guidelines to overcome these drawbacks.

CUSTOMER-TO-CUSTOMER E-COMMERCE

Customer-to-customer (C2C) e-commerce refers to e-commerce in which both the buyer and the seller are individuals (not businesses). C2C is conducted in several ways on the Internet; the best-known C2C activities are auctions.

C2C AUCTIONS

Selling and buying on auction sites is exploding throughout the world. Most auctions are conducted by intermediaries like eBay.com. However, many individuals are conducting their own auctions. For example, greatshoop.com provides software to create C2C reverse-auction communities online. Consumers can select general sites such as eBay.com or auctionanything.com, or can use specialized sites such as buyit.com or bid2bid.com.

CLASSIFIED ADS

People sell to other people every day through classified ads. Internet-based classified ads have several advantages over newspaper classified ads: They offer a national rather than a local audience. This greatly increases the supply of goods and services available and the number of potential buyers. For example, infospace.com/info.cls2k contains a list of 3 million job openings and about 500,000 cars, compared with the much smaller numbers you might find locally. Another example is recycler.com. Often, placing an ad

TABLE 14.4   The Benefits of E-Learning

Benefit	Description
Shorter training time	Training time has been reduced by 50% and more (e.g., at Cisco Systems).
Can train more people	Saving on facility space and doing training faster means more people can be trained.
Cost reduction	One study reported that the cost of providing a learning experience can be reduced by 50 to 70 percent when classroom lectures are replaced by e-learning sessions (see Urdan and Weggen, 2000).
Higher content retention	E-learning students are usually self-initiated and self-paced. Their motive for acquiring more knowledge may be to widen their scope of view or to develop career skills. Urdan and Weggen (2000) contend that such self-motivation results in content retention that could be 25 to 60 percent higher than that of lecturer-led training.
Flexibility	Students can be learn from any place and at any time, at their own pace. Easy references (links) to sources and past material. Can be used in universities and corporations.
Updated and consistent material	Material in e-learning is more consistent (Urdan and Weggen, 2000). Can be most-up-to-date.
Risk-free environment	People can express themselves more freely to their peers and the instructors. Can be privacy protected.
Creation and delivery of content	Content can be created by third-party experts and delivered by experts as well, thus freeing corporate HR employees to do developmental work.

on one Web site brings it automatically into the classified sections of numerous partners. This increases ad exposure, at no cost. Shoppers can use search engines to narrow the search for a particular item on several sites. Internet-based classifieds often can be placed for free by private parties, can be edited or changed easily, and in many cases display photos of the product offered for sale.

Classified Web sites accept no responsibility for the content of any advertisement. Advertisers are identified by e-mail address. A password is used to authenticate the advertiser for future changes in an ad. Most classified ads are provided for free.

The major categories of classified ads are similar to those found in a newspaper: vehicles, real estate, employment, general merchandise, collectibles, computers, tickets, and travel. Classified ads are available through most Internet service providers (AOL, MSN, etc.), in some portals (Yahoo!, etc.), and from Internet directories, online newspapers, and more. Once users find an ad and get the details, they can e-mail or call the other party for additional information or to make a purchase. Classified sites generate revenue from affiliate sites, especially when the sellers are businesses.

PERSONAL SERVICES

Numerous personal services are available on the Internet (lawyers, handy helpers, tax preparers, investment clubs, dating services). Some are in the classified ads, but others are listed in specialized Web sites and directories. Some are for free, some for a fee. Be very careful before you purchase any personal services. Fraud or crime could be involved (e.g., a lawyer online may not be an expert or may not deliver the service at all).

SUPPORT SERVICES FOR C2C

When individuals buy products or services from individuals, they usually buy from strangers. The issues of ensuring quality, receiving payments, and preventing fraud are critical to the success of C2C. One service that helps C2C is payments by companies such as paypal.com (see Section 14.11).

14.10 M-COMMERCE, L-COMMERCE, AND PERVASIVE COMPUTING

Mobile commerce and its variants are one of the most interesting developments in electronic commerce.

MOBILE COMMERCE

Mobile commerce (m-commerce) refers to the conduct of e-commerce from mobile computing devices (e.g., cell phones, PDAs), usually on wireless networks. The number of cell phones in use worldwide, according to the GartnerGroup, topped 1.3 billion by 2004. Scores of millions of PDAs are also sold each year. These devices can be connected to the Internet, making it possible to conduct transactions from anywhere the users are. In addition, many corporate employees are mobile—working at home, on clients' sites, or on the road. GartnerGroup projected that 30 to 50 percent of all employees in developed countries will be mobile, at least part of the time, by 2010. These employees need to collaborate and communicate with in-office employees and to access corporate data, rapidly and conveniently. Such a capability is provided by m-commerce.

THE ADVANTAGES OF M-COMMERCE

Two main characteristics are driving the interest in m-commerce: mobility and reachability. *Mobility* implies that Internet access travels with the customer. M-commerce is appealing because wireless offers customers information from any location. This enables employees to contact the office from anywhere they happen to be, and allows customers to act instantly on any shopping impulse. *Reachability* means that people can be contacted at any time, which most people see as a convenience of modern life. (Of course, you can block certain times or certain messages.) These two characteristics, mobility and reachability, break the barriers of geography and time. As a result, mobile devices can be used to obtain real-time information and to communicate from anywhere, at any time. For details on m-commerce, see Sadeh (2002) and Kalakota and Robinson (2001).

Mobile devices make possible *location-based commerce*, also known as **L-commerce**. L-commerce delivers information about goods and services based on where you (and your mobile device) are located. For example, in San Francisco, NextBus service (nextbus.com) knows, by the use of global positioning systems (GPS), where the buses are, in real-time; when you call on your cell phone to ask about a particular bus stop, the system will compute when the bus will actually arrive there. Other localization systems will find where you are located, and based on this information will send you advertisements for vendors located nearby.

APPLICATIONS OF M-COMMERCE

Here are some representative applications of m-commerce.

- *Online banking.* Mobile banking is taking off rapidly. For example, the Swedish Postal Bank allows customers to make payments from their headsets, and MaritaNordabanken in Sweden allows several other types of banking transactions. Citibank has mobile banking services in Singapore, Hong Kong, and other countries.
- *Micropayments.* Consumers in Japan can use their mobile phones to pay for purchases from vending machines. In the Scandinavian countries, consumers pay for parking in unattended parking lots, for car washes, for gasoline, and for soft drinks in vending machines. Similar capabilities exist in France and in several other countries worldwide. In Germany, customers can pay for transportation, including taxis, from their mobile phones.
- *Online gambling.* Eurobet, a large vendor in Britain, allows online gambling. In Hong Kong you can use your cell phone to bet on horse races.
- *Ordering and service.* Barnes and Noble has created a service for PDA devices and cell phones that allows users to download their favorite music clips to the devices. You can order books online as well.
- *Online auctions.* QXL.com, an online British auction company, lets users open accounts on its Web sites and bid for items, using cell phones. EBay also conducts online auctions that can be accessed by cell phones.
- *B2B applications.* Remote employees can handle tasks like checking inventory or submitting orders while in the field. The Internet thus becomes a repository of corporate information, and a virtual warehouse of goods and services.
- *Online stock trading.* Online stock trading can be done all over the world via a cell phone. Dagens Industri of Sweden allows subscribers to trade on the Stockholm Stock Exchange and receive financial data using a PDA. E*Trade allows trading from mobile devices in several countries; in Korea, a million customers trade stocks from their cell phones. i-mode, discussed below, offers online stock trading plus various other m-commerce activities.
- *Mobile Portal.* i-mode (nttdocomo.com) is a pioneering wireless service that took Japan by storm as of 1999. With a few clicks of a handset, i-mode users can conduct a large variety of m-commerce activities, ranging from online stock trading and banking to purchasing travel tickets and booking karaoke rooms. You can also send and receive color images via i-mode. The service had over 40 million users by the end of 2003. i-mode users can access train and bus timetables, guides to shopping areas, and automatic notification of train delays; get discount coupons for shopping and restaurants; purchase music online; send or receive photos; buy airline tickets; and find information about best-selling books.

TECHNOLOGY AND LIMITATIONS

The implementation of m-commerce requires a multitude of infrastructures: hardware (cell phones, PDAs, etc.), software (microbrowsers, operating systems, application software), and wireless transmission media (e.g., satellites). Some of the major limitations on m-commerce relating to these technologies are insufficient bandwidth, lack of standard security protocols, high cost of 3G licenses, high power consumption (i.e., the need to charge batteries frequently), and possible health hazards. For details see Sadeh, 2002.

PERVASIVE COMPUTING

With pervasive computing, we envision a future in which computation becomes part of the environment. The computer forms (workstations, personal computers, personal digital assistants, game players) through which we now relate to computation will occupy only a small niche in this new computational world. Our relationship to pervasive computing will differ radically from our current relationship with computers. When computation becomes part of the environment, most human-computer interaction will be implicit, and it will have to take account of physical space. Physical space rarely matters in current human-computer interaction; but as computational devices become part of furniture, walls, and clothing, physical space becomes a necessary consideration. In pervasive computing computation will be embodied in things, not computers. We can already put computation almost anywhere. Embedded computation controls braking and acceleration in our cars, defines the capability of medical instruments, and runs virtually all machinery. Hand-held devices (especially cell phones and pagers) are commonplace; serious computational wristwatches and other wearables are becoming practical; computational furniture and rooms are demonstrable. Relentless progress in semiconductor technology, low-power design, and wireless technology will make embedded computation less and less obtrusive. Computation is ready to disappear into the environment.

Pervasive computing is closely related to intelligent systems and DSS. For example, in the Elite-Care Project (see Stanford, 2002 and the Opening Vignette to Chapter 15), patients are monitored by portable or wearable devices, and such decisions as directing a patient or issuing an alert are made by the system.

Pervasive computing (Burkhardt et al., 2002) is based on advances in intelligent systems, mobile computing, and distributed computing. This futuristic technology will enable the automation of many decisions (Amor, 2001).

14.11 E-COMMERCE SUPPORT SERVICES

The implementation of EC may require several support services. B2B and B2C applications require payments and order fulfillment. Portals require content. And so on. Figure 14.5 portrays the the major EC services. Among them are *e-infrastructure* (technology consultants, system developers and integrators, hosting, security, and networks), *e-processes*, mainly payments and logistics, and *e-markets*, dealing with marketing and advertising. *E-communities* includes the different business partners. *E-services* includes CRM, PRM, and directory services. *E-content* refers to content providers. All these services support the applications in the center. All the services need to be managed.

We will discuss here only two topics; payments and order fulfillment. For details on the other services see Turban et al., 2004.

ELECTRONIC PAYMENTS

Payments are an integral part of doing business, whether in the traditional way or online. Unfortunately, in most cases traditional payment systems are not effective for EC, especially in B2B.

LIMITATIONS OF TRADITIONAL PAYMENT INSTRUMENTS

Non-electronic payment methods, such as using cash, writing a check, sending a money order, or giving your credit card number over the telephone, have several limitations in e-commerce. Cash cannot be used because there is no face-to-face contact. It takes time for payments sent by mail to be received. It also takes time to process a credit card number provided by phone or fax, and it is inconvenient to have to switch from the

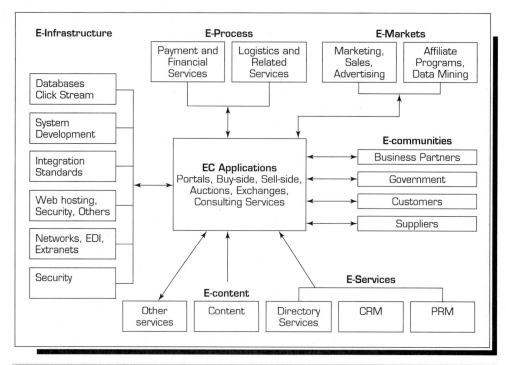

E-Infrastructure

- Databases Click Stream
- System Development
- Integration Standards
- Web hosting, Security, Others
- Networks, EDI, Extranets
- Security

E-Process
- Payment and Financial Services
- Logistics and Related Services

E-Markets
- Marketing, Sales, Advertising
- Affiliate Programs, Data Mining

EC Applications
Portals, Buy-side, Sell-side, Auctions, Exchanges, Consulting Services

E-communities
- Business Partners
- Government
- Customers
- Suppliers

E-content
- Other services
- Content

E-Services
- Directory Services
- CRM
- PRM

FIGURE 14.5   MAJOR EC SERVICES

computer to the phone to complete a transaction, especially if the same telephone line is used. Furthermore, not everyone accepts credit cards or checks, and some buyers do not have credit cards or checking accounts. Finally, contrary to what many people believe, it may be less secure for the buyer to use the telephone or mail to arrange or send payments, especially from another country, than to finish a secure transaction on a computer.

Another issue is that many EC transactions are valued at only a few dollars or even cents. The cost of processing such **micropayments** needs to be very low; you would not want to pay $5 to process a purchase valued at only a few dollars. The cost of making micropayments offline is just too high. For all of these reasons, a better way is needed to pay in cyberspace. This better way is an *electronic payment system*.

ELECTRONIC PAYMENT SYSTEMS

As in the traditional marketplace, so too in cyberspace, the diversity of payment methods allows customers to choose how they wish to pay. The following instruments are acceptable means of payment: electronic checks, electronic credit cards, purchasing cards, electronic cash, stored-value smart cards, person-to-person payments, electronic funds transfer (EFT), wireless payments, and e-wallets. Here we will look at some of these payment mechanisms. Later on we will see how to make them secure.

Electronic Checks.   Electronic checks (e-checks) are similar to regular checks, and they are used mostly in B2B. Here is how they work:

Step 1:   The customer establishes a checking account with a bank.

Step 2:   The customer contacts a seller, buys a product or a service, and e-mails an encrypted electronic check.

Step 3:   The merchant deposits the check; money is debited from the buyer's account and credited to the seller's account.

Like regular checks, e-checks carry a signature (in digital form) that can be verified (see paybycheck.com). Properly signed and endorsed e-checks are exchanged between financial institutions through electronic clearing houses (see echeck.org and nacha.org for details).

Electronic Credit Cards. Electronic credit cards make it possible to charge online payments to one's credit card account. It is easy and simple for a buyer to e-mail her or his credit card number to the seller. The risk here is that hackers will be able to read the card number and use it illegally if it is not encrypted. Sender authentication is also difficult. (New technologies will solve this problem in two or three years.) Therefore, for security, only encrypted cards should be used. (Credit card details can be encrypted by using the SSL protocol in the buyer's computer, which is available in standard browsers and is described online.) When you buy a book from Amazon.com, your credit card information and purchase amount are *encrypted* in your browser. So the information is safe while on the Internet. When this information arrives at Amazon.com, it is not opened but is transferred automatically (encrypted) to VISA, MasterCard, or some other credit card company for authorization.

Virtual Credit Cards. A virtual credit card is a service that allows you to shop with an ID number and a password instead with a credit card number (see americanexpress.com). The bank provides you with a transaction number valid for a short period. This way your loss, if any occurs, is limited. Credit cards are used mainly in B2C and in shopping by SMEs. Purchasing cards are used for B2B.

Purchasing Cards. In some countries, such as Britain, United States, and Hong Kong, companies use purchasing cards to pay other companies. Unlike credit cards, where credit is provided for 30 to 60 days for free before payment is made to the merchant, payments made with purchasing cards are settled within a week. Purchasing cards are used for unplanned B2B purchases, and corporations generally limit the amount per purchase (usually $1,000 to $2,000). Purchasing cards can be used on the Internet much like regular credit cards. They expedite the process of unplanned purchases, usually as part of *desktop e-purchasing* described in Section 14.6.

Electronic Cash. Cash is the most prevalent consumer-payment instrument. Traditional brick-and-mortar merchants prefer cash because they do not have to pay commissions to credit card companies and can put the money to use as soon as it is received. Some buyers pay with cash because they do not have checks or credit cards, or because they want to preserve their anonymity. It is logical therefore, that EC sellers and some buyers may prefer electronic cash (e-cash). Electronic cash appears in three major forms:

a. **Electronic payment cards with e-cash.** A typical e-payment card is known as a *stored-value* money card. It is the one you use to pay for photocopies in your library, for transportation, or for telephone calls. It allows a fixed amount of prepaid money to be stored on it. Each time you use the card, the amount is reduced. One successful example is used by the New York Metropolitan Transportation Authority (MTA), which operates buses, trains, interstate toll bridges, and tunnels. Nearly 5 million customers present cards to card-reader machines on buses, subways, and road tollbooths each day. In January 2003 the MTA decided to discontinue the use of tokens in public transportation (they had been in use for over 50 years) in favor of stored-value cards. Similar cards are used in many cities around the world. Some of these cards are reloadable, and some are discarded when the money is depleted. The Octopus transportation card in Hong Kong is used in trains, buses, and for shopping in stores and from vending machines.

Cards with stored-value money can be also purchased for Internet use. You enter a third-party Web site and provide an ID number and a password, much as you do when you use a prepaid phone card. The money can be used only in participating stores.

b. Smart cards. Some people refer to stored-value cards as smart cards, but they are not really the same. True smart cards contain a microprocessor (chip) and can store a considerable amount of information (more than 100 times what is in a stored-value card) and can conduct processing. Such cards are frequently multipurpose; they can be used as credit cards, debit cards, and stored-value cards, and when used in department-store chains as loyalty cards they contain purchasing information about shoppers.

Advanced smart cards have the ability to transfer funds, pay bills, buy from vending machines, or pay for services such as those offered on television or PCs. Money values can be loaded at ATMs, kiosks, or from your PC. For example, the VISA Cash Card allows you to buy goods or services at participating gas stations, fast-food outlets, pay phones, discount stores, post offices, convenience stores, coffee shops, and even movie theaters. Smart cards are ideal for micropayments.

Smart cards can also be used to transfer benefits from companies to their employees, as when retirees get their pension payments, and from governments that pay citizens different entitlements. The money is transferred electronically to a smart card at an ATM, kiosk, or PC.

c. Person-to-person payment. Person-to-person payments (P2P) are one of the newest and fastest-growing payment schemes. They enable the transfer of funds between two individuals for a variety of purposes, like repaying money borrowed from a friend, sending money to a student at college, paying for an item purchased at an online auction, or sending a gift to a family member. One of the first companies to offer this service is PayPal (paypal.com). PayPal (an eBay company) claimed, in 2003, to have about 20 million customer accounts, handling more than 35 percent of all eBay transactions and funneling $8.5 billion in payments through its servers annually. Citibank c2it (c2it.com), AOL QuickCash, Bank One's eMoneyMail, Yahoo! PayDirect, and WebCertificate (webcertificate.com) are all PayPal competitors.

Virtually all P2P systems work the same way. Assume you want to send money to someone over the Internet. First, you select a service and open up an account with it. Basically, this entails creating a user name, a password, giving the service your e-mail address, and providing the service with a credit card or bank account number. Next, you add funds from your credit card or bank account to your account. Once the account has been funded you're ready to send money. You access PayPal (for example) with your user name and password. Now you specify the e-mail address of the person to receive the money, along with the dollar amount you want to send. An e-mail is sent to the payee's e-mail address. The e-mail will contain a link back to the service's Web site. When the recipient clicks on the link, he or she will be taken to the service and asked to set up an account to which the money that was sent will be credited. The recipient can then credit the money from this account to his or her credit card or bank account. The payer pays a small amount (around $1) per transaction.

Electronic Bill Presentment and Payment.   An increasing number of people prefer to pay monthly bills online, such as telephone, utilities, credit cards, and cable TV. The recipients of are even more enthusiastic about this service than the payers, since online payment enables them to reduce processing costs significantly. The following are the major existing payment systems in common use: automatic payment of mortgages, automatic transfer of funds to pay monthly utility bills, paying bills from an online bank account, merchant-to-customer direct billing, and use of an intermediary to aggregate bills into one payable Web site.

SECURITY IN ELECTRONIC PAYMENTS

Two main issues need to be considered under the topic of payment security: what measures are necessary in order to make EC payments safe (security requirements), and the methods that can be used (security protection).

Security Requirements.   The security requirements for conducting EC are:

1. *Authentication.* The buyer, the seller, and the paying institutions must be assured of the identity of the parties with whom they are dealing.
2. *Integrity.* Data and information transmitted in EC, such as orders, replies to queries, and payment authorizations, must be protected against accidental or malicious alteration or destruction during transmission.
3. *Non-repudiation.* Merchants need protection against the customer's unjustified denial of placing an order. On the other hand, customers need protection against the merchant's unjustified denial of payments made. (Both types of denials are called repudiation.)
4. *Privacy.* Many customers want their identity to be secured. They want to make sure others do not know what they buy. Some prefer the same complete anonymity that is possible with cash payments.
5. *Safety.* Customers want to be sure that it is safe to provide a credit card number on the Internet.

Security protection.   Several methods and mechanisms can be used to fulfill these security requirements. The primary mechanism is encryption, which is often part of the most useful security schemes. Intelligent systems are extremely useful in facilitating Internet security. For details see DSS Online 14.2.

ORDER FULFILLMENT IN EC

A company that sells direct to customers is involved in various-order fulfillment activities. It must:

1. Quickly find the products to be shipped and pack them.
2. Arrange for the packages to be delivered speedily to the customer's door.
3. Collect the money from every customer, either in advance, by Cash On Delivery (COD), or by individual bill.
4. Handle the return of unwanted or defective products.

It is very difficult to effectively and efficiently accomplish these activities in B2C, since a company may need to ship small packages to many customers, and do it quickly. For this reason, both online companies and click-and-mortar companies have difficulties in their B2C supply chains. Here we provide only a brief overview; more detailed discussion is provided in Turban et al. (2004), and in Bayles (2001).

Order fulfillment refers not only to providing customers with what they ordered and doing it on time, but also to providing all related customer services. For example, the customer must receive assembly and operating instructions for a new appliance. (A nice example is available at livemanuals.com.) In addition, if the customer is not happy with a product, an exchange or return must be arranged (see fedex.com for how returns are handled). Order fulfillment is basically a part of the back-office operations.

In the last few years, e-tailers have faced continuous problems in order fulfillment, especially during the holiday season. Such problems result in inability to deliver on time, delivery of wrong items, high delivery costs, and the need to heavily compensate unhappy customers. Several factors can be responsible for delayed deliveries. They range from inability to forecast demand accurately to ineffective supply chains. Problems of this kind also exist in offline businesses. One factor that is typical of EC, though, is that it is based on the concept of "pull" operations, which begin with an order, frequently a customized one. This is in contrast with traditional retailing, which begins with a production to inventory that is then "pushed" to customers (see DSS Online 14.3). In the pull case it is more difficult to forecast demand, due to the unique demands of customized orders and lack of sufficient years of experience. For many e-tailers, taking orders over the Internet could well be the easy part of B2C e-commerce. Fulfillment to the customer's door is the sticky part. Fulfillment is less complicated in B2B, where several effective methods are in use (see Bayles, 2001).

14.12 LEGAL AND ETHICAL ISSUES IN E-COMMERCE

Ethical standards and their incorporation into law frequently trail technological innovations. E-commerce is taking new forms and enabling new business practices that may bring numerous risks—particularly for individual consumers—along with their advantages. Before we present some specific issues, we discuss the topic of market practices and consumer/seller protections.

MARKET PRACTICES AND CONSUMER AND SELLER PROTECTION

When buyers and sellers do not know each other and cannot even see each other (they may even be in different countries), there is a chance that dishonest people will commit fraud and other crimes over the Internet. During the first few years of e-commerce, the public witnessed many instances of this, ranging from the creation of a virtual bank that disappeared along with the investors' deposits, to manipulation of stock prices on the Internet. Unfortunately, fraudulent activities on the Internet are increasing faster even than the use of the Internet.

FRAUD ON THE INTERNET

Internet fraud has become more sophisticated, and has grown as much and even faster than the Internet itself. For example, stock promoters falsely spread positive rumors about the prospects of the companies they touted. In other cases the information provided might have been true, but the promoters did not disclose that they were paid to talk up the companies. Stock promoters specifically target small investors who are lured by the promise of fast profits.

Stocks are only one of the many areas where swindlers are active. Auctions are especially conducive to fraud, both by sellers and buyers. Other areas of potential fraud include selling bogus investments and phantom business opportunities. Financial criminals now have access to far more people, mainly due to the availability of electronic mail. The U.S. Federal Trade Commission has published a list of scams most likely to arrive via e-mail and popup screens (ftc.gov).

There are several ways buyers can be protected against EC fraud. Representative methods are described next.

BUYER PROTECTION

Buyer protection is critical to the success of any commerce where buyers do not see the sellers, and this is especially true for e-commerce. Some tips for safe electronic shopping are shown in Table 14.5. In short, do not forget that you have shopper's rights. Consult your local or state consumer-protection agency for general information on your consumer rights.

SELLER PROTECTION

Sellers, too, may need protections. They must be protected against consumers who refuse to pay or who pay with bad checks, and from buyers' claims that the merchandise did not arrive. They also have the right to protect against the use of their name by others as well as use of their unique words and phrases, slogans, and Web addresses (trademark protection). Another seller protection applies particularly to electronic media: sellers have legal recourse against customers who download without permission copyrighted software and/or knowledge, and use it or sell it to others.

ETHICAL ISSUES

Many of the ethical and global issues related to IT and DSS apply also to e-commerce (see Chapter 15 for details). Here we touch on issues particularly related to e-commerce.

PRIVACY

Most electronic payment systems know who the buyers are; therefore, it may be necessary to protect the buyers' identities. Another privacy issue may involve tracking of Internet user activities by intelligent agents and cookies. A privacy issue related to employees also involves tracking. Many companies monitor employees' e-mail and have installed software that performs in-house monitoring of Web activities; many employees feel as if they are under the watchful eye of "Big Brother" while at work.

TABLE 14.5 Tips for Safe Electronic Shopping

- Look for reliable brand names at sites like Wal-Mart Online, Disney Online, and Amazon.com. Make sure that the sites are authentic before purchasing, by entering the site directly and not from an unverified link.
- Search any unfamiliar selling site for the company's address and phone and fax numbers. Call up and quiz the employees about the sellers.
- Check out the vendor with the local Chamber of Commerce or Better Business Bureau (bbbonline.org). Look for seals of authenticity such as TRUSTe.
- Investigate how secure the seller's site is by examining the security procedures and by reading the posted privacy notice.
- Examine money-back guarantees, warranties, and service agreements.
- Compare prices to those in regular stores. Too-low prices are too good to be true, and some "catch" is probably involved.
- Ask friends what they know. Find testimonials and endorsements in community sites and well-known bulletin boards.
- Find out what your rights are in case of a dispute.
- Consult the National Fraud Information Center (fraud.org).
- Check consumerworld.org for a listing of useful resources.

WEB TRACKING

By using tracking software, companies can track individuals' movements on the Internet. Cookies raise a batch of privacy concerns. With cookies, the tracking history is stored on your PC's hard drive, and any time you revisit a certain Web site, the computer knows it. Programs such as Cookie Cutter are designed to allow users to have some control over cookies (for further discussion see commerceNet.com).

DISINTERMEDIATION

The use of EC may result in the elimination of some of a company's employees, brokers, and agents. This result is called disintermediation—that is, "eliminating the intermediary." The manner in which unneeded workers, especially employees, are treated may raise ethical issues, such as how to handle the displacement.

LEGAL ISSUES SPECIFIC TO E-COMMERCE

There are many legal issues related to e-commerce (Cheeseman, 2001). Representative examples are:

DOMAIN NAMES

Internet addresses are known as **domain names**. Domain names appear in levels. prenhall.com or stanford.edu are top-level names. prenhall.com/turban and ibm.com.hk (for IBM in Hong Kong) are second-level names. Top-level domain names are assigned by central nonprofit organizations that check for conflicts and possible infringement of trademarks. Obviously, companies that sell goods and services over the Internet want customers to be able to find them easily, so the URL must match the company's name. Problems arise when several companies with similar names compete over a domain name. For example, if you want to book reservations at a Holiday Inn hotel and you go to holidayinn.com, you get the Web site for a hotel in Niagara Falls, New York; to get to the hotel chain's Web site, you have to go to holiday-inn.com. Several cases of disputed names are already in court. An international arbitration organization is available as an alternative to the courts. The problem of domain names was alleviated somewhat in 2001 after several upper-level names were added to "com" (such as "info" and "coop").

TAXES AND OTHER FEES

Federal, state, and local authorities are scrambling to figure out how to get a piece of the revenue created electronically. The problem is particularly complex for interstate and international commerce. For example, some claim that the state in which a server is located deserves to receive some sales tax from an e-commerce transaction. Others say that the state in which the seller is located deserves the entire sales tax (or value-added tax, VAT, in some countries).

In addition to sales tax, there is a question about where (and in some case, whether) electronic sellers should pay business license taxes, franchise fees, gross-receipts taxes, excise taxes, privilege taxes, and utility taxes. Furthermore, how should tax collection be controlled? Legislative efforts to impose taxes on e-commerce are opposed by an organization named the Internet Freedom Fighters. Its efforts have been successful so far. As of this writing, there was a ban on taxing Internet business in the United States and many other countries (sales tax only) that would remain valid until the fall of 2006. Another disputed area is tax on Internet access.

COPYRIGHT

Intellectual property, in its various forms, is protected by copyright laws and cannot be used freely. Copyright issues and protection of intellectual property are discussed in Chapter 15.

❖ CHAPTER HIGHLIGHTS

- E-commerce can be conducted on the Web, by e-mail, and on private networks. It has several major forms: business-to-consumer, consumer-to-consumer, business-to-business, e-government, collaborative commerce, and intrabusiness. In each of these there are several business models. E-commerce offers many benefits to organizations, consumers, and society, but it also has limitations (technical and nontechnical). The current technical limitations are expected to lessen with time.

- The Internet provides an infrastructure for executing auctions at lower cost, and with many more involved sellers and buyers, including both individual consumers and corporations. Forward auctions and reverse auctions are the two major types.

- The major service application areas of B2C commerce are in direct retailing, banking, securities trading, job markets, travel, and real estate. Several issues slow the growth of B2C, notably channel conflict, order fulfillment, and customer acquisition. B2C e-tailing can be "pure play" (e.g., Amazon.com) or part of a click-and-mortar organization. Direct marketing is done via solo storefronts or in malls. It can be done by using electronic catalogs or auctions.

- Understanding consumer behavior is critical to e-commerce. Finding out what customers want can be determined by asking them in questionnaires or by observing what they do online. Other forms of market research can be conducted on the Internet by using intelligent agents. Like any commerce, EC requires advertising support, much of which can be done online by methods such as banner advertisements and customized ads. Permission marketing, interactive and viral marketing, pop ups, using electronic catalogs, and online coupons offer ways for vendors to reach more customers. Customer service occurs before purchase,

while purchasing, after purchasing, and during disposal of products.

- The major B2B applications are selling from catalogs and by forward auctions, buying in reverse auctions and in group purchasing, and trading in exchanges. In addition, most organizations employ collaborative commerce, usually along the supply chain.

- EC activities can be conducted inside organizations. Three types are recognized: between business and its employees, between units of the business, and among employees of the same organization. All of these utilize many methods and tools.

- E-government commerce can take place between government and citizens or between businesses and governments. It makes government operations more effective and efficient. Using a wireless environment allows new mobile commerce applications as well as more convenient access to the Internet. EC can also be done between consumers (C2C), but should be undertaken with caution. Auctions are the most popular C2C mechanism.

- Traditional nonelectronic payment systems are insufficient or inferior for doing business on the Internet, so electronic payment systems are used. Electronic payments can be made by e-checks, e-credit cards, e-cash, smart cards, and EFT. Order fulfillment is especially difficult in B2C.

- Protection of customers, sellers, and intellectual property is a major concern, but so are the value of contracts, domain names, and how to handle legal issues in a multicountry environment. Implementing e-commerce is not simple, and multiple financial, organizational, technological, and managerial issues must be addressed.

❖ KEY WORDS

- auction
- autoresponder
- banners
- brick-and-mortar organization
- business-to-business (B2B)
- business-to-consumer (B2C)
- business-to-employees (B2E)
- business models
- buy-side marketplace
- channel conflict
- click-and-mortar organizations
- collaborative commerce (c-commerce)
- collaborative filtering

- collaborative workflow management
- customer-to-customer (C2C)
- cyberbanking
- desk-top purchasing
- domain names
- relectronic auctions
- electronic banking
- electronic bartering
- electronic benefits transfer (EBT)
- electronic business (e-business)
- electronic cash (e-cash)
- electronic commerce (e-commerce, EC)

- electronic exchange
- electronic funds transfer (EFT)
- electronic retailing (e-tailing)
- electronic storefronts
- e-government
- e-learning
- e-procurement
- forward auction
- group purchasing
- intelligent agent
- internet communities
- intrabusiness
- keyword banner
- L-commerce

- micropayments
- mobile commerce (m-commerce)
- mobile portal
- order fulfillment
- permission marketing
- person-to-person (P2P)
- pervasive computing
- pop-under ad

- pop-up ad
- private exchange
- public exchange
- pure play companies
- random banner
- reverse auction
- search engine
- segmentation

- sell-side marketplace
- smart cards
- spamming
- systematic sourcing
- viral marketing
- virtual banks
- virtual organizations

❖ QUESTIONS FOR REVIEW

1. Define e-commerce and distinguish it from e-business.
2. List the major types of EC (by type of transaction).
3. Distinguish between business-to-consumer, business-to-business, and intrabusiness EC.
4. List some organizational, societal, and consumer benefits of EC (five each).
5. List the major technical and nontechnical limitations of EC (three each).
6. Describe electronic storefronts and malls.
7. List the benefits of cyberbanking.
8. Describe electronic securities trading.
9. Describe the online job market.
10. Explain how electronic auctions work and list their benefits.
11. Describe the EC consumer-behavior model.
12. Describe EC market research and its tools.
13. Describe the major support areas of intelligent agents in EC.
14. Describe online advertising, its methods, and benefits.
15. Describe pop-up and pop-under ads and the issues surrounding them.
16. Briefly describe the sell-side marketplace.
17. Describe the various methods of e-procurement.
18. Describe how forward and reverse auctions are used in B2B commerce.
19. Describe the role of exchanges in B2B.
20. Describe c-commerce and its various activities.
21. Describe e-government and its benefits.
22. What makes m-commerce so appealing?
23. Describe some C2C activities.
24. Describe intrabusiness and B2E commerce.
25. List the various electronic payment mechanisms.
26. List the security requirements for EC.
27. Describe customization in EC.
28. Describe the issues in EC order fulfillment.
29. Describe some of the potential frauds on the Internet.
30. Describe buyer protection in EC.
31. List some ethical issues in EC.
32. List the major legal issues of EC.

❖ DISCUSSION QUESTIONS

1. Discuss the major limitations of e-commerce. Which of them are likely to disappear? Why?
2. Why is the electronic job market popular, especially in the high-tech professions?
3. Distinguish between business-to-business forward auctions and buyers' bids for RFQs.
4. Some say that the major benefit of EC occurs in c-commerce. Why?
5. Discuss the benefits to sellers and buyers of a B2B exchange.
6. What are the major benefits of e-government?
7. Why is m-commerce attracting a great deal of attention?
8. Why are online auctions becoming popular?
9. Discuss the contribution DSS can make to an online storefront and to an electronic mall.
10. Discuss the online consumer-behavior model and explain why is it needed.
11. Discuss the contribution that EC can make in decision support and analysis.
12. Relate e-learning to decision support.
13. Distinguish between value-added cards and smart cards.

❖ EXERCISES

1. Assume you're interested in buying a car. You can find information about cars at autos.msn.com. Go to autoweb.com or autobytel.com for information about financing and insurance. Decide what car you want to buy. Configure your car by going to the car manufac- turer's Web site. Finally, try to find the car from autobytel.com. What information is most supportive of your decision-making process? Write a report about your experience.

❖ INTERNET EXERCISES

1. Access etrade.com and register for the Internet stock-simulation game. You will be bankrolled with $100,000 in a trading account every month. Play the game and relate your experiences to DSS.
2. Access hsbc.com.hk/hk/hexagon.default.htm and us.hsbc.com/corporate/cashmgmt/hexagon/payments, and find information about Hexagon. What are its advantages to the bank? To the customers?
3. Access realtor.com. Prepare a list of services avail- able on this site. Then prepare a list of advantages for users and for realtors. Are there any disadvantages? For whom?
4. Enter alibaba.com. Identify the site's capabilities. Look at the site's private trading rooms. Write a report. How can such a site help a purchasing deci- sion-maker?
5. Try to find a unique gift on the Internet for a friend. Several sites help you do it. You might try shopping.com and amazon.com, for example. Describe your experience with such a site.
6. Enter campusfood.com. Explore the site. Why is it so successful? Could you start a competing one? Why or why not?
7. Enter dell.com, go to "desktops" and configure a sys- tem. Register to "my cart" (no obligation). What cal- culators are used there? What are the advantages of this process as compared to buying a computer in a physical store? What are the disadvantages?
8. Enter bizrate.com and fill out one of the question- naires that entitles you to participate in the site's rewards and receive information. What data are col- lected? Why?
9. Enter microstrategy.com and look for the EC/DSS (or EC/BI) products like BPM. Prepare a report on such products.

❖ GROUP ASSIGNMENTS AND ROLE-PLAYING

1. Have each team study a major bank with an exten- sive EC strategy. For example, Wells Fargo Bank is well on its way to being a cyberbank. Hundreds of brick-and-mortar branch offices are being closed. In late 2003 the bank served more than 1.3 million cyberaccounts (see wellsfargo.com). Other banks are Citicorp, Netbank, and HSBC (Hong Kong). Each team should attempt to convince the class that its e- bank is the best.
2. Assign each team to one industry. Each team will find five real-world e-DSS-related applications of the major business-to-business models listed in the chap- ter. (Try success stories about vendors in EC-related magazines.) Examine the problems they solve or the opportunities they exploit.

AMAZON.COM:
THE KING OF E-TAILING

THE OPPORTUNITY

It was not a business problem but rather an opportunity that faced entrepreneur Jeff Bezos. He saw the huge potential for retail sales over the Internet and selected books as the most logical product for e-tailing. In July 1995, Bezos started Amazon.com, an e-tailing pioneer, offering books via an electronic catalog from its Web site. Over the years, the company has recognized that it must continually enhance its business models and electronic store by expanding product selection, improving the customer's experience, and adding services and alliances. The company also recognized the importance of order fulfillment and warehousing. It invested hundreds of millions of dollars in building physical warehouses designed for shipping small packages to hundreds of thousands of customers. Amazon's problem was, and remains, how to succeed where many have failed—namely, how to compete in selling consumer products online, showing a profit and a reasonable rate of return on the huge investment it has made.

THE PROJECT

In addition to its initial electronic bookstore, Amazon.com has expanded in a variety of directions. It now offers specialty stores, such as its professional and technical store. It has expanded its editorial content through partnerships with experts in certain fields. It has increased product selection with the addition of millions of used and out-of-print titles. It also is expanding its offerings beyond books. For example, in June 2002 it became an authorized dealer of Sony Corp. for selling Sony products online. Key features of the Amazon.com superstore are easy browsing, searching, and ordering; useful product information, reviews, recommendations, and personalization; broad selection; low prices; secure payment systems; and efficient order fulfillment.

The Amazon.com Web site has a number of features that make the online shopping experience more enjoyable. Its "Gift Ideas" section features seasonally appropriate gift ideas and services. Its "Community" section provides product information and recommendations shared by customers. Through its e-cards section, customers can send free animated electronic greeting cards to friends and family, and much, much more.

Amazon.com also offers various marketplace services. Amazon Auctions hosts and operates auctions on behalf of individuals and small businesses throughout the world. The zShops service hosts electronic storefronts for a monthly fee, offering small businesses the opportunity to have customized storefronts supported by the richness of Amazon.com's order-fulfillment processing.

Amazon.com is recognized as an online leader in creating sales through customer intimacy and customer-relationship management (CRM), which are cultivated by informative marketing front-ends and one-to-one advertisements. For example, in May 2002, to support CRM, Amazon started posting, at no cost, restaurant menus from thousands of restaurants. In addition, sales are supported by highly automated, efficient back-end systems. When a customer makes a return visit to Amazon.com, a cookie file identifies the user and says, for example, "Welcome back, Sarah Shopper," and then proceeds to recommend new books from the same genre of previous customer purchases. The company tracks customer purchase histories and sends purchase recommendations via e-mail to cultivate repeat buyers. It also provides detailed product descriptions and ratings to help consumers make informed purchase decisions. These efforts usually result in satisfactory shopping experiences and encourage customers to return. The site has an efficient search engine and other shopping aids.

Customers can personalize their accounts and manage orders online with the patented "One-Click" order feature. This personalized service includes an *electronic wallet*, which enables shoppers to place an order in a secure manner without the need to enter their address, credit card number, and other information each time they shop. One-Click also allows customers to view their order status, cancel or combine orders that have not yet entered the shipping process, edit the shipping options and addresses on unshipped orders, modify the payment method for unshipped orders, and more.

In 1997, Amazon started an extensive affiliates program. By 2002, the company had more than 500,000 partners that refer customers to Amazon.com. Amazon pays a 3 to 5 percent commission on any resulting sale. Starting in

---

Sources: Compiled from Bayers (2002), Daisey (2002), and press releases from Amazon.com (2001–2003).

2000, Amazon.com has undertaken alliances with major "trusted partners" that provide knowledgeable entry into new markets. For example, Amazon's alliance with carsdirect.com allows it to sell cars online. Clicking "Health and Beauty" on the Amazon.com Web site takes the visitor to a site Amazon.com operates jointly with Drugstore.com. Clicking on "Wireless Phones" will suggest a service plan from an Amazon.com partner in that market. In yet another extension of its services, in September 2001 Amazon signed an agreement with Borders Group Inc., providing Amazon's users with the option of picking up books, CDs, and other merchandise at Borders physical bookstores. Amazon.com also is becoming a Web-fulfillment contractor for national chains like Target and Circuit City.

THE RESULTS

According to Retail Forward's study, *Top E-Retail 2001* (emarketer.com; news, August 1, 2002), Amazon was the number-one e-tailer in 2001, generating $3.12 billion. This level of sales represented 22 percent of the total online sales for all 50 companies in the study. According to Bayers (2002), Amazon.com is very successfully reducing its costs and increasing its profitability.

Annual sales for Amazon.com have trended upward, from $15.7 million in 1996 to $600 million in 1998 to over $5 billion by 2003. This pioneer e-tailer now offers over 17 million book, music, and DVD/video titles to some 20 million customers. Amazon.com also offers several features for international customers, including over 1 million Japanese-language titles.

In January 2002, Amazon.com declared its *first* ever profit—for the 2001 fourth quarter—and followed that by a profitable first quarter in 2002. Yet the company's financial success is by no means assured: The company sustained operating losses in the second and third quarters of 2002, although those losses were smaller than the losses in the same quarters in preceding years. In the fourth quarter of 2002 the company made a profit again. Like all businesses, and especially all e-tailing businesses, Amazon .com, the king of e-tailers, will continue to walk the fine line of profitability.

QUESTIONS FOR THE CASE

1. Enter Amazon.com and find this textbook. Comment on the search process. Try to order a copy, stop before you pay. Summarize your experience.
2. Identify all the decisions aids provided on this site.

3. What are the advantages of a pure e-tailer like Amazon.com over Wal-Mart online? What are the disadvantages?

CHAPTER 15

INTEGRATION, IMPACTS, AND THE FUTURE OF MANAGEMENT-SUPPORT SYSTEMS

LEARNING OBJECTIVES

❖ Understand the need for systems integration for MSS

❖ Describe the difficulties in integrating systems

❖ Describe major models of MSS integration

❖ Define intelligent DSS and explain the sources of intelligence

❖ Understand the concept of intelligentmodelling and the issues in model management

❖ Describe MSS integration with enterprise and Web systems

❖ Describe organizational impacts of MSS

❖ Learn the potential impacts of MSS on individuals

❖ Describe societal impacts of MSS

❖ List and describe major ethical and legal issues of MSS implementation

❖ Define the digital divide and discuss how to close it

❖ Describe Internet communities

❖ Provide an overview regarding the future of MSS

Building MSS is the first phase of supporting decision-making and problem-solving. Perhaps it is more important to introduce these systems into organizations and use them for their intended purpose. In this chapter, we introduce several topics. First, we discuss the issue of implementation, including the integration of MSS technologies with one another and with other information systems. Then we discuss the organizational, personal, legal, ethical, and societal impacts of support systems.

15.1 OPENING VIGNETTE: ELITE CARE SUPPORTED BY INTELLIGENT SYSTEMS

Delivering health services to the elderly is becoming a major societal problem in many countries, especially in countries where there are relatively fewer and fewer young people to take care of more and more elderly. The problem is already acute in Japan, and it is expected to be very serious in 10–15 years in several European countries and in China. The specific delivery depends on the health status of the individual, and it is provided in different facilities ranging from home care to nursing homes.

Managing and delivering such care involves large number of diversified decisions, ranging from allocation of resources to determining what treatment to provide to each patient at each given time.

Elderly residents in assisted-living facilities require different levels of care. Some residents need minimal assistance, others have short-term memory problems, and yet others have more severe problems like Alzheimer's disease, and so require more supervision and help. At Elite Care's Estates Cluster Residential Care Facility in Milwaukee, Wisconsin, pervasive computing and intelligent systems are being used to increase the autonomy and care level of all of the residents, regardless of their individual needs.

Elite Care is a family-owned business (elite-care.com), built from the ground up to provide "high-tech, high-touch" programs. Its advisory committee, which include, among others, representatives from the Mayo Clinic, Harvard University, the University of Michigan, the University of Wisconsin, and Sandia National Laboratory, has contributed a number of ideas that have been put into practice.

The entire facility is wired with a 30-mile network (wireline and wireless) of unobtrusive sensors and other devices, including:

- Biosensors (e.g., weight sensors) attached to each resident's bed.
- Movement sensors embedded in badges worn by the residents and staff (wearable computers).
- Panic buttons used to call for help.
- Internet access accessible via touch screens in each room.
- Video conferencing using Webcams.
- Climate control, lights, and other regulated appliances.

The results collected by the monitoring devices are interpreted by intelligent systems, allowing the staff to determine:

- Patient location; indicating whether the resident is in an expected area of the facility.
- Weight loss; indicating conditions like impending congestive heart failure.
- Restlessness at night; indicating conditions like insufficient pain medication.
- Frequency of trips to the bathroom; indicating medical problems like infection.
- Length of absence from bed; indicating that the patient may have fallen or been incapacitated in other ways.

Close monitoring of conditions also allows for giving medicine and/or other treatments *as needed*, rather than at a predetermined time. This enables true one-to-one care, which is both more effective and less expensive.

One of the initial concerns with the monitors was that the privacy of the residents would be unnecessarily invaded. To alleviate these concerns, residents and their families are given the choice of participating or not. Most of them choose to participate because the families believe that the monitors provide better tracking and care. The monitors also increase the autonomy of the patients, since they lessen the need for staff to constantly monitor residents in person, especially those with more acute care needs.

All of the sensors and intelligent systems are connected through a high-speed ethernet. The data produced by thee sensors and systems is stored in an SQL database and can be used to alert the staff in real-time if necessary. The data are analyzed to determine patients' health status and to develop individualized care programs. The same database is also used for administrative purposes, such as monitoring staff performance in timely delivery.

A similar concept is used in Swan Village of Care in Bentley, Australia. At the present time such projects are experimental and expensive, but someday they will be affordable to many.

❖ QUESTIONS FOR THE OPENING VIGNETTE

1. Identify the devices that support decision-making.
2. What are the benefits of automatic monitoring over manual monitoring?
3. What were the privacy concerns?
4. The system uses both wireless and wireline networks. Can decision support be improved this way? How?

WHAT CAN WE LEARN FROM THE VIGNETTE

- MSS are integrated with other information systems, or even embedded in them.
- MSS may be only a small part of large information systems, yet they are a necessary component.
- MSS, and/or the larger systems in which they are contained, may have a significant impact on organizations, employees, and users of the systems.
- Such systems may raise ethical and legal issues, such as privacy.
- Such systems may have significant societal impacts, such as reengineering the delivery of elderly care.

These points and related ones are the subject of the concluding chapter of our book. We will also discuss here the issues of Internet communities and the future of management-support systems.

15.2 SYSTEM INTEGRATION: AN OVERVIEW

Integration of computer-based systems means that the constituent parts of an integrated system function as one entity, as opposed to each being used separately, so that it is necessary to manually input their outputs as inputs to the other parts. Integration can be at the development level or at the *application system level* (known as *application*

Sources: Compiled from Stanford, 2002, elite-care.com, and ECC.online.wa.gov.au/news, January 14, 2003.

integration, our main area of interest). There are several types of integration: data, applications, methods, processes (for details see Linthicum, 2001). Integration can also be viewed from two aspects: functional and physical.

Functional integration implies that different applications are provided as a single system. For example, working with electronic mail, using a spreadsheet, communicating with external databases, creating graphical representations, and storing and manipulating data, can all be accomplished at the same workstation. Similarly, working with a DSS and an ES is done from one interface, with one menu, resulting in one output. A user can access the appropriate facilities through a single consistent interface, usually a Web browser and a portal, and can easily and quickly switch from one task to another and back again.

Physical integration refers to packaging the hardware, software, and communication features required to accomplish functional integration.

The discussion in this chapter deals primarily with functional-application integration, which can be done in two ways:

- Integration of two or more MSS applications, creating a unified application.
- Integration of one or more MSS with other information systems, such as knowledge management, databases, or a financial system. Integration can occur within a company (internal integration) or between systems of different companies (external integration).

WHY INTEGRATE?

There are three major objectives for MSS software integration:

- ***Increasing the capabilities of the MSS applications.*** In this case the tools complement each other. Each tool performs the subtasks at which it is the best. For example, a DSS can be used to recommend a resource-allocation plan, and an attached ES can provide expert advice on the minimum resources required in certain areas. Here we may wish to integrate several DSS applications (or other MSS).
- ***Enhance the capabilities of non-MSS applications.*** For example, business intelligence tools are added to ERP systems to provide analytical capability. Similarly, an intelligent agent is added to a forecasting system or to an electronic auction system.
- ***Enhancements by intelligent tools.*** Here the purpose of the integration is to enhance other tools. For example, ES can enhance DSS, and ANN can enhance the knowledge acquisition of an expert system. Expert systems are often used as intelligent agents to enhance other tools or applications. On a specific level, a major reason for integrating DSS and expert systems is the benefits that each technology provides to the other. These are organized in Table 15.1, which shows benefits by major component, as well as the overall benefits. Enable the conduct a MSS-based business-to-business electronic commerce.

Integration of different MSS technologies combines the strengths of each individual technique. For example, Li and Love (1999) present an integration of ES and ANN for estimating a contractor's mark-up percentage in the construction industry. Li (2000) describes a hybrid intelligent system for developing market strategy by combining the strengths of ES, fuzzy logic, and ANN.

LEVELS OF MSS INTEGRATION

Functional integration, discussed above, can be considered at two different levels: across different MSS, and within MSS (Figure 15.1, p. 804). Integration of MSS at these

TABLE 15.1   Summary of Integrating Expert Systems and Decision-Support Systems

	ES Contribution	*DSS Contribution*
Database and database management systems	Improves construction, operation, and maintenance of DBMS Improves accessibility to large databases Improves DBMS capabilities Permits symbolic representation of data Advises on data warehouse	A database is provided to the ES Provides numeric representation of data
Models and model base management systems	Improves model management Helps in selecting models Provides judgmental elements to models Improves sensitivity analysis Generates alternative solutions Provides heuristics Simplifies building simulation models Makes the problem structure incrementally modifiable Speeds up trial-and-error simulation	Provides initial problem structure Provides standard model computations Provides facts (data) to models Stores specialized models constructed by experts in the model base
Interface	Enables friendlier interface Provides explanations Provides terms familiar to user Acts as a tutor Provides interactive, dynamic, visual problem-solving capability	Provides presentations to match individual cognitive and decision styles
System capabilities (synergy)	Provides intelligent advice (faster and cheaper than human) to the DSS or its user Adds explanation capability Expands computerization of the decision-making process	Provides effectiveness in data collection Provides effective implementation Provides individualized advice to users to match their decision styles

levels is appropriate for systems that can be used to solve repetitive and/or sequential decision problems. MSS can also be used to facilitate integration by assisting in the transformation of the outputs of one system to the inputs to another system.

Combining several management-support systems, each addressing a specific portion of a complex decision problem, is an example of integration across MSS. For example, a DSS for supporting marketing-campaign decisions can be combined with a production-planning DSS, with certain outputs of the first system as the inputs to the second system. Atanackovic et al. (1997) present an integrated knowledge-based model to support various activities associated with the planning and design of electric power systems, integrating several expert systems with simulation tools.

An integrative framework proposed by Dutta et al. (1997) can be helpful in understanding the extended role of MS, with an emphasis on learning to improve decisions and the decision making process, and with a focus on the process of decision-making in addition to the traditional emphasis on the final decision. Their framework also guides the design of integrated MSS that facilitate different modes of decision support. An integrated approach to synthesizing an organization's computing infrastructure to sup-

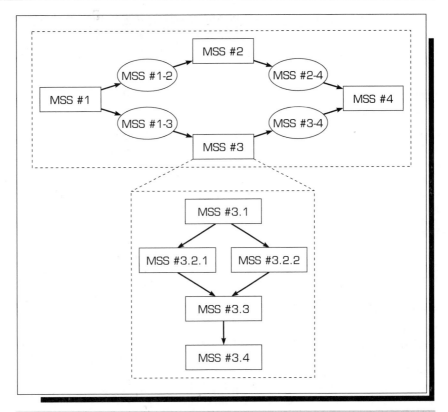

FIGURE 15.1   MSS INTEGRATION AT DIFFERENT LEVELS

port various tasks performed by users is presented by Nezlek et al. (1999). Different models of integration of DSS and ES are described later in this section.

The second level of integration refers to the integration of appropriate MSS technologies in building a specific MSS, especially to take advantage of the strengths of specific MSS technologies. For example, artificial neural networks can be used for pattern recognition as part of the intelligence phase of the decision-making process, or for data mining, and an ES can be used to assess the recommended solution generated by a DSS. This type of integration can be either in the form of a mix of different technologies (e.g., fuzzy logic and AHP, see Kuo et al., 1999) or in the form of supporting different phases or activities in decision-making (e.g., ANN for pattern recognition in the intelligence phase, and ES for the design and choice phases). Several examples of MSS integration at this level are described later in the chapter.

EMBEDDED SYSTEMS

Over the last few years we have seen an increasing number of systems that include embedded intelligent systems. For their evolution, see Grabowski and Sanborn (2001). In such systems, the intelligent part is nontransparent to the user, and the intelligent part (an expert system or an agent) works in real time.

INTEGRATING MSS WITH OTHER INFORMATION SYSTEMS

There is an increasing trend to embed intelligent systems in larger information systems, as shown in the following examples:

AIS IN ACTION 15.1

INTELLIGENT PRICE SETTING IN RETAILING

Pricing of the several thousands items offered at Long's Drug Stores (a U.S. chain of about 400 drug stores) is decentralized. Each store is empowered to price each of the items it carries so it can compete locally. Pricing traditionally was done manually by modifying the manufacturer's suggested retail price. Similar practices existed in all other retail chains, including supermarkets. Furthermore, when a price war occurred, or when seasonal sale time arrived, prices were slashed across the board, without paying attention to demand forecast, profitability, pricing strategy, or price consistency across stores.

Now it is all changing. Following what airlines and car-leasing companies were doing for years, the retail industry is introducing *price-optimization* programs, as Long's and about half of all other U.S. retailers are doing. How does a price-optimization program work? Such programs (offered by Demand-Tech Inc., and others) combine information-support systems, such as DSS, intelligent systems, data warehouse, and more, to form a system that recommends for each store a price for each item. The input data used in the system are seasonal sales figures, actual sales at each store (in real time),

each product price-demand curve, competitors' prices, profitability metrics, and more.

Using the program, retailers can identify the most price-sensitive products; they can change prices and see the impact on profit margin or another desired goal (e.g., sales volume), in a second. Using each store's priorities, strategies can be developed and tested.

The models used are similar to the *yield management* models pioneered by the airline industry in the 1980s and since adopted by car-leasing companies, financial services, consumer electronics, transportation, and many more industries. Even casinos are introducing similar programs to determine the optimal payout for slot machines.

Initial results at Long's, Shop Ko stores and others show volume, revenue and profit increases of 2–10 percent. While the software is fairly expensive, so that only large retailers can use it at present, it will become cheaper in the future when more competitors will be producing similar software.

Source: Condensed from Cortese, 2002.

- Computer telephony integration at "intelligent" call centers to select and assign a human agent for a specific customer call in real-time (Marlin, 1999).
- Real-time decision-making built around online transaction-processing systems, such as collaborative planning, forecasting, and replenishment in supply-chain management (MMH, 2000), and real-time scheduling decision-support systems (Bistline et al., 1998).
- Carlsson and Walden (2000) developed an intelligent agent-based DSS for supporting strategic management planning and analysis.
- Incorporating intelligent DSS for process enhancements and management to support group decision-making (Pervan, 1999).
- Incorporating an intelligent optimization system for determining item prices at large retail chains (see AIS in Action 15.1).

The last example illustrates a trend for building integrated enterprise systems. This is done by using the integration approaches shown in MSS in Focus 15.2.

15.3 MODELS OF MSS INTEGRATION

There are several configurations of integration. We will present only two here: 1) ES and DSS; 2) EIS, DSS, and ES

MSS IN FOCUS 15.2

INTEGRATING THE ENTERPRISE

Several approaches exist for integrating MSS applications with other applications across the enterprise. Here are four common ones:

1. *Second-Generation ERP Systems*   The second-generation ERP systems from SAP, Oracle, PeopleSoft, and other vendors add business intelligence capabilities. For example, they all provide for OLAP, query tools, data mining, and more. In addition, they provide supply-chain management (SCM) tools. There are DSS tools, for example, for scheduling, inventory control, and production scheduling.

2. *Enterprise Application Integration*   Instead of using a package from one vendor, as the preceding item, a company can use systems from various vendors that may better fit its needs. For example, the ERP of vendor A may not include appropriate

business intelligence tools, which are available from vendor B. In such a case, a company will take both A and B, trying to assemble a "best-of-breed" system. However, to do this one needs integration tools, which are considered to be *middleware*. In such cases, one uses an integration approach called Enterprise Application Integration (EAI), provided by vendors like ibm.com, tibco.com and Oracle.com.

3. *Comprehensive Systems*   Since 2001 there has been a trend for using "all in one stop" systems. Here is an example.

ORACLE 9i PLATFORM

Oracle 9i platform provides an all-in-one approach. It is a complete e-business platform composed of three parts:

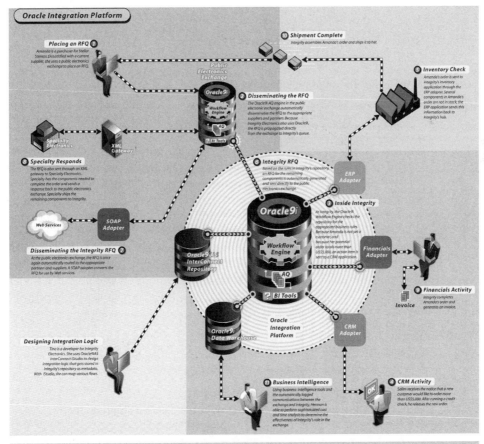

FIGURE 15.U1   THE ORACLE 9i SYSTEM

a. 9i Database and data *warehouse* manage all the required data.

b. 9i Application server runs all applications (e.g., business intelligence, order placing, e-procurement).

c. 9i Developer suite is a one-platform and one-tool set for developing customized applications (using Oracle InterConnect SDK).

The architecture of the platform, which is programmed in Java, is illustrated in Figure 15.U1. The platform integrates diverse applications and business processes (e.g., placing RFQ requests or conducting inventory checks).

In the center of the system, a workflow engine called Advanced Queuing (AQ), provides the integration capabilities. It is totally integrated with the Oracle database, which is very scalable and allows the adding of many applications. The AQ provides coordination of disparate business processes, applications, and systems, so they operate as a unified whole. This is extremely important in today's complex business environments, which require interactions with customers, suppliers and other business partners. The integration is done via a set of application *adopters* to major vendors' products (e.g., SAP, Siebel, PeopleSoft) and a set of supporting messaging (IBM, Tibco, etc.). For business processes integration one can use workflow tools. These include a variety of functions (e.g., authorizations and notifications). The workflow component allows for seamless messaging and collaboration. The system also allows integration of applications with databases. Finally, the system includes a comprehensive *business intelligence* set of tools (data mining, querying, online analysis). All the above is done through the *9i Portal*, which provides personalized views, search, and more.

1. *Web Services*   There are several definitions of Web Services. Here is a simple one: **Web Services** are self-contained, self-describing business and consumer modular applications, delivered over the Internet, that users can select and combine through almost any device from personal computers to mobile phones. By using a set of shared protocols and standards, these applications permit disparate systems to "talk" with one another— that is, share data and services—without requiring human beings to translate the conversation. The result promises to be "on-the-fly" and in real-time links among the online processes of different systems and companies. These links could shrink corporate IT departments, foster new interactions among businesses, and create a more user-friendly Web for consumers.

Web Services provide for inexpensive and rapid solutions for application integration, access to information, and application development. For details see Hagel (2002).

Sources: compiled from Lipson (2001) and Oracle.com (March, 2003).

INTEGRATING ES AND DSS

Several models have been proposed for integrating expert systems (or other intelligent systems) and decision-support systems. Integration of this kind appears under several names, ranging from expert support systems to intelligent DSS (discussed later in the chapter). The following models are described in this chapter: expert systems attached to DSS components, ES as a separate DSS component sharing in the decision-making process, ES generating alternative solutions for DSS, and a unified approach. Watkins et al. (1992) take the view that one should investigate to determine where a particular intelligent system could enhance a DSS. Their model is *problem-driven*, and they suggest that MSS integration is a process of matching problems with appropriate methods that can then be integrated to provide enhanced decision support.

EXPERT SYSTEMS ATTACHED TO DSS COMPONENTS

Expert systems can be integrated into any or all DSS components. The arrangement shown in Figure 15.2 includes five expert systems:

- *ES 1:* Database intelligent component.
- *ES 2:* Intelligent agent for the model base and its management.
- *ES 3:* System for improving the user interface.
- *ES 4:* Consultant to DSS builders. In addition to giving advice on constructing the various components of the DSS, this ES gives advice on how to structure a DSS,

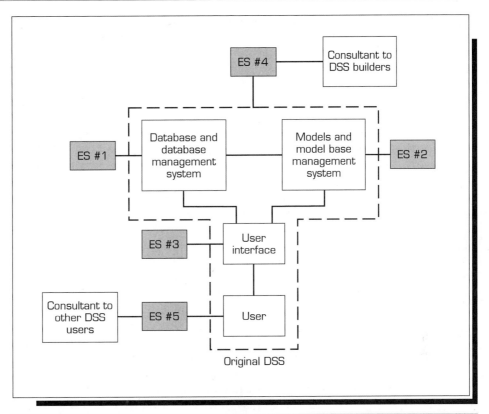

FIGURE 15.2   INTEGRATION OF ES INTO ALL DSS COMPONENTS

how to join the various parts together, how to conduct a feasibility study, and how to execute the many activities involved in the construction of a DSS.

- *ES 5:* Consultant to users. The user of a DSS may need the advice of an expert for complex issues such as the nature of the problem, the environmental conditions, or possible implementation problems. A user also may want an ES that will offer guidance on how to use the DSS and its output.

In most cases not all five systems are considered. Often it is beneficial to attach only one or two expert systems (or other intelligent systems). There are many variations of this model. For example, one can have a natural language interface adjust to the user interface and an intelligent inference agent that operates between the database and the model base.

ES AS A SEPARATE DSS COMPONENT
An ES can be added as a separate component. The integration is tight because the ES shares the interface as well as other resources. Such integration is also available via a communication link over the Internet or an intranet. Three possible configurations for such integration follow.

ES Output as Input to a DSS.   The ES output is used as input to the DSS. For example, the ES is used during the initial phase of problem-solving to determine the importance of the problem or to classify it. Then the problem is transferred to a DSS for analysis.

DSS Output as Input to ES.   Often the results of computerized quantitative analysis provided by a DSS are forwarded to an individual or a group of experts for the purpose of interpretation. Therefore, it would make sense to direct the output of a DSS to an ES that can perform the same function as an expert, whenever it is cheaper or faster to do so (especially if the quality of the advice is also superior).

Feedback.   According to this configuration, the output from the ES goes to a DSS, and then the output from the DSS goes back to the original ES.

The three possibilities are illustrated in Figure 15.3.

SHARING IN THE DECISION-MAKING PROCESS

According to this approach, ES can complement DSS in one or more of the steps in the decision-making process. Decision-making can be viewed as a multistep process consisting of such activities as specification of objectives and parameters, retrieval and management of data, generation of decision alternatives, predicting the consequences of decision alternatives, evaluation of the impact of consequences, selecting an alternative, explanation and implementation of the alternative, and strategy formulation.

Some of these activities can best be supported by DSS analysis, while those that require expertise (e.g., strategy formulation, interpretation of results) are better executed by an intelligent system.

Such sharing can be visualized as follows: The user works with the DSS following those activities amenable to DSS. Upon reaching the strategy-formulation phase or any other activity that requires expertise, the user calls on the ES, which will be a completely separate system (loose integration), although it may share a database and perhaps use some of the capabilities of the model base. This can be done on the Web using Web Services (see Cerami, 2002). To better understand this type of integration, we assume that the ES plays the role of a human expert whom the user can call upon when in need of expertise. The expert may give an answer immediately or may conduct further analysis (e.g., forecasting). The analysis can be accomplished by using the DSS database and its forecasting model.

The ES/DSS integration can be expanded to include other intelligent systems, such as neural computing, case-based reasoning, and genetic algorithms. These can substitute for or supplement the ES. For an example of case-based integrated systems, see Gan and Yang (1994). An example of an expanded system is provided by Liberatore and Stylianou (1995), who proposed a DSS/ES system that includes management-science models for deciding on new-product development. Lane et al. (1999) present

FIGURE 15.3   INTERFACE POSSIBILITIES BETWEEN EXPERT SYSTEMS AND DECISION-SUPPORT SYSTEMS

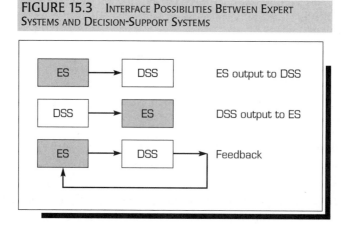

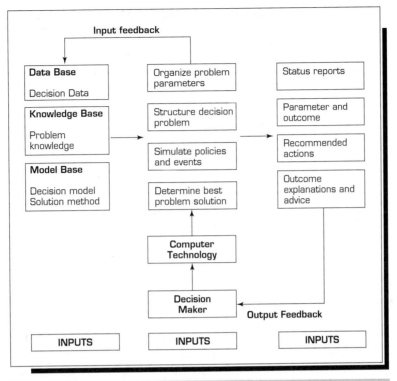

FIGURE 15.4   GLOBAL INTEGRATION

Source: Forgionne et al. (2002); Fig 2., p. 161.

an expert-simulation system integrating ES and a simulation system for supporting local area network configuration decisions.

An example of an integrated system in the health care environment is provided by Forgionne et al. (2002). The system, illustrated in Figure 15.4, shows the integration of knowledge and DSS models. The input includes data (for the DSS), knowledge (for an intelligent component and the decision-maker), and a model base to process them. The processing capability organizes the problem and structure and then generates a solution in concert with the decision-maker. The proposed solution returns as a feedback to the system input. After several iterations the system reaches stability and can generate reports, proposed actions, explanation and advice. The output returns to the decision-maker, which may change some of the problem parameters (e.g., assumptions), and the process iterates again, until stability is reached.

INTEGRATING EIS, DSS, AND ES

As indicated earlier, an EIS can be integrated with a DSS. For example, a large drug company encourages brand managers to download EIS data to a spreadsheet-based DSS forecasting model to predict monthly sales and upload them back to the EIS. EIS is commonly used as a data source for PC-based modeling.

The integration of EIS and DSS can be done in several ways. Most likely, the information generated by the EIS is used as an input to the DSS. More sophisticated systems include a DSS feedback to the EIS and possibly an interpretation and explanation capability performed by an ES.

FEEDBACK LOOPS IN INTEGRATED SYSTEMS

Feedback from the processing provides additional data, knowledge, and enhanced decision models that may be useful in current as well as future decision-making. Output feedback (often in the form of sensitivity analyses) is used to extend or modify the original analyses and evaluations. Multiple expert systems or intelligent agents are a special case of intelligent EIS/DSS; for details see Chi and Turban (1995). For further information on EIS/DSS/ES integration, see King (1996).

To connect the MSS to other organizations, an EDI can be used (Figure 15.5). The EDI can be Internet-based and supplemented by Web Services. The corporate MSS includes DSS and ES, an Internet-based video-conferencing system for groupwork, and EDI for transaction processing. For details on an architectural framework for integrating systems to provide access through information portals, see the articles at intelligententerprise.com/000301/feat3.shtml and intelligententerprise.com/991611/feat1.shtml.

15.4 INTELLIGENT DSS

Several models of intelligent DSS have been developed over the years. Representative examples are described briefly in this section. Intelligent DSS are reported to be very successful (see Matsatsinis and Siskos, 1999; Ozbayrak and Bell, 2003).

ACTIVE (SYMBIOTIC) DSS

Regular DSS play a passive role in human–computer interactions. The DSS executes computations, presents data, and responds to standard commands. But it cannot play the role of an intelligent assistant to the decision-maker. This restricts the use of some DSS to well-defined, unambiguous tasks.

However, certain tasks in problem-solving are ambiguous and complex, and then an intelligent DSS is needed. For example, the DSS should be able to take the initiative or at least respond to nonstandard requests and commands. This type of DSS is called **active or symbiotic DSS**. Modern systems use learning intelligent agents for this purpose (see Liu, 2001).

According to Mili (1990), an active DSS is an application that follows the tasks of:

- *Understanding the domain (terminology, parameters, interactions).* Here the active DSS can provide explanations.
- *Formulating problems.* Here an active DSS can help in determining assumptions, abstracting reality, deciding what is relevant, and so on.
- *Relating a problem to a solver.* The active DSS can assist with proper problem-solver interaction, advise about what procedures to use and what solution techniques to follow, and so on.
- *Interpreting results.*
- *Explaining results and decisions.*

For these tasks, one needs an intelligent component(s) in the DSS (see AIS in Action 15.3).

For details on an intelligent DSS capable of assisting decision-makers in substantiating their decisions, see Vahidov and Elrod (1999).

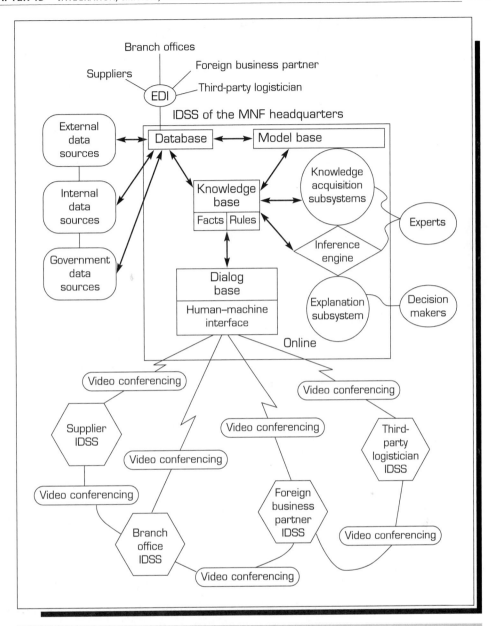

FIGURE 15.5   A GLOBALLY INTEGRATED MSS

Source: Min and Eom (1994, p. 3).

SELF-EVOLVING DSS

A self-evolving DSS is a DSS design approach whose basic premise is that a DSS should be "aware" of how it is being used and should then automatically adapt to the evolution of its users. To do so it needs the following capabilities:

- A dynamic menu that provides different hierarchies to fulfill different user requirements.

- A dynamic user interface that provides different output representations for different users.
- An intelligent model base management system that can select appropriate models to satisfy different preferences.

The purposes of a self-evolving DSS are to increase the flexibility of the DSS, reduce the effort required to use the system, enhance control over the organization's information resource, and encourage system sharing.

PROBLEM MANAGEMENT

Most DSS revolve around Simon's design and choice phases of decision-making. The intelligence phase, which includes problem finding, problem representation, and information surveillance, is difficult to automate for most DSSs. Furthermore, several activities in the design and choice phases, such as model management, are usually executed manually. To make DSS more effective, it is necessary to automate as many tasks as possible. Weber and Konsynski (1987/88) suggested dividing the decision-making process into five steps and proposed an architecture to support the functional requirements of these steps. They called their approach **problem management**. The suggested support involves several intelligent agents.

For more details on intelligent DSS in different types of decision-making environments, see DePold and Gass (1999), Matsatsinis and Siskos (1999), and Palma-dos-Reis and Zahedi (1999).

Some examples of intelligent decision-support systems (IDSS) accessible on the Internet are listed below:

- Assessing the severity of an illness in the management of health care resources (bgsm.edu/bgsmneonatal/test/projectsummary.html).
- Assisting help-desk personnel at a consumer loan company by answering customers' queries (shai.com/projects/helpdesk.htm).
- Assisting a space crew on a deep-space mission in diagnosing problems with, and maintaining, their life-support systems (shai.com/projects/spacecrafthealth.htm).

15.5 INTELLIGENT MODELING AND MODEL MANAGEMENT

Adding intelligence to the process of modeling (building models or using existing models) and to their management makes lots of sense because some of the tasks involved (e.g., modeling and selecting models) require considerable *expertise*. The topics of intelligent modeling and intelligent model management attracted significant academic attention during the 1990s (Blanning, 1993; Chang et al., 1993) because the potential benefits could be substantial. However, it seems that the implementation of such integration is fairly difficult and slow. For a survey of the early approaches, see Suh et al. (1995) and Eom (1999). However, the introduction of Web Services may solve many of the integration problems (see Cerami, 2002). For a detailed study on computer-based modeling environments from the perspectives of modelers (analysts) and model users (decision-makers), see Wright et al. (1998).

ISSUES IN MODEL MANAGEMENT

Wu (2000) developed a model management system for helping nonexperts make decisions related to test construction. The system consists of four components: problem analysis, model-type selection, model formulation, and model solver. This system proved to be very user-friendly and efficient.

We discuss here four similar interrelated subtopics of model management: problem diagnosis and selection of models, construction of models (formulation), use of models (analysis), and interpretation of the output of models.

PROBLEM DIAGNOSIS AND SELECTION OF MODELS
Several commercial ES are now helping to select appropriate statistical models (e.g., Statistical Navigator, at static.elibrary.com). Goul et al. (1984) have developed a model selection of ES to be used in mathematical programming, and Courtney et al. (1987) have produced an expert system for problem diagnosis. Liang and Konsynski (1993) have suggested using analogy as a source of knowledge for modeling. Dutta (1996) claims that model selection is a major area of AI and optimization integration. Venkatachalam and Sohl (1999) have presented an application of ANN for forecasting model selection. Lu et al. (2000) have proposed a guidance framework for designing intelligent systems to help a typical decision-maker in selecting the most appropriate method for solving various multiobjective decision-making problems.

CONSTRUCTION OF MODELS
The construction of models for decision-making involves the simplification of a real-world situation so that a less complex representation of reality can be made. Models can be normative or descriptive, and they can be used in various types of computer-based information systems (especially DSS). Finding an appropriate balance between simplification and representation in modeling requires expertise. The definition of the problem to be modeled, the attempt to select a standard model (e.g., linear programming), the data collection, the model validation, and the estimation of certain parameters and relationships are not simple tasks. For instance, data can be tested for suitability for a certain statistical distribution (e.g., does the arrival rate in queuing follow a Poisson distribution?). The ES could guide the user in selecting an appropriate test and interpreting its results, which in turn can help in appropriate modeling of the situation.

Knowledge-discovery techniques, such as decision-rule discovery, offer intelligent support in decision modeling using input and output attribute values of past decisions.

Such an approach can minimize the effort required for model builders (or analysts) to model the decision-making processes of decision-makers. For details see Bolloju (1999).

USE OF MODELS

Once models are constructed, they can be put to use. The application of models may require some judgmental values (e.g., setting an alpha value in exponential smoothing). Experience is also needed to conduct a sensitivity analysis as well as to determine what constitutes a significant difference (e.g., is project A really superior to project B?). Expert systems can provide the user with the necessary guidelines for the use of models.

INTERPRETATION OF RESULTS

Expert systems are able to provide explanations of the models used and interpretations of the derived results. For example, an ES can trace anomalies in the data. Furthermore, sensitivity analysis may be needed, or it may be necessary to convert information to a certain format. An ES can advise in all of the above cases.

QUANTITATIVE MODELS

Most experimental ES are *not* developed according to the four model management issues just discussed. Instead, they are based on the type of quantitative model used. Then some portion of one or more of the four issues may be considered.

Human experts often use quantitative models to support their experience and expertise. For example, an expert may need to forecast the sales of a certain product or to estimate future cash flow using a corporate-planning model. Similarly, many models are used by experts in almost all aspects of engineering.

ES contributions in the area of quantitative models and model management can be demonstrated by examining the work of a consultant. A consultant is involved in the following steps:

1. Discussing the nature of the problem with the client.
2. Identifying and classifying the problem.
3. Constructing a mathematical model of the problem.
4. Solving the model.
5. Conducting sensitivity analyses with the model.
6. Recommending a specific solution.
7. Assisting in implementing the solution.

The system involves a decision-maker (client), a consultant, and a computer.

If we can codify the knowledge of the consultant in an ES, we can build an intelligent computer-based information system capable of the same process. Unfortunately, little is known about the nature of the cognitive skills that consultants use.

15.6 INTEGRATION WITH THE WEB, ENTERPRISE SYSTEMS, AND KNOWLEDGE MANAGEMENT

Most MSS integration today is conducted in a Web-based environment and with enterprise systems, such as an ERP, data warehouses, and business intelligence. The objectives of such integration are:

- Increase the functionalities of the enterprise systems by adding intelligent components or a computational engine.

- Make the use of the enterprise systems more user-friendly.
- Allow greater flexibility in accessing dynamic data.
- Save money for the users by providing them with integrated systems from several vendors (there is no need for integration by users).
- Enabling an easier integration of the functional systems with electronic markets and/or business partners.

A summary of the Web-integration connection is provided in Table 15.2.

INTEGRATION WITH ERP AND SUPPLY-CHAIN SYSTEMS

One of the major solutions to supply-chain problems is to use optimization tools, which are part of supply-chain management (SCM) software. Such software is provided by i2, Manugetics, Computer Associates, Oracle, PeopleSoft, and other vendors. SCM software often includes DSS optimization models for scheduling and resource allocation.

DSS models are now integrated with supply chains (Shapiro, 2001) and ERPs. ERPs (e.g., SAP R|3) consists of dozens of applications (e.g., finance, accounting) integrated via the ERP software. Since these systems are transaction-oriented, adding decision-support capabilities can greatly enhance their capabilities. This is usually done by adding supply-chain management and/or business intelligence software.

Most ERP and enterprise vendors integrate some analytical capabilities into their products. For example, Grimes (2003) reports that PeopleSoft offers Enterprise Scorecard with Activity Based Management that presents a process-centric view. The company provides a prepackaged analytical content in its Enterprise Warehouse.

The U.S. Navy's SMART program is an example of integrating ERP with decision-support tools (Clarke, 2003). The SMART program (Supply Maintenance Aviation

TABLE 15.2 The Web-Integration Connection	
Topic of Integration	*Description*
Provision of infrastructure	Intranets for internal integration. Extranets for external integration.
New technologies	Web Services could provide a breakthrough in facilitating difficult internal and external integration. Wireless infrastructure make it less expensive and easier to integrate systems.
Integration methods	Use of ASP over the Web makes it cheaper and faster to integrate. Some integration can be done by the ASP vendor.
Improve technologies	Expensive and/or complex and inflexible technologies can be made simpler and cheaper to use. Most notably, moving from EDI to Internet/EDI.
Connecting business partners	The Web makes it cheaper, faster and easier to connect applications and databases among several partners.
Flexibility and adoptability to change	Traditional integration tools/methods, such as middleware, are inflexible. It is necessary to adopt modify applications to fit them. Using Web-based tools, one can integrate systems without modification, and change integrated systems to adopt to changing business environment.
Opportunities and challenges	The Web enables integration of applications in different locations, faster and easier. Connection to legacy systems is simpler.
Rich multi-media integration, Web tools, and usability	The Web enables integration of rich media applications. The support of Internet tools (hyperlinks, search engines) makes the integrated systems more usable.

Reengineering Team) allows rapid decision support for complex maintenance-management activities.

Finally, SCM can benefit through integration with knowledge-management systems (KMS) because knowledge is frequently required for solving problems along the supply chain.

INTEGRATION WITH KNOWLEDGE-MANAGEMENT SYSTEMS

INTEGRATION OF KMS WITH OTHER BUSINESS INFORMATION SYSTEMS

Since a knowledge-management system is an enterprise system, it must be integrated with other information systems. Obviously, when it is designed and developed, it cannot be perceived as an add-on application. It must be truly integrated into other systems. Through the structure of the organizational culture, a knowledge-management system and its activities can be directly integrated into a firm's business processes. For example, a group involved in customer support can capture its knowledge to provide help on customers' difficult problems.

Since a KMS can be developed on a knowledge platform consisting of communication, collaboration, and storage technologies, and most firms already have many such tools and technologies in place, it is often possible to develop a KMS in the organization's existing tools (e.g., Lotus Notes/Domino Server). Or an *enterprise knowledge portal* can provide universal access and an interface into all of an individual's relevant corporate information and knowledge.

INTEGRATING DSS AND KNOWLEDGE MANAGEMENT

While DSS and knowledge management (KM) are independent activities in many organizations, they are interrelated in many others. For example, knowledge creation may be done by evaluating historical decisions. Alternatively, decision-makers may use stored knowledge for making decisions. Bolloju et al. (2002) proposed a framework for integrating decision support and KM processes using knowledge-discovery techniques. The framework is based on the relationship shown in Figure 15.6. The decision-maker is using applications fed by data warehouse and marts, and is also using various sources of knowledge (right side of figure). The DSS information and the knowledge are integrated in a DSS, where the knowledge can be stored in the model base.

A study reported by Heinriches and Lim (2003) demonstrated the positive interaction obtained by integrating data-mining tools to enhance the decision capability of knowledge workers who used Web-based DSS models for improving strategic performance capabilities.

INTEGRATION OF INTELLIGENT SYSTEMS AND KNOWLEDGE MANAGEMENT

Knowledge management has a natural relationship with intelligent systems methods and software. There are a number of ways in which knowledge management and intelligent systems can integrate. For example, if the knowledge stored in a knowledge-management system is to be represented and used as a sequence of if-then-else rules, then an expert system becomes part of the KMS (see Rasmus, 2000). An expert system could also assist a user in identifying how to apply a chunk of knowledge in the KMS.

Much work is being done in the field of artificial intelligence relating to knowledge engineering, tacit-to-explicit knowledge transfer, knowledge identification, understanding, dissemination, and so on. Companies are attempting to realign these technologies and resultant products with knowledge management. The AI technologies most often integrated with knowledge management are intelligent agents, expert systems, neural networks, and fuzzy logic.

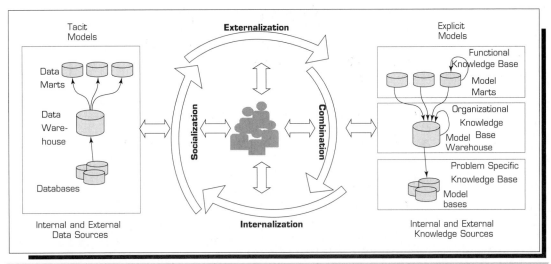

FIGURE 15.6   FRAMEWORK FOR INTEGRATING DECISION SUPPORT AND KNOWLEDGE MANAGEMENT SYSTEMS

Source: Bolloju, N. et al., "Integrating Knowledge Management into Enterprise environments for the next generation of decision support," *Decision Support Systems,* vol. 33 #2, June 2002, pp. 163–176.

OTHER KM-RELATED INTEGRATION

The number of application integrations of MSS and KM has been growing recently. Examples are:

- Integration of data-mining tool and business modeling for knowledge management (Heinriches and Lim, 2003).
- An integration of intelligent data-mining tools with manufacturing systems (Lau et al., 2001).
- DSS integration with learning and training systems (Mitri, 2002).

INTEGRATION WITH OTHER SYSTEMS

DSS and intelligent systems are integrated with other types of systems. In many cases they are embedded in the systems to provide intelligent interface, calculating engines, and so on. As such they are basically invisible to the user and do not appear as MSS.

Another type of integration is where decision support is provided to many processes in the system. In contrast with ERP, where the SCM analytical tools support few processes, here a customized DSS is the center of the system into which either standard or custom applications are integrated. An example is provided in DSS in Action 15.4, which describes the integration of the purchasing, stores, and user departments into a DSS-enabled materials management process.

A framework for integrating intelligent systems in the context of design and control of modern manufacturing system was proposed by Zaremba and Morel (2003). The framework recognizes different integrations and different intelligent systems at different stages in a product life-cycle. The authors also consider ubiquitous systems involving multisensory systems (see Opening Vignette).

ISSUES IN INTEGRATION

Many other factors should be considered when integrating MSS. Some major representative problems and issues are summarized in Table 15.3.

DSS-ENABLED MATERIAL MANAGEMENT IN A HOSPITAL

MP Trust Hospital in the state of Gujarat, India, provides special care for patients with kidney-related ailments. Established in 1978, the hospital has treated about 70,000 patients and performed about 800 kidney transplants.

General administration provides the necessary support services by coordinating the activities of the material stores, purchase, personnel, accounts departments, and so on. Hospital management became concerned about its ability to continue offering cost-effective, high-quality medical services.

Managing hospital-supplies inventory is critical. Fixed expenses account for 75 percent of the hospital's operating expenses; stores' expenses for hospital supplies account for most of the hospital's variable expenses. Thus, ensuring the availability of supplies to the user departments on time and at the lowest cost is necessary to deliver cost-effective, high-quality medical care.

A study recommended a major change. Change requires energy, enthusiasm, and dedication from all participants in the inventory systems, namely, stores, purchase, accounts, and user departments. The first step was to form a project team. The project team decided to keep hospital staff informed about the project and its development. A meeting was held that included representatives of all the departments. The user departments shared a number of problem areas, described constraints faced in providing quality medical services, and gave suggestions for improvements and changes.

THE OLD INVENTORY-MANAGEMENT PROCESS

The purchase officer handles all regular purchases as well as emergency requisitions through direct purchases from the open market for immediate delivery to user departments. The accounts department, on receipt of relevant documents from the purchase department, makes payments to the suppliers. The stores officer maintains a stores inventory records only for surgical and medical items, and relies entirely on the stock status reported by the user departments for all other items. There is very little coordinated effort by the stores, purchase, accounts, or user departments.

Since the unit of measurement for purchase (in bulk) is usually different from the unit of measurement for consumption, the total quantity ordered by the purchase officer is invariably larger than the total quantity requisitioned by all the user departments. This excess quantity remains in the stores, without the knowledge of either the purchase officer or the user departments. Availability of this excess stock is therefore not recognized by the user departments, which then place expensive emergency requisitions for items the hospital has in stock.

THE NEW MATERIALS-MANAGEMENT PROCESS

In the case of MP Trust Hospital, a decision-support system (DSS), known as an enabled materials-management process (MMP) was introduced. The objectives were to:

- Reduce expenses incurred on stores and purchase.
- Ensure delivery of hospital supplies to the user departments (wards, laboratories, etc.).
- Decrease lead times within the system and therefore stocks held.
- Reduce the number of suppliers and purchase costs.

Computer support for decision-making was central to the proposed MMP; however, there was practically no integration of information across departments, and therefore computer support for planning, monitoring, and controlling the inventory of hospital supplies was necessary.

The team designed and developed a DSS linking the coordinators to the DSS components as well as to models providing consumption, requisition, procurement, and accounts payable analyses.

At the end of every day, the heads of each of the user departments interact with the data-entry menu of the DSS interface, which is made available to them on their own PCs. Then they each enter the "quantity withdrawn." The stores coordinator updates the stock status on receipt of materials by the user department at the time the materials are issued.

Implementation. Top management agreed with all the observations the project team made and was fully convinced about the benefits likely to accrue to the hospital as a result of adopting the proposed MMP.

The DSS was implemented on the existing hardware resources. Software developments included the design and development of a centralized database and new software systems as well as modifications and extensions to the existing systems that were done in-house.

RESULTS

The total value of the items the user departments requisitioned decreased by about 10 percent in the first two months of DSS use even though the load on hospital services did not decrease in those months. This may have been due to (1) decision support for the user departments from the MMP, and (2) user awareness about MMP support to the hospital administration in monitoring the user departments' performance. The major positive results of the DSS were:

- Savings in materials purchase costs through annual contracts negotiated for quantity purchases on a 30-day/60-day credit period.
- Savings in the clerical cost of placing purchase orders as a result of drastically reducing the number of suppliers (from 200 to 35) and negotiating annual contracts with a specified monthly delivery schedule.

- Rationalizing inventory holdings, minimizing emergency purchases, and managing hospital supplies better.
- Staff operating at various levels in an ambiguous environment now work together across functional and project boundaries.

QUESTIONS FOR THE CASE

1. In what ways does the DSS facilitate collaboration among the different departments?

2. Identify the applications that needed to be integrated in order to provide data for the DSS models.

3. The system was connected to the supply chain as well (not described here due to lack of space). Identify potential connections between the DSS and the supply chain.

4. Explain how the four objectives could have been achieved by the MMP.

Source: Condensed from Ramani (2001).

TABLE 15.3   Problems and Issues of Integration

Issue	*Description*
Justification	Conduct a cost-benefit and need assessment; Rosenstein (1999)
Feasibility	Conduct a technological, economical, organizational, and behavioral analysis. Conduct an impact study, if needed
Architecture	Examine the best possible architecture
Infrastructure	What types of hardware, software, etc., will be involved. What commercially available components to use
Outsourcing	Who will do the integration? How to select and manage the vendors?
Supporting the project	Who is committed to the project? What is the support of top management, especially if several departments are involved?
Support of business partners	Many MSS involve connecting to business partners, especially along the supply chain. Do they collaborate?
Development process and tools	Depending on the architecture, infrastructure, etc., one needs to decide on a development process and selection of tools
Data issues	How is symbolic processing handled when combined with algorithms?
Legal and privacy	How secure are data in integrated systems, especially when several departments/organizations are involved? Is privacy protected?
Connectivity	Which options are available to assure the connectivity? Are Web Services going to be used?
Web-based integration	How to ensure that the integrated system will be Web-based? How are legacy systems, ERP, etc., connected?
Introducing new technologies	How to deal with Web Services and Microsoft.Net, adoption strategy, justification

15.7 THE IMPACTS OF MSS: AN OVERVIEW

Management-support systems are important participants in the information, Web, and knowledge revolution, a cultural transformation with which most people are only now coming to terms. Unlike the slower revolutions of the past, such as the industrial revolution, this revolution is taking place very quickly and affecting every facet of our lives. Inherent in this rapid transformation is a host of managerial and social problems: impact on organizational structure, resistance to change, rapidly increasing unemployment levels, and so on. According to Gartner.com, the MSS share of the computer industry, including embedded systems and business intelligence, are expected to grow at a 20% compound annual growth rate, reaching over $1.5 billion in 2006 (per Lurhq, 2003), and so their impact may be substantial.

Separating the impact of MSS from that of other computerized systems is a difficult task, especially because of the trend toward integrating, or even embedding, MSS with other computer-based information systems. There is very little published information about the impact of pure MSS technologies because the techniques are frequently integrated with other information systems. Another problem is the rapid changes in MSS implementation. Thus, some of our discussion must relate to computer systems in general. We recognize, however, that MSS technologies do have some unique implications, which are highlighted throughout the remainder of this chapter.

MSS can have both micro and macro implications. It can affect particular individuals and jobs, the work structure of departments, and units within an organization. It can

FIGURE 15.7   FRAMEWORKS FOR ORGANIZATIONAL AND SOCIETAL IMPACTS OF AI TECHNOLOGY

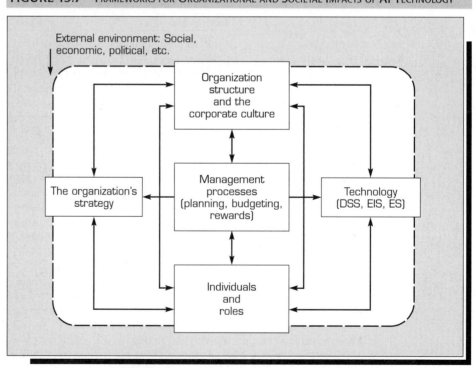

Source: M. Scott Morton, "DSS Revisited for the 1990s," paper presented at DSS 1986, Washington, DC, April 1986. Used with permission.

TABLE 15.4 Social Impacts of Computer Technology	
Area of Impact	*Section in This Chapter*
Changing role of home bound people	15.14
Computer crime	15.14
Consumers	15.14
Digital Divide	15.14
Electronic communities	15.13
Employment levels	15.12
Opportunities for the disabled	15.14
Quality of life	15.14
Telecommuting (working at home)	15.8
Work in hazardous environments	15.14

also have significant long-term effects on total organizational structures, entire industries, communities, and society as a whole (see the Opening Vignette).

Figure 15.7 presents a framework that shows a complete management system. Such a system stays in equilibrium as long as all of its parts are unchanged. If there is a major change in one of the components or in the relevant environment, the change will probably affect some of the other components. The major change stimuli (relevant to MSS) are strategy and technology, especially when computerized systems such as a DSS or ES are introduced. For further discussion, see Gill (1996) and Grudin and Wellman (1999).

One of the major changes now occurring is the emergence of the Web and its impact on MSS (Sikder and Gangopadhyay, 2002) and the relationship of DSS and knowledge management. (Holsapple 2003). Both are related to the organizational transformation. Information technology plays a major role in supporting this change, especially some intelligent systems.

The impact of computers and MSS technology can be divided into three general categories: *organizational*, *individual*, and *societal*. Computers have had an impact on organizations in many ways. We cannot possibly consider all of them in this chapter, and so we have selected the topics we feel are most relevant to MSS.

Computer technology has already changed our world, and much more change is anticipated. In addition to the effect on individuals, there are significant societal effects. Table 15.4 summarizes some of the major areas of social impact and lists the sections in which they are discussed.

15.8 MSS IMPACTS ON ORGANIZATIONS

NEW ORGANIZATIONAL UNITS

One change in organizational structure is the possibility of creating a DSS department, management-support department, business intelligence department, AI department, or knowledge-management department in which MSS plays a major role. The additional unit can be combined with or replace a management science unit, or can be a completely new entity.

There are separate DSS departments in several large corporations. For example, many major banks have a DSS department in their financial services division. Mead Corporation has a special corporate DSS applications department (see DSS in Action 15.5), although it is integrated with other enterprise activities. Many companies have a small DSS unit. Several large corporations have already created AI departments. Boeing operates a large AI department. In both cases, the departments are involved in extensive training in addition to research, consulting, and application activities. A number of firms have created knowledge-management departments headed by a chief

---

DSS IN ACTION 15.5

DECISION SUPPORT AT MEAD CORPORATION

Mead Corporation created a DSS department in the mid-1980s that included an interactive help center, office systems, decision analysis, and financial modeling. In the 1990s, a new function was added: local area experts. These people report directly to users departments and indirectly to the director of the DSS department. They assist users in developing and maintaining DSS applications.

The system has been modified several times. A major change occurred in the late 1990s when DSS was

integrated with enterprise systems. The latest available structure (2001) is shown in Figure 15.U2. Note that the hierarchical organizational structure has been changed to a hub.

_____

Source: Compiled from B. C. McNurlin, and R. H. Sprague, Jr., *Information Systems in Practice*, 5th ed. Englewood Cliffs, NJ: Prentice Hall, 2001, pp. 21–33.

FIGURE 15.U2   MEAD CORPORATION'S 2001 CORPORATE INFORMATION RESOURCES STRUCTURE

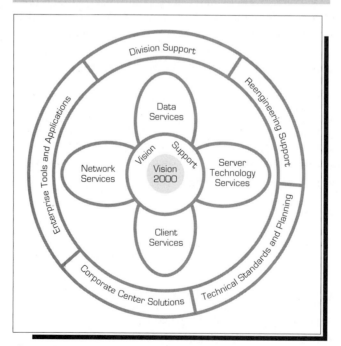

Source: Courtesy of Mead Corporation.

knowledge officer. Others have empowered a chief technology officer over business intelligence, intelligent systems, and e-commerce applications.

ORGANIZATIONAL CULTURE AND VIRTUAL TEAMS

Organizational culture can affect the diffusion rate of technology and can be influenced by it. For example, the use of Lotus Notes changed the organizational climate of a large CPA firm by making employees more cooperative and willing to share information and use computers. There is also some dissolution of organizational structure. Virtual teams can meet anytime and anyplace. People can join a virtual team for as long as the project lasts or whenever their expertise is needed. When the project is completed, the team can disband. For changes in organizational culture due to MSS, see Watson et al. (2000).

RESTRUCTURING BUSINESS PROCESSES

In many cases it is necessary to restructure business processes before introducing new information technologies. For example, before IBM introduced e-procurement it restructured all related business processes, including decision-making, searching inventories, reordering, and shipments. Such changes are often necessary for profitability or even survival. Restructuring is especially needed when major IT projects, such as ERP or EC, are undertaken. Sometimes an organization-wide, major restructuring is needed, and then it is referred to as reengineering. Reengineering involves changes in structure, organizational culture, and processes. In its extreme form, the process is referred to as **business-process reengineering**, or BPR (Hammer and Stanton, 1995).

Several concepts of BPR greatly change organizational structure: team-based organization, mass customization, empowerment, and telecommuting. In these cases, MSS are used extensively as an enabler (Turban et al., 2004b). MSS also plays a major role in BPR (El Sawy, 2001). MSS (especially ES, DSS, AI, and EIS) allow business to be conducted in different locations, providing flexibility in manufacturing, permit quicker delivery to customers, and support rapid, paperless transactions among suppliers, manufacturers, and retailers.

Expert systems can enable organizational changes by providing expertise to nonexperts (Yu et al., 1996). An example is shown in Figure 15.8. The upper part shows a bank before reengineering. A customer who needs several services must go to several departments. The bank keeps multiple records and provides the customer with several monthly statements. The reengineered bank is shown in the lower part. A customer makes contact with only one person, an account manager, who is supported by an expert system. The new arrangement is cheaper, and customers save time and receive only one statement. See Min et al. (1996) for a description of an intelligent bank-reengineering system. For additional examples of ES in BPR in real-world situations, see Strischeck and Cross (1996) and Sugumaran and Bose (1996).

SIMULATION MODELING AND ORGANIZATIONAL RESTRUCTURING

It is difficult to carry out restructuring calculations even with a computer spreadsheet. For this reason, consultants and IT specialists are turning to an expanding class of products called *business simulation tools*. Many of these programs let users set up flowcharts to diagram the movement of resources through manufacturing or other business processes. El Sawy (2001) provides a comprehensive description of how to use simulation modeling for BPR.

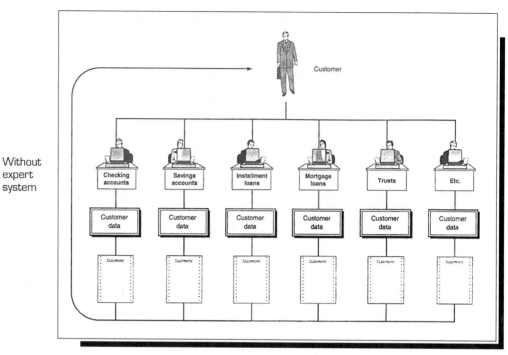

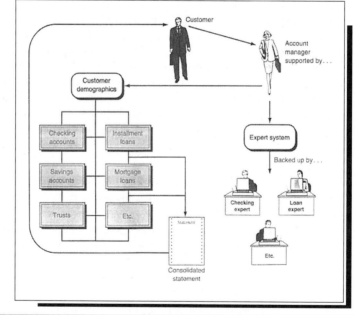

Without expert system

With expert system

FIGURE 15.8   Restructuring a Bank with Expert System

Source: Turban et al. (2001). *Information Technology Management,* 3rd ed. New York: Wiley

OTHER ORGANIZATIONAL IMPACTS

Many other organizational impacts can be attributed to management support systems. As we have seen throughout the book, MSS are expected to increase productivity, speed, customer satisfaction, quality, and supply-chain improvements. This results in cost reduction and increased profits. Much of this comes about in integrated systems in which a DSS or an expert system is a component. For a comprehensive description of the benefits of the introduction of data warehouses and business intelligence, see Watson et al. (2000).

The impact goes beyond one company or one supply chain. It is an impact on entire industries. The use of profitability models and optimization is reshaping retailing, real estate, banking, transportation, airlines, and car renting, just to mention a few. Even fields like architecture are changing (Huang, 2001). For more on organizational issues, see Mora (2002).

15.9 IMPACT ON INDIVIDUALS

MSS systems may affect individuals in various ways. What is a benefit to one individual may be a curse to another. What is an added stress today can be a relief tomorrow. Some of the areas where MSS systems may affect individuals, their perceptions, and behaviors are described next.

JOB SATISFACTION

Although many jobs may be substantially enriched by MSS, other jobs may become more routine and less satisfying. For example, more than 30 years ago, Argyris (1971) predicted that computer-based information systems would reduce managerial discretion in decision-making and thus create dissatisfied managers. A study by Ryker and Ravinder (1995) showed that IT has had a positive effect on four of the five core job dimensions: identity, significance, autonomy, and feedback. No significant effect was found on skill variety.

INFLEXIBILITY AND DEHUMANIZATION

A common criticism of traditional data-processing systems is their negative effect on people's individuality. Such systems are criticized as being impersonal: They dehumanize and depersonalize activities that have been computerized because they reduce or eliminate the human element that was present in noncomputerized systems. Many people feel a loss of identity; they feel like just another number. On the bright side, one of the major objectives of MSS is to create flexible systems and interfaces that will allow individuals to share their opinions and knowledge. Despite all these efforts, some people are simply afraid of computers.

JOB STRESS AND ANXIETY

An increase in workload and/or responsibilities can trigger job stress. Although computerization has benefited organizations by increasing productivity, it has also created an ever-increasing workload. Some workers feel overwhelmed and begin to feel anxious about their jobs and their performance. These feelings of anxiety can adversely affect their productivity. Management's responsibility is to alleviate these feelings by redistributing the workload among workers or by hiring more individuals.

One of the negative impacts of the information age is information anxiety. This disquiet can take several forms, such as frustration with our inability to keep up with the amount of data present in our lives. Other forms of information anxiety are:

- Frustration with the quality of the information available on the Web. This information is frequently not up-to-date or is incomplete.
- Too many online sources.
- Frustration due to guilt associated with not being better informed or being informed too late. "How come everyone else knew before we did?"

COOPERATION OF EXPERTS

Human experts who are about to give their knowledge to an organizational or a problem-specific knowledge base may have reservations. Consider these examples of thoughts that might enter an expert's mind:

- The computer may replace me.
- The computer may make me less important.
- Why should I tell the computer my secrets? What will I gain?
- The computer may reveal that I am not as great an expert as people think.

This kind of thinking may cause the expert not to cooperate, or even to give incorrect knowledge to the computer. To deal with such situations, management should motivate (and possibly compensate) the experts.

15.10 DECISION-MAKING AND THE MANAGER'S JOB

Computer-based information systems have had an impact on the job of manager for over three decades. However, this impact was felt mainly at the lower- and middle-managerial levels. Now MSS are affecting top managers as well.

The most important task of managers is making decisions. MSS technologies can change the manner in which many decisions are being made and consequently change managers' jobs. The impacts of MSS on decision-making are numerous; the most probable areas are the following:

- Automation of routine decisions or phases in the decision-making process (e.g., for frontline decision-making).
- Less expertise (experience) required for making many decisions.
- Faster decision-making because of the availability of information and the automation of some phases in the decision making process.
- Less reliance on experts and analysts to provide support to top executives; managers can do it by themselves with the help of intelligent systems.
- Power redistribution among managers.
- Support for complex decisions, making them faster and of better quality.
- Information for high-level decision-making is expedited or even self generated.

Many managers report that the computer has finally given them time to get out of the office and into the field (EIS can save an hour a day for every user). They also find that they can spend more time planning activities instead of putting out fires because they can be alerted to potential problems well in advance (via EIS with intelligent agents, expert systems, OLAP, and other analytical tools). Another aspect of the managerial challenge lies in the ability of MSS to support the decision process in general and strategic planning and control decisions in particular. MSS could change the decision-making process and even decision-making styles. For example, information gathering for decision-making is completed much more quickly. Enterprise information systems are extremely useful in supporting strategic management (Liu et al., 2002). AI technologies are now used to improve environmental scanning of information. As a result, managers can change their approach to problem-solving. Research indicates that most managers tend to work on a large number of problems simultaneously, moving from one to another as they wait for more information on their current problem (Mintzberg et al., 2002). MSS tend to reduce the time required to complete tasks in the decision-making process and eliminate some of the nonproductive waiting time by providing knowledge and information. Therefore, managers will work on fewer tasks during each day but will complete more of them. The reduction in start-up time associated with moving from task to task could be the most important source of increased managerial productivity.

Another possible impact on the manager's job could be a change in leadership requirements. What are now generally considered good leadership qualities may be significantly altered by the use of MSS. For example, as face-to-face communication is replaced by electronic mail and computerized conferencing, thus, leadership qualities attributed to physical appearance could become less important.

Even if managers' jobs do not change dramatically, the methods managers use to do their jobs will. For example, an increasing number of CEOs no longer use intermediaries; instead, they work directly with computers and the Web. Once voice understanding is of high quality, we may see a real revolution in the way managers use computers.

IMPACT ON PERFORMANCE OF MANAGERS AND EMPLOYEES

According to Perez-Cascante et al. (2002), an ES-DSS was found to improve the performance of both existing and new managers and employees. It helped managers to gain more knowledge, experience, and expertise, and consequently enhanced the quality of their decision-making.

15.11 ISSUES OF LEGALITY, PRIVACY, AND ETHICS

LEGAL ISSUES

The introduction of management-support systems, and especially of ES, may compound a host of legal issues already relevant to computer systems. The expensive, prolonged litigation of the IBM and Microsoft antitrust cases are prominent examples. Questions concerning liability for the actions of intelligent machines are just beginning to be considered. The issue of computers as a form of unfair competition in business was already raised in the 1990s with the well-known dispute over the practices of airline reservation systems.

In addition to resolving disputes about the unexpected and possibly damaging results of some MSS systems, other complex issues may surface. For example, who is liable if an enterprise finds itself bankrupt as a result of using the advice of an MSS? Will the enterprise itself be held responsible for not testing the system adequately before entrusting it with sensitive issues? Will auditing and accounting firms share the liability for failing to apply adequate auditing tests? Will the manufacturers of intelligent systems be jointly liable? Consider the following specific legal issues:

- What is the value of an expert opinion in court when the expertise is encoded in a computer?
- Who is liable for wrong advice (or information) provided by an ES? For example, what happens if a physician accepts an incorrect diagnosis made by a computer and performs an act that results in the death of a patient?
- What happens if a manager enters an incorrect judgment value into an MSS and the result is damage or a disaster?
- Who owns the knowledge in a knowledge base?
- Should royalties be paid to experts who provide knowledge to an ES or a knowledge base, and if so, how much?
- Can management force experts to contribute their expertise?

For a discussion of these and other ethics-related issues, consult Celik (2001), Charles (1995), and Warkentin et al. (1994).

PRIVACY

Privacy means different things to different people. In general, **privacy** is the right to be left alone and the right to be free from unreasonable personal intrusions. Privacy has long been a legal, ethical, and social issue in many countries. The right to privacy is recognized today in every state of the United States and by the federal government, either by statute or by common law. The definition of privacy can be interpreted quite broadly. However, the following two rules have been followed fairly closely in past court decisions: (1) The right of privacy is not absolute. Privacy must be balanced against the needs of society. (2) The public's right to know is superior to the individual's right to privacy. These two rules show why it is difficult, in some cases, to determine and enforce privacy regulations (see Buchholz and Rosenthal, 2002). Privacy issues online have their own characteristics and policies (Rykere et al., 2002).

COLLECTING INFORMATION ABOUT INDIVIDUALS

The complexity of collecting, sorting, filing, and accessing information manually from numerous government agencies was, in many cases, a built-in protection against misuse of private information. It was simply too expensive, cumbersome, and complex to invade a person's privacy. The Internet, in combination with large-scale databases, has created an entirely new dimension of accessing and using data. The inherent power in systems that can access vast amounts of data can be used for the good of society. For example, by matching records with the aid of a computer, it is possible to eliminate or reduce fraud, crime, government mismanagement, tax evasion, welfare cheats, family-support filchers, employment of illegal aliens, and so on. The question is: What price must the individual pay in terms of loss of privacy so that the government can better apprehend criminals?

The Internet offers a number of opportunities to collect private information about individuals. Here are some of the ways it can be done:

- By reading an individual's newsgroup postings.
- By looking up an individual's name and identity in an Internet directory.
- By reading an individual's e-mail.

DSS IN FOCUS 15.6

OUTSMARTING THE COOKIE MONSTER

The cookie controversy is about privacy and the way a technology is being used—or abused—by some Web site owners. Cookies are simply strings of text stored on hard-drive files to record the history of a particular user's actions at a particular Web site, including what links are followed, what sections of the site are visited, and what ads are clicked. The problem—and the controversy—is how they get on the hard drive and how they are used. The cookie can record actions, and when the user returns, the cookie may tell the server where the user has been before, what areas were accessed, and what links he or she has followed.

Cookies are viewed by some as a helpful way of narrowcasting, or providing specific information to a particular audience, based on past browsing. Then the Web server can direct a user to material or products of interest. The cookie problem is twofold: Most users do not know that a cookie has been written to their hard disk (when active, they can be detected and the user is warned by some browsers), and cookies can be used to target both content and advertising.

- By wiretapping wireline and wireless communication lines and listening to employees (Ghosh and Swaminatha, 2001).
- By conducting surveillance on employees (Steinberg, 2001).
- By asking an individual to complete a Web site registration.
- By recording an individual's actions as he or she navigates the Web with a browser, usually using *cookies*.

Users can protect themselves against cookies; they can delete them from their computers or they can use anticookie software, such as Pretty Good Privacy's Cookie Cutter or Luckman's Anonymous Cookie. Anti-cookie software disables all cookies and allows the user to surf the Web anonymously. The problem with deleting or disabling cookies is that the user will be forced to keep reentering information and in some instances may be blocked from viewing particular pages. See DSS in Focus 15.6 for a discussion of cookies.

A Microsoft component called Passport is beginning to raise some of the same concerns as cookies. Passport is an Internet strategy that lets consumers permanently enter a profile of information along with a password and use this information and password repeatedly to access services at multiple sites. Critics say that Passport affords the same opportunities as cookies to invade an individual's privacy.

The use of AI technologies in the administration and enforcement of laws and regulations may increase public concern regarding privacy of information. These fears, generated by the perceived abilities of AI, will have to be addressed at the outset of almost any AI development effort. For further discussion, see Exercise 4 at the end of this chapter. Also see Berghel (2000), Cranor (1999), Denning (1998), and Mizell (1998).

Fortunately, users can take steps to improve their privacy. Tynan (2002) provides 34 tips that show you how to do it (also, go to pcworld.com/26702). While privacy protection is the major concern for individuals, *intellectual property* protection is the major concern of those who own it (see later discussion).

ETHICS

The ethical issues for MSS are similar to those for other information systems (Table 15.5).

TABLE 15.5   A Framework for Ethical Issues

Privacy	*Accuracy*
• What information about oneself should a person be required to reveal to others? • What kind of surveillance can an employer use on its employees? • What things can people keep to themselves and not be forced to reveal to others? • What information about individuals should be kept in databases and how secure is the information there?	• Who is responsible for the authenticity, fidelity, and accuracy of information collected? • How can we ensure that information will be processed properly and presented accurately to users? • How can we ensure that errors in databases, data transmissions, and data processing are accidental and not intentional? • Who is to be held accountable for errors in information, and how is an injured party compensated?

Property	*Accessibility*
• Who owns the information? • What are the just and fair prices for its exchange? • Who owns the channels of information? • How should one handle software piracy (copying copyrighted software)? • Under what circumstances can one use proprietary databases? • Can corporate computers be used for private purposes? • How should experts who contribute their knowledge to create expert systems be compensated? • How should access to information channels be allocated?	• Who is allowed to access information? • How much should be charged for permitting access to information? • How can accessibility to computers be provided for employees with disabilities? • Who will be provided with equipment needed for accessing information? • What information does a person or an organization have a right or a privilege to obtain, under what conditions, and with what safeguards?

Source: Turban et al. (2001); compiled from Mason et al. (1995) by E. Turban.

Representative issues that could be of interest in MSS implementations are the following:

- Computer abuse and misuse
- Electronic surveillance (Diffie and Landau, 1998)
- Ethics in DSS design (Carlson et al, 1999; Chae et al., 2002)
- Software piracy (Smith and Parr, 1998)
- Invasion of individuals' privacy (Mizell, 1998)
- Use of proprietary databases
- Use of intellectual property (Harris, 1998; Yueng, 1998)
- Exposure of employees to unsafe environments related to computers
- Computer accessibility for workers with disabilities
- Accuracy of data, information, and knowledge
- Protecting the rights of users (Karat, 1998)
- Accessibility to information
- Use of corporate computers for private purposes (Andries et al., 2002; Simmers, 2002)
- How much decision-making to delegate to computers.

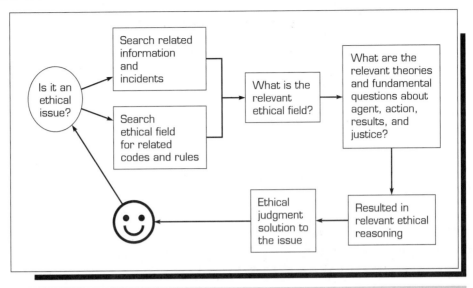

FIGURE 15.9 A MODEL FOR ETHICAL REASONING PROCESS

Personal values constitute a major factor in the issue of ethical decision-making. For a comprehensive study, see Fritzsche (1995). The study of ethical issues in MSS is complex because of its multidimensionality. Therefore, it makes sense to develop models to describe ethics processes and systems. Mason et al. (1995) explain how technology and innovation expand the size of the domain of ethics and discuss a model for ethical reasoning that involves four fundamental focusing questions: Who is the agent? What action was actually taken or is being contemplated? What are the results or consequences of the act? Is the result fair or just for all stakeholders? (Figure 15.9). They also describe a hierarchy of ethical reasoning in which each ethical judgment or action is based on rules and codes of ethics, which are based on principles, which in turn are grounded in ethical theories.

Loch and Conger (1996) describe a study evaluating ethical decision-making and computer use based on the theory of reasoned action (TRA) and its extensions. The TRA relates an individual's attitudes and social norms to intentions to act. Attitudes and norms are expected to differ from situation to situation. Their results indicate that deindividuation (a feeling of being separated from others that can lead to behavior violating established norms of appropriateness), self-image, ethical attitude, computer literacy, and social norms impact ethical decision-making and computer use. Other interesting information on MSS and ethics can be found in Conger et al. (1995) and in "Ethics and Computer Use," *Communications of the ACM*, December 1995.

For a MSS ethical debate, see online materials, plus Online AIS in Action 15.1.

INTELLECTUAL PROPERTY RIGHTS

Intellectual property rights are one of the foundations of modern society. Without these rights, the movie, music, software, publishing, pharmaceutical, and biotech industries would collapse (Claburn, 2001). According to the World Intellectual Property Organization (WIPO; wipo.org), **intellectual property** refers to "creations of the mind: inventions, literary and artistic works, and symbols, names, images, and designs used in commerce." There are four main types of intellectual property related to MSS: copyrights (see Cherry, 2002a), trademarks, domain names, and patents.

NON-WORK-RELATED USE OF THE INTERNET

Employees are tempted to use e-mail and the Web for non-work-related purposes. In some companies this use is tremendously out of proportion with the work-related uses (see Anandarajan, 2002). The problem has several dimensions. For example, e-mail can be used to harass other employees or to pose a legal threat to a company. It can also be used to conduct illegal gambling activity (e.g., betting on results of a football game). Some employees may use the e-mail to advertise their own businesses. Using other corporate computing facilities for private purposes may be a problem too. Last but not least is the time employees waste surfing non-work-related Web sites during working hours.

For further discussion of the ethical issues, see Chae et al. (2002) and Spinello and Tavani (2001).

15.12 INTELLIGENT SYSTEMS AND EMPLOYMENT LEVELS

There is very little information on the relationship of MSS to employment levels. However, MSS and especially intelligent systems have the potential to significantly affect the productivity and employment of many types of employees as well to completely automate jobs. The material in this section summarizes the positions of some of the world's top experts with regard to the potential impact of intelligent systems on productivity and unemployment.

Although the impact of AI may take decades to fully materialize, there is agreement among researchers that intelligent systems are increasing the productivity of knowledge workers. Technology is getting less expensive and more capable, and thus is bringing about substantial changes in jobs and job content. However, researchers disagree about the potential impact of intelligent systems on the aggregate employment

TABLE 15.6   Is Mass Unemployment Coming?

Massive Unemployment Will Come	*No Massive Unemployment*
• Benefit/cost advantage of computers increases with time.	• New occupations and jobs have always been created by automation.
• Less skillful employees are needed.	• There is much less unemployment in countries that use more automation.
• Shifting displaced employees to services is getting difficult.	• Work can be expanded to accommodate everyone.
• Many employees lost their jobs in the 1990s.	• Conversion to automation is slow, and the economy can adjust.
• Hidden unemployment exists in many organizations.	• Many tasks cannot be fully automated.
• Millions of help-desk employees will be replaced by intelligent agents.	• There will always be some areas where people are better than machines.
• Electronic commerce will cause millions of intermediaries and agents to lose their jobs.	• People will work less but will have more money.
• Unemployment levels in certain countries is high and is increasing.	• Electronic commerce reduces the cost of many goods and services; thus their consumption will increase, resulting in more buying and more jobs.
• There is an upper limit to customer consumption.	

AIS IN ACTION 15.7

ROBOTS CLEAN TRAIN STATIONS IN JAPAN

With growing amounts of rubbish to deal with at Japanese train stations and fewer people willing to work as cleaners, officials have started turning the dirty work over to robots. The central Japan Railway Company and Sizuko Company, a Japanese machinery maker, have been using robots programmed to vacuum rubbish. A railway official said that the robots, which are capable of doing the work of 10 people, each have been operating two or three days a week at the Sizuko station in central Japan. The robots are about 1.5 meters wide and 1.2 meters long. The railway and Sizuko spent 200 million yen ($2 million) to develop the machines and are planning to program them for other tasks, such as sweeping and scrubbing. Similar robots are now cleaning many major railway stations in Japan.

More than any other country, Japan has made extensive use of robots in industry. It also uses them to assist the blind and the elderly, as well as to diagnose some illnesses.

level. The two extreme positions are *massive unemployment* and *increased employment* (or at least no change in the employment level). These positions have been supported by two Nobel Prize winners, Wassily Leontief (1986), who supports the massive unemployment argument, and Herbert Simon, who takes the opposite position. Table 15.6 summarizes the main arguments of each side.

The debate has been going on for many years. It is true that many people have lost their jobs to intelligent systems. But many new jobs and job categories have been created.

The following is a list of newly created MSS-related jobs: terrorists fighting using AI, biometric specialist, security expert, AI computer lawyer, BI headhunter, BI project manager, BI hardware-architecture specialist, BI venture capitalist, BI user-training specialist, MSS tool developer and vendor, industrial robotics supervisor/manager, knowledge acquisition and maintenance specialist, robotics maintenance engineer, system integrator, ANN software developer, software-agent developer and vendor, chief knowledge officer (CKO), MSS system integrator, knowledge maintainer, and intelligent agent builder.

The debate about how intelligent systems will affect employment raises a few other questions: Is some unemployment really socially desirable? (People could have more leisure time.) Should the government intervene more in the distribution of income and in determination of the employment level? Can the "invisible hand" in the economy, which has worked so well in the past, continue to be successful in the future? Will AI make most of us idle but wealthy? (Robots will do the work; people will enjoy life (see Teresko, 2002 and AIS in Action 15.7). Should the issues of income and employment be completely separated? The issue of how to handle unemployment both at the organizational and the national level is beyond the scope of this book.

15.13 INTERNET COMMUNITIES

A *community* is a group of people with some interest in common who interact with one another. A **virtual community** is one in which the interaction is done by using the Internet. Virtual communities, also known as *electronic communities* or *Internet communities*, parallel typical physical communities such as neighborhoods, clubs, or associations, but the people do not meet face-to-face; rather they meet online. Virtual com-

TABLE 15.7	Elements of Interactions in Virtual Communities
Category	**Element**
Communication	Bulletin boards (discussion groups)
	Chat rooms/threaded discussions (string Q&A)
	E-mail and instant messaging
	Private mailboxes
	Newsletters, "netzines" (electronic magazines)
	Web postings
	Voting
Information	Directories and yellow pages
	Search engines
	Member-generated content
	Links to information sources
	Expert advice
E-commerce element	Electronic catalogs and shopping carts
	Advertisements
	Auctions of all types
	Bartering online
	Classified advertisement

munities offer several ways for members to interact, collaborate, and trade (see Table 15.7). Many *physical communities* have a Web site for Internet-related activities.

CHARACTERISTICS AND TYPES OF COMMUNITIES

Pure-play Internet communities may have thousands or even millions of members. This is one major difference from purely physical communities, which are usually smaller. Another difference is that offline communities are frequently confined to one geographical location, whereas only a few online communities are of this type.

Many thousands of communities exist on the Internet. Some communities are independent and are growing rapidly. For instance, GeoCities grew to 10 million members in less than two years, and had close to 50 million members in 2002 (geocities .yahoo.com). GeoCities members can set up personal home pages on the site, and advertisers buy ad space targeted to community members. In order to understand the economic impact of electronic communities, let us see what they really are.

Virtual communities are spreading quickly over the Internet. Most of the successful ones have been purchased by Yahoo, AOL, and Google. Hagel and Armstrong (1997) recognize four types of electronic communities, described below.

COMMUNITIES OF TRANSACTIONS
These communities facilitate buying and selling. Members include buyers, sellers, intermediaries, and so on. Typical examples are the EC exchanges presented in Chapter 14.

COMMUNITIES OF INTEREST
Here people have the chance to interact with each other on a specific topic. For example, if you are interested in gardening, try gardenWeb.com. The Motley Fool (fool.com) is a forum for individual investors. City411 provides comprehensive information about local communities, and many topics, such as entertainment, traffic, and

weather reports, are displayed. The community for IT professionals can be found at planetit.com.

The many million members of Geocities (geocities.com) are organized into dozens of communities such as MotorCity (car lovers) and Nashville (country music). Members have a marketplace for buying and selling goods and services. Another community is talkcity.com with millions of chatterers.

Some successful communities of interest are actually based on transactions. An example is the Australian Fishing Shop (ausfish.com.au). For a comprehensive information about Internet communities see usinfo.state.gov/journals/itgic/1100/ijge/ijge1100.htm.

COMMUNITIES OF RELATIONS

These communities are organized around certain life experiences. For example, the cancer forum on CompuServe contains information and exchange of opinions regarding cancer. Parent Soup is a favorite gathering spot for parents; seniors like to visit SeniorNet, and Women's Wire is a well-known online community aimed at women, with regular celebrity chats and discussions.

Many communities are organized according to professional business interests. For example, plasticsnet.com is used by thousands of engineers in the plastics industry. A related extranet, comerx.com, provides a cybermarket for the industry.

COMMUNITIES OF FANTASY

Here participants create imaginary environments. For example, AOL subscribers can pretend to be medieval barons at the Red Dragon Inn. On ESPNet (go.espn.com) participants can create competing teams and "play" with Michael Jordan. Related to this is a large number of games that thousands of people play each simultaneously.

THE BUSINESS SIDE OF THE COMMUNITY

Interactive Week (May 11, 1998) provides the following suggestions on how to transform a community site into a commerce site:

1. Understand a particular niche industry, its information needs, and the step-by-step process by which it does the research needed to do business.
2. Build a site that provides this information, either through partnerships with existing publishers and information providers or by gathering it independently.
3. Set up the site to mirror the steps a user goes through in the information-gathering and decision-making processes, for example, how a chip designer whittles down the list of possible chips that will fit a particular product.
4. Build a community that relies on the site for decision support.
5. Start selling products and services that fit into the decision-support process, like sample chips to engineers.

Forrester Research conducted a survey in 1998 that found the following expected paybacks in order of importance:

- Customer loyalty increases.
- Sales increase.
- Customer participation and feedback increase.
- Repeat traffic to site increases.
- New traffic to site increases.

For further discussion, see Turban et al. (2004a) and Wellman (1999).

15.14 OTHER SOCIETAL IMPACTS AND THE DIGITAL DIVIDE

Several positive and negative social implications of management support systems, and especially of artificial intelligence systems, could be far-reaching (for an overview see Grudin and Wellman, 1999; Kosko, 2000; Papazafeiropoulou and Pouloudi, 2001). MSS have already had many direct beneficial effects on society; they are used for complicated human and social problems such as medical diagnosis, computer-assisted instruction, government-program planning, environmental quality control, and law enforcement. Problems in these areas could not have been solved economically (or solved at all) by other types of computer systems. Furthermore, the spread and benefits of electronic commerce are greatly enhanced with the help of intelligent agents (Wyckoff et al., 2000). Specific examples of potential impact are described next.

REPRESENTATIVE POSITIVE EFFECTS

Of the many positive effects we mention some below.

WORK IN HAZARDOUS ENVIRONMENTS

Expert systems, especially when combined with sensors and robots, can reduce or even eliminate the need for a human presence in dangerous or uncomfortable environments. See Oxman's (1991) work on cleaning up chemical spills.

OPPORTUNITIES FOR THE DISABLED

The integration of some AI technologies (speech recognition, vision recognition) into a CBIS could create new employment opportunities for disabled people. For example, those who cannot type would be able to use a voice-operated keyboard, and those who cannot travel could work at home. Boeing is developing several ES to help disabled employees perform useful tasks. Adaptive equipment permits disabled people to do ordinary tasks by using computers. Lazzaro (1993) describes AI support for deaf, blind, and motor-disabled people. Su et al., (2001) describe support to deaf-blind people, and Konrad (2001) describes services to the visually impaired. For further discussion, see Turban et al. (2004a).

CHANGING ROLE OF SINGLE PARENTS AND HOME-BOUND PEOPLE

MSS could change the traditional workplace role of home-bound people. For example, the opportunity to work at home and the need for less travel (because of the Internet and computer teleconferencing) could help single parents with young children and even home-bound people to assume more responsible (and demanding) managerial positions in organizations.

WORKING AT HOME (TELECOMMUTING)

Another trend gaining momentum is working at home via telecommuting (Khalifa and Davidson, 2000; Niles, 1998). The advantages are flexible hours, reduced travel time, less office and parking space needed, and employment for the home-bound. There are some disadvantages, however, including supervision difficulties, lack of human interaction, and increased isolation. Despite the promising benefits, the spread of telecommuting has been slow.

IMPROVEMENTS IN HEALTH

Several early expert systems (e.g., MYCIN) were designed to improve the delivery of health care. Since they were first developed, we have seen an increased role for AI technologies in supporting various tasks carried out by physicians and other health-care workers. Of special interest are expert systems that support the diagnosis of diseases and systems involving the use of machine vision in radiology. Advancements in simulation and robotics enable surgeons to guide and perform surgeries from a distance (see Noonan, 2001).

MSS technologies are supporting wired health-care hospitals (see Austen, 2002) and other facilities (see the Opening Vignette). The digital hospital (Weiss, 2002) includes many intelligent systems and EDSS. Finally, physicians are using MSS models for faster and better diagnosis (Landro, 2002). For an overview, see Staff (2002).

AIDS FOR THE CONSUMER

Several AI products are already on the market, and many more are being developed, to help ordinary people perform skilled or undesirable tasks. For example, Taxcut is an ES that assists in tax preparation, Willmaster is an ES that helps laypeople draft simple wills, and Wines on Disk provides advice on how to select wines. Intelligent robots could clean the house and mow the lawn (see the lawnmower at friendlyrobotics.com and run the simulator). Fuzzy logic has already provided blur-free video cameras, improved antilock brakes, and toasters that do not burn toast. Other advances include more realistic video games and virtual reality systems. Large numbers of intelligent agents provide comparisons and evaluations for consumers (see mysimon.com). These and many other improvements will contribute to an improved quality of life (Hanson and Stork, 1999).

QUALITY OF LIFE AT HOME AND IN THE WORKPLACE

On a broader scale, MSS have implications for the quality of life in general. Improved organizational efficiency may result in more leisure time. The workplace can be expanded from the traditional nine-to-five at a central location to 24 hours a day at any location. This expansion provides flexibility that can significantly improve the quality of leisure time (see relax-guide.com) even if the total amount of leisure time is not increased. MSS and other IT can change the workplace for the better, if designed properly (see Drucker, 2002; Jackson and Suomi, 2001).

LAW ENFORCEMENT

Computers and especially some AI technologies excel in supporting law-enforcement agencies (Wright, 2001). For example, using computer-mapping systems, police can track the location of 911 callers who use cell phones (Fujimoto, 2002). For an overview of DSS methods used in law enforcement, see Brown and Hagen (2003).

POTENTIAL NEGATIVE EFFECTS

The introduction of MSS technologies may be accompanied by some negative effects (Baatz, 1996). In addition to unemployment and the creation of large economic gaps among people, MSS technologies may result in other problems, some of which are common to other computer systems.

COMPUTER CRIME

Computer fraud and embezzlement are increasing. The American Bar Association estimates that losses from the theft of tangible and intangible assets (including software), destruction of data, embezzlement of funds, and fraud total $100–150 billion annually. With ES, there is a possibility of deliberately providing bad advice (e.g., advising employees to opt for early retirement when they should not). On the other hand, DSS, ES, and neural computing are being used to detect and prevent computer crimes. Neural computing systems can detect stolen credit cards and cellular phones almost instantaneously once they are used illegally. Fraud on the Web is becoming a major problem (see ftc.gov) and intelligent systems can help.

TOO MUCH POWER

Distributed MSS allows greater centralization of organizational decision-making and control. This may give some individuals or government agencies too much power over other people. Power may be used in an unethical manner (Dejoie et al., 1995).

THE DANGERS OF THE WEB

Extensive use of the Web has caused some people to neglect their families and friends, and sometimes has even caused divorces. A Web game addict in Korea died in February 2000 because he was too busy to break a nonstop playing record in order to eat. In Japan, two people died in 1999 after purchasing over the Web poison and information on how to kill themselves.

BLAMING THE COMPUTER PHENOMENON

Many people tend to blame computers to cover up human errors or wrongdoing. You may hear someone say, "But the expert system told us to do it," to justify an action that otherwise would be unjustifiable.

SOCIAL RESPONSIBILITY

Organizations need to be motivated to use MSS to improve the quality of life in general. They should design their MSS to minimize negative working conditions. This challenge should be met not only by companies that produce MSS hardware and software but also by companies that use these technologies. Properly designed systems can be implemented and used in ways that are either positive or negative (Papazafeiropoulou and Pouloudi, 2001).

THE DIGITAL DIVIDE

Despite the factors and trends that contribute to future IT growth, we have witnessed a growing gap, since the introduction of IT technology including MSS, between those who have and those who do not have the ability to use the technology (see Adams, 2001; Venkat, 2002). This gap is referred to as the **digital divide**. According to United Nations and International Telecommunication Union (ITU) reports, more than 90 percent of all Internet hosts are in developed countries, where only 15 percent of the world's population resides. In 2001, the city of New York, for example, had more Internet hosts than the whole continent of Africa. For possible societal problems, see Compaine (2001).

The gap exists both *within* and *between* countries. Federal and state governments in the United States are attempting to close this gap within the country by encouraging training and supporting education and infrastructure (see ecommerce.gov). The gap among countries, however, may be widening rather than narrowing. Many governments and international organizations are trying to close the digital divide. On strategies for closing the divide, see Iyer et al., 2002.

15.15 THE FUTURE OF MANAGEMENT-SUPPORT SYSTEMS

Where are MSS in general and DSS in particular going? Are they mature enough to be classified as mainstream IT? Are they still evolving? Are they taking new directions? Experts answer these questions differently, but most of them agree that MSS is migrating toward mainstream IT but is still evolving in certain areas (see the papers in Carlsson and Turban, 2002). The following is a summary of the major developments:

- As described throughout the book, MSS is certainly becoming a *Web-based* technology. This can be seen not only in the dissemination but also in the increasing use of the Web for MSS development and applications.
- Business intelligence is being combined with other Web-based applications, such as CRM, EC, and knowledge management.
- Business intelligence is integrated with ERP and other enterprise systems.
- Intelligent systems, ranging from face recognition to scenario interpretations, will be a major contributor in the fight against terrorism.
- Web-based advisory services that provide self-diagnosis and resulting prognoses will mushroom on the Internet. Quality control is needed to ensure quality and prevent fraud.
- More complex MSS applications are expected.
- The trend toward making MSS systems more intelligent will continue. The major technologies that will make this happen are intelligent agents, expert systems, case-based reasoning, neural networks, and fuzzy logic (Carlsson and Walden, 2001).
- Advancements in pervasive computing, such as the Elite Care projects, require the use of a greater number of intelligent devices.
- Management-support systems will be available for dissemination via application service providers (ASPs). For a reasonable fee, specifically constructed centers will provide solutions to a large number of potential users (Wagner, 2001). The trend toward utility computing (Greenemeier, 2003) will accelerate the use of MSS.
- Natural language–based search engines, such as about.com and askjeeves.com, will populate the Internet, frequently specializing in a certain domain. This feature will facilitate MSS construction by reducing costs.
- Similarly, the *semantic Web* (Cherry, 2002b) will increase the use of MSS.
- The use of voice technologies and natural language processing will further facilitate the usage of MSS.
- Frontline decision-support technologies that mostly support customer-relationship management will become an integral part of IT in most medium-sized and large organizations.
- MSS will continue to be integrated with ERP to provide better supply-chain management, including manufacturing planning and control.
- Large numbers of experts will offer expertise on the Internet. Web sites such as expertcentral.com and allexperts.com (which allow experts to bid on requests for expertise) will become an important part of knowledge dissemination.
- More and more companies will initiate formal *knowledge-management* programs. Some will sell the knowledge accumulated in their knowledge bases to others.
- With the greater usage of *wireless* technologies and the ability to access the Web with wireless devices, employees will be able to access MSS and knowledge bases anytime and from anywhere. Therefore, the usage of MSS will increase considerably. For example, hand-held devices already help customers to compare prices available on the Internet while they shop in physical stores.
- Intelligent agents will roam the Internet and intranets, assisting decision-making in the monitoring and interpretation of information. These agents will alert decision-makers and provide alternative courses of action.
- Groupware technologies for collaboration and communication will become easier to use, more powerful, and less expensive. They will make electronic group support a viable initiative even in small organizations.

- Decision-support tools for electronic commerce, currently limited to recommendations of certain products and brands, and to providing comparing agents, will expand to include more and better applications.

SUMMARY AND CONCLUSIONS

MSS are clearly having far-reaching and dramatic impacts on society and organizations. These range from providing rapid information access, to instantaneous communication around the world, to artificial intelligence assisting and even replacing human effort. Today we consider not the evolution of technology but the revolution of technology because of the nature and reach of the impact. MSS effects can often be predicted, planned for, and used to benefit us all.

❖ CHAPTER HIGHLIGHTS

- Integrating MSS technology with conventional computer-based information systems increases the functionality of the latter.
- Functional integration differs from the physical integration required to accomplish it.
- A major area of integration is databases (and database-management systems) with expert systems and natural language processors. The result is easy access to information.
- Expert systems can be used to improve accessibility to databases, either corporate or commercial (online).
- The second major area of integration is the use of expert systems to interpret results of data generated by models, particularly quantitative models.
- Expert systems can be used to enhance knowledge management, database management, and model management.
- Expert systems are being successfully integrated with decision-support systems; many useful applications have resulted.
- Several conceptual models of integration are applicable to expert systems and decision-support systems.
- MSS technologies are being integrated with many computer-based information systems, ranging from CAD/CAM to ERP.
- There are many problems with respect to the integration of AI technology, including technical, behavioral, and managerial factors.
- MSS can affect organizations in many ways, as standalone systems or integrated with other computer-based information systems.

- MSS supports business process reengineering as an enabler.
- MSS could reduce the need for supervision by providing more guidelines to employees via electronic means.
- The impact of MSS on individuals is unclear; it can be either positive, neutral, or negative.
- Management should motivate experts to contribute their knowledge to knowledge bases.
- Serious legal issues may develop with the introduction of AI; liability and privacy are the dominant problem areas.
- In one view, intelligent systems will cause massive unemployment because of increased productivity, lower required skill levels, and impacts on all sectors of the economy.
- In another view, intelligent systems will increase employment levels because automation makes products and services more affordable and so demand increases; the process of disseminating automation is slow enough to allow the economy to adjust to intelligent technologies.
- Many positive social implications can be expected from MSS. These range from providing opportunities to disabled people to leading the fight against terrorism.
- Quality of life, both at work and at home, is likely to improve as a result of MSS.
- Virtual communities are evolving and changing the way we live and work.
- Managers need to plan for the MSS of the future so as to be ready to make the most of them.

❖ KEY WORDS

- active (symbiotic) DSS
- business process reengineering (BPR)
- cookies
- digital divide
- functional integration
- information revolution
- intellectual property
- intelligent DSS
- intelligent interface
- Internet communities
- knowledge workers

- pervasive computing
- physical integration
- privacy
- problem management
- project management

- self-evolving DSS
- semantic Web
- symbiotic DSS
- telecommuting
- top management support

- user commitment
- user resistance
- virtual corporations (enterprises)
- virtual communities
- Web Services

❖ QUESTIONS FOR REVIEW

1. What is the difference between functional and physical integration?
2. Describe the two levels of functional integration.
3. DSS and ES integration may result in benefits along what three dimensions?
4. It is said that an ES is an intelligent DSS. Describe the common characteristics of ES and DSS. Do you agree with this statement? Why or why not?
5. How can synergy result when decision-support systems and expert systems are integrated?
6. Summarize the benefits a DSS can gain in terms of its database when it is integrated with an ES.
7. How can the knowledge base of an ES help a DSS?
8. What is a model base management system?
9. Summarize the benefits an ES can provide to a DSS in the area of models and their management.
10. Summarize the benefits that an ES can provide to a human–machine interface.
11. List the possibilities of integrating decision-support systems and expert systems.
12. Give an example of an ES output that can be used as an input to a DSS. Also give an example of the reverse relationship.

13. List some reasons why an expert may be unable or unwilling to contribute expertise to an ES.
14. Why will managers in the future work on fewer problems simultaneously?
15. List the major ethical issues related to MSS.
16. Describe some of the legal implications of ES advice.
17. List three reasons why intelligent systems could result in massive unemployment.
18. Give three arguments to counter the reasons in the preceding question.
19. Define the Internet (virtual) community.
20. List the four types of Internet communities.
21. List some potential social impacts of MSS.
22. Define the digital divide.
23. How can telecommuting improve the quality of life?
24. List some possible negative effects of MSS technologies.
25. Could MSS provide more managerial opportunities for disabled people and minorities? Why or why not?

❖ QUESTIONS FOR DISCUSSION

1. Why may it be difficult to integrate an expert system with an existing information system? Comment on data, people, hardware, and software.
2. Explain the following statement and give an example of both cases: Integration of a DSS and an ES can result in benefits during the construction (development) of the systems and during their operation.
3. Discuss the potential benefit of Web services to MSS integration.
4. One expert system can be used to consult several decision-support systems. What is the logic of such an arrangement? What problems may result when two or more decision-support systems share one expert system?
5. Why is visual modeling considered an integration of decision-support systems and expert systems?

6. Explain how the addition of an ES capability can improve the chances of successfully implementing a DSS.
7. Review current journals and surf the Web to identify a system that you believe is an MSS integration. Analyze the system according to the integration frameworks suggested in this chapter.
8. Discuss why the Web facilitates the integration of business intelligence and ERP.
9. Some say that MSS in general, and ES in particular, dehumanize managerial activities, and others say they do not. Discuss arguments for both points of view.
10. Should top managers who use ES instead of a human assistant be paid more or less for their jobs? Why?
11. The following excerpt is from the November 1974 issue of *InfoSystems*:

I've seen the ablest executives insist on increased productivity by a plant manager, lean on accounting for improved performance, and lay it on purchasing in no uncertain terms to cut its staff. But when these same executives turn to EDP (Electronic Data Processing) they stumble to an uncertain halt, baffled by the blizzard of computer jargon. They accept the presumed sophistication and differences that are said to make EDP activities somehow immune from normal management demands. They are stopped by all this nonsense, uncertainty about what's reasonable to expect, and what they can insist upon. They become confused and then retreat, muttering about how to get a handle on this blasted situation.

Can MSS technologies change a situation that has existed for about 30 years? Why or why not?

12. The Department of Transportation in a large metropolitan area has an expert system that advises an investigator about whether to open an investigation of a reported car accident. (This system, which includes 300 rules, was developed by T. J. Nagy at George Washington University.) Discuss the following questions:

a. Should the people involved in an accident be informed that a machine is deciding the future of an investigation?

b. What are some of the potential legal implications?

c. In general, what do you think of such a system?

13. Diagnosing infections and prescribing pharmaceuticals are the weak points of many practicing physicians (according to E. H. Shortliffe, one of the developers of MYCIN). It seems, therefore, that society would be better served if MYCIN (and other expert systems) were used extensively, but few physicians use expert systems. Answer the following questions:

a. Why do you think ES are little used by physicians?

b. Assume that you are a hospital administrator whose physicians are salaried and report to you. What would you do to persuade them to use ES?

c. If the potential benefits to society are so great, can society do something that will increase the use of ES by doctors?

❖ EXERCISES

1. Given below is a DSS success-factor questionnaire developed by Sanders and Courtney (1985). Administer the questionnaire to 10 users of DSS in your organization. Assign a 5 to strongly agree, a 4 to agree, a 3 to neutral, a 2 to disagree, and a 1 to strongly disagree. Compute the average results and rank the factors in order of their importance. Comment on the results.

Overall Satisfaction
- I have become dependent on DSS.
- As a result of DSS, I am seen as being more valuable to this organization.
- I have personally benefited from the existence of DSS in this organization.
- I have come to rely on DSS in performing my job.
- All in all, I think that DSS is an important system for this organization.
- DSS is extremely useful.

Decision-Making Satisfaction
- The use of DSS has enabled me to make better decisions.
- As a result of DSS, I am better able to set priorities in decision-making.
- The use of data generated by DSS has enabled me to present arguments more convincingly.

- DSS has improved the quality of the decisions I make in this organization.
- As a result of DSS, the speed with which I analyze decisions has increased.
- As a result of DSS, more relevant information has been available to me for decision-making.
- DSS has led me to greater use of analytical aids in my decision-making.

2. Certain key factors strongly influence the success level of a DSS or ES. The IS/IT/ES literature abounds with cases of failure because key success factors were missing. Likewise, many more studies indicate what is actually meant by success (user satisfaction, level of use, money saved, payback period, etc.). Interview someone who was involved in either sponsoring or using (or both) a real-world DSS or ES. If possible, interview several people, including the system developers or maintainers. Guide your interviews to determine the following:

a. What is the nature of the system? What problem is it intended to solve? Who is using it and why? Is its use mandatory or optional? Why?

b. How was the system implemented? Did the implementation procedure contribute to its success in any way? If so, how? If not, why not?

c. What measures are being used to determine the value of the system to the organization?

    d. What success measures are being used?

    e. Was the system deemed a success? Why?

    f. What are the future plans for the system?

3. Identify a failed DSS or ES (or one slated for replacement or a major upgrade because of problems) in an organization and evaluate why the system failed.

4. Several hospitals are introducing or considering the introduction of an intelligent bedside assistant that provides physicians and staff with a patient's medical-record database for diagnosis and prognosis. The system supplies any information required from the patient's medical records, makes diagnoses based on symptoms, and prescribes medications and other treatments. The system includes an expert system as well as a DSS. The system is intended to eliminate some human error and improve patient care. You are a hospital administrator and are very excited about the benefits for the patients. However, when you called a staff meeting, the following questions were raised: What if the system malfunctions? What if there is an undetected error in the program or the rules? The system, once implemented, takes full responsibility for patient care because physicians rely on it. A loss of data or an error in the program may result in disaster. For example, suppose there is a bug in the database program, and as a result a critical piece of information is missing from the patient's record. A physician who relies on the system could prescribe a drug on the basis of incomplete data. The consequence of this mistake may be life-threatening. Another possibility is that some of the rules in the knowledge base may not be accurate for all patients. Would you implement such a system? Why or why not?

5. One of the major complaints about the Olympic Games is that the judges are biased. We see this especially in figure skating and gymnastics. Would it be possible to use a computerized judge to do the job or at least to supplement the human judges? (Disregard the cost issue.)

    a. Is it possible to delegate such a task to a Robo-Judge? If your answer is no, explain in detail why not.

    b. If your answer to part (a) is yes, explain how this could be done. Specifically, what tools and techniques could be used and how?

    c. There are two possible options: supporting the judges with a computer and replacing them with a computer. Explain what could be done in each case and how (list the tools and techniques as well).

6. Comment on the cookie controversy (see DSS in Focus 15.6). How do you feel about a Web server being able to attach an ID number to you, track your visits on its site, and later learn more about you? How do you feel about directed advertising being sent to you using such information on the Web? How do you feel about such information being sold to other organizations? Could an intelligent agent use cookie information? Explain.

7. Perform a literature search on electronic voting, including allowing the general public voting via the Internet (see polls at cnn.com and cnnfn.com). Write a report describing the advantages and disadvantages of electronic voting.

8. Investigate developments in robotic vacuum cleaners and lawn mowers. Are these devices practical? Why or why not? Would you like to have one? Why or why not?

❖ GROUP EXERCISES AND TEAM PLAYING

1. Each team is assigned to a major DSS/business intelligence company (e.g., Microstrategy, SAS, Brio). Identify integrated products and prepare a list of their capabilities.

2. Meet with your group and discuss ways in which intelligence could be integrated into your university's advising and registration system. Are there any concrete ways in which it could be accomplished quickly and at low cost? Explain.

3. Intelligent advisory systems of all kinds are now available on the Web for fee or free. Experts are selling services, and corporations are selling access to their knowledge bases (e.g., Webmd.com, guru.com). Each team is assigned to one area of expertise (include training and education). Prepare a report on the legal issues that may be involved in such a venture.

❖ INTERNET EXERCISES

1. Identify Internet communities that are related to MSS. Start your search with DSSresources.com.

2. In an attempt to achieve efficiency, there is a trend toward producing expert systems and other intelligent systems on a chip. These chips can be embedded in other CBIS. Visit the Web sites of Motorola, Intel, and other chip manufacturers and find the newest smart chips on the market.

3. Several EIS, ES, and other vendors have development tools that support the construction of inte-

grated systems. Identify vendors that make such tools, prepare a representative list, and download and try some available demos.

4. Enter tradeportal.com and view its TradeMatrix. Explain why it is advertised as a powerful decision-support tool. Identify integration points.

5. Search the Internet to identify failures of management-support systems during implementation and prepare a report describing how such failures can be prevented.

6. Your mission is to identify ethical issues related to managerial decision-making. Search the Internet, join chat rooms, and read articles from the Internet. Prepare a report.

7. There is considerable talk about the impact of the Internet on society. Concepts such as global village, Internet community, digital divide, Internet society, and the like are getting much attention (Hanson and Stork, 1999; Kosko 2000; Magid, 1999). Search the Internet and prepare a short report on the topic. How does this concept relate to managerial decision-making?

8. Search the Internet to find examples of how intelligent systems (especially expert systems and intelligent agents) facilitate activities such as empowerment, mass customization, and teamwork.

9. Access the Business Resource Software Web site (brs-inc.com). Read the case studies and product information. How are these products helping businesses to

reengineer? Download the demo of Business Insight, install it, and try it. What does it do, and how effective do you think it could be in practice?

10. Access scout.cs.wisc.edu. Find the Scout Report. Look for information on social sciences, business, and economics. Find the issues discussed in the last six months that are related to the topics considered in this chapter.

11. Visit the Web sites minds.com, geocities.com, siNo.net, and others to find the latest developments on electronic communities and virtual teams. Write a short report relating this subject to corporate decision-making.

12. Investigate the American Bar Association's artificial intelligence Web site. What are the major legal and societal concerns and advances addressed there? How are they being dealt with?

13. The value of telecommuting and its slow adoption are the subject of extensive research (Khalifa and Davidson, 2000). Surf the Internet to find out what is happening. Join a relevant news group (or access postings via an archive on the Web) and identify some frequently asked questions (FAQs). Write up your results in a report.

14. Explore several sites related to health care (e.g., Webmd.com, who.int, medicalert.com, and cyberdocs.com). Write a report on how these sites improve health care.

HYBRID INTELLIGENT SYSTEM FOR DEVELOPING MARKETING STRATEGY

MSS has been used for years to support market strategy (see references in Li, 2000). Since marketing strategy involves several stages, it is necessary to develop MSS support for each. The major stages are:

- SWOT (strength, weakness, opportunities, and threat analysis)
- Portfolio summary of current product/market status
- Setting marketing objectives and strategies

To support the above three stages effectively, the system needs to:

- provide a logical process for strategic analysis
- support group assessment of strategic marketing factors
- help the coupling of strategic analysis with managerial judgment
- help managers handle uncertainty and fuzziness
- provide intelligent advice on developing marketing strategy

To attain the above objectives, a hybrid intelligent system has been developed. It integrates the strengths of ES, fuzzy logic, ANN, and DSS with different strategic-analysis models. The system consists of five relatively independent, self-contained processing subsystem modules that share and exchange information, as well as undertaking distinct functions to help solve parts of the strategic marketing-decision problems to which they are best suited. These modules are coordinated by intercommunicating software-control mechanisms. The system architecture is illustrated in Figure 15.10.

The ANN is used to analyze and forecast market growth and market share to support managers' assessment of market attractiveness and business strengths. The output of the ANN is an input to the *individual/group assessment model*, which is designed to evaluate internal and external strategic factors, based upon the opinions of an individual or a group of managers. A *fuzzification component* is used to deal with the fuzziness and imprecision

of information. It works jointly and cooperatively with the expert system module to handle imprecise linguistic concepts, fuzzy terms, and uncertainty in the assessment of market attractiveness and business strengths. A *fuzzy expert system model* is developed mainly to represent expertise on marketing-strategy development. Other components provide standard MSS support (database, interface, etc.).

To combine the advantages of different strategy-analysis models, Porter's five-forces model and the directional policy matrices (DPM) are integrated into the hybrid system. The DPM models offer a detailed methodological approach to analyze strategic factors and establish marketing objectives and strategy.

The following benefits are recognized:

1. It provides managers with an organized method to conduct strategic analysis.
2. It supports the group assessment of marketing strategy factors based upon the opinions of a panel of managers.
3. It employs an ANN forecasting model to help managers assess market growth and market share.
4. It helps the coupling of strategic analysis with managerial judgment.
5. It harnesses fuzzy logic to handle fuzziness and uncertainty in evaluating criteria.
6. It utilizes a fuzzy expert system to conduct fuzzy reasoning for developing marketing strategy.

The system has been evaluated with marketing directors in five large British companies. Their responses to the system were very favorable. Empirical evidence indicates that the hybrid system is useful and helpful in support of the key aspects of marketing-strategy development. The advice or outputs generated by the hybrid systems were reported to be mostly sound, surprisingly accurate, and clearly reflecting managerial judgment. The system has potential as an effective means for developing marketing strategy.

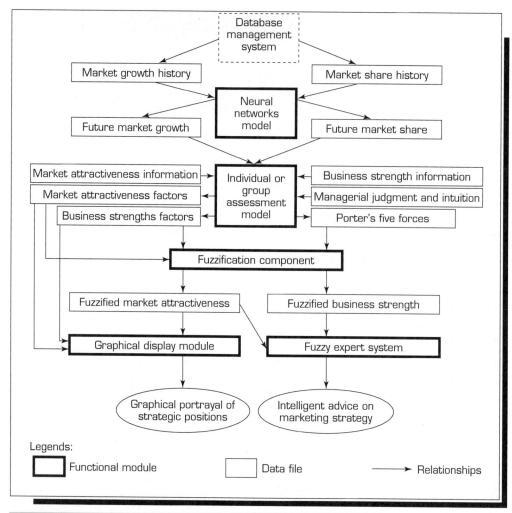

FIGURE 15.10   THE ARCHITECTURE OF A HYBRID INTELLIGENT SYSTEM.

Source: Li, 2000.

QUESTIONS FOR THE CASE

1. What are the contributions of each of the MSS components?

2. What are the benefits of having an integrated system? Why not use individual systems for each decision phase?

3. Based on the description and the fact that the system was evaluated successfully by five different companies, do you believe it can be general, or will it work better in one industry, or one company? Why?

active (symbiotic) DSS A special type of intelligent DSS that can respond to changes and is viewed as proactive rather than reactive.

ad hoc DSS DSS that deals with specific problems that are usually neither anticipated nor recurring.

advanced planning and scheduling (APS) A software package that can be integrated with ERP or SCM software to help optimize software integration.

agency The degree of autonomy vested in a software agent.

agent A computer software that performs certain tasks by its own rules automatically, such as monitoring a set of data and generate alerts when abnormality is found.

AI workstations *See* LISP machines.

algorithm A step-by-step search in which improvement is made at every step until the best solution is found.

analog model An abstract, symbolic model of a system that behaves like the system but looks different.

analogical reasoning Determining the outcome of a problem with the use of analogies. A procedure for drawing conclusions about a problem by using past experience.

analytical techniques Methods that use mathematical formulas to derive an optimal solution directly or to predict a certain result, mainly in solving structured problems.

anonymity Being able to remain anonymous while contributing at a meeting.

application service provider (ASP) A software vendor that offers leased software applications to organizations.

approximate reasoning A computational modeling of processes (or parts of processes) used by humans to reason about natural phenomena.

artificial intelligence (AI) The subfield of computer science concerned with symbolic reasoning and problem-solving.

artificial neural networks (ANN) Computer technology that attempts to build computers that will operate like a human brain. The machines possess simultaneous memory storage and works with ambiguous information. *See* neural computing.

associative memory The ability to recall complete situations from partial information.

asynchronous Occurring at different times.

auction A market mechanism by which sellers place offers and buyers make sequential bids.

automated translation A process that a computer software translates a document from one language to another without the intervention of human.

automatic methods Automatic knowledge acquisition methods: Using computer software to automatically discover knowledge from a set of data.

autonomous agent A software agent with learning capability.

autoresponders intelligent agents that answer customers' e-mails.

avatars Computer representations of users in an animated, three-dimensional format; also known as *computer characters*.

axon An outgoing connection (terminal) from a biological neuron.

backbone Long-distance, high-capacity, high-speed networks that link major Internet computer centers.

backpropagation The best-known learning algorithm in neural computing. Learning is done by comparing computed outputs to desired outputs of historical cases.

backtracking A technique used in tree searches. The process of working backward from a failed objective or an incorrect result to examine unexplored alternatives.

backward chaining A search technique (employing IF-THEN rules) used in production systems that begins with the action clause of a rule and works backward through a chain of rules in an attempt to find a verifiable set of condition clauses.

banners An electronic "billboard" that typically contains a short text or graphical message to advertise a product or a vendor.

belief function The representation of uncertainty without the need to specify exact probabilities.

best practices In an organization, the best methods for solving problems. These are often stored in the knowledge repository of a knowledge-management system.

blackboard An area of working memory set aside for the description of a current problem and for recording intermediate results in an expert system.

blind search A search approach that does not make use of knowledge or heuristics to help speed up the search process. A time-consuming, arbitrary search process that attempts to exhaust all possibilities.

bots Intelligent software agents; an abbreviation of *robots*. Usually used as part of another term, as in *knowbots*, *softbots*, or *shopbots*.

brainstorming (electronic) A methodology of idea generation by association. This group process uses analogy and synergy. In GSS, it is computer supported.

breadth-first search A search technique that evaluates every item at a given level of the search space before proceeding to the next level.

brick-and-mortar Pure physical organizations (corporations).

business (system) analyst An individual whose job is to analyze business processes and the support they receive (or need) from information technology.

business activity monitoring (BAM) systems These systems consist of real-time systems that alert managers to potential opportunities, impending problems, and threats, and then empower them to react through models and collaboration. Situations are detected in real-time, quickly analyzed, and solved.

business analytics (BA) The application of models directly to business data. Using DSS tools (*see* business intelligence), especially models, in assisting decision-makers. Essentially OLAP/DSS.

business intelligence (BI) The use of analytical methods, either manually or automatically, to derive relationships from data. See business analytics, data-mining, decision-support systems, online analytical processing (OLAP).

business intelligence tools An information system that allows users to view data in databases and interpret them easily and quickly. It is usually related to an EIS.

business process reengineering (BPR) A methodology for introducing a fundamental change in specific business processes. It is usually supported by an information system.

business process management (BPM) system This type of system integrates data, applications, and people together through a common business process. It aims to streamline and automate business processes, thus offsetting the administrative burden of the organization and creating an environment where processes can be leveraged for strategic value. (See Datz, 2002; and CKB, 2003.)

buy-side marketplace A model in which electronic commerce technology is used to streamline the purchasing process in order to reduce the cost of items purchased, the administrative cost of procurement, and the purchasing cycle time.

career ladders Different career paths that individuals may take in an organization. For example, there are management paths and technical paths.

case library The knowledge base of a case-based reasoning system.

case-based reasoning (CBR) A methodology in which knowledge and/or inferences are derived from historical cases.

case-management system (CMS) A system for managing the large volume of cases in an organizational decision-support system.

certainty A condition under which it is assumed that future values are known for sure and only one result is associated with an action.

certainty factor (CF) A percentage supplied by an expert system that indicates the probability that the conclusion reached by the system is correct. Also, the degree of belief an expert has that a certain conclusion will occur if a certain premise is true.

certainty theory A framework for representing and working with degrees of belief of true and false in knowledge-based systems.

channel conflict When one method (or channel) of reaching customers hinders or impedes another method of reaching customers.

chief knowledge officer (CKO) The person in charge of a knowledge-management effort in an organization.

choice phase The third phase in decision-making, in which an alternative is selected.

chromosome A candidate solution for a genetic algorithm.

chunking Divide and conquer, or dividing complex problems into subproblems.

class A term used in object-oriented programming to designate a group of items with the same characteristics (e.g., the Fiat car is in a class of transportation).

classification model For ES, a model employed in building expert systems that uses production rules and covers a highly bounded problem with a few known possible solutions.

click-and-mortar (or click-and-brick organizations) Organizations that conduct some e-commerce activities but their primary business is done in the physical world.

client/server architecture A network system in which several PCs (clients) share the memory and other capabilities of a larger computer or those of printers, databases, and so on (servers).

cognitive limits The limits of the ability of the human mind to process, store, and recall information.

cognitive style (cognition) The subjective process through which individuals organize and change information during the decision-making process.

collaborating multiagents Multiple agents working on the same task.

collaborative commerce (c-commerce) A type of electronic commerce where business partners, usually along the supply chain, collaborate electronically.

collaborative computing The shared computerized work when two or more people work together (e.g., by using screen sharing). *See* groupware; group-support systems.

collaborative filtering A method for generating recommendations from user profile. It uses preferences of other users of similar behavior to predict the preference of the particular user.

collaborative workflow management A major tool for collaborating in processes of business activities and functions including: planning and scheduling, design, new product information, product-content management, order management, and sourcing and procurement.

community of practice (COP) A group of people in an organization with a common professional interest, often self-organized for managing knowledge in a knowledge-management system.

complete enumeration   The process of checking every feasible solution to a problem.

complexity   A measure of how difficult a problem is in terms of its formulation for optimization, its required optimization effort, or its stochastic nature.

component model   A model that contains a functional description of all components and their interactions.

computer-aided instruction (CAI)   In general, the use of computers as teaching tools. Synonymous with *computer-based instruction, computer-assisted learning,* and *computer-based training.*

computer-based information system (CBIS)   An information system specifically designed to run on computers.

computer supported cooperative work (CSCW)   *See* collaborative computing.

conceptual graph (CG)   A diagram that describes how and when an expert's knowledge will come into play as an expert system operates.

conflict resolution (of rules)   Selecting a procedure from a conflicting set of applicable competing procedures or rules.

connection weights   The weight associated with each link in a neural network model. They are assessed by neural networks learning algorithms.

consistency enforcer   The component of the inference engine in an expert system that attempts to maintain a consistent representation of the emerging solution.

consultation environment   The part of an expert system that is used by a nonexpert to obtain expert knowledge and advice. It includes the workplace, inference engine, explanation facility, recommended action, and user interface.

content management system (CMS)   An *electronic document management system* that produces dynamic versions of documents, and automatically maintains the current set for use at the enterprise level.

control structure   *See* inference engine.

controllable variables   Decision variables, such as quantity to produce, amounts of resources to be allocated, and so on, that can be changed and manipulated by the decision-maker.

cookies   Text strings stored on a user's hard drive files to record the history of his or her actions at particular Web sites.

corporate portal   A system that integrates internal applications, such as database management, document management, and e-mail, with external applications, such as news services and customer Web sites. It is a Web-based interface that gives users access to such applications.

cost–benefit analysis   A method of determining the viability of a project by comparing estimated costs with anticipated benefits.

courseware   A software system that supports learning.

creativity   The human trait that leads to the production of acts, items, and instances of novelty; and the achievement of creative products.

creativity support system (CSS)   A group support system that helps users develop creative solutions to problems.

critical success factors (CSFs)   The factors that are most critical to the success of an organization.

crossover   The combining of parts of two superior solutions by a genetic algorithm in an attempt to produce an even better solution.

customer relationship management (CRM)   An organizational initiative whose objective is to properly deliver various services to customers, ranging from Web-based call centers to loyalty programs, such as rewarding frequent fliers.

customer-to-customer (C2C)   e-commerce in which both the buyer and the seller are individuals (not businesses).

cyberbanking   *See* Electronic banking.

data   Raw facts that are meaningless by themselves (e.g., names or numbers).

data integrity   The accuracy and accessibility of data. It is a part of data quality.

data marts   Departmental data warehouses that only store relevant data.

data mining   The activity of looking for very specific, detailed, but unknown information in databases. A search for valuable yet difficult to find data. Formerly called *data dipping.*

data quality (DQ)   The quality of data, including their accuracy, precision, completeness, and relevance.

data visualization   A graphical animation or video presentation of data and the results of data analysis.

data warehouse   The physical repository where relational data are specially organized to provide enterprise-wide, cleaned data in a standardized format.

data warehousing   A relational database specially organized to provide data for easy access.

database   The organizing of files into related units which are viewed as a single storage concept. The data are then made available to a wide range of users.

database management systems (DBMS)   Software for establishing, updating, and querying (e.g., managing) a database.

decision analysis   Methods for determining the solution to a problem, typically when it is inappropriate to utilize iterative algorithms.

decision room   An arrangement for a group support system in which PCs are available to some or all participants. The objective is to enhance groupwork.

decision style   The manner in which a decision-maker thinks and reacts to problems. It includes perceptions, cognitive responses, values, and beliefs.

decision table   A table used to represent knowledge and prepare it for analysis.

decision tree   A graphical presentation of a sequence of interrelated decisions to be made under assumed risk.

decision variables *See* controllable variables.

decision-making The action of selecting among alternatives.

decision-support systems (DSS) Computer-based information systems that combine models and data in an attempt to solve nonstructured problems with extensive user involvement through a friendly user interface.

declarative knowledge The representation of facts and assertions.

declarative rules Rules that state all the facts and relationships involved in a problem.

deductive reasoning In logic, reasoning from the general to the specific. Consequent reasoning in which conclusions follow premises.

deep knowledge A representation of information about the internal and causal structure of a system that considers the interactions among the system's components.

deep representation A model that captures all the forms of knowledge used by experts in their reasoning.

defuzzification Creating a crisp solution from a fuzzy logic solution.

deindividuation A feeling of being separated from others that can lead to behavior violating established norms of appropriateness.

Delphi Method A qualitative forecasting methodology using anonymous questionnaires. Effective for technological forecasting and for forecasting involving sensitive issues.

demand chain The flow of materials from an operation to the final demand. It includes order generation, taking, and fulfillment and has been integrated into the supply chain.

demon (or daemon) A procedure that runs if a specific predefined state is recognized.

demonstration prototype A small-scale prototype of a (usually expert) system that demonstrates some major capabilities of the final system on a rudimentary basis. It is used to gain support among users and managers.

dendrite The part of a biological neuron that provides inputs to the cell.

dependent variables A system's measure of effectiveness.

depth-first search A search procedure that explores each branch of a search tree to its full vertical length. Each branch is searched for a solution; if none is found, a new vertical branch is searched to its depth, and so on.

descriptive models Models that describe things as they are.

design phase The second decision-making phase: finding possible alternatives in decision-making and assessing their contribution.

desktop purchasing A variation of e-procurement in which suppliers' catalogs are aggregated in an internal master catalog on the buyer's server, so that the company's purchasing agents or even end-users can shop more conveniently.

deterministic models Models constructed under assumed certainty, namely, there is only one possible (and known) result of each alternative course of action.

development environments Parts of expert systems that are used by builders. They include the knowledge base, the inference engine, knowledge acquisition, and improving reasoning capability. The knowledge engineer and the expert are considered part of these environments.

development strategies Methods used to analyze, design, and implement computer systems.

directory A catalog of all the data in a database or all the models in a model base.

disbelief The degree of belief that something is not going to happen.

distance learning (DL) The process of learning when it involves tools or technologies designed to overcome the restrictions of either same-time or same-place learning. Students are not in a classroom but use telecommunication networks, groupware, telephones, faxes, and television to learn.

distributed artificial intelligence (DAI) A multiple-agent system for problem-solving. Splitting of a problem into multiple cooperating systems in deriving a solution.

document management The automated management and control of digitized documents throughout their life-cycle.

document management systems (DMS) Information systems (e.g., hardware, software) that allow the flow, storage, retrieval, and use of digitized documents.

documented knowledge For ES, stored knowledge sources not based directly on human expertise.

domain An area of expertise.

domain names The official name assigned to an Internet site, consisting of multiple parts, separated by dots, which are translated from right to left in locating the site.

domain-specific tools Software shells designed to be used only in the development of a specific area; for example, a diagnostic system.

drill down The investigation of information in detail; for example, finding not only total sales but also sales by region, by product, or by salesperson.

DSS application A DSS program built for a specific purpose; for example, a scheduling system for a specific company. *See* specific DSS.

DSS generator (engine) Computer software that provides a set of capabilities for quickly building a specific DSS.

DSS integrated tool A toolkit for DSS development. It includes a spreadsheet, a database management system, graphics, and other features.

DSS primary tools Features that facilitate the development of either a DSS generator or a specific DSS, such as programming languages, graphics, editors, query systems, and random-number generators.

DSS technology levels A framework for understanding DSS development: specific DSS, DSS generators, and DSS tools.

DSS tools Software elements (e.g., languages) that facilitate the development of a DSS or a DSS generator.

dynamic explanation In ES, an explanation facility that reconstructs the reasons for its actions as it evaluates rules.

dynamic models Models whose input data are changed over time; for example, a five-year profit (or loss) projection.

e-business A broad definition of electronic commerce that refers not just to buying and selling, but also to servicing customers, collaborating with business partners, and conducting electronic transactions within an organization.

effectiveness The degree of goal attainment. Doing the right things.

efficiency The ratio of output to input. Appropriate use of resources. Doing the things right.

E-government The use of Internet technology in general and electronic commerce in particular to deliver information and public services to citizens, business partners and suppliers, and those working in the public sector.

E-learning The online delivery of information for purposes of education, training, or knowledge management.

electronic brainstorming *See* Brainstorming (electronic).

electronic commerce (EC) Buying and selling products and services using computers and networks.

electronic communities Groups of people with similar interests who use the Internet to communicate, collaborate, discuss issues of mutual concern, or conduct business. Also called *virtual communities*.

electronic customer relationship management (e-CRM) Customer service, self-service web applications, sales force automation tools, and analysis of customers' purchasing behaviors on the Internet initiatives that enable an organization to more effectively respond to its customers' needs and to market to them on a one-to-one basis.

electronic document management (EDM) A method for processing documents electronically, including capture, storage, retrieval, manipulation, and presentation.

electronic Internet communities *See* electronic communities.

electronic meeting (Emeeting) A meeting that is enhanced by a group-support system.

electronic meeting systems (EMS) An information technology–based environment that supports group meetings (groupware), which may be distributed geographically and temporally.

electronic retailing (e-tailing) Direct selling to consumers through electronic storefronts or malls, usually designed around an electronic catalog format.

electronic solo storefronts Electronic businesses that maintain their own Internet name and Web site; may be extensions of physical stores or may be new businesses started by entrepreneurs who saw a niche on the Web.

electronic storefronts *See* electronic solo storefronts

elicitation of knowledge *See* knowledge elicitation.

empowering employees Providing employees with access to information needed for decision-making and with computer programs that generate recommended decisions for specific scenarios.

EMYCIN (Empty MYCIN) The nonspecific part (called the shell) of MYCIN consisting of what is left after the knowledge is removed. EMYCIN becomes a new problem-solver when the knowledge (using rules) for a different problem domain is added.

encapsulation In object-oriented programming, the coupling of data and procedures and embedding them in an object.

end user computing Developing one's own information system.

end user development *See* end-user computing.

enhanced product realization (EPR) An Internet-based, state-of-the-art distributed system that allows manufacturers to make fast product modifications anywhere and accelerates the time to market for new products and services. EPR integrates and leverages the Internet with other existing and emerging information technologies to enable a host of collaborative manufacturing and electronic commerce applications. It is a kind of extranet.

enterprise computing *See* enterprise information system (EIS).

enterprise information portal *See* enterprise portal.

enterprise information system (EIS) An organization-wide system that enables people to communicate with one other and access appropriate data throughout an enterprise. It includes a number of enterprise-wide systems: content management systems (CMS), knowledge management systems (KMS), supply chain management systems, (SCM), enterprise resource planning (ERP)/enterprise resource management (ERM) systems, etc.

enterprise knowledge portal (EKP) An electronic doorway into a knowledge management system.

enterprise portal A corporate internal Web site (on its intranet) that integrates many internal applications with external ones. Users access them via standard Web browsers.

enterprise resource management (ERM) *See* enterprise resource planning (ERP).

enterprise resource planning (ERP) A process that integrates the information processing of all routine activities inside an organization (e.g., ordering, billing, production scheduling, budgeting, staffing) and among business partners. Also known as *enterprise resource management (ERM)*.

enterprise systems *See* enterprise computing.

enterprise-wide collaboration systems Group support systems that support entire enterprises.

enterprise-wide computing *See* enterprise computing.

enumeration (complete) A listing of all possible solutions and a comparison of their results in order to find the best solution.

environmental scanning and analysis Conducting a search for and an analysis of information in external databases and flows of information.

e-procurement Purchasing by using electronic support.

evaluation The activity of assessing the overall value of an expert system in terms of acceptable performance levels, usefulness, flexibility, efficiency, and cost-effectiveness.

evolutionary development A systematic process for system development that is used in DSS. A portion of the system is quickly constructed and then tested, improved, and enlarged in steps. Similar to prototyping.

exception reporting Calling attention to a deviation larger than an agreed-on threshold (e.g., 10 percent or $200,000).

executive information system (EIS) A computerized system specifically designed to support executive work.

executive support system (ESS) An executive information system that includes some analytical and communication capabilities.

expectation-driven processing A reasoning method, used with frames, that attempts to identify data to confirm expectations.

expert A human being who has developed a high level of proficiency in making judgments in a specific, usually narrow, domain.

expert support system An expert system whose primary mission is to support problem-solving and decision-making.

expert system (ES) A computer system that applies reasoning methodologies to knowledge in a specific domain to render advice or recommendations, much like a human expert. A computer system that achieves a high level of performance in task areas that, for human beings, require years of special education and training.

expert system shell A computer program that facilitates relatively easy implementation of a specific expert system. Analogous to a DSS generator.

expert tool user A person who is skilled in the application of one or more types of specialized problem-solving tools.

expert-driven knowledge acquisition A situation in which an expert captures her or his own knowledge without the help of a knowledge engineer.

expertise transfer system (ETS) A computer program that interviews experts and helps them build expert systems.

expertise The set of capabilities that underlines the performance of human experts, including extensive domain knowledge, heuristic rules that simplify and improve approaches to problem-solving, metaknowledge and metacognition, and compiled forms of behavior that afford great economy in a skilled performance.

explanation and justification The design and programming of an explanation capability.

explanation facility The component of an expert system that can explain the system's reasoning and justify its conclusions.

explanation subsystem *See* explanation facility.

explanation-based learning A machine-learning approach that assumes that there is enough existing theory to rationalize why one instance is or is not a prototypical member of a class.

explicit knowledge Knowledge that deals with objective, rational, and technical material (data, policies, procedures, software, documents, etc.).

extended supply chain A supply chain that includes business partners, such as customers and suppliers.

extract To capture data from several sources, synthesize them, summarize them, determine which of them are relevant, and organize them.

extranet A combination of corporate intranets and the Internet, specifically used in enhanced product realization (EPR).

facet An attribute or a feature that describes the content of a slot in a frame.

facilitator (in GSS) A person who plans, organizes, and electronically controls a group in a collaborative computing decision-making environment (e.g., a decision room).

facts Declarative knowledge: the true and false statements in an artificial intelligence system.

feasibility study A preliminary investigation for developing plans to construct a new information system. The major aspects of the study are cost vs. benefit, technological, human, organizational, and financial.

feedforward-backpropagation Allows all neurons to link the output in one layer to the input of the next layer, but does not allow any feedback linkage.

fifth-generation languages (5GL) Artificial intelligence computer programming languages. The best known are PROLOG and LISP.

firewall A method for protecting an organization's computers from outsiders.

firing a rule Obtaining information on either the IF or the THEN part of a rule that makes the rule an assertion (true or false).

forecasting Predicting the future.

forward auctions Used mainly as a selling channel; a single seller auctions item(s) to many potential buyers.

forward chaining A data-driven search in a rule-based system.

fourth-generation languages (4GLs) Nonprocedural, user-oriented languages that enable quick programming by specifying only the desired results.

frame A knowledge representation scheme that associates one or more features with an object in terms of slots and particular slot values.

frame-based system An expert system whose knowledge is represented as frames (object-oriented) in the knowledge base.

frontline decision-making A process of automating decision processes and pushing them down the organization to empower employees who are in contact with customers. It includes evaluation matrices and ready-made DSS.

functional integration Providing different support functions as a single system through a single, consistent interface.

fuzzification A process that converts an accurate number into a fuzzy description, such as converting from an exact age into young or old.

fuzzy logic Logically consistent ways of reasoning that can cope with uncertain or partial information; characteristic of human thinking and many expert systems.

fuzzy sets A set theory approach in which set membership is less precise than having objects strictly in or out of the set.

game playing A domain that has been investigated in artificial intelligence, including checkers and chess.

general-purpose problem-solver (GPS) A procedure developed by Alan Newell and Herb Simon in an attempt to create an intelligent computer. Although unsuccessful, the concept made a valuable contribution to the AI field.

genetic algorithms Software programs that learn in an evolutionary manner similar to the way biological systems evolve.

geographic information system (GIS) An information system that uses spatial data, such as digitized maps. A combination of text, graphics, icons, and symbols on maps.

goal seeking analysis Asking a computer what values certain variables must have in order to attain desired goals.

graphical user interface (GUI) An interactive user-friendly interface in which, by using icons and similar objects, the user can control communication with a computer.

group DSS *See* group-support systems.

group purchasing The requirements of many buyers are aggregated so that they make up a large volume.

group support systems (GSS) Information systems that support the work of groups (communication, decision-making) generally working on unstructured or semistructured problems.

groupthink In a meeting, continual reinforcement of an idea by group members.

groupware Computerized technologies and methods that aim to support the work of people working in groups.

groupwork Any work being performed by more than one person.

heuristic programming The use of heuristics in problem-solving.

heuristics Informal, judgmental knowledge of an application area that constitutes the "rules of good judgment" in the field. Heuristics also encompasses the knowledge of how to solve problems efficiently and effectively, how to plan steps in solving a complex problem, how to improve performance, and so forth.

hidden layer The middle layer of an artificial neural network with three or more layers.

hidden unemployment A situation in which people are considered employed but work only part of the time. In such cases the same amount of work could be performed by fewer people.

hierarchical reasoning A reasoning method, based on a tree search, in which certain alternatives, objects, or events can be eliminated at various levels of the search hierarchy.

human–machine interface *See* user interface.

hybrid (integrated) computer systems Different computer programs or tools that are integrated to perform a complex task.

hybrid systems (environments) Software packages for expediting the construction of expert systems that include several knowledge representation schemas.

iconic model A scaled physical replica.

idea generation The process by which people generate ideas, usually supported by software; for example, developing alternative solutions to a problem. *See* brainstorming.

IF-THEN A conditional rule according to which a certain action is taken only if a particular condition is satisfied.

implementation phase The fourth decision-making phase, involving actually putting a recommended solution to work.

independent variables Variables in a model that are controlled by the decision-maker and/or the environment and which determine the result of a decision (also called *input variables*).

induction table A table that facilitates rule induction for expert systems.

inductive learning A machine learning approach in which rules are inferred from facts or data.

inductive reasoning In logic, reasoning from the specific to the general. Conditional or antecedent reasoning.

inexact (approximate) reasoning A type of reasoning used when an expert system must make decisions based on partial or incomplete information.

inference The process of drawing a conclusion from given evidence. To reach a decision by reasoning.

inference engine The part of an expert system that actually performs the reasoning function.

inference tree A schematic view of the inference process showing the order in which rules are being tested.

inferencing Performing the inference function.

inferencing rules In ES, rules that direct the inference engine.

influence diagram A diagram that shows the various types of variables in a problem (decision, independent, result) and how they are related to each other.

information Data that are organized in a meaningful way.

information revolution The changes created by computers that have revolutionized our life. A concept similar to the industrial revolution, which changed the world when machines were introduced.

inheritance The process by which one object takes on or is assigned the characteristics of another object higher up in a hierarchy.

inputs The resources introduced into a system for transformation into outputs.

instantiation The process of assigning (or substituting) a specific value or name to a variable in a frame (or in a logic expression), making it a particular "instance" of that variable.

institutionalization The process through which an MSS system is incorporated as an ongoing part of organizational procedures.

institutional DSS (or MSS) A system that is a permanent fixture in an organization with continuing financial support. It deals with decisions of a recurring nature.

intellectual asset A specific part of the know-how of an organization. Intellectual assets often include the knowledge that employees possess.

intellectual capital The know-how of an organization. Intellectual capital often includes the knowledge that employees possess.

intellectual property The intangible property created by individuals or corporations, which is protected under copyright, trade secret, and patent laws.

intelligence A degree of reasoning and learned behavior, usually task- or problem-solving–oriented.

intelligence phase The initial phase of problem definition in decision-making.

intelligent agent (IA) An expert or knowledge-based system embedded in computer-based information systems (or their components) to make them smarter.

intelligent computer-aided instruction (ICAI) The use of AI techniques for training or teaching with a computer.

intelligent database A database management system exhibiting artificial intelligence features that assist the user or designer; often includes ES and intelligent agents.

intelligent DSS A DSS that includes one or more components of an expert system or other AI technology. With this component, the DSS behaves in a better (more "intelligent") manner.

intelligent interface A user interface exhibiting artificial intelligence features that assist the user; often includes ES and intelligent agents. It may learn the usage style of the decision-maker.

intelligent software agent *See* intelligent agent.

intelligent tutoring system (ITS) Self-tutoring systems that can guide learners in how best to proceed with the learning process.

intellimedia systems Intelligent multimedia systems.

interactive induction A computer-based means of knowledge acquisition that directly supports an expert in performing knowledge acquisition by guiding the expert through knowledge structuring.

interfaces The parts of computer systems that interact with users, accepting commands from the computer keyboard and displaying the results generated by other parts of the systems.

intermediary A person who uses a computer to fulfill requests made by other people; for example, a financial analyst who uses a computer to answer questions for top management.

Internet A global network of hundreds of thousands of local networks.

Internet communities *See* electronic (virtual) communities.

Internet softbot A software agent that can learn and be used on the Internet.

interpreter (rule interpreter) *See* inference engine.

interview analysis An explicit, face-to-face knowledge-acquisition technique involving a direct dialog between the expert and the knowledge engineer.

intrabusiness (intraorganizational) EC Electronic business transactions that take place within an organization, in an attempt to increase productivity, speed, and quality, and to cut costs.

intranet An internal network that uses Internet capabilities, such as browsing, search engines, and e-mail.

iterative design *See* evolutionary prototyping process; prototyping.

iterative process *See* evolutionary prototyping process; prototyping.

job content The specific tasks and responsibilities involved in a job.

justification facility (or justifier) *See* explanation facility.

justifier *See* explanation facility.

key performance indicators (KPIs) Specific measures of the critical success factors in an executive information system.

key word search A method of looking for important terms in document- or Web-based systems.

key words Important terms in a document-based (or Web-based) system. Used for searching.

key word banners   Electronic advertisements that appear when a predetermined word is queried from the search engine; used to target customers with particular interests.

knowbots   A software product for implementing mobile agents (see http://www.cnri.reston.va.us/home/koe/)

knowledge   Understanding, awareness, or familiarity acquired through education or experience. Anything that has been learned, perceived, discovered, inferred, or understood. The ability to use information. In a knowledge-management system, knowledge is information in action.

knowledge acquisition   The extraction and formulation of knowledge derived from various sources, especially from experts.

knowledge audit   The process of identifying the knowledge an organization has, who has it, and how it flows (or does not) through the enterprise.

knowledge base   A collection of facts, rules, and procedures organized into schemas. The assembly of all the information and knowledge about a specific field of interest.

knowledge diagram   A graphical representation of knowledge.

knowledge discovery in databases (KDD)   A machine learning process that performs rule induction, or a related procedure to establish knowledge from large databases.

knowledge discovery   A machine learning process that performs rule induction, or a related procedure for establishing knowledge from large databases or textual sources.

knowledge elicitation   The act of extracting knowledge, generally automatically, from nonhuman sources; machine learning.

knowledge engineer   An AI specialist responsible for the technical side of developing an expert system. The knowledge engineer works closely with the domain expert to capture the expert's knowledge in a knowledge base.

knowledge engineering (KE)   The engineering discipline in which knowledge is integrated into computer systems to solve complex problems normally requiring a high level of human expertise.

knowledge inferencing   *See* inferencing.

knowledge interchange format (KIF)   A computer-oriented language used in the interchange of knowledge among disparate programs.

knowledge management   The active management of the expertise in an organization. It involves collecting, categorizing, and disseminating knowledge.

knowledge management suites   Knowledge-management software that consists of a comprehensive set of tools.

knowledge management system (KMS)   A system that facilitates knowledge management by ensuring knowledge flow from the person(s) who know to the person(s) who need to know throughout the organization; knowledge evolves and grows during the process.

knowledge map   *See* induction table.

knowledge queries, and manipulation language (KQML)   A language and protocol for exchanging information and knowledge.

knowledge refining system   A system that has the ability to analyze its own performance, learn, and improve itself for future consultations.

knowledge repository   The actual storage location of knowledge in a knowledge management system. Similar in nature to a database, but generally text-oriented.

knowledge representation   A formalism for representing facts and rules in a computer about a subject or specialty.

knowledge validation   Testing to determine whether the knowledge in an AI system is correct and whether the system performs with an acceptable level of accuracy.

knowledge warehouse   A repository for an organization's expertise.

knowledge workers   Employees who use knowledge as a significant input to their work.

knowledge-based economy   The modern, global economy which is driven by what people and organizations "know" rather than only by capital and labor.

knowledge-based system   A typically rule-based system for providing expertise. Identical to ES, except that the source of expertise may include documented knowledge.

knowledge-poor procedures   Standard methods for dealing with shallow knowledge domains,

knowledgeware   Artificial intelligence software.

Kohonen self-organizing feature maps   A type of neural network model for machine learning.

L-commerce   E-commerce delivered information about goods and services based on the location of you and your mobile device.

leaky knowledge   *See* explicit knowledge.

learning algorithm   The training procedure used by an artificial neural network.

learning organization   An organization capable of learning from its past experience, implying the existence of an organizational memory and a means to save, represent, and share it through its personnel.

learning rate   A parameter for learning in neural networks. It determines the portion of the existing discrepancy that must be offset.

life-cycle   In system development, a structured approach to the development of information systems in several distinct steps.

linear programming (LP)   A mathematical model for the optimal solution of resource allocation problems. All the relationships among the variables are linear.

LISP (list processor) An AI programming language, created by AI pioneer John McCarthy, that is especially popular in the United States. It is based on manipulating lists of symbols.

LISP machines A single-user computer designed primarily to expedite the development of AI programs. Also called *AI workstations*.

list A written series of related items. Used to represent knowledge.

logic A science of deriving relationships among propositions and arguments. It includes propositional logic and predicate calculus.

machine learning The process by which a computer learns from experience (e.g., using programs that can learn from historical cases).

management science (MS) The application of the scientific approach and mathematical models to the analysis and solution of managerial decision problems.

management-information system (MIS) A business information system designed to provide past, present, and future information appropriate for planning, organizing, and controlling the operations of an organization.

management support system (MSS) The application of any type of decision-support technology to decision-making.

manual methods Manual methods for knowledge acquisition: Knowledge engineers use interviews and observations to elicit knowledge from experts.

manufacturing requirements planning (MRP) A computerized integrated plan for purchasing and/or buying parts and subassemblies used for several items so that inventories are minimized but product deliveries are met on schedule.

massive parallel processing A fine-grained, parallel computing environment in which many small, limited-capability processing elements are used; describes artificial neural networks.

mathematical (quantitative) model A system of symbols and expressions representing a real situation.

mathematical programming An optimization technique for the allocation of resources subject to constraints.

metadata Data about data. In a data warehouse these describe the contents of the data warehouse and the manner of its use.

metaknowledge In an expert system, knowledge about how the system operates or reasons. More generally, knowledge about knowledge.

metarule A rule that describes how other rules should be used or modified.

metasearch engines Search engines that combine results from several different search engines.

microelectronics Miniaturization of electronic circuits and components.

micropayments Payments of small dollar-amounts for goods and services.

mobile agents Intelligent software agents that move from one Internet site to another, retrieving and sending information.

mobile portal Portals that are accessible from mobile devices.

mobility The degree to which agents travel through a computer network.

model base A collection of preprogrammed quantitative models (e.g., statistical, financial, optimization) organized as a single unit.

model base management system (MBMS) Software for establishing, updating, combining, and so on (e.g., managing), a DSS model base.

model building blocks Preprogrammed software elements that can be used to build computerized models. For example, a random-number generator can be employed in the construction of a simulation model.

model marts Small, generally departmental repositories of knowledge created by employing knowledge-discovery techniques on past decision instances. Similar to *data marts. Also see* model warehouses.

model warehouses Large, generally enterprise-wide repositories of knowledge created by employing knowledge-discovery techniques on past decision instances. Similar to *data warehouses. Also see* model marts.

model-based reasoning *See* model-based system.

model-based system (or reasoning) An application whose knowledge is derived by a mathematical (or other type of) model.

modeling tools Software programs that enable the building of mathematical models quickly. Spreadsheets and planning languages are modeling tools.

modified Turing test A test in which a manager is shown two solutions, one derived by a computer and one by a human, and is asked to compare them.

modus ponens An inference rule type which the rule "A implies B" justifies B by the existence of A.

modus tollens An inference rule type in which the rule "A implies B" may be true, but B is known to be false, implying that A is false.

momentum A learning parameter in feedforward-back-propagation neural networks.

Monte Carlo simulation A mechanism that uses random numbers to predict the behavior of an event whose probability is known.

multiagent system A system with multiple cooperating software agents.

multiagents *See* multiagent system.

multicriteria modeling *See* multiple goals.

multidimensional analysis An analysis of data by three or more dimensions. *See* multidimensionality.

multidimensional modeling A modeling method that involves data analysis in several dimensions. *See* multidimensional analysis.

multidimensional scaling A method that identifies various dimensions of knowledge and then arranges it in the form of a distance matrix. It uses least-squares fitting regression to analyze, interpret, and integrate the data.

multidimensional spreadsheets Spreadsheet software systems that manipulate spreadsheets in more than two dimensions. Multidimensional spreadsheets work with data cubes.

multidimensionality Organizing, presenting, and analyzing data by several dimensions, such as sales by region, by product, by salesperson, and by time (four dimensions).

multiple-criteria problem (multicriteria problem) *See* multiple goals.

multiple experts Two or more experts used as the source of knowledge for an expert system.

multiple goals Refers to a decision situation in which alternatives are evaluated with several, sometimes conflicting, goals.

multiple knowledge representation The use of two or more representations of knowledge in an expert system; for example, frames and rules.

multiple-objective problem (multiobjective problem) *See* multiple goals.

mutation A genetic operator that causes a random change in a potential solution.

MYCIN An early rule-based expert system, developed by Edward H. Shortliffe, that helps to identify types of blood infections and prescribe appropriate antibiotics.

natural language A language spoken by humans on a daily basis, such as English, French, Japanese, or German.

natural language interface A user interface that uses a natural (human) language for interaction.

natural language processing (NLP) Using a natural language processor to interface with a computer-based system.

natural language processor An AI-based user interface that allows the user to interact with a computer-based system in much the same way that he or she would converse with another human.

need assessment An analysis to determine whether an MSS is worth developing.

neural computing (networks) An experimental computer design aimed at building intelligent computers that operate in a manner modeled on the functioning of the human brain. *See* artificial neural networks (CANN).

neural network *See* artificial neural networks (ANN).

neurons Cells (processing elements) of a biological or artificial neural network.

nominal group technique (NGT) A simple brainstorming process for nonelectronic meetings.

nonprogrammed problem *See* unstructured decisions.

normative models Models that prescribe how a system should operate.

nucleus The central processing portion of a neuron.

numeric processing The traditional use of computers to manipulate numbers.

O-A-V triplet A knowledge representation using objects, attributes, and values.

object A person, place, or thing about which information is collected, processed, or stored.

object-oriented database management system (OODBMS) A database that is designed and manipulated using the object-oriented approach.

object-oriented model base management system (OOMBMS) An MBMS constructed in an object-oriented environment.

object-oriented programming A language for representing objects and processing these representations by sending messages and activating methods.

online (commercial) databases External databases provided to organizations and individuals for a fee.

online analytical processing (OLAP) An information system that enables the user, while at a PC, to query the system, conduct an analysis, and so on. The result is generated in seconds.

open systems Computer systems on a network that permit the software and hardware of any vendor to be used by any user.

operational models Models that represent problems for the operational level of management.

operations research (OR) *See* management science.

optimal solution The best possible solution to a modeled problem.

optimization The process of identifying the best possible solution to a problem.

organizational agent *See* public agent.

organizational computing Organization-wide information systems and knowledge management.

organizational culture The aggregate attitudes in an organization concerning a certain issue (e.g., technology, computers, DSS).

organizational decision-support system (ODSS) A networked DSS that serves people at several locations, usually dealing with several decisions.

organizational intelligence *See* knowledge warehouse.

organizational knowledge base An organization's knowledge repository.

organizational learning The process of capturing knowledge and making it available enterprise-wide.

organizational memory That which an organization "knows."

ossified cases Cases that have been analyzed and have no further value.

outcome variable *See* result variable.

overexpectations   Assumptions that a system can deliver more than it actually can; especially common in regard to early AI systems.

paradigmatic cases   A case that is unique that can be maintained to derive new knowledge for the future.

parallel processing   An advanced computer processing technique that allows a computer to perform multiple processes at once—in parallel.

parallelism   In a group-support system, a process gain in which everyone in a group can work simultaneously (in brainstorming, voting, ranking, etc.).

parameters   Fixed factors, not under the control of the decision-maker, that affect the result variables in a decision situation.

pattern matching   *See* pattern recognition. Sometimes this term refers specifically to matching the IF and THEN parts in rule-based systems. In this case, pattern matching can be considered one area of pattern recognition.

pattern recognition   The technique of matching an external pattern to one stored in a computer's memory; used in inference engines, image processing, neural computing, and speech recognition (in other words, the process of classifying data into predetermined categories).

perceptron   Early neural network structure that uses no hidden layer.

personal agent   *See* private agent.

personal construct theory   An approach in which each person is viewed as a "personal scientist" who seeks to predict and control events by forming theories, testing hypotheses, and analyzing results of experiments.

personal digital assistant (PDA)   A (usually) handheld device that employs agent technology to help handle an individual's day-to-day activities (appointments, etc.).

personality (temperament) type   A person's general attitude. It influences the person's orientation toward goal attainment, selection of alternatives, treatment of risk, and reactions under stress.

person-to-person payments   Enables the transfer of funds between two individuals for a variety of purposes.

phased development   A methodology that involves breaking a system up into a series of versions that are developed sequentially. Each version has more functionality than the previous one, and they evolve into a final system.

physical integration   The seamless integration of several systems into one functioning system.

pop-under/pop-up ad   An ad that appears underneath the current browser window and is seen by the user when the active window is closed.

practice approach   The practice approach toward knowledge management focuses on building the social environments or communities of practice necessary to facilitate the sharing of tacit understanding. *See* personalization strategy.

predicate logic (calculus)   A logical system of reasoning used in AI programs to indicate relationships among data items. The basis of the computer language PROLOG.

principle of choice   The criterion for making a choice among alternatives.

privacy   Privacy means different things to different people. In general, *privacy* is the right to be left alone and the right to be free of unreasonable personal intrusions. *Information privacy* is the right to determine when, and to what extent, information about oneself can be communicated to others.

private agent   An agent that works for only one person.

problem management   Dividing a decision-making process into steps and supporting the functional requirements of these steps.

problem ownership   The jurisdiction (authority) to solve a problem.

problem-solving   A process in which one starts from an initial state and proceeds to search through a problem space to identify a desired goal.

procedural (numeric) reasoning   A reasoning method that utilizes a numeric rather than a symbolic approach.

procedural knowledge   Information about courses of action; contrasts with declarative knowledge.

procedural rules   Rules that advise on how to solve a problem, given that certain facts are known.

process approach   The process approach to knowledge management attempts to codify organizational knowledge through formalized controls, processes and technologies. *See* codification strategy.

process gain   In GSS, improvements in the effectiveness of the activities of a meeting.

process loss   In GSS, degradation in the effectiveness of the activities of a meeting.

process tracking   Trace the reasoning process for reaching a conclusion by expert systems.

processing elements (PEs)   The neurons in a neural network.

product life-cycle   The process that starts with the creation of a product and ends with its disposal.

product life-cycle management (PLM)   An integrated, information-driven approach to all aspects of a product's life, from its design through manufacture, deployment, and maintenance, culminating in the product's removal from service and final disposal.

production rules   A knowledge representation method in which knowledge is formalized into rules containing an IF part and a THEN part (also called a condition and an action, respectively).

productivity   The ratio of outputs (results) to inputs (resources).

programmed problem   Well-structured problems that are repetitive and routine and for which there are standard models.

project management The activity and methods of directing and controlling a project.

PROLOG A high-level computer language based on the concepts of predicate calculus.

propositional logic A formal logical system of reasoning in which conclusions are drawn from a series of statements according to a strict set of rules.

protocol analysis A set of instructions governing the format and control of data in moving from one medium to another.

prototyping In system development, a strategy in which a scaled-down system or portion of a system is constructed in a short time, tested, and improved in several iterations.

public agent An agent that serves any user.

public exchanges E-marketplaces in which there are many sellers and many buyers.

pure play companies *See* virtual organizations.

qualitative reasoning (QR) A means of representing and making inferences using general physical knowledge about the world.

quality of life A usually descriptive measure of how well life is treating people in the workplace and the home; often used to describe the impact of MSS.

quantitative software packages Preprogrammed (sometimes called ready-made) models and optimization systems; sometimes they serve as building blocks for other quantitative models.

query facility The mechanism that accepts requests for data, accesses them, manipulates them, and queries them.

query language A language provided as part of a DBMS for easy access to data in the database.

query tools A DBMS subsystem that provides easy access to data in the database.

rapid application development (RAD) A development methodology that adjusts a system development lifecycle so that parts of the system can be developed quickly, thereby enabling users to obtain some functionality as soon as possible. It includes methods of phased development, prototyping, and throwaway prototyping.

rapid prototype In expert systems development, an initial version of an expert system (usually one with 25 to 200 rules) that is quickly developed to test the effectiveness of the proposed knowledge representation and inference mechanisms in solving a particular problem.

ready-made expert systems Mass-produced expert system packages that can be purchased from software companies. They are fairly general in nature.

ready-made quantitative models Mass-produced quantitative analysis models for specific vertical markets, such as vehicle routing and product mixing.

ready-made systems Mass-produced system packages that can be purchased from software companies. They are fairly general in nature.

real-time The actual occurrence of events; refers to results given rapidly enough to be useful in directly controlling a physical process or guiding a human user.

real-time system A system that is synchronized to run in real time. *See* real-time.

recommendation systems A computer system that can suggest new items to a user based on his revealed preference. It may be content-based or collaborative filtering to suggest items that match the preference of the user. An example is that Amazon.com's function of "Other people bought this book also bought . . ." function.

recommender systems *See* recommendation systems.

recurrent network A particular type of artificial neural networks that allows the recurrent connections of neurons.

regression analysis A trend analysis method based on a statistical forecasting model.

relational database A database whose records are organized into tables that can be processed by either relational algebra or relational calculus.

relational model base management system (RMBMS) The relational approach (as in relational databases) to the design and development of a model base management system.

repertory grid analysis A tool used by psychologists to represent a person's view of a problem in terms of its elements and constructs.

reproduction The creation of new generations of improved solutions with the use of a genetic algorithm.

resolution A reasoning approach in artificial intelligence.

result (outcome) variable A variable that expresses the result of a decision (e.g., one concerning profit), usually one of the goals of a decision-making problem.

reverse auctions One buyer who wants to buy a product or a service; suppliers are invited to submit bids; lowest bid wins; several rounds can take place if the lowest bid is not satisfactory to the seller.

reverse logistics A flow of material or finished goods back to the source; for example, the return of defective products by customers.

risk A probabilistic or stochastic decision situation.

risk analysis A decision-making method that analyzes the risk (based on assumed known probabilities) associated with different alternatives. Also known as *calculated risk*.

robotics The science of using a machine (a robot) to perform manual functions without human intervention.

role ambiguity A situation in which the role to be performed by an employee is not clear. Lack of a job description and changing conditions often result in role ambiguity.

rule A formal way of specifying a recommendation, directive, or strategy, expressed as an IF premise and a THEN conclusion and possibly an ELSE conclusion.

rule induction The creation of rules by a computer from examples of problems for which the outcome is known. These rules are then generalized to other cases.

rule interpreter The inference mechanism in a rule-based system.

rule-based system A system in which knowledge is represented completely in terms of rules (e.g., a system based on production rules).

SAP R/3 The most widely used ERP product, from SAP A.G. (Germany). It is a highly integrated package.

satisficing A process by which one seeks a solution that will satisfy a set of constraints. In contrast to optimization, which seeks the best possible solution, satisficing simply seeks a solution that will work (well enough).

scenario A statement of assumptions and configurations concerning the operating environment of a particular system at a particular time.

script A framelike structure representing a stereotyped sequence of events (e.g., eating at a restaurant).

search engines Program that finds and lists Web sites or pages (designated by URLs) that match some user-selected criteria.

segmentation Dividing markets into specific groups.

self-evolving DSS A special type of intelligent DSS.

self-organizing A neural network architecture that uses unsupervised learning.

semantic network A knowledge representation method consisting of a network of nodes, representing concepts or objects, connected by arcs describing the relations between the nodes.

semantic Web *See* semantic web services.

semantic Web services An extension of XML that allows semantic information to be represented in web services.

semiautomatic methods Knowledge acquisition methods that use computer-based tools to support knowledge engineers in order to facilitate the process.

semistructured decisions Decisions in which some aspects of the problem are structured and others are unstructured.

sensitivity analysis A study of the effect of a change in one or more input variables on a proposed solution.

shallow knowledge A representation of only surface-level information that can be used to deal with very specific situations.

shallow (surface) representation A model that does not capture all the forms of knowledge used by experts in their reasoning. Contrasts with deep representation.

shell Software for systems development that consists of the basic structure of the system without the details related to a specific problem. A complete expert system stripped of its specific knowledge. In rule-based systems, it is a kind of expert system development tool consisting of two standalone pieces of software—a rule-set manager and an inference engine capable of reasoning with the rule set built with the rule-set manager.

sigmoid (logical activation) function An S-shaped transfer function in the range of zero to one.

simulation An imitation of reality.

slot A subelement of a frame of an object. A particular characteristic, specification, or definition used in forming a knowledge base.

social computing The use of computing and telecommunications for socialization, discussion, and so on, instead of face-to-face interaction.

soft information Fuzzy, unofficial, intuitive, subjective, nebulous, implied, or vague information.

softbots (intelligent software robots) Software agents with learning capabilities.

software agents *See* softbots and intelligent agent (IA).

software intelligent agent (IA) *See* softbots; intelligent agent.

spamming Indiscriminate distribution of e-mail messages (junk e-mail).

specific DSS (application) A system that actually accomplishes a specific task. It is similar to application software in conventional MIS.

specific expert systems An expert system that advises users on a specific issue.

speech recognition Translation of the human voice into individual words and sentences understandable by a computer.

speech understanding An area of AI research that attempts to allow computers to recognize words or phrases of human speech.

spreadsheet add-in Software programs designed to work with spreadsheets, such as optimization or decision trees.

staff assistant An individual who acts as an assistant to a manager.

static explanation In an ES, associating a fixed explanation text with a rule to explain the rule's meaning.

static models Models that describe a single interval of a situation.

statistical methods Mathematical methodologies based on probability and statistical theory.

status access A rapid access to current information, provided by a computer.

sticky knowledge *See* tacit knowledge.

stories Cases with rich information and episodes. Lessons may be derived from this kind of cases in a case base.

strategic models Models that represent problems for the strategic level (executive level) of management.

structured decisions Standard or repetitive decision situations for which solution techniques are already available.

structured interview A systematic goal-oriented interviewing process that forces organized communication between the knowledge engineer and the expert.

structured problem *See* structured decisions.

structured query language (SQL)   A data definition and management language of relational databases. It front-ends most relational DBMS.

subjective probability   A probability estimated by a manager without the benefit of a formal model.

suboptimization   An optimization-based procedure that does not consider all the alternatives for or impacts on an organization.

summation function   *See* transformation function.

supervised learning   A method of training artificial neural networks in which sample cases are shown to the network as input and the weights are adjusted to minimize the error in its outputs.

supply chain   The flow of material, information, and money, from the creation of raw materials to their final processing into a product (or service) and the delivery of the product to end-users. It includes all the necessary organizational units, people, and procedures that support the flow.

supply chain management (SCM)   The activities involved in managing supply chains: planning, organizing, staffing, and control.

symbiotic DSS   *See* Active DSS.

symbol   A string of characters that represents a real-world concept.

symbol structures   The meaningful relationships represented in an AI program.

symbolic processing   The use of symbols, rather than numbers, combined with rules of thumb (or heuristics) to process information and solve problems.

synapse   The connection (where the weights are) between processing elements in a neural network.

synchronous   Occurring at the same time.

system   A set of elements considered to act as a single goal-oriented entity.

system advocate   The sponsor who initiates a project.

system analysis   The investigation and recording of existing systems and the conceptual design and feasibility study of new systems.

system builder   A person responsible for the implementation of a system.

system design   The specification of appropriate hardware and software components required to implement an information system.

system development life cycle (SDLC)   A systematic process for the effective construction of large information systems.

tabu search   A memory- and intelligence-based search procedure for computer problem-solving.

tacit knowledge   Knowledge that is usually in the domain of subjective, cognitive, and experiential learning. It is highly personal and hard to formalize.

tactical models   Models that represent problems for the tactical level (mid-level) of management.

team-developed DSS   A team assembled to build a large, usually interdisciplinary DSS.

technology levels of DSS (or ES)   The classification of software as basic development tools, integrated development tools, and completed applications (DSS or ES).

telecommuting   An arrangement whereby employees work at home, generally using a computer or a terminal linked to their place of employment.

teleconferencing   The use of telecommunication for a meeting held in different locations.

temporal reasoning   The ability to reason about the time relationships between events.

threshold value   A hurdle value for the output of a neuron to trigger the next level of neurons. If an output value is smaller than the threshold value, it will not be passed to the next level of neurons.

throwaway prototyping   A development methodology that creates design prototypes to increase understanding of a system that is not clearly understood. These help the user learn about requirements and the final system to be deployed.

time-series analysis   A technique that analyzes historical data over several time periods and then makes a forecast.

toolkit   A collection of related software items that assist a system developer.

top management support   The presence of a top-level manager as a system advocate; one of the most important factors necessary for the introduction of any organizational change.

topologies   The type neurons are organized in a neural network.

training set   A set of data for inducing a knowledge model, such as a rule base or a neural network.

transaction processing system (TPS)   The system that processes an organization's routine, repetitive, basic transactions such as ordering, billing, or paying.

transformation (transfer) function   In a neural network, the function that sums and transforms inputs before a neuron fires. The relationship between the internal activation level and the output of a neuron.

Turing test   A test designed to measure the "intelligence" of a computer.

uncertainty   In expert systems, a value that cannot be determined during a consultation. Many expert systems can accommodate uncertainty; that is, they allow the user to indicate whether he or she does not know the answer.

uncertainty avoidance   The omission of uncertainty from a stochastic model.

uncertainty processing   Estimating and aggregating uncertainties in rule inferencing.

uncontrollable variables   Factors that affect the result of a decision but are not under the control of the decision-maker. They can be internal (e.g., related to technology or to policies) or external (e.g., related to legal issues or to climate).

undocumented knowledge   Knowledge that comes from nondocumented sources, such as human experts.

unstructured decisions   Complex decisions for which no standard solutions exist.

unstructured (informal) interview   An informal interview that acquaints a knowledge engineer with an expert's problem-solving domain.

unstructured problems   *See* unstructured decisions.

unsupervised learning   A method of training artificial neural networks in which only input stimuli are shown to the network, which is self-organizing.

user commitment   The extent to which a user buys into an MSS. A critical success factor in developing MSS.

user-developed DSS   A DSS developed by one user or by a few users in one department.

user interface (or human–machine interface)   The component of a computer system that allows bidirectional communication between the system and its user.

user interface management system (UIMS)   *See* dialog generation; management system.

user interface objects   In a Windows or other object-oriented environment, menus, hot keys, buttons, and other icons used by the user interface.

user resistance   The behavioral aspects of the refusal of users to use new technology or of their attempts to sabotage it.

validation   Determination of whether the right system was built.

value chain   The actual steps an item follows as it moves along the supply chain. *See* value chain model.

value chain model   A model developed by Michael Porter that describes how value is added when a product moves along the supply chain. There are primary activities that add value directly (e.g., manufacturing, testing, storage) and secondary activities that support the primary activities (e.g., accounting, personnel, engineering).

value system   In a firm's value chain, the suppliers and other business partners and their supply chains.

verification   Confirmation that a system was built to specifications (correctly).

virtual community   *See* electronic communities

virtual corporation   An organization in which people work wherever and whenever it is appropriate. Also called *virtual enterprise.*

virtual learning   *See* distance learning.

virtual organization (pureplay companies)   A partnership of several organizations created for a specific accomplishment (usually short-term). Each partner stays with a permanent organization and communicates and collaborates electronically.

virtual reality (VR)   A three-dimensional interactive technology that gives the user a sense of being physically present in a real world.

virtual reality markup language (VRML)   An Internet language for the Web that enables coding of three-dimensional graphics.

virtual workspace (virtual workplace)   The "place" where virtual meetings occur.

visual interactive modeling (VIM)   Graphical animation in which systems and processes are presented dynamically to the decision-maker. It enables visualization of the results of different potential actions.

visual interactive simulation (VIS)   A special case of VIM in which a simulation approach is used in the decision-making process.

visual recognition   The addition of some form of computer intelligence and decision-making to digitized visual information, received from a machine sensor such as a camera.

visual simulation   *See* visual interactive simulation.

walk-through (or talk-through)   In knowledge engineering, a process whereby the expert walks (or talks) the knowledge engineer through the solution to a problem.

Web   Abbreviation for World Wide Web.

Webcasting   Customized broadcasting over the Web where the information, as it becomes available, appears on the user's screen in a ticker-tape format (push technology).

Web analytics   The application of business analytics activities to Web-based processes, especially electronic commerce.

Web intelligence   The application of business intelligence activities to Web-based processes, especially electronic commerce.

Web-mining   Data mining on the Internet via intelligent agents. It involves information discovery, extraction, summarization, and generalization.

weights   Values assigned to each connection at the input to a neuron. Analogous to a synapse in the brain. Weights control the inflow to the processing elements in neural networks.

what-if analysis   Asking a computer what the effect of changing some of the input data or parameters would be.

wizards   Software agents that conduct routine tasks for users.

World Wide Web   A set of standard protocols for organizing, storing, and retrieving information on the Internet. Also called *the Web.*

REFERENCES

"2002 Decision Analysis Survey" in *OR/MS Today*, June 2002.

Abbott, B. (2000, October 2). "Software Failure Can Lead to Financial Catastrophe." *InfoWorld*.

Abramson, G. (1998, June 15). "Measuring Up." *CIO*.

Abramson, G. (1999, May 15). "On the KM Midway." *CIO* (Enterprise Section 2).

Adams, A. R. (2001, September). "Beyond Numbers and Demographics: 'Experience-Wear' Exploration of the Digital Divide." *Computers & Society*.

Adams, K. C. (2001, October 24). "Peak Performance." *Intelligent Enterprise*.

Adeli, H., and S. Hung. (1995). *Machine Learning: Neural Networks, Genetic Algorithms and Fuzzy Systems*. New York: John Wiley.

Adelman, L. (1992). *Evaluating Decision Support and Expert Systems*. New York: John Wiley.

Adelman, S., and L. Moss. (2001, Winter). "Data Warehouse Risks." *Journal of Data Warehousing*, Vol. 6, No. 1.

Agans, D. J. (2002). *Debugging: The 9 Indispensable Rules for Finding Even the Most Elusive Software and Hardware Problems*. Amacom Books.

Agatstein, K., and J. B. Rieley. (1998, Winter). "Using Simulation to Improve the Decision-making Process." *National Productivity Review*, Vol. 18, No. 1.

Agosta, L. (2002). *The Essential Guide to Data Warehousing*. Upper Saddle River, NJ: Prentice Hall PTR.

Agosto, D. E. (2002, January). "Bounded Rationality and Satisficing in Young People's Web-Based Decision Making." *Journal of the American Society for Information Science and Technology*, Vol. 53, No. 1.

Agrawal, M., et al. (2001). "The False Promise of Mass Customization." *McKinsey Quarterly*, No. 3.

Agrew, M. (2000, July 10). "Collaboration on the Desktop." *InformationWeek*.

AI Letter. (1988, June; 1989, April). Dallas: Texas Instruments.

Aiba, H., and T. Terano. (1996). "A Computational Model for Distributed Knowledge Systems with Learning Mechanisms." *Expert Systems with Applications*, Vol. 10, Nos. 3 and 4.

Ainscough, T. L., and J. E. Aronson. (1999). "A Neural Networks Approach for the Analysis of Scanner Data." *Journal of Retailing and Consumer Services*, Vol. 6.

Ainscough. T. L., J. E. Aronson, and T. M. Seiler. (1997, June). "Neural Network Applications in Business." *Journal of Applied Management and Entrepreneurship*, Vol. 3, No. 2.

Akarte, M. M., N. V. Surendra, B. Ravi, and N. Rangaraj. (2001, May). "Web Based Casting Supplier Evaluation Using Analytical Hierarchy Process." *Journal of the Operational Research Society*, Vol. 52, No. 5.

Akkermans, H., and K. van Helden. (2002, March). "Vicious and Virtuous Cycles in ERP Implementation: A Case Study of Interrelations Between Critical Success Factors." *European Journal of Information Systems*, Vol. 11, No. 1.

Aksoy, Y., and A. Derbez. (2003, June). "Supply Chain Management." *OR/MS Today*, Vol. 30, No. 3.

Alavi, M. (2000). "Managing Organizational Knowledge." Chapter 2 in W. R. Zmud, (ed.). *Framing the Domains of IT Management: Projecting the Future*. Cincinnati: Pinnaflex Educational Resources.

Alavi, M., and D. Leidner. (1999, February). "Knowledge Management Systems: A Descriptive Study of Key Issues, Challenges, and Benefits." *Communications of the AIS*.

Alavi, M., and D. Leidner. (2001, March). "Knowledge Management and Knowledge Management Systems: Conceptual Foundation and An Agenda for Research." *MIS Quarterly*, 107-136.

Alavi, M., and E. A. Joachimsthaler. (1992, March). "Revisiting DSS Implementation Research: A Meta-analysis of the Literature and Suggestions for Researchers." *MIS Quarterly*, Vol. 16, No. 1.

Alavi, M., T. Kayworth, and D. Leidner. (2003). "An Empirical Investigation of the Impact of Organizational Culture on KM Initiatives." Working Paper, Baylor University, Waco, TX.

Alavi, M., et al. (1995, September). "Using IT to Re-engineer Business Education: An Exploratory Investigation of Collaborative Telelearning." *MIS Quarterly*.

Albaum, G., and J. Herche. (1999). "Management Style Comparisons Among Five European Nations." *Journal of Global Marketing*, Vol. 12, No. 4.

Alexander, S. (2003, February 24). "Web Site Adds Inventory Control and Forecasting." *Computer World*.

Allan, J., G. Fairtlough, and B. Heinzen. (2002). *Decision Making: The Power of the Tale: Using Narratives for Organizational Success*. New York: John Wiley.

Allard, S. (2003). "Knowledge Creation." Chapter 18 in C. W. Holsapple (ed.). *Handbook of Knowledge Management: Knowledge Matters*, Vol. 1. Heidelberg, Germany: Springer Verlag.

Allee, V. (1997, November). "12 Principles of Knowledge Management." *Training and Development*, Vol. 51, No. 11.

Allee, V. (1999, September). "Are You Getting Big Value from Knowledge?" *KMWorld,* pp. 16–17.

Allen, B. P. (1994, March). "Case-Based Reasoning: Business Applications." *Communications of the ACM,* Vol. 37, No. 3.

Allan, R. G. (2001, Summer). "Data Models for a Registrar's Data Mart." *Journal of Data Warehousing.* Vol. 6, No. 3.

Alpar, P., and W. Dilger. (1995, October). "Market Share Analysis and Prognosis Using Qualitative Reasoning." *Decision Support Systems,* Vol. 15, No. 2.

Alter, S. L. (1980). *Decision Support Systems: Current Practices and Continuing Challenges.* Reading, MA: Addison-Wesley.

Althoff, K. D., et al. (1995). *A Review of Industrial Case-Based Reasoning Tools.* San Francisco: AI Intelligence Publishing.

Altier, W. J. (1999). *The Thinking Manager's Toolbox.* Oxford, UK: Oxford University Press.

Alwast, T., and I. Miliszewska. (1995). "An Agent-Based Architecture for Intelligent DSS for Natural Resource Management." *New Review of Expert Systems.*

Al-Zobaidie, A., and J. B. Grimson. (1987, February). "Expert Systems and Database Systems: How Can They Serve Each Other?" *Expert Systems.*

Ambrosio, J. (2000, July 3). "Knowledge Management Mistakes." *ComputerWorld,* Vol. 34, No. 27.

Amor, D. (2001). *How Pervasive Computing Services Will Change the World.* Upper Saddle River, NJ: Prentice Hall/PTR.

Anandarajan, M. (2002, January). "Internet Abuse in the Workplace." *Communications of the ACM.*

Anders, U., O. Korn, and C. Schmitt. (1998, September/November). "Improving the Pricing of Options: A Neural Network Approach." *Journal of Forecasting,* Vol. 17, Nos. 5 and 6.

Anderson, E. E. (1990, Spring). "Choice Models for the Evaluation and Selection of Software Packages." *Journal of MIS.*

Andries, F., et al. (2002). "The Use of Computers Among the Works in the European Union and Its Impact on the Quality of Work." *Behavior and Information Technology,* Vol. 21, No. 6.

Andreu, R., and C. Ciborra. (1996, June). "Organisational Learning and Core Capabilities Development: The Role of IT." *Strategic Information Systems,* Vol. 5, No. 2.

Andrews, J., and D. C. Smith. (1996, May). "In Search of the Marketing Imagination: Factors Affecting the Creativity of Marketing Programs for Mature Products." *Journal of Marketing Research,* Vol. 33.

Andrienko, G., N. Andrienko, and P. Jankowski. (2002, July). "Building Spatial Decision Support Tools for Individuals and Groups." *Proceedings of DSIage 2002,* Cork, Ireland.

Angele, J., D. Fensel, and R. Studer. (1993). "Formalizing and Operationalizing Models of Expertise with KARL." Research Report. Karlsruhe, Germany: Institute für Angewandte Informatik und Formale Beschreibungsverfahren, University of Karlsruhe.

Angelov, P. P., and R. A. Buswell. (2003). "Automatic Generation of Fuzzy Rule–Based Models from Data by Genetic Algorithms." *Information Sciences,* Vol. 150, pp. 17–31.

Anguita, D., A. Boni, and G. Parodi. (2000, March). "A Case Study of a Distributed High-Performance Computing System for Neurocomputing." *Journal of Systems Architecture,* Vol. 46, No. 5.

Angus, J. (2001, May). "To Tell the Truth." *Knowledge Management.*

Angus, J., J. Patel, and J. Harty. (1998, March 16). "Knowledge Management: Great Concept . . . But What Is It?" *InformationWeek.*

Anonymous. (1999a, September 15). "The Means to an Edge: Knowledge Management: Key to Innovation." Special Supplement, *CIO.*

Anonymous. (1999b, November). "Credit Risk Analysis Software Makes E-commerce Safer." *ABA Banking Journal,* Vol. 91, No. 11.

Anonymous. (1999c, December). "Tools for Conferences, Meetings, and Distance Learning. *Presentations,"* Vol. 13, No. 12.

Anonymous. (2000, March). "Fuzzy Logic Predicts Accident Risk." *Civil Engineering,* Vol. 70, No. 3.

Anonymous. (2001, March). "Herman Miller Creates Virtual Enterprise with Suppliers." *I/S Analyzer Case Studies.* Vol. 40, No. 3.

Anonymous. (2002a, January/February) "Emerging Trends in Technology." *Financial Executive.* Vol. 18, No. 1.

Anonymous. (2002b, April) "D&B Online Decision-Maker Takes Strain Out of Credit Conundrums." *Information World Review,* No. 179.

Anonymous. (2002d, July). "Conferencing Technologies to Enjoy Robust Year, Sustain Growth Through 2005." *High-Speed Internet Access.* Vol. 18, No. 7.

Anonymous. (2002e, September 30). "35 Years of IT Leadership: The Best and the Worst." *ComputerWorld,* Vol. 36, No. 40.

Anonymous. (2002c, June 13). "EBizinsights Tries to Take the Clickstream Bull by the Horns." *IntelligentEnterprise.*

Ansari, A., S. Essegaier, and R. Kohli. (2000). "Internet Recommendation Systems.", Vol . 37, pp. 363–375.

Anthes, G. H. (2000, June 26). "Software Development Goes Global." *ComputerWorld.*

Anthes, G. H. (2002, April 15). "The Search Is On." *ComputerWorld.*

Anthes, G. H. (2003a, April 14). "The Forecast Is Clear." *ComputerWorld.*

Anthes, G. H. (2003b, June 30). "Hilton Checks into New Suite." *ComputerWorld.*

Anthony, R. N. (1965). *Planning and Control Systems: A Framework for Analysis.* Cambridge, MA: Harvard University Graduate School of Business.

Aparico, G. (1995). "The Role of Intelligent Agents in the Information Infrastructure." IBM's *White Paper,* ctivist.gpl.com:81/WhitePaper/ptc2.htm.

Applegate, D., W. Cook, S. Dash, and A. Rohe. (2002). "Solution of a Min-Max Vehicle Routing Problem." *INFORMS Journal on Computing.* Vol. 14, No. 2.

Appleton, E. L., (1997, March). "How to Survive ERP." *Datamation.*

April, C. A. (2002, November 4). "BAM to Speed App Reports." *InfoWorld.*

April, C. A., and H. Harreld. (2002, September 2). "Seeking CRM Integration." *InfoWorld,* No. 35.

Argyris, C. (1971, February). "Management Information Systems: The Challenge to Rationality and Emotionality." *Management Science,* Vol. 17, No. 6.

Arinze, B., and S. Banerjee. (1992, May). "A Framework for Effective Data Collection, Usage, and Maintenance of DSS." *Information and Management.*

Arisha K. A., et al. (1999, March/April). "Impact: A Platform for Collaborating Agents." *IEEE Intelligent Systems.*

Armstrong, J. S. (ed.). (2001). *Principles of Forecasting.* Norwell, MA: Kluwer Academic Publishers.

Aronson, J. E. (1989). "A Survey of Dynamic Network Flows." *Annals of Operations Research,* Vol. 20.

Aronson, J. E., R. M. Myers, and R. B. Wharton, (2000, June). "Time Pressure Impacts on Electronic Brainstorming in a Group Support System Environment." *Informatica,* Vol. 24, No. 2.

Arsham, H. (2003a). "Applied Management Science: Making Good Strategic Decisions." www.ubmail.ubalt.edu/~harsham/opre640/opre640.htm.

Arsham, H. (2003b). "Decision Science Resources." www.ubmail.ubalt.edu/~harsham/refop/Refop.htm.

Ashling, J. (2003, March) "International Report." *Information Today.* Vol. 20, No. 3.

Aspect Communications. (2003). "Seven Powerful Strategies for Increased CRM Profitability." White Paper, Aspect Communications, San Jose, CA.

Atanackovic, D., D. T. McGillis, F. D. Galiana, J. Cheng, and L. Loud. (1997, July/August). "An Integrated Knowledge-Based Model for Power System Planning." *IEEE Expert.*

Athappilly, K. (1985, February). "Successful Decision Making Starts with DSS Evaluation." *Data Management,* Vol. 23, No. 2.

Atre, S. (2003, June 30). "The Top 10 Critical Challenges for Business Intelligence Success." *ComputerWorld,* White Paper/Special Advertising Supplement, Vol. 37, No. 26.

Ausubel, D. P. (2000). *The Acquisition and Retention of Knowledge: A Cognitive View,* Boston: Kluwer Academic Publishers.

Austen, L. (2002, August 24–25). "Information at Hand: Hospitals Are Adapting to Computers." *International Herald Tribune.*

Austin, M., et al. (1997). "Security Market Timing Using Neural Network Models." *Review of Applied Expert Systems.*

Avouris, M., and L. Gasser. (1992). *Distributed Artificial Intelligence: Theory and Praxis.* Boston: Kluwer Academic.

Avritzer, A., J. P. Ros, and E. J. Weyuker. (1996). "Reliability Testing of Rule-Based Systems." *IEEE Software,* Vol. 13, No. 5.

Awad, E. M. (1996). *Building Expert Systems: Principles, Procedures, and Applications.* Minneapolis/St. Paul: West Publishing.

Azuaje, F., W. Dubitzky, N. Black, and K. Adamson (1999, October). "Improving Clinical Decision Support through Case-Based Data Fusion." *IEEE Transactions on Biomedical Engineering,* Vol. 46, No. 10.

Ba, S., et al. (1997). "Enterprise Decision Support Using Intranet Technology." *Decision Support Systems,* Vol. 20, No. 2.

Baatz, E. B. (1996, May/June). "Will the Web Eat Your Job?" *Webmaster,* Vol. 1. No. 1.

Babyak, R. J. (1999, February). "Brainstorming." *Appliance Manufacturer,* Vol. 47, No. 2.

Bacheldor, B. (2003a, March 3). "Supply on Demand." *InformationWeek.*

Bacheldor, B. (2003b, April 14). "Keep Supply Chains Flowing." *InformationWeek.*

Back, B., T. Laitinen, and K. Sere. (1996). "Neural Networks and Genetic Algorithms for Bankruptcy Predictions." *Expert Systems with Applications,* Vol. 11, No. 4.

Badaracco, J. L. (1991). *The Knowledge Link.* Boston: Harvard Business School Press.

Baer, T. (2002, April). "Analyzing Data in Real Time." *Application Development Trends.*

Bagnoli, C., and H. C. Smith. (1998). "The Theory of Fuzzy Logic and Its Application to Real Estate Valuation." *Journal of Real Estate Research,* Vol. 16, No. 2.

Baker, B. M., and M. A. Syechew. (2003). "A Genetic Algorithm for the Vehicle Routing Problem." *Computers and Operations Research,* Vol. 30, pp. 787–800.

Baker, E.H. (2003). "Project Management." *CIO Insight/Research.*

Baker, T., and N. N. Murthy. (2002, Summer). "A Framework for Estimating the Benefits of Using Auctions in Revenue Management." *Decision Sciences.* Vol. 33, No. 3.

Baker, T. K., and D. A. Collier. (1999, Winter). "A Comparative Revenue Analysis of Hotel Yield Management Heuristics." *Decision Sciences,* Vol. 30, No. 1.

Balabanovic, M., and Y. Shoham, Y. (1997). "Fab: Content-Based Collaborative Recommendaiton." *Communications of the ACM*, Vol. 40, No. 3, pp. 66–72.

Balen, H. (2000, December). "Deconstructing Babel: XML and Application Integration." *Application Development Trends.*

Balentine B., et al., (1999). *How to Build a Speech Recognition Application.* San Francisco: Enterprise Integration Group.

Ballantine, J., et al. (1996, Fall). "The 3-D Model of Information Success: The Search for the Dependent Variable Continues." *Information Resources Management Journal,* Vol. 9, No. 4.

Bankes, A. (2003, April). "Taking on the Challenge of ECM." *KMWorld*, Special Supplement.

Banks, J., J. S. Carson, B.L. Nelson, and D.M. Nicol. (2001). *Discrete-Event System Simulation.* Upper Saddle River, NJ: Prentice Hall.

Bannan, K. J. (2003, January). "The Pulse of the Supply Chain." *Internet World.*

Barba-Romero, S. (2001, July/August). "The Spanish Government Uses a Discrete Multicriteria DSS to Determine Data Processing Acquisitions." *Interfaces.*

Barker, V., and D. O'Connor. (1989, March). "Expert Systems for Configuration at Digital, XCON and Beyond." *Communications of the ACM,* Vol. 32, No. 3.

Barki, H., and J. Hartwick. (1994, March). "Measuring User Participation, User Involvement, and User Attitude." *MIS Quarterly,* Vol. 18, No. 1.

Barquin, R., and H. Edelstein. (eds.). (1997a). *Planning and Designing the Data Warehouse.* Upper Saddle River, NJ: Prentice Hall PTR.

Barquin, R., and H. Edelstein. (eds.). (1997b). *Building, Using, and Managing the Data Warehouse.* Upper Saddle River, NJ: Prentice Hall PTR.

Barquin, R., and H. Edelstein. (1997c). *Data Mining Techniques for Marketing, Sales and Customer Support.* New York: Wiley.

Barquin, R. C., A. Paller, and H. Edelstein. (1997). "Ten Mistakes to Avoid for Data Warehousing Managers." Chapter 7 in R. Barquin and H. Edelstein. (eds.). *Building, Using, and Managing the Data Warehouse.* Upper Saddle River, NJ: Prentice Hall PTR.

Barrett, A. R., and J. S. Edwards. (1994). "Knowledge Elicitation and Knowledge Representation in a Large Domain with Multiple Experts." *Expert Systems with Applications,* Vol. 8.

Barsanti, J. B. (1990, Winter). "Expert Systems: Critical Success Factors for Their Implementation." *Information Executive,* Vol. 3, No. 1.

Barth, P. S. (1997). "Mining for Profits in the Data Warehouse." Chapter 8 in R. Barquin, and H. Edelstein. (eds.). *Planning and Designing the Data Warehouse.* Upper Saddle River, NJ: Prentice Hall PTR.

Barth, S. (2000a, February). "Knowledge as a Function of X." *Knowledge Management.*

Barth, S., (2000b, October). "KM Horror Stories." *Knowledge Management.*

Barth, S. (2001, April). "Learning from Mistakes." *Knowledge Management.*

Bartholomew, D. (2003, May 13). "Backers of PLM Claim the Software Speeds Manufacturing, Cuts R&D Costs and Boosts Sales." *CFO.*

Bartos, F. J. (1999, May). "Motion Control Tunes into AI Methods." *Control Engineering,* Vol. 46, No. 5.

Basden, A. (1994, May). "Three Levels of Benefits in Expert Systems." *Expert Systems,* Vol. 11, No. 2.

Bauer, T., and D. Leake. (2002). "Using Document Access Sequences to Recommend Customized Information." *IEEE Intelligent Systems*, Vol. 17, No. 6, pp. 27–33.

Baum, D. (1996, November). "U.N. Automates Payroll with AI System." *Datamation,* Vol. 42, No. 17.

Bayles, D. (1996). *Intranets: Planning and Implementing the Enterprise.* Upper Saddle River, NJ: Prentice Hall.

Bayles, D. L. (2001). *E-Commerce Logistics and Fulfillment.* Upper Saddle River, NJ: Prentice Hall.

Bazerman, M.H. (2001). *Judgment in Managerial Decision Making.* 5th ed. New York: John Wiley.

Beach, L. R. (1997). *The Psychology of Decision Making: People in Organizations.* Thousand Oaks, CA: Sage Publications.

Bean, R., and R. Radford. (2001). *The Business of Innovation: Managing the Corporate Imagination for Maximum Results.* Amacom Books, New York.

Beazley, H., J. Boenisch, and D. Harden. (2002). *Continuity Management: Preserving Corporate Knowledge and Productivity When Employees Leave.* New York: John Wiley.

Bebenham, J. (1998). *Knowledge Engineering.* Berlin: Springer-Verlag.

Beck, D. F., et al. (1999, June). "Landscapes, Games, and Maps for Technology Planning." Chemtech.

Becker, G. (1999). "Knowledge Discovery." In J. Liebowitz (ed.). *Knowledge Management Handbook.* Boca Raton, FL: CRC Press.

Beckley, G. B., and M. Gaines. (1990, August 6). "12 Tips for Better Systems Implementation." *ComputerWorld*, Vol. 24, No. 32.

Bednarz, A. (2003, March 31). "EAI Vendors Move Beyond Integration." *Network World*, Vol. 20, No. 13.

Beer M., et al. (1999). "Negotiation in Multi-Agents Systems." *Knowledge Engineering Review,* Vol. 14, No. 3.

Beerel, A. (1993). *Expert Systems in Business: Real World Applications.* New York: Ellis Horwood.

Belange, F., and J. Deannett. (2000). *Evaluation and Implementation of Distance Learning: Technologies, Tools and Techniques.* Hershey, PA: Idea Group Publishing.

Belenguer, J. M., M. C. Martinez, and E. Mota. (2000, September/October). "A Lower Bound for the Split Delivery Vehicle Routing Problem." *Operations Research.* Vol. 48, No. 5.

Bell, D. E., and A. Schleifer, Jr. (1996). *Decision Making Under Uncertainty.* Cambridge, MA: Course Technology.

Bell, L. (2003, June). "For Pfizer, AlphaBlox Is Just What the Doctor Ordered." *What Works: Best Practices in Business Intelligence and Data Warehousing*, Vol. 10. Chatsworth, CA: Data Warehousing Institute.

Bell, L. D. (2001, Spring). "MetaBusiness Meta Data for the Masses: Administering Knowledge Sharing for Your Data Warehouse." *Journal of Data Warehousing*, Vol. 6, No. 2.

Bell, P. C., C. K., Anderson, D. S. Staples, and M. Elder. (1999, April). "Decision-Makers' Perceptions of the Value and Impact of Visual Interactive Modeling." *Omega*, Vol. 27, No. 2.

Beltratti, A., S. Margarita, and P. Terna. (1996). *Neural Networks for Economic and Financial Modeling.* London: International Thomson Computer Press.

Belz, R., and P. Mertens. (1996, May 21). "Combining Knowledge-Based Systems and Simulation to Solve Rescheduling Problems." *Decision Support Systems*, Vol. 17, No. 2.

Benaroch, M., and V. Dhar. (1995, October). "Controlling the Complexity of Investment Decisions Using Qualitative Reasoning Techniques." *Decision Support Systems*, Vol. 15, No. 2.

Benders, J., and F. Manders. (1993, October). "Expert Systems and Organizational Decision Making." *Information and Management*, Vol. 25, No. 4.

Benjamin, C. O., and J. Bannis. (1990, May). "A Hybrid Neural Network/Expert System for the Property Casualty Insurance Industry." *Proceedings of the Fourth International Conference on Expert Systems in POM.* Chapel Hill: University of North Carolina Press.

Benjamin, C. O., and J. Bannis. (1991). "A Hybrid Neural Network/Expert System for the Property Casualty Insurance Industry." *Proceedings of the IJCNN,* Seattle.

Benjamins, V. R., D. Fensel, S. Decker, and A. G. Perez. (1999). "Building Ontologies for the Internet: A Mid-Term Report." *International Journal of Human–Computer Studies.*

Bennet, D., and A. Bennet. (2003a). "The Rise of the Knowledge Organization." Chapter 1 in C. W. Holsapple (ed.). *Handbook of Knowledge Management: Knowledge Matters*, Vol. 1. Heidelberg: Springer Verlag.

Bennet, A., and A. Bennet. (2003b). "The Partnership Between Organizational Learning and Knowledge Management." Chapter 23 in C. W. Holsapple (ed.). *Handbook of Knowledge Management: Knowledge Matters*, Vol. 1. Heidelberg: Springer-Verlag.

Bennett, D. L. (2002, September 23). "City Fed Up With Computer System." *Atlanta Journal-Constitution.*

Berens, L.V. (2000). *Dynamics of Personality Type: Understanding and Applying Jung's Cognitive Processes.* Huntington Beach, CA: Telos Publications.

Berens, L.V., et al. (2002). *Quick Guide to the 16 Personality Types in Organizations: Understanding Personality Differences in the Workplace.* Huntington Beach, CA: Telos Publications.

Berg, D., and C. Heagele. (1997). "Improving Data Quality: A Management Perspective and Model." Chapter 5 in R. Barquin, and H. Edelstein. (eds.). *Planning and Designing the Data Warehouse.* Upper Saddle River, NJ: Prentice Hall PTR.

Berg, M., and R. K. Wong. (2000, January). "A Multi-Agent Architecture for Cooperative Query Answering." *Proceedings of the Thirty-third Hawaii International Conference on Systems Sciences HICSS–33,* Los Alamitos, CA: IEEE Computer Society.

Berger, N. S. (1999, December). "Pioneering Experiences in Distance Learning: Lessons Learned." *Journal of Management Education*, Vol. 23, No. 6.

Bergeron, B. (2003). *Essentials of Knowledge Management.* New York: Wiley.

Berghel, H. (2000, February). "Identity Theft, Social Security Numbers, and the Web." *Communications of the ACM*, Vol. 43, No. 2.

Berglas, A., and P. Hoare. (1999, July/August). Spreadsheet Errors: Risks and Techniques." *Management Accounting*, Vol. 77, No. 7.

Berinato, S. (2001, July 1). "The Secret to Software Success." *CIO.*

Berkman, E. (2001, April 1). "When Bad Things Happen to Good Ideas." *Darwin.*

Berkman, E. (2001, September 1). "Project Win for J.P. Morgan Partners." *CIO.*

Berkman, E. (2002, May 15). "How to Use the Balanced Scorecard." *CIO.*

Berkowitz, J. (2001, Winter). "Customer Relationship Management (CRM): The Defining Business Initiative of the New Millennium." *Journal of Data Warehousing.* Vol. 6, No. 1.

Berman, S. L., J. Down, and C. W. L. Hill. (2002). "Tacit Knowledge as a Source of Competitive Advantage in the National Basketball Association." *Academy of Management Journal*, Vol. 45, No. 1.

Berndsen, R., and H. Daniels. (1994, January). "Causal Reasoning and Explanation in Dynamic Economic Systems." *Journal of Economic Dynamics and Control,* Vol. 18, No. 1.

Berners-Lee, T., et al. "The Semantic Web." *Scientific American,* Vol. 284, No. 5, pp. 34–43.

Berry, M. J. A. (2000). *Mastering Data Mining: The Art and Science of Customer Relationship Management.* New York: John Wiley.

Berry, M. J. A. (2002). *Mastering Data Mining MS with Data Mining Set.* New York: John Wiley.

Berry, M. J. A. (2003a). *Survey of Text Mining: Clustering, Classification, and Retrieval.* Berlin: Springer-Verlag.

Berry, M. J. A. (2003b). *Data Mining Techniques with Mastering with Data Mining Set.* New York: John Wiley.

Berry, D., and A. Hart (eds.). (1990). *Expert Systems: Human Issues.* New York: Chapman & Hall.

Berry, M. J. A., and G. Linoff. (1997). *Data Mining Techniques: For Marketing, Sales and Customer Support.* New York: John Wiley.

Berson, A., et al. (2000). *Building Data Mining Applications for CRM.* New York: McGraw-Hill.

Berson, A., and S. J. Smith. (1997). *Data Warehousing Data Mining and OLAP.* New York: McGraw-Hill.

Betts, M. (2003, April 14). "Unexpected Insights." *ComputerWorld.*

Bhandari, I., E. Colet, J. Parker, Z. Pines, R. Pratap, and K. Ramanujam. (1997). "Advanced Scout: Data Mining and Knowledge Discovery in NBA Data." *Data Mining and Knowledge Discovery,* Vol. 1. No. 1.

Bhargava, H. K., and R. Krishnan. (1993, January). "Computer-Aided Model Construction." *Decision Support Systems,* Vol. 9, No. 1.

Bhatt, A., and J. Fenner. (2001, July 23). "A Portal Odyssey." *Network Computing.*

Bidgoli, H. (1995, May/June). "Geographic Information Systems: A New Strategic Tool for the 90's and Beyond." *Journal of Systems Management.*

Bieber, M. (1992). "Automating Hypermedia for Decision Support." *Hypermedia,* Vol. 4, No. 2.

Bieber, M. (1995, July). "On Integrating Hypermedia into Decision Support and Other Information Systems." *Decision Support Systems,* Vol. 14, No. 3.

Bielli, M. (1992, August 25). "A DSS Approach to Urban Traffic Management." *European Journal of Operational Research,* Vol. 61, Nos. 1 and 2.

Biggs, M. (1999, July 26). "Enterprise Application Integration Offers Great Benefits After Careful Consideration." *InfoWorld,* Vol. 21, No. 30.

Bigus, J. P. (1996). *Data Mining with Neural Networks.* New York: McGraw-Hill.

Birkman, R. (1995). *True Colors.* Nashville: Thomas Nelson.

Bisby, A. (1999, October 1). "Microsoft Examines Digital Dashboard." *Computer Dealer News,* Vol. 15, No. 37.

Bishopp, F. T., Jr. (1991). "Automated Airline Control Systems: Existing Methodology, Technology Review, and a Suggested Solution Method." Master's thesis, Terry College of Business, University of Georgia, Athens.

Bistline, W. G., Sr., S. Banerjee, and A. Banerjee. (1998, November). "RTSS: An Interactive Decision Support System for Solving Real Time Scheduling Problems Considering Customer and Job Priorities with Schedule Interruptions." *Computers & Operations Research,* Vol. 25, No. 11.

Blachars, D. xyz, at ITWorld. (accessed March 8, 2003).

Blair, J. (2003, June). "Grid Application Design." *eAI Journal.*

Blanning, R. W. (1993, January). "Model Management Systems: An Overview." *Decision Support Systems,* Vol. 9, No. 1.

Bloom, C. P., and R. B. Loftin. (1998). *Facilitating the Development and Use of Interactive Learning Environments.* New York: Erlbaum Associates.

Blodgett, M. (2000, February 1). "Prescription Strength." *CIO.*

Bochner, P. (2003, May). "Dashboards Come into View." *Application Development Trends.*

Bodily, S. E. (1985). *Modern Decision Making.* New York: McGraw-Hill.

Bogarin, J. A. G., and N. F. F. Ebecken. (1996). "Integration of Knowledge Sources for Flexible Pipe Evaluation and Design." *Expert Systems with Applications,* Vol. 10, No. 1.

Boguslavsky, J. (2000, September). "Visualize Large Data Sets Online." *Research & Development.* Vol. 42, No. 9.

Boisvert, L. (2000, Winter). "Web-Based Learning: The Anytime Anywhere Classroom." *Information Systems Management,* Vol. 17, No. 1.

Bolen, A. (2001, November/December). "Data Mining for Text." *SAS.com.*

Bolen, A. (2003, Second Quarter). "Now They're Cooking." *SAS.com.*

Bolles, G. A. (2003, May). "Order Out of Chaos." *CIO Insight.* No. 26.

Bolloju, N. (1999, August). "Decision Model Formulation of Subjective Classification Problem-Solving Knowledge Using a Neuro-Fuzzy Classifier and its Effectiveness." *International Journal of Approximate Reasoning,* Vol. 21.

Bolloju, N., M. Khalifa, and E. Turban. (2002, June). "Integrating Knowledge Management into Enterprise Environments for the Next Generation of Decision Support." *Decision Support Systems,* Vol. 33.

Bonabeau, E., and C. Meyer. (2001, May 1). "Swarm Intelligence: A Whole New Way to Think About Business." *Harvard Business Review.*

Bonczek, R. H., C. W. Holsapple, and A. B. Whinston. (1980). "The Evolving Roles of Models in Decision Support Systems." *Decision Sciences,* Vol. 11, No. 2.

Bond, A. H., and L. Gasser (eds.). (1988). *Readings in Distributed AI.* San Mateo, CA: Morgan Kaufman.

Bonissone, P. P. (1993). "Knowledge Representation and Inference in First-Generation Knowledge-Based Systems." In M. Grabowski and W. A. Wallace (eds.). *Advances in Expert Systems for Management,* Vol. 1. Greenwich, CT: JAI Press.

Bonissone, P. P., and H. E. Johnson, Jr. (1985). "Expert System for Diesel Electric Locomotive Repair." *Human Systems Management,* Vol. 4.

Booker, E. (2000, April 3). "Enterprise Software Projects Rarely Satisfy." *InternetWeek.*

Boonnoon, J. (2000, March 28). "Phone Technology Is Boon for Visually-Impaired." *Nation.*

Boose, J. H. (1989, March). "A Survey of Knowledge Acquisition Techniques and Tools." *Knowledge Acquisition,* Vol. 1.

Boose, J. H., and J. M. Bradshaw. (1993). "Expertise Transfer and Complex Problems: Using AQUINAS as a Knowledge-Acquisition Workbench for Knowledge-Based Systems." In B. G. Buchanan and D. Wilkins (eds.). *Readings in Knowledge Acquisition and Learning: Automating the Construction and Improvement of Expert Systems.* San Mateo, CA: Morgan Kaufmann.

Boose, J. H., and J. M. Bradshaw. (1999, August). "Expertise Transfer and Complex Problems: Using AQUINAS as a Knowledge-Acquisition Workbench for Knowledge-Based Systems." *International Journal of Human–Computer Studies.*

Boose, J. H., and B. R. Gaines (eds.). (1990). *The Foundations of Knowledge Acquisition.* New York: Academic Press.

Borenstein, D. (1998, July). "IDSSFLEX: An Intelligent DSS for the Design and Evaluation of Flexible Manufacturing Systems." *Journal of the Operational Research Society,* Vol. 49, No. 7.

Borges, M. R. S., J. A. Pino, and C. Valle. (2002, July). "On the Implementation and Follow-up of Decisions." *Proceedings of DSIage 2002,* Cork, Ireland.

Borgulya, I. (2002, September). "A Cluster-Based Evolutionary Algorithm for the Single Machine Total Weighted Tardiness-Scheduling Problem for Machine Sequencing." *Journal of Computing and Information Technology.* Vol. 10, No. 3.

Bort, J. (1996, April 29). "Data Mining's Midas Touch." *InfoWorld,* Vol. 18, No. 18.

Bose, R. (1996). "Intelligent Agents Framework for Developing Knowledge-Based DSS for Collaborative Organizational Processes." *Expert Systems with Applications,* Vol. 11, No. 3.

Boslet, M. (2001, August 6–13). "CRM: The Promise, the Peril, the Eye-Popping Price." *Industry Standard.*

Bossaerts, P., L. Fine, and L. Ledyard. (2000, March 27). "Inducing Liquidity in Thin Financial Markets through Combined-Value Trading Mechanisms." Working Paper, California Institute of Technology, Pasadena CA.

Bostrom, R. P., C. Kadlec, and D. Thomas. (2002). "Implementation and Use of Collaboration Technology in e-Learning: The Case of a Joint University-Corporate MBA." In B.E. Munkvold (ed.). *Implementing Collaboration Technologies in Industry: Case Examples and Lessons Learned.* London: Springer.

Bostrom, R. P., R. Watson, and S. T. Kinney (eds.). (1993). *Computer Augmented Teamwork: A Guided Tour.* Florence, KY: Van Nostrand Reinhold.

Boswell, C. (1999, September 27). "Process Simulation Software Offers Efficiency and Savings." *Chemical Market Reporter,* Vol. 256, No. 13.

Bourbaki, N. (1990, July). "Turing, Searle and Thought." *AI Expert.*

Bourjolly, J-M., L. Dejoie, K. Ding, O. Dioume, and M. Lominy. (2001, April). "Canadian Telecom Makes the Right Call." *OR/MS Today.*

Bowden, P. R., P. Halstead, and T. G. Rose. (1996). "Extracting Conceptual Knowledge from Text Using Explicit Relation Markers." In N. Shadbolt, K. O'Hara, and G. Schreiber (eds.). *Advances in Knowledge Acquisition.* Berlin: Springer-Verlag.

Boyd, A. (1998, October). "Airline Alliances." *OR/MS Today.*

Boyd, J. (2001, July 16). "Data Searches Get More Intelligent." *InternetWeek.*

Boyd, J. (2001a, October 8). "Navy to Add Web to Its Battle Plan." *InternetWeek.*

Boyd, J. (2001b, November 12). "Finance Portal Extended: Bank One's FX Trader to Let Third Parties Deal in Foreign Currencies Online." *InternetWeek.*

Brachman, R. J., et al. (1999, October). "Reducing CLASSIC to Practice: Knowledge Representation Theory Meets Reality." *Artificial Intelligence.*

Bradshaw, J. (ed.). (1997). *Software Agents,* Menlo Park, CA: AAAI Press/MIT Press.

Brailsford, T. W. (2001, September/October). "Building a Knowledge Community at Hallmark Cards." *Research Technology Management,* Vol. 44, No. 5.

Brancheau, J. C., et al. (1996, June). "Key Issues in Information Systems Management: 1994–95 SIM Delphi Results." *MIS Quarterly,* Vol. 20, No. 2.

Bratko, I. (2000). *Prolog Programming for Artificial Intelligence,* 3rd ed. Reading, MA: Addison-Wesley.

Brenner, W., et al. (1998). *Intelligent Software Agents.* New York: Spring-Verlag.

Brewin, B., and M. Hablem. (2001, September 10). "Pocket PC OS Gains Enterprise Features." *ComputerWorld,* Vol. 35, No. 37.

Brezillon P., and J. C. Pomeral. (1997, February). "Lessons Learned on Success and Failures of KBSs." *Failures and Lessons Learned in IT Management.*

Briccarello, P., G. Bruno, and E. Ronco. (1995). "REBUS: An Object-Oriented Simulator for Business Processes." *Proceedings of the IEEE Annual Simulation Symposium,* Los Alamitos, CA.

Briggs, D., and D. Arnott. (2002, July 4–7). "Decision Support Systems Failure: An Evolutionary Perspective." *Proceedings of DSIage 2002*, Cork, Ireland.

Brooking, A. (1999). *Corporate Memory: Strategies for Knowledge Management.* London: International Thomson Business Press.

Brooks, D. W., D. E. Nolan, and S. M. Gallagher. (2001). *Web-Teaching: A Guide to Designing Interactive Teaching for the World Wide Web.* 2nd ed. New York: Kluwer Academic/Plenum Publishers.

Brown, D. E., and S. Hagen. (2003, March). "Data Association Method with Applications to Law Enforcement." *Decision Support Systems.*

Brown, J. S., and P. Duguid. (2002). "Organizational Learning and Communities of Practice: Toward a Unified View of Working, Learning, and Innovation." Chapter 7 in Lesser, E.L., M.A. Fontaine, and J.A. Slusher. (eds.). *Knowledge and Communities.* Woburn, MA: Butterworth-Heinemann.

Brown, S. J., and P. Duguid. (2000, May/June). "Balancing Act: How to Capture Knowledge Without Killing It." *Harvard Business Review*, 73–80.

Brun A., and A. Portioli. (1999, October). "Agent-Based Shop-Floor Scheduling of Multi Stage Systems." *Computers and Industrial Engineering.*

Buchanan, G., P. Daunais, and C. Micelli (2000, February) "Enterprise Resource Planning: A Closer Look." *Purchasing Today.*

Buchanan, B. G., and E. H. Shortliffe. (1984). *Rule-Based Expert Systems: The MYCIN Experiments of the Stanford Heuristic Programming Project.* Reading, MA: Addison-Wesley.

Buchanan, B. G., and D. Wilkins (eds.). (1993). *Readings in Knowledge Acquisition and Learning: Automating the Construction and Improvement of Expert Systems.* San Mateo, CA: Morgan Kaufmann.

Buchholz, R. A., and S. B. Rosenthal. (2002, Winter). "Internet Privacy: Individual Rights and the Common Good." *SAM Advanced Management Journal.*

Buck, J. (2001). "Assuring Quality in Distance Education." *Higher Education in Europe*, Vol. 26, No. 4.

Buck, N. (2000, December). "Eureka! Knowledge Discovery." *Software Magazine.*

Buede, D. (1998, August). "Decision Analysis Software Survey: Aiding Insight IV." *OR/MS Today.*

Buehlmann, U., C. T. Ragsdale, and B. Gfeller. (2000). "A Spreadsheet-Based Decision Support System for Wood Panel Manufacturing." *Decision Support Systems.* Vol. 29.

Bui, T., and J. Lee. (1999, April). "An Agent-Based Framework for Building Decision Support Systems." *Decision Support Systems*, Vol. 25, No. 3.

Bunker, E. (1999). "History of Distance Education." Center for Excellence in Distance Learning (CEDL). Lucent Technologies, www.lucent.com/cedl/.

Bunker, P. (2002, June 13). "The Dream Team." *Intelligent Enterprise.*

Burden, K. (1999, January 11). "Coming into Focus." *Computerworld,* 91–94.

Burger, J. (1995). *Multimedia for Decision Makers: A Business Primer.* Reading, MA: Addison-Wesley.

Burke, K. (2002, May). "E-Collaboration: Working Together, Being Apart." *e-Services Journal*, Vol. 1. No. 3.

Burke, R. R. (1996, March/April). "Virtual Shopping." *Harvard Business Review.*

Burkhardt, J., et al. (2002). *Pervasive Computing: Technology and Architecture of Mobile Internet Applications.* Boston: Addison-Wesley.

Burns, R. B. (2000). *Introduction to Research Methods.* London: Sage.

Burrough, P., et al. (1998). *Principles of GIS.* London: Oxford University Press.

Burzinski, T. (2002, July). "The Case for Business Intelligence Assessments." *DM Review.*

Bushko, D., and M. Raynor. (1998, November). "Knowledge Management: New Directions for IT (and Other) Consultants." *Journal of Management Consulting,* Vol. 10, No. 2.

Bustamente, G. G., and K. Sorenson. (1994). *Decision Support at Land's End—An Evolution*, Vol. 33, No. 2.

Byrd, T. A. (1995). "Expert Systems Implementation: Interviews with Knowledge Engineers." *Industrial Management and Data Systems,* Vol. 95, No. 10.

Cabena, P., et al. (1997). *Discovering Data Mining from Concept to Implementation.* Upper Saddle River, NJ: Prentice Hall.

Cahill, T. (1996). *How the Irish Saved Civilization.* New York: Anchor.

Callaghan, D. (2001, November 19). "Armed Services Turn to Portals." *eWeek.*

Callaghan, D. (2002, December). "BI Standards Emerging." *EWeek.*

Callaghan, D. (2003d, January 13). "Software Updates Analysis Dashboard." *eWeek.*

Callaghan, D. (2003a, April 14). "CRM Offerings Focus on SMBs." *eWeek.*

Callaghan, D. (2003a, May 26). "SPSS, SAS Take Predictive Paths." *eWeek.*

Callaghan, D. (2003b, June 2). "IBM Builds Bridge for DB2." *eWeek.*

Callaghan, D. (2003b, June 30). "Celequest Releases BAM Application." *eWeek.*

Callaghan, D. (2003c, July 21). "Oracle Pushes Collaboration." *eWeek.*

Callaghan, D. (2003c, June 30). "New Apps Buttress Businesses' Goals." *eWeek.*

Canter, J. (2002, Spring). "Today's Intelligent Data Warehouse Demands Quality Data." *Journal of Data Warehousing*. Vol. 7, No. 2.

Calvanese, D., G. de Giacomo, M. Lenzerini, D. Nardi, and R. Rosati. (2001, September). "Data Integration in Data Warehousing." *International Journal of Cooperative Information Systems*. Vol 10, No. 3.

Camacho, D., et al. (2001). "Intelligent Travel Planning: A MultiAgent Planning System to Solve Web Problems in the e-Tourism Domain." *Autonomous Agents and Multi-Agent Systems*, No. 4.

Camm, J. D., and J. R. Evans (2001). *Management Science and Decision Technology*. Cincinnati, OH: South-Western College Publishing.

Carlson, J. R., et al. (1999, Summer). "On the Relationship Between DSS Design Characteristics and Ethical Decision Making." *Journal of Managerial Issues*.

Carlsson, C., and E. Turban (eds.). (2001, February). "Decision Support Systems in the First Decade of the 21st Century." Special Issue. *Decision Support Systems*.

Carlsson C., and E. Turban (eds.). (2002, June). "The Future of DSS: Special Issue." *Decision Support Systems*.

Carlsson, C., and P. Walden. (1995, July/August). "AHP in Political Group Decision: A Study in the Art of Possibilities." *Interfaces*, Vol. 25, No. 4.

Carlsson, C., and P. Walden. (2001a, February). "Intelligent Support Systems—The Next Few DSS Steps." *Human Systems Management*, Vol 19, no. 2.

Carlsson, C., and P. Walden. (2001b, February). "Soft Computing and Decision Support." *Decision Support Systems*.

Carr, D. F. (2002, December). "Sweet Victory." *Baseline 2.0*.

Carrico, M. A., et al. (1989). *Building Knowledge Systems: Developing and Managing Rule-Based Applications*. New York: McGraw-Hill.

Cass, K., and T. Lauer. (2002, August). "What Is the Relationship in Customer Relationship Management?" *Proceedings of the America's Conference on Information Systems-AMCIS 2002*, Dallas.

Castelli, V., and L. D. Bergman. (eds.). (2002). *Image Databases: Search and Retrieval of Digital Imagery*. New York: John Wiley.

Castillo, L., and A. Gonzalez. (1998, August 1). "Distribution Network Optimization: Finding the Most Economic Solution by Using Genetic Algorithms." *European Journal of Operational Research*, Vol. 108, No. 3.

Catalano, C. (1999, June 7). "Web-Based Groupware." *Computerworld*, Vol. 33, No. 23.

Caudill, M. (1991, January). "Neural Network Training Tips and Techniques." *AI Expert*.

Cavoukian, A., and D. Tapscott. (1997). *Who Knows: Safeguarding Your Privacy in a Networked World*. New York: McGraw-Hill.

Cawsey, A. (1995). "Developing an Explanation Component for a Knowledge-Based System: Discussion." *Expert Systems with Applications*, Vol. 8, No. 4.

Celik, M. (2001, July). "Catching Up with Expert Systems." *Pharmaceutical Technology*.

Cerami, E. (2002). *Web Services Essentials*. Sebastopol, CA: O'Reidy Assoc.

Cercone, N. (1999, January/February). "Rule-Induction and Case-Based Reasoning: Hybrid Architectures Appear Advantageous." *IEEE Transactions on Knowledge and Data Engineering*, Vol. 11, No. 1.

Cercone, N., A. An, and C. Chan. (1999). "Rule-Induction and Case-Based Reasoning: Hybrid Architectures Appear Advantageous." *IEEE Transactions on Knowledge and Data Engineering*, Vol. 11, No. 1.

Cerpa, N. (1995). "Pre-physical Data Base Design Heuristics." *Information Management*, Vol. 28, No. 6.

Chae, B., et al. (2002, July 4–7). "Incorporating an Ethical Perspective into DSS Design." In F. Adam (ed.). *Proceedings, DSlage 2002*, Cork, Ireland.

Chaffee, D. (1998). *Groupware, Workflow and Intranets: Reengineering the Enterprise with Collaborative Software*. Boston: Digital Press.

Champy, J. (2001, June 25). "The Other Legacies." *ComputerWorld*. Vol. 35, No. 26.

Champy, J., et al. (1996, June 10). "Creating the Electronic Community." *Information Week*.

Chandra, A., et al. (eds.). (Forthcoming). "Business Applications of Data Mining." Special Issue: *International Journal of Intelligent Systems in Accounting, Finance, and Management*.

Chandra, N., and D. M. Reeb. (1999, January). "Neural Networks in a Market Efficiency Context." *American Business Review*, Vol. 17, No. 1.

Chang, A. M., et al. (1993, January). "Model Management Issues and Directions." *Decision Support Systems*, Vol. 9, No. 1.

Chang, Y-L. (1997). *QSB1 for Windows*. New York: John Wiley.

Chang, Y-L. (2000). *Win QSB*. New York: John Wiley.

Charkrabarti, S. (2002). *Mining the Web: Analysis of Hypertext and Semi-Structured Data*, San Francisco: Morgan Kaufmann.

Charles, R. B. (1995, January 23). "Online Libel: A $200 Million Bug." *ComputerWorld*, Vol. 29, No. 4.

Chau, M., et al. (2003). "Design and Evaluation of a Multi-Agent Collaborative Web Mining System." *Decision Support Systems*, Vol. 35, No. 1, pp. 167–183.

Chau, P. Y. K., and P. C. Bell. (1994, November). "Decision Support for the Design of a New Production Plant using Visual Interactive Simulation." *Journal of the Operational Research Society*, Vol. 45, No. 11.

Chau, P. Y. K., and P. C. Bell. (1996, May). "A Visual Interactive Decision Support System to Assist the Design of a New Production Unit." *INFOR*, Vol. 34, No. 2.

Chaudhri, A. B., and M. Loomis (eds.). (1998). *Object Databases in Practice.* Upper Saddle River, NJ: Prentice Hall.

Chaudhri, V. K., and J. D. Lowrance, (1998). "Generic Knowledge-Base Editor." www.ai.sri.com/~gkb/welcome.shtml.

Chaudhury, A., et al. (2001, January). "Web Channels in E-Commerce." *Communications of the ACM.*

Cheeseman, H. R. (2001). *Business Law: Ethical, International, and E-Commerce Environments,* 4th ed. Upper Saddle River, NJ: Prentice Hall.

Chen, H. (1996). "An Inventory Decision Support System Using the Object-Oriented Approach." *Computers & Operational Research,* Vol. 23, No. 2.

Chen H. (2003a, February). "Digital Government: Technologies and Practices." *Decision Support Systems,* Special Issue.

Chen, H. (2003b, April). "Web Retrieval and Mining." *Decision Support Systems,* Special Issue.

Chen, H., et al. (1995). "Intelligent Meeting Facilitation Agents: An Experiment on GroupSystems." Tucson: University of Arizona, ai.bpa.arizona.edu/papers/agent95/agent95.html.

Chen, H., et al. (1997, January). "Intelligent Spider for Internet Searching." *Proceedings of the Thirtieth Hawaii International Conference on Systems Sciences.* Wailea, HI. Los Alamitos, CA: IEEE Computer Society Press.

Chen, Z. (1996). "Role-Limiting Methods for Automated Knowledge Acquisition: A Problem-Solving Perspective." *Information Processing & Management,* Vol. 32, No. 2.

Cheng, P. C-H. (1996). "Diagrammatic Knowledge Acquisition: Elicitation, Analysis and Issues." In N. Shadbolt, K. O'Hara, and G. Schreiber (eds.). *Advances in Knowledge Acquisition.* Berlin: Springer-Verlag.

Cheng, R., M. Gen, and Y. Tsujimura. (1999, October). "A Tutorial Survey of Job-Shop Scheduling Problems Using Genetic Algorithms: Part II. Hybrid Genetic Search Strategies." *Computers & Industrial Engineering,* Vol. 37, Nos. 1 and 2.

Cherry, S. M. (2002a). "Getting the Copy-Right." *IEEE Spectrum.*

Cherry, S. M. (2002b, September). "Weaving a Web of Ideas." *IEEE Spectrum,* pp. 65–69.

Cheung, K. W., et al. (2003). "Mining Customer Product Ratings for Personalized Marketing." *Decision Support Systems,* Vol. 35, No. 2, pp. 231–243.

Chi, R. J., and E. Turban. (1995, June). "Distributed Intelligent Executive Information Systems." *Decision Support Systems,* Vol. 14, No. 2.

Chiasson, M.W., and C.Y. Lovato. (2001, Summer). "Factors Influencing the Formation of a User's Perceptions and Use of a DSS Software Innovation." *The Data Base for Advances in Information Systems.*

Chidambaram, L. (1996, June). "Relational Development in Computer-Supported Groups." *MIS Quarterly.*

Chiem, P. X. (2001a, May). "Trust Matters." *Knowledge Management.*

Chiem, P. X. (2001b, August). "Government Employees Also Need Motivation to Share." *Knowledge Management.*

Chin, K. (1999, April). "Capturing The Power of the Human Mind." *Chemical Engineering,* Vol. 106, No. 4.

Chiu, C. (2001). "A Case-Based Customer Classification Approach for Direct Marketing." *Expert Systems with Applications,* Vol. 22, No. 2, pp. 163–168.

Cholewinski, P., V. W. Marek, and A. Mikitiuk. (1999, August). "Computing with Default Logic." *Artificial Intelligence.*

Chorafas, D. N. (1994). *Chaos Theory in the Financial Markets.* Chicago: Probus Publishing.

Choy, K. L., et al. (2002). "Development of a Case Based Intelligent Customer-Supplier Relationship Management System." *Expert Systems with Applications,* Vol. 23, No. 3, pp. 281–297.

Chuang, T-T., M. Bernard, and A. Shahid. (2002, Spring). "Computer-Supported Collaborative Learning Performance and Satisfaction: A Multistage Study." *Journal of International Technology and Information Management.* Vol. 11, No. 1.

Chung, Q.B. (2000, August). "Influence of Model Management Systems on Decision Making: Empirical Evidence and Implications." *Journal of the Operational Research Society.* Vol. 51, No. 8.

Churchman, C. W. (1975). *The Systems Approach,* rev. ed. New York: Delacorte.

Churchman, C. W. (1982). *Prediction and Optimal Decision.* Westport, CT: Greenwood Publishing Group.

CIO.com. (1999, November 1). "Supply Chain Integration: The Name of the Game Is Collaboration." Special Advertising Supplement. *CIO.*

CIO. (1999, September 15). "The Means to an Edge: Knowledge Management: Key to Innovation." Special Supplement, *CIO.*

CIO Insight. (2003, May 23). "The 2003 CIO Insight Business Intelligence Research Study: Are Your BI Systems Making You Smarter?" *CIO Insight,* No. 26.

Cippola, E. (2001, Spring). "Use of a DW and BI to Support CRM Initiatives." *Journal of Data Warehousing.* Vol. 6, No. 2.

CKB. (2003). CKB: Workflow & Document Management Specialists Web Site www.ckb.co.za/ework.htm.

Claburn, T. (2001, December 1). "Intellectual Property: Harder to Protect Than Ever." *Smart Business,* Vol. 14.

Clarke, K. (2003, April 9). "EDS and Navy Activate New Aviation Supply Chain Maintenance Management." *PR Newswire.*

Clarke, K. C. (1997). *Getting Started with Geographical Information Systems.* Upper Saddle River, NJ: Prentice Hall.

Clarke, P. (1998 March/April). "Implementing a Knowledge Strategy for Your Firm." *Research Technology Management.*

Clemen, R. T., and T. Reilly. (2000). *Making Hard Decisions with Decision Tools Suite.* Belmont, MA: Duxbury Press.

Cliff D., et al. (1999) "Making Money from Agents." *Knowledge Engineering Review,* Vol. 14, No. 3.

Close, W. (2002, April 1). "The CRM Buy-In Challenge." *CIO.*

Clyman, J. (2002, September 17). "From Chaos to Control." *PC Magazine.*

Coddington, P. D., et al. (1999). "Web-Based Access to Distributed High Performance GIS for Decision Support." *Proceedings of the Thirty-second Annual Hawaii International Conference on System Sciences HICSS-32.* Maui, HI. Los Alamitos, CA: IEEE Computer Society.

Coe, L. R. (1996, Fall). "Five Small Secrets to Success." *Information Resources Management Journal,* Vol. 9, No. 4.

Coffee, P. (2003, June 23). " 'Active' Warehousing." *eWeek.*

Cognos Inc. (2000). "OLAP Reporting for the Enterprise." Cognos, Inc., www.cognos.com.

Cohen, M., et al. (2001, March/April). "Decision Support with Web-Enabled Software." *Interfaces.*

Cohen, M-D., C. B. Charles, and A. L. Medaglia. (2001, March/April). "Decision Support with Web-Enabled Software." *Interfaces.* Vol. 31, No. 2.

Cohen, T. (2002, May 16). "Nonprofits Target Donor Relations." *Philanthropy Journal.*

Cohn, A. G. (1995, September). "The Challenge of Qualitative Spatial Reasoning." *ACM Computing Surveys,* Vol. 27, No. 3.

Cohn, M. (2002, June). "Out Load via Phone." *InternetWorld.*

Cole, B. (1996, November 4). "Oracle and Powersoft Ease Move to Web Applications." *NetworkWorld.*

Coleman, K. G., and S. Watenpool. (1992, January). "Neural Networks in Knowledge Acquisition." *AI Expert.*

Collett, S. (2002, April 15). "Incoming!" *ComputerWorld.*

Collins, H. (2001). *Corporate Portals: Revolutionizing Information Access to Increase Productivity and Drive the Bottom Line,* AMACOM.

Compaine, B. M. (2001). *The Digital Divide: Facing a Crisis or Creating a Myth?* Cambridge, MA: MIT Press.

Compton, J. (2001, July). "Climbing Out of the Abyss." *Knowledge Management.*

Compton, J. (2002, January). "Product Lifecycle to the Rescue." *CRM Magazine.*

Compton, J. (2003, April). "The 10 Best Things to Do With Your Data." *Customer Relationship Management.*

Cone, E. (2001, March 19). "Factory Incentive: DaimlerChrysler Apps Program Brings Savings." *Interactive Week.*

Conger, S., et al. (1995). "Ethics and Information Technology Use: A Factor Analysis of Attitudes Toward Computer Use." *Information Systems Journal,* Vol. 5.

Connolly, P. J. (2001, December 3). "Videoconferencing Adds Depth." *InfoWorld.* No. 49.

Connors, K. (1999, December). "Inspection Gadgets." *Software Magazine.*

Conway, D. G., and G. J. Koehler. (2000, January). "Interface Agents: Caveat Mercater in Electronic Commerce." *Decision Support Systems.*

Conway, S. (2003). "Valuing Knowledge Management Behaviors: Linking KM Behaviors to Strategic Performance Measures." Chapter 24 in C. W. Holsapple (ed.). *Handbook of Knowledge Management: Knowledge Matters,* Vol. 1. Heidelberg: Springer-Verlag.

Cook, D. (2002). *Robot Building for Beginners.* Berkeley, CA: Apress.

Cook, M. A. (1996). *Building Enterprise Information Architectures: Reengineering Information Systems.* Upper Saddle River, NJ: Prentice Hall.

Cope, J. (2002, April 1). "Tuning into Travel Savings." *ComputerWorld.*

Copeland, M. V. (2003, May). "TV Finally Gets Depth." *Business 2.0.*

Copeland, L. (2001, October 22). "Developers Approach Extreme Programming with Caution." *ComputerWorld.* Vol. 35, No. 43.

Copeland, R. (2001, May 21). "More Than a Pretty Interface." *InformationWeek.*

Copeland, R. (2001, May 21). "Innovation: Genetic Gold Mine." *InformationWeek.*

Cortese, A. (2002, September). "The Power of Optimal Pricing." *Business 2.0.* business2.com/articles/mag/0,1640,42875,00.html.

Cothrel, J., and R. L. Williams. (1999a). "On-line Communities: Helping Them Form and Grow." *Journal of Knowledge Management,* Vol. 3, No. 1.

Cothrel, J., and R.L. Williams. (1999b, January/February). "On-Line Communities: Getting the Most Out of On-Line Discussion and Collaboration." *Knowledge Management Review,* No. 6.

Courtney, J. F., and D. B. Paradice. (1993, June). "Studies on Managerial Problem Formulation Systems." *Decision Support Systems.* Vol. 3, No. 4.

Courtney, J. F., Jr., et al. (1987, Summer). "A Knowledge-Based DSS for Managerial Problem Diagnosis." *Decision Sciences,* Vol. 18, No. 3.

Covington, M. A., D. Nute, and A. Vellino. (1997). *Prolog Programming in Depth,* 2nd ed. Upper Saddle River, NJ: Prentice Hall.

Cox, E. (1999, September/October). "A Data Mining and Rule Discovery Approach to Business Forecasting with Adaptive, Genetically-Tuned Fuzzy System Models." *PC AI.*

Cox, E. (2001). Building Intelligent Business Applications with Semantic Nets and Business Rules." *PC AI,* Vol. 15, No. 1.

Cox, E. (2002). "Seeing the Invisible: Computational Intelligence." *PC AI,* Vol. 16, No. 1, pp. 17–22.

Cox, E., and R. Terlaga. (1992, Fall). "A Clear Approach to Fuzzy Logic." *Chief Information Officer Journal,* Vol. 5, No. 2.

Craig, R. (1998, December). "Analyzing the OLIVE Branches." *Entonline.*

Craig, R. S., J. A. Vivona, and D. Bercovitch. (1999). *Microsoft Data Warehousing.* New York: John Wiley.

Cramond, B. (1995). "The Torrance Tests of Creative Thinking: From Design Through Establishment of Predictive Validity." In *Beyond Terman: Contemporary Studies of Giftedness and Talent,* R. F. Subotnik and K. D. Arnold (eds.). Norwood, NJ: Ablex Publishing Co., pp. 229–254.

Cranfield University. (1998). "The Cranfield/Information Strategy Knowledge Survey: Europe's State of the Art in Knowledge Management." London: *Economist Group.*

Cranor, L. F. (1999, February). "Internet Privacy." Special Issue. *Communications of the ACM.*

Croasdell, D., D. Paradice, and J. Courtney. (1997, January). "Using Adaptive Hypermedia to Support Organizational Memory and Learning." *Proceedings of the Thirtieth Annual Hawaii International Conference on Systems Sciences HICSS-30,* Wailea, HI. Los Alamitos, CA: IEEE Computer Society Press.

CRMguru.com. (2002a, June). "The Customer Relationship Solutions Guide." Front Line Solutions, at CRMGuru.com.

CRMguru.com. (2002b, July). "The Customer Relationship Management Primer: What You Need to Know to Get Started." Front Line Solutions, at CRMGuru.com.

Cross, R., and L. Baird. (2000, Spring). "Technology Is Not Enough: Improving Performance by Building Organizational Memory." *Sloan Management Review.*

Cross, R. G. (1997). *Revenue Management: Hard-Core Tactics for Market Domination.* New York: Broadway Books.

Cross, V. (2001, May/June) "Ready for Some Decision-Making Help?" *EDUCAUSE Review,* Vol. 36, No. 3.

Cuena, J., and M. Molina. (1996). "KSM: An Environment for Design of Structured Knowledge Models." In S. G.

Tzafestas (ed.). *Knowledge-Based Systems: Advanced Concepts, Techniques and Applications.* Singapore: World Scientific Publishing.

Cule, P., R. Schmidt, K. Lyytinen, and M. Keil. (2000, Spring). "Strategies for Heading Off IS Project Failure." *Information Systems Management,* Vol. 17, No. 2.

Culpepper, R. B. (2002, October). "Quick-Take Reviews: ComminityViz 1.3." *GeoWorld.*

Cupit, J., and N. Shadbolt. (1996). "Knowledge Discovery in Databases: Exploiting Knowledge-Level Redescription." In N. Shadbolt, K. O'Hara, and G. Schreiber, *Advances in Knowledge Acquisition.* Berlin: Springer-Verlag.

Currid, C., et al. (1994). *Computer Strategies for Reengineering Your Business.* Rocklin, CA: Prima.

Cyre, W. R. (1997). "Capture, Integration, and Analysis of Digital System Requirements with Conceptual Graphs." *IEEE Transactions on Knowledge and Data Engineering,* Vol. 9, No. 1.

D'Agostino, D. (2003, May). "Water from Stone." *CIO Insight,* No. 26.

D'Amico, (2003, February 19). "PLM Market Expected to Double by 2008." *Chemical Week,* Vol. 165, No. 7.

Dasu, T., and T. Johnson. (2003). *Exploratory Data Mining and Data Cleaning.* New York: John Wiley.

Datz, T. (2002, August 15). "Strategic Alignment." *CIO.*

Datz, T. (2002, December 1). "Integrating America." *Framingham,* Vol. 16, No. 5.

Davenport, D., and M. Sena. (2003). "Technologies for Knowledge Derivation." Chapter 40 in C. W. Holsapple (ed.). *Handbook of Knowledge Management: Knowledge Directions,* Vol. 2. Heidelberg: Springer-Verlag.

Davenport, T. (1998, July/August). "Putting the Enterprise in the Enterprise System." *Harvard Business Review,* Vol. 76, No. 4.

Davenport, T., D. W. DeLong, and M. C. Beers. (1998, Winter). "Successful Knowledge Management Projects." *Sloan Management Review,* Vol. 39, No. 2.

Davenport, T., et al. (1998, Winter). "Successful Knowledge Management Projects." *Sloan Management Review,* Vol. 39, No. 2.

Davenport, T. H. (1994, March/April). "Saving IT's Soul: Human-Centered Information Management." *Harvard Business Review.*

Davenport, T. H., and L. Prusak. (1998). *Working Knowledge: How Organizations Manage What They Know.* Boston: Harvard Business School Press.

Davids, M. (1999, May/June). "Smiling for the Camera." *Journal of Business Strategy,* Vol. 20, No. 3.

Davies, J., et al. (eds.) (2003). *Towards the Semantic Web: Ontology-Driven Knowledge Management.* Wiley.

Davis, F. D. (1989, September). "Perceived Usefulness, Perceived Ease of Use, and User Acceptance of Information Systems." *MIS Quarterly.*

Davis, J. T., et al. (2001). "Predicting Direction Shifts on Canadian-US Exchange Rates with Artificial Neural Networks." *International Journal of Intelligent Systems in Accounting, Finance and Management*, Vol. 10, pp. 83–96.

Davis, M. (1998, Fall). "Knowledge Management." *Information Strategy: The Executive's Journal.*

Davis, R. (1993). "Interactive Transfer of Expertise: Acquisition of New Inference Rules." In B. G. Buchanan and D. Wilkins (eds.). *Readings in Knowledge Acquisition and Learning: Automating the Construction and Improvement of Expert Systems.* San Mateo, CA: Morgan Kaufmann.

Day Group. (2002, July). "Newsletter." *CIO Analysts Outlook.* Day Group.

De La Maza, M., and D. Yuret. (1994, March). "Dynamic Hill Climbing." *AI Expert.*

De Long, D. W., and L. Fahey. (2000, November) "Diagnosing Cultural Barriers to Knowledge Management." *Academy of Management Executive*, Vol. 14, No. 4.

De Vreede, G. J., R. O. Briggs, R. van Duin, and B. Enserink. (2000). "Athletics in Electronic Brainstorming: Asynchronous Electronic Brainstorming in Very Large Groups." *Proceedings of the Thirty-third Annual Hawaii International Conference on System Sciences HICSS-33.* Los Alamitos, CA: IEEE Computer Society Press.

Dearlove, D., and S. Crainer. (2001, April 16). "A Whole New B School." *Industry Standard.*

Deboeck, G. (1999, January/February). "Public Domain vs. Commercial Tools for Creating Neural Self-Organizing Maps." *PC AI.*

Deboeck, G., and T. Kohonen. (1997). *Visual Explorations in Finance with Self-Organizing Maps.* Berlin: Springer-Verlag.

Decision Analysis Society. (2003). Decision Tree & Influence Diagram Software." Decision Analysis Society, faculty. fuqua.duke.edu/daweb/dasw6.htm.

Deck, S. (1999a, May 17). "Mining Your Business." *ComputerWorld*, Vol. 33, No. 20.

Deck, S. (1999b, May 24). "A Service to Combat Fraud." *ComputerWorld*, Vol. 33, No. 21.

Deck, S. L. (2001, September). "CRM Made Easy." *CIO.*

Decker K., et al. (1999, March). "Continuing Research in Multi-agent System." *Knowledge Engineering Review.*

Decker, S., et al. (2000)." Framework for the Semantic Web: An RDF Tutorial." *IEEE Internet Computing*, Vol. 4, No. 6, p. 68.

DeFanti, T. A. (1997). "Deep Learning and Visualization Technologies." National Science Foundation, www.her.nsf.gov/lis/defanti.htm.

Dejoie, R. M., et al. (1995). *Ethical Issues in Information Systems*, 2nd ed. Cincinnati: Boyd & Fraser.

DeLeon, W. H., and E. R. McLean. (1992, March). "Information System Success: The Quest for the Dependent Variable." *Information Systems Research*, Vol. 3, No. 1.

Delic, K.A., and U. Dayal. (2003, June 30). "A New Analytic Perspective." *Intelligent Enterprise*,

DeLong, D. W., and L. Fahey (2000, November). "Diagnosing Cultural Barriers to Knowledge Management, *Academy of Management Executive*, Vol. 14, No. 4, pp. 113–127.

DeJesus, E.X. (2000, October 30). "XML Enters the DBMS Arena." *ComputerWorld.*

Dembo, R., A. Aziz, D. Rosen, and M. Zerbs. (2000). "Mark-to-Future: A Framework for Measuring Risk and Reward." Report, Algorithmics Publications, Toronto, Canada.

Demetriadis, S., et al. (1999, May). "Graphical Jog Through: Expert-Based Methodology for User Interface Evaluation, Applied in the Case of an Educational Simulation Interface." *Computers and Education.*

den Haan, A. (2001, March). "Tearing Down the Software Tower of Babel." *eAI Journal.*

Denardo, E.V. (2001, August). "The Science of Decision Making." *OR/MS Today.*

Deng, R. (2003, Quarter 2). "Effective Indexes for Data Warehouses." *DB2 Magazine.*

Deng, P. S., and E. G. Tsacle. (2000). "Coupling Genetic Algorithm and Rule-Based Systems for Complex Decisions." *Expert Systems with Applications*, Vol. 19, No. 3, pp. 209–218.

Denning, D. E. (1998). *Information Warfare and Security.* Reading, MA: Addison-Wesley.

Denning, S. (2000). *The Springboard: How Storytelling Ignites Action in Knowledge-Era Organizations.* Burlington, MA: Butterworth-Heinemann.

Dennis, A., et al. (1988, December). "Information Technology to Support Electronic Meetings." *MIS Quarterly.*

Dennis, A. R. (1996). "Information Exchange and Use in Group Decision Making: You Can Lead a Group to Information But You Can't Make It Think." *MIS Quarterly*, Vol. 20, No. 4.

Dennis, A. R., J. E. Aronson, W. G. Heninger, and E. D. Walker II. (1999, March). "Structuring Time and Task Decomposition in Electronic Brainstorming." *Management Information Systems Quarterly*, Vol. 23, No. 1.

Dennis, A. R., and M. J. Garfield. (1999, November 12). "Breaking Structures: The Adoption and Use of GSS in Project Teams." Department of MIS Working Paper, Terry College of Business, The University of Georgia, Athens.

Dennis, A. R., and T. A. Carte. (1998, June). "Using GIS for Decision Making." *Information Systems Research.*

Dennis, A. R., K. M. Hilmer, and N. J. Taylor. (1997/1998). "Information Exchange and Use in GSS and Verbal Group Decision Making: Effects of Minority Influence." *Journal of Management Information Systems,* Vol. 14, No. 3.

Dennis, A. R., S. K. Pootheri, and V. L. Natarajan (1998, Spring). "Lessons from the Early Adopters of Web Groupware." *Journal of Management Information Systems,* Vol. 14, No. 4.

Dennis, A. R., J. S. Valacich, T. C., M. Garfield, B. Haley, and J. E. Aronson. (1997, June). "The Effectiveness of Multiple Dialogues in Electronic Brainstorms." *Information Systems Research,* Vol. 8, No. 2.

Dennis, A., and B. Wixom. (2003). *Systems Analysis and Design.* 2nd ed. New York: John Wiley.

Dennis, A., B. Wixom, and D. P. Tegarden. (2002). *Systems Analysis and Design: An Object-Oriented Approach with UML.* New York: John Wiley.

Dennis, A. R., B. H. Wixom, and R. J. Vandenberg. (2001, June). "Understanding Fit and Appropriation Effects in Group Support Systems Via Meta-Analysis." *MIS Quarterly.* Vol. 25, No. 2.

DePold, H. R., and F. D. Gass. (1999, October). "The Application of Expert Systems and Neural Networks to Gas Turbine Prognostics and Diagnostics." *Journal of Engineering for Gas Turbines and Power,* Vol. 121, No. 4.

Deris, S., et al. (1999, February 1). "Ship Maintenance Scheduling by Genetic Algorithm and Constraint-Based Reasoning." *European Journal of Operational Research,* Vol. 112, No. 3.

Derra, S. (1999, April). "Refocusing AI Research on Real-world Applications." *Research & Development,* Vol. 41, No. 5.

DeSanctis, G., and R. B. Gallupe. (1987). "A Foundation for the Study of Group Decision Support Systems." *Management Science,* Vol. 33, No. 5.

DeSanctis, G., and R. B. Gallupe. (1985, Winter). "Group Decision Support Systems: A New Frontier." *Data Base.*

Despres, S., and C. Rosenthal-Sabroux. (1992, August 25). "Designing DSS and Expert Systems with Better End-User Involvement: A Promising Approach." *European Journal of Operational Research,* Vol. 61, Nos. 1 and 2.

Desouza, H.C. (2001). "Intelligent Agents for Competitive Intelligence: Survey of Applications." *Competitive Intelligence Review,* Vol. 12, No. 4.

Detlor, B., and M. Glacomin. (2002). "Web Information Seeking and Retrieval in Digital Library Contexts: Towards an Intelligent Agent Solution." *Online Information Review,* Vol. 26, No. 6, pp. 404–412.

Devedzic, V., J. Debenham, and D. Radovic. (1996, October). "Object-Oriented Modelling of Expert System Reasoning Process." *Proceedings, IEEE Conference on Systems, Man, and Cybernetics,* Beijing, China, pp. 2716–2721.

Devlin, B. (2003, Quarter 2). "Solving the Data Warehouse Puzzle." *DB2 Magazine.*

Dhar, V., and R. Stein. (1997). *Intelligent Decision Support Methods.* Upper Saddle River, NJ: Prentice Hall.

Diamantidis, N. A., and E. A. Giakoumakis. (1999, February). "An Interactive Tool for Knowledge Base Refinement." *Expert Systems.*

Dias, L.C., and J.N. Climaco. (2002, July 4-7). "A Multi-Criteria DSS for Group Decisions Using Value Functions with Imprecise Information." *Proceedings of DSIage 2002,* Cork, Ireland.

DiBella, A. J. (1995). "Developing Learning Organizations: A Matter of Perspective." *Academy of Management Journal.* Best Papers Proceedings 1995.

Dickson, G., and R. Powers. (1973). "MIS Project Management: Myths, Opinions, and Realities." In F. W. McFarlan et al. (eds.). *Information Systems Administration.* New York: Holt, Rinehart & Winston.

Dienes, Z., and J. Perner. (1999, October). "A Theory of Implicit and Explicit Knowledge." *Behavioral and Brain Sciences.*

Dieng, R. (1995). "Agent-Based Method for Building a Cooperative Knowledge-Based System." *Proceedings of the FGSC 1994 Workshop on Heterogeneous Cooperative Knowledge Bases: Lecture Notes in Computer Science.* Berlin: Springer-Verlag.

Diffie, W., and S. Landau (1998). *Privacy on the Line: The Politics of Wiretapping and Encryption.* Boston: MIT Press.

diPiazza, J. S., and F. A. Helsabeck. (1990, Fall). "Laps: Cases to Models to Complete Expert Systems." *AI Magazine.*

Dolk, D. R. (2000, April 16). "Integrated Model Management in the Data Warehouse Era." *European Journal of Operational Research.* Vol. 122, No. 2.

Dollar, G. (2000, August). "Web-Based Course Delivery: An Empirical Assessment of Student Learning Outcomes." *Proceedings of the Americas Conference of the Association for Information Systems,* Milwaukee.

Dologite, D. G., and R. J. Mockler. (1989, Winter). "Developing Effective Knowledge-Based Systems: Overcoming Organizational and Individual Behavioral Barriers." *Information Resource Management Journal.*

Domaszewicz, A. (2002 August). "Online Tools Drive Health Care Decisions." *HRMagazine,* Vol. 47, No. 8.

Dong, J., D. Sundaram, and A. Srinivasan. (2002, July). "A Framework and Prototype for Web-Enabled Decision Systems." *Proceedings of DSIage 2002,* Cork, Ireland.

Donlon, J. J., and K. D. Forbus. (1999). "Using a Geographic Information System for Qualitative Spatial Reasoning about Trafficability." *Proceedings of the Qualitative Reasoning Workshop,* Loch Awe, Scotland.

Donovan, J. J., and S. E. Madnick. (1977). "Institutional and Ad Hoc DSS and Their Effective Use." *Data Base,* Vol. 8, No. 3.

Donston, D. (2002, July 1). "Web Conference Call." *eWeek.*

Dorrington, P. (2003, Second Quarter). "Innovative, Industrious and Nefarious Fraudsters!" *SAS com.*

Dotti, F.L., et al. (2000). "Design and Implementation of Cooperative Optimization Centers." *16th International Conference on CAD/CAM, Robotics and Factories of the Future.* University of the West Indies, Trinidad and Tobago.

Downes, L. (2001, July 9–16). "Man, Plan, Canal." *Industry Standard.*

Downing, C. E., and A. S. Clark. (1999, Spring). "Groupware in Practice." *Information Systems Management,* Vol. 16, No. 2.

Dragoon, A. (2003a, May 15). "Putting IT on the Map." *CIO.*

Dragoon, A. (2003b, July 1). "All for One View." *CIO.*

Drake, K. C., and P. Hess. (1990, September/October). "Abduction: A Numeric Knowledge Acquisition Approach." *PC AI.*

Dravis, F. (2002, Spring). "Information Quality: The Quest for Justification." *Journal of Data Warehousing,* Vol. 7, No. 2.

Dresner, H. (1993, June 3). *Multidimensionality: Ready or Not, Here It Comes, Research Note.* Boston: Gartner Group.

Dronzek, R. (2001, November). "Improving Critical Care." *IIE Solutions.*

Drucker, D. (2001, January 29). "Knowledge Mgm't Revised—Theory Doesn't Equal Practice." *InternetWeek,* No. 846.

Drucker, P. (2002). *Managing in the Next Society.* New York: Truman Talley Books.

Drummond, H. (2001). *The Art of Decision Making.* New York: John Wiley.

Dryden, P. (1996, July 29). "Help for Harried Help Desk." *ComputerWorld,* Vol. 30, No. 31.

Du, T. C. (2001, April). "Using Object-Oriented Paradigm to Develop an Evolutional Vehicle Routing System." *Computers in Industry,* Vol. 44, No. 3.

Dubois, D., et al. (2003). "On the Representation of Fuzzy Rules in Terms of Crisp Rules." *Information Sciences,* Vol. 151, pp. 301–326.

Dubois, D., and H. Prade. (1995, September). "What Does Fuzzy Logic Bring to AI?" *ACM Computing Surveys,* Vol. 27, No. 3.

Duchessi, P., and R. H. O'Keefe. (1992, August 25). "Constructing Successful and Unsuccessful Expert Systems." *European Journal of Operational Research,* Vol. 61, Nos. 1 and 2.

Duffy, D. (1998, November). "Knowledge Champions." *CIO* (Enterprise–Section 2).

Duffy, D. (1999, November 15). "A Capital Idea." *CIO* (Enterprise–Section 2).

Duffy, D. (2002, August 1). "GIS Goes Worldwide." *CIO.*

Dugan, S. M. (1999, July 5). "Groupware Still Going Strong." *InfoWorld,* Vol. 21, No. 27.

Dunham, K. J. (2003, January 28). "Career Journal: Online-Degree Programs Surge, But Do They Pass Hiring Tests?" *Wall Street Journal.* Eastern Edition.

Dunham, M. (2003). *Data Mining: Introductory and Advanced Topics.* Upper Saddle River, NJ: Prentice Hall.

Dupuy, F. (2002). *The Chemistry of Change: Problems, Phases, and Strategy.* New York: Houndmills; Basingstoke, UK: Palgrave-Macmillan.

Durkin, J. (1994). *Expert Systems: Design and Development.* New York: Macmillan.

Durkin, J. (1996, April). "Expert Systems: A View of the Field." *IEEE Expert.*

Dutta, A. (1996, November). "Integrating AI and Optimization for Decision Support." *Decision Support Systems,* Vol. 18, Nos. 3 and 4.

Dutta, S., B. Wierenga, and A. Dalebout. (1997, June). "Designing Management Support Systems Using an Integrative Perspective." *Communications of the ACM.* Vol. 40, No. 6.

Dwinnell, W. (2002, March/April). "Putting Fuzzy Logic to Work: An Intro to Fuzzy Logic." *PC AI,* pp. 33–36.

Dyche, J. (1999, February 1). "The Big Bang of Business Intelligence." *Telephony*

Dyché, J. (2001). *The CRM Handbook: A Business Guide to Customer Relationship Management.* Reading, MA: Addison-Wesley.

Dyche, J. (2002, Winter). "Choosing the Right CRM Tool." *Journal of Data Warehousing.* Vol. 7, No. 1.

Dyer, G. (2000, March). "Knowledge Management Crosses the Chasm." *Knowledge Management.*

e-optimization.com. (2002, April 12). "How Airlines Manage Ticket Prices : An Introduction to Revenue Management and Dynamic Pricing." Video of a Seminar on Revenue Management, www.e-optimization.com (e-optimization community).

Earl, M., and B. Khan.(2001). "E-Commerce Is Changing the Face of IT." *Sloan Management Review,* Vol. 43, No. 1.

Easton, F. F., and M. Nashat. (1999, November). "A Distributed Genetic Algorithm for Deterministic and Stochastic Labor Scheduling Problems." *European Journal of Operational Research,* Vol. 118, No. 3.

Eckerson, W. (2002a, May). "Data Quality and the Bottom Line." *Application Development Trends*.

Eckerson, W. (2002b, May). "Four Ways to Build a Data Warehouse." *Application Development Trends*.

Eckerson, W. (2003a, January). "The Rise of Analytic Packages." *Application Development Trends*. Vol. 10, No. 1.

Eckerson, W. (2003b, June). "Four Ways to Build a Data Warehouse." *What Works: Best Practices in Business Intelligence and Data Warehousing*, Vol. 15, Chatsworth, CA: Data Warehousing Institute.

Edelstein, H. (1996, January 8). "Mining Data Warehouses." *InformationWeek*.

Edelstein, H. A. (1997). "An Introduction to Data Warehousing." Chapter 3 in R. Barquin and H. Edelstein. (eds.). *Building, Using, and Managing the Data Warehouse*. Upper Saddle River, NJ: Prentice Hall PTR.

Edelstein, H. A. (2001, March 12). "Pan for Gold in the Clickstream." *InformationWeek*.

Eden, C., and F. Ackerman. (2002). "Emergent Strategizing." In A. Huff and M. Jenkins (eds.). *Mapping Strategic Thinking*. Thousand Oaks, CA: Sage Publications.

Edman, A., and Hamfelt, A. (1999, November) "A System Architecture for Knowledge-Based Hypermedia." *International Journal of Human–Computer Studies*.

Edwards, J. (2000, March 1). "3-D Finally Gets Serious." *CIO*.

Edwards, J. (2003a, February 15). "Tag, You're It." *CIO*.

Edwards, J. (2003b, July 1). "Smooth Talkers." *CIO*.

Ehrgott, M., and X. Gandibleaux. (eds.). (2002). *Multiple Criteria Optimization*. Norwell, MA: Kluwer Academic Publishers.

Eisenhart, M. (2000, October) "Around the Virtual Water Cooler: Sustaining Communities of Practice Takes Plenty of Persistence." *Knowledge Management*.

Eisenhart, M. (2001, April). "Gathering Knowledge While It's Ripe." *Knowledge Management*.

El Sawy, O. (1998). *The Business Process Reengineering Workbook*. New York: McGraw-Hill.

El Sawy, O. (2001). *Redesigning Enterprise Processes for E-Business*. New York: McGraw-Hill.

Eldabi, T., R. J. Paul, and S. J. Taylor. (1999, October). "Computer Simulation in Healthcare Decision Making." *Computers & Industrial Engineering*, Vol. 37, Nos. 1 and 2.

Elkins, J. (2000). *How to Use Your Eyes*. London: Routledge.

Ellingsworth, M., and D. Sullivan. (2003, July). "Text Mining Improves Business Intelligence and Predictive Modeling in Insurance." *DM Review*, Vol. 13, No. 7.

Elofson, G., et al. (1997, May). "An Intelligent Agent Community Approach to Knowledge Sharing." *Decision Support Systems,* Vol. 20, No. 1.

Elofson, G. S., and B. R. Konsynski. (1990, January). "Supporting Knowledge Sharing in Environment Scanning." In *Proceedings of the Twenty-third Annual Hawaii International Conference on System Sciences HICSS-23, Wailea, HI*. Los Alamitos, CA: IEEE Computer Society Press.

Englemore, R., and T. Morgan (eds.). (1989). *Blackboard Systems*. Reading, MA: Addison-Wesley.

Eom, S.B. (1999). "Decision Support Systems Research: Current State and Trends." *Industrial Management Data Systems*. Vol. 99, No. 5.

Eom, S. (2002, July). "Extended Enterprise Decision Support Systems: A New Frontier in the Internet Age." *Proceedings of DSIage 2002*, Cork, Ireland.

Eom, S. B. (1996, September/October). "A Survey of Operational Expert Systems in Business (1980–1993)." *Interfaces,* Vol. 26, No. 5.

Erickson, W. (2003, June). "The Evolution of ETL." *What Works: Best Practices in Business Intelligence and Data Warehousing*, Vol. 15. Chatsworth, CA: Data Warehousing Institute.

Ericson, J. (2002, October). "Portal with a Pulse." *Portals Magazine*.

Ericson, J. (2003, July). "Content Collaborators." *Portals Magazine*. Vol. 33, No. 22.

Ericsson, K. A., and H. A. Simon. (1984). *Protocol Analysis, Verbal Reports and Data*. Cambridge, MA: MIT Press.

Eriksson, H. (1992, September). "A Survey of Knowledge Acquisition Techniques and Tools and their Relationship to Software Engineering." *Journal of Systems & Software*.

Eriksson, H. (1996, June). "Expert Systems as Knowledge Servers." *IEEE Expert*.

Erlebach, T., H. Kellerer, and U. Pferschy. (2002, December). "Approximating Multiobjective Knapsack Problems." *Management Science,* Vol. 48, No. 12.

Estes, D. (2001, January). "Disciplined XML." *eAI Journal*.

Etzioni, O. (1996, November). "The WWW: Quagmire or Gold Mine." *Communications of the ACM,* Vol. 39, No. 11.

Etzioni, O., and D. S. Weld. (1994, July). "A Softbot-Based Interface to the Internet." *Communications of the ACM,* Vol. 37, No. 7.

Etzioni, O., and D. S. Weld. (1995, August)."Intelligent Agents on the Internet: Fact, Fiction, and Forecast." *IEEE Expert,* Vol. 10, No. 4.

Evans, B. (2003, January 13). "Supply Siders." *InformationWeek*.

Evans, J. R., and D. L. Olson. (2002). *Introduction to Simulation and Risk Analysis*, 2nd ed. Upper Saddle River, NJ: Prentice Hall.

Evans, S. (1997). *The PACE System: An Expert Consulting System for Nursing.* New York: Springer-Verlag.

Ewalt, D. M. (2002, September 30). "Pinpoint Control." *InformationWeek.*

Ewalt, D. M. (2003a, June 30). "PDAs Make Inroads into Businesses." *InformationWeek.*

Ewalt, D. M. (2003b, July 14–21). "Wal-Mart Shelves RFID Experiment." *InformationWeek.*

Eysenck, H. J. (1994). "The Measurement of Creativity." In M. A. Boden (ed.). *Dimensions of Creativity.* Cambridge, MA: MIT Press, pp. 199–242.

Fadlalla, A. and C. Lin (2001). "An Analysis of the Applications of Neural Networks in Finance." *Interfaces,* Vol. 31, No. 4, pp. 112–122.

Fahey, L., and L. Prusak (1998, Spring). "The Eleven Deadliest Sins of Knowledge Management." *California Management Review,* Vol. 40, No. 3.

Faigle, U., W. Kern, and G. Still. (2002). *Algorithmic Principles of Mathematical Programming.* Norwell, MA: Kluwer Academic Publishers.

Fakas, G., and B. Karakotas. (1999). "A Workflow Management System Based on Intelligent Collaborative Objects." *Information and Software Technology,* Vol. 41.

Far, B. H., and Z. Koono. (1996). "Ex-W-Pert System: A Web-Based Distributed Expert System for Groupware Design." *Expert Systems with Applications,* Vol. 11, No. 4.

Far, B. H., et al. (1996, September). "Merging CASE Tools with Knowledge-Based Technology for Automatic Software Design." *Decision Support Systems,* Vol. 18, No. 1.

Faraj, S., and L. Sproull. (2000, December). "Coordinating Expertise in Software Development Teams." *Management Science.* Vol. 46, No. 12.

Farhoomand, A., and P. Lovelock. (2001). *Global E-Commerce.* Singapore: Prentice Hall.

Fayyad, U., et al. (1996a). "From Knowledge Discovery in Databases." *AI Magazine,* Vol. 17, No. 3.

Fayyad, U. M. (1997). "Editorial." *Data Mining and Knowledge Discovery,* Vol. 1. No. 1.

Fayyad, U. (2003, May). "Optimizing Customer Insight." *Intelligent Enterprise.*

Fayyad, U., G. Grinstein, and A. Wierse (eds.). (2002). *Information Visualization in Data Mining and Knowledge Discovery.* San Francisco: Morgan Kaufman.

Fayyad, U. M., G. Piatetsky-Shapiro, P. Smyth, and R. Uthurusamy. (1996b). *Advances in Knowledge Discovery and Data Mining.* Menlo Park, CA: AAAI Press/MIT Press.

Fayyad, U. M., and R. Uthurusamy (eds.). (1995). *KDD-95: Proceedings of the First International Conference on Knowledge Discovery and Data Mining.* Menlo Park, CA: AAAI Press.

Fedorowicz, J., and A. O. Villeneuve. (1999, June). "Surveying Object Technology Usage and Benefits: A Test of Conventional Wisdom." *Information & Management,* Vol. 35, No. 6.

Feigenbaum, E., and P. McCorduck. (1983). *The Fifth Generation.* Reading, MA: Addison-Wesley.

Feldman, R., and I. Dagan (1995). "Knowledge Discovery in Textual Databases (KDT)." In U. M. Fayyad and R. Uthurusamy (eds.). (1995). *KDD-95: Proceedings of the First International Conference on Knowledge Discovery and Data Mining.* Menlo Park, CA: AAAI Press.

Feldman, S. (2002, June). "What Technologies Are KM Professionals Buying?" *KMWorld.*

Fensel, D. (1996). *The Knowledge Acquisition and Representation Language KARL.* Amsterdam: Kluwer Academic.

Fensel, D., J. Angele, and R. Struder. (1998, July/August). "The Knowledge Acquisition and Representation Language KARL." *IEEE Transactions on Knowledge and Data Engineering,* Vol. 10, No. 4.

Ferguson, M. (2001, April). "Corporate and E-Business Portals." *MyITadviser.*

Ferguson, R. B. (2002, December 23). "Oracle Provides Greater Visibility into Financials." *eWeek.*

Ferguson, R. B. (2003, January 6). "Small-Firm ERP Suite Ready for Mac OS X." *eWeek.*

Ferguson, R. W., and K. D. Forbus. (1999). "GeoRep: A Flexible Tool for Spatial Representation of Line Drawings." *Proceedings of the Qualitative Reasoning Workshop,* Loch Awe, Scotland.

Ferguson, R. B., and L. Vaas. (2003, July 21). "PeopleSoft Seals Deal." *eWeek.*

Ferrar, R., and W. King. (1999, August). "Rip First or Cut First? Use 'Evolution' to Choose." *Wood Technology,* Vol. 126, No. 7.

Ferris, N. (1999, July). "ERP: Sizzling or Stumbling." *Government Executive,* Vol. 31, No. 7.

Fickel, L. (2000, August 15). "Power to the People." *CIO.*

Finin, T., et al. (1997). "KQML as an Agent Communication Language." In J. Bradshaw (ed.). *Software Agents.* Menlo Park, CA: AAAI Press/MIT Press.

Finlay, D. (2001, April 15). "Real-Time Intelligence Scores Over OLAP." *Software Development Times.*

Finnie, G., and Z. Sun. (2003). "R5 Model for Case-Based Reasoning." *KSB,* Vol. 16, pp. 59–65.

Firestone, J. (2003, April). "Portal Progress and Knowledge Management: eKnowledge Portal." *KMWorld.*

Fisher, B. (1999, Spring). "Mellon Creates Fraudwatch to Predict and Manage Risk Using Neural Technology." *Journal of Retail Banking Services,* Vol. 21, No. 1.

Fjermestad, J. (2000/2001, Winter). "Group Support Systems: A Descriptive Evaluation of Case and Field Studies." *Journal of Management Information Systems.* Vol. 17, No. 3.

Fjermestad, J., and S. R. Hiltz. (1998, Winter). "An Assessment of Group Support Systems Experimental Research: Methodology and Results." *Journal of Management Information Systems,* Vol. 15, No. 3.

Flash, C. (2001a, May). "Who Is the CKO?" *Knowledge Management.*

Flash, C. (2001b, Aug). "Personal Chemistry" *Knowledge Management.*

Florida, R. (2000a, May). "The Rise of the Creative Class." *Optimize.*

Florida, R. (2000b). *The Rise of the Creative Class.* : Basic Books.

Follett, J. H. (2003, June 23). "HP Gives Partners an OpenView of Adaptive Enterprises." *CRN.*

Fonseca, B. (2003a, February 3). "BI Titans Bolster Integration." *InfoWorld.*

Fonseca, B. (2003b, June 9). "Consolidation Transforms ERP Landscape." *InforWorld.*

Forgionne, G., M. Mora, F. Cervantes, and O. Gelman. (2002, July). "I-DMSS: A Conceptual Architecture for the Next Generation of Decision Making Support Systems in the Internet Age." *Proceedings of DSIage 2002,* Cork, Ireland.

Forman, E. H., and M. A. Selly. (2001). *Decision by Objectives.* Singapore: World Scientific Publishing Co.

Forsyth, D. A. and J. Ponce. (2002). *Computer Vision: A Modern Approach.* : Prentice Hall.

Foulds, L. R., and D. G. Johnson. (2000). "SlotManager: A Microcomputer-Based DSS for University Course Timetabling." *Decision Support Systems.* Vol. 27.

Foulds, L. R., and C. Thachenkary. (2001, June). "Empower to the People." *OR/MS Today.*

Fourer, R. (2001, August). "Linear Programming Survey." *OR/MS Today,* Vol. 28, No. 4.

Fourer, R., and J-P. Goux. (2001, March/April). "Optimization as an Internet Resource." *Interfaces,* Vol. 31, No. 2.

Fox, J. (2003, May). "Active Information Models for Data Transformation." *eAI Journal.*

Francis, P., and N. Capon. (1996, May). "BPR Software for Financial Services Industry." *Management Services,* Vol. 40, No. 5.

Franklin, D. (2002, November). "Any Way You Slice It." *Credit Union Management.*

Franklin, S., and A. Graesser. (1996). "Is It an Agent, or Just a Program? A Taxonomy for Autonomous Agents." *Proceedings of the Third International Workshop on Agent Theories, Architecture and Languages.* Berlin: Springer-Verlag.

Frappaolo, C. (1998). "Defining Knowledge Management: Four Basic Functions." *ComputerWorld,* Vol. 32, No. 8.

Fraser, J. C. (2002, January). "Groundwork for Project Success." *WebTechniques.*

Freeman, D. (1996, May). "How to Make Spreadsheets Error-Proof." *Journal of Accountancy,* Vol. 181, No. 5.

Freiling, M., et al. (1985, Fall). "Starting a Knowledge Engineering Project: A Step by Step Approach." *AI Magazine.*

Frenzel, L. (1987). *Crash Course in Artificial Intelligence and Expert Systems.* New York: Howard W. Sams.

Friley, M. (2002, February). "Human Language Technologies." *myITadviser.*

Fritz, M. B. W., S. Narasimhan, and H-S. Rhee. (1998, Spring). "Communication and Coordination in the Virtual Office." *Journal of Management Information Systems,* Vol. 14, No. 4.

Fritzsche, D. (1995, November). "Personal Values: Potential Keys to Ethical Decision Making." *Journal of Business Ethics,* Vol. 14, No. 11.

Frolick, M. N., and N. K. Ramarapu. (1993, July). "Hypermedia: The Future of EIS." *Journal of Systems Management,* Vol. 44, No. 7.

Frolick, M. N., and B. P. Robichaux. (1995, June). "EIS Information Requirements Determination: Using a Group Support System to Enhance the Strategic Business Objectives Method." *Decision Support Systems,* Vol. 14, No. 2.

Frye, C. (2002a, October). "IT Still Spending on Portals." *Application Development Trends.*

Frye, C. (2002b November). "Can IT Developers Work Together?" *Application Development Trends.*

Fujimoto, L. (2002, December 14). "Police Can Track Emergency-Call Location Using New Technology." *Maui News.*

Frye, C., and H. Mason. (2001, September). "Project Management Simplified." *WebTechniques.*

Fryer, B. (1997, October 15). "Home Field Advantages." *CIO.*

Fu, L-M. (1999, November). "Knowledge Discovery Based on Neural Networks." *Communications of the ACM,* Vol. 42, No. 11.

Fuerst, W., et al. (1994/1995, Winter). "Expert Systems and Multimedia: Examining the Potential for Integration." *Journal of Management Information Systems,* Vol. 11, No. 3.

Fulton, S. L., and C. O. Pepe. (1990, January). "An Introduction to Model-Based Reasoning." *AI Expert.*

Gabriel, S. A., A. S. Kydes, and P. Whitman. (2001, January/February). "The National Energy Modeling System: A Large-Scale Energy-Economic Equilibrium Model." *Operations Research.* Vol. 49, No. 1.

Gachet, A. (2002, July). "A New Vision for Distributed Decision Support Systems." *Proceedings of DSIage 2002*, Cork, Ireland.

Gale, S. F. (2002, September). "For ERP Success, Create a Culture Change." *Workforce*, Vol. 81, No. 9.

Gallagher, S. (2002, November). "Grand Test Auto." *Baseline*. No. 012.

Gallagher, S. (2003, January 1). "Product Lifecycle Management: A Primer." *Baseline Magazine*.

Gamble, P. R., and J. Blackwell. (2002). *Knowledge Management: A State of the Art Guide*. London: Kogan Page.

Gaines, B. (2003). "Organizational Knowledge Acquisition." Chapter 16 in C. W. Holsapple (ed.). *Handbook of Knowledge Management: Knowledge Matters*, Vol. 1. Heidelberg: Springer-Verlag.

Gaines, B. R., and M. L. G. Shaw. (1993). "Basing Knowledge Acquisition Tools in Personal Construct Psychology." *Knowledge Engineering Review*, Vol. 8, No. 1.

Gan, R., and D. Yang. (1994, September). "Case-Based DSS with Artificial Neural Networks." *Computers and Industrial Engineering*, Vol. 27, Nos. 1–4.

Gareiss, R. (2002, December 2). "Ralph Szygenda." *InformationWeek*.

Garson, G. P. (1995). *Computer Technology and Societal Issues*. Harrisburg, PA: Idea Group.

Garvin, D. A. (1993, July/August). "Building a Learning Organization." *Harvard Business Review*.

Garvin, D.A. (2000a, October). "Learning to Lead." *CIO*.

Garvin, D.A. (2000b). *Learning in Action*. Boston: Harvard Business School Press.

Gaskin, J. E. (1997). *Corporate Politics and the Internet: Connection Without Controversy*. Upper Saddle River, NJ: Prentice Hall.

Gates, L. (2000, September). "Testing Smoothes Path to Integration." *Application Development Trends*.

Gates, L. (2001, February). "Analysis and Design: Critical ... Yet Complicated." *Application Development Trends*.

Gates, L. (2002, July). "Getting Control of Data." *Application Development Trends*.

Gates, L. (2003). "Project Management Tools: A New Look." *Application Development Trends*.

Gatignon, H., M. L. Tushman, W. Smith, and P. Anderson. (2002, September). "A Structural Approach to Assessing Innovation: Construct Development of Innovation Locus, Type and Characteristics." *Management Science*, Vol. 48, No. 9.

Gaud, W. S. (1999, November/December). "Assessing the Impact of Web Courses." *Syllabus*.

Geigle, D. S., and J. E. Aronson. (1999, November/December). "An Artificial Neural Network Approach to the Valuation of Options and Forecasting of Volatility." *Journal of Computational Intelligence in Finance*, Vol. 7, No. 6.

Gendreau, M., G. Laporte, C. Musaraganyi, and E. D. Taillard. (1999, October). "A Tabu Search Heuristic for the Heterogeneous Fleet Vehicle Routing Problem." *Computers & Operations Research*, Vol. 26, No. 12.

Genesereth, M. R. (1997). "An Agent-Based Framework for Interoperability." In J. Bradshaw (ed.). *Software Agents*. Menlo Park, CA: AAAI Press/MIT Press.

Genesereth, M. R., and R. E. Fikes. (1992, June). "Knowledge Interchange Format: Version 3.0 Reference Manual." Stanford, CA: Computer Science Department, Stanford University.

Geng, G., et al. (1999, January). "Applying A1 to Railway Freight Loading." *Expert Systems with Applications*.

Gensym. (2000). "Gensym's Intelligent G2 Software Optimizes Calciner Throughput at Aughinish Alumina." *Success Stories*, Gensym Corporation, www.gensym.com.

Geoffrion, A.M., and R. Krishnan. (2001, March/April). "Prospects for Operations Research in the E-Business Era." *Interfaces*, Vol. 31, No. 2.

George, J. F. (1991/1992). "The Conceptualizations and Development of Organizational Decision Support Systems." *Journal of MIS*, Vol. 8, No. 3.

Georgia, B. (2001, March 12). "Building a Better Project." *NetworkWorld*. Vol. 18, No. 11.

Ghafoor, A. (1995). "Multimedia Database Management Decision Systems." *ACM Computing Surveys*, Vol. 27, No. 4.

Ghanea-Hercock, R. and R. K. Ghanea-Hercock. (2003). *Applied Evolutionary Algorithms in Java*. Berlin: Springer-Verlag.

Gharajedaghi, J. (1999). *Systems Thinking*. Woburn, MA: Butterworth-Heinemann.

Giarratano, J., and G. Riley. (1998). *Expert Systems: Principles and Programming*, 3rd ed. Pacific Grove, CA: PWS Publishing Co.

Gibson, S. (2003, July 14). "MasterCard Is Charging Ahead." *eWeek*.

Gilbert, D., and P. Janca. (1997, February). *IBM Intelligent Agents*. IBM White Paper. Raleigh, NC: IBM Corporation, www.networking.ibm.com/iag/iagwp1.html.

Gennari, J. H., et al. (2003). "The Evolution of Protégé: An Environment for Knowledge-Based Systems Development." *International Journal of Human-Computer Studies*, Vol. 58, no. 1, pp. 89–123.

Ghoash, A. K., and T. M. Swaminatha. (2001, February). "Software Security and Privacy Risks in Mobile E-Commerce." *Communications of the ACM*.

Gilbert, S.D. (2001). " How to Be a Successful Online Student." New York: McGraw-Hill.

Gill, K. S. (ed.). (1996). *Information Society*. London: Springer.

Gill, P. J. (1996a, June 3). "Retooling for the Web." *InformationWeek*, 1A–8A.

Gill, P .J. (2001, May). "Once Upon an Enterprise." *Knowledge Management.*

Gill, T. G. (1995, March). "Early Expert Systems: Where Are They Now?" *MIS Quarterly,* Vol. 19, No. 1.

Gill, T. G. (1996b, September). "Expert Systems Usage: Task Change and Intrinsic Motivation." *MIS Quarterly,* Vol. 20, No. 3.

Gimes, S. (2001, June 13). "Mining a Demographic Mother Lode." *Intelligent Enterprise.*

Ginzberg, M. J. (1981). "Key Recurrent Issues in the MIS Implementation Process." *MIS Quarterly,* Vol. 5, No. 2.

Gladwin, L.C. (2001, April 2). "Volvo Delves into Web-Based Car Design." *ComputerWorld.* Vol. 35, No. 14.

Glaser, B., and H. Kobayashi. (2002). *Efficiency Versus Sustainability in Dynamic Decision Making.* Berlin: Springer-Verlag.

Glover, F., and G.A. Kochenberger. (2001). *Handbook of Metaheuristics.* Norwell, MA: Kluwer Academic Publishers.

Glover, F., and M. Laguna. (1997). *Tabu Search.* Norwell, MA: Kluwer Academic Publishers.

Glymour, C., D. Madigan, D. Pregibon, and P. Smyth. (1997). "Statistical Themes and Lessons for Data Mining." *Data Mining and Knowledge Discovery,* Vol. 1, No. 1.

Goettl, B. (ed.). (1998 August). *Proceedings of Intelligent Tutoring Systems Fourth International Conference,* San Antonio, TX.

Gold, A.H., A. Malhotra, and A.H. Segars. (2001, Summer). "Knowledge Management: An Organizational Capabilities Perspective." *Journal of Management Information Systems,* Vol. 18, No. 1.

Goldberg, D. E. (1989). *Genetic Algorithms in Search Optimization and Machine Learning.* Reading, MA: Addison-Wesley.

Goldberg, D. E. (1994, March). "Genetic and Evolutionary Algorithms Come of Age." *Communications of the ACM,* Vol. 37, No. 3.

Goldbogen, G., and G. A. Howe. (1993). "Integrating Artificial Intelligence into Existing Software Applications." In M. Grabowksi and W. A. Wallace (eds.). *Advances in Expert Systems for Management.* Greenwich, CT: JAI Press.

Golding, A. R., and P. S. Rosenbloom. (1996, November). "Improving Accuracy by Combining Rule-Based and Case-Based Reasoning." *Artificial Intelligence,* Vol. 87.

Goldman, J., R. Nagel, and K. Preiss. (1994). *Agile Competitors and Virtual Organizations: Strategies for Enriching the Customer.* New York: Van Nostrand Reinhold.

Goldstein, D. (2002). "Automating Large Business Rule and Expert Systems Verification: Easy Approach Simplifies Maintenance." *PC AI,* pp. 47–48.

Gonzales, M.L. (2001, June 13). "Fear and Loathing in Project Management." *Intelligent Enterprise.*

Gonzales, M. L. (2003, February 1). "The New GIS Landscape." *Intelligent Enterprise.*

Gonzales, M., and G. Robinson. (2003, Quarter 2). "The OLAP Aware Database." *DB2 Magazine.*

Goodie, A. (2001, September). "Paradoxical Betting on Items of High Confidence with Low Value: The Effects of Control on Betting." *Proceedings of the Annual Meeting of the Society for Judgment and Decision Making,* Orlando, FL.

Goodman, P. S., and E. D. Darr. (1998). "Computer-aided Systems and Communities: Mechanisms for Organizational Learning in Distributed Environments." *MIS Quarterly,* Vol. 22, No. 4.

Goodridge, E. (2001a, April). "GM Drives E-Learning." *InformationWeek.*

Goodridge, E. (2001b, October 22). "Virtual Meetings Yield Real Results." *InformationWeek.*

Goodridge, E. (2001c, November 19). "Portal Gives Workers Cruise Control." *InformationWeek.*

Goodridge, E. (2002, January 28). "IBM and Microsoft Send Employees Back to School." *InformationWeek.*

Goodwin, P., and G. Wright. (2000). Decision Analysis for Management Judgment. 2nd ed. New York: John Wiley.

Goralski, W. M., et. al. (1997). *VRML: Exploring the Virtual World on the Internet,* Upper Saddle River, NJ: Prentice Hall.

Gorry, G. A., and M. S. Scott Morton. (1971). "A Framework for Management Information Systems." *Sloan Management Review,* Vol. 13, No. 1.

Gorry, G. A., and M. S. Scott Morton. (1989, Spring). "A Framework for Management Information Systems-Revisited." *Sloan Management Review.*

Gottinger, H. W., and H. P. Weimann. (1995, September). "Intelligent Inference Systems Based on Influence Diagrams." *Decision Support Systems,* Vol. 15, No. 1.

Gottschalk, P. (2000, January). "Knowledge Management in the Professions: The Case of IT Support in Law Firms." *Proceedings, 33rd HICSS.*

Goul, M., B. Shane, and F. Tong. (1984, May). "Designing the Expert Component of a Decision Support System." *ORSA/TIMS Joint National Meeting,* San Francisco.

Goul, M., et al. (1992, November/December). "The Emergence of AI as a Reference Discipline for Decision Support Systems Research." *Decision Sciences.*

Goulet, M., and D. Wishart. (1996, June). "Classifying a Bank's Customers to Improve Their Financial Services." *Conference of the Classification Society of North America (CSNA).* Amherst, MA.

Gourdin, E. (2001, April). "Optimizing Internet Networks." *OR/MS Today.*

Grabowski, M., and S. D. Sanborn. (2001, Winte5r). "Evaluation of Embedded Intelligent Real-Time Systems." *Decision Sciences,* Vol. 32, No. 1.

Grabowski, M., and W. W. Wallace. (1993). *Advances in Expert Systems for Management.* Vol. 1. Greenwich, CT: JAI Press.

Grady, S. M. (1998). *Virtual Reality.* New York: Facts on File.

Gray, P. (1999). "Tutorial on Knowledge Management." *Proceedings of the Americas Conference of the Association for Information Systems,* Milwaukee.

Gray, P., and D. Meisters. (2003). "Knowledge Sourcing Effectiveness." Working Paper, University of Pittsburgh.

Gray, P., and S. Tehrani. (2003). "Technologies for Knowledge Distribution." Chapter 38 in C. W. Holsapple (ed.). *Handbook of Knowledge Management: Knowledge Directions,* Vol. 2. Heidelberg: Springer-Verlag.

Green, H., and P. Katz. (2002, Sept). "Arrow Takes Aim at Supply Chain." *Optimize.*

Green, J. (1999, March). "Deluxe Beefs Up Its Debit Bureau." *Credit Card Management,* Vol. 11, No. 12.

Greenberg, P. (2002). *CRM at the Speed of Light: Capturing and Keeping Customers in Internet Real Time,* 2nd ed. New York: McGraw-Hill.

Greenemeier, L. (2003, April). "Utility Computing Meets Real Life." *Information Week.*

Greenhalgh, C. (1999). *Large Scale Collaborative Virtual Environments.* Berlin: Springer-Verlag.

Gregg, D. G., and Goul, M. (1999, November). "A Proposal for an Open DSS Protocol." *Communications of the ACM,* Vol. 42, No. 11.

Gregg, D.G., et al. (2002, January). "Distributing Decision Support Systems on the WWW: The Verification of a DSS Metadata Model." *Decision Support Systems.*

Griffith, T. L., M. A. Fuller, and G. B. Northcraft. (1998, March). "Facilitator Influence in Group Support Systems: Intended and Unintended Effects." *Information Systems Research,* Vol. 9, No. 1.

Grimes, S. (2003, April 23). "Declaration Support: The B.P.M. Drumbeat." *Intelligent Enterprise.*

Grimshaw, D. J. (1999). *Bringing Geographical Information Systems into Business.* New York: John Wiley.

Grodner, K. (2003, July). "Creating Virtual Communities." *Portals Magazine,* Vol. 33, No. 22.

Grogono, P., et al. (1991, November). "Expert System Evaluation Techniques: A Selected Bibliography." *Expert Systems,* Vol. 8, No. 4.

Grossman, T. A. (2002, August). "Spreadsheet Add-Ins for OR/MS." *OR/MS Today.* Vol. 29, No. 4.

Groth, R. (1998). *Data Mining: A Hands-On Approach for Business Professionals.* Upper Saddle River, NJ: Prentice Hall PTR.

Gruber, T. R., and P. R. Cohen. (1987). "Design for Acquisition Principles of Knowledge System Design to Facilitate Knowledge Acquisitions." *International Journal of Man-Machine Studies,* No. 2.

Grudin J., and B. Wellman. (1999, February). "The Changing Relationship Between Information Technology and Society." *IEEM Intelligent Systems.*

Grunther, H. O. (1996). *Evolutionary Search and the Job Shop: Investigations on Genetic Algorithms for Production Scheduling.* New York: Springer-Verlag.

Grupe, F. H., R. Urwiler, and N. K. Ramarapu. (1998). "The Application of Case-Based Reasoning to the Software Development Process." *Information and Software Technology,* Vol. 40, No. 9.

Guha, R. V., and D. B. Lenat. (1994, July). "Enabling Agents to Work Together." *Communications of the ACM,* Vol. 37, No. 7.

Guimaraes, T., et al. (1992, March/April). "The Determinants of DSS Success: An Integrated Model." *Decision Sciences,* Vol. 23, No. 2.

Guimaraes, T., Y. Yoon, and A. Clevenson. (1996, June). "Factors Important to Expert Systems Success: A Field Test." *Information & Management,* Vol. 30, No. 3.

Guimaraes, T. O., M. Igbaria, and M-t. Lu. (1992). "The Determinants of DSS Success: An Integrated Model." *Decision Sciences.* Vol. 23, No. 2.

Gung, R. R., Y. T. Leung, G. Y. Lin, and R. Y. Tsai. (2002, December). "Demand Forecasting Today." *OR/MS Today,* Vol. 29, No. 6.

Gungor, Z., and F. Arikan. (2000, January 15). "Application of Fuzzy Decision Making in Part-Machine Grouping." *International Journal of Production Economics,* Vol. 63, No. 2.

Gupta, A., and R. Jain. (1997, May). "Visual Information Retrieval." *Communications of the ACM.*

Gupta, B., L. Iyer, and J. E. Aronson. (1999, August). "An Exploration of Knowledge Management Techniques." *Proceedings of the Americas Conference of the Association for Information Systems,* Milwaukee.

Gupta, B., L. Iyer, and J. E. Aronson. (2000). "Knowledge Management: A Taxonomy, Practices and Challenges." *Industrial Management and Data Systems,* Vol. 100, Nos. 1 and 2.

Gupta, B., et al. (2000). "Knowledge Management: A Taxonomy, Practices and Challenges/" *Industrial Management and Data Systems,* Vol. 100, Nos. 1 and 2.

Gupta, B., et al. (1999, August). "An Exploration of Knowledge Management Techniques." *Proceedings of the Americas Conference of the Association for Information Systems,* Milwaukee.

Gupta, M. (1995). *Fuzzy Logic and Intelligent Systems.* Norwell, MA: Kluwer.

Gupta, S., and D. R. Lehmann. (2002, May). "What Are Your Customers Worth?" *Optimize.*

Guptill, B. (2003, April). "Customer Metrics That Matter." *Optimize.*

Guth, M. (1999). "An Expert System for Curtailing Electric Power." www.wvjolt.wvu.edu.

Ha., S. H. (2002). "Helping Online Customers Decide Through Web Personalization." *IEEE Intelligent Systems*, Vol. 17, No. 6, pp. 34–43.

Hackathorn, R. D., and P. G. W. Keen. (1981, September). "Organizational Strategies for Personal Computing in Decision Support Systems." *MIS Quarterly*, Vol. 5, No. 3.

Hackbarth, G., and V. Grover. (1999, Summer). "The Knowledge Repository: Organizational Memory Information Systems." *Information Systems Management*.

Hagel, J., III. (2002). *Out of the Box*. Boston: Harvard Business School Press.

Hagel, J., III, and A. G. Armstrong. (1997). *Net Gain: Expanding Markets through Virtual Communities*. Boston: Harvard Business School Press.

Hahn, U., M. Klenner, and K. Schnattinger. (1996). "A Quality-Based Terminological Reasoning Model for Text Knowledge Acquisition." In N. Shadbolt, K. O'Hara, and G. Schreiber (eds.). *Advances in Knowledge Acquisition*. Berlin: Springer-Verlag.

Haimila, S. (2000, April). "Knowledge Helps Scotland Yard Nab Criminals." *KMWorld*, Vol. 9, No. 3.

Haley, B. J., and H. J. Watson. (1996, Winter). "Using Lotus Notes in EISs." *Information Systems Management*.

Hall, J., G. Mani, and D. Barr. (1996). "Applying Computational Intelligence to the Investment Process." *Proceedings of CIFER-96: Computational Intelligence in Financial Engineering*. Washington, DC: IEEE Computer Society.

Hall, M. (2002a, April 1). "Web Analytics: Get Real." *ComputerWorld*, Vol. 36, No. 14.

Hall, M. (2002b, July 1). "Decision Support Systems." *ComputerWorld*, 36, No. 27.

Hall, N. (1987). "A Fuzzy Decision Support System for Strategic Planning." In E. Sanchez and L. Zadeh (eds.). *Approximate Reasoning in Intelligent Systems, Decision and Control*. Oxford: Pergamon Press.

Hall, R. H., et. al. (1999, Winter). "The Effects of Graphical Post-Organization Strategies on Learning from Knowledge Maps." *Journal of Experimental Education*.

Hall, M. (2002, April 15). "Seeding for Data Growth." *ComputerWorld*.

Hallett, P. (2001, June). "Web-Based Visualization." *DM Review*.

Halpern, J. J., and R. N. Stern. (1998). *Debating Rationality: Nonrational Aspects of Organizational Decision Making*. Ithaca, NY: Cornell University Press.

Hamey, J. (2003, January). "Predictive Analytics: Forecasting Future Trends from Existing Data." *KMWorld*. Vol 12, No. 1.

Hamilton, D. M. (1996a). "Knowledge Acquisition for Multiple Site, Related Domain Expert Systems: Delphi Process and Applications." *Expert Systems with Applications*, Vol. 11, No. 3.

Hamilton, J. M. (1996b, March 15). "A Mapping Feast." *CIO*.

Hammer, M., and J. Champy. (1993). *Reengineering the Corporation*. New York: Harper Business.

Hammer, M., and S. Stanton. (1995). *The Reengineering Revolution: A Handbook*. New York: HarperCollins.

Hamscher, W., M. Y. Kiang, and R. Lang. (1995). "Qualitative Reasoning in Business, Finance, and Economics: Introduction." *Decision Support Systems*, Vol. 15, No. 2.

Han, J., and M. Kamber. (2000). *Data Mining: Concepts and Techniques*. San Francisco: Morgan Kaufmann.

Hand, D. J. (1984, October). "Statistical Expert Systems Design." *Statistician*, Vol. 33, No. 4.

Hand, D.J., H. Mannila, and P. Smyth. (2001). *Principles of Data Mining*. Cambridge, MA: MIT Press.

Handzic, M., and M. Cule. (2002. July 4-7). "Creative Decision Making: Review, Analysis and Recommendations." Proceedings of DSIage2002, Cork, Ireland.

Hanley, S., and G. Malafsky. (2003). "A Guide for Measuring the Value of Knowledge Management Investments." Chapter 49 in C. W. Holsapple (ed.). *Handbook of Knowledge Management: Knowledge Directions*, Vol. 2. Heidelberg: Springer-Verlag.

Hansen, F. (2002, May). "Global Economic and Business Data for Credit Managers." *Business Credit*, Vol. 104, No. 5.

Hansen, M., et al. (1999, March/April). "What's Your Strategy for Managing Knowledge?" *Harvard Business Review*, Vol. 77, No. 2.

Hanson, M. A., and R. L. Brekke. (1988). "Workload Management Expert System Combining Neural Networks and Rule-Based Programming in an Operational Application." Special Report. Triangle Park, NC: Instrument Society of America.

Hanson R. D., and D. G. Stork. (1999, May/June). "Building Intelligent Systems: One E-Citizen at a Time." *IEEM Intelligent Systems*.

Hapgood, F. (2001a, August 15). "Smart Decisions." *CIO*.

Hapgood, F. (2001b, November 15). "Point of Reference: Geographic Information Systems Gave Us a New Look at the World." *CIO*.

Harel, D., and M. Politi. (1998). *Modeling Reactive Systems with Statecharts: The STATEMATE Approach*. New York: McGraw-Hill.

Hargadon, A. B. (1998, Spring). "Firms as Knowledge Brokers: Lessons in Pursuing Continuous Innovation." *California Management Review*, Vol. 40, No. 3, pp. 209–227.

Harmon, P. (ed.). (1993, March) "Precisely Fuzzy, Part I." *Intelligent Software Strategies*, Vol. 9, No. 4.

Harmon, P., et al. (1988). *Expert Systems Tools and Applications*. New York: John Wiley.

Harreld, H. (2002, December 2). "BI Analytics with Brains." *InfoWorld*.

Harrell, C. R., B. K. Ghosh, and R. Bowden. (2000, November-December). *Simulation Using PROMODEL w/CD-ROM*. New York: McGraw-Hill.

Harris, L. E. (1998). *Digital Property*. New York: McGraw-Hall.

Harris, P. (2003, February). "ROI of E-learning: Closing In." *T + D*. Vol. 57, No. 2.

Harrison, A. (2000, October 30). "Online Voting Moves Closer to Acceptance." *ComputerWorld*.

Hart, A. (1992). *Knowledge Acquisition for Expert Systems*. New York: McGraw-Hill.

Hartman, P. J. (1993, March). "Finding Cost-Effective Applications for Expert Systems." *Transactions of the ASME*, Vol. 115.

Hashemi, R. R., L. A. Le Blanc, C. T. Rucks, and A. Rajaratnam. (1998, September 1). "A Hybrid Intelligent System for Predicting Bank Holding Structures." *European Journal of Operational Research*, Vol. 109, No. 2.

Haskett, M. (2000a, April). "An Introduction to Data Mining, Part 1: Understanding the Critical Data Relationship in the Corporate Data Warehouse." *Enterprise Systems Journal*.

Haskett, M. (2000b, May.). "An Intro to Data Mining, Part 2: Analyzing the Tools and Techniques." *Enterprise Systems Journal*.

Haskin D. (1998, February). "Leveraging Your Knowledge Base." *Internet World*.

Hastings, J., et al. (2002). "CARMA: A Case-Based Rangeland Management Adviser." *AI Magazine*, pp. 49–62.

Hatcher, D. (2003, June 30). "Sharing the Info Wealth." *ComputerWorld*.

Hauser, R. D., Jr., and F. J. Hebert. (1992, Winter). "Managerial Issues in Expert System Implementation." *SAM Advanced Management Journal*, Vol. 57, No. 1.

Havenstein, H. (2003a, April 28). "Real-Time Smarts." *InfoWorld*.

Havenstein, H. (2003b, May 26). "BAM Bolsters Data Visibility." *InfoWorld*.

Havenstein, H. (2003c, June 2). "BI Vendors Seek to Tap End-User Power." *InfoWorld*.

Hayes, M. (2001, January 30). "The Model Customer." *Intelligent Enterprise*.

Hayes-Roth, B., et al. (1998, March). "Staffing the Web with Interactive Characters." *Communications of the ACM*.

Hayes-Roth, B., et al. (1999, March/April). "Web Guides" *IEEE Intelligent Systems*. (Animated agents).

Haykin, S. S. (1999). *Neural Networks: A Comprehensive Foundation*, 2nd ed. Upper Saddle River, NJ: Prentice Hall.

Heinriches, J. H., and J. S. Lim (2003). "Integrating Web-Based Data Mining Tools with Business Models for Knowledge Management." *Decision Support Systems*, Vol. 35, No. 2.

Hellriegel, D., and J. W. Slocum, Jr. (1992). *Management*, 6th ed. Reading, MA: Addison-Wesley.

Hendler, J. (2001). "Agents and the Semantic Web." *IEEE Intelligent Systems*, Vol. 16, No. 2, pp. 30–37.

Hendler, J., and K. Stoffel. (1999, May/June). "Back-End Technology for High-Performance Knowledge Representation Systems." *IEEE Intelligent Systems and Their Applications*, Vol. 14, No. 3.

Hendriks, L. (2002, June). "Customers in Sight: Supporting Corporate Accommodation Decisions with Real Estate Data." *Journal of Corporate Real Estate*, Vol. 4, No. 3.

Henfridsson, O., and A. Söderholm. (2000). "Barriers to Learning: On Organizational Defenses and Vicious Circles in Technological Adoption." *Accounting, Management and Information Technologies*, Vol. 10, No. 1, pp. 33-51.

Hengl, T. (1995). *AI on the Internet*. Phoenix: Knowledge Technology.

Hengl, T. (2002). "Fuzzy Logic and Evolutionary Electronics." *PC AI*, Vol. 16, No. 3, pp. 44–46.

Hernandez-Serrano, J., and D. H. Jonassen. (2003). "The Effect of Case Libraries on Problem Solving." *Journal of Computer-Assisted Learning*, Vol. 19, No. 1, pp. 103–114.

Herschel R. T., and H. R. Nemati. (1999). "Knowledge Management: The Role of the CKO." *Proceedings of the Americas Conference of the Association for Information Systems*, Milwaukee.

Herschel, R. T., and H. R. Nemati. (2000, Summer). "Chief Knowledge Officer: Critical Success Factors for Knowledge Management." *Information Strategy*, Vol. 16, No. 4.

Hess T. J., et al. (2000, July). "Using Autonomous Software Agents to Create the Next Generation DSS." *Decision Sciences*.

Hibbard, J. (1998, September 21). "Cultural Breakthrough." *InformationWeek*.

Hickey, E. (2002, May). "New Tricks." *SmartBusiness*.

Hicks, M. (2001, November 26). "Getting Pricing Just Right." *eWeek*.

Hill, T. R., and W. E. Remus, (1994, June). "Neural Network Models for Intelligent Support of Managerial Decision Making." *Decision Support Systems*, Vol. 11, No. 5.

Hill, R. B., D. C. Wolfram, and D. E. Broadbent. (1986, October). "Expert Systems and the Man–Machine Interface." *Expert Systems*.

Hillier, F. S., and G. J. Lieberman. (2003). *Introduction to Operations Research*. 7th ed. New York: McGraw-Hill.

Hillman, D. V. (1990, June). "Integrating Neural Networks and Expert Systems." *AI Expert*.

Hilmer, K. M., and A. R. Dennis. (2000). "Stimulating Thinking in Group Decision Making." *Proceedings of the Thirty-third Annual Hawaii International Conference on System Sciences HICSS-33.* Los Alamitos, CA: IEEE Computer Society Press.

Hinds, R. S., and J. E. Aronson. (2002, August). "Developing the Requisite Organizational, Attitudinal, and Behavioral Conditions for Effective Knowledge Management." *Proceedings of the Americas Conference for Information Systems*, Dallas.

Hoch, S. J. (2001a). "Combining Models with Intuition to Improve Decisions." Chapter 5 in S. J. Hoch, H. C. Kunreuther, with R. E. Gunther, ed. (2001). *Wharton on Making Decisions.* New York: John Wiley

Hoch, S. J., and H. C. Kunreuther. (2001b). "A Complex Web of Decisions." Chapter 1 in S. J. Hoch, H. C. Kunreuther, with R. E. Gunther, ed. (2001). *Wharton on Making Decisions.* New York: John Wiley.

Hoch, S. J., H. C. Kunreuther, with R. E. Gunther. (2001c). *Wharton on Making Decisions.* New York: John Wiley.

Hoffer, J., M. Prescott, and F. McFadden. (2002a). *Modern Database Management.* 6th ed. Upper Saddle River, NJ: Prentice Hall.

Hoffer, J. A., M. B. Prescott, and F. R. McFadden. (2002b). *Modern Database Design.* 6th ed. Upper Saddle River, NJ: Prentice Hall.

Hoffman, T. (2002, December 2). "Automaker Goes 'Digital.'" *ComputerWorld.* Vol. 36, No. 49.

Holland, R. (2000, October 16). "XML Standards Are Gaining a Foothold." *eWeek.*

Holloway, P. (2000, January). "Sharing Knowledge and Other Unnatural Acts." *Knowledge Management* (White Paper).

Hollowell, T., and G. Verma. (2002, July 24). "Customers Want the Personal Touch." *InformationWeek.*

Holsapple, C. W. (ed.). (2003a). *Handbook of Knowledge Management: Knowledge Matters*, Vol. 1. Heidelberg: Springer-Verlag.

Holsapple, C. W. (ed.). (2003b). *Handbook of Knowledge Management: Knowledge Directions*, Vol. 2. Heidelberg: Springer-Verlag.

Holsapple, C. W. (2003c). "Knowledge and Its Attributes." Chapter 9 in C. W. Holsapple (ed.). *Handbook of Knowledge Management: Knowledge Matters*, Vol. 1. Heidelberg: Springer-Verlag.

Holsapple, C. W., and K. D. Joshi (1999). "Description and Analysis of Existing Knowledge Management Frameworks." *Proceedings of the Thirty-second Annual Hawaii International Conference on System Sciences HICSS-32,* Los Alamitos, CA: IEEE Computer Society.

Holsapple, C. W., and A. B. Whinston. (1996). *Decision Support Systems: A Knowledge-Based Approach.* St. Paul: West Publishing.

Holt, K. (2002, August 5) "Nice Concept: Two Days' Work in a Day," *Meeting News*, Vol. 26, No. 11.

Holweg, M., and F. Pil. (2001, Fall). "Successful Build-to-Order Strategies Start with the Customer." *MIT Sloan Management Journal*, Vol. 43, No. 1.

Homburg, V., and A. Meijer. (2001, January). "Why Would Anyone Want to Share His Knowledge?" *Proceedings, 34th HICSS.*

Hong, K. K., and Y-G. Kim. (2002, October). "The Critical Success Factors for ERP Implementation: An Organizational Fit Perspective." *Information & Management*, Vol. 40, No. 1.

Hopper, E., and B. Turton (1999, October). "A Genetic Algorithm for a 2D Industrial Packing Problem." *Computers & Industrial Engineering,* Vol. 37, Nos. 1 and 2.

Horgan, D. J. (2003, April 1). "Knowledge Preservation." *CIO.*

Horner, P. (2000, June). "The SABRE Story." *OR/MS Today.*

Horowitz, A. S. (2003, January 13). "Biting Back." *ComputerWorld.* Vol. 37, No. 2.

Housel, T., and A.H. Bell (2001). *Measuring and Managing Knowledge.* Boston: McGraw-Hill/Irwin.

Hsiang, T. (2002, June). "How to Conduct Product Mix Analysis." *OR/MS Today.*

Huang, H. J. (1999, Fall). "Intelligent Diagnose Learning Agents for Intelligent Tutoring Systems." *Journal of Computer Information System.*

Huang, J. (2001, April). "A New Blueprint for Business Architecture." *Harvard Business Review.*

Huang, K. T. (1998a). "Knowledge Is Power: So Use It or Lose It." IBM Corp. www.ibm.com/services/articles/.

Huang, K. T. (1998b). "Capitalizing on Intellectual Assets, Not Infrastructure." *IBM Systems Journal*, Vol. 37, No. 4.

Huang, K. T., Y. W. Lee, and R. Y. Wang. (1999). *Quality Information and Knowledge.* Upper Saddle River, NJ: Prentice Hall.

Huang, S. H., and H. C. Zhang. (1995, May). "Neural–Expert Hybrid Approaches for Intelligent Manufacturing: A Survey." *Computers in Industry,* Vol. 26, No. 2.

Huber, G. P. (1990). "A Theory of the Effects of Advanced Information Technologies on Organizational Design, Intelligence, and Decision Making." *Academy of Management Review,* Vol. 15, No. 1.

Hudnell, M., and H. Kitayama. (2000, November/December). "Transforming Business with Data Mining." *SAS.com.*

Hudson, M. J. (2001, October). "Don't Make Me Repeat Myself." *Intelligent Enterprise.*

Hudson, M. J. (2002, June 28). "Popularity Contest." *Intelligent Enterprise.*

Huff, S. L., et al. (2001). *Cases in Electronic Commerce.* New York: McGraw-Hill.

Hugos, M. H. (2003). *Essentials of Supply Chain Management*. New York: John Wiley.

Huh, S-Y. (2000, November). "Collaborative Model Management in Departmental Computing." *INFOR*. Vol. 38. No. 4.

Huhns, M. N. (2002). "Agents as Web Services." *IEEE Internet Computing*, Vol. 6, No. 4, pp. 93–95.

Humphrey, M. C. (1999, February). "A graphical notation for the design of information visualisations." *International Journal of Human–Computer Studies*.

Humphrey, W. S. (2002). *Winning With Software: An Executive Strategy*. Reading, MA: Addison-Wesley.

Humphreys, P., et al. (2003). "Using Case-Based Reasoning to Evaluate Supplier environmental Management Performance." *Expert Systems with Applications*, Vol. 25, pp. 141–153.

Hung, S-Y. (1999). "Expert Versus Novice Use of the Executive Support Systems: An Empirical Study." *IEEE Conference on Systems Sciences*.

Hung, Y-F., C-C. Shih, and C-P. Chen. (1999, August). "Evolutionary Algorithms for Production Planning Problems with Setup Decisions." *Journal of the Operational Research Society*, Vol. 50, No. 8.

Hunt, J. (1997, February). "Case-Based Diagnosis and Repair of Software Faults." *Expert Systems*, Vol. 14, No. 1.

Hunter, G., and J. E. Beck. (2000, March). "Using Repertory Grids to Conduct Across Cultural Information Systems Research." *Information Systems Research*.

Huntington, D. (1997, March/April). "Web-Based AI: Expert Systems on the WWW." *PC AI*.

Huntington, D. (2002). "Back to Basics—Backward Chaining: An Expert System Fundamental." *PC AI*, Vol. 16, No. 4, pp. 27–32.

Hurley, W. J. and D. U. Lior. (2002). "Combining Expert Judgment: On the Performance of Trimmed Mean Vote Aggregation Procedures in the Presence of Strategic Voting." *European Journal of Operational Research*, Vol.140, No. 1, pp. 142–147.

Hutchinson, M. O. (1998, Summer). "The Use of Fuzzy Logic in Business Decision-Making." *Derivatives Quarterly*, Vol. 4, No. 4.

Hurwicz, M. (2002, August). "Attack of the Space Data: Down-to-Earth Data Management at ISS EarthKAM." *New Architect Magazine*.

Hwang, C-P., B. Alidaee, and J. D. Johnson. (1999, August). "A Tour Construction Heuristic for the Travelling Salesman Problem." *Journal of the Operational Research Society*, Vol. 50, No. 8.

Hyperion. (2003). Hyperion Solutions Corporation Web site, www.hyperion.com.

Iacobucci, D, P. Arabie, and A. Bodapati. (2000). "Recommendation Agents on the Internet." *Journal of Interactive Marketing*, Vol. 14, No. 3, pp. 2–11.

IBM Corporation. (1995). *Intelligent Agent Strategy*. IBM Corporation White Paper.

Imhoff, C. (2001, May). "Power Up Your Enterprise Portal." *E-Business Advise*.

Information Advantage. (1997). "Putting the Data Warehouse on the Internet." White Paper www.inforadvan.com/1f.4_int.html.

InfoWorld. (2000, December 4). "Enterprise Knowledge Portals Wise Up Your Business." *InfoWorld*, Vol. 22, No. 49.

Inmon, W. H. (1998, May). "Data Mart Does Not Equal Data Warehouse." *DM Review*.

Inmon, W.H. (2002). *Building the Data Warehouse*. 3rd ed. New York: John Wiley.

Inmon, W. H., C. Imhoff, and R. Sousa (2002). *Corporate Information Factory*, 2nd ed. (E-Book). New York: John Wiley.

Inmon, W. H., R. H. Terdeman, and C. Imhoff. (2000). *Exploration Warehousing: Turning Business Information into Business Opportunity*. New York: John Wiley.

Inmon, W. H., R. H. Terdeman, J. Norris-Montanari, and D. Meers (2001). *Data Warehousing for E-Business*. New York: John Wiley.

Ishman, M. D. (1996, Fall). "Measuring Information Success at the Individual Level in Cross-cultural Environments." *Information Resources Management Journal*, Vol. 9, No. 4.

Ives, B., and M. H. Olson. (1984, May). "User Involvement in Information System Development: A Review of Research." *Management Science*, Vol. 30, No. 5.

Iwasaki, Y. (1997, May/June). "Real-World Applications of Qualitative Reasoning." *IEEE Expert*, Vol. 12, No. 3.

Iyer, L. S., et al. (2002). "Global E-Commerce: Rationale, Digital Divide, and Strategies to Bridge the Divide." *Journal of Global Information Technology Management*, Vol. 5, No. 1.

Jackson, P., and R. Suomi. (2001). *eBusiness and Workplace Redesign*. : Routledge.

Jacob, M., and G. Ebrahimpur. (2001). "Experience vs. Expertise: The Role of Implicit Understandings of Knowledge in Determining the Nature of Knowledge Transfer in Two Companies." *Journal of Intellectual Capital*, Vol. 2, No. 1.

Jacobs, A. (1996, August 5). "Mapping Software Finds the Net." *Computerworld*, Vol. 20, No. 32, p. 44.

Jacobs, F. R., and D. C. Whybark. (2000). *Why ERP?* Boston: McGraw-Hill.

Jacobson, I., and M. L. Griss. (2001, June). "Approaching the Promised Land of Component Reuse." *Application Development Trends*.

Jacobson, I., G. Booch, and J. Rumbaugh. (1998). *The Unified Software Development Process*. Reading, MA: Addison-Wesley.

Jacobson, I., M. Griss, and P. Jonsson. (1998). *Software Reuse: Architecture, Process and Organization for Business Success.* Reading, MA: Addison-Wesley.

Jacso, P. (1999, December). "New Web Technology: Shopping Agents." *Information Today.* Vol. 16, No. 11.

Jamali, N., et al. (1999, March/April). "An Actor-Based Architecture for Customizing and Controlling Agent Ensembles." *IEEE Intelligent Systems.*

James, R. (2000, March). "Open Wide for the Latest Automation Advances." *PPI,* Vol. 42, No. 3.

Jamshidi, M., A. Titli, L. Zadeh, and S. Boverie (eds.). (1997). *Applications of Fuzzy Logic: Towards High Machine Intelligent Quotient Systems.* Upper Saddle River, NJ: Prentice Hall.

Jana, R. (1999, September 13). "Getting the Most Out of Online Learning." *InfoWorld,* Vol. 21, No. 37.

Janvrin, D., and J. Morrison. (2000, January). "Using a Structured Design Approach to Reduce Risks in End User Spreadsheet Development." *Information & Management,* Vol. 37, No. 1.

Jeng, B., T. P. Liang, and M. Hong. (1996). "Interactive Induction for Knowledge Acquisition." *Expert Systems with Applications*, Vol. 10, Nos. 3 and 4, pp. 393–401.

Jenkins, M. (2002). "Cognitive Mapping." In D. Partington (ed.). *Essential Skills for Management Research.* Thousand Oaks, CA: Sage Publications.

Jennex, M., and L. Olfman. (2003). "Organizational Memory and Its Management." Chapter 11 in C. W. Holsapple (ed.). *Handbook of Knowledge Management: Knowledge Matters*, Vol. 1. Heidelberg: Springer-Verlag.

Jennings N. R., et al. (eds.). (1998). *Agent Technology: Foundation, Applications, and Markets.* New York: Springer-Verlag.

Jerez-Aragones, J. M., et al. (2003). "A Combined Neural Network and Decision Trees Model for Prognosis of Breast Cancer Relapse." *Artificial Intelligence in Medicine*, Vol. 27, No. 1, pp. 45–63.

Jessup, L. M., and D. van Over. (1996, July/August). "When a System Must Be All Things to All People: The Functions, Components and Costs of a Multi-Purpose Group Support System Facility." *Journal of Systems Management*, Vol. 47, No. 4.

Jia, J. (2002, November 6). "Four Keys to Content Management." *Knowledge Management.*

Jiang, J. J., G. Klein, and J. L. Balloun. (1998, Fall). "Systems Analysts' Attitudes Toward Information Systems Development." *Information Resources Management Journal,* Vol. 11, No. 4.

Jiang, J. J., G. Klein, J. L. Balloun, and S. M. Crampton. (1999, January 25). "System Analysts' Orientations and Perceptions of System Failure." *Information and Software Technology,* Vol. 41, No. 2.

Jiang, J. J., W. A. Muhanna, and G. Klein. (2000, January). "User Resistance and Strategies for Promoting Acceptance Across System Types." *Information & Management,* Vol. 37.

Johnson, A. H. (2002, September 30). "A New Supply Chain Forged." *ComputerWorld.*

Johnson, D. G., and J. M. Mulvey. (1995, December). "Accountability and Computer Decision Making." *Communications of the ACM,* Vol. 38, No. 12.

Johnson, J. (1999, December). "Turning Chaos into Success." *Software Magazine.*

Johnson, J. (2001, April/May). "Microproject Methodology Defined." *Software Magazine.*

Johnson, R. C. (1999, August 16). "Genetic Algorithms Adapt Fast ICs to Fab Variations." *Electronic Engineering Times,* No. 1074.

Jones, C. (2000a, July). "Spotting the Best, and Worst, Software Development Practices." *Application Development Trends.*

Jones, C. (2000b). *Software Assessments, Benchmarks, and Best Practices.* Reading, MA: Addison-Wesley.

Jones, J. (2001, December 19). "Examining PLM's Benefits." *InfoWorld.*

Jones, M., et al. (1995). "An Agent-Based Approach to Spacecraft Mission Operations." In N. J. I. Mars (ed.). *Towards Very Large Databases.* Amsterdam: IOS Press.

Joukhadar, K. (2001, March 19). "Programming in the Extreme." *InformationWeek.*

Jovanovic, N. (2002, September). "Task Scheduling in Distributed Systems by Work Stealing and Mugging—A Simulation Study." *Journal of Computing and Information Technology*, Vol. 10, No. 3.

Juan, P., Morant, J., and Gonzalez, L. (1999, October). "Knowledge-Based Systems' Validation: When to Stop Running Test Cases." *International Journal of Human–Computer Studies.*

Jung, C. (1923). *Psychological Types.* New York: Harcourt Brace.

Kalakota, R., and M. Robinson. (2001). *M-Business: The Race to Mobility.* New York: McGraw-Hill.

Kaliebe, K. (2003, Second Quarter). "Within Reach." *SAS.com.*

Kalifa R., and R. Davidson. (2000, March) "Exploring the Telecommuting Paradox." *Communications of the ACM,* Vol. 43, No. 3.

Kallman, E. A., and J. P. Grillo. (1996). *Ethical Decision Making and Information Technology,* 2nd ed. New York: McGraw-Hill.

Kandel, H. (1996). *Fuzzy Expert Systems Tools.* New York: John Wiley.

Kaneshige, T. (2000, February 1). "The Importance of Being Outrageous." *CIO.*

Kaneshige, T. (2002, October). "A Government First." *Portals Magazine.*

Kaneshige, T. (2003, July). "Counter Culture." *Portals Magazine*, Vol. 33, No. 22.

Kaplan, D., et al. (1998, February). "Assessing Data Quality in Accounting Information Systems." *Communications of the ACM.*

Kaplan, P. J. (2002). *F'D Companies: Spectacular Dot.com Flameouts*. New York: Simon & Schuster.

Kaplan, R. S., and D. P. Norton. (1992, January/February). "The Balanced Scorecard—Measures That Drive Performance." *Harvard Business Review.*

Kaplan, S. (2001, November 1). "Easter in November, Christmas in July." *CIO.*

Kaplan S. (2002, July 15). "KM the Right Way." *CIO.*

Kaplan, S., and M. Sawhney. (2000, May 1). "E-Hubs: The New B2B Marketplaces." *Harvard Business Review*.

Kappelman, L. A., and E. R. McLean. (1991). "The Respective Roles of User Participation and User Involvement in Information System Implementation Success." *Proceedings of the Twelfth International Conference on Information Systems,* New York.

Kappelman, L. A., and E. R. McLean. (1994). "User Engagement in the Development, Implementation, and Use of Information Technologies." *Proceedings of the Twenty-seventh Annual Hawaii International Conference on System Sciences HICSS-27,* Wailea, HI, Los Alamitos, CA: IEEE Computer Society Press.

Kapur, G.K. (2001, September). "How to Kill a Troubled Project: A Decision Process." Whiteboard in *CIO Insight*, No. 5.

Karaboga, D., and D. T. Pham. (1999). *Intelligent Optimization Techniques: Genetic Algorithms, Tabu Search, Simulated Annealing and Neural Networks.* Heidelberg: Springer-Verlag.

Karacapilidis, et al. (2003). "Applying Intelligent Agent Technology in a Collaborative Work Environment." *International Transactions in Operational Research*, Vol. 10, No. 1, pp. 13–31.

Karat, C. M. (1998, December). "Guaranteeing Rights for the User." *Communications of the ACM.* Vol. 41, No. 12.

Karimi, J., and P. L. Briggs. (1996, September). "Software Maintenance Support for Knowledge-Based Systems." *Journal of Systems and Software,* Vol. 34, No. 3.

Karimi, J., and M. K. Zand. (1998). "Asset-Based System and Software Development—A Frame-Based Approach." *Information and Software Technology,* Vol. 40, No. 2.

Kaski, S., J. Kargas, and T. Kohonen. (1997). "Bibliography of Self-Organizing Map (SOM) Papers." www.icsi.berkeley.edu.

Kassam, S. (2002, April 16). "Freedom of Information." *Intelligent Enterprise.*

Kaula, R. (1994). "Integrating DSS in Organizations: A Three-Level Framework." *Industrial Management and Data Systems,* Vol. 94, No. 4.

Kay, R. (2000, July 17). "Programming Languages." *ComputerWorld.*

Kayworth, T., and D. Leidner. (2003). "Organizational Culture as a Knowledge Resource." Chapter 12 in C. W.

Holsapple (ed.). *Handbook of Knowledge Management: Knowledge Matters*, Vol. 1. Heidelberg: Springer Verlag.

Kearney, M. (1990, July). "Making Knowledge Engineering Productive." *AI Expert.*

Keating, W. (2003, March). "Fast Tracking." *Optimize.*

Keen, P. G. W. (1980, Fall). "Adaptive Design for Decision Support Systems." *Data Base,* Vol. 12, Nos. 1 and 2.

Keen, P. G. W., and M. S. Scott Morton. (1978). *Decision Support Systems: An Organizational Perspective.* Reading, MA: Addison-Wesley.

Keirsey, D. (1998). *Please Understand Me II: Temperament, Character, Intelligence.* Del Mar, CA: Prometheus Nemesis.

Keirsey, D., and M. Bates. (1984). *Please Understand Me: Character & Temperament Types.* Del Mar, CA: Prometheus Nemesis.

Kelly, A. (2002). *Decision Making Using Game Theory: An Introduction for Managers*. Cambridge: Cambridge University Press.

Kelly, A. L. (1999, July 1). "Working Smart: United Airlines' Passenger Demand Forecasting System." *CIO.*

Kemp, T. (2000, July, 10). "When Teams Don't Talk." *InternetWeek*.

Kemp, T. (2001, January 8). "Covisint to Put Supplier Data Online." *InternetWeek.*

Kephart, J., J. Hanson, and A. Greenwald. (2000, May 30). "Dynamic Pricing by Software Agents." *Computer Networks*. Vol. 32, No. 6.

Kepner, C., and B. Tregoe. (1965). *The Rational Manager.* New York: McGraw-Hill.

Keskinocak, P., and S. Tayur. (2001, March/April). "Quantitative Analysis for Internet-Enable Supply Chains." *Interfaces*, Vol. 31, No. 2.

Kestelyn, J. (2002, July 28). "Microsoft's New Methodology Will Further Validate Balanced Scorecards." *Intelligent Enterprise.*

Keyes, J. (1989, November). "Why Expert Systems Fail." *AI Expert,* Vol. 4, No. 11.

Khalifa R., and R. Davidson. (2000, March) "Exploring the Telecommuting Paradox." *Communications of the ACM*, Vol. 43, No. 3.

Khan, A. S., and A. Horrman. (2003). "Building a Case-Based Recommendation Systems without a Knowledge Engineer." *Artificial Intelligence in Medicine*, Vol. 27, No. 2, pp. 155–179.

Khoshafian, S., et al. (1998). *The Jasmine Object Database: Multimedia Applications on the Web.* San Francisco: Morgan Kaufmann.

Kidd, A. L., and M. B. Cooper. (1985). "Man–Machine Interface Issues in the Construction and Use of an Expert System." *International Journal of Man–Machine Studies,* Vol. 22.

Kilov, H., and L. Cuthbert. (1995). "Model for Document Management." *Computer Communications,* Vol. 18, No. 6.

Kim, J., et al. (2002). "Document-Based Workflow Modeling: A Case-Based Reasoning Approach." *Expert Systems with Applications*, Vol. 23, No. 2, pp. 77–93.

Kim, K., and I. Han. (2003). "Application of a Hybrid Algorithm and Neural Network Approach in Activity-Based Costing." *Expert Systems with Applications*, Vol. 24, No. 1, pp. 73–77.

Kim, S. K., and J. I. Park. (1996). "A Structured Equation Modeling Approach to Generate Explanation for Induced Rules." *Expert Systems with Applications*, Vol. 10, Nos. 3 and 4.

Kim, Y., and W. N. Street. (2003). "An Intelligent System for Customer Targeting: A Data Mining Approach." *Decision Support Systems*.

Kim, Y. J., et al. (2002). "A Knowledge Management Perspective to Evaluation of Enterprise Information Portals." *Knowledge and Process Management*, Vol. 9, No. 2.

Kim, Y. J., Y. K. Kim, and Y. Cho. (1998, February). "A Heuristic-Based Genetic Algorithm for Workload Smoothing in Assembly Lines." *Computers & Operations Research*, Vol. 25, No. 2.

Kimball, R. (2003, July 18). "RFID Tabs and Smart Dust." *Intelligent Enterprise*.

Kimball, R., L. Reeves, M. Ross, and W. Thornwaite. (2001). *The Data Warehouse Life Cycle Toolkit*. New York: John Wiley.

Kimball, R., and K. Strehlo. (1994, June 1). "Why Decision Support Fails and How to Fix It." *Datamation*, Vol. 40, No. 11.

King, D. (1990). "Intelligent Decision Support: Strategies for Integrating Decision Support, Database Management and Expert System Technologies." *Expert Systems with Applications*, Vol. 1. No. 1.

King, D. (1996). "Intelligent Support Systems." In R. H. Sprague and H. J. Watson, *Decision Support for Management*. Upper Saddle River, NJ: Prentice Hall.

King, D., and K. Jones. (1995, January). "Competitive Intelligence, Software Robots and the Internet: The NewsAlert Prototype." *Proceedings of the Twenty-eighth Hawaii International Conference on Systems Sciences HICSS-28*, Wailea, HI. Los Alamitos, CA: IEEE Computer Society Press.

King, J. (1993). "Editorial Notes." *Information Systems Research*, Vol. 4, No. 4.

King, J. (2001, July/August). "Shell Strikes Knowledge Gold." *ComputerWorld*.

King, J. (2002, April 22). "Back to Basics." *ComputerWorld*.

King, J. (2003, June 30). "Taming Data Complexity." *ComputerWorld*.

King, J. A. (1995, February). "Intelligent Agents: Bringing Good Things to Life." *AI Expert*, Vol. 10, No. 2.

King, J. L., and S. L. Star. (1990). "Conceptual Foundations for the Development of Organizational Support Systems." *Proceedings of the Twenty-third Annual Hawaii International Conference on System Sciences HICSS-23*. Los Alamitos, CA: IEEE Computer Society Press.

King, N. (2002, May 9). "The Golden Rules." *Intelligent Enterprise*.

Kirkwood, C. W. (1997). *Strategic Decision Making: Multiobjective Decision Analysis with Spreadsheets*, Duxbury Press, Belmont, CA.

Kirsch, L. J., V. Sambamurthy, D-G. Ko, and R. L. Purvis. (2002, April). "Controlling Information Systems Development Projects: The View from the Client." *Management Science*. Vol. 48, No. 4.

Kiser, K. (1999, November). "10 Things We Know So Far about Online Training." *Training*, Vol. 36, No. 11.

Kitamura, Y., et al. (1996). "A Method of Qualitative Reasoning for Model-Based Problem Solving and Its Application to a Nuclear Plant." *Expert Systems with Applications*, Vol. 10, Nos. 3 and 4.

Kivijarvi, H. (1997). "A Substance-Theory-Oriented Approach to the Implementation of Organizational DSS." *Decision Support Systems*, Vol. 20, No. 3.

Klahr, P. (1997, January/February). "Getting Down to Cases." *PC AI*.

Klahr, P., and E. Byrnes (eds.). (1993). *Innovative Applications of Artificial Intelligence 5*. Cambridge, MA: AAAI Press/MIT Press.

Klein, G., and J. J. Jiang. (1999, October 15). "User Perception of Expert System Advice." *Journal of Systems and Software*, Vol. 48, No. 2.

Klein, G., and J. J. Jiang. (2001, March 1). "Seeking Consonance in Information Systems." *Journal of Systems and Software*, Vol. 56, No. 2.

Klein, M. R., and L. B. Methlie. *Knowledge-Based DSS with Applications in Business*, 2nd ed. Chichester, UK: John Wiley.

Kleindorfer, P.R. (2001). "Decision Making in Complex Environments: New Tools." Chapter 7 in S. J. Hoch, H. C. Kunreuther, with R. E. Gunther, ed. (2001). *Wharton on Making Decisions*. New York: John Wiley.

Klir, G. J., and B. Yuan. (1995). *Fuzzy Sets and Fuzzy Logic: Theory and Applications*. Upper Saddle River, NJ: Prentice Hall.

Klusch, K. (1999). *Intelligent Information Agents: Agent-Based Information Discovery and Management on the Internet*. New York: Springer Computer Science.

Knapp, E. M. (1998, July/September). "Knowledge Management." *Business and Economic Review*, Vol. 44, No. 4.

Koch, C. (2002a, July 15). "It's Time to Take Control." *CIO*.

Koch, C. (2002b, December 1). "Covisint's Last Chance." *CIO*.

Koch, C. (2002c, February 7). "The ABC's of ERP." *CIO* Web Site, www.cio.com.

Koenig, M. (2001, September). "Codification vs. Personalization." *KMWorld.*

Kogan, J. M. (1986). "Information for Motivation: A Key to Executive Information Systems That Translate Strategy into Results for Management." In J. Fedorowicz (1986, April). *DSS-86 Transactions,* Washington, DC: Institute of Management Sciences.

Kohli, R., et al. (November 2001). "Managing Customer Relationships Through E-Business Decision Support Applications: A Case of Hospital-Physician Collaboration." *Decision Support Systems.*

Kohonen, T. (1990). "The Self-Organizing Map." *Proceedings of the IEEE,* Vol. 78.

Kohonen, T. (1997). *Self-Organizing Map,* 2nd ed., Berlin: Springer-Verlag.

Koksalan, M., and S. Zionts (eds.). (2001). *Multiple Criteria Decision Making in the New Millennium.* Berlin: Springer-Verlag.

Koller, G. R. (2000). *Risk Modeling for Determining Value and Decision Making.* Boca Raton, FL: CRC Press.

Kolonder, J. (1993). *Case-Based Reasoning.* Mountain View, CA: Morgan Kaufmann.

Konicki, S. (2000, May 1). "Powerful Portals Evolve into Something Essential." *InformationWeek.*

Konicki, S. (2001a, June 11). "Ryder Trucks Into New E-logistics Strategy." *InformationWeek.*

Konicki, S. (2001b, November 12). "Collaboration Is the Cornerstone of $19B Defense Contract." *InformationWeek.*

Konicki, S. (2002a, January 3). "Time Trials." *InformationWeek.*

Konicki, S. (2002b, January 14). "Groupthink Gets Smart." *InformationWeek.*

Konicki, S. (2002c, July 1). "Shopping for Savings." *InformationWeek.*

Konsynski, B. R., and E. A. Stohr. (1992). "Decision Processes: An Organizational View." Chapter 2 in E. A. Stohr and B. R. Konsynski, eds. (1992). *Information Systems and Decision Processes.* Los Alamitos, CA: IEEE Computer Society Press.

Kontoghiorghes, E.J., B. Rustem, and S. Siokos. (2002). *Computational Methods in Decision-Making, Economics and Finance.* Boston: Kluwer Academic Publishers.

Konzer, T. (2002, October 7). "Come Together." *InformationWeek.*

Kopcso, D., et al. (1988, Summer). "A Comparison of the Manipulation of Certainty Factors by Individuals and Expert Systems Shells." *Journal of Management Information Systems,* Vol. 5, No. 1.

Korte, G. (2001). *The GIS Book.* 5th ed. Portland, OR: Book News.

Kosko B. (2000). *The Fuzzy Future: From Society and Science to Heaven in a Chip.* New York: Harmony Books.

Koundis, T. (2000, May 9). "The Six C's of Corporate Portals." *MetaKM.com.* www.metakm.com.

Koutsoukis, N. S., G. Mitra, and C. Lucas. (1999, July). "Adapting On-line Analytical Processing for Decision Modeling: The Interaction of Information and Decision Technologies." *Decision Support Systems,* Vol. 26, No. 1.

Kowal, K. C. (2002, October). "Tapping the Web for GIS and Mapping Technologies: For All Levels of Libraries and Users." *Information Technology and Libraries.* Vol. 21, No. 3.

Koza, J. (1992). *Genetic Programming.* Cambridge, MA: MIT Press.

KPMG Management Consulting. (1998). *Knowledge Management: Research Report.*

KPMG Consulting. (2000). Press release. kpmgconsulting.com/kpmgsite/service/km/publications.htm.

KPMG Consulting. (2002). "Virtual Close—A Financial Management Solution." cisco.com/warp/public/756.

Kraff, A., et al. (2000, January). "Agent-Driven Online Business in Virtual Communities." *Proceedings of the thirty-third Hawaii International Conference on Systems Sciences HICSS-33,* Hawaii, Los Alamitos, CA: IEEE Computer Society Press.

Kreie, J., and T. P. Cronan. (1998, September). "How Men and Women View Ethics." *Communications of the ACM.* Vol. 41, No. 9.

Kroening, M. (1999, March/April). "Weather on the Web." *PC AI.*

Kroenke, D. (2002). *Database Concepts.* Upper Saddle River, NJ: Prentice Hall.

Krogh, G. V., et al. (2000). *Enabling Knowledge Creation.* Oxford University Press.

Krovvidy, S. (1999, July/August). "Successful Knowledge Management Systems: An Expert Systems Approach." *PC AI.*

Krutchten, P. (1998). *The Rational Unified Process: An Introduction.* Reading, MA: Addison-Wesley.

Kuechler, W. L., N. Lim, and V. K. Vaishnavi. (1995). "A Smart Object Approach to Hybrid Knowledge Representation and Reasoning Strategies." *Proceedings of the Twenty-eighth Annual Hawaii International Conference on System Sciences HICSS-28,* Hawaii, Los Alamitos, CA: IEEE Computer Society Press.

Kuhn, D., and A. Zohar (1995). *Strategies of Knowledge Acquisition.* Chicago: University of Chicago Press.

Kuipers, B. (1994). *Qualitative Reasoning and Simulation with Incomplete Knowledge.* Cambridge, MA: MIT Press.

Kuipers, B. J., and J. M. Crawford. (1994). *Short Algernon Reference Manual* (Version 1.3.0). Austin: The University of Texas at Austin.

Kulik, P. (1992, November/December). "Automating the Helpdesk." *PC AI.*

Kumar, A., and Y. P. Gupta. (1995, January). "Genetic Algorithms." *Computers & Operations Research.*

Kunnathur, A. S., M. U. Ahmed, and R. J. S. Charles. (1996, January). "Expert Systems Adoption: An Analytical Study of Managerial Issues and Concerns." *Information & Management,* Vol. 30, No. 1.

Kuo, R. J., and C. A. Chen. (2003). "A Decision Support System for Order Selection in Electronic Commerce Based on Fuzzy Neural Network Supported by Real-Coded Genetic Algorithm." *Expert Systems with Applications.*

Kuo, R. J., S. C. Chi, and S. S. Kao. (1999, October). "A Decision Support System for Locating Convenience Store Through Fuzzy AHP." *Computers & Industrial Engineering,* Vol. 37, Nos. 1 and 2.

Kurtyka, J. (2003, June). "The Limits of Business Intelligence: An Organizational Learning Approach." *DM Review.*

Kurtzman, J. (2003). "The Knowledge Economy." Chapter 5 in C. W. Holsapple (ed.). *Handbook of Knowledge Management: Knowledge Matters,* Vol. 1. Heidelberg: Springer-Verlag.

Kusiak, A. (ed.). (1988). *Artificial Intelligence, Implication for CIM, IFS.* New York: Springer-Verlag.

Kvassov, V. (2000, January). "Strategic Decisions and Intelligent Tools." *Proceedings of the Thirty-third Hawaii International Conference on Systems Sciences HICSS-33,* Hawaii, Los Alamitos, CA: IEEE Computer Society Press.

Kwon, O. B., and N. Sadeh. (2003, Summer). "Applying Case-Based Reasoning and Multi-Agent Intelligent Systems to Context-Aware Comparative Shopping." *Decision Support Systems.*

Lach, J. (1999, July). "Fraud Detectives." *American Demographics,* Vol. 21, No. 7.

Lais, S. (1999, December 13). "CA Advances Neural Network System." *Computerworld,* Vol. 33, No. 50.

Lais, S. (2000, November 20). "Where Is It Exactly?" *ComputerWorld.*

Lais, S. (2001, June 25). "GIS: More Than Just a Map." *ComputerWorld.*

Lalkaka, R., and P. Albetti. (1999, September). "Business Incubation and Enterprise Support Systems in Restructuring Countries." *Creativity and Innovation Management,* Vol. 8, No. 3.

Lam, S. S. Y., K. L. Petri, and A. E. Smith. (2000, January). "Prediction and Optimization of a Ceramic Casting Process Using a Hierarchical Hybrid System of Neural Networks and Fuzzy Logic." *IIE Transactions,* Vol. 32, No. 1.

LaMonica, M. (2003, January 1). "Process Power." *CIO.*

Lamont, J. (2000, May). "Software Agents: Proactive Help for Web Users." *KMWorld.*

Lamont, J. (2003a, April). "Prognosis Good for KM in Patient Treatment and Diagnostics." *KMWorld.*

Lamont, J. (2003b, May). "Dynamic Taxonomies: Keeping Up With Changing Content." *KMWorld.*

Landro, L. (2002, June 14–16). Is There a Doctor in the House?" *Wall Street Journal Europe.*

Lane, P., and M. Lubatkin. (1998, May). "Relative Absorptive Capacity and Interorganizational Learning." *Strategic Management Journal,* Vol. 19, No. 5.

Lane, P. G., D. E. Doughlas, and T. P. Cronan. (1999, Fall). "LAN Configuration Decisions: An Expert Simulation (ESS) Approach." *Journal of Computer Information Systems.*

Lang, K. R., J. C. Moore, and A. B. Whinston. (1995). "Computational Systems for Qualitative Economics." *Computational Economics,* Vol. 8.

Langenwalter, G. (2000). *Enterprise Resources Planning and Beyond: Integrating Your Entire Organization.* Boca Raton, FL: St. Lucie Press.

Langseth, J., and N. Vivatrat. (2002, November). "Outward Bound." *Intelligent Enterprise,* Vol. 5, No. 18.

Laporte, G., F. V. Louveeaux, and L. Van Hamme. (2002, May/June). "An Integer L-Shaped Algorithm for the Capacitated Vehicle Routing Problem with Stochastic Demands." *Operations Research,* Vol. 50, No. 3.

Larsen, N. C. (1999, December). "Distance Learning: Linking the Globe through Education." *World Trade,* Vol. 12, No. 12.

Larson, J. A. (1995). *Database Directions: From Relational to Distributed, Multimedia and Object-oriented Systems.* Upper Saddle River, NJ: Prentice Hall.

Larson, M. (1999, November). "New Software Tools Speed Analysis: Trade Your DOE Shotgun for a Rifle." *Quality,* Vol. 38, No. 12.

Larsson, S-O. (2002, July). "Decision Process and Decision Support." *Proceedings of DSIage 2002,* Cork, Ireland.

Lau, H. C. W., et al. (2001, September). "Development of an Intelligent Data-Mining System for a Dispersed Manufacturing Network." *Expert Systems.*

Lau, L. (2000). *Distance Learning Technologies: Issues, Trends, and Opportunities.* London: Idea Group Publishing.

Lavington, S., N. Dewhurst, and E. Wilkins. (1999, June). "Interfacing Knowledge Discovery Algorithms to Large Database Management Systems." *Information and Software Technology.*

Law, A. M., D. W. Kelton, W. D. Kelton, and D. M. Kelton. (2000). *Simulation Modeling and Analysis.* 3rd ed. New York: McGraw-Hill.

Lawton, G. (1999). "Chatterbots: the Web Gets Help from AI." *Computer,* Vol. 32, No. 7.

Lazzaro, J. J. (1993, July). "Computers for the Disabled." *Byte*.

Le Roux, B. (1996, September). "Knowledge Acquisition as a Constructive Process: A Methodological Issue." *Decision Support Systems*, Vol. 18, No. 1.

Leahy, T. (2003, March). "5 Moves Toward Better BPM." *Business Finance*. Vol. 9, No. 3.

Leake, D. B. (ed). (1996). *Case-Based Reasoning: Experiences, Lessons and Future Directions*. Menlo Park, CA: AAAI Press/MIT Press.

Leatham, L. (2000). *Getting Started with GIS*. Upper Saddle River, NJ: Prentice Hall.

LeBlanc, L. J., D. R. Randalls, and T. K. Swann. (2000). "Heery International's Spreadsheet Optimization Model for Assigning Managers to Construction Projects." *Interfaces*, Vol. 30, No. 6.

Lechner, U., et. al. (1998). "Structuring and Systemising Knowledge on the Internet—Realising the Encyclopedia Concept as a Knowledge Medium." Institute for Media and Communications Management, University of St. Gallen, www.netacademy.org.

Ledlow, G. R., D. M. Bradshaw, and M. J. Perry. (1999, March/April). "Animated Simulation: A Valuable Decision Support Tool for Practice Improvement." *Journal of Healthcare Management*, Vol. 44, No. 2.

Ledman, T. (2003, June). "TCF Bank." *What Works: Best Practices in Business Intelligence and Data Warehousing*, Vol. 15. Chatsworth, CA: Data Warehousing Institute.

Lee H., et al. (1999, April/June). "A View-Based Hypermedia Design Methodology." *Journal of Database Management*.

Lee, H-Y., H-L. Ong, and L-H. Quek. (1995). "Exploiting Visualization in Knowledge Discovery." In V. M. Fayyad and R. Uthurusamy (eds.). *Proceedings of the First International Conferences on Knowledge Discovery and Data Mining (KDD-95)*. Menlo Park, CA: AAAI Press.

Lee, K. Y., et al. (2003). "MOCAAS: Auction Agent System Using a Collaborative Mobile Agent in Electronic Commerce." *Expert Systems with Applications*, Vol. 24, No. 2, pp. 183–187.

Lee, J. K., and J. K. Kim. (2002). "A Case-Based Reasoning Approach for Building a Decision Model." Expert Systems, Vol. 19, No. 3.

Lee, J. W., et al. (1997, January). "Intelligent Agents for Matching Information Providers and Consumers on the Web." *Proceedings of the Thirtieth Hawaii International Conference on Systems Sciences HICSS-30*, Hawaii, Los Alamitos, CA: IEEE Computer Society Press.

Lee, L. K., and H. G. Lee. (1987, June). "Integration of Strategic Planning and Short-Term Planning: An Intelligent DSS Approach by the Post Model Analysis Approach." *Decision Support Systems*. Vol. 3, No. 2.

Lee., P. Y., et al. (2002, September/October). "Neural Networks for Web Content Filtering." *IEEE Intelligent Systems*, pp. 48–57.

Lee, W. P., et al. (2002). "Intelligent Agent-Based Systems for Personalized Recommendations in Internet Commerce." *Expert Systems with Applications*, Vol. 22, No. 4, pp. 275–284.

Lee-Young, J., and M. Barnett. (2001, June 11). "Furiously Fast Fashions." *Industry Standard*.

Legare, T. L. (2002, Fall). "The Role of Organizational Factors in Realizing ERP Benefits." *Information Systems Management*, Vol. 19, No. 4.

Leidner D., et al. (1999, Summer). "Mexican and Swedish Managers' Perceptions of the Impact of EIS on Organizational Intelligence, Decision Making and Structure." *Decision Sciences*, Vol. 30, No. 3.

Leidner, D. E. (2003). "Understanding Information Culture: Integrating Knowledge Management Systems into Organizations." In R. Galliers and D. Leidner (eds.). *Strategic Information Management*. Oxford: Butterworth Heinemann.

Leifer, R., et al. (2000). *Radical Innovation: How Mature Companies Can Outsmart Upstarts* Boston: Harvard Business School Press.

Lemken, B., et al. (2000, January). "Sustained Knowledge Management by Organizational Culture." *Proceedings, 33rd HICSS*. Wailea, HI, Los alamitos, CA: IEEE Computer Society Press.

Lemmon, H., and N. Chuk. (1995, May 15–18). "Cotton 11: A Cotton Crop Model and Expert System to Support On-Farm Decisions." *Proceedings of PACES*. Huangshan, China.

Lenat, D. B. (1982). "The Ubiquity of Discovery." *Artificial Intelligence*, Vol. 19, No. 2.

Lenat, D. B., and R. V. Guha. (1990). *Building Large Knowledge-Based Systems. Representation and Inference in the Cyc Project*. Reading, MA: Addison-Wesley.

Lenz, M., et al. (1996). "CBR for Diagnosis and Decision Support." *AI Communications*, Vol. 9.

Leon, M. (2001, October 29). "From the Lab: Math Theory Aids Code Debugging." *InfoWorld CTO Supplement*, p. S12.

Leon, M. (2003a, April 14). "Keys to the Kingdom." *ComputerWorld*.

Leon, M. (2003b, June 16). "Dashboard Democracy." *ComputerWorld*.

Leonard, D., and S. Sensiper. (1998, Spring). "The Role of Tacit Knowledge in Group Innovations." *California Management Review*, Vol. 40. No. 3.

Leonard, N. H., R. W. Scholl, and K. B. Kowalski. (1999, May). "Information Processing Style and Decision Making." *Journal of Organizational Behavior*, Vol. 20, No. 3.

Leontief, W. (1986). *The Future Impact of Automation on Workers*. Oxford: Oxford University Press.

Lesser, E., and L. Prusak. (2001, Fall). "Preserving Knowledge in an Uncertain World." *Sloan Management Review.*

Lesser, E., and L. Prusak. (2002). "Communities of Practice, Social Capital and Organizational Knowledge." Chapter 8 in E. L. Lesser, M. A. Fontaine, and J. A. Slusher (eds.). *Knowledge and Communities.* Woburn, MA: Butterworth-Heinemann.

Lesser, E. L., M. A. Fontaine, and J. A. Slusher (eds.). (2000). *Knowledge and Communities.* Woburn, MA: Butterworth-Heinemann.

Leu, S-S., and H. Y. Chung. (1999, November). "A GA-Based Resource-Constrained Construction Scheduling System." *Construction Management and Economics,* Vol. 17, No. 6.

Levasseur, R. E. (2001, July/August). "People Skills: Change Management Tools—Lewin's Change Model." *Interfaces,* Vol. 31. No. 4.

Levasseur, R. E. (2002, July/August). "People Skills: Change Management Tools—Ideal State Analysis." *Interfaces,* Vol. 32. No. 4.

Levinson, M. (2002a, April 1). "Cleared for Takeoff." *CIO.*

Levinson, M. (2002, April 15). "The Art of the Shmooze." *CIO.*

Levinson, M. (2000b, August 15). "Slices of Lives." *CIO.*

Levinson, M. (2002c November 1). "Portal U." *CIO.*

Lewin, K. (1947). "Group Decision and Social Change." In N. T. Newcomb and E. L. Hartley (eds.). *Readings in Social Psychology.* Troy, MO: Holt, Rinehart, & Winston.

Lewis, S. (2001, September 25). "Online Playmates Get a Virtual Life." *International Herald Tribune.*

Li, H., and P. E. D. Love. (1999, March). "Combining Rule-Based Expert Systems and Artificial Neural Networks for Mark-up Estimation." *Construction Management and Economics,* Vol. 17, No. 2.

Li, J., and R. S. K. Kwan (2003). "A Fuzzy Genetic Algorithm for Driver Scheduling." *European Journal of Operational Research,* Vol. 147, pp. 334–344.

Li, S. (2000, January). "The Development of a Hybrid Intelligent System for Developing Marketing Strategy." *Decision Support Systems,* Vol. 27, No. 4.

Liang, D. B. (2000). *Applied Knowledge Acquisition.* San Francisco: Morgan Kaufmann.

Liang, T. P. (1992). "A Composite Approach to Automated Knowledge Acquisition." *Management Science.*

Liang, T. P., and H. S. Doong. (2000, Spring). "Effect of Bargaining Agents in Electronic Commerce." *International Journal of Electronic Commerce,* Vol. 4, No. 3, pp. 23–44.

Liang, T. P., and C. V. Jones. (1987, Summer). "Design of a Self-Evolving Decision Support System." *Journal of Management Information Systems.*

Liang, T. P., and B. R. Konsynski. (1993, January). "Modeling by Analogy: Use of Analogical Reasoning in Model Management Systems." *Decision Support Systems,* Vol. 9, No. 1.

Liang, T. P., and E. Turban, eds. (1993, January/March). "Case-Based Reasoning and Its Applications." Special Issue. *Expert Systems with Applications.*

Liao, J., et al. (2000). "Application of a System for the Automatic Generation of Fuzzy Neural Networks." *Engineering Applications of Artificial Intelligence,* Vol. 13, No. 3, pp. 293–302.

Liao, T. W. (2003). "Classification of Welding Flaw Types with Fuzzy Expert Systems." *Expert Systems with Applications,* Vol. 25, No. 1, pp. 101–111.

Liao, Z., and R. Landry, Jr. (2000). "An Empirical Study on Organizational Acceptance of New Information Systems in a Commercial Bank Environment." *Proceedings of the Thirty-third Hawaii International Conference on System Sciences HICSS-33.* Wailea, HI, Los Alamitos, CA: IEEE Computer Society Press.

Liautaud, B., and M. Hammond. (2000). *E-Business Intelligence: Turning Information into Knowledge into Profit.* New York: McGraw-Hill.

Liaw, S., and H. Huang. (2000, Winter). "How Web Technology Can Facilitate Learning." *Information Systems Management.*

Liberatore, M. J., and A. C. Stylianou. (1995, August). "Expert Support Systems for New Product Development Decision Making." *Management Science,* Vol. 41, No. 8.

Liedtka, J. (2002). "Linking Competitive Advantage with Communities of Practice." Chapter 9 in E. L. Lesser, M. A. Fontaine, and J. A. Slusher. (eds.). *Knowledge and Communities.* Woburn, MA: Butterworth-Heinemann.

Lientz, B. P., and K. P. Rea. (2000). *Project Management: Planning and Implementation.* New York: Harcourt Brace Professional Publishing.

Lightfoot, J. M. (1999, August). "Expert Knowledge Acquisition and the Unwilling Expert: A Knowledge Engineering Perspective." *Expert Systems.*

Lin, C-T., and C. S. G. Lee. (1996). *Neural Fuzzy Systems: A Neuro-Fuzzy Synergism to Intelligent Systems.* Upper Saddle River, NJ: Prentice Hall.

Linden, A. (1999, July 7). "CIO Update: Data Mining Applications of the Next Decade." Gartner Group-Inside Gartner Group.

Linden, G., B. Smith, and J. York. (2003). "Amazon.com Recommendations: Item-to-Item Collaborative Filtering." *IEEE Intelligent Systems,* pp. 76–80.

Linoff, G. S., and M. J. A. Berry. (2002). *Mining the Web: Transforming Customer Data.* New York: John Wiley.

Lindquist, C. (2003, May 15). "Real Timing." *CIO.*

Lindsey, C. S. (1998). "Neural Networks in Hardware: Architectures, Products and Applications." Royal

Institute of Technology, Stockholm, www.particle.kth.se/~lindsey/HardwareNNWCourse/home.html.

Lindstone, H., and M. Turroff. (1975). *The Delphi Method: Technology and Applications.* Reading, MA: Addison-Wesley.

Ling, X., and W. G. Rudd. (1989). "Combining Opinions from Several Experts." *Applied AI,* Vol. 3.

Linthicum, D. S. (2001). *B2B Application Integration.* Boston: Addison-Wesley.

Lipp, A., and C. Y. Carver. (2000, January). "Using Web Groupware and Cognitive Mapping in a CIS Department to Review and Revise the Assessment Process and Document Reasoning." *Proceedings of the Thirty-third Annual Hawaii International Conference on System Sciences HICSS-33.* Los Alamitos, CA: IEEE Computer Society Press.

Lipschutz, R. (2003, July). "Look Who's Talking." *Portals Magazine.* Vol. 33, No. 22.

Lipson, S.(2001, November/December). "Integration Building Blocks." *Oracle Magazine.*

Little, J. D. C. (1970, April). "Models and Managers: The Concept of a Decision Calculus." *Management Science,* Vol. 16, No. 8.

Liu, F-H. F., and S. Y. Shen. (1999, October). "An Overview of a Heuristic for Vehicle Routing Problem with Time Windows." *Computers & Industrial Engineering,* Vol. 37, Nos. 1 and 2.

Liu, J. (2001). *Autonomous Agents and Multi-Agent Systems.* Singapore: World Scientific Publishing.

Liu, J., and L. Tang. (1999, October). "A Modified Genetic Algorithm for Single Machine Scheduling." *Computers & Industrial Engineering,* Vol. 37, Nos. 1 and 2.

Liu, N. K., and K. K. Lee (1997, August). "An Intelligent Business Advisor System for Stock Investment." *Expert Systems.*

Liu, S. (1998). "Data Warehousing Agent: To Make the Creation and Maintenance of Data Warehousing Easier." *Journal of Data Warehousing,* No. 1.

Liu, S., et al. (2000, May) "Software Agents for Environmental Scanning in Electronic Commerce." *Information Systems Frontiers.*

Liu, S., et al. (2002, July). "Mobile E-Services: Creating Added Value for Working Mothers." *Proceedings DSI AGE 2002.* Cork, Ireland.

Lloyd, B. (1996). "Knowledge Management: The Key to Long-Term Organizational Success." *Long Range Planning,* Vol. 29, No. 4.

Loch, K. D., and S. Conger. (1996, July). "Evaluating Ethical Decision Making and Computer Use." *Communications of the ACM,* Vol. 39, No. 7.

Lockwood, S., and Z. Chen. (1994). "Modeling Experts' Decision-Making Using Knowledge Charts." *Information and Decision Technologies,* Vol. 19, No. 4.

LoFrumento, T. (2003, April). "How Profitable Are Your Customers?" *Optimize.*

Lopez, M.A., et al. (2003). "An Intelligent Tutoring System for Turban Startup Training of Electronic Power Plant Operators." *Expert Systems with Applications,* Vol. 24, No. 1, pp. 95–101.

Loshin, D. (2001). *Enterprise Knowledge Management: The Data Quality Approach.* San Francisco: Morgan Kaufman.

Loshin, D. (2003). *Business Intelligence: The Savvy Manager's Guide.* San Francisco: Morgan Kaufman.

Low, L., and M. Goldberg. (2002, November 15). "Hershey's Bittersweet Lesson." *CIO.*

Lowry, P. B., and D. C. Wilson. (2000, April). "The Potential of Group Support Systems (GSS) to Enhance Systems Analysis and Design Processes and Outcomes" *3rd Annual Conference of the Southern Association for Information Systems,* Atlanta.

Lu, H-P., H-J. Yu, and S. S. K. Lu. (2001). "The Effects of Cognitive Style and Model Type on DSS Acceptance: An Empirical Study." *European Journal of Operational Research,* 131

Lu, J., M. A. Quaddus, and R. Williams. (2000). "Developing a Knowledge-Based Multi-Objective Decision Support System." *Proceedings of the Thirty-third Hawaii International Conference on System Sciences HICSS-33.* Wailea, HI, Los Alamitos, CA: IEEE Computer Society Press.

Lucas, H. C. (1981). *Implementation: The Key to Successful Information Systems.* New York: Columbia University Press.

Luce, M. F., J. W. Payne and J. R. Bettman. (2001). "The Emotional Nature of Decision Trade-Offs." Chapter 2 in S. J. Hoch, H. C. Kunreuther, with R. E. Gunther, ed. (2001). *Wharton on Making Decisions.* New York: John Wiley.

Lui, H. C., et al. (1991). "Practical Application of a Connectionist Expert System—The Inside Story." In J. K. Lee, et al. (eds.). *Operational Expert Systems Applications in the Far East.* New York: Pergamon Press.

Lukose, D. (1996). "MODEL-ECS: Executable Conceptual Modelling Language." *Proceedings of the Tenth Knowledge Acquisition for Knowledge-Based Systems Workshop.* www.ksi.cpsc.ucalgary.ca/KAW/KAW96/KAW96Proc.html.

Lummus, R. R., and R. J. Vokura. (2002, January/June). "Making the Right E-Fulfillment Decision." *Production and Inventory Management Journal.*

Lunt, P. (2001, July). "Know the Score." *Customer Support Management.*

Luther, R. K. (1998, Spring). "An Artificial Neural Network Approach to Predicting the Outcome of Chapter 11 Bankruptcy." *Journal of Business and Economic Studies,* Vol. 4, No. 1.

Luu, D. T., et al. (2003). "A Case-Based Procurement Advisory System for Construction." *Advances in Engineering Software*, Vol. 34, No. 7, pp. 429–438.

Lyczak, R., and S. Weber-Russel. (1992). "An Expert Natural Language Interface for Statistical Packages." *Expert Systems with Applications,* Vol. 5, Nos. 1 and 2.

Machacha, L. L., and P. Bhattacharya. (2000, February). "A Fuzzy-Logic-Based Approach to Project Selection." *IEEE Transactions on Engineering Management,* Vol. 47, No. 1.

Mack, R., et al. (2001). "Knowledge Portals and the Emerging Digital Knowledge Workplace." *IBM Systems Journal.* Vol. 40, No. 4.

MacSweeney, G. (2002, June). "The Knowledge Management Payback." *Insurance & Technology.*

Madden, J. (1999, August 9). "KPMG Sharing Knowledge." *PCWeek.*

Madhaven, R., and R. Grover. (1998, October). "From Embedded Knowledge to Embodied Knowledge: New Product Development as Knowledge Management." *Journal of Marketing,* Vol. 62, No. 4.

Madsen, M. (2003, May 31). "Data As It Happens." *IntelligentEnterprise.*

Maes, P. (1994, July). "Agents That Reduce Work and Information Overload." *Communications of the ACM,* Vol. 37, No. 7.

Maes, P. (1995). "Artificial Life Meets Entertainment: Life-Like Autonomous Agents." *Communications of the ACM,* Vol. 38, No. 11.

Maes, P., et al. (1999, March). "Agents That Buy and Sell." *Communications of the ACM.*

Magid, I. (1999, December). "The Driving Forces in the Virtual Society." *Communications of the ACM.*

Mahapatra, R. K (1997/1998, Winter). "Case-Based Reasoning: Extending the Frontiers of Knowledge-Based Systems." *Journal of Computer Information Systems.*

Malafsky, G. (2003). "Technology for Acquiring and Sharing Knowledge Assets." Chapter 36 in C. W. Holsapple (ed.). *Handbook of Knowledge Management: Knowledge Directions,* Vol. 2. Heidelberg: Springer-Verlag.

Malhotra, A., A. Majchrzak, R. Carman, and V. Lott. (2001, June). "Radical Innovation without Collocation: A Case Study at Boeing-Rocketdyne." *MIS Quarterly,* Vol. 25, No. 2.

Malhotra, Y. (2003). "Why Knowledge Management Systems Fail: Enablers and Constraints of Knowledge Management in Human Enterprises." Chapter 30 in C. W. Holsapple (ed.). *Handbook of Knowledge Management: Knowledge Matters,* Vol. 1. Heidelberg: Springer-Verlag.

Manago, M., and E. Auriol. (1995). "Integrating Induction and Case-Based Reasoning for Troubleshooting CFM-56 Aircraft Engines." *XPS'95. Fourth German Conference on Expert Systems.* Kaiserslautern, Germany: University of Kaiserslautern.

Mandry, T., et al. (1999, June). "Mobile Agents on Electronic Markets: Opportunities, Risks, and Protection." *Proceedings of the Twelfth International Bled EC Conference.*

Manheim, M. L. (1989). "Issues in the Design of Symbiotic DSS." *Proceedings of the Twenty-second Hawaii International Conference on System Sciences HICSS-22.* Wailea, HI, Los Alamitos, CA: IEEE Computer Society Press.

Maniezzo, V., et al. (1993, August). "D-KAT: A Deep Knowledge Acquisition Tool." *Expert Systems.*

Mannino, M.V. (2001). *Database Application Development & Design.* New York: McGraw-Hill.

Mapleston. P. (1999, August). "Real-Time Process Control Is Said to Provide Perfect Shots." *Modern Plastics,* Vol. 29, No. 8.

Marakas, G. M. (2003a). *Decision Support in the 21st Century.* 2nd ed. Upper Saddle River, NJ: Prentice Hall.

Marakas, G. M. (2003b). *Modern Data Warehousing, Mining, and Visualization: Core Concepts.* Prentice Hall, Upper Saddle River, NJ.

Marchant, B. (2002, October). "Virtual Tune-Up: Simulated Design and Upkeep for a Fighter-Jet Engine." *AV Video Multimedia Producer.*

Marco, D. (2001, September). "Getting It Right with Meta Data." *Application Development Trends.*

Markel, M. (1999, April). "Distance Education and the Myth of the New Pedagogy." *Journal of Business and Technical Communication,* Vol. 13, No. 2.

Markova, D. (1996). *The Open Mind: Exploring the 6 Patterns of Intelligence.* Berkeley, CA: Conari Press.

Markus, M. L. (1983, June). "Power, Politics and MIS Interpretation." *Communications of the ACM,* Vol. 26, No. 6.

Marlin, S. (1999, June). "Intelligent Telecentres." *Bank Systems & Technology.* Vol. 36, No. 6.

Marling, C., et al. (2002, Spring). "Case-Based Reasoning Integrations." *AI Magazine,* pp. 69–86.

Mars, N. J. I. (ed.). (1995). *Towards Very Large Knowledge Bases.* Amsterdam: IOS Press.

Marshall, L. (1997, September/October). "Facilitating Knowledge Management and Knowledge Sharing: New Opportunities for Information Professionals." *Online,* Vol. 21, No. 5.

Martin, B. (2000). "Knowledge Management Within the Context of Management: An Evolving Relationship." *Singapore Management Review,* Vol. 22, No. 2.

Martin, D., and M. Ryan. (2002). "Pop-Ups Abound But Most Advertisers Remain Inline." *NetRatings.*

Martin, P. (1996). "CGKAT: A Knowledge Acquisition Tool and an Information Retrieval Tool Which Exploits Conceptual Graphs and Structured Documents." INRIA, France, www.inria.fr/acacia/personnel/phmartin/cgkat.html.

Martin, P., and P. Eklund (1999, May) "Embedding Knowledge in Web Documents." *Computer Networks.*

Maselli, J. (2002, June 24). "Making CRM Fit." *InformationWeek*.

Mason, R. O., F. M. Mason, and M. J. Culnan. (1995). *Ethics of Information Management*. Thousand Oaks, CA: Sage.

Massetti, B. (1996, March). "An Empirical Examination of the Value of Creativity Support Systems on Idea Generation." *MIS Quarterly*, Vol. 20, No.1.

Matsatsinis, N. F., and Y. Siskos. (1999, March 1). "MARKEX: An Intelligent Decision Support System for Product Development Decisions." *European Journal of Operational Research*, Vol. 113, No. 2.

Matskin, M., and A. Tveit. (2001). "Mobile Commerce Agents in WAP-Based Services." *Journal of Database Management*, Vol. 12, No. 3, pp. 27–35.

Matthews, D. (1999, September). "The Origins of Distance Education and Its Use in the United States." *T.H.E. Journal*, Vol. 27, No. 2.

Matthews, W. (2002, April 25). "Knowledge Management's Worst Nightmare." *Federal Computer Week*.

Maxwell, D.T. (2002, June). "Decision Analysis: Aiding Insight VI—'It's Not Your Grandfather's Decision Analysis Software.' "*OR/MS Today*.

May, J. H., and L. G. Vargas. (1996, January 20). "SIMP-SON: An Intelligent Assistant for Short Term Manufacturing Scheduling." *European Journal of Operations Research*, Vol. 88, No. 2.

Maybury, M. (2001, December) "Collaborative Virtual Environments for Analysis and Decision Support." *Communications of the ACM*.

Maybury, M. T. (1997). *Intelligent Multimedia Information Retrieval*. Boston: MIT Press.

McAmis, D. (2003, July 18). "The Bigger Picture." *Intelligent Enterprise*.

McBride, B. (2002). "Jena: A Semantic Web Toolkit." *IEEE Internet Computing*, Vol. 6, No. 6, pp. 55.

McCaffrey, M. J. (1992). "Maintenance of Expert Systems: The Upcoming Challenge." In E. Turban and J. Liebowitz (eds.). *Managing Expert Systems*. Harrisburg, PA: Idea Group.

McCann, D. W. (1999, May/June). "Aircraft Icing Forecasts from Neural Networks." *PC AI*.

McCarthy, J., and M. McCarthy. (2002). *Software for Your Head: Core Protocols for Creating and Maintaining Shared Vision*. Boston: Addison-Wesley.

McCarthy, R.V., K. Mazouz, and J.E. Aronson. (2001, August). "Measuring the Validity of Task-Technology Fit for Knowledge Management Systems." *Proceedings of the America's Conference on Information Systems (AMCIS 2001)*. Boston, MA.

McCarthy, V. (1996, February 15). "Nifco Lets Businesses Deal with NAFTA." *Datamation*, Vol. 42, No. 4.

McClenahen, J. (2002, April). "The Book on the One-Day Close." *industryweek.com*, pp. 31–33.

McCright, J. S. (2001, May 7). "XML Eases Data Transport." *eWeek*.

McCright, J. S. (2003a, June 9). "Oracle Pulls PeopleSoft Shocker." *eWeek*.

McCright, J. S. (2003b, June 9). "Switching Gears." *eWeek*.

McCullough, S. (1999, October 15). "On the Front Lines." *CIO*.

McDaniel., C., and R. H. Gates. (2001). *Marketing Research: The Impact of the Internet*. Cincinnati: South-Western Publishing.

McDermott, R. (2002). "Why Information Technology Inspired But Cannot Deliver Knowledge Management." Chapter 2 in E. L. Lesser, M. A. Fontaine, and J. A. Slusher. (eds.). *Knowledge and Communities*. Woburn, MA: Butterworth-Heinemann.

McDonald, M., and D. Shand. (2000, March). "Request for Proposal: A Guide to KM Professional Services." *Knowledge Management*.

McDonough, B. (2003a, March). "Enterprise Portals: Adding Value Through Workflow." *KM World*.

McDonnough, B. (2003b, July). "The State of Enterprise Portal Initiatives: Portal Adoption Trends 2003." Special IDC Report, *Portals Magazine*, Vol. 33, No. 22.

McFetridge, L., and M. Y. Ibrahim. (1998, December). "New Technique of Mobile Robotic Navigation Using a Hybrid Adaptive Fuzzy-potential Field Approach." *Computers & Industrial Engineering*, Vol. 35, Nos. 3 and 4.

McGee, M.K., and C. Murphy. (2001, December 10). "25 Innovators in Collaboration." *Information Week*.

McGraw, K. L., and B. K. Harbison-Briggs. (1989). *Knowledge Acquisition, Principles and Guidelines*. Englewood Cliffs, NJ: Prentice Hall.

McGuire, C. (1999, January). "The Next Level of Proprietary Protection." *Wall Street & Technology*, Vol. 17, No. 1.

McKeen, J., and S. Staples. (2003). "Knowledge Managers: Who Are They and What Do They Do?" Chapter 2 in C. W. Holsapple (ed.). *Handbook of Knowledge Management: Knowledge Matters*, Vol. 1. Heidelberg: Springer Verlag.

McKeen, J. D. (1997, Fall). "Successful Strategies for User Participation in Systems Development." *Journal of MIS*, Vol. 14, No. 2.

McKellar, H. (2000, March 8). "KPMG Releases KM Report." *KMWorld.*.

McKenna, B. (1999, February). "Growing Knowledge Organically." *Information World Review*, No. 144.

McKie, S. (2003, July 18). "The Big Bam." *Intelligent Enterprise*, Vol. 6, No. 12.

McNeill, D., and P. Freiberger. (1993). *Fuzzy Logic*. New York: Simon & Schuster.

McNurlin, B. C., and R. H. Sprague, Jr. (2001). *Information Systems Management in Practice*, 5th ed. Upper Saddle River, NJ: Prentice Hall.

McQuaid, M. M., et al. (2000). "Tools for Distributed Facilitation." *Proceedings of the Thirty-third Annual Hawaii International Conference on System Sciences HICSS-33.* Los Alamitos, CA: IEEE Computer Society Press.

McRoy, S.W., et al. (2002, Summer). "Creating Natural Language Output for Real-Time Systems." *Intelligence,* pp. 21–34.

McVicker, D. (2001, March 12). "HANDS-ON DECISION MAKING—Logistics and Warehousing Executives Led the Way with PDAs." *InternetWeek.*

Meador, C. L., M. J. Guyote, and P. G. W. Keen. (1984a, June). "Setting Priorities for DSS Development." *MIS Quarterly,* Vol. 8, No. 2.

Meador, C. L., P. G. Keen, and M. J. Guyote. (1984b, May 7). "Personal Computer and Distribution Decision Support." *ComputerWorld,* Vol. 18, No. 19.

Mearian, L. (2002, February 28). "Sears Triples Its Storage Capacity." *ComputerWorld.*

Meehan, M. (2002, April 15). "Data's Tower of Babel." *ComputerWorld.*

Medsker, L., and E. Turban. (1994). "Integrating Expert Systems and Neural Computing for Decision Support." *Expert Systems with Applications,* Vol. 7, No. 4.

Medsker, L., and J. Liebowitz. (1994). *Design and Development of Expert Systems and Neural Networks.* New York: Macmillan.

Medsker, L., et al., (1995). "Knowledge Acquisition from Multiple Experts: Problems and Issues." *Expert Systems with Applications,* Vol. 9.

Melymuka, K. (1999, June 21). "Coca-Cola: Marketing Partner." *ComputerWorld,* Vol. 33, No. 25.

Melymuka, K. (2000, November 6). "The Crucible." *ComputerWorld.*

Melymuka, K. (2001a, April 30). "Profiting from Mistakes." *ComputerWorld.*

Melymuka, K. (2001b, September 24). "Engaging Users." *ComputerWorld.*

Melymuka, K. (2002a, February 25). "How to Choose an IT Vendor." *ComputerWorld.*

Melymuka, K. (2002b, July 8). "Knowledge Management Helps Cut Errors by Half." *ComputerWorld.*

Melymuka, K. (2002c, July 22). "Taking Projects to the Extreme." *ComputerWorld,* Vol. 36, No. 30.

Melymuka, K. (July 21, 2003). "Ready, Set…" *ComputerWorld.*

Menczer, F. (2003). "Complementing Search Engines with Online Web Mining Agents." *Decision Support Systems,* Vol. 35, No. 2, pp. 195–212.

Menezes, J. (2000, June 9). "Post Enterprise ERP: Data to Knowledge." *Computing Canada,* Vol. 26, No. 12.

Menninger, D. (1997). "Building Object-Oriented OLAP Applications: Not Just Any Object-oriented Tool Will Do." Chapter 7 in R. Barquin and H. Edelstein (eds.). *Planning and Designing the Data Warehouse.* Upper Saddle River, NJ: Prentice Hall PTR.

Meredith, J. R. (1981, October). "The Implementation of Computer-Based Systems." *Journal of Operational Management.*

Meredith, R. (2002, July). "Design of a Multimedia, Internet-Enabled Decision Support System for Patients and Physicians." *Proceedings of DSIage 2002,* Cork, Ireland.

Meso, P. N., and J. O. Liegle. (2000, August). "The Future of Web-Based Instruction Systems." *Proceedings of the Americas Conference of the Association for Information Systems,* Milwaukee.

Microsoft Corp. (2001). "Practicing Knowledge Management." microsoft.com/business/km/casestudies/jdedward.asp.

Microsoft Corp. (2002, October). "Industry Solutions: Manufacturing—Maybelline." Thinque.com. www.thinque.com/pdfs/ThinqueMaybellineCS.pdf.

Miettinen, K., and M.M. Makela. (2000). "Interactive Multiobjective Optimization Systems WWW-NIMBUS on the Internet." *Computers and Operations Research.* Vol. 27, Nos. 7–8.

Milberg, S., et al. (1995, December). "Values, Personal Information Privacy, and Regulatory Approaches." *Communications of the ACM,* Vol. 38, No. 12.

Mili, F. (1990, May). "Active DSS: Issues and Challenges." *TIMS/ORSA Joint National Meeting,* Las Vegas.

Mili, H., and F. Pachet. (1995). "Regularity, Document Generation, and Cyc." In R. Rada and K. Tochtermann (eds.). *Expertmedia: Expert Systems and Hypermedia.* Singapore: World Scientific.

Mimno, P. R. (1997). "Data Warehousing Architectures." Chapter 8 in R. Barquin and H. Edelstein. (eds.). *Building, Using, and Managing the Data Warehouse.* Upper Saddle River, NJ: Prentice Hall PTR.

Min, D. M., et al. (1996, September). "IBRS: Intelligent Bank Reengineering System." *Decision Support Systems,* Vol. 18, No. 1.

Min, H., and S. B. Eom. (1994). "An Integrated Decision Support System for Global Logistics." *International Journal of Physical Distribution and Logistics Management,* Vol. 24, No. 1.

Mingers, J., and J. Rosenhead. (eds.). (2001). *Rational Analysis for a Problematic World Revisited.* New York: John Wiley.

Mintzberg, H., et al. (2002). *The Strategy Process,* 4th ed. Upper Saddle River, NJ: Prentice Hall.

Mintzberg, H. A. (1980). *The Nature of Managerial Work.* Englewood Cliffs, NJ: Prentice Hall.

Mintzberg, H. A. (1989). *Mintzberg on Management.* New York: Free Press.

Mintzberg, H. A. (1993). *The Rise and Fall of Strategic Planning.* New York: Free Press.

Miranda, S. M., and R. P. Bostrom. (1997, January). "Meeting Facilitation: Process Versus Content Interventions." *Proceedings of the Thirtieth Annual Hawaii International Conference on Systems Sciences, HICSS-30* Wailea, HI, Los Alamitos, CA: IEEE Computer Society Press.

Mirchandani, D., and R. Pakath. (1999). "Four Models for a DSS." *Information Management.* Vol. 35, No. 1

Mitchell, M. (1999). *An Introduction to Genetic Algorithms.* Cambridge, MA: MIT Press.

Mitchell, T. M., et al. (1986). "Explanation-Based Generalization: A Unifying View." *Machine Learning,* No. 1.

Mitri, "DSS Integration with Learning and Training System."

Miyake, D. (2002, July 26). "Beyond the Numbers." *Intelligent Enterprise.*

Mizell, I. R. (1998). *Invasion of Privacy.* Berkley, CA: Berkley Publishing.

MMH (2000, February). "Real Time Decisions, Instant Response." *Modern Materials Handling,* Vol. 55, No. 2.

Moloney, J., and S. Tello. (2003, February). "Principles for Building Success in Online Education." *Syllabus.*

Monahan, G. E. (2000). *Management Decision Making: Spreadsheet Modeling, Analysis, and Applications.* Cambridge: Cambridge University Press.

Money, A., et al. (1988, June). "The Quantification of Decision Support Benefits Within the Context of Value Analysis." *MIS Quarterly,* Vol. 12, No. 2.

Montana, J. C. (2000, July). "The Legal System and Knowledge Management." *Information Management Journal,* Vol. 34, No. 3.

Montaner, M., et. al. (2003). "A Taxonomy of Recommender Agents on the Internet." *Artificial Intelligence Review,* Vol. 19, pp. 285–330.

Montgomery, A. L. (2001, March/April). "Applying Quantitative Marketing Techniques to the Internet." *Interfaces.* Vol. 31, No. 2.

Montgomery, S. (2002). *People Patterns: A Modern Guide to the Four Temperaments.* Archer Publications.

Montaldo, E., et al. (2003). "Enhancing Workflow Management in the Manufacturing Information System of a Small–Medium Enterprise: An Agent-Based Approach." *Information System Frontiers,* Vol. 5, No. 2, pp. 195–205.

Moody, J. W., et. al. (1998/1999, Winter). "Capturing Expertise from Experts: The Need to Match Knowledge Elicitation Techniques with Expert System Types." *Journal of Computer Information Systems.*

Moon, Y. B., C. K. Divers, and H-J. Kim. (1998, March). "AEWS: An Integrated Knowledge-Based System with Neural Networks for Reliability Prediction." *Computers in Industry,* Vol. 35, No. 2.

Mooney, S. F. (2000, December 18–25). "P-C 'Knowledge Capital' Can Be Measured." *National Underwriter,* Vol. 104, Nos. 51–52.

Moore, C. (1999, October). "Eureka! Xerox Discovers Way to Grow Community Knowledge." *KMWorld.*

Moore, C. (2002, October 8). "Knowledge Management Offers Hope for Homeland Security." *InfoWorld.*

Moore, J. H., and M. G. Chang. (1980, Fall). "Design of Decision Support Systems." *Data Base,* Vol. 12, Nos. 1 and 2.

Mora, M. (2002, October/December). "Management and Organizational Issues for Decision Making Support Systems." *Information Resources Management Journal,* Special Issue.

Mora, M., G. A. Forgionne, and J. N. D. Gupta, (eds.). (2002). *Decision Making Support Systems: Achievement and Challenges for the New Decade.* Hershey, PA: Idea Group Publishing.

Moran, P., and S. Ghoshal. (1996, January). "Theories of Economic Organization: The Case for Realism and Balance." *Academy of Management,* Vol. 21, No. 1.

Morris, B. A. (2003, February). "The Fast Track to CE Credits." *Rough Notes.* Vol. 146, No. 2.

Morris, H. (2003, January). "Build vs. Buy." *DM Review.*

Morris, M. G., C. Speier, and J. A. Hoffer. (1999, Winter). "An Examination of Procedural and Object-Oriented Systems Analysis Methods: Does Prior Experience Help or Hinder Performance?" *Decision Sciences,* Vol. 30, No. 1.

Motiwalla, L. F. (1995, Spring). "An Intelligent Agent for Prioritizing E-Mail Messages." *Information Resources Management Journal,* Vol. 8, No. 2.

Mottl, J. N. (2000, January 3). "Learn at a Distance." *Informationweek,* No. 767.

Moundridou, M., and M. Virvou. (2002). "Evaluating the Persona Effect of an Interface Agent in a Tutoring System." *Journal of Computer-Assisted Learning,* Vol. 18, No. 3, pp. 253–261.

Moyle, S., and M. Watts. (2003, January/February). "Neural Networks Raise the Roof." *IEEE Intelligent Systems,* pp. 8–10.

Mukherjee, A. (2001, August 9–11). "Advanced Decision Support Tools in Airline Scheduling, Planning and Operations." *Proceedings of the PRISM Symposium.*

Mullin, T. (2002, Winter). "Deploying Enterprise Information Management in Conjunction with a Data Warehouse." *Journal of Data Warehousing,* Vol. 7, No. 1.

Munakata, T., and Y. Jani. (1994, March) "Fuzzy Systems: An Overview." *Communications of the ACM,* Vol. 37, No. 3.

Murphy, C. (2002, May 20). "Technology Nudges Managers to Do Better." *InformationWeek,* No. 889.

Murthy, S., et al. (1999, September/October). "Cooperative Multiobjective Decision Support for the Paper Industry." *Interfaces,* Vol. 29, No. 5.

Murthy, U. S., and D. S. Kerr. (2000). "Task/Technology Fit and the Effectiveness of Group Support Systems: Evidence in the Context of Tasks Requiring Domain Specific Knowledge." *Proceedings of the Thirty-third Annual Hawaii International Conference on System Sciences HICSS-33.* Los Alamitos, CA: IEEE Computer Society Press.

Musen, M. A., et al. (1995). "PROTÉGÉ-II: Computer Support for Development of Intelligent Systems from Libraries of Components." *Proceedings of MEDINFO 1995, Eighth World Congress on Medical Informatics,* Vancouver, BC.

Musen, M. A., et. al (1999, August)."Use of a Domain Model to Drive an Interactive Knowledge-Editing Tool." *International Journal of Human–Computer Studies.*

Mustajoki, J., and R.P. Hamalainen. (2000, August). "Web-HIPRE: Global Decision Support by Value Tree and AHOP Analysis." *INFOR,* Vol. 3, No. 3.

Myers, I. B. (1998). *Introduction to Type: A Guide to Understanding Your Results on the Myers-Briggs Type Indicator,* 6th ed.. Gainesville, FL: Center for Applications of Psychological Type.

Myers, I. B., and P. B. Myers. (1995). *Gifts Differing: Understanding Personality Type,* reprint ed. Palo Alto, CA: Consulting Psychologists Press.

Mykytyn, K., et al. (1990, March). "Expert Systems: _A Question of Liability?" *MIS Quarterly,* Vol. 14, No. 1.

Myron, D. (2003, July). "Service on Steroids." *Customer Relationship Management.*

Nagy, G. (2000, January). "Twenty Years of Document Image Analysis in PAMI." *IEEE Transactions on Pattern Analysis and Machine Intelligence,* Vol. 22, No. 1.

Nahapiet, J., and S. Ghoshal. (1998, April). "Social Capital, Intellectual Capital, and the Organizational Advantage." *Academy of Management Review,* Vol. 23, No. 2.

Nance, B. (2001, April 23). "Managing Tons of Data." *ComputerWorld.*

Nance, R. E., and R. G. Sargent. (2002, January/February). "Perspectives on the Evolution of Simulation." *Operations Research,* Vol. 50, No. 1.

Nardi, B. A., et al. (1998, March). "Collaborative, Programmable, Intelligent Agents." *Communications of the ACM,* Vol. 41, No. 3.

Nash, K. S. (2000, October 30). "Companies Don't Learn from Previous IT Snafus." *ComputerWorld.*

Nash, K. S. (2002, July). "Chemical Reaction." *Baseline.*

Nash, K. S. (2002a, April 15). "Merging Data Silos." *ComputerWorld.*

Nash, K. S. (2002b, December). "Pinpointing a Gusher." *Baseline.*

Nault, B. R., and V. C. Storey. (1998). "Using Object Concepts to Match Artificial Intelligence Techniques to Problem Types." *Information and Management,* Vol. 34, No. 1.

Navigli, R., et al. (2003, January/February). "Ontological Learning and Its Application to Automated Terminology Translation." *IEEE Intelligent Systems,* pp. 22–31.

Nedovic, L. and V. Devedzic (2002). "Expert Systems in Finance: A Cross-Section of the Field." *Expert Systems with Applications,* Vol. 23, No. 1, pp. 49–66.

Nelson, B., and M. Wawiorka. (1999). *1001 Ways to Take Initiative at Work.* New York: Workman Publishing Co.

Nemati, H. R., and C. D. Barko. (2001, Winter). "Issues in Organizational Data Mining: A Survey of Current Practices." *Journal of Data Warehousing,* Vol. 6, No. 1.

Neo, B. S. (1996). *Exploiting Information Technology for Business Competitiveness: Cases and Insights from Singapore-Based Organizations.* Reading, MA: Addison-Wesley.

Neumann, S. (1994). *Strategic Information Systems.* New York: Macmillan.

Nevis, E. C., A. J. DiBella, and J. M. Gould. (1995, Winter). "Understanding Organizations as Learning Systems." *Sloan Management Review.*

Newell, A., and H. A. Simon. (1972). *Human Problem Solving.* Englewood Cliffs, NJ: Prentice Hall.

Newman, C. (2002, Quarter 3). "Teradata: Your Next Best Action with Your Customers." *Teradata Magazine.*

Newquist, H. P. (1996, September). "Data Mining: The AI Metamorphosis." *Database Programming & Design* (Supplement).

Nezlek, G. S., H. K. Jain, and D. L. Nazareth. (1999, November). "An Integrated Approach to Enterprise Computing Architectures." *Communications of the ACM,* Vol. 42, No. 11.

Nguyen H. T., and E. A. Walker. (1999). *A First Course in Fuzzy Logic.* Boca Raton, FL: CRC Press.

Ngwenyama, O. K., et al. (1996). "Supporting Facilitation in Group Support Systems: Techniques for Analyzing Consensus Relevant Data." *Decision Support Systems,* Vol. 16, No. 1.

Nick, Z., and P. Themis. (2001). "Web Search Using a Genetic Algorithm." IEEE Internet Computing, Vol. 5, No. 2, pp. 18–26.

Nielsen, K. (ed.). (2003). *Uncertainty in Economic Decision Making: Ambiguity Mental Models and Institutions.* Northampton, MA: Edward Elgar.

Niettinen K., et al. (1999). *Recent Advances in Genetic Algorithms.* New York: John Wiley.

Niles, J. M. (1998). *Making Telecommuting Happen: A Guide for Telemanagers and Telecommuters.* New York: John Wiley.

Nilson N. J. (1998). *Artificial Intelligence: A New Synthesis.* San Francisco: Morgan Kaufmann.

Ninios, P., K. Vlahos, and D. W. Bunn. (1995). "Industrial Simulation: System Modeling with an Object Oriented/DEVS Technology." *European Journal of Operational Research,* Vol. 81.

Nissen, M. E. (2001) "Agent-Based Supply Chain Integration." *Information Technology and Management*, No. 2.

Nobel, C. (2003, July 21). "Treo E-mail Options Grow." *eWeek*.

Nonaka, I., and H. Takeuchi. (1995). *The Knowledge-Creating Company: How Japanese Companies Create the Dynamics of Innovation.* New York: Oxford University Press.

Noon, D. (2001, June 25). "Surgery of the Future: The Ultimate Remote Control." *Newsweek*.

Nord, J. H., and D. Nord. (1995, August). "Executive Information Systems: A Study and Comparative Analysis." *Information & Management*, Vol. 29, No. 2.

Nord, J. H., and D. Nord. (1996, Winter). "Why Managers Use Executive Information Systems." *Information Strategy: Executive's Journal*, Vol. 12, No. 2.

Norman, B. A., and J. C Bean. (2000, May). "Scheduling Operations on Parallel Machine Tools." *IIE Transactions*, Vol. 32, No. 5.

Nunamaker, J. F., Jr. (1991). "Electronic Meeting Systems to Support Group Work: Theory and Practice at Arizona." *Communications of the ACM*, Vol. 34, No. 7.

Nurminen, J., et al. (2003). "What Makes Expert Systems Survive Over 10 Years: Empirical Evaluation of Several Engineering Applications." *Expert Systems With Applications*, Vol. 24, No. 1, pp. 199–211.

Nute, D. E., et al. (1995). "A Toolkit Approach to Developing Forest Management Advisory Systems in Prolog." *AI Applications*, Vol. 9, No. 3.

Nwana, H. S., and D. T. Ndumu. (1999). "A Perspective on Software Agent Research." *Knowledge Engineering Review*, No. 2.

Nwosu, K. C., et al. (1997, July/September). "Multimedia Database Systems: A New Frontier." *IEEE Multimedia*.

O'Brien, G., and J. Opie. (1999, October). "What's Really Doing the Work Here? Knowledge Representation or the Higher-Order Thought Theory of Consciousness." *Behavioral and Brain Sciences*.

Ocken, V. (2002; Sep 30). "Making the Most of Online Databases." *Marketing News*, Vol. 36, No. 20.

O'Dell, C., S. Elliot, and C. Hubert. (2003). "Achieving Knowledge Management Outcomes." Chapter 44 in C. W. Holsapple (ed.). *Handbook of Knowledge Management: Knowledge Directions,* Vol. 2. Heidelberg: Springer-Verlag.

O'Dell, C., and C. J. Grayson. (2003). "Identifying and Transferring Internal Best Practices." Chapter 31 in C. W. Holsapple (ed.). *Handbook of Knowledge Management: Knowledge Matters,* Vol. 1. Heidelberg: Springer-Verlag.

O'Dell, C., C. J. Grayson, Jr., and N. Essaides. (1998). *If Only We Knew What We Know: The Transfer of Internal Knowledge and Best Practice.* New York: Free Press (Simon & Schuster).

O'Dell, C., et al. (2003). "Successful KM Implementations: A Study of Best Practice Organizations." Chapter 51 in C. W. Holsapple (ed.). *Handbook of Knowledge Management: Knowledge Directions,* Vol. 2. Heidelberg: Springer-Verlag.

O'Donnell, P., D. Arnott, and M. Gibson. (2002, July 4–7). "Data Warehousing Methodologies: A Comparative Analysis." *Proceedings of DSIage 2002*, Cork, Ireland.

O'Hare, G., and N. Jennings (eds.). (1996). *Foundations of Distributed Artificial Intelligence.* New York: John Wiley.

O'Hare, G. M. P., and M. J. O'Grady. (2003). "Gulliver's Genie: A Multi-Agent System for Ubiquitous and Intelligent Information Content Delivery." *Computer Communications*, Vol. 26, No. 11, pp. 1177–1187.

O'Keefe, R. M., and O'Leary, D. E. (1993). "Performing and Managing Expert System Validation." In M. Grabowski and W. A. Wallace (eds.) *Advances in Expert Systems for Management.* Vol. 1. Greenwich, CT: JAI Press.

O'Keefe, R. M., and T. McEachern. (1998, March). "Web-Based Customer Decision Support System." *Communications of the ACM*.

O'Keefe, R. M., et al. (1987, Winter). "Validating Expert System Performance." *IEEE Expert*.

O'Leary, D. (1996, April). "AI and Navigation on the Internet and Intranet." *IEEE Expert*.

O'Leary, D. (1998, May). "Knowledge Management Systems: Converting and Connecting." *IEEE Intelligent Systems and Their Applications,* Vol. 13, No. 1.

O'Leary, D. (2003). "Technologies for Knowledge Storage and Assimilation." Chapter 34 in C. W. Holsapple (ed.). *Handbook of Knowledge Management: Knowledge Directions,* Vol. 2, Heidelberg: Springer-Verlag.

O'Leary, D. E. (1993, March/April). "Determining Differences in Expert Judgment: Implications for Knowledge Acquisition and Validation." *Decision Sciences,* Vol. 24, No. 2.

O'Leary, D. E. (1995, April). "Some Privacy Issues in Knowledge Discovery: The OECD Personal Privacy Guidelines." *IEEE Expert*, Vol. 10, No. 2.

O'Leary, D. E., et al. (1997, January). "Artificial Intelligence and Virtual Organizations." *Communications of the ACM*, Vol. 40, No. 1.

Oliver, J. R. (1996, January). "On Artificial Agents for Negotiation in Electronic Commerce." *Proceedings of the Twenty-ninth Hawaii International Conference on Systems Sciences HICSS-29,* Wailea, HI. Los Alamitos, CA: IEEE Computer Society Press.

Olson, J. E. (2003a). *Data Quality: The Accurate Dimension.* San Francisco: Morgan Kaufman Publishers.

Olson, J. E. (2003b, June). "The Business Case for Accurate Data." *Application Development Trends*.

OR/MS Today. (1999, December). "2000 OR/MS Resource Directory." *OR/MS Today*, Vol. 26, No. 6.

Orman, L. V. (1998, Summer). "A Model Management Approach to Business Process Reengineering." *Journal of Management Information Systems,* Vol. 15. No. 1.

Orovic, V. (2003, June). "To Do & Not To Do." *eAI Journal.*

Orzech, D. (1998, June). "Call Centers Take to the Web." *Datamation.*

Osyk, B. A., and B. S. Vijayaraman. (1995, Spring). "Integrating Expert Systems and Neural Nets." *Information Systems Management,* Vol. 12, No. 2.

Overby, S. (2003, March 1). "Bringing I.T. Back Home." *CIO.*

Owen, S. (1990). *Analog for Automated Reasoning.* New York: Academic Press.

Owrang, M. M., and F. J. Groupe. (1996). "Using Domain Knowledge to Guide Database Knowledge Discovery." *Expert Systems with Applications,* Vol. 10, No. 2.

Oxman, S. W. (1991, May). "Reporting Chemical Spills: An Expert Solution." *AI Expert,* Vol. 6, No. 5.

Ozbayrak, M., and R. Bell. (2003, May). "A Knowledge Based DSS for the Management of Parts and Tools in FMS." *Decision Support Systems.*

Pal, K., and O. Palmer. (2000). "A Decision Support System for Business Acquisitions." *Decision Support Systems,* Vol. 27, No. 4.

Pallatto, J. (2002a, February). "Business Tools Get Smart." *Internet World.*

Pallatto, J. (2002b, February). "Interview: Colleen Challenger." *InternetWorld.*

Pallatto, J. (2003, January). "Data Tools Expose Sales Opportunities." *InternetWorld.*

Palma-dos-Reis, A., and F. Zahedi. (1999, July). "Designing Personalized Intelligent Financial Decision Support Systems." *Decision Support Systems,* Vol. 26, No. 1.

Palmer, B. (1999, May 10). "Click Here for Decisions." *Fortune,* Vol. 139, No. 9.

Palopoli, L., and R. Torlone. (1997, November/December). "Generalised Production Rules as a Basis for Integrating Active and Deductive Databases." *IEEE Transactions on Knowledge and Data Engineering,* Vol. 9, No. 6.

Palshikar, G. K. (2001, April 16). "Matching Patterns." *Intelligent Explorer.*

Panko, R. R. (1998, Spring). "What We Know About Spreadsheet Errors." *Journal of End User Computing,* Vol. 10, No. 2.

Panko, R. R. (1999, Fall). "Applying Code Inspection to Spreadsheet Testing." *Journal of Management Information Systems.* Vol. 16, No. 2.

Papazafeiropoulou, A., and A. Pouloudi. (2001, October/December). "Social Issues in Electronic Commerce: Implications for Policy Makers." *Information Resources Management Journal.*

Papazoglou, M. P. (2001). "Agent-Oriented Technology in Support of e-Business." *Communications of the ACM,* Vol. 44, No. 4, pp. 71–77.

Park, C., and I. Han. (2002). "A Case-Based Reasoning with the Feature Weights Derived by Analytic Hierarchy Process for Bankruptcy Prediction." *Expert Systems with Applications,* Vol. 23, No. 3, pp. 255–264.

Parker, S., et al. (1994, September). "A DSS for Personnel Scheduling in a Manufacturing Environment." *Computers and Industrial Engineering.*

Parsaye, K., and M. Chignell. (1988). *Expert Systems.* New York: John Wiley.

Parsaye, K., and M. Chignell. (1993). *Intelligent Database: Object-Oriented, Deductive Hypermedia Technologies.* New York: John Wiley.

Pasahow, E. (2000, Spring). "How Can you Improve the Odds for Successful ERP Implementation?" *Digital Systems Reports,* Vol. 22, No. 1.

Patton, S. (2002a, May 1). "Get the CRM You Need at the Price You Want." *CIO.*

Patton, S. (2002b, December 15 / 2003, January 1). "Ideas2003: 14. Still Searching (After All These Years)." *CIO.*

Pauly, M.V. (2001). "Split Personality: Inconsistencies in Private and Public Decisions." Chapter 2 in S. J. Hoch, H. C. Kunreuther, with R. E. Gunther, ed. (2001). *Wharton on Making Decisions*, Wiley, New York.

PC AI. (1997, April 15). "Blackboard Technology." www2.primenet.com/pcai/New_Home_Page/ai_info/blackboard_technology.html.

PC Magazine. (2000, February 8). "Pipeline: Enter the Third Dimension." *PC Magazine.*

PC Magazine. (2002, September 3). "The Future in Gear." *PC Magazine.*

Pearman, R.R. (1998). *Hardwired Leadership: Unleashing the Power of Personality to Become a New Millennium Leader.* Palo Alto, CA: Davies-Black.

Pederson & Larsen. 2001.

Peffers, K., and V. K. Tunnainen. (1998). "Expectations and Impacts of Global Information System: The Case of a Global Bank in Hong Kong.*"* Global Information Technology Management*, Vol. 1, No. 4.

Pelletier, S-J., S. Pierre, and H. H. Hoang. (2003, March). "Modeling a Multi-Agent System for Retrieving Information from Distributed Sources." *Journal of Computing and Information Technology*, Vol. 11, No. 1.

Pender, L. (2000, August 15). "CRM from Scratch." *CIO.*

Pendergast, M., and S. Hayne. (1999, April 25). "Groupware and Social Networks: Will Life Ever Be the Same Again?" *Information and Software Technology,* Vol. 41, No. 6.

Peppers, D., et al. (1999). *The One-to-One Fieldbook.* New York: Bantam Books.

Perez, I., et al. (2003). "Extracting and Re-using Design Patterns from Genetic Algorithms Using Case-Based Reasoning." *Engineering Optimization*, Vol. 35, No. 2, pp. 121–141.

Perez-Cascante, L. P., et al. (2002, October/December). "The Impact of Expert Decision Support Systems on the Performance of New Employees." *Information Resources Management Journal.*

Pervan, G. P. (1999, July). "Intelligent Group Support Systems: Some Suggestions." *Proceedings of the Fifth International Conference of the Decision Sciences Institute,* Athens, Greece.

Peterson, T. (2003, April 21). "Getting Real About Real Time." *ComputerWorld.*

Pham, D. T., and R. M. Setchi. (2003). "Case-Based Generation of Adaptive Product Manuals." *Journal of Engineering Manufacturing,* Vol. 217, No. 3, pp. 313–322.

Phillips-Wren, G. E., and G. A. Forgionne. (2002, July). "Evaluating Web-Based Real-Time Decision Support Systems." *Proceedings of DSIage 2002,* Cork, Ireland.

Piatetsky-Shapiro, G., et al. (1996). "An Overview of Issues in Developing Industrial Data Mining and Knowledge Discovery Applications." In M. J. Han and E. Ptyra (eds.). *Fuzzy Logic: Implementation and Applications.* New York: John Wiley.

Picarille, L. (2003, July). "CRM World Domination." *Customer Relationship Management.*

Piccoli, G., et al. (2001, December). "Web-Based Virtual Learning Environments." *MIS Quarterly.*

Pinsonneault, A., and K. Kraemer. (1993, September). "The Impact of Information Technology on Middle Mangers." *MIS Quarterly,* Vol. 17, No. 3.

Pinto, N. B., L. M. Stephens, and R. D. Bonnell. (1995). "A Case Study in the Use of Large-Scale Knowledge-Based Technology for an Environmental Application." In N. J. I. Mars, (ed.). *Towards Very Large Knowledge Bases.* Amsterdam: IOS Press.

Piramuthu, S., et al. (1993, January). "Integration of Simulation Modeling and Inductive Learning in an Adaptive Decision Support System." *Decision Support Systems,* Vol. 9, No. 1.

Plamonden, R., and S. N. Srihari. (2000, January). "On-Line and Off-Line Handwriting Recognition: A Comprehensive Survey." *IEEE Transactions on Pattern Analysis and Machine Intelligence,* Vol. 22, No. 1.

Pooley, R., and P. Wilox. (2000, April). "Distributing Decision Making Using Java Simulation Across the World Wide Web." *Journal of the Operational Research Society.* Vol. 41, No. 4.

Poe, V. (1996). *Building a Data Warehouse for Decision Support.* Upper Saddle River, NJ: Prentice Hall.

Poh, H. L. (1994). "A Neural Network Approach for Decision Support." *International Journal of Applied Expert Systems,* Vol. 2. No. 3.

Poirier, C. C., (1999). *Advanced Supply Chain Management: How to Build a Sustained Competition.* Berkeley, CA: Publishers' Group West.

Polanyi, M. (1958). *Personal Knowledge.* Chicago: University of Chicago Press.

Polanyi, M. (1966). *The Tacit Dimension.* London: Routledge & Kegan Paul.

Port, O., and J. Carey. (1997, November 10). "Getting to Eureka!" *BusinessWeek.*

Portals Magazine. (2002, October) "Big Returns for IRS Portal." *Portals Magazine,* Vol. 3, No. 19.

Portals Magazine. (2003, July). "Covisint Resets Strategy." *Portals Magazine,* Vol. 33, No. 22.

Porter, M. E., (1985). *Competitive advantage, creating and sustaining superior performance,* New York: Free Press.

Post, G. V. (2002). *Database Management Systems.* 2nd ed. New York: McGraw-Hill.

Powell, A. L. (2000, August). "Commitment in a Virtual Team." *Proceedings of the Americas Conference of the Association for Information Systems,* Milwaukee.

Powell, P. L., and J. E. V. Johnson, (1995, May). "Gender and DSS Design: The Research Implications." *Decision Support Systems,* Vol. 14, No. 1.

Power, D.J. (2002). *Decision Support Systems: Concepts and Resources for Managers.* Westport, CT: Quorum Books.

Preece, A., and S. Decker. (2002). "Intelligent Web Services." *IEEE Intelligent Systems,* Vol. 16, No. 1, pp. 15–17.

Prerau, D. S. (1990). *Developing and Managing Expert Systems.* Reading, MA: Addison-Wesley.

Price, J., and T. Schweitzer. (2002, October). "Before the Deluge FEMA, Floodplains, and GIS." *Geospatial Solutions.* Vol. 12, No. 10.

Principe, J. C., N. R. Euliano, and W. C. Lefebvre. (2000). *Neural and Adaptive Systems: Fundamentals Through Simulations.* New York: John Wiley.

Probst, G., S. Raub, and K. Romhardt. (2002). *Managing Knowledge.* New York: John Wiley.

Proudlove, N. C., S. Vadera, and K. A. H. Kobbacy. (1998, July). "Intelligent Management Systems in Operations: A Review." *Journal of the Operational Research Society,* Vol. 49, No. 7.

Ptak, C., and E. Schragenheim. (2000). *ERP: Tools, Techniques, and Applications for Integrating the Supply Chain.* Boca Raton, FL: St. Lucie Press.

Ptyra, M. J. (ed.). (1996). *Fuzzy Logic: Implementation and Applications.* New York: John Wiley.

Puls, T. L. (2002). "Prolog Fundamentals: A Logic Programming Tutorial." *PC AI,* Vol. 16, No. 6, pp. 28–33.

Qi, M. (1999, October). Nonlinear Predictability of Stock Returns Using Financial and Economic Variables." *Journal of Business & Economic Statistics,* Vol. 17, No. 4.

Qi, M., and G. S. Maddala. (1999, May). "Economic Factors and the Stock Market." *Journal of Forecasting,* Vol. 18, No. 3.

Quah, T-S., et al. (1996, May 21). "Towards Integrating Rule-Based Expert Systems and Neural Networks." *Decision Support Systems,* Vol. 17, No. 2.

Quarantiello, L. E. (1996, January). "Gangs: Tracking the Homeboys." *Law and Order.*

Quenk, N. L. (1999). *Essentials of Myers-Briggs Type Indicator Assessment Essentials of Psychological Assessment Series.* New York: John Wiley.

Quinn, P. (2003, May). "Inventory Optimization: Lean But Not Mean." *SCS Magazine.*

Quiroga, L. A., and L. C. Rabelo. (1995, September). "Learning from Examples: A Review of Machine Learning, Neural Networks and Fuzzy Logic Paradigms." *Computers & Industrial Engineering,* Vol. 29, Nos. 1–4.

Rada, R., and K. Tochtermann, eds. (1995). *Expertmedia: Expert Systems and Hypermedia.* Singapore: World Scientific.

Raden, N. (1997). "Choosing the Right OLAP Technology." Chapter 10 in R. Barquin, and H. Edelstein. (eds.). *Planning and Designing the Data Warehouse.* Upper Saddle River, NJ: Prentice Hall PTR.

Raden, N. (2003a, June 17). "Real Time: Get Real." *Intelligent Enterprise.*

Raden, N. (2003b, June 30). "Real Time: Get Real, Part II." *Intelligent Enterprise.*

Rafea, A., et al. (2003). "Automated Knowledge Acquisition Tool for Irritation and Fertilization Expert Systems." *Expert Systems With Applications,* Vol. 24, pp. 49–57.

Raghunathan, A. (2002, December 8). "Texas Hopes to Ease Teacher Shortage with Internet, Distance Learning Programs." *Knight Ridder Tribune Business News.*

Raghunathan, N. (1994, Summer). "An Application of Qualitative Reasoning to Derive Behavior from Structure of Quantitative Models." *Journal of Management Information Systems,* Vol. 11, No. 1.

Ragsdale, C.T. (2000). *Spreadsheet Modeling and Decision Analysis.* 3rd ed. Cincinnati, OH: South-Western.

Ragusa, J. M., et al. (2001, December). "Collaborative Virtual Design Environments." *Communications of the ACM.*

Rainer, R. K., Jr., and H. J. Watson. (1995a, June). "What Does It Take for Successful Executive Information Systems?" *Decision Support Systems,* Vol. 14, No. 2.

Rainer, R. K., Jr., and H. J. Watson. (1995b, Fall). "The Keys to Executive Information System Success." *Journal of Management Information Systems,* Vol. 12, No. 2.

Rainone, S. H., et al. (1998, Spring). "Ethical Management of Employee E-mail Privacy." *Information Strategy: The Executive Journal.*

Raju, K. S., and C. R. S. Pillai. (1999, January 16). "Multicriterion Decision Making in River Basin Planning and Development." *European Journal of Operational Research,* Vol. 112, No. 2.

Ralha, C. G. (1996). "Structuring Information in a Distributed Hypermedia System." In N. Shadbolt, K. O'Hara, and G. Schreiber (eds.). *Advances in Knowledge Acquisition.* Berlin: Springer-Verlag

Ram, S., and S. Ram (1996, January). "Validation of Expert Systems for Innovation Management: Issues, Methodology, and Empirical Assessment." *Journal of Product Innovation Management,* Vol. 13, No. 1.

Ramakrishnan, R., and J. Gehrke. (2002). *Database Management Systems.* New York: McGraw-Hill, 2002.

Ramani, K. V. (2001, January/March). "DSS-Enabled Material Process at MP Trust Hospital." *Production and Inventory Control Management Journal.*

Ramsay, A. M. (ed.). (1996). *Artificial Intelligence: Methodology, Systems, Applications.* Amsterdam: IOS Press.

Ranganathan C., and V. Sethi. (2002, Winter). "Rationality in Strategic Information Technology Decisions: The Impact of Shared Domain Knowledge and IT Unit Structure." *Decision Sciences,* Vol. 33, No. 1.

Ranjan, A., et al. (2002) "From Process Experts to a Real-Time Knowledge-Based System." *Expert Systems,* Vol. 19, No. 2, pp. 69–79.

Rao, S. S. (1998, January 12). "Evolution at Warp Speed." *Forbes,* Vol. 161, No. 1.

Rapoza, J. (2002, September 16). "Web Services–Portal is on Tap for New Mexico." *eWeek.*

Rapoza, J. (2003a June 9). "Content Management at High and Low Ends." *eWeek.*

Rapoza, J. (2003b, July 21). "EIPs More Compelling Than Ever." *eWeek.*

Rappaport, A., and R. Smith (eds.). (1990). *Innovative Applications of Artificial Intelligence 2.* Cambridge, MA: MIT Press.

Rapport, M. (2001, July). "Unfolding Knowledge." *Knowledge Management.*

Rasmus, D. W. (1995). "Creativity and Tools." *PC AI,* Pt. 1: May/June; Pt. 2: July/August; Pt. 3: September/ October

Rasmus, D. W. (2000, March/April). "Knowledge Management: More Than AI But Less Without It." *PC AI,* Vol. 14, No. 2.

Ratner, R. K., B. E. Kahn, and D. Kahneman. (1999, June). "Choosing Less-Preferred Experiences for the Sake of Variety." *Journal of Consumer Research.* Vol. 26, No. 1.

Rayham, A. F. R., and M. C. Fairhurst. (1999, February). "Enhancing Multiple Expert Decision Combination Strategies Through Exploration of A Priori Information Sources." *IEE Proceedings—Vision, Image and Signal Processing,* Vol. 146, No. 1.

Raynor, W. (1996). *The International Dictionary of Artificial Intelligence.* London: Glenlake Publishing.

Rayward-Smith, V. J., I. H. Osman, and C. R. Reeves (eds.). (1996). *Modern Heuristic Methods.* New York: John Wiley.

Reamy, T. (2002a, June). "Imparting Knowledge Through Storytelling." *KMWorld,* Vol. 11, No. 6.

Reamy, T. (2002b, July/August). "Imparting Knowledge Through Storytelling—Part 2." *KMWorld,* Vol. 11, No. 7.

Redman, T. C. (1998, Feb). "The Impact of Poor Data Quality on the Typical Enterprises." *Communications of the ACM.*

Reed, R. D., and R. J. Marks II. (1999). *Neural Smithing: Supervised Learning in Feedforward Artificial Neural Networks.* Cambridge, MA: MIT Press.

Rees, J., and G. Koehler. (1999). "Brainstorming, Negotiating and Learning in Group Decision Support Systems: An Evolutionary Approach." *Proceedings of the Thirty-second Annual Hawaii International Conference on System Sciences HICSS-32.* Los Alamitos, CA: IEEE Computer Society.

Reeves, C. R., and J. E. Rowe. (2002). *Genetic Algorithms: Principles and Perspectives.* Norwell, MA: Kluwer Academic Publishers.

Reichheld, F. F., and Bain and Co.. (1997). *The Loyalty Effect.* Cambridge, MA: Harvard Business School Press.

Reid, K. A. (1999). "Impact of Technology on Learning Effectiveness." Center for Excellence in Distance Learning (CEDL). Lucent Technologies, www.lucent.com/cedl.

Reimers, B. D. (2003, April 14). "Too Much of a Good Thing." *ComputerWorld.*

Reinig, B. A., R. O. Briggs, and J. F. Nunamaker, Jr. (1997/1998, Winter). "Flaming in the Electronic Classroom." *Journal of Management Information Systems,* Vol. 14, No. 3.

Reinig, B. A., and B. Shin. (2002, Fall). "The Dynamic Effects of Group Support Systems on Group Meeting." *Journal of Management Information Systems,* Vol. 19, No. 2.

Reiter E., and R. Dale. (2000). *Building Natural Language Generation Systems.* Cambridge: Cambridge University Press.

Reiter, R. (1980). "A Logic for Default Reasoning." *Artificial Intelligence,* Vol. 13, 81–132.

Respicio, A., M. E. Captivo, and A. J. Rodrigues (2002, July 2002). "A DSS for Production Planning and Scheduling in the Paper Industry." *Proceedings of DSIage2002,* Cork, Ireland.

Rettig, H. (2000). "3D Business Data Utilization VARs Are Helping Their Customers See Business Data More Clearly." pubs.cmpnet.com/vb/case/167drill.htm.

Rheingold, H. (1993). *The Virtual Community: Homesteading on the Electronic Frontier.* Reading, MA: Addison-Wesley.

Rhey, E. (2002, September 3). "Tech Frontiers." *PC Magazine.*

Ribeiro, R., et al. (1995, February). "Uncertainty in Decision Making: An Adductive Perspective." *Decision Support Systems,* Vol. 13, No. 2.

Riccardi, G. (2003). *Database Management.* Boston: Pearson Education.

Ricci, F. (2002). "Travel Recommender Systems." *IEEE Intelligent Systems,* Vol. 17, No. 6, pp. 55–57.

Rich, E., and K. Knight. (1991). *Artificial Intelligence,* 2nd ed. New York: McGraw-Hill.

Ridell, J., et al. (2002). *Word of Mouse: The Marketing Power of Collaborative Filtering.* New York: Warner Books.

Riesbeck, C. K., and R. L. Schank. (1989). *Inside Case-Based Reasoning.* Hillsdale, NJ: Erlbaum Associates.

Riffee, W. H. (2003, February). "Putting a Faculty Face on Distance Education Programs." *Syllabus.*

Riekki, J., et al. (2003). "Genie of the Net: An Agent Platform for Managing Services on Behalf of the User." *Computer Communications,* Vol. 26, pp. 1188–1198.

Roberts, B. (2001, September). "A Balanced Approach." *Knowledge Management.*

Roberts, J. (2000, December). "From Know-How to Show-How? Questioning the Role of Information and Communication Technologies in Knowledge Transfer." *Technology Analysis & Strategic Management,* Vol. 12, No. 4.

Roberts-Witt, S. L. (2000, October). "Portal Pitfalls." *Knowledge Management.*

Roberts-Witt, S. L. (2002, November). "The @HP Way." *Portals Magazine.*

Robey, D. (1979, September). "User Attitudes and MIS Use." *Academy of Management Journal,* Vol. 22, No. 3.

Robin, M. (2000, March). "Learning by Doing." *Knowledge Management.*

Robinson, W. N. (1997). "Electronic Brokering for Assisted Contracting of Software Applets." *Proceedings of the Thirtieth Annual Hawaii International Conference on Systems Sciences HICSS-30,* Wailea, HI. Los Alamitos, CA: IEEE Computer Society Press.

Rockart, J. F., and A. D. Crescenzi. (1984, Summer). "Engaging Top Management in Information Technology." *Journal of Systems Management.*

Rockart, J. F., and D. W. DeLong. (1988). *Executive Support Systems: The Emergence of Top Management Computer Use.* Homewood, IL: Dow Jones–Irwin.

Roe, A. (1998, July 27/August 3). "Water Distribution Engineers Apply Darwin's Theory to System Design." *Engineering News Record,* Vol. 241, No. 4.

Roiger, R. J., and M. Geatz. (2003). *Data Mining: A Tutorial-Based Primer.* Reading, MA: Addison-Wesley.

Romano, N. C., Jr., J. F. Nunamaker, Jr., and R. O. Briggs. (1997). "User Driven Design of a Web-Based Group Support System." *Proceedings of the Thirtieth Annual Hawaii International Conference on Systems Sciences HICSS-30,* Wailea, HI, Los Alamitos, CA: IEEE Computer Society Press.

Rosenschein, J. S., and G. Zlotkin. (1994, Fall). "Designing Conventions for Automated Negotiation." *AI Magazine,* Vol. 15, No. 3.

Rosenstein, A. H. (1999, Spring). "Measuring the Benefits of Clinical Decision Support: Return on Investment." *Health Care Management Review,* Vol. 24, No. 2.

Rosenwald, G. W., and C-C. Liu. (1997, January). "Rule-Based System Validation Through Automatic

Identification of Equivalence Classes." *IEEE Transactions on Knowledge and Data Engineering,* Vol. 9, No. 1.

Ross, S.M. (2003). *Simulation.* 3rd ed. New York: Academic Press.

Rossetti, M.D., and F. Selandar. (2001, December). "Multiobjective Analysis of Hospital Delivery Systems." *Computers & Industrial Engineering,* Vol. 41, No. 3.

Roth, B. M., and J. D. Mullen. (2002). *Decision Making: Its Logic And Practice.* Lanham, MD: Rowman & Littlefield.

Rothrock, D. (2002, September 30). "Decision Management Hits the Road." *National Underwriter,* Vol. 106, No. 39.

Rouse, W. B. (1993, November/December). "Enterprise Support Systems: Training and Aiding People to Plan and Manage." *Industrial Management,* Vol. 35, No. 6.

Rubenfeld, S., et al. (1994, Winter). "Caveat Emptor: Avoiding Pitfalls in Data-Based Decision Making." *Review of Business.*

Ruber, P. (2001, January 11). "Build a Dynamic Business Portal With XML." *Knowledge Management.*

Ruber, P. (2003, June). "Analytics Improve Merchandising." *InternetWorld.*

Rublin, L. R. (1999, December 13). "Neglected Gems." *Barron's,* Vol. 79, No. 50.

Rudenstein, R. (2000, January). "A Bright Idea: HR Portal Helps Osram Sylvania See the Light." *Enterprise Systems Journal,* pp. 24–30.

Ruggiero, M. A., Jr. (1999, March). "Birth of a Neural Network." *Futures,* Vol. 28, No. 3.

Ruggles, R. (1998). "The State of the Notion: Knowledge Management in Practice." *California Management Review,* Vol. 40, No. 3.

Rumizen, M. C. (2002). *The Complete Idiot's Guide to Knowledge Management.* Madison, WI: Alpha Books.

Russ, K., and A. Wetherelt, (1999, March/April). "Large Scale Mine Visualization Using VRML." *IEEE Computer Graphics and Applications.*

Russel, S. J. and P. Norvig, P. (2002). *Artificial Intelligence: A Modern Approach,* 2nd ed. Prentice Hall.

Russell, I. F., and A. N. Kumar (eds.). (2000, February). "Special Issue: Tools and Techniques of Artificial Intelligence." *International Journal of Pattern Recognition and Artificial Intelligence,* Vol. 14, No. 1.

Russell, S., and P. Norvig. (1995). *Artificial Intelligence: A Modern Approach.* Upper Saddle River, NJ: Prentice Hall.

Ryan, J. (1988, November). "Expert Systems in the Future: The Redistribution of Power." *Journal of Systems Management,* Vol. 39, No. 11.

Ryker, R., and N. Ravinder. (1995, October). "An Empirical Examination of the Impact of Computer Information Systems on Users." *Information and Management,* Vol. 29, No. 4.

Rykere R., et al. (2002, Summer). "Online Privacy Policies: An Assessment." *Journal of Computer Information Systems.*

Saarenvirta, G. (2001, Quarter 2). "Operation Data Mining." *DB2 Magazine.*

Saaty, T. L. (1995). *Decision Making for Leaders: The Analytic Hierarchy Process for Decisions in a Complex World,* rev. ed. Pittsburgh: RWS Publishers.

Saaty, T. L. (1996). *Decision Making for Leaders,* Vol. 2. Pittsburgh: RWS Publishers.

Saaty, T. L. (1999). *The Brain: Unraveling the Mystery of How It Works (The Neural Network Process).* Pittsburgh: RWS Publications.

Saaty, T. L. (2000). *The Brain: Unraveling the Mystery of How it Works.* Pittsburgh: University of Pittsburgh Press.

Sabri, H. (2003, July 18). "CRM: The Power of Prediction." *Intelligent Enterprise.*

Sadaranda, R., and S. K. Acharya. (1993, October). "Modeling the Negotiation Paradigm for the Banking Industry." *Computers in Industry,* Vol. 22, No. 3.

Sadeh, N. (2002, April). *Mobile Commerce: New Technologies, Services and Business Models.* New York: John Wiley.

Saitta, L. (1996). "Representation Change in Machine Learning." *AI Communications,* Vol. 9.

Saltzman, R.M., and V. Mehrotra. (2001, May/June). "A Call Center Uses Simulation to Drive Strategic Change." *Interfaces,* Vol. 31, No. 3.

Sandahl, K. (1994). "Transferring Knowledge from Active Experts to End-User Environments." *Knowledge Acquisition,* Vol. 6.

Sanders, G. L., and J. F. Courtney. (1985, March). "A Field Study of Organizational Factors Influencing DSS Success." *MIS Quarterly,* Vol. 9, No. 1.

Sandoe K., and A. Saharia. (2001). *Enterprise Integration.* New York: John Wiley.

Sangster, A. (1994). "The Adoption of IT in Management Accounting: The Expert Systems Experience." *Journal of Information Technology,* Vol. 9.

Santosus, M., and J. Surmacz. (2001, May 23). "The ABCs of Knowledge Management," *CIO.*

Santosus, M. (2001, September) "A Penny for Your Thoughts." *In the Know* at cio.com.

Sarin, R. (1999, September). "Debating Rationality: Nonrational Aspects of Organizational Decision Making." *Journal of Economic Literature,* Vol. 37, No. 3.

Sarker, R., M. Mohammadian, and X. Yao. (eds.). (2002). *Evolutionary Optimization.* Norwell, MA: Kluwer Academic Publishers.

Satzinger, J. W., M. J. Garfield, and M. Nagasundaram. (1999, Spring). "The Creative Process: The Effects of

Group Memory on Individual Idea Generation." *Journal of Management Information Systems,* Vol. 15, No. 4.

Satzinger, J. W., R. Jackson, and S. Burd. (2002). *Systems Analysis and Design in a Changing World.* Cambridge, MA: Course Technology.

Satzinger, J.W., and T.U. Orvik. (2002). *The Object-Oriented Approach: Concepts, Systems Development, and Modeling with UML.* 2nd ed., Cambridge, MA: Course Technology.

Savage, H. (2001, Winter). "Democratizing Data Exchange." *edirections.*

Sawyer, D. C., (1999). *Getting It Right: Avoiding the High Cost of Wrong Decisions.* Boca Raton, FL: St. Lucie Press.

Scalet, S. (2000, August 15). "Repairing the Trust." *CIO.*

Scannell, E., and C. Moore. (2002, October 14). "Microsoft Touts Office Vision." *InfoWorld.*

Schantz, H. F. (1991, Spring). "An Overview of Neural OCR Networks." *Journal of Information Systems Management,* Vol. 8, No. 2.

Scheier, R. L. (2003, June 23). "Tools for Tough Times." *Computerworld.*

Schein, E. (1997). *Organizational Culture and Leadership,* 2nd ed., San Francisco: Jossey-Bass.

Schein, E. (1999). *The Corporate Culture Survival Guide.* San Francisco: Jossey-Bass.

Schein, E. H. (1956). "The Chinese Indoctrination Program for Prisoners of War." *Psychiatry,* Vol. 19, No. 1.

Scheiner, M. (2003, January 1). "Neiman Marcus Uses Natural Language Search to Boost Online Sales." *Customer Relationship Management.*

Schell, G. P. (2000, August). "The 'Introduction to Management Information' Course Goes Online." *Proceedings of the Americas Conference of the Association for Information Systems,* Milwaukee.

Schlegel, K. (2003, June). "Web Analytics Essentials." *InternetWorld Special Report.*

Schmidt, R., K. Lyytinen, M. Keil, and P. Cule. (2001, Spring). "Identifying Software Project Risks: An International Delphi Study." *Journal of Management Information Systems,* Vol. 17.

Schmitt, B. H., and L. Brown. (2001). *Build Your Own Garage: Blueprints and Tools to Unleash Your Company's Hidden Creativity.* New York: Free Press.

Schmitt, L. J., and M. M. Amini. (1998, August 1). "Performance Characteristics of Alternative Genetic Algorithmic Approaches to the Traveling Salesman Problem Using Path Representation: An Empirical Study." *European Journal of Operational Research,* Vol. 108, No. 3.

Schocken, S., and G. Ariav. (1994, June). "Neural Networks for Decision Support: Problems and Opportunities." *Decision Support Systems,* Vol. 11, No. 5.

Schoder, D., and T. Eymann. (2000). "The Real Challenges of Mobile Agents." *Communications of the ACM,* Vol. 43, No. 6, pp. 111–112.

Schrage, L. (1997). *Optimization Modeling with LINDO,* 5th ed. Pacific Grove, CA: Duxbury Press.

Schrage, M. (1995). *No More Teams!: Mastering the Dynamics of Creative Collaboration.* New York: Doubleday.

Schrage, M., and T. Peters. (1999). *Serious Play: How the World's Best Companies Simulate to Innovate.* Boston: Harvard Business School Press.

Schroek, M. (2001, December). "The Next Generation of Balanced Scorecards." *DM Review.*

Schultheis, R., and M. Sumner. (1994, Spring). "The Relationship of Application Risks to Application Controls: A Study of Microcomputer-Based Spreadsheet Applications." *Journal of End User Computing,* Vol. 6, No. 2.

Schulz, M. (2001, August). "The Uncertain Relevance of Newness: Organizational Learning and Knowledge Flows." *Academy of Management Journal,* Vol. 44, No. 4.

Schwartz, H. (1998). *Rationality Gone Awry? Decision Making Inconsistent with Economic and Financial Theory.* Westport, CT: Praeger.

Schweitzer, H. (1999). *Designing and Teaching an Online Course: Spinning Your Web Classroom.* Needham Heights, MA: Allyn & Bacon.

Scofield, M. (2002, December). "CRM: Reigning in Unrealistic Expectations." *DM Review.*

Scott Morton, M. (1984, May 21–22). "Expert Decision Support Systems." Paper presented at a special DSS conference. New York: Planning Executive Institute and Information Technology Institute.

Scott, A. C., J. E. Clayton, and E. L. Gibson. (1991). *A Practical Guide to Knowledge Acquisition.* Reading, MA: Addison-Wesley.

Scott Morton, M. (ed.). (1991). *The Corporation of the 1990's.* Oxford: Oxford University Press.

Scott Morton, M. S. (1971). *Management Decision Systems: Computer-Based Support for Decision Making.* Cambridge, MA: Harvard University, Division of Research.

Sebell, M.H., J. Yocum, and C.K. Prahalad. (2001). *Ban the Humorous Bazooka.* Chicago: Dearborn Trade Publishing.

Seila, A., P. Tadikamalla, and V. Ceric. (2003). *Applied Simulation Modeling.* Belmont, CA: Duxbury Press.

Seiler, T. M., and J. E. Aronson. (1995, June). "Using Interest Rate Parity in Simulated Artificial Neural Networks to Forecast the Movement of the Yen with Respect to the U.S. Dollar." *Proceedings of the Academy of International Business South Pacific Regional Meeting,* Perth, Australia.

Selden, L., and G. Colvin. (2002, September 30). "Will This Customer Sink Your Stock?" *Fortune.*

Selic, B. (1999, October). "Turning Clockwise: Using UML in the Real-Time Domain." *Communications of the ACM,* Vol. 42, No. 10.

Sen, S., and J. L. Higle. (1999, March/April). "An Introductory Tutorial on Stochastic Linear Programming Models." *Interfaces,* Vol. 29, No. 2.

Senker, P. (1989). "Implications of Expert Systems for Skill Requirements and Working Life." *AI and Society,* Vol. 3.

Sgarioto, M. S. (1999, November 29). "Object Databases Move to the Middle." *InformationWeek,* No. 763.

Shachtman, N. (2000, October 23). "E-Learning Moves Out of the Office." *InformationWeek.*

Shadbolt, N., K. O'Hara, and L. Crow. (1999, October). "The Experimental Evaluation of Knowledge Acquisition Techniques and Methods: History, Problems and New Directions." *International Journal of Human–Computer Studies.*

Shadbolt, N., K. O'Hara, and G. Schreiber (eds.). (1996). *Advances in Knowledge Acquisition.* Berlin: Springer-Verlag.

Shafer, G. (1976). *A Mathematical Theory of Evidence.* Princeton, NJ: Princeton University Press.

Shafer, G. (1996). *Probabilistic Expert Systems.* Philadelphia: Society for Industrial and Applied Mathematics.

Sharma, R. S., and D. W. Conrath. (1992, August). "Evaluating Expert Systems: The Socio-Technical Dimensions of Quality." *Expert Systems.*

Sharma, R. S., and D. W. Conrath. (1993). "Evaluating Expert Systems: A Review of Applicable Approaches." *AI Review,* Vol. 6.

Shaw, M. L. G., and B. R. Gaines. (1996). "WebGrid: Knowledge Elicitation and Modeling on the Web." KSI, University of Calgary, ksi.cpsc.ucalgary.ca.

Shawver, T., and J.E. Aronson. (2003). "A Neural Network Approach To Determine Accurate Bank Merger Premiums." Working paper, Department of MIS, Terry College of Business, The University of Georgia, Athens, Georgia.

Sheetz, S. D., D. P. Tegarden, L. F. Tegarden, L. Poppo, and D. Gynwali. (2000, August). "A WWW-Based Group Cognitive Mapping Approach to Support Case-Based Learning." *Proceedings of the Americas Conference of the Association for Information Systems,* Milwaukee.

Sheetz, S. D., et al. (1994, Summer). "A Group Support Systems Approach to Cognitive Mapping." *Journal of Management Information Systems,* Vol. 11, No. 1.

Sheikh, K. (2003). *Manufacturing Resource Planning (MRP II) with Introduction to ERP, SCM, and CRM.* New York: McGraw-Hill Professional.

Shelton, S. (2000, March) "Breathing New Life into a Dead Language: Teaching Latin Online." *T.H.E. Journal.*

Shen, Q. and Chouchoulas, A. (2002). "A Rough-Set Approach for Generating Classification Rules." *Pattern Recognition,* Vol. 35, No. 11, pp. 2425–2438.

Sherif, K., and M. Mandviwalla. (2000). "Barriers to Actualizing Organizational Memories: Lessons from Industry." *Proceedings of the Thirty-third Annual Hawaii International Conference on System Sciences HICSS-33.* Los Alamitos, CA: IEEE Computer Society Press.

Sherman, L. (2000, October). "Creating Useful Knowledge Structures: Lessons from Library Science and Architecture Inform Today's Web Designs." *Knowledge Management.*

Sheth, A. (2003, July). "Semantic Meta Data for Enterprise Information Integration." *DM Review,* Vol. 13, No. 7.

Sheth J. N., and R. S. Sisodia. (1999, November 15). "Are Your IT Priorities Upside Down?" *CIO.*

Shih, W., and K. Srihari. (1995). "DAI in Manufacturing Systems Control." *Computers and Industrial Engineering,* Vol. 29, Nos. 1–4.

Shim, J.P., M. Warkentin, J.F. Courtney, D.J. Power, R. Sharda, and C. Carlsson. (2002). "Past, Present and Future of Decision Support Technology." *Decision Support Systems,* Vol. 33, pp. 111–126.

Shim, S. J. (1999, Spring). "Exploring the Benefits of Expert Systems use in Organizations." *Journal of Computer Information Systems.*

Shin, K., and Y. Lee. (2002). "A Genetic Algorithm Application in Bankruptcy Prediction Modeling." *Expert Systems with Applications,* Vol. 23, No. 3, pp. 321–328.

Shirani, A. I., M. H. A. Tafti, and J. F. Affisco. (1999, September). "Task and Technology Fit: A Comparison of Two Technologies for Synchronous and Asynchronous Group Communication." *Information & Management,* Vol. 36, No. 3.

Shoemaker, P. J. H., and J. E. Russo. (2001). "Managing Frames to Make Better Decisions." Chapter 9 in S. J. Hoch, H. C. Kunreuther, with R. E. Gunther, ed. (2001). *Wharton on Making Decisions,* New York: John Wiley.

Siau, K., and J. Messersmith. (2002). "Enabling Technologies for E-Commerce and ERP Integration." *Quarterly Journal of Electronic Commerce,* Vol. 3, No. 1.

Siegel, D. L. (1990, Summer). "Integrating Expert Systems for Manufacturing." *AI Magazine,* Supplement.

Sikler, I. U., and A. Gangopadhyay. (2002, October/December). "Design and Implementation of a Web-Based Collaborative Spatial Decision Support System: Organizational and Managerial Implications." *Information Resources Management.*

Silverman, B. G., et al. (2001). "Implications of Buyer Decision Theory for Design of E-Commerce Web Sites." *International Journal of Human Computer Studies,* Vol. 55, No. 5.

Simon, J. L. (2000). *Developing Decision Making Skills for Business.* Armonk, NY: M.E. Sharpe.

Silver, C.A. (2000, November/December). "Where Technology and Knowledge Meet." *Journal of Business Strategy*, Vol. 21, No. 6.

Silverman, B. (1995, November/December). "Knowledge-Based Systems and the Decision Sciences." *Interfaces*.

Silverstone, S. (1999, December). "Innovate Creatively." *Knowledge Management*.

Simmers, C. A. (2002, January). "Aligning Internet Usage with Business Priorities." *Communications of the ACM*.

Simon, H. (1977). *The New Science of Management Decision*. Englewood Cliffs, NJ: Prentice Hall.

Sistek-Chandler, C. (2001, July). "Learning Portals for Education and Beyond." *Converge*.

Skalak, D. (2001, Quarter 2). "Data Mining Blunders Exposed!" *DB2 Magazine*.

Skinner, D. (1999). *An Introduction to Decision Analysis*. 2nd ed.

Skyrme, D. J. (1997, September). "Knowledge Management: Oxymoron or Dynamic Duo?" *Managing Information*, Vol. 4, No. 7.

Skyrme, D. J. (1999). *Knowledge Networking: Creating the Collaborative Enterprise*. Woburn, MA: Butterworth-Heinemann.

Skyrme, D. J., and D. M. Amidon. (1998, January/February). "New Measures of Success." *Journal of Business Strategy*, Vol. 19, No. 1.

Slade, S. (1991, Spring). "Case-Based Reasoning: A Research Paradigm." *AI Magazine*.

Slade, S. (1997). *Object-Oriented Common LISP*. Upper Saddle River, NJ: Prentice Hall.

Slater, D. (2000, February 1). "Loan Star." *CIO*, Vol. 13, No. 8.

Sleeman, D., and F. Mitchell. (1996). "Towards Painless Knowledge Acquisition." In N. Shadbolt, K. O'Hara, and G. Schreiber (eds.). *Advances in Knowledge Acquisition*. Berlin: Springer-Verlag.

Sliwa, C. (2002, March 18). "Users Warm up to Agile Programming." *ComputerWorld*.

Sliwa, C. (2003, January 20). "Retailers Explore Price Optimization." *ComputerWorld*, Vol. 37, No. 3.

Small, R. D., and H. A. Edelstein. (1997). "Scalable Data Mining." Chapter 9 in R. Barquin, and H. Edelstein. (eds.). *Planning and Designing the Data Warehouse*. Upper Saddle River, NJ: Prentice Hall PTR.

Smeaton, A. F., and F. Crimmins. (1996). "Using a Data Fusion Agent for Searching the WWW." Glasnevin, Dublin, Ireland: School of Computer Applications, Dublin City University, lorca.compapp.dcu.ie/fusion/papers/fusion-wwwb.html.

Smith, B. C., D. P. Gunther, B. V. Rao, and R. M. Ratliff. (2001, March/April). "E-Commerce and Operations Research in Airline Planning, Marketing, and Distribution." *Interfaces*, Vol. 31, No. 2.

Smith, G. V., and R. L. Parr. (1998). *Intellectual Property*. New York: John Wiley.

Smith, H., and P. Fingar (2003). *Business Process Management (BPM): The Third Wave*. Tampa, FL: Meghan-Kiffer Press.

Smith, H., and J. McKeen. (2003). "Creating and Facilitating Communities of Practice." Chapter 20 in C. W. Holsapple (ed.). *Handbook of Knowledge Management: Knowledge Matters*, Vol. 1. Heidelberg: Springer-Verlag.

Smith, H., and J. McKeen. (2003). "Knowledge Management in Organizations: The State of Current Practice." Chapter 50 in C. W. Holsapple (ed.). *Handbook of Knowledge Management: Knowledge Directions*, Vol. 2. Heidelberg: Springer-Verlag.

Smith, H., and J. McKeen. (2003). "Valuing the Knowledge Management Function." Chapter 48 in C. W. Holsapple (ed.). *Handbook of Knowledge Management: Knowledge Directions*, Vol. 2. Heidelberg: Springer-Verlag.

Smith, K. T., and L. M. Smith. (1996, April). "A Software Tool for Internet Operations Risk Analysis." *CPA Journal*, Vol. 66, No. 4.

Smith, M. (1999, July/August). "Gender, Cognitive Style, Personality and Management Decision-Making." *Management Accounting—London*, Vol. 77, No. 7.

Smith, M. (2001). "Business-Critical Prism: A Strategic Assessment Guide for BI Products." *Intelligent Enterprise*.

Smith, P., et al. (1996). "Forecasting Short Term Regional Gas Demand Using an Expert System." *Expert Systems with Applications*. Vol. 10, No. 2.

Smoliar, S. W., and R. Sprague. (2002, July 4-7). "Communication and Understanding for Decision Support." *Proceedings of DSIage2002*, Cork, Ireland.

Sodhi, M. S. (2001, March/April). "Applications and Opportunities for Operations Research in Internet-Enabled Supply Chains and Electronic Marketplaces." *Interfaces*, Vol. 31, No. 2.

Sodhi, M. S., and M. Aichlmayr. (2001, September). "Intelligent Software and the Web: The Brain Behind the Brawn." *Transportation & Distribution*, Vol. 42, No. 9.

Solomon, M. R. (2002). *Consumer Behavior*. Upper Saddle River, NJ: Prentice Hall.

Songini, M. (2002, April 15). "Collections of Data." *ComputerWorld*.

Songini, M. L. (2003a, February 17). "Data Analysis Vendors Add Supply Chain Tools." *ComputerWorld*.

Songini, M. L. (2003b, March 10). "CRM Projects Continue to Inspire Caution, Users Say." *ComputerWorld*.

Songini, M. L. (2003c, March 31). "Revenue Optimization Software." *ComputerWorld*.

Songini, M. (2003d, June 9). "Buyout Bids Rock ERP Landscape: Oracle Makes Hostile Offer for PeopleSoft." *ComputerWorld*.

Songini, M. L. (2003e, June 9). "Buyout Bids Rock ERP Landscape: Baan Sale Breathes Life into Struggling Vendor." *ComputerWorld*.

Songini, M. L. (2003f, July 21). "Boehringer Cures Slow Reporting." *ComputerWorld*.

Songini, M. (2003g, April 28). "Business Objects Upgrades Its Data Analysis Software." *ComputerWorld*.

Sonka, M., et al. (1998). *Image Processing: Analysis and Machine Vision*. Pacific Grove, CA: Brooks/Cole.

Sonnen, D. (1999, October 25). "SIM: Fitting in with Everything Else." *Directions Magazine*.

Soo, C., T. Devinney, D. Midgley, and A. Dering. (2002, Summer). "Knowledge Management: Philosophy, Processes, and Pitfalls." *California Management Review*, Vol. 44, No. 4.

Sowa, J. F. (1997). *Principles of Semantic Networks: Exploration in the Representation of Knowledge*. San Francisco: Morgan Kaufmann.

Sparacino, D., and C. O'Reilly. (2000, October). "Leveraging Customer Metrics for Strategic Decision Making." *Call Center CRM Solutions*, Vol. 19, No. 4.

Spector, L., et al. (eds.). (1999). *Advances in Genetic Programming*. Cambridge, MA: MIT Press.

Spice, B. (2002, November 4). "CMU Work Aims to Change Relationship Between Vehicle, Driver." *Pittsburgh Post-Gazette* (post-gazette.com).

Spinello, R. A., and H. T. Tavani. (2001). "The Internet, Ethical Values and Conceptual Framework: An Introduction to Cyberethics." *Computer and Society*.

Spivey, J. M. (1996). *Logic Programming: The Essence of Prolog*. Upper Saddle River, NJ: Prentice Hall.

Sprague, R. H., Jr., and E. D. Carlson. (1982). *Building Effective Decision Support Systems*. Englewood Cliffs, NJ: Prentice Hall.

Sprague, R. H., Jr., and H. J. Watson (eds.). (1996a). *Decision Support Systems*, 4th ed. Englewood Cliffs, NJ: Prentice Hall.

Sprague, R. H., Jr., and H. J. Watson. (1996b). *Decision Support for Management*. Upper Saddle River, NJ: Prentice Hall.

Srivihok, A. (1999). "Understanding Executive Information Systems Implementation: An Empirical Study of EIS Success Factors." *IEEE Conference on Systems Sciences*.

Staab, S. (2003). "Web Services: Been There, Done That?" *IEEE Intelligent Systems*, Vol. 17, No. 1, pp. 72–77.

Stack, R. (1997). "Boston Central Artery/Tunnel Traffic Management Using an Expert System." www.transdyn.com/HTML/Papers/Traffic_Management_Expert_Sys.htm.

Stackpole, B. (2001, February 15). "Dirty Data Is the Dirty Little Secret That Can Jeopardize Your CRM Effort." *CIO*.

Stackpole, B. (2003, May 15). "There's a New App in Town." *CIO*.

Staff. (2002, July 16–29). "Technology Inspires Multitude of Health Care Innovations." *Long Beach Business Journal*.

Stahl, S. (1999, April 5). "Knowledge Yields Impressive Returns." *InformationWeek*.

Stamberg, R. (2002, November) "Of Course: Which Distance-Learning Approach Best Fits Your Business?" *AV Videeo Multimedia Producer*.

Stamen, J. P. (1993, October). "Structuring Databases for Analysis." *IEEE Spectrum*.

Stanford, V. (2002, January/March). "Using Pervasive Computing to Deliver Elder Care." *Pervasive Computing* (also in *Healthcare Review*, July 2, 2002, and *IEEE Distributed Systems Online*, March 2002).

Staten, M. (2001, Fall). "Customer Relationship as a Privacy Enhance." *Journal of Data Warehousing*, Vol. 6, No. 4.

Stefanowski, J. and S. Wilk. (2001). "Evaluating Business Credit Risk by Means of Approach-Integrating Decision Rules and Case-Based Reasoning." *International Journal of Accounting, Finance, and Management*, Vol. 10, pp. 97–114.

Stein, E. W. (1992, Fall). "A Method to Identify Candidates for Knowledge Acquisition." *Journal of Management Information Systems*, Vol. 9, No. 2.

Stein, L. A. (1996, Winter). "Science and Engineering in Knowledge Representation and Reasoning." *AI Magazine*, Vol. 17, No. 4.

Steinberg, D. (2001, December 1). "Privacy: Surveillance vs. Freedom." *Smart Business*, Vol. 12.

Sterne, J. (2002). *Web Metrics*. New York: John Wiley.

Stevens, L. (2000, October). "Incentives for Sharing." *Knowledge Management*.

Stevens, L. (2000, December). "Knowing What Your Company Knows." *Knowledge Management*.

Stewart, T. A. (1996, November 27). "Getting Real About Brainpower." *Fortune*, Vol. 132, No. 11.

Stewart, T. A. (2002, November). "How to Think with Your Gut." *Business 2.0*.

Stewart, V., and Mayes, J. (2000). "Business Applications of Repertory Grid" *Enquire Within*, www.EnquireWithin.co.nz/business.htm.

Stith, B. (2000, March). "Web-Enhanced Lecture Course Scores Big with Students and Faculty." *T.H.E. Journal*.

Stodder, D. (2002, June 28). "Quality is Job One." *Intelligent Enterprise*.

Stojkovic, M., and F. Soumis. (2001, September). "An Optimization Model for the Simultaneous Operational Flight and Pilot Scheduling Problem." *Management Science*, Vol. 47, No. 9.

Stone, D., and S. Warsone. (2003). "Does Accounting Account for Knowledge?" Chapter 13 in C. W. Holsapple (ed.). *Handbook of Knowledge Management: Knowledge Matters*, Vol. 1. Heidelberg: Springer-Verlag.

Stone-Gonzalez, J. (1998). *The 21st Century Intranet*. Upper Saddle River, NJ, Prentice Hall.

Storck, J., and P. A. Hill. (2002). "Knowledge Diffusion Through Strategic Communities." Chapter 5 in E. L. Lesser, M. A. Fontaine, and J. A. Slusher. (eds.).

Knowledge and Communities. Woburn, MA: Butterworth-Heinemann.

Strassmann, P.A. (2001, July). "KM and Profits." *Knowledge Management.*

Strauss, J., et. al. (2003). *Internet Marketing,* 3rd ed. Upper Saddle River, NJ: Prentice Hall.

Strischeck, D., and R. Cross. (1996, January). "Reengineering the Credit Approval Process." *Journal of Commercial Lending,* Vol. 78, No. 5.

Strong, D. M., et al. (1997, May). "Data Quality in Context." *Communications of the ACM.*

Studt, T. (1994, May). "Rapid Prototyping: Key to Fast Development." *R&D (RDV).*

Studt, T. (1998, November). "Stat Systems Focus on Decision Making." *R&D,* Vol. 40, No. 12.

Sturman, M. C., and G. T. Milkovich. (1995, January/February). "Validating Expert Systems: A Demonstration Using Personal Choice Expert, a Flexible Employee Benefit System." *Decision Sciences,* Vol. 26, No. 1.

Stylianou, A. C., G. R. Madley, and R. D. Smith. (1992). "Criteria for the Selection of Expert System Shells: A Sociotechnical Framework." *Communications of the ACM,* Vol. 35, No. 10.

Stylianou, A. C., R. D. Smith, and G. R. Madey. (1995). "An Empirical Model for the Evaluation and Selection of Expert System Shells." *Expert Systems with Applications,* Vol. 8, No. 1.

Su, M. C., et al. (2001, February). "Portable Communication Aid for Deaf-Blind People." *Computing and Control Engineering Journal.*

Sugumaran, V., and R. Bose. (1996, February). "Expert System Technology in Organisational Process Domain Modeling." *Expert Systems,* Vol. 13, No. 1.

Suh, C. K., and E. H. Suh. (1993, August). "Using Human Factor Guidelines for Developing Expert Systems." *Expert Systems,* Vol. 10, No. 3.

Suh, C. K., et al. (1995, April). "Artificial Intelligence Approaches in Model Management." *Computers and Industrial Engineering,* Vol. 28, No. 2.

SuJeong, K., and L. JungHyun. "User Preference Mining Through Collaborative Filtering and Content-Based Filtering in Recommender Systems." *E-Commerce and Web Technologies,* pp. 244–254.

Sullivan, D. (2001a). *Document Warehousing and Text Mining: Techniques for Improving Business Operations, Marketing and Sales.* Wiley.

Sullivan, D. (2001b, August 31). "5 Principles of Intelligent Content Management." *Intelligent Enterprise.*

Sullivan, D. (2002, May 28). "Vision of Intelligence." *Intelligent Enterprise.*

Sullivan, G., and K. Fordyce. (1990). "IBM Burlington's Logistics Management System." *Interfaces,* Vol. 20, No. 1.

Sun, M., J. E. Aronson, P. G. McKeown, and D. Drinka. (1998). "A Tabu Search Procedure for the Fixed Charge Transportation Problem." *European Journal of Operational Research,* Vol. 106, pp. 441–456.

Sun R., and C.L. Giles. (2001, July/August). "Sequence Learning: From Recognition and Prediction to Sequential Decision Making." *IEEE Intelligent Systems.*

Sutton, R.I. (2001, October) "The Creativity Dilemma." *CIO Insight.* Telecomworldwire. (2003, March 4). "Polycom Provides Distance Learning Capabilities to Schools in Edinburgh." *Telecomworldwire.*

Sviokla, J. J. (1990, June). "An Examination of the Impact of Expert Systems on the Firm: The Case XCON." *MIS Quarterly,* Vol. 13, No. 1.

Sviokla, J. J. (1996, Summer). "Knowledge Workers and Radically New Technology." *Sloan Management Review,* Vol. 37, No. 4.

Sviokla, J. J. (2001, February 15). "Knowledge Pays." *CIO.*

Sviokla, J., and A. Wong. (2003, April 1). "CRM Is Not for Micromanagers." *CIO.*

Swan, J., et al. (2000, January). "Knowledge Management—When Will People Management Enter the Debate?" *Proceedings, 33rd HICSS.* Vol. 3. Los Alamitos, CA: IEEE Computer Society Press.

Swanson, B. D., E. Ralls, and J. E. Aronson. (1999, February). "The Challenge of Information Systems Planning for Outcomes Systems in Managed Care." *Journal of Rehabilitation Outcomes Measurement,* Vol. 3, No. 1.

Swanson, E. B. (1988). *Information System Implementation.* Homewood, IL: Irwin.

Swanson, E. B., and R. Zmud. (1990, January). "Distributed Decision Support Systems: A Perspective." *Proceedings of the Twenty-third Annual Hawaii International Conference on System Sciences HICSS-33,* Vol. 3. Los Alamitos, CA: IEEE Computer Society Press.

Swap, W., D. Leonard, M. Shields, and L. Abrams. (2001, Summer). "Using Mentoring and Storytelling to Transfer Knowledge in the Workplace. *Journal of Management Information Systems.*" Vol. 18, No. 1.

Swanson, S. (2000, September 4). "Schwab to Use E-Learning for Call-Center Reps." *InformationWeek.*

Swartz, A. (2002). "MusicBrainz: A Semantic Web Service." *IEEE Intelligent Systems,* Vol. 17, No. 1, pp. 76–77.

Swartz, N. (2003, March/April). "Data-Mining Initiatives." *Information Management Journal,* Vol. 37, No. 2.

Sweiger, M., et al. (2002). *Clickstream Data Warehousing.* New York: John Wiley.

Swenson, J. (1996, July 8). "Maps on the Web." *InformationWeek.*

Swift, R. S. (2001). *Accelerating Customer Relationships: Using CRM and Relationship Technologies.* Upper Saddle River, NJ: Prentice Hall PTR.

Swink M., and C. Speier. (1999, Winter). "Presenting Geographical Information." *Decision Sciences.*

Swissler, M.A. (2001, May). "Merging Knowledge with Companies." *Knowledge Management.*

Taboada, M., et al. (1996, November). "Integrating Medical Expert Systems, Patient Databases and User Interfaces." *Journal of Intelligent Information Systems,* Vol. 7, No. 3.

Taft, D. K. (2003, June 16). "SAP Soaks Up Java." *EWeek.*

Taha, H. (2003). Operations Research: An Introduction, 7th ed. Upper Saddle River, NJ: Prentice Hall.

Tanier, D. (1997). "Inheritance and Parallelization: Emerging Object-Oriented and Parallel Technologies for High Performance Database Systems." *Proceedings of the High-Performance Computing on the Information Superhighway,* HPC—Asia 1997. Piscataway, NJ: Institute of Electrical and Electronics Engineers.

Tannenbaum, A. (2002, Spring). "Identifying Meta Data Requirements." *Journal of Data Warehousing,* Vol. 7, No. 2.

Targowski A. (2001, January/June). "From ERP to CRM: A New Trend in Decision Support Architecture." *Information Management.*

Tavakkoli-Moghaddain, R., and E. Shayan. (1998, December). "Facilities Layout Design by Genetic Algorithms." *Computers & Industrial Engineering,* Vol. 35, Nos. 3 and 4.

Tavana, M., and S. Banerjee. (1995). "Strategic Assessment Model (SAM): A Multiple Criteria Decision Support System for Evaluation of Strategic Alternatives." *Decision Sciences,* Vol. 26, No. 1.

Taylor, B. (2002). *Introduction to Management Science.* 7th ed. Upper Saddle River, NJ: Prentice Hall.

Taylor, C. (2001, March 12). "Intellectual Capital." *Knowledge Management.* Vol. 35, No. 11.

Tecuci, G. (1998). *Building Intelligent Agents.* New York: Academic Press.

Tedechi, B. (2002, September 2). "Scientifically Priced Retail Goods." *New York Times.* Late Edition–Final.

Teece, D. (2003). "Knowledge and Competence as Strategic Assets." Chapter 7 in C. W. Holsapple (ed.). *Handbook of Knowledge Management: Knowledge Matters,* Vol. 1. Heidelberg: Springer-Verlag.

Teng, J. T. C. (1988, January). "A Unified Architecture for Intelligent DSS." *Proceedings of the Twenty-first Hawaii International Conference on Systems Science HICSS-21.* Wailea, HI, Los Alamitos, CA: IEEE Computer Society Press.

Tennant, R. (2002, May 15). "The Importance of Being Granular." *Library Journal.* Vol. 127, No. 9.

Teradata. (2003). "Burlington Northern Santa Fe." Teradata Web site: www.teradata.com.

Teresko, J. (2002, April). "Robots Revolution." *Industry Week.*

Thaler, S. L. (2002, January/February). "AI for Network Protection: LITMUS—Live Intrusion Tracking Via Multiple Unsupervised STANNOs." *PC AI,* pp. 23–30.

Theodoratos, D., and M. Bouzeghoug. (2001, September). "Data Currency Quality Satisfaction in the Design of a Data Warehouse." *International Journal of Cooperative Information Systems,* Vol 10, No. 3.

Theodore, J. (1998, June). "Turn Data Puzzles into Perfect Pictures." *Business Geographies.*

Thomas, H., et al. (1997, November/December). "New Technology in Large Customer Call Center." *PC AI.*

Thomsett, R. (2002). *Radical Project Management.* Upper Saddle River, NJ: Prentice Hall PTR.

Thoreson, K. (2003, July 14). "CRM as a Development Tool." *Customer Relationship Management Magazine* Web Site, www.destinationcrm.com.

Thuraisingham, B. (1989, October). "Rules to Frames and Frames to Rules." *AI Expert.*

Tillett, L. S. (2000, September 25). "Banks Mine Customer Data." *InternetWeek.*

Tillett, S. (2000, November 20). "Will Internet Improve Voting?" *InternetWeek.*

Tobia, P. (2000, December). *Decision Making in the Digital Age: Challenges and Responses.* Princeton, NJ: Kepner-Tregoe Report.

Tobin, T. (2003, October). "Eight Lessons for Knowledge Management Success." *CIO,* White Paper.

Tochtermann, K., and M. Fathi. (1994). "Making Use of Expertext to Enhance the Process of Knowledge Acquisition." In J. Liebowitz (ed.). *Proceedings of the Second World Congress on Expert Systems,* Lisbon.

Tochtermann, K., and V. Zink. (1995). "Artificial Intelligence and Hypermedia." In R. Rada and K. Tochtermann (eds.). *Expertmedia: Expert Systems and Hypertext.* Singapore: World Scientific Publishing.

Toffler, A. (1970). *Future Shock,* New York: Random House.

Toffler, A. (1991). *Powershift.* New York: Bantam Books.

Tolun, M. R., and S. M. Abu-Soud. (1998, April). "ILA: An Inductive Learning Algorithm for Rule Extraction." *Expert Systems with Applications,* Vol. 14, No. 3.

Torrance, E. P. (1988). "The Nature of Creativity as Manifest in Its Testing." In R. J. Sternberg (ed.). *The Nature of Creativity,* Sternberg. Cambridge: Cambridge University Press.

Touchton, R. A., and S. D. Rausch. (1993, July/August). "Putting Expert Systems to the Test." *PC AI.*

Trepper, C.H. (2000a, August). "A Project Management Primer." *Application Development Trends.*

Trepper, C. H. (2000b, August 28). "Getting an Edge on the Competition." *InformationWeek.*

Trick, M. (2003, January). "Best Possible Outcome." *Optimize Magazine.*

Trippi, R., and E. Turban. (1996a). *Neural Computing Applications in Investment and Financial Services.* Burr Ridge, IL: Irwin.

Trippi, R., and E. Turban. (1996b). *Neural Network Applications in Investment and Financial Services,* rev. ed. Chicago: Probus Publishers.

Trippi, R., and E. Turban. (1996c). *Neural Networks in Finance and Investing*. Burr Ridge, IL: Irwin.

Trippi, R. R., and E. Turban (eds.) (1996d). *Neural Networks in Finance and Investing: Using Artificial Intelligence to Improve Real-world Performance,* 2nd ed. Chicago: Irwin.

Trommer, D. (2003, May 26). "PLM Software Helps OEM Play in the Big Leagues." *EBN.*

Tsai, N., C. R. Necco, and G. Wei. (1994a, October). "Implementing an Expert System: A Report on Benefits Realized (Part 1)." *Journal of Systems Management,* Vol. 45, No. 10.

Tsai, N., C. R. Necco, and G. Wei. (1994b, November). "An Assessment of Current Expert Systems: Are Your Expectations Realistic?" *Journal of Systems Management.*

Tsai, Y-C. (2001, April). "Comparative Analysis of Model Management and Relational Database Management." *Omega,* Vol. 29, No. 2.

Tschang, F. T., and T. D. Senta. (2001). *Access to Knowledge: New Information Technologies and the Emergence of the Virtual University*. Kidlington, UK: Elsevier Science.

Tsumoto, S. (2003). "Automated Extraction of Hierarchical Decision Rules from Clinical Databases Using Rough Set Model." *Expert Systems with Applications*, Vol. 24, No. 2, pp. 189–197.

Tung, L. L., and E. Turban. (1996, March). "Expert Systems Support Container Operations in the Port of Singapore." *New Review of Applied Expert Systems.*

Tung, Y., R. D. Gopal, and J. R. Marsden. (1999, October). "HypEs: An Architecture for Hypermedia-enabled Expert Systems." *Decision Support Systems,* Vol. 26, No. 4.

Turban, E. (1992). *Expert Systems and Applied Artificial Intelligence.* New York: Macmillan.

Turban, E., et al. (2000). *Electronic Commerce: A Managerial Perspective*. Upper Saddle River, NJ: Prentice Hall.

Turban, E., J. K. Lee, D. King, and M. Chung. (2000). *Electronic Commerce: A Managerial Perspective.* Upper Saddle River, NJ: Prentice Hall.

Turban, E., et al. (2001). *Information Technology for Management,* 2nd rev. ed. New York: John Wiley.

Turban, E., et al. (2004a). *Electronic Commerce*, 3rd ed. Upper Saddle River, NJ: Prentice Hall.

Turban, E., and D. King. (2003). *Introduction to E-Commerce.* Upper Saddle River, NJ: Prentice Hall.

Turban, E., and J. Liebowitz (eds.). (1992). *Managing Expert Systems.* Hershey, PA: Idea Group.

Turban, E., and J. Meredith. (1994). *Fundamentals of Management Science,* 6th ed. Homewood, IL: Irwin.

Turban, E., and P. Watkins. (1986, June). "Integrating Expert Systems and Decision Support Systems." *MIS Quarterly,* Vol. 10, No. 2.

Tversky, A., P. Slovic, and D. Kahneman. (1990, March). "The Causes of Preference Reversal." *American Economic Review,* Vol. 80, No. 1.

Tynan, D. (2002, June). "How to Take Back Your Privacy (34 Steps)." *PC World.*

Tyo, J. (1996, July 15). "Slicing Data on the Desktop." *InformationWeek,* pp. 59–72.

Tyran, C. K., and J. F. George. (1993, Winter). "The Implementation of Expert Systems: A Survey of Successful Implementations." *Data Base.*

Tyran, C. K., and M. Shepherd. (2000, August). "Collaborative Technology in the Classroom: A Research Framework." *Proceedings of the Americas Conference of the Association for Information Systems,* Milwaukee.

Ulfelder, S. (2000a, June 5). "Undercover Agents." *ComputerWorld.*

Ulfelder, S. (2000b, September 25). "Data Visualization Tools Catch On for Business Analysis." *ComputerWorld.*

Ulrich, D. (1998, Winter). "Intellectual Capital 5 Competence 3 Commitment." *Sloan Management Review,* Vol. 39, No. 2.

Umble, E. J., R. R. Haft, and M. M. Umble. (2003, April 16). "Enterprise Resource Planning: Implementation Procedures and Critical Success Factors." *European Journal of Operational Research*, Vol. 146, No. 2.

Umble, E. J., and M. M. Umble. (2002, January/February). "Avoiding ERP Implementation Failure." *Industrial Management*, Vol. 44, No. 1.

Ursem, R. K., B. Filipic, and T. Krink. (2002, September). "Exploring the Performance of an Evolutionary Algorithm for Greenhouse Control." *Journal of Computing and Information Technology*, Vol. 10, No. 3.

Vaas, L. (1999, May 31). "Brainstorming." *PCWeek,* Vol. 16, No. 22.

Vaas, L. (2003a, January 6). "Road to Open Source." *eWeek.*

Vaas, L. (2003b, April 14). "Services in Demand." *eWeek.*

Vaduva, A., and T. Vetterli. (2001, September). "Metadata Management for Data Warehousing: An Overview." *International Journal of Cooperative Information Systems.* Vol 10, No. 3.

Vahid, F., S. Narayan, and D. Gajski. (1991). "SpecCharts: A Language for System Level Synthesis." *Proceedings Computer Hardware Description Languages.*

Vahidov, R., and Elrod, R. (1999, September). "Incorporating Critique and Argumentation in DSS." *Decision Support Systems,* Vol. 26, No. 3.

Van Bruggen, G., and B. Wierenga. (2001). "Matching Management Support Systems and Managerial Problem-Solving Modes: The Key to Effective Decision Support." *European Management Journal,* Vol. 19, No. 3.

Van der Heijden, M.C., A. van Harten, and M. J. R. Ebben. (2002, July/August). "Using Simulation to Design an Automated Underground System for

Transporting Freight Around Schiphol Airport." *Interfaces*, Vol. 32.

Van Harmelen, F., et al. (1996, February). "Evaluating a Formal KBS Specification Language." *IEEE Expert,* Vol. 11, No. 1.

Van Horn, M. (1986). *Understanding Expert Systems.* Toronto: Bantam Books.

Van Weelderen, J. A., and H. G. Sol. (1993, May/June). "MEDESS: A Methodology for Designing Expert Support Systems." *Interfaces,* Vol. 23, No. 3.

Vance, M., and D. Deacon (1997). *Think Out of the Box.* Franklin Lakes, NJ: Career Press.

Vance, M., and D. Deacon (1999). *Raise the Bar: Creative Strategies to Take Your Business and Personal Life to the Next Level.* Franklin Lakes, NJ: Career Press.

Varon, E. (2002, December 1). "Portals (Finally) Get Down to Business." *CIO.*

Vaughan, J. (2002, December). "Technologies to Watch." *Application Development Trends.*

Vaughan, J. (2003, January). "XML Meets the Data Warehouse." *Application Development Trends.*

Vedder, R. G., T. P. Van Dyke, and V. R. Prybutok. (2002, Spring). "Death of an Expert System: A Case Study of Success and Failure." *Journal of International Technology and Information Management*, Vol. 11, No. 1.

Vedder R. G., et al. (1999, July). "An Expert System That Was." *Proceedings of DSI International,* Athens, Greece.

Venkat, K. (2002, February). "Delving into the Digital Divide." *IEEE Spectrum.*

Venkatachalam, A. R., and J. E. Sohl. (1999, May). "An Intelligent Model Selection and Forecasting System." *Journal of Forecasting,* Vol. 18, No. 3.

Verhoef, P. C., et al. (2003, March). "The Commercial Use of Segmentation and Predictive Modeling Techniques for Database Marketing in the Netherlands." *Decision Support Systems.*

Verma, N., and C. W. Churchman. (1998). *Similarities, Connections and Systems: The Search for a New Rationality for Planning and Management*, Lanham, MD: Lexington Books.

Verton, D. (2003, May 26). "Feds Plan Biometrics for Border Control. *ComputerWorld.*

Vieira, P., and F. Gomide. (1996, July). "Computer-Aided Train Dispatch." *IEEE Spectrum,* Vol. 33, No. 7.

Vijayan, J. (2003a, February 24). "The Data Builds the Products." *Computerworld.* Vol. 37, No. 8.

Vijayan, J. (2003b, April). "GEIS to Centralize Data for Product Design, Manufacturing." *ComputerWorld.*

Villa, A. (2002). "Emerging Trends in Large-Scale Supply Chain Management." *International Journal of Production Research*, Vol. 40, No. 15, pp. 3487–3496.

Vitiello, J. (2001, July 16). "Fast Track into Management." *ComputerWorld.*

Vitt, E., M. Luckevich, and S. Misner. (2002). *Business Intelligence: Making Better Decisions Faster*. Redmond, WA: Microsoft Press.

Vizard, M., and B. Darrow. (2003, February 2). "SAP to Bring Business One to U.S., Will Sell Via Channel." *CRN.*

Vlahavas, et al. (2002). "ExperNet: An Intelligent Multiagent System for WAN Management." *IEEE Intelligent Systems*, pp. 62–71.

Volonino, L., H. J. Watson, and S. Robinson. (1995). "Using EIS to Respond to Dynamic Business Conditions." *Decision Support Systems,* Vol. 14, No. 2.

Von Altrock, C. (1996). *Fuzzy Logic and Neurofuzzy Applications in Business and Finance.* Upper Saddle River, NJ: Prentice Hall.

Von Krogh, G., K. Ichijo, and I. Nonaka. (2000). *Enabling Knowledge Creation: How to Unlock the Mystery of Tacit Knowledge and Release the Power of Innovation.* New York: Oxford University Press.

Von Krogh G., et al. (2000). *Knowledge Creation: A Source of Value.* New York: St. Martin's Press.

von Oech, R. (1998). *A Whack on the Side of the Head.* New York: Warner Books.

von Oech, R. (2002). *Expect the Unexpected or You Won't Find It: A Creativity Tool Based on the Ancient Wisdom of Heraclitus.* San Francisco: Berrett-Koehler.

Vranes, S., et al. (1996, May). "INVEX: Investment Advisory Expert System." *Expert Systems,* Vol. 13, No. 2.

Wagner, H. M. (1995, November/December). "Global Sensitivity Analysis." *Operations Research.*

Wagner, J. (2001, February). "Delivering DSS via ASP's." *Decision Support Systems.*

Wagner, W. P., and C. W. Holsapple. (1997, February). "An Analysis of Knowledge Acquisition Roles and Participants." *Expert Systems,* Vol. 14, No. 1.

Wagner, W.P., et al. (2003). "The Impact of Problem Domains and Knowledge Acquisition Techniques: A Content Analysis of P/OM Expert System Case Studies." *Expert Systems with Applications*, Vol. 24, pp. 79–86.

Walbridge, C. T. (1989, June). "Genetic Algorithms: What Computers Can Learn from Darwin." *Technology Review.*

Walczak, S., et al. (2002). "A Decision Support Tool for Allocating Hospital Bed Resources and Determining Required Acuity of Care." *Decision Support Systems*, Vol. 34, No. 4, pp. 445–456.

Walden, P., C. Carlsson, and O. Kollonen. (2000). "Active Decision Support and Strategic Management—the Kirkniemi Fine Paper Mill Case." *Decision Support Systems.*

Walker, E. (2002, November/December). "Innovation and Social Responsibility in Financial Services." *SAS com.*

Wallace, B. (2000, September 11). "Industry Optimizes Supply Chains." *InformationWeek.*

Wallace, D. J. (2000, April). "Illuminating Corporate Knowledge." *Knowledge Management.*

Wallach, S. L. (2001, June). "Feeding Corporate Portals." *Knowledge Management.*

Waltner, C. (2001, January 29). "CRM Makes Online Shopping Personal." *InformationWeek.*

Wang, H., and H. K. O. Lee (1998, March). "Consumer Privacy Concern about Internet Marketing." *Communications of the ACM,* Vol. 41, No. 3.

Wang, J. (1994, June). "Artificial Neural Networks vs. Natural Neural Networks." *Decision Support Systems,* Vol. 11, No. 5.

Wang, K., et al. "A Hybrid Intelligent Method for Modeling the EDM Process." *International Journal of Machine Tools and Manufacture,* Vo. 43, No. 10, pp. 995-999.

Wang, R. Y. (1998, February). "Total Data Quality Management." *Communications of the ACM.* Vol. 41, No. 2.

Wang, S. (1999, Winter). "Analyzing Agents for Electronic Commerce." *Information Systems Management.*

Wang, W., S. Zhong, Q. Tian, and T. Wang. (1996). "An Agent Belief System for Multiagent Systems." *Proceedings of the Twenty-ninth Annual Hawaii International Conference on Systems Sciences HiCSS-29,* Wailea, HI. Los Alamitos, CA: IEEE Computer Society Press.

Wang, Y. (2002). "An Application of Genetic Algorithm Methods for Teacher Assignment Problems." *Expert Systems with Applications,* Vol. 22, No. 4, pp. 295–302.

Wang, Y. (2003). "Using Genetic Algorithm Models to Solve Course Scheduling Problems." *Expert Systems with Applications,* Vol. 25, No. 1, pp. 39–50.

Wareham, E. (1999, July 9). "Fraud-Buster App Raises Concerns." *Computing Canada,* Vol. 25, No. 27.

Warkentin, M. (ed.). (2001). *B2B Electronic Commerce: Challenges and Solutions.* Hershey, PA: Idea Group.

Warkentin, M., et al. (1994, November/December). "AI in Business and Management: Law and Legal Application (of AI)." *PC AI,* Vol. 8, No. 6.

Warkentin, M., L. Sayeed, and R. Hightower. (1999). "Virtual Teams Versus Face-to-Face Teams." In K. E. Kendell (ed.). *Emerging Information Technologies.* Thousand Oaks, CA: Sage Publications.

Warnock, S., M. R. Baren, and M. Barchilon. (2000, August). "Collaborative Problem-Solving with Listservs in a Long-Distance Engineering Classroom." *Proceedings of the Americas Conference of the Association for Information Systems,* Milwaukee.

Warren, J. R., et al. (1995, Fall). "Simulation Modeling for BPR." *Information Systems Management,* Vol. 12, No. 4.

Warren, J.R., et al. (2002). "Supporting Special-Purpose Health Care Models via Adaptive Interfaces to the Web." *Interacting With Computers,* Vol. 14.

Waterman, D. A. (1985). *A Guide to Expert Systems.* Reading, MA: Addison-Wesley.

Watkins, P. R., T. W. Lin, and D. E. O'Leary. (1992). "AI Integration for Enhanced Decision Support." *Proceedings of the Twenty-fifth Annual Hawaii International Conference on System Sciences HICSS-25,* Wailea, HI, Los Alamitos, CA: IEEE Computer Society Press.

Watson, H. J., et al. (1996, Summer). "Including Soft Information in EISs." *Information Systems Management,* Vol. 13, No. 3.

Watson, H. J., et al. (2000, Winter). "The Effects of Technology-Enabled Business Strategy at First American Corporation." *Organization Dynamics.*

Watson, H. J., J. E. Aronson, R. H. Hamilton, L. S. Iyer, M. Nagasundaram, H. R. Nemati, and J. Suleiman. (1996). "Assessing EIS Benefits: A Survey of Current Practices." *Journal of Information Technology Management,* Vol. 7, Nos. 1 and 2.

Watson, H., J. Gerard, L. Gonzalez, M. Haywood, and D. Fenton. (1999, Spring). "DataWarehousing Failures: Case Studies and Findings." *Journal of Data Warehousing.*

Watson, H. J., G. Houdeshel, and R. K. Rainer, Jr. (eds.) (1997). *Building Executive Information Systems and Other Decision Support Applications.* New York: John Wiley.

Watson, H. J., and B. J. Haley. (1998, September). "Managerial Considerations." *Communications of the ACM,* Vol. 41, No. 9.

Watson, R. T. (1990). "A Design for and infrastructure to organizational Decision Making." *Proceedings of the Twenty-third Hawaii International Conference on System Sciences HICSS-23,* Los Alamitos, CA: IEEE Computer Society Press.

Watson, R. T. (2001). *Data Management: Databases and Organizations.* 3rd ed. New York: John Wiley.

Weaver, P. (2002, August). "Preventing E-Learning Failure." *Training and Development,* Vol. 56, No. 8.

Weber, A. (1996, October). "Advanced Technology Propels Citgo Refinery Toward 21st Century." *Control Magazine.* Also at www.gensym.com.

Weber, E. S., and B. R. Konsynski. (1987/88, Winter). "Problem Management: Neglected Elements in Decision Support Systems." *Journal of Management Information Systems.*

Weinberger, J. (2003, January 1). "Establishing Proof of Life(Cycle)." *Baseline Extras Online.*

Weir, R. (2002, Winter). "Best Practices for Implementing a Data Warehouse." *Journal of Data Warehousing,* Vol. 7, No. 1.

Weiss, G. (2002, March). "Welcome to the (Almost) Digital Hospital." *IEEE Spectrum.*

Weiss, T. (2003, September 9). "Hershey Upgrades R/3 ERP System Without Hitches." *ComputerWorld.*

Weiss, G., and S. Sen (eds.). (1995). *Adaptation and Learning in Multi-Agent Systems.* Berlin: Springer-Verlag.

Weitz, R. R. (1990, Summer). "Technology, Work and the Organization: The Impact of Expert Systems." *AI Magazine,* Vol. 11, No. 2.

Wellman, B. (ed.). (1999). *Networks in the Global Village.* Boulder, CO: Westview Press.

Wenger, E. (2002a). *Communities of Practice: Learning, Meaning, and Identity.* New York: Cambridge University Press.

Wenger, E. (2002b). "Communities of Practice: The Key to Knowledge Strategy." Chapter 1 in E. L. Lesser, M. A. Fontaine, and J. A. Slusher (eds.). *Knowledge and Communities.* Woburn, MA: Butterworth-Heinemann.

Wenger, E., R. McDermott, and W. M. Snyder. (2002a). *Cultivating Communities of Practice.* Boston: Harvard Business School Press.

Wenger, E., R. McDermott, and W.M. Snyder. (2002b, May 15). "It Takes a Community." *CIO.*

Wenger, E.C., and W.M. Snyder. (2000, January/February). "Communities of Practice: The Organizational Frontier." *Harvard Business Review,* pp. 139–145.

Werner, V., and C. Abramson (2001, Summer). "Managing Clickstream Data." *Journal of Data Warehousing,* Vol. 6, No. 3.

Wesphal C., and T. Blaxton (1998). *Data Mining Solutions: Methods and Tools for Solving Real-World Problems.* New York: John Wiley.

Westerman, P. (2000). *Data Warehousing: Using the Wal-Mart Model.* San Francisco: Morgan Kaufmann.

Westland, J. C. (2002, May). "Transaction Risk in Electronic Commerce." *Decision Support Systems.*

Wheatley, M. (2000, August 1). "Her Majesty's Flying I.T. Circus." *CIO.*

White, A. P. (1995). "An Expert System for Choosing a Statistical Test." *New Review of Applied Expert Systems,* Vol. 1. No. 1.

White, C. (2002, December). "Enterprise Portals: State of the Art." *DM Review.*

White, S., and G.P. Wright. (2002). *New Ideas About New Ideas.* Cambridge, MA: Perseus Publishing.

Whitehead, S. D. (1995, December). "Auto-FAQ: An Experiment in Cyberspace Leveraging." *Computer Networks and ISDN Systems,* Vol. 28, Nos. 1 and 2.

Whiting, R. (2000, December 4). "Database Grudge Match." *InformationWeek.*

Whiting, R. (2001, January 22). "Seagate Offering Analyzes Multidimensional Data." *InformationWeek.*

Whiting, R. (2002, April 1). "Companies Unify Data Sources." *InformationWeek.*

Whiting, R. (2003, May 12). "Business-Intelligence Buy-In." *InformationWeek.*

Whiting, R. (2003, January 13). "Look Within." *InformationWeek.*

Whittaker, D. (1999, October). "Spreadsheet Errors and Techniques for Finding Them." *Management Accounting,* Vol. 77, No. 9.

Whitten, J. L., L. D. Bentley and K. C. Dittman. (2001). *Systems Analysis and Design Methods.* 5th ed., Columbus, OH: McGraw-Hill.

Whitting, R. (2003, January 13). "Warehouse Worries." *InformationWeek.*

Wick, M. R., and J. R. Slagle. (1989). "An Explanation Facility for Today's Expert Systems." *IEEE Expert,* Vol. 4, No. 1.

Wierenga, B., and G. H. van Bruggen. (1998, March). "The Dependent Variable in Research into the Effects of Creativity Support Systems: Quality and Quantity of Ideas." *MIS Quarterly,* Vol. 11, No. 1.

Wierenga, B., and G. H. van Bruggen. (2001, June). "Developing a Customized Decision-Support System for Brand Managers." *Interfaces.*

Wiig, K. M. (1993). *Knowledge Management Foundations.* Arlington, TX: Schema Press.

Williams, C., and B. D. Clayton. (1994). "Case Base Retrieval." White Paper. Inference Corporation, www.inference.com: m5.inference.com/products/cbrwp.html.

Williams, G. (2002, September) "Innovative Model." *Entrepreneur.*

Williams, J. (1991). "Negative Consequences of Information Technology." In *Management Impacts of Information Technology: Perspectives of Organizational Change and Growth.* Harrisburg, PA: Idea Group.

Williams, J. D. (2000, September). "Raising Components." *Application Development Trends.*

Williams, S. R., and R. L. Wilson. (1999). "Group Support Systems, Power and Influence in an Organization." In K. E. Kendell (ed.). *Emerging Information Technologies.* Thousand Oaks, CA: Sage Publications.

Wilson, R. L., and R. Sharda. (1994, June). "Bankruptcy Prediction Using Neural Networks." *Decision Support Systems,* Vol. 11, No. 5.

Winarchick, C., and R. D. Caldwell. (1997, May). "Physical Interactive Simulation: A Hands-On Approach to Facilities Improvements." *IIE Solutions,* Vol. 29, No. 5.

Winslow, J., and A. Lea. (2002, April). "Location Maximizes Return on Investment." *GeoWorld.*

Winston, W. L., and S. C. Albright. (2000). *Practical Management Science: Spreadsheet Modeling Applications.* Belmont, MA: Duxbury Press.

Wise E. (1999). *Applied Robotics.* Indianapolis: H.W. Sams.

Witzerman, J. P. (2001, August 9–11). "Using Robotic Simulation to Support General Motors Paint Shops." *Proceedings of the PRISM Symposium.*

Wixom, B., and H. Watson. (2001, March). "An Empirical Investigation of the Factors Affecting Data Warehousing Success, *MIS Quarterly*, Vol. 25, No. 1.

Wolf, G. (1994, May). "Schedule Management: An Object Oriented Approach." *Decision Support Systems,* Vol. 11, No. 4.

Wolfe, W. J., and S. E. Sorensen. (2000, January). "Three Scheduling Algorithms Applied to the Earth Observing Systems Domain." *Management Science,* Vol. 46, No. 1.

Wolfgram, D. D., et al. (1987). *Expert Systems.* New York: John Wiley.

Wolsey, L. A. (2002, December). "Solving Multi-Item Lot-Sizing Problems with an MIP Solver Using Classification and Reformulation." *Management Science.* Vol. 48, No. 12.

Wong, B. K. (1996, July/August). "The Role of Top Management in the Development of Expert Systems." *Journal of Systems Management.*

Wong, B. K., and J. K. S. Chong. (1992, Winter). "Averting Development Problems (in ES)." *Information Systems Management,* Vol. 9, No. 1.

Wong, B. K., and J. A. Monaco. (1995, September). "Expert Systems in Business: A Review and Analysis of the Literature." *Information and Management.*

Wong, F. S., et al. (1992 January/February). "Fuzzy Neural Systems for Stock Selection." *Financial Analysts Journal.*

Worthen, B. (2001a, May 1). "Rock in a Hard Place." *CIO.*

Worthen, B. (2003b, July 15). "Future Results Not Guaranteed." *CIO.*

Worthen, B. (2001c, December 15). "How to Kill an Enterprise Project." *CIO.*

Wright, B. (2002, Fall). "The Legal Risk of Computer Pests and Hacker Tools." *Information Strategy: The Executive's Journal.*

Wright, G. P., A. R. Chaturvedi, R. V. Mookerjee, and S. Garrod. (1998, March). "Integrated Modeling Environments in Organizations: An Empirical Study." *Information Systems Research,* Vol. 9, No. 1.

Wright, J. (2001, July). "High-Tech Holmes." *Security Management.*

Wu, D. J. (1999, November). "Discovering Near-Optimal Pricing Strategies for the Deregulated Electric Power Marketplace Using Genetic Algorithms." *Decision Support Systems,* Vol. 27, Nos. 1 and 2.

Wu, I-L. (2000, January). "Model Management System for IRT-Based Test Construction Decision Support Systems." *Decision Support Systems.* Vol. 27, No. 4.

Wu, X., (1995). *Knowledge Acquisition from Databases.* Norwood, NJ: Ablex Publishing.

Wyckoff A., et al. (2000). *The Economic and Social Impacts of Electronic Commerce.* Washington DC: Brookings Institute Press.

Xiang, Y.P., and K.L. Poh. (2002, January). "Knowledge-Based Time-Critical Dynamic Decision Modelling." *Journal of the Operational Research Society,* Vol. 53, No. 1.

Xianzhong, M. X., and G. R. Kaye. (2002, Winter). "Knowledge Workers for Information Support: Executive's Perceptions and Problems." *Information Systems Management,* Vol. 19, No. 1.

Xu, X. M., and G. R. Kaye. (2002, Winter). "Knowledge Workers for Information Support: Executives' Perceptions and Problems." *Information Systems Management.*

Yager, R. R. (2003). "Fuzzy Logic Methods in Recommender Systems." *Fuzzy Sets and Systems,* Vol. 136, pp. 133–149.

Yager, R. R., M. Fedrizzi, and J. Kacprzyk. (1994). *Advances in the Dempster-Shafer Theory of Evidence.* New York: John Wiley.

Yamada, K. (2003, July). "Jersey Online." *Portals Magazine,* Vol. 33, No. 22.

Yan, Y., et al. (2000, January). "A Multi-Agent Based Negotiation Support System for Distributed Transmission Cost Allocation." *Proceedings of the Thirty-third Annual Hawaii International Conference on Systems Sciences HICSS-33,* Wailea, HI. Los Alamitos, CA: IEEE Computer Society Press.

Yang, J. B. (2002). "A Rule Induction–Based Knowledge System for Retaining Wall Selection." *Expert Systems with Applications,* Vol. 23, pp. 273–279.

Yang, Z. R., M. B. Platt, and H. D. Platt. (1999, February). "Probabilistic Neural Networks in Bankruptcy Prediction." *Journal of Business Research,* Vol. 44, No. 2.

Ye, L. R., and P. E. Johnson. (1995, June). "The Impact of Explanation Facilities on User Acceptance of Expert Systems Advice." *MIS Quarterly,* Vol. 19, No. 2.

Yen, J. (1999, January/February) "Fuzzy Logic—A Modern Perspective." *IEEE Transactions on Knowledge and Data Engineering,* Vol. 11, No. 1.

Yen, J., and R. Langari. (1998). *Fuzzy Logic: Intelligence, Control, and Information.* Upper Saddle River, NJ: Prentice Hall.

Yongbeom, K., and E. A. Stohr. (1998, Spring). "Software Reuse: Survey and Research Directions. *Journal of Management Information Systems,* Vol. 14, No. 4.

Yoon, Y., et al. (1994, January). "Integrating ANN with Rule-Based Expert Systems." *Decision Support Systems,* Vol. 11, No. 5.

Yoon, Y., T. Guimaraes, and Q. O'Neal. (1995, March). "Exploring the Factors Associated with Expert System Success." *MIS Quarterly,* Vol. 19, No. 1.

Yorman, D. (1988, May). "Success Factors for Expert Systems." *Capital PC Monitor,* Vol. 7.

Young, J. (1987, November 4). "Ways to Win Top Brass Backing." *ComputerWorld.*

Yourdon, E. (2000, May 15). "'Viewing' the Project." *ComputerWorld.*

Yourdon, E. (2001, May 21). "Mastering Contracts." *ComputerWorld,* Vol. 35, No. 21.

Yu, E. S. K., et al. (1996, August). "AI Models for Business Process Reengineering." *IEEE Expert,* Vol. 11, No. 4.

Yuan, S. T. (2003, January). "A Personalized and Integrative Comparison-Shopping Engine and Its Applications." *Decision Support Systems.*

Yuan, S. T., and Y. W. Tsao. (2003). "A Recommendation Mechanism for Contextual Mobile Advertising." *Expert Systems with Applications,* Vol. 24, No. 4, pp. 399–414.

Yuan, Y., et al. (2002). "The Development and Evaluation of a Fuzzy Logic Expert System for Renal Transplantation Assignment: Is This a Useful Tool?" *European Journal of Operational Research,* Vol. 142, No. 1, pp. 152–173.

Yueng, M. M. (ed.). (1998, July). "Digital Watermarking." Special Issue. *Communications of the ACM,* Vol. 41, No.7.

Yun, W. Y., and Y. S. Choi. (1999, March 20). "A Simulation Model for Container-Terminal Analysis Using an Object-Oriented Approach." *International Journal of Production Economics,* Vol. 59, Nos. 1–3.

Zack, M. H. (1999, Spring). "Developing a Knowledge Strategy." *California Management Review.*

Zadeh, L. A., (1994, March). "Fuzzy Logic, Neural Networks, and Soft Computing." *Communications of the ACM,* Vol. 37, No. 3.

Zahedi, F. (1987). "Qualitative Programming for Selection Decisions." *Computers and Operations Research,* Vol. 14, No. 5.

Zahedi, F. (1993). *Intelligent Systems for Business: Expert Systems with Neural Networks.* Belmont, CA: Wadsworth.

Zaima, A. (2003, June). "The Five Myths of Data Mining." *What Works: Best Practices in Business Intelligence and Data Warehousing,* Vol. 15. Chatsworth, CA: Data Warehousing Institute.

Zand, D.E., and R.E. Sorenson. (1975). "Theory of Change & Effective Use of Management Science." *Administrative Science Quarterly,* Vol. 20. No. 4.

Zaremba, M. B., and G. Morel. (2003, February). "Integration and Control of Intelligence in Distributing Manufacturing." *Journal of Intelligent Manufacturing.*

Zarri, G. P. (1995). "Knowledge Acquisition from Natural Language Documents for Large Knowledge Bases." In N. J. I. Mars (ed.). *Towards Very Large Knowledge Bases.* Amsterdam: IOS Press.

Zarri, G. P., and S. Jacqmin (1999). "WWW, Metadata and Knowledge Representation: A New Version, RDF-Compliant, of the Conceptual Language NKRL." www.apim.ens.fr/workshop_text_99/zarri_abstract. html.

Zellen, B. (2001, June). "Changing IT Culture: Can Component Management Tools Make a Difference?" *Application Development Trends.*

Zhang, G., M. Y. Hu, B. E. Patuwo, and D. C. Indro. (1999, July 1). "Artificial Neural Networks in Bankruptcy Prediction: General Framework and Cross-Validation Analysis." *European Journal of Operational Research,* Vol. 116, No. 1.

Zhang, G. P. (2001). "An Investigation of Neural Networks for Linear Time-Series Forecasting." *Computers and Operations Research,* Vol. 28, No. 12, pp. 1183–1202.

Zhu, K., et al. (2000, January). "Air Cargo Transport by Multi-Agent Based Planning." *Proceedings of the Thirty-third Annual Hawaii International Conference on Systems Sciences HICSS-33,* Wailea, HI. Los Alamitos, CA: IEEE Computer Society Press.

Zimmermann, K.A. (2002, June). "Portals Help Insurers and Their Customers." *KMWorld.*

Zimmermann, K.A. (2003a, April). "Can You Measure Return on Knowledge?" *KMWorld.*

Zimmermann, K.A. (2003b, May). "Happy Together: Knowledge Management and Collaboration Work Hand-in-Hand to Satisfy the Thirst for Information." *KMWorld.*

Zimmerman, K. A. (2003c, June). "Coming Full Circle: Gathering Knowledge Throughout the Supply Chain Improves Decision-Making." *KM World.*

Zipkin, P. (2001, Spring). "The Limits of Mass Customization." *MIT Sloan Management Review.*

Zipperer, J. (2002, September). "Supply Chain Knowledge Is the Answer." *InternetWorld.*

Zurada, J. M. (1995). *Introduction to Artificial Neural Networks.* Boston: PWS Publishing.

Note: Page numbers followed by t and f refer to tables and figures. Those followed by A and F refer to DSS in Action and DSS in Focus boxes, repectively.

at Arrow Electronics, 436A
at Aviall Inc., 443A
at Diageo plc, 439A
evolution of computerized, 447
goal of, 436
intelligent agents for, 720
inventory reduction and, 439A, 440A
at John Deere, 440A
at Littlewoods Stores, 445A
MSS technologies and the Web in, 21t
at PBS, 441, 442A
problems and solutions in, 442–446
Supply chain management systems
(SCMS)
ERP and, 451–452
integrating with EIS, 444
integrating with KMS, 515
MSS integration and, 815–816
at Nike, 444A
Web impacts and, 412t
Supply chains, 435–442
automobile industry, 437–439
benefits of, 436
components of, 436–439
concept of, 435
decision-making and, 441
definition of, 436
extended, 441
integrating, 448, 449A
problems and solutions for, 442–446
value chain and, 439–441
of wine making, 437f
Support
for creativity, 394
DSS, 132–133
for e-commerce, 786–791
for group communication, 367–368,
369f
personal, 132
Sustainable Computing Consortium,
317A
Symbiotic DSS, 812
Symbolic processing, 541–542
Symbolic reasoning, 550
Symbolic representation of uncertainty,
629
Symbols, 541
Synapses, 663, 664f
Synchronous communication, 370
System analysts, 126
Systematic sourcing, 775
System development life cycle (SDLC),
309–327, 313F
agile development and XP, 328–331
alternative methodologies for,
327–331
analysis/design tools in, 315–316
CASE tools in, 314–315
code debugging/testing in, 316–317
for e-commerce/Web projects, 320–321
expertise in, 320
implementation failure and, 321–324
parallel development, 327

project management in, 317–320,
323A, 324–327
prototyping in, 327–328, 331–334
RAD, 327–328
traditional, 310–327
Systems, 41–47
closed/open, 44–45
definition of, 41
development of, 20t
effectiveness/efficiency of, 45–46
information, 46–47
interfaces in, 42
structure of, 43–45

Tabu search heuristics, 183
Tacit knowledge, 492–494, 500
Tactical models, 116
Tags, 30
Taxes, in e-commerce, 793
TCF Bank, 259A
Team-developed DSS, 346–347
Teams, virtual, 823. *See also*
Collaboration
Team skills, 246
Technology. *See also individual technologies*
C2C and, 785
collaborative, 361–407
emerging/trends in, 28–30
group support systems, 361–407,
379–382
impacts of, 820–822
in knowledge management, 504–508
levels of, 339–340
pervasive computing, 785–786
supporting decision-making, 77–78
tools for DSS, 339–340
Web impacts and, 339t
TEIRESIAS, 593–594
Telecommuting, 837
Temperament types, 78–81, 83, 84F
Temporal continuity, 708
Temporal reasoning, 617t
Temtec Executive Viewer, 260, 261f, 262f,
418
Term extraction, 272F
Testing
in agile systems development, 331
artificial neural networks, 678–679
black-box, 678–679
in case-based reasoning, 658
code, 316–317
neural networks, 678–679
Texaco, 501A
Text mining, 270–273, 276–277
Text-oriented DSS, 127, 129A
Theory of reasoned action, 831–832
"Think small, strategize big" philosophy,
306–309
ThoughtPath, 399
3Ga Corporation, 76A
3NF schemas, 285F
Threshold values, 667

Throwaway prototyping, 328
TIGON, 593
Time compression, 185
Time-dependent simulation, 188
Time-independent simulation, 188
TIREDDX, 579A
T&N, 130A
Toffler, Alvin, 709
Toolboxes, 758
Toolkits, 637
Top-level financials, 419
Topologies, 664–665
Total Information Awareness (TIA) project, 275F
TPS (transaction processing systems), 4,
45
Trace/line of reasoning, 627
Training. *See also* Learning
e-learning, 781–782
neural network, 677–678
via distance learning, 385–394
Training sets, 599
Transaction processing systems (TPS), 4,
45
Transformation/transfer functions,
666–667
Transport layer, XML, 727
Travel, e-commerce in, 762–763
Trial and error, 176
Tri Valley Growers, 454A
TRIZ, 398
True Colors personality typing, 78, 80F
Trust, semantic Web, 730
Turing test, 540–541

UltraEx, 288A
Uncertainty, 153–154
in decision tables, 162
expert systems and, 563
inferencing with, 627–633
representing, 628–629
in the supply chain, 443–444, 446
Uncertainty processing, 558
Uncontrollable variables/parameters,
164, 165t
Undocumented sources of knowledge,
579–580
Unemployment, 336A, 826–827, 833–834
Uniformity checks, 222
Union Pacific Railroad, 74A
United Airlines, 148A
United Sugars Corporation, 28A
Unity Trust Bank, 277A
Universal Resource Identifiers (URIs),
728
University of Georgia, 131A, 133,
389A
University of Southern California,
548A
Unstructured decisions, 14
Unstructured interviews, 587–588
Unstructured problems, 12
Unstructured processes, 12